THE PAPERS OF
THOMAS JEFFERSON

THE PAPERS OF
Thomas Jefferson

Volume 25
1 January to 10 May 1793

JOHN CATANZARITI, EDITOR

EUGENE R. SHERIDAN, SENIOR ASSOCIATE EDITOR

J. JEFFERSON LOONEY, ASSOCIATE EDITOR

GEORGE H. HOEMANN AND RUTH W. LESTER,
ASSISTANT EDITORS

ELIZABETH PETERS BLAZEJEWSKI, EDITORIAL ASSISTANT

PRINCETON, NEW JERSEY

PRINCETON UNIVERSITY PRESS

1992

DEDICATED TO THE MEMORY OF

ADOLPH S. OCHS

PUBLISHER OF THE NEW YORK TIMES

1896-1935

WHO BY THE EXAMPLE OF A RESPONSIBLE

PRESS ENLARGED AND FORTIFIED

THE JEFFERSONIAN CONCEPT

OF A FREE PRESS

ACKNOWLEDGMENTS

As INDICATED in the first volume, this edition was made possible by a grant of $200,000 from The New York Times Company to Princeton University. Since this initial subvention, its continuance has been assured by additional contributions from The New York Times Company and The New York Times Company Foundation; by grants of the Ford Foundation and the National Historical Publications and Records Commission; by grants of the Andrew W. Mellon Foundation, the Pew Charitable Trusts, and the Charles E. Culpeper Foundation to Founding Fathers Papers, Inc.; by benefactions from the Charlotte Palmer Phillips Foundation, Time Inc., the Dyson Foundation, the Lucius N. Littauer Foundation; and by gifts from James Russell Wiggins, David K. E. Bruce, and B. Batmanghelidj. In common with other editions of historical documents, THE PAPERS OF THOMAS JEFFERSON is a beneficiary of the good offices of the National Historical Publications and Records Commission, tendered in many useful forms through its officers and dedicated staff. For these and other indispensable aids generously given by librarians, archivists, scholars, and collectors of manuscripts, the Editors record their sincere gratitude.

FOREWORD

Faithful readers of this and earlier volumes may remember that twenty years ago Ruth W. Lester's name appeared for the first time on the title page of this edition. Mrs. Lester had joined the Jefferson Office in 1962 as secretary to Julian P. Boyd, but with the publication of Volume 18 in 1971 she ascended to the place on the title page that she would hold even after her retirement as Assistant Editor in December 1987, completing a quarter century of loyal service to the edition. The tireless vitality, infectious enthusiasm, and determined persistence Mrs. Lester brought to editorial tasks large and small during her long and productive tenure—one transcended only by that of Mr. Boyd himself—were no less evident in the contributions she made to the early preparations for this volume. Although this is the last volume that will bear Mrs. Lester's name, the present Editors and their successors will long benefit from the tangible evidences of her work accumulated in the editorial files; and the former are especially privileged to be able to record this tribute with equal measures of esteem and affection. The Editors also extend their good wishes to George H. Hoemann, who after nearly four years at Princeton took up his new position as Associate Editor of The Papers of Andrew Jackson at the Knoxville campus of the University of Tennessee in 1988, and whose final participation in the edition is reflected in this volume.

Publication of the present installment in this series also provides the Editors with the welcome opportunity of acknowledging the expertise and assistance graciously tendered by the following individuals: David J. Furley, Anthony T. Grafton, William C. Jordan, and Jean-Yves Le Saux of Princeton University; the late Sara Dunlap Jackson, Donald L. Singer, and Timothy Connelly of the archival staff of the National Historical Publications and Records Commission; Louis L. Tucker, Peter Drummey, and the staff of the Massachusetts Historical Society; James H. Hutson and his staff at the Manuscript Division of the Library of Congress, especially Paul H. Smith, Gerard W. Gawalt, Charles Kelly, and Mary Wolfskill; James Gilreath of the Rare Book and Special Collections Division at the Library of Congress; Lucia C. Stanton of the Thomas Jefferson Memorial Foundation at Monticello; Whitfield J. Bell, Jr., Beth Carroll-Horrocks, and Martin L. Levitt of the American Philosophical Society; John Van Horne of the Library Company of Philadelphia; Edmund Berkeley, Jr., Michael Plunkett,

FOREWORD

and William Runge of the Special Collections Department at the University of Virginia; Margaret Heilbrun of the New-York Historical Society; John J. McCusker of the University of Maryland; Dorothy W. Twohig and Philander D. Chase of The Papers of George Washington at the University of Virginia; Elaine W. Pascu of The Papers of Albert Gallatin at Baruch College of the City University of New York; Robert E. Parks of the Pierpont Morgan Library; Peter Michel of the Missouri Historical Society; Daniel Preston of Ash Lawn-Highland; and Cynthia M. Gessele, Mary-Jo Kline, and Barbara Stein. To these and other friends of the enterprise the Editors extend their cordial thanks.

JOHN CATANZARITI

15 August 1991

GUIDE TO EDITORIAL APPARATUS

1. TEXTUAL DEVICES

The following devices are employed throughout the work to clarify the presentation of the text.

[. . .], [. . . .]   One or two words missing and not conjecturable.

[. . .]¹, [. . . .]¹   More than two words missing and not conjecturable; subjoined footnote estimates number of words missing.

[   ]   Number or part of a number missing or illegible.

[roman]   Conjectural reading for missing or illegible matter. A question mark follows when the reading is doubtful.

[*italic*]   Editorial comment inserted in the text.

⟨*italic*⟩   Matter deleted in the MS but restored in our text.

2. DESCRIPTIVE SYMBOLS

The following symbols are employed throughout the work to describe the various kinds of manuscript originals. When a series of versions is recorded, *the first to be recorded is the version used for the printed text.*

Dft   draft (usually a composition or rough draft; later drafts, when identifiable as such, are designated "2d Dft," &c.)

Dupl   duplicate

MS   manuscript (arbitrarily applied to most documents other than letters)

N   note, notes (memoranda, fragments, &c.)

PoC   polygraph copy

PrC   press copy

RC   recipient's copy

SC   stylograph copy

Tripl   triplicate

All manuscripts of the above types are assumed to be in the hand of the author of the document to which the descriptive symbol pertains. If not, that fact is stated. On the other hand, the following types of manuscripts are assumed *not* to be in the hand of the author, and exceptions will be noted:

FC file copy (applied to all contemporary copies retained by the author or his agents)

Lb letterbook (ordinarily used with FC and Tr to denote texts copied into bound volumes)

Tr transcript (applied to all contemporary and later copies except file copies; period of transcription, unless clear by implication, will be given when known)

3. LOCATION SYMBOLS

The locations of documents printed in this edition from originals in private hands and from printed sources are recorded in self-explanatory form in the descriptive note following each document. The locations of documents printed from originals held by public and private institutions in the United States are recorded by means of the symbols used in the National Union Catalog in the Library of Congress; an explanation of how these symbols are formed is given in Vol. 1: xl. The symbols DLC and MHi by themselves stand for the collections of Jefferson Papers proper in these repositories; when texts are drawn from other collections held by these two institutions, the names of those collections will be added. Location symbols for documents held by institutions outside the United States are given in a subjoined list. The lists of symbols are limited to the institutions represented by documents printed or referred to in this volume.

CSmH The Huntington Library, San Marino, California
CtY Yale University Library
DLC Library of Congress
DNA The National Archives, with identifications of series (preceded by record group number) as follows:
  CD Consular Dispatches
  DCI Diplomatic and Consular Instructions
  DCLB District of Columbia Letter Book
  DD Diplomatic Dispatches
  DL Domestic Letters
  FL Foreign Letters
  LGS Letters from the Governors of the States
  MD Miscellaneous Dispatches
  MDC Miscellaneous Duplicate Consular and Diplomatic Dispatches
  MLR Miscellaneous Letters Received

NL	Notes from Legations
PBG	Public Buildings and Grounds
PC	Proceedings of the Board of Commissioners for the District of Columbia
PCC	Papers of the Continental Congress
PDL	Printing and Distribution of the Laws
SDC	State Department Correspondence: Copy books of George Washington's Correspondence with the Secretaries of State
SDR	State Department Reports: A Record of the Reports of Thomas Jefferson, Secretary of State for the United States of America
TR	Transcribed Reports
ICHi	Chicago Historical Society
InHi	Indiana Historical Society, Indianapolis
MH	Harvard University Library
MHi	Massachusetts Historical Society, Boston
MWA	American Antiquarian Society, Worcester, Massachusetts
MeB	Bowdoin College, Brunswick, Maine
MoSHi	Missouri Historical Society, St. Louis
NHi	New-York Historical Society, New York City
NHyF	Franklin D. Roosevelt Library, Hyde Park, New York
NN	New York Public Library
NNC	Columbia University Library
NNP	Pierpont Morgan Library, New York City
NcU	University of North Carolina Library, Chapel Hill
Nj	New Jersey State Library, Trenton
NjGbS	Glassboro State College, Glassboro, New Jersey
NjP	Princeton University Library
PHarH	Pennsylvania Historical and Museum Commission, Harrisburg
PHi	Historical Society of Pennsylvania, Philadelphia
PPAmP	American Philosophical Society, Philadelphia
PPL	Library Company of Philadelphia
PWacD	David Library of the American Revolution, Washington Crossing, Pennsylvania
R-Ar	Rhode Island State Archives, Providence
ScHi	South Carolina Historical Society, Charleston

TxAuLBJ   Lyndon Baines Johnson Library, Austin, Texas
Vi   Virginia State Library, Richmond
ViFreJM   James Monroe Memorial Foundation, Fredericks-
           burg, Virginia
ViHi   Virginia Historical Society, Richmond
ViU   University of Virginia Library, Charlottesville
ViW   College of William and Mary Library, Williams-
           burg, Virginia

The following symbols represent repositories located outside of the
United States:

AHN   Archivo Histórico Nacional, Madrid
AMAE   Archives du Ministère des Affaires Étrangères,
           Paris, with identification of series as follows:
           CPEU   Correspondance Politique, États-Unis
AN   Archives Nationales, Paris
AR   Algemeen Rijksarchief, The Hague
PRO   Public Record Office, London, with identification
           of series as follows:
           FO   Foreign Office

4. OTHER SYMBOLS AND ABBREVIATIONS

The following symbols and abbreviations are commonly employed
in the annotation throughout the work.

Second Series   The topical series to be published as part of this
    edition, comprising those materials which are best suited to a
    topical rather than a chronological arrangement (see Vol. 1: xv-
    xvi)
TJ   Thomas Jefferson
TJ Editorial Files   Photoduplicates and other editorial materials in
    the office of *The Papers of Thomas Jefferson*, Princeton University
    Library
TJ Papers   Jefferson Papers (applied to a collection of manuscripts
    when the precise location of an undated, misdated, or otherwise
    problematic document must be furnished, and always preceded
    by the symbol for the institutional repository; thus "DLC: TJ
    Papers, 4: 628-9" represents a document in the Library of Con-
    gress, Jefferson Papers, volume 4, pages 628 and 629. Cita-
    tions to volumes and folio numbers of the Jefferson Papers at the
    Library of Congress refer to the collection as it was arranged at the
    time the first microfilm edition was made in 1944-45. Access to

the microfilm edition of the collection as it was rearranged under the Library's Presidential Papers Program is provided by the *Index to the Thomas Jefferson Papers* [Washington, D.C., 1976])

RG   Record Group (used in designating the location of documents in the National Archives)

SJL   Jefferson's "Summary Journal of Letters" written and received for the period 11 Nov. 1783 to 25 June 1826 (in DLC: TJ Papers). This register, kept in Jefferson's hand, has been checked against the TJ Editorial Files. It is to be assumed that all outgoing letters are recorded in SJL unless there is a note to the contrary. When the date of receipt of an incoming letter is recorded in SJL, it is incorporated in the notes. Information and discrepancies revealed in SJL but not found in the letter itself are also noted. Missing letters recorded in SJL are, where possible, accounted for in the notes to documents mentioning them or in related documents. A more detailed discussion of this register and its use in this edition appears in Vol. 6: vii-x

SJPL   "Summary Journal of Public Letters," an incomplete list of letters and documents written by TJ from 16 Apr. 1784 to 31 Dec. 1793, with brief summaries, in an amanuensis's hand. This is supplemented by six pages in TJ's hand, compiled at a later date, listing private and confidential memorandums and notes as well as official reports and communications by and to him as Secretary of State, 11 Oct. 1789 to 31 Dec. 1793 (in DLC: TJ Papers, Epistolary Record, 514-59 and 209-11, respectively; see Vol. 22: ix-x). Since nearly all documents in the amanuensis's list are registered in SJL, while few in TJ's list are so recorded, it is to be assumed that all references to SJPL are to the list in TJ's hand unless there is a statement to the contrary

V   Ecu

f   Florin

£   Pound sterling or livre, depending upon context (in doubtful cases, a clarifying note will be given)

s   Shilling or sou (also expressed as /)

d   Penny or denier

tt   Livre Tournois

℔   Per (occasionally used for pro, pre)

5. SHORT TITLES

The following list includes only those short titles of works cited frequently, and therefore in very abbreviated form, throughout this edition. Since it is impossible to anticipate all the works to be cited in very abbreviated form, the list is appropriately revised from volume to volume.

Adams, *Diary*   L. H. Butterfield and others, eds., *Diary and Auto-biography of John Adams*, Cambridge, Mass., 1961, 4 vols.

Adams, *Works*   Charles Francis Adams, ed., *The Works of John Adams*, Boston, 1850-56, 10 vols.

AHA   American Historical Association

AHR   *American Historical Review*, 1895-

Ammon, *Monroe*   Harry Ammon, *James Monroe: The Quest for National Identity*, New York, 1971

Annals   *Annals of the Congress of the United States: The Debates and Proceedings in the Congress of the United States . . . Compiled from Authentic Materials*, Washington, D.C., Gales & Seaton, 1834-56, 42 vols. All editions are undependable and pagination varies from one printing to another. The first two volumes of the set cited here have "Compiled . . . by Joseph Gales, Senior" on the title page and bear the caption "Gales & Seatons History" on verso and "of Debates in Congress" on recto pages. The remaining volumes bear the caption "History of Congress" on both recto and verso pages. Those using the first two volumes with the latter caption will need to employ the date of the debate or the indexes of debates and speakers.

APS   American Philosophical Society

Archives Parlementaires   *Archives Parlementaires de 1787 à 1860: Recueil Complet des Débats Législatifs & Politiques des Chambres Françaises*, Paris, 1862- , 222 vols.

ASP   *American State Papers: Documents, Legislative and Executive, of the Congress of the United States*, Washington, D.C., Gales & Seaton, 1832-61, 38 vols.

Bear, *Family Letters*   Edwin M. Betts and James A. Bear, Jr., eds., *Family Letters of Thomas Jefferson*, Columbia, Mo., 1966

Bemis, *Jay's Treaty*   Samuel Flagg Bemis, *Jay's Treaty: A Study in Commerce and Diplomacy*, rev. ed., New Haven, 1962

Bemis, *Pinckney's Treaty*   Samuel Flagg Bemis, *Pinckney's Treaty: America's Advantage from Europe's Distress, 1783-1800*, rev. ed., New Haven, 1960

Betts, *Farm Book*   Edwin M. Betts, ed., *Thomas Jefferson's Farm Book*, Princeton, 1953

Betts, *Garden Book*   Edwin M. Betts, ed., *Thomas Jefferson's Garden Book, 1766-1824*, Philadelphia, 1944

Biog. Dir. Cong.   *Biographical Directory of the United States Congress, 1774-1989*, Washington, D.C., 1989

Brant, *Madison*   Irving Brant, *James Madison*, Indianapolis, 1941-61, 6 vols.

Brigham, *American Newspapers*   Clarence S. Brigham, *History and Bibliography of American Newspapers, 1690-1820*, Worcester, Mass., 1947, 2 vols.

Bryan, *National Capital*   W. B. Bryan, *History of the National Capital*, New York, 1914-16, 2 vols.

Burnett, *Letters of Members*   Edmund C. Burnett, ed., *Letters of Members of the Continental Congress*, Washington, D.C., 1921-36, 8 vols.

Butterfield, *Rush*   L. H. Butterfield, ed., *Letters of Benjamin Rush*, Princeton, 1951, 2 vols.

CVSP   William P. Palmer and others, eds., *Calendar of Virginia State Papers . . . Preserved in the Capitol at Richmond*, Richmond, 1875-93, 11 vols.

DAB   Allen Johnson and Dumas Malone, eds., *Dictionary of American Biography*, New York, 1928-36, 20 vols.

DeConde, *Entangling Alliance*   Alexander DeConde, *Entangling Alliance: Politics & Diplomacy under George Washington*, Durham N.C., 1958

Dexter, *Yale*   Franklin B. Dexter, *Biographical Sketches of the Graduates of Yale College with Annals of the College History*, New York, 1885-1912, 6 vols.

DNB   Leslie Stephen and Sidney Lee, eds. *Dictionary of National Biography*, 2d ed., New York, 1908-09, 22 vols.

DSB   Charles C. Gillispie, ed., *Dictionary of Scientific Biography*, New York, 1970-80, 16 vols.

Evans   Charles Evans, Clifford K. Shipton, and Roger P. Bristol, comps., *American Bibliography: A Chronological Dictionary of all Books, Pamphlets and Periodical Publications Printed in the United States of America from . . . 1639 . . . to . . . 1820*, Chicago and Worcester, Mass., 1903-59, 14 vols.

Ferguson, *Power of the Purse*   E. James Ferguson, *The Power of the Purse: A History of American Public Finance, 1776-1790*, Chapel Hill, 1961

Fitzpatrick, *Writings*   John C. Fitzpatrick, ed., *The Writings of George Washington*, Washington, D.C., 1931-44, 39 vols.

Ford   Paul Leicester Ford, ed., *The Writings of Thomas Jefferson*, Letterpress Edition, New York, 1892-99, 10 vols.

Freeman, *Washington*   Douglas Southall Freeman, *George Washington*, New York, 1948-57, 7 vols.; 7th volume by J. A. Carroll and M. W. Ashworth

HAW   Henry A. Washington, ed., *The Writings of Thomas Jefferson*, New York, 1853-54, 9 vols.

Hening   William Waller Hening, ed., *The Statutes at Large; Being a Collection of All the Laws of Virginia*, Richmond, 1809-23, 13 vols.

Henry, *Henry*   William Wirt Henry, *Patrick Henry, Life, Correspondence and Speeches*, New York, 1891, 3 vols.

Humphreys, *Humphreys*   F. L. Humphreys, *Life and Times of David Humphreys*, New York, 1917, 2 vols.

Hunt, *Madison*   Gaillard Hunt, ed., *The Writings of James Madison*, New York, 1900-10, 9 vols.

JCC   Worthington C. Ford and others, eds., *Journals of the Continental Congress, 1774-1789*, Washington, D.C., 1904-37, 34 vols.

Jefferson Correspondence, Bixby   Worthington C. Ford, ed., *Thomas Jefferson Correspondence Printed from the Originals in the Collections of William K. Bixby*, Boston, 1916

JEP   *Journal of the Executive Proceedings of the Senate of the United States ... to the Termination of the Nineteenth Congress*, Washington, D.C., 1828

JHD   *Journal of the House of Delegates of the Commonwealth of Virginia* (cited by session and date of publication)

JHR   *Journal of the House of Representatives of the United States*, Washington, D.C., Gales & Seaton, 1826, 9 vols.

JS   *Journal of the Senate of the United States*, Washington, D.C., Gales, 1820-21, 5 vols.

JSH   *Journal of Southern History*, 1935-

Kimball, *Jefferson, Architect*   Fiske Kimball, *Thomas Jefferson, Architect*, Boston, 1916

L & B   Andrew A. Lipscomb and Albert E. Bergh, eds., *The Writings of Thomas Jefferson*, Washington, D.C., 1903-04, 20 vols.

Library Catalogue, 1783   Jefferson's MS list of books owned or wanted in 1783 (original in Massachusetts Historical Society)

Library Catalogue, 1815   *Catalogue of the Library of the United States*, Washington, D.C., 1815

Library Catalogue, 1829   *Catalogue: President Jefferson's Library*, Washington, D.C., 1829

List of Patents   *A List of Patents granted by the United States from April 10, 1792, to December 31, 1836*, Washington, D.C., 1872

Madison, *Papers*   William T. Hutchinson, Robert A. Rutland, J. C. A. Stagg, and others, eds., *The Papers of James Madison*, Chicago and Charlottesville, 1962-   , 17 vols.

Malone, *Jefferson*   Dumas Malone, *Jefferson and his Time*, Boston, 1948-81, 6 vols.

Marshall, *Papers*   Herbert A. Johnson, Charles T. Cullen, Charles F. Hobson, and others, eds., *The Papers of John Marshall*, Chapel Hill, 1974- , 5 vols.

Mathews, *Andrew Ellicott*   Catharine Van Cortlandt Mathews, *Andrew Ellicott, His Life and Letters*, New York, 1908

Mayo, *British Ministers*   Bernard Mayo, ed., "Instructions to the British Ministers to the United States 1791-1812," American Historical Association, *Annual Report*, 1936

MB   James A. Bear, Jr., and Lucia C. Stanton, eds., *Jefferson's Memorandum Books: Accounts, with Legal Records and Miscellany, 1767-1826*, Princeton, forthcoming as part of *The Papers of Thomas Jefferson*, Second Series

Miller, *Treaties*   Hunter Miller, ed., *Treaties and other International Acts of the United States of America*, Washington, D.C., 1931-48, 8 vols.

Mitchell, *Hamilton*   Broadus Mitchell, *Alexander Hamilton*, New York, 1957-62, 2 vols.

Moore, *Digest*   John B. Moore, *A Digest of International Law*, Washington, D.C., 1906, 8 vols.

Morris, *Diary*   Beatrix C. Davenport, ed., *A Diary of the French Revolution by Gouverneur Morris, 1752-1816*, Boston, 1939, 2 vols.

MVHR   *Mississippi Valley Historical Review*, 1914-

National State Papers   Eileen D. Carzo, ed., *National State Papers of the United States, 1789-1817. Part II: Texts of Documents. Administration of George Washington, 1789-1797*, Wilmington, Del., 1985, 35 vols.

Notes, ed. Peden   Thomas Jefferson, *Notes on the State of Virginia*, ed. William Peden, Chapel Hill, 1955

Nussbaum, *Commercial Policy*   Frederick L. Nussbaum, *Commercial Policy in the French Revolution: A Study of the Career of G. J. A. Ducher*, Washington, D.C., 1923

OED   Sir James Murray and others, eds., *A New English Dictionary on Historical Principles*, Oxford, 1888-1933

Peterson, *Jefferson*   Merrill D. Peterson, *Thomas Jefferson and the New Nation*, New York, 1970

PMHB   *Pennsylvania Magazine of History and Biography*, 1877-

Randall, *Life*   Henry S. Randall, *The Life of Thomas Jefferson*, New York, 1858, 3 vols.

Randolph, *Domestic Life*   Sarah N. Randolph, *The Domestic Life of*

Thomas Jefferson, Compiled from Family Letters and Reminiscences by His Great-Granddaughter, 3d ed., Cambridge, Mass., 1939

Scott and Rothaus, *Historical Dictionary*   Samuel F. Scott and Barry Rothaus, eds., *Historical Dictionary of the French Revolution, 1789-1799*, Westport, Conn., 1985, 2 vols.

Setser, *Reciprocity*   Vernon G. Setser, *The Commercial Reciprocity Policy of the United States*, Philadelphia, 1937

Shipton-Mooney, *Index*   Clifford K. Shipton and James E. Mooney, comps., *National Index of American Imprints through 1800: The Short-Title Evans*, [Worcester, Mass.], 1969, 2 vols.

Sowerby   E. Millicent Sowerby, comp., *Catalogue of the Library of Thomas Jefferson*, Washington, D.C., 1952-59, 5 vols.

Sparks, *Morris*   Jared Sparks, *Life of Gouverneur Morris With Selections from His Correspondence and Miscellaneous Papers*, Boston, 1832, 3 vols.

Syrett, *Hamilton*   Harold C. Syrett and others, eds., *The Papers of Alexander Hamilton*, New York, 1961-87, 27 vols.

Taxay, *Mint*   Don Taxay, *The U.S. Mint and Coinage: An Illustrated History from 1776 to the Present*, New York, 1966

Terr. Papers   Clarence E. Carter and John Porter Bloom, eds., *The Territorial Papers of the United States*, Washington, D.C., 1934- , 28 vols.

Thomas, *Neutrality*   Charles M. Thomas, *American Neutrality in 1793: A Study in Cabinet Government*, New York, 1931.

TJR   Thomas Jefferson Randolph, ed., *Memoir, Correspondence, and Miscellanies, from the Papers of Thomas Jefferson*, Charlottesville, 1829, 4 vols.

Tucker, *Life*   George Tucker, *The Life of Thomas Jefferson*, Philadelphia, 1837, 2 vols.

Turner, *CFM*   Frederick Jackson Turner, "Correspondence of French Ministers, 1791-1797," American Historical Association, *Annual Report*, 1903, II

U.S. Statutes at Large   Richard Peters, ed., *The Public Statutes at Large of the United States ... 1789 to March 3, 1845*, Boston, 1855-56, 8 vols.

VMHB   *Virginia Magazine of History and Biography*, 1893-

Washington, *Diaries*   Donald Jackson and others, eds., *The Diaries of George Washington*, Charlottesville, 1976-79, 6 vols.

Washington, *Journal*   Dorothy Twohig, ed., *The Journal of the Proceedings of the President, 1793-1797*, Charlottesville, 1981

Whitaker, *Frontier*   Arthur P. Whitaker, *The Spanish-American Frontier: 1783-1795*, Boston, 1927

White, *Federalists*   Leonard White, *The Federalists: A Study in Administrative History*, New York, 1948

Windham Papers   *The Windham Papers: The Life and Correspondence of the Rt. Hon. William Windham, 1750-1810*, Boston, 1913, 2 vols.

WMQ   *William and Mary Quarterly*, 1892-

Woods, *Albemarle*   Edgar Woods, *Albemarle County in Virginia*, Charlottesville, 1901

CONTENTS

CONTENTS

CONTENTS

CONTENTS

CONTENTS

[xxv]

CONTENTS

CONTENTS

CONTENTS

CONTENTS

CONTENTS

CONTENTS

CONTENTS

CONTENTS

[xxxiii]

CONTENTS

CONTENTS

CONTENTS

CONTENTS

ILLUSTRATIONS

Following page 400

JEFFERSON'S "ADAM AND EVE" LETTER ON THE FRENCH REVOLUTION

Jefferson's celebrated letter to William Short of 3 Jan. 1793, the second page of which is illustrated in this volume, represented a profound shift in his attitude toward the French Revolution. During his ministry to France and for approximately the first thirty months of his tenure as Secretary of State, Jefferson's hopes for the French Revolution were tempered by his belief that centuries of royal despotism and religious authoritarianism made a constitutional monarchy along British lines the most desirable outcome of the revolutionary turmoil in France. But with the overthrow of the Bourbon monarchy in August 1792 and the establishment of the French Republic in the following month, his enthusiasm for the Revolution became almost unbounded, and the conviction grew in his mind that the success of French republicanism in Europe was necessary to thwart what he regarded as the monarchical designs of the Federalists in America. Despite the ensuing changes of regime in France, it took Napoleon Bonaparte's rise to power to convince Jefferson that his enthusiasm for the French Republic had been mistaken and that his earlier support for a French constitutional monarchy had been well founded. (*Courtesy of the College of William and Mary*)

THE EXECUTION OF LOUIS XVI

The guillotining of Louis XVI on 21 Jan. 1793 shortly after the National Convention tried and convicted him as a traitor to the nation was the most vivid symbol of the demise of the old regime in France. During the king's trial Maximilien Robespierre, the Jacobin leader, was the leading advocate of the view that the execution of Louis was necessary for the French Revolution to survive. This graphic depiction of the monarch's severed head and Robespierre's accompanying commentary expressed the Jacobin belief in the revolutionary justice and necessity of this act of regicide. At first Jefferson neither regretted nor rejoiced in Louis's execution, but looking back on this event in his autobiography, written in 1821, he attributed the king's problems to the nefarious influence of Marie Antoinette and stated that if he had been a member of the National Convention he would have voted to confine the queen to a convent and make Louis a strictly limited constitutional monarch. (*Courtesy of the Bibliothèque nationale*)

THE FIRST MANNED BALLOON FLIGHT IN AMERICA

Jefferson manifested his zealous patronage of scientific and technological advances by purchasing a ticket to watch Jean Pierre Blanchard make America's first successful manned balloon ascension on the morning of 9 Jan. 1793. Blanchard, the first aeronaut to cross the English Channel in a balloon and the earliest to make a living entirely from admission fees and subscriptions connected with his flights, rose from the courtyard of Philadelphia's Walnut Street Prison before an immense crowd headed by President Washington and flew about fifteen miles in three-quarters of an hour. Blanchard soon published a pamphlet describing his exploit, the frontispiece of which is depicted here. Jefferson had displayed keen interest in balloons even before viewing an unmanned release in Philadelphia in May 1784, and was one of the only ones at Blanchard's launch who had already witnessed manned flights, in Paris in September 1784 and June 1786. On the day of Blanchard's ascension Caspar Wistar, Jr., wrote Jefferson about the scientific experiments to be conducted while the balloon was aloft, and around the same time Jefferson spoke with Blanchard and took notes on the methods the aviator employed to produce the hydrogen which propelled his craft. (*Courtesy of the American Antiquarian Society*)

SUBSCRIPTION AGREEMENT FOR ANDRÉ MICHAUX'S PROPOSED
WESTERN EXPEDITION

This subscription agreement, written on behalf of the American Philosophical Society, in whose vault the signed text was discovered only in 1979, represented a fortunate conjuncture between Jefferson's longstanding interest in western exploration and the personal and professional needs of the distinguished French botanist, André Michaux. With his status as a French royal botanist in America thrown into doubt by the overthrow of the Bourbon monarchy, Michaux sought the support of the American Philosophical Society in December 1792 for an expedition designed to find an overland water route to the Pacific. Jefferson, who had proposed a similar venture to the Society months before, took the lead in dealing with Michaux on the Society's behalf, drafting this subscription agreement, soliciting subscribers to it, and drawing up detailed instructions for the expedition itself. In the end, despite Jefferson's painstaking preparations, Michaux never undertook this expedition, preferring instead to serve as an agent of Edmond Charles Genet, the French Republic's first minister to the United States, in an unsuccessful effort to organize a filibustering expedition from Kentucky to free Louisiana from Spanish rule. (*Courtesy of the American Philosophical Society*)

TENCH COXE (1755-1824)

When Jefferson assumed office as Secretary of State in 1790 it seemed unlikely that he would develop any kind of working relationship with Coxe, a Philadelphia merchant and former loyalist who served under Alexander Hamilton in the Department of the Treasury as assistant secretary and commissioner of the revenue. But the two men became close collaborators throughout Jefferson's tenure in office because of their shared belief in the need for retaliation against British restrictions on American trade—a viewpoint that placed them sharply at variance with Hamilton. Drawing upon his access to private and official sources of information, Coxe provided Jefferson with vital economic data pertaining to some of his reports to Congress as Secretary of State. He was especially helpful in collecting information for and commenting in detail on Jefferson's December 1793 Report on Commerce, as evidenced by the notes on a draft of this famous state paper that he sent to the Secretary of State on 5 Feb. 1793.

Engraving by Samuel Sartain. (*Courtesy of the Historical Society of Pennsylvania*)

ILLUSTRATIONS

WILLIAM BRANCH GILES (1762-1830)

This staunchly Republican congressman from Virginia, who graduated from the College of New Jersey and studied law with George Wythe, was the ostensible leader of an effort by Republicans in the House of Representatives to censure Alexander Hamilton's administration as Secretary of the Treasury and thereby drive him from office. The House inquiry culminated at the end of February and the beginning of March 1793 in the overwhelming defeat of censure resolutions against Hamilton introduced by Giles on 27 Feb. Although Federalists had long suspected that Jefferson was the guiding spirit behind this Republican attempt to undermine Hamilton, there was no documentary evidence for Jefferson's involvement until 1895, when Paul L. Ford announced his discovery of an even more strongly worded set of draft resolutions in Jefferson's hand among a collection of papers owned by his great-granddaughter, Sarah Nicholas Randolph. This collection was dispersed after the death of Miss Randolph, and the manuscript resolutions have since disappeared.

Portrait by Gilbert Stuart, ca. 1792. (*Courtesy of the Frick Art Reference Library*)

JEFFERSON'S NOTES ON THE DEFEAT OF THE GILES RESOLUTIONS

On this page from what came to be called the "Anas," Jefferson recorded privately in three separate entries his reaction in March 1792 to the crushing defeat in the House of Representatives of a series of resolutions introduced by William Branch Giles attacking the probity of Alexander Hamilton's stewardship as Secretary of the Treasury. Despite his veiled involvement in this episode, Jefferson maintained a curious air of detachment in describing their legislative history. Initially he contented himself with a general statement that Hamilton had weathered the attack only because a corrupt cadre with a vested interest in supporting his fiscal policies had rejected self-evident truths abetted by a combination of staunch Federalists, indifferent moderates, and vacillating Republicans. However, Jefferson soon attempted to document the pivotal role of stockholders in the defeat of the resolutions by compiling lists of congressional holders of stock in the Bank of the United States and of government securities, an enterprise in which other Republicans were equally active. (*Courtesy of the Library of Congress*)

WASHINGTON AND JEFFERSON AVOID EUROPEAN ENTANGLEMENTS

This draft of Jefferson's dispatch of 23 Mch. 1793 to William Carmichael and William Short, the commissioners of the United States in Madrid, signaled an important shift in American policy toward Spain. During the Nootka Sound crisis in 1790, Jefferson had instructed Carmichael to explore with Spain the possibility of ceding its possessions east of the Mississippi to the United States in exchange for an American guarantee of Spanish lands to the west of that boundary. The easing of tension between Spain and Britain ended any realistic prospect of reaching such an agreement, but authorization to discuss it was not withdrawn until Jefferson wrote this letter, which grew out of a report from William Stephens Smith that France contemplated sending an army to free Spain's transatlantic colonies. Jefferson initially favored diluting the offer

ILLUSTRATIONS

to a trade of the Floridas to the United States in exchange for an American guarantee of Louisiana against British attack, but not against a movement for independence within that Spanish colony. In this form he showed the draft on 22 Mch. 1793 to the President, who withheld his assent. Evidently Washington concluded that a guarantee that could lead to war with Britain was unduly risky, even if accompanied by major territorial gains. When Jefferson resubmitted the draft two days later, amended to withdraw the offer of any form of guarantee, the President formally endorsed it with his approval, an unusual step in his dealings with his Secretary of State. (*Courtesy of the Library of Congress*)

JEFFERSON'S RESIDENCE ON THE SCHUYLKILL

Although Jefferson reluctantly abandoned his plan to resign as Secretary of State at the end of George Washington's first term as president, he sought to forestall a lengthy continuance by sending most of his furniture to Virginia and leasing a summer cottage outside Philadelphia owned by Moses Cox. At the beginning of April 1793 he moved to this house near Gray's Ferry on the east bank of the Schuylkill River, which by that time was the site of a floating bridge with a pleasure garden situated on the opposite bank. During the summer Jefferson ate, read, wrote, and received company under the plane trees which encompassed the small three-room building, going inside only to sleep. On 17 Sep. 1793 he left Philadelphia to visit Monticello and, having determined to take lodgings in the city on his return, urged his landlord to take up residence at the Gray's Ferry house during the yellow fever epidemic then raging in the metropolis.

Watercolor by David J. Kennedy, executed after Jefferson's death from a 1793 sketch by John Andrews, Jr. (*Courtesy of the Historical Society of Pennsylvania*)

WASHINGTON'S PROCLAMATION OF NEUTRALITY

The French Revolution took on a maritime dimension affecting vital American commercial and diplomatic interests when France declared war on Great Britain and the Netherlands on 1 Feb. 1793. Although Washington and the Cabinet unanimously agreed on the overriding need to keep the United States neutral in the midst of this epochal conflict, Jefferson initially opposed a presidential declaration of neutrality, arguing during a Cabinet meeting on 19 Apr. 1793 that the executive was not constitutionally authorized to make such a declaration and that it would be wise to withhold one anyway in the hope of extracting concessions on the recognition of neutral rights from the belligerents. But he acquiesced in the majority opinion of the Cabinet in favor of the issuance of a proclamation by the President declaring American neutrality, which was subsequently drafted by Attorney General Edmund Randolph, who in deference to Jefferson's sensibilities did not use the word *neutrality* in it. Despite this omission, the substance of the proclamation issued by the President on 22 Apr. 1793 was in fact a declaration of neutrality, and it was recognized as such almost immediately both inside and outside the Washington administration. (*Courtesy of the Massachusetts Historical Society*)

ILLUSTRATIONS

This document, which illustrates Jefferson's methodical working habits, is an outline of a masterly opinion that he submitted to the President on 28 Apr. 1793 in favor of the continued validity of the 1778 treaties of alliance and commerce with France even after the establishment of the French Republic and its declaration of war on Britain and the Netherlands. The opinion itself was called forth by Alexander Hamilton's attempt to persuade Washington during a Cabinet meeting on 19 Apr. 1793 that the change in government in France and the altered international situation justified the United States government in informing Edmond Charles Genet, the first minister from the French Republic, that it reserved the right to suspend or terminate these treaties as circumstances dictated. Faced with such a threat to the French alliance, the sheet anchor of his diplomacy, Jefferson mustered all of his persuasive powers in a successful effort to convince the President to reject Hamilton's arguments and to honor the treaties. (*Courtesy of the Library of Congress*)

Volume 25

1 January to 10 May 1793

JEFFERSON CHRONOLOGY
1743 · 1826

1743	Born at Shadwell, 13 Apr. (New Style).
1760	Entered the College of William and Mary.
1762	"quitted college."
1762-1767	Self-education and preparation for law.
1769-1774	Albemarle delegate to House of Burgesses.
1772	Married Martha Wayles Skelton, 1 Jan.
1775-1776	In Continental Congress.
1776	Drafted Declaration of Independence.
1776-1779	In Virginia House of Delegates.
1779	Submitted Bill for Establishing Religious Freedom.
1779-1781	Governor of Virginia.
1782	His wife died, 6 Sep.
1783-1784	In Continental Congress.
1784-1789	In France as Minister Plenipotentiary to negotiate commercial treaties and as Minister Plenipotentiary resident at Versailles.
1790-1793	Secretary of State of the United States.
1797-1801	Vice President of the United States.
1801-1809	President of the United States.
1814-1826	Established the University of Virginia.
1826	Died at Monticello, 4 July.

VOLUME 25
1 January to 10 May 1793

3 Jan.	Defends French Revolution in letter to William Short.
ca. 4 Jan.	Notes on Hamilton's Report on Foreign Loans.
21 Jan.	Execution of Louis XVI.
ca. 22 Jan.	Subscription agreement for André Michaux's western expedition.
26 Jan.	Informs daughter of his decision to defer retirement as Secretary of State.
1 Feb.	France declares war on Great Britain and the Netherlands.
7 Feb.	Notifies Washington of his decision to continue as Secretary of State.
12 Feb.	Observations on the American debt to France.
20 Feb.	Defers submission of Report on Commerce to House of Representatives.
27 Feb.-1 Mch.	Resolutions censuring Hamilton introduced and defeated in the House of Representatives.
7 Mch.	France declares war on Spain.
12 Mch.	Decides to rent house on the Schuylkill from Moses Cox.
12 Mch.	Instructs Gouverneur Morris to resume payments on the debt to France.
15 Mch.	Instructions concerning Lafayette's captivity.
ca. 17 Mch.	New form for United States patents.
23 Mch.	Withdraws offer to guarantee Spanish possession of Louisiana.
7 Apr.	Notifies Washington of war between Great Britain and France.
8 Apr.	Arrival of Edmond Charles Genet in Charleston.
9 Apr.	Moves into house on the Schuylkill.
22 Apr.	Washington's Proclamation of Neutrality.
28 Apr.	Opinion defending the validity of the French treaties.
ca. 30 Apr.	Instructions for André Michaux's western expedition.
6 May	Validity of the treaties with France accepted by Washington.
8 May	Criticizes Hamilton's plan for enforcing neutrality.

THE PAPERS OF
THOMAS JEFFERSON

·◄▬▬▬▬▬▬▬▬▬►·

From James Brown

Dear Sir   Richmond 1st: Janry 1792 [i.e. 1793]
  I am honord with your letter of the 20th. Uto. covering two Letters
to the Consul of U S at Marseilles for which Accept my best thanks.
Both Ships will sail in course of this Week and I hope will meet a
good Reception. My advices from France are of Old dates 20h: Septr.
in which there is little encouragement for Shipments of Tobacco every
Port being glutted. At Havré alone not less than 15,000 Hhds: part
of which the Owners have begun to export to Other Markets.
  Should Col: Eppes deposite any Money with Me it will be attended
to and brought to your Credit. No late arrivals in this Quarter, should
advices at any Period justify a Purchase or Shipment of Produce I will
take it Kind your communicating the same. Mean time I am D Sir
Your very Hle Sr   James Brown

RC (MHi); misdated; endorsed by TJ as received 8 Jan. 1793 and so recorded in
SJL.

From George Divers

Dr Sir   Albemarle County Virginia 1st. Jany 1793
  I have been favord with yours of the 26th. Novemr. I would advise
you to purchase One Still that will work 85 one of 45 and a Copper
Kettle of Sixty Gallons. With these Stills and Boiler you may make
from 70 too 80 Gallons of whisky ♏ Week and feed 60 or 70 Hogs.
The feeding that number of Hogs will be an object to you as it will
save a considerable quantity of Indian Corn, from which Consideration
I have been induced to recommend it to you to purchase Stills of the
above size, that you may be able to keep them at work for 7 months
in the year in which time they will Distill about 900 Bushls. of grain.
If you wish to carry on the business to a greater extent you can add
10 or 15 Galls. to each Still but I would not exceed 100 Galls. for

[3]

the large or 70 Galls. for the small one. A pewter worm is better than Copper.

I am sorry to hear that wheat and Flour is not in demand to the Northward hope it will be Higher in the spring. Your friends in this part of the Country are well, Doctr. Gilmer I think in a better state of health than he has been since his attack of the palsy. I am Dr. Sir Yr. friend & Servt.   GEORGE DIVERS

RC (MHi); endorsed by TJ as received 26 Jan. 1793 and so recorded in SJL.

From Gouverneur Morris

DEAR SIR   Paris 1 January 1793

I transmit herewith a Duplicate of what I had the Honor to write on the twenty first of last Month. Since that Period this Government, perceiving that they had been Wholly deceiv'd respecting the british Nation, have made Advances towards Conciliation. At least so I am inform'd, and also that these Advances are by a Declaration that however general the Terms of their Decree they had no Idea of exciting Revolt except in the Dominions of the Powers leagu'd against them. That as these Powers had entered into France with Design to change the established Government, they are justified in turning against them the Weapons of Revolt which they had intended to use. If this should ever become an Object of diplomatic Controversy, it will perhaps be objected that, untill the asserted Meaning of a general Decree be declared by some other Decree, the Words must be taken in their plain and natural Import. Should such new Decree be passed, which by the bye would take from France a very powerful Engine, the Case of Savoy will be quoted where, whatever may have been the supposed Intentions, no Facts existed to support the Conduct which has been pursued, in such Manner as to shew a Consistency with the limited Interpretation put upon the Decree. Lastly as to the Austrian Netherlands, it will, I presume be alledg'd that not only the Aggression was on the Part of France, but that it was avowedly made with a View to excite Revolt in that Country. But I do not beleive that we shall have any such War of Words, for I am convinc'd that France must, to avoid a War, do Something more than make Professions and Explanations. I say Nothing about the Navigation of the Scheld and the projected Invasion of Holland. I shall not either make any Remarks on the Unanimity in the British Parliament which your Good Sense and Knowlege of that People had certainly anticipated.

[4]

Enclos'd is the Copy of a Letter receiv'd from Mr. de la Motte (or rather an Extract therefrom) with Copy of my Answer of the twenty seventh of December. Accept I pray you Sir the Compliments of this Season and beleive me truly yours   Gouv Morris

P.S. The french Armies are at length permitted to go into Winter Quarters; that under Dumouriez amounted, by the last Returns, to 35000 Effectives after the Junction of Valence and Miranda.

RC (DNA: RG 59, DD); at head of text: "No. 15"; at foot of first page: "Thomas Jefferson Esqr. Secretary of State"; endorsed by TJ as received 22 Apr. 1793 and so recorded in SJL. FC (Lb in DLC: Gouverneur Morris Papers). Tr (DNA: RG 46, Senate Records, 3d Cong., 1st sess.). Tr (Lb in DNA: RG 59, DD). Enclosures: (1) Morris to TJ, 21 Dec. 1792. (2) Extract from Delamotte to Morris, Havre, 25 Dec. 1792, asking if he should grant permission to use the American flag to Captain McFaden, a United States citizen resident in Philadelphia and owner as well as commander of L'Euphrasie, a ship with American registration papers that arrived from New Orleans under a Spanish flag and the name L'Esperance and now wishes to sail to New York flying American colors (Tr in DNA: RG 59, DD, in French; Trs in DNA: RG 46, Senate Records, 3d Cong., 1st sess., in French and English; Trs in Lb in DNA: RG 59, DD, in French and English). (3) Morris to Delamotte,

27 Dec. 1792, suggesting the likelihood of fraud in Captain McFaden's voyage, "since he arrives as a Spaniard and sail'd as an American," but advising that he be allowed to hoist American colors because little can be done to prevent it and he cannot be presumed guilty of breaking the navigation law before conviction on trial, and that Delamotte report the transaction to the Secretary of State (Tr in DNA: RG 59, DD, signed by Morris; Tr in DNA: RG 46, Senate Records, 3d Cong., 1st sess.; Tr in Lb in DNA: RG 59, DD).

The National Convention's DECREE of 19 Nov. 1792 offered French assistance to all peoples seeking to recover their liberty (Archives Parlementaires, 1st ser., LIII, 474). Eight days later, in response to the appeal of certain Savoyards, the National Convention annexed SAVOY to France (same, 357-8, 506-8, 610-15).

TJ submitted this letter to the President on 23 Apr. 1793, and he returned it the same day (Washington, Journal, 118).

From Timothy Pickering

SIR   Genl. Post Office Jany. 1. 1793.

I have received your note of this date. It will certainly be most eligible for the Messenger destined to Georgia to take a passage from New-York in a vessel bound to Savannah or Charleston—perhaps preferably to Charleston, where on his arrival he can find a vessel destined to return to New York by the time he can go to Augusta and get back to Charleston—the trade of Charleston requiring so many more vessels than Savannah. I will give him a letter to the Postmaster at Charleston, who is a very excellent one to render him all necessary aid. Yr. most obedt Servt.   Timothy Pickering

RC (DNA: RG 59, MLR); at foot of text: "Honble. Thomas Jefferson Esqr."; endorsed by TJ as received 1 Jan. 1793 and so recorded in SJL.

TJ's NOTE OF THIS DATE is not recorded in SJL or SJPL and has not been found.

To Thomas Pinckney

DEAR SIR   Philadelphia Jan. 1. 1793.

I have it in charge from the President of the United States, to desire you to be very attentive to the embarkation of troops from the British dominions in Europe, to those in America, and particularly to Quebec—and to give us the earliest advice of their numbers, destination, object and other material circumstances.[1] I have the honor to be with great and sincere esteem, Dear Sir Your most obedient and most humble servt   TH: JEFFERSON

RC (DLC); with sentence in code; at foot of text: "Mr. Pinckney"; endorsed by William A. Deas. FC (Lb in DNA: RG 59, DCI); entirely *en clair*.

The CHARGE FROM THE PRESIDENT was Washington to TJ, [31 Dec. 1792].

[1] This sentence is written in unidentified code; the text has been supplied from the FC.

To George Washington

SIR   Philadelphia Jan. 1. 1793.

I have duly considered the translation of the letter of Dec. 27. from M. de la Forest[1] stating that the French Consuls here have a right to recieve their salaries at Paris, that under the present circumstances they cannot dispose of their bills, and desiring that our government will take them as a remittance in part of the monies we have to pay to France. No doubt he proposes to let us have them on such terms as may ensure us against loss either from the course of exchange of cash for cash at Philadelphia, Amsterdam and Paris, or from the difference between cash and assignats at Paris, in which latter form they will probably be paid. I do not observe any objection from the treasury that this channel of remittance would be out of their ordinary line and inadmissible on that account.—Taking it therefore on the ground merely of an advance unauthorised by the French government, I think the bills may be taken. We have every reason to believe the money is due to them, and none to doubt it will be paid, every creditor being authorised to draw on his debtor. They will be paid indeed in assignats, at the nominal value only, but it is previously understood that these will procure cash on the spot of the real value we shall have paid for them. The risk, if any, is certainly very small, and such as it would be expedient in us to encounter in order to oblige these gentlemen. I think it of real value to produce favorable dispositions in the agents of foreign nations here. Cordiality among nations depends very much on the representations of their agents mutually, and cordiality once established, is of immense value, even counted in money, from the favors it produces in commerce, and the good understanding it preserves in matters merely political. I have the honor to be with sentiments of the most perfect respect & attachment, Sir, your most obedient & most humble servt   TH: JEFFERSON

RC (DNA: RG 59, MLR); at foot of first page: "The President of the U.S."; endorsed by Tobias Lear. PrC (DLC); partly overwritten in a later hand. Tr (Lb in DNA: RG 59, SDC). Recorded in SJPL.

No text has been found of the letter to Alexander Hamilton from Antoine René Charles Mathurin de LA FOREST, the French consul general in Philadelphia, requesting the payment of French consular salaries through advances on the American debt to France. Hamilton had submitted a translation of La Forest's letter to Washington, who referred it in turn to TJ. The President immediately submitted TJ's letter to Hamilton, and although there is no record of the Secretary of the Treasury's response, he must have temporarily withheld his approval from the course of action recommended by TJ. For on 8 Jan. 1793 the French minister, Jean Baptiste Ternant, called TJ's attention to the subject of La Forest's request, and two days later TJ submitted Ternant's letter to Washington, who promptly referred it to the Secretary of the Treasury. Hamilton advised the President that although the Treasury was able to comply with the French consul general's request, it was advisable to consider this issue at a Cabinet meeting in view of the uncertain political situation in France and the fact that the United States had already made its scheduled debt payments to that nation. As a result, the Cabinet met on 12 Jan. 1793 and approved the payment of French consular salaries (Ternant to TJ, 8 Jan. 1793; Syrett, *Hamilton*, XIII, 386, 440; Washington, *Journal*, 7, 9, 11; Turner, *CFM*, 168).

[1] Preceding five words interlined.

From Thomas Barclay

Cadiz, 2 Jan. 1793. Contrary winds having detained the vessel by which he intends to proceed to Setúbal on his way to Lisbon, he may go by way of Ayamonte. He encloses "a letter of some Consequence" he has just received from Gibraltar and hopes to reach that place this month.

RC (DNA: RG 59, CD); 1 p.; endorsed by TJ as received 25 Feb. 1793 and so recorded in SJL. FC (disassembled Lb in same); mutilated. Enclosure not found.

To Benjamin Smith Barton

[*Ed. Note*: This letter, printed in Vol. 24: 687-8 under its inscribed date of 2 Dec. 1792, was almost certainly written on 2 Jan. 1793. See note to Barton to TJ, 4 Jan. 1793.]

From Francis Eppes

DR SIR   Eppington Janry. 2d. 1793

Yours of 19th. of last month I received the day before yesterday. Carys Exr. has mentiond no particular sum tho' told me it woud be considerable, its the whole amount of the hire of 180 Negros for the last year. I expect to see the Exr. on the tenth of this month after which I will write you more particularly, in the mean time, shou'd he make me a payment, it shall be deposited in Mr. Browns hands, subject to your order; that is your proportion of what ever I receive. I am at present unable to inform you what will be the amount of the whole debt tho hope after seeing Mr. Hay the Commisioner shall be furnishd with the papers and will then inform you, from what Idea I have of the payments it cant be far short of £3000 however this is mear conjecture for I have had no papers in my possession for several years. I am glad to hear of the Dukes retreat. I cant help Flatering myself its preparatory to his being Cornwallis'd or Burgoind a circumstance that will give me highest gratification. Wheat fluctuates here from a dollar to 6/8 but by no means fixd. The Merchants seam determin'd to take every advantage of the planter-necessities. You will oblige me very much by informing what you think of this business, whether the European prices will justify[1] more than the above prices and whether then it will be prudent to keep wheat until spring. Tell Jack he has grown lazy. We think he might write oftner. We are all well and unite in our best affections to yourself Polly and Jack. I am Dr Sir Your Friend   FRANS. EPPES

P.S. Tell Jack I shall write him on the tenth from Richmond.

RC (ViU); endorsed by TJ as received   [1] Manuscript appears to read "iustify."
10 Jan. 1793 and so recorded in SJL.

To David Humphreys

DEAR SIR   Philadelphia Jan. 2. 1793.

My last to you was of the 6th. of November, since which the papers have been duly forwarded to you by every opportunity from my office, as Mr. Taylor assures me, to whom I am obliged to confide that duty. Your last received was No. 59. as acknoleged in mine. With the present you will recieve newspapers for yourself, Mr. Carmichael and Mr. Short whom we expect by this time to be at Madrid: also half a dozen plans of the city of Washington in the district of Columbia, to be displayed wherever they will be most likely to be seen by that class of people who might be attracted to it.—Congress is in session as you will see by the papers, which will give you the details of their proceedings. The Western Indians have proposed to meet us in the spring in the neighborhood of Sanduskey to treat of peace. The result is far from being certain.—The late election of President and Vice President has given us the former unanimously, the latter by a great majority.—We have now been a considerable time without hearing from Mr. Barclay, and shall always be glad to be informed by you on his subject, as he may be in a situation not to find means of conveying letters to us. We are anxious to know too whether the monopoly of grain mentioned in your letter threatens really to take place. We wonder that we hear nothing of the Minister of Portugal. Wheat has been in great demand here lately. The price has been consequently high, and will be so again. The French West Indies become more and more dependant on us for subsistence. There is at present some glimmering of hope that the efforts of the free inhabitants will be directed with more efficacy to the reduction of the common enemy. However we are far from certainty on that subject.—Referring you for details on these subjects to the papers which accompany this, I am with great & sincere esteem Dear Sir Your most obedt. and most humble servt   TH: JEFFERSON

RC (NjP: Andre deCoppet Collection); addressed: "A Monsieur Monsieur Humphreys Ministre Resident des Etats Unis d'Amerique à Lisbonne"; endorsed by Humphreys. PrC (DLC); dated 3 Jan. 1793. FC (Lb in DNA: RG 59, DCI); dated 3 Jan. 1793. Recorded in SJL under 3 Jan. 1793.

TJ wrote this letter after receiving one of 2 Jan. 1793 from Tobias Lear advising that a vessel was about to sail for Lisbon the following day by which TJ might write to Humphreys, and that he would send one of the "plans of the City of Washington" Humphreys had requested from him if they had not already been forwarded (RC in DLC; endorsed by TJ as received 2 Jan. 1793).

To the Speaker of the House of Representatives

SIR   Philadelphia, January 2nd 1793.

According to the Resolution of the House of Representatives of the 31st of December, delivered to me yesterday, I have the honor to lay before you a list of the several persons employed in my Office, with the Salaries allowed to each, as follows

	Dollars
George Taylor Jr. (of New York) Chief Clerk, his salary fixed by law	800
Jacob Blackwell (of New York) Clerk	500
George Pfeiffer (of Pennsylvania) Clerk	500
Philip Freneau (of New York[1]) Clerk for foreign Languages	250
Sampson Crosby (of Massachusetts) messenger and office keeper	250

The Act of Congress of June 4th. 1790. c. 18, allowed me an additional Clerk with the same salary as the chief Clerk. After the retirement of the person first appointed, whose services had been particularly desirable because of his long and intimate acquaintance with the papers of the Office, it did not appear necessary to make further use of the indulgence of that Law. No new appointment, therefore, has been made.

The Clerk for foreign Languages has but half the usual Salary. I found his clerkship on this establishment when I came into office, and made no change in it, except that, in the time of his predecessor, where translations were required from any language with which he was unacquainted, they were sent to a special translator and paid for by the public. The present Clerk is required to defray this expense himself. I have the honor to be, with the most perfect respect, Sir, Your most obedient & most humble servt.

PrC (DLC); in the hand of George Taylor, Jr., unsigned; at foot of text: "The Speaker of the House of Representatives." FC (Lb in DNA: RG 59, DL). Tr (Lb in DNA: RG 233, House Records, TR). Not recorded in SJL.

The RESOLUTION of 31 Dec. 1792 directed the Secretaries of State, Treasury, and War to submit to the House "lists of the several persons employed in the offices of their respective Departments, with the salaries allowed to each" (JHR, I, 658). Henry Remsen had been TJ's first CHIEF CLERK in the Department of State.

[1] Word written over "Jersey," erased.

To Harry Innes

SIR   Philadelphia January 3rd. 1793.

No list of the Votes of the Electors of your district for a President and Vice President at the last election having yet been received by the President of the Senate, I do, in obedience to the law, send the Bearer hereof   as special messenger, to desire that you will be pleased to transmit by him to the Seat of Government the list of the said Votes lodged in your hands by the Electors of your District. I have the honor to be with the most perfect respect Sir, Your most obedient and most humble servant

PrC (DLC); in the hand of George Taylor, Jr., unsigned; at foot of text: "The Judge of the District of Kentucky." FC (Lb in DNA: RG 59, DL).

A statute of March 1792 stipulated that each state's presidential and vice-presidential electors meet and vote on the first Wednesday in December. The electors were to sign three certificates listing all the votes cast, two to be sent to the President of the Senate (one delivered in person, the other by the Post Office) and the third to be deposited with the state's

District Judge. The Secretary of State was to send a special messenger to obtain the judge's copy when any state's tally had not reached the national capital by the first Wednesday in January. Congress was to open the certificates and count the votes on the second Wednesday in February (Annals, III, 1341-3). John Adams, the President of the Senate, informed TJ on Wednesday, 3 Jan. 1793, that he had not received the votes from the electors of Kentucky, but no letter to that effect has been found or is recorded in SJL (see TJ to Adams, 1 Mch. 1793).

From James Monroe

DEAR SIR   Phila. Jany. 3. 1793
My St. Croix friends have mentioned that it might reach you, that a Mr. Durant would be more acceptable there as Mr. Yards successor than any other person. The enclosed letter respects the pretensions of another Gentleman for another place and which I have thought expedient to submit to your inspection. Sincerely I am yr. affectionate friend & servt   JAS: MONROE

RC (DLC); endorsed by TJ as received 2 Jan. 1793 and so recorded in SJL; noted by TJ beneath endorsement: "Furant. to be Consul at St. Croix."

For the recommendations to succeed James Yard as consul at St. Croix and

the ENCLOSED LETTER of James Yard to Monroe of 27 Dec. 1792 recommending William Stevenson for consul at St. Eustatius, see TJ's Memorandum on Consuls and Consular Appointments, 15 Feb. 1793, and note.

From Thomas Pinckney

DEAR SIR   London 3d Janry 1793
Your several letters of the 6, 8th and 13th November (under one cover) and 20th of the same month by Mr. Tellier together with your private favor of the 3d December by packet with their several inclosures reached me in the course of yesterday and the day preceeding. I have only time to say by the present opportunity that their contents

shall be duly attended to. I have strongly urged the adoption of equitable regulations concerning seamen and from a conference with Lord Grenville this day I have greater hope of a favorable termination of this negociation than I hitherto entertained. My expectations on this head are however only founded on what Lord Grenville declares to be his own ideas of the subject at present, but as this business particularly concerns another department nothing conclusive can be relied on from a declaration thus expressly confined. There is every appearance of grain bearing a high price in Europe through the present year. Immense preparations are making for the next campaign; even the Pope is said to have a considerable body of forces on foot. This Country appears to be on the Eve of embarking in the general contest, their naval preparations are going on with vigour though the decisive measure of issuing press warrants has not yet been adopted. The most important intelligence you will find in the few Gazettes I send by the packet is the formal declaration of neutrality made by the Court of Spain to the Executive of the French Government through the avowed diplomatic Agent of his Catholic Majesty at Paris.

I have at length despaired of procuring proper persons in this Country[1] for undertaking the offices of Chief Coiner and Engraver in our mint for the salaries proposed; I have therefore refer'd the Matter to Mr. Morris: and this with the greater readiness as upon investigation I find that Mr. Droze who both on account of his integrity and ability would be a most valuable acquisition to us is employed in Paris not greatly to his satisfaction. With respect to an Assayer I have a prospect of soon engaging one here with such recommendations as will be satisfactory. I shall be very glad to be occasionally informed of the Progress of your negociation with Mr. Hammond, for though I carefully avoid every thing that may tend to remove the discussion to this side of the Atlantic yet the communication may be useful for the purpose of a more exact cooperation. The Dutch minister here (whom I consider very much in the same light with one of the Ministry of this Government) told me a few days ago that he knew Monr. Genest who is going in a diplomatic character from France to our Country, that he was artful and intriguing and he apprehended would endeavor to induce us in case of a naval[2] war to furnish the french West India Islands with provisions and to attempt to protect them in case of an attack. I answerd that it was evidently our interest and I could assure him our inclination to avoid all interference in the present disputes:— that we should undoubtedly sell to the French as much provision as they might have occasion for and as for anything farther it was always in the power of this country to induce us to be neuter. I have the honor to be with the utmost respect Dear Sir Your most obedient and most humble Servant   THOMAS PINCKNEY

RC (DNA: RG 59, DD); at foot of text: "The Secretary of State"; endorsed by TJ as received 12 Apr. 1793 and so recorded in SJL. PrC (ScHi: Pinckney Family Papers). Tr (Lb in DNA: RG 59, DD).

Pinckney allowed more than two months to elapse before he transmitted to TJ a fuller account of his proposals to Lord Grenville on the subject of EQUITABLE REGULATIONS CONCERNING SEAMEN (see Pinckney to TJ, 13 Mch. 1793). For a discussion of the background of TJ's interest in employing Jean Pierre Droz as chief coiner for the United States Mint, see Editorial Note on report on copper coinage, in Vol. 16: 335-42. At this time Pinckney was engaged in an effort

to employ a certain Mr. Marriot, who "has been 17 years in the Assay Office of the Goldsmiths Company, at London," as ASSAYER of the Mint. But this effort came to naught when Pinckney decided that he could not offer Marriot better terms of employment than those set by law (J. Alchorne to Pinckney, 3 Jan. 1793, DLC: Pinckney Family Papers; Pinckney to Marriot, 21 Jan. 1793, ScHi: Pinckney Family Papers). See also Pinckney to TJ, 12 Mch. 1793.

TJ submitted this letter to the President on 18 Apr. 1793, and Washington returned it the next day (Washington, *Journal*, 110, 114).

[1] Preceding three words interlined.
[2] Word interlined.

To John M. Pintard

SIR   Philadelphia. Jan. 3. 1793.

Your favor of Oct. 5. has been duly recieved. The Consular fees recieved at Madeira and Lisbon had before been the subject of application to me by some of our merchants. I thereupon wrote to Colo. Humphreys to inform me what those fees were and on what foundation they were taken. I have not yet recieved his answer. I shall be glad if you will also give me information on the subject. It would be of some consequence to know which of these fees would be given to some other person by the laws of the land, if our Consul refused them. As soon as full information could be obtained, I proposed that the whole should be laid before the Attorney general, with the act relative to Consuls, in order to have his opinion thereon. I am, with great esteem, Sir your most obedt. humble servt   TH: JEFFERSON

PrC (DLC); at foot of text: "J. M. Pintard, esq. Consul at Madeira." FC (Lb in DNA: RG 59, DCI).

Pintard's FAVOR OF OCT. 5, recorded in SJL as received 28 Dec. 1792, has not been found. The dispute over what fees

American consuls in Portuguese territory could legitimately charge seems not to have been settled while TJ was Secretary of State (see Pintard to TJ, 4 July 1793, and TJ to Pintard, 12 Sep. 1793). No letter from TJ to David Humphreys seeking information on this point has been found.

To William Short

DEAR SIR   Philadelphia Jan. 3. 1793.

My last private letter to you was of Oct. 16. since which I have recieved your[1] No. 103. 107. 108. 109. 110. 112. 113. and 114. and yesterday your private one of Sep. 15. came to hand. The tone of your[2] letters had for some time given me pain,[3] on account of the extreme warmth with which they censured the proceedings of the Jacobins of France. I considered that sect as the same with the Republican patriots, and the Feuillants as the Monarchical patriots, well known in the early part of the revolution, and but little distant in their views, both having in object the establishment of a free constitution, and differing only on the question whether their chief Executive should be hereditary or not. The Jacobins (as since called) yeilded to the Feuillants and tried the experiment of retaining their hereditary Executive. The experiment failed completely, and would have brought on the reestablishment of despotism had it been pursued.[4] The Jacobins saw this, and that the expunging that officer was of absolute necessity, and the Nation was with them in opinion, for however they might have been formerly for the constitution framed by the first assembly, they were come over from their hope in it, and were now generally Jacobins. In the struggle which was necessary, many guilty persons fell without the forms of trial, and with them some innocent. These I deplore as much as any body, and shall deplore some of them to the day of my death. But I deplore them as I should have done had they fallen in battle. It was necessary to use the arm of the people, a machine not quite so blind as balls and bombs, but blind to a certain degree. A few of their cordial friends met at their hands[5] the fate of enemies. But time and truth will rescue and embalm their memories, while their posterity will be enjoying that very liberty for which they would never have hesitated to offer up their lives. The liberty of the whole earth was depending on the issue of the contest, and was ever such a prize won with so little innocent blood? My own affections have been deeply wounded by some of the martyrs to this cause, but rather than it should have failed, I would have seen half the earth desolated. Were there but an Adam and an Eve left in every country, and left free, it would be better than as it now is. I have expressed to you my sentiments, because they are really those of 99 in an hundred of our citizens. The universal feasts, and rejoicings which have lately been had on account of the successes of the French shewed the genuine effusions of their hearts. You have been wounded by the sufferings of your friends, and have by this circumstance been hurried into a temper of mind which would be extremely disrelished if known to your countrymen. The reserve of *the Prest. of the U.S.*[6] had never permitted me to discover the light in which he viewed it, and as I was more anxious that you should satisfy him than me, I had still avoided explanations with you on the subject. But your 113. induced him to break silence and to notice the extreme acrimony of your expressions. He added that he had been informed the sentiments you expressed *in your conversations*[7] were equally offensive to our allies, and that you should consider yourself as the representative of your country and that what you say[8] might be imputed to your constituents. He desired me therefore to write to you on this subject. He added that he considered *France as the sheet anchor of this country and its friendship as a first object.* There are in the U.S. some characters of opposite principles; some of them are high in office, others possessing great wealth, and all of them hostile to France and fondly looking to England as the staff of their hope. These I named to you on a former occasion. Their prospects have certainly not brightened. Excepting them, this country is entirely republican, friends to the constitution, anxious to preserve it and to have it administered according to it's own republican principles. The little party above mentioned[9] have espoused it only as a stepping stone to monarchy, and have endeavored to approximate it to that in it's administration, in order to render it's final transition more easy. The successes of republicanism in France have given the coup de grace to their prospects, and I hope to their projects.—I have developed to you faithfully the sentiments of your country, that you may govern yourself accordingly. I know your republicanism to be pure, and that it is no decay of that which has embittered you against it's votaries in France, but too great a sensibility at the partial evil by which it's object has been accomplished there. I have written to you in the stile to which I have been always accustomed with you, and which perhaps it is time I should lay aside. But while old men feel sensibly enough their own advance in years, they do not sufficiently recollect it in those whom they have seen young. In writing too the last private letter which will probably be written under present circumstances, in contemplating that your correspondence will shortly be turned over to I know not whom, but certainly to some one not in the habit of considering your interests with the same fostering anxieties I do, I have presented things without reserve, satisfied you will ascribe what I have said to it's true motive, use it for your own best interest, and in that fulfill completely what I had in view.

With respect to the subject of your letter of Sep. 15. you will be sensible that many considerations would prevent my undertaking the reformation of a system of which I am so soon to take leave. It is but common decency to leave to my successor the moulding of his own business.—Not knowing how otherwise to convey this letter to you with certainty, I shall appeal to the friendship and honour of the Spanish commissioners here, to give it the protection of their cover, as a letter of private nature altogether. We have no remarkeable event here lately, but the death of Dr. Lee: nor have I any thing new to communicate to you of your friends or affairs. I am with unalterable affection & wishes for your prosperity, my dear Sir, your sincere friend and servant.

P.S. Jan. 15. Your Nos. 116. 117. and Private of Nov. 2 are received.—Congress have before them a statement of the *paiments to France*.[10] It appears none were made from *Dec. till Aug. nine*. This long previous suspension and *paiment* the day before the *tenth August begot suspicions on Gov. Morrise. Hamilton cleared* him and leaves it *on you by denying that Morris* had any thing to do with it, and *he clear[s]*[11] *himself by saying that you had no order[s]*[12] *from hence either for the suspension or paiment. Contrive to convey to me the truth of this* and I will have it so used for your justification as to clear you with all and injure you with *none*.[13]

RC (ViW); unsigned; partly in code, with Short's interlinear decipherment (see note 6 below), except for encoded passages in postscript supplied from accompanying Tr; at head of text: "Private"; at foot of first page: "Mr. Short"; endorsed by Short as received 25 Mch. 1793. PrC (DLC). Tr (ViW); undated; entirely in Short's hand; consists of small slip interfiled with RC bearing only cipher for encoded passages in postscript and Short's interlinear decipherment (see note 10 below). Enclosed in TJ to Josef Ignacio de Viar and Josef de Jaudenes, the Spanish agents in Philadelphia, 15 Jan. 1793, forwarding "a letter to Mr. Short which covers one from his brother on their private affairs, and one from Th:J. also entirely of a private nature," and requesting them to give the latter "the protection of their cover to some of their friends who will be so good as to deliver it" (PrC in DLC; Tr in DLC, 19th-century copy).

For the FORMER OCCASION, see note to TJ's second letter to Short of 28 July 1791. Short's SEP. 15 1792 letter had proposed reform of the American diplomatic establishment. DR. LEE:

Arthur Lee, the controversial Revolutionary diplomat and propagandist who had died the previous month in Virginia.

The STATEMENT OF THE PAIMENTS TO FRANCE was contained in Alexander Hamilton's report on foreign loans, which was submitted to the House of Representatives on 4 Jan. 1793 (Syrett, *Hamilton*, XIII, 451-62). Since Hamilton's remarks about Short and Gouverneur Morris did not appear in any of the reports he submitted to Congress at this time, they must have been made in private conversations (see Monroe to TJ, and TJ to Monroe, both 14 Jan. 1793). Despite TJ's suspicions, however, Hamilton's version of the roles played by Short and Morris in the matter of the French debt was basically correct. In January 1792, Short, who had been authorized by Washington and Hamilton to oversee the payment of the United States debt to France, decided of his own accord to suspend payments in anticipation of a formal request by the French government to use part of the American debt for the relief of Saint-Domingue, which was in the midst of a massive slave revolt. Before such a request could be made Short learned that he had been appointed minister to The Hague and Morris minister to Paris, in consequence of which he mistakenly assumed that Morris was now responsible for transacting the debt payments to France. Accordingly he relinquished this responsibility to Morris immediately upon the new minister's arrival in Paris in May 1792 and did not learn until the middle of August that Hamilton still regarded him as being responsible for the payment of the debt. In the meantime, owing to ministerial instability in France and differences over exchange rates, Morris and the Commissioners of the French Treasury were unable to agree on a resumption of payments until a few days before the downfall of the French monarchy on the TENTH AUGUST 1792, at which time Morris agreed to the payment of 1,625,000 florins to the French government. Morris thereupon directed Short, who by then was in the Netherlands, to instruct the American bankers in Amsterdam to transfer this sum to another banking firm in that city representing the French government, and although Short was initially reluctant to deal with the new revolutionary regime in Paris because of doubts about its legitimacy, he finally completed all arrangements for the payment early in September 1792. In the following month TJ and Hamilton respectively instructed Morris and Short to suspend further debt payments to France in view of the uncertain political situation in that country (TJ to Morris, 15 Oct. 1792; Hamilton to Short, 1-15 Oct. 1792, Syrett, *Hamilton,*

XII, 513-14; see also same, X, 479-80, 566, XI, 182-3, 400-2, 519, 594-6, XII, 104-5, 171-8, 293-6, 425-75, 624-6, 636-44, XIV, 432-6).

[1] Here TJ canceled "public letters."
[2] Here TJ canceled "public."
[3] Here TJ canceled "at least."
[4] TJ canceled "in a crisis" at the beginning of the next sentence.
[5] Preceding three words interlined.
[6] Except as noted below, these and subsequent words in italics are written in code and have been supplied from Short's decipherment, which has been verified by the Editors using partially reconstructed Code No. 10, the most significant discrepancies being recorded below.
[7] Words written *en clair* and underscored by TJ.
[8] Preceding three words interlined in place of "your sentiments."
[9] Here TJ canceled "composed of monocrats and aristocrats."
[10] TJ added the postscript in such a minuscule hand at the foot of the last page that Short copied the ciphers for this and subsequent encoded passages onto a separate slip and deciphered them.
[11] TJ encoded this word in the singular.
[12] Short inadvertently copied the code for this word onto the separate slip in the singular rather than in the plural used by TJ and deciphered it accordingly.
[13] Word written *en clair* and underscored in PrC; underscoring in RC eliminated by slight clipping at foot of page.

From Benjamin Smith Barton

SIR   Jan: 4th: 1793.

In consequence of your note, I have waited on Mr. Michaux. He assures me, that he will relinquish all thoughts of his journey to South-Carolina, and that he will engage in his scheme, as soon as you think proper. He seems much pleased with the prospect of having so valuable a guide, to Kaskaskia,[1] as the one you have pointed out, and will be happy to have an opportunity of conversing with the Indian, whenever you shall appoint a time, for the purpose.

I have ventured, this morning, to be very explicit with my friend on the *pecuniary* head. He seems content to undertake the arduous task (for such it, undoubtedly, is) with a very moderate assistance in the off-set. This assistance he does not even ask for until his arrival at Kaskaskia, where, he thinks, it would be p[roper] that he should have the "power" of drawing for the sum of One hundred guineas. Upon his return, he supposes (provided he shall make discoveries of any interesting importance) he shall be entitled to something handsome. In consequence of some conversation which I had with my uncle (Mr. D. Rittenhouse), last evening, I ventured to tell Mr. Michaux that I did not doubt his expectation would be gratified.

I shall be happy to have an opportunity of conversing with the Indian, on the subject of the journey. Meanwhile, I remain, with great respect, Sir, Your obliged and very humble Servant, &c.

B: S: BARTON

RC (MHi); one word partly torn away; endorsed by TJ as received 4 Jan. 1793 and so recorded in SJL.

Although clearly dated 2 Dec. 1792 and printed under that date in Vol. 24, it now seems clear that TJ's NOTE to Barton was actually written on 2 Jan. 1793. TJ obviously wrote this note when the French botanist André Michaux was in Philadelphia, but Michaux did not return to the city from a scientific expedition to Canada until 8 Dec. 1792, after which he waited another two days before first broaching the idea of a western expedition to members of the American Philosophical Society, to which TJ and Barton both belonged. Moreover, nothing in Barton's response indicates that a significant amount of time had elapsed between TJ's request that Barton confer with Michaux about his plans for western exploration

and Barton's compliance with it. Finally, the GUIDE TO KASKASKIA mentioned here and in TJ's note was undoubtedly Jean Baptiste Ducoigne, a Kaskaskia Indian chief who arrived in Philadelphia with other Western Indians late in December 1792 for a peace conference with the President. In light of this evidence, there can be no doubt that TJ misdated his note to Barton (see note to Minutes of a Conference with the Illinois and Wabash Indians, [1-4 Feb. 1793]; and C. S. Sargent, ed., "Portions of the Journal of André Michaux, Botanist, written during his Travels in the United States and Canada, 1785 to 1796," APS, *Proceedings*, XXVI [1889], 89-90). Barton's UNCLE, David Rittenhouse, was president of the American Philosophical Society.

[1] Preceding two words interlined.

To J. P. P. Derieux

DEAR SIR   Philadelphia Jan. 4. 1793.

We have been so long without a conveyance to Bordeaux that in the mean time I have recieved a letter from Mr. Fenwick dated Bordeaux Sep. 28. 1792. wherein he says 'The bill Mr. Derieux drew for 5000.^{tt} *is paid*, and which closes the account of his legacy, his brother or uncle having received the other 10,000.^{tt}'

I sincerely congratulate you on the triumphs of France over her enemies, and am with great esteem Dr. Sir Your most obedt. humble servt   TH: JEFFERSON

P.S. I return your letter for Mr. Fenwick, and Mr. Vaughan's memorandum.

PrC (DLC); at foot of text: "Mr. Derieux." Tr (ViU: Edgehill-Randolph Papers); 19th-century copy.

TJ enclosed this letter in one to Robert Gamble of the same date, asking him to seal and forward the missive after perusing it, "as it concerns a bill in which Colo. Gamble as well as Th:J. were interested" (PrC in DLC).

The LETTER for Joseph Fenwick, not found, had been enclosed in Derieux to TJ, 19 Nov. 1792. The MEMORANDUM by John Vaughan, also not found, is briefly described in Derieux to TJ, 10 Jan. 1793.

To Francis Eppes

DEAR SIR   Philadelphia Jan. 4. 1793.

The greatest council of Indians which has been or will be held in our day, is to be at the river Au glaise, about the South-West corner of L. Erie early in the spring. Three Commissioners will be appointed to go there on our part. Jack is desirous of accompanying them, and, tho' I do not know who they will be, I presume I can get him under their wing. The route I expect will be through Hudson's river, the Mohawks river, Lake Ontario and Lake Erie, and to return by Fort Pitt, Winchester &c. I imagine he can be at home in July. The expence will probably be 300. Dollars, rather more than less. He says you had agreed he should go to Boston in the spring which would cost within 100. Dollars as much. He can go there at any time, but will never have another chance for seeing so great a collection of Indians (probably 3000.) of nations from beyond the lakes and Missisipi: it is really important that those who come into public service should know more of those people than we generally do, and such a knowlege may often give a man a preference over competitors otherwise equal. I think it will be 4. or 5. months profitably employed, and know no reason against it but that Mrs. Eppes will be thinking about his scalp. However you may safely trust his where the Commissioners will trust theirs. I think both will be in perfect safety. We shall await your determination. I am with best affections to Mrs. Eppes & the family, Dear Sir your affectionate friend & servt   TH: JEFFERSON

P.S. They will set out early in February.

PrC (DLC); at foot of text: "Mr. Eppes." Tr (MHi); 19th-century copy.

For the background of the COUNCIL OF INDIANS planned for Auglaize, see Notes for a Conversation with George Hammond, [ca. 10 Dec. 1792], and note.

From Alexander Hamilton

SIR   Treasury Department Jany: 4 1792 [i.e. 1793]

I have the honor to inclose you the Copy of a letter I have received from Mr. Geo. Latimer of this City, relating to some concerns of his, with the Govt. of St. Domingo, to which I have answered in substance as heretofore communicated to you on a similar subject. I have the honour to be With Respect Sir Your Obed Servt   A HAMILTON

RC (DLC); misdated; in a clerk's hand, signed by Hamilton; at foot of text: "The Secretary of State"; endorsed by TJ as received 4 Jan. 1793 and so recorded in SJL. Enclosure: George Latimer to Hamilton, Philadelphia, 2 Jan. 1793, complaining of the refusal of French Consul General La Forest to honor bills of exchange for $7,927.37 drawn on him to pay for 1,500 barrels of flour Latimer had supplied to the government of Saint-Domingue in July 1792 (Tr in DLC; text printed in Syrett, *Hamilton*, XIII, 445-7).

For Hamilton's communication on a SIMILAR SUBJECT, see Hamilton to TJ, 14 Dec. 1792; see also Syrett, *Hamilton*, XIII, 443-5. There is no evidence that TJ ever corresponded with Latimer on the subject of his protested bills.

Notes on Alexander Hamilton's Report on Foreign Loans

[after 4 Jan. 1793]

The most prominent suspicion excited by the Report of the S. of the T. of Jan. 3. 1793. is that the funds raised in Europe and which ought to have been applied to the paiment of our debts there, in order to stop interest, have been drawn over to this country and lodged in the bank,[1] to extend the speculations and increase the profits of that institution.

To come at the truth of this, it becomes necessary to[2] arrange the articles of this Report into two accounts. viz.

1. An account of the funds provided *in Europe*, for which the treasury is to be debited: while it is to be credited for the application of these funds to such disbursements as they were by law appropriated to. The balance remaining on hand there, must still belong to the same purposes.
2. An account of the funds provided *in America* for the objects which are entered in this report, or may be brought forward to support it; which are to be Debited to the Treasury, while it is Credited for the applications of them to the purposes to which they have been appropriated by law.

The two following Accounts are raised on these principles.

The Treasury, for Receipts & Disbursements *in Europe*, in account

	Dr.		with the U.S. of America		Cr.

Dr.

(pa. 2.) To nett amount of monies borrowed in Amstdm. & Antwerp.

florins ƒ   D
18,678,000 (@ 99 = 40)

D
7,545,912

with the U.S. of America

By disbursements for the purposes to which the loans were appropriated by law. vz (bank law §.11.) To the bank for the subscription of the U.S.

Cr.

D
2,000,000

(pa. 2.)   To France
(pa. 3.)   for other foreign loans
Commission &ca
postage, & advertizing
interest to foreign officers
To Spain

ƒ   s
10,083,116–9
1,733,189–2–8
19,172.
613–8–8
105,000
680,000

12,621,091 =

balance stated to be in hands of the Commissioners
407,287–7–8 = 164,544 =
Deficit not found in their hands
282,447.24

5,098,920.76

446,991.24

7,545,912

Note. We have here admitted that the whole 2,000,000 D subscribed to the bank might have been paid out of the funds in Europe. Whereas in truth their subscription being on the 1st. Jan. 1792. there should have been paid on that day the first instalment only of 500,000 D. and before any other other instalment became due, there was the loan of 2,000,000 D. from the bank, on the same day, which might have been applied, so as to spare the European fund. There would then have remained 1,500,000 D. more in Europe to pay off the French debt and stop it's interest, instead of lying dead in the bank.[3] But wave this, because it admits some cavil.

The Treasury, for Receipts & Disbursements *in America* in Account with the U.S. of America

	Dr		Cr.
To Deficit in the *European* fund as per contra	282,447.24	(pa. 5.) By Departmt. of state for Barbary & foreign transactions [acts 90. July 1. c.22. 92. May 8. c.41.]	D 128,766.67
To loan from the bank	2,000,000	By paid to France for St. Domingo	445,263.83
To Surplusses of revenues approprd to Purchase of Public debt. (suppose)	967,821.65	By paid in purchase of Public debt [see Report of Commrs. of Nov. 17. 92. pa. 4.]	967,821.65
	3,250,268.89		1,541,852.15
		Balance remaining in bank ought to be 1,708,416.74. but if to avoid cavil, we admit the 191,316.90 D rightly drawn from Europe into the hands of the bank to pay *certain foreign officers* in Europe as by contract, then we must credit that sum	191,316.90
		the Balance in bank will then be 1,517,099.84	1,517,099.84[4]
			3,250,268.89
		The only possible deduction which could be made from[5] this balance further would be so much of the 967,821.65 D paid in purchase of the public debt as exceeds the Surplusses of Revenue applicable to that purchase. If there has been no surplus at all then from	1,517,099.84
		we must deduct the whole	967,821.65
		which would leave a balance in the bank still of	549,278.19

There being certainly then a balance of 549,278.19 D. and probably much more in the bank, there must have been a balance of 39,278.19 D. before[6] the last draughts for 510,000 D. were made in it's favor. Why then were they made? But to put these matters out of question two further statements are requisite. viz

1. The account of the U.S. with the bank, from which we may see whether the state of the account was such as to require this paiment?

2. a statement of the surplusses of revenue which actually arose, and might have been applied to the purchase of the publick debt. The amount of these surplusses are to be added to our balance against the bank.

MS (DLC: Madison Papers); entirely in TJ's hand; undated; brackets in original except in dateline; consists of one long sheet folded to make four pages, with notes on first page and accounts on second and third pages, the fourth being blank. PrC (DLC: TJ Papers, 96: 16478-80). PrC of Dft (same, 16481-2); undated; consists of two pages of entries forming a worksheet for accounts.

These notes, obviously intended for James Madison, consist of TJ's analysis of Alexander Hamilton's 3 Jan 1793 report on foreign loans; the House of Representatives received the report on the following day. TJ's references indicate that he used the text of the report printed by order of the House (Evans, No. 26350; Syrett, *Hamilton*, XIII, 451-62). At Washington's direction, Hamilton drew up the report in response to a 27 Dec. 1792 resolution of the House requesting a detailed statement of the disposition of foreign loans negotiated under presidential authority. The resolution had been prompted by debates over a Hamilton-inspired bill to pay the government's debt to the Bank of the United States (*Annals*, III, 753-61). TJ's MOST PROMINENT SUSPICION that Hamilton was guilty of misapplying foreign loans in the interest of the Bank of the United States was aroused by

Hamilton's revelation in this report that he had drawn to America and LODGED IN THE BANK some of the funds negotiated in Europe to discharge the foreign debt. Hamilton's subsequent explanation and defense of his action (Syrett, *Hamilton*, XIV, 46-57) failed to convince TJ and led to his involvement with House Republicans in the preparation of censure resolutions which severely criticized the Secretary of the Treasury on this issue. For the hypothesis that TJ set down and transmitted these notes to Madison sometime before 23 Jan. 1793, see Editorial Note on Jefferson and the Giles resolutions, at 27 Feb. 1793. REPORT OF COMMRS.: Report of the Commissioners of the Sinking Fund, [17 Nov. 1792].

[1] TJ first completed the sentence with "to enable them to extend their speculations and increase their profits" before altering the passage to read as above.

[2] Here TJ canceled "divide the."

[3] TJ appears to have added the following sentence after first ending the paragraph here and drawing the line underneath.

[4] Reworked from "1,541,852.15."

[5] Preceding six words interlined in place of "obligation which might discount."

[6] Word interlined in place of "when."

From the Commissioners of the Federal District

We have your two favors of the 13th and that of the 17th of last month before us. It appears to us more and more desirable to expedite the Stone-cutting by machinery, not more on account of the expence, which the State of our funds require to be attended to, than to insure the quantity wanted in time for we have as yet only about $\frac{1}{5}$ done of what would be wanted on the large scale of the President's house, to the water table of it. Mr. Harbaugh who is very ingenious and chearfully renders us every assistance in his power after seeing the Schetch inclosed by you a draft by Mr. Hallet and having, as it appears to us a perfect idea of Mr. Mullikin's plan, has made and shewn us a model of a Stone saw mill to be worked with horses or oxen on the principle of giving motion to the Saws by a Spiral Line, the Simplicity and cheapness of it and our hope of its effectual operation have induced us to desire him to set up one instantly which he has undertaken. We do not however rely on the success of this effort. We have agreed on the most generous Terms for the introduction of Foreigners and inclose you a Copy of them as well as our Letter open to Mr. Traquair. If the whole number, which we do not expect, should be engaged, we should be rather over burthened for the too probable State of our finances, otherwise we could wish to have the cut stone so forward that a sufficient number might be early spared to assist private buildings, which would tend to beautify the City. Messrs. Mason & Fenwick will have the charge of this business in France assisted by a Letter from Mr. Hallet. Mr. Delius's house, in Bremen, for Germany. Mr. Hoben has fallen on measures for some from Dublin as Mr. Williamson has for some from Scotland and we hope Mr. Traquair may succeed in part.

As it is not expected to get higher next year than the Water Tables, that is, 13 feet in elivation there are Carpenters enough who may be had on the spot and we shall want but a few additional Masons next season, for some in each line have already purchased and agreed to sink the price by their work, so that we think it can be no object to introduce others from Connecticut. Yet we are almost certain that there will be employment for a great many Mechanics in the City and Geo. Town next season in private building on Connecticut wages which are rather lower than here. The provisioning the workmen draws after it so many expences and so much waste that we have hitherto left them to provide for themselves. We are under the necessity of doing otherwise with the labourers, a part of whom we can easily make up of negroes and find it proper to do so. Those we have employed this summer have proved a very useful check and kept our affairs cool.

We have agreed with Mr. Blodget for his services and hope that his assistance will be very useful. He has great confidence in a Lottery. We find ourselves at liberty and agree to it. Our communications with him go into some particulars which we suppose need not be repeated here. Mr. Walker we understand will go soon to Scotland, any thing he could do there for us, we imagine may be done at least as well by Mr. Traquair through his correspondent, and we must be excused from giving signs of approbation and confidence that we do not feel.

Mr. Hallet looses nothing of our estimation of him: he has not been able to finish his plan so soon as he hoped, but says it shall be ready in about three weeks.

The survey seems to us very tedious and we know it is very expensive. We have had some explanations with Majr. Ellicott but do not yet know how they may end. Indeed in the other parts of our business we have necessarily not profusely entered into engagements to a great amount with officers, which will be thought extravigant unless our funds hold out to fill up with actual labour. Much depends on the next sales. On weighing every thing we think one sale the 17th Septr. gives the best chance. We are Sir With Regard & Respect Your most obedt. Servants

TH. JOHNSON
DD. STUART
DANL. CARROLL

RC (DLC); in a clerk's hand except for complimentary close and signatures; at foot of text: "Mr Jefferson"; endorsed by TJ as received 10 Jan. 1793 and so recorded in SJL. FC (DNA: RG 42, DCLB); contains minor variations in wording. Enclosures: (1) "Terms for Mechanics," [3 Jan. 1793], offering to advance up to 30/ sterling to mechanics in Europe for expenses and to pay their passage upon arrival in the Federal District, and to make the same advances for wives in some instances; promising to pay the same wages as mechanics of similar skills in the United States, namely the daily wage of 4/6 to 5/ sterling presently earned by stonecutters and good masons; giving assurances from the projected expenditure of $2,000,000 over eight years that there was "no probability of any considerable

decline of wages"; and stipulating that half their weekly wages would be retained until the advance and passage were repaid (FC in same, PC). (2) Commissioners to James Traquair, 2 Jan. 1793, requesting him to induce fifty plain stonecutters in Great Britain to emigrate to the United States to work in the Federal District, enclosing the "Terms for Mechanics," and inviting him to visit the Federal District for consultation (FC in same, DCLB).

Only one letter from TJ to the Commissioners of 13 Dec. 1792 is recorded in SJL and has been found. On 5 Jan. 1793 the Commissioners appointed Samuel BLODGET, Jr., "Supervisor of the Buildings" and their agent for the day-to-day business of the Federal District at £600 per annum in lots or money (DNA:

RG 42, PC; Commissioners to Blodget, 5 Jan. 1793, same, DCLB; Bryan, *National Capital*, I, 193-4).

TJ submitted the above letter and enclosures to the President on 10 Jan. 1793, and Washington returned them the next day "together with a draft of the Survey" of the Federal District and a request for TJ's opinion "whether they should be laid before Congress or not" (Washington, *Journal*, 6-7, 10).

From Alexander Donald

DEAR SIR   London 5th. January 1793

This day I have recieved your much esteemed favour of the 11th. Novemr. I am sorry that you should think it necessary to offer any apology for commanding my services. I will only say once for all, that the oftner you do so, the more you will oblige me. The window sashes will be ordered tomorrow and sent to Virginia the ensueing Spring if possible.

I will immediately apply to some of my Friends in Scotland to procure you if possible a good stone mason. There are plenty of them in that Country, but it is growing so rich that Fine Houses cannot be so fast built as they are wanted, nothing can induce a good workman therefore to leave his Country but some tempting offer. I wish you had given me some Idea of the wages you was willing to give. I shall be able to write you more fully on this subject by next Packet.

Great Preparations are making here for War. I still hope that such an event will not take place. I am very confident that our Ministry will do every thing in their power consistent with the honor and dignity of the Nation to avoid it, but it is impossible to reason on the measures which the National Convention of France may think proper to adopt. I hope however they will provoke this Country to go to war.[1] I have frequently been asked what part America would take in case of such an event. I have always said, that I am positive She will not take any part in it if she can possibly avoid it. She knows her own Interest better. I wish you most truely, the Compliments of the Season, & I remain with great consideration Dear Sir Your mo: obt. humb. St.

                                                                    A DONALD

RC (DLC); endorsed by TJ as received 23 Feb. 1793 and so recorded in SJL.

[1] Sentence thus in manuscript.

To James Carey

SIR   Philadelphia Jan. 6. 1793.

I will beg the favor of you to furnish the office of the Secretary of
state with your paper, sending it by post sealed up, and addressed to
the Secretary of state, not mentioning the name as that might produce
confusion in the accounts of the *office* and the *man*. Be so good as to let
me know the price, time of payment &c and it will be duly attended
to by Mr. George Taylor, chief clerk of the office. If you can send the
papers from the 1st. day of January, our year may as well begin then.
I am Sir Your very humble servt   TH: JEFFERSON

PrC (DLC); at foot of text: "Mr.
Carey. printer Richmond." Tr (DLC);
19th-century copy.

James Carey (d. ca. 1801), younger
brother of Mathew Carey, had begun publication of the *Virginia Gazette: and Richmond Daily Advertiser* on 1 Oct. 1792.
Shortly thereafter the PAPER became a tri-
weekly, ceasing publication early in 1793.
In March of that year Carey removed
to Charleston, South Carolina, where he
established another short-lived newspaper.

In the next seven years Carey started six
other papers, in Georgia, the Carolinas,
and Pennsylvania, none surviving longer
than two years. A radical Jeffersonian, by
1797 he had settled in Philadelphia where,
in the last years of his life, he published
successively the *Daily Advertiser, Carey's
United States' Recorder*, and the *Constitutional Diary* (Brigham, *American Newspapers*, II, 1149, 1388; PMHB, XCIV [1970],
333n, 334; *Bulletin of the New York Public
Library*, LIII [1949], 340).

From Gouverneur Morris

DEAR SIR   Paris 6 January 1793

Mr. Short, who is so kind as to take Charge of my Letters as far
as Bourdeaux, will go he says this Day. I therefore take the latest
Opportunity to write, and to inform you that the Appearances have
not at all changed since mine of the first. Dumouriez has been some
Days in Paris; He stays at Home under Pretence of Illness, but in
Fact to receive and consider the Propositions of the different Parties.
It would seem that he is not reconcild to Pache the Minister of War.
Pache is very strong in Paris, and that Circumstance renders him
formidable both to his Colleagues and to the Convention. I am told
that the Majority of the latter Body expect soon to be supported by
a considerable Number of Volunteers from the Departments. I am
also told, that it cannot be long before the Bursting of the Storm
which has been so long brewing. This last Intelligence is from one
of those who, tho a Promoter of the last Revolution, is now marked
as one of the Victims. He says he will die hard but laments the

Feebleness of Temper which he experiences among those who, like him, are doom'd to Destruction. On the other Hand, a Person of cool discerning Temper and Understanding, who is in the Confidence of those who direct the Jacobines, told me when I last saw him that *they* are determin'd to rule or perish. You will easily suppose that this Prevision of Horrors is far from pleasant. I have, I assure you, been not a little tempted to spend a few Days with some of my friends in the Country during the Festive Season, which would render such an Excursion natural, but the critical State of Things with Great Britain might take a Turn which it would be important for you to know and therefore it is right that I stay here. I am Sir with Esteem and Respect your obedient Servant   Gouv Morris

RC (DNA: RG 59, DD); at head of text: "No. 16"; at foot of first page: "Thomas Jefferson Esqr."; endorsed by TJ as received 22 Apr. 1793 and so recorded in SJL. FC (Lb in DLC: Gouverneur Morris Papers). Tr (DNA: RG 46, Senate Records, 3d Cong., 1st sess.). Tr (Lb in DNA: RG 59, DD).

TJ submitted this letter to the President on 23 Apr. 1793, and he returned it the same day (Washington, *Journal*, 118).

From John Bulkeley & Son

Sir   Lisbon 7th. January 1793.

We had the honour to receive the original and copy of your esteem'd favour 11th. October L. Y. the latter via London on the 10th. Ulto. and the other the 24th. Do. by the Ship Dominick Terry, Capn. De Hart, from your Port. It affords us pleasure to find you approv'd of the quality of the Termo white wine, we sent you, and desiring us to Ship for you three pipes of the same, by first conveyance bound to Richmond addressed to the care of Mr. James Brown, which will be complied with, and each Pipe cas'd as you direct. We also receiv'd your Bill of 225 Dollars your Currency, on Messrs. Donald & Burton of London, which we sent forward, and when we are advis'd the English Sum that will be given for it, as it mentioned no Exchange, will credit you the amount in Portse. Currency. We sincerely thank you for your friendship and politeness in recommending our Wines to your friends, and you may depend on our doing all justice, and Credit, in that or any other recommendations, you may honour us with. The present situation of the most part of Europe, anxiously looks towards the U.S. for supplies of grain as they all will be in want of bread towards next Spring. We receivd two Cargoes lately from Philadelphia, of wheat and Indian Corn, which we sold at about 420 rs. the one and 260 rs. the other 🜲 alqr. on board, which are as good prices as any of the surrounding Markets, would afford at present. Wishing you the Compliments of the Season & a series of happy years, we remain with Esteem.

Tr (MHi); at head of text: "Mr. Thomas Jefferson Monticello near Charlotteville Virginia"; conjoined to the firm's letter to TJ of 20 Feb. 1793; endorsed by TJ as received 12 Apr. 1793 but recorded in SJL as received 17 Apr. 1793. The missing RC is recorded in SJL as received 14 Mch. 1793.

TJ's FAVOUR of 11TH. OCTOBER L. Y. was his letter to Bulkeley & Son of 11 Oct. 1792, recorded in SJL but not found, which evidently enclosed the BILL

of exchange for $225 (see note to TJ to Alexander Donald, 11 Oct. 1792). The proceeds of the TWO CARGOES received from Philadelphia are quoted in réis per alquire, respectively the Portuguese unit of money and the Portuguese measure for dry commodities (see P[atrick] Kelly, *The Universal Cambist and Commercial Instructor* ..., 2d ed., 2 vols. [London, 1821], I, 210, 215). The Editors wish to thank Professor John J. McCusker of the University of Maryland for supplying this reference.

From David Humphreys

Lisbon, 7 Jan. 1793. He has received TJ's letter of 6 Nov. 1792, with postscript of the 7th, acknowledging receipt of his letters numbered 54 to 59. He presumes TJ meant to acknowledge receipt of numbers 44 to 59 or else the miscarriage of so many of his letters would not have gone unnoticed. "The last public Dispatch I had the honour to receive, previous to that which I now acknowledge, was dated the 9th.[1] of April 1792." Upon the receipt of the enclosed letter from Captain O'Bryen a few days ago, he interviewed Pinto, the Secretary of State for Foreign Affairs, about the report that Portugal was on the verge of signing a treaty with Algiers. The Secretary replied that, although the matter fell within the domain of the Minister of Marine, it was impossible for negotiations to be carried on without his knowledge, that he had often heard that minister declare he "would suffer his head to be cut off" before concluding a peace with Algiers that involved the payment of any money, which would be better employed in keeping a fleet than in bribing those pirates, and that there was no truth to the report. Although he had already believed this to be the case—a reliable gentleman having informed him a short time before that the Minister of Marine had told the last Portuguese ambassador who negotiated with Algiers that "'if he made a peace he would do well, but if he did not he would do better'"—he writes in this detail to prevent the alarm which the report would produce in America. He plans to answer O'Bryen's letter, the first he has received from him, as soon as possible, though communication is infrequent, difficult, and likely to be unproductive. P.S. He will also send Carmichael a copy of his letter to O'Bryen in order to learn whether the debts due for the subsistence of the prisoners in Algiers have been ascertained and if their future subsistence has been arranged, so that the money may be paid.

RC (DNA: RG 59, DD); 4 p.; at head of text: "(No. 63.)"; at foot of text: "The Secretary of State &c. &c. &c."; with notations in TJ's hand (see note 1 below);

endorsed by TJ as received 14 Mch. 1793 and so recorded in SJL. Tr (Lb in same). For the letter from Richard O'Bryen, which Humphreys forgot to enclose, see Humphreys to TJ, 23 Jan. 1793, and note.

TJ submitted this letter to the President on 14 Mch. 1793 (Washington, *Journal*, 90).

[1] TJ attached an asterisk to the beginning of this date to serve as a key to a note he penciled lengthwise in the margin: "My letter of July 12. acknoleged the receipt of his Nos. 45. to 53. This must have miscarried. It was merely a letter of common intelligence."

To Thomas Mann Randolph, Jr.

DEAR SIR   Philadelphia Jan. 7. 1793.

Our news from France continues to be good, and to promise a continuance. The event of the revolution there is now little doubted of, even by it's enemies. The sensations it has produced here, and the indications of them in the public papers, have shewn that the form our own government was to take depended much more on the events of France than any body had before imagined. The tide which, after our former relaxed government, took a violent course towards the opposite extreme, and seemed ready to hang every thing round with the tassils and baubles of monarchy, is now getting back as we hope to a just mean, a government of laws addressed to the reason of the people, and not to their weaknesses. The daily papers shew it more than those you recieve.—An attempt in the house of representatives to stop the recruiting service has been rejected. Indeed the conferences for peace, agreed to by the Indians, do not promise much, as we have reason to believe they will insist on taking back lands purchased at former treaties.—Maria is well. We hope all are so at Monticello. My best love to my dear Martha and am most affectionately Dear Sir your's &c.   TH: JEFFERSON

RC (DLC); at foot of text: "Mr. Randolph." PrC (DLC).

On 20 Dec. 1792 John Steele, a Federalist representative from North Carolina, introduced a resolution in the House of Representatives to reduce the size of the regular army, citing the need for a more effective form of frontier defense and the desirability of applying the resultant savings to the reduction of the public debt so as to avoid new taxes. During the ensuing debates on this resolution, Steele urged that greater reliance be placed on the militia to defend the western frontier against Indian attacks. At the same time, Hugh Williamson, another North Carolina Federalist, offered an amendment to Steele's resolution that proposed to STOP THE RECRUITING SERVICE at a specified date instead of immediately reducing the size of the army. Williamson's amendment and Steele's resolution were both rejected in committee of the whole on 5 Jan. 1793 and in the full House three days later (*Annals*, III, 750, 762-8, 773-90, 791-802).

To David Rittenhouse

Jan. 7. 1793.

Th: Jefferson, beginning to pack his useless furniture, finds nothing more so than the article he now sends to Mr. Rittenhouse. He wishes he could propose it to his acceptance for a better reason: but if two bad reasons will make one good one, to that of the *uselessness of the thing* he will add (what will be equally useless to him) *the sincere affection of the giver*; as a testimony of which he desires Mr. Rittenhouse to give it house-room.

PrC (DLC); addressed: "Mr. Rittenhouse." Tr (DLC); 19th-century copy.

The ARTICLE sent by TJ was undoubtedly one of the plaster busts of himself executed by Houdon, which TJ had purchased in 1789. The bust remained in the Rittenhouse family until 1811 when Elizabeth Rittenhouse Sergeant donated it to the American Philosophical Society, which had it bronzed and placed on exhibit (MB, 3 July 1789; Alfred L. Bush, *The Life Portraits of Thomas Jefferson*, rev. ed. [Charlottesville, 1987], 11-14; APS, *Proceedings*, XXII, pt. 3 [1885], 427, 430; Fiske Kimball, "The Life Portraits of Jefferson and their Replicas," same, LXXXVIII [1944], 505-7, with illustration; Brooke Hindle, *David Rittenhouse* [Princeton, 1964], 336).

From David Rittenhouse

SIR   Januy. 7. 1793.

I have herewith enclosed the result of our Assays &c. of the Coins of France, England, Spain, and Portugal. In the course of the Experiments a very small source of Error was detected, too late for the present occasion, but which will be carefully guarded against in future. I am with the most perfect esteem, Your most obedient humble servant

DAVD. RITTENHOUSE
Director of the Mint

Tr (DNA: RG 59, MLR); in the hand of George Taylor, Jr.; marked "(Copy)"; at head of text in a different ink: "A."; at foot of text: "T. Jefferson, Secretary of State." PrC (DLC). PrC of another Tr (DNA: RG 59, MLR); in Taylor's hand; marked "(Copy)." Tr (Lb in same, SDR). Enclosed in Report on Foreign Coinage, 8 Jan. 1793, and TJ to George Washington, 8 Jan. 1793.

ENCLOSURE
Assay of Foreign Coins
Assay of Gold coins

	Date	Fine Gold		Alloy		specific gravity
		Grs.	32d Parts	grs.	32d parts	
French Guineas	1726	21.	16	2.	16	17. 48
	1734	21.	19	2.	13	17. 38
	1742	21.	26	2.	6	17. 58
	1753	21.	3	2.	29	17. 23
	1775	21.	22	2.	10	17. 57
Double do.	1786	21.	22	2.	10	17. 51
	1789	21.	22	2.	10	17. 50
	1790	21.	25	2.	7	17. 57
Spanish Pistoles	1776	21.	21	2.	11	17. 53
	1780	21.	0	3.	0	17. 57
	1786	21.	18	2.	14	17. 63
	1788	21.	2	2.	30	17. 0

	Date	Fine Gold		Alloy		specific gravity
		Grs.	32d parts	Grs.	32d parts	
English Guineas	1755	21.	28	2.	4	17. 78
	1777	21.	31	2.	1	17. 75
	1785	21.	30	2.	2	17. 78
	1788	21.	31	2.	1	17. 79
	1789	22.	3	1.	29	17. 78
	1791	22.	1	1.	31	17. 74
Half Joannes' of Portugal	1739	21.	31	2.	1	17. 63
	1770	22.	5	1.	27	17. 78
	1776	22.	5	1.	27	17. 87
	1785	21.	30	2.	2	17. 68
	1788	21.	31	2.	1	17. 78

Silver Coins

		In 12 Ounces		
		Fine Silver	Alloy	
		Oz. dwt. grs.	Oz. dwt. grs.	
English half Crown of Willm. III	1787	10. 19. 9½	1. 0. 14½	
Engl. Shillg.	1791	11. 0. 0	0. 19. 21½	
French Crown	1739	10. 16. 0	1. 4. 0	
do. Half Crown	1792	10. 17. 0	1. 3. 0	
do.		10. 16. 19	1. 3. 5	

		In 12 Ounces		
		Fine silver	Alloy	
		Oz. dwt. grs.	Oz. dwt. grs.	
Spanish Dollar of	1772	10. 15. 5	1. 4. 19	
do.	1782	10. 14. 2½	1. 5. 21½	
do.	1790	10. 14. 0	1. 6. 0	
do.	1791	10. 14. 21½	1. 5. 2½	

Assayed by Mr. David Ott, under my Inspection, at the Mint, in pursuance of a resolution of Congress of Nov. 29th. 1791. I have added the specific gravity of each piece of Gold Coin.

DAVD. RITTENHOUSE Director of the Mint

Mint January 7. 1793.

Tr (DNA: RG 59, MLR); in the hand of George Taylor, Jr.; marked "(Copy)"; at head of text in a different ink: "B." PrC (DLC). PrC of another Tr (DNA: RG 59, MLR); in a clerk's hand. Tr (Lb in same, SDR). Enclosed in Report on Foreign Coinage, 8 Jan. 1793, and TJ to George Washington, 8 Jan. 1793. TJ also sent the assays to Congressman John Page of Virginia, for he wrote a brief note of this date to his longtime friend covering "the result of Mr. Rittenhouse's experiments" (Tr in DLC: TJ Papers, 81: 13968; undated; 19th-century copy).

From Jean Baptiste Ternant

MONSIEUR   Philadelphie 7. de Janvier 1793.

J'ai l'honneur de vous addresser la copie d'une réquisition que vient de me faire parvenir la Commission nationale, chargée d'exercer l'autorité suprême de la Métropole à St. Domingue. Dans des circonstances assez interessantes au salut de la colonie pour avoir pû nécessiter une réquisition de cette nature, j'estime que, malgré le défaut d'instructions ministerielles ad hoc, et malgré les justes observations contenues dans votre reponse officielle du 20 Nove. dernier, je n'en dois pas moins renouveller mes sollicitations auprès du Gouvernement des Etats Unis, et le presser de venir complettement au secours de St. Domingue sur la base du decret dont j'ai eû l'honneur de vous donner connoissance, en pourvoyant, tant au payement des traites Coloniales non encore acceptées qu'à la solde du complément des quatre millions, de maniere à ce que ce dernier objet puisse être employé aussitôt à des achats de vivres pour la Colonie.

D'après les dispositions favorables dans lesquelles j'ai toujours trouvé le gouvernement des Etats Unis, j'ose esperer que dans la circonstance actuelle, il ne se refusera pas de concourir efficacement au salut d'une colonie utile à son propre commerce, en fournissant à nos Commissaires nationaux les moyens qu'ils requierent comme indispensables au succès de leurs opérations.

J'ai l'honneur de joindre ici un etat des traites non acceptés, avec un tableau indicatif des epoques de payment; d'où il resulte que sauf erreur dans l'evaluation des traites inconnues, il ne restera à employer pour un envoy immédiat de vivres à St. Domingue, qu'environ trente six mille piastres formant le complément des quatre Millions, au pair de change précédemment convenu entre nous.

Je vous prie, Monsieur, de vouloir bien, en mettant cette lettre sous les yeux du President, solliciter une décision favorable au voeu de la réquisition qui s'y trouve jointe. J'ai l'honneur d'être avec les sentimens les plus parfaits d'estime et de respect, Monsieur, Votre très humble et très obeissant serviteur   TERNANT

Tr (NNC: Gouverneur Morris Papers); in the hand of George Taylor, Jr.; at foot of text: "(copy)" and "Monsieur Jefferson, Secretaire d'Etat." PrC (DLC); dateline torn. Tr (AMAE: CPEU, xxxvii); at head of text: "Duplicata"; contains variations in wording not recorded here. Tr (same, Supplément, xx); contains variations in wording not recorded here. Tr (MHi); 19th-century copy. Recorded in SJL as received 7 Jan. 1793. Enclosures: (1) Requisition by Léger Félicité Sonthonax, Saint-Domingue, 9 Dec. 1792, urgently requesting Ternant, on the basis of a 26 June 1792 decree of the French Legislative Assembly and despite the lack of express ministerial instructions, to obtain from the United States government a further sum of money for the purchase of provisions for Saint-Domingue and especially for the bills of exchange already issued by the government of the colony for such purchases (Tr in NNC: Gouverneur Morris Papers, in French, in Taylor's hand, at head of text: "Copie," at foot of text: "pour copie conforme à l'original Ternant"; PrC in DLC; Tr in AMAE: CPEU, xxxvii, in a clerk's hand on printed form, at head of text: "Duplicata"). (2) Statement by Antoine René Charles Mathurin de La Forest, 6 Jan. 1793, listing unpaid drafts by the government of Saint-Domingue amounting to $237,999.84, with a table indicating the dates of payment (Tr in AMAE: CPEU, xxxvii; in French). Letter and Enclosure No. 1 enclosed in TJ to Gouverneur Morris, 12 Mch. 1793.

Léger Félicité Sonthonax, Etienne Polverel, and Jean Antoine Ailhaud formed the COMMISSION NATIONALE which the Legislative Assembly had appointed in the spring of 1792 to take control of the government of Saint-Domingue and suppress the slave revolt on the island (Thomas O. Ott, *The Haitian Revolution, 1789-1804* [Knoxville, 1973], 65-6). The Legislative Assembly's DECRET of 26 June 1792 had authorized the French executive to negotiate an agreement with the American minister in Paris to use 4,000,000 livres of the United States debt to France for the relief of Saint-Domingue, but no such agreement was ever made (*Archives Parlementaires*, 1st ser., XLV, 594-5). For a discussion of the problems caused by the refusal of the French consul general in Philadelphia to honor TRAITES drawn on him by the government of Saint-Domingue for the purchase of supplies from American merchants, see Syrett, *Hamilton*, XIII, 443-5. The previous arrangements with Ternant for relieving the embattled French regime on Saint-Domingue are described in notes to TJ to Ternant, 7 Mch. and 20 Nov. 1792. See also TJ to Ternant, 14 Jan. 1793.

From Ernst Frederick Guyer

SIR   Philadelphia January 8th. 1793.

I do not know how to apologize for the boldness wherewith I again intrude upon your weightier concerns. The affability wherewith you have received me before; the approbation you have been pleased to bestow upon some of my work; and the disagreeable situation I find myself in at present, will, I trust, plead in my behalf with a Man, who is the avowed patron of arts and in whom the distressed have always found a protector. My Situation is really distressing: I have tried these two years past all what laid in my power to establish myself either as a mathematical instrument maker, or in erecting a type foundary. In the first profession I find it in vain to attempt any thing; and in the second, I have met with such and so many obstacles, as to render all my endeavours unsuccessful.

It is well known that the type founding business is a most profitable one when once established; but that it requires both time and money to bring it to any degree of perfection, and without that it is impossible to do any thing. I experience this at present in a high degree, as I have not as much work as is sufficient to maintain myself, whereas if I had once a beginning, I should be able in a reasonable time to make such an establishment as would yield an ample competence to me and be of benefit to the public. It is true, partnerships for the typefounding business have been offered to me, but the terms were such, that I should have been the slave of others, with hardly a prospect of a competence for myself: I could therefore not possibly accept them. I am now quite out of work, but if I had a sufficient sum to begin a typefoundary with, I am sure of encouragement, as the most eminent printers here in town have made me promises to that purpose. A moderate sum would be sufficient to begin with. To finish the punches &c. for Long Primer would take nine months and a fount of 2000 ℔. might be cast during the same time, which would cost about 420 Doll: and the value thereof would be about 800 Dollars. A sum of six hundred Dollars would therefore be sufficient to begin with (some money being required for the purchase of some tools and for my maintenance during the first nine months) and in case the sale of the types was as rapid, as I have reason to expect, these six hundred Dollars might be sufficient to erect a compleat foundary, which would take about 8 years. If I could find a generous man who would assist a young man who wishes to establish himself but who now is obliged to waste his best time in doing nothing, or at least little better than nothing, and would advance him six hundred Dollars, he might depend upon being repaid in a few years with a good interest, besides the godlike pleasure of being the cause of the happiness of a young man and perhaps of a future family. I have had honor to work for you, and as I flatter myself was so fortunate as to meet with your approbation: Whom could I then implore for assistance with more hopes of success, than you, Sir; have pity on my situation, have pity on a young artist, who wishes to render himself useful, and who is capable of being so, if the means to begin with are only granted him; grant him these means, and his gratitude can only end with his life. It would be his constant endeavour to merit this favor by his industry, strict attention to business and the goodness of his work, and to shew by the general tenor of his conduct, that this favor has not been bestowed unworthily. I have the honor to be with utmost respect Sir Your most obedient and most humble servant   ERNST FREDERICK GUYER

RC (DLC); addressed: "The Honorable Thomas Jefferson Esquire Secretary of State of the United States of North-America"; endorsed by TJ as received 8 Jan. 1793 and so recorded in SJL.

On 12 Dec. 1792 Guyer had sent a similar letter to Alexander Hamilton, praying for his patronage in establishing a type foundry (Syrett, *Hamilton*, XIII, 316-17).

To Ernst Frederick Guyer

SIR   Philadelphia Jan. 8. 1793

I am really sorry that I cannot, by the advance of 600 Dollars enable you to set up the Type-founder's business: but it is entirely out of my power for reasons respecting my private affairs which need not be explained. Your wish to set out on a plan which would require capital, but would produce profit in proportion, is natural to a young artist. I wish you may be able to do it: but you will surely not be discoraged should the ordinary course of young artists prove to be yours, that of struggling against difficulties, and having patience till time, industry and talents can enable them to set up for themselves. I am with wishes for your success Sir your most humble servt   TH: JEFFERSON

PrC (DLC); at foot of text: "Mr. Frederick Gayer." Tr (ViU: Edgehill-Randolph Papers); 19th-century copy.

From David Humphreys

MY DEAR SIR   Lisbon Janry 8th. 1793

Although I was well acquainted with your reluctance to come into the office you hold, having seen the letters which passed on the subject; yet I cannot avoid being much distressed by your determination to quit it so soon. I entertained hopes that a desire to assist the President in the execution of his important office, together with some other motives resulting from a consciousness of your abilities and dispositions to render service to your Country, would have withheld you from your favourite retirement, at least, a few years longer. Since you have judged otherwise, be assured, my dear Sir, my best wishes and real friendship will attend you to the domestic and philosophic walks of life. I will not say how much I envy the situation of those who are competent to retire from the noise and jarrings of the great world at a reasonably early hour. But I will say, that the strong feelings I possess in favour of my Country and its Government are every day heightened by what I see or hear in other Countries. If I was a true Republican, when I left America, I flatter myself I shall not become the less so by my absence from it. However I study most earnestly to avoid giving offence to the Government or People where I reside. And for this purpose the virtues of silence are uncommonly necessary.

I have attended to your intimation respecting the admission of our flour, and I can only promise that zeal on my part in attempting to promote the interests of the U.S. shall not be wanting. This Country affords little curious for your amusement, but in case I may find any thing I apprehend will contribute towards it, I shall take a particular pleasure in the communication. And in all events shall be extremely happy to hear from you whenever your leisure will permit. In sincerely wishing that your successor in office may be as useful to the Public, as acceptable to the President, and as friendly to myself, as I have ever found you; I conclude by offering the heartfelt homage of esteem & respect, with which I have the honour to be, My dear Sir, Your most obedient & Most humble Servant   D. HUMPHREYS

P.S. If I can be any ways useful to you while abroad, or whenever I may return home, I beg you will command my services with unlimited confidence of being cheerfully obeyed.

RC (DLC); at head of text: "(Private.)"; below signature: "Mr. Jefferson &c. &c. &c." endorsed by TJ as received 14 Mch. 1793 and so recorded in SJL.

Humphreys had been privy to the LET-TERS exchanged between TJ and Washington concerning TJ's appointment as Secretary of State because at the time he was serving as one of the President's secretaries.

Report on Foreign Coinage

The Secretary of State, to whom was referred by the President of the United States, the Resolution of the House of Representatives of the 29th. of Novr. 1792. on the subject of Experiments on the Coins of France, England, Spain, and Portugal,
REPORTS
          That assays and experiments have been accordingly made at the Mint by the Director, and under his care and inspection, of sundry Gold and Silver Coins of France, England, Spain and Portugal, and a statement of the quantity of fine metal and Alloy in each of them, and the specific gravities of those of Gold given in by the Director, a

copy of which, and of the letter covering it, are contained in the papers marked A. and B.   TH: JEFFERSON

Jan. 8. 1793.

Pr C (DNA: RG 59, MLR); in the hand of George Taylor, Jr., signed and dated by TJ in ink. Tr (same); in Taylor's hand, signature and date by TJ clipped; endorsed by Tobias Lear. Pr C (DLC). FC (Lb in DNA: RG 59, SDR). Recorded in SJPL. Enclosure: David Rittenhouse to TJ, 7 Jan. 1793, with enclosed Assay of Foreign Coins. Enclosed in TJ to the Speaker of the House of Representatives, 8 Jan. 1793, and TJ to George Washington, 8 Jan. 1793.

This report grew out of a recommendation in the President's fourth annual message to Congress of 6 Nov. 1792 that the legislature complete its consideration of regulations to fix the value of foreign coins in connection with the establishment of the United States Mint the previous April. On 16 Nov. the House received from the Senate a bill to regulate the value of foreign coins in the United States. After reading and amending the bill, the House decided on 28 Nov. to recommit it to the committee of the whole on the first Monday in January 1793. In the meantime, in order to obtain information on the coins, the House resolved on the following day to request the President "to cause assays and other proper experiments to be made, at the Mint of the United States, of the gold and silver coins of France, England, Spain, and Portugal; and a report of the quantity of fine metal, and of alloy, in each of the denominations of the coins, to be laid before this House" (JHR, I, 620-1, 626, 627, 629, 630; JS, I, 454, 458). Washington referred this resolution to

TJ, whose department had jurisdiction over the Mint, and the assays were carried out by David Ott, a temporary employee of the Mint, under the supervision of David Rittenhouse, the Mint's director. Rittenhouse sent the results of the assays to TJ on 7 Jan. 1793, the day the House was supposed to reconsider the foreign coinage bill, but lacking the assays, the House took no action on the measure. Meanwhile, TJ prepared the above report and drafted a covering message to the House for the President (see note to TJ to Washington, 8 Jan. 1793); the message was not used, however, and TJ submitted the report to the House this day with his own covering letter to the Speaker.

The House read and tabled TJ's report the same day it was submitted and did not resume consideration of the foreign coinage bill until 29 Jan. After amendments were made in the House and Senate, the bill received Washington's approval on 9 Feb. 1793. In its final form the act established the value at which certain British, French, Portuguese, and Spanish coins would circulate as legal tender in the United States for three years after the Mint began to issue coinage, beyond which period all but the Spanish milled dollar would have to be recoined by the Mint, and stipulated that no foreign coins issued after 1791 could be legal tender unless their value was shown by assay to meet the required standards (JHR, I, 663, 685, 687, 688, 695, 698; JS, I, 476, 477, 480, 481, 482; Annals, III, 1412-13; Taxay, Mint, 102-3).

To the Speaker of the House of Representatives

SIR   Philadelphia Jan. 8. 1793.

I have the honor to inclose you a Report of the assays and experiments made on the gold and silver coins of France, Spain, England and Portugal, in pursuance of the resolution of the House of Representatives of Nov. 29. 1792. and of assuring you of those sentiments of respect & esteem with which I am Sir Your most obedient & most humble servt   TH: JEFFERSON

PrC (DLC); at foot of text: "The Speaker of the H. of Representatives." FC (Lb in DNA: RG 59, SDR). Not recorded in SJL. Enclosure: Report on Foreign Coinage, 8 Jan. 1793.

From Jean Baptiste Ternant

Philadelphie 8 Janvier L'an 2 de la Republique

Deux objets qui intéressent le service de ma nation m'obligent de recourir encore au Gouvernement des Etats unis. Il sagit de pourvoir aux besoins pressans que la difficulté[1] de placer des traites sur france fait éprouver depuis longtems à nos agens consulaires et de mettre celui d'entr'eux qui reside à Boston, en état de Solder un envoy de vivres qu'il a été ministeriellement autorisé de faire à St. Pierre et Miquelon,[2] et qu'il va ne pouvoir acquitter à l'échéance du contrat, par l'impossibilitè actuelle de faire valoir à cet effet une traite sur notre trésor national. Pour remplir convenablement le premier de ces objets, il faudroit huit mille deux cens piastres, et le second en exigeroit dix huit cens. Je crois ne pouvoir mieux faire dans la circonstance, que de proposer au Gouvernement des Etats unis,[3] d'avancer encore ces deux sommes aux conditions stipulées pour les fonds relatifs au Service de St. Domingue, et d'en mettre le montant à la disposition[4] du Sieur Laforest qui l'employera sur sa responsibilité.

Voulez vous bien, Mr. mettre cette proposition sous les yeux du Président, et l'assurer[5] que je ne me Suis déterminé à la faire que dans l'intime persuasion, que le Gouvernement français verra avec satisfaction un mode circonstanciel de remboursement qui pourvoit au maintien de Ses agens et de Son Service national au dehors.

Signé TERNANT

Tr (AMAE: CPEU, xxxvii); at head of text: "Lettre du Ministre plenipo. au Sécrétaire d'Etat Américain." Tr (same, Supplément, xx); contains variations in wording, the most important of which are noted below. Recorded in SJL as received 8 Jan. 1793.

For the background of this letter, see TJ to Washington, 1 Jan. 1793.

[1] Tr in Supplément: "l'impossibilité."
[2] Remainder of sentence in Tr in Sup-

plément: "et que la défaveur des traites l'empecher a d'acquitter à l'echeance du contrat."
[3] Tr in Supplément: "à votre gouvernement."
[4] Remainder of sentence in Tr in Supplément: "du Consul General Laforest."
[5] Remainder of sentence to "un mode" in Tr in Supplément: "de l'intime persuasion où je suis que le gouvernement francois ne peut manquer d'approuver."

To George Washington

8 January 1793.

Th: Jefferson has the honor to inclose to the President 3 copies of the papers on the subject of the Coins. He does not see however that it is necessary to send one to the Senate, unless usage has rendered it so.

He has retained the Directors *original* statement, thinking it ought to be of record in his Office, as it may be the foundation of a Law.

Tr (Lb in DNA: RG 59, SDC); at head of text: "The President of the United States." Not recorded in SJL. Enclosures: (1) David Rittenhouse to TJ, 7 Jan. 1793, with enclosed Assay of Foreign Coins. (2) Report on Foreign Coinage, 8 Jan. 1793. (3) Washington to the House of Representatives, [8 Jan. 1793]: "According to the request expressed in your Resolution of the 29. of November, I have caused Assays and other proper experiments to be made at the mint of the united States, of the gold and silver coins of France, England, Spain, and Portugal, and now lay before you the result" (MS in DNA: RG 59, MLR; undated text prepared by TJ but in the hand of a clerk, with "Gentlemen of the House of Representatives" at head of text and endorsement by Tobias Lear: "From The Secretary of State Jany 8th: 1793"; PrC of Tr in same, undated and in a clerk's hand; not sent by the President).

From John Butler

SIR   St. Christopher January 9th. 1793.

I have taken the Liberty of inclosing a Sketch of the Affairs of Martinique and Guadeloupe, as they Stood About the 20th. Ulto. Since that time a Parcell of Vagabonds who Call themselves Patriots, headed by Some Merchants, have forced Gouvernor D'Arot, to quit the Island, and he is now here. The other Islands and this, Swarm, with the old Men, Women and Children of the Most opulent Planters who have been forced away by the Rabble. Of all the Revolutions ever heared of this of France (if their Gasconades are to be attend to,) portends most towards bringing the World under their Dominion. I think it is fortunate your Republick happens to be so far away from those Alexanders!

I hope you will forgive this trouble from one who has not the Honor of Knowing you but by your fame, and your Labours for the good of Mankind and your Country. I wish you Long Life & good Health & am Sir Your Very obedient Servant

JOHN BUTLER
Barrister at Law at St. Kitts

RC (DLC); endorsed by TJ as received 25 Feb. 1793 and so recorded in SJL. The enclosure was probably "A Friend to Liberty," *A Vindication of the planters of Martinique & Guadaloupe against the charges made on them by their enemies. In a letter addressed to His Excellency the* *Viscount d'Arot Governor of Guadaloupe* (1793). See Sowerby, No. 2564.

From C. W. F. Dumas

The Hague, 9 Jan. 1793. The lessons offered by the quarrelsome Europeans can make the good American people thankful for the wisest and most virtuous government in the world and the constitutions which assure it. Behold the king of England, who seems determined to add to the disorder by joining with his hereditary Continental cousins and risks drowning with them like Pharoah, thus atoning for the war of 1779-84. Here it has been decided to increase the land force by 18,000 men. He encloses the French newspapers left behind by Short, who departed from here again; he has continued them for the next six months and will send them as often as possible. P.S. 9 Jan. Having just received TJ's letter of 14 Nov. 1792, he is grieved by the news of his approaching retirement, although consoled by TJ's kind recollection of him, and hopes TJ will recommend him to his successor as a faithful servant of the United States, in the certainty of whose continuing happiness he will die contentedly.

FC (AR: Dumas Letterbook); 1 p.; in French; at head of text: "No. 92" and "A S.E.M. Ths. Jefferson, Min. d'Et. & des Affes. etr. en Congrès des Et. Un." Recorded in SJL as received 13 Mch. 1793 with a "private" letter from Dumas, a designation TJ may have assigned to the postscript.

From Andrew Ellicott

SIR   Geo. Town Jany. 9th 1793

From a conversation which I had with you some time ago, I remember you was desirous of discovering the Indian name of the Eastern Branch of the Potomak: by some old surveys it appears to be *Annakostia.*

The reasons of my disagreement with the Commissioners, and ultimate determination to quit the business of the City of Washington, on the first day of May next, shall be published immediately after that date: And I have no doubt, but that from a clear investigation of facts, my conduct, and exertions, will be approved of, by the candid and discerning. I am with much esteem Your Real Friend

ANDREW ELLICOTT

RC (DLC); at foot of text: "Honble Thomas Jefferson Esqr"; endorsed by TJ as received 12 Jan. 1793 and so recorded in SJL. The often strained relationship between Ellicott and the Commissioners of the Federal District threatened to reach a breaking point early in January 1793 when the Commissioners criticized his survey of the Federal District as having been too dilatory and sometimes erroneous. Despite the DETERMINATION to resign as chief surveyor of the Federal District and publicly criticize the Commissioners that Ellicott expressed in the present letter, which the Secretary of State shared with the President, TJ and Washington were averse to any controversy that might delay work on the new capital. They dissuaded Ellicott from following this course and convinced him to continue as chief surveyor, even though the Commissioners actually dismissed him from their employ in March 1793. Soon after Ellicott's reinstatement in April, however, he accepted a surveying commission from the government of Pennsylvania and never worked again in the Federal District (Ellicott to the Commissioners, 4, 5, 8 Jan. 1793, DNA: RG 42, PBG; Commissioners to Ellicott, 8 Jan. 1793, and to Washington, 9 Jan. 1793, DLC: Washington Papers; Washington, *Journal*, 15; Tobias Lear to TJ, 11, 15 Jan. 1793, and notes; TJ to Ellicott, 15 Jan., 22 Mch. 1793; Commissioners to TJ, 7 Feb. 1793, and note; TJ to Washington, 17 Mch. 1793, and note; Bryan, *National Capital*, I, 208-11; William Tindall, *Standard History of the City of Washington* [Knoxville, 1914], 151-7).

TJ submitted this letter to the President on 13 Jan. 1793, and Washington returned it the next day (Washington, *Journal*, 15, 16).

Note on Balloons

[ca. 9 Jan. 1793]

Blanchard tells me that it takes

$\left.\begin{array}{l}\text{3000 lb vitriolic acid}\\\text{2000 lb iron[1] filings}\end{array}\right\}$ for a single person to ascend in a baloon.

the vitriolic acid costs in London 4d. sterl. per lb.

the baloon he ascended in was 22. feet French in diam.

calculating this without regard to fractions, and on supposition it was equal to a sphere of that diameter, it would contain 6800. cub. feet. this is about $\frac{3}{10}$ lb of iron to every cub. foot of air.

MS (DLC: TJ Papers, 234: 41865); written entirely in TJ's hand on a small scrap; undated; endorsed by TJ: "Baloons."

[1] Word written over what appears to be "steel," erased.

From Thomas Mann Randolph, Jr.

DEAR SIR   Monticello Jan: 9: 1793.

Since the 26. of October I have not passed 6 successive days at Monticello and consequently have not paid that attention to the work you requested me to direct, which I could have wished. It is by no means so forward as it might have been. The Window frames which you ordered were prepared immediately. A quantity of Stone which appears to me to be about $\frac{2}{3}$ of what will be required has been brought to the top of the Mountain. Jupiter from what I can learn has not raised more than $\frac{1}{4}$ of the lime-stone you ordered: he is now at work with 2 assistants. The 2 men who were with Colvard return on the 17: when with 2 others they will begin to get timber for the stables &c. I was grieved on my arrival last night to find poor little Anna much indisposed again. She looks pale today but we are comforted by finding a large jaw-tooth which has just pierced the gum. We have no reason to apprehend a return of her former disorder. Patsy and the little boy are well. We are extremely anxious to be assured that you and Polly are in good health. Your most affectionate friend & hble Servt.   TH: M. RANDOLPH

RC (MHi); endorsed by TJ as received 19 Jan. 1793 and so recorded in SJL.

From Caspar Wistar, Jr.

Wednesday Morning [9 Jan. 1793]

Dr. Wistars respectful Compliments to Mr. Jefferson and sends the Vials for which he requests Mr. J. to procure a passage in the Balloon. Three facts may be ascertained by bringing down some of the upper Atmosphere—viz The proportion of pure air; The proportion of fixed air, or the absence of it; and the Comparative state of Expansion of the Atmosphere. To ascertain this last Circumstance the temperature of the air at the time of inclosing it should be noted. The State of the Barometer must of course be marked.

P.S. Mr. Blanchard must be requested to empty the Bottles and Cork them well at the greatest height.

RC (MHi); partially dated; dateline between body of letter and postscript; endorsed by TJ as received 9 Jan. 1793 and so recorded in SJL.

TJ's purchase of a $5 admission ticket for the event indicates that he, along with President Washington, French minister Jean Baptiste Ternant, and an "immense number of people," was present this morning in the courtyard of the Walnut Street Prison in Philadelphia to witness the balloon ascent of Jean Pierre BLAN-CHARD (1750-1809), the veteran French aeronaut who had come to the United States exactly a month before to "convince the New World that man's ingenuity is not confined to earth alone, but opens to him new and certain roads in the vast expanse of heaven." During this flight, the first successful manned ascent in America, Blanchard traveled some fifteen miles from Philadelphia to Deptford in Gloucester County, New Jersey, in forty-six minutes and performed scientific experiments for a number of Philadelphia physicians and

[43]

natural scientists, including Wistar, who actually placed the six VIALS in question in Blanchard's balloon car (Blanchard, *Journal of my Forty-Fifth Ascension, being the First Performed in America, On the Ninth of January, 1793* [Philadelphia, 1793], 7-27; MB, 9 Jan. 1793). The ever-curious TJ closely questioned Blanchard shortly afterward about methods of producing hydrogen and subsequently contributed $20 to help cover the cost of his flight and $1 to watch the aeronaut's parachute experiments with animals (Note on Balloons, [ca. 9 Jan. 1793]; TJ to Martha Jefferson Randolph, 14 Jan. 1793, and note; MB, 9 Apr., 17 June 1793). Howev-er, TJ subsequently rejected Blanchard's request that he ask the President for a loan of $400 and regretted his own inability to assist the balloonist privately (Blanchard to TJ, 16 Oct. 1793; TJ to Blanchard, 15 Dec. 1793). For Blanchard's prior aeronautical career in France, which began in 1784 and included a successful flight across the English Channel the following year, see *Dictionnaire de biographie française*, 15 vols. [Paris, 1933-], VI, 604-5; and Charles C. Gillispie, *The Montgolfier Brothers and the Invention of Aviation, 1783-1784* (Princeton, 1983), 87, 95, 97, 119-20.

From J. P. P. Derieux

Charlottesville, 10 Jan. 1793. Owing to the carelessness of the Richmond courier, TJ's letters of 22 Nov. and 14 Dec. arrived simultaneously. He has now received from Gamble another 250 dollars obtained by TJ as an advance from Vaughan, which relieves him of some financial difficulty because, his bill of exchange having been returned to Gamble protested, Gamble had credited the first 250 dollars to his account. Since Gamble needs the money loaned in March, there might be a way of concluding his business if Vaughan did not plan to accept the profit for the 25 cases of glass window panes in Homassel's hands, for which he has received an order from Darcel via Boston that he encloses. But if TJ believes that any awkwardness would result for Vaughan, he should not comply in this matter, and Derieux will arrange to settle his account with Gamble with the first remittance from TJ. Gamble has notified him to prepare for the settlement of protest charges, which clearly occurred either because Gamble forgot to denote Fenwick as the person to whom first application was to be made or because his correspondents were negligent. He assumes that he will have to pay at least the greater part of the charges because Gamble wishes to settle this transaction on liberal principles. He asks TJ to forward the enclosed letters to his uncle and to Mme. Bellanger. Although he has written to the latter several times since TJ left Virginia, he has received but one letter from her dated June. He hopes that with news improving, communication will be easier, and the letters will not be examined by the government. Having joyfully learned from the latest gazette of the enemy's evacuation of France, they hope that the Republic will take shape and carry on to the satisfaction of all. He and his wife present their respects. [P.S.] He requests a copy of the memorandum Vaughan must have given TJ about the best goods from Bordeaux and Nantes because, his uncle having written some time ago about power of attorney for the settlement of a small inheritance expected soon because of the imminent death of an old aunt in Tours, he desires him to have an account beforehand of goods that will sell more promptly and surely in Philadelphia than feathers and other fantasy items that have only a fashionable appeal and momentary value.

RC (MHi); 3 p.; in French; addressed: "The Honble. Ths. Jefferson Esqr. Secretary of State Philadelphia"; dateline between signature and postscript; endorsed by TJ as received 19 Jan. 1793 and so recorded in SJL. Enclosures not found.

From Tobias Lear

Thursday January 10th: 1793

The President orders T. Lear to return to the Secretary of State the letter from Mr. Pinckney—the one from Mr. Johnson and that from Mr. Livingston, which have been submitted to the President's perusal; and to observe that the President thinks it is to be regretted that Mr. Pinckney does not say anything in his letters relative to certain matters which he was instructed to be particularly attentive to.

RC (DLC); endorsed by TJ as received 10 Jan. 1793. FC (DNA: RG 59, MLR); in Lear's hand. FC (Lb in same, SDC). Enclosures: (1) Henry Livingston to TJ, 5 Oct. 1792 (not found; but see Washington, *Journal*, 5). (2) Thomas Pinckney to TJ, 5 Oct. 1792. (3) Joshua Johnson to TJ, 9 Oct. 1792.

From Tobias Lear

Friday January 11th: 1793

T. Lear is ordered by the President of the U.S. to transmit to the Secretary of State a letter and its enclosures, together with a draft of the Survey of the federal District, which he has received from the Commissioners.

The President requests that the Secretary will take this matter into consideration and report to the President his opinion whether it should be laid before Congress or not.

TOBIAS LEAR
Secretary to the President
of the United States

RC (DLC); inadvertently endorsed by TJ as received 8 Jan. 1793. FC (Lb in DNA: RG 59, SDC); undated. Enclosure: Commissioners of the Federal District to George Washington, 5 Jan. 1793, enclosing several lists of squares in the Federal District in various stages of division, copies of letters from Andrew Ellicott, and Ellicott's survey of the Federal District with accompanying certificates; indicating that Ellicott may be leaving their service and voicing concern over his temper in dealings with them; informing that the accounts of expenses for the surveys of the District and the City would soon be prepared in the expectation that Congress will defray them; detailing various expenses associated with the proprietors' claims and the President's house; announcing their appointment of Samuel Blodget, Jr., as superintendent; and advising in a postscript that Ellicott's survey would be delivered separately by Joseph Wailes of Massachusetts (FC in DNA: RG 42, DCLB). Concerning Ellicott's survey, see TJ to the Commissioners, 15 Jan. 1793, and note.

From David Rittenhouse

Dʀ Sɪʀ   Jany. 11th. 1792 [i.e. 1793]

Mrs. Rittenhouse is greatly obliged to you for your Valuable present. To me it is more acceptable than any other thing of its kind in existence, but the pleasure it wou'd otherwise afford is greatly abated by an expression in the note accompanying it, That you are packing up your useless furniture: by which I suppose I am to understand that you are going to take your flight to the summit of the South-Mountain. On this occasion I feel most sensibly the misfortune of contracting so very few friendships in youth, which is certainly the proper season for providing whatever will be necessary to us in old age. However on recollection I do not find cause to reproach myself much on this account. When I have Voluntarily forborn to take advantage of opportunities[1] that offered of cultivating intimate friendships, it has been for reasons that still appear sufficently Weighty, such as too great a dissimularity of Views and pursuits, perhaps of vices. I am indeed in a fair way of doing what many a selfish old fellow has done, to give up all expectations of social happiness out of the limits of my own family, but I shall ever remember with pleasure, whilst memory continues to perform its office, that I have counted the name of Mr: Jefferson in the very short list of my friends. I am, Dr Sir, with great sincerity Yours

D. Rɪᴛᴛᴇɴʜᴏᴜꜱᴇ

I was complaisant enough to walk an hour thro' the Mud with Dr. Smith a few days ago, and the consequence is a Violent Cold.

RC (DLC); misdated; endorsed by TJ as received 12 Jan. 1793 and so recorded in SJL, where, as in TJ's endorsement, it is incorrectly registered as a letter of 11 July.

on 15 Jan. 1793, recorded in SJL as received the same date, but it has not been found.

[1] Preceding two words interlined.

Rittenhouse wrote another letter to TJ

To George Washington

Sunday Jan. 13. 93.

Th: Jefferson has the honor to send to the President a sketch which he has submitted to a gentleman or two in the legislature on the subject of Indian purchases.

He sends him also two letters received last night from Mr. Gouverneur Morris. The correspondence referred to in one of them, is in French, and being improper to go into the hands of a clerk, Th:J. is translating it himself for the use of the President. It is lengthy, and will require a good part of to-day to do it.

RC (DNA: RG 59, MLR); endorsed by Tobias Lear. PrC (DLC). Tr (Lb in DNA: RG 59, SDC). Not recorded in SJL. Enclosures: Gouverneur Morris to TJ, 19 and 27 Sep. 1792. Third enclosure printed below.

The CORRESPONDENCE between Gouverneur Morris and French Foreign Minister Lebrun is described in Morris to TJ, 19 Sep. 1792, and note. TJ's translations of these letters, in DLC: TJ Papers, 81: 13986-95, are recorded in SJPL under 13 Jan. 1793; see also Washington, *Journal*, 12-15. TJ sent the translations to the President this day, and Washington returned them the following day. Since these letters dealt among other things with the payment of the American debt to France, Washington decided that they ought to be shown to the Secretary of the Treasury, and therefore he had Tobias Lear write the following note to TJ on 15 Jan. 1793: "If the Secretary of State has not already sent to the Secretary of the Treasury the letters from Mr. G. Morris, relative to the French debt, the President will thank the Secretary to send them to him (the President) as he expects to see the Secretary of the Treasury this morning and will give them to him" (RC in DLC; endorsed by TJ as received 15 Jan. 1793; see also Washington, *Journal*, 16, 18). TJ immediately complied with this request and subsequently wrote this brief note to Washington on 16 Jan. 1793: "Th: Jefferson finding the inclosed letter out of it's place, suspects it may have escaped him when he sent the others to the President. Lest that should have been the case he now sends it with his respects" (RC in DNA: RG 59, MLR, addressed "The President of the U.S.," endorsed by Lear; Tr in Lb in same, SDC; not recorded in SJL). The letter in question was the one Morris wrote to TJ on 10 Sep. 1792, which Lear returned to TJ in a brief note of 17 Jan. 1793 with the President's thanks and with the information that TJ had previously sent it to the President (RC in DLC; endorsed by TJ as received 17 Jan. 1793).

ENCLOSURE

Clause for Bill Regulating Trade with the Indians

[13 Jan. 1793]

Be it enacted &c that no person shall be capable of acquiring any title, in law or equity, to any lands beyond the Indian boundaries and within those of the U.S. by purchase, gift, or otherwise, from the Indians holding or claiming the same: and that it shall be a misdemeanor in any person, punishable by fine and imprisonment[1] at the discretion of a jury, to obtain, accept, or directly or indirectly to treat for, any title to such lands from the said Indians or any other for them.   But where any such Indians shall of their own accord desire to sell any part of their lands, and it shall be deemed the interest of the U.S. that a purchase shall be made, the same shall be done by treaty or convention, to be entered into by the President of the U.S. and ratified by two thirds of the Senate according to the constitution: to enure to the use of the states respectively, where the said lands lie within the limits of any state, they paying the price, and to the use of the U.S. where such lands lie within any territory ceded to them by particular states.

[47]

MS (DNA: RG 59, MLR); entirely in TJ's hand; undated. PrC (DLC: TJ Papers, 96: 16477). Recorded in SJPL under 13 Jan. 1793: "draught of clause for law rgt buying Indian lands."

This document was intended to serve as an amendment to a bill for regulating trade and intercourse with the Indians, which was then under consideration by the House of Representatives, and was designed to prevent the unauthorized purchase by American citizens of lands which by treaty the United States government had recognized as belonging to the Indians. Under the the terms of an act for the regulation of trade and intercourse with the Indians passed in 1790, which was to last for only two years, Congress declared invalid all purchases of Indian lands except those made by treaty with the United States. With the time drawing near for the expiration of this act, which failed to end private purchases of Indian lands, the House appointed a committee on 14 Nov. 1792 to draft a new trade and intercourse bill. The committee reported a new bill at the end of November, which over the next month and a half the House read and amended. Since this bill, like its predecessor, merely invalidated illicit purchases of Indian lands, TJ sought to strengthen it by drafting a clause that provided criminal penalties for such acquisitions. James Madison, no doubt one of the congressmen to whom the Secretary of State submitted the document, offered TJ's amendment to the House in modified form on 15 Jan. 1793, leaving the first sentence intact but altering the second to read as follows: "*And that, where any such Indians shall, of their own accord, desire to sell any part of their lands, and it shall be deemed for the interest of the United States, that a purchase shall be*

made, the same shall be done no otherwise than by treaty or convention, to be entered into pursuant to the constitution; the lands so purchased, to enure to the use of whoever may have the right of pre-emption thereto, and shall pay the price thereof" (Madison, *Papers*, XIV, 442). Two days later the House approved the amendment as offered by Madison after first deleting TJ's phrase AT THE DISCRETION OF A JURY in the first sentence—specifying instead a maximum fine of $4,000 and a maximum prison term of one year for violators of the act—and omitting the passage "Indians shall . . . that a" in the second sentence as revised by Madison. The House then passed the trade and intercourse bill on 18 Jan. 1793 and sent it to the Senate. The Senate made still more changes in the TJ-Madison amendment, substantially altering the wording (though not the meaning) and specifying a maximum fine of $1,000 and a maximum term of imprisonment of one year for offenders. The House accepted these amendments, which remained faithful to TJ's objective of employing criminal sanctions to deter unauthorized Indian land purchases, and the trade and intercourse bill became law on 1 Mch. 1793 (JHR, I, 629, 652, 656, 671, 674, 675, 719, 720, 722, 723; JS, I, 472, 473, 489-90, 491-2, 493, 495, 498, 499, 501; *Annals*, II, 2301-3, III, 827-8, 1442-5; *National State Papers*, XVII, 117-28). For a discussion of the role of unauthorized land purchases in exacerbating relations with the Indians during the Washington administration, see Francis P. Prucha, *American Indian Policy in the Formative Years: The Indian Trade and Intercourse Acts, 1790-1834* (Cambridge, Mass., 1962), 139-58.

[1] TJ here interlined and erased "and by incapaci."

From Robert Gamble

SIR   Richmond 14th. Jany. 1793.

I am honored with your favor of the 4th. enclosing letters to Monsr. De Reaux, and informing that the 5,000^{tt} which we were concerned in *is paid.*

I forwarded to London a Bill for 4,000 to J. & T. Gilliat, leaving the date of payment, after presenting, *blank* for them to fill up, as appeared most advantagiously suited to obtain the money. 21 days was the sight they inserted, and it was returned protested, to me the 20th. of June with 8/ sterlg. Cost. As the Executors had paid 10,000^{tt} the balance of the Legacy was not then in their hands or due, and protested for want of effects. I presume the second of exchange was never presented by that house as I have letters of Various dates till the 9th. of Novemr. from them and no farther notice taken of that matter.

Necessity compelled me to be endeavoring to remit to that House, otherwise from the insolent disposition of some of the *Anglois* towards the French and Americans both, I should not have put it in their power to act so Cavalierly and filling up the sight at 21. days was either injudiciously, or designedly done, that I might not be induced to have further Connections with that nation.

I apprehend in Consequence of the powers Vested in Mr. Fenwick he has obtained for the use of Monsr. De Rieux the 4,000^{tt} livers thus protested, and holds it subject to his order—and that the remaining 1,000^{tt} has been paid to his order in my favor to the House of Mess. P. Changuer & Co. of Bordeaux from whom I ordered some Merchandize as a sample.

To-morrow I will forward your Letter and the enclosure to Charlotsville as directed. I am with consideration & regard Your mo. obt Hu st.   Ro. Gamble

RC (DLC); endorsed by TJ as received 23 Jan. 1793 and so recorded in SJL.

From Tobias Lear

United States, January 14th: 1793

By the President's command T. Lear has the honor to return to the Secretary of State the letter to the Minister of France, relative to the supply of money to pay certain Bills drawn by the administration of St. Domingo, which has been submitted to the President; and to inform the Secretary, that the President, presuming that the contents of said letter is conformable to the arrangements made on that subject, approves of the same.   Tobias Lear
                                                 Secretary to the President
                                                 of the United States

RC (DLC); endorsed by TJ as received 14 Jan. 1793. PrC (DNA: RG 59, MLR). FC (Lb in same, SDC). Enclosure: TJ to Jean Baptiste Ternant, 14 Jan. 1793.

From James Monroe

Dear Sir   Phila. Jany 14. 1793
I have just heard it stated here that the suspension of the payments
to France was in the first instance by Mr. Short before the commencement of Mr. Morris's service and without orders from this place[1]
and that the latter only conformed to a rule shewn him, implicating
strongly that there never had been any direction from this quarter on
the subject. This statement was given by Cabot upon an interrogatory
of Mr. Adams. If you can give me the facts (without your appearing
in it) they may be communicated here. Yrs affecy   Jas. Monroe

RC (DLC); endorsed by TJ as received   [1] Preceding six words interlined.
14 Jan. 1793 and so recorded in SJL.

To James Monroe

Th:J. to Col: Monroe   Jan. 14. 93.
I am a stranger to the instructions given to Mr. Short on the subject
of money, the correspondence thereon having been [direct?] between
the Sec. of the Treasury and him, without any mediary. Neither do
I know whether any authority was given or not to G. Morris on that
subject. The payment of the 19th. of Aug. was made in consequence
of a letter from G. Morris as I have reason to believe. Whether that
letter could be an order or not I am uninformed, but it probably was
either authoritative or of decisive influence.

PrC (DLC); faded.

To Martha Jefferson Randolph

My dear Martha   Philadelphia Jan. 14. 1793.
Mr. Randolph's letter of Dec. 20. from Richmond is the only one
come to hand from him or you since your's from Bizarre of two months
ago. Tho' his letter informed me of the re-establishment of Anne, yet I
wish to learn that time confirms our hopes. We were entertained here
lately with the ascent of Mr. Blanchard in a baloon. The security of
the thing appeared so great that every body is wishing for a baloon
to travel in. I wish for one sincerely, as instead of 10. days, I should
be within 5 hours of home. Maria will probably give you the baloon

details, as she writes to-day.—Have you recieved the package with the servants clothes? My best attachments to Mr. Randolph. Adieu my dear Your's affectionately   TH: JEFFERSON

RC (NNP); at foot of text: "Mrs. Randolph." PrC (MHi). Tr (ViU: Edgehill-Randolph Papers); 19th-century copy.

The LETTER OF DEC. 20 from Thomas Mann Randolph, Jr., recorded in SJL as received 28 Dec. 1792, has not been found. Maria reported that she had been "very much entertained" by Jean Pierre Blanchard's BALOON ascent on 9 Jan. 1793 (Maria Jefferson to Thomas Mann Randolph, Jr., 13 Jan. 1793, RC in DLC).

To Jean Baptiste Ternant

SIR   Philadelphia January 14th. 1793.

I have laid before the President of the United States your Letter of the 7th. instant, desiring a supply in money, on account of our debt to France, for the purpose of paying certain Bills drawn by the Administration of St. Domingo, and for procuring necessaries for that Colony, which supply you wish should, with those preceding, make up the amount of four millions of Livres. You are sensible of the difficulty of the situation in which this places our Government, between duty to it's own constituents, on the one side, which would require that large payments of their money should be made on such sanction only as will establish them beyond the reach of all question, and, on the other side, their sincere friendship to the nation of France heightened in the case of the colony by motives of neighborhood and Commerce. But having, in a former letter expressed to you our desire that an authentic and direct sanction may be obtained from the Government of France for what we have done, and what we may hereafter be desired to do, I proceed to inform you that motives of friendship prevailing over those of rigorous caution, the President of the United States, has acceded to your present desire.—Arrangements will consequently be taken at the Treasury for furnishing money for the calls and at the epochs stated in your letter of the 7th. and also for those expressed in your other letter of the 8th.[1] relating to the Consuls of France.

I have however, Sir, to ask the favor of you to take arrangements with the Administration of St. Domingo, so as that future supplies from us, should they be necessary, may be negotiated here, before they are counted on and drawn for there. Bills on the French Agents here to be paid by us, amount to Bills on us; and it is absolutely necessary that we be not subject to calls, which have not been before calculated and provided for.

In enabling you to get rid of the present embarrassment, you are more at ease to take measures against any similar one in future from the same source. I have the honor to be, with sentiments of the most perfect respect, Sir, Your most obedient and most humble servant

TH: JEFFERSON

RC (AMAE: CPEU, Supplément, xx); in the hand of George Taylor, Jr., except for addition by TJ and his signature; at foot of first page: "The Minister of France." PrC (DLC); unsigned. FC (Lb in DNA: RG 59, DL). Tr (AMAE: CPEU, xxxvii); French translation. Not recorded in SJL. Enclosed in Tobias Lear to TJ, 14 Jan. 1793.

The FORMER LETTER, in which TJ noted the failure of the French government to authorize the use of the American debt to France for the relief of Saint-Domingue, was the one he wrote to

Ternant on 20 Nov. 1792. Washington, to whom TJ submitted the above letter this day, approved payment of the bills of exchange drawn by the government of that colony on the French consul general in Philadelphia, Antoine René Charles Mathurin de La Forest, through advances on the French debt after deciding that this course of action was consistent with a recent Cabinet decision to pay French consular salaries in the same way (Washington, *Journal*, 11, 16-17).

[1] Date in TJ's hand. Date left blank in PrC and FC.

To the Commissioners of the Federal District

GENTLEMEN   Philadelphia Jan. 15. 1793.

The President, thinking it would be better that the outlines at least of the city and perhaps of Georgetown should be laid down in the plat of the Territory, I have the honor now to send it, and to desire that Mr. Ellicot may do it as soon as convenient that it may be returned in time to be laid before Congress. I have the honor to be with perfect esteem, Gentlemen your most obedt & most humble servt   TH: JEFFERSON

PrC (DLC); at foot of text: "Messrs. Johnson, Stewart & Carrol." FC (Lb in DNA: RG 59, DL). Enclosure not found.

The enclosed PLAT, or survey, of the Federal District that Andrew Ellicott submitted to the Commissioners on the first of the month was the product of the instructions he had received from the Secretary of State nearly two years before (TJ to Ellicott, 2 Feb. 1791, in Vol. 19: 68-70; Ralph E. Ehrenberg, "Mapping the Nation's Capital: The Survey-

or's Office, 1791-1818," *Quarterly Journal of the Library of Congress*, xxxvi [1979], 282). The survey, which had been forwarded to the President by the Commissioners in a letter of 5 Jan. 1793, has not been found (Tobias Lear to TJ, 11 Jan. 1793, and note; Washington, *Journal*, 7, 10). For its return to TJ with Ellicott's corrections and its submission to Congress, see Commissioners to TJ, 11 Feb. 1793; and TJ to George Washington, 18 Feb. 1793, and note.

From Delamotte

Le Havre, 15 Jan. 1793. He encloses a report of ships entering this port for the last half of 1792. Coffyn will send a similar report for Dunkirk. No ships came to the other ports in his department, except perhaps for Rouen, where he has no agent owing to the refusal of Le Couteulx, who was recommended by Barrett, to accept the appointment offered him, preferring apparently a vice-consular appointment by the government itself. Not wishing to counter Barrett's views, or seemingly those of the American government to establish a consul in Rouen, he awaits TJ's orders before appointing an agent there. This report will come in a roll containing some tables of France's financial state, which has already been changed four times since they were written—so unstable is the current government. He believes a very great majority of the French people hope the king, who was to have been judged yesterday, will be spared. France is on the verge of declaring war on England. The opening of the Escaut is a pretext; the real cause is France's wish to liberate all nations, even against their will. France's finances, navy, and army are in such disarray that he does not know how it can hope to sustain a war that will surely involve Spain and Holland. The war will be a fortunate one if an Anglo-Spanish mediation ends the state of anxiety that has existed for four years. The rate of exchange on London is 15¾, with others in the same proportion. Fear of war has brought a large inflation in prices in all types of commodities, but not yet so much as one might fear. Tobacco is worth 60 to 65ᵗᵗ, rice 40 to 45ᵗᵗ, flour 55 to 60ᵗᵗ per barrel, and wheat 60ᵗᵗ per six-bushel sack of 60 pounds each. American ships will make a fortune in case of war, and he will pay close attention to the fraudulent use of American colors. He will urge merchants to encourage the French government to allow neutral ships trading with the French colonies to enter French ports; if the flag exempts the merchandise, this arrangement will benefit both France and the neutrals, and it is the only means by which France can exploit what is left of trade in the colonies. If the United States wishes to have a consul at Ostend, it could find no one more suitable than George Gregorie—a wealthy Ostend merchant born to a Scotsman in Dunkirk and brother of a merchant with Gregorie, Maitland & Company in Petersburg, Virginia—who wishes to become vice-consul in the Austrian Netherlands. TJ's letter of 10 Oct. did arrive, and he will send the books Froullé dispatched, and the macaroni, by the first ship bound for Virginia or Philadelphia.

RC (DLC); 4 p.; in French; in a clerk's hand, signed by Delamotte; at foot of first page: "Mr. Jefferson Secretaire d'Etat à Philadelphie"; conjoined to text of Delamotte to TJ, 9 Mch. 1793; endorsed by TJ as received 4 May 1793 and so recorded in SJL. Dupl (DNA: RG 59, CD); in a clerk's hand, signed by Delamotte; at head of text: "Duplicata"; conjoined to text of Delamotte to TJ, 9 Mch. 1793.

The report from Francis Coffyn, the American consular agent at Dunkirk, may have been enclosed in a missing letter to TJ of 18 Jan. 1793 recorded in SJL as received from "Coffyn" on 4 May 1793. Three other letters written from Dunkirk and dated January 1793 and 26 Feb. and 11 Apr. 1793 were recorded in SJL as received 10 June 1793 from "L. Coffyn," possibly Laben Coffin, master of a whaling vessel operating out of Dunkirk, but they have not been found (Massachusetts Historical Society, *Proceedings*, 3d ser., LIII, [1920], 224).

To Andrew Ellicott

DEAR SIR   Philadelphia Jan. 15. 1793.

I have duly recieved your favor of the 9th. The President thinking it would be better that the outlines at least of the city, and perhaps of George-town should be laid down in the plat of the territory, I have sent it back to the Commissioners from whom it came, that you may do this. Suppose you were to consult them on the propriety of adding to *the Eastern branch*, the words '*or [Anna]kostia.*' This would probably revive the antient Indian name instead of the modern one. I am extremely sorry to learn that there has arisen any dissatisfaction between the Commissioners and yourself. I am sure it is without a fault on either side, such is my confidence in both parties. The work you are employed in must be slow from it's nature: and it is not wonderful if the Commissioners should think it too much so. However I hope you will change your mind about bringing it before the public. This cannot be done without injuring the expectations built on the city, nor can it be necessary in a case unknown beyond the circle of George-town. Within that circle, verbal explanations will certainly answer equally well as a justification to you. Indeed I hope nothing will take place to render your future services there unobtaineable with the Commissioners, and that you will suspend any resolution you may have taken on this subject.—I thank you for your almanac. But why have you adopted the name of Georgium sidus, which no nation but the English took up, while justice and all other nations gave it that of Herschel? I have oftened wished we could have published in America an Almanac, which without going beyond the purchase of the people in general, might answer some of[1] the purposes of those a little above them in information. The declination and right ascension of the sun, the equation of time, places of those of the remarkable stars which are above our horizon *in the night*, and some other little matter might be substituted in place of the weather, and other useless articles without increasing the bulk or price of the Almanac. I know nobody but yourself from whom we could hope such a thing. What say you to it? I am with great esteem Dear Sir Your very humble servt   TH: JEFFERSON

PrC (DLC); faded in part; at foot of first page: "Mr. Andrew Ellicot." Tr (DLC); 19th-century copy; with gaps in transcription.

Ellicott had sent TJ a copy of his ALMANAC for 1793 with his letter of 26 Nov. 1792. GEORGIUM SIDUS, or George's Star, now known as the planet Uranus, was discovered in 1781 by Sir William HERSCHEL and named by him for George III (DSB, VI, 328-9).

TJ evidently sent the President a copy of this letter to Ellicott (Washington,

Journal, 52). The surveyor's reply, presumably the letter dated at Washington on 24 Jan. 1793 and recorded in SJL as received two days later, has not been found.

[1] Preceding two words interlined.

From Alexander Hamilton

SIR   Treasury Department January 15th 1793

Major Rochefontaine has presented at the Treasury an authenticated copy of a Register Certificate in his favour, from which it appears, that the original has been deposited with Mr. Delamotte, vice consul of the united States at Havre in France.

It being necessary, that the Treasury should be in possession of the original certificate, I have in the enclosed letter desired Major Rochefontaine to cause it to be forwarded hither. This letter will probably be transmitted to Havre, and will therefore require to be authenticated by your signature; it being presumed, that mine is not familiar to the Consul. I request some proper Memorandum on the inclosed for this purpose.[1]

It will be requisite, that Mr. Delamotte and other consuls and Vice Consuls of the U States[2] should be directed to forbear in future taking any deposits of original certificates of the like nature. This direction I conceive will come properly from your department. I have the honor to be very respectfully Sir Your obedt Servt

ALEXANDER HAMILTON

RC (DLC); in a clerk's hand, with additions by Hamilton and signed by him; at foot of text: "The Secretary of State." Enclosure not found. Enclosed in the following letter.

Instead of affixing SOME PROPER MEMORANDUM ON THE INCLOSED, TJ apparently decided to send a letter to Delamotte of this date (see note to Rochefontaine to TJ, [15 Jan. 1793]). No instructions from TJ to American consuls regarding their receipt of DEPOSITS OF ORIGINAL CERTIFICATES has been found.

[1] Preceding sentence in Hamilton's hand.
[2] Preceding ten words interlined by Hamilton.

From Alexander Hamilton

Jany 15. 1792 [i.e. 1793]

Mr. Hamilton presents his Compliments to Mr. Jefferson. The inclosed letter written by his Clerk will, it is hoped, express his wish sufficiently to render it unnecessary to remodel it. As Col. Rochefontane informs him the vessel, by which the letter is intended to be sent, departs tomorrow Morning he will be obliged by its being returned to him with the proper certificate this Evening.

RC (DLC: TJ Papers, 69: 12074); misdated; endorsed by TJ as received 15 Jan. 1793. Enclosure: Hamilton's first letter of this date to TJ.

From Alexander Hamilton

Jany. 15. 1793

The Secretary of the Treasury presents his respectful compliments to The Secretary of the State—requests he will meet the Comms. of the Sinking Fund at ten 'oClock tomorrow forenoon[1] at the house of the Secy. of the Treasury. The V President has been so obliging as to accommodate the place to the indifferent state of Mr. Hamilton's health.

RC (DLC); endorsed by TJ as received 15 Jan. 1793 and so recorded in SJL.

The minutes of the Commissioners of the Sinking Fund for 16 Jan. 1793 are in ASP, *Finance*, I, 237.

[1] Word written in the margin.

From Tobias Lear

15 Jany 1793.

As the Secretary of State may be about to write to the Commissioners respecting the additions of the City to be marked in the survey of the federal territory, the President sends him the enclosed which he has just recieved from Mr. Forrest, that he may see more particularly the situation of matters between Mr. Ellicott and the Commissioners.

RC (DLC); endorsed by TJ as received 15 Jan. 1793. Enclosures: (1) Uriah Forrest to Washington, Georgetown, 10 Jan. 1793, informing that Andrew Ellicott has determined to attack the Commissioners of the Federal District in the newspapers and given notice of his intention to resign as surveyor of the Federal District in May 1793, recounting his efforts to resolve the acrimonious dispute between Ellicott and the Commissioners, enclosing a copy of an answer from Ellicott, and expressing the hope that an accommodation between the disputants can be reached to avoid impeding progress on the city, which "has infinitely more to dread from the discord and want of union in its friends than from all the power of its Enemies" (RC in DNA: RG 59, MLR). (2) Andrew Ellicott to [Forrest], n.d., defending himself against the criticisms of the Commissioners, refusing to reconsider his decision to resign as surveyor in May 1793, but promising to delay until then his public criticism of the Commissioners (Tr in same). See also Washington, *Journal*, 20, 21; and TJ to Ellicott, 15 Jan. 1793, and note.

From Lebrun

MONSIEUR   Paris le 15 Janvier 1793 L'an 2e de la république.
Le Citoyen Ternant qui a rempli les Fonctions de Ministre plénipotentiaire de la Nation Française près des Etats-unis, ayant donné une nouvelle preuve de son patriotisme en manifestant le desir
d'etre employé dans les armées de la République, le Conseil éxécutif
n'a pas voulu négliger cette occasion de tirer parti des connoissances
de cet officier dans l'art de la guerre et de lui témoigner, en même
tems, la Satisfaction que lui ont donné ses services. Le ministre de la
Guerre lui destine, en consequence, un commandement dans l'armée
à son retour en France. Le Citoyen Genet qui le remplace près des
Etats-unis joint à une longue experience des affaires le patriotisme le
plus pur et l'avantage d'etre particulierement instruit des dispositions
amicales et Fraternelle de la République Française pour les Etats-unis.
En considerant les preuves réïterées qu'il a donné de ses bons principes
et de son caractere dans plusieurs missions importantes, je ne doute
aucunement qu'il ne se rende agréable au Gouvernement des Etats-
unis et qu'il ne contribuë à resserer des liens trop longtems négligés
entre deux Nations dont les principes et les interets ont la plus parfaite
analogie.
    Au moment de ce changement heureux de mesures, qui, indu-
bitablement seront reciproques, je dois me féliciter, Monsieur, que le
Citoyen Genet ait pour interprete de nos Sentimens près des Etats
unis, un ministre qui pendant un long Séjour en France à pu se con-
vaincre de l'attachement de la nation pour les Américains libres et qui
a travaillé lui même avec autant de zéle que de pénétration à consolider
les liaisons d'amitié et de commerce entre les deux Peuples.
    Les Obstacles que vous aves rencontrés Sont heureusement écartés.
Ils le sont pour toujours. Les Français se livreront désormais, sans
réserve à leurs sentimens pour une Nation qui les à dévancés, avec
tant de Succès dans la recherche des vrais principes de l'ordre Social.
Le Citoyen Genet qui vous exposera, avec une confiance entiere, les
vües et les principes de la République Française, vous Fera part, en
même tems, des moyens qui paroissent les plus efficaces pour établir,
sur des bases inebranlables et mutuellement avantageuses, les rapports
d'amitié et de commerce entre les deux Nations.
    Il ne dépendra pas de nous, Monsieur, que les Francais et les Amer-
icains libres, unis par les liens les plus étroits, ne confondent entierement leurs interets politiques et commerciaux et que les deux Peuples
les plus libres du monde et les plus éclairés ne donnent l'exemple
touchant d'une Fraternité complette. Ce seroit la premiere Fois qu'une

alliance aurait été formée pour le bonheur des hommes et non pour les enchainer ou les detruire. J'ai l'honneur d'être avec un très Sincère attachement Monsieur Votre très-humble et très obeïssant Serviteur.

LeBrun

RC (DNA: RG 59, MLR); in a clerk's hand, signed by Lebrun; at foot of first page: "M Jefferson Secretaire d'Etat"; endorsed by TJ as received 16 May 1793 and so recorded in SJL. Dft (AMAE: CPEU, xxxvii); in a clerk's hand; dated 13 Jan. 1793. Tr (DLC: Genet Papers); dated 13 Jan. 1793. Enclosed in Edmond Charles Genet to TJ, 16 May 1793.

Pierre Henri Hélène Marie Lebrun (1754-93), a Girondist, was the French foreign minister from August 1792 to June 1793. He was arrested that month during the purge of the Girondins and guillotined in December (J. C. F. Hoefer, ed., *Nouvelle biographie générale depuis les temps les plus reculés jusqu'a nos jours*, 46 vols. [Paris, 1855-66], xxx, 160-1; Frédéric Masson, *Le Département des Affaires Étrangères pendant La Révolution,*

1787-1804 [Paris, 1877], 237-84). Lebrun's wish that the replacement of Ternant by Edmond Charles Genet be regarded by the United States as a CHANGEMENT HEUREUX DE MESURES, QUI, INDUBITABLEMENT SERONT RECIPROQUES, was of course a request for the recall of Gouverneur Morris, whose antipathy to the French Revolution had earned him the displeasure of the French government. As early as the preceding September Lebrun had instructed Ternant to notify United States government of the revolutionary regime's grave dissatisfaction with Morris's conduct as minister to France (Lebrun to Ternant, 13, 19 Sep. 1792, AMAE: CPEU, xxxvi). See also Notes on Conversations with William Stephens Smith and George Washington, 20 Feb. 1793.

Notes on the French Revolution

1793. Jan. 15. M. Blacon, member from Dauphiné, of the 1st. National assembly of France is now[1] here. He was one of those who met at my house in Paris when the Monarchical patriots (afterwards called Feuillants) and the Republican patriots (afterwards called Jacobins) were[2] about to form a schism. At a dinner at Mr. Hammond's to-day he recalls to my mind the names of all the members of both parties who met, to wit, la Fayette, Duport, Barnave, Alexr. La Meth, Blacon, Mounier, Maubourg, and Dagout. The result of that conference was that they made mutual sacrifices of opinion, and prevented the schism. The Republicans gave up their opposition to *a king*, the Monocrats theirs to a *single branch of legislature*.

MS (DLC); entirely in TJ's hand; written on same sheet as "Anas" entries for 13 and 17 Dec. 1792 and 16 Jan. 1793. Recorded in SJPL under 15 Jan. 1793: "Blacon on the caucus at my house in Paris." Included in the "Anas."

Henri François Lucrecius d'Armand de Forest, Marquis de Blacons, a liberal member of the Estates General in 1789 who thereafter became progressively more royalist in his political views, left France, apparently in 1792, and did not return

until 1801 (Jean François Eugène Robi-
net and others, eds., *Dictionnaire His-
torique et Biographique de La Révolution et
de L'Empire, 1789-1815*, 2 vols. [Paris,
1899], I, 195-6). For a fuller account of
the meeting at TJ's HOUSE IN PARIS, see

Lafayette to TJ, [25 Aug. 1789], and
note.

[1] Word interlined.
[2] Word written over "agreed."

From Rochefontaine

[15 Jan. 1793]

Col: Rochefontaine Came to begg Mr. Gefferson to write to M.
delamotte vice consul of america at havre de Grace, to order him
to send immediately to M. hamilton secretary of the treasury of the
United states of america, the original title of M. Rochefontaine against
the United states; which has been deposited by him in the Consul's
office last February. M. hamilton had agreed with M. Rochefontaine
to Speack to Mr. Gefferson on the subject, and M. Rochefontaine hope
he has done it; but as he has an opportunity of a Gentleman sayling
Wednesday next, from this port to proceed by the way of Belfast to
france, M. Rochefontaine will be much obliged to Mr: Gefferson to
write the said letter, and he will call to morrow morning to get it.

RC (DNA: RG 59, MLR); undated; at
foot of text in the hand of George Taylor,
Jr.: "(recd. in the office 15 Jany. 1793)";
on verso: (in TJ's hand) "to be filed" and
(in Taylor's hand) "(filed in case No. 2.
Box No. 7)."

Etienne Nicolas Marie Béchet, Chevalier de Rochefontaine (1755-1814), a
French volunteer who rose to the rank of
brevet major as an engineer in the Continental Army during the American Revolution, subsequently became a colonel
in the French army and settled in the
United States in 1792 after a short term
of service with the expeditionary force
that the French government had sent to
Saint-Domingue in 1791 to quell the great
slave revolt that was raging there (André
Lasseray, *Les Français sous les Treize
Etoiles (1775-1783)*, 2 vols. [Mâcon and

Paris, 1935], I, 124-7). In order to facilitate Rochefontaine's effort to secure payment of the debt the United States owed
him for his wartime services, TJ wrote
the following note this day to Delamotte,
the American vice-consul at Le Havre: "I
am informed by Colo. Rochefontaine that
he deposited with you in February last
the original certificate from the treasury of
the U.S. of the sum of money due from
them to him. As the rules of the Treasury
office require that these originals should be
returned on paiment, I am to desire that
you will transmit the same by some safe
conveyance to Mr. Hamilton, Secretary of
the Treasury, for which this will be your
warrant" (PrC in DLC; at foot of text:
"M. de la Motte, V. Consul of the U.S.
at Havre"). Rochefontaine received payment of his claim in January 1794 (Syrett,
Hamilton, XVII, 538).

From William Short

I address this letter to you in your private character. It is merely to inform you of my being thus far on my way to Madrid. It will probably find you at Monticello. My last from the Hague will have informed you of the causes of my delay there after recieving your despatches for Spain. Nothing induced me to pass through France, but the inevitable desire to see the distressed and unfortunate family of le Rocheguyon. I could not resist their pressing sollicitations, altho' everybody thought there was real danger in the present situation of France to traverse it. To my great astonishment I have found the people on the roads from Valenciennes here as calm, and as peaceable as ever I saw them. The roads however from total neglect have become almost impassable. No carriage passes without breaking down between Angouleme and this place. This has happened to mine daily, notwithstanding it is of the best and strongest kind of English carriages. This has occasioned a good deal of delay on the road unavoidably—another delay of eight days, which I may call unavoidable also, was at Le Rocheguyon, for I had not morally force enough to get away sooner. After making all their wounds bleed afresh I could not stay less and at length did violence to myself in forcing myself away from them. Their situation is so peculiarly distressing—and their friendship for me is such that nothing but the irresistible sense of my duty could have torn me away from them in their unexampled situation. I hope and trust the loss of these eight days exactly passed at le Rocheguyon (where this unhappy family has been ever since their catastrophe) will not be of any consequence and indeed it is impossible it can—nothing less than the certainty could have enabled me to have staid less. I inclose you two letters—one from the old lady which she desired me to send to you, without its[1] appearing to have gone through my hands—from which I infer there is something in it respecting me, although I have told her and repeated to her an hundred times that nothing depends on you—and at present probably on no body else, I mean of the kind she wishes. If I were sure there was nothing else in the letter I would not send it. You will recieve it such as it is—the other was sent to me for you from Clerici.

My letters to you since I received yours with the instructions for Madrid on the 28th. of Nov. have been as follows. Nos. 120 to 122. inclusive dated Nov. 30. Dec. 8. and Dec. 18. Private dated Nov. 30. Dec. 18.

I say nothing to you of the affairs of this country because it would require a great deal to give you an idea of them. You will have received also up to the present date from M. Morris—as I brought with me and gave to M. Fenwick a great number of letters and packets for you. My ideas also are all agog—in the hurry and impatience of being at the end of this long journey from whence I will write to you *à tête reposée*. Ever your sincere friend & faithful servant   W Short

RC (DLC); at head of text: "*Private*"; addressed: "Mr. Jefferson Monticello"; endorsed by TJ as received 20 Apr. 1793 and so recorded in SJL. Enclosures: (1) Gaudenzio Clerici to TJ, 26 Dec. 1792. (2) Madame d'Enville to TJ, 30 Dec. 1792.

Short had recently visited Madame d'Enville and Duchesse Alexandrine de La Rochefoucauld, who was simultaneously her granddaughter and daughter-in-law, at their estate, La ROCHEGUYON,

forty miles northwest of Paris. During this visit Short asked the recently widowed Duchesse, with whom he had been carrying on an affair, to marry him, but she refused (George Green Shackelford, "William Short, Jefferson's Adopted Son, 1758-1849" [Ph.D. diss., University of Virginia, 1955], 328-59, 384-97). For the CATASTROPHE suffered by these two women, see Madame d'Enville to TJ, 30 Dec. 1792, and note.

[1] Here Short canceled "passing thro."

From Jean Baptiste Ternant

Tuesday 15th. Jany. 1793

Mr. ternant returns many thanks to Mr. Jefferson for the french papers now sent back—he incloses the letter received from Savanna, and begs Mr. Jefferson will return it with a duplicata of the letter of 9th. novr. to the district Judge of Georgia. The letter announced yesterday by Mr. Jefferson, on my colonial application, is not yet come to hand.

RC (DNA: RG 59, NL); at foot of text in the hand of George Taylor, Jr.: "sent the above papers same morng. to Mr. Ternant." Enclosure not found.

TJ's LETTER OF 9TH. NOVR. 1792 to Matthew McAlister concerned the theft of certain slaves from Martinique.

To George Washington

SIR   Philadelphia Jan. 15. 1793.

On further consideration I have thought it may be as well to omit the proposition for making any *addition* however small to the foreign fund, till the next session of Congress, by which time it will be more evident whether it is necessary or not. I have the honor to be with the greatest respect Sir your most obedt. & most humble servt

TH: JEFFERSON

PrC (DLC). Tr (DLC); 19th-century copy. Not recorded in SJL.

FOREIGN FUND: The money appropriated by Congress to meet the expenses of the diplomatic establishment. In February

1793 Congress passed an act continuing in force for another year a 1790 act which authorized the expenditure of $40,000 a year for this purpose (*Annals*, II, 2292, III, 1411-12).

From Etienne Clavière

Paris le 16. Janvier 1793 L'an 2e. de La Republique

J'ai reçu, Monsieur, La Lettre que vous m'avés écrite, le 16. aout dernier. Elle m'a été remise par M. Cassinave à qui j'aurois voulu prouver le cas, tout particulier, que je fais de votre recommandation. Les circonstances ne se sont pas trouvées favorables à des arrangemens avec lui pris en france même: mais ce qui est différé, peut très bien n'être pas perdu: Le Citoyen Genet, ministre plenipotentiaire de la republique francoise, auprès des Etats unis, est chargé de traitter à son arrivée de tous Les objets qui nous intéressent dans ce moment; Il a vu M. Cassinave et a pris de lui[1] des renseignemens qui pourront conduire à quelques marchés qu'il eut été difficile de conclure ici.

Le Citoyen Genet est chargé des pouvoirs Les plus amples et d'instructions toutes tendantes à resserrer Les Liens qui doivent subsister entre La france et Les Etats unis,[2] et à fonder des relations commerciales qui puissent prendre une consistance solide et rendre L'union, entre Les deux républiques, toute à La fois utile et amicale. Je ne doute point, Monsieur, que ce Citoyen estimable ne trouve auprès de vous un ami; qui S'empressera à lui aplanir toutes les difficultés, et à répondre aux intentions de fraternité et de concorde qu'il manifestera.

Je vous remercie, de tout ce que vous me dites d'obligeant sur la place que j'occupe. Si La bonne volonté, L'amour du travail et quelque courage, sont des titres; j'ai du Là mériter, mais La nature de La place que j'occupe reduit à bien peu de chose Le merite que vous voulez bien me suposer. Je fais des vœux pour votre bonheur et votre Conservation, et vous prie d'agréer L'assurance de mon sincère attachement.

CLAVIERE

RC (DLC); in a clerk's hand, signed by Clavière; at head of text: "Clavière Ministre des Contributions Publiques à Th Jefferson membre du Congrès des Etats unis"; endorsed by TJ as received 16 May 1793 and so recorded in SJL. Dupl (DLC); in a clerk's hand, signed by Clavière; endorsed by TJ as received 31 Mch. 1794 and so recorded in SJL.

Dft (AN); contains emendations, the most important of which are noted below.

[1] Preceding five words substituted in Dft for "avec la maison duquel il pourra tres bien s'arranger."

[2] Here in Dft Clavière first wrote "entre nations libres" before altering and completing the phrase to read as above.

To Francis Eppes

DEAR SIR   Philadelphia Jan. 16. [1793]
Your favor of the 2d. inst. is duly recieved, and in answer to your
enquiries about the prospect of foreign demand for wheat I answer
that it will be undoubtedly great. Something like a famine may be
apprehended thro' the greater part of France. Spain is buying largely.[1]
And I am assured from good authority that England will want a good
deal. Her ports were opened to the reception of it for home consumption in November, which was very early indeed for the price to be
already up to the importation price. The demands in the West Indies
are always considerable: but we now furnish the whole consumption
to the French West Indies which used to be chiefly supplied from
France. In addition to this the military they have sent over require
40,000 dollars worth of provisions a month, which is regularly purchased for them here. So that the price cannot but be high. I think the
best rule is, never to sell on a rising market. Wait till it *begins* to fall.
Then indeed one will lose a penny or two, but with a rising market
you never know what you are to lose. My love to Mrs. Eppes and the
family. Jack is well. Adieu your's affectionately   TH: JEFFERSON

RC (NcU: Southern Historical Collection, Hubard Family Papers); partially
dated; at foot of text: "Mr. Eppes." Pr C
(DLC). Tr (DLC); 19th-century copy.

[1] Preceding sentence interlined, TJ having previously abandoned two attempts to
interline it at other points below.

Notes on John Adams and the
French Revolution

Jan. 16. At a meeting of the board for the sinking fund, in a conversation after business was over, Mr. Adams declared that 'men could
never be governed but *by force*' that neither virtue prudence, wisdom nor any thing else sufficed to restrain their passions. That the
first National convention of France had established a constitution, had
excluded themselves from it's administration for certain time, a new
set of successors had come, had demolished their constitution, put to
death all the leading characters concerned in making it, were now
proceeding to make a new constitution, and to exclude themselves for
6. years from it's administration. That their successors would in their
turn demolish, hang them, and make a new constitution, and so on

eternally till[1] force could be brought into place to restrain them.—E.R. took notice of this declaration.

MS (DLC); entirely in TJ's hand; partially dated; written on same sheet as "Anas" entries for 13 and 17 Dec. 1792 and 15 Jan. 1793. Recorded in SJPL under 15 Jan. 1793: "Mr. Adams on French revoln." Included in the "Anas."

[1] TJ here canceled "a."

From Martha Jefferson Randolph

Monticello January 16 1793

With infinite pleasure I date once more from Monticello tho for the third time since my return[1] but from the negligence of the servant that carried the letters once and the great hurry of the post another time they never got farther than Charlottesville. Our dearest Anne has had an attack of a different nature from her former ones which the doctor imagines to proceed from her fatening too quickly. She is far from being well yet, tho considerably better. She is at present busily employed *yiting* to you a thing she has never missed doing whenever her health has permitted her. Her memory is uncommonly good for a child of her age. She relates many circumstances that happened during her travels with great exactitude but in such broken language and with so many gestures as renders it highly diverting to hear her. Her spirits have as yet been proof against ill health so far as to recover them with the least inter mission of it tho I much fear that will not long be the case if she does not mend speedily. The little boy continues well and is little inferior to his sister in point of size. He also begins to take a great deal of notice and bids fair to be as lively. I am afraid you will be quite tired of hearing so much about them but a fond Mother never knows where to stop when her children is the subject. Mr. Randolph did not recieve the letter in which you mentioned the books and stalactite till after he had left Richmond with 4 or 5 other Letters of yours which had been detained by some accident. Peter desires to be remembered to you and wishes to know if you have recieved one he wrote you from Richmond. Adieu dearest Papa. My Love to dear Maria. I will write to her by the next post. Believe me to [be][2] with tenderest affection yours   M. RANDOLPH

RC (ViU: Edgehill-Randolph Papers); endorsed by TJ as received 26 Jan. 1793 and so recorded in SJL.

[1] Preceding three words interlined.
[2] Word supplied.

From Francis Eppes

DR SIR   Eppington Janry. 17th. 1793
   Your favour of Janry. 2 is come to hand. I have consulted Betsey
on the subject of it, it will give her as well as myself great pleasure for
Jack to accompany the Commissioners to the Council of Indians, as we
wish at all times he shoud do what you think best for his improvement
and also to comply with all his reasonable requests, there is therefore
only one objection. I fear it will be impossible for me to procure the
money in time, as you inform me they will set off early in February.
I have the promis of as much cash as woud answer his purpos on the
28th of this month. Shoud I be fortunate enough to receive it will remit
it immediately. If the money cant be got Jack must indevour to put
up with the disappointment. I am offerd some Bonds of E Randolph's
the Attorney General. If you think you can make them answer your
purposes in Philadelphia I will send them to you. I am Dr Sir Your
Friend   FRANS. EPPES

Mrs. E. joins in respects to your self and Polly and complains heavily
of Pollys neglect.   F E

RC (ViU: Edgehill-Randolph Papers);
endorsed by TJ as received 26 Jan. 1793
and so recorded in SJL.

YOUR FAVOUR OF JANRY. 2 is undoubt-

edly a reference to TJ's letter of 4 Jan.
1793. Eppes probably confused the letter
from TJ with one he had written to him
on 2 Jan. 1793.

To Robert Gamble

SIR   Philadelphia Jan. 17. 1793.
   Our mutual friend Colo. Bell was to pay me a sum of about 200.
dollars and I think he said it would be through your channel. If he
has taken any arrangements with you on the subject, I should be glad
to recieve the remittance in any way most convenient. If he has not,
I will take the liberty of troubling you to forward him this letter in
order to avoid a delay which it would be convenient to me to avoid. I
am with much esteem, Sir, Your most obedt. humble servt
                                        TH: JEFFERSON

PrC (DLC); at foot of text: "Mr. Richard Gamble." Tr (ViU: Edgehill-Randolph
Papers); 19th-century copy.

From Gouverneur Morris

DEAR SIR   Paris 17 January 1793

I have already had the Honor to inform you that the Statue of General Washington by Houdon is finish'd and to ask to what Place it is to be sent. I have since been applied to by the Statuary in Regard to the last Payment for that Object. He tells me that "he hopes the State of Virginia will do as other foreigners pay him the Difference of Exchange a Thing the more easy to them as in Fact it can only cost them the Sum Stipulated. The Sum which they would have paid two Years ago and which eight Years ago would have been specially secur'd against Depreciation could the Emission of Assignats have been then foreseen." I have said to him that I am by no Means competent to decide on the Subject but would forward to the State his Application. I hope you will pardon me Sir for troubling you with it but as you agreed with Mr. Houdon in the first Instance it is (as well for that as for other Reasons) most proper that I should address myself to you. I am with Esteem and Respect Dear Sir your obedient Servant

GOUV MORRIS

RC (DNA: RG 59, DD); at head of text: "No. 17"; at foot of first page: "Thomas Jefferson Esqr."; endorsed by TJ as received 1 May 1793 and so recorded in SJL. FC (Lb in DLC: Gouverneur Morris Papers). Tr (DNA: RG 46, Senate Records, 3d Cong., 1st sess.) Tr (Lb in DNA: RG 59, DD).

Jean Antoine Houdon's statue of Wash-

ington had been commissioned in 1784 by the Virginia General Assembly, which requested TJ, then an American commissioner in France, to select a sculptor. See Vol. 15: xxxvii-ix; and Freeman, *Washington*, VI, 40-2.

TJ submitted this letter to the President on 1 May 1793, and Washington returned it the next day (Washington, *Journal*, 124, 125).

To Aaron Burr

Jan. 20. 1793.

Th: Jefferson presents his respectful compliments to Colo. Burr and is sorry to inform him it has been concluded to be improper to communicate the correspondence of *existing ministers*. He hopes this will, with Colo. Burr, be his sufficient apology.

RC (MWA); addressed: "Colo. Burr." Not recorded in SJL.

The provenance of TJ's first written communication to Aaron Burr (1756-1836), his future Vice President, who had

been chosen in 1791 to represent New York in the Senate, is obscure. According to his earliest biographer, Burr, in an effort to improve his understanding of American diplomacy, had obtained permission from TJ to examine the records of the Department of State in the morning hours before it opened each day. Burr is said to have availed himself of this privilege during the winter session of the Senate in 1791-92, taking notes and extracts from the records, until Washington issued a peremptory order denying him further access. Subsequently during this period, according to the same account, Burr wrote a note to TJ asking permission to consult departmental records relating to "a surrender of the western posts by the British," to which TJ returned the above reply (Matthew L. Davis, *Memoirs of Aaron Burr, with Miscellaneous Selections from his Correspondence*, 2 vols. [New York, 1836-37], I, 331). But there is no other evidence that TJ granted Burr access to departmental records as Davis claimed, no other record exists of Washington's order denying Burr such access, no text of Burr's note to TJ on the western posts has been found, and TJ's note to Burr was written a full year later than Davis assumed.

Nevertheless, although Davis's account is seriously flawed, TJ's reply shows that Burr did seek access to the CORRESPONDENCE OF EXISTING MINISTERS, probably on the subject of British retention of the western posts, and it may perhaps be inferred from TJ's note that he had already obtained access to the department's prefederal diplomatic records. Although Burr was not at this time involved in any Senate business relating to foreign affairs, he was interested in the maintenance of peaceful relations with the Western Indians, and Britain's occupation of the posts was widely regarded in America as a significant factor in inciting hostilities between these tribes and the United States (Burr to George Washington, 13 Mch. 1792, DNA: RG 59, MLR, printed conjecturally as a letter to TJ in Mary-Jo Kline and others, eds., *Political Correspondence and Public Papers of Aaron Burr*, 2 vols. [Princeton, 1983], I, 101-3; same, 145-6; see also George Hammond to TJ, 30 Jan. 1792).

To J. P. P. Derieux

DEAR SIR   Philadelphia Jan. 20 1793

I recieved yesterday your favor of the 9th. Mine of the 4th. would reach you about five days after the date of yours, and consequently would shew you that your bill in Mr. Fenwick's hands having been paid, all your funds transmitted by me through Colo. Gamble are free from that incumbrance. There remains nothing further to be done therefore than to wait till the sales here are closed, and settle and remit you the balance.—I sent, in mine of the 4th. the paper specifying the best articles of sale here, which you desired, and I shall forward the two letters you last inclosed to me. I am with compliments to Mrs. Derieux, Dear Sir your most obedt. humble servt   TH: JEFFERSON

PrC (DLC); at foot of text: "Mr. Derieux." Tr (ViU: Edgehill-Randolph Papers); 19th-century copy.

Derieux's FAVOR OF THE 9TH was actually dated 10 Jan. 1793.

From Joseph Fenwick

SIR   Bordeaux 20 Jany. 1793.

I have the honor to own your favors of the 31st. May and the 16 Octor. 1792—the latter covering letters for Mr. Morris and Mr. Short which were forwarded and held as you desired—answers to which go by this opportunity via St. Eustatius by the American Brigg the Mermaid as the best opportunity now offering from hence. The first I only received in November accompanying the Laws of Congress of the Session closing the 8 May. I herewith send you a Bond required by the Law relative to the functions of Consuls. Mr. John Mason of Virginia will be my security and who will procure another person satisfactory to you that will join him in the same as required by the Law.

I shall profit of the different occasions that present to communicate to you such information as you may require and that I think will be acceptable.

I shall also correspond with the minister of the United States that may reside in this country.[1]

Grain is now very scarce here and demanded at the prices below also all articles of provision, and the demand likely to continue during the war or until a plentiful crop supplies the real and immaginary wants. The value of the assignats have considerably depreciated lately and exchange on England is now 5d$\frac{1}{4}$ stg. ⅌ Livre uncertain and fluctuating. Articles of subsistence do not fluctuate with the Exchange, tho' it is the Thermometer for most others. This may be attributed to the system adopted by the Government for procuring their supplies thro' agents of Government and not in the ordinary chanel of Commerce. Wheat and Flour are not higher now than in Novemr. when Exchange was 7d ⅌ Livre or thereabouts. Tobacco is ready sale and not a great provision in market.

There is a late decree of the Convention to arm immediately 30 sail of the line and 20 Frigates which added to this number already equipped of 22 sail of the Line and 30 Frigates will make a considerable Fleet. The sailors, Carpenters, Rope Makers &ca. &ca. are classed as under the former Government and they have heretofore gone off without murmuring to the Dockyards and I think they will continue to go at least from this and the neighboring places without difficulty. A war with England and Holland is thought inevitable—the Underwriters refuse all premiums of Insurance. I have the honor to be Sir Your most Obedient and most humble Servant   JOSEPH FENWICK

Exchange London 15¾ a ½
Amsterdam 30 a 29¾
Madrid 27
Wheat 23 a 24^{tt} ℔ Boisseau
Flour 52 a 55^{tt} ℔ barrl.
Indian Corn 12 ℔ Boisseau
Rice 36 a 38^{tt} ℔ Ct.
Tobacco 40 a 60^{tt} ℔ do.
Whale Oil 50 a 55^{tt} ℔ Ct.
Sperm do. 80 a 85
Whale Bone common short 160 a 200 ℔ Ct.
Beef 60 a 80^{tt} ℔ barrl.
Pork 90 a 110 ℔ do.
Pot ash 70 a 76 ℔ Ct.
Pearl do. 70. a 80 ℔ do.

RC (DNA: RG 59, CD); addressed: "Thomas Jefferson Esqre Secretary of State Philadelphia"; endorsed by TJ as received 20 Apr. 1793 and so recorded in SJL; portion of text marked in pencil by TJ for publication (see note 1 below). Enclosure: Fenwick's consular bond, 20 Nov. 1792 (MS in same).

At Fenwick's request, JOHN MASON, his partner in the mercantile firm of Fenwick, Mason & Company, wrote a brief note to TJ from Georgetown on 22 Jan. 1793 asking how he and his friends could post the required security for Fenwick's consulship (RC in DLC; addressed: "Thomas Jefferson Esqr."; endorsed by TJ as received 26 Jan. 1793 and so recorded in SJL).

1 Except for the complimentary close and signature, the remainder of the letter and the subjoined list of prices were printed as the "Extract of a Letter from Bourdeaux, dated January 20, 1793," in the *National Gazette* of 1 May 1793.

To Richard Hanson

SIR   Philadelphia Jan. 20. 1793.

I received yesterday a letter from Mr. D. Hylton informing me that he has compleated the sale of my Elkhill lands to Doctor Taylor and Banks. He says 'he has taken their bonds jointly and severally backed with the Greenbriar lands, all which patents with the several bonds are now in my possession, subject to your orders. In the mortgage or deed of trust for the Greenbriar lands, you have the power, as the bonds become due, to act on the bonds by instituting a suit, or on giving three months notice in the Philadelphia and Richmond gazette to sell so much of the lands for cash as will discharge the bonds as they become due. This precaution I think secures the debt equally as well as could be done by mortgage on Elkhill. Those whom I have mentioned the lands given in trust, who appear to be acquainted with that part of the country, agree they are of much more value than the debt Banks and Taylor are bound for.'—So far Mr. Hylton's letter.— As soon as I come to Virginia I will deliver the bonds and deed of trust or mortgage to you, and then shall be glad to make a conjectural calculation whether (supposing none of my bonds to prove bad) any and what sum will be yet wanting to compleat the paiment of my part of the debt to Farrell & Jones. I am Sir your very humble servt

TH: JEFFERSON

PrC (MHi); at foot of text: "Mr. Richard Hanson." Tr (ViU: Edgehill-Randolph Papers); 19th-century copy.

For the sale of TJ's ELKHILL LANDS, see TJ to Daniel L. Hylton, 3 June 1792, and note.

To Daniel L. Hylton

DEAR SIR   Philadelphia Jan. 20. 1793.

I recieved yesterday your favor of the 9th. inst. and am happy that the sale of Elkhill is at length compleated. I would at once renew the deed here, but that there exists no such law of Congress as you suppose which could make a record here effectual to pass lands in Virginia. There is I believe some law of Virginia allowing a considerable time for the probat of deeds executed out of the state. Quere whether this would not admit the deed executed here last year to be still recorded? Be this as it may, I shall be in Virginia ere long, and will then do whatever is necessary to compleat the title. Till then also, I would rather you should either keep the bonds and other[1] papers which are in your hands, or deliver them to Mr. T. Randolph whenever you see him, and he will deposit them at Monticello. In the mean time, if the papers I before sent you did not authorize you to deliver possession of the lands to the purchasers, I do it fully by this letter, and further, to remove any tenant who may be on it, except the old woman (if she be living) who has her life in the 50. acres on the back of one of the tracts.—I pray you not to fail having the mortgage immediately recorded.—With many thanks for the trouble you have had in this business, and with my best respects to Mrs. Hylton I am Dear Sir your friend & servt   TH: JEFFERSON

PrC (MHi); at foot of text: "Mr. Hylton." Tr (ViU: Edgehill-Randolph Papers); 19th-century copy misdated 20

Jan. 1788 and erroneously printed under the date of 20 Jan. 1783 in Vol. 6: 220-1.

Hylton's FAVOR OF THE 9TH. from Richmond, recorded in SJL as received 19 Jan. 1793, has not been found. His previous letter of 26 Dec. 1792, recorded in SJL as recieved 7 Jan. 1793, is also missing.

[1] Preceding three words interlined.

From Benjamin Joy

Boston, 20 Jan. 1793. In accordance with the Consular Act, he submits the names of John Coffin Jones and Christopher Gore, Esqrs., Joseph Russell, Jr., merchant, and John Joy, Jr., gentleman, all of Boston, as sureties for his bond, and asks for instructions relating to the care of shipwrecked, sick, or captive mariners, as well as on any other matters TJ may deem fit. The daily allowance made by Congress for the relief of sick seamen is inadequate in the case of India, where many of them can be expected from the frequent sales of American ships and the unhealthiness of the climate. There is an excellent hospital at Calcutta supported at great expense by the East India Company "to which all white men that are sick are admitted on their paying after the rate of ten sicca rupees per month"; if he could pay the same rate for sick seamen, they would be more comfortably cared for there. Alternatively, a law might be passed enabling him to charge every ship arriving in Calcutta a fee for the relief of distressed seamen based on tonnage or size of the crew, a custom in Madeira and other places, or perhaps the wages of deserting seamen, who without a home are most likely to get sick in the hot climate of India, might be appropriated for this purpose, a practice followed in some parts of Europe.

RC (DNA: RG 59, CD); 2 p.; at foot of text: "Honble Thomas Jefferson Secretary of State"; endorsed by TJ as received 28 Jan. 1793 and so recorded in SJL.

Benjamin Joy (ca. 1755/57-1828), a merchant from Newburyport, Massachusetts, who was appointed United States consul at Calcutta and other Indian ports in November 1792, had resided in that country and participated in its trade for a number of years before his appointment.

When the East India Company refused to recognize his consular authority after he arrived in Calcutta in April 1794, Joy returned to Massachusetts late in 1795 and resigned his consulship in January of the following year. Thereafter he prospered as a Boston merchant (Tobias Lear to TJ, 17 Nov. 1792, and note; TJ to Joy, 12 Mch. 1793; G. Bhagat, *Americans in India, 1784-1860* [New York, 1970], 72, 86-9).

André Michaux's Observations on His Proposed Western Expedition

Observations sur le Voyage a l'Ouest du Misissipi

1°. Afin d etre plus libre d'agir et de prendre le parti auquel je serois forcé par les Circonstances je préfere entreprendre ce Voyage a mes Dépens. Ma delicatesse ne me permet pas d accepter la Somme proposée pour une Entreprise qui peut être ne pourra pas être éxécutée entierement.

2°. Pour ne pas differer ce Voyage et remedier aux difficultés que j'éprouve actuellement de tirer sur l'Administration je considereray comme une grande faveur l'acceptation de mes Traites jusqu a la concurrence de trois mille six cens livres tournois sur celle de dix sept mille cinq cens vingt livres due pour mes Appointemens et mes Avances[1] par l'Administration. Si Mr. De la forest ne veut pas endosser mes traites pour cette Somme de 3600^{tt} non obstant qu il y ait été authorisé par le Ministre de la Marine et si je ne suis pas assuré du montant avant de partir de Philadelphie, je n'entreprendray pas ce Voyage.

3°. Il me sera donné toutes les Lettres de recommandation necessaires pour les Negocians aux Illinois, Chefs Indiens &c.

4° Toutes les Connoisssances, Observations et Informations Geographiques seront communiquées a la Societé Philosophique.

5° Les autres Découvertes en histoire Naturelle seront a mon profit immediat et ensuite destinées a l'Utilité Générale.

6° Je n'entreprendray pas ce Voyage que je nay reglé mes Affaires en Caroline et je ne demande que trois jours apres la reception de Lettres que j attends de Charleston.[2]

A Philadelphie le 20 Janvier 1793
A. Michaux

RC (ViW); endorsed by TJ. Tr (PPAmP: Miscellaneous Manuscripts); in Michaux's hand; docketed by Michaux: "Copie des Conditions remise a Mr. Jefferson Secretaire d'Etat le 20 Janvier 1793." Tr (DLC: Genet Papers); in Michaux's hand; incomplete text quoted in 22 May 1793 statement of Michaux to Edmond Charles Genet.

For a discussion of Michaux's projected western expedition, see Editorial Note on Jefferson and André Michaux's proposed western expedition, at 22 Jan. 1793.

[1] Remainder of paragraph omitted from Tr in DLC.
[2] Paragraph omitted from Tr in DLC.

To Thomas Mann Randolph, Jr.

DEAR SIR Philadelphia Jan. 21. 1793.

I received the day before yesterday your's of the 9th. From an expression in that, as well as the preceding one, I fear you may not have received my letters which have been regular and constant once a week, except once when the post day was perceived to be changed. I then accomodated the day of my writing to the day of the departure of the Western post from Richmond.—I have received information from Mr.

Hylton that he has compleated the sale of Elk hill, and has the bonds and mortgage in his possession, which I desired him to keep till he shall see you, and give them to you to be deposited safe at Monticello. I wish to hear of the sale in Bedford.—I thank you for information of the work done at Monticello, and shall be happy to have the further progress noted in every letter. I now inclose you a bill of scantling to be got by the sawyers. It is material that the stocks should be got as soon as possible, lest the sap should begin to rise, which would occasion the timber to rot very soon. By getting the stocks now too, they may find employment for the oxcart and waggon when the roads from the stone quarry shall be rendered too miry and laborious. In laying off the stocks for the triangular sleepers, as mentioned in the paper, the sawyers will probably need to be shewn by you once or twice how to do it.—The bringing slabs from Henderson's is another job, when the others cannot be proceeded on. My love to my dear Martha, and am Dear Sir yours most affectionately   TH: JEFFERSON

RC (DLC); addressed: "Thos. M. Randolph junr. esq. Monticello." PrC (CSmH). Tr (ViU: Edghill-Randolph Papers); 19th-century copy.

ENCLOSURE

Instructions on Timber for Monticello

[ca. 21 Jan. 1793]

Scantling for the operations of 1793

10. Sleepers.	23. feet long:	10 Inches deep. 4. Inches thick.
30. do.	12. feet long.	same depth and breadth.
17. do.	18. feet long.	same depth and breadth.
10. do.	23. feet long	
30. do.	12. feet long	all these are to be triangular, and to be got in
17. do.	18. feet long.	the manner pointed out on the next page.
10. do.	16. feet long.	
15. Joists.	25. feet long.	
15. do.	11. f. long	for the depth and thickness of these, measure
20. do.	31. f. long	those of the Study at Monticello.
24. do.	24. f. long	
180. Rafters	16. f. long.	of the same depth and thickness of those over the Study.

The Sleepers, joists and rafters must, I presume, be got of Pine. But they must be absolutely clear of sap. Poplar is not strong enough for sleepers: it would do for joists or rafters; but I imagine there is not enough of it to be had at Monticello. Chesnut is bad, because it very soon corrodes the nails. Oak is bad, because it springs so as to throw the floors into swells and hollows.

5000. square feet of bastard plank, for sheeting. No matter of what breadth or length. The stocks need not be hewed.

Manner of getting and laying off the Triangular sleepers.

Cut down a tree, of at least 18. Inches diameter besides the sap and take off the bark. It is not to be hewed.

Cross-cut it as square as possible to it's proper lengths.

When laid on the pit, strike a circle of 9. Inches radius at each end.

hang a plumb-line over the center c. and mark the points a. and b. where the line intersects the circle.

then with the same opening of the compasses with which the circle was struck, that is to say, with the radius, mark the circle at d. and e. on one side, and at f. and g. on the other side.

draw the three diameters ab. dg. ef.

lay off the other end of the stock in the same manner. Indeed it will be best, immediately after marking the points a.b. with the plumb-line at one end, to mark corresponding points with the plumb line at the other end, lest the stock should by any accident be justled a little, in which case the corresponding diameters at the two ends would not be in the same plane.

this done at both ends, the stock will be lined[1] from a. to the corresponding point at the other end,[2] from d. to it's corresponding point, and so on, and then sawed through.

the convexity of one side of the sleeper, or any roughnesses it may have, will be of no consequence, as that side will lie between the floor and cieling. The sap may be left on till we come to work: but all pieces which will not yeild a triangle of 9. I. on every side, clear of sap, will be to be rejected.

I imagine it will be best to bring the stocks home before they are sawed, that (a slab cover being put over the pit) they may be sawed even in wet weather.

MS (DLC: TJ Papers, 79: 13723); undated; written entirely in TJ's hand on two sides of one sheet; docketed on recto at a later date by Thomas Mann Randolph, Jr.: "Th: Jefferson Instructions respecting timber for his house Nov: '92."

[1] TJ here canceled "at top."
[2] TJ here canceled "and at bottom."

Jefferson and
André Michaux's Proposed
Western Expedition

EDITORIAL NOTE

Discovered in the vault of the American Philosophical Society in 1979 with supporting financial papers described below, this signed text of the subscription for André Michaux, together with the instructions to the French botanist printed under 30 Apr. 1793, represents the fullest expression, previous to the expedition of Lewis and Clark, of Jefferson's longstanding interest in promoting American exploration of the vast territory beyond the Mississippi that he was destined as President to add to the national domain and that he came to regard as the foundation of an "empire for liberty" (APS, *Year Book* [1979], 158-60; TJ to James Madison, 27 Apr. 1809).

Jefferson's efforts to promote American exploration of the trans-Mississippi West with a view toward finding a convenient water route to the Pacific began at the close of the Revolutionary War. In 1783, while serving in the Confederation Congress, he sought unsuccessfully to induce the conqueror of the Old Northwest, George Rogers Clark, to lead an exploring party from the Mississippi to California in order to counter a British expedition that was reportedly being prepared for this purpose. Three years later, as minister to France, he supported the abortive effort of the Connecticut adventurer John Ledyard to explore this region from the opposite direction by way of Russia. Then, in 1792, against a background of growing British and American interest in the Pacific Northwest stemming from the voyages of Captain James Cook, the Nootka Sound crisis of 1790, and the beginning of American involvement in the region's fur trade, Jefferson proposed to the American Philosophical Society, according to his later recollection, that it "should set on foot a subscription to engage some competent person to explore that region ... by ascending the Missouri, crossing the Stony mountains, and descending the nearest river to the Pacific" (TJ to George Rogers Clark, 4 Dec. 1783; TJ to Paul Allen, 18 Aug. 1813; Donald Jackson, *Thomas Jefferson & the Stony Mountains: Exploring the West from Monticello* [Urbana, Ill., 1981], 42-56, 74).

Although there is no mention of this proposal in Jefferson's surviving papers of that period, other evidence substantiates his recollection. In June 1792, Caspar Wistar, Jr., a fellow member of the American Philosophical Society, informed the American botanist Moses Marshall—who had earlier shown an interest in exploring the western United States, possibly with the Society's support, and who was already aware of "the wishes of some gentlemen here to have our continent explored in a western direction"—that "Mr. Jefferson and several other gentlemen are much interested, and think they can procure a subscription sufficient to insure one thousand guineas as a compensation to any one who undertakes the journey and can bring satisfactory proof of having crossed to the South Sea." Wistar invited Marshall, who lived in Chester County, to come to Philadelphia at once and meet with Jefferson, who, he reported, "seems principally interested" in the expedition, which was to make its way by the Missouri, but nothing came of this suggestion (Wistar to Marshall, 20 June 1792, in John W. Harshberger, *The Botanists of Philadelphia and Their Work* [Philadelphia, 1899], 106; see also same, 102, 105-6).

Since the plan for a western expedition apparently had been contemplated by Jefferson and other members of the Society for some time, it may well have come to the attention of André Michaux, a French botanist who was visiting Philadelphia during the spring of 1792. Born in 1746 on the royal domain of Satory, a part of Versailles, Michaux had for a number of years joined with his father in farming this land for the French crown before abandoning agriculture after the sudden death of his wife in 1770 and dedicating the rest of his life to botany. He underwent rigorous professional training in this science at the royal gardens of Trianon in Versailles and the Jardin du Roi in Paris and gained valuable practical experience in botanical field expeditions to England, the Auvergne, Spain, and Persia. Upon his return to France from his Persian expedition in 1785, Michaux received an appointment as royal botanist from Louis XVI, a prestigious position that gave him the same status as regular French diplomats. As part of a government effort to revitalize French agriculture and animal husbandry, as well as to reinvigorate French forestry, Michaux was instructed to repair to America and ship back to France such trees, plants, fruits, seeds, and animals as would contribute to these ends (Henry Savage, Jr., and Elizabeth J. Savage, *André and François André Michaux* [Charlottesville, 1986], 3-39).

Michaux arrived in New York in November 1785 and was struck by the plenitude of natural riches he encountered in the New World, later exclaiming to a French correspondent, "I cannot desire a situation more fortunate than that of having an immense country to visit, immense collections to make, for which I would devote all my life, my time, my fortune" (Michaux to Comte d'Angiviller, 18 Aug. 1786, translated and quoted in Savage, *Michaux*, 52). Between 1785 and 1792, Michaux applied himself to his mission with unflagging industry and zeal, establishing nurseries first in Bergen, New Jersey, and then outside Charleston, South Carolina, which served as his bases of operations in America. Pursuing his botanical researches, often under the most arduous conditions, in virtually every state from New York to Georgia, as well as in Florida, the Bahamas, and Canada, he dispatched prodigious numbers of American specimens to France, including 60,000 trees. At the same time, he introduced many Asian and European trees and plants to the United States.

During his sojourn in North America Michaux became acquainted with various members of the American Philosophical Society, although not—as far as the record shows—with Jefferson. Michaux, however, was in Philadelphia between 25 Apr. and 27 May 1792, a period when Jefferson and others had a western expedition under consideration, visiting with various members of the Society before embarking on an expedition to Canada (C. S. Sargent, ed., "Portions of the Journal of André Michaux, Botanist, written during his Travels in the United States and Canada, 1785 to 1796," APS, *Proceedings*, XXVI [1889], 68). After completing his Canadian expedition, Michaux arrived in Philadelphia on 8 Dec. 1792, his future very much in doubt because of the overthrow of the French monarchy. Uncertain of continued employment by the French Republic, and unable to have drafts on his delinquent back salary accepted, yet unwilling to discontinue his scientific work in America, he decided to seek the sponsorship of the nation's leading scientific institution. Thus, two days later, he met with several otherwise unidentifed members of the American Philosophical Society and offered to explore the sources of the Missouri River and search for rivers that flowed into the Pacific in return for the Society's endorsement of his drafts in the amount of 3,600 livres tournois. Although Michaux emphasized the increase in accurate geographical knowledge that would accrue to the United States, there can be no doubt that his proposed expedition was also designed to enable him to pursue his official botanical researches, even in the absence of support from the French government. Nevertheless, the similarities between Michaux's proposition and the expedition Jefferson and others were considering earlier in the year— especially when it is considered that the French botanist previously had evinced no interest in purely geographical exploration—lead almost irresistibly to the conclusion that Michaux was not only aware of Jefferson's idea, but may have been inspired by it. In any event, Michaux's interlocutors approved his plan and offered to form a subscription of $5,000 in order to finance it (Savage, *Michaux*, 42-124, 167-8; Michaux's Observations on His Proposed Western Expedition, 20 Jan. 1793; Michaux, "Memoire abregé concernant mes Voyages dans l'Amerique Septentrionale," 21 May 1793, DLC: Genet Papers; Michaux, Statement to Edmond Charles Genet, 22 May 1793, same; Sargent, "Journal of Michaux," 89-90).

Although it remains unclear whether Jefferson was one of the members of the American Philosophical Society to whom Michaux first broached his plan for a western expedition, it is not surprising that he thereafter took the lead in dealing with Michaux on the Society's behalf (Benjamin Smith Barton to TJ, 4 Jan. 1793, and note). Unwilling to surrender the freedom of action to which he had grown accustomed during his stay in America, Michaux submitted to Jefferson on 20 Jan. 1793 a list of six conditions under which he would make the journey. In this document, obviously written to Jefferson in his capacity as an officer of the American Philosophical Society, Michaux made several stipulations: that to preserve his freedom of action he would prefer to travel at his own expense rather than accept the proffered subscription of $5,000 for an expedition he might not be able to complete; that the Society facilitate his departure by accepting as a favor his bills of exchange for 3,600 livres tournois, this loan to be repaid from the 17,520 livres owed him in salary and advances by the French government, but that he would not undertake the expedition unless the French consul general in Philadelphia endorsed his bills and he was assured of the whole amount before leaving the city; that he be given letters of recommendation to ease his passage with any Indians he encountered; that he would communicate to the Society all geographical knowledge arising from the expedition; that he would reserve other discoveries in natural history for his immediate profit before making them available to the public; and that he would not begin the expedition until he had first settled his affairs in Charleston (Michaux's Observations on His Proposed Western Expedition, 20 Jan. 1793; Michaux, Statement to Genet, 22 May 1793, DLC: Genet Papers; Sargent, "Journal of Michaux," 90). Jefferson thereupon prepared a draft of the subscription that incorporated elements of all but the third and sixth of Michaux's conditions but deviated significantly from his stipulations by providing for an advance and by qualifying the terms under which the Society would accept his bills, thus undercutting Michaux's status as a free agent and placing him under the Society's exclusive employ. He then submitted either the draft or the final text to the President on 22 Jan. 1793—hence the conjectural date assigned to the document.

The President immediately indicated his willingness to contribute to the proposed expedition, and Jefferson soon began to seek other subscribers in Philadelphia. Soliciting members and nonmembers of the American Philosophical Society alike, Jefferson proceeded according to a hierarchical order, as evidenced by the sequence of signatories (TJ to George Washington, 22 Jan. 1793; Washington to TJ, 22 Jan. 1793). Thus, the first column of signatures consists of the President, the Vice President, and seven Senators, four of whom (Washington, Adams, Izard, and Morris) were members of the Society; the second of three Cabinet officials, five Senators, and the governor of Pennsylvania, four of whom (the Cabinet officers and the governor) were members of the Society; the third of thirteen Representatives, two of whom (Madison and Kittera) belonged to the Society; and the fourth of one Representative who was not a member of the Society (Mercer), five other subscribers who did belong to it, and two more who did not (Norris and Ross). Gathering thirty-seven signatures besides his own, including those of fifteen members of the Society, Jefferson garnered pledges of support amounting to $870. All those listed in the first three columns and Mercer, whose name appears at the head of the fourth column on the verso, must have signed no later than 2 Mch. 1793, the date Congress adjourned and apparently the last day Mercer could have left Philadelphia (Syrett, *Hamilton*, xiv, 178-9, 189-90). Nor is there any reason to doubt, judging from the physical appearance of the manuscript, that the remaining seven subscribers signed their names to the agreement at approximately the same time.

The American Philosophical Society officially approved the subscription agreement for Michaux and accepted sponsorship of the expedition at a meeting on 19 Apr. 1793 that Jefferson did not attend, doubtless because of his participation in the Cabinet meeting of that day on the urgent question of neutrality. At the same time the Society appointed two committees to oversee subscriptions—one to solicit further subscriptions and another to collect them (Rough Minutes of the American Philosophical Society, 19 Apr. 1793, PPAmP; Cabinet Opinion on Washington's Questions on Neutrality and the Alliance with France, [19 Apr. 1793]). Nicholas Collin, a member of the second committee, made a copy of the text of the agreement and obtained the signatures of thirty-one additional subscribers, among them approximately eighteen members of the Society, who pledged $389. Collin also compiled an undated list of the names and pledges of the first thirty-four signatories of Jefferson's manuscript, below which he penciled the names and pledges of six new subscribers from the Society, and John Ewing, another member of the Society, signed again, evidently pledging another $10. Thanks to the combined efforts of Jefferson and the American Philosophical Society, seventy-five subscribers, including approximately thirty-nine members of the Society, pledged to contribute $1,569 to the French botanist's proposed journey of western exploration. Before the month was out Jefferson paid his advance of $12.50 toward the expedition along with a number of other subscribers (MB, 28 Apr. 1793; see list of money collected as described below).

Jefferson's efforts on Michaux's behalf did not end with the preparation of the subscription agreement and the solicitation of contributors. During the same meeting at which the American Philosophical Society approved the agreement, it also appointed a committee consisting of Jefferson and five other members, or any three of them, to confer with Michaux, "frame Instructions for his observance" in order "to promote the Advantages of his Tour," and report thereon at the Society's next session. This action was prompted by Michaux himself, who had recently asked David Rittenhouse, the Society's president, for such instructions before he embarked on the expedition (Rough Minutes of the American Philosophical Society, 19 Apr. 1793, PPAmP; see also Rittenhouse to TJ, [10 Apr. 1793]; and TJ to Rittenhouse, 11 Apr. 1793). Jefferson, who had been requested by Rittenhouse to undertake this task more than a week before the committee was appointed, thereupon drew up detailed instructions governing the conduct of Michaux's expedition and showed them to the French botanist. While not rejecting the instructions out of hand, Michaux had serious reservations about them. By this time Michaux was aware that the French Republic had decided to employ him in the same capacity and entrust him with the same scientific mission in America he had been given by Louis XVI. Consequently, with his status as an officer of the French government now reconfirmed, he criticized the instructions for regarding him solely as an agent of the American Philosophical Society to the exclusion of his responsibilities to the French nation. Accordingly, on 30 Apr. 1793, he submitted a memorandum to Rittenhouse setting forth a revised set of conditions under which he would undertake his proposed journey of western exploration for the Society. Emphasizing that his duties to France took precedence over his mission for the Society, he insisted that in order to preserve his freedom of action he would only accept financial help from the Society upon completion of his western journey, and therefore bound himself to do no more than strive to fulfill the first, fourth, and fifth conditions he had stipulated to Jefferson on 20 Jan. 1793. Since these conditions were still compatible with the goals of the expedition, the Society approved Jefferson's instructions for Michaux, with several amendments, during a special meeting Jefferson attended on 30 Apr. 1793 (Michaux's Observations on His Proposed Western Expedition, 20 Jan. 1793; American Philosophical Society's Instructions to André Michaux, [ca. 30 Apr. 1793]; Michaux, "Expositions des Motifs sur les quels je suis déterminé a entreprendre le Voyage a l'Ouest du Misissipi," 29-30 Apr. 1793, PPAmP: Miscellaneous Manuscripts; Rough Minutes of the American Philosophical Society, 30 Apr. 1793, PPAmP; Michaux, Statement to Genet, 22 May 1793, DLC: Genet Papers; Sargent, "Journal of Michaux," 90). With the Society's approval of the subscription agreement and instructions, Jefferson's vision of exploring the trans-Mississippi West in order to find a convenient continental water route to the Pacific seemed on the verge of realization—and this through the agency of an accomplished French botanist who was fluent in English, inured to the hardships of wilderness travel, and sponsored by the new American nation's most prestigious scientific institution.

Notwithstanding all these painstaking preparations, Michaux soon became engulfed in the maelstrom of revolutionary French diplomacy and failed to carry out his intended mission of western exploration. Instead of leaving Philadelphia immediately after the American Philosophical Society approved his instructions, Michaux delayed his departure so that he could first confer with

Edmond Charles Genet, the new French minister to the United States. Shortly after Genet's arrival in Philadelphia on 16 May 1793, Michaux informed him that, though he still considered his western expedition essential to the completion of his official botanical mission in America, he nevertheless stood ready to serve France in any way Genet deemed best suited to advance the Republic's interests (Michaux, "Memoire abregé," 21 May 1793, DLC: Genet Papers). Genet took advantage of this offer by enlisting Michaux in a grandiose plan, authorized by the Girondist ministry in Paris, to liberate Louisiana from Spanish rule by means of a joint attack by a French naval force and an American volunteer corps to be raised in Kentucky and commanded by the Revolutionary War veteran George Rogers Clark. By this time an ardent republican, Michaux readily accepted a commission as Genet's liaison agent with Clark and other Kentucky leaders. Toward the end of June Genet unofficially informed Jefferson of the French botanist's assigned role in the projected liberation of Louisiana and won his qualified support for it, since the Secretary of State then believed that it was more important to acquiesce in a plan which might force Spain to concede the right of the United States to navigate the Mississippi than to insist on Michaux's adherence to his original design of exploring the lands and rivers beyond it. Jefferson, however, refused to confirm Genet's appointment of Michaux as French consul for Kentucky, though he granted Genet's request that he write a letter recommending Michaux to the governor of that state. On 15 July, armed with instructions from the American Philosophical Society and Genet, Michaux left Philadelphia on his redefined mission (TJ to Isaac Shelby, 28 June 1793; "Anas" entry, 5 July 1793; Turner, *CFM*, 220-3; AHA, *Annual Report*, 1897, p. 986, 990-6; Sargent, "Journal of Michaux," 90-1; Frederick J. Turner, "The Origins of Genet's Projected Attack on Louisiana and the Floridas," AHR, III [1897-98], 650-71).

In the end, Jefferson was forced to witness the demise of both ventures. While Michaux was in Kentucky planning the expedition with Clark, the Washington administration petitioned the French government to recall the troublesome Genet. Unaware of this development, in November Michaux set out for Philadelphia to report to the French minister and obtain additional funding for the operation against Louisiana. He arrived on 12 Dec., conferred with Genet the following day, and called upon Rittenhouse and Jefferson on 14 Dec., but the substance of these interviews, as well as visits to Rittenhouse on 26 Dec. and to Jefferson two days later, is not recorded. Although Genet had not abandoned his plans for a French attack on Louisiana, the arrival from Paris in January 1794 of the order for his recall and the cancellation in March of his commissions by Jean Antoine Joseph Fauchet, his successor, effectively aborted the undertaking. With the collapse of the project, Michaux returned to Charleston in March 1794 and resumed his official botanical researches for the French government, returning to his native land two years later and dying in Madagascar in 1802 while on a botanical expedition to the South Seas (Sargent, "Journal of Michaux," 96-103; AHA, *Annual Report*, 1897, p. 1007-10, 1012-14, 1016, 1024-6; Richard Lowitt, "Activities of Citizen Genet in Kentucky, 1793-1794," *Filson Club Quarterly*, XXII [1948], 256-67; Savage, *Michaux*, 146-79). Despite the disappointing outcome of this episode, Jefferson's involvement in the planning of Michaux's proposed western enterprise was a crucial link in the chain of events that led a decade later to the more celebrated Lewis and Clark expedition, not only in terms of the shared objectives of both ventures, but perhaps more importantly for the lesson Michaux's failure taught Jefferson about the need for federal support to ensure the success of American exploration of the trans-Mississippi West.

American Philosophical Society's Subscription Agreement for André Michaux's Western Expedition

[ca. 22 Jan. 1793]

Whereas Andrew Michaux,[1] a native of France, and inhabitant of the United States has undertaken to explore the interior country of North America from the Missisipi along the Missouri, and Westwardly to the Pacific ocean, or in such other direction as shall be advised by the American Philosophical society, and on his return to communicate to the said society the information he shall have acquired of the geography of the said country it's inhabitants, soil, climate, animals, vegetables, minerals[2] and other circumstances of note: WE THE SUBSCRIBERS, desirous of obtaining for ourselves relative to the land we live on, and of communicating to the world, information so interesting to curiosity, to science, and to the future prospects of mankind, promise for ourselves, our heirs executors[3] and administrators, that we will pay the said Andrew Michaux, or his assigns, the sums herein affixed to our names respectively, one fourth part thereof on demand, the remaining three fourths whenever, after his return, the said Philosophical society shall declare themselves satisfied that he has performed the said journey and that he has communicated to them freely all the information which he shall have acquired and they demanded of him: or if the said Andrew Michaux shall not proceed to the Pacific ocean, and shall reach the sources of the waters running into it, then we will pay him such part only of the remaining three fourths, as the said Philosophical society shall deem duly proportioned to the extent of unknown country explored by him, in the direction prescribed, as compared with that omitted to be[4] so explored. And we consent that the bills of exchange of the said Andrew Michaux, for monies said to be due to him in France,[5] shall be recieved to the amount of two hundred Louis, and shall be negociated[6] by the said Philosophical society, and the proceeds thereof[7] retained in their hands,[8] to be delivered to the said Andrew Michaux, on his return, after having performed the journey to their satisfaction, or, if not to their satisfaction, then[9] to be applied towards reimbursing the subscribers the fourth of their subscription advanced to the said Andrew Michaux. We consent also that the said Andrew Michaux shall take[10] to himself all benefit arising from the publication of the[11] discoveries he shall make in the three departments of Natural history, Animal, Vegetable and Mineral, he concerting[12] with the said Philosophical society such measures for securing to himself the said benefit, as shall be consistent with the due publication of the said discoveries.[13] In witness whereof we have hereto subscribed our names and affixed the sums we engage respectively to contribute.

[Column 1]

Go: WASHINGTON one hundred Dollars
JOHN ADAMS Twenty Dollars
BENJAMIN HAWKINS Twenty Dollars
RA. IZARD Twenty Dollars
SAM JOHNSTON Twenty Dollars
ROBT MORRIS Eighty Dollrs.
JNO. HENRY ten dollars
G CABOT Ten Dollars
JOHN RUTHERFURD Twenty dollars

[Column 2]

H KNOX fifty dollars
TH: JEFFERSON fifty dollars
ALEXANDER HAMILTON Fifty Dollars
RUFUS KING Twenty Dollars
JOHN LANGDON Twenty Dollars
JOHN EDWARDS Sixteen Dollars
JOHN BROWN Twenty Dollars
THO MIFFLIN Twenty Dollars

[Column 3]

JONA: TRUMBULL Twenty Dollrs.
JAMES MADISON JR. Twenty dollars
J: PARKER Twenty dollars
ALEXR WHITE Twenty Dollars
JOHN PAGE twenty Dollars
JOHN B. ASHE 10 Drs.
WM SMITH Twenty Dollrs.
JERE WADSWORTH Thirty Dollars
RICHARD BLAND LEE ten dollars
THOS. FITZSIMONS ten dollars
SAML. GRIFFIN Ten dollars
WM B. GILES Ten Dollars
JNO W: KITTERA Ten Dollars

[Column 4]

JOHN F. MERCER twelve Dollars
SAM. MAGAW Sixteen Dollars
NICHOLAS COLLIN sixteen dollars
JONA WILLIAMS Twenty Dollars
JOHN BLEAKLEY Ten Dollars
JOS PARKER NORRIS Ten Dollars
WM: WHITE ten Dollars
JOHN ROSS Twenty Dollars

MS (PPAmP: Miscellaneous Manuscripts); undated; entirely in TJ's hand, except for signatures of thirty-seven other subscribers with amounts pledged arranged in four columns, three at foot of text and a fourth on verso. Dft (DLC: TJ Papers, 81: 14061); undated; entirely in TJ's hand, unsigned; significant variations and emendations are noted below. Tr (PPAmP: Miscellaneous Manuscripts); undated; in the hand of Nicholas Collin, except for thirty-one signatures, all different from those in MS, arranged in no apparent order in three columns, two at

foot of text and another on endorsement page, and quoted here as follows:

[Column 1]

J: ROSS Twenty Dollars
J BEALE BORDLEY Twenty Dollars
JOHN PENN Twenty Dollars
JOHN EWING ten Dollars
MATH: McCONNELL ten ds.
JOHN NIXON ten dollars
THOS WILLING ten dollars
CHRISTIAN FEBIGER ten Dls.
ROBT. BLACKWELL sixteen dols.
J HUTCHINSON ten Dollars
W. SHIPPEN JR Ten Dollars

[*Column 2*]
JOHN D COXE Ten Dollars
JARED INGERSOLL Eight Dollars
MATTH CLARKSON Eight Dollars
J B SMITH Eight dollars
SAMUEL POWEL Ten Dollars
WALTER STEWART Ten Dollars
J DORSEY eight Dols
W. HAWES ten dollars
THOS RUSTON 20 Dollars
CASPAR WISTAR 30 Dollars
PETER S. DU PONCEAU 16 Dollars

[*Column 3*]
BENJN. FRANKLIN BACHE 8 dolls
A. KUHN 20 dollars
SAML M FOX ten dollars
KEARNY WHARTON ten dollars
DAVID LEWIS Ten Dollars
SAM. COATES Nine Dollars
CASPAR W MORRIS Eight Dolls
JOSA GILPIN Ten dollars
REUBEN HAINES JUNR 20 Dollars

endorsed in an unidentified hand: "Papers relative to Subsn. to Michaud." Tr (same); undated; entirely in Collin's hand, except for signature of John Ewing; lacks text and consists solely of names and pledges of first thirty-four signatories to TJ's MS, followed by names in pencil of six members of the American Philosoph-

ical Society and Ewing's signature, evidently pledging another $10, quoted here as follows:

JOHN NICHOLSON
DAVID RITTENHOUSE
HENRY HILL
DR THORNTON
JN VAUGHAN
WILLIAM BINGHAM
} fifty Dollars each

JOHN EWING ten Dollars

at head of text: "Copy of subscriptions." Recorded in SJPL under 23 Jan. 1793: "subscription for Michaux' mission." Enclosed in TJ to George Washington, 22 Jan. 1793. Also found in the vault of the American Philosophical Society with the subscription papers listed above was a signed certification by President David Rittenhouse, dated 23 Apr. 1793, of the appointment four days before of a committee consisting of Collin, Charles Willson Peale, and John Vaughan to collect "one fourth part of the Subscriptions for Mr. Michaud's Expedition, or the whole, of such subscribers as chuse to pay, in order to enable Mr. Michaud to proceed immediately," with a list of the advances received toward the subscription in Collin's hand, except for the last entry in Vaughan's hand, as follows:

Received by me Nicholas Collin

Apr. 23d. from Mr. Hamilton			Twelve and ½ dollars
from General Washington			Twenty five dollars
Gen. Walter Stewart	52.50	{	five dollars
John Ross Merchant			five dollars
Mr. J. B. Bordley			five Dollars
Bishop White			two and one half
Mr. Robert Morris			Twenty dollars
Doctor Ewing	40	{	two dollars–half
Samuel Powel			two–half
Mr. Vaughn			twelve–half
Mathew McConnel			two–half
John Nixon			two–half
Benjamin Beach [Bache]			two
Samuel Coats			two–quarter
Robert Blackwell	18.00	{	four dollars
Jared Ingersol			two dollars
Mathew Clarcson			two dollars
John Dorsey			two dollars
Received by John Vaughan			
Dr. Thornton	12.50		Twelve & one half Dolls
	123.00		

[83]

(MSS in PPAmP: Miscellaneous Manuscripts; on verso of certificate in Vaughan's hand: "NB July 22. 1796 Recd from Mr Rittenhouse $128\frac{25}{100}$"; on verso of list in Vaughan's hand: "Money Collected"). Comparison of this list with a statement Collin submitted to the Society in April 1800 on behalf of a committee appointed in February 1799 to report and recommend disposition of the sums received for the Michaux expedition indicates that the two rosters are not identical, the MS omitting the $12.50 advance by TJ and the $4 advance by Collin reported in 1800 but including the payment by Thornton not reported in 1800. The ultimate disposition of the money is not recorded (APS, *Proceedings*, XXVI [1889], 278, 298).

¹ Here and throughout the Dft TJ first wrote "_____ Michaud" before inserting the first name and, except in one case, altering the surname.
² Preceding three words interlined in Dft in place of "productions."
³ Word written over "and," erased, in Dft.
⁴ Preceding three words interlined in Dft in place of "not."
⁵ Here in Dft TJ interlined and then canceled "to the amount of 200 louis."
⁶ Here in Dft TJ first wrote "shall be accepted and negociated" before he altered the passage to read as above.
⁷ Preceding two words interlined in Dft in place of "money."
⁸ Preceding three words interlined in Dft.
⁹ Preceding six words interlined in Dft in place of "otherwise."
¹⁰ Word interlined in Dft in place of "enjoy" and an interlined and canceled "have."
¹¹ Word interlined in Dft in place of "any discov botanical."
¹² Preceding thirteen words inserted in Dft.
¹³ In Dft TJ first wrote "the publication of the discoveries producing it" and then altered the phrase to read as above.

From James Cole Mountflorence

SIR   Norfolk 22d. Jany. 1793

This Day I put into the Post office, agreeable to Mr. Morris's Request to me at Paris, his Dispatches to you. We arrived here Yesterday in the french Ship L'aimable Antoinette in 61 days passage from Havre de Grace. When we Sailed from france, nothing was yet determined on the fate of the King and Queen, but the Republican Armies of france were triumphing in every Quarter. I have given to the Printer of this Place a circumstantial and impartial Account of the Great Events that have taken place in france during the Year 1792, and as soon as the same be printed, I shall have the Honor of transmitting A Copy to you.

If You have any Dispatches for Governer Blount, or the Governer of Kentuckey, by forwarding them to me at Richmond, I would take charge of them with great Pleasure. I shall be in Richmond before the 1st. feby.; shall only stay there a few days, and proceed to Govr. Blount and the South Western Territory, therefore your Orders to those places would meet with an immediate Conveyance. I have the Honor to be respectfully Sir Yr. most Obedt. & most humble Servant

J: C. MOUNTFLORENCE

RC (ViW); endorsed by TJ as received 1 Feb. 1793 and so recorded in SJL.

For Mountflorence's ACCOUNT OF THE GREAT EVENTS of the French Revolution as he sent it to TJ, see enclosure to Mountflorence to TJ, 1 Feb. 1793.

To George Washington

Jan. 22. 1793.

Th: Jefferson has the honor to inclose to the President the subscription paper he has prepared for enabling the Philosophical society to send Mr. Michaux on the mission through the country between the Missisipi and South sea, and he will have that of waiting on him tomorrow morning on the subject.

RC (DNA: RG 59, MLR); addressed: "The President of the U.S."; endorsed by Tobias Lear. PrC (DLC). Tr (Lb in DNA: RG 59, SDC). Not recorded in SJL. Enclosure: American Philosophical Society's Subscription Agreement for André Michaux's Proposed Western Expedition, [ca. 22 Jan. 1793].

From George Washington

DEAR SIR   Philadelphia 22d. Jan. 1793

Nothing occurs to me as necessary to be added to the enclosed project.

If the Subscription is not confined to the members of the Philosophical Society, I would readily add my mite to the means for encouraging Mr. Michaud's undertaking—and do authorize you to place me among, and upon a footing with the respectable sums which may be Subscribed. I am always Yours.   Go: WASHINGTON

RC (DLC); addressed: "Mr. Jefferson"; endorsed by TJ as received 22 Jan. 1793. Dft (DLC: Washington Papers); contains minor variations in phraseology; docketed by Washington. FC (Lb in DLC: Washington Papers); wording follows Dft. Recorded in SJPL under 23 Jan. 1793. Enclosure: American Philosopical Society's Subscription Agreement for André Michaux's Proposed Western Expedition, [ca. 22 Jan. 1793].

Washington evidently forgot that he had been elected to membership in the American Philosophical Society in 1780 (Fitzpatrick, *Writings*, XVIII, 11-12).

From James Currie

DR. SIR Richmond Jany. 23d. 1793

I had the honor of recieving your favor of the 19th. of Octr. –92 inclosing that of Mr. Barton's to you of the 26th of Sepr 1792. I observe what he mentioned to you in his letter and the conversation held with him afterwards in regard to it and where to point his interrogatories particularly. I am under very great Obligations to you on this Occasion and beg leave here to Thank you once more for the Sollicitude you express to have it finishd before you leave Philadelphia, and unless it happens before that Period I shall despond in regard to it. I should be happy to hear from you soon on this Subject and I pray it may be equal to your warm and friendly wishes. With the most Sincere & Respectfull Attachment I have the Honor to be Sir your Most Ob. & Hble Serv. JAMES CURRIE

RC (DLC); endorsed by TJ as received 16 Feb. 1793 and so recorded in SJL.

From David Humphreys

SIR Lisbon Janry 23d. 1793.

My last public letter to you was dated Janry. 7th. and acknowledged the receipt of yours of Novr. 6th. Since that time, I have received your previous Dispatch in date July 12th, by way of Madeira. By these it appears that all my letters, except No. 52. had come to hand. Should that have finally miscarried, I will send a copy that the series may be complete.

The Papers transmitted herewith relate to our Captives at Algiers. No. 1. is the letter from Captn. Obrian, which I omitted by mistake to enclose in my last. No. 2. is the extract of a letter of Novr. 2nd. 1792 from him to Messrs. John Bulkeley & Son. No. 3. is my answer to Captn. Obrian. And No. 4. my last letter to Mr. Carmichael. From these, and former communications an adequate idea may be formed of the state of the subject. And I hope by this ulterior arrangement the Captives cannot fail to receive all the relief of which, in their situation, they are susceptable; and that my proceedings will meet the approbation of Government.

Mr. Barclay, Consul for Morocco, who arrived here from Cadiz on tuesday last, died on Saturday. His sudden death is supposed to have been occasioned by an inflamation of the lungs. After having received Dispatches from Mr. Pinkney, by a special Messenger, he informed you from Cadiz of the necessity he found himself under of coming here to obtain the Money he had occasion for, and that he could probably effect it without informing any Person but myself of the business. Two days before his death, we went to the Exchange together, and entered into arrangements for drawing the Money. He complained of a slight fever, costiveness and raging thirst for water, for some time. That night he took Medicine. On friday he mostly kept his bed; I conversed with him, however, a good deal on business; and when I left him he told me he hoped to be well in two or three days. Next morning I was sent for early, and finding his life despaired of by the Physicians, I immediately took possession of all the Papers contained in the Dispatches from Mr. Pinkney to him. And I am fully certain, no Person in Europe (except Mr. Pinkney and myself) is acquainted with their contents. I have written to Mr. Pinkney, that I shall await your or his orders for their disposal; of which I take the earliest occasion to advise you.

Happily we had not proceeded so far in the Money transaction, but that I have been able to break it off without incurring loss. For had the business proceeded there must have been some loss in the Exchange.

From the time Mr. Barclay was apprehended to be in danger, he was never able to pronounce more than a word or two at a time; or to give the least information respecting the public affairs or his own. After his death, upon searching (with the assistance of Mr. Harrison Consular Agent for the U.S.) the Papers which he brought here, I have not been able to find any Invoice, Receipt, Memorandum or Document, relative to the Property of the U.S. which was destined for the Morocco negociation; nor any Key except one which appears to belong to a small Portfeuille. I am confident the Presents &c. are at Gibralter, but I do not know in whose possession they are. To ascertain this, and prevent their being lost or embezzled, I propose making use of the earliest possible opportunity to go myself to Gibralter. In taking this step without waiting for orders, I hope my zeal may not be imputed to me as a fault: since it must be known, I could not have any motive, but a desire to serve the public interest even beyond the line of my immediate duty, in encountring the inconvenience and expence of the voyage, at this very inclement Season. With Sentiments of sincere respect & esteem I have the honour to be Sir, Your most obedt. & most hble Servt   D. HUMPHREYS

RC (DNA: RG 59, DD); at head of text: "(No. 64.)"; at foot of text: "The Secretary of State &c. &c. &c."; endorsed by TJ as received 16 Mch. 1793 and so recorded in SJL. Dupl (same, MDC); at head of text: "(Duplicate)"; note at foot of text: "N.B. I have not time to copy the enclosures sent in the original, or a letter addressed to the President in the same; I shall, therefore, be anxious to hear of their arrival. D.H." Tr (Lb in same, DD). Enclosures: (1) Richard O'Bryen to Humphreys, Algiers, 12 Nov. 1792, describing efforts by the Spanish consul in Algiers to bring about a treaty between Algiers and Portugal, reflecting on the adverse consequences such a treaty would have on the fate of the American captives in Algiers and on American commerce, noting attempts by the same consul to persuade Algiers to break its peace with France so as to engross the Mediterranean trade, and bitterly lamenting the failure of efforts to free the American seamen (RC in same; Tr in Lb in same). (2) Extract from O'Bryen to [John Bulkeley & Son], Algiers, 2 Nov. 1792, stating that, since receiving William Carmichael's letter of November last acknowledging Congress's orders to pay the captives' debts and continue their usual pay, he has written "many letters but can obtain no answer," and that on the basis of Carmichael's letter he has tried to procure some monthly subsistence for the most desperate of his fellow prisoners, "but as we can have no farther account on this subject, our credit has entirely failed." (3) Humphreys to O'Bryen, 19 Jan. 1793, stating that there was no prospect of an Algerine-Portuguese peace treaty, expressing surprise at the failure of Carmichael and Robert Montgomery to provide subsistence for the captives, and authorizing O'Bryen to contract for the supply of provisions and clothing to the prisoners for-

merly furnished by the Spanish consul, to collect the accounts of bona fide debts due for their subsistence and maintenance, and to draw bills of exchange for both purposes on Humphreys's bankers, John Bulkeley & Son. (4) Humphreys to Carmichael, 20 Jan. 1793, authorizing him to pay the bills of exchange for the debt the United States owes to Don Joseph Torino in the event Humphreys is in Gibraltar attending to the property of the United States relating to the Moroccan business left by the recently deceased Thomas Barclay, and enclosing a copy of his letter to O'Bryen (Trs in same; Trs in Lb in same).

For the DISPATCHES FROM MR. PINKNEY, see TJ to John Paul Jones, 1 June 1792, and Washington to Thomas Barclay, 11 June 1792, and note. Concerning the MOROCCO NEGOCIATION, see Instructions for Thomas Barclay, 13 May 1791. The 23 Jan. 1793 "letter addressed to the President" that Humphreys mentioned in his note on the Dupl consisted for the most part of an appeal for the appointment of someone to take custody of the goods entrusted to Barclay for his mission to Morocco (DLC: Washington Papers).

TJ submitted this letter and its enclosures to the President on 16 Mch. 1793, and Washington returned them the next day (Washington, *Journal*, 91-2, 93).

George Washington to Charles Carroll of Carrollton

DEAR SIR   Philadelphia Jan. 23. 1793.

The Western Indians having proposed to us a conference at Au Glaise[1] in the ensuing spring, I am now about to proceed to nominate three Commissioners to meet and treat with them on the subject of peace. What may be the issue of the conferences is difficult to foresee, but it is extremely essential that, whatever it be, it should carry with it the perfect confidence of our citizens that every endeavor will have been used to obtain peace which their interests would permit. For this reason it is necessary that characters be appointed who are known to our citizens for their talents and integrity; and whose situation in life places them clear of every suspicion of a² wish to prolong the war, or say rather whose interest, in common with that of their country, is clearly to produce peace. Characters uniting these desiderata do not abound, some of them too are in offices inconsistent with the appointment now in question, others under impediments of health or other circumstances so as to circumscribe the choice within a small circle. Desirous in the first instance that you should be in this commission, I have mentioned these difficulties to shew you, in the event of your declining, how serious they are, and to induce you to come forward and perform this important service to your country, a service with which it's prosperity and tranquility are intimately connected. It will be necessary to set out from this place about the _____ of _____.³ The route will be by the North river, and the lakes,⁴ it will be safe, and the measures for your comfortable⁵ transportation and subsistence taken as effectually as circumstances will admit. Will you then permit me, Sir, to nominate you, as one of the Commissioners, with a certain reliance on your acceptance? Your answer to this by the first or second⁶ post will oblige, Dear Sir &c.

Dft (DLC: Washington Papers); in TJ's hand except for revisions by Washington as noted below; at foot of first page in TJ's hand: "Mr. Carrol of Carrolton"; docketed in part by Washington. PrC (DLC); entirely in TJ's hand; with two notations added at a much later date in pencil by TJ to correct an error in placement after text had been bound, probably as part of the "Anas": (at foot of first page) "[turn back 3 pages]" and (at head of second page) "from [p.?] 60, further on." Entry in SJPL: "draught of letter from G.W. to Commrs. for Indn. treaty."

Carroll, the noted Maryland Revolutionary leader who had recently resigned his seat in the United States Senate, rejected his proposed appointment as peace commissioner to the Western Indians on the grounds of age and health (Washington to Carroll, 23 Jan. 1793, and Carroll to Washington, 28 Jan. 1793, in Kate M. Rowland, *The Life of Charles Carroll of Carrollton, 1737-1832, with His Correspondence and Public Papers*, 2 vols.

[New York, 1898], II, 197-9). Washington also sent the same letter to Charles Thomson, the former secretary of the Continental Congress, who declined the appointment for the same reasons (Washington to Thomson, 31 Jan. 1793, DLC: Washington Papers; Thomson to Washington, 31 Jan. 1793, DNA: RG 59, MLR). The texts Washington sent to Carroll and Thomson reflected the changes he made to TJ's Dft. See also TJ to Beverley Randolph, 18 Feb. 1793, and note.

¹ Washington here interlined "not far distant from Detroit."
² Preceding three words interlined by TJ.
³ Sentence interlined by TJ. Washington altered the end of the sentence to read "1st of May."
⁴ Preceding two words canceled by Washington and replaced with "Niagara."
⁵ Word interlined by TJ.
⁶ Washington here underlined "first" and canceled "or second."

From Robert Gamble

SIR Richmond Jany. 24. 1793

Your letter of the 17th. is at hand, by this nights post—and in reply; I inform you, our friend Colo. Bell has not put any money into my hands to be remitted, you, nor has he intimated to me any thing on that subject; Agreeably to your directions, I will forward your letter to me—*enclosed to him*, and will with pleasure take first oportunity to remit you any payment he may forward to me for that purpose. I am with much Esteem & regard Sir Your mo. ob Hume servt

Ro. GAMBLE

(Note—my name is Robert Gamble)

RC (DLC); opposite complimentary close: "Honbl. T. Jefferson"; endorsed by TJ as received 1 Feb. 1793 and so recorded in SJL.

In SJL TJ had recorded Gamble's name as "Richard," rather than ROBERT, and had so addressed letters to him.

To John Wilkes Kittera

SIR Philadelphia Jan. 24. 1793.

My letter of Nov. 5 to Mr. Chambers, which was directed to him at Mercersburg and that of Dec. 12. addressed according to his particular directions, and both sent by post, having miscarried, I take the liberty of observing to him, through you, that if he wishes to secure a right to his discovery, relative to firearms, in America, it will be necessary for him to petition the Patent board for that purpose, accompanying his petition with a *Specification*, that is to say, a written description of his invention. If he wishes to avail himself of it in France, I do not know that he could do better than to consult with the Minister of France here as to the manner of proceeding. I have the honor to be with great respect Sir your most obedt. humble servt   TH: JEFFERSON

PrC (DLC); at foot of text: "Mr. Kittera." Tr (ViU: Edgehill-Randolph Papers); 19th-century copy.

John Wilkes Kittera (1752-1801), a Lancaster County lawyer who graduated from the College of New Jersey in 1776, was a staunchly Federalist member of the House of Representatives for Pennsylvania from 1791 to 1801 (Richard A. Harrison, *Princetonians, 1776-1783: A Biographical Dictionary* [Princeton, 1981], 59-62).

From Thomas Mann Randolph, Jr.

Dear Sir   Monticello Jan: 24: 1793.

In consequence of your letter to Mr. Randolph Jefferson a Mr. James Kinsolving applied to Clarkson on the 16: inst: for Dinah and her children. Their value was fixed by Colo. Lewis and Colo. Bell, 139:17.6 for which sum he has given his bonds on the terms of your sale in Bedford. He is a very substantial planter himself: one John Burnley a man allso in very good circumstances is joined with him. The bonds are in my hands. The works which you desired me to direct are going on briskly. 426 bushels of limestone are raised: nearly the whole of the timber for the buildings you ordered is ready: the business of bringing it in goes on and in 8 days we shall begin to rear the Stable. 2 laborers are constantly employed in grubing the orchard of which about 4 acres are allready clean. Patsy told you last week of the fire in Charlottesville: 3 dwelling houses only were destroyed and those of no great value: in one of them there was a parcel of goods belonging to Dyvers & Lindsey which raised the sum of the loss to 1200£; by the estimates I have heard. The houses consumed are not missed in our prospect. I am told that they will be rebuilt immediately. I have not been in Richmond since I received your letter concerning the Stalactite: as there is no likelihood of my being there soon I shall inform Mr. Hylton of your wish. The package of servants cloathes has not arrived at Monto. nor have we heard of its being in Mr. Browns hands: I shall make inquiry for it.

Our little Anna is not yet in firm health. She has an ulcer on her which Gilmer thought once to have a very bad aspect tho' now it promises to heal speedily. He imputes it to our having continued too long the very nutritive aliments which were necessary during the Diarrhea. A sudden fatness and extreme gross habit was produced by this. She has 3 jaw-teeth just coming out which I am convinced occasion allmost entirely her indisposition.

Assure Polly of my most tender regard and tell her that I decline answering her letter this week as her sister writes.

The whole neighbourhood is in transport at the success of the French arms. Your most aff. friend   Th: M. Randolph

Patsy reminds you thro me of her warm and constant affection.

RC (ViU: Edgehill-Randolph Papers); addressed: "Thomas Jefferson. Secretary of State Philada."; franked; endorsed by TJ as received 6 Feb. 1793 and so recorded in SJL.

TJ's letter to Randolph Jefferson is dated 25 Sep. 1792.

From Robert Dick

SIR Bladensburgh 25th. January 1793

The inclosed Letter addressed to You, together with the Book refered to in it, I have just received from a friend in Glasgow (who is related to Mr. Stewart,) along with a copy for myself.

It gives me pleasure to have so early and good an opportunity of forwarding it by my friend Mr. John Campbell. I have the honour to be respectfully Sir Your Most Obedt. hum. Servant ROBT. DICK

RC (MHi); endorsed by TJ as received 31 Jan. 1793 and so recorded in SJL. Enclosure: Dugald Stewart to TJ, 1 Oct. 1792, covering a copy of Stewart's *Elements of the Philosophy of the Human Mind*.

Robert Dick (b. ca. 1736) was a Scottish factor in Bladensburg, Maryland, since before the American Revolution (Gaius Marcus Brumbaugh, ed., *Maryland Records: Colonial, Revolutionary, County and Church from Original Sources*, 2 vols. [Baltimore, Md., and Lancaster, Pa., 1915-28; repr. Baltimore, 1967], I, 20; *Maryland Historical Magazine*, LXII [1967], 144n).

To Albert Gallatin

SIR Philadelphia Jan. 25. 1793.

Mr. Legaux called on me this morning to ask a statement of the experiment which was made in Virginia by a Mr. Mazzei for the raising vines and making wine, and desired I would address it to you. Mr. Mazzei was an Italian and brought over with him about a dozen laborers of his own country, bound to serve him 4. or 5. years. We made up a subscription for him of £2000. sterling, and he began his experiment on a peice of land adjoining to mine. His intention was, before the time of his people should expire, to import more from Italy. He planted a considerable vineyard, and attended to it with great diligence for three years. The war then came on. The time of his people soon expired; some of them enlisted, others chose to settle on other lands and labor for themselves; some were taken away by the gentlemen of the country for gardeners, so that there did not remain a single one with him, and the interruption of navigation prevented his importing others. In this state of the thing he was himself employed by the state of Virginia to go to Europe as their agent to do some particular business. He rented his place to General Riedesel, whose horses in one week destroyed the whole labour of three or four years, and thus ended an experiment, which, from every appearance, would in a year or two more have established the practicability of that branch of culture in America. This is the sum of the experiment as exactly as I am able to state it from memory, after such an interval of time, and I consign it to you in whose hands I know it will be applied with candor, if it contains any thing applicable to the case for which it has been asked. I have the honor to be with great esteem & respect Sir Your most obedt & most humble servt

TH: JEFFERSON

RC (NHi: Gallatin Papers): addressed: "Mr. Gallatin": endorsed by Gallatin at a later date: "Jany. 25th 1793 Ths. Jefferson (first letter from him)." PrC (DLC). Tr (DLC): 19th-century copy.

With the exception of a brief note of 14 Jan. 1791 that will appear in a supplement planned for Vol. 27, this is TJ's first letter to his future Secretary of the Treasury, the rising Pennsylvania Republican leader Albert Gallatin (1761-1849). The state's House of Representatives had appointed Gallatin on 23 Jan. 1793 one of a committee of five to consider a memorial and plan from Peter LEGAUX, a French immigrant who was a member of the American Philosophical Society, requesting approval for the "incorporation of a society for the pro-

motion of the culture of the vine, and the raising of silkworms and silk." On the very day TJ wrote the above letter the committee urged the House to authorize an "association of persons" to promote viniculture in Pennsylvania, and a bill to this effect, drafted by another committee composed of the same five legislators, was enacted into law in March 1793 (*Journal of the First Session of the Third House of Representatives of the Commonwealth of Pennsylvania* [Philadelphia, 1792-93], 119, 124, 129, 141; Syrett, *Hamilton*, XXVI, 738). TJ was already familiar with Legaux's proposals, having been present on 18 Jan. 1793 when the American Philosophical Society had considered a text of Legaux's plan respecting viniculture (APS, *Proceedings*, XXII, pt. 3 [1885], 174, 212).

From David Humphreys

SIR   Lisbon Janry. 25th. 1793

The enclosed Papers from No. 1. to No. 6. inclusive may serve to shew the proceedings I conceived myself authorised in taking, with respect to American flour and grain. The crisis is as favorable for obtaining a liberal policy as perhaps ever can be expected; and I have endeavoured to avail myself of it in as delicate and efficacious a manner as I was able. Some names of great authority, I know, approve of the systems I have proposed. Still the success is very precarious. Should the answers which Government will be under the necessity of giving not prove favorable, perhaps hereafter some statements of facts in the American News Papers may have a tendency to rouse this nation from its present torpid state to insist upon a wiser and better policy.

I have concerted with the Secretary of State for foreign affairs the mode of transacting our business during my absence. And I am determined that absence shall be of as short duration as possible. With sincere & great esteem, I have the honour to be, Sir, Your most obedt. & Most humble Servt   D. HUMPHREYS

P.S. I have but just this moment received the Box of Papers from the Custom House which came with your[1] of July 12th. by way of Madeira. It is impossible to send such unweildy Packets on Horseback by the Spanish Ambassador's ordinary Courier. And this is the only conveyance which offers. I have however sent to Mr. Carmichael all but such as appear to contain the large volumes of Laws and Journals. For this I have given a Moidore to the Courier. I have also informed Mr. Carmichael, that, not knowing where Mr. Short is at present, I must await his and Mr. Short's information and dispositions for obtaining the remainder.

RC (DNA: RG 59, DD); at head of text: "(No. 65.)"; at foot of first page: "The Secretary of State"; endorsed by TJ as received 19 Mch. 1793 and so recorded in SJL, where TJ erroneously listed it as No. 63 dated 23 Jan. 1793. Tr (Lb in same). Enclosures: (1) Memorial of Humphreys to Foreign Minister Luis Pinto de Sousa Coutinho, 27 Dec. 1792, setting forth the mutual advantages of permitting the importation of American flour into Portugal before the conclusion of a treaty of commerce with the United States. (2) Humphreys to same, 16 Jan. 1793, requesting an answer to his memorial so that he can inform his government by a ship about to sail for Philadelphia, noting that after some difficulty a cargo of American flour had recently been admitted for sale in Lisbon by a temporary measure, and emphasizing the mutual benefits of regularizing such admissions. (3) Pinto de Sousa Coutinho to Humphreys, 17 Jan. 1793, stating that he would respond to Humphreys's memorial as soon as the council to which the Prince of Brazil referred it had considered the matter. (4) Samuel Harrison to same, 16 Jan. 1793, reporting that the administrator of the corn market has denied to three American ships recently arrived in Lisbon with wheat the privilege of "franquia to proceed to the Ports of their destination" and has ordered them to "come up and discharge." (5) Memorial of Humphreys to Pinto de Sousa Coutinho, 18 Jan. 1793, enclosing Harrison's letter regarding the abolition of the customary "indulgence of Franquie" at Lisbon, so far at least as it applies to the American vessels recently arrived, pointing out that he will be required to announce this innovation in American newspapers so that merchants trading to Europe have the opportunity to order vessels not destined to unload in Portugal to go instead to England, Ireland, or other countries, whence they could proceed to their final destinations, and asking whether the new measure would not divert surpluses of cargoes wanted in Portugal. (6) Same to same, 21 Jan. 1793, reminding him of the papers he had left concerning the government's rejection of the accustomed "indulgence of Franquiæ" at Lisbon, noting that British merchants have been alarmed by reports of a declaration from a high official that the government had decided not to permit cargoes of grain to leave until a six months' supply had been obtained, protesting that this policy would be "assuming a power to reduce the price in Portugal below what it is in the Ports of the neighbouring Nations," and asking whether it would not "create the scarcity it means to avert" (Trs in same, with No. 3 in Portuguese filed with translation in TJ's hand; Trs in Lb in same).

TJ submitted this letter and its enclosures to the President on 19 Mch. 1793, and Washington returned them the same day (Washington, *Journal*, 94-5).

[1] Thus in manuscript.

From Gouverneur Morris

DEAR SIR   Paris 25 January 1793

My last No. 17 was of the seventeenth Instant. The late King of this
Country has been publickly executed. He died in a Manner becoming
his Dignity. Mounting the Scaffold he express'd anew his Forgiveness
of those who persecuted him and a Prayer that his deluded People
might be benefited by his Death. On the Scaffold he attempted to
speak but the commanding Officer Santerre ordered the Drums to be
beat. The King made two unavailing Efforts but with the same bad
Success. The Executioners threw him down and were in such Haste
as to let fall the Axe before his Neck was properly placed so that he
was mangled. It would be needless to give you an affecting Narrative
of Particulars. I proceed to what is more important having but a few
Minutes to write by the present good Opportunity.

The greatest Care was taken to prevent an Affluence of People.
This proves a Conviction that the Majority was not favorable to that
severe Measure. In Effect the great Mass of the parisian Citizens
mournd the Fate of their Unhappy Prince. I have seen Grief such
as for the untimely Death of a beloved Parent. Every Thing wears
an Appearance of Solemnity which is awfully distressing. I have been
told by a Gentleman from the Spot that putting the King to Death
would be a Signal for disbanding the Army in Flanders. I do not
believe this but incline to think it will have some Effect on that Army
already perishing by Want and mouldering fast away. The People of
that Country if the french Army retreats will I am perswaded take
a severe Vengeance for the Injuries they have felt and the Insults
they have been expos'd to. Both are great. The War against France
is become popular in Austria and is becoming so in Germany. If my
Judgment be good the Testament of Louis the sixteenth will be more
powerful against the present Rulers of this Country than an Army of
an hundred thousand Men. You will learn the Effect it has in England.
I beleive that the English will be wound up to a Pitch of enthusiastic
Horror against France which their cool and steady Temper seems to
be scarcely susceptible of.

I enclose you the Translation of a Letter from Sweden which I
have receivd from Denmark. You will see thereby that the jacobine
Principles are propagated with Zeal in every Quarter. Whether the
Regent of Sweden intends to make himself King is a moot Point. All
the World knows that the young Prince is not legitimate altho born
under Circumstances which render it *legally speaking* impossible to
question his Legitimacy.

[95]

I consider a War between Britain and France as inevitable. The Continental Powers opposed to France are making great and prompt Efforts while on this Side I as yet see but little done to oppose them. There is a Treaty on Foot (I beleive) between England and Austria whose Object is the Dismemberment of France. I have not Proof but some very leading Circumstances. Britain will I think suspend her Blow till she can strike very hard, unless indeed they should think it adviseable to seize the Moment of Indignation against late Events for a Declaration of War. This is not I think improbable because it may be coupled with those general Declarations against all Kings under the Name of Tyrants which contain a Determination to destroy them and the Threat that if the Ministers of England presume to declare War an Appeal shall be made to the People at the Head of an invading Army. Of Course a Design may be exhibited of entering into the Heart of Great Britain to overturn the Constitution destroy the Rights of Property and finally to dethrone and murder the King. All which are Things the English will neither approve of nor submit to.

Yours of the seventh of November is just receiv'd. I will reply to it by the first good Opportunity. With sincere Esteem I am my dear Sir Your obedient Servant   Gouv Morris

RC (DNA: RG 59, DD); at head of text: "No. 18"; at foot of first page: "Thomas Jefferson Esqr Secretary of State." FC (Lb in DLC: Gouverneur Morris Papers). Tr (DNA: RG 46, Senate Records, 3d Cong., 1st sess.); copy made early in 1794 by State Department; with omissions. PrC (DNA: RG 59, MD). Tr (Lb in same, DD). Recorded in SJL as received 1 May 1793. Enclosure: "Translation of a letter from Stockholm dated 28 Debr. 1792," stating that abuses of freedom of the press had led the Swedish government to reimpose restrictions on printers, one of whom was arrested for printing a Jacobinical pamphlet; that excesses in the playhouses and the existence of "Revolution Clubs" demonstrated that "french Subversion Frenzy" had already taken deep root in Sweden; that various false reports had obliged the Duke Regent to make a public declaration of the policies he was following on behalf of the young Swedish king and to take other steps to stifle opposition to his administration; that it is not known whether all this was the

result of a letter from Dean Widen or a discovery made by the government, although suspicion falls on a large club of followers of Gustavus III reportedly supported from abroad; and that all was now quiet (Tr in same; Tr in DNA: RG 46, Senate Records, 3d Cong., 1st sess.; PrC in DNA: RG 59, MD; Tr in Lb in same, DD).

Duke Karl of Södermanland (1748-1818) served as REGENT OF SWEDEN from 1792 to 1796 in consequence of the assassination of his brother Gustavus III and the minority of Gustavus's heir, the YOUNG PRINCE Gustav IV Adolf (1778-1837), whose paternity was a matter of frequent speculation among contemporaries (Byron J. Nordstrom, ed., *Dictionary of Scandinavian History* [Westport, Conn., 1986], 244-6, 319).

TJ submitted this letter and its enclosure to the President on 1 May 1793, and Washington returned them the next day (Washington, *Journal*, 124, 125).

From George Gilmer

My dear Sir   26 Jany 1793 Pen Park
As your return to Monticello shortly is determined on discover my
nerves begin to vibrate with more vigor and can declare to you that
they have not had their tone stimulated by any auxilliary for some
time, having prior to the new year totally abandoned one atom of the
Brownonian stimulant power and have been uniform in an innocent
simple regimen though increased in fibres not equally so in strength;
our illuminations in Charlottesville were not designd for the news
of the Armies retreating Brunswick we expected would have been
Burgoined, the conflagration in town was large for the little City but
will soon grow up again. Our winter has appeard a spring a few days
past a small sprinkle of snow which soon disappeard heavenly weather
after it that our old feild will smile spring on your return. Your Grand
daughter has become robust and appears too abound in health. A
report prevails that a body of french have gon to Ireland. Will they
know at what point to stand, or are for obliterating monarchs? With
the best affections of Cousin Lucy & the Park, your friend

GEO GILMER

RC (MHi); endorsed by TJ as received   For an explanation of the BROWNON-
13 Feb. 1793 and so recorded in SJL.   IAN STIMULANT, see Gilmer to TJ, 9 Oct.
1792, and note.

To Martha Jefferson Randolph

My dear Martha   Philadelphia Jan. 26. 93.
    I received two days ago your's of the 16th. You were never more
mistaken than in supposing you were too long on the prattle &c. of
little Anne. I read it with quite as much pleasure as you write it. I
sincerely wish I could hear of her perfect reestablishment.—I have for
some time past been under an agitation of mind which I scarcely ever
experienced before, produced by a check on my purpose of returning home at the close of this session of Congress. My operations at
Monticello had been all made to bear upon that point of time, my
mind was fixed on it with a fondness which was extreme, the purpose firmly declared to the President, when I became assailed from
all quarters with a variety of objections. Among these it was urged
that my retiring just when I had been attacked in the public papers,
would injure me in the eyes of the public, who would suppose I either

withdrew from investigation, or because I had not tone of mind sufficient to meet slander. The only reward I ever wished on my retirement was to carry with me nothing like a disapprobation of the public. These representations have, for some weeks passed, shaken a determination which I had thought the whole world could not have shaken. I have not yet finally made up my mind on the subject, nor changed my declaration to the President. But having perfect reliance in the disinterested friendship of some of those who have counselled and urged it strongly, believing that they can see and judge better a question between the public and myself than I can, I feel a possibility that I may be detained here into the summer. A few days will decide. In the mean time I have permitted my house to be rented after the middle of March, have sold such of my furniture as would not suit Monticello, and am packing up the rest and storing it ready to be shipped off to Richmond as soon as the season of good sea-weather comes on. A circumstance which weighs on me next to the weightiest is the trouble which I foresee I shall be constrained to ask Mr. Randolph to undertake. Having taken from other pursuits a number of hands to execute several purposes which I had in view for this year, I can not abandon those purposes and lose their labour altogether. I must therefore select the most important and least troublesome of them, the execution of my canal, and (without embarrassing him with any details which Clarkson and George are equal to) get him to tell them always what is to be done and how, and to attend to the levelling the bottom. But on this I shall write him particularly if I defer my departure.—I have not received the letter which Mr. Carr wrote to me from Richmond nor any other from him since I left Monticello. My best affections to him, Mr. Randolph & your fireside and am with sincere love my dear Martha yours   Th:J.

RC (NNP); at foot of first page: "Mrs. Randolph"; endorsed by Mrs. Randolph. PrC (DLC). Tr (ViU: Edgehill-Randolph Papers); 19th-century copy.

To Joseph Fay

DEAR SIR   Philadelphia Jan. 27. 1793
I have not for a long time been so much mortified as on calling at your lodgings to-day, for the third time, to be told you had left town. The first and second time of my calling, you were gone out, as I unfortunately happened to be when you were so good as to call on me. The constant confinement to which my office holds me prevented

my repeating my early efforts to have the pleasure of seeing you, but I should have broke through this had I not been told you would not leave town till the middle or end of the ensuing week, and I called this day to propose your meeting with Mr. Madison and some other[1] friends at dinner with me. My feelings will not permit me to withold these expressions of my concern, and of my hope that you will not think me capable of neglecting a person of whose civilities I had been so sensible in passing thro' his residence. I hoped that the acquaintance, which these civilities gave me the occasion of making, would not terminate with them, but that I might be permitted to cultivate and retain it: and tho' we are far distant, and shall ere long be farther, permit me to assure you that I valued your attentions too much to consider them as merely transient and that I shall continue to cherish those sentiments of esteem and attachment with which I am Dear Sir your most obedt. & most humble servt   TH: JEFFERSON

PrC (DLC); at foot of text: "Colo. Fay." Tr (DLC); 19th-century copy.

[1] Preceding six words interlined in place of "some."

From Christopher Greenup

SIR   Arch Street No. 28. January 28th. 1793

The Representatives from Kentucky have lately received a Letter from the Governor of that State, inclosing a Resolution of the General Assembly directing an application to be made to Congress for a reimbursement of the Expence incurred in carrying on expeditions against the Indian Tribes since the first of January 1785.

On examination I find this business was brought before Congress the second day of August 1787 by request of Governor Randolph, and a Committee on that day brought in a report which has never been decided on.

I must therefore beg of you Sir to favour me with the original papers which I am informed are filed in the Office of the Department of State, or Copies of them for the purpose of supporting the present application; this being now a Debt to be paid by the State of Kentucky by the Compact with Virginia. I have the honour to be Sir with great respect Your Very Hble Servt.   CHRISTO. GREENUP

RC (DNA: RG 59, MLR); at foot of text: "Honble Mr. Jefferson"; endorsed by TJ as received 28 Jan. 1793 and so recorded in SJL.

Christopher Greenup (1750-1818), a lawyer and Revolutionary War military officer who had participated in several Indian expeditions during the Confederation period, was a member of the House of Representatives from Kentucky, 1792-97 (*Biog. Dir. Cong.*). In a report submitted to the House in April 1794, Alexander Hamilton rejected Kentucky's claim for REIMBURSEMENT, contending that the costs for the expeditions had been covered by the settlement of accounts between the federal government and Virginia, of which Kentucky had been part until 1792 (Syrett, *Hamilton*, XVI, 244-5).

From Samuel Stearns

Taunton, 28 Jan. 1793. He encloses a copy of the *Free Mason's Calendar*, asking that it be deposited according to the copyright law, and that a receipt be given to William Foster, the bearer.

RC (DNA: RG 59, MLR); 1 p.; addressed: "Hon. Thomas Jefferson, LL.D. Secretary of State, Philadelphia Honrd. by the Hon. Mr. Foster"; endorsed by George Taylor, Jr., as received 11 Feb. 1793.

Samuel Stearns (1747-1819), a native of Bolton, Massachusetts, was a physician, astronomer, and author of several books, including *The Free Mason's Calendar, and Continental Almanac; for the Year of our Lord 1793* ... (New York, [1792]), enclosed here, and *The American Oracle. Comprehending an Account of Recent Discoveries In the Arts and Sciences* ... (New York, 1791), which he had submitted for copyright registry the previous year (Stearns to TJ, 21 Mch. 1792, RC in DNA: RG 59, MLR; at foot of text: "Hon. Mr. Jefferson"). For a sketch, see James Grant Wilson and John Fiske, eds., *Appletons' Cyclopædia of American Biography*), 7 vols. (New York, 1888-1901), V, 656.

From C. W. F. Dumas

The Hague, 29 Jan. 1793. He regards the unfortunate fate of the last of the kings of France as a human tragedy but a political necessity, there being no middle ground between his ruin and the destruction of civil liberties. The discourse by Paine in the enclosed *Journal des Débats* shows that his ideas on natural law are infinitely superior to his politics. Louis would have given no cause for alarm had he been banished to Holland, but the same cannot be said of the intriguing émigrés who would have followed him. Grenville, the British foreign secretary, prepared an invasion plan at Nijmegen in 1787 and advised a certain lady to make a famous journey to Holland, which, when prevented, was to serve as a pretext for Prussian intervention. Now he presumes to count on a similar outcome to the escapade in which he seems to want to involve England, but the United States will benefit whatever happens.

RC (DNA: RG 59, MLR); 1 p.; in French; at head of text: "No. 93. A Son Excellence M. Le Secretaire d'Etat, & Minre. des Affes. Etr. en Congrès des Et. Un. d'Am."; endorsed by TJ as received 3 May 1793 and so recorded in SJL. Dupl (same, MDC); at head of text: "Dupl."; endorsed by TJ as received 17 May 1793 and so recorded in SJL. Enclosure not found.

From Thomas Bell

DEAR SIR   30. Jany. 1793

Yours of the 17th. is now at hand. Exclusive of Mr. Browns account the Sherriff has called upon me for your taxes, that with other accounts that I have paid and assumed which Colo. Lewis tells me are Just, and cannot be put off, nearly ballances our account exclusive of the hire of Marey and children. I applied to one of the Gentlemen who Valued her to meet the other and Say what I Should give for the hire. He Seemd of opinion, that as She had so many, I ought not to pay thing.[1] On finding that to be his opinion, I could not think of doing any thing more in the business untill your return.

However Sir, I assure you this is not the reason why I cannot with propriety give you a draft on Colo. Gamble. The high price my customers expect for their produce in the Spring induces them to hold back their Tobacco &c. for the Spring market. Of course I have nothing as yet in the hands of Colo. Gamble.

I applied to our friend Mr. De Reux who has long wishd to have it in his power to make me a payment. He tells me that what he has already received is in advance and cannot with any propriety draw upon you at present.

If the Sale of his Goods (before you leave Philadelphia) will Justify a draft that will be of service to you, I am well assured he will give it with pleasure. And I would in that case endeavor to refund him and wait untill his last payment comes to hand.

I will that you to write me[2] what prospects there are like to be through this channel, without advising Mr. De Reux any thing about it, as it would hurt his feelings in case of a disapointment.

He has not yet fixed upon a piece of land to his mind.

If our worthy friend Mr. Monroe should have it in his power, Any advances he might make would be perfectly agreeable. I am Sir with due respect your most ob. Svt.   THOS BELL

Snow now about 12 inches deep on level ground—the first we have had this winter.   T. B.

RC (DLC); addressed: "The Honl. Thomas Jefferson Esqr Secretary of State Philadelphia"; franked; endorsed by TJ as received 13 Feb. 1793 and so recorded in SJL.

YOURS OF THE 17TH. was undoubtedly TJ to Robert Gamble of 17 Jan. 1793, which TJ had asked Gamble to forward to Bell.

[1] Thus in manuscript.
[2] Sentence to this point thus in manuscript.

From Nathaniel Cutting

Philadelphia, 30 Jan. 1793. Knowing "the wish and intention of the political Fathers of our Country to cherish and protect its Commerce, that great source of Federal Revenue," he represents the need for a consul or vice-consul at Cadiz, a port as heavily frequented by American vessels as any other on the Continent. American citizens have incurred considerable expense there without a consular representative, as he himself did some years ago when dealing with Spanish officials in connection with a collision between his ship and another vessel. Knowing of no American resident at Cadiz who intends to seek the office of consul there, and observing that the Constitution authorizes the appointment of foreigners as vice-consuls, he recommends Don Joseph Yznardi, a Spaniard who has just arrived here with letters of recommendation from Carmichael. Well qualified for the post he seeks, Yznardi has not only "lived long enough in England to acquire the language and manners of that Country so perfectly that he might naturally be mistaken for a native of it," and been employed for two or three years in the counting house of Mr. Duff, a respectable merchant who is English "Pro-Consul" at Cadiz, but his family is influential at the Spanish court.

RC (DLC: Washington Papers, Applications for Office); 2 p.; at head of text: "Thomas Jefferson Esqr. Secretary of State, &c. &c."; endorsed by TJ as received 31 Jan. 1793 and so recorded in

SJL. FC (Lb in MHi: Cutting Papers); in Cutting's hand.

Washington submitted Yznardi's nomination as consul at Cadiz to the Senate on 19 Feb. 1793, and the Senate confirmed it on the following day (JEP, I, 130, 131).

From James Monroe

DEAR SIR   [30 Jan. 1793]

Mr. Gunn has mentioned to Major Butler the report that his conduct at New York upon some publick questions was influenc'd by some expectations of a foreign mission. He has called on Hamilton whom he did not see but means to chastise those concerned in the charge. Hamilton informed him at the time it took place[1] that the appointment of Short was at your instance contrary to his wishes, and that he wanted the President to appoint him (viz. Majr. Butler). As he means to call on you immediately[2] as a friend to confer on this subject I have thought proper to apprize you of the above. Yrs. affecy.

JAS. MONROE

RC (DLC); undated; endorsed by TJ as received 30 Jan. 1793 and so recorded in SJL.

[1] Preceding six words interlined.
[2] Word interlined.

From Thomas Pinckney

DEAR SIR   London 30th Janry. 1793

In my letter of the third of the present month I acknowledged your several favors of the 6th., 8th., 13th. and 20th. of November and 3d. of December; and I now avail myself of the present opportunity of adverting to some parts of them not answered in my last. Mr. Pintards representation of the conduct of Captain Hargood of the British Frigate Hyana at Madeira has been submitted to the Secretary of State for the foreign department as one of the several cases which call loudly for the interposition and redress of this Government; on this subject after various personal conferences I have brought forward my objections in a written Note and have been assured by Lord Grenville that the business is in a train for decision.

Not finding upon enquiry a mode of conveyance on which I could place confidence for forwarding your letter to our Commissioners at Madrid I sent it by a safe opportunity to Mr. Morris at Paris, with an extract from your letter relating to it, and as I understand the communication between the two countries has of late been tolerably free I have little doubt of his being able to transmit it in safety to its destination.

I am happy to find that my rejection of Mr. Sayre's demand met your approbation; he afterwards however returned to the charge on new and more important ground, but as my first answer was given on principle no change of circumstances could justify a deviation therefrom. The particulars of his last application I will forward by a safe private conveyance.

I have as yet heard nothing from the agent of the State of Pensylvania on the subject of Mr. Galloways letter. Mr. Morris in his last letter from Paris informed me that he had sent to Mr. Droz but had not then seen him. The Person whom I thought myself almost certain of engaging as an Assayer now raises objections and makes new demands with which I can not comply, so that I doubt whether he will accept the appointment which I regret on account of his unexceptionable recommendations. With him as an Assayer and Droz as Engraver and chief Coiner under the respectable direction of the Officer appointed in America I flattered myself our Mint would be perfectly well established.

The news papers herewith will convey the public news up to this date. The melancholic fate of the unfortunate Louis has made a forcible impression on the public mind here which was before considerably irritated against the French nation, owing I believe in a great measure to their apprehensions for their own internal tranquillity. Mr. Chavelin has been formally[1] notified to depart as you will perceive by the official note herewith a copy of which was sent to each of the foreign ministers, so that it now appears almost inevitably that this country and Holland will be involved in the War against France. As this will of course be a naval war our Vessels will I presume be provided with proper passports to intitle them to those advantages which our commercial treaties with some of the belligerent powers will afford. I wish we had similar articles in a treaty with this country for altho the administration[2] appear sensible of the importance of our trade and profess an inclination to cultivate our friendship yet they are adopting a measure respecting the French which in its execution may lead to disagreeable consequences with respect to us, I mean their plan of distressing by preventing them from receiving supplies of provisions; now as we shall be the people who must principally supply them, and as we[3] have no treaty with Great Britain respecting our inter course with countries with whom she may be at war, and (although our claim to a free inter course is founded in reason and our natural rights yet)[4] as we have no armed neutrality the members whereof this people have to fear, I am apprehensive they may stop our Vessels bound to the French Ports with Provisions: if such should be the case you may rely on my remonstrating with that temperate firmness which the magnitude of the object and our clear Right will justify and that in this as well as in every other instance no argument I can adduce or exertion I can make shall be wanting to protect our commercial interests. As however I have no instructions particularly relating to circumstances which may arise from this Country being engaged in War I have earnestly to request that my line of conduct may be as accurately marked out as possible, directing it in circumstances which may suggest themselves as probable to take place from our relation to the contending parties and giving general rules to be applied in unforeseen events. I have the honor to be with the utmost respect & sincere esteem Dear Sir Your most faithful & obedient Servant   TH: PINCKNEY

RC (DNA: RG 59, DD); at foot of text: "The Secretary of State"; endorsed by TJ as received 20 Apr. 1793 and so recorded in SJL. PrC (ScHi: Pinckney Family Papers); consists of all but last page. FC (same); consists of last page only written in ink in Pinckney's hand on verso of last page of PrC; unsigned. Tr (Lb in DNA: RG 59, DD). Enclosure not found.

Pinckney's 7 Jan. 1793 NOTE to Lord Grenville on the removal of seven allegedly British seamen from the American ship *Illustrious President* by the captain of H.M.S. *Hyena* is in ScHi: Pinckney Family Papers. See also John M. Pintard to TJ, 15 May 1792. The circumstances surrounding Stephen SAYRE'S DEMAND for a temporary appointment as Pinckney's secretary are described in Pinckney to

TJ, 8 Sep. 1792, and note. On 24 Jan. 1793, the day after news of the execution of Louis XVI reached London, the British government ordered the Marquis de CHAUVELIN, the French ambassador, to leave England by 1 Feb. (John Ehrman, *The Younger Pitt: The Reluctant Transition* [London, 1983], 254).

TJ submitted this letter to the President on 20 Apr. 1793 (Washington, *Journal*, 115).

[1] Pinckney here canceled "dismissed."
[2] Pinckney here canceled "of this country"; phrase not canceled in PrC.
[3] Preceding two words interlined; they are omitted in PrC.
[4] Parentheses not in PrC.

From John Carey

SIR   January 31: 1793.

Before I proceed in the business of copying the records, which your kindness has enabled me to resume, I request your permission to suggest a few hints—on paper rather than otherwise, as being less likely to trespass on your time.

1. The task before me is weighty; and the time, for the performance, being short, the loss of two or three hours' writing every day, and of one whole day every week, becomes a serious object with me. Various concurring causes will prevent me from staying in your office much later than 8 o'clock at night; whereas I could write till 10 or 11, if I had your permission to carry home with me *a few* letters, which I would take back next morning. Thus also I could usefully employ sundays. And if the apprehension of danger, in the removal of the papers, can only be got over, I think I can undertake to obviate *every* other objection.

2. Possibly, at a future day, some of the passages that I copy, or even the existence of entire letters, may be controverted; in which case, should your successor in office refuse access to the originals, it will be difficult to prove the truth. Such an event may be guarded against, by a certificate, at the head of my publication, setting forth that "*J: C has, under the proper authority, obtained access, &c*" and "*has made oath, that he has faithfully copied, &c without wilfully altering or perverting the sense* &c."

3. Willing as I am to share my scanty finances in order to procure assistance in expediting the work; I cannot venture to make any offer whatever, until I be acquainted with the extent of my resources. Hence it would be useful to me to know what sum I may probably receive for the Index to the laws; and *when* my present employment (which I understood to be but temporary) is likely to cease; as this knowledge would the better enable me to judge, whether I can safely venture to call in the necessary aid.

[105]

4. As Mr. Brown, the printer, must have an Index to his edition of the laws; and will probably pay somebody for compiling one, I would beg to be informed, whether I may, without impropriety, furnish him with a copy of that which I make for the United States, and receive payment from him, on the best terms that I can obtain.

Whenever you are pleased to command my attendance, to learn your pleasure respecting these points, I shall be ready to wait on you; and have the honor to be, with due respect, Sir, your most obliged, humble servant, JOHN CAREY

RC (DLC); endorsed by TJ as received 31 Jan. 1793 and so recorded in SJL.

Although Andrew BROWN, a Philadelphia printer, had published an edition of the laws passed during the first session of the second Congress, there is no record of a subsequent volume (see Evans, No. 24869).

From Thomas Pinckney

DEAR SIR   London 31st. Janry. 1793

Altho I write fully by the William Penn which will sail in a day or two for Philadelphia yet as I am informed that there is a Vessel in the Downs bound to New York I send this to Mr. Auldjo at Cowes to endeavor to get it on board in order to acknowledge the receipt of your favors of the 30th. of Decr. 1792 and 1st. Janry. 1793—to say that the contents of the first should receive due attention; but to inform you that I am prevented from obtaining the contents of the second by the loss of my Cypher, an accident for which I can not account. I took the precaution in order to secure such of my Papers as ought to be kept secret to put them into a heavy desk which could not easily be removed and had a patent lock put on the drawer, which the Mechanics here assert can not be picked, and the Key I have never intrusted to any person; notwithstanding which this paper is gone and I have in vain bewildered myself with conjectures to account for it. I have had no servant whom I have discovered to be guilty of other thefts; indeed this does not appear to have been taken by a common thief because I have always kept money both in bank bills and coin in the same drawer, none of which I have missed; neither has it much the appearance of being taken by a person employed particularly for the purpose of purloining papers of consequence as my instructions and indeed all my papers which require any degree of secrecy were there and still remain untouched. The only way in which I think it possible that I can myself have put it out of the way is that when I was making up Mr.

B's dispatches his cypher being with mine I may have inclosed both together to him. Of this however I may not get any immediate account as I have only received one letter from him by post dated at Cadiz 25th. Decr. 1792 in which he mentions that great attention should be paid to what I had written. I need not, Sir, perplex you as I have myself with any farther conjectures on this accident, nor describe the anxiety I suffer lest beneficial measures may be thereby retarded. I do not think either of your last favors has been opened. They were secured by a single wafer which I conceive the safest way; at least it is easier to discover when letters fastened in that mode have been opened than those secured in any other way. I purpose immediately to inform Mr. Morris of this circumstance, requesting him to communicate by a confidential conveyance any thing he may have received or shall receive from home which he may judge it at all important for me to be acquainted with. The danger of this cypher having fallen into improper hands is obviously so great that you will doubt less send a different one by the first safe opportunity and it will be necessary to transmit a copy of the old one unless you send duplicates written in the new Cypher, of yours of the 1st. Janry. and of any other you may in the mean time write in the former. Mr. de Chavelin has been cavalierly ordered away since the execution of the late King and immediate war seems almost inevitable and yet a doubt still remains on this subject. Before the next packet sails this doubt will either be strengthened or removed. With the utmost respect I remain Dear Sir Your faithful & obedient Servant   THOMAS PINCKNEY

RC (DNA: RG 59, DD); at foot of first page: "The Secretary of State"; endorsed by TJ as received 8 Apr. 1793 and so recorded in SJL. PrC (ScHi: Pinckney Family Papers). Tr (Lb in DNA: RG 59, DD).

MR. B: Thomas Barclay. TJ submitted this letter to the President on 18 Apr. 1793, and Washington returned it the next day (Washington, *Journal*, 110, 114).

George Washington to the Commissioners of the Federal District

Jan. 31. 93.

I have had under consideration Mr. Hallet's plans for the capitol, which undoubtedly have a great deal of merit. Doctor Thornton has also given me a view of his. These last come forward under some very advantageous circumstances. The grandeur, simplicity, and beauty of the exterior, the propriety with which the apartments are distributed, and economy in the mass of the whole structure, will[1] I doubt not give it a preference in your eyes, as it has done in mine, and those of several others whom I have consulted.[2] I have therefore thought it better to give the Doctor time to finish his plan, and for this purpose to delay till your next meeting a final decision. Some difficulty arises with respect to Mr. Hallet, who you know was in some degree led into his plan by ideas we all expressed to him. This ought not to induce us to prefer it to a better: but while he is liberally rewarded for the time and labor he has expended on it, his feelings should be saved and soothed as much as possible. I leave it to yourselves how best to prepare him for the possibility that the Doctor's plan may be preferred to his. Some ground for this will be furnished you by the occasion you[3] will have for recourse to him as to the interior of the apartments, and the taking him into service at a fixed allowance, and I understand that his necessities render it material that he should know what his allowance is to be.

Dft (DLC: Washington Papers); in TJ's hand except for additions by Washington noted below; mutilated upper right portion supplied from Pr C; at head of text in Washington's hand: "(Private)" and "Gentlemen"; at foot of text in TJ's hand: "Private. to Dr. Stewart. or to all the gentlemen," which Washington lined through and replaced with "The Commr. Fedl. District"; on verso in TJ's hand: "Dr. Thornton has given more views of his"; endorsed by Bartholomew Dandridge, Jr. Pr C (DLC); entirely in TJ's hand, but lacks his notation on verso. Recorded in SJPL; only one letter to the Commissioners of this date is recorded in SJL. The text Washington sent to the Commissioners reflected the changes he made to TJ's Dft (DLC: Presidential Manuscripts General; Fitzpatrick, *Writings*, XXXII, 324-5).

This clear expression of presidential preference for Dr. William Thornton's plan FOR THE CAPITOL, which was reinforced by TJ's letter on the following day to Daniel Carroll, induced the Federal District Commissioners in March 1793 to award the West Indian-born, Scottish-educated physician and self-taught architect a prize of $500 and a lot in the Federal District as the winner of the competition that had begun in March 1792 for the best design of the United States Capitol (Commissioners to Washington, 11 Mch., to Stephen Hallet, 13 Mch., and to Thornton, 5 Apr. 1793, in DNA: RG 42, DCLB; Glenn Brown, *History of the United States Capitol*, 2 vols. [Washington, D.C., 1900-03], I, 4-9). Although Thornton's prize-winning plan no longer exists, its character and evolution have been imaginatively reconstructed on the basis of contemporary comments and related manuscripts and drawings in Fiske Kimball and Wells Bennett, "William Thornton and the Design of the United States Capitol," *Art Studies: Medieval, Renaissance and Modern*, I (1923), 76-92, which argues that important elements of it were derived from a design for the Capitol drawn by Stephen Hallet, a French-born architect whose Capitol plan had heretofore been the one most favored by the Commissioners. For the subsequent modifications of Thornton's design, see Brown, *History*, I, 9-31.

[1] Word interlined in place of "would."
[2] Washington here interlined "and are deemed men of Skill and taste in Architecture."
[3] Washington here interlined "probably."

George Washington to the Commissioners of the Federal District

GENTLEMEN   Philadelphia Jan. 31. 1793.

The regular course which the affairs of the Federal city are likely to move in by the appointment of a Superintendant, who may relieve you from details, and from all sacrifices of time except your periodical meetings, enables me now[1] to proceed, on more certain grounds to the subject of compensation. That a proper compensation should be made you must undoubtedly be the public expectation as well as your own.[2] In proposing the sum, I do not see that I can take a better guide than that of the legislature, which in fixing the compensation for members of Congress has furnished a kind of standard to which services and qualifications in a certain line may be referred. I should therefore propose to you six dollars a day for the days of actual service, and milage for travelling, in lieu of service and all expences[3] to commence from the first day of the present year.

With respect to the past I have more difficulty to name a sum, because I do not know the time you have actually sacrificed, and perhaps it would not be practicable for yourselves to state it. On the best judgment I am able to form of it however I should propose the sum of 1500.[4] dollars, each, for your services preceding the commencement of the present year. Should these propositions not exactly meet your own ideas, I shall be very happy to receive your observations on them.[5]

Dft (DNA: RG 59, MLR); in TJ's hand except for revisions by Washington and Bartholomew Dandridge, Jr., noted below; Washington's signature clipped; at foot of text: "Messrs. Johnson, Stewart & Carrol"; endorsed by Dandridge. Pr C (DLC); entirely in TJ's hand, but partially faded and overwritten in a later hand. Recorded in SJPL; only one letter to the Commissioners of this date is recorded in SJL. In addition to the changes noted below, Washington added the following postscript to the text he sent to the Commissioners: "My meaning is, that the above sum of One thousand dolrs.

should be exclusive of your expencies" (DLC: Presidential Manuscripts General; Fitzpatrick, *Washington*, XXXII, 323-4).

[1] Word interlined. TJ interlined it in ink on the Pr C.

[2] Washington here interlined "although the Law is silent thereupon."

[3] Preceding seven words interlined.

[4] Thus in Dft and Pr C before being reworked to "1000" in Dft.

[5] Here the complimentary close is inserted in Dandridge's hand: "With great esteem, I am, Gentn. your mo: obt. Servt."

To Daniel Carroll

DEAR SIR   Philadelphia Feb. 1. 1793.

Doctr. Thornton's plan of a Capitol has been produced, and has so captivated the eyes and judgment of all as to leave no doubt you will prefer it when it shall be exhibited to you; as no doubt exists here of it's preference over all which have been produced, and among it's admirers no one is more decided than him whose decision is most important. It is simple, noble, beautiful, excellently distributed, and moderate in size.[1] The purpose of this letter is to apprise you of this sentiment. A just respect for the right of approbrobation in the Commissioners will prevent any formal decision in the President till the plan shall be laid before you and be approved by you. The Doctor will go with it to your meeting in the beginning of March. In the mean time, the interval of *apparent* doubt, may be improved for soothing the mind of poor Hallet, whose merit and distresses interest every one for his tranquility and pecuniary relief. I have taken the liberty of making these private intimations, thinking you would wish to know the true state of the sentiments here on this subject, and am with sincere respect & esteem for your collegues & yourself Dear Sir your most obedt. humble servt

TH: JEFFERSON

PrC (DLC); at foot of text: "Mr Car-   [1] Preceding sentence interlined.
rol."

From Daniel Carroll

DEAR SIR   Geo Town feby 1st. 1793

Your favor of the 15th Ulto. with the plat of the Territory of Columbia reachd this as I am informed on the 25th Ulto. It came to my hands the monday following and I disired Mr. Gantt to deliver it to Mr. Ellicot for the purposes desired. Your Note with Mr. Traquairs to you is just receivd. I expect Messrs: Johnson and Stuart this Evening & remain Dear Sir, with very great esteem & respect, Your Most Obt hble Servt

DANL. CARROLL

RC (DLC); endorsed by TJ as received 6 Feb. 1793 and so recorded in SJL.

TJ's NOTE has not been found, nor is it recorded in SJL. MR. TRAQUAIRS TO YOU was undoubtedly James Traquair to TJ of 22 Jan. 1793, recorded in SJL as received 23 Jan. 1793, but also not found.

From Alexander Hamilton

SIR   Treasury Department Febry 1st 1793
   The following is an extract from a letter of Mr. Short to me, dated
Hague November 2. 1792.

   "I should repeat perhaps what I formerly mentioned to you, that Mr.
Jefferson on his departure from Paris left with me bills of exchange
to the amount of I think 66,000^{tt}. This was destined to a particular
object with which You are acquainted. He expected it would be immediately applied and therefore wished me to be the instrument instead
of deposing it in a Bankers hands to avoid the Commission. When
the term of these bills arrived, finding less probability of their being
immediately applied, and not chusing to keep by me such a sum at my
risk in an house which was robbed regularly two or three times a year,
I gave the bills to Mr. Grand to receive their amount, and to hold it
appropriated to the object in question. It remains still in his hands,
having never been called for. I wrote more than once respecting it on
finding the depreciation commencing but never received an answer. It
remains now to be considered whether You would chuse to receive it
in its depreciated State—or wait for the change of circulating medium
in France."

   This communication is made with a request to Know, whether the
fund in question continues to be necessary for its original purpose or
may be withdrawn. I have the honor to be very respectfully Sir Your
obedient Servant   ALEX. HAMILTON

RC (DLC); in a clerk's hand, with signature and complimentary close by Hamilton; at foot of text: "The Secretary of
State"; endorsed by TJ as received 2 Feb.
1793 and so recorded in SJL.

The PARTICULAR OBJECT of the funds in
question is explained in TJ to Hamilton,
4 Feb. 1793.

From Benjamin Hawkins

                                              1 Feby. 93.
   I send you your share of the white bent grass, so much valued by
Mr. Bassett. I have sent the half of the remainder to the President.
Mr. B. being a farmer, we may count with certainty on its being a
valuable acquisition from the experience he has had.
   If you have formd any thing interesting from the name I sent you,

you can communicate it to the President with a translation of the botanical discription. Yours sincerely BENJAMIN HAWKINS

RC (MHi); addressed: "Mr. Jefferson"; endorsed by TJ.

Minutes of a Conference with the Illinois and Wabash Indians

[1-4 Feb. 1793]

Feb. 1. 1793. The President having addressed the Chiefs of the Wabash and Illinois Indians, John Baptist De Coin, chief of Kaskaskia, spoke as follows.

Father. I am about to open to you my heart. I salute first the Great Spirit, the master of life, and then you.

I present you a black pipe on the death of[1] our chiefs who have come here and died in your bed. It is the calumet of the dead. Take it and smoke in it in remembrance of them. The dead pray you to listen to the living and to be their friends. They are gone, we cannot recall them, let us then be contented; for, as you have said, tomorrow perhaps it may be our turn. Take then their pipe, and as I have spoken for the dead, let me now address you for the living. [He delivered the black pipe]

[Here Three-legs, a Piankishaw chief, came forward and carried round a white pipe from which every one smoked.]

John Baptist De Coin spoke again.

Father. The sky is now cleared. I am about to open my heart to you again: I do it in the presence of the Great Spirit, and I pray you to attend.

You have heard the words of our father General Putnam. We opened our hearts to him, we made peace with him, and he has told you what we said.

This pipe is white. I pray you to consider it as of the Wiatonons, Piankeshaws, and the people of Eel river.

The English at Detroit are very jealous of our father. I have used my best endeavors to keep all the red men in friendship with you: but they have drawn over the one half, while I have kept the other. Be friendly then to those I have kept.

I have long known you, General Washington, the Congress, Jefferson, and Sinclair. I have laboured constantly for you, to preserve peace.

You see your children on this side: [pointing to the friends of the dead chiefs] they are now[2] orphans. Take care then of the orphans of our dead friends.

Father, your people of Kentuckey are like Musketoes, and try to destroy the red men: the red men are like Musketoes also, and try to injure the people of Kentuckey. But I look to you as to a good being. Order your people to be just. They are always trying to get our lands. They come on our lands. They hunt on them; kill our game and kill us. Keep them then on one side of the line, and us on the other. Listen, father, to what we say, and protect the nations of the Wabash and Missisipi in their lands.

The English have often spoken to me, but I shut my ears to them. I despise their money. It is nothing to me. I am attached to my lands. I love to eat in tranquility, and not like a bird on a bough.

The Piankeshaws, Wiatenons, Piorias and all the Indians of the Missisipi and Wabash, pray you to open your heart and ears to them, and as you befriend them, to give them Capt. Prior for their father. We love him, men, women and children of us, he has always been friendly to us, always taken care of us, and you cannot give us a better proof of your friendship than in leaving him with us.

[Here Three legs handed round the White pipe to be smoked]
De Coin then, taking a third pipe, proceeded.
This pipe, my father, is sent you by the great chief of all the Wiaws, called Crooked legs. He is old, infirm, and cannot walk. Therefore he is not come. But he prays you to be his friend and to take care of his people. He tells you there are many red people jealous of you. But you need not fear them. If he could have walked he would have come; but he is old, and sick and cannot walk. The English have a sugar mouth: but Crooked legs would never listen to them. They threatened us send the red men to cut off him and his people, and they sent the red men who threatened to do it unless he would join the English. But he would not join them.

The Chiefs of the Wabash, father, pray you to listen. They send you this pipe from afar. Keep your children quiet at the Falls of Ohio. We know you are the head of all. We appeal to you. Keep the Americans on one side of the Ohio from the Falls downwards, and us on the other; that we may have something to live on according to our agreement[3] in the treaty which you have. And do not take from the French the lands we have given them.

Old crooked legs sends you this pipe [here he presented it] and he prays you to send him Capt. Pryor for his father, for he is old and you ought to do this for him.

Father, I pray you to listen. So far I have spoken for others, and now will speak for myself. I am of Kaskaskia, and have always been a good American from my youth upwards. Yet the Kentuckians take my lands, eat my stock, steal my horses, kill my game, and abuse our persons. I come far with all these people. My nation is not numerous. No people can fight against you father, none but the Great god himself. All the red men together cannot do it. But have pity on us. I am now old.[4] Do not let the Kentuckians take my lands nor injure me; but give me a line to them to let me alone.

Father, the Wiatonons, Piankeshaws, Piorias, Powtewatomies, Musketons, Kaskaskias have now made a road to you. It is broad and white: take care of it then and keep it open.

Father, you are powerful. You said you would wipe away our tears. We thank you for this. Be firm and take care of your children.

The hatchet has been long buried. I have been always for peace, I have done what I could, given all the money I had, to procure it.

The half of my heart, father, is black. I brought the Piorias to you, half of them are dead. I fear they will say it was my fault. But father, I look upon you, my heart is white again and I smile.

The Shawanese, the Delawares, and the English are always persuading us to take up the hatchet against you, but I have been always deaf to their words.

[Here he gave a belt]

Great Joseph, who came with us, is dead. Have compassion on his neice, his son in law, and his chiefs [pointing to them].[5] It is a dead man who speaks to you, father, accept therefore these black beads. [Here he presented several strands of dark coloured beads]

I have now seen Genl. Washington, I salute and regard him next after the Great Spirit.

Como, a Poughtewatomy chief then said that as the President had already been long detained, and the hour was advanced, he would reserve what he had to say to another day.

Shawas, the little Doe, a Kickapou chief, tho' very sick, had attended the Conference, and now carried the pipe round to be smoked. He then addressed the President.

Father. I am still very ill and unable to speak. I am a Kickapou, and drink of all the waters of the Wabash and Missisipi. I have been to the Wabash and treated with General Putnam: and I came here, not to do ill, but to make peace. Send to us Capt. Prior to be our father, and no other. He possesses all our love.

Father, I am too ill to speak. You will not forget what the others have said.

Feb. 2. The day being cloudy, the Indians did not chuse to meet.

Feb. 4. The morning was cloudy. They gave notice that if it should clear up they would attend at the President's at 2. aclock. Accordingly, the clouds having broke away about Noon, they attended a little after two; except Shawas and another who were sick, and one woman.

Como, a Powtewatomy chief spoke.[6]

Father, I am opening my heart to speak to you. Open yours to recieve my words. I first address you from a dead chief, who, when he was about to die, called us up to him and charged us 'never to part with our lands so I have done for you, my children, and so do you for yours. For what have we come so far? Not to ruin our nation, nor yet that we might carry goods home to our women and children: but to procure them lasting good, to open a road between them and the Whites. Sollicit our father to send Capt. Prior to us. He has taken good care of us and we all love him.'

Now, father, I address you for our young people. But there remains not much to say; for I spoke to you through Genl. Putnam, and you have what I said on paper. I have buried the hatchet for ever: so must your children. I speak the truth and you must believe me. We all pray you to send Capt. Pryor to us, because he has been so very kind to us all.

[Here he delivered strands of dark colored beads.]

Father, hear me and believe me. I speak the truth and from my heart; recieve my words then into yours. I am come from afar, for the good of my women and children, for their present and future good. When I was at home in the midst of them, my heart sunk within me, I saw[7] no hope for them. The heavens were gloomy and lowering and I could not tell why. But General Putnam spoke to us, and called us together. I rejoiced to hear him, and determined immediately to come and see my father. Father, I am happy to see you. The heavens have cleared away, the day is bright, and I rejoice to hear your voice. These beads [holding up a bundle of white strands] are a road between us. Take you hold[8] at one end. I will at the other, and hold it fast. I will visit this road every day, and sweep it clean. If any blood be on it, I will cover it up; if stumps, I will cut them out. Should your children and mine meet in this road they shall shake hands and be good friends. Some of the Indians who belong to the English will be trying to sow harm between us: but we must be on our guard and prevent it.

Father, I love[9] the land on which I was born, the trees which cover it, and the grass growing on it. It feeds us well. I am not come here to ask gifts. I am young, and by hunting on my own land, can kill what I want and feed my women and children in plenty. I come not to beg. But if any of your traders would wish to come among us, let them come. For who will hurt them? Nobody. I will be there before them.

Father, I take you by the hand with all my heart, I will never forget you; do not you forget me.

[Here he delivered the bundle of white strands]

The Little beaver, a Wiatonon, on the behalf of Crooked legs, handed round the pipe, and then spoke.

Father, listen now to me, as you have done to others. I am not a very great chief: I am a chief of war, and leader of the young people.

Father, I wished much to hear you: you have spoken comfort to us, and I am happy to have heard it. The sun has shone out, and all is well. This makes us think it was the great spirit speaking truth through you. Do then what you have said:[10] restrain your people if they do wrong, as we will ours if they do wrong.

Father, we gave to our friend (Pryor) who came with us, our name of Wiatonon, and he gave us his name of American. We are now Americans. Give him then to us for a father. He has loved us and taken care of us. He had pity on our women and children and fed them. Do not forget to grant us this request. You told us to live in quiet and to do right. We will do what you desire. Then do you what we desire, and let Pryor come to us.

Now that we are come so far to hear you, write a line to your people to keep the river open between us, that we may go down it in safety, and that our women and children may work in peace. When I go back, I will bear to them good tidings, and our young men will no longer[11] hunt in fear for the support of our women and children.

Father, all of us who have heard you, are made happy. All are in the same sentiment with me; all are satisfied. Be assured that, when we return, the Indians and Americans will be one people, will hunt, and play, and laugh together. For me, I will never depart one step from Pryor.

We are come from afar to make a stable peace to look forward to our future good. Do not refuse what we sollicit. We will never forget you.

Here I will cease. The father of life might otherwise think I babbled too much; and so might you. I finish then, in giving you this pipe. It is my own and from myself alone. I am but a warrior. I give it to you to smoke in. Let it's fumes ascend to the great Spirit in heaven.

[He delivered the pipe to the President.]

The wife of the Souldier, a Wiatonon, speaks.

Father I take you by the hand with all my heart because you have spoken comfort to us. I am but a woman: yet you must listen.[12]

The Village-chiefs, and Chiefs of war have opened their bodies and laid naked their hearts to you. Let them too see your heart and listen to them.

We have come, men and women, from afar to beseech you to let no one take our lands. That is one of your children [pointing to Genl. Putnam] it was he who persuaded us to come. We thought he spoke the truth: we came, we hope that good will come of it.

Father. We know you are strong. Have pity on us. Be firm in your words. They have given us courage. The father of life has opened our hearts on both sides for good.

He, who was to have spoken to you, is dead, great Joseph. If he had lived, you would have heard a good man, and good words flowing from his mouth. He was my uncle, and[13] it has fallen to me to speak for him. But I am ignorant. Excuse then these words. It is but a woman who speaks.

[She delivers white strands]

Three legs, a Piankasha spoke.

I speak for a young chief whom I have lost here. He came to speak to you, father, but he had not that happiness. He died. I am not a Village-chief, but only a chief of war.

We are come to seek all our good, and to be firm in it. If our father is firm we will be so. It was a dark and gloomy day in which I lost my young chief. The master of life saw that he was good, and called him to himself. We must submit to his will.

[He gave a black strand]

I pray you all who are present to say, as one man, that our peace is firm, and to let it be firm. Listen to us if you love us. We live on the river;[14] on one side, and shall be happy to see capt. Pryor on the other, and to have a lasting peace.

Here is our father Putnam. He heard me speak at Au Poste. If I am false, let him say so.

My land is but small. If any more be taken from us, I will come again to you and complain, for we shall not be able to live. Have pity on us father. You have many red children there and they have little whereon to live. Leave them land enough to labour, to hunt and to live on: and the lands which we have given to the French, let them be to them for ever.

Father, we are very poor. We have traders among us, but they sell too dear. We have not the means of supplying our wants at such prices. Encourage your traders then to come, and to bring us guns, powder and other necessaries: and send Capt. Prior also to us.

[He gave a string of white beads.]

De Coin spoke.

Jefferson, I have seen you before, and we have spoken together.

Sinclair, we have opened our hearts to one another.

Putnam, we did the same at Au Poste.

Father, you have heard these three speak of me, and you know my character. The times are gloomy in my town. We have no commander, no souldier, no priest. Have you no concern for us father? If you have, put a magistrate with us to keep the peace. I cannot live so. I am of French blood. When there are no priests among us, we think that all is not well. When I was small we had priests. Now that I am old, we have none. Am I to forget then how to pray? Have pity on me and grant what I ask. I have spoken on your behalf to all the nations. I am a friend to all, and hurt none. For what are we on this earth? but as a small and tender plant of corn;—even as nothing. God has made this earth for you as well as us: we are then but as one family, and if any one strikes you, it is as if he had struck us. If any nation strikes you father, we will let you know what nation it is.

Father, we fear the Kentuckians. They are headstrong, and do us great wrong. They are not content to come on our lands to hunt on them, to steal and destroy our stocks,[15] as the Shawanese and Delawares do, but they go further and abuse our persons. Forbid them to do so. Sinclair, you know that the Shawanese and Delawares came from the Spanish side of the river, destroyed our corn and killed our cattle. We cannot live, if things go so.

Father, you are rich, you have all things at command, you want for nothing. You promised to wipe away our tears. I commend our women and children to your care.

[He gave strands of white beads][16]

The President then assured them that he would take into consideration what they had said, and would give them an answer on another day, whereupon the Conference ended for the present.[17]

PrC (DLC: TJ Papers, 81: 14068-81); consists of 14 pages entirely in TJ's hand, but partly faded and overwritten in a later hand; brackets in original. Recorded in SJPL under 1 Feb. 1793: "Indian Speeches."

This document consists of TJ's minutes of a conference with various Illinois and Wabash Indian chiefs who had been invited to Philadelphia by General Rufus PUTNAM to discuss a peace treaty Putnam had concluded with their tribes on 27 Sep. 1792. The Indian leaders, who arrived at the capital near the end of December and did not leave until early in May 1793, met with Washington, TJ, Secretary of War Knox, Attorney General Randolph, and other administration officials at the President's house on 1 and 4 Feb. 1793. TJ sent the first six pages and subsequently the complete MS of his minutes to Washington, who requested the addition of a final paragraph (see note 17 below) and sent them thus amended, together with the "Pipes & wampum" presented by the Indians, to Knox on 8 Feb. for deposit in the archives of the Department of War. This text has not been found, however, leaving the PrC printed here as the only extant version of TJ's minutes and an unparalleled record of these proceedings with the Indians. On 13 Feb. 1793, nine days after the conference ended, Washington submitted the treaty to the Senate, which finally rejected it in January 1794 because the agreement did not give the United States the right of preemption to Wabash and Illinois tribal lands (ASP, *Indian Affairs*, I, 319-20, 338-40; Washington, *Journal*, 39, 40, 42-3, 44-5, 129, 130; JEP, I, 128, 134, 135, 144, 145-6; *National Gazette*, 29 Dec. 1792, 2, 12 Jan. 1793; TJ to Washington, 1, 7 Feb., Tobias Lear to TJ, 2, 4 Feb. 1793).

DE COIN: Jean Baptiste Ducoigne, a Kaskaskia Indian chief who had first met TJ in 1781 and to whom TJ as governor of Virginia addressed his first known Indian speech (Vol. 6: 60-4). SINCLAIR: Arthur St. Clair, governor of the Northwest Territory. PRIOR: Abner Prior, a United States Army captain who had escorted a group of Wabash chiefs from the Northwest Territory to the Philadelphia conference (ASP, *Indian Affairs*, I, 319; Francis B. Heitman, comp., *Historical Register and Dictionary of the United States Army...*, 2 vols. [Washington, D.C., 1903], I, 808).

[1] Preceding four words interlined in place of what appears to be "because."
[2] Here and before "orphans" in the next sentence TJ canceled "widows and."
[3] TJ here canceled "with General Putnam."
[4] Preceding sentence interlined.
[5] Bracketed passage interlined.
[6] Sentence interlined.
[7] TJ here canceled "nothing."
[8] TJ here canceled "of it."
[9] TJ here canceled "my nation."
[10] TJ here canceled "and if any of your people."
[11] TJ here canceled "fish and."
[12] TJ first wrote "but you must listen to me" and then altered it to read as above.
[13] Sentence to this point interlined.
[14] TJ here canceled "and shall be happy."
[15] TJ here canceled "but they abuse our persons."
[16] Bracket inserted in ink by TJ after he canceled "and the conference ended]."
[17] This paragraph subsequently added by TJ at Washington's request (see Tobias Lear to TJ, 7 Feb. 1793).

From James Cole Mountflorence

SIR   Norfolk the 1st. february 1793

I have the Honor to transmit to you herewith the Manuscript relative to the Events of the French Revolution of last year. You will find, Sir, that I have been pretty circumstancial respecting what regards the unhappy Marquis De la Fayette: It was the Opinion of a Number of his friends in Paris that the United States of America would probably interfere in his Behalf, and that the Supreme Executive could demand him as a Citizen of those States which he has served with so much Honor and Zeal; they suggested that such Interference would meet with Success in consideration of the friendly terms subsisting between America and Prussia, and that at all Events should it not have the desired Effect, it would evince to the World the Gratitude of the United States to their Meritorious Officers.

My Stay in the Territory South of the Ohio, Sir, will be only of two or three Weeks at most, Some private Business making it necessary for me to return to Europe most immediately, and Should any thing be determined on by the United States in favor of that Patriotic Nobleman, which might render an Application to the Court of *Berlin* necessary, I would deem myself exceedingly happy to be intrusted with an official Negociation to that Effect, and no Zeal would be wanting from me to fulfill the Wish of the United States to liberate that unfortunate officer. With great Respect I have the Honor to be Sir your most Obedt & most humble Servt.

J. C. MOUNTFLORENCE

I will not leave Richmond before the 15th. inst., for Holston.

RC (ViW); endorsed by TJ as received 14 Feb. 1793 and so recorded in SJL.

The Washington administration ignored Mountflorence's offer to act on its behalf in securing the Marquis de Lafayette's release from Prussian captivity, preferring instead to refer this matter to the American ministers in London and Paris (TJ to Gouverneur Morris and Thomas Pinckney, 15 Mch. 1793).

ENCLOSURE

James Cole Mountflorence's Account of the French Revolution

Copy of a Letter from an American Officer in Paris to his friend in Virginia, brought by the Amiable Antoinette.

DEAR SIR   Paris 11th. Novbr. 1792

I have not written to you since the memorable 10th. of August, but do not accuse me of neglect, The tyrannical proceedings of the Municipality of Paris who had erected themselves into one of the most tremendous inquisitorial courts, ten times more arbitrary than the star chamber, or the Dominicans Inquisition in Spain and sicily made it unsafe even for a stranger to trust his thoughts to paper locked up in his desk; much more dangerous would it therefore have been to send a letter by post containing any political intelligence.[A] No doubt you have had in America such various and different reports concerning the french Revolution, that you must be at a loss to find out the truth from the many opposit accounts you have received; and indeed I will

[A] The Days following the 10th. August, the Municipality ordered the Several Sections to appoint confidential Persons, that is to say hot headed Jacobins, to search in the Dead of the Night Every house in Paris, to examine Papers, and to take up every Person whom they might have suspected of not favoring their party; this order was executed with so much Zeal, that Thousands in less than four or five Days filled up the Jails of Paris, who were afterwards murdered at the General Massacre of the 2d., 3d. and 4th. September; A Pamphlet, a Letter, or any piece of Writing reflecting on the Jacobins, or expressing an Attachment to the King, or to the Constitution, or to Mr. Lafayette, found in the Possession of any man, was sufficient to Send him to Prison, had he been happy enough not to be butchered on the Spot.

[120]

confess to you that it is a difficult matter for a man even on the spot and who is attatched to none of their parties, not to be mislead by the persons from whom he gets his information. When the late french constitution was adopted in 1791 contrary to the Wish and opinion of a large number of the then Legislators, who wanted a republican form of government, a party was immediately formed in the jacobin Club, determined to overthrow the constitution and abolish Royalty. The members of this Club (disseminated in Societies establish'd on the same principles, in every Town of France corresponding with each other, but of which the Paris club seems to be the head or great council) contributed very much to the Revolution, and to their Exertions France is indebted for the Destruction of arbitrary Power and for the Constitution of 1791, most of the Legislators of the first national Assembly, belonging to that Club; But this Constitution having retained a hereditary King, a Schism immediately took place, and those who were averse to Monarchy combined together in order to overset it; Most of the Societies of *Marseilles* and of other Towns in the South of France joined that Party who preserved the Name of Jacobin, and may be compared to the most furious *Roundheads*(B) under the Reign of Charles the first, the others who were for maintaining the Constitution lately adopted, were distinguished by the Name of "*Feuillants*." The most violent Spirit of Party broke out at the first Meeting of the Second Legislature, when the jarring Interests of the two most powerful Factions, the Jacobin and Feuillant, together with the ineffectual Efforts of those Members who were still attached to the Clergy, Nobility and all the Errors of the old Government produced that unwise Measure of declaring War to the Emperor, without the least Necessity and almost without Provocation. All Parties were for War, tho' actuated by very different motives; the Jacobins desirous of rendering the King odious and of throwing him into every Embarassment, flattered themselves that the Influence of the Queen in the Council would prevent the King from *Sanctioning*(C) the Legislature Decree for War; in that case they would have taken pains to represent to the People that he was inimical to the Welfare and Glory of the Nation, and thereby alienate more and more from him the Affections of the People; on the other hand, should he Sanction the Decree, as he really did, they would have an Opportunity of accusing him as head of the Executive Department

(B) They have in truth and in fact surpassed in Cruelties and Horrors any thing of the Kind that has ever happened; they have not yet, it is true, put their Sovereign to Death, but they are thirsty of his Blood; and with Difficulty will it be Spared. It is a self evident truth, that any Nation or People have an imprescriptible Right of being governed as they please, and it is equally true, that a Republican form of Government is more analogous to the Rights of Men; Therefore if a great Majority of the french are tired of a Kingly Government and wish a Democratical one, they have an undoubted Right to Send their King about his Business, the former Contract being annulled; at the Same time it is unnecessary to accuse him of Crimes never committed, and it is dishonoring the glorious Cause of Liberty, to make use of falsities, Murders and the most abominable Cruelties in order to serve it.
(C) The Constitution had left to the King the power of ratifying and negativing the Decrees of the Legislature, before they became Laws; the King's Ratification or Approbation was called his *Sanction*, and his Negative, was distinguished by his *Veto*; from which the Blackguards of Paris, designed under the Appellation of "*Sans-culottes*" (without Breeches) in their infamous Songs made against the King, called him *Monsieur Veto*.

for all the unavoidable Misfortunes of the War, charging him with the Bad Situation of Warlike and other Supplies, the frontier Towns were in, the Want of Discipline in the Army, and the Divisions subsisting between the Officers of all Rank; altho those Circumstances were the natural Consequences of Three Years Anarchy and Confusion produced by the Revolution; yet they Knew well that the People in general do not reflect, but believe implicitly what is told them by those Persons who have gained their Confidence, by pretending to be their Friends; The feuillants[d] voted for the War, in the Belief that it would give Stability and Energy to the new form of Government, it being natural to suppose that those who were still displeased at some Articles of the Constitution, would nevertheless rally themselves under its Banners to oppose a foreign foe; the Royalists, who sighed for the old Arbitrary Government, and the Aristocrats desirous of restoring the Priviledges and Immunities of the Nobility and Clergy, were satisfied with the War, expecting that the confused Situation France was in, would have made it impossible for her to carry on the War without restoring to the King, Nobility and Clergy their former insufferable Power; all Parties therefore concurred to the adopting of a Measure so impolitical and so contrary to the true Interest of the Nation.

War was therefore undertaken with all possible Disadvantage, and the Marquis De la Fayette was appointed to the Command of one of the Armies. The Jacobins Kept Agents and Emissaries in every Army and in every Regiment, in order to gain Proselytes, to alienate the Affections of the Soldiers from the Prince, and to induce them to mistrust such of their officers as were of a noble Descent, preaching up the Doctrine of universal Equality. The Insubordination produced by their Machination caused the Miscarriage of the first Attack upon Mons, on the Retreat from which Place, the mislead Soldiery cut to [. . .]¹ General Dillon, who had served with so much honor and Courage in the American War. The Experienced Count De Rochambeau, who commanded the french forces at the taking of Lord Cornwallis's Army at York, resigned the Command of the Army on the Rhine, not being able to put up with the Indiscipline so industriously introduced in his Army; but La Fayette remained at his Post, and with his well Known Activity and conciliating manners, he succeeded in reestablishing Good Order and Discipline in his Army, having taken the judicious Precaution of expelling from it all the Jacobins and Every Person who held Discourses against the Constitution, him and his Army had sworn to maintain.

The Jacobins persuing their favorable Plan of susciting Difficulties upon Difficulties to the King, their Adherents in the National assembly promoted a Decree to call under the Wall of Paris a Camp of 30,000 Men, to be composed of "*Federés*"[E] of every *Department*;[F] and another submitting the

[d] The feuillants had already divided themselves into two Parties, since their Seperation from the Jacobins; towitt those who were Constitutionalists, or wished to maintain the Constitution in all its Points, and those who tho' attached to the Constitution, wanted an Alteration in it to establish an Upper house of Legislature; even these last thought that a War would favor their Design.
[E] Such is the name made use of to distinguish the National Guards of the Several Departments from the National Guards of Paris.
[F] France which was formerly divided into Provinces and Military Governments, is since the Revolution divided into Eighty three Districts, called *Departements*.

Clergy who had not taken the new test-Oath,(G) to be apprehended at the Demand of several Persons not even on Oath, and to be transported out of the Country. The King's Council discovered the Precipice which the sanction of the [co]up-decree would have precipitated him in, as this intended Army near Paris would have been composed only of such Féderés as were Jacobins; or influenced by them, by the uncommon Pains they had taken throughout the Kingdom to procure themselves Adherents, and to place them in most of the Civil public Offices; therefore Not only the King's Existence would have been endangered by Such measure, but the Constitution itself would have run the Risk of being subverted. As to the other Decree respecting the Clergy non-conformist, it was unconstitutional in its Principles, and would have given lieu to the most arbitrary Proceeding against One Portion of the Citizens of france, and a pretty considerable one too. The King's Refusal to sanction those two Decrees was made use of to represent to the People that he was not their friend, nor had the good of the Nation at heart, since he opposed their Wishes expressed by their Representatives in the national Assembly; With similar Sophistry and some more powerful Means, the Jacobins caused the Inhabitants of the Suburbs of St. Anthony and St. Marceau to repair to the Number of Several Thousand Men, armed with all kind of Weapons to the King's Palace on the 20th. June; Resistance would have been vain, as the Municipality took no Pains to prevent this Insurrection, which they had the appearance of rather favoring; As all the News papers must have given you a Circumstancial Account of the Events of that day, in which the spirited Conduct of the King gained him so many Partisans, I shall only add on that Subject that it is now evident that the Scheme of the Jacobins for that Day was twofold, that is to say to terrify the King into a Sanction of the two above recited Decrees, otherwise to carry matters to the last Extremities with him; But his Firmness and Courage on this Occasion imposed in so wonderful manner on the Multitude, that they departed without having done any bodily hurt to the King, after having abominably insulted the Queen with the most opprobrious Language. Upwards of Seventy Departments out of the 83, sent affectionate and respectful Adresses to the King, congratulating him on his spirited Conduct, his miraculous Escape from the imminent Dangers he had been exposed to, and devoting to Execrations the Authors and Promoters of the indecent Scenes of that Day. The Jacobins having thus failed in this attempt, used every Effort to march to Paris, without any order from Government, all the Féderés, they could possibly raise in the Departments where they had the most Influence, in which they partly succeeded; but the Army of Lafayette(H) were

(G) The Constitution had established a liberty of Worship for all Religions, but had preserved a National One, the Ministers of which had Revenues and livings; but none of the Clergy could have these Livings without taking a particular Oath for that purpose; those who held any of the Livings and refused to take the Oath were to be removed from them, and others substituted in their places.
(H) Never was Patriotism, Courage and Virtue persecuted with more Virulence, than in the Case of this brave General, a Son of Liberty, and who fought so nobly in America for her Rights the Calumny the most absurd and Pamphlets the most scurrilous were propagated, and every base Subterfuge resorted to, in order to ruin him in the Minds of the People; in the National assembly he was accused as the only Cause of the french Arms bad Success in the Austrian Netherlands by not cooperating with Genl. Luckner's

moved with Indignation at the Events of the 20th. June; they presented very spirited Adresses to their General, and some of the Regiments even expressed their Resolution of marching to Paris to protect the King's Person; The Marquis in order to prevent a Step of which the Consequences might have involved the Kingdom in a open civil War, and left the frontiers exposed to the Ravages of the Enemy, came to Paris with only some of his Aids-de-Camp, presented himself at the Bar of the National Assembly, informed them of the Sentiments of his Army on the Events of the 20th. June, denounced the Jacobins as Enemies to the Government and Constitution, and declared to them that he would maintain the Constitution of the Nation against all Parties and Factions whatsoever. This Spirited Measure of the Marquis, irritated more than ever the Jacobins who directed all their Fury against him, and from that Moment his Ruin seemed unavoidable; With the Greatest acrimony they moved in the Assembly for a Decree of Accusation against him, that is to say an Impeachment of high Treason, but the Virtue and Innocence of this

Army, and that by his inaction he had obliged the french troops to evacuate that Country; Lafayette published in his Defence, his whole Correspondence with Luckner, by which it appeared that when Genl. Luckner marched against Courtray, the Marquis acting in concert with that General, advanced with his Army another Way in the Enemy's Country, in order to make a Diversion and favor thereby his Operations; that Correspondence contained likewise a letter from the Marquis to that General, after the taking of Courtray, offering to join their forces in order to reduce all the low Country before the Arrival of the Prussian Army, that were on their March; Luckner's Answer was his Refusal to adopt that plan, and ordering a Retreat back to france, to cover that Country. Sometime before the 10th. August, Genl. Luckner came to Paris, and it was reported that being at Dinner with some of the Leaders of the Jacobins he had Said that Genl. La Fayette had proposed to him to march both their Armies to Paris to free the King from the Tyranny and Persecutions of the Jacobins; and that Monsieur De Puzy, la fayette's Aid-de-Camp, was the officer who brought him that Proposal; Information of this Circumstance having been given to the Assembly by Some of the Members who declared that they were present at this Conversation, the Assembly Ordered that De Puzy should appear at the Bar of the house to Answer the Charge exhibited against him, and that the Marquis should answer in Writing. In Every other Country than France, the Event of that Accusation which proved to be malicious false and without any Ground, would have conciliated to the Marquis the Esteem and Affections of his fellow Citizens covering at the Same time his base Accusers with Shame and Infamy; but it happened otherwise. La Fayette's Answer was that of a Gallant officer and a Virtuous Patriot moved with Indignation at the Injustices and Persecution of a violent Party; "Ce n'est pas vrai" (it is false) was the Laconic Defense of this Brave Man, and his only Answer to so heinous a Charge. Mr. De Puzy his Aid-de-camp and coaccused appeared at the Bar of the Assembly with that Serenity and Firmness which are the Appendages of a virtuous man conscious of his own Innocence and shocked at the Presence of his Enemies and vile Accusers; But what must have been their Confusion, could Such Monsters blush when he produced all the Letters that passed between the two Generals since the pretended Conversation that gave Rise to the Accusation, in Several of which Luckner denies positively, with that frankness So common to an old Veteran of four Score that Knows more about fighting than of the pitiful Intrigues of political Parties, that he ever did Say or think any thing of his Colleague like the Charge preferred against him, giving him at the Same time the greatest Assurance of his Respect and Esteem. Notwithstanding this Ample Justification of a Charge exhibited on a Hearsay Testimony, the Base Calumniators remained unpunished, and continued their Diabolical Machinations against The M[. . . .]

brave Patriot triumphed of his factious Enemies in a very glorious Manner on the Day that was set apart by the Assembly to determine whether there should be a Decree of Accusation against the Marquis or not; Two Thirds of the Legislature having voted that there was no Ground for Such a Decree, to the great Mortification of the Jacobins; this did happen in the first Week of August. But Some time before in the latter part of July, the Jacobins expected that with the assistance of the *Fœderés* (who were still flocking to Paris, without any Legal Order to that Effect, but by the mere Influence of that violent Party) they would be able to seize upon the Royal family and Such of the Members of the Assembly who were attached to the Constitution: Santerre Commandant of the Paris National Guards and one of them, promised to raise forty Thousand Men; accordingly a Plan of Operations was fixed upon and reduced into Writing by Mr. Barbaroux of Marseilles and now one of the Members of the Convention, and Signed at "*Charenton*" (a Village about Six Miles from Paris) by Such of the Members of the Assembly who were of that party and other Persons of Influence; the 28th. of July was the Day fixed upon to carry this Scheme into Execution; a large Party of *Federés* from Marseilles were to arrive that Day, and it had been agreed that Santerre would contrive to march his Men out as far as Charenton, as if to meet the Marseillois, and welcome them with a Treat; all the Conspirators were to Assemble at the same place, and Santerre men were each of them, that is to say as many as there would have been of the Marseillois, take one of them home with him, in order to carry him at Midnight at the Several Stations and Posts agreed upon in the Vicinity of the King's Palace, to attack it on all Sides all at Once; but to the great Dismay of the Conspirators, Santerre could only parade about Fifteen hundred Men; that Number joined to the Marseillois did not appear sufficient for the Purpose, and therefore they once more postponed the Execution of their Design.[1] The King well knew all the Designs of his Enemies, but could not guard himself against them; for Some time before the 10th. August, the most abominable Songs were Sung Night and Day under the Windows of his Apartments and those of the Queen, and they were insulted upon every occasion. It is very probable that he had thought of retiring to Rouen, as part of the Swiss-guards had been sent there, and Great Numbers of the Nobility and Clergy had taken Shelter in that town, where they were less exposed by the Urbanity and Moderation of the Inhabitants to personal Insults and Dangers than in any other town of France. Nothing was more natural and less criminal even for an Individual who finds himself in the Midst of his Enemies, and Knowing his Life to be in the greatest Danger, to endeavor to Save himself, by escaping to another Place, yet it was reported in Paris that the King had a Design of flying out of that City, and it was looked upon by

---

[1] This Conspiracy was related in my presence by Mr. Barbaroux himself, and Now it is a Matter frequently talked of in the Convention, where the Conspirators who signed the said Articles, will not suffer any Man to plume himself of having contributed to bring about the Counter-revolution of the 10th. August, but such as met at Charenton. As this is now a Matter of Notoriety not only acknowledged but even boasted of by Some of the principal Characters in the Convention, What Opinion can we form of Men that published and circulated thro' all france that they had the most Evident Proofs of the Designs of the King to massacre all the Jacobins and Patriots on the 10th. August, whilst on the Contrary it was themselves who put into Execution a premeditated Plan conceived long before, and often postponed by the Circumstances?

the Mob as a very Great Crime. I believe tho' that if He had been able to get to Rouen, the Counter-revolution would not have happened; the Greatest part of the Army would have remained in his Interest, and all those who were attached to the Constitution would have flocked to him; the Jacobins were well aware of this, and therefore they had him watched in the strictest manner and hurried the Execution of their Plan.

On the 9th. of August a little before Midnight, the Allarm-bells rung all over Paris, and the General war beat in every Street; Three or Four Days before, this Event had been advertised and posted up in Every Street of Paris, recommending to all Good Citizens who wished to maintain the Constitution; to rally themselves near the King and Protect him and Royal family from the premeditated Massacre; What Noblemen and Officers were in Paris had repaired to the King's Palace on the 9th., in order to defend the hereditary Representative of the People; the Bataillon of National Guards on Duty with two field Pieces promised to defend the King's Persons, and Similar Assurances he received from Several Corps of the Same troops; In the Night Some of the Municipal officers at the King's Request came to him, and promised to use their Efforts to preserve Order and prevent Any Violence; During the Night all Paris was under arms, and Mr. Roederer (a Jacobin) one of the Municipal officers having been called upon for Orders by the officers of the Swiss and National Guards, could not help ordering to repell force by force; for which Order he was afterwards impeached. The 10th. Early in the Morning the King himself reviewed his Swiss-Guards, gave them some Money and had Some Extraordinary Drink distributed to them. About Eight oClock Some of the Municipal officers returned to the King, informed him that their Efforts to contain the People in order had been vain, and insisted upon his going with the Royal family into the house of Assembly then Sitting, as the only safe place for them. Arrived in the Middle of the Legislature, Some Members represented that all Paris was in Arms, that Order and Law were intirely out of Question, that the People was so inraged that not only the Life of the King but even the Existence of the Legislature itself were in Danger; that there was no way left to quell the People that Surrounded the Palace to the Number of Thirty or forty Thousands with all the field pieces that were in the City, but Enacting immediately a Decree suspending the King from all his Functions as head of the Executive, till the Meeting of a Convention. The Decree was enacted in a few Minutes in the presence of the King and Royal family, and as a Députation of 12 Members were repairing from the Assembly to the People around the Palace with a Copy of the Decree, the Fœderés of Marseilles who were nearest to the Gates of the Palace-Yard, attempted to force them; the Swiss Guards who were there on Duty repulsed them with a well directed fire; I never heard a better Platoon fire on a field day; upwards of Eleven Hundred of the Assaillants in a few Minutes fell to the Ground; the Swiss finding that the Company of Artillery and the Bataillon of National Guards on Duty did not join them in the Defense of the Palace, Seized upon the two field pieces that were in the Yard loaded with Grape shots, and fired them with great Execution; they pursued their Advantage, Sallied out of the Yard into the Place "*des Carouzels*" crowded with National Guards and Fœderés, took two of their field-pieces, and brought them into the Yard; they acted with so much Spirit and Bravery, that they would have undoubtedly scattered[2] and dispersed the Numerous Bands of their Enemies, if Several thousand Men coming into the Place by all the Avenues (at the general Cry uttered with Design through all the Streets of Paris, "*that the*

Swiss were murdering the People") pressing forward those that were in the Place, drove them along Pall-mall with the Swiss into the Palace Yard, where a Dreadful Slaughter ensued; after expending all their Amunition they retired into the Palace where they were most inhumanely Massacreed; In vain they cried for Quarters, not One of them was Spared, except about 150 who had the Good luck to escape by the tops of Houses to the National Assembly, where they were with great Difficulty protected for several Days from the Fury of the People. The Palace having been ransacked, Every man of the Swiss Nation was hunted after in Paris with the greatest Industry, and as many as they found they put to instant Death; they did the Same with most of the Nobility and Such of the Regular Clergy and Monks who had not taken the Test-Oath. Such of the Nobility, Clergy and People of the King's household who were Spared, were confined in the Several Prisons, which were soon filled up.

The Constitution thus violated, Law and Order having given Way to Anarchy, Confusion and Horror, the King and his family whose lives were sought after by the Misguided Parisians and *Fœderés*, were sent Prisoners under a strong Guard to the Temple, formerly a Palace of his Brother. The Municipality usurped the sovereign Command, and suffered the Assembly to continue their Sittings till the Meeting of the Convention for form-sake only, and in order to enact such Decrees as suited their Views and Interest; Guards were ordered on all the Avenues to Paris; not a Soul was permitted to go out of the City whose Streets were every hour[3] sullied with Some of the most horrid and atrocious Murders; The Jacobins had very industriously circulated a Report throughout the Kingdom (which tho' ever so absurd, gained Credit with the People at large) that the King had formed the Design of murdering all the Patriots; that the Aristocrats, the Nobility and the Clergy were of his Party, that they begun the Execution of this Plan on the 10th. August, but that the Bravery and Spirit of the Parisians and Fœderés in defending themselves defeated the Intents and Purposes of the Court who became the Victims of their own Perfidy and Treachery against the Nation. What contributed much to the implicit faith given to this false Representation of Facts, was the Tyrany of the ruling Party; Any One who would had dared to contradict the Report by relating what he had seen with his own Eyes, who could have been so unmindful of his own personal Safety as to offer even an Argument to show the Improbability or rather the Impossibility of such Designs in the King, would have had immediately his throat cut, Such being the arbitrary Proceedings of those Days, which are not much altered even now; People then of the mildest Dispositions, out of fear, or out of Confidence in the false Recitals of the Events of the 10th., were heard to say that the People did take a terrible Vengeance both of the Evils formerly done to them and of those attempted against them. It was enough to be put to Death on the Spot[4] without Trial or Jury, that any ill looking or Shabily drest fellow who met You in the Streets, said that you were an Aristocrat, or a friend of Genl. La Fayette; the Rights of Individuals and then of Nations[(L)5] were equally violated; the Dwellings of Ambassadors and Envoys of foreign Nations and Princes were no longer

[(L)] Some Gentlemen of the United States of America, who happened then to be in Paris, were taken up on the 10th. August, compelled to be armed, and were dragged along to the Attack of the Palace on the 10th. August, without any Consideration or Respect for their Country. No Redress has been given for Such Violation of the Rights of Nations insulted in the persons of their Citizens.

held sacred, nor their Persons free from Insults, trying to escape from those Scenes of repeated Horrors; Most of them retired to their Respective Courts; Our Worthy Representative "Mr. *Governeur Morris*" stood his Ground, not without running the greatest Danger for his Personal Safety, tho' he had always conducted himself with the greatest Caution and Prudence, but the Jacobins never admitted of any Neutrality, and whoever did not join them and approve of all their Measures, was sure to be devoted to the Fury of their Satellites; tho' it was certainly the Only Conduct that a foreign Minister could with any Degree of Propriety adopt, that of being of no party and not to intermeddle with the Jarring Interests of the Contending Parties. Some few of the Departments at first had Spirit enough to disapprove of the Events of the 10th., and to declare their Resolutions of maintaining the Constitution they had sworn to preserve, but they were compelled by the Numbers who gave their Assent to what had been done[6] to the Measures that were pursued, to acquiesce to them also.

At First, Genl. La Fayette's Army were struck with Amazement and Indignation, but the Emissaries of the Jacobins worked up so effectually the Minds of the Soldiery, that the General finding that he could not with what few men remained staunch to the Constitution, oppose the Torrent of the Counter-revolutionists, he left his mislead Army, and repaired to Germany where he was taken up by the Austrian Troops, detained Prisoner by Order of the Emperor, and sent into Confinement at Wezel where he remains still. What a Folly! What an Absurdity then to suppose that the Brave La Fayette, One of the Champions of Liberty, was a Traitor to his Country, bribed by its Enemies and sold to the Emperor? Would he now be a Prisoner among them, had he been so base a Villain? The Shadow of the Legislature intirely influenced by the all Powerful Jacobins offered a Reward to whoever should bring to them la Fayette, or put him to Death. A more horrid Motion was at that time made in the Assembly and had like to be carried into Effect; that was to raise a Body of Twelve hundred Regicides or King's Murderers, who were to be well paid and equiped; their Services were to introduce themselves in Disguise or otherwise in the Enemy's Camps, and Countries; to[7] Assassinate the Emperor, the King of Prussia, the Duke of Brunswick, the Austrian and Prussian Generals, the Princes of France, and the Marquis De la Fayette; this Motion was seconded and heard with Patience and without Indignation in the Assembly of about Seven hundred Representatives of the People of France, a Nation but a little ago reknowned thro' the World for its humanity and Benevolence.

The Fury of the People being somewhat abated, as Murders became less Frequent, The Monsters who had prompted them to all Kind of Crimes, at the Beginning of September, instigated them with the Design of slaughtering all the Prisoners detained in the Several Jails of Paris to the number of several Thousands, those detained for Debt excepted.[(M)] This diabolical Scheme was put into Execution by not more than Three or Four hundred Men in a [. . .][8]

[(M)] About this time the Duke of Brunswick at the head of an Army of about Eighty thousand Men had entered france, taken the Town of Longwy, and was marching towards the Center of the Kingdom; the Cruel Murderers made the Invasion of the Prussian Army their Pretence for Killing the Prisoners alledging that as it was necessary that most of the National Guards should march from Paris to Stop the Progress of the Enemy, in their Absence the Prisoners might revolt and put to Death their Wives and Children. A very plausible Story indeed to justify the Murder of near Ten Thousand defenceless Victims in cold Blood!

never attempted to prevent this unnecessary and abominable Effusion of human blood, altho' the Massacre lasted pretty near a Week, the Murderers not being numerous enough to go to all the Prisons at Once, but they went on deliberately from One Jail to another, destroying coolly and deliberately all those who had the Misfortune to be therein confined. The Kennels of all Streets in Paris were tinged with Blood, but the most Cruel Sight that shocked my Eyes, was the head of the Princess Lamballe full of Blood, with all the hair on it, carried in Triumph through the Streets of Paris, on the Spear of a Pike, at the general Acclamation of the Populace and Boys shouting, "*Vive la Nation*"![N] Some Days previous to the general Massacre of the Prisoners, this unhappy Princess a near Relation to the King, had been confined in one of the Jails, because it was known that she was very much in the Confidence of the Queen, or rather that she might experience the Same horrible Fate designed for the other Prisoners. The Day before the Slaughter at the Jail where she was, it was well Known by Every body in Paris, that the infernal blood thirsty Executioners were [. . .][9] remove this devoted[10] Princess, nor was even the ordinary Guard reinforced.[O] After cutting off her head in the Street before the Prison's Gate, they mangled her[11] naked Body by cutting her open, taking out her Heart and Intrails, and cutting off her privy parts, which after having washed at a neighbouring Fountain, they carried also exulting On the Point of a Pike through the Streets of Paris.[P]

The Assembly having decreed that Members should be elected in every Department to meet in Convention at Paris by the latter End of September, to pronounce on the fate of the King, the same Tyrany that[12] directed Every Measure of the Municipality of Paris, presided at the Elections of Delegates to the Convention. Matters were carried so far, that all those who were Known or suspected of pitying the King's Confinement and that of the royal family, all those who preserved an Attachment to Genl. La Fayette and to the Constitutions, all those who had signed Petitions to the King subsequent to the 20th. June reprobating the Insults offered to him on that Day, and all those who were suspected of detesting the Horrors and Violences daily committed, were excluded from the [. . .][13] place in Several Departments, yet it was not the Case all over the Kingdom. Can therefore the present Convention be properly called the free Representatives of the French Nation?[14] whilst in Several of the most populous Cities, the principal Characters, the Land holders, monied men, Merchants and Gentlemen were excluded from Voting and from being elected. About that time Attempts were made in Paris to promote what they improperly called an "*Agrarian Law*," but which in fact was nothing else but to divide equally all the Properties and Riches of France between the Jacobins and their Adherents.[Q]

[N] That is to Say Huzza for the Nation, or Long live the Nation!

[O] She was a Person of the greatest Affability; Kind, generous and compassionate; and spent great part of her Revenue in Deeds of Charity. The Unhappy and the Persecuted were always sure to find Protection and Relief from her benevolent Hand.

[P] All the Prisoners of Paris having been thus massacred, the Same Murderers, repaired to Orleans; where the State Prisoners against whom there had been Decrees of Accusation were confined, among whom were Several Ministers of State and Some of the first Nobility of the Kingdom; they carried them to Versailles, where they were all put to Death in the same Cruel Manner as those of Paris.

[Q] Immediately after the 10th. August, they erected a New Tribunal to judge in a Summary manner all suspected Persons; this new Set of Judges of the Jacobins Tribe,

Before I entertain you with the Proceedings of the Convention it will not be amiss to relate to you the Warlike Operations of Austria and Prussia. Those two Powers had agreed together that the Duke of Brunswick at the head of the Prussian Army should endeavor to penetrate to Paris to deliver the King, and facilitate thereby the assembling of the french Royalists, without losing any time by besieging Places or fighting pitched Battles; that the Austrian Army should follow the Duke at three or four Days March Distance, in order to [. . .] the [french] [. . .] in [. . .] to facilitate the Supplies of the Prussians, and protect their Retreat in case of Necessity.(R) The Prussian Army after taking Longwy and Verdun which made no Resistance, advanced into the Province of Champaign, the Duke of Brunswick having got between Genl. Kellermann's and Dumourier's Armies. Paris was open to him, at about only one hundred Miles Distance, without a Single fortified Town on his Way, or any Troops to oppose him, but a few unarmed Bataillons of newly levied National Guards unarmed; but the Austrians had not followed the Duke as it had been agreed, which rendered his Situation exceedingly critical; his Army had already suffered very much by Sickness, Scarcity of Provisions, and Want of almost Every Necessary; his Cavalry was almost intirely ruined; in that Situation, had he pursued his March to Paris, abandonned by the Austrians, in case of a Repulse, His whole Army must have been sacrificed, being so far ingaged in His Enemy's Country, destitute of Supplies, and two formidable Armies on his Rear, besides Numberless fortified Towns. The King of Prussia was himself with his Army; and probably directed the Operations; he was moved with Resentment at the Conduct of the Austrians; Flags begun to pass and repass between the french and Prussian Armies, the Consequences of which were, as it is generally thought now, an Agreement entered into by the french and Prussians that the Prussians should immediately evacuate all the french territory, and that the french [. . .]¹⁵ Retreat; that is the more probable as they were suffered to retire into Germany without any Attempts being made upon them by the French, the first day excepted (which was the Effect of a Misunderstanding) and that they evacuated Verdun, longwy, all Lorain

---

condemned to Death Mr. La Porte, the King's Intendant for having obeyed the King's Orders, which he was bound to do; Mr. Du Rosoy a Man of Letters, who had redacted a Newspaper previous to the 10th. August under the Title of the *"Gazette de Paris,"* which was distributed and read all over Paris, france and Europe, was also condemned on account of his Same Gazette, for his Opinions of Attachment to the Constitution, and Dislike of the Jacobins and their proceedings. Those two unhappy Gentlemen were immediately executed with several others; it was enough to be brought before that Tribunal to be condemned to Death; the Massacre at the Prisons put an End for that time to their bloody Operations.

(R) On the first Approach of the Enemies to the Frontiers of France, Genl. La Fayette had ordered Genl. Dumourier, who commanded a detached Body of his Army at the Camp of Maulde, to evacuate that Camp, and to join him with all his forces; Dumourier devoted to the Jacobins and who had flattered himself before he left Paris to join the Army that he would ruin the Marquis, refused to comply with this Order and wrote to the National Assembly to justify his Disobedience, representing the Marquis's Order as impolitical, and tending to favor the Entry of the Enemies into France. He was not punished for his Disobedience, tho' the Moment he succeeded Genl. Lafayette in his command, he Ordered himself the Evacuation of the Camp of Maulde. This will give an Idea of the Principles of this now Commander in Chief of the french Armies.

and Alsatia, where it is very evident they might have with Safety taken up Winter Quarters; Besides the King of Prussia, after his Retreat from France, having taken Possession with his Troops of the strong City of Luxemburg, notified the Emperor that he would Keep in his hands that town, untill he should be indemnified of his Expences and Losses marching at his Sollicitations into France. Whatever may have been the true Cause of the Prussians sudden Retreat, Dumourier[(S)] had the whole honor and Merit of driving the Prussians out of France.

The Convention a few days after making an House, took upon themselves, without consulting their Constituents to pass a Decree abolishing at once "*Royalty*" in France, which they declared to be a Republic; Afterwards they Resolved that another new Constitution or Form of Government, should be prepared and redacted by their Body, which should be offered to the People at Large for their Approbation or Refusal; A Committee of Nine Members of the Convention was appointed to that Effect, and Thomas Paine, the Author of "*Common-Sense*," who wrote so much in favor [. . .][16] astonishing that the Convention should have declared absolutely the Extinction of the Constitution of 1791, without referring their Opinion to the People at Large for their Assent, and at the same time enact that a New plan or form of Government should be submitted to them for their Approbation, as if it required a different or a greater Power to Create than to abolish? But Contradictions have marked every Step of the French Revolution, and it seems to be One of the Characteristics of that Nation.

Two Parties seem now to be formed among the Republican Members of the present Convention; the One desirous of reestablishing Order and Law, putting an End to all further arbitrary Proceedings, and wishing in order to provide for the legal Protection of Persons and Properties to bring to condign Punishments the Authors and Promoters of all the atrocious and unnecessary Murders perpetrated for some time Past to the great Contempt of Law and good Government; the other Party conscious of their own Guilt, by the Share they have had in those horrible Deeds, endeavor to throw Difficulties in the Way of the others, and pursue with great Earnestness the Plan of bringing the King and Queen to Trial, seeking after their Blood, whilst the other party wish to Save their Lives. Indeed there's very little Harmony in the Convention, and the Dissentions there prevailing, may possibly occasion some very great Trouble in Paris. The Constitution Committee have not yet made any Report, intending to present to the Convention an intire Plan of a form of Government to be accepted or rejected in toto.

Having given you an impartial Account of this Year's transactions in Paris, permit me to remark to You, that the Noble and Glorious Cause of[17] Liberty, for which You and I have so often fought and bled in America, is almost

---

[(S)] This Mr. Dumourier is the Same Man who being Minister and Secretary of State, wormed himself into the King's Confidence and induced him to turn out of the Ministry the Patriot and popular Ministers, Roland, Claviere and Servan; this Change of Ministry was made use of by the Jacobins to discredit more and more the King with the People, and as soon as Dumourier had made the King commit that "*faux-pas*," he resigned himself his place as Secretary of State, leaving the King without hardly a Single Minister, after having plunged him in the greatest Embarrassment—this is the Man who has been preferr'd to the brave General La Fayette, who supplanted him in his Command, and who now enjoys all the Confidence of the French Nation.

dishonored in France by the Horrors and Cruelties committed by designing and ferocious Men, who make use of the Word only, as a Pretence to violate in the most flagrant Manner all the most precious and unalienable Rights of Men.[18] Under a free Government like ours, the Liberties of Individuals cannot nor ought not to be infringed; the Citizen is to find Security for his Person and Property under the protection[19] of the Law which abhors all tyranical Proceedings. In my Next I will inform you of the Progress of the Convention. Yours

MS (DLC: Rare Book and Special Collections); entirely in Mountflorence's hand, unsigned; see below for discussion of date; consists of 27 numbered pages of narrative and footnotes written on both sides of 14 folio sheets bound and folded, with some trimming, into a volume in TJ's library; torn at several folds, resulting in detached and frayed pieces and the loss of several lines of text; sequential lettering of author's footnotes broken (see note 5 below).

Though written in the guise of one in a series of personal letters from Paris to a private citizen in Virginia, James Cole Mountflorence's narrative of some of the most dramatic episodes of the French Revolution was evidently produced in response to a personal request from TJ for intelligence about the rapidly changing political situation in France. Obviously intended for publication, it was in fact the only such document Mountflorence wrote for TJ.

A North Carolina militia officer during the Revolutionary War, Mountflorence was a lawyer, land speculator, and businessman associated with a North Carolina mercantile firm run by John Gray Blount and Thomas Blount in association with their brother, William Blount, the governor of the Southwest Territory. Mountflorence first came to TJ's attention in the summer of 1791 when he was deputed by Governor Blount to provide TJ with information about the boundaries of the Southwest Territory for the Secretary of State's Report on Public Lands of 8 Nov. 1791. Later that year, as he was preparing to undertake a business trip to France in order to sell some of his own western lands as well as to act as an agent for the Blount firm, Mountflorence pre-

vailed upon TJ to write a letter of recommendation for him to William Short, then serving as American chargé d'affaires in Paris. At the same time, according to a pamphlet written by Mountflorence more than a decade later to refute certain "unfavorable reflections" on his political principles and conduct and to support a claim for compensation from the United States, TJ also asked him "to procure the best information possible respecting the political events which then succeeded each other so rapidly in France" (James Cole Mountflorence, *A Short Sketch of the Public Life of Major J. C. Mountflorence* [Paris, 1804], 3-7; enclosed with Mountflorence to James Monroe, Paris, 8 July 1817, DNA: RG 59, MLR; see also Alice Barnwell Keith, ed., "Letters from Major James Cole Mountflorence to Members of the Blount Family (William, John Gray, and Thomas) from on Shipboard, Spain, France, Switzerland, England, and America, January 22, 1792-July 21, 1796," *North Carolina Historical Review*, XIV [1937], 251-4; and TJ to Short, 16 Nov. 1791).

Arriving in Paris near the end of May 1792, Mountflorence remained in France for six tumultuous months. In the midst of his generally unsuccessful efforts in Paris to dispose of his western lands and obtain government contracts for the Blount firm, he witnessed the overthrow of the French monarchy, the September Massacres, and the proclamation of the French Republic, while becoming acquainted with some of the leading figures in the National Convention in order to obtain for TJ "the most accurate information possible, of the views, designs, spirit, and means of the several parties which engrossed and distracted the public attention" (*Short Sketch*, 7). But Mountflorence regretted the failure of the French experiment in constitutional monarchy and abhorred the accompanying radicalization of the Revolution, complaining in 1795 that "the Inroads of the Vandals, Goths, Visigoths & of the Northern Tribes have never caused such a general destruction" as that wrought in Europe by the French Republic ("Letters from Mountflorence," 284; see also same, 264-9; and "Anas" entry, 18 July 1793). Mountflorence's hostility to the phases of the French Revolution he personally witnessed suffuses his narrative, which, notwithstanding its place and date, his later testimony indicates was actually written aboard the *Amiable Antoinette* between the time of his departure from France on 20 Nov. 1792 and his arrival at Norfolk on 21 Jan. 1793 (*Short Sketch*, 7-8).

Although Mountflorence initially planned to have the narrative printed in Norfolk and sent to TJ in published form, he soon sent the original manuscript instead, possibly because he was unable to find a printer for an account so critical of the French Revolution. In any event, no evidence of its publication in pamphlet or newspaper form has been found. TJ did not share Mountflorence's perspective on the events described above, and he neither acknowledged receipt of the narrative nor made any official use of it. Nevertheless, TJ apparently did value it as a vivid account of a pivotal turning point in French history, for he carefully preserved it and had it bound (as "Mountflorence's lre relative to La Fayette. M.S.") with a collection of sixteen French pamphlets published between 1787 and 1792 that

he later included in the sale of his personal library to the Library of Congress in 1815 (*Short Sketch*, 8; Mountflorence to TJ, 22 Jan., 1 Feb. 1793; Sowerby, No. 2563).

[1] MS torn; one line illegible.
[2] Mountflorence here canceled "the whole."
[3] Preceding word written over "day," interlined.
[4] Preceding three words interlined.
[5] Author's note so designated by Mountflorence, thus omitting "J" and "K."
[6] Mountflorence here canceled "and was a doing."
[7] Mountflorence here canceled "Kill the."
[8] MS torn; one line illegible.
[9] MS torn; one line illegible.
[10] Before this word Mountflorence canceled "hap."
[11] Mountflorence here canceled "body."
[12] Mountflorence here canceled "dictated."
[13] MS torn; one line illegible.
[14] Mountflorence here canceled "I will leave this Point to others to determine."
[15] MS torn; approximately six words illegible.
[16] MS torn; one line illegible.
[17] Mountflorence here canceled "Universal."
[18] Mountflorence here canceled an incomplete continuation of this sentence: "which they do not understand, or rather which."
[19] Word interlined in place of "Despotism."

To George Washington

Feb. 1. 1793.

Th: Jefferson has the honor to send to the President the speech of De Coin, written at length from his notes, very exactly. He thinks he can assure the President that not a sentiment delivered by the French interpreter is omitted, nor a single one inserted which was not expressed. It differs often from what the English Interpreter delivered, because he varied much from the other who alone was regarded by Th:J.

RC (DNA: RG 59, MLR); addressed: "The President of the U.S."; endorsed by Tobias Lear. PrC (DLC); partially faded and overwritten in a later hand. Not recorded in SJL.

Jean Baptiste Ducoigne, a Kaskaskia chief, was a member of the delegation of Illinois and Wabash Indians currently conferring with Washington about the peace treaty General Rufus Putnam had negotiated with their tribes the previous September. TJ undoubtedly sent the President the SPEECH of Ducoigne as set down in the first six manuscript pages of his minutes of the first day of the conference with this delegation (Minutes of a Conference with the Illinois and Wabash Indians, printed under 1 Feb. 1793, and note). The NOTES TJ took at the conference have not been found.

To Samuel Clarkson

SIR   Philadelphia. Feb. 2. 1793

It has been by my direction that my servant has offered the horse for sale, which is the subject of your letter. He had told me yesterday that he had found a purchaser, but I did not enquire who it was. At present, presuming, if the purchase is either for yourself or a friend, you may be glad of information respecting the horse which may be relied on, I take the liberty of mentioning that I purchased him in Oct. 1790. for 5. years old the preceding spring, and I gave $116\frac{2}{3}$ Doll. for him in Virginia. He is high blooded, a most excellent creature and I believe perfectly sound. [Goes well?] in a carriage, for which purpose I bought him, and I now sell him for no reason but that the horses I have since purchased for my set, render it necessary to get a larger in his stead. My price is as mentioned in your letter £45. Pensylva. currency, for which, payment to the bearer will be a discharge. I am with esteem Sir Your very humble servt   TH: JEFFERSON

PrC (DLC); partly faded; at foot of text: "Mr. Samuel Clarkson." Tr (ViU: Edgehill-Randolph Papers); 19th-century copy; varies slightly in wording.

Samuel Clarkson, a Philadelphia merchant, resided at 42 Union Street (James Hardie, *The Philadelphia Directory and Register* [Philadelphia, 1793], 24). His LETTER to TJ of 2 Feb. 1793, recorded in SJL as received that day, has not been found. Another letter from Clarkson of 2 Feb. 1793, recorded in SJL as received 3 Feb. 1793 but also not found, probably enclosed his payment of $120 for Brimmer, the horse in question (MB, 3 Feb. 1793; Betts, *Farm Book*, 97; TJ to Thomas Mann Randolph, Jr., 18 Feb. 1793).

To C. W. F. Dumas

DR. SIR   Philadelphia Feb. 2. 1793.

Taking for granted that before the arrival of the vessel by which this goes, Mr. Short will have left the Hague on a temporary mission to Madrid, I have taken the liberty of addressing to you a packet of plans of the city of Washington on the Potomak, with a desire that they may be exhibited (not for sale) but in such shops, houses, or other places, where they may be most seen by those descriptions of people who would be the most likely to be attracted to it, and who would be worth attracting. The sea-port towns are the most likely to possess persons of this description. With every wish for your health and happiness, I am with great esteem, Dear Sir your most obedt. humble servt   TH: JEFFERSON

RC (Terry B. O'Rourke, La Jolla, California, 1989); at foot of text: "Mr. Dumas." PrC (DLC). Tr (DLC); 19th-century copy. Enclosure: *Plan of the City of Washington in the Territory of Columbia,* ceded by the States of Virginia and Maryland to the United States of America, and by them established as the Seat of their Government, after the Year MDCCC (Philadelphia, 1792).

To George Washington Greene

DEAR SIR   Philadelphia Feb. 2. 1793.

Mr. Peale the bearer of this letter proposing to go to Georgia to collect curiosities in Natural history, for his father's Museum, now become considerable and worthy of encouragement, I take the liberty of recommending himself and his object to you. If I did not mistake symptoms in an early part of your life, your dispositions and your attention to these subjects will be in his favor.

Permit me to take this opportunity of congratulating you on your return to America, and to hope that neither the time you have been abroad, nor the scenes which have past under your eye will have lessened your attachment to your own country nor to those principles on which it's present government is founded. It is no small consolation to see those just entering on a stage from which we are about to withdraw, bring into public life dispositions for improving and completing that system of public happiness to which their predecessors have devoted their lives. I am with very sincere wishes for your success and happiness, my dear Sir, Your friend & servt   TH: JEFFERSON

PrC (DLC); torn at foot of text: "Mr. Geo[rge W. Gr]eene." Tr (DLC); 19th-century copy.

George Washington Greene (ca. 1776-93) was the first child of the deceased Revolutionary War general Nathanael Greene and the godson of President Washington. Although Washington had expressed an interest in educating Greene, his parents accepted instead a similar offer from the Marquis de Lafayette. Greene journeyed to France in 1789 and returned to Georgia early in 1793, where shortly afterwards he drowned in the Savannah River (Richard K. Showman and others, eds., *The Papers of General Nathanael Greene,* 5 vols. [Chapel Hill, 1976-], I, 188n; Francis Vinton Greene, *General Greene* [New York, 1893], 302; John F. Stege-

[135]

man and Janet A. Stegeman, *Caty: A Biography of Catharine Littlefield Greene* [Athens, Ga., 1985], 161-2). Raphaelle Peale, the BEARER OF THIS LETTER and the eldest son of Charles Willson Peale, did not return from his trip to Georgia to collect specimens for his father's natural history museum in Philadelphia until the fall of 1793 (Charles Coleman Sellers, *Charles Willson Peale*, 2 vols. [Philadelphia, 1947], II, 42, 53-4).

From Tobias Lear

Saturday 2d feby 1793

T. Lear has the honor to inform the Secretary of State that as it is a cloudy day the Indians decline doing business. Their meeting is therefore put off till monday 12 O'clock.

RC (DLC); endorsed by TJ as received 2 Feb. 1793.

The BUSINESS that brought a delegation of Wabash and Illinois Indians to Philadelphia is described in Minutes of a Conference with the Illinois and Wabash Indians, printed under 1 Feb. 1793, and note.

To George Washington

Feb. 2. 93.

Th: Jefferson has the honor to inclose for the President's notice a small pamphlet sent to Th:J. by the author, containing some ideas which may merit attention, in due time, at the Federal city.

RC (DNA: RG 59, MLR); addressed: "The President of the U.S."; endorsed erroneously by Tobias Lear as a letter of 2 Mch. 1793, but corrected in another hand. Tr (Lb in same, SDC). Not recorded in SJL. Enclosure: [Tench Coxe], *A Plan for encouraging Agriculture, and increasing the value of farms in the Midland and more Western Counties of Pennsylvania, applicable to several other Parts of that State, and to many Parts of the United States* [Philadelphia, 1793], which detailed a scheme for construction of a town on the Susquehanna River and suggested that such an enterprise or similar ones on other bodies of water would increase commerce so greatly as to yield a substantial profit quickly (Sowerby, No. 3631; see also TJ to Coxe, 8 Feb. 1793).

The President sent Coxe's pamphlet to the Commissioners of the Federal District with a letter of 3 Mch. 1793 (Fitzpatrick, *Writings*, XXXII, 373).

From C. W. F. Dumas

The Hague, 3 Feb. 1793. Since his last of 29 Jan. each day becomes more critical for France on one side and the dominant parties here and in London on the other. He is unable to give an account of some propositions with which Maulde, the former French minister plenipotentiary who had been recalled to Paris, is said to have returned here, and to which it is said the Grand Pensionary has unofficially given evasive responses, because he has been unable to see Maulde, who is incognito here and suspected by both parties, and because there is a secretary of the French legation, accredited but not admitted by the government, who seems unaware of Maulde's business and whom he has just begun to see. This secretary has been ordered to join Dumouriez's army as soon as it enters the Republic. *4 Feb.* This morning the Grand Pensionary informed the commercial agent of Amsterdam and Rotterdam here that France has declared war on the British government. The threat is being circulated here that patriots will be slaughtered as soon as the French set foot in the Republic; also being considered is a plan to tax foreign funds on a fourth of the interest they bring in, which would reduce the appeal of the Dutch funds and climax the misfortunes of this country. *5 Feb.* News arrived this morning that on 1 Feb. the National Convention unanimously declared war against the king of England and the Stadtholder of the United Netherlands.

RC (DNA: RG 59, MLR); 2 p.; in French; at head of text: "No. 94. A Son Excl. Mr. _____ le Secrétaire d'Etat & des Affes. Etr. en Congrès Génl. des Et. Unis d'Amériqe."; endorsed by TJ as received 14 May 1793 and so recorded in SJL. Dupl (same, MDC); at head of text: "Dupl."; endorsed by TJ as received 17 May 1793 and so recorded in SJL.

To Thomas Mann Randolph, Jr.

DEAR SIR   Philadelphia Feb. 3. 1793.

In my letter to my daughter, of the last week, I suggested to her that a possibility had arisen that I might not return home as early as I had determined. It happened unfortunately that the attack made on me in the newspapers came out soon after I began to speak freely and publicly of my purpose to retire this spring, and, from the modes of publication, the public were possessed of the former sooner than of the latter: and I find that as well those who are my friends, as those who are not, putting the two things together as cause and effect, conceived I was driven from my office either from want of firmness or perhaps fear of investigation. Desirous that my retirement may be clouded with no imputations of this kind, I see not only a possibility, but rather a probability that I shall postpone it for some time. Whether for weeks or months I cannot now say. This must depend in some degree on the will of those who troubled the waters before. When they suffer them to get calm, I will go into port.—My inclinations never before suffered such violence; and my interests also are materially affected. I had digested a plan of operation too complicated to be pursued by any one less interested in it than my self: and there seems no way to save myself from great loss and disappointment but to change the order of the objects, and to take up first that one which is the most simple and the most important, I mean, my canal. And here, my dear Sir, I am under the necessity of giving you a trouble for which that necessity alone must be my apology: that is, to undertake to direct the manner of carrying it on. George, aided by Clarkson, will be sufficient to see that the work is done, and to take all details off of your hands. But they will need to be instructed in what manner to conduct it. I think the mouth of the canal is already indicated by what has been done. The bottom of it should be a foot lower than the common surface of the river in winter, and it may be carried on at a dead level, as it will then be easy for me when I come home to dress off the bottom to the fall which may be necessary. I propose that it shall be 6. feet wide at bottom, and to slope at the sides so as to permit grass to grow on them. It was my intention that the Carpenters should join in this work, so that the whole force will consist of the following. George, Davy, John, Abram, Phill, Lewis, Johnny, Jupiter, King, Goliah, Mingo, Fanny, and Moses. The invalids to work only when they shall be able. They will probably be equal to the hauling away the earth and forming it into a bank on the side next the river. I consider George rather as their foreman, and should not require him to lay his hand to the hardest work. The time for the carpenters joining them will depend on the rise of the sap, as they should cease then to get stocks for the house, and having sawed up what they shall have gotten, will then only join the canal people. You will be so good as to judge whether one or more strikers and blowers will be necessary, and indeed to govern the whole matter according as you shall think circumstances render best. The bringing home stocks, common stone and limestone too will influence the commencement of this work, at least it's commencement in full force. I am in hopes that the canal may be so far got over in time to make that part of the addition to my house in the fall which I had meditated to have made in the present spring. Therefore it is that I wish the timber, stone, and limestone to be prepared before the season is open enough for the Canal. I am not without hopes that I may find a tenant here for my mill. Mr. Brown at Richmond will furnish the gunpowder and iron necessary. I think the Rafter level, accurately adjusted is the safest to use in levelling the bottom. Were there to be times when water or other circumstances should hinder the working *in* the canal there is a great deal of earth which has been very unwisely thrown on the upper bank, and which they will be well employed at *such times* in throwing over on the lower bank, in order to fence out the river in flood-times.—Committing all this to your kind direction, I must conclude with assurances to my dear Martha and yourself of the sincere affections of Dear Sir your's sincerely   Th: Jefferson

RC (DLC); addressed: "Thomas M. Randolph junr. Monticello." PrC (MHi). Tr (DLC); 19th-century copy.

From William Short

Dear sir   Madrid Feb. 3. 1793

My letter from the Hague of the 18th. of Dec. will have informed you of my intention to set out from that place the next day and proceed to this by the way of France. This I have accordingly done, and have now the honor to inform you of my arrival here the day before yesterday, after completing my journey of 400 leagues. I was singularly and unexpectedly fortunate in meeting with no impediment in my route through France except what arose from the present state of the roads. These occasioned a very considerable delay, having become from a total neglect of four years almost impracticable for carriages of any kind, and rendering unavoidable frequent stoppages for repairs to those which get through. From Bayonne to this place there being no regular post I came with the same horses the whole way, and was therefore twelve days on the road, owing in some measure also to the advanced season and several of the mountains which I had to pass being covered with snow, so as to render the assistance of oxen necessary to draw my carriage over them.

The court having lately gone to Aranjuez, Mr. Carmichael wrote yesterday to the Duke de la Alcudia, the present minister of foreign affairs, who is there also, to inform him of my arrival and to know when we can wait on him: we are expecting his answer and shall immediately on recieving it, repair to that residence.

I have delivered to M. Carmichael the two packets you addressed to him containing the journals of Congress and gazettes—and also the several papers I had received at the Hague addressed to us jointly containing the instructions relative to our business here.[1]

In your letter of January 5th. 1792. you say "see the three lines of the second page[2] of that letter beginning *some* and ending *letter*"[3]— since then I have not had the honor of receiving any letter from you on that subject addressed to me except that of January 23d. 1792 simply saying "—see the last page—the sentence beginning *The* and ending *orders*"—as these are the only circumstances you have ever mentioned respecting this business in your letters to me and as you said nothing in those addressed to us jointly which I received *of*[4] *the Causes which induced the President to form the Commission for treating at this place* I remained absolutely ignorant of them. I took it for granted however that *this Court had given assurances of their desire that persons should be sent to treat here* [and][5] imagined you had omitted mentioning it *as being known to Mr. Carmichael from whom I might learn it.* I find however on speaking with him that he has no knowledge of it. He takes it for granted *that the Spanish Agents in America must have been instructed to give such assurances* although you have not thought it worth while *to mention it to us* and yet it seems to me by no means indifferent *for us to know with precision and particularly in the present situation of affairs on what our mission was grounded. Mr. Carmichael knows of no other ground than a letter of Count Florida to him, sent to you, saying the King had resolved to send* [*to America*][6] *a person authorised to treat and verbal assurances from the same Minister of the good dispositions of this Court—he was told by Ct*[7] *Aranda during his short administration*, in speaking on this subject, *that the assurances given by one Minister were not an obligation on his successor. I cannot yet know in what light the present Minister* who is a remove further from the *Count Florida will consider the assurances he gave.* I am fully persuaded however he will give *no weight to them further than as they correspond with his own sentiments, being his personal enemy and desirous to find out all means of staining and counteracting his administration.* Besides this *Change of Administration (since the assurances given to Mr. Carmichael which can't but be unfavorable to our business at present as far as depends on negotiation)*[8] *I can't dissemble to you my fear also that there will be a Change of Circumstances which will be still more unfavorable. The news of the assassination*[9] *of Louis the sixteenth arrived here three days ago; This seems to render war certain between France and this Country—between France and England war is still more certain—of course these two Countries will unite in their exertions against the Common Enemy. An union between two Countries, situated, governed and disposed of like these two is nothing less than Spain putting itself in the dependence of England.* They will pay this dear in the end and repent of it, but in the mean time they will probably consider themselves *fortified with respect to us, they will be forced in many instances to obey English influence* in doing what they do not chuse. They will be happy in listening to it therefore in those cases when it shall dictate *what they do chuse. We can't doubt of the real sentiments of Spain as to the Missisippi and their territorial claim[s]*[10] nor can we suppose that the *English Minister is so* changed as to become a *Missionary of peace* and desire to see *these subjects of Contention removed from between Spain and us.* As it is not in the power of the *United States to prevent Spain and England having a Common Enemy nor to prevent their being more or less united,* it becomes our business it seems to me to await the developement of this union and not increase it by increasing alarm here. *My opinion will be for holding on every occasion that language* which I conceive will be conformable to the sentiments of the *President, namely of our real desire of living on terms of close friendship with Spain. It would not be difficult to prove to a Minister of Information that Spain since the loss of France will have in future, more than ever, need of our friendship, that she*[11] *may hope finally to oppose a Balance to the English Marine and prevent the advantages of transmarine possessions and the remains of her commerce being swallowed up by that power. These however are considerations for the time to come—and most Ministers are for the time present. He who governs every thing* [*at present*][12] *here being young and without experience will be less apt to be suspicious of English professions and promises, and as young men believe readily what they desire, he will believe perhaps that the English affection will be real and will be a protection for this Country.* Mr. Carmichael tells me he has good reason to believe that vague propositions have already passed *between the two Countries, which ultimately regard us* but in what manner *they regard us* he does not know. *These circumstances will sufficiently suggest to us the propriety of aiming at peace at present, but of being prepared for events.*

The system of the English in case of War with France will be to cut off all foreign supplies from them, and particularly of provision and this will be the most distressing mode of warfare they can exercise against a[13] Country under their present wants. [*They*][14] *will probably sieze neutral vessels going into their*[15] *ports—what they will do with them is for time to determine. I think they would prefer having us for enemy*[16] *to allowing us to carry them supplies of provision, if they can prevent it no other way.*[17] I have the honor to be with the most perfect respect & sincere attachment Dr. Sir &c &c   W: SHORT

PrC (DLC: Short Papers); entirely *en clair*; consists of first page only, bearing dateline, salutation, and first three paragraphs, pasted onto a longer sheet containing part of subjoined FC, remainder of letter being supplied from Tr (see note 1 below); at head of text: "*1.* No. 123." Tr (Lb in DNA: RG 59, DD); partially encoded copy, with interlinear decipherment, made from missing RC; several words and part of last paragraph supplied from FC; paragraphing varies from PrC and FC; at head of text: "No. 123 To the Secy. of State"; text beginning with first deciphered word repeated, with minor variations, *en clair* at foot of text. FC (DLC: Short Papers); written *en clair* in Short's hand in 1795; consists of all but the first three paragraphs subjoined to PrC and continued on two additional pages; note by Short in margin at foot of first page: "This part of the letter was written on a *brouillon* from which it was reduced to a partial cypher, being forwarded by post. It is now transcribed here from that *brouillon*.—Note on transcribing this part of the letter at Madrid Jan. 22. 95. The original was addressed thus Thomas Jefferson, Secretary of State Philadelphia"; at foot of text on third page is a note by Short relating to a subjoined copy, continued on a fourth page, of a letter in Short's hand from William Carmichael and Short to the Duke de la Alcudia of 17 Feb. 1793 headed "2" (for a discussion of this letter, see Carmichael and Short to TJ, 19 Feb. 1793). Recorded in SJL as received 8 May 1793.

TJ's INSTRUCTIONS to Short and William Carmichael regarding their mission to Spain are embodied in his 18 Mch. 1792 Report on Negotiations with Spain. Short's forebodings about the diplomatic consequences of a UNION between Spain and Great Britain proved to be well founded. The conclusion of an alliance between these two countries in May 1793, making them partners in the first coalition against France, strengthened Spain's determination to make no concessions to the United States on the various issues Short and Carmichael had been authorized to resolve (Bemis, *Pinckney's Treaty*, 168-70). Manuel Godoy, Duque de la Alcudia, the young Spanish first secretary and the favorite and suspected paramour of Queen María Luisa, was the person WHO GOVERNS EVERY THING AT PRESENT HERE (Richard Herr, *The Eighteenth-Century Revolution in Spain* [Princeton, 1958], 316-18).

TJ submitted this letter to the President on 11 May 1793, and Washington returned it two days later (Washington, *Journal*, 136).

[1] PrC ends here; remainder supplied from Tr.

[2] FC: "see the three last lines."

[3] This and the next quotation are bracketed in FC.

[4] This and subsequent words in italics are written in code and have been supplied from the interlined decipherment, which has been verified by the Editors using partially reconstructed Code No. 10 and collated with the conjoined PrC and FC, the most significant variations and discrepancies being recorded below.

[5] Word supplied from FC.

[6] Preceding two words, encoded but not deciphered interlinearly, supplied from FC.

[7] Word deciphered thus, but encoded as "Count."

[8] Parentheses not in FC.

[9] Word omitted in FC.

[10] Word encoded as "claims," but deciphered as "claim." FC: "claims."

[11] FC: "that it is by us that she."

[12] Preceding two words, encoded but not deciphered interlinearly, supplied from FC.

[13] Word interlined in place of "that." FC: "that."

[14] Sentence to this point supplied from FC. Corresponding section of Tr is mistakenly encoded as "Ther will probably siise neutral ve need," decoded interlinearly as "These will probably si fight ise ve need," and repeated at foot of text as "These will probably si sight ise neutral ve need."

[15] FC: "those."

[16] FC: "enemies."

[17] A variant text of this paragraph is quoted in Short to TJ, 16 Oct. 1793.

From George Washington

Sunday Morng. 3d. Februy. [1793]

The enclosed,[1] containing some things which are not in Gouvr. Morris official letter, the President sends it for Mr. Jeffersons perusal.

RC (DLC); partially dated; addressed: "Mr. Jefferson"; with notation by TJ (see note 1 below); endorsed by TJ as received [3] Feb. 1793. Recorded in SJPL. Enclosure: Gouverneur Morris to Washington, 23 Oct. 1793, which, in addition to the subjects dealt with in his official letter of the same date to TJ, also discussed the French government's suppression of Louis XVI's correspondence with the Marquis de Lafayette and Morris's negative reply to William Short's proposal about an American diplomatic effort to secure Lafayette's release from Austrian captivity (RC in DLC: Washington Papers; erroneously endorsed by Tobias Lear as received 12 Feb. 1793).

[1] TJ attached an asterisk to the beginning of this word to serve as a key to the note he added at the foot of text: "of Oct. 23. 92."

To Alexander Hamilton

SIR   Philadelphia, February, 4th. 1793.

The details respecting the Sum of 66,000^{tt}, which are the subject of Mr. Short's letter of Nov. 2d. 1792, and of yours of the 1st. instant, and which he observes still remain in the hands of Mr. Grand, are as follow.

On the 14th. of February 1785, Congress appropriated a sum of 80,000 Dollars, for the purpose of effecting Treaties with the Barbary States. The missions of Mr. Barclay to Morocco, and of Mr. Lamb, to Algiers, were made on this fund. On the 18th. of July, and 12th. of October 1787, they gave orders to their Minister Plenipotentiary at Versailles to take measures, through the agency of a particular religious order, for ransoming their citizens in captivity at Algiers, and constituted the Balance of the appropriation of February 14. 1785, as a fund for this purpose. On the 21st. of February 1789, the Commissioners of the Treasury, drew an Order on their Bankers in Holland in favor of the minister Plenipotentiary of the United States, at Versailles for 30,000 florins, supposed to be the Balance aforesaid, which order came to my hands, on the 5th. of April. I left Paris in September following, at which time a part of the Bills for this sum, had been remitted to me, but were not yet due. These I delivered to Mr. Short, to whom bills for the residue were also sent by the Bankers: and the Religious order, which I had engaged to commence the negotiation were notified that the business had devolved on Mr. Short. Letters received in 1790, left little to hope from their agency.   The State of this business was reported by me to Congress December 28. 1790, and I submitted the expediency of adopting some more promising measures, without relinquishing the chance of success by the former: of which, however, having little hope, you will recollect that I proposed to you the application of this money to the payment of our foreign Officers at Paris, rather than let it lie idle there, and, more especially, as we might then presume on commanding that sum at any time, should the negotiations at Algiers, call for it, contrary to expectations. You observed to me that you did not think yourself authorized to change the appropriation of this money, without an Act of Congress, but that you were then preparing a Report for Congress, which would necessarily comprehend this object.   I accordingly wrote to Mr. Short, on the 23rd. of January 1791, in these words 'We must still pursue the redemption of our captives, through the same channel, till some better means can be devised. The money, however, which is in Mr. Grand's hands, will be the subject of a letter to you from the Secretary of the Treasury, as soon as he can have an act of Congress, authorizing the application of it, to the debt of the foreign officers.'   Mr. Short, in a letter of March 30. 1791, acknowledged the receipt of this letter of mine, which, probably had escaped his recollection, when in that to you of Nov. 2d. 1792. he said he had never received an answer, unless he meant a definitive answer. The subsequent appropriation of 50,000 Dollars by Congress in their act of May 8. –92. c.41.§.3. being a substitute for the sum in the hands of Mr. Grand, the latter became unnecessary for it's original purpose, and therefore open to any other application.

I must apologize for the minuteness of these details, by the desire I felt of availing myself of the occasion furnished by your letter of possessing the Treasury Office with a full statement of a transaction, in which I, among others, had been entrusted, while the particulars are yet in my mind, and on papers in my possession. I am, with due respect Sir, Your most obedt. servant,   TH: JEFFERSON

RC (DLC); in the hand of George Taylor, Jr., signed by TJ; addressed: "The Secretary of the Treasury"; written on address sheet by Comptroller Oliver Wolcott, Jr.: "To be transmitted to the Audr., that a statement in which a proper Entry may be made, may be prepared in his Office—OW." PrC (DLC); unsigned. FC (Lb in DNA: RG 59, DL).

The object of the ACT OF MAY 8. –92 was to finance a mission to Algiers by John Paul Jones for the purpose of concluding a peace treaty with that country and ransoming the captive American seamen held there (see TJ to Pierce Butler, 2 Dec. 1791, and note; TJ to John Paul Jones, 1 June 1792).

From Tobias Lear

Monday 4th feby 1793

T Lear has the honor to inform the Secretary of State, that if the weather continues cloudy the Indians will not do business to day; but if it should clear off they will meet the President at *two* O'clock.

RC (DLC); addressed: "The Secretary of State"; endorsed by TJ as received 4 Feb. 1793.

For the administration's conference with the Indians, see Minutes of a Conference with the Illinois and Wabash Indians, printed under 1 Feb. 1793.

From Tench Coxe

Tuesday February 5th. [1793]

Mr. Coxe has the honor to return to Mr. Jefferson the report, on which he has taken the liberty to make marks (to connect his notes)[1] with a pencil. These notes apply very unreservedly to questions of fact—and to modes of expression. There are some Ideas of importance in relation to the subject in general, and to this present moment or state of thing's on which Mr. C. will communicate his Ideas this afternoon at any hour between 4 and 7, when Mr. J. will be disengaged, being himself particularly engaged till four and at 7.

Mr. Coxe proposes therefore to wait on Mr. Jefferson about 4 oClock this day. Should he inform Mr. Coxe that he will be unable to see him to day Mr. Coxe will call tomorrow a little before 8 in the Morning.

RC (DLC); partially dated.   [1] Opening parenthesis supplied.

ENCLOSURE

Tench Coxe's Notes on Jefferson's Draft Report on Commerce

[5 Feb. 1793]

Notes on the Report of the Secretary of State, made in consequence of the reference of the House of Representatives of the   day of   1791

[pa]ge	1	1	*Nations*[1]—substitute *Countries*—or change the words "*Spain* &ca."[2]
	2		Quere the difference between *Breadstuff* and *meals*
page	2	1	*its Dominions*[3]—to prevent mistakes might be inserted as above
			so of the rest.
	3	1	The Tonnage of last year from the French Islands must be much reduced—but the exchange of supplies of American produce & foreign Merchandise with them for returns of Sugar, Coffee &ca., have been very great, and highly beneficial to the United States. We have even shipt large quantities of them to foreign Countries. It is best however and fair to bottom the

report upon the preceding state of things—that is upon the french laws in times of order.[4]

		2	Spain receives also grain, I believe.[5]
page	4	1	They do not obtain from us any of the advantages of a circuitous foreign Trade—and this applies to France and Portugal.
		2	—"—[6]
		3	Does France receive our Bread Stuff. How is it in the new Tariff?
page	5	1	It[7] would be more generally understood, if the words (nearly equal to the same Number of Cents) were added.
		2	Did not Tobacco pay duty at places other than the free Ports?
		3	What is supposed to be the reason of this.[8]
page	6.	1.	*Incidental* to the[9] legal mode of securing the collection of the Duty—and not to the *Commerce* of the Article.
	6	2	*Pickled meats*[10]—or *wet provisions*—for Bacon is *salted* provisions: the Merchants term is *wet provisions*.[11]
		3	are 50*l.* Sterling the limited price
		4	Will it not be well to strike out the word "*even*" and
		5	to insert after "*purchased*" the words—*and Navigated*—[12]
page	6	6	*an equal participation of the privilege*—for there are foreign Goods which no ship can carry to Britain.
page	6&7	1	Quere—The Aspect in which this is presented—Does the mode of proceeding arise from favor or the reverse, or from caution in a new and particular Case—Quere—Does the report of the privy Council explain the principle.
			A Question may be raised whether this may not be deemed too
page	7	3	strong? I think not, for if a serious possibility of changes were not contemplated, why should *the power to make them* be purposely created in a manner very Questionable in a Government possessing even the portion of freedom that is to be found in the British.
page	8	1	What are the duties in Holland on grain Spirits, and on what Authority are they ascertained. I understand they are not mentioned in their Tariffs.[13]
		2	What[14] details are known of the exports of our produce from the Dutch Netherlands to foreign Markets. Germany takes some, but the Amsterdam and Rotterdam are among the natural portals of Germany, and we take many goods through those two Cities from Germany. They are so far, as it were, mere market Houses and among the most natural ones.
page	9	1	Is it known why the Danes prohibit our Indigo producing none, and not having any Indian ports from whence they can obtain it—This appears to be a great misconception of their own Interests. I suspect it must be the fruit of some Monopoly, or the consequence of some law passed before our Independency. I believe from some such laws our Ships or produce, or manufactures, or all are on a worse footing than those of some other Nations in their European Ports.

2 If[15] the divisions of a dollar intended by the figures .6 and .25 are Cents the passage may be more generally understood by expressing them so.

3 To avoid mistakes this perhaps had best be changed for "*meats.*"[16]

4 more unfavorable to us and to them.[17]

page   10   1 Do not the laws and practice of the European Kingdoms run in the same line. Will it not be argued that Individuals and Nations in their political relations are often considered differently from what would prevail in a state of Nature— and that the laws of nature cannot apply absolutely either to associated *Man*—or to associated *Bodies* (or *Nations*) *of Men*—Yet a modification of this clause may be preferable to striking it out.

2 May not the words "from time to time" be properly exchanged for—*occasionally.*

Page.   10.   3. Live[18] stock and live provisions.[19]

page.   11.   1. Livres of the Colonies.[20]

2. As[21] free as theirs.

3. Live[22] stock and live provisions.[23]

4. Quere, as to this limitation.

5. grain vizt. *indian Corn, oats &ca.*[24]

6. *as is all intercourse in our vessels.*[25]

7. It is required I believe by the British Kings proclamation that all importations and exportations shall be made by British subjects, which prevents our being *factors* in their *West India Islands*, but I do not know of anything which prevents our being Merchants there, tho' the factorage line is all that we desire or should pursue.[26] In Britain and Ireland we may be Merchants as well as factors.

8. should[27] not this be unmanufactured.[28]

9. Qu:[29] *freely.*

page.   12.   1. *Our grain requires to be specially mentioned in this summary.*[30]

2. The footing of our intercourse with Ireland is more favorable than that with Britain and appears to require notice (W. Knox.)

3. Ships built in the United States may be used in the Trade between the British European Dominions and the United States, I *think.*[31]

4. Are[32] prohibited by France and received under temporary colonial laws relaxing those of the dominant Country.

5. but long after the peace our Vessels and the French participated equally in the carrying trade between the United States, and their Dominions in Europe and the West Indies. We laid a duty of 10 ⅌ Cent advance on our impost, and upon their Vessels an extra tonnage of 44 Cents. They followed with the extra duty on Tobacco since reduced to   livres.[33]

Page.   14.   2. Will it not be well to omit "and vexations"—and to say— *numerous restrictions rigidly executed.*

[147]

15. | 1. *general* "peace."[34]
16. | 1. *May*.[35]
17. | 1. Note the State Governments 1 and 1.
     | 2. See former note.
18. | 1 or impose a duty on their Negociations.[36]
     | 2. See draught of the bill reported in 1791 by the Committee.
     | 3. Article 4 how would it operate among the Nations in general. It would make a common cause among the British, Spaniards, Portuguese, who together take   of our produce, and the two latter of whom make our Vessels free—one without a fine or duty.[37]
19. | 1. See State of the Trade from United States to the British American Islands and Colonies.
     | 2. Are they necessary to an efficient Navigation system.
     | 3. Is discrimination a general practice.
     | 4. Nations who favor our *productions* and Navigation.[38]
20. | 1. *better in fact*—query—in what respect.
     | 2. This gives a clear Direction to the report.

MS (DLC); undated; consists of five pages in a clerk's hand, with emendations by Coxe and check marks and notations by TJ described below; first page slightly torn; printed literally. Dft (PHi: Coxe Papers); undated; consists of four tattered pages entirely in Coxe's hand with numerous emendations not noted here.

The text of TJ's draft Report on Commerce to which these notes relate is in DLC: TJ Papers, 69: 11981-91. The several drafts and final state of the Report will be printed at 16 Dec. 1793, where the relationship between Coxe's notes and TJ's emendations to the text cited above will be fully described.

[1] TJ inserted a check before this word.
[2] Closing quotation mark supplied. Beneath this line in Dft Coxe canceled "[page] 2—interline *respective* before American." In the margin next to it he also canceled "(Chinese trade)."
[3] TJ inserted a check before these two words.
[4] In the margin next to this paragraph in Dft Coxe wrote two notes separated by a line before canceling both of them: "What is the cause or true meaning of the apparent increase of the British Tonne.— Enquire of all our foreign Minrs. especially Pinckney. Qu. forn. Ships—should they do this" and "The [first?] [. . .] increase of french W. I. Demand."

[5] In the margin next to the succeeding eight lines in Dft Coxe canceled "G. R. Each foreign Nation appears closely to move in that line in which, according to their best Judgment, the combined force of their ⟨best⟩ own several interests impel them. We should not blame them for so doing neither should they presume to censure us for a Similar conduct, produced entirely by their regulations; for we should be ready to annul all commercial restrictions & [will with those who will impose?] none upon us."
[6] Here in Dft Coxe canceled "qu. *Beeswax* also." He subsequently wrote the same words again without italics and then canceled them.
[7] TJ inserted a check before this word.
[8] "1." interlined here in a clerk's hand.
[9] Preceding three words canceled on previous line and interlined here by Coxe with page and number.
[10] Above these two words TJ wrote "qu? dried beef."
[11] Here TJ wrote "is dried beef either pickled or wet? are salted fish wet provisions?"
[12] TJ inserted a check before these two words.
[13] Preceding sentence, not in Dft, inserted in Coxe's hand.
[14] TJ inserted a check before this word.
[15] TJ inserted a check before this word.
[16] Beneath this sentence TJ wrote "this would not include fish."

[17] Here TJ wrote "qu. to omit whole passage."

[18] TJ inserted a check before this word.

[19] Here TJ wrote "= fresh provisions."

[20] Here TJ wrote "qu. the par with the livre of France? The dollar is 8.^ħ 5s colonial."

[21] TJ inserted a check before this word.

[22] TJ inserted a check before this word.

[23] Here TJ wrote "= fresh provisions."

[24] Here TJ wrote "+ wheat, flour, biscuit."

[25] Here TJ wrote "could we not import thence in our vessels?"

[26] Here TJ interlined "it is the Navigation act."

[27] TJ inserted a check before this word.

[28] Here TJ wrote "may not even manufactures be carried to St. Eustatius?"

[29] TJ inserted a check before this abbreviation.

[30] Here TJ wrote "breadstuff comprehends grain."

[31] Here TJ wrote "no."

[32] TJ inserted a check before this word.

[33] Beneath this section TJ wrote "in Sweden, as it is also in France since our act &c."

[34] TJ inserted a check before these two words.

[35] TJ inserted a check before this word.

[36] Here TJ wrote "= or modify their transactions."

[37] In the margin next to this paragraph in Dft Coxe canceled "Measures not proper now ⟨should⟩ may be adopted *gradatim*."

[38] Underneath this line in Dft Coxe wrote "Abolish the drawback on [Beer?] —it is dangerous." Opposite this additional line in the margin he canceled "Qu. Modifications of Drawbacks."

To Tench Coxe

Feb. 5. 1793.

Th: Jefferson presents his compliments to Mr. Coxe and his thanks for his Notes, which are exactly in the way he wished. But Mr. Coxe having omitted to return the report, Th:J cannot as yet understand the whole of them. He will be glad to receive the report now, and devote this evening to the examination of them, and would be happy to see Mr. Coxe tomorrow morning at the hour he proposes, as he has company to dine with him to-day which will probably engage him from 4. to 7.

RC (DLC); endorsed by Coxe. Not recorded in SJL.

From Thomas Pinckney

DEAR SIR   London 5th. Febry. 1793

I had just concluded mine of the 30th. ulto. herewith, when your favors of the 30th. of December and 1st. January were brought to me, seeing the latter was in cypher I immediately opened the Drawer in which I kept all my confidential papers when to my great mortification I saw that my counterpart of the Cypher was missing; after the most accurate search I can not find it, nor can the strictest investigation enable me to discover what is become of it. Neither money nor other papers of equal or perhaps greater consequence which had always been kept in the same drawer were missing. No precaution for its security was neglected as I had placed it in a drawer of a piece of furniture so cumbersome as not to be easily removed, and had a lock of a construction particularly calculated to prevent frauds put on the drawer, the key of which I never intrusted to any person. My servants are such as are usually met with here; but I have not known either of them guilty of stealing. In short unless I have sent mine together with Mr. B's Cypher to him (as they were both before me when I was making up his packet) uncommon pains must have been taken to purloin it and that by no common persons. I can not describe to you, Sir, the uneasiness I feel on this account—an opportunity may be lost which can not be retrieved and the worst consequences may ensue from the discovery of measures which ought to be secret.

You will doubtless, Sir, take such measures as may be best calculated to obviate the ill consequences which may be expected from this event; in the mean time I have written to request Mr. Morris to send me a copy of his cypher with a hope that it may be a duplicate of mine; but lest that should fail I have desired him to furnish me with all the intelligence he may receive from home which he may conceive it of importance for me to be apprised of. I have also written to Mr. B: requesting him to return my cypher if I inclosed it with his, or at any rate a duplicate of his own—but to this letter I know not when I may receive an answer. I had a few lines from him by post dated 25th. of Decr. in which he only mentions that he has received mine and that every attention shall be paid to its contents.

An event has taken place which renders me less apprehensive of the Ships of War of this country preventing Vessels with Provisions from going into the French Ports in case of war, which is that the Custom house officers at Falmouth[1] had stopped an American Brig loaded with American flour and bound to Havre de Grace, but orders were immediately given that no American Vessels should be detained, and she was accordingly released, before I could obtain an audience of Lord Grenville for which I had applied. I however availed myself of the opportunity offered by the conference I had on that occasion to bring forward Mr. Hammonds negociation. His lordship assigned as reasons for the delay hitherto the pressure of business here on account of the present state of Europe, and mentioned that part of it had been submitted to Mr. Bond, but said that he would forward his dispatches to Mr. Hammond by the March[2] packet. He seemed sensible of the propriety of preventing every move in the negociation from crossing the Atlantic but promised nothing. Due attention shall be paid to the order for Copper. I have forwarded the letter for Mr. Lamotte to Mr. Morris at Paris by a confidential conveyance. We are about to try in the Court of Admiralty the right to recover the wages of British Seamen who desert from on board American Vessels and enter in his Majesty's Ships of War. The Attorney General is to give his opinion whether an American Master of a Vessel can by legal process in this country compell an American seaman to comply with his shipping contract. These are measures adopted by this Government which indicate an inclination to pay some attention to our rights. By the Pigou which will sail in the course of the present month I hope to give farther information on this subject. With great respect & sincere esteem I have the honor to be Dear Sir Your faithful & obedient Servant

THOMAS PINCKNEY

RC (DNA: RG 59, DD); at foot of text: "The Secretary of State"; endorsed by TJ as received 20 Apr. 1793 and so recorded in SJL, which erroneously describes it as a letter of 7 Feb. 1793. PrC (ScHi: Pinckney Family Papers). Tr (Lb in DNA: RG 59, DD).

MR. B: Thomas Barclay. TJ's NEGOCIATION with George Hammond related to the enforcement of the disputed provisions of the Treaty of Paris, on which TJ and the British minister had exchanged lengthy statements of the positions of their respective governments (Hammond to TJ, 5 Mch. 1792; TJ to Hammond, 29 May 1792). Hammond had submitted TJ's statement of the American case to Lord GRENVILLE, the British foreign secretary, who in August 1792 instructed

Hammond to suspend all negotiations on this issue pending a thorough review of this state paper. The harsh critique of TJ's complaints about British infractions of the peace treaty that Grenville received from Phineas BOND, the British consul at Philadelphia, who was on leave in England at this time, was one of the reasons why Hammond was never instructed to resume these negotiations during TJ's tenure as Secretary of State (see Notes of a Conversation with George Hammond, 4 June 1792, and note).

TJ submitted this letter to the President on 20 Apr. 1793 (Washington, *Journal*, 115).

[1] Word interlined in place of "Cowes."
[2] Word interlined in place of "next."

From John M. Pintard

Madeira, 5 Feb. 1793. Acknowledging receipt of the letter of 14 Nov. 1792 wherein TJ announces his intention to resign on 3 Mch. 1793, he expresses regret, "as I think our Country will Sensibly feel the loss of your distinguished abilities," and wishes him well in retirement. He will observe TJ's directions for addressing public letters and encloses "the American Ship list" from 30 June to 31 Dec. 1792. He has communicated the latter part of TJ's letter to the island's governor, who is "thankfull and pleased" at being so noticed.

RC (MoSHi: Bixby Collection); 1 p.; in a clerk's hand except for complimentary close and signature; endorsed by TJ as received 16 Mch. 1793 and so recorded in SJL as a "private" letter. Enclosure not found. According to SJL, a public letter from Pintard of 5 Feb. 1793 was also received 16 Mch. 1793, but it has not been found.

From the Commissioners of the Federal District

SIR   George Town 7th. Feby. 1793

The plat of the Territory was sent by Mr. Carroll as soon as it arrived, to Mr. Ellicott who has informed us that he will have the Additions required by the President, completed by Sunday; so as to be in readiness to be sent by the post on Tuesday. We are sorry to mention, that Mr. Ellicott still continues in a very ill humor with us, and has refused to give us any information relative to his department, untill May next, when he means to dismiss himself. If he persists in this temper, we shall certainly not wait till that period: Should this happen, we have no doubt but his place will be well supplied by Mr. Briggs. From some indisposition in his family, we have not the pleasure of Mr. Johnson's company at this meeting, we expect him next week, when we shall come to some final decision on this subject. It is our wish to wait his own time, if it be possible. We have as yet received only ten thousand dollars on the Presidents second draft on Virginia. We have to day, written to the executive of Virginia requesting a payment of the ballance. Governor Lee, who is in Phila. can probably inform you of the success to be expected from thence. As a disappointment will be very embarrasing, and prevent us from commencing our opperations the approaching season, with the spirit we could wish, we think it advisable that the President should send us his Draft on the Treasurer of Maryland, for the third Instalment. We have information that most of the money is ready.

We shall send you by the first opportunity to be met with, some of the samples of Marble from the Patomac, which we have had polished.

Tho' we are much pleased, that we shall at length be furnished with the plan of a Capitol so highly satisfactory to the President, and all who have seen it, we feell sensibly for poor Hallet, and shall do every thing in our power to sooth him. We hope he may be usefully employed notwithstanding.

Not to discourage Mr. Traquair from corresponding with us by the expence of postage, we take the liberty of sending the inclosed Letter

for him to your Address, it being on business relating to the public. We are with great respect Your Obt: Servts: Dd. Stuart
Danl. Carroll

P:S: We are this moment informed by a gentleman, (who had it from Mr. Ellicot himself) that he is appointed, Superintendant general of the in land navigation of Pennsylvania.

RC (DLC); in a clerk's hand except for complimentary close and postscript in the hand of David Stuart and signatures; addressed: "Secretary of State"; endorsed by TJ as received 13 Feb. 1793 and so recorded in SJL. FC (DNA: RG 42, DCLB). Enclosure: Commissioners to James Traquair, 7 Feb. 1793, thanking him for his efforts in securing workmen for the Federal District; agreeing that, though it would be more convenient if European workmen were to land at Washington, the greatest difficulty would be removed if they arrived at any American port; and requesting his continuing assistance (FC in same).

Isaac BRIGGS was one of Andrew Ellicott's assistants in surveying the Federal District (Bryan, *National Capital*, I, 209). Ellicott's rumored appointment as SUPERINTENDANT GENERAL OF THE IN LAND NAVIGATION was, in reality, a commission from the government of Pennsylvania to survey a road from Reading to Presque Isle, in western Pennsylvania, formally conferred on 15 Apr. 1793. Ellicott's acceptance of the commission effectively ended his service as surveyor of the Federal District (same, 209-10; Mathews, *Andrew Ellicott*, 107-8; Commissioners to George Washington, 23 Dec. 1793, DLC: Washington Papers).

From Tobias Lear

Thursday 7th feby 1793
The President requests the Secretary of State to add words to the effect of those marked by the President with a pencil at the end of the Indians' Speeches to the President, and return the paper to the President.

RC (DLC).

For TJ's record of the Indians' speeches, see Minutes of a Conference with the Illinois and Wabash Indians, printed under 1 Feb. 1793. See note 17 to that document for the words TJ added at Washington's behest.

Notes of a Conversation with George Washington

Feb. 7. 1793. I waited on the President with letters and papers from Lisbon. After going through these I told him that I had for some time suspended speaking with him on the subject of my going out of office because I had understood that the bill for intercourse with foreign nations was likely to be rejected by the Senate in which case the remaining business of the department would be too inconsiderable to make it worth while to keep it up. But that the bill being now passed I was freed from the considerations of propriety which had embarrassed me: that &c. [nearly in the words of a letter to Mr. T. M.[1] Randolph of a few days ago] and that I should be willing, if he had taken no arrangements to the contrary to continue somewhat longer, how long I could not say, perhaps till summer, perhaps autumn. He said, so far from taking arrangements on the subject, he had never mentioned to any mortal the design of retiring which I had expressed to him, till yesterday having heard that I had given up my house and that it was rented by another, whereupon he mentioned it to Mr. E. Randolph and asked him, as he knew my retirement had been talked of, whether he had heard any persons suggested in conversations to succeed me. He expressed his satisfaction at my change of purpose, and his apprehensions that my retirement would be a new source of uneasiness to the public. He said Govr. Lee had that day informed of the general discontent prevailing in Virga., of which he never had had any conception, much less sound information. That it appeared to him very alarming. He proceed[2] to express his earnest wish that Hamilton and my self could coalesce in the measures of the government, and urged here the general reasons for it which he had done to me on two former conversations. He said he had proposed the same thing to Ham. who expressed his readiness, and he thought our coalition would secure the general acquiescence of the public.—I told him my concurrence was of much less importance than he seemed to imagine: that I kept my self aloof from all cabal and correspondence on the subject of the government, and saw and spoke with as few as I could. That as to a coalition with Mr. Hamilton, if by that was meant[3] that either was to sacrifice his general system to the other, it was impossible. We had both no doubt[4] formed our conclusions after the most mature consideration and principles conscientiously adopted could not be given up on either side. My[5] wish was to see both houses of Congr. cleansed of all persons interested in the bank or public stocks: and that a pure legislature being given us, I should always be ready to acquiesce under their determinations[6] even if contrary to my own opinions, for that I subscribed to the principle that the will of the majority honestly expressed should give law. I confirmed him in the fact of the great discontents to the South, that they were grounded on seeing that their judgments and interests were sacrificed to those of the Eastern states on every occasion, and their belief that it was the effect of a corrupt squadron of voters in Congress at the command of the Treasury, and they saw that if the votes of those members who had an interest distinct from and contrary to the general interest of their constituents had been withdrawn, as in decency and honesty they should have been, the laws would have been the reverse of what they are in all the great questions. I instanced the new assumption carried in the H. of Repr. by the Speaker's vote. On this subject he made no reply.—[7]He explained his remaining in office to have been the effect of strong sollicitations after he returned here declaring that he had never mentioned his purpose of going out but to the heads of departments and Mr. Madison; he expressed the extreme wretchedness of his existence while in office, and went lengthily into the late attacks on him for levees &c.—and explained to me how he had been led into them by the persons he consulted at New York, and that if he could but know what the sense of the public was, he would most chearfully conform to it.

MS (DLC); entirely in TJ's hand; brackets in original. Entry in SJPL: "Notes of a conversn with G.W. on my retiremt from office." Included in the "Anas."

The official LETTERS AND PAPERS TJ submitted to Washington consisted of Thomas Barclay to TJ, 1 Oct. 1792, and David Humphreys to TJ, 23 Dec. 1792 (Washington, *Journal*, 44). The Senate passed the BILL FOR INTERCOURSE WITH FOREIGN NATIONS on 5 Feb. 1793 (see TJ to Washington, 1 Dec. 1792, and note). The LETTER TO T. M. RANDOLPH was that of 3 Feb. 1793. For the TWO FORMER CONVERSATIONS, see Notes of a Conversation with George Washington, 10 July and 1 Oct. 1792. In regard to the NEW ASSUMPTION, the House of Representatives, with the aid of a tie-breaking vote cast by Speaker Jonathan Trumbull, passed a bill on 25 Jan. 1793 authorizing a loan to be subscribed in the certificates or notes of such states as had balances due to them upon a final settlement of accounts with the United States. The Senate rejected this bill on 4 Feb. 1793 by a vote of 17 to 11 (JHR, I, 681-2; JS, I, 479; Notes on Levees and Assumption, 16 Feb. 1793). In an essay published in the *National Gazette* on 2 Feb. 1793,

"A Farmer" attacked LEVEES as the "legitimate offspring of inequality, begotten by aristocracy and monarchy upon corruption," and warned, in an obvious reference to Washington, that "it is dangerous in the extreme to set up any man as an idol, to suppose that he alone is capable of dispensing the blessings of liberty; to prostrate your entire confidence, and security before him; to hail him as your political saviour; for however deserving he may be, there is a magic in power which assimilates every thing to itself, & the more implicit your confidence, the more easily will you become dupes to his views." TJ recorded two other documents relating to Hamilton and the Hamiltonian system in SJPL around this time: "history of A. Hamilton" under 2 Feb. 1793; and "Th:J. to G.W. on the funds of the treasury" between entries of 3 and 7 Feb. 1793. Neither has been found.

[1] Initials interlined.
[2] Thus in MS.
[3] Here TJ canceled "a concurrence of sentimen."
[4] Here TJ canceled "adopted."
[5] Here TJ canceled "object."
[6] Here TJ canceled "however."
[7] Here TJ canceled "He detailed to me."

From Thomas Mann Randolph, Jr.

DEAR SIR   Monticello Feb: 7. 1793.

We find by your letters not coming as usual that the Northern mail has been delayed by the Snow. Monticello and the country adjacent were covered with it to the depth of 12 inches at least and yet today not a particle is to be seen the Weather has been so uncommonly warm. The farmers say, it has been of great service to the Wheat which really suffered from drought in the middle of Winter. For the navigators of Rivanna it has been very fortunate the river having been too shallow for boats to pass the greater part of the Winter. George the black-smith tells me that he wants principally files and screw-plates and that the bellows he has at present is too small for such work as the Mill will require. The carpenters began this morning to raise the stable the snow having prevented their seting about it sooner. I fear you will find the work which was to be done by the teams very backward. The horses have been employed a part of two days only, in bringing two loads of slabs, the oxen have brought two more and these are all we have. Indeed I am much afraid that the quantity you desired cannot be got as the saw is frequently stoped and the slabs are in great demand. The store of them which you saw at the saw-mill was exhausted by a neighbouring black-smith who took it into his head to make Charcoal of them, and those which the waggons brought away were such as had just fallen from the saw. Your directions concerning the scantling will be exactly attended to, alltho' I am apprehensive that it will not be brought in before your return as it must be sawed on the other side of the river there being no timber fit on this side.

Patsy and the children are well and we are all extremely impatient for your return. Your most sincere friend & hble Servant

THS: M. RANDOLPH

Diary.

Feb:			
1. 30	f	36.	c.
2. 36.	r.	40.	f.
3. 42.	f.	45.	f.
4. 37.	f.	44.	f.
5. 48.	clouds.	55.	very cloudy
6. 50.	c.	54.	rain
7. 50.	f.		

RC (MHi); addressed: "Thomas Jefferson Secretary of State Philada."; franked. Recorded in SJL as received 26 Feb. 1793.

A continuation of the weather diary, written by Randolph on the verso of a separate address cover directed to TJ, almost certainly accompanied this letter.

Endorsed by TJ as indicated below, the diary bears wax imprints matching those of the letter and its cover, which evidently missed the post and may have accompanied Randolph's missing letter to Maria Jefferson of 14 Feb. 1793 (see TJ to Martha Jefferson Randolph, 24 Feb. 1793; TJ to Thomas Mann Randolph, Jr., 3 Mch. 1793):

"Diary

M. ob:		Even: Ob:	
Feb:	7. 50. c	50. f.	
	8. 38. c	45. c. a. r.	
	9. 54. f.	53. f.	
	10. 48. f.	47. f.	
	11. 34. c.	35. snow falling	
		Therm. 29. at	
		10 P.M.	
	12. 32. snowing	31. snowing yet.	
	13. 33. f. Wind	34. f. Wd. N.W.	
	N.W.	high.	
	14. 35. f. Wind		
	N.W."		

(RC in MHi; addressed: "Thomas Jefferson, Secretary of State Philada"; franked; endorsed by TJ: "Randolph T. M. jr. Mont. Feb. 7. 93. recd. Feb. 26.").

The previous installment of the weather diary, written by Randolph on the verso of an address cover directed to TJ, may have been sent with Randolph's missing letter to Maria Jefferson of 30 Jan. 1793 that presumably was not posted until 31 Jan. or later (see TJ to Thomas Mann Randolph, Jr., 18 Feb. 1793; TJ to Martha Jefferson Randolph, 24 Feb. 1793):

"Diary.

Jan: M.		E.
19. 44. f.		
20. 43. f.		
21. 45. f.	45. f.	
22. 37. f.	40. f.	
23. 34. c.	42. c.	
24. 40. c.	44. c.	
25. 39. f.		
26. 44. f.		
27. 39. c. Snow		
28. 44. f.	49. f.	
29. 41. f.		
30. 32. Snow.		
31. 35 f"		

(RC in MHi; addressed: "Thomas Jefferson Secretary of State Philada."; franked).

From Winthrop Sargent

Cincinnati County of Hamilton, and Territory of the
United States north west of the Ohio Feby: the 7th: 1793.

I conceive it my duty Sir, in the absence of Governour St: Clair to represent to the General Government, that considerable public embarrassments, and injury, accrue to this Territory, from the absence of the Judges thereof.

Our Code of laws materially deficient to promote the welfare and happiness of the people (as observation must evince) can know no alteration from this cause, at the same time that the judicial trusts of their Honours must be suspended.

Complaints upon this subject having already been transmitted with my recent official communications, would not again be laid before the Sovereign Authority, but for the sudden departure of the honourable Judge Symmes from the Government—thereby virtually effecting a total present abdication upon[1] the Supreme Bench of this Territory. Some of the probable consequences of which, together with my solicitation and remonstrances to avert them, in the enclosed copy of

[157]

a letter to his Honour, upon the 6th: instant, I deem it incumbent to submit by this the earliest opportunity. I have the honour to be, Sir, with every sentiment of respect, Your most obedt: humble servant,

WINTHROP SARGENT

PrC of Tr (DLC); in a clerk's hand; at foot of text: "Honble: Secretary of State." Tr (Lb in DNA: RG 76, Yazoo Land Claims). Recorded in SJL as dated 6 Feb. 1793 and received 27 Mch. 1793. Enclosure: Sargent to John Cleves Symmes, 6 Feb. 1793, asking Symmes to delay his intended visit to Philadelphia until either he or Judges Rufus Putnam or George Turner, who were already absent from the Northwest Territory, held "the next terms of the Supreme Court in the two western counties," so as to avoid further antagonizing the people of those districts, who have made their dissatisfaction known to the President as "a very great grievance," and inducing them "to remove to the Spanish Government" (PrC of Tr in DLC; in a clerk's hand; at head of text: "Copy of a letter to Judge Symmes"). Letter and enclosure enclosed in TJ to George Turner, 30 Mch. 1793.

Winthrop Sargent (1753-1820), a graduate of Harvard, brevet major in the Continental Army, and secretary of the Ohio Company, was secretary and sometime acting governor of the Northwest Territory from 1787 to 1798, when he became the first territorial governor of Mississippi, an office to which TJ refused to reappoint him in 1801 because of his staunch Federalism and autocratic methods of government (DAB). The ABSENCE OF THE JUDGES from the Northwest Territory had been a matter of concern to TJ for some time (TJ to George Turner, 9 Nov. 1792, and note).

[1] Word canceled and "of" interlined in pencil by an unidentified hand. Tr: "upon."

To George Washington

Feb. 7. 93.

Th: Jefferson has the honor to return the Indian proceedings with the addition proposed, and to mention to the President that he did not send him in writing the proposition for enquiring into their boundaries, because having spoken to Genl. Knox on the subject it was found that their claims had been perfectly explained to Genl. Putnam.

RC (DNA: RG 59, MLR); addressed: "The President of the U.S."; endorsed by Tobias Lear. Tr (Lb in same, SDC). Not recorded in SJL. Enclosure: Minutes of a Conference with the Illinois and Wabash Indians, printed under 1 Feb. 1793.

To Tench Coxe

Feb. 8. 93.

Th: Jefferson presents his compliments to Mr. Coxe and incloses a letter from which he gets a hint which may serve as a clue to the unfavorable distinction made by the British as to our vessels. He suspects that they permit vessels *belonging* to other countries,[1] tho' not *built in those countries* to carry to Engld. the produce of those countries. They certainly did this for us till lately. In this case[2] it is a favorable connivance to other nations refused to us.

Th:J. having given the pamphlet containing plan for establishing a town, to the Presidt. will thank him for 2 more, one to be sent to the Commrs. at Geo. town, the other for his own use.

RC (MoSHi: Bixby Collection); date-line between body of letter and postscript; addressed: "Mr. Coxe"; endorsed by Coxe, with additional notation in his hand, possibly of a later date: "Plan of Town on Susquehannah: *Exempli gratia.*" Not recorded in SJL. Enclosure not found.

For the PAMPHLET, see TJ to George Washington, 2 Feb. 1793, and note.

[1] Word interlined in place of "nations."
[2] Preceding three words written over "I suspect [. . .]," erased.

From Tench Coxe

Feby. 8th. 1793.

Mr. Coxe has the honor to inform the Secretary of State that he has applied to those whom he considers as the first mercantile authorities here, and that their statements vary so materially that he is not able to furnish any materials on which a reliance can be placed either in regard to Ireland, or foreign built ships owned by British subjects. On the latter point he relies upon the British Statutes, but not having them before him he is unable to point out the Sections.

Mr. Coxe has written to New York and Providence on the subject of the Danish European Trade.

RC (DLC).

From David Humphreys

Gibraltar, 8 Feb. 1793. His letter No. 64, a duplicate of which went by a second conveyance, described Barclay's sudden death and the reasons he felt it necessary to come here to take care of the public property. Upon his arrival last Sunday he found the packages Barclay had brought from Lisbon safely in the hands of the Russian consul, James Simpson, who promptly told all he could about them but does not appear to have given any receipt to Barclay. After examining with Simpson all the papers relating to Barclay's mission and making a list, he enclosed the papers under his seal stating they were to be opened by the person appointed to take charge of Barclay's effects and left them in Simpson's custody. He sends six enclosures pertaining to the expenditure of the 32,175 current guilders that were obtained from the bills of exchange he had drawn on our Amsterdam bankers and were received by Barclay. He has had the boxes with the most perishable items opened in his presence and found the velvets and muslins in good condition but the broadcloths and silks in various states of disrepair. Since damaged articles will be useless as presents in Morocco, they should be aired immediately and put under someone's care. P.S. He has taken from Barclay's papers only two ciphers, which he holds pending TJ's orders.

Tr (Lb in DNA: RG 59, DD); 3 p.; at head of text: "No. 66."; in the margin: "The Secretary of State." Recorded in SJL as received 18 Mch. 1793. Enclosures: (1) Account of funds paid to Thomas Barclay by John Bulkeley & Son through bills of exchange drawn by Humphreys on Willink, Van Staphorst & Hubbard, 11-27 Oct. 1791 (same; in the margin: "No. 1. Copy from Mr. Bulkeley's Books"). (2) James Simpson, "Account of sundry Articles purchased and disbursements made by order of Thomas Barclay Esqr." for the period 26 Dec. 1791-14 June 1792, Gibraltar, 26 Sep. 1792 (same; in the margin: "No 2. Invoice sundry articles provided by order of Mr. Barclay for public service"). (3) Simpson, "Inventory of sundry Articles remaining in my possession, which by certain written Memorandums found among the late Thos. Barclay Esqr's papers, appear to have been destined for public Service," Gibraltar, 7 Feb. 1793 (same; in the margin: "No. 3. Inventory of Articles provided at Gibraltar, and found in

Mr. Barclay's small Leather Trunk for public service"). (4) Simpson, List of Purchases "Extracted from Mr. Thomas Barclay's Book Lisbon 5th. November 1791," Gibraltar, 7 Feb. 1793 (same; in the margin: "No. 4. Receipt for Packages brought from Lisbon"). (5) Simpson, "Statement of Expenditure of Four thousand Mexican Dollars delivered to me by the late Thomas Barclay Esqr. on the 26th. December 1791," Gibraltar, 7 Feb. 1793 (same; in the margin: "No. 5."). (6) "Copy of a Memorandum found among Mr. Barclay's papers—in his own hand writing—no date, or signature," listing expenditure of money received from John Bulkeley & Son, with attestation by Humphreys and Simpson, Gibraltar, 8 Feb. 1793 (same; in the margin: "No. 6.").

TJ submitted this letter and its enclosures and the next letter from Humphreys to the President on 18 Mch. 1793, and Washington returned them the next day (Washington, *Journal*, 93-4).

From David Humphreys

Gibraltar, 8[1] Feb. 1793. The fortuitous arrival here of the British consuls for Morocco, Algiers, and Tripoli and the French consul for Morocco has enabled him to obtain valuable information about Barbary affairs. Mr. Matra, the British consul for Morocco, has been summoned to Tangier to consult with Messrs. Mace and Lucas, who are enroute from England to Algiers and Tripoli. He says that the parties of the two pretenders to the throne there continue much as they have in the past, that confusion is increasing, that the mountaineers have descended close to Tangier, that two small camps have been formed to protect that town, that depredations to agriculture from the civil war have led to a great scarcity of grain in several provinces, and that the defeat of either of the pretenders will probably cause one or more to arise in his place, making it impossible to predict when peace will be reestablished. Some of this information is confirmed by a British officer who returned yesterday from

Tetuán. "A great want of rain" exists in Barbary and southern Europe. Besides the enclosed extract from a letter for Barclay, which "treats allegorically of the Competitors for the Empire," James Simpson, the Russian consul here, will periodically give TJ further information about the Moroccan conflict. Having visited Mr. Mace, who is going to relieve Mr. Logie at Algiers, and received his offer to be of service there to him or the United States, he has called Mace's attention to the plight of the American captives in Algiers, with whom Mace's secretary is acquainted. Mace offered to open a correspondence with him on that subject, but not having instructions as to a treaty, he could in his private capacity only recommend the captives to Mace's protection, indicate that he would probably accept the offer to correspond, and suggest that in the meantime Mace could render the best service to the United States "by impressing upon the Dey and Regency the idea of our being a new Nation, possessed of small pecuniary resources, and which could never hereafter treat but upon very reasonable and moderate terms," which Mace appeared to regard as "a useful Line" and promised to try to inculcate. Although he has been unable to meet with Mr. Lucas, the British consul for Tripoli, who is ill, he can say that political affairs of Algiers and Tripoli, "as to negociations &c, are totally seperate and distinct." Official news has just arrived of an Algerine declaration of war against the Dutch, with captures due to begin on 13 Feb., in consequence of which the Dutch consul has dispatched a cutter to stop all Dutch vessels.

RC (DNA: RG 59, DD); 5 p.; at head of text: "(No. 67.)"; at foot of text: "The Secretary of State &c. &c. &c."; endorsed by TJ as received 18 Mch. 1793 and so recorded in SJL. Tr (Lb in same). Enclosure: Extract of Unknown to Thomas Barclay, Mogador, 31 Dec. 1792: "Apropos the 2 trees which you know have not yet made great vegetative progress, and I cannot discern which of the two will produce its fruit, which leads me to say that we must not yet submit to the expense of cultivation of one or the other before we know p[h]ysically which [of] the two will take root. A mexican wound would be necessary to their flourishing—but truly we lament here the want of water which makes us fear on account of the approaching harvest. The tree exposed to the northern wind promises the best; the blossoms begin to appear—however till this moment nothing can be relied on" (Trs in same, English translation in the hand of George Taylor, Jr., subjoined to French text, with bracketed letters supplied from Tr in Lb; Trs in Lb in same, in French and English).

[1] Reworked from "9."

From William Stephens Smith

SIR   New York Feby 8th. 1793.

I have the honor of informing you of my arrival last night from England in the Portland Packett, which sailed from Falmouth on the 23d. of Decr., and shall take the earliest opportunity that my private affairs will allow, to present myself to you at Philadelphia, not doubting but it will be satisfactory, to have a detail of the present political State of Europe, from one who has been personally attentive for some months past, to their opperation particularly, as he supposed they might in some degree effect his own Country. I left Paris, on the 9th. of November and have the satisfaction to inform you, that your friends there are well, and pursuing attentively the interests of that great and rising Republic, which notwithstanding the immense combination against them, I doubt not will be firmly established, and the principles which gave it birth will expand and effect more or less every European State. Concluding the Letters from Mr. Pinckney, which I have the honor of forwarding will sufficiently detail the present state of affairs, it will be superfluous for me to enter minutely into them. I have the honor to be, with great regard, Sir, Your most obedt. Humble Servt.

W. S. SMITH

RC (DLC); at foot of text: "Thos. Jefferson Esqr. Secretary of State &c. &c."; endorsed by TJ as received 9 Feb. 1793 and so recorded in SJL.

From Jean Baptiste Ternant

Philadelphia. Feb. 8. 1793.
The Minister of France to the Secretary of state of the U.S.

I am enjoined by the government of France to lay before the government of the U.S. the indispensable want[1] under which we are to draw from abroad subsistences of first necessity, and the advantage which would arise to the two nations to recieve these provisions from hence, in deduction of our credit with you. This mode of payment would procure to America a vent for superfluous commodities, useful to it's commerce as well as to it's agriculture, and at the same time, an occasion of keeping up mutual offices of friendship between two nations which the cause of liberty first united, and into which the same public spirit, and similar principles of government ought to inspire at this time a mutual interest stronger than ever. These considerations induce me to hope that your government will not refuse to place in my power a sum equal to three millions tournois, which I am instructed to ask from it to ensure the purchase here and shipment of provisions of which some parts of France have the most urgent want.

I pray you to place my application under the eyes of the President, and to sollicit a decision sufficiently prompt for that the shipments which I may have to make in consequence may arrive in France at the time when there will probably be the most pressing occasion to recieve them.

TERNANT

Tr (DNA: RG 59, NL); entirely in TJ's hand; at foot of text: "Translation." Pr C (DLC). Tr (AMAE: CPEU, Supplément, xx); in French. Recorded in SJL as received 8 Feb. 1793.

Ternant wrote this letter a day after receiving a dispatch from French foreign minister Lebrun instructing him to apply to the United States government for 3,000,000 livres on account of the debt to France in order to purchase provisions in America for the use of the French republic (Turner, *CFM*, 170-1; TJ to George Washington, 25 Feb. 1793). TJ submit-

ted Ternant's original letter and his own translation of it in a brief note of this date to Washington in which he stated that he would call on the President about this matter the following day (RC in DNA: RG 59, MLR, endorsed by Tobias Lear; Pr C in DLC; Tr in Lb in DNA: RG 59, SDC; recorded in SJPL). For the sequel, see the Editorial Note on Jefferson's questions and observations on the application of France, at 12 Feb. 1793.

[1] Word interlined in place of "necessity."

From John Nancarrow

Philada 2mo. 9. 1793

On dipping into the second Vol. of Desaguliers' experimental Philos. I find that his 5th. size Engine which worked with 22 men, threw Water to the height of 55 yards or 165 feet, which if I am not mistaken exceeds the largest Engines made in Philada. altho' a greater number of hands were employed. The Machine of Newsham in England expended 870 Gallons per minute with 22 men and the largest in this place about 200 Galls. with 25 or 26 men. This difference may be attributed to the different densities of the Atmosphere here and in England, it being an acknowledged fact that there is at least half an inch difference in the height of the mercury in this Country where the Air is generally denser than in the more northerly latitudes. It may be observed that the construction of these machines in Philada. and London is essentially the same.

Newshams first size Garden Engine at which 2 men are employed, which expends 30 Gallns. per minute and throws the water to the distance of 25 yards or 75 feet in a dispersed column may be a very proper size for the use of a private Gentleman, but where there are a large number of servants, I should prefer a machine which would require 4 hands to work it, furnished with hose both for the spout and tail of the Engine tho' the expence might be more considerable.

I have thrown the above hints together with no other view than to submit them to thy better judgement & am with much respect Thy real Friend   JNO. NANCARROW

[163]

Since writing the above I called on Richd. Mason (one of our best Engine-makers who works in 3d. Street a little below Chesnut) who handed me the enclosed which confirms me in my opinion that a machine requiring 4 men will prove the most effectual—if JN can be of further service, please to command him freely.

RC (DLC); dateline between signature and postscript; endorsed by TJ: "fire engine." Enclosure: Richard Mason's notes on fire engines, n.d.: "An Engine that will discharge 30 Gals. water per Minute and throw the water 60 feet to work with two men Price £20 without Hose. One that will discharge 40 Galls. per Minute and throw the water 80 feet to work with four men Price £35. Suctions are an additional Expence of £6 to Each Engine and Hose at 3/9 per foot with Brass Screws and Everything complete" (MS in DLC: TJ Papers, 236: 42372).

DESAGULIERS' EXPERIMENTAL PHILOS.: John Theophilus Desaguliers, A Course of Experimental Philosophy, 2 vols. (London, 1734-44; 2d ed. of Vol. 1, 1745). See Sowerby, No. 3738. NEWSHAM: Richard Newsham (d. 1743), an early English maker of fire engines whose models were copiously described and illustrated by Desaguliers (DNB). Richard MASON of Philadelphia reputedly built the first fire engine in America (PMHB, XVI [1892], 95, LVI [1932], 374, 376-7).

From Jean Baptiste Ternant

Philadelphie 9 fevrier 1793

J'ai l'honeur d'envoyer à Monsieur Jefferson le tableau de notre créance, ainsi que l'extrait qu'il a desiré à ce sujet. Il verra que l'exposé de notre Ministre des contributions correspond assez avec celui de Monsieur hamilton; mais que les remboursemens ont eté faits jusqu'ici en valeurs nominales, et sans egard à la compensation promise par la lettre que Monsieur Jefferson m'ecrivit le 1r. Sepe. 1791 et qu'en ajoutant même aux payemens faits en Europe, les avances fournies ou à fournir encore ici, il en resultera à peine une extinction complette de l'exigible jusqu'à ce moment.   TERNANT

RC (DLC); endorsed by TJ as received 10 Feb. 1793 and so recorded in SJL. Enclosures: (1) "Tableau redigé en decembre 1789. de la créance de France, sur les Etats unis. Avec la diminution graduelle des interets en raison des remboursemens, conformément aux contrats Signés le 16 Juillet 1782 et le 25 fevrier 1783," n.d. (MS in DLC: TJ Papers, 70: 12234, endorsed by TJ: "Ternant"; PrC of Tr in same, 82: 14226-7, in a clerk's hand, with note at foot of text by TJ: "Feb. 1793. given in by Mr. Ternant to Th:J."). (2) Extract of Clavière

to Lebrun, 10 Sep. 1792, summarizing Enclosure No. 1 and concluding that the United States remained in arrears in its debt to France, even if the calculation was made in depreciated money, and was much further behind if it chose to be just and compensate for the depreciation (Tr in Ternant's hand, on verso of MS of Enclosure No. 1, same, 70: 12333; PrC of Tr in same, 77: 13370).

TJ submitted a text of the enclosures on the American debt to France to the President in a letter of 14 Feb. 1793 as part of his effort to win approval of Ter- nant's request to use the debt to pur- chase provisions for France in the United States. Washington in turn sent it to the Secretary of the Treasury on the follow- ing day (Washington, *Journal*, 54; Ter-

nant to TJ, 8 Feb. 1793, and note). For Hamilton's statement on the current sta- tus of the American debt to France, see his 3 Jan. 1793 report to the House of Representatives on foreign loans in Syrett, *Hamilton*, XIII, 453-4.

From Joseph Fenwick

SIR   Bordeaux 10 Feby. 1793.

I have none of your favors to reply to. On the first Inst. the National Convention declared war against England and Holland. This declara- tion was preceded by an embargo in all the ports of France on English, Dutch, Russian, Prussian and Austrian vessels. The commerce with the two last, altho' in war with France, had not before been interupted.

This circumstance has given great favor to the American vessels. All that were in port were immediately taken up at their own terms for different quarters, and a great number might now procure very advan- tageous freights for the north, the West or East Indias. The prices of American produce have considerably rose, and there is no doubt that while the war lasts all the products of America will command high and advantageous prices in France and their vessels obtain very profitable freights. The National Convention has also revoked the Decree that prevented the American vessels from being sold in France and con- verted into French. Thus when peace takes place the Americans may expect to find a sale for their vessels in this Country.

The French are arming a great number of privateers in all their ports. Most of their seamen are at home out of employ from the injury their commerce has sustained by the situation of the west Indias, therefore the privateers as well as the Ships of the Nation will be more easily armed and equipped. Sailors, and all Tradesmen necessary to the Dock yards are going from hense daily to Brest Rochfort and Toulon and they continue to go without discontent.

France may now be said to be perfectly quiet. The funds and Exchange have risen since the declaration of war. The commercial and common opinion seem to give the W. India Colonies up for lost—but they expect the united Netherlands in exchange.

I send you herewith a price current and have the honor to be Sir Your most Obedient Servant   JOSEPH FENWICK

12 feby.

I hope that the united States will preserve a respected neutrality, and that the President will take measures to make their intention manifest for the advantage of their commerce and carrying trade.

RC (DNA: RG 59, CD); at foot of first page: "Thomas Jefferson Esquire Secretary of State Philadelphia"; endorsed by TJ as received 6 May 1793 and so recorded in SJL. Enclosure not found.

From Thomas Pinckney

DEAR SIR   London 10th February 1793

The Masters of the American Vessels in this port homeward bound have applied for passports conformable to our treaties of Commerce; stating that they can not get their insurance done on moderate terms unless they are furnished therewith. I have doubts of the strict right of any person out of America to grant these Passports, but as war has been declared by France against Great Britain and Holland I thought it best to grant the Passports in the best manner I could—if the underwriters at Lloyd's are satisfied with them, I have little doubt but that they will be respected by the French, they may therefore be of some service and I hope will do no harm.

The detention of these Vessels affords me an opportunity of informing you of the loss we have sustained by the death of Mr. Barclay who had gone to Lisbon in order to put his money matters in a train to enable him to proceed to his destination. He was carried off by an illness of two days continuance. Fortunately he had imparted the purport of his business to Colo. Humphreys who took possession of his papers. This gentleman writes that he is well assured that the purport of the business is known to no person but himself and that he has written to you on the Subject. I have requested him to retain the papers in his hands till we have your direction concerning them. A Parcel sent by Mr. Arthur Young to the President is on board of the William Penn. I likewise inclose to You a packet addressed to Mr. Genest the French Minister at Philadelphia, which was transmitted to me by Mr. Marit the day on which he left London.

Although I have written twice on the subject lately yet in order to insure your having the earliest information I must here repeat the misfortune that has happened to me by the loss of my Cypher. On the receipt of your favor of the 1st. Janry. I immediately went to the place where I kept my Cypher, but to my great mortification discovered it to be missing; from the precautions I had taken in having a patent lock of a secure construction fixed to the drawer in which it was kept, in never trusting the key to any person, but particularly from the circumstance of my having lost nothing else from the same drawer, though my most confidential papers and my money, both in cash and bank bills, was constantly kept therein I am induced to think this paper is not stolen. The only way in which I can account for its absence is that when I landed from America I kept about my person certain papers which I was determined should not be seen, among these were Mr. Morris's Cypher, Mr. Barclays and mine which in order to render this packet of as small bulk as possible I took from among other papers of less importance with which they had been originally placed. The three cyphers by this arrangement came together. After my arrival in London I forwarded Mr. Morris's to him, but in making up Mr. Barclays dispatches I think it possible I may have sent both the remaining cyphers to him. I have stated this circumstance to Colonel Humphreys but it may be a considerable time before I shall receive his answer. I have likewise mentioned it to Mr. Morris requesting him to send me a copy of his cypher and to communicate to me by confidential conveyance any important intelligence he shall receive from home of which it may be proper for me to be informed. A sense of[1] the vast advantages I conceive our country may derive from our being able to remain neuter during the present situation of Europe and the possibility that these advantages may be endangered through my misfortune convey sensations to my mind that I cannot describe. You will of course, Sir, adopt such measures as will be best calculated to prevent or remedy the evils I apprehend. I have the honor to be with the utmost respect Dear Sir Your most obed & most humble Servt.   THOMAS PINCKNEY

RC (DNA: RG 59, DD); at foot of text: "The Secretary of State"; endorsed by TJ as received 9 Apr. 1793 and so recorded in SJL. PrC (ScHi: Pinckney Family Papers). Tr (Lb in DNA: RG 59, DD).

Article 25 of the 1778 Treaty of Amity and Commerce between France and the United States stipulated that if one of the contracting parties became involved in war, the ships and vessels of the other "must be furnished with Sea Letters or Passports expressing the name, Property and Bulk of the Ship as also the name and Place of habitation of the Master or Commander of the said Ship, that it may appear thereby, that the Ship really & truely belongs to the Subjects of one of the Parties, which Passport shall be made out and granted according to the Form annexed to this Treaty" (Miller, *Treaties*,

II, 23-4, 28-9). There was a similar article in American treaties of amity and commerce with the Netherlands, Sweden, and Prussia (same, 80-1, 131-2, 172-3). The parcel from ARTHUR YOUNG, the noted English agricultural writer, consisted of a letter to Washington of 17 Jan. 1793 containing numerous queries about various aspects of American farming (DLC: Washington Papers). Washington referred this letter to TJ and then submitted TJ's observations to Young (Washington to TJ, 13 May 1793; TJ to Washington, 28 June 1793; Washington to Young, 1 Sep. 1793, Fitzpatrick, *Writings*, XXXIII, 78-9).

TJ submitted Pinckney's letter to the President on 18 Apr. 1793, and Washington returned it the next day (Washington, *Journal*, 110, 114).

[1] Preceding three words interlined.

From Thomas Pinckney

DEAR SIR   London 10th Febry. 1793
     This will convey to you the assurance of my sincere regret on being
informed by your favor of the 8th. of November that you purpose
relinquishing your situation at the head of the department of State.
I truly lament the loss the public will suffer from your retirement
but I must confess myself selfish enough to feel most sensibly the
apprehension of the removal of those kind attentions and that friendly
mode of conducting business I have experienced in my relation with
your office.
     After many inquiries I have found one of the threshing Machines at
no great distance from this City. I went to the place where it is and
prevailed on the owner to let me see it work. I liked the performance
so well that I have engaged a Mechanic to make a compleat model of
it and hope to send it you in good time for you to have one erected to
thresh out your next crop. With the force of three horses to work it
and three men to feed and attend it from 8 to 16 bushels of Wheat are
threshed by it and other grain in proportion. This account I received
from the owner having only seen a few sheaves threshed.
     I feel some consolation for your loss in Office from the latter part of
your letter wherein you give me cause to hope that I may sometimes be
favord with a line from your retirement, of which I shall be ever happy
to shew a grateful sense, being with sincere respect & attachment Dear
Sir Your faithful & obed Servant   THOMAS PINCKNEY

RC (DLC); at head of text: "(Private)"; at foot of text: "Thomas Jefferson Esqr.";
endorsed by TJ as received 9 Apr. 1793 and so recorded in SJL. PrC (ScHi: Pinckney
Family Papers).

To George Washington

                                                        Feb. 10. 93.
     Th: Jefferson has the honor to submit to the judgment of the Pres-
ident the rough draught of the Report he has prepared on commerce.

RC (DNA: RG 59, MLR); endorsed
by Tobias Lear. Tr (Lb in same, SDC).
Not recorded in SJL.

     The text sent to Washington, in the
hand of George Taylor, Jr., with revisions made by TJ in response to comments he had solicited from Tench Coxe,

is in DLC: TJ Papers, 69: 11981-91;
see also Coxe to TJ, 5 Feb. [1793], and
enclosure. It was received by the President
on 11 Feb. (Washington, *Journal*, 50).
The drafts and final state of the Report
will be printed and discussed at 16 Dec.
1793.

From the Commissioners of the Federal District

SIR   George Town 11th February 1793

We have the pleasure to send you, by Mr. Ellicott, the plat of the Territory, executed according to the President's request. We are happy to inform you, that we have had some explanations with him, which render us better satisfied with him, than we were, at the time of our last. We are, Sir, with respect your mo. Obt Servts

DD: STUART }
DANL. CARROLL } Commrs

RC (DLC); in a clerk's hand except for signatures; endorsed by TJ as received 18 Feb. 1793 and so recorded in SJL. FC (DNA: RG 42, DCLB); place given in dateline: "City of Washington." Enclo-

sure: Andrew Ellicott's corrected plat of the Federal District (not found).

TJ submitted this letter to the President on 19 Feb. 1793, and Washington returned it the next day (Washington, *Journal*, 59, 60).

From Thomas Pinckney

DEAR SIR   Great Cumberland Place London 11 Febry. 1793

Within these few days I have written to you by the Packet, the William Penn and the George Barclay; by the harmony which will convey this to you I have only to inclose a copy of the Passports I have given to our homeward bound Vessels, being the highest evidence we can give of their being American bottoms and as near the Passports required by our treaties of Commerce as the circumstances of their being issued here and the very inaccurate copy (the only one I can immediately procure here) of the form annexed to the treaties enable me to make them. In future I presume none of our Vessels will leave America unprovided but as stragling Vessels from distant parts may continue to drop in here for some time I would submit the propriety of a few Passports properly signed and sealed but in other respects blank being lodged with our Consuls at the different Ports.

To insure the earliest intelligence I must here repeat the information of the loss of my Cypher on which I have written fully in my three last letters and have assigned my reasons why I think it is not stolen but sent through mistake to Mr. Barclay. I must likewise repeat the news of this gentlemans sudden death at Lisbon. Col. Humphreys has taken possession of his Papers. The French declaration of War is in the

Gazettes herewith. With sentiments of sincere respect I remain Dear Sir Your most faithful and obedient Servant   THOMAS PINCKNEY

RC (DNA: RG 59, DD); at foot of text: "The Secretary of State"; endorsed by TJ as received 9 Apr. 1793 and so recorded in SJL. PrC (ScHi: Pinckney Family Papers). Tr (Lb in DNA: RG 59, DD).

Pinckney was unable to send a sample ship passport to TJ until the following month (Pinckney to TJ, 13 Mch. 1793). TJ submitted this letter to the President on 18 Apr. 1793, and Washington returned it the next day (Washington, *Journal*, 110, 114).

To Martha Jefferson Randolph

MY DEAR MARTHA   Phila Feb. 11. 1793.

The hour of post is come and a throng of business allows me only to inform you we are well, and to acknolege the receipt of Mr. Randolph's letter of Jan. 24. With hopes that you are all so accept assurances of[1] constant love to you all from your's my dear most affectionately   TH:J.

RC (NNP); at foot of text: "Mrs. Randolph"; endorsed by Mrs. Randolph. PrC (CSmH). Tr (ViU: Edgehill-Randolph Papers); 19th-century copy.

[1] Here TJ canceled "my."

From the Commissioners of the Federal District

SIR   George Town Feby 12th. 1793

From the short notice we had of Mr. Ellicotts intentions to go to Philadelphia, we omitted sending the Account of the Expences, incurred in running the out lines of the Territory. We now send it, that if it is thought proper, we may be reimbursed.

The original from whence the present Account is taken, was signed by Mr. Ellicott, who, if it be necessary will no doubt sign this.

The specimens of marble, alluded to, in a former letter were sent by Mr. Ellicott. We are Sir, with great respect Your Obt. Svts.

                                              DD: STUART
                                              DANL. CARROLL

RC (DLC); in a clerk's hand except for signatures; endorsed by TJ as received 18 Feb. 1793 and so recorded in SJL. FC (DNA: RG 42, DCLB). Enclosure: "Expences Incured on Surveying the Experimental and Permanent Lines of the District of Columbia," 12 Feb. 1793, listing expenses from 1 Mch. 1791 to 8 Jan.

1793 amounting to $2,986.25 (MS in DLC; in a clerical hand, attested and signed by Stuart and Carroll; endorsed by George Taylor, Jr., as enclosed in the Commissioners to TJ of 12 Feb. 1793).

TJ submitted this letter and its enclosure to the President on 19 Feb. 1793, and Washington returned them the next day (Washington, *Journal*, 59, 60).

From James Currie

DR SIR   Richmond Feby. 12th. 1793

I some time ago took the liberty of writing you a line enquiring into the situation of my debt and suit vs. Dr. Griffin and solliciting your further friendly agency therein. I hope you have received the letter before or at this period and anxiously hope and wish for favorable Accounts of the business; as soon as convenient, and agreeable to yourself, to write me. I have been this forenoon with Messrs. Jnos. Harvie and Marshall and the Act of Congress passd the 10th. of Aug 1790. came on the Carpet in regard to the Officers and Soldiers of the Virginia line on Continental Establishment, to obtain titles to certain Lands laying N West of the River Ohio between the little Miami and Sciota. I beg leave to refer you to the above act and to be (if not asking a favor you cannot grant being, I am afraid, some what troublesome and difficult) fully informed in what Situation I stand in as An Assignee, of Original Grantees, Officers and Soldiers (to the amount 11.400 Acres) on the Continental Establishment therefore, included in the Act alluded to, and which has cost me a Very considerable Sum of money, in the first instance as a purchaser, and then by act of the Virga. Assembly 1 Dr. per 100 Acres over and above what it would cost the Original Grantee to have it secured and added to that the considerable Sums advanced to the Surveyor of the Continental Line when the warrants were delivered here and afterwards answering his Bills drawn upon me on that account. Their is not One Word in the act referred to in regard to the Assignee of any Original Grantee. I wish to know whether it is the intention and meaning of Congress that every or any Assignee shall lose his lands and money, so advanced on that account altogether, or that the Word Assigns means to embrace those who have purchased as I have done anterior to the passing of that Act. Many Others of your friends and acquaintances here Are under the Same Anxiety in regard to this matter as myself being circumstanced precisely as I am on that account. Your friendly and full information on this head, accompanied (if you please) with your best advice how to act, will be regarded as highly obliging by me. We have nothing new here, political or Otherwise Worth Communicating: Only we are likely to have [a?] Winter in the Spring. The 2d. deep Snow is now on the Ground Within this fortnight and is still snowing fast. Wm. Ronald of Powhatan died Suddenly a few days [ago] of a Paralytick Stroke. I never heard whether your a[gent] here did any thing with him in the land business you mentioned when in Virginia. All your friends are well here, Mrs. Currie joins me in our best wishes for your health and happiness. I am Dr Sir Ever most respectfully yr m Ob & Very Hble. Servt   JAMES CURRIE

RC (DLC); several illegible words conjectured in brackets; endorsed by TJ as received 19 Feb. 1793 and so recorded in SJL. In the margin of the first page of text, now torn, TJ wrote lengthwise: "['gran]ting to such person so ori[ginall]y entitled to bounty lands, to his use [and] to the use of his heirs or assigns, or his or their legal representative or [repres]entatives, his her or their heirs [or ass]igns, the lands designated in the said entries [P]rovided &c. that the Secretary at war shall have indorsed thereon [on the patent] that the *grantee* therein named was *originally* entitled to such bounty lands.' Act. Aug. 10. 1790. c.40.§.5." (last pair of brackets in the original; all others supplied).

For a discussion of the 10 Aug. 1790 ACT OF CONGRESS regarding land bounties in the Northwest Territory for Virginia veterans of the Revolutionary War, see John Harvie to TJ, 20 Sep. 1791, and note.

Jefferson's Questions and Observations on the Application of France

I. STATEMENT OF THE AMERICAN DEBT TO FRANCE, [CA. 12 FEB. 1793]

II. THOMAS JEFFERSON TO GEORGE WASHINGTON, 12 FEB. 1793

III. QUESTIONS ON THE APPLICATION OF FRANCE, 12 FEB. 1793

IV. OBSERVATIONS ON THE QUESTIONS ABOUT THE APPLICATION OF FRANCE, 12 FEB. 1793

EDITORIAL NOTE

The four documents printed below illuminate an obscure episode in the Secretary of State's continuing political contest with his great antagonist in the Treasury Department. As Republican critics in the *National Gazette* and the House of Representatives mounted their assault on Alexander Hamilton's management of public finances, this chapter in Jefferson's conflict with the Treasury Secretary quietly played itself out within the confines of the Cabinet. Jefferson's renewed thrust against Hamilton began on 8 Feb. 1793, when the Secretary of State received from French minister Jean Baptiste Ternant a request authorized by the French foreign minister for an advance of 3,000,000 livres on the debt to France for the purchase of provisions in America to relieve a critical food shortage in the war-torn French Republic. Responding to the urgency of this matter, Jefferson on the same day submitted a translation of Ternant's request to Washington, who immediately sent a copy to Hamilton and asked for his advice on it. Hamilton met with Washington on 9 Feb. and recommended that he take no action until the Senate passed the general appropriations bill for the federal government, whereupon the President instructed the Secretary of State to inform Ternant that a decision on his request would soon be forthcoming. Meanwhile, presumably in response to a request Washington made when he met with the Secretary of State that same day, Jefferson tabulated a statement of the American debt to France for his own use in evaluating the feasibility of complying with the French minister's appeal and then prepared the questions and observations about Ternant's application that he submitted with a covering letter to the President on 12 Feb. (Ternant to TJ, 8 Feb. 1793, and note; Tobias Lear to Hamilton, 8 Feb. 1793, Syrett, *Hamilton*, XIV, 16; Washington, *Journal*, 45-6; Documents I-IV below).

Jefferson obviously designed the documents he sent Washington to serve a double purpose. In the first instance, they were intended to secure presidential approval for Ternant's request so that the French minister could begin to purchase provisions in the United States. Perhaps even more significantly, however, they were also calculated to raise doubts in Washington's mind about the probity of Alexander Hamilton's handling of foreign loans contracted in Europe to pay the foreign debt, thus reinforcing the criticisms of the Secretary of the Treasury being made by Republican congressmen in the House of Representatives and by Republican critics in the *National Gazette* (see Editorial Note on Jefferson and the Giles resolutions, at 27 Feb. 1793; Notes on Conversations with Tobias Lear and John Beckley, 7 Apr. 1793).

Instantly recognizing the gravity of Jefferson's insinuation that the United States government might not have enough money on hand to meet the French minister's request because of Hamilton's mishandling of the foreign loans, and his thinly veiled call for a presidential investigation of the Treasury Secretary, Washington turned almost immediately for counsel to Attorney General Edmund Randolph. After examining the three documents Jefferson had sent Washington, Randolph on 14 Feb. suggested a course of action by which the President could satisfy the French minister without appearing to protect the Secretary of the Treasury or to countenance the Secretary of State. He advised Washington to approve the payment to Ternant of only what was due on the French debt at the end of 1792 and to defer a decision on the remainder of the sum requested by the French minister until after Congress had passed the general appropriations bill. In this way, the Attorney General argued, Washington could avoid a presidential examination of the Department of the Treasury, which was bound to reflect adversely on Hamilton in the eyes of his critics, gain time to determine whether the current House inquiry into Hamilton's conduct at the Treasury uncovered any evidence that warranted bringing Jefferson's suspicions to the Secretary's attention, and still enable Ternant to begin buying food supplies for the French government (Randolph to Washington, 14 Feb. 1793, DLC: Washington Papers).

Meanwhile, having learned that $100,000 was on hand in the Treasury from a European loan that had been contracted to help pay the foreign debt, Ternant made an oral request to Jefferson for an initial advance of $100,000 against the American debt to France so that he could begin purchasing provisions. The Secretary of State quickly relayed the appeal to Washington, who approved the payment even before receiving the Attorney General's advice on the documents Jefferson had submitted (Ternant to the Minister of Foreign Affairs, 13 Feb. 1793, Turner, *CFM*, 173-4; Washington, *Journal*, 52; Washington to TJ, 13 Feb. 1793; TJ to Ternant, 14 Feb. 1793).

In the end, Jefferson succeeded in obtaining the advance requested by the French minister, but not in undermining the President's confidence in the Secretary of the Treasury. The Cabinet considered Ternant's application for funds on 25 Feb., six days after the Senate passed the general appropriations bill. At this meeting Randolph and Secretary of War Henry Knox joined Jefferson in advising the President to grant the full amount requested by Ternant, whereas Hamilton only favored the payment of $318,000, the arrears the United States still owed on its debt payments to France for 1792. Washington sided with the majority in the Cabinet and approved Ternant's request in full, but he refrained from launching an executive investigation of the Department of the Treasury or referring to its head the substance of Jefferson's allegations against him. Jefferson immediately notified Ternant of the government's decision on his application (Cabinet Opinions on the Debt to France, 25 Feb. 1793; TJ to Ternant, 25 Feb. 1793; Notes on Cabinet Opinions, 26 Feb. 1793; Washington, *Journal*, 54, 56, 63, 68-9, 70, 74; JS, I, 490). If the Secretary of State had achieved his principal aim, his success was qualified when Ternant evidently took offense at his cautionary request, inspired by the arrival of William Stephens Smith from France with a proposal from the Revolutionary government for securing payment of the entire debt, that he produce authorization to obtain the payment approved by the Cabinet (Notes on Conversations with William Stephens Smith and George Washington, 20 Feb. 1793; TJ to James Monroe, 5 May 1793, and note).

I. Statement of the American Debt to France

[ca. 12 Feb. 1793]

	Loan of 18. Millns.		6. Millns.	10. Millions		Total due in Dollars.	Payments made each year.	Balance unpaid at end of each year.
	Principal payable	Interest payable	Interest payable	Principal payable	Interest payable			
	day of paiment Sep. 3.		day of payment Jan. 1.	day of payment Nov. 5.				
1784.		900,000	300,000		this interest was paid for 1784. & 1785. qu. if for any years since till 1790?			
1785.		900,000	300,000					
1786.	1,500,000	900,000	300,000	1,000,000	400,000			
1787.	1,500,000	900,000	300,000	1,000,000	400,000			
1788.	1,500,000	900,000	300,000	1,000,000	400,000			
1789.	1,500,000	900,000	300,000	1,000,000	400,000			
1790.	1,500,000	900,000	300,000	1,000,000	400,000			
1791.	1,500,000	900,000	300,000	1,000,000	400,000	4,788,333	3,372,717	1,415,616
	9,000,000	7,200,000	2,400,000	5,000,000	2,400,000			
1792.	1,500,000	450,000[1]	300,000	1,000,000	26,000,000 / 200,000 / 3,450,000[2]	635,375	626,500 / 726,000[3]	668,491[4]
1793.	1,500,000	450,000	300,000	1,000,000	160,000[5] / 3,410,000	⟨5,423,708⟩ / 628,008		

Note, if any sums of interest on the 10. Millions were paid after 1785. and before the remittance of Dec. 3. 1790. such sums will be to be deducted from the balance stated to be unpaid, that is to say, they will diminish that balance so much.

D ₶ ƒ
1. = 5.43 = 2.5

₶ D
1. = .1841²⁄₃ = .46

ƒ D ₶
1. = .4 = 2.1719

Hamilton makes par of metals ₶ 1 = .1815[6]

MS (DLC: TJ Papers, 81: 14120); undated; entirely in TJ's hand; with one notation added at a later date (see note 6 below).

TJ prepared this statement of the American debt to France in connection with Document IV below, probably working from a table he had recently received from the French minister (see Enclosure No. 1 listed at Jean Baptiste Ternant to TJ, 9 Feb. 1793). For a discussion of this debt, on which no principal or interest payments were made AFTER 1785. AND BEFORE THE REMITTANCE OF DEC. 3. 1790, see Samuel F. Bemis, "Payment of the French Loans to the United States, 1777-1795," *Current History*, XXIII (1926), 824-31.

[1] First digit written over "2." Second and third digits written over illegible

digits.
[2] Second digit written over "2."
[3] Number and braces apparently inserted subsequently.
[4] Number written over erased seven-digit number beginning with a "1," possibly "1,394,491," a change which the insertion of the second number in the adjacent entry would have dictated (see preceding note).
[5] Number written on top of erased eight-digit number, possibly "29,450,000," the sum of the three numbers above before the last was emended (see note 2 above) and the equivalent in livres of the dollar figure erased in the next column.
[6] Judging from the smaller handwriting, TJ added this notation at a later date, probably around 5 June 1793, when he used this rate of exchange in his opinion on opening a new foreign loan.

II. Thomas Jefferson to George Washington

SIR   Philadelphia Feb. 12. 1793.

According to the desire you expressed the other day when speaking of the application of France for 3. millions of livres, I have the honour to inclose a statement of the Questions which appear to me to enter into the consideration of that application. After putting them on paper, I saw that some developements and observations would be necessary to explain their propriety and connection. These therefore I put down summarily on another paper, also inclosed. As they relate to the affairs of another department, some of these ideas may be wrong. You will be readily able however to correct them from the information you possess, or may procure from that department. Still however, combining and weighing them with the ideas of others, and, most of all, trying them by your own judgment, they may contribute to enable you to form an ultimate decision of what is right; in which decision no man on earth has more entire confidence than he who has the honor to be with sincere and affectionate respect, Dear Sir Your most obedt & most humble servt   TH: JEFFERSON

RC (DLC: Washington Papers); at foot of text: "The President of the U.S."; endorsed by Washington: "The Secrety of State Mr. Jefferson's Opinion on the Appln of France for 3,000000 of Livres 12th. Feby. 1793." PrC (DLC); torn. Recorded in SJPL. Enclosures printed below.

III. Questions on the Application of France

Questions arising on the application of France for 3. millions of
    livres to be sent in Provisions to France.
I.   1. Has the Legislature furnished the money?
      2. is that money in it's place, or has it been withdrawn for other
         purposes?
      3. if it has, should we not take the first proper occasion of rectify-
         ing the transaction by repaying the money to those for whom
         the law provided it?
      4. is the application from France for an *arrearage*, or an *advance*?
      5. have we money any where at command to answer this call?
      6. if we have not, should we not procure it by loan under the act
         for borrowing 12. Millions?
II. Whether and How far we may venture to pay in advance?

Feb. 12. 1793.

MS (DLC: Washington Papers); entirely in TJ's hand. PrC (DLC). Enclosed in
Document II above.

IV. Observations on the Questions about the Application of France

I. The First[1] question is Whether the application of the Executive of
    France for 3. millions of livres = 544,500 Doll. is to be com-
    plied with?
    But to be in condition to solve this, some preliminary Queries
    and Observations are necessary.
  Qu. Has the Legislature done their part, by providing the money?
      The act of 1790. Aug. 4. c.34. §.2. authorized the President
      to borrow 12. Millions of dollars, and appropriated them to
      payment first of arrears and instalments of the *foreign debt*,
      and then to the *residue* of that debt.
      The act of 1790. Aug. 12. c.47. authorized the Presidt. to
      borrow 2,000,000. D. to purchase up the public debt. It
      appropriated certain surplusses of revenue to the same object,
      and put the application of the whole under the direction of
      a board with the approbation of the President.

[177]

19,550,000 florins were borrowed under the authority of the two acts, so that any part of them might be applied to either purpose. But the surplusses of revenue having sufficed for the orders of the Board for the sinking fund they never called for any part of the loans. *The whole therefore of their nett produce may be considered as appropriated to the foreign debt.[2]

The Treasury Report of Jan. 3. 1793. states the application of the whole of this to it's proper purposes except (page. 3) a balance of 5,649,621f–2s–8d which is carried on to page 5. and there stated as equal to 2,304,769D.13. Part[3] of it is stated there to have been applied to purposes[4] to *which it was not[5] applicable by law*[6] part transferred to the Bank for purposes not explained. We must therefore consider it as a loan by one fund to another, to be replaced afterwards.

There follow however in the same page two Items, fairly chargeable on the Foreign fund. So that on the whole the Account stands thus.

	D
Borrowed from the Foreign for the Domestic funds	2,304,769.13

Paid by the Domestic for the	D	
Foreign fund to St. Domingo	726,000	
to foreign officers	191,316.90	917,360.90
Balance in favor of Foreign fund		1,387,452.23

It appears then that the Legislature has furnished and appropriated the money, and if it is not in hand, it is by the act of the Executive departments.

The Executive (into whose hands the money is confided) has the power, tho not the right, to apply it contrary to it's legal appropriations.

Cases may be imagined however where it would be their duty to do this. But they must be cases of *extreme necessity*.

The *paiment of interest to the Domestic creditors* has been mentioned as one of the causes of diverting the foreign fund. But this is not an object of greater necessity than that to which it was legally appropriated.[7] It is taking the money from our *foreign creditors* to pay it to the *domestic ones*, a preference

[*In the margin:*] *The bank law authorised a temporary use of these funds to pay the subscription of the U.S. to that institution. It is not noticed here because the permission was never used. See Treasury Report Feb. 4. pa. 7.

which neither justice, gratitude nor the estimation in which[8] these two descriptions of creditors are held in this country, will justify.

The *payment of the army* and the *daily expences of the government* have been also mentioned as objects of withdrawing this money. These indeed are pressing objects, and might produce that degree of distressing necessity which would be a justification.

But the possibility that our domestic finances can be in such a state of distressing necessity as to oblige us to recur to borrowed money for our daily subsistence, will be *doubted* on the ground of the[9] communications to the last and present session of Congress.

It will be *denied* on the ground of the Treasury Report of Feb. 4. pa. 5. and 13. where it appears that 614,593. Dollars of this money has been drawn away, not to furnish present necessities, but to be put out of our power for 3, 6, and 9 months. It was ready money there; it was payable there; it has been drawn here; and the draughts (which are always a ready money article) have been parted with on long credit. Why?

If it should appear that the Legislature has done their part in furnishing the money for the French nation, and that the Executive departments have applied it to other purposes, then it will certainly be desireable that we get back on legal[10] ground as soon as possible, by pressing on[11] the Domestic funds[12] and availing ourselves of any proper opportunity which may be furnished of replacing the money to the foreign Creditors. Does the present application from the French government furnish such an occasion? If it be an *arrearage*, it does? If it be an *advance*, we shall be more[13] free to calculate our own necessities against theirs. The next Question then is

Are we in *arrears* for instalments or interest with France?

On this head I cannot pretend to accurate information.

From the best I can get at, it would appear that we were in arrears with France at the close of 1792. 668,491. Doll.

But it is possible that certain sums of interest for the years 1786, 7, 8, 9, or some of them, may have been paid. Of this I am not informed.

If they have been all paid,
    it will make a deduction of   294,666 D.
and will reduce the balance
    at the close of 1792 to about   373,825
then add instalments and interest
    payable in 1793. about   <u>628,008</u>
makes the whole sum payable
    now, and shortly to France   1,001,833

Still this statement may be liable to corrections from the treasury, but I think they cannot be considerable.

The next question then is

Have we the money on hand?

The balance remaining in Amster- f D
    dam [see Report Jan. 3. pa. 3.] 407,287 = 166,153
Cash in the Banks and Treasury [see
    Rept. Feb. 4. pa. 13.[14] first 3. articles]   <u>1,567,325</u>
makes the whole sum actually in hand   1,733,478

But[15] if the Treasury from impending calls of more distressing necessity cannot repay to the Foreign fund the sum of 378,347 D. [which with the 166,153. D. in Amsterdam will amount to[16] 544,500. D.][17] in part of what it has borrowed from that then it becomes a question

Whether the President should not instantly set on foot a loan for the 378,347. D.[18] under the authority of the act for borrowing 12. Millions, in order to comply with the application, *if it be an arrearage?*

A famine is probable in France.

The Ministers there will throw the blame[19] on any shoulders to clear their own.

They will shift it[20] on us before the tribunal of their own people.

We have interests[21] which will be injured by this.

Such a charge on their part, may raise one in this country on the Executive.

To what extent this may be pressed, will depend on the[22] events which will happen.

The diversion of this money from it's legal appropriation offers a flaw against the Executive which may place them in the wrong.

II. The Second Principal question is Whether and How far we may undertake to pay in *advance* of the exigible part of our debt to France?

The law authorizes the President to pay the whole, if it can be done on terms advantageous to the U.S.—yet it is left discretionary in him, and the point of *discretion* is the one to be considered.

Before a judgment can be formed as to future payments, it seems necessary to disentangle the Foreign from the Domestic fund, that the balance of the former may be known, and in hand, to be operated on.

This done, we shall see our way clear,[23] to judge When and to What extent to open a new loan.

The annual instalments and interest will, for some years to come, be between 5 and 600,000. Doll.

Perhaps it may be found no bad rule (subject however to the circumstances of the time) to borrow the preceding year what is to be paid the next, and to pay as fast as we borrow. This will keep us part of a year in advance, will be grateful to our creditors, and honorable to ourselves.

Circumstances may arise which may render it expedient to borrow and pay faster, perhaps the whole.

The state and prospect of things in France at the time[24] will materially influence this question.

Feb 12. 1793.

MS (DLC: Washington Papers); entirely in TJ's hand; with note written lengthwise in margin; brackets in original. PrC (DLC); right margin torn and clipped; contains variations noted below. Enclosed in Document II above.

The reports to the House of Representatives by the Secretary of the Treasury of 3 Jan. and 4 Feb. 1793 to which TJ refers in this document are in Syrett, *Hamilton*, XIII, 451-62, 542-79.

[1] Word written over "Main," erased. PrC: word interlined in ink in place of "Main."

[2] TJ inserted a large bracket at the beginning of the preceding paragraph and another at the end of this paragraph to indicate that his marginal note applied to these paragraphs of his observations.

[3] Word written over "The whole," erased. TJ did not make this revision in PrC.

[4] Here TJ canceled "*to none of*" and

added the next word, which he added to the PrC in ink.

[5] Word interlined.

[6] Remainder of sentence interlined.

[7] TJ first wrote "But this is not a case of greater necessity than the legal appropriation" before altering the sentence to read as above.

[8] TJ here canceled "the [necessity?] of."

[9] Remainder of sentence written over "President's speech at the opening of the two last sessions of Congress," erased. In PrC remainder of sentence interlined in ink in place of canceled passage.

[10] Word interlined in place of "safe."

[11] Word interlined.

[12] TJ here separately canceled "to" and "on behalf of any justifiable occasion."

[13] TJ here canceled "at ease."

[14] Page citation interlined.

[15] Word written over "Lastly," erased. PrC: word interlined in ink in place of "Lastly."

[16] The passage "378,347 . . . amount to" is interlined.

¹⁷ "D" reworked from "d" and bracket added by TJ after he interlined the passage described in the preceding note.
¹⁸ This sum and the two words preceding it were finally substituted by TJ after he twice reworked the passage. He initially wrote "[for that?] amount," but then substituted "for 378.347 D. [which with the 166,153 in Amsterdam will amount to the sum asked]" (brackets in original) before expunging the passage and reducing it to read as above. He subsequently incorporated the second revision a few

lines up (see notes 16 and 17 above). The second revision is interlined in ink on the PrC, but TJ neglected to insert the final wording in that text.
¹⁹ Preceding two words interlined in place of "it."
²⁰ Word interlined in place of "the blame."
²¹ Word written over an erased and illegible word.
²² Word interlined.
²³ Word interlined.
²⁴ Preceding three words interlined.

From James Simpson

Gibraltar, 12 Feb. 1793. He encloses two dispatches from Humphreys and a duplicate of one he had forwarded from the late Thomas Barclay some weeks ago by the English ship *Norfolk*, Wilson master, bound for Baltimore. By the death of his "much esteemed Friend" Barclay he has been placed in "a very particular situation," since Barclay after arriving from Lisbon did not take a receipt for the money left with him nor for several packages containing articles left in his charge and intended for the public service in Morocco. Humphreys came to Gibraltar with the first news of Barclay's death and allowed him to be present at the opening of the papers Barclay left with him. The public papers that have been selected and sealed up state exactly the sum he received from Barclay and the details of the packages containing the presents. He has delivered to Humphreys the statements and accounts for immediate transmittal to TJ, and anything else TJ needs will be sent at once. He had been sharing with Barclay news that he collected for Russia regarding the disputed Moroccan succession. Predicting when the matter will be settled is impossible, since other pretenders besides Muleys Ischem and Suliman are quiet now but are certain to press their claims when opportunity permits. In accordance with Humphreys's request, he will advise TJ of any interesting news from Morocco and gladly render any acceptable service in his power. Humphreys sailed for Lisbon on an English ship this morning, with weather that promises a very short passage.

RC (DNA: RG 59, CD); 4 p.; at foot of first page: "The Honble Thomas Jefferson"; endorsed by TJ as received 18 Mch. 1793 and so recorded in SJL. Enclosures: David Humphreys to TJ, 8 Feb. 1793, nos. 66-7. The letter from Barclay has not been identified.

Simpson, the Russian consul at Gibral-

tar, became United States consul at the same place on 29 May 1794 and United States consul for the kingdom of Morocco on 20 May 1796 (JEP, I, 157-8, 209).

TJ submitted this letter to the President on 18 Mch. 1793, and Washington returned it the next day (Washington, *Journal*, 93, 94).

From Fulwar Skipwith

DEAR SIR Boston 12th. Feby. 1793

In order to save the remnant of a little property, which, from the Situation of Martinique, I have been obliged to leave behind me, I am under the necessity of returning once more to that unhappy Island. What the posture of affairs there, may be on my arrival I can hardly hazard a conjecture; should, however, its Inhabitants have been brought under obedience to the reigning Government of France, with Mr. *Rochambeau* as their Governor, I should expect, if not formally acknowledged in my capacity of Consul from the U. States, that my representations would receive the same attention, as if I were—and more especially, could I obtain through you, a letter from the french Minister to Mr. Rochambeau.

Pardon, Sir, the repetition of my letters, and believe, that the peculiar hardship of my Situation, added to a wish not to return among my connexions in Virginia poor and dependent, alone could lead me to importune you.

Accept my most ardent wish for your health and happiness, and assurances, that no one feels a greater zeal for your prosperity than your poor Huml Servant FULWAR SKIPWITH

RC (DLC); endorsed by TJ as received 18 Feb. 1793 and so recorded in SJL.

From George Washington

DEAR SIR Feby. 12th. 1793

Taking it for granted that the several matters enumerated in the Report,[1] herewith returned, are supported by authenticated facts thoroughly investigated—the statement of them, and the observations thereupon, accord with the sentiments of Dear Sir Yours &ca.

GO: WASHINGTON

RC (DLC); at foot of text: "Secretary of State"; with marginal note by TJ (see below); endorsed by TJ as received 12 Feb. 1793. FC (DLC: Washington Papers, Journal of the Proceedings of the President). Recorded in SJPL. The enclosed Report on Commerce is identified in note to TJ to Washington, 10 Feb. 1793.

[1] At the beginning of this word TJ inserted a cross to serve as a key to the note he wrote in the margin: "Report on the commerce of the US."

From Joseph Fay

Dear Sir   Bennington 13th. Feby. 1793

I had this day the honor of your letter of the 27th. Ulto. in which you lay me under too much obligation by your friendly apology for not shewing me that attention which you really meant while I was in Phila. Be assured sir, that I was so far from entertaining a thought of any Neglect on your part, that I felt as tho I had committed an *error* in not paying that attention to you which I conceived due to your Station. Mr. Bradley informed me of your friendly intention which you express in your letter, and I desired Mr. Robinson to be particular in making my best Compliments to you, and to excuse my not Calling on you again, as business required my immeadiate return to N. York. I took the Liberty a few days ago of enclosing you the last Canada papers, and shall send you more as they come to hand. Please to accept the best wishes of your Sincere friend and Servant   JOSEPH FAY

RC (MHi); at foot of text: "Mr Jefferson"; endorsed by TJ as received 1 Mch. 1793 and so recorded in SJL.

Fay must have enclosed the Canadian newspapers in a letter to TJ of 10 Feb. 1793, which is recorded in SJL as received 1 Mch. 1793 but has not been found.

Circular to Foreign Ministers in the United States

Sir   Philadelphia Feby. 13. 1793.

The House of Representatives having referred to me to Report to them, the nature and extent of the privileges and restrictions on the Commerce of the united States with foreign nations, I have accordingly prepared a Report on that subject. Being particularly anxious that it may be exact in matters of fact, I take the liberty of putting into your hands, *privately and informally*, an extract of such as relate to our commerce with your nation in hopes that if you can either enlarge or correct them you will do me that favor. It is safer to suppress an error in its first conception, than to trust to any after correction; and a confidence in your sincere desire to communicate or to reestablish any truths which may contribute to a perfect understanding between our two nations, has induced me to make the present request. I wish it had been in my power to have done this sooner and thereby have obtained the benefit of your having more time to contemplate it: but circumstances have retarded the entire completion of the report till the Congress is approaching its end, which will oblige me to give it in within three or four days. I am with great and sincere esteem Sir Your most obedient & most humble Servant   TH: JEFFERSON

P.S. The Report having been prepared before the late diminution of the duties on our tobacco, that circumstance will be noted in the letter which will cover the Report.

Pr C (DLC); in a clerk's hand, except for signature, postscript, and words at foot of text in TJ's hand; at foot of text in ink: "Circular" and "To Messrs. Ternant Van Berckel Hammond Viar & Jaudenes." FC (Lb in DNA: RG 59, DL); at head of text: "Messrs. Ternant, Van Berckel, Hammond, Viar & Jaudenes." Pr C of RC (DLC); in a clerk's hand, except for signature in ink and words in ink at head and foot of text in TJ's hand; at head of text: "Dup"; at foot of text: "Mr. Van Berkel." Pr C (DLC); in a clerk's hand, except for signature in ink and words in ink at head and foot of text in TJ's hand; at head of text: "Dup."; at foot of text: "Mr. Hammond." Pr C (DLC); in a clerk's hand, except for signature in ink and words in ink at head and foot of text in TJ's hand; at head of text: "Dup"; at foot of text: "Messrs. Viar & Jaudenes." Tr (Lb in PRO: FO 116/3). Tr (same, 5/1). Tr (AHN: Papeles de Estado, legajo 3895); Spanish translation; in Viar's hand, attested by Jaudenes and Viar. The Pr Cs of RCs sent to F. P. Van Berckel, George Hammond, and Josef Ignacio de Viar and Josef de Jaudenes and the Trs derived from them, lack the postscript, indicating that by reason of substance it was only included in the text of the letter sent to Jean Baptiste Ternant. Enclosed in TJ to

George Washington, 14 Feb. 1793. Each of the enclosures printed below was compiled from portions of a draft of the Report on Commerce in the hand of George Taylor, Jr., that included revisions TJ made in light of comments he had solicited from Tench Coxe and that TJ bracketed in pencil with marginal notations—from "No. 1." to "No. 4."—to denote those appertaining to each country. The extracts are printed here in the order TJ designated (DLC: TJ Papers, 69: 11981-91; Coxe to TJ, 5 Feb. [1793], and enclosure). This and the other texts of the Report will be printed at 16 Dec. 1793.

TJ on the following day submitted a text of this letter to Washington, having previously sent the President the "rough draught" of his Report on Commerce and received it back with his approval (Washington, *Journal*, 52; TJ to Washington, 10 Feb. 1793; Washington to TJ, 12 Feb. 1793). The House of Representatives had requested the Secretary of State to prepare this report on 23 Feb. 1791, but TJ did not submit a final version to Congress until 16 Dec. 1793 (JHR, I, 388; TJ to the Speaker of the House of Representatives, 22 Mch. 1792, 20 Feb. 1793, 16 Dec. 1793).

ENCLOSURES

Extracts from Jefferson's Draft Report on Commerce

I
Spain

OF our commercial objects, Spain receives favorably our Bread-stuff, salted Fish, wood, Ships, Tar, Pitch, and Turpentine. On our meals, however, when re-exported to their Colonies, they have lately imposed Duties, of from half a dollar to two dollars the Barrel, the Duties being so proportioned to the current price of their own Flour, as that both together are to make the constant sum of nine Dollars per Barrel.

THEY do not discourage our Rice, Pot and Pearl ash, Salted provisions, or whale Oil: but these Articles, being in small demand at their markets, are carried thither but in a small degree. Their demand for Rice, however, is increasing. Neither Tobacco, nor Indigo are received there.

THEMSELVES and their Colonies are the actual consumers of what they receive from us.

OUR navigation is free with the Kingdom of Spain, foreign Goods being received there in our Ships on the same Conditions as if carried in their own, or in the vessels of the Country of which such Goods are the manufacture or produce.

SPAIN and PORTUGAL refuse, to those parts of America which they govern, all direct intercourse with any people but themselves. The commodities in mutual demand, between them and their neighbors, must be carried to be exchanged in some port of the dominant Country, and the transportation between that and the subject State, must be in a domestic bottom.

PrC (DLC: TJ Papers, 81: 14136); undated; in the hand of George Taylor, Jr. FC (Lb in DNA: RG 59, DL). Tr (AHN: Papeles de Estado, legajo 3895); Spanish translation in Viar's hand, attested by Jaudenes and Viar.

II
France

FRANCE receives favorably our Bread-stuff, Rice, wood, Pot and Pearl ashes.

A duty of 5 Sous the Kental, or nearly $4\frac{1}{2}$ Cents, is paid on our Tar, Pitch and Turpentine. Our whale Oils pay six livres the Kental, and are the only foreign whale oils admitted. Our Indigo pays 5 livres the Kental, their own two and a half. But a difference of quality, still more than a difference of duty prevents it's seeking that market.

SALTED BEEF is received freely for re-exportation; but, if for home-consumption, it pays 5 Livres the Kental. Other salted provisions pay that duty in all cases, and salted fish is made lately to pay the prohibitory one of 20 Livres the Kental.

OUR SHIPS are free to carry thither all foreign goods, which may be carried in their own or any other Vessels, except Tobaccos not of our own growth: and they participate with theirs, the exclusive carriage of our whale oils.

DURING their former government, our Tobacco was under a monopoly, but paid no duties; and our Ships were freely sold in their ports and converted into national bottoms. The first national assembly took from our Ships this privilege. They emancipated Tobacco from it's monopoly, but subjected it to duties of 18 Livres 15 Sous the Kental, carried in their own Vessels, and 25 Livres, carried in ours; a difference more than equal to the freight of the article.

THEY and their Colonies consume what they receive from us.

FRANCE by a standing Law, permits her west India possessions to receive directly our Vegetables, Live Provisions, Horses, wood, Tar, Pitch, and Turpentine, Rice and maize, and prohibits our other Bread stuff: but a suspension of this prohibition having been left in the colonial Legislature, in times of scarcity, it was formerly suspended occasionally, but latterly without interruption.

OUR Fish and salted Provisions (except Pork) are received in their Islands, under a Duty of 3 Colonial Livres the Kental, and our Vessels are as free as their own to carry our Commodities thither, and to bring away Rum and molasses.

PrC (DLC: TJ Papers, 81: 14128-9); undated; in the hand of George Taylor, Jr. FC (Lb in DNA: RG 59, DL).

III
Great Britain

GREAT BRITAIN receives our Pot and Pearl Ashes free, while those of other Nations pay a duty of 2s/3d the Kental. There is an equal distinction in favor of our Bar-iron; of which Article, however, we do not produce enough for our own use. Woods are free, from us, whilst they pay some small duty from other Countries. Indigo and Flaxseed are free, from all Countries. Our Tar and Pitch pay 11d. sterling the Barrel. From other alien Countries they pay about a penny and a third more.

OUR Tobacco, for their own Consumption, pays 1/3 Sterling the pound, custom and Excise, besides heavy expenses of collection; and rice, in the same case, pays 7/4 sterling the hundred-weight, which, rendering it too dear as an Article of common food, it is consequently used in very small quantity.

OUR salted fish, and other salted provisions, except Bacon, are prohibited. Bacon and whale oils are under prohibitory duties: so are our Grains, Meals, and Bread, as to internal Consumption, unless in times of such scarcity as may raise the Price of wheat to 50/. sterling the quarter; and other Grains and meals in proportion.

OUR Ships, though purchased and navigated by their own Subjects, are not permitted to be used; even in their trade with us.

WHILE the Vessels of other nations are secured by standing Laws, which cannot be altered but by the concurrent will of the three Branches of the British legislature, in carrying thither any produce or manufacture of the Country to which they belong, which may be lawfully carried in any Vessels, ours, with the same prohibition of what is foreign, are further prohibited by a standing law (12. Car. 2. 18. §. 3.) from carrying thither all and any of our domestic productions and manufactures. A subsequent Act, indeed, has authorized their Executive to permit the carriage of our own productions in our own bottoms, at it's sole discretion: and the permission has been given from year to year by Proclamation; but subject every moment to be withdrawn on that single Will, in which event, our Vessels having any thing on board, stand interdicted from the Entry of all british ports. The disadvantage of a tenure, which may be so suddenly discontinued, was experienced by our merchants on a late occasion, when an official notification that this law would be strictly enforced, gave them just apprehensions for the fate of their Vessels and cargoes dispatched or destined to the Ports of Great Britain. It was privately believed, indeed, that the Order of that Court went further than their intention, and so we were, afterwards, officially informed: but the embarrassments of the moment were real and great, and the possibility of their renewal lays our commerce to that Country under the same species of discouragement, as to other Countries, where it is regulated by a single Legislator: and the distinction is too remarkable not to be noticed, that our navigation is excluded from the security of fixed Laws, while that security is given to the navigation of others.

OUR Vessels pay in their ports 1/9 Sterling per ton, light and Trinity dues, more than is paid by British Ships, except in the port of London, where they pay the same as British.

THE greater part of what they receive from us, is re-exported to other Countries, under the useless charges of an intermediate deposite and double Voyage.

FROM Tables published in England, and composed, as is said, from the Books of their Custom houses, it appears that of the Indigo imported there in the Years 1773, –4. –5, one third was re-exported, and from a document of Authority, we learn that of the Rice and Tobacco imported there before the War, four fifths were re-exported. We are assured, indeed, that the Quantities sent thither for re-exportation since the war, are considerably diminished: Yet less so than reason and national interest would dictate. The whole of our Grain is re-exported, when wheat is below 50/. the Quarter, and other Grains in proportion.

GREAT BRITAIN admits in her Islands our Vegetables, Live Provisions, Horses, Wood, Tar, Pitch and Turpentine, Rice, and Bread-stuff, by a Proclamation of her Executive limited always to the term of a Year but hitherto renewed from Year to Year. She prohibits our salted fish and other salted Provisions. She does not permit our Vessels to carry thither our own produce. Her Vessels alone, may take it from us, and bring in exchange, Rum, Molasses, Sugar, Coffee, Cocoa-nuts, Ginger, and Pimento. There are, indeed, some freedoms in the Island of Dominica, but under such circumstances as to be little used by us. In the British Continental Colonies, and in Newfoundland, all our productions are prohibited, and our vessels forbidden to enter their ports. Their Governors, however, in times of distress, have power to permit a temporary importation of certain Articles, in their own Bottoms, but not in ours.

OUR citizens cannot reside as merchants or Factors within any of the British Plantations, this being expressly prohibited by the same Statute of 12. Car. 2. c. 18. commonly called their navigation act.

PrC (DLC: TJ Papers, 81: 14131-3); undated; in the hand of George Taylor, Jr. FC (Lb in DNA: RG 59, DL). Tr (Lb in PRO: FO 116/3).

IV
United Netherlands

THE UNITED NETHERLANDS prohibit our pickled Beef and Pork, Meals and Bread of all sorts, and lay a prohibitory duty on Spirits distilled from Grain.

ALL other of our productions are received on varied duties, which may be reckoned on a medium, at about 3 per cent.

They consume but a small proportion of what they receive. The residue is partly forwarded for consumption in the inland parts of Europe, and partly reshipped to other maritime Countries. On the latter portion, they intercept, between us and the consumer so much of the value as is absorbed by the charges attending an intermediate deposit.

FOREIGN goods, except some East India Articles are received in the vessels of any nation.

OUR ships may be sold and naturalized there, with exceptions of one or two privileges, which scarcely lessen their value.

IN the american Possessions of the United Netherlands, and Sweden, our Vessels and produce are received, subject to duties, not so heavy as to have been complained of.

PrC (DLC: TJ Papers, 81: 14130); undated; in the hand of George Taylor, Jr. FC (Lb in DNA: RG 59, DL).

From Gouverneur Morris

DEAR SIR   Paris 13 feby. 1793

My last No: 18 was of the 25th. of January. Since it was written I have had every Reason to beleive that the Execution of Louis XVI has produced on foreign Nations the Effect which I had imagin'd. The War with England exists and it is now proper perhaps to consider it's Consequences to which Effect we must examine the Objects likely to be pursued by England for in this Country notwithstanding the Gasconades a defensive War is prescrib'd by Necessity. Many suppose that the french Colonies will be attack'd but this I do not beleive. It is indeed far from improbable that a british Garrison may be thrown into Martinique but as to St. Domingo it would require more Men than can be spard to defend it and as much Money as it is worth. Besides which there are higher Considerations to be attended to. In one Shape or other this Nation will make a Bankruptcy. The Mode now talk'd of is to pay off the Debt in a Species of Paper Money which shall be receivable for the Sales of confiscated Property and which shall bear no Interest. When once the whole of the Debt shall be fairly afloat the single word Depreciation will settle all Accounts. You will say perhaps that this Measure is unjust but to this I answer that in popular Governments strongly convuls'd it is a sufficient Answer to all Arguments that the Measure proposd is for the public Good. Supposing then the Debt of France thus liquidated She presents a rich Surface coverd with above twenty Millions of People who love War better than Labor. Be the Form of Government what it may Administration will find War abroad necessary to preserve Peace at Home. The Neighbors of France must therefore consider her as a great Power essentially beligerent and they must measure themselves by the Scale of her Force. In this View of the Object to take her Islands is to possess but the paring of her Nails and therefore more serious Efforts must be made. Strange as it may seem, the present War is on the Part of France a War of Empire and if she defends herself she commands the World. I am persuaded that her Enemies consider this as the real State of Things and will therefore bend their Efforts towards a Reduction of her Power and this may be compased in two Ways, either by obliging her to assume a new Burthen of Debt to defray the Expence they are at on her Account or else by a Dismemberment. The latter appears the more certain Mode. In this Case it will I presume be attempted to make the Saome her northern Boundary as far as the Ardennes and then along the Ardennes to the Vosges Mountains to Mount Jura and along Mount Jura to the Alpes. This will throw French Flanders Artois and a Part of Picardy into the Circle of Austrian Flanders which may be erected into an independent State and the Country lying East of the Vosges and Mount Jura may be a Compensation to the Elector Palatine for the Cession of Bavaria. On such a Project, if it exists, the first Question is as to the Means of Execution and these are well prepar'd if the Enemy knows how to make Use of them. Alsace is attach'd to the German Empire and to the Cause of Religion. The only Thing which pleases them in the Revolution is the Abolition of the Tithes and they are as much disgusted by the Banishment of their Priests. I speak here of the Roman Catholicks only. The Sentiments of this People cannot be unknown to the Enemy. As to french Flanders and Artois the Cause of Religion is with them the first Care but as yet they have not had a fair Opportunity to shew themselves because they are awed by the numerous Garrisons spread thro their Country. I think as I mention'd in my last that there exists a Treaty respecting Flanders between England and Austria but I cannot find out the exact Purport. Prussia is (I think) to find her Account in Poland.

As to the Conduct of the War I beleive it to be on the Part of the Enemy as follows. First the maritime Powers will try to cut off all Supplies of Provisions and take France by Famine that is to say excite Revolt among the People by that Strong Lever. Give us again our Bread and our Chains might perhaps be the Language of Paris. I think I can perceive some Seeds already sown to produce that Fruit. It is not improbable that our Vessels bringing Provisions to France may be captured and taken into England the Cargoes paid for by the Government. Secondly Britain may perhaps land a Body of Troops in Normandy with Intention to penetrate to Rouen and cause the royal

Standard to be erected by the French Emigrants. If a large Body of the People flock to it they might come on towards the Capital if not they may move to the left along the Coast to Abbeville and thence form a Junction with the Army acting in Flanders for this Descent if it takes Place is but a secondary Operation; the main Stress will be in Flanders for there the Troops of Britain Holland Hanover Austria and Prussia can be fed from the Ocean at a very cheap Rate and the more their Operations be confind to the Sea Coast the more will it be difficult for France to oppose them because the Provisions must in such Case be carried to an extreme Corner of the Country. Thirdly An Attack of great Energy will be made on the Side of Mayntz in the View to destroy totally the Army under Custine and penetrate into lower Alsace but the real Attack of that çij devant province will I think be on the Side of upper Alsace for which Purpose nothing will be left undone to bring the Swiss into Action as thereby the Fire of War will extend all along from the German Ocean to the Mediterranean Sea. Fourthly the Efforts on the Side of Savoy will probably be confind to the Recovery of that Country and such Diversion as may occupy a Part of the french Army for their own Defense. [Fifthly]¹ on the Side of Provence and Languedoc there will be only a predatory War or War of Alarm such as may encrease the Want of Bread by multiplying the Consumers for I do not beleive in a serious Attempt on either Toulon or Marseilles. Under this Chapter as an incidental Consideration are the Intrigues with the Turk to engage the barbary Powers. I think a British Squadron in the Mediteranean will do more towards this than a dozen Embassadors. Lastly on the Side of Spain there will be I beleive Nothing more than Diversion. How great that may be will depend on Contingencies not within the Compass of human foresight. A Revolution at Court which should dismiss the Queen and her Paramour might give some Energy to the Administration which at present is extremely feeble.

Having thus ran through the Probabilities on the Side of the Adversary I come now to what appear to be the Views of France. You will have seen that the effective Army for 1793 is fixed at Something more than 500000 Men. These they will be able to get together. The recruiting Service goes on well and altho many of the last Year's Men return with Design not to reengage their Places will be supplied so that by the Beginning of June that immense Army (barring Accidents) will be compleated. The main Object at present is to overrun Holland a Thing which might have been effected six Weeks ago but at present I beleive it is not to be done. If the Prussian and Hanoverian Troops advance rapidly it will hardly be attempted. It is however expected that Maestricht may fall as suddenly as Mayntz and perhaps by similar Means. If this should happen it would greatly impede the Confederates and of Course they will exert themselves to prevent that Misfortune. Never were the Moments more precious than they are to both Parties in that Quarter for there the first Blow will be more than Half of the Battle. Should the Enemy become speedily superior in the Field there is Nothing to stop them till he comes to Valenciennes and at every Step he would gather new Force: besides he need not embarrass himself with Convoys because he would soon receive Abundance from the Side of the Sea. As to the Colonies I believe that France will not attempt to defend them and their whole Commerce falls naturally into the Lap of America unless the british prevent it and I think they will find it more convenient to neglect that small Object to pursue the great ones which open themselves to View in this Quarter.

What I have just said leads me very naturally to your Letter of the seventh of November. You had previously instructed me to endeavor to transfer the Negotiation for a new Treaty to America, and if the Revolution of the tenth of August had not taken Place but instead thereof the needful Power and Confidence been restor'd to the Crown I should perhaps have obtain'd what you wish'd as a Mark of Favor and Confidence. Tempora mutantur et nos mutamur in illis. A Change of Circumstances rendered it necessary to change entirely my Conduct so as to produce in one Way what was impracticable in another. As I saw clearly or at least thought I saw that France and England would at length get by the Ears it seem'd best to let them alone untill they should be nearly pitted. When I found this to be the Case I ask'd an Interview with the Minister of foreign Affairs and mention'd to him my Wish that an Exception should be made in the Decree against Emigrants in Favor of those who were in the United States. I told him truly that I wish'd the Alliance between the two Nations to be strictly preservd. I told him with great Frankness that notwithstanding Appearances and the flattering Accounts transmitted by some of his Agents Britain was in my Opinion hostile and an Attempt at Alliance with her idle. He assur'd me that he was of the same Opinion. I then observ'd to him that in such Case there could be no Doubt but Mr. Hammond would exert himself to inculcate the Opinion that our Treaty having been made with the King was void by the Revolution. He said that such an Opinion was absurd. I told him (premising in this Place, that the whole Conversation was inofficial and unauthoriz'd on my Part from Circumstances he was well acquainted with) that my private Sentiments were similar to his but I thought it would be well to evince a Degree of Good Will to America which might prevent disagreable Impressions and had therefore taken the Liberty to suggest the Exception in Favor of Emigrants &ca. Here I left it and chang'd the Conversation. Now I knew well that some of the Leaders here who are in the diplomatic Committee hate me cordially tho it would puzzle them to say why, and I was determin'd rather to turn that Disposition to account than to change it because I see some Advantages to result from it. Thus I contributed indirectly to the Slight put on me by sending out Mr. Genest without mentioning to me a Syllable either of his Mission or his Errand both of which nevertheless I was early and sufficiently inform'd of. The Pompousness of this Embassy could not but excite the Attention of England and my Continuance at Paris notwithstanding the many Reasons which might have induc'd me to leave it would also I thought excite in some Degree their Jealousy and I have good Reason to beleive that this Effect was produc'd. From all this I conjectur'd that both Parties might be brought to bid at your Auction. At any Rate the Thing you wish'd for is done and you can treat in America if you please. Whether you will or not is another Affair. Perhaps you will see that all the Advantages desir'd do already exist that the Acts of the constituent Assembly have in some Measure set us free from our Engagements and that encreasing daily in Power we may make quite as good a Bargain some Time hence as now.

It remains to add a few Words in Reply to what regards me personally in your Letter. I am very happy indeed to find that my Conduct as far as it was known is approv'd of. This is the Summit of my Wish for I candidly acknowlege that the Good Opinion of the Wise and Virtuous is what I prize beyond all earthly Possessions. I have lately debated much within myself what to do. The Path of Life in Paris is no longer strew'd with Roses as you may well imagine, indeed it is extremely painful. I have already given my Reasons for staying here but now the Scene is chang'd and I had Thoughts of making a Tour to the different Consulates: there are however some pretty solid Objections to that Plan, for the present. The next Thing which suggested itself was to hire a Country House, for the Summer Season, in the Neighbourhood. At length, that my leaving the City might give no Offence to any Body, I have bought a Country House in an out of the Way Place where it is not likely that any Armies will pass or repass even should the Enemy penetrate. If I loose the Money paid for it I will put up with the Loss. The Act in itself shews a Disposition freindly to France and as it is between twenty and thirty Miles from Paris I shall be at Hand should Business require my Presence. Mr. Livingston my Secretary will continue in Town unless driven out of it by War or Famine. In this Way I hope to avoid those Accidents which are almost inseperable from the present State of Society and Government and which should they light on the Head of a public Minister might involve Consequences of a disagreable Nature. It is more proper also I conceive to make Arrangements of this Kind in a Moment of Tranquility than when Confusion is awakened into Mischief. In all this my Judgment may err but I can truly say that the Interest of the United States is my sole Object. Time alone can tell whether the Conduct be as right as I know the Intentions to be.

Before I close this Letter I must pray your Indulgence for referring to the enclos'd Copy of what I wrote on the twenty seventh of last Month to the Bankers of the United States in Amsterdam. I make no Comment thereon only as I had no Right to give the order in Question I consider it as of Course that if disapprov'd of I must replace the Money which may be advanc'd on it. This is one of the Cases in which not to act is taking a Part and in which it is vain to ballance. I am with sincere Respect Dr Sir your Obedient Servant

GOUV MORRIS

RC (DNA: RG 59, DD); at head of text: "No. 19"; endorsed by TJ as received 4 May 1793 and so recorded in SJL. FC (Lb in DLC: Gouverneur Morris Papers); with corrections in Morris's hand. Tr (DNA: RG 46, Senate Records, 3d Cong., 1st sess.); copy made early in 1794 by State Department; with omissions. Pr C (DNA: RG 59, MD); more complete text containing page not corresponding to Tr. Tr (Lb in same, DD). Enclosure: Morris to Willink, Van Staphorst & Hubbard, 27 Jan. 1793, stating that he does not believe the assertion made by friends of Lafayette that no provision is made for his comfortable subsistence at Magdeburg, where he is held in close confinement, but in case it is true he directs the firm to instruct its correspondents there to supply up to 10,000 florins for that purpose, noting that "it is not in my Contemplation to furnish the Means of Escape, for I cannot enter into Intrigues of that Sort directly nor indirectly because it is not becoming the Dignity of the United States to act in an underhanded Manner" (Tr in same, DD; Tr in DNA: RG 46, Senate Records, 3d Cong., 1st sess.; Pr C in DNA: RG 59, MD; Tr in Lb in same, DD).

The Spanish foreign minister Manuel Godoy, Duque de la Alcudia, was the sus-

pected PARAMOUR of Queen Maria Luisa (see William Short to TJ, 3 Feb. 1793, and note). TJ's effort to TRANSFER THE NEGOTIATION FOR A NEW TREATY of commerce with France to the United States is discussed in TJ to Gouverneur Morris, 28 Apr. 1792, and note. Owing in part to this effort the French government was sending Edmond Charles Genet to America with instructions to negotiate such a treaty (see Genet to TJ, 23 May 1793). TEMPORA ... ILLIS: "The times have changed and we have changed with them." Although it has not been possible to identify to which of the many French decrees AGAINST EMIGRANTS Morris was referring, he was concerned that the various penalties imposed on émigrés were impeding his efforts to pay the debts owed by the United States government to French officers who had served in America during the Revolutionary War (Morris to Hamilton, 16 Feb. 1793, Syrett, *Hamilton*, XIV, 85-6).

TJ submitted the above letter and its enclosure to the President on 4 May 1793, and Washington returned them two days later (Washington, *Journal*, 128, 129).

On this date Morris also wrote a brief note to TJ enclosing "a Letter which I have receivd from a Monsieur Duchesne with the Copy of my Answer. I know not whether any Use can be made of such Offers but think it right to forward them in order that Government may decide thereon" (RC in DNA: RG 59, DD, at head of text: "No. 20," at foot of text: "Thomas Jefferson Esqr. Secretary of State," endorsed by TJ as received 4 May 1793 and so recorded in SJL; FC in Lb in DLC: Gouverneur Morris Papers; Tr in DNA: RG 46, Senate Records, 3d Cong., 1st sess.; Pr C in DNA: RG 59, MD; Tr in Lb in same, DD). In his lengthy 6 Feb. 1793 letter to Morris, Duchesne, who described himself as "cy devant commissaire du roy prés le tribunal civil de Blois," proposed that, for the tranquility, prosperity, and interest of the United States, the Indians in the Mississippi region could be delivered from the savagery to which they had descended under English control by the establishment of a colony at the mouth of the Mississippi, as well as others among the Indians at existing towns along the river north to the Illinois country, and by the erection of missions, schools, and seminaries run by French émigré priests under the aegis of the bishop of Baltimore with authorization by the United States government (RC, in French, in DNA: RG 59, DD, endorsed by TJ; Trs, in French and English, in DNA: RG 46, Senate Records, 3d Cong., 1st sess.; Pr Cs in DNA: RG 59, MD; Trs, in French and English, in Lb in same, DD). In his 12 Feb. 1793 reply, Morris promised to forward Duchesne's letter to the Secretary of State and noted the likelihood of opposition to his plan from Spain, which contested the right of the United States to navigate the Mississippi (Tr, in French, in same, DD; Trs, in French and English, in DNA: RG 46, Senate Records, 3d Cong., 1st sess.; Pr Cs in DNA: RG 59, MD; Trs, in French and English, in Lb in same, DD).

[1] Word supplied from FC, where it is interlined by Morris in place of "Fourthly." Tr in DD: "Fifthly." RC: "Fourthly."

From Gouverneur Morris

DEAR SIR   Paris 13 feby. 1793

I am to acknowlege yours of the seventh of last November which I cannot do without expressing my Concern at a Resolution which will deprive the United States of an able and faithful Servant. Since you declare your determination to be unalterable it would be idle to offer Reasons to dissuade you besides which it seems probable that e'er this can arrive you will have acted. But were it otherwise I know not whether in my present Feelings I could attempt to divert from the Sweets of private and domestic Life one who has so long been deprivd of them. Every Day makes me contemplate with additional Pleasure the Prospect of Retirement and that Tranquility whose Loss is not perhaps to be compensated by any Thing else. If however the Die be not cast permit me to express one Wish. It is that you would hold your Place untill a Successor can be fixed on whom you think fully equal to the Duties of the Office. This may perhaps be a painful Sacrifice but it is one which I hope you will make to the Interests of our Country in the present very critical Moment. If you shall have quit or persist in doing it give me I pray your Opinions and Advice. These so long as I stay here will be very useful to me and I trust not quite useless to the United States. In whatever Situation you may be beleive I pray you in that respectful Esteem with which I am yours

Gouv Morris

RC (DLC); at head of text: *"private"*; at foot of text: "Thomas Jefferson Esqr"; endorsed by TJ as received 4 May 1793 and so recorded in SJL. FC (Lb in DLC: Gouverneur Morris Papers).

From William G. Sydnor

SIR   [before 13 Feb. 1793]

The inclosed from Mr Thomas Randolph jr will explain to you my wishes and situation in The army of The United States, altho' I confess I have no right to expect Promotion, (nor do I wish it) until I have served sufficiently to gain a proper Knowledge in the Military line to entitle me to a superior rank. Yet wishing to take advantage of any Vacancy which may happen, I have Forwarded the letter alluded to above to you, and sundry others differently directed tending in some measure to the same effect. My wish to remain in the Army induces me to hope promotion, and a consciousness that no endeavour of mine to merit the Recommendations herewith sent, makes me hope to receive every benefit from the same. I have the honor to be with every sentiment of Respect Yr Ob Servt.   WM. G Sydnor

RC (ViW: Tucker-Coleman Collection); undated; at head of text: "The honle. Thomas Jefferson Secretary of State Philadelphia"; endorsed by TJ as received 13 Feb. 1793 and so recorded in SJL. Enclosure: Thomas Mann Randolph, Jr., to TJ, 28 Dec. 1792. Other enclosures not identified.

Sergeant Sydnor failed to attain the promotion he sought (JEP, passim).

From George Washington

SIR   Philadelphia Feb. 13th. 1793.

Arrangements may be made with the Secretary of the Treasury for the immediate payment of One hundred thousand dollars on account of the debt due from the United States to France.

The statement of the Account between these Countries will, it is expected, be compleated tomorrow; and the balance up to the last of December be ascertained; when the propriety of further, and to what extent advances shall be made will be the subject of further consideration.

The Secretary of the Treasury knows of no settlement between Mr.

Jay and Mr. Otto in the year 1789; and conceives if such did take place the document respecting it must be in the Secretary of States Office.   Go: WASHINGTON

RC (DLC); endorsed by TJ as received 13 Feb. 1793. FC (Lb in DNA: RG 59, SDC). Recorded in SJPL.

Jean Baptiste Ternant's request for an

advance of $100,000 on the DEBT DUE FROM THE UNITED STATES TO FRANCE is discussed in the Editorial Note on Jefferson's questions and observations on the application of France, at 12 Feb. 1793.

From Benjamin Hawkins

Senate Chamber 14 Feby. 1793

Mr. Strong
Mr. Rutherford
Mr. Hawkins   The committee on the enclosed bill reported verbally in substance as follows. That the line to be run would be exparte, as the President of the United States was authorized to appoint the officers to be employed in running the line, although such line would have affected the jurisdiction of the States of Virginia and Kentuckey, and perhaps, would have affected the property of their citizens. That the inhabitants of the territory south of the Ohio, being now entitled by their numbers to a Legislature, should be left to establish their boundary with the adjoining States, that any interferance on the part of the general government is unnecessary, and that the expense of running the line ought to be paid by the States particularly interested. Yours sincerely   BENJAMIN HAWKINS

RC (DLC); at foot of text: "Mr Jefferson"; endorsed by TJ. Enclosure: *An Act for determining the Northern Boundary of the Territory ceded to the United States, by the State of North-Carolina* [Philadelphia, 1793] (printed bill in Vi: Executive Papers; filed with TJ to Henry Lee, 11 Mch. 1793).

The ENCLOSED BILL was inspired by a 9 Nov. 1792 message from President Washington to Congress transmitting a letter and enclosures from TJ on the subject of the Southwest Territory's unsettled northern boundary with Virginia and Kentucky and recommending that the legislature take this matter under consideration (see TJ to Washington, 2 Nov. 1792, and note). In response the House of Rep-

resentatives appointed a committee on 28 Nov. 1792 to prepare a bill requesting and authorizing the President, with the concurrence of Virginia and Kentucky, to have this boundary surveyed at federal expense. The committee submittted a bill to this effect on 3 Dec. 1792 that was passed by the House and sent to the Senate on 18 Jan. 1793. Three days later the Senate referred the bill to a committee consisting of John Rutherford of New Jersey, Benjamin Hawkins of North Carolina, and Caleb Strong of Massachusetts, whose report on the measure, described above by Hawkins and REPORTED VERBALLY to the Senate by Rutherford on 8 Feb. 1793, led to its rejection on the same day by the upper house (JHR, I, 629, 631, 632, 674-5, 697; JS, I, 473, 482).

To Jean Baptiste Ternant

SIR   Philadelphia Feb. 14. 1793

It will require some few days yet to estimate the probable calls which may come on the treasury, and the means of answering them; till which is done a final answer can not be given to your application for the three millions of livres. But in the mean time that your purchases of provision may be begun, arrangements may be made with the Secretary of the Treasury for the immediate payment of one hundred thousand dollars on account of our debt to France. I can assure you that we[1] have every possible wish and disposition to find ourselves able to comply with the residue of the application, and as early as possible. I have the honour to be with great respect & esteem Sir Your most obedt. humble servt

TH: JEFFERSON

RC (AMAE: CPEU, Supplément, xx); addressed: "M. de Ternant Minister Plen. of France." PrC (DLC). FC (Lb in DNA: RG 59, DL). Tr (AMAE: CPEU, xxxvii); French translation.

Ternant's APPLICATION FOR THE THREE

MILLIONS OF LIVRES is discussed in the Editorial Note on Jefferson's questions and observations on the application of France, at 12 Feb. 1793.

[1] Here TJ canceled "shall."

To George Washington

Feb. 14. 93.

Th: Jefferson with his respects to the President sends him a letter from Mr. Short.

Also a circular letter he has written to the foreign ministers at Philadelphia, in order to place his Report on commerce on safe ground as to them.

Also a copy of the statement of the French debt as furnished me by Mr. Ternant.[1]

RC (DNA: RG 59, MLR); dateline at foot of text; addressed: "The President of the U.S."; endorsed by Tobias Lear, whose notation at foot of page—"a letr ⟨from⟩ To Mr. Ellicott"—in fact pertains to TJ's other letter of this date to Washington. Tr (Lb in same, SDC). Not recorded in SJL. Enclosures: (1) William

Short to TJ, 16 Nov. 1792. (2) Circular to Foreign Ministers in the United States, 13 Feb. 1793. (3) Enclosures to Jean Baptiste Ternant to TJ, 9 Feb. 1793.

[1] Sentence interlined above dateline at foot of text.

To George Washington

Feb. 14. 93.

Th: Jefferson presents his respects to the President and returns him the letters from the Commissioners. He does not recollect whether he shewed him his letter to Ellicot[1] the only one he has written to him since last Summer. Lest he should not have done it he now incloses it. He thinks it impossible that any thing in that could have produced ill humour in Ellicot towards the Commissioners and if the President should be of the same opinion, and could recollect it in answering Dr. Stewart, he would be glad he should be informed so.

Th:J. having a petition referred to him by the House of Representatives which renders it necessary for him to examine a little the extent of the claims of the 6. nations Southwardly, in former times, he will thank the President for an hour's use of Evans's analysis.

RC (DNA: RG 59, MLR); addressed: "The President of the U.S."; endorsed by Tobias Lear. Tr (Lb in same, SDC). Not recorded in SJL. Enclosures: (1) TJ to Andrew Ellicott, 15 Jan. 1793. (2) Commissioners of the Federal District to Washington, 8 Feb. 1793, deferring the question of compensation for their services, stating that they would be unable to continue Ellicott as surveyor if he persisted in his refusal to give an account of his work until May, indicating the need for more money from the second installment of the Virginia grant for the Federal District to expedite their work, and suggesting that Washington obtain payment of the third Maryland installment for that purpose (DNA: RG 42, DCLB). (3) David Stuart to Washington, 8 Feb. 1793 (not found, but see note below).

TJ's concern over his enclosed LETTER TO ELLICOT was prompted by David Stuart's letter to Washington of 8 Feb. 1793,

which has not been found but apparently expressed the belief that the Secretary of State had somehow encouraged Ellicott's complaints against the Commissioners of the Federal District. Stuart reiterated the complaint to the President ten days later (Stuart to Washington, 18 Feb. 1793, DLC: Washington Papers; for the sequel, see TJ to Washington, 4 Mch. 1793, and note). The PETITION referred to TJ by the House of Representatives concerned the case of John Rogers, on which see Report on the Petition of John Rogers, 16 Feb. 1793. EVANS'S ANALYSIS: Lewis Evans, *Geographical, Historical, Political, Philosophical and Mechanical Essays. The First, Containing an Analysis of a General Map of the Middle British Colonies in America; And of the Country of the Confederate Indians* . . . (Philadelphia, 1755). See Sowerby, No. 3850.

[1] Remainder of sentence interlined.

From George Hammond

SIR   Philadelphia 15 February 1793

I had not the honor of receiving your letter of the 13th curt., until yesterday afternoon. This circumstance, added to the near approach of the period, at which you propose giving in your Report to the House of

Representatives, renders it expedient, on my part, to decline entering into any general examination of the facts advanced in the extract you have transmitted to me, or of the inferences which you have deduced from them. Yet having prepared some time ago a statement of the difference of duties on particular articles imported into Great Britain from the United States or from other foreign parts, I deem it not altogether improper to communicate this statement to you, as being more minute and definite with respect to the principle and extent of the discriminations in question than the brief enumeration which you have specified in the commencement of the extract from your report.

Of one assertion however, Sir, it is incumbent upon me to take some notice, as it refers to a transaction in which I was a party principally concerned and some particulars of which you appear to have either overlooked or forgotten. In reasoning upon the King's proclamation, regulating the commercial intercourse between Great Britain and this country, you advert to an *official notification*, which I communicated to you in the month of April last. You then add, "It was *privately* believed, indeed, that the order of that court went further than their intention, and so we were, *afterwards*, officially informed." You will, I hope, Sir, recollect that in delivering to you that notification, I accompanied it with a *formal* assurance of my conviction that "it was not intended to militate against the order of the King in Council, regulating the commercial intercourse between the two countries." In that assurance the members of the executive government of the United States reposed entire confidence; under their sanction it was announced *to the public*, and in consequence thereof I have reason to imagine (from the best information I can collect) that the commerce of this country sustained no embarrassment or obstruction whatsoever. Whilst I am upon this subject, I must also recall to your recollection that, in your letter to the President of the 13th. April, which he communicated to the two houses of the legislature, you say, "The Minister moreover assured me verbally that he would immediately write to his court for an explanation, and in the mean time is of opinion that the usual intercourse of commerce between the two countries (Jersey and Guernsey excepted) need not be suspended." That explanation, approving the conduct I had held, and stating the views of his Majesty's government in regard to the notification alluded to, I received from my Court whilst I was at New York, and transmitted to you by letter on the 3rd. of August last. And I must now beg leave to repeat the enquiry which I addressed to you verbally about six weeks ago: viz. whether you ever received that letter and whether you ever laid it before the two houses of the legislature, which (from the passage in your letter to the President above-cited) might be induced to expect some ulterior communication from me on so important a subject? I have the honor to be with great respect, Sir, Your most obedient humble servant

GEO. HAMMOND

RC (DNA: RG 59, NL); in Edward Thornton's hand, signed by Hammond; at foot of first page: "Mr Jefferson"; endorsed by TJ as received 15 Feb. 1793 and so recorded in SJL. FC (Lb in PRO: FO 116/3). Tr (same, 115/2). Tr (same, 5/1). Tr (Lb in DNA: RG 59, NL).

Enclosed in TJ to George Washington, 16 Feb. 1793.

In regard to the subject of the KING'S PROCLAMATION of December 1783, see Hammond to TJ, 11 Apr. 1792, and note.

ENCLOSURE

Table of British Import Duties

Table
shewing the discrimination of duties upon certain articles imported into Great Britain from the United States and from all other foreign countries. Column 1st. marks the duties on importations, from the United States or British colonies in vessels belonging to the citizens of the United States or to British subjects. Column 2nd. duties on importations from other foreign countries in British vessels. Column 3rd. duties on importations from foreign countries in vessels belonging to subjects of those countries.

	Col. 1	Col. 2	Col. 3
Pot & Pearl Ashes per cwt.	free	2/3	2/3
Tar & Pitch per 12 Barrels of $31\frac{1}{2}$ Galls:	11	$12/4\frac{1}{2}$	13/1
Turpentine per cwt.	2/3	12/9	12/9
Rosin per cwt.	1/6	2/3	2/4
Bar iron per ton	free		
Do. of Ireland £1.10.10			
Do. of Russia		56/2	69/1
Do. not of Ireland or Russia		56/2	67/2
Pig iron per ton	free	5/6	5/6
Rice per cwt.	7/4		
Do. by East India Company		8/10	
Tobacco per lb.	1/3	3/6	3/6
Beaver Skins per piece	/1.	$/8\frac{1}{4}$	$/8\frac{1}{4}$
Beech Boards under 15 feet in length per 120	free	26/5	27/6
Do. above Do. per Do.	free	52/10	53/11
Oak Boards under Do. per Do.	free	52/10	55/
Do. above Do. per Do.	free	105/8	107/8
Oak Plank per 50 Cubic feet	free	19/10	20/8

Oak Timber per Do.	free	9/11	10/4
All timber not otherwise enumerated per Do.	free	6/8	6/10
Deals under 20 feet in length nor exceeding 3¼ inches in thickness per 120	free	53/	54/10
Do. above 20 feet & exceeding 3¼ inches per Do.	free	106/	107/5
Do. above 20 feet nor exceeding 4 inches per Do.	free	119/	123/2
Do. above Do. & exceeding 4 inches per Do.	free	238	242/2
Barrel Staves of various dimensions per 120	free		
Do. in Col. 2. from 4/, 7/6, 10/, 15/, 17/6, 20/, 30/, a 60/			
Do. in Col. 3. from 4/1, 7/7, 10/1, 15/1, 17/7, 20/2, 30/3, a 60/3			
Oars per 120	free	39/8	41/3
Handspikes under 7 feet per 120	free	6/8	6/11
Do. above Do. per Do.	free	13/4	13/7
Masts from 6 to 8 inches diameter	1/1½	1/1½	1/2
Do. from 8 to 12 Do.	3/4	3/4	3/6
Do. above 12	6/8	6/8	6/11
Woods generally (except Yards, Masts & Bowsprits)	free	Various	high duties

Indigo } free generally
Flaxseed }

Snuff per lb. from United States
  or British Colonies   1/6
Do. from the East Indies   3/3
Do. from any other place   2/2

GEO. HAMMOND

MS (DNA: RG 59, NL); undated; in Edward Thornton's hand, signed by Hammond. FC (Lb in PRO: FO 116/3). Tr (Lb in DNA: RG 59, NL).

Memorandum on Consuls and Consular Appointments

Consuls remaining in office. Feb. 15. 1793.
Marseilles. Stephan Cathalan of France. vice-consul
Bordeaux. Joseph Fenwick. of Maryland. Consul
Havre. M. de la Motte of France. vice consul

London. Joshua Johnson. of Maryland. Consul. He refuses to give
    bond.
                qu. therefore if a successor must be appointed?
Bristol. Elias Vanderhorst of S. Carolina. Consul

Liverpool. James Maury of Virginia. Consul.
Pool. Thomas Auldjo of Gr. Britain. vice consul.

Lisbon. Edward Church. of Massachusets. Consul.
Madeira. John Marsden Pintard of New York. Consul.
Fayal. John Street of Fayal. vice consul.

Copenhagen. Hans Rodolph Saabye of Denmark. Consul.
Morocco. Thomas Barclay of Pensylva. Consul.
Calcutta. Benjamin Joy. of Massachusets. Consul.
Canton. Samuel Shaw. of Massachusets. Consul.
Martinique. Fulwar Skipwith of Virginia. Consul.

Consuls &c. who have resigned or abandoned their Consulates.
Nantes. Burrel Carnes. resigned.
Rouen. Nathaniel Barrett. abandoned, and settled at New York.
Dublin. William Knox. resigned.
St. Domingo. Sylvanus Bourne. resigned.[1]
Santa Cruz. James Yard. resigned.
Surrinam. Ebenezer Brush. abandoned.

	Candidates for appointments.
Havre.	Nathaniel Cutting of Massachusets to be Consul.
Falmouth.	Edward Fox. of Gr. Britain. to be Consul. Our ships often touch at Falmouth for orders, and have occasion for patronage to prevent their being forced to enter. A safe person there also for taking care of letters, is important. Fox recommended by Mr. Morris and Mr. Meade.
Cadiz.	Joseph Yznardi. of Spain. to be Consul. One very much wanting both for commerce and intelligence. He is recommended by Mr. Harison (Auditor) and N. Cutting. See the letter of the latter. He speaks English very well, and appears to Th:J. to be sensible and discreet.
Alicant.	Robert Montgomery. of ___ to be Consul.[2] This candidate has been very pressing for many years. His zeal has prompted him to try to serve us with the Barbary states, where however he has done us more harm than good. His character and circumstances are understood to be good, and an appointment at Barcelona becomes less indifferent since Mr. Barclay's information of the number of our vessels which now venture into the Straights.

Teneriffe.[3]

Hamburg.   John Parish of Gr. Britain. to be Consul. He was formerly appointed viceconsul, but would not accept that. A consul at that port is of some importance to our commerce; and may be so to our mint, as the convenient port for obtaining copper from Sweden.

Santa Cruz.   M. Furant. of   to be Consul. Mentioned by Mr. Yard.

Henry Cooper.   Recommended by John Wilcocks. See his letter.

St. Eustatius.   David Matthew Clarkson. Pennsylva. to be Consul. Recommended by his father in Philadelphia and by a Mr. Godin, whose letter is to be noted.

William Stevenson. of New Jersey. to be do. Recommended by Mr. Wilcocks, Mr. Gouverneur, Mr. Yard, and objected to by Godin.

Curaçoa.   Benjamin Hamnell Philips of Pensylvania. to be Consul. Strongly recommended by Messrs. Meade, Wolne, Vaughan, Nesbitt, Pickering and others. See the letters.   Th: JEFFERSON

Philadelphia. Feb. 15. 1793.

PrC (DLC). Entry in SJPL: "Consuls."

TJ prepared this document for the use of the President, to whom he submitted it this day. Washington returned it on the 16th, and two days later TJ prepared another memorandum for the President in which he recommended the appointment of consuls for all the places listed above except Tenerife (Washington, *Journal*, 55; Memorandum on Consuls Recommended for Appointment, 18 Feb. 1793, and note).

Nathaniel Cutting's letter to TJ recommending Joseph Yznardi is dated 30 Jan. 1793. Concerning the candidacy of Furant, see note to James Monroe to TJ, 3 Jan. 1793. The letter from John Wilcocks to TJ on behalf of Henry Cooper is dated 17 Sep. 1792 (Tr in DLC: Washington Papers, Applications for Office; in Wilcocks's hand and signed by him; at foot of text: "(Copy) Original forwarded to Monticello"; endorsed by TJ as received 6 Oct. 1792 and so recorded in SJL). P. N. Godin's 28 June 1791 letter to

Robert Morris on the subject of a consular appointment for St. Eustatius is in Vol. 20: 581-2. Isaac Gouverneur's letter of recommendation in favor of William Stevenson was enclosed in Richard Harrison to TJ, 28 Nov. 1792. James Yard's 27 Dec. 1792 letter to James Monroe on Stevenson's behalf (DLC: Washington Papers, Applications for Office) was enclosed in Monroe to TJ, 3 Jan. 1793. George Meade's letter to TJ in favor of Benjamin Hamnell Philips is dated 24 Jan. 1792. The other letters of recommendation mentioned by TJ have not been found.

[1] Beneath this line TJ canceled "Martinique Fulwar Skipwith resigned."
[2] Preceding three words interlined.
[3] Here TJ canceled "John Culnan. of   to be Consul. Recommended by John and James Moylan and others. See the papers. There is rather more reason for than against the appointment, tho it is not very important." Culnan was not nominated and confirmed as consul at Tenerife until May 1794 (JEP, I, 158).

From Josef Ignacio de Viar and Josef de Jaudenes

SIR   Philadelphia Feb. 15. 1793.

We have received with due acknolegement your favor of the 13th. inst. and from it a new proof of your sincere desire and good disposition to contribute to the reciprocal advantages of Spain and the U.S.

Moved with equal zeal, and encouraged by your very polite attention, we have examined with all possible care the Statement which you have been pleased to inclose to us, relative to the extent of the privileges and restrictions in the commerce of the US. with Spain.

In the short interval which this occasion has furnished us, those objects only have occurred to us which, confiding in your indulgence, we take the liberty to mention, to wit.

If the Canary islands (of which the statement makes no mention) are understood to be comprehended under the generic name of Spain, the remark is taken away. Nevertheless it would enhance the sum of advantages, to call the attention to them separately, in considering the conditions of commerce, good and bad, which the US. carry on with them without restraint.

If they are understood to be comprehended under the title of America, or the Colonies, in such case it would be proper to except them, as we know that the commerce with them is not subject to the same restrictions.

Also it may not be superfluous to make some mention on the subject of the island of Trinidad, with which these states carry on some lucrative commerce.

Nor would it be less proper, in mentioning the duty lately imposed in Spain on flour re-exported to the colonies, to insert some expression giving to understand that the duty is general on all foreign flours. It might soften the impression, which might otherwise be made, that this duty is only directed against the produce of the US: to whom, if prejudice accrues, it is only indirect; the same calculation taking place which you make of the price which the barrel of flour may bear when exported to the colonies. This loss falls on the Spaniard, and not on the American.

We submit the preceding observations to your better judgment, with the same liberality with which you have been pleased to confide to us your statement in order that if they may contribute to the favorable advancement of the object you will have the goodness to give them a place in the draught, and if you find them superfluous, you will pass them by with frankness.

[205]

We are sorry that the time is not less limited, as perhaps the receipt of further advice from our court, and some private informations might apprise us more fully of the object, and suggest to us circumstances which on the sudden we do not know, or do not recollect. Pardon the liberty we have taken and be assured that we are with the most sincere good will & profound respect, Sir, your most obedt & most humble servts.   JOSEPH IGNACIO DE VIAR   JOSEPH DE JAUDENES

Tr (DNA: RG 59, NL); entirely in TJ's hand; at head of text: "Translation." PrC (MoSHi: Bixby Collection). RC (DNA: RG 59, NL); in Spanish; in Viar's hand, signed by Viar and Jaudenes; at foot of text: "Sor. Don Thomas Jefferson &ca. &ca"; endorsed by TJ as received 16 Feb. 1793 and so recorded in SJL. Tr (AHN: Papeles de Estado, legajo 3895); in Spanish; in Jaudenes's hand, attested by Jaudenes and Viar.

To George Hammond

SIR   Philadelphia Feb. 16. 1793.

I have duly recieved your letter of yesterday with the statement of the duties payable on articles imported into Great Britain. The Object of the Report, from which I had communicated some extracts to you, not requiring a minute detail of the several duties on every article, in every country, I had presented both articles and duties in groups, and in general terms, conveying information sufficiently accurate for the Object. And I have the satisfaction[1] to find, on reexamining the expressions in the Report, that they correspond with your statement as nearly as generals can with particulars.[2] The differences which any nation makes between our commodities and those of other countries, whether favorable or unfavorable to us, were proper to be noted: but they were subordinate to the more important questions What countries *consume* most of our produce? exact the lightest duties? and leave to us the most favorable balance?

You seem to think that in the mention made of your *official* communication of Apr. 11. 1792.[3] that the clause in the Navigation act (prohibiting our own produce to be carried in our own vessels into the British European dominions) would be strictly inforced in future, and the *private belief* expressed at the same time that the intention of that court did not go so far, that the latter terms are not sufficiently accurate. About the fact it is impossible we should differ, because it is a written one. The only difference then must be a merely verbal one. For thus stands the fact.[4] In your letter of Apr. 11. you say you have recieved by a circular dispatch from your court directions to inform this government that it had been determined in future strictly

[206]

to inforce this clause of the navigation act. This I considered as an *official* notification. In your answer of Apr. 12. to my request of explanation, you say 'in answer to your letter of this day, I have the honor of observing that I have no other instructions upon the subject of my communication than such as are contained in the circular dispatch of which I stated the purport in my letter dated yesterday. I have however no difficulty in assuring you that the result of my *personal conviction* is that the determination of his Majesty's government to inforce the clause of the act &c. is not intended to militate against the Proclamation &c.' This *personal conviction* is expressed in the Report as a *private belief* in contradistinction to the *official* declaration. In your letter of yesterday you chose to call it 'a formal assurance of your conviction.' As I am not scrupulous about words, when they are once explained, I feel no difficulty in substituting, in the Report, your own words '*personal conviction*' for those of '*private belief*' which I had thought equivalent. I cannot indeed insert that it was a *formal* assurance, lest some readers might confound this with an *official* one, without reflecting that you could not mean to give[5] *official* assurance that the clause would be enforced, and *official* assurance at the same time of your personal conviction that it would not be enforced.

I had the honor to acknowledge verbally the receipt of your letter of the 3d. of August, when you did me that of making the enquiry verbally about six weeks ago:[6] and I beg leave to assure you that I am with due respect, Sir your most obedt. & most humble servt

TH: JEFFERSON

PrC (DLC); at foot of text: "Mr. Hammond M. P. of G. Britain." PrC of Dft (DLC); at head of text in ink: "not sent"; enclosed in TJ to George Washington, 16 Feb. 1793, and subsequently amended (see below); recorded in SJPL as "not sent." FC (Lb in DNA: RG 59, DL). Tr (Lb in PRO: FO 116/3). Tr (same, 5/1). Only the most significant differences between the PrC and the PrC of Dft are recorded below.

TJ this day submitted the Dft of this letter to Washington, who advised him to omit his reply to Hammond's query as to whether the British minister's letter of 3 Aug. 1792 had been laid before Congress "because it was a request which Mr. H. had no right to make." TJ accepted the President's advice and amended the letter accordingly (Washington, *Journal*, 55; see also note 6 below). In fact Hammond's let-

ter had not been submitted to Congress. For an explanation of the dispute that had arisen over the announcement of the British government's intention to enforce the CLAUSE IN THE NAVIGATION ACT, see Hammond to TJ, 11 Apr. 1792, and note.

[1] Preceding three words interlined in place of "am happy" in PrC of Dft.
[2] Remainder of paragraph not in PrC of Dft.
[3] All the words from this point to the first comma are within parentheses in PrC of Dft.
[4] This sentence not in PrC of Dft.
[5] PrC of Dft: "could not give."
[6] Here the PrC of Dft contains the following passage: "But to the remaining interrogatory Whether I 'ever laid it before the two houses of legislature'? I will take my answer from an authority to which I am sure you will subscribe, and which is

so replete with good sense, and it's terms so well chosen, that I need seek nothing out of it. 'I must therefore observe to you, Sir, that in my quality of Secretary of state to the United States, I cannot receive any communication on the part of a foreign minister but for the purpose of laying it before the President, and of taking his orders upon it; and that the deliberations of the two houses of legislature, as well as the communications, which it may please the President to make to them, relative to the affairs of this country, are objects entirely foreign from all diplomatic correspondence, and upon which it is impossible for me to enter into any discussion whatever with the ministers of other countries.' I have the honor to be with great consideration Sir your most obedient & most humble servt." In the margin alongside this passage TJ wrote lengthwise: "The Presidt. thought that it would be [. . .], to avoid irritation."

Notes on Levees and Assumption

Feb. 16. 93. E.R. tells J. Mad. and myself a curious fact which he had from Lear. When the Presidt. went to N.Y. he resisted for 3. weeks the efforts to introduce *levees*. At length he yeilded, and left it to Humphreys and some others to settle the forms. Accordingly an Antichamber and Presence room were provided, and when those who were to pay their court were assembled, the President set out, preceded by Humphreys, after passing thro' the Antichamber the door of the inner room was thrown in and Humphreys entered first calling out with a loud voice 'the President of the US.' The President was so much disconcerted with it that he did not recover it the whole time of the levee, and when the company was gone he said to Humphreys 'well, you have taken me in once, but by god you shall never take me in a second time.'

There is reason to believe that the rejection of the late additional[1] assumption by the Senate was effected by the President thro Lear, operating on Langdon. Beckley knows this.

MS (DLC); entirely in TJ's hand; second paragraph written in a different shade of ink and possibly at a later date. Included in the "Anas."

For an account of the current newspaper controversy in Philadelphia occasioned by the *National Gazette*'s attacks on presidential LEVEES as a form of monarchism, see Freeman, *Washington*, VII, 5-6. The Senate vote on ADDITIONAL ASSUMPTION is described in Notes of a Conversation with George Washington, 7 Feb. 1793, and note.

[1] Word interlined.

Report on the Petition of John Rogers

The Secretary of State, to whom was referred by the House of Representatives of the United States, the Petition of John Rogers, setting forth that as an Officer of the State of Virginia, during the last war, he became entitled to Two thousand Acres of Lands on the North east side of the Tennessee at it's confluence with the Ohio, and to 2400 Acres in different parcels, between the same River and the Missisippi, all of them within the former limit of Virginia, which lands were allotted to him under an Act of the Legislature of Virginia before it's Deed of cession to the United States; that by the Treaty of Hopewell in 1786 the part of the country comprehending those Lands was ceded to the chickasaw Indians; and praying compensation for the same.
REPORTS.

That the portion of country comprehending the said parcels of Land has been ever understood to be claimed, and has certainly been used, by the Chickasaw and cherokee Indians for their hunting grounds. The chickasaws holding exclusively from the Missisippi to the Tennissee, and extending their claim across that River, Eastwardly, into the claims of the cherokees, their conterminous neighbors.

That the government of Virginia, was so well apprised of the Rights of the Chickasaws to a portion of country within the limit of that State, that about the year 1780, they instructed their Agent, residing with the southern Indians, to avail himself of the first Opportunity which should offer, to purchase the same from them, and that, therefore, any act of that Legislature allotting these Lands to their Officers and Soldiers must probably have been past on the supposition that a purchase of the Indian right would be made, which purchase, however, has never been made.

That, at the Treaty of Hopewell, the true boundary between the United States, on the one part, and the Cherokees and Chickasaws on the other, was examined into and acknowledged, and, by consent of all parties, the unsettled limits between the Cherokees and Chickasaws, were at the same time ascertained, and in that part, particularly, were declared to be the Highlands dividing the Waters of the Cumberland and Tennessee, whereby the whole of the petitioner's locations were found to be in the Chickasaw country.

That, the right of occupation of the Cherokees and Chickasaws, in this portion of Country, having never been obtained by the United States, or those under whom they claim it cannot be said to have been ceded by them, at the treaty of Hopewell, but only recognised as belonging to the Chickasaws, and retained to them.

That the Country South of the Ohio was formerly contested between the six Nations and the Southern Indians for hunting-grounds.

That the six nations sold for a valuable consideration to the then Government, their right to that Country, describing it as extending from the mouth of the Tennessee upwards. That no evidence can at this time and place be procured, as to the right of the Southern Indians, that is to say, the Cherokees and Chickasaws, to the same Country; but it is believed that they voluntarily withdrew their claims within the Cumberland River, retaining their right so far, which consequently could not be conveyed from them or to us, by the act of the six nations, unless it be proved that the six nations had acquired a right to the Country between the Cumberland and Tennessee rivers by conquest over the Cherokees and Chickasaws, which, it is believed cannot be proved.

That, therefore, the locations of the Petitioner must be considered as made within the Indian Territory, and insusceptible of being reduced into his possession, till the Indian right be purchased.

That this places him on the same footing with Charles Russel and others, Officers of the same State, who had located their bounty Lands in like manner, within the Chickasaw lines, whose Case was laid before the House of Representatives of the United States at their last Session, and remains undecided on; and That the same and no other measure should be dealt to this Petitioner, which shall be provided for them.

TH: JEFFERSON

Feb. 16. 1793.

PrC (DNA: RG 59, MLR); in the hand of George Taylor, Jr., signed and dated in ink by TJ. PrC (DLC); in a clerk's hand, with dateline in Taylor's hand; unsigned. FC (Lb in DNA: RG 59, SDR). Tr (Lb in DNA: RG 233, House Records, TR). Recorded in SJPL. Enclosed in TJ to George Washington, 16 Feb. 1793.

On 6 Feb. 1793 the House of Representatives read and referred to a committee a petition from John Rogers, a Virginia captain of dragoons during the War for Independence, "praying compensation for certain lands on the Mississippi and Tennessee rivers, granted him by the State of Virginia, for his services as an officer in the line of the said State, prior to the cession made to the United States, of the territory Northwest of the river Ohio; the title to which lands has since been

ceded to the Chickasaw Indians, by the treaty of Hopewell" (JHR, I, 692; WMQ, 1st ser., VIII [1899], 100-4). Two days later the House discharged this committee and instead requested TJ to submit a report on the petition (JHR, I, 696). After first laying it before Washington this day (Washington, Journal, 55), TJ submitted the present report with a brief covering letter of 18 Feb. 1793 to the Speaker of the House of Representatives (PrC in DLC, at foot of text: "The Speaker of the H. of Representatives"; FC in DNA: RG 59, SDR). The House read and tabled TJ's report on the following day (JHR, I, 706). Here the matter rested until 1807 when, in response to a petition from one of Rogers's heirs, the House approved a committee report stating that Virginia land grants to Rogers and other Revolutionary War veterans remained valid, despite the Treaty of Hopewell, on the grounds that the Indian land titles recognized by the United States in this and other treaties did not abrogate the prior fee simple land titles of the states (JHR, V, 536, 555; ASP, *Public Lands*, I, 582). For further information on this subject, see Report on Case of Charles Russell, 22 Jan. 1792, and note.

From Jean Baptiste Ternant

JOHN TERNANT TO TH: JEFFERSON [16 Feb. 1793]

I have found the statement which you have taken the trouble to address to me with your private letter of the 13th. of the month, conformable with what is known to me of our present regulations on commerce and the duties of importation. But I remark that you have passed over in silence that the importation of tobaccos into France is exclusively reserved to American and French bottoms. When you shall have reflected that this exclusion of other nations will result to the sole advantage of your commerce, considering the recent reduction of the duties, and the known state of our merchant shipping, I hope you will think it right to make mention of it in your Report. Since the changes which have taken place in our government, and the dispositions of the French nation, towards United America there is no doubt that the relations subsisting between our two nations will become closer[1] than ever, and that there will result from it new advantages to the American commerce which cannot be long in realizing themselves. Your judgment will decide if this reflection is not of a nature to be communicated in your report. I thank you for the knolege you have been so good as to give me of this part of the Report which concerns France and I pray you to accept the homage of my respect & esteem.

TERNANT

Tr (DLC); undated; entirely in TJ's hand; at head of text: "Translation." PrC (MoSHi: Bixby Collection). Recorded in SJL as a letter of 16 Feb. 1793 received the same day. Enclosed in TJ to Washington, 17 Feb. 1793.

[1] Word interlined in place of "stricter."

To George Washington

Feb. 16. 93.

Th: Jefferson has the honor to send to the President the copy of a Report he proposes to give in to the H. of Representatives on Monday on the subject of a Petition of John Rogers referred to him.

The President will see by Mr. Hammond's letter, now inclosed, that he has kindled at the facts stated in Th:J's report on commerce. Th:J. adds the draught of an answer to him, if the President should think that any answer should be given. It is sometimes difficult to decide whether indiscretions of this kind had better be treated with silence, or due notice. The former perhaps would be best, if it were not that his letter would go unanswered to his court, who might not give themselves the trouble of seeing that he was in the wrong. Th:J. will wait on the President immediately.

RC (DNA: RG 59, MLR); endorsed by Tobias Lear. PrC (DLC). Tr (Lb in DNA: RG 59, SDC). Recorded in SJPL. Enclosures: (1) Report on the Petition of John Rogers, 16 Feb. 1793. (2) George Hammond to TJ, 15 Feb. 1793. (3) Dft of TJ to George Hammond, 16 Feb. 1793.

From Stephen Cathalan, Jr.

SIR   Marseilles the 17th. Febrûary 1793

Since my Last Respects of the 10th. Last Septr. from Bordeaux, I have the honour of acknowledging you, your most esteemed favours of the novber. 6th. 14th. and Decber. 2d. of which I have duly noted the Contents;

The Letter you may have wrotte to me via London, at the Same time you wrotte to Consuls, Fenwick and Edwd. Church, which they received the 20th. october Last at Bordeaux, (when I was there,) by a Vessel from London, I have ever not received, nor there nor here; it is however necessary for this Consulate to have the full Collection of the Laws of America, to Consult them when Occasion occûrs.

Gouvr. Morris Minister of the U. States has Sent me a Copy, (hand's Writing), of the Act Concerning Consuls and Vice-Consuls, Passed in that Session, but being not Signed, it Can't be reckowned in Case of need, as an Official Piece;

That has then Prevented me to present you in Conformity of that Act and Give you, Sir, the Bound with such Securities, as shall be approved by you, in a Sum not Less than Two Thousand Dollards, Conditionned for the Trûe discharge of my office, according to Law— however I writte now to Messrs. Fenwick Mason & co. of Georges-Town Potomack to offer you, Sir, that Bond, in my Behalf; I hope they will be my Secûrity. In Case you, or they, Should not find it Convenient, Messrs. Robt. Gilmor & Co. of Baltimore, Willm. Bingham, or Willing Morris & Swanwick of Philadelphia, on my demand to them, would I hope offer them Selves, for that Purpose; at Lenght, I Could here or at Paris offer to Your Minister Plenipotentiary any Securities at your Both Satisfaction and for a Larger Sum, if you desire it. This Matter would be done already, if I had the Proper Instructions to do it as you may desire it.

I have Delivered to this Municipality of Marseilles, the 4th. Inst. the Letter you adressed them, and Inclosed in yours of the Novber. 6th. in Answer to their Letter of the 24th. Last august, to the President of the U. States, of America; it was a Fortunate Circumstance for me, that the Day Before the American Sckoenner Madison Capn. Saml. Cassan arived in this harbour from Philada. to my address, with 659. Barrels of Flour; (it is till now, the only one who has been dispatched from the U.S. in this harbour, on my Encouragments and those of this Municipality). You have here inclosed the Verbal of that enterview, to which I Beg your Refference.

I find my Self also very happy for having obtained your Approbation for my Conduct Mentionned in my dispatch of the 1st. August Last.

Some French Vessels dispatched from this Place to U.S. Last Summer, are Returned with wheat or Flour, but that quantity was So Small or Tryflyng, for the Great Consumption of this and others neighbouring Places, that we are actûaly in the Greatest Need, having Approvisionment Scarcely for Two Months, *for this Place only*, and nothing to Provide the neighbouring ones, who can't obtain from this one charge of wheat or a Barrel of Flour, Prices have risen of Course, New York wheat has been Sold at £75 a £80. per charge, flour £75. 80. and 85.^{tt} per Barl. none Remains unsold; the 1st. arivals will obtain £5 a £10.^{tt} more, and God knows what Price, they will offer in Two or three Months! £110.^{tt} perhaps £120.^{tt} per Bel. fortunate they will be if they find to Purchase!

I agrée with you that the apprehensions of the Barbarian Cruisers have Lessen very much the Supplies, we might otherwise have received from your Plentifûll harvest; but now those apprehensions Can't be Compared with the Risk the French Vessels rûn now by the war they have declared to England, holland, Russia &ca. &ca. and the other Maritime Powers, who will take a Part in this Great Contest; in[1] Such a Circumstance if you remain Neutrals, your Trade and Vessels will Procure to U.S. Large Benefit; now the duty on Tobacco, on American vessels is reduced, and at a very Small difference, of that imported on french Bottoms, Forèeing Vessels may be Purchased by the French, The Americans are allowed to trade freely with the French West Indies; The French not Going this year, to the new found land fishery, your Baccalao will obtain Great Price, this fall and next winter, and I am Confident that the Prohibitive duty imposed on foreing Baccalao will be moderated as it has been during all the Last warr;

your Ships will be the Carriers of all the Belligerant Powers, and now I could freight here fifty americans vessels, and the Shippers or their Insurors here would make a very trifling difference of your Colours, with the Swedish or danish ones on account of your war with algiers, Thirty Dollards Freight per Ton only to Go to Philadelphia are offered to me, on American Bottom. It is a Pity that in this Circumstance a Treaty Could not be made yet between you and algiers, or Two or Three Frigates fitted out to Protect your Flag in the Mediteranean Sea; now I find that all I had Foreseen in my Memoir of the 15th. Janûary 1791. happens, and I reffer you to it, for the advantages you may now draw by the Public affairs in Europe.

29. Privateers have been already fitted out at this Port against the English, Dutch &ca. Some prises are arived here.

Tobacco is worth of £65 a 75^{tt} per ql. Marc taken in the entrepot, Carolina Rice £45. per ql. of ℔ 90. english, Baccalao will obtain £55 per ql. of 90 ℔. next fall.

I have not the Time to answer you about the olive Tries, and I Conclude in haste,[2] Capn. Casson being on his departure. I have the honour to be with great Respect Sir your most obedient humble Servant   STEPHEN CATHALAN JUNR.

The French armed Vessels which will be in number in the Mediteranean Sea will always take under their Protection, the American vessels they will Meet.

RC (DNA: RG 59, CD); at foot of first page: "To the Secretary of State Philadelphia"; with notations in pencil by TJ, including (lengthwise in margin of second page) "Extract of a letter dated Marseilles Feb. 17. 1793" and (at foot of text) "to be offered to Freneau & Fenno"; endorsed by TJ as received 1 May 1793 and so recorded in SJL. Dupl (same); in a clerk's hand, signed by Cathalan; lacks part of final paragraph and postscript; at head of text: "Copy"; enclosed in Cathalan to TJ, 19 Mch. 1793. Four extracts—consisting of paragraph seven, part of paragraph eight (see note 1 below), paragraph ten, and the postscript—were marked in pencil by TJ for publication and printed with slight revisions in the *National Gazette*, 4 May 1793. Enclosure not found.

TJ submitted this letter to the President on 1 May 1793, and Washington returned it the next day (Washington, *Journal*, 125).

[1] Beginning with this word, TJ marked the remainder of the sentence for extraction and lined through the next two words, substituting in pencil "the present," an alteration reflected in the extract published in the *National Gazette*.

[2] Remainder of sentence not in Dupl.

From Angelica Schuyler Church

London February the 17th. 1793

You will say my dear Sir after the Long silence I have observed that a line from me has lost its effect. But remember that I plead guilty to the charge of Idleness only; for when my friends require my assistance few are more willing than myself and there is no occasion in which I take more pleasure than in warmly recommending to your Attention the Count de Noailles, one great object of his visit to America is to render service to his Brother the Marquis de La Fayette, whose fate America must see with sorrow and indignation.

Catherine unites with me in best remembrances to yourself and daughters she hopes to see her young friend in a few years.

Accept my dear Sir of my grateful remembrances for the pleasure you procured me at Paris, and the assurances of my friendship.

ANGELICA CHURCH

RC (DLC); at foot of text: "Mr. *Jefferson*"; endorsed by TJ as received 5 May 1793 and so recorded in SJL, which notes that it was delivered "by M. de Noailles."

To George Clinton

SIR   Philadelphia Feb. 17. 1793

As it is possible and perhaps probable that at the ensuing conferences on Lake Erie with the Northern and Western Indians they may be disposed to look back to antient treaties, it becomes necessary that we should collect them, in order to be in a state of preparation. This can only be done with the aid of the several state-offices where these treaties have been deposited, which, in New York I am told, was in the office of the Secretary for Indian affairs under the old government. Will you permit me, Sir, to hope for your aid so far as to receive through you the several treaties between the six nations and the Governors of New York from the year 1683, and especially those with Colo. Dongan, authenticated under seal in the most formal manner. The necessity of compleating all the arrangements on this subject before the close of Congress, which will be probably on Saturday sennight, obliges me to ask for these papers under the shortest delay possible. On sending me a note of the expences of the copies they shall be immediately remitted. I confide in the candor and zeal for the public service which I am sure you feel, in asking your interposition in this business, and have the honor to be with sentiments of the most perfect esteem & respect Your Excellency's most obedt & most humble servt Th: Jefferson

PrC (DLC); at foot of text: "[. . .] Govr. Clinton." FC (DNA: RG 59, DL).

colo. dongan: Thomas Dongan, the proprietary and royal governor of New York, 1683-88, who was noteworthy for his assertion of English suzerainty over the Iroquois (DAB).

From Tobias Lear

Sunday February 17t: 1793

The President of the United States requests that the Secretary of State will write to the Governor of New York, by the post of tomorrow, for authenticated Copies, under Seal, of the several treaties between the Six nations and the Governors of New York from the Year 1683; and especially those with Colo. Dongan. They were preserved under the old Government of New York, in the Office of the Secretary for Indian Affairs.

The Attorney General of the United States having been directed by the President to go into an examination of the several treaties which have been made with the Northern and Western Indians, from the earliest period that they can be obtained, has desired that the foregoing application may be made to obtain a copy of those which are preserved in New York—and the President conceiving it proper that the application should be made through the Secretary of State, has therefore sent him this request; and wishes that the Copies may be had as early as possible, that all arrangements necessary for the Commissioners should be made, if possible, before the Close of the present Session of Congress.

If in the Secretary's opinion the expense of taking said Copies should be paid by the U.S. he will let the Governor know that it will be done by them, that no delay or difficulty may arise from that source.

RC (DLC); endorsed by TJ as received 17 Feb. 1793. FC (DNA: RG 59, MLR); in the hand of Benjamin Bankson; endorsed by Lear. FC (Lb in same, SDC).

From John Syme

Dear Sir   Virginia, Rockey Mills, 17th. Feby 1793.

Your Very Freindly attention to Mrs. Barclay, induces Me, to ask the Favor of You, to give the inclos'd, a safer Conveyance, than either

Her, Or Myself can do, and as it Contains Matters of importance, the Obligation Would be greatly added to, by forwarding the Answer, which is speedily wanted. We Experience so Many disapointments by private Oportunitys, that, it is Hop'd, the Freedom will not be taken Amiss.

Not Hearing of Late, of your Farther intintions of resigning, We wish You may alter your Mind, as be assur'd, You Will shortly have, an Addition to the Number of Your Freinds, and particularly some of My Connections. It is said by Gentlemen who Visit your part of the World, They do not like the going on of Things, any More than Yourself. Please Accept, the best Wishes, and Blessings, of all at the retreat and this place, which Concludes me for present, Dear Sir, Your Sincere Freind & Servt.   J SYME

RC (MHi); endorsed by TJ as received 26 Feb. 1793 and so recorded in SJL.

The INCLOS'D, not found, was undoubtedly a letter from Mary Barclay to her husband, Thomas Barclay, who had died in Lisbon the previous month while on his way to a special mission to Algiers.

On 8 Mch. 1793 Syme sent a duplicate of the enclosure to TJ with a covering letter expressing the hope that one or the other, going by separate conveyances, would soon be forwarded and that he would soon hear from his "Old Freind" TJ (RC in MHi; endorsed by TJ as received 16 Mch. 1793 and so recorded in SJL).

To Jean Baptiste Ternant

SIR   Philadelphia Feb. 17. 1793.

I have duly received your letter of yesterday, and am sensible of your favor in furnishing me with your observations on the Statement of the commerce between our two nations, of which I shall avail myself for the good of both. The omission of our participation with your vessels[1] in the exclusive transportation of our tobacco was merely that of the copy, as it was expressed in the original draught where the same circumstance respecting our whale oil was noted: and I am happy that your notice of it has enabled me to reinstate it before the Report goes out of my hand.

I must candidly acknolege to you that I do not foresee the same effect in favor of our navigation from the late reduction of duties on our tobaccos in France which you seem to expect. The difference in favor of French vessels is still so great as in my opinion to make it their interest to quit all other branches of the carrying business, to take up this: and as your stock of shipping is not adequate to the carriage of all your exports, the branches which[2] you abandon will be taken up[3] by other nations. So that this difference thrusts us out of the tobacco carriage to let other nations in to the carriage of other branches of your commerce. I must therefore avail myself of this occasion to express my hope that your nation will again revise this subject and place it on more equal grounds. I am happy in concurring with you more perfectly in another sentiment, that as the principles of our governments become more congenial, the links of affection are multiplied between us. It is impossible they should multiply beyond our wishes. Of the sincere interest we take in the happiness and prosperity of your nation you have had the most unequivocal proofs. I pray you to accept assurances of sincere attachment to you personally, and of the sentiments of respect & esteem with which I am, Sir, Your most obedient & most humble servt   TH: JEFFERSON

PrC (DLC); at foot of first page: "M. de Ternant." FC (Lb in DNA: RG 59, DL). Enclosed in TJ to Washington, 17 Feb. 1793.

[1] Preceding three words interlined.
[2] Preceding three words interlined in place of "what."
[3] Preceding two words interlined in place of "gained."

From Jean Baptiste Ternant

Philadelphie 17 fevrier 1793, L'an 2 de la Republique française

Conformément à des ordres que je viens seulement de recevoir, je m'empresse de notifier au Gouvernement des Etats unis, au nom du Conseil Exécutif provisoire, chargé de l'administration de notre gouvernement, que la nation française s'est constituée en République. Cette notification eut été accompagnée de nouvelles lettres de créance, si les arrangemens qu'on est occupé de prendre à ce sujet, eussent été définitivement arrêtés, et Si le Conseil exécutif n'eut désiré manifester au plutot la resolution prise par la nation entiére, et par ses délégués réunis en convention nationale, de déclarer l'abolition de la Royauté, et la création de la République en france. Indépendamment de l'intéret que doit inspirer ici cette grande détermination d'un peuple qui a lui même concouru à la défense de la liberté et à l'établissement de l'indépendance de l'amerique, elle sera sans doute aussi envisagée par les Etats unis comme un nouveau garant de l'étroite amitié qui subsiste entre nos deux nations. C'est dans cette persuasion, que le Conseil exécutif de la République française m'a chargé d'assurer votre Gouvernement de ses dispositions qui sont aussi celles de toute ma nation, à resserrer nos liens d'amitié avec vous, et à multiplier entre les deux peuples des rapports commerciaux réciproquement utiles. Je me félicite d'avoir à vous transmettre l'expression de Sentimens que je partage dans toute leur étendue, et dont ma conduite ici ne cessera de porter invariablement l'empreinte.   Signé TERNANT

Tr (AMAE: CPEU, xxxvii); at head of text: "Le Ministre de france, au sécrétaire d'Etat des Etats unis." Recorded in SJL as received 18 Feb. 1793.

Ternant wrote this letter immediately after receiving official news from France this day of the abolition of the monarchy and the establishment of the republic (Turner, *CFM*, 176).

To Josef Ignacio de Viar and Josef de Jaudenes

GENTLEMEN   Philadelphia Feb. 17. 1793.

I have duly received your favor of the 15th. and return you my thanks for the observations you are so good as to make. The Canary islands shall be specially noted in the Report, and the duty on flour re-exported to the colonies shall be stated, as I know it to be, common to the flour of all foreign nations, and not confined to ours alone. I will make enquiries as to the nature of the commerce we carry on with the island of Trinidad, as I do not possess any information which made it worthy of particular remark. If you can furnish me with any, I shall be particularly thankful.

The session of Congress approaching so nearly to it's close, as to render it doubtful whether they will enter on the subject of this report, permit me to sollicit your further attention to that part of it which respects Spain and the US. and a friendly communication of any information you may be able to obtain on the subject between this and the next session of the legislature, and be assured that it is among my first wishes to cultivate with sincerity mutual interests, good offices and friendship between our nations. I have the honor to be with great & sincere respect & esteem, Gentlemen Your most obedt & most humble servt   TH: JEFFERSON

Pr C (DLC); at foot of text: "Messrs. de Viar & Jaudenes." FC (Lb in DNA: RG 59, DL). Tr (AHN: Papeles de Estado, legajo 3895); Spanish translation in Viar's hand, attested by Jaudenes and Viar. Enclosed in TJ to Washington, 17 Feb. 1793.

To George Washington

Feb. 17. 1793.

Th: Jefferson has the honor with his respects to the President to communicate the answers he has received from the Representatives of France and Spain with his replies.

RC (DNA: RG 59, MLR); addressed: "The President of the US."; endorsed by Tobias Lear. Tr (Lb in same, SDC). Not recorded in SJL. Enclosures: (1) Josef Ignacio de Viar and Josef de Jaudenes to TJ, 15 Feb. 1793. (2) Jean Baptiste Ternant to TJ, 16 Feb. 1793. (3) TJ to Ternant, 17 Feb. 1793. (4) TJ to Viar and Jaudenes, 17 Feb. 1793.

George Washington to the Cabinet

SIR   United States, February 17th. 1793.

I transmit you a Copy of a letter from the Secretary of War to me, with the heads of Instructions proposed to be given to the Commissioners who may be appointed to hold a Treaty with the Western Indians, in the spring.

As I intend, in a few days, to call for the advice and opinion of the Heads of the Departments on the points touched upon in the enclosed paper, I must request you will give it an attentive and serious consideration, and note such alterations, amendments or additions, in writing, as may appear to you proper to be introduced into the instructions proposed to be given to the Commissioners.

I shall likewise request the opinion of the same Gentlemen upon the expediency of asking the advice of the Senate, before the end of their present Session, as to the propriety of instructing the Commissioners to recede from the present boundary, provided peace cannot be established with the Indians upon other terms. I therefore desire you will turn you attention to this matter also, in order that you may be able to give a deliberate opinion thereon, when the Gentlemen shall be called together.   GO: WASHINGTON

RC (DLC); in the hand of Tobias Lear, signed by Washington; at head of text: "(Private)"; at foot of text: "The Secretary of State"; endorsed by TJ as received 17 Feb. 1793 and so recorded in SJL. FC (Lb in DLC: Washington Papers); at head of text: "The Secretary of State; The Secretary of the Treasury, and The Attorney General, of the U.S. (Circular)."

Recorded in SJPL between 16 and 18 Feb. 1793. Enclosure: Henry Knox to Washington, 16 Feb. 1793: "I have the honor respectfully to submit to your consideration certain general ideas which may be proper for the heads of the Instructions to the Commissioners for treating with the hostile Indians. After you shall have decided upon the general principles of the

Instructions, the details may be formed and submitted to your judgment" (Tr in DLC; in the hand of Benjamin Bankson; at head of text: "Copy"). Second enclosure printed below.

ENCLOSURE

Henry Knox's Heads of Instructions for the Commissioners to the Western Indians

[ca. 16 Feb. 1793]

The Commissioners[1] to be fully informed upon the subject of all the Treaties which have been held by the United States, or which have been held under their authority with the Northern and western Indians—particularly of the Treaty of Fort Harmar in the year 1789, and of the boundaries then described. That the Commissioners possess themselves fully of all the proceedings of said Treaty, and of the tribes and principal Characters who formed the same. The Indians to be informed by the Commissioners, that the United States consider the said Treaty to have been formed with the Tribes who had a right to relinquish the lands which were then ceded to the United States. That, under this impression, part of the said lands have been sold to individuals, and parts assigned to the late army of the United States.

That the lands acquired by the said Treaty were by purchase, as well as a confirmation of the former treaties. That if the consideration then given was inadequate, or if other tribes, than those who formed the said Treaty, should have a just right to any of the lands in question, a particular compensation should be made them. That in both instances the United States were disposed to be liberal in granting additional compensations.

That the[2] remaining lands of the Indians within the limits of the United States, shall be guaranteed solemnly, by the general Government.

That[3] if the Commissioners can get the former boundaries established, that they be directed, besides compensation in gross to the amount of   Dollars, to promise payment of ten thousand dollars per annum in such proportions to the several tribes as shall be agreed upon.

That the Commissioners be directed, further[4] to relinquish the reservations marked upon the map as trading places—provided the same would satisfy the Indians so as to confirm the remainder of the boundary, always, however, reserving[5] as much land about the several British Posts, within the United States, as are now occupied by the several Garrisons, or[6] which shall be necessary for the same.

That the Commissioners be[7] instructed to use their highest exertions, to obtain the boundary now fixed, the reservations excepted, as before explained— and that for this purpose they be entrusted with   dollars to be used to influence certain white men to favour their measures.

But if, after every attempt, the assembled Indians should refuse the boundaries aforesaid, then the Commissioners are to endeavour to obtain from the Indians a description of the best boundary to which they will agree, the Commissioners always endeavouring to conform the same, as nearly as may be, to the one described in the Treaty of Fort Harmar.[8]

On obtaining this information from the Indians, they are to be informed by the Commissioners, that the President of the United States, conceiving the boundary established by the Treaty of Fort Harmar, to have been made with the full understanding and free consent of the parties having the right to make the same, had not invested them (the Commissioners) with power to alter the same, excepting as to the reservations before described. But that now possessing the final and full voice of the Indians upon the subject, the same should be reported to the President, who would give a definitive answer thereon, at a period to be fixed, which period should not be earlier than four months[9] after the Senate should be assembled at their next Session—and this would fix the period about one year from the time the Commissioners should obtain this information.

The Commissioners should further inform the Indians, that until the answer should be received, a solemn truce should be observed on both sides. The Indians to be answerable for their young warriors—and the President to be answerable for our's.

If the idea of a Truce should be relished, perhaps it might be extended, by the Commissioners, to three or seven years, all things to remain in the same state. If so, the effect would be a peace to all intents and purposes.

The Commissioners to be particularly instructed to do nothing which should in the least impair the right of pre-emption or general sovereignty of the United States over the Country, the limits of which were established by the peace of 1783. But, at the same time, to impress upon the Indians that the right of pre-emption in no degree affects their right to[10] the soil, which the United States concedes unlimitedly, excepting that when sold,[11] it must be to the United States, and under their authority, and no otherwise.

Tr (DLC); undated; in the hand of Tobias Lear. Recorded in SJPL between 16 and 18 Feb. 1793: "Instructions for Commrs. to treat with hostile Indians." See notes below for TJ's suggested amendments to this document.

Knox's heads of instructions for the commissioners to negotiate with the hostile Western tribes at the Lower Sandusky conference were considered by the Cabinet on 25 Feb. 1793 (Cabinet Opinions on Indian Affairs, 25 Feb. 1793; Notes on Cabinet Opinions, 26 Feb. 1793). In anticipation of this meeting, TJ set down on a separate sheet a series of proposed amendments, keyed sequentially by page and line numbers to the Tr he received from the President, and several notes on the subject (MS in DLC: TJ Papers, 82: 14153; undated; recorded in SJPL between 16 and 18 Feb. 1793: "amendmts proposed to [Instructions]"). The textual notes below record only the amendments and notes in this MS, as TJ wrote nothing on the Tr of the instructions. The final text of the instructions, which was not

completed until 26 Apr. 1793, incorporated the substance of all but paragraphs 8-10 of the heads of instructions (ASP, Indian Affairs, I, 340-2).

The treaty of FORT HARMAR, concluded between the United States and various Western tribes in 1789, established a boundary between the contracting parties west of the Ohio River line that these tribes were currently insisting on as a condition of peace (same, 6-7).

[1] TJ suggested the insertion here of "after due enquiry into the earlier treaties."

[2] TJ suggested the insertion here of "occupation of the." He interlined this amendment between those described in notes 1 and 3.

[3] TJ suggested that the next eleven words be replaced by: "in consideration of the wants of the Indians and the reduced limits of their hunting grounds, the Commissioners."

[4] TJ suggested the insertion here of "if the Indns. should make a point of it, stipulate against our selling or settling."

[5] TJ suggested that "provided . . . re-

serving" be replaced by "save only."

⁶ TJ suggested that the remainder of the sentence be replaced by "by white inhabitants."

⁷ TJ suggested the deletion of "instructed . . . they be."

⁸ TJ suggested that the preceding paragraph be replaced with: "That if their confirmation of the boundary cannot be otherwise obtained, the Commrs. may agree on an interior line, beyond which we will neither sell nor settle, tho' we retain the property; and that this shall form a ⟨margin⟩ border between them and us, within which neither party shall enter with arms."

⁹ In regard to this point TJ made the following comment: "quere expediency of short truce?" He interlined this comment between the amendments described in notes 8 and 10.

¹⁰ TJ suggested the insertion here of "occupy."

¹¹ TJ suggested that "when sold" be replaced by "if they should ever sell." Below this amendment TJ drew a line and wrote below it:

"1. right to cede?
       not to exercise right of selling or
            settling.
2. short truce?
3. Communication to Senate?"

These were obviously points he thought should be raised when the Cabinet met to consider the heads of instructions.

To Martha Jefferson Carr

DEAR SISTER   Philadelphia Feb. 18. 1793.

I recieved some days ago your favor of Dec. 15. and have so long delayed answering it because I was in daily expectation of receiving information of a considerable sum of money being lodged for me in Richmond. Tho I think this cannot fail to take place, and that very shortly, yet I have thought it necessary to acknolege in the mean time the receipt of your letter, and to mention to you my prospect of doing what you desire, I think with so much certainty as that Mr. Myers may be satisfied. It would not be in my power to pay it from any resources I have here, as these are far from supplying my wants here. The moment I can receive any information, I will give you notice. I had intended from the same fund to pay the balance on my bond to Mr. Carr's estate, as, your children are now arrived to that period when it may enable you to help them with it, as far as it will go. I give joy to yourself, my new married neice and Mr. Terrel on the occasion, and wish them all possible happiness and success in their pursuits in a new country.—I have been over-persuaded¹ to stay here somewhat longer than I had determined. I must therefore write to Dabney how to employ himself till I come. I am with sincere love to yourself & the family, dear sister yours affectionately   TH: JEFFERSON

PrC (CSmH); added in ink at foot of text: "Mrs. Carr." Tr (ViU: Carr-Cary Papers); 19th-century copy.

¹ First four letters and hyphen interlined.

From George Hammond

Sir   Philadelphia 18 February 179[3]

I should feel a considerable degree of reluctance in troubling you again on the subject of your communication of the 13th curt., were I not solicitous to justify an expression in my answer, which, from the letter I received from you this morning, appears to you exceptionable in point of accuracy.

I was induced to regard the *assurance* of my *personal* conviction &ca. as a *formal* one, by the recollection of the circumstances, under which the letter containing it, was written. On delivering to you the notification of the 11th. of April, I waited upon you in person, and informed you that, though I had felt it my duty to make the official communication nearly in the words of my instructions, I entertained the strongest personal conviction that it was not intended to militate against the King's proclamation. After I had stated some considerations, explanatory of the grounds of this opinion, you expressed your apprehensions that this government would not esteem my *oral* exposition as sufficient to counterbalance the effect of my *official* notification: And you then asked me if, upon your addressing a letter to me upon the subject, I should have any objection to repeating the same opinions in *writing*. To this I replied that I could certainly have no objection to confirming in writing any sentiments which I had advanced in conversation. I then returned home, and, on the receipt of your letter, immediately sent you an answer, conformable to the desire you had manifested. For these reasons I then considered, and have ever since considered that answer as a *formal* "assurance of my conviction," not as a *private* individual, but as the Kings Minister in this country.

I flatter myself, Sir, that your recollection of the particulars of our conversation will corroborate my present statement. At all events I desire you to be persuaded that the terms, of the expression alluded to, were not intended as a quibble, upon words; as I could unquestionably entertain no expectation of deceiving you, and much less of endeavoring to make you the instrument of deceiving others. I am, with great respect, Sir, Your most obedient humble Servant,

Geo. Hammond

RC (DNA: RG 59, NL); dateline torn; at foot of first page: "Mr Jefferson & & &."; endorsed by TJ as received 18 Feb. 1793 and so recorded in SJL. FC (Lb in PRO: FO 116/3). Tr (same, 115/2). Tr (same, 5/1). Tr (Lb in DNA: RG 59, NL).

To Jacob Hollingsworth

SIR   Philadelphia Feb. 18. 1793

You desired in a former letter to be informed when Congress should provide for lost certificates which might be proved by other vouchers. I am not certain whether the inclosed act passed and printed a few days ago may come up to your view. But under the possibility that it might, I send it to you by the first post since it was printed.

I have not yet received any letter from Mr. Biddle. I wish he could find tenants enough for 2000 acres, that being the whole I wish to rent in that part of the country. It would enable them too to settle the different lots among themselves more to their mind, and to proportion the rent of each to it's comparative value, so as that while I should receive a quarter of a dollar the acre upon the whole, they should pay some more some less according as their lot should be more or less good. In like manner, they might then have the whole of the laborers now on the lands, paying me 50. dollars a year[1] for every man and woman of the whole, but they dividing them to their mind, and contributing more or less according as each should have the more or the less valuable laborers in their lot. This I think would be just and satisfactory to all. I shall not pass Elkton so early as March but will give Mr. Biddle notice when I do pass, in time to meet me. I will trouble you to communicate these things to him and to let him know I shall be glad to receive information from him by letter. I am Sir your very humble servt   TH: JEFFERSON

PrC (DLC); at foot of text: "[Mr.] Hollingsworth." Tr (ViU: Edgehill-Randolph Papers); 19th-century copy. Enclosure: *An Act relative to claims against the United States, not barred by any act of limitation, and which have not been already adjusted* . . . (Philadelphia, 1793). See Evans, No. 26305.

Hollingsworth had mentioned the subject of LOST CERTIFICATES in his [9] Dec. 1792 letter to TJ. The INCLOSED ACT, approved on 12 Feb. 1793, dealt with the disposition of unsettled claims for various services rendered to the United States before 4 Mch. 1789 (*Annals*, III, 1413-14).

[1] Preceding two words interlined.

From Jean Baptiste Le Roy

De Paris ce 18 Fevrier 1793

Quoique J'aye de grands torts avec vous Monsieur d'avoir tant tarde à vous accuser La récéption des lettres que vous m'avez fait l'honneur de m'écrire Cependant me confiant dans Les Sentimens que vous avez bien voulu me témoigner dans plus d'une occasion J'ai pensé que vous me permettriez de vous présenter M. D Hauterive mon ami qui va habiter votre heureuse contrée pendant quelques années étant nommé Consul. Je n'aurois pas L'honneur de vous le présenter Si à des Sentimens très [Civiques?] il ne joignoit pas beaucoup de qualités essentielles et des connoissances très étendues dans plus d'un genre. A ces titres J'espere que vous voudrez bien L'accueillir favorablement. Je vous en aurai la même obligation que Si cette bonne reception me regardoit moi même. Je le trouve bien heureux Monsieur de pouvoir espérer Jouïr de votre entretien car avec Les connoissances qu'il a Ce Sera un grand plaisir pour lui de pouvoir S'entretenir avec un des hommes les plus instruits des deux Mondes. Après vous avoir parlé de mon ami J'en viens à ce qui regarde *M Churchman*. Vous aurez bien imaginé Monsieur qu'a la multitude d'evenemens qui ont eu lieu L'année derniere et dans celle-cy[1] Les Sciences ont beaucoup Souffert parmi nous aussi notre pauvre Académie ne fait elle presque rien et Si ce n étoit l'affaire des poids et mesures qui l'occupe elle Seroit presque dans l'inactivité. Incertain Si vous avez eu connoissance d'un mémoire que mon Confrère M De Borda a lu au nom de l'Académie à la Convention nationale à ce Sujet Je le Joins à ma Lettre il vous instruira du point où nous en Sommes Sur cette grande entreprise.

Une raison m'a fait diffèrrer de Semaine en Semaine et de mois en mois de répondre à la lettre que vous m'avez fait L honneur de m'écrire, au Sujet de M Church-man, c'est que je n'ai reçu que près d'un an après, La Carte et L'ouvrage de M. Churchman et que Je voulois en[2] outre vous mander ce qui S étoit passé à ce Sujet dans L'Académie, mais Le rapport n en ayant pas eté encore fait J'ai èté obligé de differrer Cependant comme je compte qu'il Sera fait ce mois cy ou au commencement de l'autre vous pouvez être Sur que vous aurez tous aussitôt de mes nouvelles, et que Je vous en manderai le résultat.

Ah Monsieur que J'ai fait de réfléxions Sur la marche Sure et mesurée du congrès dans tout ce qui S'est passé depuis La déclaration de L'indépendance de l'Amèrique Septentrionale Sur tous les avantages de votre heureuse révolution. Qui nous auroit dit Lorsque nous causions ensemble dans l'assemblée constituante de Versailles qu'elle eut donnè lieu à une telle multitude d'evenemens et Si extraordinaires, et Si incroyables. Je ne Sais Si On l'a dit mais cela me paroit aujourd-hui parfaitement démontré que le Caractère d'une Nation est toûjours le même et que Ses grandes[3] assemblées n'agissent le plus Souvent qu'avec L'esprit qui la caractérise.

Recevez Monsieur Les assurances les plus Sincères de tous les Sentimens d'attachement et de la plus haute estime que vous m'avez Inspirés depuis que J'ai eu l'honneur de vous connoitre.

LeRoy de l Acad. des Sciences

RC (DLC); at foot of first page: "M. Jefferson"; endorsed by TJ as received 30 May 1793 and so recorded in SJL.

Alexandre Maurice Blanc de Lanautte, Comte d'HAUTERIVE, served as French consul at New York from 1793 to 1794 (Frances S. Childs, "The Hauterive Journal," *New-York Historical Society Quarterly*, XXXIII [1949], 69-86). The MÉMOIRE of the French Academy of Sciences on a unit of measure, submitted to the National

Assembly in March 1791, is printed as an enclosure to Condorcet to TJ, [ca. 3 May 1791]. TJ's 24 Nov. 1790 LETTRE to Le Roy concerning John Churchman is quoted in the note to his letter of that date to Churchman.

[1] Preceding three words interlined.
[2] Preceding two words interlined in place of "differois."
[3] Word interlined.

Memorandum on Consuls Recommended for Appointment

Havre. Nathaniel Cutting of Massachusets, Consul of the U.S. of A. for the port of Havre in France, and for such other parts of that country as shall be nearer to the said port than to the residence of any other Consul or Vice consul of the U.S. within the same allegiance.

Falmouth. Edward Fox native[1] of Great Britain. Consul of the US. of A. for the port of Falmouth in the kingdom of Great Britain, and for such other parts of the said kingdom as shall be nearer to the said port than to the residence of any other Consul or Vice consul of the US. in the same kingdom.

Cadiz. Joseph Yznardi native[2] of Spain, Consul of the US. of A. for the port of Cadiz, in the kingdom of Spain, and for such other parts of the said kingdom as shall be nearer to the said port than to the residence of any other Consul or Vice-consul of the US. within the same allegiance.

Alicant. Robert Montgomery of Alicant Consul of the US. of A. for the port of Alicant in the kingdom of Spain, and for such other parts of the said kingdom as shall be nearer to the said port than to the residence of any other Consul or viceconsul of the US. within the same allegiance.

Hamburg.   John Parish native[3] of Great Britain. Consul of the US. of A. for the port of Hamburg and for all other places within the same allegiance.

Santa Cruz.   Henry Cooper of Pensylvania Consul of the US. of A. for the island of Santa Cruz and for all other places under the same allegiance in America as shall be nearer to the said island of Santa Cruz than to the residence of any other Consul or Vice Consul of the US. within the same allegiance.

St. Eustatius. David Matthew Clarkson of Pennsylvania. Consul for the US. of A. for the island of Saint Eustatius and for all other places under the same allegiance in America which shall be nearer to the said island of St. Eustatius than to the residence of any other Consul or Viceconsul of the US. within the same allegiance.

Curaçoa.   Benjamin Hamnell Philips of Pensylvania. Consul for the US. of A. in the island of Curaçoa and for all other places under the same allegiance in America which shall be nearer to the said island of Curaçoa than to the residence of any other Consul or Vice consul of the US. within the same allegiance.

TH: JEFFERSON
Feb. 18. 1793.

PrC (DLC). Entry in SJPL: "Consuls."

President Washington incorporated this memorandum into a message that he submitted on 19 Feb. 1793 to the Senate, which confirmed all of his consular nominees the following day (JEP, I, 129-30). For the background, see Memorandum on Consuls and Consular Appointments, 15 Feb. 1793, and note. The appointment of Edward Fox to be consul at Falmouth was a mistake, and the intended candidate, Robert W. Fox, was not nominated and confirmed until May 1794 (same, 158, 159).

On 25 Feb. 1793 Thomas Hartley of Philadelphia, unaware that the Senate had already confirmed John Parish as consul for Hamburg, wrote a letter to TJ in which he recommended the appointment of Caspar Voght, "a Man of great respectability as a Merchant at Hamburg" (RC in DLC: Washington Papers, Applications for Office; at foot of text: "Mr. Jefferson Secretary of State"; endorsed by TJ as received 25 Feb. 1793 and so recorded in SJL).

[1] Word interlined.
[2] Word interlined.
[3] Word interlined.

To Beverley Randolph

DEAR SIR   Philadelphia Feb. 18. 1793.

A great assembly of the Northern and Western Indians is to be held at Sanduskey in the approaching spring, to be met by three Commissioners from the general government to treat of peace. It is highly important that some person from the Southward, possessing the public confidence, should be in the commission: and a person too who has firmness enough to form opinions for himself. Though I knew that your health was sometimes in default, yet I have ventured to propose you to the President who joined at once in the wish that you would undertake it, and I expect he writes to you by this post. It will be the greatest collection of Indians (about 3000) which has ever taken place, and from very distant and various parts. The route thither will be through N. York, the Hudson, the Mohawk, L. Ontario, Niagara, and L. Erie, and you could return by Fort Pitt. The season the finest of the year, and I presume every accomodation will be provided which the nature of the service admits. I am not able to say what the allowance will be, but I believe it has usually been 6. or 8. Doll. a day exclusive of expences. But this is guess-work in me.—I hope you will resolve to undertake it, as I conceive the public interest intimately concerned in the conducting of this treaty, and on that consideration I am confident you will sacrifice any private disinclination to it. Be pleased to present my best respects to Mrs. Randolph & to be assured of the esteem with which I am Dear Sir, your friend & servt   TH: JEFFERSON

RC (ViU); addressed: "Beverley Randolph esq. Cumberland by the Richmond post"; franked; postmarked. PrC (DLC). Tr (DLC); 19th-century copy.

Acting on the advice of Edmund Randolph, Washington had requested the Attorney General on 17 Feb. to inform Beverley Randolph that he would be nominated to serve as a commissioner to the forthcoming Sandusky Indian conference. Randolph was also asked to induce the acceptance of the former governor of Virginia and to request that he be in Philadelphia early in April. The following day the President asked Postmaster General Timothy Pickering to serve as a commissioner. He undoubtedly made a similar request to Benjamin Lincoln of Massachusetts, the former Revolutionary War general who was currently serving as federal customs collector in Boston. Lincoln, like Pickering, was in Philadelphia at this time and had had extensive experience in Indian negotiations (Washington, *Journal*, 40, 57, 58, 76). Washington submitted the nominations of Lincoln, Pickering, and Randolph to the Senate on 1 Mch. 1793 and they were confirmed the following day, even before Randolph received TJ's letter (Beverley Randolph to TJ, 14 Mch. 1793; JEP, I, 135, 136).

[229]

To Thomas Mann Randolph, Jr.

Dear Sir   Philadelphia Feb. 18. 1793.

I recieved about a fortnight ago your favor of Jan. 24. and by this week's post Maria received the one addressed to her. I am extremely pleased with the progress of the work at Monticello, and indebted to you for it, as also for communicating it, as well as the account of the sales in Bedford. I am in hopes of procuring tenants in Maryland for all my lands on the Shadwell side of the river at a quarter of a dollar the acre, to be rented for 7. years, and to hire the negroes on the same lands for 25. dollars averaged, from year to year only, so that I may take them away if ill treated. The business is not yet concluded, and therefore I would wish it to be not at all known. I mention it to you, because I think you have sometimes expressed a disposition to rent Edgehill, in which if you still are, and like these terms, perhaps it might be possible for me to engage a further number of tenants. As soon as Congress is over I shall go, if I have time, into the neighborhood (at the head of Elk) where the business is on the carpet, and try to conclude for myself. I propose to parcel the lands in tenements of from 200 to 400. acres each. If I succeed in this, I should expect to be able to extend the same system to Bedford. The husbandry about the head of Elk is in wheat and grazing: little corn, and less pork. This I think is what would suit us best, for which reason I turned my attention to that quarter, and also because the labour there being performed by slaves with some mixture of free labourers, the farmers there understand the management of negroes on a rational and humane plan.

I sometime ago sold my horse Brimmer for what he cost me. A few days after, Joseph took it into his head to take an airing, on Matchless, let him run away with him, in doing which he run full speed against the shaft of a cart and killed himself. So that I am now reduced to my old pair, and to Tarquin, whom also I must sell before I come home, as his hoofs are not firm enough for our stones. I have offered him for 100. Doll. and he is in better condition than when I bought him.— I hope you have heard of the servants clothes. They went from here the 12th. of Dec. by a Capt. Swaile of the schooner Mary bound to Norfolk and Richmond. The box was addressed to you, to the care of Mr. Brown. If he has not received it, enquiries will be necessary at Norfolk.—Give my love to my dear Martha and be assured of the best affections of Dear Sir Your's sincerely   Th: Jefferson

RC (DLC); at foot of first page: "Mr. Randolph." Tr (ViU: Edgehill-Randolph Papers); 19th-century copy. Not recorded in SJL.

To George Washington

S<small>IR</small>   Philadelphia February[1] 18th. 1793.

The Commissioners of the Territory of the United States on the Potomac having, according to law, had the said Territory surveyed and defined by proper metes and bounds, and transmitted their report with a plat of the boundary, I have now the honor to lay them before you. As this work has been executed under the Authority of the Legislature, I presume it would be proper to communicate the report to them, and to submit the Plat also to their inspection, that they may be duly informed of the progress of the Work.

I have to add that these papers, being original, are again to be deposited with the Records in the Office of the Department of State. I have the honor to be, with Sentiments of the most perfect esteem and attachment, Sir, Your most obedient and Most humble servant,

T<small>H</small>: J<small>EFFERSON</small>

PrC (DLC); in the hand of George Taylor, Jr., with emendation and signature in ink by TJ; at foot of text: "The President of the United States." FC (Lb in DNA: RG 59, DL). Tr (Lb in DLC: Washington Papers). Not recorded in SJL. Enclosures: (1) Report of the Commissioners of the Federal District on the survey of the Federal District, 1 Jan. 1793 (DNA: RG 42, PC). (2) Andrew Ellicott's corrected plat of the Federal District (not found).

On this day TJ wrote a brief note to Washington transmitting the above letter, "the plan of the Federal territory just received by Mr. Ellicot," and a covering message to Congress he had written for the President (RC in DNA: RG 59, MLR, addressed: "The President of the US.," endorsed by Tobias Lear; Tr in Lb in same, SDC; not recorded in SJL). Washington, in turn, submitted TJ's letter and its two enclosures to the Senate and the House of Representatives the same day with the message drafted by the Secretary of State: "I now lay before you a Report and Plat of the Territory of the United States, on the Potomac, as given in by the Commissioners of that Territory, together with a letter from the Secretary of State which accompanied them. These papers being original, are to be again deposited with the Records of the Department of State, after having answered the purpose of your information" (PrC in DLC: TJ Papers, 82: 14064, undated, in the hand of George Taylor, Jr., at foot of text: "que—should this be recorded with am. letters"; FC in Lb in DLC: Washington Papers, dated 18 Feb. 1793). Since only one copy of the plat of the Federal District was available, however, the President sent it to the House of Representatives and requested that it be forwarded to the Senate (Washington, *Journal*, 58; JHR, I, 705; JS, I, 489, 490). For a discussion of the new map Andrew Ellicott made after his corrected plat was returned by Congress, see Ralph E. Ehrenberg, "Mapping the Nation's Capital: The Surveyor's Office, 1791-1818," *Quarterly Journal of the Library of Congress*, XXXVI (1979), 282; see also Commissioners of the Federal District to TJ, 25 June 1793.

[1] "Febr-" interlined in ink by TJ in place of "Jan."

From William Carmichael and
William Short

Sir   Aranjuez Feb. 19.[1] 1793

It has been our intention for some time past to have commenced our joint correspondence with you—and we have only deferred it because we flattered ourselves from day to day that we should be able at the same time to inform you of some step taken in the negotiation with which the President has been pleased to charge us.

Although our commission was recieved at Madrid so long ago as the 1st. of this month, and this circumstance immediately announced to the Duke de la Alcudia the present minister of foreign affairs, yet it is not until to-day that we are enabled to inform you that a person has been named to treat with us, having just learned by a letter from that minister that His Majesty has destined for that purpose M. de Gardoqui Minister of finance.

We are happy that you yourself are acquainted with the usage converted into system in most of the European courts, (and in none more than this) of always beginning by searching for all the pretexts of procrastination, and never proceeding to business until they are exhausted. Hitherto these pretexts with respect to us, have been derived from the form of our commission, and the manner in which we are accredited by the President being different from the diplomatic usages established here.

On our first interview with the minister we delivered him a copy of our commission, it being the only document we had recieved from you. He made use of the ordinary expressions of civility and added conformably to usage that he would take His Majesty's orders thereon and communicate them to us.

As a considerable time elapsed much to our surprize without our hearing further from him, M. Carmichael waited on him, having to speak to him on other business, in order to give him an opportunity of explaining the cause of the silence. He began by apologizing in mentioning their embarassment as to the manner in which we were to be recieved and treated. Our commission partaking both of the second and third order of ministers they were at a loss in which to range us. It was probably thought necessary to decide on this beforehand as the laws of etiquette are observed with unrelaxing rigor here, and as there are very marked and humiliating distinctions established at this court between these two orders not only as to the manner of their being recieved, but also as to that of their being treated afterwards. He concluded by assuring that some decision should be taken in a few days.

We conceived that we should act conformably to the intention of the President and the nature of the commission we had recieved, in not interfering in any way in this decision and in subscribing to whatever it might be.

It was notified to us two days afterwards in the usual manner that we were to be presented the day after and have an audience of the King, in a way which shewed that they had decided to consider us as of the second order—a circumstance which could not have failed to have given weight to our negotiation and have facilitated us in it. We observed however in the letter of the Introductor of Ambassadors announcing this audience an expression which supposed our having delivered a copy of our *credentials* to the Duke. Although he had been informed at our first interview and also at the second which Mr. Carmichael had with him alone, that we had no other credentials than the commission of which we gave him a copy—and although this was fully ascertained from our having given him copies of no other, (it being the constant usage to give to the minister previously, copies of all papers intended to be put into the King's hands) still as plenipotentiary powers in European courts are always accompanied by letters of credence, we judged it would be proper to repeat to him the peculiar circumstance of our having none, lest any embarassment should result to him, if perchance he had directed that mode of presentation without attending to it. We accordingly wrote him a note observing at the same time on the expression of the Introductor which had suggested to us the propriety of repeating this circumstance. To this he answered the same evening, that he had conceived we should be certainly provided with a letter of some kind for the King though not in the usual form, and that His Majesty had determined to recieve it as a letter of credence and give us the audience which had been notified to us. But that as we had no letter of any kind addressed to His Majesty, the presentation in the manner he had proposed was absolutely precluded by the etiquette established at this court. He added that we should be presented in some manner corresponding to our commission about which he should speak to us.

Fearing with reason that this would be made an additional pretext for procrastination, we determined to leave nothing undone to abridge it as far as depended on us. We therefore wrote to him immediately, reminding him of the length of the delay which had already taken place since our arrival here—expressing our disposition to subscribe to whatever kind of presentation he might judge proper—our hope that it would be no impediment to our proceeding at present to business— and our desire to be informed of the intention of His Majesty with respect to the designation of a person to treat with us. In answer to which we have just recieved the letter mentioned above, informing us of the nomination of M. de Gardoqui.

We should not have thought it worth while to have troubled you with these details of mere form if they had not been made the cause of so considerable a delay. We do not add copies of the letters alluded to because we have cited their substance and because we shall annex them to the journal of our proceedings under our joint commission. We have &c.[2]

PrC (DLC: Short Papers); in Short's hand, unsigned; at head of text in ink: "*C & S*"; at foot of first page: "The Secretary of State for the United States—Philadelphia"; at foot of text in ink: "*end*"; lacks final page with remainder of complimentary close. Recorded in SJL as received 8 May 1793.

Diego de GARDOQUI was no stranger to Spanish-American diplomacy. He had served as Spain's chargé d'affaires to the United States from 1785 to 1789 and since then had been frequently consulted by the Spanish government on American affairs. For an account of his previous career, see Bemis, *Pinckney's Treaty*, 60-148, 157-9.

TJ submitted this letter to the President on 8 May 1793, and Washington returned it the same day (Washington, *Journal*, 131).

[1] Second digit reworked, probably from "8."

[2] Abbreviation, written in ink, added in lieu of remainder of complimentary close.

From James Simpson

Gibraltar, 19 Feb. 1793. He encloses a duplicate of his letter of 12 Feb. that went by the ship *Perseverance* of Philadelphia. He opened a box of velvets, silks, and broadcloth left with him by Barclay. The velvets are undamaged, the cloth received only trifling injury from moths, and three pieces of the satin are a little mildewed, but a good airing stopped this deterioration. After one box of the muslins was opened and judged undamaged, the rest were left alone. Several cases of "Angelica and Cinamon Waters" are on the inventory of presents. Muley Yezid welcomed such gifts, but it is improper to carry them "in so great a quantity to that Country." If a treaty with Muley Suliman becomes politic, "nothing of that Kind must be offerd." Barclay probably informed TJ of the ferment in the mountains near Tetuán. The inhabitants have been pacified and are paying the annual tribute, in arrears since the death of Sidi Muhammad, to Muley Teib for his brother Suliman's use. Yesterday Mr. Classon, the Danish consul at Tangier, arrived from Kena, and says that Suliman is still at Mequinez, Ischem continues quiet at Morocco, and reports current some weeks ago of revolt against Ischem in the middle provinces have not been confirmed. France has declared war on Russia, England, and Holland. He reiterates his disposition to be helpful by forwarding news until Barclay's successor arrives.

RC (DNA: RG 59, CD); 3 p.; at foot of first page: "The Honble Thomas Jefferson &ca. &ca."; endorsed by TJ as received 9 Apr. 1793 and so recorded in SJL. Enclosure: Simpson to TJ, 12 Feb. 1793.

From Caleb Alexander

Mendon, Massachusetts, 20 Feb. 1793. In compliance with the copyright law he sends a copy of his book, "A Grammatical system of the English language: comprehending a plain and familiar scheme of teaching young gentlemen and ladies the art of speaking and writing correctly their native tongue." Before publication the book was properly entered by Mr. Goodale, clerk of the Massachusetts district court, and to secure copyright protection he asks that it be recorded in the Secretary of State's office.

RC (DNA: RG 59, MLR); 1 p.; addressed: "The Hon. Thomas Jefferson, Esq. Secretary of State. Philadelphia"; note on address cover: "To be carried in the mail"; endorsed by George Taylor, Jr.

Caleb Alexander (1755-1828), a Yale graduate and Congregational minister, held various pastorates in Massachusetts and Connecticut. *A Grammatical System of the English Language* ... (Boston, 1792), which appeared in ten editions through 1811, was one of many works written by Alexander, who in 1800 helped to produce the first Greek New Testament printed in the United States, a copy of which TJ acquired (Dexter, *Biographical Sketches*, III, 644-9; Isaac H. Hall, *A Critical Bibliography of the Greek New Testament as Published in America* [Philadelphia, 1883], 8-10; Sowerby, No. 1486).

From John Bulkeley & Son

SIR   Lisbon 20 Febry 1793

The foregoing is Copy of what we had the honour of writing you 7th. Uto. by the Aurora Captn. O'Brien, via Philadelphia, and on the 26 Do. we received via London, a Triplicate Copy of your Esteemd favour 11 Octr. L. Y., and agreeable to your directions, we have ship'd the 3 Pipes best Termo Wine cased, on board the Ship Four Friends Capn. Joseph Volans, bound to Norfolk, consignd to Mr. James Brown Mercht. in Richmond, and recommend to Messrs. Wm. & Jas. Douglas of Norfolk, to forward them to Richmond by a safe conveyance, which no doubt will be complied with. For their cost we debit you Rs. 222$000 as ℔ note at foot, and we flatter ourselves that the quality will prove to your Entire satisfaction, being of the vintage 88., and when you please to renew the like orders, we will be carefull to send of the very best quality. We remain with perfect regard & Esteem Sir Your most obedt. & very Hble. Serts.

JOHN BULKELEY & SON

London 7½ ℔ $[1]

3. Pipes Lisbon Wine vintage 88—@ 70 $ ℔ Pipe 210$000
3 Cases 12$000
222$000 Rs.

RC (MHi); subjoined to Tr of the firm's letter to TJ of 7 Jan. 1793; with notation by TJ (see note 1 below); endorsed by TJ as received 12 Apr. 1793 but recorded in SJL as received 17 Apr. 1793.

Throughout this letter the Editors have used the dollar sign to represent the cifrão, the Portuguese symbol for milréis. This conventional notation of Portuguese money is conveniently discussed in John J. McCusker, *Money and Exchange in Europe and America, 1600-1775: A Hand-book* (Chapel Hill, 1978), 107; see also note to Bulkeley & Son to TJ, 7 Jan. 1793, where TJ's missing FAVOUR of 11 OCTR. L. Y. was first acknowledged. Two additional letters from Bulkeley & Son to TJ of 22 and 28 Feb. 1793, recorded in SJL as received 14 Apr. 1793, have not been found.

[1] Below this line TJ wrote: "1793. Apr. 21. to Curson for freight 3. pipes wine 12.D. James Brown frt. from Baltimore and duties."

From John Carey

SIR   Feb: 20. [1793]

Whenever you are pleased to favor me with my transcripts of the state-papers, I wish to proceed to the copying of many of the enclosures, which I omitted at first to insert in their proper places. I cannot indeed help regretting, that so many of the originals are missing, and, I fear, irrecoverably lost, unless the President has preserved copies of them. The want of them will oblige me to omit the resolutions of Congress, to which they gave birth—it being my intention to add the resolutions, at the bottom of the page, by way of note to each letter, on which they were founded. I have the honor to be, with due respect, Sir, your most obliged & humble servt.   JOHN CAREY

RC (DLC); partially dated; endorsed by TJ as received 20 Feb. 1793 and so recorded in SJL.

From Tench Coxe

Feby. 20. 1793.

Mr. Coxe has the honor to inclose a further letter to Mr. Jefferson, on the subject of the Danish Trade received this day. He has not yet heard from R. Island, but he presumes the two houses will concur in the substance of their Information.

Mr. Coxe finds the Dutch Consul to think that the U.S. being within the limits of their E. India Company Spirits can be imported at the Companys duties $3\frac{1}{2}$ to $4\frac{1}{2}$ ℔ Ct. This may be the case *on sufferance*, which is a very bad footing; and it may be the Case in regard to Spirits distilled from *Molasses*, a *west Indian* raw material: but Mr. Coxe does not believe it would be the case on an experiment of *Grain* Spirits or *fruit* Spirits, of which it is agreed no trial in holland has yet been made. It is admitted by Mr. Heineken that the prohibition of flour, bread and pealed Barley, tho our produce, could not be avoided by the cover of the West India Company—nor could the prohibitory duties of Beef nor the great duties on butter be so avoided.

RC (DLC); endorsed by TJ.

In connection with the preparation of TJ's Report on Commerce, Coxe elicited two letters of 9 Feb. 1793 on DANISH TRADE with the United States from the New York City mercantile firm of Samuel Ward & Brothers. In the first, which he passed on to TJ sometime before writing the above letter, Ward & Brothers dealt with Danish purchases of American ships, Danish alien, commercial, and port duties, and American exports to Denmark, not-

ing that Copenhagen was the only Danish port in which Americans traded. In the second, which he enclosed with the above letter, the New York merchants continued their discussion of Danish alien duties and also dealt with Danish tonnage duties (RCs in DLC; both addressed to Coxe; both endorsed by TJ: "Denmark"). These letters did not cause TJ to alter the draft of the Report on Commerce that he had recently asked Coxe to review (see Coxe to TJ, 5 Feb. [1793], and enclosure).

From Tobias Lear

February 20th: 1793

By the President's command T. Lear has the honor to return to the Secretary of State, the enclosed letter addressed to the Speaker of the House of Representatives, and to inform the Secretary that the President approves the same.

The President was engaged with the Secretary of War when the enclosed was put into his hands which prevented him from looking at it 'till this moment.

2 o'clock

RC (DLC); endorsed by TJ as received 20 Feb. 1793. Enclosure: TJ to the Speaker of the House of Representatives, 20 Feb. 1793.

To Robert Montgomery

SIR   Philadelphia, February 20th. 1793

The President of the United States desiring to avail the public of your services as Consul of the United States for the Port of Alicant, in the Kingdom of Spain, I have now the honor of inclosing the Commission and a copy of the Laws of the United States, together with the copy of a Circular letter written to our Consuls and Vice-Consuls, the 26th. of August 1790, to serve as their standing Instructions. I am with sentiments of perfect respect, Sir, &c.   TH: JEFFERSON

FC (Lb in DNA: RG 59, DCI); at head of text: "To Robert Montgomery Esqre."; note at foot of text: "A similar Letter to the foregoing was written to the following Gentlemen, and a copy of the Laws of the United States, and Circular Letter mentioned therein, transmitted to each:

To Edward Fox, as Consul for the Port of Falmouth, in the Kingdom of Great Britain.
Nathaniel Cutting, for the port of Havre de Grace, in France.
John Parish, for the port of Hamburgh.
Joseph Yznardi, for the port of Cadiz, in the Kingdom of Spain.
David Matthew Clarkson, for the Island of St. Eustatia.
Benjamin Hamnell Phillips, for the Island of Curracao."
Not recorded in SJL. Enclosures: (1) Circular to American Consuls, 26 Aug. 1790. (2) Consular Commission for Montgom-

ery, 20 Feb. 1793 (FC in same, Commissions of Consuls and Consular Agents).

TJ this day wrote a variant text of this letter to Henry Cooper, notifying him of his appointment as consul at Santa Cruz but not enclosing a copy of the laws (PrC in DLC, in the hand of George Taylor, Jr., unsigned, at foot of text: "Henry Cooper Esqr."; FC in DNA: RG 59, DCI). Joseph Yznardi, Jr., acknowledged TJ's letter in a brief note from Philadelphia of 2 Apr. 1793 accepting the appointment as consul at Cadiz and promising his endeavors to serve satisfactorily (RC in same, CD; at foot of text: "Thomas Jefferson Esqr Secratary of State &ca. &ca."; endorsed by TJ as received 3 Apr. 1793). For the background of these appointments, see Memorandum on Consuls and Consular Appointments, 15 Feb. 1793, and Memorandum on Consuls Recommended for Appointment, 18 Feb. 1793.

Notes on Alexander Hamilton's Report on Foreign Loans

[ca. 20 Feb. 1793]

Extracts from Colo. Hamilton's letters to Mr. Short,
laid before the H. of Representatives. Feb. 1793.

A.H.'s letter to W.S. Nov. 26. 92. in the observations on it[1] to justify
his idea of a suspension of payment for 6. months,
a year, or much longer he says the Executive here
had considered and admitted the propriety of a suspension of payments.

The opinion given in the first week of Nov. to
the Presidt. by those whom he consulted was *unanimously* that after the dethronement of the king the
government was become incomplete and incompetent to give a valid discharge for any payment, that
therefore payments should be suspended till there
was some legitimate body authorized to receive and
discharge. Three out of four were of opinion the
National convention, about to meet, would be such
a body, but as we did not know whether it's meeting might not be prevented by the D. of Brunswick
then marching directly on Paris, it was thought
safest to suspend payment *till further orders*. Before
such orders could be renewed, it was found there
was no money left for them to operate on. They
now await for money.

do. Aug. 29. 90. he confirms the loan made by our bankers without
previous authority. (It[2] was for 3. Milln. flor.) He
destines $1\frac{1}{2}$ Milln. of it to French debt. Why was not
the whole so destined? What other foreign purposes
could be adequate to such a defalcation?

do. 91. May. 9. directions to Treasurer to draw 800,000
24. to reserve in the hands of bankers $1\frac{1}{2}$ milln. of the
next succeeding loan, and one million of the one
immediately succeeding that for completing the
purposes of the act for borrowing 12. Milln.

Nov. 1. has directed Treasurer to draw for 1. Milln. flor.
and at the close of this month shall direct him to
draw for another milln.

30. the prices of the public debt here rendering it questionable whether to purchase with monies borrowed @ 5. per Ct. and there being *reasons of the moment* against beginning the redemption of the 6. per Cts. I shall forbear drawing for the 2d. milln. mentioned in my letter of 1st. inst. Payments for interest on Dutch loans for 92. to be out of monies borrowed abroad, which will leave in the Treasy. the sums which ought to be remitted for interest as part of the 2. Mills. authorised to be borrowed by the act for the redemption of the public debt.

1792. Apr. 2. the Treasurer will draw for 500,000*f*—I consider it as for the interest of the U.S. to prosecute purchases of the public debt with monies borrowed on the terms of the last loan, and mean as fast as it can be done with safety to draw for a further sum of 2½ millns. florins to complete the 3 millns. intended by my last mentioned letter

July 25. has drawn for 500,000*f* and shall draw for 500,000*f*

by my letter of June 4. last your agency in the whole of the pecuniary business to continue and Mr. Morris as representative of the U.S. at France instructed to cooperate. I understand the Secy. of state that this instruction has been forwarded.

Sep. 13. Mr. Morris authorised to pay interest to foreign officers and to draw 105,000*f* for that

Dec. 31. has drawn for 1,237,500*f* and 24,750*f*

1790. Aug. 8. the Presidents instructions to A.H. committing to him the charge of borrowing under the two acts for 12. Mills. and 2 Millns.

to employ W.S. except where otherwise specially directed.

to borrow (within the limitations prescribed by law as to time of repayment and rate of interest) so much as necessary to pay instalments and interest of foreign debt becoming due before end of 1791. to apply the money to that with all convenient dispatch.

not to extend the loan beyond that amount unless it

can be done on terms more advantageous to U.S. than those on which residue of said debt shall stand or be.

but if residue can be paid off on terms of advantage you are to borrow and apply accordingly.

empowers him to make the necessary contracts.

if any negociation with any prince or state to whom any part of the debt is due be requisite he shall carry it on thro' the Minister &c of the U.S. with that prince or state 'for which purpose I shall direct the Secy. of state, with whom you are on this behalf to consult and concert, to co-operate with you.'

MS (DLC: TJ Papers, 82: 14225); entirely in TJ's hand; undated. Recorded in SJPL under 20 Feb. 1793: "Extracts from Hamilton's lres to Mr Short."

This document, consisting of TJ's notes on some of the letters and papers appended to the first of two reports on foreign loans that Alexander Hamilton submitted to the House of Representatives on 13-14 Feb. 1793, marks the continuation of the Secretary of State's efforts to document what he believed to be Hamilton's maladministration of the nation's finances (TJ's notes on Hamilton's earlier report on foreign loans are printed under 4 Jan. 1793). Hamilton drew up the February reports in response to two resolves, introduced by Congressman William B. Giles and passed by the House on 23 Jan. 1793, calling upon the President to provide it with copies of the authorities under which he had arranged for the negotiation of European loans under two acts of Congress—one of 4 Aug. 1790 authorizing the loan of up to $12,000,000 to pay the foreign debt, and another of 12 Aug. 1790 authorizing the loan of up to $2,000,000 to redeem the domestic debt—and with statements of the payments made on the American debts to France, Spain, and investors in the Netherlands with the proceeds of these loans. In response, Hamilton included in the first report copies of the authorizations he had received from the President in August 1790 to negotiate these loans, as well as his correspondence about them with William Short, the

agent he appointed to transact the loans, and Willink, Van Staphorst & Hubbard, the bankers of the United States government in Amsterdam. Both reports sought to refute Republican charges that he had corruptly drawn some of the borrowed funds to America for the benefit of the Bank of the United States (*Annals*, III, 835-40; Syrett, *Hamilton*, XIV, 17-67).

As these notes reveal, TJ concluded that the documentation appended to the first report substantiated Republican suspicions that Hamilton had exceeded his authority from the President and failed to comply with the express intent of Congress in regard to the negotiation of the loans and the disposition of their proceeds. This document, therefore, forms an important link in the chain of events that soon led to TJ's involvement in the effort by Congressman William B. Giles to censure Hamilton and call for his dismissal by the President (Editorial Note on Jefferson and the Giles resolutions, at 27 Feb. 1793). About this time James Madison wrote a series of observations on the same set of documents, with special emphasis on Hamilton's correspondence with Short, in which he also concluded that they supported Republican charges against the Secretary of the Treasury ("Notes as to Charges vs Secy Treasury brought in by Mr Giles' Resolns," undated but filed at 31 Dec. 1792 in DLC: Madison Papers and calendared in Madison, *Papers*, XIV, 450-1, under the conjectural date of 15-19 Feb. 1793).

Hamilton's OBSERVATIONS on his 26

Nov. 1792 letter to Short are in Syrett, *Hamilton*, XIV, 23-6. The President and the Cabinet approved the SUSPENSION OF PAYMENTS on the American debt to France in the middle of October rather than in THE FIRST WEEK OF NOV. 1792 (see TJ to Gouverneur Morris, 15 Oct. 1792, and note).

The LOAN MADE BY OUR BANKERS WITHOUT PREVIOUS AUTHORITY was a provisional loan of 3,000,000 florins negotiated on behalf of the United States government in January 1790 by Willink, Van Staphorst & Hubbard in order to forestall a plan under consideration by the beleaguered French finance minister Jacques Necker to allow a group of private speculators to purchase the American debt to France. Hamilton retrospectively approved this loan under the authority of the aforementioned debt acts of August 1790 empowering the President to borrow up to $14,000,000 in order to discharge the foreign debt and redeem the domestic debt (Syrett, *Hamilton*, VI, 210-18, 580-6). Then, as he explained in his second 13 Feb. 1793 report to the House on foreign loans, which TJ evidently did not read before he wrote these notes and which failed to persuade him afterwards, he decided for what he regarded as urgent reasons of national interest to apply part of this loan to the payment of the foreign debt as well as to the redemption of the domestic debt. Invoking the principle of executive discretion and insisting that his actions were consistent with the terms of the two 1790 debt acts, Hamilton informed the House that although in August 1790 he had regarded it as important to resume debt payments to France, he had considered it no less vital to maintain the government's credit by ensuring that in the event of an unanticipated deficiency in ordinary revenues it had adequate funds on hand to make the first scheduled interest payments to holders of the domestic debt in April 1791. He revealed, therefore, that he had used only half of the 3,000,000 florins to help pay the French debt, that he had drawn about 800,000 florins to the United States to help redeem the domestic debt, and that he had reserved the remainder for payment of the Dutch debt (same, XIV, 30-7; Edito-

rial Note on Jefferson and the Giles resolutions, at 27 Feb. 1793; TJ to Hamilton, 27 Mch. 1793).

TJ based his belief that Hamilton was guilty of a DEFALCATION in the handling of this loan on two documents contained in the Secretary of the Treasury's first report to the House of 13 Feb. 1793 on the subject of foreign loans. These were Hamilton's letter of 29 Aug. 1790 to William Short, which directed him to apply only half of the 3,000,000 florins from this loan to the FRENCH DEBT, and the PRESIDENTS INSTRUCTIONS to Hamilton, actually dated 28 Aug. 1790, on the negotiation of the loans in pursuance of the two debt acts—instructions which TJ construed as confining the loan strictly to the payment of the foreign debt. TJ's reading of these documents was influenced, in turn, by his own involvement in the original approval of this loan and the drafting of Hamilton's instructions. On or about 26 Aug. 1790 Hamilton wrote a letter to the President recommending that the government retrospectively approve the loan for 3,000,000 florins under the authority the debt acts, that it apply two-thirds of the proceeds, to be borrowed under the first act, to the payment of the debt to France, Spain, and Dutch investors, and the remainder, to be borrowed under the second act, to the redemption of the domestic debt. Hamilton also sent the President drafts of the powers and instructions Washington was to issue to him for negotiating loans under the acts. The President thereupon submitted Hamilton's letter and instructions to the Secretary of State for his opinion. In a 26 Aug. 1790 opinion for the President, TJ approved all of Hamilton's recommendations, suggesting only that the 1,000,000 florins be used in Amsterdam to purchase the domestic debt held by Europeans instead of drawing this money to the United States, and recommending that the instructions be amended to forbid Hamilton's agent in Europe to borrow more than $1,000,000 at a time. Although TJ had signified his support for Hamilton's proposals to sanction the January 1790 loan and to divide its proceeds between the foreign and domestic debts, he did not see the President's final instructions to Hamilton of 28 Aug. 1790, which pertained to both debts, until they appeared in the Secretary of the Treasury's first 13 Feb. 1793 report to the House on foreign loans. When he finally did read them he concluded that their failure specifically to approve Hamilton's proposed division of the loan meant that the Secretary of the Treasury had not received presidential authorization for applying part of it to the domestic debt. In contrast, Hamilton in this case apparently operated on the assumption that the Secretary of the Treasury might do what the President did not explicitly forbid, for immediately after he received these instructions from Washington he notified Willink, Van Staphorst & Hubbard that he intended to apply the loan to both debts in the same proportions he had originally suggested to the President (Syrett, *Hamilton*, VI, 566, 568-70, 579-86, XIV, 30-7;

Jefferson's Opinion on Fiscal Policy, 26 Aug. 1790; TJ to Hamilton, 27 Mch. 1793). In any case, Hamilton's alleged deviation from the President's instructions in the commingling of funds borrowed under the authority of the two acts figured prominently in the resolutions of censure in TJ's hand that have since been lost (see Editorial Note on Jefferson and the Giles resolutions, at 27 Feb. 1793).

THE ACT FOR THE REDEMPTION OF THE PUBLIC DEBT was the 12 Aug. 1790 act mentioned above (*Annals*, III, 2369-70). The LETTER OF JUNE 4 mentioned in Hamilton's 25 July 1792 letter to Short was actually a letter of 14 June 1792 (Syrett, *Hamilton*, XI, 519-20, XII, 104).

[1] TJ here canceled "he says to support."
[2] Before this word TJ canceled "I think."

Notes on Conversations with William Stephens Smith and George Washington

Feb. 20. 1793. Colo. W. S. Smith called on me to communicate intelligence from France. He had left Paris Nov. 9. He says that the French Ministers are entirely broken with Gouvr. Morris, shut their doors to him and will never receive another communication from him. They wished Smith to be the bearer of a message from the Presidt. to this effect, but he declined and they said in that case they would press it thro' their own minister here. He says they are sending Genet here with full powers to give us all the privileges we can desire in their countries, and particularly in the W. Indies, that they even contemplate to set them free the next summer: that they propose to emancipate S. America, and will send 45. ships of the line there in the spring, and Mirande at the head of the expedition: that they desire our debt to be paid them in provisions, and have authorised him to negociate this. In confirmation of this he delivers a letter to the Presidt. from Le brun, Minr. for forn. affrs., in which Le brun says that Colo. Smith 'will communicate plans worthy of his (the Pr.'s) great mind, and he shall be happy to receive his opinion as to the means the most suitable to effect it.'[1]

I had 5. or 6. days ago received from Ternant extracts from the letters of his ministers, complaining of both G. Morris and Mr. Short. I sent them this day to the Presidt. with an extract from a private letter of Mr. Short's justifying himself, and I called this evening on the Presidt. He said he considered the extracts from Ternant as very serious, in short as decisive: that he saw that G. Morris could be no longer continued there consistent with the public good, that the moment was critical in our favor and ought not to be lost: that he was extremely at a loss what arrangement to make. I asked him whether G. Morris and Pinckney might not change places. He said that would be a sort of remedy, but not a radical one. That if the French ministry conceived G. M. to be hostile to them, if they had been jealous merely on his proposing to visit London, they would never be satisfied with us at placing him at London permanently. He then observed that tho' I had unfixed the day on which I had intended to resign, yet I appeared fixed in doing it at no great distance of time: that in this case, he could not but wish that I would go to Paris, that the moment was important, I possessed the confidence of both sides and might do great good; that he wished I could do it were it only to stay there a year or two. I told him that my mind was so bent on retirement that I could not think of launching forth again in a new business, that I could never again cross the Atlantic: and that as to the opportunity of doing good, this was likely to be the scene of action, as Genet was bringing powers to do the business here, but that I could not think of going abroad. He replied that I had pressed him to a continuance in public service and refused to do the same myself. I said the case was very different: he united the confidence of all America, and was the only person who did so: his services therefore were of the last importance: but for myself my going out would not be noted or known, a thousand others could supply my place to equal advantage. Therefore I felt myself free: and that as to the mission to France I thought Pinckney perfectly proper. He desired me then to consider maturely what arrangement should be made.

Smith in speaking of Morris said that at his own table in presence of his company and servants he cursed the French ministers as a set of damned rascals, said the king would still be replaced on his throne: he said he knew they had written to have him recalled, and expected to be recalled. He consulted Smith to know whether he could bring his furniture here duty free. Smith has mentioned the situation of G. Morris freely to others here.

Smith said also that the ministers told him they meant to begin their attack at the mouth of the Missi., and to sweep along the bay of

Mexico Southwardly, and that they would have no objections to our incorporating into our government the two Floridas.

MS (DLC); entirely in TJ's hand; last paragraph written in a different shade of ink and possibly at a later date. Entry in SJPL: "notes relative to G. Morris, French affairs—G.W's proposn to me to go to Paris." Included in the "Anas."

William Stephens Smith, the son-in-law of John Adams, had been authorized by the Provisional Executive Council of France in November 1792 to negotiate the immediate payment of the United States debt to France and to use some of the resultant funds to purchase food and war supplies for the French. Lebrun, the French foreign minister, commended this plan in a letter to Washington of 8 Nov. 1792 (DLC: Washington Papers). The Washington administration subsequently declined to negotiate with Smith, who nevertheless found other means of procuring supplies in the United States for France (Cabinet Opinion on the American Debt to France, 2 Mch. 1793; Nussbaum, *Commercial Policy*, 212-25). When Smith left Paris early in November 1792 the French government was planning to dispatch an expedition to liberate South America under the leadership of Francisco de Miranda, a Venezuelan revolutionary leader who had recently become a general in the French army, but it abandoned this

plan shortly thereafter (William S. Robertson, *The Life of Miranda*, 2 vols. [Chapel Hill, 1929], I, 120-30).

Washington did not abandon his efforts to persuade TJ to replace Gouverneur Morris as minister to France after this conversation. Instead he asked Attorney General Edmund Randolph to second them. Randolph sought first to convince TJ and then apparently James Madison to serve as Morris's successor in Paris, but to no avail. He then advised Washington to take no action on Morris for the moment, arguing that a simple exchange of diplomatic assignments between Morris and Thomas Pinckney in London would be unpopular in France and America alike, and suggested that it would be expedient to await the arrival of Edmond Charles Genet in order to determine the true depth of French dissatisfaction with Morris (Randolph to Washington, 22 Feb. 1793, DLC: Washington Papers). Washington accepted this advice, and in the long run his failure to find a satisfactory alternative to Morris at this time was one of the primary reasons why Morris remained as minister to France until James Monroe arrived in Paris to replace him in August 1794.

[1] Closing quotation mark supplied.

From Thomas Mann Randolph, Jr.

DEAR SIR   Monticello Feb: 20: 1793.

Your letter by the post before last has not yet reached Monto. and consequently we did not know of your having changed your resolution to retire in the spring till last week. The information throws a gloom over our prospects of happiness this summer and of course gives no joy at Monto. but your determination was received with much applause by the county at large where the interest in your fame is greater than that in your person. The different works over which you request my superintendance shall be forwarded with all my power and directed with all the little ability I have. My Gratitude and affection are so strong that they will come near to Self-love alltho it is impossible for any *motive* to equal it in force.

The children and Patsy are in perfect health. Your sincere friend & hble Servt.   Th: M. Randolph

Diary.

M. Ob. Th.	E. Ob. Th.
Feb: 14. 35. fair.	34. f.
15. 38. f.	43. f.
16. 39. r.	45. rain
17. 44. r.	53. f.
18. 43. c.	50. cloudy
19. 44. r.	43. rain
20. 52. light clouds	

RC (MHi); endorsed by TJ as received 9 Mch. 1793 and so recorded in SJL.

To the Speaker of the House of Representatives

Sir   Philadelphia, February 20th. 1793.

The House of Representatives, about the close of the Session before the last, referred to me the Report of a Committee on a message from the President of the United States of the 14th. of Feb. 1791, with directions to report to Congress the nature and extent of the privileges and restrictions of the commercial intercourse of the United States with foreign Nations, and measures for it's improvement. The report was accordingly prepared during the ensuing recess ready to be delivered at their next Session, that is to say, at the last. It was thought possible at that time, however, that some changes might take place in the existing state of Things, which might call for corresponding changes in measures. I took the liberty of mentioning this in a letter to the Speaker of the House of Representatives, to express an opinion that a suspension of proceedings thereon for a time, might be expedient, and to propose retaining the Report 'till the present session, unless the House should be pleased to signify their pleasure to the contrary. The changes then contemplated, have not taken place, nor, after waiting as long as the term of the session will admit, in order to learn something further on the subject, can any thing definite thereon be now said. If, therefore, the House wishes to proceed on the subject,[1] the Report shall

[246]

be delivered at a moments warning. Should they not chuse to take it up till their next Session, it will be an advantage to be permitted to keep it by me till then, as some further particulars may perhaps be procured relative to certain parts of our commerce, of which precise information is difficult to obtain. I make this suggestion, however, with the most perfect deference to their will, the first intimation of which shal! be obeyed on my part so as to occasion them no delay. I have the honor to be, with sentiments of the most perfect respect and Esteem, Sir, Your most obedient and most humble servant

PrC (DLC); in the hand of George Taylor, Jr., unsigned; with cancellation made in ink (see note 1 below); at foot of first page: "The Speaker of the house of Representatives of the united States." FC (Lb in DNA: RG 59, DL). Tr (Lb in DNA: RG 233, House Records, TR). Not recorded in SJL. Enclosed in TJ to Washington, 20 Feb. 1793, and Tobias Lear to TJ, 20 Feb. 1793.

Three days later TJ reported to Washington, who had approved the letter this day, that a House committee had called upon him to discuss the Report on Commerce. Although TJ advised the committee of his willingness to submit the report "upon the shortest notice," he had argued in favor of delaying submission until the next session of Congress because "circumstances might occur to render a material alteration in the Report necessary—and moreover, that its being now given in might have an effect unfriendly

[to] the U.S. in the proposed treaty with the Western Indians" (Washington, *Journal*, 64-5; Tobias Lear to TJ, 20 Feb. 1793). As the last part of his remark and the cancellation recorded in note 1 below indicate, TJ was obviously concerned that his criticism of British commercial policy in the report would provoke the British to disrupt the forthcoming Lower Sandusky conference between the United States and the Western tribes. In keeping with TJ's recommendation, the House resolved on 25 Feb. 1793 that it would be inexpedient to submit the Report on Commerce during the current session (JHR, I, 718; Tr of House resolve in DLC, signed by John Beckley and endorsed by TJ). TJ's earlier LETTER TO THE SPEAKER on this report was that of 22 Mch. 1792.

[1] Here the following words are lined out in ink: "and I know of no circumstance at present but their own convenience which need enter into the consideration."

To George Washington

Feb. 20. 1793.

Th: Jefferson, with his respects to the President, has the honor of inclosing him a letter he proposes to send to the Speaker to-day, if approved by the President: also the translation of some papers given him by Mr. Ternant three or four days ago, which he has not before had time to prepare: also extract of a private letter from Mr. Short. Th:J. will have the honor of waiting on the President at one aclock on these subjects.

RC (DNA: RG 59, MLR); addressed: "The President of [...]"; endorsed by Tobias Lear. PrC (DLC). Tr (Lb in DNA: RG 59, SDC). Recorded in SJPL.

Enclosures: (1) Extract of William Short   20 Feb. 1793. Other enclosure printed
to TJ, 20 Nov. 1792. (2) TJ to the   below.
Speaker of the House of Representatives,

ENCLOSURE

Extracts of Letters concerning
Gouverneur Morris and William Short

[20 Feb. 1793]

Pro memoriâ. Different extracts relative to the Minister Plen. of the U.S. in
France.

Letter from M. Le Brun Minister of foreign affairs to the Minister of France
with the U.S. dated Sep. 13. 1792.

'We have been as much astonished, as piqued at the forms, and tone assumed
by the American Minister. We expected to find in him dispositions which
would manifest the close union which should prevail between two people
animated by the same principles of liberty, made to esteem and love one another
reciprocally on account of the connections and relations of interest which
subsist between them. It has appeared that Mr. Morris is in no wise penetrated
with these truths. He has on the contrary demonstrated *humour* [indisposition
or dislike] towards us. The Provisory Executive council, informed of these
facts, charges you to speak of it to Mr. Jefferson in suitable terms, and to
express to him our discontent at the conduct of the American minister.'

Letter from the Minister of public contributions to the Minister of foreign
affairs, a copy of which was inclosed in the preceding. dated Sep. 10. 1792.

'It is impossible not to see in the scruples manifested by Mr. Morris, on the
subject of our present government, the man accused of giving counsels at the
Palace, while they were plotting there against the principles of the constitution.
I wish you, my dear collegue, to reflect very attentively on this Minister. His
ill will is proved. It is in vain that he conceals it under diplomatic forms, which
cannot be admitted between two nations who will not submit their liberty to
the dangers of Royalty. In this point of view, the Americans of the U.S. are our
brothers, and their Minister holding himself back from that candor which our
situation exacts on their part, betrays them as well as us. I think it necessary
then to inform the U.S. of his conduct, and to endeavor seriously to preserve us
from the artifices of a man dangerous by his talents and the ill use he appears
disposed to make of them.'

Letter from the Minister of foreign affairs to the Minister of France with the
U.S. dated Sep. 19. 1792.

'I have sufficiently informed you, in my last dispatch, of the ill-dispositions
of the American minister.

The resolution of Mr. Morris to chuse to quit Paris to go to London, appears
to us extraordinary enough: and I do not dissemble to you that it gives room
for suspicions as to the views and designs of this minister. But as he has since
resumed the determination of remaining in France, and of waiting there the
orders of his court, you may abstain from all reflections, and from taking any
steps with Mr. Jefferson on the subject of that journey.'

Pro memoriâ. Extract relative to Mr. Short.

Letter from the Minister of foreign affairs to the Minister of France with the U.S. dated Sep. 19. 1792.

'We complain with reason of the conduct of Mr. Morris. But you will see by the letter inclosed of our Minister at the Hague, that we are not less founded in reason to complain of Mr. Short. We charge you specially to ask satisfaction from the American ministry on a fact so much the more serious as the object of Mr. Short was to hinder a banking house of Amsterdam to remit to our national treasury a sum which the U.S. had deposited in the hands of the banker to be there subject to our disposal. We suppose that in submitting this maneuvre of Mr. Short to the judgment of his employers they will not hesitate to manifest to him their dissatisfaction at it, and to prescribe to him to be more prudent and more circumspect in future.'

Letter from the Minister of France at the Hague to the Minister of foreign affairs. dated Sep. 11. 1792.

'Messrs. William & John Willink, merchants of Amsterdam, were charged by the U.S. to deposit in the hands of the house of Hoguer, Grand & co. a sum of 15, or 1600,000 florins. The American Minister Mr. Short repaired lately to Amsterdam, and pressed in strong terms the banker Hoguer, to engage by his receipt not to pay the remittance to the National treasury but on an approbation signed by the king. The discussion was as lively as long, and at length Mr. Hoguer held himself to the ordinary forms. This conduct of Mr. Short is perfectly consistent with his language, as well as the intimacy of his connections with the enemy-ministers.'

MS (DNA: RG 59, MLR); entirely in TJ's hand; undated; at head of text: "Translation"; brackets in original; endorsed in part by Tobias Lear: "laid before the President Feby 20th. 1793." PrC (DLC: TJ Papers, 77: 13376-9).

The FORMS and TONE of Gouverneur Morris that so offended Lebrun are described in Morris to TJ, 30 Aug. 1792, and note, and enclosures summarized in note to Morris to TJ, 19 Sep. 1792. Etienne Clavière was the MINISTER OF PUBLIC CONTRIBUTIONS. For Morris's COUNSELS AT THE PALACE, see note to Morris to TJ, 10 June 1792.

Concerning William Short's delayed payment to the French government's bankers in Amsterdam of an installment of 1,625,000 florins on the American debt to France, see note to TJ to Short, 3 Jan. 1793.

Although Ternant received these letters on 7 Feb. 1793, he did not submit them to TJ until about the middle of the month when he was reasonably confident that their submission would not jeopardize his efforts to persuade the United States government to allow him to use 3,000,000 livres tournois of the debt to France for the purchase of supplies in America for the French nation (Turner, *CFM*, 170-1, 173).

To Pierre Billet

SIR   Philadelphia, February 21st. 1793.

A petition signed by a number of persons at Post Vincennes, of whom you are first named, has been presented to the President of the

United States, complaining 1st. of duties imposed on all merchandize which raise them to exorbitant prices with you: and 2. that you are not permitted to sell or trade in any thing but on paying immense sums. The President has had this petition under consideration, and I am[1] charged by him to observe that if by the Duties complained of, you mean those imposed by the Spanish Government on supplies through the Missisippi, these are not subject to alteration by this Government. Relief from this must depend on the result of negotiations with Spain on behalf of our Western citizens for the free navigation of the Missisippi: but if by these duties is meant the impost paid on foreign importations on their entrance into our Atlantic ports, this depends on the Legislature of the United States, who would probably see great doubt and difficulty in taking off the imposts from those particular Articles of importation which are sent forward to your settlement.

As to the second Complaint, it is supposed to have in view the regulations established by the Legislature for the Indian trade. Some regulations were found to be necessary; those established were the result of the best information which could be obtained but might still be revised by the Legislature if it can be shewn that hardship and injustice result from any particular part of them: But such proofs should be brought forward and well articulated. In the mean time these regulations do not prohibit the disposal of any thing which is of the produce of your farms, the President will at all times feel peculiar happiness in contributing to relieve your settlement from any well-founded grievances. After desiring you to communicate this to your fellow petitioners, I subscribe myself Sir, Your most humble servant

PrC (DLC); in the hand of George Taylor, Jr., with additions in ink in TJ's hand; unsigned; at foot of first page in ink in TJ's hand: "Mr. P. Billet." FC (Lb in DNA: RG 59, DL). Enclosed in TJ to George Washington, 22 Feb. 1793.

On 30 Jan. 1793 Tobias Lear wrote a brief note transmitting to the Secretary of State "two petitions from Sundry Inhabitants of Post Vincennes, which the President requests the Secretary will take into consideration and report to him his opinion of what ought to be done respecting them" (RC in DLC, endorsed by TJ as received 30 Jan. 1793; PrC in DNA: RG 59, MLR; FC in Lb in same, SDC). See also Washington, *Journal*, 39-40. The first of these petitions, addressed to Presi-

dent Washington, dated 5 Oct. 1792 and signed by Billet and twenty-eight other French residents of Post Vincennes in the Northwest Territory, set forth the complaints described above by TJ (DNA: RG 59, MLR; in French). On the petition TJ wrote the following undated note: "Genl. Sinclair knows of no duties on the merchandize of the petitioners, unless they mean either our own Impost, or the duties imposed by the Spaniards down the river. By the paiment of these immense sums on the sales and bargains, he knows nothing which can be meant but that they are not allowed to trade with the Indians but on taking out a license which costs 100.D." For the second petition on which the President solicited TJ's opinion, see TJ to Paul Gamelin, 21 Feb. 1793.

For the REGULATIONS ESTABLISHED BY THE LEGISLATURE in 1790 requiring all those trading with the Indians to obtain a license, see *Annals*, II, 2301-3.

¹ Word written in the margin in ink by TJ.

To Paul Gamelin

SIR   Philadelphia Feby. 21. 1793.

The President has had under consideration the Petition of yourself and others, complaining of illegal acts committed on you by a body of armed men from Virginia in the year 1786, stating that you are pursuing redress through the channel of the Courts of Kentucky, have not yet been able to obtain it, and are unequal to a continuation of the expenses necessary for the object. Injuries for which the laws have provided a remedy, do not admit of any other interference; for what might be done in addition to the law to help the one party, would be considered as an oppression of the other. We are bound to believe that the Courts of Justice are equally open and impartial to both. If either party is too poor to prosecute or defend themselves, the laws in most of the States, and particularly as is believ'd in that of Kentucky, provide for the maintenance or defence of the suit *in formâ pauperis*, and nothing is necessary to obtain this protection but an application to the Court and proof of the Condition of the party applying. I have it in charge from the President to assure you of the interest he feels in your situation, of his wishes that you may receive substantial justice, and his confidence that you will; regretting at the same time that the occasion does not admit of his being instrumental towards it. I beg the favor of you to communicate this to your fellow Petitioners, and am, Sir, Your very humble servt.

PrC (DLC); in a clerk's hand; unsigned; at foot of text: "Mr. Paul Gamelin. Post Vincennes." FC (Lb in DNA: RG 59, DL). Enclosed in TJ to George Washington, 22 Feb. 1793.

Paul Gamelin, who died about a month before this letter was written, had been a militia captain, justice of the peace, and treasurer in Knox County in the Northwest Territory (*History of Knox and Daviess Counties Indiana* [Chicago, 1886], 204; *Terr. Papers*, III, 316, 384, 405). He and Pierre Gamelin, a judge of the Knox County Court of Com-

mon Pleas, had witnessed a 6 Oct. 1792 petition of Laurence Baradone, John Darguilleur, John Toulon, and Peter Trousserau, four French merchants at Post Vincennes, asking President Washington to consider their complaint against General George Rogers Clark and other military officers for confiscating property of theirs worth almost 70,000 livres while leading a detachment of Kentucky militia against hostile Indians in the vicinity of Vincennes in 1786. According to the four merchants, who had come to Post Vincennes from New Orleans in 1783, Clark had them arrested and imprisoned and their property condemned by court martial and forfeited to the United States in retaliation for a similar action taken by Spanish officials against an American citizen on the Mississippi. Reduced to indigence and thus far unable to obtain legal redress in Kentucky, the four petitioners urged the President to "obtain for them from the United States such Relief as they in their Wisdom may find equitable" (DNA: RG 59, MLR; signed by the Gamelins and Darguilleur, and with marks by Baradone, Toulon, and Troussereau). TJ, however, apparently failed to realize that Gamelin had merely signed as a witness to the PETITION OF YOURSELF AND OTHERS. Washington had referred the petition to the Secretary of State on 30 Jan. 1793 (see note to TJ to Pierre Billet, 21 Feb. 1793). For a fuller explanation of Clark's actions, see James Alton James, *The Life of George Rogers Clark* (Chicago, 1928), 352-62.

From Wakelyn Welch

SIR   London 21 Feby 1793

In 1786 when I had the pleasure of settling and adjusting your account which left a Balance in favor of the Partnership of R. Cary & Co. £88.13.4 flattered myself you would before now have sent me a Remittance for the debt arose from Goods shipd on Commission which only came to £1.1.6. We ought not to sustain any loss. I have inclosed a Copy of the last settlement with the Interest £24 making together £112.13.4 which I hope you will favor me with and if inconvenient to procure a Remittance may trouble Mr. Waller to receive it.

As to Mr. Wayles debt you assured me was very safe and partly owing to Mr. Waller's Father that it had not been before discharged. Mr. Eppes was the acting Executor during your absence and on your return you would be enabled to favor me with farther particulars but as yet, nothing has transpired. Relying on your promise & friendship am Your Excellcys Much Obliged Servt   WAKE. WELCH

RC (MoSHi: Bixby Collection); at foot of text: "His Excellcy Thos. Jefferson"; endorsed by TJ as received 18 July 1793 and so recorded in SJL. Enclosure not found.

From Robert Crew

SIR   London Feby 22d 1793

I take the liberty of enclosing for you the morning chronicle for this day; it contains a motion by Mr. Gray for an address to the King against the War with France, which paper may be acceptable to you, should the subject it contains not have reached you before.

In order the better to enable me to serve my friends, and that neither their interest nor my own may suffer should business at any time cause me to be absent from London, I have given Mr. Thos. Allport of this City a concern in my business, and formed a copartnership with him which commenced the 1st. of last month. I shall think myself very much favoured should you at any time give us your commands.

This government offer 7/ ℔ bus. for American Wheat that may touch in England for orders, in order to prevent the French from being supplied. At the same time British Wheat is only 5/10 ℔ bus. I am, with the greatest Respect Sir Your most Obedt Servt

ROBT CREW

RC (DLC); endorsed by TJ as received 24 Apr. 1793 and so recorded in SJL.

In a MOTION defeated in the House of Commons on 21 Feb. 1793, Charles Grey, a Whig follower of Charles James Fox, proposed the adoption of an address to the king questioning the advisability of war with France and urging a prompt restoration of peace (Thomas C. Hansard, comp.,

The Parliamentary History of England . . ., 36 vols. [London, 1806-20], xxx, 454-60; DNB). At some point TJ also received a printed circular letter of 10 Dec. 1792 from Crew and Thomas Allport announcing the formation of their COPARTNERSHIP (RC in DLC; addressed: "Thomas Jefferson Secretary of State Philadelphia"; see also Vol. 18: 309n).

From F. P. Van Berckel

High Street Feby. 22 1793.

Mr. vanBerckel presents his Compliments to Mr. Jefferson, and has the honor of Sending herewith two or three remarks on Mr. Jefferson's Letter of the 13th. of this month. Should any thing worth noticing, occur on the Same Subject, Mr. vBerckel will have the honor of Communicating it in the same private and informal manner.

RC (DLC).

ENCLOSURE

Notes on Jefferson's Draft Report on Commerce

[22 Feb. 1793]

By resolve of January 16th. 1786 the States General have determined, that no foreign built Vessel Can obtain a Mediterranean pass, which lessens the value of Such Ships materially.

At St. Eustatius, St. Martins and Curaçao, the duties on American and all other foreign Vessels are but trifling, but at Surinam, Demerary and the other Dutch possessions in America, they are heavy, tho' it Cannot be exactly ascertained to what amount.

Letters have been received from Amsterdam dated 24th. October last, in which it is mention'd, that the export duties there on Goods to North America were by agreement entered into with the Dutch West India Company augmented one half perCent. Of this however no official account has been received.

MS (DLC); in Van Berckel's hand; undated; endorsed by TJ as received 23 Feb. 1793.

To George Washington

[22 Feb. 1793]

Th: Jefferson with his respects to the President, incloses him a letter he received from Mr. Short yesterday, by which he expected to leave the Hague on the 12th. of December: also the answers he has prepared to the two petitions from Post Vincennes.

RC (DNA: RG 59, MLR); undated; addressed: "The President of the US."; endorsed by Tobias Lear as a letter of 22 Feb. 1793. Tr (Lb in same, SDC). Not recorded in SJL. Enclosures: (1) William Short to TJ, 8 Dec. 1792. (2) TJ to

Pierre Billet, 21 Feb. 1793. (3) TJ to Paul Gamelin, 21 Feb. 1793.

Washington approved the ANSWERS ... TO THE TWO PETITIONS FROM POST VINCENNES and returned them to TJ this day (Washington, *Journal*, 62).

To Jean Baptiste Ternant

SIR   Philadelphia Feb. 23. 1793

I have laid before the President of the US. your notification of the 17th. instant, in the name of the Provisory Executive council, charged with the administration of your government, that the French nation has constituted itself into a Republic. The President receives with great satisfaction this attention of the Executive council, and the desire they have manifested of making known to us the resolution entered into by the National convention, even before a definitive regulation of their new establishment could take place. Be assured Sir that the government and the citizens of the US. view with the most sincere pleasure every advance of your nation towards it's happiness, an object essentially connected with it's liberty, and they consider the union of principles and pursuits between our two countries as a link which binds still closer their interests and affections. The genuine and general effusions of joy which you saw overspread our country on their seeing the liberties of yours rise superior to foreign invasion and domestic trouble have proved to you that our sympathies are great and sincere, and we earnestly wish on our part that these our mutual dispositions may be improved to mutual good by establishing our commercial intercourse on principles as friendly to natural right and freedom as are those of our governments. I am with sincere esteem & respect, Sir, your most obedient & most humble servant   TH: JEFFERSON

PrC (DLC); at foot of text: "The Minister of France." FC (Lb in DNA: RG 59, DL). Tr (AMAE: CPEU, xxxvii); French translation.

This day TJ submitted the above letter to Washington, together with letters from William Short of 9 Nov. and 18 Dec. 1792 and from Elias Vanderhorst of 24 and

31 Dec. 1792. Washington immediately approved the letter to Ternant, and on 24 Feb. 1793 Tobias Lear wrote a brief note to TJ, informing him of the President's approval and returning all five letters (RC in DLC; addressed: "The Secretary of State"; endorsed by TJ as received 24 Feb. 1793). See also Washington, *Journal*, 64, 65.

Tobias Lear to the Cabinet

United States, February 24th: 1793

The President of the United States requests the attendance of the Secretary of State,[1] at *nine O'clock tomorrow morning*, at the President's House, on the subject of the Note sent to the Secretary[2] from the President, on the 17th Inst. and that the Secretary will bring with him such remarks as he may have committed to writing in pursuance of said Note.

At the same time the President will lay before the heads of the Departments[3] some communications which he has just received from General Hull.

RC (DLC); endorsed by TJ as received 24 Feb. 1793. FC (Lb in DLC: Washington Papers); at head of text: "(Circular) The Secretary of State: The Secretary of the Treasury; The Secretary of War, and The Attorney General of the U.S."; with blanks as noted below.

For the ensuing meeting of the Cabinet,

see Cabinet Opinions on Indian Affairs, 25 Feb. 1793, and note.

[1] Blank space in FC for preceding three words.
[2] Blank space in FC for this word here and below.
[3] FC here adds "and the Attorney General."

From Tobias Lear

Feby 24th: 1793

The enclosed letter came under cover to the President, and is by his direction transmitted to Mr. Jefferson.

The President sends likewise a letter from Mr. Vall Travers to him, with a request that Mr. Jefferson will peruse the same, and if it requires an acknowledgement that Mr. Jefferson would give it to Mr. Vall Travers.

RC (DLC); dateline precedes postscript; addressed: "Mr. Jefferson"; erroneously endorsed by TJ as received 23 Feb. 1793. Enclosures: (1) Rodolph Vall-Travers to the President of the "honble. Society for promoting Arts and Manufactures throughout the United States of N. America" [American Philosophical Society], Amsterdam, 13 Dec. 1792, reporting that in Europe's unsettled state "useful Emigrants and Artists of all Denominations" can be persuaded to move to "your Land of legal Liberty, Peace and Industry"; announcing his intention, once appointed agent, of settling in Brussels and there using the liberty of the press and his own extensive European connections to second the Society's wishes; enclosing a description and samples of a new method invented by Dandiran, a French fugitive from Guienne now in the Netherlands, of carding, spinning, and weaving raw hemp cheaper and better than linen; promising to support Dandiran and his family until he hears whether the Society wishes to sponsor him; and directing that correspondence be sent to the care of Beerenbroek & Van Dooren at Amsterdam under TJ's protection (RC in PPAmP). (2) "Mr. Dandiran's Succinct Account of the respective Charges and Profits, in manufacturing Hemp, after his improved Method, compared with the common Method of manufacturing Flax; ... Imparted to Rh. Vall Travers, at the

Hague, by the Inventor Decr. 9th. 1792" (MS in same; entirely in Vall-Travers's hand). (3) Vall-Travers to Washington, Amsterdam, 10 Dec. 1792, acknowledging TJ's reply to his earlier letters to the President, requesting an appointment as United States "Agent, Consul, or Resident" at Brussels, suggesting that the paper on hemp can serve as an example of the useful immigration to America he could encourage if given this post, and recommending the Amsterdam firm of Beerenbroek & Van Dooren if the United States needs to borrow additional money in Europe (RC and Dupl in DLC: Washington Papers).

The first two enclosures (identified in Washington, *Journal*, 65-6) were submitted on 15 Mch. 1793 to a meeting of the American Philosophical Society chaired by TJ. The Society immediately appointed a committee on hemp, which recommended at the next meeting that American manufacturing societies be notified of the new invention and that Vall-Travers be informed of "the American system of patent rights," of the abundance of hemp in America, and of the readiness of several persons to employ Dandiran if his invention answered the description (APS, *Proceedings*, XXII, pt. 3 [1885], 213-14). No reply by TJ to Vall-Travers's 10 Dec. 1792 letter to Washington has been found.

To Martha Jefferson Randolph

MY DEAR DEAR DAUGHTER   Philadelphia Feb. 24. 1793.

We have no letter from Monticello since Mr. Randolph's of Jan. 30. to Maria. However we hope you are all well and that there are letters on the road which will tell us so. Maria writes to-day. Congress will rise on Saturday next, a term which is joyous to all as it affords some relaxation of business to all. We have had the mildest winter ever known, having had only two snows to cover the ground, and these remained but a short time. Heavy rains now falling will render the roads next to impassable for the members returning home. Colo. Monroe will stay some days after the rising of Congress.—Bob was here lately, and as he proposed to return to Richmond and thence to Monticello I charged him with enquiring for the box with the servants clothes, should Mr. Randolph not yet have heard of it. It went from hence the 12th. of December by the Schooner Mary, Capt. Swaile, bound for Norfolk and Richmd. The capt. undertook to deliver it to Mr. Brown in Richmond. From these circumstances it may certainly be found. Perhaps however an enquiry at Norfolk may be necessary. Present me affectionately to Mr. Randolph. Kiss dear Anne and ask her if she remembers me and will write to me. Health to the little one and happiness to you all. Your's affectionately my dear

TH: JEFFERSON

RC (NNP); at foot of text: "Mrs. Randolph"; endorsed by Mrs. Randolph. PrC (ViU: Edgehill-Randolph Papers). Tr (same); 19th-century copy.

To Peyton Short

DEAR SIR   Philadelphia Feb. 24. 1793.

I have the pleasure to inclose you a letter from your brother. I had that of recieving one from yourself dated July 22. 1792. and mentioning that it covered one for him; as also a copy of the constitution of Kentuckey. But neither object was in the letter. Afterwards I received the Kentuckey constitution under another cover, but still no letter for your brother. I informed him of this circumstance and have his answer since. I shall be happy at all times to forward your mutual communications, and to be otherwise useful to you when any occasion arises, being with sentiments of perfect esteem Dear Sir Your most obedt. humble servt   TH: JEFFERSON

PrC (DLC); at foot of text: "Mr. Peyton Short." Tr (ViU: Edgehill-Randolph Papers); 19th-century copy. Enclosure: William Short to Peyton Short, 18 Dec. 1792 (DLC: Short Papers).

From George Washington

Sunday 24th. Feb. 1793.

Enclosed is a letter from poor Madam La Fayette! How desirable it would be, if something could be done to relieve that family from their present unhappy Situation.

Colo. Smith, yesterday, gave me the enclosed extract of a Letter from the House of Warder & Co. to one of their Partners in this City. Whether it is founded in fact, or with design to affect the prices of provision in this County, I know not. Nor whether it was a Communication for public or private information to myself, I am equally uncertain.

RC (DLC); unsigned; addressed: "Mr. Jefferson." Enclosure: Marquise de Lafayette to Washington, Chavaniac near Brioude, 8 Oct. 1792, requesting the dispatch of an American envoy to secure the Marquis de Lafayette's release from Prussian captivity at Spandau (Tr in DLC: Washington Papers; English translation in the hand of Tobias Lear). Other enclosure not found.

Cabinet Opinions on Indian Affairs

[25 Feb. 1793]

The President having required the attendance of the heads of the three departments and of the Attorney general at his house on Monday the 25th. of Feb. 1793. the following questions were proposed and answers given.

1. The Governor of Canada having refused to let us obtain provisions from that province or to pass them along the water communication to the place of treaty with the Indians, and the Indians having refused to let them pass peaceably along what they call the bloody path, the Governor of Canada at the same time proposing to furnish the whole provisions necessary, Ought the treaty to proceed?

Answer unanimously, it ought to proceed.

2. Have the Executive, or the Executive and Senate together authority to relinquish to the Indians the right of soil of any part of the lands North of the Ohio, which has been validly obtained by former treaties?

The Secretary of the Treasury, Secretary at war and Attorney general are of opinion that the Executive and Senate have such authority, provided that no grants to individuals nor reservations to states be thereby infringed. The Secretary of state is of opinion they have no such authority to relinquish.

3. Will it be expedient to make any such relinquishment to the Indians if essential to peace?

The Secretaries of the Treasury and War and the Attorney general are of opinion it will be expedient to make such relinquishment, if essential to peace, provided it do not include any lands sold or reserved for special purposes (the reservations for trading places excepted).

The Secretary of state is of opinion that the Executive and Senate have authority to stipulate with the Indians and that if essential to peace it will be expedient to stipulate that we will not settle any lands between those already sold or reserved for special purposes, and the lines heretofore validly established with the Indians.

4. Whether the Senate shall be previously consulted on this point?

The Opinion unanimously is that it will be better not to consult them previously.

TH: JEFFERSON
ALEXANDER HAMILTON
H KNOX
EDM: RANDOLPH

MS (DLC: Washington Papers); undated; in TJ's hand, signed by TJ, Hamilton, Knox, and Randolph; written with Cabinet opinions on the debt to France of same date on one sheet folded to make four pages; endorsed by Tobias Lear. PrC (DLC); unsigned; overwritten in part by a later hand. Entries in SJPL: "[Opins of heads of deptmts.] on proceeding in treaty with the hostile Indians" and "on previous consultation with Senate."

The President put these QUESTIONS to the Cabinet because on the previous day he had received dispatches from General William Hull to the Secretary of the Treasury and the Secretary of War containing two critically important pieces of intelligence about the forthcoming Lower Sandusky peace conference with the hostile Western tribes. In the first place Hull reported that Lieutenant Governor John Graves Simcoe of Upper Canada had refused his request to purchase supplies in Canada and transport them to the Indians attending this conference. Hull had been dispatched on this mission by Hamilton after the Treasury Secretary received assurances from George Hammond that Simcoe would be amenable to such a request. At the same time, moreover, Hull enclosed various documents which made it clear for the first time to the Washington administration that the Western Indians were demanding an Ohio river boundary as a condition of peace with the United States (Washington, *Journal*, 66-7; Syrett, *Hamilton*, XIII, 382-3, 479, XIV, 9-13). As a result, the Cabinet decided to allow the TREATY TO PROCEED in order to mollify domestic critics of the Indian war and not from any genuine hope that a peaceful settlement was possible as long as the Western tribes sought to interpose an Ohio river boundary between themselves and the United States (Notes on Cabinet Opinions, 26 Feb. 1793). For a discussion of the origins of the Lower Sandusky conference, see Notes for a Conversation with George Hammond, [ca. 10 Dec. 1792], and note.

In addition to the intrinsic historical importance of the subjects with which they deal, this document and the one that follows are also significant in American constitutional history as the first written corporate opinions that the Cabinet submitted to the President. Hitherto Cabinet members had either submitted individual written opinions in response to specific requests by Washington or made their views known during group meetings held in his presence. The combination of a formal consultation of the heads of the three executive departments and the Attorney General with the President and the subsequent submission to the chief executive of a corporate opinion embodying the views of these officers was an important milestone in the development of the American Cabinet system. See Mary L. Hinsdale, *A History of the President's Cabinet* (Ann Arbor, Mich., 1911), 7-16, for a generally useful account of the evolution of the Cabinet during Washington's administration that nevertheless overlooks the significance of these two documents.

Cabinet Opinions on the Debt to France

Feb. 25. 1793. The President desires the opinions of the heads of the three departments and of the Attorney General on the following question, to wit.

Mr. Ternant having applied for money equivalent to three millions of livres to be furnished on account of our debt to France at the request of the Executive of that country, which sum is to be laid out in provisions within the US. to be sent to France, Shall the money be furnished?

The Secretary of the Treasury stated it as his opinion that making a liberal allowance for the depreciation of assignats, (no rule of liquidation having been yet fixed) a sum of about 318,000 Dollars may not exceed the arrearages equitably due to France to the end of 1792. and that the whole sum asked for may be furnished, within periods capable of answering the purpose of Mr. Ternant's application, without a derangement of the Treasury:

Whereupon the Secretaries of State and War and the Attorney General are of opinion that the whole sum asked for by Mr. Ternant ought to be furnished: the Secretary of the Treasury is of opinion that the supply ought not to exceed the abovementioned sum of 318,000. Dollars.

Th: Jefferson
Alexander Hamilton
H Knox
Edm: Randolph

MS (DLC: Washington Papers); in TJ's hand, signed by TJ, Hamilton, Knox, and Randolph; endorsed by Tobias Lear. PrC (DLC); unsigned. PrC of Dft (DLC: TJ Papers, 82: 14197); undated; badly faded; consists solely of third paragraph, and possibly fourth paragraph, in Hamilton's hand. Entry in SJPL: "Opins of heads of deptmts. on paying money to France."

For a discussion of the issue considered by the Cabinet at this meeting, see Editorial Note on Jefferson's questions and observations on the application of France, at 12 Feb. 1793.

Commissioners of the Sinking Fund to the Speaker of the House of Representatives

SIR   Philadelphia, February 25, 1793.

In pursuance of a resolution of the House of Representatives, bearing date the 19th day of this instant, we lay before them a Copy of the Journal of our Board, and a statement of the purchases made since our last Report to Congress. We have the honor, Sir, to be Your most obedient Servants.

                                        JOHN ADAMS
                                        TH. JEFFERSON
                                        ALEXANDER HAMILTON
                                        EDM. RANDOLPH

MS not found; reprinted from *Report of the Board of Trustees of the Sinking Fund: Containing their Journals, and a Statement of the Purchases Made since their Last Report to Congress* [Philadelphia, 1793], 3; at foot of text: "To the Speaker of the House of Representatives." Enclosures: (1) Journal of the Commissioners of the Sinking Fund, 26 Aug. 1790-21 Feb. 1793. (2) Records relating to purchases of the public debt by the Commissioners since 17 Nov. 1792 (same, 3-29; texts printed in ASP, *Finance*, I, 234-48).

In connection with its investigation of Alexander Hamilton's management of public finance, the House of Representatives on 19 Feb. 1793 had requested copies of all hitherto unfurnished records of the Commissioners of the Sinking Fund, the body created by Congress to carry out the 12 Aug. 1790 act for the redemption of the domestic debt (JHR, I, 706-8, 717; see also Editorial Note on Jefferson and the Giles resolutions, at 27 Feb. 1793). LAST REPORT: see Report of the Commissioners of the Sinking Fund, [17 Nov. 1792].

From Joseph Fenwick

SIR   Bordeaux 25 feby. 1793.

I had the honor of writing you the 10th. Inst. by the Pensylvania Capt. Harding, inclosing the declaration of war against England and Holland. I now have the pleasure to inform you that the national Convention of France on the 19th. Inst. decreed; that the vessels of the U.S. of America shoud be admitted into all their ports; both in the East and west Indias as well as in France, on the same terms with their own, and that all goods imported or exported to or from France and her Colonies by American vessels shoud be subject to the same duties as in french vessels. This offers singular advantages to the Americans in the carrying trade, and will add to the present great demand for their vessels in the ports of France.

France is at present perfectly quiet. There is a decree for raising 300,000 men more than already in pay and every appearance of an immediate war with Spain. American produce is in great demand here at the prices quoted in a price current I inclose, with every prospect of their augmenting.

I have the honor to Inclose you a report of the American vessels at this port for the last six months of the past year—also a Copy of a Bond sent some time past for the faithful execution of the Consular functions. Mr. John Mason will be my security and will point out such other person as you may deem sufficient. With the greatest consideration I am Sir your most obedt & hble Servt.   JOSEPH FENWICK

RC (DNA: RG 59, CD); at foot of first page: "Thomas Jefferson Esquire Secretary of State Philadelphia"; endorsed by TJ as received 17 May 1793 and so recorded in SJL. Enclosure: "Prices Current at Bordeaux," 25 Feb. 1793 (printed form in same; with date and prices inserted by Fenwick). Fenwick's bond had been enclosed in his letter to TJ of 20 Jan. 1793. Other enclosure not found.

The decree of THE NATIONAL CONVENTION OF FRANCE of 19 Feb. 1793 admitted American vessels to trade with France and her colonies on the same terms as French vessels, directed the Provisional Executive Council to negotiate a corresponding reduction in American duties in favor of French merchants, and per-

mitted goods from the East Indies to be landed at any port in France during the war (*Archives Parlementaires*, 1st ser., LIX, 18-19; see also Edmond Charles Genet to TJ, 23 May 1793). Fenwick wrote a brief letter to TJ on 28 Feb. 1793 in which he mentioned having written on "the 20 Inst.," enclosed a copy of the decree, and took note of the fall of Breda to Dumouriez (RC in DNA: RG 59, CD; at foot of text: "Thomas Jefferson Esquire Secretary of State Philadelphia"; endorsed by TJ as received 1 June 1793 and so recorded in SJL; Trs of decree in French, signed by Fenwick on 28 Feb. 1793, filed in same). There is, however, no other record of a 20 Feb. 1793 letter from Fenwick.

From Peregrine Fitzhugh

Indian Queen, 25 *Feb.* 1793. The enclosed will explain his embarrassing situation and the expedient adopted for his relief. The success of his lottery entirely depends on the exertions of relatives and friends as well as the support of a "Humane Public." He would patiently accept his disappointment if only his happiness were at stake, but he can leave no means untried when his beloved wife and numerous infant childen are affected. Every husband and parent must applaud, even if they cannot help. He appeals to his military and other friends, "in which number my Feelings demand that you should be included," to patronize a venture designed to assist one whose sacrifices in the war against Britain were as great as any other person's. He entered military service at the age of nineteen "pretty early" in the war and thereby was deprived of the benefit of his intended profession, a loss he still feels keenly. The active role that his father and brothers played in the war cost his father an office worth £2,500 per annum and led British cruisers in Chesapeake Bay to lay waste to his father's plantations, causing extensive property damage and the taking away of fifty of his most "valuable Servants." Unable therefore to turn to his father for relief, he is compelled to solicit further support for his lottery, which has already been well patronized in Annapolis and its environs, as the enclosed list reveals, and also in Baltimore and various Maryland counties. Though initially reluctant to resort to a lottery, he is gratified by the discovery of so many supportive friends and the ease with which the majority of tickets have been disposed. The number of tickets and the need for timeliness, however, has induced him to approach his friends in the neighboring states.

RC (DLC); 1 p.; printed circular signed and dated by Fitzhugh; endorsed by TJ as received 5 Mch. 1793 and so recorded in SJL. Enclosures not found, but see below.

Peregrine Fitzhugh (1759-1811), son of Colonel William Fitzhugh of Maryland, attained the rank of captain in Baylor's Light Dragoons and served as an aide to Washington during the Revolution. He married Elizabeth Chew in 1782 and lived in Maryland until 1799, when he and his family moved to upstate New York (VMHB, VIII [1900], 316).

This printed circular was a revision of one dated 9 Dec. 1792 that Fitzhugh had sent to the President on 19 Feb. 1793 with a covering letter of the same date and two enclosures that must have been substantially the same as those enclosed to TJ: an undated broadside entitled "A Lottery," which listed prizes and detailed the circumstances which led to the offering; and an undated manuscript list of patrons of Fitzhugh's lottery in Annapolis (DLC: Washington Papers). There is no evidence to indicate that TJ purchased a ticket.

From Jacob Hollingsworth

Sr   Elkton 25 Feby. 1793

Yours of 18 inst. I Receved with the inclosed act of Congress, Providing for Lost Certificates, as I am Reather unfortunate in that way, tho from the meany Proofes which I now, have Sent to my Brother, in Philada. and authorising him, that I shall Recive Justice, Did it not intrude on your Office; or too Great a Favour to ask you, I would Request your assistance in the Business, I have forwarded all my Pappers to my Brother Stephen Hollingsworth now in Philada. at Mr. Live Hollingsworth.

Sr. Mr. Biddle has your Letter to me with the Directions to your Farmes or Lands, and if you pleis Send me a Line of Directions, as there has two Young Men of Reaputable Famalys gon Last weak to See your Lands, and they Say if the Like it, Several famalys out of the Neighbourhood will go, Sum of which is Reconed good Farmars and good Livers tho Renters, as Rents are so High on the Eastern Side of Elk River that they are Ditirmined to Leave the County, thise Peopple are well aquainted with the Management of Small Stocks of Neagros, and the Meathod of Raising wheat, Coarn, and a number of them of Sowing Small Seed, I am fully of opinion if Mr. Taylor and

[263]

his frind Likis your Land you will Soon git your Lands Settled. Your vry Humb Sevt   JACOB HOLLINGSWORTH

I will indeavour to git Mr. Biddle to Go to Philada. while your there.
JH

RC (DLC); addressed: "Thomas Jefferson Esqr. Philada. pr Post"; posted at Elkton, 27 Feb. 1793; endorsed by TJ as received 28 Feb. 1793 and so recorded in SJL.

LIVE HOLLINGSWORTH was a half brother of Jacob Hollingsworth (this corrects the statement about Levi Hollingsworth in note to TJ to Jacob Hollingsworth, 6 Nov. 1792). YOUR LETTER TO ME was TJ's 12 Dec. 1792 letter to Hollingsworth enclosing one of the same date to Samuel Biddle.

To Jean Baptiste Ternant

SIR   Philadelphia Feb. 25. 1793.
    In my letter of the 14th. inst. I had the honor to mention to you that it would take some days to estimate the probable calls on the treasury of the U.S. and to judge whether your application for three millions of livres to be laid out in provisions for the supply of France, could be complied with; but that in the mean time an hundred thousand dollars could be furnished in order to enable you to commence your operations. I have now to add that the residue of the three millions can be furnished on account, if you will be so good as to arrange with the Secretary of the Treasury such epochs as may be accomodated to the circumstances of the Treasury and to your operations also. We have very sincere pleasure in shewing on every possible occasion our earnest desire to serve your nation, and the interest we take in it's present situation. I have the honor to be with sentiments of perfect esteem Sir Your most obedt. & most humble servt   TH: JEFFERSON

RC (AMAE: CPEU, Supplément, xx); addressed: "M. de Ternant Minister of France." PrC (DLC). FC (Lb in DNA: RG 359, DL). Tr (AMAE: CPEU, xxxvii); French translation. Enclosed in the following letter.

Concerning Ternant's APPLICATION FOR THREE MILLIONS OF LIVRES, see the Editorial Note on Jefferson's questions and observations on the application of France, at 12 Feb. 1793.

To Jean Baptiste Ternant

Feb. 25. 93.
    Th: Jefferson presents his best compliments to M. de Ternant, and incloses him the letter he was to write him on the subject of the 3. millions.

He has attentively perused the report in the Newspaper which appeared to give Mr. Ternant so much uneasiness[1] and is candidly of opinion that, in the U.S. at least, not a single person will apply it to M. de Ternant, or suppose it concerns him. He hopes therefore that M. de Ternant will not commit himself with his country by a measure as unnecessary here as it would be injurious to him there. Th:J. hopes M. Ternant will perceive that nothing can dictate the liberty Th:J. now takes but a solicitude for the interests of M. de Ternant.

PrC (DLC). Tr (DLC); 19th-century copy. Enclosure: TJ to Ternant, 25 Feb. 1793.

Although this REPORT cannot be identified with certainty, Ternant was probably offended by an accusation by "Franklin" in the 23 Feb. 1793 *National Gazette* that the Secretary of the Treasury had engaged in the "pretence of relieving a French island." This charge indirectly impugned the arrangements Ternant had made with Hamilton to use the American debt to France for the purchase of supplies in the United States for Saint-Domingue (TJ to Ternant, 7 Mch. 1792, and note). For the identification of "Franklin" as Senator John Taylor of Virginia, a political ally of the Secretary of State, see James Madison to TJ, 11 Aug. 1793.

[1] Preceding three words interlined.

To George Washington

Feb. 25. 93.

Th: Jefferson, with his respects to the President has the honor to inclose him

1. letters from Mr. Barclay.
2. a letter from the Govr. of N. York and an act of that legislature ceding certain lands on Montack point.
3. Dr. Smith's letter, against whom one of the Indians, in a peice read today, has entered a Caveat under the description of a Land-monger.

RC (DNA: RG 59, MLR); endorsed by Tobias Lear. Tr (Lb in same, SDC). Not recorded in SJL. Enclosures: (1) Thomas Barclay to TJ, 17, 19, 27 Dec. 1792, 2 Jan. 1793. (2) George Clinton to TJ, New York, 21 Feb. 1793, enclosing "an Exemplification of an Act of the Legislature of this State, ceding the Jurisdiction of certain Lands on Montaack Point to the United States of America for the purposes in the said Act mentioned" (Tr in Lb in DNA: RG 46, Senate Records, TR; recorded in SJL as received 25 Feb. 1793). (3) Exemplification of New York's act of cession, 18 Dec. 1792, signed by Clinton on 21 Feb. 1793 and counter-signed by Lewis A. Scott on 22 Feb. 1793 (Tr in Lb in same, certified as a true copy by TJ on 27 Feb. 1793; MS, owned by Forest Sweet, Battle Creek, Michigan, 1958, consisting solely of certification in TJ's hand). (4) William Smith to Washington, Philadelphia, 25 Feb. 1793, praising effusively Washington's efforts to promote peace with the Western tribes and requesting an appointment as commissioner or secretary to the forthcoming peace conference with them (DNA: RG 59, MLR).

Washington submitted a copy of the New York ACT with TJ's certification to

Congress on 27 Feb. 1793 (for a description of the statute and its constitutional implications, see Washington, *Journal*, 70, 72n). William Smith, an Anglican clergyman who was the first provost of the College of Philadelphia, was currently involved in land speculation and the development of canals in Pennsylvania (DAB).

To George Washington

Feb. 25. 1793.

Th: Jefferson has the honor to inform the President that he called this evening on M. de Ternant, who produced to him the original letter of M. Le Brun instructing him to apply to our government for two millions of livres to be laid out in flour and one million in salted provisions.

RC (DNA: RG 59, MLR); addressed: "The President of the U.S."; endorsed by Tobias Lear. PrC (DLC). Not recorded in SJL.

Lebrun's ORIGINAL LETTER to Ternant is discussed in Ternant to TJ, 8 Feb. 1793, and note.

From Andrew Ellicott

DEAR SIR   Philadelphia Feby. 26th. 1793

Some weeks ago I gave you to understand that a disagreement had taken place between the commissioners of the public buildings in the City of Washington, and myself; without any other information on that subject. I shall now be more particular with respect to the cause, which appears to be the remains of the former difference with Major L'Enfant, added to the want of confidence, constantly manifested by the original proprietors, of the lands, in the City of Washington, in the requisite qualifications of the commissioners. I have taken up this opinion for the following reasons. *First*; because several of those, who were the most attached to Major L'Enfant, embraced an idea that I had been concerned in the dismission of that gentleman, and immediately on my return to Geo. Town last spring, commenced my enemies, and used every misrepresentation in their power to injure me; which succeeded so well, that they actually drew the commissioners into the *vortex*. This I foresaw, and endeavoured to prevent, but to no purpose: their dissatisfaction became so manifest, that my situation was rendered too disagreeable, to be borne with patience. *Secondly*, A number, (too considerable,) of the original proprietors, who want confidence in the commissioners, considered me as an enemy to the whole business, because I advocated their measures on several occa-sions, which some of the proprietors concieved to be injurious to the City. For this opinion I have more than mere conjecture, I have some of the proprietors own declarations.

I can assure you, that after the disagreement was known in the district, the proprietors generally manifested the most perfect satisfac-tion with the execution of the business in which I was engaged: And Mr. George Walker, who has now gone to Europe, fearing that his name might be made use of to my disadvantage during his absence, furnished me with the certificate No. 1.

Among all the complaints, there is but one, that merits attention; which is *delay*. In answer to this charge, I must refer you to the certifi-cates No. 2, and 3, given by gentlemen, more particularly acquainted with my exertions, and the nature of the business, than all the inhab-itants in the district together—they are too independent both in their circumstances, and principles, to deviate from the strictest integrity; and I am authorized to say, that every gentleman concerned in the executive business of the City, will certify to the same effect.

After the publication appeared against me in the Baltimore Journal, I requested the commissioners to join in an investigation, that I might have an opportunity of either standing fair in the eye of the public, or meet the reward due to a neglect of duty;—but this request was denied!

From a consciousness that I have faithfully discharged my duty, and from a conviction that *time* will not only make it manifest; but likewise prove my attachment to the district of columbia, as the most proper situation for the permanent seat of the government of the United States, I shall retire from the business with perfect satisfaction.

I wish you to acquaint the President of the United States, that he has my most sincere thanks, for the attention which I have received from him, and for the favours which he has conferred upon me, and that I shall always endeavour to deserve his approbation. I am Sir with much esteem, your real Friend, ANDW. ELLICOTT

RC (DNA: RG 59, MLR); at foot of text: "Honble. Thomas Jefferson Esqr."; endorsed by TJ as received 26 Feb. 1793 and so recorded in SJL. Enclosures: (1) Certificate of George Walker, 10 Jan. 1793, stating that Ellicott had acted in conformity with the instructions given him by the Commissioners of the Fed-eral District, praising his scientific knowl-edge, and noting his own satisfaction with Ellicott's work. (2) Certificate of George Fenwick, 26 Jan. 1793, testify-ing to Ellicott's industriousness and atten-tiveness during the survey of the Federal District boundary. (3) Certificate of Isaac Briggs, 12 Jan. 1793, describing Elli-cott's dedication to the survey, noting his attentiveness to duty, and commending his conduct to "the esteem and approbation of every unprejudiced mind" (Trs in same).

GEORGE WALKER was one of the proprietors in the Federal District; George Fenwick and Isaac Briggs were two of Ellicott's assistants in surveying it (Bryan, *National Capital*, I, 144, 209). In a PUBLICATION printed in the 29 Jan. 1793 issue of the *Maryland Journal and Baltimore Advertiser*, "A Citizen of Columbia" applauded Ellicott's announced intention to resign as surveyor of the Federal District and criticized the allegedly inaccurate, dilatory, and unduly expensive manner in which he had discharged this office.

On the day of their receipt, TJ communicated this letter and its enclosures to the President, who returned them the same day (Washington, *Journal*, 69).

From Joseph Fay

DEAR SIR   Bennington 26th. Feby. 1793

I feel so sensibly the many obligations you have laid me under by your expressions of friendship, that like others who wish to be mutually attached, I am induced to offer you my services in a matter of Interest, provided on a Stating you judge it an object worthy your Notice, and provided it will not interfere with your official situation.

I have formed a Company for the purpose of procuring a Grant of two Millions of acres of Land in the Province of upper Canada, where the lands are Granting on very advantageous termes vizt. on paying the one half of the expence of surveying—Two seventh parts to be reserved for the *Crown* and *Clergy*—to be settled within five Years from next July. The *Situation Soil* and *Climate* are Good; And from the Great increase of population in this Country, joined with the Numerous Emigrants which we may expect from Urope, in consequence of the tumults in that Country, there remains little doubt but a rapid settlement will ensue. In addition to this, there is the highest probability that Great sums[1] in Specia will also be drawn to this Country to be vested in lands which I judge cannot fail of rendering them in high demand. Should you join in Opinion with me, and find your Self at Liberty and inclined to undertake, I shall be happy to join your Name to the Company, to consist of about fifteen (a list of which I enclose—all Gentlemen of known and approved Characters, and of strict integrity. I have wrote my friend in Canada advising him of this business requesting him to send me returns immediately, of which I shall give you the earliest Notice.

You would be surpised to see what prodigeous numbers of people are Crouding into this State from the Lower Country, and even many are going quite to upper Canada, and many in this State are Selling their Farms and removing on to those New Grants. There has not been Scarsly a day since my return home from Phila. in which there has not between four and five hundred persons passed my house on their way to make settlement to the Northward. I mention this Circumstance for your information, that you may be better able to judge of the prospects of this Country, and the advantages which will arise from obtaining my proposed Grant. Permit me to hope for your Opinion on this Subject, and to excuse the trouble I am Giving You, in the meantime please to accept the most friendly wishes of Dear Sir your most Obedient and very Humble Servant   Jos. Fay

RC (DLC); at foot of text: "Hona. T. Jefferson"; endorsed by TJ as received 12 Mch. 1793 and so recorded in SJL. Enclosure not found.

[1] Word interlined in place of "Wealth."

To Elbridge Gerry

Dear Sir   Philadelphia Feb. 26. 1793.

I am just now favored with your note of to-day. The wine you enquire after is called Sauterne, and costs about 1/ sterling the bottle, (included) at 3. years old, earlier than which it should not be tasted, and still much better not to drink it till 4. years old, one year then makes great odds in the flavor. The best crop is that of the Countess de Luz-Saluce. But you had better address yourself to Mr. Fenwick our Consul at Bordeaux to whom I gave a note of this wine, and have obtained it since through him, so that he knows well the means of getting it. Let it be bottled by the maker and packed. No other introduction will be needed than to mention my having advised you to apply to Mr. Fenwick. From this circumstance he will know exactly the quality of the wine wanted.

To feed a horse with chopt rye and cut straw, put 6 quarts of the latter to 3. quarts of the former, and it makes a meal for him, two of which suffice for the day if not much used: but waggon horses worked hard thro' the day require three such meals. The cut straw filling the stomach more than grain alone, supplies the place, in some degree, of hay, so that a horse will eat somewhat less of hay in this way.—Your servant shall see the process when you please. But tell him to come to me before he goes to the coachman. I am Dear Sir your's affectionately

Th: Jefferson

RC (NNP); addressed: "Mr. Gerry 105. N. Front"; endorsed by Gerry. PrC (DLC); badly faded and partially illegible. Tr (ViU: Edgehill-Randolph Papers); 19th-century copy; with blanks for words illegible in PrC. Recorded in SJL under 25 Feb. 1793.

The NOTE from Representative Gerry of Massachusetts has not been found and is not recorded in SJL.

From Tobias Lear

February 26th: 1793

By the President's command T. Lear has the honor to send[1] to the Secretary of State a Copy of the proceedings of the Executive Department of the Government of the North Western Territory—and a copy the laws passed there from the 1st. day of July to the 31st. of december 1792, which the President requests the Secretary to look over, and to report to him any thing that may therein appear to require the agency of the President, or[2] that may be necessary to be known to him.

The President wishes to know whether Judge Turner has gone to the Territory or not. And if he should not be gone, that he may be pressed to go immediately.

The President likewise wishes to know when Governor St. Clair intends to go to his Government, as he conceives it highly proper that he should repair thither without delay.

TOBIAS LEAR
Secretary to the President
of the United States

RC (DLC); endorsed by TJ as received 26 Feb. 1793. Dft (DNA: RG 59, MLR); contains several emendations, the most significant of which are noted below; endorsed by Lear. FC (Lb in same, SDC); wording follows Dft. Enclosures: (1) Journal of Executive Proceedings in the Northwest Territory, July-December 1792 (printed in *Terr. Papers*, III, 380-90). (2) Laws of the Northwest Territory, July-December 1792 (printed in Theodore Calvin Pease, ed., *The Laws of the Northwest Territory, 1788-1800*, Illinois State Historical Library, *Collections*, XVII [1925], 57-119).

The PROCEEDINGS OF THE EXECUTIVE DEPARTMENT of the Northwest Territory and the LAWS PASSED for the period had been received this day by the President from Winthrop Sargent (Washington, *Journal*, 69). See also Report on the Proceedings of the Northwest Territory, 2 Mch. 1793.

[1] Sentence to this point interlined in Dft in place of "The President sends."
[2] In the Dft Lear initially wrote the remainder of the sentence as "to be made known to him" before interlining "that is necessary" at the beginning of the passage.

From Adam Lindsay

DEAR SIR   Norfolk 26th. Feby. 1793

By this time I hope you have received 6 Boxes Candles by the Schooner ———[1] Capt Simpson.[2] I intended them in Philadelphia two months ago—but Myrtle Wax is only bought at Market in small Quantities of 4 to 10 ℔. from the Country people and their prices vary so much I was under the necessity to limit the maker to a certain price to avoid imposition. Respecting mixing Tallow with the Wax the maker says that some is absolutely necessary—but provided they cou'd be made without any mixture they wou'd run so much in burning as to be very unprofitable. There is a small proportion to what was in the others; inclosed is the Bill which is larger than your order, hope it will be of no consequence. Our European intelligence is such as you have received by the December packet—only one vessel from Rotterdam Last night which she left the 4th. Jany.—says that Demourier had resigned in consequence of the National Convention protesting his bills and censureing him for Loseing 6000 Men in the battle before Mans. From the West Indies we hear that the Governors of Martinique and Gaudaloupe have fled to the English Islands, carrying the public money with them—an armed schooner pursued the former but was three hours too late and finding this she stood to Trinidad after certain Characters fled there—that the Emigrations was so great to Dominica and St. Vincents that the beach was lined with tents and Huts and the Government rather uneasy at the Great Numbers arriving constantly—letters in town from the Cape say they have had a severe conflict with a large party of Negroes which were conquered and all put to the Sword—shou'd I receive any interesting intelligence from Europe or the West Indies by a short passage shall do myself the pleasure to inform you. I am Dear Sir with every Mark of Esteem Yr. Very Hbl. Servt.   ADAM LINDSAY

RC (DLC); at head of text: "Thomas Jefferson Esqr."; with notation and alteration by TJ; endorsed by TJ as received 9 Mch. 1793 and so recorded in SJL. Enclosure not found.

[1] At this point TJ interlined "Richmond."

[2] TJ altered this word to "Sampson."

Notes on Cabinet Opinions

Feb. 26. 1793. Notes on the proceedings of yesterday. [see the formal opinions given to the President in writing and signed]

1st. Question. we were all of opinion that the treaty should proceed merely to gratify the public opinion, and not from an expectation of success. I expressed myself strongly that the event was so unpromising that I thought the preparations for a campaign should go on without the least relaxation, and that a day should be fixed with the Commrs. for the treaty beyond which they should not permit the treaty to be protracted, by which day orders should be given for our forces to enter into action. The President took up the thing instantly after I had said this, and declared he was so much in the opinion that the treaty would end in nothing that he then in the presence of us all gave orders to Genl. Knox not to slacken the preparations for the campaign in the least but to exert every nerve in preparing for it. Knox[1] said something about the ultimate day for continuing the negociations; I acknoleged myself not a judge on what day the campaign should begin, but that whatever it was, that day should terminate the treaty. Knox said he thought a winter campaign was always the most efficacious against the Indians.—I was of opinion since Gr. Britain insisted on furnishing provisions, that we should offer to repay. Hamilton thought we should not.

2d. Question. I considered our right of preemption of the Indian lands, not as amounting to any dominion, or jurisdiction, or paramountship whatever, but merely in the nature of a remainder after the extinguishment of a present right, which gave us no present right whatever but of preventing other nations from taking possession and so defeating our expectancy: that the Indians had the full, undivided and independant sovereignty as long as they chose to keep it and that this might be for ever: that as fast as we extended our rights by purchase from them, so fast we extended the limits of our society, and as soon as a new portion became encircled within our line, it became a fixt limit of our society: that the Executive with either or both branches of the legislature could not alien any part of our territory: that by the Law of nations it was settled that[2] the Unity and indivisibility of the society was so fundamental that it could not be dismembered by the Constituted authorities except 1. where *all power* was delegated to them (as in the case of despotic governments) or 2. where it was expressly delegated. That neither of these delegations had been made to our general government, and therefore that it had no right to dismember or alienate any portion of territory once ultimately consolidated with us: and that we could no more cede to the Indians than to the English or Spaniards, as it might according to acknoleged principles remain as irrevocably and eternally with the one as the other. But I thought that as we had a right to sell and settle lands once comprehended within our lines, so we might forbear to exercise that right, retaining the property, till circumstances should be more favorable to the settlement, and this I agreed to do in the present instance if necessary for peace.

Hamilton agreed the doctrine of the law of nations as laid down in Europe, but that it was founded on the universality of settlement there, consequently that no lopping off of territory could be made

without a lopping off of citizens, which required their consent: but that
the law of nations for us must be adapted to the circumstance of our
unsettled country, which he conceived[3] the Presidt. and Senate may
cede: that the power of treaty was given to them by the constitution,
without restraining it to particular objects, consequently that it was
given in as plenipotentiary a form as held by any sovereign in any other
society.—E. R. was of opinion there was a difference between a cession
to Indns. and to any others, because it only restored the ceded part to
the condition in which it was before we bought it, and consequently
that we might buy it again hereafter. Therefore he thought the Exec.
and Senate could cede it.   Knox joined in the main opinion. The
Presidt. discovered no opinion, but he made some efforts to get us to
join in some terms which could unite us all, and he seemed to direct
those efforts more towards me: but the thing could not be done.

3d. Qu. we agreed in idea as to the line to be drawn, towit so as to
retain all lands appropriated, or granted or reserved.

4th. Qu. we all thought if the Senate should be consulted and consequently apprised of our line, it would become known to Hammond,
and we should lose all chance of saving any thing more at the treaty
than our Ultimatum.[4]

Qu. whether we should furnish the 3. millions of livres desired by
France to procure provisions?

I was of opinion we ought to do it, the one part as an arrearage
(about 318,000) the residue as an advance towards our payments to
be made in Paris in Sep. and Nov. next.

E.R. was for furnishing the whole sum asked but under such blind
terms, that if the present[5] French government should be destroyed and
the former one reestablished, it might not be imputed to us as a proof
of our taking part with the present, but might be excused under a
pretext that we thought we might owe it.   Knox of the same
opinion.

Hamilton saw the combination of powers against France so strong,
as to render the issue very doubtful. He therefore was against going
beyond the 318,000.D. understood to be in arrear.

The Presidt. at this meeting mentioned the declaration of some person
in a[6] paper of Fenno that he would commence an attack on the character of Dr. Franklin; he said the theme was to him excessively disagreeable on other considerations, but most particularly so as the party
seemed to do it as a means of defending him (the Presidt.) against the
late attacks on him. That such a mode of defence would be peculiarly
painful to him, and wished it could be stopped. Hamilton and E. R.

undertook to speak to Fenno to suppress it, without mentioning it as the President's wish. Both observed that they had heard this declaration mentioned in many companies and that it had excited universal horror and detestation.

The paper in Fenno must lie between two persons, viz Adams and Izard, because they are the only persons who could know such facts as are there promised to be unfolded. Adams is an enemy to both characters, and might chuse this ground as an effectual position to injure both. Izard hated Franklin with unparalleled bitterness but humbly adores the Presidt. because he is in loco regis. If the paper proceeds, we shall easily discover which of these two gentlemen is the champion. In the mean time the first paper leads our suspicions more towards Izard than Adams from the circumstance of stile, and because he is quite booby enough not to see the injury he would do to the President by such a mode of defence.

MS (DLC); entirely in TJ's hand; brackets in original; last two paragraphs, in a smaller hand and in a different shade of ink, possibly written at a later date; part of entry written on the other side of a sheet bearing "Anas" entry for 28 Feb. 1793 (see note 4 below). Recorded in SJPL between entries for 25 Feb. 1793 on the Cabinet opinions of that date and entry for notes of 28 Feb. 1793 on the President's second inauguration:
"Notes on these opinions.
  do. on paiments to France.—attack on
    Dr. Franklin."
Included in the "Anas."

For further information about the Cabinet's deliberations on treating for peace with the Western Indians and allowing the French minister to use part of the debt to France for the purchase of supplies for the French Republic, see Cabinet Opinions on Indian Affairs, and Cabinet Opinions on the French Debt, both 25 Feb. 1793. In its 23 Feb. 1793 issue, the *Gazette of the United States*, the PAPER OF FENNO referred to by TJ, printed an unsigned letter to Benjamin Franklin Bache, Benjamin Franklin's grandson and the printer of *Dunlap's American Daily Advertiser* in Philadelphia, threatening to expose Franklin's servility at the court of Versailles in retaliation for various attacks on Washington in Bache's paper. IN LOCO REGIS: "in place of the king."

[1] Here TJ canceled "expressed an opinion."
[2] Here TJ canceled "this right."
[3] Here TJ canceled "we had."
[4] Remainder of text written on the other side of a sheet bearing "Anas" entry for 28 Feb. 1793.
[5] Word interlined.
[6] Here TJ canceled "letter of F."

To John Pendleton, Jr.

SIR   Philadelphia Feb. 26.[1] [1793]

I have duly received your favor of the [13th. inst. and am?] sorry I cannot furnish you from hence with [what?] you desire, as it is lodged at Monticello, [where no other?] person can turn to it but myself. I

[274]

will [keep it?] in mind, and on my first return [there endeavor?] to send it to you. I am with great esteem Sir your most obedt. servt.

TH: JEFFERSON

PrC (MHi); badly faded in part; at foot of text: "Mr. John Pendleton." Tr (ViU: Edgehill-Randolph Papers); 19th-century copy with blanks for words illegible in PrC. Recorded in SJL as a letter of 25 Feb. 1793 (see note 1 below).

John Pendleton, Jr. (ca. 1749-ca. 1807) of Henrico County, a nephew of the Virginia jurist Edmund Pendleton,

was Virginia state auditor from 1783 until 1796 (Madison, *Papers*, I, 190n; CVSP, VIII, 391-2, 398). His FAVOR OF THE 13TH. INST. from Richmond, recorded in SJL as received 21 Feb. 1793, has not been found.

[1] Digits overwritten in ink by TJ, possibly at a later date.

From David Stuart

DEAR SIR   Hope-Park 26th: Febry: 93

The Bearer of this letter is Mr. Kennedy from King and Queen County, whose claim to the estate and title of Earl of Cassilis in Scotland, you have probably heard of. His chief object in going to Philadelphia, is to obtain proper credentials of his Father's marryage. He thinks, it may be of some service to him, to be made acquainted with the British Minister. Not doubting your disposition to render this, or any other service in your power, I take the liberty of introducing him to your notice. I must observe, that tho' my acquaintance with him has been but short, I have heard him mentioned with respect, by several of his neighbours from King and Queen. I am with great esteem Your most Obt. Serv   DD: STUART

RC (MoSHi: Bixby Collection); endorsed by TJ as received 5 Mch. 1793 and so recorded in SJL as delivered "by Mr. Kennedy."

MR. KENNEDY has not been identified. After the tenth earl, David Lord Kennedy, died in December 1792 without direct heirs, the title and estates of the

Earl of Cassillis devolved through entail to Captain Archibald Kennedy of the Royal Navy, a distant cousin whose father of the same name had been a noted British official and pamphleteer in colonial New York (George E. Cokayne, Vicary Gibbs, and others, eds., *The Complete Peerage* . . ., new ed., 13 vols. in 14 [London, 1910-59], III, 79-80; DAB).

From George Washington

SIR   Philadelphia Feb: 26th 1793.

The Minister of France may, as soon as he pleases, make arrangements with the Secretary of the Treasury for the payment of Three

Million of Livres on account of the debt due from the U: States to France (including the one hundred thousand dollars already ordered, in part) agreeably to the requisition of M. Le Brun Minister for Foreign Affairs in that Country, and In such manner as will comport with the State of the Treasury.   Go: WASHINGTON

RC (DLC); at foot of text: "The Secretary of State"; endorsed by TJ as received 26 Feb. 1793. Dft (TxAuLBJ); varies slightly in wording; docketed by Washington. FC (Lb in DNA: RG 59, SDC); wording follows Dft. Recorded in SJPL.

This day TJ wrote a brief note to Wash-

ington enclosing "the Decypher of a Note from Mr. Barclay expressed in Cypher" (RC in DNA: RG 59, MLR, addressed "The President of the US.," endorsed by Tobias Lear; Tr in Lb in same, SDC; not recorded in SJL). The enclosure was the decipherment of Thomas Barclay's second letter to TJ of 27 Dec. 1792.

To George Wythe

DEAR SIR   Philadelphia Feb. 26[1] 17[93]

I have just now received your favor of [15 Feb. 1793. A?] law is passed on the subject of patents which [will require Mr.?] Clarke to present his petition anew. This [will appear?] in the newspapers within a few days. Having [only given?] it a slight reading in the Roll, I am unable [to give you a?] particular account of it.

Your seal is promised in time to [be given to Mr.?] Giles on his return from Congress. Should the [engraver?] fail in punctuality you may still [count on it?] in [a few?] more days. Adieu my dear Sir your's affectionately   TH: JEFFERSON

P.S. Mr. Clarke's letter with Meredith's affidavit is just received. By the new law, when a question arises on the *priority of invention* the parties are to name referees to decide it.

PrC (DLC: TJ Papers, 28: 4873); badly faded in part; at foot of text: "Mr. Wythe." Tr (DLC); 19th-century copy with blanks for words illegible in PrC. Recorded in SJL as a letter of 25 Feb. 1793.

Wythe's letter to TJ of 15 Feb. 1793, recorded in SJL as received 26 Feb. 1793, has not been found. For the new LAW ... ON THE SUBJECT OF PATENTS, see A Bill to Promote the Progress of the Use-

ful Arts, [1 Dec. 1791], and note. John CLARKE'S LETTER WITH MEREDITH'S AFFIDAVIT is not recorded in SJL and has not been found. On 31 Dec. 1793 Clarke was awarded a patent on a disputed claim for the invention of "a machine to work in a current of water" (*List of Patents*, 8). The ENGRAVER was James Poupard, who was engraving a seal for the Virginia Court of Chancery, of which Wythe was chancellor.

[1] Numbers added or overwritten in ink.

To William Carmichael

Philadelphia Feby. 27. 1793

In a letter from Mr. Jay of Mar. 14. 1786. papers were inclosed to you on the subject of the Dover cutter, taken out of the hands of certain citizens of this country by a Spanish governor in the Western islands for the use of the Spanish government, and no compensation made, and you were desired to apply for compensation. Mr. Jay addressed you afterwards on the same subject on the 24th. of Nov. 1786. the 14th. of May 1787. the 23d. of Sep. and 24th. of Nov. 1788. and I sent you new copies of all the papers in a letter of Apr. 11. 1791. and afterwards addressed you on it in letters of Nov. 29. 1791. and Apr. 24. 1792. No answer has ever been received from you on the subject. The persons interested now undertaking to look into the matter themselves and to convey the present letter,[1] I have only to observe that your assistance to them will be no more than a compliance with the multiplied letters which have been written to you on this subject. I inclose you an original letter of theirs retracing the outlines of the case and informing you of the change in the parties interested, and am Sir Your very humble servt   Th: Jefferson

PrC (DLC); dateline in a clerk's hand; at foot of text: "Mr. Carmichael." FC (Lb in DNA: RG 59, DCI). Enclosure not found.

The case of the DOVER CUTTER is fully described in TJ to Carmichael, 11 Apr. 1791, and note. TJ also wrote a brief note of 27 Feb. 1793 to James Hillhouse, a Federalist member of the House of Representatives from Connecticut, enclosing the above letter "which he desired in the case of the Dover cutter" (PrC in DLC; Tr in ViU: Edgehill-Randolph Papers, 19th-century copy).

[1] Preceding six words interlined.

From Stephen Cathalan, Jr.

DEAR SIR   Marseilles the 27th. February 1793

I have received in time your Public as well as your Private Letters you did me the honour of writing me the 22 Last June, 8 october by your recommended Gentn. Doctor Watters who is Still in this Place Since Two Months and to whom all the Services in my Power, I render; as well as on your honoured Recommendation, as on his Merit; of the 6th. 9ber. Last, of the 14th. do. these Learning me your determination of Retiring in the next Month of your office of Secretary of State, which new I Learn with Great Concern, tho', it is Just after having So Much laboured for the welfare of your Country to take

Some Repos, in a Private Caracter, but I wish your Successor may be able of Filling that Emminent Post as well as you have done it, and I regret, that this event will deprive me of Corresponding So often with you; however I am and will be always at your Commands, and ask of you the favour of Some of your agreable Letters when you will have nothing else or Better to do. I hope Some days or other, you will be Placed by the unanimous votes to the most eminent Post of the united States. I have answered to your Public Letters, as you desired, to the Secretary of State at Philadelphia.

I have also received the Letter of the Society of Charlestown for the agricultur inclosed in yours of the 2 Dbr. Last, I will take Some Shorter and Less expensive Means to execute your orders, than to hire one acre of Land &ce., I will not forgett it, Please to assure that respectuble Society to which I have not now the Time of answering.

All what I mentioned in my Private Letter one year ago, is then arived! what effect may have Produced that unfortunate and Shamefûll event for F–ce in your Country! now is no more Remedy and I can't enlarge on Such a Sorrowfull Subject!

France is now in war with almost all the european Powers; I reffer you to my Memoir or reflexions on algerian affairs dated the 15th. Janûary 1791—if you may remain neutral US. will reap the great advantages to Carry on in their Ships almost all the Trade of the west Indies, and Europe, you will Supply us with wheat and flour. We apprehend an horid Famin before 3 Months; I could now freight to Sundry Merchants fifty american vessels if they were in this harbour, at very extravagant terms; the national Convention has reddressed the difference in the duty on Tobacco on your Bottom, and you may easily Concûre with the French even in time of Peace, they have also allowed you the free trade with west Indies, and they have allowed the French to Purchase foreing vessels. An other object worth of the attention of america as Soon as this will reach you, it is that our new found Land fishers will not Go to the fishery, as they never Go when at war, with england; Last war the Duty Prohibitive on foreing Baccalao, was taken of and a very new dcreete toock place, it will be the Same, on the 1st. Reppresentation made; Then you may encourage your fish vessels to Come to this Markett next fall and winter, they will obtain monstruos Prices for their Baccalao here; at Lenght in any Line of Trade the Americans will undertake this way now; their Risk of the algerians, is not to be Compared with that the French and English will run by the war; it is now high time to fitt out 3 Frigattes for the Meditan. to Protect your Trade, and at the Same time try strongly for Peace with algiers, I regret very much, you have not honoured me of that negotiation, I would have perhaps more advanced than Ths. Barclay Esqr.

All what I mention you, is only by the desire I have to See america become Soon a very Great and Powerfull Nation; matters presents now a fair aspect for that if England, by Jalousy does not, prevent you to enjoy of that Benefit. I have only time to add that I have the honour to be with great Respect is for ever Dear Sir Your most obedt. hum Serv   STEPHEN CATHALAN JUNR.

Many respects and Kind Compliments from all my Family
   at 1 o Clock of the Morning
Flour £90^{tt} per Barrel, and Soon £100 a 120^{tt} Wheats in Proportion
Carolina Rice £45 per ql. 90 ℔ english
Tobacco £65 a 75^{tt} per ql. Marc Weight.

RC (DLC); addressed: "Thos. Jefferson Esqr. Philadelphia pr. the Sckoener Madison Capn. Saml. Cassan"; endorsed by TJ as received 1 May 1793 and so recorded in SJL, where it is described as "private."

The PRIVATE LETTER to TJ to which Cathalan refers is that of 11 Mch. 1792. Cathalan's 15 Jan. 1791 MEMOIR on an Algerine peace treaty was actually a 20 Jan. 1791 enclosure to a letter of 22 Jan. 1791 to TJ.

To Francis Eppes

DEAR SIR   Philadelphia Feb. 27. 1793.

The Commissioners to the Indian treaty will not leave this place till the 1st. of April, which gives more time to provide for Jack. I shall not return home as soon as I expected, tho' I shall not extend the term of my service long. I shall ship off my furniture about the beginning of April; and find in fact that my provision for winding up my affairs here, removing bag and baggage will fall short some hundred dollars. If therefore Mr. Cary's executor can be pushed to make good his promise, some part of my portion of it will be not only seasonable but necessary to me. With every wish for the health & happiness of Mrs. Eppes yourself & family I am Dear Sir Your's affectionately   TH: JEFFERSON

PrC DLC); at foot of text: "Mr. Eppes." Tr (ViU: Edgehill-Randolph Papers); 19th-century copy.

Jefferson and the Giles Resolutions

I. RESOLUTIONS ON THE SECRETARY OF THE TREASURY, [BEFORE 27 FEB. 1793]

II. WILLIAM BRANCH GILES'S RESOLUTIONS ON THE SECRETARY OF THE
TREASURY, [27 FEB. 1793]

EDITORIAL NOTE

The draft resolutions printed below as Document I represent Thomas Jefferson's climactic contribution to the unsuccessful Republican effort in the House of Representatives early in 1793 to censure Alexander Hamilton's administration as Secretary of the Treasury and bring about his removal from office. This drive against Jefferson's great antagonist was the high point of the first phase of the political conflict between Republicans and Federalists, the debate over the merits of Hamiltonian finance, which was soon to be superseded by an even more serious controversy over the American attitude toward the wars of the French Revolution sweeping through Europe. Virginia Congressman William Branch Giles ostensibly led the Republican assault on Hamilton, culminating in his submission to the House on 27 Feb. 1793 of a significantly modified version of Jefferson's draft resolutions (Document II below). Federalist critics, however, soon charged that Jefferson was actually the prime mover in the episode, an assertion echoed by John C. Hamilton, the Secretary's son and biographer, in 1860 (John C. Hamilton, *History of the Republic of the United States of America, as Traced in the Writings of Alexander Hamilton and of his Cotemporaries*, 7 vols. [New York and Philadelphia, 1857-64], v, 173-4; George Gibbs, *Memoirs of the Administrations of Washington and John Adams, Edited from the Papers of Oliver Wolcott, Secretary of the Treasury*, 2 vols. [New York, 1846], i, 91; "Fair Play," *National Gazette*, 24 July 1793). The evidence now available, though admittedly fragmentary because of the loss of Giles's personal papers, fails to substantiate the claim that Jefferson originated this effort, but it does indicate that he was far more deeply involved in it than his own contemporary comments on the subject in the "Anas" and in private correspondence would suggest, though even now many of the details remain obscure.

Conclusive documentary evidence of Jefferson's involvement with House Republicans first appeared in 1895. That year Paul Leicester Ford, the most accomplished nineteenth-century editor of Jefferson's papers, simultaneously announced his discovery of the draft resolutions in an article in *The Nation*, where he printed a partial text, and in the sixth volume of his edition of Jefferson's writings, where he published them in full, having first verified that this crucial document was in Jefferson's hand (Paul L. Ford, "The Authorship of Giles's Resolutions," *The Nation*, LXI [1895], 164-5; Ford, VI, 168-71; see also Ford, I, 222n). Ford discovered the resolutions in a family collection of Jefferson's papers made available to him by Sarah Nicholas Randolph, Jefferson's great-granddaughter and the author of a charming memoir of his family life. Miss Randolph had inherited the manuscripts from her father,

EDITORIAL NOTE

Thomas Jefferson Randolph, Jefferson's favorite grandson, the executor of his estate, and the first editor of his papers, who died in 1875. Ironically, though the papers held by Miss Randolph had once been in federal custody as part of the large collection of Jefferson manuscripts sold to the United States government by her father in 1848 and now housed in the Library of Congress, the government returned them to him after the Civil War because they were private in nature and did not fall within the purview of the 1848 purchase, which embraced only Jefferson's public papers (Merrill D. Peterson, *The Jefferson Image in the American Mind* [New York, 1960], 29-36, 231-3; Paul G. Sifton, "Introduction," *Index to the Thomas Jefferson Papers* [Washington, D.C., 1976], ix-xiii; Ford's correspondence with Sarah N. Randolph, 1890-92, concerning his use of Jefferson's papers, is in NN: Paul L. Ford Papers). This proved to be an unfortunate turn of events for the preservation of the draft resolutions. Miss Randolph, who died in 1892, bequeathed her manuscript collection to her sister, Caroline Ramsay Randolph, and although major parts of it were eventually acquired by the Massachusetts Historical Society and the University of Virginia Library, the original manuscript of the resolutions has disappeared, perhaps destroyed in a fire that consumed most of the Jefferson papers inherited by one of Caroline Ramsay Randolph's nieces, Mrs. William Mann Randolph, after her aunt's death in 1902 (Helen Duprey Bullock, "The Papers of Thomas Jefferson," in Constance E. Thurlow and Francis L. Berkeley, Jr., comps., *The Jefferson Papers of the University of Virginia*, University of Virginia Bibliographical Series, No. 8 [Charlottesville, 1950], 279-83). The loss of this manuscript is particularly unfortunate because Ford routinely ignored cancellations and interlineations except in Jefferson's most important state papers. In addition to the possible loss of these often revealing revisions, a comparison of the resolutions as printed by Ford in *The Nation* and in his edition of Jefferson's writings suggests that he supplied all numbering and italicization. Despite these caveats, Ford's printed text of the resolutions and other collateral evidence make it possible to reconstruct tentatively Jefferson's role in the Republican attempt in 1793 to undermine Hamilton.

Jefferson's involvement in the Republican attack on Hamilton stemmed in great measure from his conviction that the Secretary of the Treasury and the fiscal system he represented threatened the future of American republicanism. Despite his early support for Hamilton's plan to assume the state debts, which he later regretted as his greatest political error, by the end of 1792 Jefferson had been convinced for more than a year that his hopes for the survival of a virtuous agrarian republic were endangered by the underlying social and political implications of Hamilton's advocacy of a funded debt, a national bank, an excise, government encouragement of manufacturing, and loose construction of the Constitution. In this program Jefferson espied nothing less than a settled design to anglicize American society, subvert the Constitution, and prepare the way for the transition to a monarchical form of government along British lines. He was especially concerned by what he perceived to be the rise of a corrupt monied interest in Congress whose views and interests were directly at variance with those of the agrarian majority. In particular, he feared the presence in Congress of directors of the Bank of the United States, as well as holders of Bank stock and public securities, because he believed they formed a pliant instrument in the hands of Hamilton for compromising the independence of the legislature and rendering it subordinate to the executive—or at any rate to the Secretary of the Treasury. In a September 1792 letter to the President, which was but one of a series of unsuccessful efforts he made that year to undermine Washington's confidence in the Secretary of the Treasury, Jefferson accused Hamilton of corruptly favoring speculators by "the dealing out of Treasury-secrets among his friends in what time and measure he pleases," and denounced the Secretary of the Treasury in the strongest terms as one whose life "is a tissue of machinations against the liberty of the country which has not only recieved and given him bread, but heaped it's honors on his head" (TJ to George Washington, 9 Sep. 1792; see also Jefferson's Account of the Bargain on the Assumption and Residence Bills, [1792?], in Vol. 17: 205-8; Memoranda of Conversations with the President, 1 Mch. 1792; TJ to Washington, 23 May 1792; Notes of a Conversation with Washington, 10 July, 1 Oct. 1792; Notes of Agenda to Reduce the Government to True Principles, [ca. 11 July 1792]). With views such as these, which were shared to one degree or another by the emerging Republican opposition, Jefferson and his allies in Congress were naturally predisposed to be on the alert for the slightest opportunity to drive from office the man they regarded as a mortal threat to the survival of a republican social and political order in the United States (Lance Banning, *The Jeffersonian Persuasion: Evolution of a Party Ideology* [Ithaca, 1978], 126-78).

Hamilton himself triggered the chain of events that led to the Republican onslaught against him with a characteristically audacious proposal. In response to a recommendation he personally drafted for the President's annual message to Congress, the House of Representatives on 21 and 22 Nov. 1792 ordered the Secretary of the Treasury to prepare a plan to retire part of the public debt and to reimburse the loan that the Bank of the United States had made to the government. Against a rising tide of Republican criticism that he favored a perpetual debt to sustain a corrupt monied interest, Hamilton thereupon communicated a report on the public debt to the House early in December proposing, among other things, that Congress authorize the government to repay in a lump sum the $2,000,000 it had borrowed from the Bank to purchase its stock. Under the terms of the 1791 act establishing the Bank, the government had the option of repaying this loan to the Bank in ten annual installments of $200,000 at 6 percent interest, but Hamilton argued that repaying the entire loan in one installment would result in a substantial savings in interest, later estimated by him at $400,000. He also recommended that the government finance this operation by using unexpended proceeds from earlier European loans and replacing them with another loan of $2,000,000 abroad. Although Hamilton did not reveal this to the House until February 1793, he planned to pay the Bank with money borrowed in Europe to redeem the domestic debt and drawn to the United States that he had not yet used because of the sufficiency of other sources of revenue earmarked by Congress for debt redemption. In the end, Congress only approved the payment of the first installment of $200,000 to the Bank, but in the meantime Hamilton's original proposal aroused intense suspicions among Jefferson and House Republicans about his handling of foreign loans (Syrett, *Hamilton*, xii, 565, xiii, 271, xiv, 41, 100-103; *Annals*, ii, 2381, iii, 1452; Fitzpatrick, *Writings*, xxxii, 211-12; asp, *Finance*, i, 294; Banning, *Jeffersonian Persuasion*, 163-4, 168-70).

EDITORIAL NOTE

When a bill to finance the payment to the Bank through the use of money borrowed by the government for other purposes was introduced in the House, Republicans, led by Giles and James Madison, attacked the measure on four grounds. They suggested it was a form of favoritism to the Bank, expressed concern that it would affect American debt payments to France, questioned the wisdom of undertaking additional foreign loans, and asked whether it was justified by the actual status of funds in the Treasury. On 27 Dec. 1792—three days after the debate began—they succeeded in deferring further action on the bill and persuaded the House to request from the President a detailed accounting of the disposition of the foreign loans the government had thus far negotiated on his authority under acts of 4 and 12 Aug. 1790 for the payment of the foreign debt and the redemption of the domestic debt. On orders from Washington, Hamilton provided the information requested in a relatively brief 3 Jan. 1793 report on foreign loans that was submitted to the House a day later (*Annals*, III, 753-61, 836; Syrett, *Hamilton*, XIII, 451-62).

The report of the Secretary of the Treasury convinced Jefferson that there was ample reason to suspect Hamilton of misapplying public funds and led to his first recorded contact on this matter with the House Republicans opposing his Cabinet colleague. Earlier, having learned that a clause in the Bank loan bill would have reappropriated money borrowed in Amsterdam in 1790 to pay the French debt, Jefferson had echoed Republican charges to Washington by denouncing the whole measure as a "trick" to rescue the Bank from financial embarrassments at the expense of France (Notes of a Conversation with Washington on French Affairs, 27 Dec. 1792). Now, with his distrust of Hamilton raised to new heights, Jefferson carefully scrutinized the Treasury Secretary's report on foreign loans, which had been printed by order of the House. In an undated analysis of it that he sent to Madison, his close Virginia friend and ally, he argued that the facts set forth in it warranted the "suspicion" that without legal authorization Hamilton had drawn to the United States money borrowed in Europe to discharge the foreign debt and had lodged it in the Bank as part of a corrupt effort to benefit that institution at public expense (Notes on Alexander Hamilton's Report on Foreign Loans, printed under 4 Jan. 1793). Precisely when Jefferson set down these notes and sent them to Madison cannot be established categorically, but it was probably some time before 23 Jan. 1793, since Jefferson did not cite any of Hamilton's later reports to the current House on his administration of the Treasury, the first of which was submitted on 4 Feb. 1793. Moreover, it is unlikely he would have troubled to send an expression of suspicion to Madison after 23 Jan., when Giles discussed the misapplication of the foreign loans in a speech to the House on Hamilton's stewardship of the Treasury. If so, Jefferson's notes must be regarded as a clear signal to Madison, at a time when House Republicans had yet to respond to Hamilton's initial report on foreign loans, that there were strong grounds to press for an inquiry into the operations of the Secretary of the Treasury.

Whether inspired by Jefferson or not, the efforts of House Republicans to track their quarry gained momentum on 23 Jan. 1793 when Giles introduced five resolutions that called for nothing less than a comprehensive accounting of Hamilton's administration of the Treasury. The first two resolutions requested the President to furnish the House with the authorities under which loans had been negotiated under the debt acts of 4 and 12 Aug. 1790, and with an account of the payments made on the French, Spanish, and Dutch debts, with the dates and the names of persons who made and received them. The other three resolutions directed the Secretary of the Treasury to submit a statement of the balances between the United States government and the Bank of the United States, including its branch banks, down to the end of 1792, an account of the monies received and uninvested by the Sinking Fund, which had been established by the act of 12 Aug. 1790 to help redeem the domestic debt, and a calculation of the balance of all unapplied government revenues and loans as of the end of 1792 (*Annals*, III, 835-6). In his lengthy speech in support of the resolves, Giles maintained that the House needed the information requested to make a reasoned judgment on the still pending Bank loan bill, but there can be no doubt that their main purpose was to expose official misconduct by Hamilton. The report on foreign loans, Giles maintained, raised more questions than it answered about the Treasury's appropriation of the proceeds from the loans under the terms of the 1790 acts. In particular he suggested that Hamilton had drawn part of these to the United States for the benefit of the Bank and that he had never made an adequate accounting to Congress of the disposition of substantial amounts of public revenue. The information requested by the resolves might explain these difficulties, Giles concluded, but "Candor . . . induces me to acknowledge that impressions resulting from my inquiries into this subject, have been made upon my mind, by no means favorable to the arrangements made by the gentleman at the head of the Treasury Department." Both the resolutions and the speech questioning the probity of Hamilton's stewardship of the Treasury were printed in the *National Gazette*, signifying that they bore the imprimatur of the Republican opposition. Despite their partisan intent, both Federalists and Republicans voted to pass these resolves unanimously, though for wholly different reasons. Whereas Republicans hoped that the resulting inquiry would discredit Hamilton and lead to his dismissal from office, Federalists were confident that it would vindicate Hamilton and discredit his Republican critics (same, 836-40; JHR, I, 677-8; *National Gazette*, 26, 30 Jan. 1793; Syrett, *Hamilton*, XIV, 7; George Hammond to Lord Grenville, 4 Feb. 1793, PRO: FO 5/1; Gibbs, *Memoirs of Washington and Adams*, I, 85, 87).

Jefferson's putative involvement with these resolves became the subject of contemporary public discussion by Federalists, and as late as 1912 Giles's biographer concurred in the opinion advanced by John C. Hamilton in 1860 that "Jefferson was behind" this first set of resolves and that "Madison made a draft of them." The evidence for Jefferson's role is at least plausible, for if he did convey his notes on the Treasury Secretary's first report on foreign loans to Madison prior to 23 Jan., it is arguable that he indirectly inspired the resolves offered by Giles on that date. But the evidence for Madison's authorship is suspect. The younger Hamilton referred to a statement admitting Madisonian authorship of the resolves that Giles allegedly made to Senator Rufus King of New York and claimed to have seen a draft of them in Madison's hand in the Madison Papers, then in the State Department and now in the Library of Congress. Although he cited no source for Giles's statement to King, and it seems unlikely that a zealous Republican would have made such an admission to a staunch Federalist during the partisan debates in 1793, Giles might conceivably have done so in 1813-15, when he and King both served in the Senate and Giles had become a fierce opponent of Madison and often voted with the small Federalist opposition led by King. Similarly, while the Madison draft mentioned by Hamilton has never come to light, and he may have confused it with notes relating to the House investigation of the Secretary of the Treasury that Madison set down at some point in Febrary 1793, it is possible that it was lost during a later reorganization of the fourth president's papers. In any event, while there is still some question about Giles's authorship of the 23 Jan. resolves, it is indisputable that they were part of a developing Republican effort against Hamilton that enjoyed the support of both Jefferson and Madison (Dice Robins Anderson, *William Branch Giles: A Biography* [Menasha, Wis., 1915], 21-2; Hamilton, *Republic*, v, 181n, 204n; "Fair Play," *National Gazette*, 24 July 1793; Banning, *Jeffersonian Persuasion*, 164; Madison, *Papers*, xiv, 450-1, 452, 472; Notes on the Giles Resolutions, 2 Mch. 1793).

In a prodigious effort, Hamilton complied with the resolves in four comprehensive reports submitted to the House between 4 and 20 Feb. in which he vigorously defended his stewardship of the Treasury and rebutted each insinuation of maladministration Giles had made against him. He demonstrated that Giles's allegations about the existence of a large sum of unaccounted public revenue were based on a gross misunderstanding of the elementary principles of accounting, defended his handling of foreign loans and the use of part of the proceeds from them in America, and denied any impropriety in his dealings with the Bank of the United States. But four features of Hamilton's rebuttal provided further grist for the Republican mill. First, Hamilton offended some congressional sensibilities by caustically questioning Giles's motives in offering the resolves. Secondly, he admitted negotiating loans for the payment of the foreign debt and the redemption of the domestic debt under the joint authority of the two acts of 1790 for these purposes, instead of contracting separate loans under the authority of each act. But he denied that there was anything illegal in this, implied that he had acted with presidential authorization, argued that he had followed this course to maintain the high standing of American credit in Europe, and insisted that he had applied the money from the loans as the 1790 acts directed. Thirdly, Hamilton conceded that he had applied to the payment of the French and Dutch debts, as well as to the redemption of the domestic debt, a loan contracted in January 1790 by the American bankers in Amsterdam for the specific purpose of repaying the French debt. But he justified his use of this loan, which with the President's consent he had approved retrospectively soon after passage of the two 1790 debt acts, by asserting that it had been imperative for him to draw part of it to the United States under the authority of the debt redemption act to ensure that in the event of an unexpected deficiency in ordinary revenues the government had enough money on hand to begin the first scheduled interest payments on the domestic debt in April 1791. Finally, and perhaps most offensive to Republican sensibilities, Hamilton imperiously claimed for himself as Treasury Secretary a high degree of administrative discretion to depart from the strict letter of the law to deal with urgent public problems unforeseen by the legislature. Nevertheless, the cumulative force of Hamilton's defense was so strong that at first it left House Republicans divided over what step to take after the submission of the Secretary's last report on 20 Feb. Some wished to pursue the matter during the present legislative session, even though Congress was scheduled to adjourn within less than two weeks on 2 Mch. 1793, but others favored postponing further consideration of it until later in the year when the newly elected Third Congress was due to convene with what Republicans anticipated would be a significant increase in their strength in the House (Syrett, *Hamilton*, XIII, 542-79, XIV, 17-67, 93-133; Madison, *Papers*, XIV, 452, 472; TJ to Thomas Pinckney, 3 Dec. 1792).

Even as Hamilton sought to rebut his critics in the House, Jefferson attempted to undercut him with the President. Taking advantage of an application made on 8 Feb. 1793 by Jean Baptiste Ternant, the French minister in Philadelphia, for an advance of 3,000,000 livres tournois on the American debt to France for the purpose of procuring provisions in the United States for the French Republic, Jefferson tried to raise doubts in Washington's mind about Hamilton's probity in the handling of government funds and foreign loans and to persuade the President that an executive investigation of the Treasury Department was in order. But Washington refrained from undertaking such an investigation and confined himself instead to approving a majority recommendation in favor of granting Ternant's request made by the Cabinet during a meeting on 25 Feb. (Editorial Note and documents on Jefferson's questions and observations on the application of France, at 12 Feb. 1793).

The failure of this attempt to undermine Washington's confidence in Hamilton coincided with, and may have been influenced by, the efforts of Giles and other House Republicans to censure Hamilton. In this legislative contest the draft resolutions in Jefferson's hand charging the Treasury Secretary with various forms of maladministration and calling for his dismissal by the President played a veiled but primary role (Document I below). But in considering the relationship between Jefferson's resolutions and the modified ones Giles submitted to the House on 27 Feb., the disappearance of Jefferson's manuscript and the fragmentary contextual record make it appropriate to recall the warning of Dumas Malone, the most judicious student of this episode, that "conjectures based on unlabeled papers in anybody's files must be made with caution." Despite this caveat, and notwithstanding the possibility that Jefferson had copied the resolutions from another source, Malone himself noted that the similarities between the Jefferson resolves and the milder resolutions Giles submitted to the House were "so close as to lead to the reasonable surmise that one was copied in considerable part from the other," and that, whatever Giles's role in the episode may have been, it was "a fair assumption that the stronger set came first in point of time, being modified on second thought and under circumstances of which we are uninformed" (Malone, *Jefferson*, III, 31-2).

Although Jefferson's interaction with House Republicans during this episode remains unclear, it is possible to determine approximately when he drafted his resolutions. Since the resolutions were based in large measure on printed versions of the reports Hamilton submitted to the House between 4 and 20 Feb., the last of which was probably not printed for at least another day, he could not have set them down any earlier than 21 Feb. or any later than 27 Feb., when Giles presented a revised version of them to the House (see notes to Document I below). This dating is consistent with Giles's insistence on submitting censure resolutions before the end of the Second Congress and suggests perhaps that Jefferson's composition might have been dictated as much by the Virginia Congressman's imperatives as by any timetable of his own (Madison, *Papers*, XIV, 472). But it is equally consistent with the hypothesis that Jefferson's involvement occurred only after the Cabinet meeting of 25 Feb. indicated that the President would not launch an executive investigation of Hamilton's operations in the Treasury without stronger grounds for doing so than those Jefferson had thus far advanced.

If the dating of Jefferson's draft resolutions can be determined with some degree of confidence, there is no way of knowing with complete certainty whether he drafted them on his own initiative and made them available to House Republicans, or whether—as Malone suggested—he was approached and asked to do so by Madison or Giles, or perhaps both (Malone, *Jefferson*, III, 31-2). If Jefferson initiated the contact and transmitted his resolutions to Giles, the most plausible hypothesis is that he did so by way of Madison, his longtime collaborator, to whom he customarily submitted ordinary legislative proposals to the House and to whom he had first conveyed his suspicions of the Treasury Secretary after studying Hamilton's first report on foreign loans (for examples of Jefferson's reliance on Madison, see Thoughts on the Bankruptcy Bill, [ca. 10 Dec. 1792], and note; and enclosure to TJ to Washington, 13 Jan. 1793). There is no evidence, however, that Madison or Giles asked Jefferson to draft censure resolutions against Hamilton, and it seems unlikely that the former would have done so, given his reservations about the wisdom of offering them to the House during the final days of the Second Congress (Madison, *Papers*, XIV, 472). Still it is not outside the realm of possibility that Giles played the role in the episode that Malone ascribed to him. Jefferson and Madison both indicated that after the submission of Hamilton's final report to the House on 20 Feb. Giles was eager to bring censure resolutions against the Treasury Secretary, and there is no reason to doubt this testimony, especially since Giles in April 1792 had been the first Republican congressman to offer on the floor of the House a systematic ideological critique of the Hamiltonian financial system as a serious threat to the nation's republican political and social order (Banning, *Jeffersonian Persuasion*, 164). Whatever the actual interaction of the three Republican leaders in this episode, the weight of the available circumstantial evidence tends to point to the conclusion that Jefferson acted on his own initiative.

In two documents written immediately after the House rejected the censure resolutions offered by Giles, Jefferson sought to create the impression that the Virginia congressman was their sole author. In a confidential memorandum that he later had bound as part of the "Anas" he discussed the defeat of the resolves by the House with an air of detachment that belied his contribution to their authorship, and he informed his son-in-law in a private letter that Giles had "prepared" the resolutions introduced in the House of Representatives (Notes on the Giles Resolutions, 2 Mch. 1793; TJ to Thomas Mann Randolph, Jr., 3 Mch. 1793). Neither of these accounts should be accepted at face value. The resolutions in Jefferson's hand flowed directly from concerns that he had previously expressed in commentaries on Hamilton's reports to the House (see Notes on Alexander Hamilton's Report on Foreign Loans, printed under 4 Jan. 1793; Document IV in the group of documents on Jefferson's questions and observations on the application of France, at 12 Feb. 1793; Notes on Alexander Hamilton's Report on Foreign Loans, [ca. 20 Feb. 1793]). As a caustic critic of Hamilton's alleged corruption of the legislature, moreover, Jefferson had every reason to conceal his own involvement in the effort of House Republicans to drive his Cabinet colleague from office.

The drafting of these resolutions of censure against Hamilton for use

[287]

by House Republicans inevitably raises questions about Jefferson's ultimate motives. They arise because Jefferson clearly anticipated that the modified resolutions submitted by Giles would not secure House approval during the current session of Congress. He was well aware that Federalists outnumbered Republicans in the House during the Second Congress, and he was also convinced that the House and the Senate alike were under the sway of a corrupt monied interest that would inevitably support the Secretary of the Treasury because its members profited so handsomely from the financial policies he pursued. But, as he indicated soon after, he considered the charges of maladministration against Hamilton to be so incontrovertible that their very rejection by the House would vindicate Republican warnings about Hamiltonian corruption of the national legislature and thereby enhance the opposition's standing and credibility with the American public. However, the resolutions themselves suggest a further motive. Carefully crafted as they were to emphasize the charge that Hamilton lacked presidential authorization for his handling of foreign loans, the resolutions were also undoubtedly calculated to generate a debate in the House on this point that would convince Washington of its accuracy and lead to his dismissal of Jefferson's great nemesis in the Department of the Treasury—an objective they signally failed to achieve (TJ to Washington, 23 May, 9 Sep. 1792; TJ to Thomas Mann Randolph, Jr., 16 Nov. 1792, 3 Mch. 1793; Notes on the Giles Resolutions, 2 Mch. 1793; Madison, *Papers*, xv, 36).

The resolutions Giles actually submitted to the House on 27 Feb. 1793— only four days before it was due to adjourn—were significantly more moderate than the ones Jefferson drafted. Although they retained almost verbatim the second as well as the fourth through the eighth of Jefferson's draft resolutions, they omitted Jefferson's pointed allusion to Hamilton's alleged favoritism to the Bank of the United States and speculators, reworded the third resolution so as to charge Hamilton with specific violations of the 1790 act for discharging the foreign debt, and replaced the climactic ninth and tenth resolutions, with their call for fundamental reform of the Treasury and the dismissal of Hamilton from office, with a far less sweeping resolution that simply called for the transmittal of the other resolves to the President. In light of the existing documentary evidence, it is impossible to determine who was responsible for these changes. The most likely explanation is that they were the work of Madison, who was less eager than Jefferson or Giles to continue the Republican attack on Hamilton during the current legislative session, but until further evidence appears the answer to this question can only be a matter of conjecture (Madison, *Papers*, xiv, 452, 472).

In any event, the House considered the resolutions offered by Giles in three stages. It began by narrowing the scope of debate. On 28 Feb. 1793 Giles moved for House consideration of the resolutions, whereupon forty members approved a motion granting his request offered by the staunchly Federalist Fisher Ames of Massachusetts—a sure sign of Federalist confidence in their strength. South Carolina Federalist William Loughton Smith then rose to urge the House to confine itself to what he regarded as the main point at issue— "had the Secretary violated a law"—and therefore he argued that it should disregard the first, second, and ninth resolutions. The first two resolutions merely involved abstract points of political theory that would unduly delay consideration of Hamilton's alleged guilt, he contended, and furthermore in cases of extreme emergency a Cabinet member might be justified in deviating from the

EDITORIAL NOTE

express letter of the law. The ninth resolution calling for the submission of the other eight to the President was also unworthy of House consideration, he asserted, because passage of it would be tantamount to circumventing the constitutional provisions for impeachment and condemning Hamilton without giving him an opportunity to defend himself. Despite a plea from Virginia Republican John Page that the House at least consider the first resolution because it involved the weighty issue of ministerial discretion, the House voted 32 to 25 against taking up the first two resolutions, while only fourteen members voted in favor of considering the ninth. The House then referred the remaining six resolutions to the committee of the whole for immediate debate (*Annals*, III, 899-905).

Having narrowed the scope of the resolutions, House Republicans and Federalists next joined issue on the third one, which became the main subject of contention. For two days both sides heatedly debated whether Hamilton had violated the law by commingling the foreign loans contracted under the authority of the 4 Aug. 1790 act for the payment of the foreign debt and the 12 Aug. 1790 act for the redemption of the domestic debt, or whether he had exceeded his instructions from the President by drawing to the United States some of the funds borrowed in Europe to pay the foreign debt. Led by Smith and Robert Barnwell of South Carolina, Elias Boudinot of New Jersey, and John Laurance of New York, Federalists vigorously disputed these charges. Some Federalists conceded that Hamilton may have been in technical violation of the letter of the law when he contracted foreign loans under the joint authority of both acts, but most refused to concede even this much, and all insisted that he had applied the funds themselves as the laws directed. They added that the House had to presume that Hamilton had been authorized by the President to draw to the United States some of the money borrowed in Europe to pay the foreign debt, as otherwise Washington would surely have dismissed him, and they were insistent that Hamilton had acted for reasons of urgent public necessity, not for the benefit of the Bank of the United States (same, 907-18, 924-8, 929-30, 932-4, 945-6, 947-55).

In reply, Republicans, led by Giles, Madison, William Findley of Pennsylvania, and John F. Mercer of Maryland, argued with equal vigor in favor of the charges against Hamilton in the third resolution. They contended that Hamilton's commingling of the loans violated the express will of Congress, denied that he had taken this step with presidential authorization, and suggested that he had drawn funds from the loans to America to benefit the Bank, not the national interest. In sum, they maintained that the future of the republic was in peril if the discretion of a Cabinet officer was allowed to take precedence over the express will of the people's elected representatives. As Findley argued in the course of criticizing Hamilton for "assuming that power of dispensing with the laws which produced the late revolution in Britain"—a reference to the Glorious Revolution of 1688-89—"If the will of the Minister may control and give another direction to the will of the Legislature, the Sovereign Legislative authority is transferred from the Representative of the people to the temporary Minister" (same, 921; see also same, 918-24, 925, 926, 928-9, 931, 934-45, 946-7). But notwithstanding these Republican rhetorical efforts, the House overwhelmingly defeated the third resolution by a vote of 40 to 12 on the evening of 1 Mch. 1793 (same, 955-6; JHR, I, 727).

The vote on the third resolution accurately prefigured the fate of the others, which the House decided the same evening. Thus, it rejected the fourth resolution by a vote of 39 to 12 and then defeated the fifth resolution by a vote of 33 to 15 after Federalist Jonathan Dayton of New Jersey argued that it was not part of the Secretary of the Treasury's official duties to inform Congress of the drawing of funds from foreign loans to the United States because he had taken this action under the authority of a special commission from the President. The sixth and seventh resolutions went down to defeat by identical votes of 33 to 8. Finally, the House voted down the eighth resolution by a margin of 34 to 7 after a debate in which the staunchly Republican Findley declared that one of the main bases for the resolution—Hamilton's slighting allusions to Giles in one of his recent reports to the House—deserved "silent contempt" and should not be referred to the President, lest the House surrender its power to punish acts of contempt against itself (*Annals*, III, 956-63; JHR, I, 727-30; Syrett, *Hamilton*, XIII, 542, 553).

The pattern of voting in the House on the six Jefferson-inspired resolutions considered in the committee of the whole reveals several significant characteristics of the Republican opposition in this episode. First, the support Republicans mustered for the resolutions was strictly limited, the middle group of legislators who did not vote consistently with either party remaining largely unmoved by Republican arguments. Only the fifth resolution came close to garnering the votes of even as many as a third of the forty-eight members then present and voting. Moreover, the support the Republicans did mobilize was heavily sectional in nature. Except for Vermont, which voted for one of them, the resolutions received no backing from New England, and except for Findley and Andrew Gregg of Pennsylvania, who voted respectively for five and two of them, they enjoyed no support from the Middle States. With the exception of South Carolina, which voted for none of them, support for the resolutions was concentrated in the South, with Virginia and North Carolina providing the bulk of the votes in favor and Maryland, Georgia, and Kentucky offering scattered support. Finally, the votes on the resolutions revealed a striking lack of party discipline among the eighteen members of the House who have been identified as relatively firm Republicans by May 1792. Only five voted for all of the resolutions—Giles and Madison of Virginia, Nathaniel Macon and John B. Ashe of North Carolina, and Abraham Baldwin of Georgia—while others from Republican ranks missed some or all of the roll calls. Thus, the vote on the modified version of Jefferson's resolutions presented to the House by Giles basically represented a Southern agrarian protest against Hamiltonian finance, and not even a united one at that (JHR, I, 727-30; Noble E. Cunningham, Jr., *The Jeffersonian Republicans: The Formation of Party Organization, 1789-1801* [Chapel Hill, 1957], 22, 53-4).

The overwhelming defeat of the Jefferson-inspired resolutions in the House did not deter Jefferson and his Republican allies from pressing on with their charges of Hamiltonian corruption at the Treasury. While Federalists rejoiced in the vindication of their champion, Republicans countered by charging that Hamilton's exoneration merely confirmed the truth of their assertions that Congress had been corrupted by the Hamiltonian system. With Jefferson himself setting the tone in a letter to his son-in-law, Republicans charged in various forums that the Giles resolutions were quashed primarily by the votes of an unwholesome alliance in Congress among directors of the Bank of the United States, subscribers to its stock, and holders of the national debt, who formed the constituent elements of a corrupt monied interest that sought to keep Hamilton in office so that they could continue to take advantage of his policies and practices to advance their selfish interests at the expense of the common good. In short, Republican publicists proclaimed, an impartial consideration of the evidence that Hamilton himself had offered to the House in his own defense was sufficient to convince anyone without a vested interest in the Hamiltonian system that the charges made against him in the February 1793 Giles resolutions were valid (Notes on the Giles Resolutions, 2 Mch. 1793; TJ to Thomas Mann Randolph, Jr., 3 Mch. 1793; Notes on Stockholders in Congress, 23 Mch. 1793, and note; "Franklin," *National Gazette*, 20 Mch. 1793; "Fair Play," same, 24 July 1793; "Turn-Coat," same, 3 Aug. 1793; see also Syrett, *Hamilton*, XIV, 247-8, 338).

If Jefferson's appeals to the President, and Republican arguments on the floor of the House and in pamphlets and newspapers afterwards, failed to shake Hamilton's position in the Cabinet, they were not entirely without influence on both Washington and Hamilton. Although the President continued to express his faith in Hamilton's integrity and to disregard Jefferson's insistent complaint that Hamilton's administration of the finances was exerting a corrupting influence on Congress, he was moved to pay closer attention than before to the Treasury Secretary's disposition of overseas loans in relation to presidential and, ultimately, statutory authority (Washington to TJ, 4, 16 June 1793; Opinions to Washington, 5, 17 June 1793; Syrett, *Hamilton*, XIV, 516, 521-2, 550-4, XV, 9-10, 13, 21-4, 119, 125-6, 136-8; Madison, *Papers*, XV, 36). Moreover, stung by continued Republican criticism of his probity as Secretary of the Treasury, Hamilton sought another congressional investigation of his administration of his department to clear himself once and for all of imputations of official misconduct. At his insistence, in February 1794 the House appointed a fifteen-member committee, consisting largely of Giles and other Republicans unsympathetic to Hamilton, to undertake an exhaustive investigation into his stewardship of the Treasury Department. After carefully examining written and verbal testimony by Hamilton and other Treasury officials, the committee submitted a long report to Congress in May 1794 on the Treasury Department under his leadership that was severely factual in tone, devoid of any charges of maladministration against him, and buttressed by a somewhat grudging letter from Washington confirming Hamilton's statement to the committee that he had had written and verbal presidential approval for his handling of foreign loans. The submission of this report, which the House promptly tabled, marked the end of the Republican drive to censure the Secretary of the Treasury (Syrett, *Hamilton*, XV, 460-7, XVI, 230-2, 248-53; ASP, *Finance*, I, 281-301; Mitchell, *Hamilton*, II, 270-5).

In view of Jefferson's conviction that the informal influence Hamilton exerted over Congress constituted a dangerous form of executive corruption of the people's representatives, his own clandestine involvement in the House Republican effort to censure the Secretary of the Treasury reveals the depth of his apprehension at the threat Hamiltonian finance posed to his conception of American republicanism. Given Jefferson's expressed determination "to intermeddle not at all with the legislature" (TJ to Washington, 9 Sep. 1792), it is not surprising that he went to great lengths to conceal his part in this affair. Yet there may have been a deeper reason why he did not mention his draft resolutions in his personal correspondence or include them among his collection of official papers and private political memorandums as Secretary of State known as the "Anas," and this was his continued ambivalence over the assumption of a more active leadership role in the growing Republican opposition to Federalist policies, an ambivalence grounded in the aversion to political parties that he shared with most of his contemporaries and that was deeply rooted in early American political culture. Nevertheless, Jefferson's covert support of the House Republican drive against Hamilton in 1793 remains a highly significant benchmark in his public career, marking a crucial stage in his gradual shift from the role of a statesman standing above the clash of conflicting political parties to the more partisan role that eventually propelled him to the presidency, that of chief leader of the Republican party.

I. Resolutions on the Secretary of the Treasury

[before 27 Feb. 1793]

1. *Resolved*, That it is essential to the due administration of the Government of the United States, that laws making specific appropriations of money should be strictly observed by the Secretary of the Treasury thereof.

2. *Resolved*, That a violation of a law making appropriations of money is a violation of that section of the Constitution of the United States which requires that no money shall be drawn from the Treasury but in consequence of appropriations made by law.

3. *Resolved*, That the Secretary of the Treasury, in drawing to this country and lodging in the bank the funds raised in Europe, which ought to have been applied to the paiments of our debts there in order to stop interest, has violated the instructions of the President of the United States for the benefit of speculators and to increase the profits of that institution.

4. *Resolved*, That the Secretary of the Treasury has deviated from the instructions given by the President of the United States, in exceeding the authorities for making loans under the acts of the 4th and 12th of August, 1790.

5. *Resolved*, That the Secretary of the Treasury has omitted to discharge an essential duty of his office, in failing to give Congress official information in due time, of the moneys drawn by him from Europe into the United States; which drawing commenced December, 1790, and continued till January, 1793; and of the causes of making such drafts.

6. *Resolved*, That the Secretary of the Treasury has, without the instruction of the President of the United States, drawn more moneys

borrowed in Holland into the United States than the President of the United States was authorized to draw, under the act of the 12th of August, 1790; which act appropriated two millions of dollars only, when borrowed, to the purchase of the Public Debt: And that he has omitted to discharge an essential duty of his office, in failing to give official information to the Commissioners for purchasing the Public Debt, of the various sums drawn from time to time, suggested by him to have been intended for the purchase of the Public Debt.

7. *Resolved,* That the Secretary of the Treasury did not consult the public interest in negotiating a Loan with the Bank of the United States, and drawing therefrom four hundred thousand dollars, at five per cent. per annum, when a greater sum of public money was deposited in various banks at the respective periods of making the respective drafts.

8. *Resolved,* That the Secretary of the Treasury has been guilty of an indecorum to this House, in undertaking to judge of its motives in calling for information which was demandable of him, from the constitution of his office; and in failing to give all the necessary information within his knowledge, relatively to the subjects of the reference made to him of the 19th January, 1792, and of the 22d November, 1792, during the present session.

9. *Resolved,* That at the next meeting of Congress, the act of Sep 2d, 1789, establishing a Department of Treasury should be so amended as to constitute the office of the Treasurer of the United States a separate department, independent of the Secretary of the Treasury.

10. *Resolved,* That the Secretary of the Treasury has been guilty of maladministration in the duties of his office, and should, in the opinion of Congress, be removed from his office by the President of the United States.

MS not found; reprinted from Ford, VI, 168-71, where it is described as "From the original courteously loaned me by Miss S. N. Randolph," captioned by the editor as "Jefferson's Draft," and assigned the conjectural date of "[February? 1793]." Elsewhere Ford described this text more specifically as a "rough draft of the resolutions, in the handwriting of Thomas Jefferson," and printed resolutions 1, 3, 9-10 with their numbers in parentheses, the word *Resolved* in roman, and minor differences in punctuation (Paul L. Ford, "The Authorship of Giles's Resolutions," *The Nation*, LXI [1895], 164).

These resolutions were based in large measure on information provided by Alexander Hamilton himself in three of the four reports he submitted to the House of Representatives in February 1793 in defense of his administration of the Department of the Treasury. Thus, the fourth through the sixth resolutions were founded primarily on the basis of Hamilton's own defense of his handling of foreign loans in the second of his two 13 Feb. 1793 reports to the House on this subject (Syrett, *Hamilton*, XIV, 26-67). The information recited in the seventh resolution was drawn from Hamilton's 19 Feb. 1793 report on his relations

[293]

with the Bank of the United States, submitted to the House one day later (same, 94-7, 109-10). Finally, the INDECORUM to which the eighth resolution referred was the impugning, in Hamilton's 4 Feb. 1793 report to the House on his handling of public revenues, of Congressman William B. Giles's motives in offering to the House on 23 Jan. 1793 the resolves on the conduct of the Treasury that elicited the three reports from the Secretary of the Treasury, as well as another one of 13 Feb. 1793 on the subject of foreign loans (same, XIII, 542, 553, XIV, 17-26). The third resolution could have been based on either Hamilton's 3 Jan. 1793 report to the House on foreign loans or the one of 13 Feb. 1793 first mentioned above (same, XIII, 451-62; Notes on Alexander Hamilton's Report on Foreign Loans, printed under 4 Jan. 1793).

For a discussion of the 28 Aug. 1790 INSTRUCTIONS OF THE PRESIDENT referred to in the third resolution, which concerned the negotiation of foreign loans under the acts of Congress of 4 and 12 Aug. 1790, and the charge in the fourth resolution that Hamilton DEVIATED from them, see Notes on Alexander Hamilton's Report on Foreign Loans, [ca. 20 Feb. 1793]. Concerning the functions of the COMMISSIONERS FOR PURCHASING THE PUBLIC DEBT (of whom TJ was one) mentioned in the sixth resolution, see Report of the Commissioners of the Sinking Fund, [17 Nov. 1792], and note. For Hamilton's accounting to the House of his handling of the loans contracted for the redemption of the domestic debt, see Syrett, *Hamilton*, XIV, 30-2, 52-3, 60-3, 100-3.

The SUBJECTS OF THE REFERENCE in the eighth resolution concerned two requests by the House to Hamilton, the first that he supply it with such information about public finances as it would require to determine whether additional revenues were needed to fund a proposed increase in the army, and the second that he submit to it a plan for repaying the government's debt to the Bank of the United States (JHR, I, 493, 625; for Hamilton's responses, see Syrett, *Hamilton*, X, 531-6, XIII, 271). Hamilton's failure to inform the House in either case of the money he had drawn to the United States from European loans contracted to pay the foreign and redeem the domestic debt was evidently the basis for the charge in this resolution that he had not provided the House with all NECESSARY INFORMATION WITHIN HIS KNOWLEDGE.

Since the TREASURER OF THE UNITED STATES was already responsible for the keeping and disbursement of public revenues, the proposal in the ninth resolution to make this office a separate department of government independent of the Secretary of the Treasury was obviously designed to prevent what TJ and other Republicans perceived to be misapplications of public funds by Hamilton or his successors (ASP, *Finance*, I, 285). TJ had apparently favored this reform as early as the summer of 1792 (Note of Agenda to Reduce the Government to True Principles, [ca. 11 July 1792]).

II. William Branch Giles's Resolutions on the Secretary of the Treasury

[27 Feb. 1793]

Resolved, That it is[1] essential to the due administration of the government of the United States, that laws making specific[2] appropriations[3] of monies[4] should be strictly observed by the administrator of the finances thereof.

Resolved, That the[5] violation of a law[6] making appropriations[7] of monies,[8] is a violation of that article[9] of the Constitution of the United

States, which requires, that no monies[10] shall be drawn from the treasury but in consequence of appropriations made by law.

Resolved, That the Secretary of the Treasury has violated the law, passed the fourth of August, one thousand seven hundred and ninety, making appropriations of certain monies, authorized to be borrowed by the same[11] law, in the following particulars, to wit:

1. By applying a certain portion of the principal borrowed, to the payment of interest falling due upon that principal, which was not authorized by that, or any other law.

2. By drawing part of the same[12] monies into the United States, without the instructions of the President of the United States.

Resolved, That the Secretary of the Treasury has deviated from the instructions given by the President of the United States, in executing[13] the authorities for making loans, under the acts of the fourth and twelfth of August, one thousand seven hundred and ninety.

Resolved, That the Secretary of the Treasury has[14] omitted to discharge an essential duty of his office, in failing to give Congress official information in due time, of the monies drawn by him from Europe into the United States; which drawing commenced December, one thousand seven hundred and ninety, and continued till January, one thousand seven hundred and ninety-three, and of the causes of making such drafts.

Resolved, That the Secretary of the Treasury has, without the instructions of the President of the United States, drawn more monies, borrowed in Holland into[15] the United States, than the President of the United States was[16] authorized [to][17] draw, under the act of the twelfth of August, one thousand seven hundred and ninety, which act appropriated two millions of dollars only, when borrowed, to the purchase of[18] the public debt; and that he has omitted to discharge an essential duty of his office, in failing to give official[19] information to the commissioners for purchasing the public debt, of the various sums drawn from time to time suggested by him to have been intended for the purchase of the public debt.

Resolved, That the Secretary of the Treasury[20] did not consult the public interest, in negociating a loan with the bank of the United States, and drawing therefrom four hundred thousand dollars at five per centum per annum, when a greater sum of public money was deposited in various banks, at the respective periods of making the respective drafts.

Resolved, That the Secretary of the Treasury has been guilty of an indecorum to this House, in undertaking to judge of its motives in calling for information which was demandable of him, from the con-

[295]

stitution of his office, and in failing to give all[21] the necessary information within his knowledge, relatively to the subjects of reference made to him of the nineteenth of January, one thousand seven hundred and ninety-two, and of the twenty-second of November, one thousand seven hundred and ninety-two, during the present session.

Resolved, That a copy of the foregoing resolutions be transmitted to the President of the United States.

Text reprinted from *Journal of the House of Representatives of the United States, at the Second Session of the Second Congress* (Philadelphia, 1793), 147-8. Tr (DNA: RG 233, House Records, Smooth Journal, 2d Cong., 2d sess.); with omissions and variations. Collation of the text in the *Journal* with the Tr, with the texts printed in five Philadelphia newspapers— the *Federal Gazette and Philadelphia Daily Advertiser*, 1 Mch. 1793; *Dunlap's American Daily Advertiser*, 2 Mch. 1793; the *Gazette of the United States*, 2 Mch. 1793; the *General Advertiser*, 2 Mch. 1793; and the *National Gazette*, 6 Mch. 1793—and with the text printed in *Annals*, III, 900, establishes the *Journal* as the most reliable source for the resolutions. The *Daily Advertiser*, the *Gazette of the United States*, and the *Annals* number the resolutions; in the *Gazette of the United States* the third resolution is printed as the fourth, the fourth resolution as the fifth, and the fifth resolution as the third. Other significant variations are noted below; inconsequential differences in capitalization, punctuation, and spelling have been ignored.

[1] Word omitted in Tr.
[2] Word omitted in *Daily Advertiser*.
[3] Next two words omitted in *Federal Gazette, General Advertiser*, and *National Gazette.*
[4] *Annals, Daily Advertiser*, and *Gazette of the United States*: "money."
[5] *Daily Advertiser, Gazette of the United States*, and *Annals*: "a."
[6] Preceding three words omitted in Tr.
[7] Next two words given as "for monies" in *Federal Gazette* and *National Gazette.*
[8] *Daily Advertiser, Gazette of the United States*, and *Annals*: "money."
[9] *Daily Advertiser, Gazette of the United States*, and *Annals*: "section."
[10] *Daily Advertiser, Gazette of the United States*, and *Annals*: "money."
[11] *Daily Advertiser*: "said."
[12] *Daily Advertiser*: "said."
[13] *Gazette of the United States* and *Annals*: "exceeding."
[14] Word omitted in *Daily Advertiser.*
[15] *General Advertiser*: "in."
[16] Word omitted in *Daily Advertiser, Federal Gazette*, and *National Gazette.*
[17] Word, supplied, is present in all other texts.
[18] Preceding three words omitted in *General Advertiser.*
[19] Word omitted in Tr.
[20] Preceding three words omitted in Tr.
[21] *Federal Gazette* and *National Gazette*: "to all."

From Tobias Lear

27t Feby 1793.

The President refers the enclosed letter and affidavit of Messrs. Brown & Francis to the Secretary of State, to report to the President what may appear to him proper to be done in the case stated.

Mr. Bourne, the Representative from Rhode Island, handed the enclosed to the President and will be ready to give the Secretary any further information, if required.

RC (DLC); endorsed by TJ as received 27 Feb. 1793. Enclosures: (1) Brown & Francis to George Washington, Providence, 17 Feb. 1793, noting that supercargo Thomas Willing Francis had sold their American-built ship, the *President Washington*, in Calcutta in part to purchase the foreign-built *Eutrusco* (renamed the *Illustrious President*), which Francis dispatched to Ostend without American papers, and that before sending her from thence to China and back to the United States they wished the President to issue papers entitling her to fly the American flag for protection since federal customs officials were not authorized by law to do so (RC in DNA: RG 59, MLR). (2) Affidavit of John Brown and John Francis, Providence, 17 Feb. 1793, swearing to the circumstances under which the *Illustrious President* was acquired for them in Calcutta, as well as her subsequent voyage to Ostend and intended voyage to China and back to the United States, and certifying that they were the sole owners of the ship (MS in same; notarized on verso by Samuel Chace, justice of the peace and notary public in Providence, 18 Feb. 1793).

Washington had received the LETTER AND AFFIDAVIT this day (Washington, *Journal*, 71). No report from TJ to the President on this subject has been found.

From Martha Jefferson Randolph

DEAR PAPA   Monticello February 27, 1793

I have just this moment recieved yours of Jan. 26, which by the negligence of the post has remained a fortnight longer than it ought to have done upon the road. We had already Learnt your resolution of continuing in Philadelphia by a Letter of a Later date to Mr. Randolph. I concieve your anxiety by what I feel my self. It was a cruel disapointment to me who had set my heart upon the pleasure of seeing you in march never to separate again farther than Edgehill. Having never in my life been more intent upon any thing I never bore a disappointment with so little patience. My Little cherubs have both been very sick Lately. The Little boy has recoverd but My dear Anna continues extremely unwell. Poor Jenny Cary has Lost her husband and her sister Lucy is married to a Mr. Teril with whom she goes to Kentucke this spring so that Aunt Carr will have only one of her children with her it being the intention of Sam to settle imediately upon his own Land in this neighbourhood. It is so Late that I shall not have time to write to dear Maria this evening indeed I am affraid she thinks I never intend it again and that that is the reason she has left off writing to me However I hope to redeem my credit by the next post. In the mean time present my tenderest affections to her and be assured dear and much loved Father that no one breathing possesses them more entirely than your self. Yours   M. RANDOLPH

I have unintentionally hurt Petit by neglecting to mention him in my letters therefore I should be much obliged to you to say *bien des choses* to him or any other message you think proper. I am affraid you will scarcely be able to read my Letter but it is one o'clock and the post goes of by day break. Once more adieu dear Father.

RC (MHi); endorsed by TJ as received 9 Mch. 1793 and so recorded in SJL.

JENNY CARY: Jane Barbara Carr Cary, TJ's niece, whose husband was Wilson Cary. Mary (Polly) Carr was the ONLY ONE of Martha Jefferson Carr's children remaining at home (Bear, *Family Letters*, 15, 113n).

From Thomas Mann Randolph, Jr.

DEAR SIR   Monticello Feb: 27: 1793.

This morning we received your letters of the 26. Jan. and 18th. Feb.

Your plan of leasing your lands is exactly what I would wish to adopt with Edgehill after reserving a farm of 400 acres for myself and what I should put in execution immediately if I could get tenants. Do not you offer yours on very low terms? I have had very lately an application for a farm in the S.E. angle of my tract which will contain rather less than 100 acres and I am told I should require 10.£ for a term of 3 years: that rent I am certain of geting and yet the arable part will scarcely be two thirds. But still I believe $\frac{1}{4}$ of a Dollar with the maryland culture would be better and shall trouble you probably to procure 2 or 3 tenants for me if you do not find too much difficulty in bringing the scheme to bear for yourself. Longer terms than 7 years even, would be desirable with our lands particularly, if an adjustment could be made at certain intervals, of the rent to the value of the land. The rate of increase in general is known I suppose and a proportional size of the rent[1] might be bargained for beforehand but in many cases and perhaps in ours from a change in the husbandry of the country favorable to particular soils or from local advantages which are just begining to operate an irregular advancement of price might take place.

Sam Carr receives 2 dollars an acre for his low grounds this year, and has reason to expect a rent something higher the next.

Three pieces of information have lately come to my ears which it may be of some import to you in your private matters to receive and which I communicate accordingly without loss of time. 1. The death of Wm. Ronald. He died intestate and I am told his estate is deeply involved.

2. This relates to you as Attorney for Mazzei upon whom you remember Anthony Giannini had a pretended claim: he has transfered

the claim and delivered all the papers which *may* establish it to Charles Lewis who means to place it against the bond for Colle.

3. This I received from Mr. Pohatan Bolling; it may concern you as proprietor of the Natural bridge. He learnt while in that neighbourhood lately that one Captain Barclay had discovered the title by which you hold it, to be insufficient and designed to locate it himself. He did not explain the matter to me nor could I have understood it being totally ignorant of the subject but I mention it as he thought you might possibly lose the land.

The timber for your scantling is all cut down and out of danger of being spoiled by the sap. Your most aff. friend & hble Sert.

Th: M. Randolph

Diary.

Feb. 20. 52. flying clouds.	50. f. almond in bloom
21. 48. f.	51. f.
22. 43. f.	52. f.
23. 38. f.	54. f.
24. 53. c.	60. c.
25. 40. r. & hail	37. r. Sleet.
26. 38. sleet.	40. r.
27. 48. f. dom. Wagtail app.	41. f. Wd. N.W. high.
28. 25. f.	

RC (MHi); endorsed by TJ as received 9 Mch. 1793 and so recorded in SJL.

The NATURAL BRIDGE, located in Rockbridge County, had been acquired by TJ in 1774 and remained in his possession until his death (TJ to John Trumbull, 20 Feb. 1791, and note).

[1] At this point Randolph first interlined and then canceled "at certain periods."

Cabinet Opinion on Military Rations

Having considered the note of the President of the U.S. to General Knox, on the subject of increased rations; we are of opinion, that a proposition to congress at this time concerning such increase would be inexpedient, even if the question were more free from difficulty, than it is. But liable as it is to objections, the inexpediency of such a proposition *now*, acquires double force.

Th: Jefferson
H Knox
Edm: Randolph
Feby. 28. 1793.

MS (DLC: Washington Papers); in the hand of Edmund Randolph, signed by TJ, Knox, and Randolph; endorsed by Tobias Lear.

Washington's NOTE to Henry Knox, labeled "(Private)" and dated "Thursday Morning, Feby. 28. 1793," reads as follows: "It is much to be regretted that the subject of Rations (encreased) had not been thought of and considered at an earlier period! It is to be feared a proposition at this time would be received with an ill grace—probably no attention paid to it. At the meeting you are about to have it might be well to mention the matter and know what the Gentlemen there would think of bringing the matter forward at a time so Mal a propos" (DLC: Washington Papers; Fitzpatrick, *Writings*, XXXII, 362). The

Cabinet did not specify the OBJECTIONS to which a request to Congress for increased rations were liable, but there were undoubtedly two. In the first place, Washington this day approved a general appropriations bill providing funds for rations, and since Congress was on the verge of adjournment the Cabinet must have believed that there was not enough time for Congress to consider a supplemental request for appropriations. The Cabinet probably also feared that a call for increased rations would be viewed as a tacit admission that the administration expected the Lower Sandusky conference to fail and was preparing for the resumption of the politically unpopular war with the Western tribes, as indeed it was (*Annals*, III, 1437-41; Notes on Cabinet Opinions, 26 Feb. 1793).

From Tobias Lear, with Jefferson's Note

Thursday Morning 28 Feby. 1793.
The President requests the Secretary of State to call upon him this morning as he goes to the War Office so as to give him about 10 or 15 minutes conversation.

[*Note by TJ:*]
This was to consult about the premature nomination of Judge Patterson.

RC (DLC); addressed: "The Secretary of State"; with note by TJ at foot of text; endorsed by TJ as received 28 Feb. 1793.

On 16 Jan. 1793 Thomas Johnson of Maryland submitted his resignation as associate justice of the United States Supreme Court to Washington, citing his distaste for the arduous schedule of circuit court duty assigned to each justice. Washington accepted Johnson's resignation on 1 Feb. 1793 and began to search for a successor. In the course of this search Washington considered five candidates, including Governor William Paterson of New Jersey, a former United States Senator who had played a leading role in drafting the 1789 Judiciary Act that created the federal court system. Washing-

ton asked Attorney General Edmund Randolph to evaluate the candidates, and on 18 Feb. 1793 Randolph advised the President that Paterson's legal abilities made him best qualified to maintain harmony between the federal and state judiciaries. Randolph also endorsed Paterson during a personal meeting with the President on the following day and, upon Washington's urging, requested an opinion from TJ, who also strongly supported the nomination. Accordingly, Washington submitted Paterson's nomination to the Senate on 27 Feb. 1793 after first ascertaining his willingness to serve on the Supreme Court (Maeva Marcus and others, eds., *The Documentary History of the Supreme Court of the United States, 1789-1800*, 3 vols. [New York, 1985-], I, pt.

1, p. 80-9, pt. 2, p. 723n, 738-9; Washington, *Journal*, 36, 59, 60, 69, 71; JEP, I, 134).

Almost as soon as he had submitted his name to the Senate, however, Washington realized that Paterson's nomination was PREMATURE because of Article I, Section 6, of the United States Constitution, which forbade the appointment of a member of Congress to any federal post that had either been established or for which the emoluments had been increased during his term in office. Although Paterson had resigned from the Senate to become governor of New Jersey in 1790, Washington decided that this provision disqualified him from service on the Supreme Court until the term for which he had been chosen to serve in the Senate expired on 3 Mch. 1793 (Washington, *Journal*, 74). Consequently, after meeting with Washington this day, TJ drafted a message to the Senate in the President's name withdrawing Paterson's nomination and Washington submitted it to the upper house with only minor changes on the same day. Then, on 4 Mch. 1793, Washington resubmitted the nomination to the Senate, which immediately approved it (Washington to the Senate, with Jefferson's Note to Washington, 28 Feb. 1793; JEP, I, 135, 138). On the same day TJ wrote a brief covering letter notifying Paterson of his appointment and enclosing his commission as associate justice (FC in Lb in DNA: RG 59, DL, at head of text: "William Paterson Esquire"; not recorded in SJL), but he undoubtedly did not send it until Washington signed the commission on 6 Mch. (Commission for Paterson as Associate Justice of the United States Supreme Court, 4 Mch. 1793, MS in NjP, signed by Washington and TJ; FC in Lb in DNA: RG 59, Miscellaneous Permanent Commissions). See also Washington, *Journal*, 82. Paterson acknowledged receipt of his commission in a brief letter to TJ of 12 Mch. 1793 from New Brunswick, noting that he had been "initiated into office, by taking the necessary oaths before judge Cushing" (RC in DNA: RG 59, MLR; addressed: "The honorable Thomas Jefferson Secretary of State Philada."; endorsed by George Taylor, Jr., as received 14 Mch. 1793).

Notes on Washington's Second Inauguration and Republicanism

Feb. 28. Knox, E.R. and myself met at Knox's where Hamilton was also to have met, to consider the time manner and place of the President's swearing in. Hamilton had been there before and had left his opinion with Knox. To wit, that the Presid. should ask a judge to attend him in his own house to administer the oath in the presence of the heads of departments, which oath should be deposited in the Secy. of state's office. I concurred in this opinion. E.R. was for the President's going to the Senate chamber to take the oath, attended by the Marshal of the U.S. who should then make proclamation &c. Knox was for this and for adding the house of Repr. to the presence, as they would not yet be departed. Our individual opinions were written to be communicated to the Presidt. out of which he might form one. ⟨*He adopted E.R.*[. . . .]⟩[1] In the course of our conversation Knox stickling for parade, got into great warmth and swore that our government must either be entirely new modelled or it would be knocked to peices in

[301]

less than 10. years, and that as it is at present[2] he would not give a copper for it, that it is the President's character, and not the written constitution which keeps it together.

Same day. Conversation with Lear. He expressed the strongest confidence that republicanism was the universal creed of America, except of a very few, that republican administration must of necessity immediately overbear the contrary faction, said that he had seen with extreme regret that a number of gentlemen had for a long time been endeavoring to instil into the President that the noise against the administration of the government was that of a little faction, which would soon be silent and which was detested by the people, who were contented and prosperous: that this very party however began to see their error and that the sense of America was bursting forth to their conviction.

MS (DLC); entirely in TJ's hand; partially dated; includes heavily canceled text in margin (see note 1 below); written on the other side of a sheet bearing part of "Anas" entry for 26 Feb. 1793. Entry in SJPL: "[Notes] on time & manner of the President's swearing in." Included in the "Anas."

Edmund Randolph composed a report on the Cabinet's INDIVIDUAL OPINIONS respecting the ceremony for the President's second inauguration and submitted it to Washington this day (Syrett, Hamilton, XIV, 169-70; Washington, Journal, 74). The Cabinet met again on 1 Mch. 1793 to consider this issue and advised the President to be sworn in publicly in the Senate chamber by Justice William Cushing. TJ evidently did not attend this meeting and was not a signatory to the opinion prepared by Randolph and Alexander Hamilton. Washington followed the exact inaugural ceremony recommended by the Cabinet (Syrett, Hamilton, XIV, 176; Freeman, Washington, VII, 7-9).

[1] This is all that can be restored of thirteen short lines of text that TJ added here in the margin, which is now partly torn away, and that he evidently intended for insertion at this point. He later canceled the lines heavily in a different ink.

[2] Here TJ canceled "it is not worth."

From Timothy Pickering

Feby. 28: [1793]

Mr: Bradshaw has just returned with an Answer to your letter to the Judge of the district Court of Kentucky. He says he arrived at Lexington, on the 27th: of January. Mr: Innes being from home, Bradshaw was detained until the 8th: of February; and then waited three days for company through the wilderness.

The bearer Mr: Bradley will present to you the receipt for the fifty dollars which I advanced to Mr: Bradshaw, to be repaid by you.

TIMOTHY PICKERING

Tr (Lb in DNA: RG 233, House Records, TR); partially dated; at foot of text: "Honble: Thos: Jefferson, esqr: Secretary of State." Enclosed in TJ to the Speaker of the House of Representatives, 1 Mch. 1793.

To Arthur St. Clair

February 28th. 1793.

Th: Jefferson with his compliments to Govr. St. Clair, has the honor to send him the inclosed copy of a paper received from Mr. Sargent, and to repeat the President's wish that Govr. St. Clair should repair to the north western territory as soon as might be.

FC (Lb in DNA: RG 59, DL); at head of text: "Governor St. Clair." Enclosure not found.

George Washington to the Senate, with Jefferson's Note to Washington

GENTLEMEN OF THE SENATE

I was led, by a consideration of the qualifications of   Patterson of New Jersey to nominate him an associate justice of the Supreme court of the US. It has since occurred that he was a member of the Senate when the act creating that office was passed and that the time for which he was elected had[1] not yet[2] expired. I think it my duty therefore to declare that I deem the nomination to have been null by the constitution.

Feb. 28. 1793.

Th: Jefferson will immediately have letters of summons prepared to convoke the Senate on Monday according to the form used on a former occasion.

PrC of Dft (DLC); with note to Washington subjoined; entirely in TJ's hand, but partially overwritten by a later hand. Entry in SJPL: "draught of a message to Senate on the nullity of Judge Patterson's nomination, & on convening Senate. qu. if sent?"

For the background of this document, see Tobias Lear to TJ, 28 Feb. 1793, and note.

[1] Word interlined in place of "shall not expire till the 3d. of [. . .]."
[2] Word interlined in place of canceled and illegible word.

From Robert R. Livingston

DR SIR   [Feb.-Mch. 1793]

I find with great regret that a report which circulates here of your intention to resign your office gains credit. It appears to me that there are many motives as well of a public as of a private nature which should induce you to take this resolution with great deliberation. Your present station holds you up to the view of your country in the most conspicuous point of light. The attacks which your enemies in administration have made upon you have excited the public attention and served to convince those who were not acquaintd with your character of your[1] attatchment to the Liberties of your country in a station in which it might have been expected that you would have some byass to a contrary sentiment. Not to have been [redirected?] by[2] the spirit of the corps has done no little honor to your virtue and to your firmness. Will not the latter lose somewhat of its luster if by resigning at this period you suffer yourself in appearance to be drumed out of the regiment and that too when there is every reasonable ground to hope that upon the first vacancy you will be promoted to the command of the troops?

The interest that the public will derive from your continuing in your present station independant of your talents experience and knowledge of business are too obvious to have escaped your observation. In a fluctuating government where the members of the legislature are constantly changing and only part of the year in session what better check is there on the[3] encroachments of administration[4] than one of their own body who shall refuse to concur in improper measures?[5] A post in an enemies country serves at once to compell them to act with caution and as point of raliament for[6] the broken troops of the garrison. I submit these hasty thoughts to your consideration and shall rejoice if you afford me an opportunity of contradicting the report which is so little relished by your friends and those of the country.

Having hitherto spoken to you as a statesman let me ask you a question as a philosopher which I have put in vain to those of this place (tho this indeed is no wonder since you will find by the list of members of your philosophical society at *Philadelphia* that it is impossible to find a philosopher at *New York*). Some time before it snows the air is extremely cold but immediately before the snow falls the thermometer rises many degrees it after falls again during the snow storm and almost always after it is over. If as is now the received opinion the air acts as a menstruum to disolve water it would hold more in solution while it was warm than when cold and the reverse of what I have observed should take place it should be colder when the snow was about to fall than at any other time—to what cause is this to be attributed? My own Idea is that[7] water disolved in air is incapable of freezing as indeed is evident from water being held in solution in air[8] When the thermometer is many degrees below the freezing point. But as warm air will disolve much more water than cold when the air becomes cold and its volume is diminished it brings the particles of water nearer they naturally attract each other quit the menstruum in which they were disolved [shoot?] into crystals and assume those regular forms in which snow is always found. In their passage from water to snow they give out a quantity of heat which occasiones the rise of the thermometer that is always observable just before the snow falls. This accounts for the two phenomena that distinguish snow from hail its regular formation and the fall of the thermometer—its rise after the snow has fallen is natural since the cause that rendered it warm has ceased to operate and the renewed capacity of

Dft (NHi: Robert R. Livingston Papers); undated, unaddressed, and unfinished; two words illegible.

The absence in SJL of any record of a letter from Livingston in 1792-93 or of a reply by TJ indicates that this unfinished draft was never sent. Internal evidence suggests that Livingston, the chancellor of New York and a prominent Republican leader, probably wrote it late in February or early in March 1793—before news arrived in America early in April of the French declaration of war against England and Holland and the onset of the neutrality crisis—and then abandoned it when he received word of TJ's decision to continue as Secretary of State after President Washington's first term ended. Livingston's plea that TJ not retire in the face of ATTACKS by his ENEMIES IN ADMINISTRATION, a reference to the barrage of newspaper criticisms unleashed by Alexander Hamilton in the summer and fall of 1792, echoes one of the main arguments used publicly and privately by Republicans in Philadelphia early in 1793 to dissuade the Secretary of State from returning to private life. The first authoritative public announcement of TJ's decision to remain in office appeared in the 6 Mch. 1793 issue of the Philadelphia *General Advertiser* (Malone, *Jefferson*, III, 8-

10). It seems likely that this report came to Livingston's notice or that he unofficially learned even earlier of the Secretary of State's decision—first mentioned to one of his daughters late in January and to the President early in February 1793— and decided that his letter to TJ was no longer necessary (see TJ to Martha Jefferson Randolph, 26 Jan. 1793; Notes of a Conversation with George Washington, 7 Feb. 1793).

[1] Thus in manuscript. Livingston here canceled "unchanged."
[2] Preceding three words interlined in place of "felt."
[3] Before deciding on the preceding seven words, Livingston wrote what appears to be "how essential it is to prevent."
[4] Word interlined in place of "executive," which had been substituted for "the government."
[5] Livingston here canceled "Who shall be always upon duty and who [. . .]."
[6] Before settling on the preceding sixteen words, Livingston first wrote "will compel them to be always upon their guard and serve as point to which to rally."
[7] Livingston here canceled "when the air in the [upper?] is charged with vapours."
[8] Preceding two words interlined.

To John Adams

Sir   Philadelphia Mar. 1. 1793.

In consequence of the information I received from you on the first
Wednesday in January that the list of votes for President and Vice
President were received at the seat of government from all the states
except that of Kentuckey, I sent a special messenger to the District
judge of Kentuckey for the list of the votes of that state lodged in
his custody, and by the return of the messenger received yesterday[1]
the inclosed letter for you, which he informs me contains the list. I
have only to observe that tho' the term between the first Wednesday
of January, and the second Wednesday in February was obviously
insufficient at this season for the performance of the journey yet the
law made it my indispensable duty to send the messenger. I have the
honour to be with the most perfect esteem & respect Sir your most
obedt. & most humble servt.   Th: Jefferson

PrC (DLC); at foot of text: "The Vice
President of the US." FC (Lb in DNA:
RG 59, DL). Enclosures not found.

The INCLOSED LETTER and LIST undoubtedly had been transmitted in a let-

ter from Harry Innes, the district judge of
Kentucky, to TJ of 8 Feb. 1793, which is
recorded in SJL as received 28 Feb. 1793,
but has not been found.

[1] Word interlined.

From J. P. P. Derieux

Charlottesville, 1 Mch. 1793. He has received TJ's letters of 4 Jan. and 3
Feb., together with one from Mme. Bellanger, which frees him from anxiety,
since his last letter from her was dated 22 June. Upon receiving TJ's first
letter, he informed Gamble of Fenwick's 28 Sep. letter to TJ reporting that
his bill of exchange for 5,000 livres had been paid, hoping that Gamble would
repay him the surplus of the funds received from TJ for him. Gamble replied
that the bill must have been paid to Fenwick, who will presumably soon
remit specie or merchandise to TJ; since Gamble's account in London has
not been credited as late as 6 Nov., Gamble cannot be persuaded until the
bearer of the bill in Bordeaux has advised that it is paid. Until then he must be
patient and hope that his merchandise sells promptly so that TJ can send new
funds, payable to his order, so as to avoid a similar disappointment. His uncle
from Nantes wrote on 6 Oct. seeking his advice about the capital necessary to
acquire an estate that would produce net revenue of eight to ten thousand livres
tournois annually in Virginia, where he wants to settle with his family. He
seeks TJ's views, both generally and with reference to Elk Hill, which he hears
is for sale and might be suitable. Madame Derieux sends her respects. P.S. He
has promised some friends here seeds of "*Estragon*,"[1] a salad seasoning from
which a fine vinegar is made, and of "*Aubergine*, autrement dit *Mélongène*,"[2]

a tasty fruit with a flavor like artichokes, but they are unavailable in Richmond. If they are available in Philadelphia, he asks TJ to send a few of each in his next letter. TJ's onions from Mr. Washington flourished last year and he hopes for an abundance this year.

RC (MHi); 3 p.; in French; addressed: "The Honble. Ths. Jefferson Esqr Secretary of State Philadelphia"; endorsed by TJ as received 9 Mch. 1793 and so recorded in SJL; with comments by TJ in margin of postscript, as noted below.

[1] In the margin TJ wrote: "Tarragon" and "Artemisia Dracunculus."
[2] In the margin TJ wrote: "L. Solanum Melongena" and, possibly at a different time, "M. Melongena."

From John Kendrick

Port Independence, on the Island

SIR   of Heong-Kong, March 1st. 1793.

I have the honour of enclosing to you the Copies of several Deeds, by which the tracts of Land therein described, situated on Islands on the North West Coast of America, have been conveyed to me, and my heirs forever, by the resident Chiefs of those districts, who, I presume, were the only just proprietors thereof. I know not what measures are necessary to be taken, to secure the property of these purchases to me, and the government thereof to the United States; but it cannot be amiss to transmit them to you, to remain in the office of the Department of State. My claim to those territories has been allowed by the Spanish Crown: for the purchases I made at Nootka, were expressly excepted in a deed of conveyance, of the Lands adjacent to, and surrounding Nootka Sound, executed in September last, to El Señor Don Juan Francisco de la Bodega, y Quadra, on behalf of His Catholic Majesty, by Macquinnah and the other Chiefs of his tribe, to whom those lands belonged.

When I made these purchases, I did it under an impression, that it would receive the sanction of the United States; and, that should an act of the Legislature be necessary to secure them to me, I should find no difficulty in obtaining it. The future commercial advantages which may arise from the Fur Trade, besides many other branches which are daily opening to the view of those who visit the North West American Coast, may perhaps render a settlement there, worthy the attention of some associated Company, under the protection of Government. Should this be the case, the possession of Lands, previously and so fairly acquired, would much assist the carrying the plan into effect. Many good purposes may be effected by the Union having possessions on that Coast, which I shall not presume, Sir, to point out to you; and the benefits which have accrued to Individuals, by similar purchases to those I have made, in our own States, are too well known to need a remark. I have the honour to be, With the utmost respect & esteem, Sir, Your very hble servt   JOHN KENDRICK

RC (DNA: RG 59, MLR); at foot of text: "The Hon: Thomas Jefferson, Secretary for the Department of State"; endorsed by TJ as received 24 Oct. 1793 and so recorded in SJL. Enclosures: Five deeds, by which Kendrick purchased large tracts of land on Vancouver Island from various Indians in exchange for such considerations as muskets and gunpowder, executed between 20 July and 11 Aug. 1791 (Trs in same; printed in *Historical Magazine*, 2d ser., VIII [1870], 168-71).

John Kendrick (ca. 1740-94) was a Massachusetts sea captain who in 1787 led the *Columbia Rediviva* and the *Lady Washington* from Boston in the first American trading expedition to the Pacific northwest coast. Reaching Nootka Sound in September 1788, he made two voyages to China in the *Washington* between 1789 and 1793 and was en route to China a third time when he was killed in an accident at Oahu in the Hawaiian islands. The venture proved to be nearly a total loss to his backers, partly because after he sent the *Columbia* home in February 1790 Kendrick ignored the owners'

interests and treated the *Washington* and its capital as his own. Kendrick's purchase in his own name of five TRACTS OF LAND from Indians on Vancouver Island in 1791 violated express orders from his owners to buy land only in their name. Partly as a result of the disappearance of the original and notarized copies of the enclosed deeds, Kendrick's backers and heirs failed to secure title to this land, and Kendrick's action was rarely mentioned in later American claims to Oregon (DAB; F. W. Howay, "John Kendrick and His Sons," *Oregon Historical Society Quarterly*, XXIII [1922], 277-95; same, "An Early Colonization Scheme in British Columbia," *British Columbia Historical Quarterly*, III [1939], 51-63; Warren L. Cook, *Flood Tide of Empire: Spain and the Pacific Northwest, 1543-1819* [New Haven and London, 1973], 419n; Hubert H. Bancroft, *History of the Pacific States of North America*, 34 vols. [San Francisco, 1882-91], XXIII, 323).

On 2 Nov. 1793 TJ sent Kendrick's letter to the President, who returned it without comment the same day (Washington, *Journal*, 242-4).

Memorandum on Consular Appointments

Demarara. Samuel Cooper Johonnet of Massachusets to be Consul for the US. at the port of Demarara and for all parts under the same allegiance in America which shall be nearer to the said port than to the residence of any other Consul or Vice consul of the US. within the same allegiance.

Malaga. Michael Murphy of Malaga in the kingdom of Spain to be Consul for the US. at the said port of Malaga, and for such other parts of the said kingdom as shall be nearer to the said port than to the residence of any other Consul or Viceconsul of the US. within the same allegiance. TH: JEFFERSON
Mar. 1. 1793.

Amsterdam James Greenleaf of Massachusets Consul for the US. at
the port of Amsterdam in the[1] United Netherlands, and for
all parts of the said United Netherlands which shall be nearer
to the said port than to the residence of any other Consul or
Vice Consul of the US. within the same United Netherlands.

TH: JEFFERSON
Mar. 1 1793.

PrC (DLC); several words overwritten in a later hand. The repetition of the signature and date suggests the possibility that TJ letterpressed two different memorandums onto the same sheet.

TJ had previously submitted the consular appointments at Demerara and Malaga for the President's consideration in a memorandum of 28 Feb. 1793 that differed significantly from the one printed above. Although the paragraph about Demerara is virtually identical, TJ left blank the name and state of the nominee in the otherwise similar paragraph on Malaga, below which he wrote:
"The Candidates are:
⟨Samuel Cooper Johonnett. See Mr. Thayer's letter.⟩
Michael Murphy (of Ireland). See letters of Mr. Viar
Mr. Leamy.
Wm. Kirkpatrick (of Scotland) see letter of Mr. Cabot
Wm. Douglas Brodie see letter of Willing Morris & Swanwick
The President will be pleased to decide between the three above candidates for Malaga" (MS in DNA: RG 59, MLR, entirely in TJ's hand, with signature and date clipped, but endorsed by Tobias Lear as dated 1 Mch. 1793; PrC in DLC, dated 28 Feb. 1793, partially overwritten in a later hand; entry in SJPL: "Consuls"). The letter recommending Samuel Cooper Johonnet was George Thatcher to TJ, Philadelphia, 23 Feb. 1793 (RC in DLC: Washington Papers, Applications for Office; at foot of text: "Thomas Jefferson Esqr Secretary of State"; endorsed by TJ as received 26 Feb. 1793 and so recorded in SJL). The letters of recommendation for Michael Morphy were Josef Ignacio de Viar to TJ, 25 Feb. 1793 (RC in same; at foot of text: "Thomas Jefferson Esqre. &ca &ca &ca"; endorsed by TJ as re-

ceived 26 Feb. 1793 and so recorded in SJL), and John Leamy to TJ, Philadelphia, 27 Feb. 1793 (RC in same; at foot of text: "The Honorable Thomas Jefferson Esquire Secretary of State"; endorsed by TJ as received 27 Feb. 1793). The letter recommending Kirkpatrick was George Cabot to Washington, Beverly, Mass., 29 Jan. 1791 (same). The letter recommending Brodie was Willing, Morris & Swanwick to TJ, 8 Sept. 1791.

Washington nominated Johonnet, Morphy, and Greenleaf on 1 Mch. 1793 and the Senate confirmed them the next day (JEP, I, 135-6). TJ wrote a brief letter to them on 2 Mch. 1793, advising of their appointments and enclosing their commissions as well as "a copy of the Laws of the United States, together with the copy of a Circular letter written to our Consuls and Vice-Consuls the 26th. August 1790, to serve as their standing Instructions" (FC in Lb in DNA: RG 59, DCI; at head of text: "To Michael Murphy Esqr."; at foot of text: "The same to the following Gentlemen—Samuel Cooper Johonnet Junr., consul for the Port of Demarara. James Greenleaf, consul for the Port of Amsterdam in the United Netherlands"; not recorded in SJL). Morphy's commission is dated 2 Mch. 1793 (same, Presidential Commissions). Washington did not sign the commissions of Morphy, Johonnet, and Greenleaf until 9 Mch. 1793 (Washington, Journal, 83). TJ wrote a brief note to Viar on 15 Mch. 1793 asking him "to give a passage to the dispatches to Mr. Murphy, by any occasion which he may think safe" (PrC in DLC, undated but recorded under 15 Mch. 1793 in SJL; Tr in DLC, 19th-century copy). The PrC is letterpressed on the same sheet as TJ's brief notes of 15 Mch. 1793 to Leamy, asking him to forward the dispatches he had entrusted that day to Viar if an opportunity arose, and to George

Meade, requesting that he forward dispatches to Benjamin Hamnell Phillips, who had recently been appointed consul at Curaçao (PrCs in DLC; Trs in DLC, 19th-century copies transcribed on one sheet with Tr to Viar; note to Meade not recorded in SJL).

[1] TJ here canceled "republ."

To the Speaker of the House of Representatives

SIR   Philadelphia Mar. 1. 1793.
Having received information, on the first Wednesday of February, from the Vice-President of the US. that the list of Votes of the state of Kentuckey for President and Vice-President was not then received at the seat of government, I immediately, according to the injunctions of the law, dispatched to the district judge of that state a special messenger, to desire the list of votes lodged in his custody. The messenger returned yesterday. The expence incurred has been 150. Doll. as may be seen by the inclosed vouchers. No particular fund having been provided for this demand, I take the liberty of laying it before the house of representatives and have the honor to be with the most perfect respect, Sir, Your most obedt. & most humble servt   TH: JEFFERSON

PrC (DLC); at foot of text: "The Speaker of the House of Representatives." FC (Lb in DNA: RG 59, DL). Tr (Lb in DNA: RG 233, House Records, TR). Enclosures: (1) Timothy Pickering to Samuel Bradshaw, Philadelphia, 4 Jan. 1793, giving instructions for his journey to Kentucky with public dispatches, of which that from TJ to federal district judge Harry Innes is to be delivered personally and the rest put in the post at Danville, directing him to return without delay with Innes's reply containing the return of the votes of the Kentucky electors for president and vice-president, and agreeing to pay him $50 now and an additional $100 upon his return with Innes's answer within fifty days. (2) Receipt of Bradshaw to Pickering, Philadelphia, 4 Jan. 1792, for the initial payment of $50 (Trs in Lb in DNA: RG 233, House Records, TR). (3) Pickering to TJ, 28 Feb. 1793.

TJ meant to write THE FIRST WEDNESDAY of January (see TJ to John Adams, 1 Mch. 1793). The Speaker, Jonathan Trumbull, laid this letter before the House on this day (JHR, I, 726).

Cabinet Opinion on the American Debt to France

The President communicated to the Secretary of State, the Secretary of the Treasury, the Secretary of War and the Attorney General of the United States, a letter from William S. Smith Esqr. of the 28th. of

[310]

February past, to the Secretary of the Treasury, with sundry Papers No. I. II. III and IV. relating to a negotiation for changing the form of the debt to France; and required their opinion what answer should be returned to the Application.

The opinion unanimously is, that the Secretary of the Treasury shall inform Mr. Smith that the Government of the United States have made and engaged¹ payments to France to the extent which is at present consistent with their arrangements; and do not judge it adviseable to take any measures on the Subject of his Application.

Th: Jefferson

March 2nd. 1793   Alexander Hamilton
                    H Knox
                    Edm: Randolph

MS (DLC): Washington Papers); in the hand of Tobias Lear, signed by TJ, Hamilton, Knox, and Randolph; endorsed by Lear.

Smith's letter to Hamilton of 28 Feb. 1793 and the SUNDRY PAPERS relating to Smith's offer to buy the American debt to France and pay it in American goods have not been found. See note to Notes on Conversations with William Stephens Smith and George Washington, 20 Feb. 1793.

¹ Preceding two words in the margin.

Notes on the Giles Resolutions

Mar. 2. 1793. See the papers of this date, Mr. Giles's resolutions. He and one or two others were sanguine enough to believe that the palpableness of these resolutions rendered it impossible the house could reject them. Those who knew the composition of the house 1. of bank directors. 2. holders of bank stock. 3. stock jobbers. 4 blind devotees. 5 ignorant persons who did not comprehend them. 6. lazy and¹ good humored persons, who comprehended and acknoleged them, yet were too lazy to examine, or² unwilling to pronounce censure. The persons who knew these characters foresaw that the 3. first descriptions³ making $\frac{1}{3}$ of the house, the 3. latter would make $\frac{1}{2}$ of the residue, and of course that they would be rejected by a majority of 2. to 1. but they thought that even this rejection would do good, by shewing the public the desperate and abandoned dispositions with which their affairs were entrusted. The resolutions were proposed, and nothing spared to present them in the fullness of demonstration. There were not more than 3. or 4.⁴ who voted otherwise than had been expected.

It is known that Murray of Maryld. deals in paper.⁵

MS (DLC); entirely in TJ's hand; written with "Anas" entries for 23 and 25 Mch. 1793 on the other side of a sheet bearing "Anas" entries for 30 and 31 Mch. 1793. Recorded in SJPL under 2 Mch. 1793, where it is listed between entries of 25 and 30 Mch. 1793 as "Notes on Giles's resolns concerng. [T]reasury." Included in the "Anas." The line TJ drew underneath the first section raises the possibility that the sentence he wrote about Congressman William Vans Murray and the sentence he later canceled (see note 5 below) were added at a later date. In any event, the shade of ink in both sections is similar and suggests that TJ set them both down sometime between 2 and 23 Mch. 1793, when he compiled a list of stockholders in Congress. The canceled sentence very likely relates to revisions TJ made to that list.

[1] Preceding two words interlined.
[2] Preceding five words interlined.
[3] TJ here canceled "taking."
[4] TJ here canceled "votes."
[5] At this point, possibly at a later date, TJ canceled a sentence so heavily as to render it illegible.

Report on the Proceedings of the Northwest Territory

The Secretary of State has examined the Journal of the Proceedings in the Executive department of government Northwest of the Ohio from July 1. 1792. to Dec. 31. 1792. referred to him by the President of the United States, and thereupon
   Reports
     That there is nothing contained in the said Journal which calls for any thing to be done on the part of the President of the United States.   Th: Jefferson
                Mar. 2. 1793.

RC (DNA: RG 59, MLR); clipped signature and date supplied from PrC; endorsed by Tobias Lear. PrC (DLC); partially overwritten in a later hand. FC (Lb in DNA: RG 59, SDR). Tr (Lb in same, SDC). Recorded in SJPL.

To Jacob Hollingsworth

Sir   Philadelphia Mar. 3. 1793.
  I have duly received your favor of Feb. 25. and called yesterday on your brother to enquire in what state your affair was. He told me that he had, some days before, delivered the papers to the principal clerk of the Auditor, who had promised to examine them and communicate his opinion. I therefore desired your brother that if any difficulties should arise to the removal of which I could be useful, he would let me know, and I should chearfully give my aid to the obtaining justice for you.—

I am sorry the two persons you mention to have gone to look at my lands, should have gone without asking a letter from me, they will naturally fall into the hands of the overseers on the spot, who will be interested to impress them as disadvantageously as possible, and perhaps to shew the bad and hide the good. I would have given them a letter to my son in law, who would have given them a full view. Should any others wish to go, whom you would recommend, be so good as to drop me a line, and I will send them a letter to my son in law, pointing out to him precisely the lands to be shewn, and all necessary circumstances for their information.—As soon as the roads become quite[1] good in the spring I propose to take a trip to Brandywine to endeavor to procure there a tenant for a mill I am building. I may perhaps go on to Elkton, or contrive that Mr. Biddle may meet me at Brandywine. I am Sir your humble servt   TH: JEFFERSON

PrC (MHi); at foot of text: "Mr.   [1] Word interlined.
Jacob Hollingsworth." Tr (ViU: Edgehill-Randolph Papers); 19th-century copy.

To Thomas Mann Randolph, Jr.

DEAR SIR   Philadelphia Mar. 3. 1793.

Since my letter of the last week to my daughter yours of the 7th. to me and of the 14th. to Maria have come to hand and made us happy by announcing that all are well.—I informed you in my last of a scheme I had of leasing my lands on the Shadwell side of the river. Since that I have learned that, about the same time, two persons from the Head of Elk (the neighborhood where I was endeavoring to procure tenants) set out to examine my lands in order to decide for themselves and report to their neighbors. As they went without any letters from me, I am extremely afraid they may get into hands which may mislead them and, on their return, throw cold water on an operation which bid fair to succeed to any extent I might have chosen to carry it. I wish my letter to you may have got to hand in time for their arrival.   You have for some time past seen a number of reports from the Secretary of the Treasury on enquiries instituted by the H. of representatives. When these were all come in, a number of resolutions were prepared by Mr. Giles, expressing the truths resulting from the reports. These resolutions you will see in Fenno's paper. Mr. Giles and one or two others were sanguine enough to believe that the palpableness of the truths rendered a negative of them impossible, and therefore forced them on. Others contemplating the character of the present house, one third of which is understood to be made up of bank directors and stockjobbers who would be voting in the case of their chief; and another third of persons blindly devoted to that party, of persons not comprehending the papers, or persons comprehending them but too indulgent to pass a vote of censure, foresaw that the resolutions would be negatived by a majority of two to one. Still they thought that the negative of palpable truth would be of service, as it would let the public see how desperate and abandoned were the hands in which their interests were placed. The vote turned out to be what was expected, not more than 3. or 4. varying from what had been conceived of them. The public will see from this the extent of their danger, and a full representation at the ensuing session will doubtless find occasion to revise the decision, and take measures for ensuring the authority of the laws over the corrupt maneuvres of the heads of departments under the pretext of exercising discretion in opposition to law. The elections have been favorable to the republican candidates every where South of Connecticut; and even in Massachusets there is a probability that one republican will be sent who possesses the confidence of that description of men in that state (and which forms the mass of the state) and who will fulfil the only object needed, that of carrying back to them faithful accounts of what is doing here. This they have never had, and it is all they need.—My love to my dear Martha and am Dear Sir your's affectionately   TH: JEFFERSON

RC (DLC); addressed: "Thomas M. Randolph junr. esq. at Monticello near Charlottesville." PrC (DLC). Tr (ViU: Edgehill-Randolph Papers); 19th-century copy.

To Stephen Willis

SIR   Philadelphia Mar. 3. 1793.

I received yesterday yours of Feb. 13. I had ascribed the delay of an answer to a supposed miscarriage of my letter to you, otherwise I should have written again to inform you of what I shall now do. I have been prevailed on, contrary to what I thought possible, to remain here somewhat longer. How long I do not know, but sufficiently long to carry me so late into the season for brickwork that I think it rather improbable that there will be time after my return to Monticello to make the necessary preparations and to do the brick work I had meditated before winter would set in. Should this be the case, I shall employ the winter in making fuller preparations, make early in the spring of 1794. a batch of 60. or 80,000 bricks, and lay the whole in the summer of 1794. which I had meant to divide between 1793. and 1794.—Should circumstances vary my plan of operations I will keep you apprised of it.—The roof will be a compound one, consequently will need gutters of sheet lead.—You shall hear from me as soon as I return to Monticello, and decide finally what the season will permit me to undertake. I am Sir Your very humble servt   Th: Jefferson

P.S. If journeymen are not plenty with you, I might possibly send you some from here against the spring of 1794. They work here in a very masterly manner. If you should incline to this, let me know what wages you would give, and for how long a time and I will get them as much lower as possible.

PrC (DLC); at foot of text: "Mr. Stephen Willis." Tr (ViU: Edgehill-Randolph Papers); 19th-century copy. Willis's letter of 13 Feb. 1793 from New Kent, Virginia, recorded in SJL as received 2 Mch. 1793, has not been found.

From Edward Dowse

Sir   Ostend 4th. March 1793

Herewith will be deliver'd to you a Table Sett of China contain'd in Two Boxes, which I had made for you at Canton, agreeably to your Excellency's desire, when I had the pleasure to see you at the Isle of Wight in the year 89.

It is so long ago, that possibly you may have supplied yourself already, or the China may not be executed to your liking, in either case, I beg you would not think it necessary to retain it; but send it back to me at Boston, where I expect to be in about two months from this; and I shall not draw upon you for the amount, untill you inform me that China is entirely to your liking. I am, with great respect, Sir, Your Most Obedient Servant   Edward Dowse

PS As I shall sell my Ship at Ostend, I am obliged to send you the China by the way of Charleston So. C.

RC (DLC); at foot of first page: "Thomas Jefferson Esquire Secretary &c. &c"; endorsed by TJ as received 15 July 1793 and so recorded in SJL. Filed with the RC is an undated list by Dowse of 512 pieces of china headed "Governour Jefferson's Sett," at the bottom of which, evidently at a different time, Dowse wrote: "Paid Synchong for this service of Porcelane £79. 19. 4 Lawful Money. Received of Govr. Jefferson the above sum in full. Edward Dowse."

TJ's memorandum books record no payments to or from Dowse either before or after he received this letter, and Dowse's puzzling notation on the above list is probably a later acknowledgment that TJ had returned the set (MB, 18 July 1793; TJ to Dowse, 26 July 1793, and Dowse to TJ, 29 Aug. 1793).

To George Washington

March 4. 1793.

Th: Jefferson presents his respectful compliments to the President. Apprehensive that there has been some misconception of his correspondence with Mr. Ellicot, he incloses to the President full copies of the only letters he has written to Mr. Ellicot in the course of the years 1792. and 1793. The last of them was written with no other view than to prevent public altercation between Mr. Ellicot and the Commissioners, and after having received the President's opinion that it was desireable to prevent it. Th:J. will thank the President to make any use of the letters which may remove any suspicions excited by an inexact idea of them.

PrC (DLC). Tr (DLC); 19th-century copy. Enclosures: TJ to Andrew Ellicott, 3 July 1792, 15 Jan. 1793.

This was the second time TJ expressed concern about the MISCONCEPTION OF HIS CORRESPONDENCE with Andrew Ellicott by David Stuart, one of the Commissioners of the Federal District, who had complained to Washington in letters of 8 and 18 Feb. 1793 that TJ had somehow instigated or encouraged Ellicott's criticisms of the Commissioners. TJ had previously shown Washington his 15 Jan. letter to Ellicott in the expectation that the President would lay Stuart's charge to rest (see TJ to Washington, 14 Feb. 1793, and note). It was not until 3 Mch., howev-

er, that Washington wrote Stuart to say that TJ had shown him "the *only* letter which (he says) he has written to [Ellicott] for many Months" and was "at a loss to discover what could have proceeded from him to Mr. Ellicott" that should have aroused the latter's discontent with the Commissioners, and that he himself could see "nothing therein on which to found the conjecture" contained in Stuart's first letter. On the following day, after receiving the letter from TJ printed above, the President wrote a brief note to Stuart forwarding copies of both of TJ's letters to Ellicott (Washington to Stuart, 3 Mch. 1793, NjP: Andre deCoppet Collection; Fitzpatrick, *Writings*, XXXII, 374).

To George Washington

Mar. 4. 93.

Th: Jefferson, with his respects to the President, incloses him a letter from the Van Staphorsts & Hubbard quieting our apprehensions for the fate of the first dispatches sent to Mr. Short relative to our negociations with Spain.—Also another letter from Mr. Thatcher on the subject of the Marshal of Maine.

RC (DNA: RG 59, MLR); addressed: "The President of the US."; endorsed by Tobias Lear. Tr (Lb in same, SDC). Not recorded in SJL. Enclosures: (1) Van Staphorst & Hubbard to TJ, 29 Nov. 1792 (mistakenly endorsed by TJ

as received 9 Mch. 1793, but recorded in SJL as received 4 Mch. 1793). (2) George Thatcher to TJ, Philadelphia, 3 Mch. 1793, recommending the appointment of deputy marshal John Hobby as federal marshal for the district of Maine in preference to William Vaughan of Portland, who was in the capital soliciting the appointment (RC in DLC: Washington Papers, Applications for Office; at foot of text: "Thomas Jefferson Esqr Secretary of State"; endorsed by TJ as received 3 Mch. 1793 and so recorded in SJL).

TJ notified Hobby of his interim appointment as MARSHAL OF MAINE in a letter of 19 Apr. 1793 (FC in Lb in DNA:

RG 59, DL; at head of text: "John Hobby Esqre."; not recorded in SJL). Washington nominated Hobby to the post on 27 Dec. 1793, and the Senate confirmed him on 30 Dec. 1793 (JEP, I, 142-4). The other letter Thatcher wrote to TJ on this appointment was probably that dated 26 Feb. 1793, which is recorded in SJL as received the following day but has not been found.

From George Clinton

SIR   New York 5th. March 1793

I had not the honor of receiving your letter of the 17th. of February before the 28th. Since which time I have been endeavoring to discover, where the Indian Treaties that you request, are deposited but my researches have hitherto been unsuccessful. Our Indian affairs were formerly under the direction of a superintendant, the last of whom was Sir John Johnson, and I am inclined to believe that most of the papers respecting Indian Affairs were in his possession at the commencement of the Revolution and either destroyed or carried off by him within the British Lines. In our Secretary's Office there are certainly none that would be of any use. I have however reason to suppose, that there may be some Records of Antient Indian treaties in the Clerk's Office of the County of Albany, and have written to him to furnish me with copies if he should discover any. Will you please to let me know whether transcripts of those made under the State Government are required. I am With the greatest Respect and esteem Your most Obedt. humle. Servt.   GEO: CLINTON

RC (DNA: RG 59, MLR); in a clerk's hand, signed by Clinton; at foot of text: "The Honorable Thomas Jefferson Esquire Secretary of State"; endorsed by TJ as received 9 Mch. 1793 and so recorded in SJL.

TJ submitted this letter to the President on 9 Mch. 1793, and Washington returned it the next day (Washington, Journal, 83, 84).

To Alexander Donald

DEAR SIR   Philadelphia Mar. 5. 1793.

My last to you was of Nov. 11. since which I have received your several favors of Sep. 6. Nov. 7. Dec. 12. and Jan. 5. by all of which I see proofs of your friendly dispositions in your attention to the small-stuff commissions I trouble you with. The bill for £37–10 drawn by Count Andriani in favor of Mr. William B. Giles was to answer for a watch which the latter gentleman desired me to order for him from Paris. When I lodged the bill in your hands, I at the same time wrote to a friend in Paris to have the watch made and to draw on you. A change in the circumstance of price occasioned him to write back to me for new instructions: in the mean time Mr. Giles provided himself here, so that the object came to an end, and I have now to desire you to hold the proceeds of his bill subject to his order.—The winter has been remarkeably mild, and as remarkeably dry through the first half of it, insomuch that the rivers did not fill sufficiently for navigation, and I began to fear that my Bedford tobacco would not be brought down. However for 6. weeks past we have had uncommonly great rains so as to fill the rivers abundantly. A great want of cash has been experienced lately at this place. Perhaps a greater was never known. The banks have for a considerable time stopt discounts, and nothing but the generality of the distress producing a generality of indulgence has prevented a number of stoppages of payment being formally declared. This distress has occasioned a great deal of public paper to be brought to market, and a consequent depression of it's price, insomuch that the 6. per cents are now at 18/3 and as yet falling. This need not affect the confidence of those who hold the public paper. There is not upon earth a more solid property: and tho' one party here affect to charge the other with unfriendly dispositions towards the public debt, yet I believe there is not a man scarcely in the United states who is not sacredly determined to pay it; and the only difference which I can see between the two parties is that the republican one wish it could be paid tomorrow, the fiscal party wish it to be perpetual, because they find in it an engine for corrupting the legislature.   Bank property stands on very different ground; as that institution is strongly conceived to be unauthorised by the constitution, it may therefore be liable to shocks.—We expect that by this time you are at loggerheads with your neighbors. The more you fight, the more you will eat and waste, and the less you will make. Fight on then; leave us at peace, and let us feed you while you clothe us. Adieu my Dear Sir your affectionate friend   TH: JEFFERSON

PrC (DLC); at foot of first page: "A. Donald esq." Tr (ViU: Edgehill-Randolph Papers); 19th-century copy.

TJ enclosed this letter in a brief note to Henry Remsen of the same date asking him to put it "into the mail for the British packet" (RC, Bank of Manhattan Company, New York City, 1945; addressed: "Mr. Henry Remsen New York"; stamped, franked, and postmarked; not recorded in SJL; endorsed by Remsen: "N.B. put the enclosed Letter in British Mail"). The FRIEND IN PARIS was Jean Antoine Gautier (TJ to Gautier, 8 June 1792).

To George Washington

Mar. 5. 93.

Th: Jefferson with his respects to the President is sorry to inclose him an account of Mr. Barclay's death in a letter to a Mr. Callahan of this place from his brother in Lisbon.

RC (DNA: RG 59, MLR); addressed: "The President of the US"; endorsed by Tobias Lear. Tr (Lb in same, SDC). Not recorded in SJL. Enclosure: "Extract of a Letter dated Lisbon 24th. January 1793," describing the death of Thomas Barclay, "who arrived here about 10 days ago from Cadiz after being at Gibralter, I suppose could Not do anything with the Algarines or Morroqims, he came here to pass a little time, he was Suddenly taken with an inflamation in his Bowels which carried him off in 36 hours. Every attention that could be paid to him in his Sickness was done by Mr. Saml. Harrison and Col. Humphrys who attended him all the time with the best Physicians in the place, he was buryed on the 21 Inst. with the greatest Decency at the same time not in the most costly manner, all the American Merchants attended his buryel at the English burying grounds and I attended there too at the Request of the Counsil, all the American Ships were in mourning and Captns. attended. I am sorry to find this Gentn. left a Widdow and four Children, I don't Suppose his Freinds will know of his Death by this Vessel" (Tr in same, MLR).

From Francis Eppes

DR SIR   Richmond March 6th. 1793

Your favour of 27 of Febry. came to hand last Evening. I am sorry to find the prospect of procuring money for Jack to attend the Commissioners is rather more uncertain than when I wrote you last, the expectation of Cash from Carys Executor is at an end if the chancilor shou'd direct him to pay our debt (which I expect will be determind to day) he has nothing but bonds to do it with, as every Negro belonging to the Estate was sold in Janry. last at a credit of nine and twelve months, however, shou'd money be put into my hands I will remit it in time for the purposes you mention. The balance due us from Cary's Estate is £2049 with about five years and a half interest. I am Dr Sir your Friend   FRANS. EPPES

RC (ViU: Edgehill-Randolph Papers); endorsed by TJ as received 20 Mch. 1793 and so recorded in SJL.

From Tobias Lear

Wednesday 6th March 1793

The President requests that the Secretary of State will consider the enclosed letter, written in behalf of the French settlers at Gallipolis, and return an answer to the writer as favourable as circumstances can warrant.

The President wishes Govr. Paterson's commission to be made out and sent to him by the Post of this day, that he may be making his arrangements to go the Circuit allotted him. The President intends to ride out about 10 oclock, if he can conveniently—and therefore would wish to sign the Commission before he goes.

RC (DLC); endorsed by TJ as received 6 Mch. 1793.

The ENCLOSED LETTER from John Rome to Washington of 6 Mch. 1793 sought legislative relief for THE FRENCH SETTLERS AT GALLIPOLIS—who had immigrated to the Ohio territory in 1790 after purchasing land from the Scioto Company headed by William Duer—either in the form of confirmation of their land titles or compensation for damages they sustained after the Company's collapse and Duer's bankruptcy during the panic of 1792 left them holding invalid titles (*Terr. Papers,* II, 442-3). Rome subsequently commu-

nicated with the Attorney General, to whom the matter was referred by the Senate, and TJ evidently did not RETURN AN ANSWER to him. Congress provided some relief in March 1795 with a grant of 24,000 acres in southern Ohio to certain of the settlers (same, 450-1, 462-70; Shaw Livermore, *Early American Land Companies: Their Influence on Corporate Development* [New York, 1939], 138-46; Theodore T. Belote, *The Scioto Speculation and the French Settlement at Gallipolis: A Study in Ohio Valley History*, University of Cincinnati Studies, 2d ser., III [Cincinnati, 1907], 57-9).

To Thomas Pinckney

SIR
Philadelphia Mar. 6. 1793.

The bearer hereof Mr. Kennedy is a citizen of the commonwealth of Virginia, and lays claim to the estate and title of the Earl of Cassilis of Scotland, lately mentioned in the public papers to be dead. He goes to Great Britain to claim the inheritance. As this will be a private litigation before the ordinary tribunals of the country, he will of course pursue it in that line, and we have no doubt but that those tribunals will do him all the justice which his proofs shall shew him entitled to. Should the contrary happen in such a manner as to justify and call for your interposition, I recommend him to your aid and patronage so far as shall be requisite for the purposes of right, and within those general rules which limit the extent of your interference. I have the honor to

be with great respect & esteem, Sir, Your most obedt & most humble
servt   TH: JEFFERSON

PrC (DLC); at foot of text: "Mr. Pinckney. M.P. of the US. at London." Tr (DLC);
19th-century copy.

To Vicomte de Rochambeau

SIR   Philadelphia Mar. 6. 1793.
The bearer hereof, Mr. Skipwith, Consul for the United States in
Martinique, having had occasion to absent himself for some time on his
private affairs, now returns to that island. Permit me to present him to
your notice and to hope that he will recieve those aids in the exercise
of his functions, which the Convention between our two countries has
stipulated, and their friendly dispositions towards each other leave no
room to doubt. The imperfect information we receive here of what is
passing in the islands leaves me uninformed of the particular public
characters to which we may appeal for their patronage of our citizens
and their rights: but the personal acquaintance I have had the honor
of having with you, assures me that either as a public or private man,
I may put the rights of the citizens of the United states under your
protection. I have the honor to be with great & sincere esteem and
respect, Sir, Your most obedient & most humble servt
                                                        TH: JEFFERSON

PrC (DLC); at foot of text: "M. de
Rochambeau." Tr (DLC); 19th-century
copy. Enclosed in TJ to Fulwar Skipwith,
6 Mch. 1793.

Donatien Marie Joseph de Vimeur,
Vicomte de Rochambeau (1755-1813),
the son of the commander of the French

forces at the battle of Yorktown, was a
career military officer serving as lieutenant
general of the French Windward Islands
who at this time was stationed on Martinique (Laura V. Monti, *A Calendar of
Rochambeau Papers at the University of
Florida Libraries* [Gainesville, Fla., 1972],
1-4).

From William Short

DEAR SIR   Aranjuez March 6. 1793
I had the honor of writing to you on the 3d. ulto. from Madrid
announcing to you my arrival there on the 1st. Since then M.
Carmichael and myself have written to you a joint letter of the 19th.
ulto. informing you of such circumstances as had then taken place
concerning the business with which we are jointly charged—and particularly of the nomination of M. de Gardoqui to treat with us. We

shall continue to write to you jointly on those subjects in proportion as any progress may be made in them.

As[1] yet no step having been taken since the nomination of M. de Gardoqui,[2] and we being amused[3] with dilatory promises from day to day of commencing the conferences, although we know that he has not yet received[4] *either his instructions or his full powers,* I cannot help thinking that they have some *particular motive for delay in this business, over and above the standing rules of procrastination in all business.* None presents itself so naturally to my mind as the *present perhaps unsettled relation in which they stand to[5] England and France. The eve[6] of any other[7] war than one which[8] will throw them into the English scale would have been a favorable moment for our negotiation.* It is highly[9] probable this will be of a contrary tendency. I think I have seen *enough already to be convinced that they will come to no favorable conclusion[10] with us under present circumstances and I should be wrong not to express to you this my opinion—though you may rest assured we[11] shall leave no effort unemployed on our part.* In the mean time I am[12] confirmed in my opinion of its being *a personal misfortune to me to have been sent so far on this business. I count for nothing the length and fatigue of such a journey[13]* in the middle of the winter and in a state of health little adapted to such an undertaking—but as I suppose that *mission must have attracted public notice in America[14] so its producing nothing[15] cannot but be followed by public dissatisfaction. I trust the President who will have a knowlege of all the circumstances will attribute it to its true causes—but* the public will[16] only judge from events without enquiring into causes. *M. Car.[17] thinks that any time since the formation of our new government would have been more favorable than the present for our business. He is firmly persuaded he could have settled it without difficulty in 1790 if he had had the proper powers—and also that if he had been charged with standing full powers he could have[18] found opportunities of doing it since then.* Motives of[19] delicacy probably prevented his suggesting this *in time and asking to be furnished with those powers[20] without which he could certainly have had few opportunities of bringing the minister in* his crowd of business to attend to him. As it is the invariable usage of European courts (and by which European ministers will be guided in forming their opinion)[21] to have *standing plenipotentiary powers* when there are objects of *much less[22] importance in discussion between them, the minister would have inferred from the contrary either an indifference in the U.S. to the business itself or an indifference to its conclusion at that time.[23]* It might be added too that he had other grounds also which have been mentioned to me here[24] *for supposing this indifference in the U.S. or in some of them.* Independent of these considerations there are others which it will suffice simply to present to your recollection. I have frequently heard you remark the inconveniences to which were subjected at Versailles those members of the corps diplomatique even of the second order whose turn to speak to the minister came late. You could have little opportunity of observing it as to those of the third or residuary order, in which are classed chargés des affaires, residents and[25] all inferior characters, as the few who were[26] at that court were there by interim and seldom employed in any business which required their speaking to the minister—being destined for the most part only[27] to write news for the amusement of those who employed them. At this court that class of persons is separated from the first and second class[28] of foreign ministers by humiliating distinctions which did not exist at Versailles— and which cannot fail more or less to have an unfavorable influence on any negotiation they may be employed in with European ministers—so long as European ministers continue to be the same men and have the same sentiments as at present. Of this you would be sensible if I were to take up your time with mentioning them. I will only mention what will strike you more forcibly from your experience and recollection of the manner of doing business with a Minister[29] of foreign affairs on this side of the Atlantic. You cannot have forgotten[30] with how much caution a particular audience is to be asked by a foreign minister and how seldom it must be repeated—you will readily concieve that the caution must be still greater and the repetition less seldom, by a person of the inferior order—and particularly here. Mr. Carm: could therefore only have counted on the public audience day for seeing and conversing with the minister. Let him have arrived at what hour he would he could not be admitted until all of the first and second order had had their audience although they should have arrived hours after him. Thus it would often happen that the time allotted for the[31] audience expiring before[32] those of the second order had done— those of the third were accordingly put off until the next audience day—when the same thing might and often would happen again—if it did not then such of the third order as had their turn would find the minister already wearied by all those who had preceded—often out of humour—impatient to be at the end, little in condition to attend to business of the nature of that of which M. Carmichael had to speak to him—and less in a disposition to do it when he would reflect that[33] not being charged with plenipotentiary powers—conversations with him must end in nothing or could only serve to commit him (the Minister) without being binding on the U.S. Accordingly you observe how long a time *it took to obtain from him a simple letter accompanied by verbal assurances. Although this was in fact nothing more than*[34] *adjourning the business to Philadelphia yet it would*[35] *have been of importance if Ct. de Florida had remained in the Ministry and was certainly as much as could have been expected or could have been obtained by any person in the situation of Mr. Car. and with no other powers than those he had. I cannot help regretting therefore that M. Car. had not resided here with ordinary*[36] *plenipotentiary powers not only because I am persuaded that better opportunities than the present*[37] *must have occurred—but also because I am convinced* from my own observation and the practise and[38] experience of all the powers of Europe both great and small that it is the *most eligible*[39] *mode of negotiating all kinds of business*[40] *which admit of delay—and by far the most convenient*[41] *for the complaining party.*[42] *Under this mode if the business should not succeed it at worst remains in statu quo—and as there is no public evidence of an express demand*[43] *being made*[44] *so there is none of a refusal being recieved, and of course a greater facility in postponing the time of trying other modes of redress, than when a commission is formed and powers given ad hoc*[45]*—in which case*[46] *the non success of the business becomes as it were a refusal of justice of public notoriety—and of course embarassing to the party refused, unless indeed where the determination is fixed of resorting immediately*[47] *to the ultimate tribunal of redress for injured*[48] *nations.*[49] This is one of the principal reasons probably why it has grown up into established usage[50] for all the nations of Europe without any exception among those who are in the possibility of having any discussion between them *to furnish their respective agents*[51] *with standing*[52] *plenipotentiary powers.*[53] *Commissions ad hoc*[54] *are thus avoided except either in desperate cases where war is absolutely decided on in case of refusal, or where* they become indispensable from there being no ordinary minister as *in treating of peace during the war &c. or for a particular object out of the line of ministerial*[55] *functions as the fixing of limits or of*[56] *damages &c. after the principle having been established by previous treaty. The usage of employing agents with plenipotentiary powers however low the salary and of abolishing those of the third order (except by interim) has been increasing from early in the present century and has of late years as you will see by simply adverting to their*[57] *diplomatic establishments, become universal among European powers. It has been found more necessary for those who had not adopted it, in proportion as the number of those who had adopted it, increased. England has in consequence thereof for some years past made their secretaries of embassy (at the three European Courts where they keep Ambassadors) Ministers Plenipo: and other powers have in several instances adopted the same usage. I hope you will excuse my having digressed into these particularities*[58] *as it seems to me probable they* *may have escaped your notice from the particular circumstances of the Court at which you resided.*[59] *I am fully*[60] *persuaded, and*[61] *as I think, you will*[62] *be from this*[63] *view of the ground that the interests of the U.S. have suffered here from their having not conformed in this respect to the practise of all the nations with which this Country is accustomed to treat of objects of any importance.*

How far this may be remedied will depend much on the future circumstances of this country.[64] *At present I think it my duty to give you the superficial view which so short a residence has enabled me to take of their present, though a very uncertain means of judging of their future, situation.*

It is one of the characteristics of the French revolution to affect sensibly the minds and affairs of their neighbors. This country was of course not exempt from that influence.[65] *I learn since my arrival here that all the leading events which had taken place in France however various and opposite in their nature*[66] *had found each their censurers and approvers here—this together with the successive*[67] *changes which have taken place in the ministry of this country*[68] *had produced a variety of contending impressions on the public mind that rendered*[69] *it difficult to ascertain the nature and force of the public opinion. The news of the horrible catastrophe which took place at Paris on the 21st of Janry. seems to have compressed all this into one mass of sentiment, directing the feelings of all to this single event, which produces the same impressions on the mind of all. Whether a sentiment so violent will be lasting I cannot say, but it may be affirmed I think with certainty that there has been no instance of national hatred and animosity being more fully and unquestionably expressed. All orders from the highest to the lowest have given proofs of this in different ways. All*[70] *foreigners who are taken for Frenchmen are exposed to be insulted by the people. At Madrid particular kinds of dress are proscribed by them as being French—in the theatre particularly*[71] *they*[72] *exercised this kind of despotism, in the presence of the magistrate who is always there to prevent disorder and who did not interfere. Accounts from the provinces shew the same dispositions there.*[73] In some parts of Catalonia where the French supposed they had the greatest number of friends the magistrates have been obliged to exert themselves to prevent the massacre of those who resided there. At Valencia, a mob rose broke the windows of all the French houses—plundered two considerable magasines belonging to them, the proprietors having first escaped by flight, and would unquestionably have proceeded to greater excesses, but for the interference of the governor—and several ecclesiastics. The rich[74] nobility and clergy are daily making offers of assistance both in men and money, in case of war to an amount[75] beyond what could have been expected from them notwithstanding they consider it as a war for their orders, privileges and fortunes. Several have begun already to recruit from among their vassals in whom they find a readiness to enlist of which there is no example here.[76] The Kings recruiting officers are also employed and meet with the same success. The cities and corporations have followed the example of[77] the nobility and clergy in the offers they are making— emulation is excited among all orders and individuals by the lists of the offers made, being published daily with the names of the persons. All these promises will probably not be complied with in their full extent, yet they shew that the King would find resources on this occasion far[78] beyond what has taken place or[79] could be expected on any other. The government has issued orders for the expulsion of all Frenchmen [from] the Kingdom, with [the] exception of a few descriptions only.[80] These orders embracing a[81] great number of persons engaged here in various kinds of business[82] have been executed with a degree of expedition and rigor which has exposed all of them to much injury and many to ruin. They will of course return to their country[83] accompanied by despair and rage and under the present form of French government and in the present state of mens minds in that country, this circumstance cannot fail to have a very[84] considerable influence there. This measure might justly therefore be deemed impolitic if there be a desire still[85] as is supposed by some to avoid being forced into war. It must be observed however that the imprudence of some[86] of the French inhabitants in foreign countries has been carried to a degree of indecence under the present crisis that it was difficult to pass over unnoticed.

The several circumstances which have taken place between France and Spain under the administration of Ct. D'aranda and the present, of which you have been of course informed, will have served to have shewn you beyond all doubt the sincere desire which this country had to preserve peace. As they seemed at last to give up every other point and contend alone for the preservation of the life of the unfortunate monarch, it was natural to expect that the horrible event which took place would have brought this country at once to an open[87] decision. Several considerations have[88] probably contributed to prevent it as yet. The older[89] part of the ministry have grown up with prejudices against English policy and suspicions of their designs. They see that war will necessitate union between them and place this country at their mercy in future, as to their foreign possessions. It is difficult[90] to exempt themselves at once from[91] long rooted suspicions—they are therefore averse to the war as uncertain in the advantages it may procure to their interests in France and certain in its disadvantages to Spain.[92] *The Queen and the young principal minister are in fact averse to the war also for many obvious reasons. In all other cases they govern without control. But since the reciept of the*[93] *news [of the] event of the 21st.*[94] *the King's desire of revenge, added to the kind of point of honor not to be in arrear of the other monarchs of Europe, whilst he is the nearest relation and the head of the Bourbon family, have so decided him, that it is thought the Queen and the young minister not venturing to oppose openly the King's sentiment have thought it best to*[95] *subscribe to it. Still this kind of conflict would necessarily have occasioned delay. Besides it has been thought proper perhaps not to declare*[96] *before completing the preparations which are carrying on with great activity—and*[97] *the desire of bringing in Portugal with certainty if France should be the aggressor has probably also had influence on the delay here.*

The French minister who resided at Madrid was admitted to conference and treated with until the King's death was known. From that time it ceased and it having been signified to him not to come to this residence of the court he has [set][98] *out with his family for France. His Secretary of legation still remains at Madrid and has not been comprehended in the late order for the expulsion of French inhabitants.*

Under this view of circumstances war must be considered as hardly to be avoided[99] *unless by some miraculous change in affairs. Mr. Jackson the English Min. Plen. has been urging it by all the means in his power and seems confident of success. It is natural for England being engaged in the war herself to endeavour to draw in others and particularly this country.*[100] *The English Ambassad. arrived at Corunna the 26th. ulto. and is now on his road to this place.*[101] *You will have learned from London that the affair of Nootka has been finally settled there. Money has been already sent to effectuate the payment of the damages agreed on.*

In the case of war I know on unquestionable authority[102] *that [it] is the intention of this government to prohibit all kinds of French productions and manufactures, in whatever vessels they may be brought to this country. This will of course render the English commerce and*[103] *manufactures more necessary to*[104] *them.*[105]

The Algerines have declared war to[106] *the Dutch—the usual mode of pacification will no doubt ensue.*[107] *Some of their vessels having been taken by the Algerine cruisers and carried in to Algiers,*[108] *the Dey, contrary to usage,*[109] *ordered them to be released because taken before the expiration of the term he had allowed in his declaration.*[110] *It is reported that he has lately published or renewed his declaration of war against the U.S.* [I beg pardon for so long and tedious a letter and have the honor to be &c. &c W: SHORT]

Dft (DLC: Short Papers); heavily emended, *en clair* text with parts variously designated by Short for encoding (see note 1 below); at head of text: "*No. 124*"; at foot of first page: "Th. Jeff. Sec. of State"; bracketed words supplied from Tr; significant recoverable emendations are noted below. Tr (Lb in DNA: RG 59, DD); entirely *en clair* with coding included in part of one section and in several places in later sections where coding in missing RC was problematic; contains variant paragraphing and some variant wording. Recorded in SJL as received 17 May 1793. Neither text is an entirely satisfactory substitute for the missing RC, but only the Dft indicates all the parts intended by Short for encoding—albeit with two ambiguities. Evidently after completing the Dft Short went through the text to identify passages he wished to encode, ultimately dividing the letter into six sections for this purpose and employing in each a variation of one of two basic methods: drawing a brace in the margin to define a block of text and writing "not cyphered" lengthwise in the margin; or underscoring passages that were to remain *en clair*. Based on the presence or absence of braces, marginal notes, and underscoring in the Dft—as well as sporadic instances of coding in the Tr—the Editors have been able to identify the encoded portions of the missing RC with certainty in all but the two sections where Short's designations were ambiguous. Opposite the fifth section in the Dft (identified in note 73 below) Short drew a brace in the margin but offered no comment and did not employ underscoring to indicate unencoded text; it seems likely, however, that he intended this section to be entirely *en clair* and, employing the method he used in two earlier sections, simply neglected to write "not cyphered" in the margin—a hypothesis strengthened by the absence of coding anomalies in the corresponding section of the Tr in spite of their occurrence in every other section known to have been encoded. The final section of the Dft has no brace, written designation, or underscoring; given the absence of underscoring and the existence of several coding anomalies in the corresponding section of the Tr, it has been assumed that Short silently reverted to the

second method and intended to encode the entire section.

William Carmichael obviously believed that, given the PROPER POWERS, he could have taken advantage of the 1790 crisis between Spain and Great Britain over Nootka Sound to settle WITHOUT DIFFICULTY the leading points at issue between the American and Spanish governments. THE HORRIBLE CATASTROPHE: the execution of Louis XVI in Paris on 21 Jan. 1793. THE FRENCH MINISTER WHO RESIDED AT MADRID was Jean François de Bourgoing; HIS SECRETARY OF LEGATION was the Marques d'Urtubize (Charles Alexandre Geoffroy de Grandmaison, *L'Ambassade Française en Espagne Pendant La Révolution [1789-1804]* [Paris, 1892], 72n, 84n, 319). Alleyne Fitzherbert, Baron St. Helens, was the THE ENGLISH AMBASSAD. extraordinary to Spain, 1790-94 (DNB).

TJ submitted this letter to the President on 18 May 1793, and Washington returned it two days later (Washington, *Journal*, 143, 144).

[1] Except where noted, this and subsequent words in italics, both in the text and in the canceled matter quoted in textual notes below, represent passages clearly designated by Short for encoding in the Dft or tentatively identified as such by the Editors. Coding in the Tr has been verified by the Editors employing partially reconstructed Code No. 10, anomalies being recorded below.

[2] Short here canceled "*as far as can be known to us with certainty.*"

[3] Tr: word deciphered interlinearly as "and used" because of a coding anomaly.

[4] Short here canceled "*either from the department of foreign affairs.*"

[5] Tr: word deciphered as "have" because of a coding anomaly.

[6] Tr: word deciphered as "even" because of a coding anomaly.

[7] Short here canceled "*kind of.*"

[8] Above this word Short first interlined and then canceled "*like this.*"

[9] Word written over what appears to be "possible," erased.

[10] In the Tr to this point encoded passages are given in cipher with interlinear decipherment. Hereafter the Tr gives code

only in several instances where the decipherer suspected that it was defective. See notes 45 and 94-5 below.

[11] Word interlined in place of "*I.*"

[12] Sentence to this point and last four words of preceding sentence interlined in place of "*untried to satisfy the wishes of the Prest,*" which in turn replaced "*untried to obtain it.*"

[13] Short here canceled "*at such a season.*"

[14] Preceding two words interlined.

[15] Preceding two words interlined in place of "*failure.*"

[16] Word interlined in place of "can."

[17] Remainder of sentence interlined in place of "*considers this the most unfavorable moment for our business which has occurred since the formation of our new government.*"

[18] Short here canceled "*settled it at different epochs which have since occurred.*"

[19] Preceding two words interlined in place of "*I am of course unacquainted with the R.*"

[20] Preceding two words interlined in place of "*such standing powers, according to the constant practice of countries which have such objects of discussion between them and.*"

[21] Preceding four words interlined.

[22] Preceding two words interlined.

[23] Preceding three words interlined.

[24] Preceding eight words interlined in place of "too." Short initially designated the next four words to be *en clair*, but then reversed the designation.

[25] Preceding five words interlined.

[26] Short first wrote "as there were none such at that court employe" before altering the passage to read as above.

[27] Preceding five words interlined in place of "merely."

[28] Tr: "order."

[29] Short first wrote "recollection of the public audience of a Minister" before altering the passage to read as above.

[30] Short wrote "You will readily concieve that" before altering the passage to read as above.

[31] Preceding four words interlined in place of "hour of dinner."

[32] Tr: "as soon as."

[33] Short here canceled "M. C."—that is, Mr. Carmichael.

[34] Preceding three words interlined.

[35] Short here canceled "*certainly.*"

[36] Word interlined.

[37] Preceding three words interlined.

[38] Preceding seven words interlined in place of "*the.*"

[39] Short here interlined and then canceled "*and honorable.*"

[40] Word omitted in Tr.

[41] Preceding five words interlined in place of "*most honorable.*"

[42] Here in Tr, instead of the end of sentence, a comma and "because" are inserted.

[43] Tr: "total."

[44] Preceding five words interlined in place of "*a demand.*"

[45] Underscoring of preceding two words canceled by Short. The phrase is given correctly in the Tr, but the ciphers interlined beneath the words indicate that Short garbled the encoding. At the second occurrence of the phrase, at note 54 below, the ciphers are again interlined underneath to indicate that on this occasion Short had encoded it correctly.

[46] Coding garbled in Tr, where this word is deciphered as "ca grow." Below in this paragraph in Tr, where the coding for the singular of this word was similarly garbled, the clerk wrote in the margin: "suppose, *case.*"

[47] Word interlined.

[48] Word given correctly in Tr, but ciphers interlined beneath it indicate that Short encoded it incorrectly.

[49] Short wrote the remainder of this and the following paragraph on a separate sheet and keyed it by asterisk for insertion at this point to serve as a fair copy of a heavily emended section that he crossed out. Because the final state of the canceled section closely follows the fair copy which replaced it, only the most important and recoverable emendations are given below in notes 50-53, 55, 58, and 64.

[50] Here in the canceled section described in the preceding note Short initially wrote and then struck out "*since the commencement* of this century."

[51] Here in the canceled section described in note 49 Short initially wrote and then struck out "*who were formerly of the third order.*"

[52] Word interlined in the canceled section described in note 49.

[53] Word omitted in Tr, which has no sentence break here. In the canceled sec-

tion described in note 49 Short initially wrote and then lined through "—*and thus avoid the necessity of commissions ad hoc except in cases which admit of no other alternative.*" Although Short underscored *ad hoc*, he probably meant to emphasize the Latin phrase rather than to indicate words intended to be *en clair*.

[54] Preceding two words underscored, probably to emphasize the Latin phrase as he had done earlier (see note 53 and text at note 45 above), rather than to indicate words not to be encoded.

[55] Word interlined in place of "*plenipotentiary*" in the canceled section described in note 49.

[56] Preceding two words omitted in Tr.

[57] At this point Tr has "present."

[58] The sentence to this point and the one preceding it were substituted in the canceled section described in note 49 for "*Even the republic of Geneva has now adopted it in the course of the last year and England has carried it so far as to make their Secretaries of embassy ministers Plenipotentiary at the courts where they keep Ambassadors, this is done that their characters might keep pace with the agents of those countries who formerly keeping ministers of the third order had now placed them in the second by giving them plenipotentiary powers. I think it my duty to mention these circumstances to you.*"

[59] At this point Tr has "and as."

[60] Word omitted in Tr.

[61] Word omitted in Tr, and "as . . . ground" given in parentheses.

[62] Word written over "would." Tr: "would."

[63] Tr: "a."

[64] In the canceled section described in note 49 this sentence originally read "*How far this may be regained by time must depend on time and future circumstances.*"

[65] Preceding sentence interlined.

[66] Preceding three words interlined.

[67] Word interlined in place of "*late.*"

[68] Preceding three words omitted in Tr.

[69] Preceding nine words interlined in place of "*of impressions which left the public.*"

[70] Short first began the sentence as "*At Madrid all*" before altering it to read as above.

[71] Word interlined.

[72] Next twelve words interlined in place of a heavily reworked passage that in its final state read "*forced a lady to take off a cap.*"

[73] Beginning with the following sentence, Short drew a brace around a long section of text ending with "disadvantages to Spain." For reasons explained above, the Editors have assumed that Short intended this section of the missing RC to be entirely *en clair*.

[74] Word interlined.

[75] Preceding twelve words interlined. Short wrote the remainder of the sentence and the following three sentences lengthwise in the left margin, keying them to this point in the text and substituting them for a heavily emended and canceled passage of substantially the same import that in its final state included the following particulars: "one person only has within these few days carried 2 millns. of reals to the royal treasury as a free gift—others offer and effectuate various sums—others promise and are engaged in raising troops from among their vassals, in whom they find a willingness to enlist of which there is no example here—one city has promised 15000 men—and others different numbers in proportion to their population."

[76] Word interlined.

[77] Preceding five words interlined in place of "vie with."

[78] Word omitted in Tr.

[79] Preceding four words interlined.

[80] Word omitted in Tr.

[81] Short here canceled "very."

[82] Preceding thirteen words interlined.

[83] Preceding eight words interlined in place of a passage revised by Short to read as follows: "Three days only were allowed them, including the day of notification and that of departure—their houses and appartments locked up under a double key of which one was left to a person named by them—the other kept by the public officer—on this deposit a sum was to be advanced them sufficient to carry them to the frontier."

[84] Word omitted in Tr and interlined with the preceding two words in place of "produce a" in Dft.

[85] Preceding seven words interlined in place of "therefore extremely impolitic in this government if they really desire."

[86] Word interlined in place of "many."

[87] Preceding two words interlined in place of "a public."

[88] Preceding three words interlined in place of "This would probably have been the case if the King."

[89] Short here canceled "unthinking."

[90] At this point Tr adds "for them."

[91] At this point Tr adds "so."

[92] Emending as he proceeded, Short initially wrote a passage of this import—"of course they are therefore avoiding war as useless to the Bourbon French monarchy and dangerous to Spain"—before emending the passage several more times and finally settling on the wording given above.

[93] Preceding three words omitted in Tr.

[94] Date given as "21" in Tr, although two codes interlined beneath it indicate that Short encoded it incorrectly.

[95] Remainder of sentence garbled in Tr: "submit behind ibe to it." The clerk underscored "ibe" and interlined the codes for it beneath to indicate a perceived encoding error by Short.

[96] Preceding nine words interlined in place of a passage revised by Short to read "*the successes of the French in the last campaign have perhaps suggested the propriety of not declaring.*"

[97] Word omitted and sentence ended here in Tr.

[98] Dft: "*sat.*"

[99] Preceding nine words interlined in place of "*you will consider war as inevitable.*"

[100] Preceding sentence interlined.

[101] Here Short canceled the following sentence: "*He will no doubt add new weight to the representations of M: Jackson.*"

[102] Short first wrote "*I am unquestionably authoris*" before altering the phrase to read as above.

[103] Preceding two words interlined.

[104] Tr: "for."

[105] Preceding two words interlined in place of "*to them and of course tend to increase the union which a common enemy will produce between them.*"

[106] Tr: "against."

[107] Preceding nine words interlined.

[108] Preceding five words omitted from Tr.

[109] Short here canceled "*and in this giving an example of generosity to European powers.*" He had originally written *Christia*" before replacing it with "*European.*"

[110] Short here canceled "*in one instance he carried this principle so far, that the Dutch sailors having deserted their vessel and escaped.*"

To Fulwar Skipwith

DEAR SIR   Philadelphia Mar. 6. 1793.

I duly received your favor of Feb. 12. and knowing my situation you will be at no loss to ascribe the delay of my answer to the pressure of other business. I now inclose you a letter for M. de Rochambeau. I have not applied for one from the French minister lest the circumstance of his being recalled should excite some delicacies about writing official letters. We are told that a Mr. Genest may be hourly expected as his successor. Wishing you every success & happiness you can desire I am with great esteem Dear Sir your most obedt. servt

TH: JEFFERSON

PrC (DLC); at foot of text: "Mr. Fulwar Skipwith." Tr (DLC); 19th-century copy. Enclosure: TJ to Vicomte de Rochambeau, 6 Mch. 1793.

To Moses Cox

SIR   Philadelphia Mar. 7. 1793.
   Mr. Ogden informs me you propose to rent your house near Gray's
ferry the ensuing season, that the rent last year was £30. and he
supposed would still be the same. As the time it might suit me to
occupy a house in the country might be longer or shorter according to
circumstances, the price is of consequence, because even a low price
may by shortness of time become a high one. If therefore you are
disposed to rent it, and at the former price, I will beg your permission
to examine it, with it's conveniencies, and in that case must ask you
to trust me with the key, as I understand the house is not open. I will
ride there to-day, tomorrow, or next day as my business will permit,
and return you the key with an answer. I am Sir your most obedt.
servt   TH: JEFFERSON

PrC (DLC); at foot of text: "Mr. Mo-   Moses Cox (1734-1805), a Quaker
ses Cox." Tr (ViU: Edgehill-Randolph Pa-   merchant in Philadelphia, owned land at,
pers); 19th-century copy.   among other places, Gray's Ferry (PMHB,
                                             XLVI [1922], 169-70).

From Tench Coxe

                                                        March 7th. 1793
   Mr. Coxe has the honor to enclose to Mr. Jefferson, a copy of
a proceeding of the late board of Treasury, confirmed on the 21st.
April 1787 by Congress (see page 55. Vol. 12. Journal of Congress)
which he presumes to be the object of enquiry. It would have been
transmitted sooner, but the gentlemen in the Secys. office being unable
yesterday to find it, Mr. Coxe employed two of his Clerks this day on
the Subject, being convinced, that some thing of the kind must exist.

RC (DLC); endorsed by TJ: "Coxe   posing that land sales begin without wait-
Tenche. Western lands."   ing for seven ranges of townships to be
                                           surveyed, as had originally been planned
   The enclosed COPY OF A PROCEEDING   (Tr in DLC; printed in JCC, XXXII, 155-7).
was a 4 Apr. 1787 report to the Confeder- Congress approved the Board's proposals
ation Congress from the Board of Treas-   with only minor amendments on 21 Apr.
ury indicating how much western land   1787 (JCC, XXXII, 225-7). See also Report
had been surveyed by Thomas Hutchins,   on Boundaries with the Western Indians,
geographer of the United States, and pro- 10 Mch. 1793.

From Gouverneur Morris

Dear Sir   Paris 7 March 1793

Enclosed you have Copies of what I had the Honor to write on the twenty fifth of January and thirteenth of February also the Copy of a Letter of the twelfth of February from Mr. Pinkney with my Answer of the eighteenth. I send these last to the End that due Attention may be paid to such Vessels as may be furnished with his Passports and which may perhaps prove to be british Bottoms. I am so well perswaded that the United States will strictly observe the Laws of Nations and rigidly adhere to their Neutrality that I am solicitous to prevent a Practice which might expose us to Suspicion and finally involve us in War. On this Chapter it is proper also that I should communicate a fact which I have mentioned to Mr. Pinkney and desird him to transmit. Monsieur Genest took out with him three hundred blank Commissions which he is to distribute to such as will fit out Cruizers in our Ports to prey on the british Commerce. I am convinced that few of my Countrymen will be so lost to all moral Sense as to embark in a Game so abominable where the Murder of their fellow Creatures enters as a leading Chance. I am apprehensive however lest some Profligates may be led to fix a Blot on our national Character and deprive both themselves and their Countrymen of the great and certain Advantages to flow from honest Industry on the present important occasion. An Occasion which duly attended to and properly cultivated will give to our Navigation an Encrease too rapid almost for Conjecture, and place us in the happy Situation to be in two or three Years the exclusive Carriers of our immense Productions. These Considerations weigh much but they are still but a Feather in the Ballance with those of a much higher Nature which stand in Connection with the Nature of our Government and of Course with the Happiness of Generations to come. I know of Nothing so dangerous and I might say fatal to Morals as the sudden Acquisition of Wealth by bad Means. Industry is thereby discouraged and Honesty discountenanced. The Vulgar are soon dazzled by the Glare of prospering Vice and the Young are seduced from the Paths of Virtue. And Virtue once gone Freedom is but a Name for I do not beleive it to be among possible Contingencies that a corrupted People should be for one Moment free. Excuse I pray my dear Sir these Observations which I cannot restrain. They flow from the Conviction of my earliest Reason and are strengthened by the Experience of twenty Years.

In mine of the thirteenth of February I mention'd to you that this Country would procure the 500000 Men requird and at that Time there was every Reason to think so because the Recruiting Service went on well for all the new Corps which had been ordered but it now appears that this arose from little Circumstances of Dress and Flattery calculated to catch Idlers and that there is a real Scarcity of Men. The Losses of the last Campaign are sensible in the Mass of Population so that notwithstanding the Numbers thrown out of Employ by the Stagnation of some Manufactures and the Reduction of private Fortunes the Want of common Laborers is felt throughout the whole Country. Already they talk of Drafting for the Service an Experiment of very doubtful and dangerous Complection. It would however succeed just now but if delay'd it would not I beleive go down and at any Rate would not produce in Season the required Force; Especially if the Enemy should have any considerable Successes, for you must not imagine that the Appearances in this Country are all real, and you must take into your Estimation that the Convention is falling into Contempt because the Tribunes govern it imperiously. They try to save Appearances but the People cannot long be Dupes. It is the old Story of King Log and how long it may be before Jupiter sends them a Crane to destroy the Frogs and Froglings is a Matter of Uncertainty. Already they begin to cry out for a Dictator. An Insurrection also is brewing whose Object I am told is to destroy the Faction of the Gironde. I think I mentiond to you in a former Letter that the Death of the King would be but the Forerunner of their Destruction and already they see the Sword hanging over their Heads. The majority of the Convention is clearly at the Disposition of their Enemies.

The Consuls will forward to you and you will see in the Gazettes the Decree for opening all the Ports of this Nation to our Vessels on equal Terms with their own. You will be so kind as to observe that this was done on a Report of the Committee of Safety. Now you must know that the Members of this Committee or at least the Majority of them are sworn Foes to the Members of the Diplomatic Committee. This is necessary to explain a little what is said in mine of the 13th. about that latter Committee. I have receiv'd indirectly a Kind of Assurance from the former (which disposes entirely of the Convention) that they will do any Thing for the United States which I will point out but in Fact I know not any Thing which we ought to ask. The Decrees abovementioned contain I believe all that we want. The History of them is not material.

I had the Honor to mention to you also that I did not believe the Attempt against Holland would succeed and also that Time was extremely precious to both Parties especially in Regard to Maestricht in whose Fate was involvd perhaps that of the whole Campaign. This

Town had I am told offered to capitulate but Terms of such Rigor were insisted on as to induce a longer Defence and this Delay has saved them. The Seige is raisd and unless the french Army should gain a Victory I do not see how they are to escape provided the Enemy exerts himself. Dumouriez had taken Breda and was preparing to enter Holland being *ordered* by the Minister of War to whom he replied that he would go in but the Minister must find him his Way out. This latter may be no very easy Task. The Enemy on the Side of Maestricht are I beleive superior in Numbers and certainly if the french army in that Quarter is beaten the Allies may cut off the Retreat of Dumouriez in which Case his Fate must depend not only on the Strength of his Army not over numerous but also on the State of his Magazines which I beleive to be bad. Should Valence be able to make good a *gentle* Retreat then he may be join'd perhaps by Dumouriez at Louvain and together they may cover Brussels. But all these things again depend on some moral Contingencies. Such for Instance as the following questions. What will be the Temper and Spirit of those Departments nearest to the Scene of Action? What will be the Degree of Hope or Apprehension among the Inhabitants of the low Countries? As to them you will see by the Gazettes that they are fast expressing their Adherence to the french Republic *freely* pronounced. But since it has been no small Question among Metaphisicians what it is that constitutes the Freedom of the Will there is no small Question also on this Subject among Politicians as to the Case before us. Are Men actuated by Interest are they instigated by Desire are they seduced by Hope are they compelled by Fear? Alexander you know cut the Knot which he could not untie and the french have imitated the Example of that Conqueror. Some striking Examples of those who opposd the Union with France inducd all the Rest to give both their *speedy* and their *free* Consent. It is therefore a Problem to be resolvd what Degree of Force must be producd by the Allies to operate on the Free Will of this People in a Counter Sense. I think the Solution of that Problem is in Brussels. On the whole my dear Sir the Hour is big with important Events. As soon as I learn any Thing more I will communicate it. In the Mean Time accept the Assurances of that Respect with which I have the Honor to be your obedient Servant   GOUV MORRIS

RC (DNA: RG 59, DD); at head of text: "No. 21"; at foot of first page: "Thomas Jefferson Esqr Secretary of State"; endorsed by TJ as received 4 May 1793 and so recorded in SJL. FC (Lb in DLC: Gouverneur Morris Papers). Tr (DNA: RG 46, Senate Records, 3d Cong., 1st sess.); copy made early in 1794 by State Department; with omissions. PrC (DNA: RG 59, MD); more complete text containing two pages not corresponding to Tr. Tr (Lb in same, DD). Enclosures: (1) Morris to TJ, 25 Jan., 13 Feb. 1793, Nos. 18-20. (2) Thomas

Pinckney to Morris, 12 Feb. 1793, enclosing a sample of the passports he had issued to American vessels leaving British ports, requesting a better translation of the French treaty provisions relating to the form of such passports, and noting that American citizens would pay lower insurance costs if Morris could persuade the French government to issue a published order to its naval officers to observe treaty obligations respecting American vessels departing from Britain, as doubts about its adherence to the treaty are entertained at Lloyd's. (3) Morris to Pinckney, 18 Feb. 1793, arguing against their issuance of ship passports because they were being sought mainly for fraudulent purposes, particularly "to cover, under a neutral Dress, the Property of Enemies," because their absence might be used to justify seizures of American vessels whose papers were otherwise in order, and because they lacked authority to issue them (Trs in same, DD; Trs in DNA: RG 46, Senate Records, 3d Cong., 1st sess.; Pr Cs in DNA: RG 59, MD; Trs in Lb in same, DD).

THE OLD STORY OF KING LOG . . . FROG-LINGS refers to Æsop's fable of "The Frogs Desiring a King." Concerning the DECREE FOR OPENING ALL THE PORTS issued on 19 Feb. 1793, see Joseph Fenwick to TJ, 25 Feb. 1793, and note. Following a series of local plebiscites under French military pressure, Belgium's UNION WITH FRANCE was enacted piecemeal by fifteen French decrees between 1 and 30 Mch. 1793. Austrian reoccupation of the territory in the same month rendered the annexation nugatory almost immediately (Scott and Rothaus, *Historical Dictionary*, I, 88).

TJ submitted this letter and its enclosures to the President on 4 May 1793, and Washington returned them two days later (Washington, *Journal*, 128, 129).

From Joel Barlow

MY DEAR SIR   Paris 8 March 1793

I have been extremely anxious lest some of the late transactions in France should be so far misrepresented to the Patriots in America as to lead them to draw conclusions unfavorable to the cause of liberty in this hemisphere. You are sensible that in order to form a proper judgement it is necessary to combine many circumstances that cannot be well understood by men out of the country. The new Minister who is now gone to America bears a good character, I am sure the intention of sending him to replace the one that was there before is a very honest one. The nation concieves itself to have been misrepresented in every country. How far it is true in America, I cannot tell. But I am convinced that the Americans have been misrepresented here. At least I hope it is so, for I hope we are still republicans in theory and practice, tho' those of the French who know us only through the diplomatic chanel are disposed to doubt it.

These good people are now at war with all Europe. The liberation of the Spanish Colonies I think will be a speedy consequence of their war with Spain. This can scarcely fail to turn to the advantage of the United States by securing peace with our neighbours. I think now I shall sail in the month of April. This comes by a Mr. Corbin of

Virginia, a young man who appears amiable and well informed. I enclose to you a little address which I wrote to the people of Piemont While I was in Savoy. I am my dear Sir with great respect your obet. Serv.   JOEL BARLOW

RC (DLC); at foot of text: "Mr. Jefferson"; endorsed by TJ as received 4 May 1793 and so recorded in SJL. Enclosure: Joel Barlow, *Lettre adressée aux habitants du Piémont, sur les avantages de la Révolution française et la nécessité d'en* *adopter les principes en Italie* [N.p., 1793], consisting of a letter dated Chambéry, 29 Dec. 1792 (*B.N. Cat.*, VII, 828). For the London edition of 1795, an English translation by Barlow that TJ acquired, see Sowerby, No. 2845.

From Clement Biddle

SIR   Walnut Street March 8. 1793
In making an Alteration in my Office the Lists of the Domesticks of the foreign Ministers Are so defaced as not to answer the purpose intended, which obliges me to request the favour of you to direct Copies of them, to be signed by you, to be put up in my Office. I have the honour to be, with great respect Your mo: Obedt. & very humle Serv.   CLEMENT BIDDLE
                                                          Marshall in and for the
                                                          Pennsylvania district

RC (DNA: RG 59, MLR); endorsed by TJ: "Mr. Taylor will be pleased to comply with this"; endorsed by George Taylor, Jr.: "complied with."

Clement Biddle (1740-1814), a Philadelphia merchant, had served with the rank of colonel in the quartermaster and commissary departments of the Continental army and Pennsylvania militia during the Revolutionary War. After the war he became George Washington's trusted business agent in Philadelphia and was appointed United States Marshal for Pennsylvania by the President in 1789, an office he relinquished later in 1793 (DAB).

TJ had found it necessary to begin keeping LISTS OF THE DOMESTICKS OF THE FOREIGN MINISTERS after the arrest of a servant of the Dutch minister by a Pennsylvania official in June 1792 led to a protest over this violation of diplomatic immunity (Edmund Randolph to TJ, 26 June 1792, and note).

To Tench Coxe

                                                                    Mar. 8. 93
Th: Jefferson presents his compliments and thanks to Mr. Coxe for the paper sent him yesterday. It fixes a conjecture that the East and West line run from the intersection of the Pensylva. boundary with the Ohio, forms the head line of the ranges of townships. But there surely

was a partial survey of those ranges of townships. It is presumed that the sales made at New York must have been on an inspection of this partial survey. If there be such a one, Th:J. will be much obliged to Mr. Coxe for it, *immediately*, as he is at this time finishing what he was to prepare on the subject. Th:J. has the large chequer-board map, but this was a conjectural thing, and not done on actual survey.

RC (CtY); addressed "Mr. Coxe"; endorsed by Coxe. Not recorded in SJL.

Under the Land Ordinance of 1785, seven RANGES OF TOWNSHIPS west of the Ohio River were to be laid out before any of these lands were sold. Impatient at the slow pace of the surveying, Congress voted on 21 Apr. 1787 to begin sales of land situated in the four ranges already surveyed at that point, the notes and plats for which had been received from Thomas Hutchins, geographer to the

United States, earlier that year. Between 21 Sep. and 9 Oct. 1787, 72,934 acres of this land were sold in THE SALES MADE AT NEW YORK. The surveying of the seven ranges was completed by 26 July 1788, but no further sales affecting them had occurred since then (*Terr. Papers*, II, 12-18, 24-25; ASP, *Public Lands*, III, 459; William D. Pattison, "The Survey of the Seven Ranges," *Ohio Historical Quarterly*, LXVIII [1959], 131n, 132, 134n, 137). See also Report on Boundaries with the Western Indians, 10 Mch. 1793

From Tench Coxe

March 7. [i.e. 8] 1793

Mr. Coxe has the honor to inform Mr. Jefferson, that no plat, or draught of the seven ranges is to be found in the Treasury, nor do any of the gentlemen remember to have seen one. It appears highly probable that such a paper accompanied the Report of the Board to Congress, and that it may be on the old files of the late Secy. of Congress (Mr. Thompson) or possibly in the War office, as the military lands have relation to the ranges.

RC (DLC); misdated, but clearly a response to TJ's letter of 8 Mch. 1793; endorsed by TJ.

From Gouverneur Morris

DEAR SIR   Paris 8 March 1793

In reading over my Letter of Yesterday I find that I omitted to mention the War with Spain. Truth is that it was a Matter so much of Course and of so little Importance that it escap'd my Recollection. Our Commissioners will doubtless turn it to Account. Last Evening I was inform'd that the french Army in Flanders has been defeated but as this is not an official Account I meerly mention it as it is viz a Letter sent express by an Individual at Brussels on seeing sundry Run aways arrive and Stores &ca. &ca. coming in at sixes and sevens with the Report that the Enemy were at the Gates. On the other Hand you must take into Account that the Seige of Maestrecht being raisd only the third one Days Rest was necessary for the Troops which had come on by forc'd Marches. Now as the Action must have taken Place at Tongres about forty Miles from Brussels and the Courier in Question left that City in the Night of the fifth it would follow that the Enemy must have march'd from Maestrecht in the Night of the fourth and attack'd at Break of Day otherwise the Runaways could hardly have got in by the Evening of the fifth. On the whole there is but just Time enough for such an Affair to have happened and that is all. If there is any Confirmation I will mention it. I am respectfully my dear Sir your obedient Servant   GOUV MORRIS

RC (DNA: RG 59, DD); at head of text: "No. 22"; at foot of first page: "Thomas Jefferson Esqr. Secretary of State"; endorsed by TJ as received 4 May 1793 and so recorded in SJL. FC (Lb in DLC: Gouverneur Morris Papers); with correction by Morris. Tr (DNA: RG 46, Senate Records, 3d Cong., 1st sess.). PrC (DNA: RG 59, MD). Tr (Lb in same, DD).

THE WAR WITH SPAIN: France declared war on Spain on 7 Mch. 1793. Spain reciprocated on 23 Mch. 1793 (Bemis, *Pinckney's Treaty*, 168). OUR COMMISSIONERS: William Carmichael and William Short.

TJ submitted this letter to the President on 4 May 1793, and Washington returned it two days later (Washington, *Journal*, 128, 129).

From George Washington

SIR   United States March 8th: 1793

Being desireous of having a full and accurate knowledge of such things as are required to be done by or through the President of the United States, by the laws passed during the late Session of Congress, and which are[1] deposited among the Rolls[2] in your Office—I have to request, that the said laws may be examined for this purpose,[3] and that you will furnish me with extracts of such parts or clauses of them as relate to, or require the immediate or special[4] agency of the President of the United States.   GO: WASHINGTON

RC (DLC); in the hand of Tobias Lear, signed by Washington; at foot of text: "The Secretary of State"; endorsed by TJ: "Lear Tobias recd. Mar. 8." Dft (DNA: RG 59, MLR); in Lear's hand. FC (Lb in same, SDC).

[1] In Dft at this point "recorded and" is canceled.
[2] Preceding three words interlined in Dft.
[3] Preceding three words interlined in Dft.
[4] Preceding three words interlined in Dft.

From Delamotte

Havre, 9 Mch. 1793. No French ship was available to carry the above letter until now. The king, condemned to death, was executed on 21 Jan. France is at war with all the powers except the United States, Portugal, Sweden, and Denmark. The government has just opened trade with all the French colonies solely to the flag of the United States, whose ships may go between them and France directly without paying more duties than French ships. If the enclosed letter to the ministry was responsible for the decree, he is glad to have contributed. It is important that TJ spread this news as soon as possible to the entire Continent, and he will try to delay sending this letter until he can attach the decree. Tobacco and rice are now at 80 and 70 livres tournois, respectively, and the exchange rate with London is at $15\frac{1}{8}$.

RC (DLC); 1 p.; in French; in a clerk's hand, signed by Delamotte; subjoined to RC of Delamotte to TJ, 15 Jan. 1793; endorsed by TJ as received 4 May 1793 and so recorded in SJL. Dupl (DNA: RG 59, CD); in a clerk's hand, signed by Delamotte; subjoined to Dupl of Delamotte to TJ, 15 Jan. 1793. Enclosure: Extract of Delamotte to Gaspard Monge, Minister of Marine, 9 Feb. 1793, citing the applications he has refused from many French merchants to obtain American colors for their ships, recommending that American ships be permitted to carry goods from the French colonies to France on the same terms as French ships so that France can benefit from her colonies during the war, and explaining that provisions would otherwise have to be transported to America first and be subject to such heavy duties and expenses in both countries as to defeat the purpose (Tr, in French, in same; Tr, in French, in ViW).

From Delamotte

Havre, 9 Mch. 1793. He encloses a copy of a letter from Gouverneur Morris announcing that the French colonies have been opened solely to ships flying the American flag, which can ply between them and France directly and pay no more in duties than French ships. France is at war with Germany, Prussia, Holland, Savoy, England, and Spain, leaving only American flag vessels to help extract our capital from the colonies. "Les tabacs valent 80.^{tt} le %. Le Riz 70.^{tt} do. Le Change Sur Londres est à $15\frac{1}{8}$e."[1]

RC (DNA: RG 59, CD); 1 p.; in French; in a clerk's hand, signed by Delamotte; part of text torn away; at foot of text: "Mr. le Secretaire d'État à Philadelphie"; with notation by TJ (see note 1 below). Recorded in SJL as received 4 May 1793. Enclosure: Gouverneur Morris to Delamotte, Paris, 21 Feb. 1793, asking him to send word of the new French policy on American trade with the colonies to the United States by all opportunities, and especially to forward a copy of his letter to the Secretary of State (Tr in same, attested by Delamotte, at head of text: "Circular"; Tr in ViW, corrected and attested by Delamotte).

[1] TJ drew a line around the passage quoted here and penciled above it: "a letter from Havre of Mar. 9. quotes the following prices of American produce." A translation of the passage, with this preface, was printed in the 8 May 1793 issues of the *National Gazette* and the *Gazette of the United States.*

From Delamotte

Havre, 9 Mch. 1793. Having received TJ's letter of 14 Nov. a few days ago, he sees that TJ may retire and might even now be in Virginia. From what he has seen in American newspapers he is not surprised that TJ prefers a private life to a situation exposing him to the sarcasms of envy. Convinced that TJ will choose to remain in office, he congratulates him in advance on his reasons—envy must have abated and TJ must again be happy to be useful to his country. If on the other hand he has retired to Virginia, he congratulates him on the delights awaiting him there. There is no ship bound for Virginia, so he must keep TJ's books—as well as the macaroni, which might not find him in Philadelphia—until one occurs. He begs to have all his little errands, of which there will be more if TJ should indeed retire. [P.S.] They have a ship he thinks will go to Alexandria.

RC (DLC); 2 p.; in French; in a clerk's hand, signature and postscript by Delamotte; at foot of first page: "Mr. Jefferson à Philadelphie"; endorsed by TJ as received 4 May 1793 and so recorded as a private letter in SJL.

From William & Samuel Jones

Sir   London March 9th. 1793

We had the pleasure of receiving yours of the 26th. of Decr. Ulto. and have accordingly sent herewith, one of the best kind of our *Portable Orreries.* The price of the one sent is 3 Guineas, the additional half guinea is on account of its having a stand, and the plates under the earth and moon more durable, and not so liable to be loose dirty, and useless after a little while as those made of paper. We applied as you desired, to Donald & Burton, but was informed that they have stopped payment, but on being referred to Mr. Donald No. 11 Paper Buildings Temple he has undertaken to pay the money, and send the instrument by the favour of Mr. Marshall Sackville Street, Piccadilly. Mr. Martin very strongly recommends these alterations to the telescope as being himself in the way sometimes of making them. It is undoubtedly a curious contrivance but interferes too much with the construction of the instrument subjecting it to be deranged, and to be out of order somewhat, in shifting occasionally the parts. None of that construction are now made, but we could easily make you one if desired. The length would be 9 Inches, mounted in brass and to be used occasionally with or without the stand. The price will be either 4 or 5 guineas, not more; a pocket fish skin case included. Jupiter's Moons and Saturn's Ring can be distinctly seen by them.

A 12 Inch reflector, would be much more perfect, and magnify more, but not suitable for the pocket. The price of such a one will be 7 Guineas.

The $3\frac{1}{2}$ feet[1] achromatic refracter, is the best kind of achromatic telescope that can be made, the price is 16 Guineas. If with a brass tube, and rack work 22 Guineas. If with micrometrical and other apparatus the price is from 30 to 70 Guineas.

The prices of Globes you will see by our Catalogues sent and we have to inform you that we are concerned in new 18 Inch Globes that are in forwardness, that will contain many improvements and advantages not in any former ones. The names on the Terrestial &c will be in *English*. The discoveries included to the present time, and the positions of the Stars, and Constellations brought forward to the commencement of the year 1800. By the time we [have][2] the pleasure of next writing to you we hope that they will be completed. We have further to inform you that since you were in England, our father Mr. John Jones has declined business in the shopkeeping way, he lives cheifly in the country we are left to improve and manage the business entirely to our desires, our connections, and concerns, have thereby very considerably expanded, and improved, and at this moment we have the honor to do business for, and to be recommended by, the first persons of science and property.

We hope therefore to have the favour of your custom, and recommendation, and [. . .] pledge our reputations that the greatest attentions possible shall be paid to any commands that you may think proper to charge us with.

We have enclosed in the[3] a Dozen of our catalogues which we presume you will find to be more comprehensive than any hitherto published. We have the honor to be, Sir, Your Obliged, and Very Hble Servts.

WM & SAML. JONES (brothers)

RC (DLC); in the hand of William Jones; addressed: "Mr. Thos. Jefferson Philadelphia"; torn at seal; stamped and postmarked; endorsed by TJ as received 26 Aug. 1793 and so recorded in SJL.

The firm of W. & S. Jones, optical, mathematical, and scientific instrument makers, prospered at various addresses in Holborn, London, until at least 1860. William Jones (1763-1831), who received some training from Benjamin MARTIN (d. 1782), the instrument maker cited in TJ's letter, had previously published descrip-

tions of a new portable orrery and subsequently lectured and wrote on astronomy, mathematics, and electricity. At his death William left the bulk of his estate to his partner and younger brother Samuel (*Gentleman's Magazine*, CI, pt. 1 [1831], 275; Nicholas Goodison, *English Barometers 1680-1860* [New York, 1968], 156-7; note to William Jones to TJ, 2 Jan. 178[9]).

TJ's letter OF THE 26TH. OF DECR. 1792 was addressed to John Jones. The enclosed CATALOGUES were copies of this or a later edition of *A Catalogue of Optical*,

Mathematical, and Philosophical Instruments, made and sold by Willm. and Saml. Jones . . . [London, 1791?].

[1] At this point Jones canceled "reflector."

[2] Editors' conjecture for word inadvertently omitted by the authors.

[3] Thus in manuscript.

From Gouverneur Morris

DEAR SIR
                                            Paris 9 March 1793

The Intelligence communicated in mine of yesterday is fully confirm'd. The Accounts given to the Convention are so lame and blind that one is oblig'd to peice them out like a tatter'd writing where whole Sentences are wanting. It would seem then that the Enemy, tho at what Time is yet uncertain, made an Attack on the Army which had beseigd or rather bombarded Maestrecht and which was then at Tongres. The Route has I beleive been compleat and the Enemy by pushing on to St. Tron have cut off the Retreat of those who were at Leige before the Battle or who fled to it afterwards so that in all human Probability the greater Part of them have fallen with all their Artillery and Stores. They had indeed one Road open viz that along the Banks of the Meuse up to Huy and Namur but whether the Enemy in Luxembourg have detach'd on that Side seems as yet uncertain. Probably they have not. It would seem that such of the french Army as escap'd by the Way of St. Tron have been totally dissipated for it is said that the Enemy is in Possession of Brussels; and of Course he must have come on from eighty to an hundred Miles in the Space of four or five Days. The french have sent off every thing they could save to Valenciennes which is about sixty Miles on this Side of Bruxelles and in which the broken Remnants of their Army will probably be collected. Going on the Supposition that the allied Army is at Brussels it appears to me that Dumouriez is compleatly cut off unless he be possess'd of very considerable Magazines for he is you know in a horrible Country. In front a navigable River and in the Rear a pitiless Desert untill he gets back to the Neighbourhood of Antwerp Malines and Louvain. Now the Enemy could be at Malines as soon as at Brussels these Places being equi distant from Louvain thro which they must in either Case have past and the Distance from Malines to Antwerp is about one third of what Dumouriez had to pass over unless he began his March as soon as he receivd the News that the Enemy were on their way to Maestrecht. This Intelligence did not I presume reach him till the Night of the third or Morning of the fourth and it is a Question of

Moment whether he took instant Measures for his Retreat which must of Necessity be slow thro the very very bad Roads which he has to struggle with till he gets to the Pavement within about a League (if I remember right) of Antwerp. The Intention of the Enemy is I am certain to cut him off and if that be done God knows what will happen for the frontier Towns are almost without Garrisons the whole Force having been call'd off to the Expedition against Holland. The Force in the Low Countries has been stated very highly by those who counted on Success in that Quarter but I do not beleive that the whole amounted to more than fifty or at most sixty thousand and should those Events which are now probable take Place very few of that Number will get back again to France. I understand that the Militia are to be drafted immediately and what may be the Success of that Measure God only knows. I have not sufficient data on which to fix an Opinion but should it be accompanied by Delay or encounter Opposition The Safety of Paris is more in Distance than in Force. Adieu my dear Sir. I am truly yours   GOUV MORRIS

RC (DNA: RG 59, DD); at head of text: "No. 23"; endorsed by TJ as received 4 May 1793 and so recorded in SJL. FC (Lb in DLC: Gouverneur Morris Papers). Tr (DNA: RG 46, Senate Records, 3d Cong., 1st sess.). PrC (DNA: RG 59, MD). Tr (Lb in same, DD).

TJ submitted this letter to the President on 4 May 1793, and Washington returned it two days later (Washington, *Journal*, 128, 129).

To George Washington

Mar. 9. 93.

Th: Jefferson presents his respects to the President and sends him a letter put into his hands by Govr. St. Clair. He also sends him Govr. Clinton's answer, this moment received. He does not say how it happened that Th:J's letter of Feb. 17. did not get to him till Feb. 28. It was certainly put into the Post office here on the morning of Feb. 18. It must be presumed the Govr. has been absent from New York.

RC (DNA: RG 59, MLR); endorsed by Tobias Lear. Tr (Lb in same, SDC). Not recorded in SJL. Enclosures: (1) Winthrop Sargent to Arthur St. Clair, Cincinnati, 19 Jan. 1793, reporting on his efforts to end Christmas riots and disorders in the Northwest Territory in 1791 and 1792, and attributing the weakness of the territorial government to the refusal of its judges to meet to pass laws, and to the actions of Judge John Cleves Symmes in pandering to disturbers of the peace (*Terr. Papers*, III, 399-404; see also Washington, *Journal*, 83). (2) George Clinton to TJ, 5 Mch. 1793.

From George Washington

DEAR SIR   Philada. March 9th. 1793.

The enclosed from Messrs. Johnson and Carroll have this instant come to hand. Along with them you will receive the letter (this day read) from Doctr. Stuart, that the sentiments of all three of the Commrs. may appear at one view.

I pray you, before Mr. Madison leaves town, to lay all three before him and the Attorney Genl.; and give me a written Memorandum of the measures which you, and they, shall think most advisable for me to pursue—provisionally, or otherwise, in this business.

You will all recollect the points that were touched upon to day; I shall not, therefore, repeat them. I am always Yours

GO: WASHINGTON

RC (DLC); at foot of text: "Mr. Jefferson"; endorsed by TJ as received 9 Mch. 1793; below the endorsement TJ wrote: "what sacrifice to retain Johnson? sum in gross & what? if he goes, any sacrifice to retain other Commrs in town? Commrs in town, sum in gross?" Recorded in SJPL. Enclosures not found.

George Washington to the Secretaries of State, Treasury, and War

SIR   United States, March 9th: 1793

Expecting that my private Affairs will call me to Virginia on or before the 25th of this month, I have to request that you will lay before me, previous to that time, such matters within your department as may require my attention or agency before I set out; as well as those which might be necessary for me to know or act upon during my absence from the Seat of Government (which will be about four weeks) so far as such may come to your knowledge before my departure.

GO: WASHINGTON

RC (DLC); in the hand of Tobias Lear, signed by Washington; at foot of text: "The Secretary of State"; endorsed by TJ: "Lear Tobias recd. Mar 9. 93." Dft (DNA: RG 59, MLR); in Lear's hand and endorsed by him as intended for the Secretaries of State, Treasury, and War; contains minor variations in wording. FC (Lb in same, SDC); wording follows Dft.

To James Currie

DEAR SIR   Philadelphia Mar. 10. 1793.

Your letter of Feb. 12. came to hand on the 19th. Mr. Barton, who had your suit against Griffin in hand, quitted business a little before the last quarterly court without my being apprised of it, and the gentleman who succeeded to his docquet (Mr. Sergeant) not having time to be prepared, one term has been lost to you. As soon as I knew of Mr. Barton's having turned over his business to Mr. Sergeant, I waited on the latter, and he has promised me to attend to it very particularly at the term of the next month. As I have concluded to remain here somewhat longer, I hope to see this matter brought to a close for you.—I have paid due attention to what you say on the subject of the military land rights beyond the Ohio, but am not able to collect any information worth your notice. I have asked opinions on the words of the act of Congress, and on the views of those who will have to expound it, and I find the former so contradictory, and the latter so little disposed to lessen the obstacles to the right either of the assignee or original claimant, that it is impossible to give any relief to your doubts from this quarter.—I understand that W. Ronald has left his affairs much perplexed. Mine in his hands however are safe, as his debt to me was secured by a mortgage of the lands I sold him and also of one moiety of his Beverdam lands.—I am with great & sincere esteem Dear Sir, your friend & servt   TH: JEFFERSON

PrC (DLC); at foot of text: "Dr. Currie." Tr (ViU: Edgehill-Randolph Papers); 19th-century copy.

To J. P. P. Derieux

DEAR SIR   Philadelphia Mar. 10. 1793

I received yesterday your favor of the 1st. inst. I am unable to give you any explanation relative to your bill, as I have not had a word from Mr. Fenwick but those I copied in my letter to you. I think you would do well to write to him for an explanation as the matter seems to require it, and you will the sooner be placed on a certainty. I have not lately heard what progress is made in the sale of your effects here. But the scarcity of money never before paralleled among the merchants here for a month or two past, and which will not be over till the summer, will render remittances from hence slow. They shall not be retarded however by any want of my attention.

The estragon (called in English Tarragon) is little known in America. The Melongene (Solanum Melongena of the botanists) is unknown to me. I expect they will be to be found only in possession of Mr. Bartram who keeps a curious botanical garden some miles in the country. Due enquiry shall be made for them there and elsewhere. My compliments to Mrs. Derieux and am with great esteem Dr. Sir Your most obedt. servt   TH: JEFFERSON

P.S. I had omitted to answer your questions on the purchase of lands for your uncle. I think lands may be rented in Virginia for 5. per cent on their cost. The gradual increase of value is an additional profit.— My lands at Elkhill have been sold some time ago.

PrC (DLC); at foot of first page: "Mr. Derieux." Tr (DLC); 19th-century copy; lacks postscript. Tr (ViU); 19th-century copy; postscript only.

From Thomas Digges

SIR   Birmingham 10 Mar. 1793
I send You this Letter in a Book of Medals and Coins (as numberd and markd) which were done at Mr. Boultons mint at Soho near this place. Some of the trash of half pence which are in local tho' current circulation in and about the Towns to which they appertain, are added to fill up the book; And as I know You have made the American Mint and Coinage much Your study, they may serve as assistant samples towards perfection, those of Mr. Boultons being of a very superior kind.

I am at present engagd in this central part of England trying to get Leasehold or annual Tennants for my Lands fronting the Presidents on Potowmac, and adjoining the new Federal City and Bladensburgh, and I expect to Embark for America in May or June. Not knowing of a safe conveyance to You, I have made free to send the parcell to and ask the favour of Mr. Pinkney to forward it, And, as I understood from Mr. Boulton He had made some application for a Die sinker I have left open the book of Coins for his inspection.

Since my Letter to You by Wm. Pearce the Double Loom maker, and the original inventor of Arkwrights first weaving and spining Machinery, I have not had occasion to write, nor would I have likely done it before my Embarkation for America But am inducd now to do so from having accidentally seen a Birmingham production of one of the American *Cents*, the intended Coin of America and the $\frac{1}{100}$th part of the Dollar. Knowing it had been determin in Congress to have all their money minted in the States, I made it my business to seek out and inform myself all I could about this Cent coinage here and of the artists and Merchants engaged about them. I first applyd to Messrs. W. & Alxr. Walkers (who have a Partner Mr. Thos. Ketland in Philaa.) and they shewd me the Specimens No. 16. and No. 17 sent herewith and afterwards gave them to me. They said it was merely a speculation or trial to obtain the order for making the intended[1] cents here which inducd them to the attempt in 1791 and that some hundred wt. or so had been sent to America and given to the President and other public Gentlemen; But that on the determination of Congress to mint their own money, their scheme here had fallen thro'. They were close and secret as to *who* the die sinker was, *where* coind &ca. but upon further Enquirys I found Messrs. Walkers had orderd them to be done at Mr. Obediah Westwoods (a considerable maker of these kinds of money),[2] and that his die Sinker Mr. Jno. Gregory Hancock (one of the first in this place 'tho with the Character of a dissipated man) and a prentice Lad Jno. Jordan, very Clever in that line, had executed them and still hold the dies. This Lad Jordan, has two years of His time to serve, wishes much to go to America, but I suppose his time would be worth 200£. The face likeness on both are the same die and a good likeness of the President, tho' the Eagles and motto are different. The likeness was taken from a large medal struck at Phila.

Those enquirys about the American *Cent*, and my intimacy with Mr. Boulton and Mr. Watt, led me to look at and study more the apparatus and modes of Coining, the Expence attending a Copper Coinage, &ca. than I otherways should have done, and I suppose I need not inform You that Mr. Boulton is by far the neatest and best Coiner and has a more excellent Apparatus for Coining than any in Europe. It cost Him some thousands. The whole machine is moved by an improvd steam Engine which rolls the Copper for halfpence *finer* than copper has before been rolld for the purposes of money. It works the Coupoirs or screw press's, for cutting the particular peices of Copper, and coins both the faces *and edges* of the money at the same time, with such superior excellence and cheapness of workmanship, as well as with marks of such powerful machinery as must totally prevent counterfieting it. By his machinery four boys can strike thousands of Guineas in an hour. Eight presses works four ton of Copper per day— four or five presses two ton per day, and the machine by the Evolutions of the great wheel, which is of cast Iron, keeps an unerring account of the number of peices struck. It is not workd in the old way but the mettal is put into a kind of hopper, and drops out into a bag nearly as smoothly as grain in a Mill.

The Excellence of His Coinage are

1st.   The peices are perfectly round—2d. They are all precisely Equal in Diameter

3d.   The work is exactly concentric to the Edge

4   An inscription or Ornament is put round the Edge, either indented, or in relief, or partly one and partly the other, and this inscription is struck by the same blow that gives impression to the Faces; Whereas the common mode of making ornaments on the Edge, is by a seperate well known operation calld milling and which is much more easily immitated.

5.   The ground of his Coin is smooth and of a light polish.

6   Much greater quantities of money with all these perfections may be coind in less time, with fewer persons, and with more exactness and ease to those Employd, than by any mode hitherto invented.

Memorandums   A Water mill will work all the machinery as well as a steam Engine and will be better understood and managd in America—indeed the power of two or 3 horses might answer. Mr. Boulton told me He would sell the whole apparatus, *exclusive of the Steam Engine*, (which is a considerable part of the Cost) and it might be got to America (I think) for 11 or 1200£.

The whole apparatus is this.

A *Rolling Mill*;   which must be unconnected with the Coining Mill.

Mill work to work Coupoirs
   Do. Do.   Coining
   Do. Do. for turning Laths and cleaning the Blanks.
   Do. Do. for Lettering the Edges.

The Arts necessary, and which might be easily learnt are
   Hardning and polishing Dies.
   Multiplying the Dies.
   Managing the Presses.
   Improvements in presses and Coupoirs
   In annealing so as to preserve the Pollish

The *Matrasses* (which are the Adam and Eve for Casting medals or Coins) being obtaind, the *multiplication of dies*, and the hardening them, (a sort of Secret) is to be learnt. The best artists in this line are said to be in Paris; But Mr. Boulton would lend His assistance in this, and give His instruction and direction, to any confidential person sent from America for the purpose of looking after or superintending a Copper Coinage at His mint, which with the Dies &ca. &ca. He would afterwards sell for a fair price to America and on Easy terms.

—

Sheet Copper from England being Cast or rolld *Hot*, and liable to stain at Sea will not do. It may be sent over a little thicker than the money, and then put thro' a Roller to make it of exact thickness.

—

Mr. Boultons prices for Coining Copper, notwithstanding the superior beauty and Excellence to any in England, will be equally cheap.

—

The following is an Estimate given me by Mr. Obdiah Westwood for Coining half pence or Cents.

Suppose *a Cent*, made in pure Copper 29 ps/s in the ℔ of Copper. one ton would Contain 64,960 Cents; which is 649½

Dolls. a 4/6 is £146.19.9

The Copper cost say 90£ the ton ⎫ 120–
Dies & Expence of Manufactg 30 – – ⎭

Profit on the ton when paid out would be £26.19.9

But Copper is now as high as £112 per ton. At this or the above price not a less order than for twenty ton would answer for Him in finding dies, Rolling the Copper, manufacturing into Cents, Capping in paper and Casking up &ca.

According to the greater or less number of peices made from three pound of Copper, so the Expence of Coinage would alter Vizt. *for working* only.

For 40 ps/s in the ℔ it would amot. to 42£ suppose Copper a 100£ the ton

for 36 ps/s 34–

for 32 ps/s which is ½ an Oz. each ps. 32—so that in his order for half pence say of 40 ps. in the ℔ the profit would be to the Emitter £45.13.4 on the ton thus the ps/s amot. to £187.13.4

Cost of Copper 100–
87.13.4

Expence of Coining 42
45.13.4

The standard of the British half penny is three to one ounce of Copper which is 48 half pence to the ℔. an Enormous profit to the Government on Emission!

If I can obtain any other information, or hear of a person likely to serve in this Business I will write You, I am in the interim with great regard Sir Yr. Ob Hu Serv TH A DIGGES

RC (DLC); addressed: "Thomas Jefferson Esqr Philadelphia"; endorsement by TJ mutilated. Recorded in SJL as received 31 May 1793. Enclosed in Thomas Pinckney to TJ, 10 Apr. 1793, and TJ to George Washington, 12 June 1793.

Digges's LETTER TO YOU BY WM. PEARCE was dated 28 Apr. 1791. The BIRMINGHAM PRODUCTION OF ONE OF THE AMERICAN CENTS was almost certainly the large and small Eagle Cents of 1791 (William S. Baker and George Fuld, *Medallic Portraits of Washington*, rev. ed. [Iola, Wis., 1965], Nos. 15-16, p. 17-18, 20; see also Sylvester S. Crosby, *The Early Coins of America* [Boston, 1873-75; repr. Lawrence, Mass., 1974], 352-

4). The LARGE MEDAL STRUCK AT PHILA. was probably the Manly Medal, minted in Philadelphia in 1790 (Baker and Fuld, *Medallic Portraits*, No. 61, p. 40-1, 43; but see also Taxay, *Mint*, 53n, which argues that it was the "Washington before Boston" medal, minted in Paris in 1786).

[1] Word interlined.
[2] Closing parenthesis supplied.

From Alexander Donald

DEAR SIR London 10th. march 1793

I have no doubt but you will hear before this letter reaches you, that the House of D. & Burton have been obliged to stop payment. Several causes combined to bring upon us this misfortune, and none more than the rash and ill judged Speculation of my Partner in wheat and flour in the Winter of 89. 90. My mind for some months past has been in great distress, but I have the consolation to find that altho I have lost my Fortune, I still retain what is infinitely more valuable, my Character is unimpeached. This gives me firm hopes of being able very soon to go on again in a [smug?] business entirely under my own direction, for I am determined never to put it in the power of any man to bring me to ruin again.

It is impossible for me to say how the business of D. & B. will be settled. The Creditors have been proposing to accept of a composition, and to give time for collecting our debts, But in whatever way it is settled, I mean in future to do business on my own account. And being perswaded that you and my other Friends in Virga. are incapable of deserting me in my distress, I must request the favour of you to consign your Tobacco this year to Mr. John Younger, He is one of our Clerks who has been with us ever since the commencement of our Partnership, He will receive it for me in Trust, but you may depend that I will have the sole disposal of it, and the money received for it will be at yours. It gives me pain however to mention, that you will not trust to Mr. James Brown for shipping your Tobacco to me, for since I left the Country he has shewn a decided preference to Mr. Burton, notwithstanding all my kindness to him. I know Brown's disposition so well, that I have no doubt of his doing every thing he can to hurt my Interest, but he will find it is too strongly founded to be shaken by his ingratitude. I have a Nephew living in Richmond, but he is too young to take the charge of my business. He is a very fine young man, when he gets more experience, and a few more years, he will do very well. Capt. Ay. Singleton is a man in whose honour and integrity I have always had the most unbounded Confidence. To him I have written freely, and I am much mistaken if he will not do every thing he can to serve me. If you will have the goodness to order your Tobacco to be delivered to him, I am confident he will take the trouble of shipping it to me. You will very much oblige me by mentioning me to the notice of your Friends.

I will send you a letter from D. & B. by this same opportunity of Mr. Marshall, in which you will find an Invoice of the few Books you ordered sometime ago. That Blackguard Ramsden has disapointed me in not having gotten ready the Telescope, which he faithfully promised would be ready two months ago. I must get one from Dolland. A mathematical Instrument maker in Holborne came to me and produced a letter from you, ordering some thing in his line and which you had desired him to call upon me for payment. He accordingly went to the Counting House, where he was told by the Clerks, that in our situation the money would not be paid, but they gave him my direction and desired him to call upon me. He accordingly did so, when I ordered him to get the thing ready and that I would pay the money for it, which I have borrowed to prevent your being disapointed. I expect the bill will be presented to morrow. If it is, I shall inclose it herein. I remain with great consideration Dear Sir Your Faithful & obd. Sert

A DONALD

RC (MHi); at foot of text: "Thos. Jefferson Esqr."; endorsed by TJ as received 6 May 1793 and so recorded in SJL.

Donald & Burton's LETTER to TJ of 9 Mch. 1793, recorded in SJL as received from London on 6 May 1793, has not been found, but for the INVOICE see TJ to John Wayles Eppes, 12 May 1793, and note. The TELESCOPE probably accompanied Donald's letter of 30 Aug. 1793,

which has not been found; next to the SJL entry for that letter, which was received from London on 12 Nov. 1793, TJ wrote "telescope." The MATHEMATICAL INSTRUMENT MAKER IN HOLBORNE was either William or Samuel Jones (William & Samuel Jones to TJ, 9 Mch. 1793). In 1795 TJ had still not received the bill for the orrery he purchased from them or for the telescope Donald sent (TJ to Donald, 30 May 1795).

To Martha Jefferson Randolph

MY DEAR DAUGHTER   Philadelphia Mar. 10. 1793.

Your letters of the 20th. and 27th. Feb. as well as Mr. Randolph's of the same dates, came to hand only yesterday. By this I percieve that your post must be under bad regulation indeed. I am sorry to learn that your garden is dismantled, and yourself thereby discoraged from attention to it. I beg that Mr. Randolph will employ the whole force, he has been so kind as to direct, in repairing the inclosure in preference to every other work I had proposed. Nothing can be placed in competition with the loss of the produce of the garden during the season, either for health or comfort, and my own are less dear and desireable to me than the health and comfort of yourself, Mr. Randolph and the little ones. I had hoped that from the same resources your supplies of wood in the winter would not have failed. I again repeat it that I wish every other object to be considered as secondary in my mind to your accomodation and insist that Mr. Randolph make the freest use of the people under his direction for his and your convenience in the first place. When I shall see you I cannot say: but my heart and thoughts are all with you till I do. I have given up my house here, and taken a small one in the country on the banks of the Schuylkill to serve me while I stay. We are packing all our superfluous furniture and shall be sending it by water to Richmond when the season becomes favorable. My books too, except a very few, will be packed and go with the other things, so that I shall put it out of my own power to return to the city again to keep house, and it would be impossible to carry on business in the winter at a country residence. Tho' this points out an ultimate term of stay here, yet my mind is looking to a much shorter one if the circumstances will permit it which broke in on my first resolution. Indeed I have it much at heart to be at home in time to run up the part of the house the latter part of the summer and fall which I had proposed to do in the spring. Maria is well. Whether she writes or no to-day I know not. My best affections to Mr. Randolph; cherish your little ones for me, for I feel the same love for them as I did for yourself when of their age, and continue to me your own love which I feel to be the best solace remaining to me in this world. Adieu my dear your's affectionately   TH: JEFFERSON

RC (NNP); at foot of first page: "Mrs. Randolph"; endorsed by Martha Jefferson Randolph. PrC (MHi). Tr (ViU: Edgehill-Randolph Papers); 19th-century copy.

Martha Jefferson Randolph's letter to TJ of 20 Feb. 1793, recorded in SJL as received 9 Mch. 1793, has not been found.

Report on Acts of Congress

The Secretary of state, according to the requisition of the President of the US. of the 8th. instant has examined the laws passed during the late session of Congress and
Reports
That none of those laws relate to, or require the immediate or special agency of the President, except the 'Act regulating foreign coins and for other purposes,' (a copy of which is hereto annexed) whereupon it would be proper to give in charge to the Director of the Mint to take measures for collecting samples of foreign coins, issued in the year 1792, of the species which usually circulate within the United States, to examine by assays at the Mint whether the same are conformable to the respective standards required, and to report the result, that the same may be made known by proclamation.

Th: Jefferson
Mar. 10. 1793.[1]

RC (DNA: RG 59, MLR); endorsed by Tobias Lear. PrC (DLC); partially overwritten in a later hand. FC (Lb in DNA: RG 59, SDR). Tr (Lb in same, SDC). Entry in SJPL: "Th:J. to G.W. on laws requiring his agency." Enclosure: *An Act regulating Foreign Coins, and for other purposes* [Philadelphia, 1793], dated 9 Feb. 1793, specifying the rates at which certain European gold and silver coins were to be legal tender effective 1 July 1793, and providing that foreign coins issued after 1 Jan. 1792 were to become legal tender only after "samples thereof shall have been found, by assay, at the Mint of the United States, to be conformable to the respective standards required, and proclamation thereof shall have been made by the President of the United States" (printed act in same, MLR).

On this day TJ submitted this report to the President, who on the following day directed Attorney General Edmund Randolph to "examine the laws & report respectg. them" (Washington, *Journal*, 84).

[1] Last digit reworked by TJ from "2."

Report on Boundaries with the Western Indians

The Secretary of state, according to instructions received from the President of the US.
Reports
That, for the information of the Commissioners appointed to treat with the Western Indians, he has examined the several treaties entered into with them, subsequent to the declaration of Independance, and relating to the lands between the Ohio and lakes; and also the extent of the grants, reservations, and appropria-

tions of the same lands, made either by the United States, or by individual states, within the same period, and finds that the lands obtained by the said treaties and not so granted, reserved, or appropriated, are bounded by the following lines, to wit,

NORTHWARDLY, by a line running, from the fork of the Tuscarora's branch of the Muskingum, at the crossing place above Fort Laurence, Westwardly (towards the portage of the Big Miami) to the main branch of that river, then down the Miami to the fork of that river next below the old fort which was taken by the French in 1752. Thence due West to the river de la Panse, and down that river to the Wabash: which lines were established with the Wiandots, Delawares, Chippawas, and Ottawas by the treaty of fort Mc.Intosh, and with the Shawanese by that of the Great Miami.

WESTWARDLY, by the bounds of the Wabash Indians:

EASTWARDLY, by the MILLION of acres appropriated to Military claimants by the resolution of Congress of Oct. 22. 1787. and lying in the angle between the VIIth. range of townships counted Westwardly from the Pensylvania boundary, and the Xth. range counted from the Ohio Northwardly along the said VIIth. which Million of acres may perhaps extend Westwardly so as to comprehend the XIIth. range of townships, counted in that direction from the Pensylvania boundary: under which view, the said XIIth. range may be assumed for the EASTERN boundary of the territory now under consideration, from the said Xth. range to the INDIAN line.

SOUTHWARDLY, by the Northern boundary of the said Xth. range of townships to the Sioto river, and along the said river to what shall be the Northern limit of the appropriations for the Virginia line: (which two last lines are those of the lands granted to the SIOTO company): thence along what shall be the Northern limit of the said appropriations of the VIRGINIA LINE to the Little Miami, and along the same to what shall be the Northern limit of one million of acres of land purchased by John C. Symmes: thence due West along the said Northern limit of the said JOHN C. SYMMES to the Great Miami, and down the same to it's mouth: then along the Ohio to General Clarke's

lands, and round the said lands to the Ohio again, and down the same to the Wabash or the lands of the Indians inhabiting it. Which several lines are delineated on the copy of Hutchins's map accompanying this report; the dotted parts of the delineation denoting that they are conjectural. And it is further necessary to apprize the Commissioners that, tho' the points at which these several lines touch the Ohio are taken from actual surveys, yet the country included by the said lines, not being laid down from actual survey, their lengths and intersections with each other and with the watercourses, as appearing in the map, are not at all to be relied on.   No notice is here taken of the lands at the mouth of the Ohio appropriated for military bounties by the same resolution of Congress of Oct. 22. 1787. nor of the settlements of Cahokia, Kaskaskia, Post Vincennes &c. because these can concern no Indians but those of the Illinois and Wabash, whose interests should be transacted with themselves separately,[1] and not be permitted to be placed under the patronage of the Western Indians.   TH: JEFFERSON
Mar. 10. 1793.

PrC (DLC); partially overwritten in a later hand. FC (Lb in DNA: RG 59, SDR). Entry in SJPL: "Report on our boundary with Northern Indians."

Washington must have requested this report, which TJ submitted to him this day, at or after the 25 Feb. 1793 meeting of the Cabinet, when it was decided that such lands west of the Ohio as had previously been obtained from the Indians and were not yet GRANTED, RESERVED, OR APPROPRIATED could possibly be deeded back to them in exchange for peace (Cabinet Opinions on Indian Affairs, 25 Feb. 1793; Notes on Cabinet Opinions, 26 Feb. 1793; Washington, *Journal*, 84). In preparing the report TJ drew on his Report on Public Lands, 8 Nov. 1791, parts of which he followed verbatim. For his efforts to obtain additional information, see TJ to George Clinton, 17 Feb. 1793; Tench Coxe to TJ, 7, 8 Mch. 1793; TJ to Coxe, 8 Mch. 1793. This

report was among the papers Washington sent to the Cabinet, which he directed to meet during his absence from the capital and draft for his consideration instructions for the American commissioners to the Lower Sandusky peace conference with the Western Indians (Washington, *Journal*, 106; Washington to the Cabinet, 21 Mch. 1793, and note). HUTCHINS'S MAP: Thomas Hutchins, *A New Map of the Western Parts of Virginia, Pennsylvania, Maryland and North Carolina* (London, 1778). The marked copy of this map has not been found, but it was enclosed with Henry Knox's 26 Apr. 1793 instructions to the Indian commissioners, who were ordered not to agree to relinquish any lands which the map indicated had already been granted by the United States (ASP, *Indian Affairs*, I, 340-2; Washington to the Cabinet, 17 Feb. 1793, and enclosure).

[1] Word interlined.

To Dugald Stewart

DEAR SIR   Philadelphia Mar. 10. 1793.

I am to acknolege the receipt of your favor of Oct. 1. and of the valuable present which accompanied it. I reserve to myself the pleasure of perusing it when I shall be in a situation to do it without interruption from public business, which situation I place at no great distance. The subject of your book is interesting, and I am sure I shall find the manner of treating it both interesting and instructive.—In forwarding to you the inclosed diploma I have to explain the circumstances which have so long kept it here. It was ordered on the day of it's date. I happened to go into the country soon afterwards, and the diploma, when made out, was laid by to be delivered to me on my return in order to be forwarded to you. When I came back, the Secretaries happened not to recollect it, and I, taking for granted it had been transmitted during my absence, made no particular enquiry, till recieving your letter and finding no mention of it, I asked information on the subject, when it turned out to be as I have explained. I must beg your excuse of us all, and acceptance of my sincere satisfaction on the honor done our roll by the addition of your name to it.—Our distance is great, but my sense of your worth and talents, may induce me, when I become less occupied, as I contemplate soon to be, to seek sometimes occasions of renewing assurances of the great & sincere esteem with which I am Dear Sir your most obedt. & most humble servt   TH: JEFFERSON

PrC (DLC); at foot of text: "Mr. Dugald Stewart." Tr (DLC); 19th-century copy.

The INCLOSED DIPLOMA probably certified Stewart's election to membership in the American Philosophical Society, which had taken place on 21 Oct. 1791 (APS, *Proceedings*, XXII, pt. 3 [1885], 198).

From George Washington

SIR   Sunday March 10th: 1793

If, upon a due consideration of the letter from the Secretary of the N.W. Territory to Govr. St. Clair, which you sent to me yesterday, and is herewith returned, you shall be of opinion that my official interference is necessary on the subject of that letter, I must request that you will report to me wherein such interference may be necessary—as well as the authority under which the President may exercise it.

But I confess to you, that the long absence of the Governor, as well as of some of the Judges, from the Territory, appears to me, if not the cause of producing¹ the irregularities complained of by the Secretary, to be a great means of encouraging a spirit of riot and disorder, by relaxing the energy of the laws.² This, therefore, is an additional reason for me to wish that the Governor may be pressed to repair to the Territory without delay—And unless he does, I shall be under the disagreeable necessity of issuing a peremptory Order for that purpose.³

I wish to be informed whether Judge Turner has set out for the Territory.

I think it would be best for you to consult with the Atty. Genl. to determine whether transcripts of the treaties made with the Indians under the State Government of N. York should be sent for or not.

Go: WASHINGTON

RC (DLC); in the hand of Tobias Lear, signed by Washington; at foot of text: "The Secretary of State"; endorsed by TJ: "Lear Tobias. recd. Mar. 10. 93." Dft (DNA: RG 59, MLR); in Lear's hand; contains emendations, the most significant of which are noted below. FC (Lb in same, SDC). Recorded in SJPL. For the enclosure, see note to TJ to Washington, 9 Mch. 1793.

On 12 Mch. 1793 TJ sent Washington a brief note reporting that he had "en-

quired and finds that Judge Turner is not yet gone from this city" (RC in same, MLR, addressed: "The President of the US.," endorsed by Tobias Lear; Tr in Lb in same, SDC; not recorded in SJL).

¹ Word interlined in Dft.
² Word interlined in Dft in place of "government."
³ In the Dft Lear substituted this sentence for an inchoate formulation that he lined through heavily.

From Gaetano Drago di Domenico

Genoa, 11 Mch. 1793. He has been informed by Joseph Ravara, the Genoese consul to the United States, that TJ submitted to Congress his petition to be appointed American consul at Genoa, which was transmitted by his friend James Maury, the American consul at Liverpool. He is grateful and hopes TJ will support his candidacy. The courts of Austria, Russia, Sweden, and Denmark have often borrowed from monied Genoese, and Congress could easily do the same, especially with the aid of a zealous agent like himself. France's declaration of war on Britain, Spain, and Holland has idled their ships, and Holland suffers doubly by the 13 Feb. declaration of war on her by the Algerines. Now is the time for the American flag to flourish in the Mediterranean and capture the bulk of that trade; if the United States could conclude a treaty with the Barbary regencies by virtue of an annual donation, its free navigation would produce "immense and incalculable" advantages. Wheat and flour sent up the Mediterranean will fetch "an amazing Price," since the last corn crop in Sicily failed and those of the Levant, Venice, and the Papal States were so poor that they prohibited its exportation. France also needs corn and faces the threat of a famine that is likely to continue as long as her agriculture continues to be neglected during the upheavals in that republic. Exports of corn to Marseilles have kept the price excessively high in Genoa, where wheat sells for 68 shillings sterling per English quarter. France's naval forces in the Mediterranean consist of forty sail, sixteen of them ships of the line commanded by Vice Admiral Truguet, who with sixty transports and 10,000 troops has been attacking Sardinia for two months with little apparent success. The latest reports from that quarter state that Truguet has given up the siege after bombarding Cagliari and being repulsed several times in attempts to land, and that he has lost two ships of the line driven ashore in a gale, one of which was burned by the Sardinians and the other stripped by the French before they abandoned it. The French seem determined to capture Turin once the roads become passable this spring. This will cost them thousands of men if the Piedmontese and German auxiliaries defend the fortresses of Brunetta and Saorgio, the only roads the French can take into the Piedmont. The French have entered Holland, where it is reported that Dumouriez has taken two small forts on the Meuse and that besieged Maestricht is expected to surrender soon. Genoa's early declaration of neutrality has been well received by both sides and enables her to enjoy tranquility and a lively commerce that he hopes will continue unhindered. He apologizes for the length of this letter and offers to report monthly if his dispatches are found to be useful, especially now that the imminent arrival of a powerful British fleet under Lord Hood is likely to make the Mediterranean an interesting theater. Large numbers of French privateers based in Marseilles infest the Mediterranean and have already captured one Dutch and four English trading vessels.

Dupl (DLC: Washington Papers, Applications for Office); 6 p.; at head of text: "Copy"; at foot of text: "The Honorable Thomas Jefferson Minister of State of the Thirteen United Provinces of America Philadelphia"; endorsed by TJ as received 17 May 1793 and so recorded in SJL. Tripl (same); unsigned and dated 25 Mch. 1793; at head of text: "Copy"; enclosed in Drago di Domenico to TJ, 13 July 1793, and recorded in SJL as received 24 Oct. 1793.

Drago di Domenico's petition to

Congress of 30 Apr. 1792 was enclosed in James Maury's letter to TJ of 19 Sep. 1792, but there is no evidence it was ever submitted to Congress. Ravara may have been referring to an earlier Drago petition concerning a plan for a truce among the United States, Algiers, and Tunis, which was presented to Congress in January 1790. TJ had been sent copies of both petitions, but no evidence has been found of his agency in presenting the earlier one to Congress (Drago di Domenico to TJ, 4 May, 22 June 1789; JS, I, 106, 108; JHR, I, 147).

To Henry Lee

SIR   Philadelphia Mar. 11. 1793.

On receipt of the letter with which you were pleased to honor me on the subject of the unsettled boundary between Virginia and the SouthWestern territory, I laid it before the President, who communicated it to Congress. A committee was thereupon appointed by the house of representatives who reported a proposition for authorising the President with the concurrence of the states of Virginia and Kentuckey, to have the line extended, which proposition was passed by that house, but rejected by the Senate. Their motives for the rejection not being expressed, I can only add from private information that it was observed that the SouthWestern territory would be shortly entitled to a legislature of it's own, and that it would be more just to give them an opportunity of acting for themselves, and also to leave the expence of the settlement to be borne by the states interested. I inclose you a copy of the bill passed by the Representatives, and have the honor to be with great esteem and respect, your Excellency's Most obedient & most humble servt   TH: JEFFERSON

RC (Vi: Executive Papers); addressed: "His Excellency Governor Lee Richmond"; franked and postmarked. PrC (DLC). FC (Lb in DNA: RG 59, DL). For the enclosure, see note to Benjamin Hawkins to TJ, 14 Feb. 1793.

TJ was responding to Lee's LETTER of 24 Oct. 1792. For more on the boundary dispute in question, see William Blount to TJ, 26 Dec. 1791, and note.

Opinion on Compensation to the Commissioners of the Federal District

Qu. 1? What sacrifice may be made to retain Mr. Johnson in the office of Commissioner for the federal territory?
Answ. for such an object it is worth while to give up the plan of an allowance per diem, to give, instead of that, a sum in gross, and to extend that sum to 500. Dollars per annum, and expences; the latter to be rendered in account.

If Mr. Johnson persists in resigning, as it is evident Dr. Stewart will not continue even for the above allowance, and Mr. Carrol does not appear to make any conditions, the President will be free as to Mr. Carrol and two new associates to adhere to the allowance per diem already proposed, or to substitute a sum in gross.

Qu. 2? may new commissioners be chosen in the town?
Answ. it is strongly desireable that the Commissioners should not be of the town, nor interested in it; and this objection is thought a counterpoise for a sensible difference in talents. But if persons of adequate talents and qualifications cannot be found in the country, it

will be better to take them from the town, than to appoint men of inadequate talents from the country.

Qu. 3 How compensate them?

Answ. if they come from the country, the per diem allowance is thought best. If from the town, a sum in gross will be best, and this might be as far as 300. D. a year, and no allowance for expences: if partly from the town and partly from the country, then 300. Dol. a year to the former, and the same with an allowance of expences to the latter.

Mr. Madison, Mr. Randolph and Th: Jefferson having consulted together on the preceding questions, with some shades of difference of opinion in the beginning, concurred ultimately and unanimously in the above answers. TH: JEFFERSON

Mar. 11. 1793.

PrC (DLC); partially overwritten in a later hand. Entry in SJPL: "opns on compensns to Commrs. of Fedl. territory."

Congress had not provided for payment to the Commissioners of the Federal District, and they had served without compensation since their initial appointment in January 1791. On 31 Jan. 1793 President Washington offered each of the Commissioners $1,000 plus expenses for past services and, beginning 1 Jan. 1793, $6 for each day of actual service plus a mileage allowance, a rate of compensation similar to that received by Congressmen. Evidently the Commissioners regarded both proposals as inadequate, and for this and other reasons Thomas Johnson and David Stuart announced their intention to resign. Washington had solicited the opinion of TJ, James Madison, and Edmund Ran-

dolph on 9 Mch. 1793, and TJ sent the above memorandum to the President three days later. The use Washington made of it is unclear. Johnson and Stuart both remained adamant about stepping down, although in June 1794 the President was still trying to persuade Johnson to remain in his post, and they seem to have been paid by the day for attendance until they were replaced in August and September 1794. Their successors were paid $1,600 a year, an increase justified by the stipulation that they live in or near the Federal District and devote enough time to the work to make a Superintendent unnecessary (Fitzpatrick, *Writings*, XXXII, 323-4, 326, XXXIII, 415-16, 481-2; Washington, *Journal*, 85; Washington to TJ, 9 Mch. 1793; payments to Stuart and Johnson in DNA: RG 42, PC, 17 Sep., 14 Oct. 1794; Bryan, *National Capital*, I, 237).

From Benjamin Smith Barton

Tuesday-morning, 12th. [Mch. 1793]

SIR   No 119. Third-Street, between Walnut & Spruce Streets.

It is not without a great degree of pain, that I write to you on the subject of this letter. You will, however, I hope, pardon the liberty which I take, when I assure you that nothing but a very urgent case would permit me to do it. I am already indebted to you for your liberal kindness shewn to me, on various occasions. Your attention to me now, as at former times, I shall ever remember, with a large share of gratitude. The loan of Sixty-Five Dollars will relieve me from much anxiety of mind. This sum as well as that which I formerly received of you, I shall punctually pay to you, at the time I have mentioned, in the enclosed note. Nothing shall prevent me from doing it. Should you not comply with my request, I still hope, you will pardon me, and put no unfavourable construction on my[1] conduct. I am, Sir, with great respect, Your humble and much obliged servant, &c.

BENJN. S. BARTON

RC (MHi); partially dated; endorsed by TJ as received 12 Mch. 1793. Enclosure not found.

TJ seems not to have honored this request. His accounts record no such loan, and when Barton offered in 1796 to repay his debt to TJ he mentioned only the $60 loan FORMERLY RECEIVED from him on 19 Dec. 1792 (Barton to TJ, 1 Aug., 25 Oct. 1796; TJ to Barton, 10 Oct. 1796; MB, 19 Dec. 1792).

[1] Barton here canceled "request."

To Moses Cox

Mar. 12. 1793.

Th: Jefferson presents his compliments to Mr. Cox and will take[1] his house on the terms mentioned by his son, who if he could accompany Th:J. there at any time would oblige him. Th:J. would wish to commence at the beginning of April, at which time he would remove there.

PrC (DLC). Tr (ViU: Edgehill-Randolph Papers); 19th-century copy.

Sending most of his furniture to Virginia, TJ early in April moved from the Market Street residence owned by Thomas Leiper to the small summer HOUSE near Gray's Ferry on the east bank of the Schuylkill River that he leased from Cox until his temporary return to Monticello in September (MB, 9 Apr., 17 Sep. 1793; TJ to Francis Eppes, 7 Apr. 1793; TJ to Leiper, 11 Apr. 1793; TJ to Martha Jefferson Randolph, 7 July 1793; TJ to Cox, 17 Sep. 1793).

[1] TJ originally wrote "and takes" before altering the phrase to read as above.

From Delamotte

Havre, 12 Mch. 1793. This letter will be brought by the *Euphrasia*, Captain William McFaden of Philadelphia, which arrived here last October from New Orleans under the Spanish flag as *L'Espérance.* After disposing of his cargo and completing his business with the Spanish consul, McFaden came to him claiming to be American and presenting a ship's register for the *Euphrasia* dated Philadelphia, 2 Jan. 1792, which identifies McFaden as sole owner and the ship as one of two decks, three masts, and 195¾ tons. After being informed by McFaden of his wish to load the ship for New York under the American flag, he consulted the Spanish consul, who had no evidence that it was Spanish and did not object. He then wrote Gouverneur Morris, who replied that even if the captain had committed fraud, it was better to give him the benefit of his register than to stop him, provided he explained himself to TJ, who can take any appropriate action.

RC (DNA: RG 59, CD); 2 p.; in French; in a clerk's hand, signed by Delamotte; at foot of first page: "Mr. le Secretaire d'État des E.U. à Philadelphie"; endorsed by TJ as received 8 May 1793 and so recorded in SJL.

From Joseph Fay

DEAR SIR   Bennington 12th March 1793
Inclosed you will receive my latest Canada papers, by which you observe their publications begin to be more liberal, and the spirit of Liberty which rages so Vehemently in Urope begins to kindle in Canada.

I fear I am trobling you to often without furnishing any new information, as I am not informed wheather you receive the Canada papers from any other quarter or not. I hope before this you have received my letter on the Subject of Canada Lands, of which my friend in that Country writes me favourably, who I have directed not to make public use of your Name until I obtain your permission. I am Sir with much Esteem your friend and Servant   JOSEPH FAY

RC (MHi); at foot of text: "Mr. Jefferson"; endorsed by TJ as received 19 Mch. 1793 and so recorded in SJL. Enclosed in TJ to George Washington, 20 Mch. 1793.

Fay had raised THE SUBJECT OF CANADA LANDS in his letter to TJ of 26 Feb. 1793.

To Horatio Gates

DEAR GENERAL   Philadelphia Mar. 12. 1793
During the invasion of Virginia in 1780. and 1781. nearly the whole of the public records of that state were destroyed by the British. The least valuable part of these happens to be the most interesting to

me, I mean the letters I had occasion to write to the characters with whom my office in the Executive brought me into correspondence. I am endeavoring to recover copies of my letters from the hands to whom they were addressed, and have been happy to find this more practicable than I had apprehended. While you commanded in the South I had occasion to write to you sometimes on the subject of our proceedings. If you happen to have preserved these letters, you will particularly oblige me by trusting me with them till I can have them copied, when the originals shall be returned. If you could repose the same confidence in me as to the letters you addressed to me, it would increase the obligation. The whole shall be sacredly returned. I have been the more disposed to trouble you on this occasion as it furnishes me a pretext of recalling myself to your recollection, and an opportunity of renewing to you assurances of the sincere esteem & respect with which I have the honor to be Dear General your sincere friend & servt   TH: JEFFERSON

RC (NHi: Gates Papers); at foot of text: "Majr. Genl. Gates"; endorsed by Gates. PrC (DLC).   For the results of TJ's request, see note to Gates to TJ, [19 July 1780].

To George Washington Greene

DEAR SIR   Philadelphia Mar. 12. 1793.

I took occasion by young Mr. Peale, who was going to Georgia, to congratulate you on your return to your native country. I now take the liberty of troubling you on a subject in which I feel an interest. During the invasion of Virginia in the years 1780. and 1781. the greater part of the records of that state were burnt by the British. Among these were all the proceedings of the Executive during the period that I was in that administration. I have been since endeavoring to collect such parts of my correspondence as might be found in the hands to which it was addressed, and have been successful in some important parts. Your father commanded in the South at that time, and I had occasion to address frequent letters to him. If you can find these among his papers, and will be so good either as to trust me with the originals, to be returned after I shall have taken copies, or which might be safer, to have copies taken there and forwarded to me, the expence of which I will gladly replace, it would lay me under singular obligation. I would add a request for copies of his letters to me, were it not that this would be adding too much to the trouble. I content myself therefore with asking those of my own letters, and as speedily as you can make it convenient to have them taken. General Wadsworth gave me a hope that you would make choice of the college of Williamsburg for the scene of your future study. If I can render you any service there, in that state, or any where else, I shall do it with the pleasure which it will give me on every occasion to afford you proofs of the sincere esteem & attachment with which I am Dear Sir Your friend & servt

TH: JEFFERSON

PrC (DLC); at foot of first page: "Mr. Greene." Tr (DLC); 19th-century copy.

Greene died before he received this let-

ter. The family spokesman who answered it indicated that TJ's request would be honored, but evidently it never was (Phineas Miller to TJ, 3 May 1793).

To Benjamin Joy

SIR   Philadelphia Mar. 12. 1793.

I herein inclose you a blank bond to be executed and returned to my office. The gentlemen named as sureties in your letter of Jan. 20. will be entirely sufficient. I am sensible of the advantages to our seamen which might result from the regulations mentioned in your letter, and the reasons for augmenting the allowance for sick seamen in so distant and dear a country. But the law having provided no exceptions from the general rule, and the duties of my office being bound up by the precepts of the law, I have no authority to make any augmentation whatever.

As a very general war appears to be gathering in Europe I have to desire your utmost vigilance in protecting our vessels in the rights of neutrality, and in preventing the usurpation of our flag by the vessels of other nations; an usurpation which tends to commit us with the belligerant powers, to provoke rigorous examinations of the vessels truly ours in order to distinguish them from Counterfeits, and to take business from us.—You will receive herewith a copy of the laws of the US. I am with great regard, Sir, your most obedt. humble servt

TH: JEFFERSON

P.S. April 12. I have just received your letter enclosing a Bond, which being approved, the Blank one mentioned in this is not sent.
I also enclose copy of a Circular letter intended to serve as a standing instruction to our Consuls.

[365]

PrC (DLC); at foot of text: "Mr. B. Joy"; lacks postscript. FC (DLC); in the hand of George Taylor, Jr.; consists of postscript only. FC (Lb in DNA: RG 59, DCI); includes postscript. Recorded in SJPL in clerk's hand under dates of 12 and 14 Mch. 1793. Enclosure: Circular to American Consuls, 26 Aug. 1790.

On 26 Mch. 1793, not having received an answer to his letter of 20 Jan. 1793 and concluding that the sureties he named there were sufficient, Joy wrote TJ from Boston a LETTER ENCLOSING A BOND guar-anteed by them and asking him to have it "filled in by the Office of the Secretary of the Treasury" (RC in DNA: RG 59, CD; at foot of text: "Thos Jefferson Esqr Secretary of State"; endorsed by TJ as received 8 Apr. 1793 and so recorded in SJL). The bond itself, dated 22 Mch. 1793 and signed by Joy, John C. Jones, Joseph Russell, Jr., John Joy, Jr., and Christopher Gore, was endorsed as "approved" and signed by TJ (MS in DNA: RG 39, Records of the Bureau of Accounts, Surety Bonds).

To James Monroe

Mar. 12. 1793.

The following suits were put into the hands of Mr. N. Pope in 1791. to wit

		£	s	d
against Lewis & Woodson on bond. principal & interest to Sep. 30. 1791. were		192–12–9$\frac{1}{2}$		
against Woodson on his Note. do. to do.		7–14–2		
against Lewis on Account of rent. balance & interest to Sep. 30. 1791		86– 7–0$\frac{1}{2}$		
		286–14–0		

Out of these monies when recovered the following orders were given

		£	
in favr. of Donald, Scott & co. principal & int. to Sep. 30. 91.	139– 0–0		
of Wm. & James Donald. do. to do.	38–13–6	177–13–6	
left a balance to be received of		109– 0–6	

An order for this balance was given in favor of Dobson: but as his departure from the country required prompter payment, prompter resources were resorted to for him, of which I advised Mr. Pope by letter of Sep. 25. 92. so as to leave this balance free.

Mr. Pope by letter of Jan. 3. 93. informs me he has judgments against Lewis and Woodson and execution, which has been replevied: and that the suits against Lewis had been ready for trial, but delayed by the inability of Colo. N. Lewis to attend as a witness: but that he should have judgments the next term. The balances with interest will now be upwards of £120.

Mr. N. Pope, always giving priority to the orders in favor of Donald, Scott & co. and Wm. & James Donald, is desired to pay the residue of the money he may receive on the above accounts (clear of costs) to Colo. Monroe or order, or such portion of the residue as Colo. Monroe shall apply for to be disposed of for my use.   TH: JEFFERSON

P.S. No notice is taken above of the suit ordered against Lewis and Ware, because it was countermanded.

RC (NN); endorsed by Monroe. PrC (DLC); badly faded; at foot of text in ink: "Monroe James." Tr (ViU: Edgehill-Randolph Papers); undated 19th-century copy with gaps and errors in transcription. Notation in SJL: "order on Pope."

Nathaniel Pope's LETTER OF JAN. 3. 93, recorded in SJL as received 15 Jan. 1793, has not been found. Sixteen letters between Pope and TJ recorded in SJL as written between 17 Mch. 1794 and 1 June 1797 are also missing.

To Gouverneur Morris

DEAR SIR   Philadelphia. Mar. 12. 1793.[1]

Your Nos. 8. to 13. inclusive have been duly received. I am sensible that your situation must have been difficult during the transition from the late form of government to the reestablishment of some other legitimate authority, and that you may have been at a loss to determine with whom business might be done. Nevertheless when principles are well understood, their application is less embarrassing. We surely cannot deny to any nation that right whereon our own government is founded, that every one may govern itself according to whatever form it pleases, and change these forms at it's own will: and that it may transact it's business with foreign nations through whatever organ it thinks proper, whether king, convention, assembly, committee, president or any thing else it may chuse. The will of the nation is the only thing essential to be regarded. On the dissolution of the late constitution in France, by removing so integral a part of it as the king, the National assembly, to whom a part only of the public authority had been delegated, appear to have considered themselves as incompetent to transact the affairs of the nation legitimately. They invited their fellow citizens therefore to appoint a national convention. In conformity with this their idea of the defective state of the national authority, you were desired from hence[2] to suspend further payments of our debt to France till new orders, with an assurance however[3] to the acting power that the suspension should not be continued a moment longer than should be necessary for us to see the reestablishment of some person or body of persons authorized to receive paiment and give us a good acquittal; (if you should find it

[367]

necessary to give any assurance or explanation at all.) In the mean time we went on paying up the four millions of livres which had been destined by the last constituted authorities to the relief of St. Domingo. Before this was compleated we received information that a National assembly had met, with full powers to transact the affairs of the nation, and soon afterwards the Minister of France here presented an application for three millions of livres to be laid out in provisions to be sent to France. Urged by the strongest attachments to that country, and thinking it even providential that monies lent to us in distress could be repaid under like circumstances, we had no hesitation to comply with the application, and arrangements are accordingly taken for furnishing this sum at epochs accomodated to the demand and our means of paying it. We suppose this will rather overpay the instalments and interest due on[4] the loans of 18. 6. and 10. millions to the end of 1792.:[5] and we shall certainly use our utmost endeavors to make punctual payments of the instalments and interest hereafter becoming exigible, and to omit no opportunity of convincing that nation how cordially we wish to serve them. Mutual good offices, mutual affection and similar principles of government seem to destine the two nations for the most intimate communion: and I cannot too much press it on you to improve every opportunity which may occur in the changeable scenes which are passing, and to seize them as they occur, for placing our commerce with that nation and it's dependancies, on the freest and the most encouraging footing possible.

Besides what we have furnished publicly for the relief of St. Domingo, individual merchants of the U.S. have carried considerable supplies thither, which have been sometimes purchased sometimes taken by force, and bills given by the administration of the colony on the minister here, which have been protested for want of funds. We have no doubt that justice will be done to these our citizens, and that without a delay which would be ruinous to them. We wish authority to be given to the minister of France here to pay the just demands of our citizens out of the monies he may recieve from us.

During the fluctuating state of the Assignats of France, I must ask the favor of you to inform me in every letter of the rate of exchange between them and coin, this being necessary for the regulation of our customhouses.

Congress closed it's session on the 2d. instant. You will see their acts in the newspapers forwarded to you, and the body of them shall be sent as soon as the 8vo. edition is printed. We are to hold a treaty with the Western Indians in the ensuing month of May, but not under very hopeful auspices.

You will perceive by the newspapers a remarkeable fall in the price of our public paper. This is owing chiefly to the extraordinary demand for the produce of our country, and a temporary scarcity of cash to purchase it. The merchants holding public paper are obliged to part with it at any price to raise money.

The following appointment of Consuls has taken place. Nathanl. Cutting for Havre, Edward Fox for Falmouth, Joseph Yznardi for Cadiz, Robert Montgomery for Alicant, John Parish for Hamburg, Henry Cooper for Santa Cruz, Matthew Clarkson for St. Eustatius, Benjamin Hamnell Philips for Curaçoa, Samuel Cooper Johonnet for Demarara, Michael Murphy for Malaga, and James Greenleaf for Amsterdam.

I sent you by the way of London a dozen plans of the city of Washington in the Federal territory, hoping you would have them displayed to public view where they would be most seen by those descriptions of men worthy and likely to be attracted to it. Paris, Lyons, Rouen, and the seaport towns of Havre, Nantes, Bordeaux and Marseilles would be proper places to send some of them to.　　　　I trust to Mr. Taylor to forward you the newspapers by every direct occasion to France. These are rare at all times and especially in the winter: and to send them thro' England would cost too much in postage. To these circumstances as well, probably as to some miscarriages, you must ascribe the length of interval sometimes experienced in the receipt of your papers.—I have the honor to be with great esteem & respect, Dear Sir, your most obedt. & most humble servt　　　　　　　　Th: Jefferson

RC (NNC: Gouverneur Morris Papers); with altered date and other emendations, the most significant of which are noted below; addressed: "Monsieur Morris Ministre Plenipotentiaire des E.U. d'Amerique à Paris"; endorsed by Morris. PrC (DLC). FC (Lb in DNA: RG 59, DCI). Enclosure: Jean Baptiste Ternant to TJ, 7 Jan. 1793, and Enclosure No. 1.

This letter, which TJ submitted to Washington this day and received back the day after, authorized the resumption of payments on the American debt to France, which had been suspended since October 1792 because of the uncertainties attendant upon the overthrow of the French monarchy (see TJ to Morris, 15 Oct., 7 Nov. 1792; Washington, *Journal*, 85-6, 88). TJ had drafted a similar message to Morris on 30 Dec. 1792, but withheld it, choosing instead to use his letter

to Thomas Pinckney of the same date to obtain Washington's explicit approval of the policy of de facto diplomatic recognition (TJ to Morris, 30 Dec. 1792; Notes on the Legitimacy of Government, 30 Dec. 1792). The subsequent ten-week delay was caused by a vote in the House of Representatives in December 1792 to apply money set aside for payments on the French debt to pay the government's debt to the Bank of the United States. This threat to the resumption of debt payments was defeated only on 28 Feb. 1793 when the House voted to pay the Bank with other funds (Notes of a Conversation with George Washington on French Affairs, 27 Dec. 1792, and note).

It is clear from the very similar and sometimes identical wording in his unsent text of 30 Dec. 1792 that TJ had the earlier version in front of him as he penned the present dispatch. His acknowledgment of letters received as late as 1 Feb. 1793 shows that he could not have begun it at an earlier date, and internal evidence demonstrates that he could not have finished it earlier than 2 Mch. 1793. All things considered, however, and despite TJ's initial and inadvertent use of the 30 Dec. 1792 dateline (see note 1 below), the Secretary of State very likely prepared the dispatch on or about 12 Mch. 1793, although he could not have completed and sent it before the next day, when the President approved it and TJ made a final

change (see Washington to TJ, 13 Mch. 1793; and note 5 below).

[1] TJ first wrote "Dec. 30. 1792." and then altered the date to read as above. The alteration blurred the month and day in the PrC, where TJ canceled and rewrote them in ink above the line.
[2] Preceding two words interlined.
[3] Word interlined.
[4] Preceding two words interlined in place of "of."
[5] Preceding five words interlined in light of a comment by the President (see Washington to TJ, 13 Mch. 1793).

From Thomas Pinckney

DEAR SIR   London 12th. March 1793.

Mr. Albion Cox having been recommended to me to fill the Office of Assayer of our Mint I made all the requisite Enquiries concerning his Abilities and Integrity and received a satisfactory account of both, but as he has been under Misfortunes in America I thought it prudent not to make a final Agreement with him unless his Character should bear the Test of Enquiry there as well as in this Country and for this reason you will observe a Clause in our Agreement stipulating that it shall be void if not approved by the President. I inclose a Copy of his Receipt for the Money furnished him in part of Salary and for Articles bought. He had been employed some time in procuring these Articles and conceived his Salary should commence from the time in which he was so engaged. Though I saw the Equity of the Proposal yet being limitted by my Instructions I told him all I could do would be to state the Matter to you. I believe you must go on with the other Officers you have as Mr. Morris thinks he cannot procure Droze, and I cannot obtain others in conformity to my directions. I have the honor to be with the utmost respect Dear Sir Your faithful and obedient Servant

THOMAS PINCKNEY

RC (DNA: RG 59, DD); in the hand of William A. Deas, signed by Pinckney; at foot of text: "The Secretary of State"; endorsed by TJ as received 4 May 1793 and so recorded in SJL, which notes its delivery "by Albion Coxe." PrC (ScHi: Pinckney Family Papers). Tr (Lb in

DNA: RG 59, DD). Tr (DNA: RG 104, Records of the Bureau of the Mint, General Correspondence); extract in the hand of George Taylor, Jr., made on 2 Jan. 1794, consisting of all except the passage "but as he has been ... for this reason," the final sentence, and the complimentary close. Enclosures: (1) Memorandum of agreement by Pinckney and Cox, witnessed by Deas, London, 8 Mch. 1793, in which Pinckney promises that Cox will be appointed assayer of the United States Mint for three years to begin on the date he leaves London for America, Cox pledges to perform the duties of the office faithfully, to take instructions from the President and the Director of the Mint, to give such securities as the law requires, and to instruct others in the art and business of assayer as directed, and both parties agree that Cox's appointment will be null and void if the President disapproves. (2) Receipt from Cox, 8 Mch. 1793, for Pinckney's order on Bird, Savage & Bird for £50 sterling on account of salary and £34.15 sterling for articles purchased for the Mint on account. (3) Certificates of Cox, Merle & Company, refiners and bankers, Little Britain, 24 Jan. 1793, recommending Cox as an experienced assayer and refiner of "Gold, Silver, Copper, Lead, &ca." who has been in business for many years and whose knowledge is equal to that of any person in the country, and from William Cox, Piddlehenthyde, 25 Feb. 1793, stating that the losses of his relative, Albion Cox, whom he had prosecuted in America, arose chiefly from an unfortunate business connection, that his integrity was not impeached during the incident, and that his abilities are equal to the appointment

(Trs in DNA: RG 104, Records of the Bureau of the Mint, General Correspondence; in Deas's hand). Other enclosure not found, but listed in Washington, *Journal*, 129, as "List of Accts. pd. by Mr. Cox for things for the Mint." Enclosed in TJ to George Washington, 5 May 1793, and returned by Washington the next day (same).

A native of England, Cox had minted copper coinage for New Jersey in 1786 but returned to Britain after escaping from debtors' prison, to which he had been consigned as a result of a suit brought by a former business partner. Owing to concern about this incident and Cox's general reputation for carelessness, TJ, the President, and Director of the Mint David Rittenhouse met on 16 May 1793 and decided to employ Cox as an assayer for the Mint "but without a regular appointment." In April 1794, however, Washington commissioned Cox to serve as assayer, a post he held until his death in December 1795 (Taxay, *Mint*, 103-4; Washington, *Journal*, 141, 297; Tench Coxe to TJ, [11 May 1793]). The ARTICLES BOUGHT by Cox for the use of the Mint consisted of "five cases of glassware, assay scales, weights and other articles" (Frank H. Stewart, *History of the First United States Mint: Its People and Its Operations* [Camden, N.J., 1924], 88).

From Thomas Pinckney

DEAR SIR   London 12th. March 1793.

Messrs. Talon and Bonnet applied to me in the Month of October last expressing their intention to settle in the United States and requesting Information in what way it would be most advantageous to vest a considerable property they purpose placing in that Country. I recommended (what indeed I found to have been their original plan) to examine and determine for themselves. To facilitate their Access to the best channels of Information and to prevent them from falling into improper hands on their arrival I have taken the liberty of introducing

[371]

them to you, from whom a word of general Advice may prove infinitely advantageous; and this I thought due to Strangers in their unfortunate predicament who have been Men of consideration in their own Country and are now seeking an Asylum in ours. I have the honor to be with the utmost Respect dear Sir Your faithful and obedient Servant

THOMAS PINCKNEY

RC (DLC); in the hand of William A. Deas, with signature and part of complimentary close by Pinckney; at foot of text: "The Secretary of State"; endorsed by TJ as received 5 May 1793 and so recorded in SJL, which notes its delivery "by Talon & Bonnet"; also endorsed by TJ as "private." PrC (ScHi: Pinckney Family Papers).

Antoine Omer TALON, formerly a deputy to the French National Assembly who fled to England in 1792, was a founder and agent of the Asylum Company, a land venture backed by Robert Morris and John Nicholson, which established a settlement of French immigrants, largely refugees from the Revolution, on the Susquehanna River. His companion, John BONNET, a banished French clergyman who also invested in the company, became a citizen of the United States but returned to Europe by December 1794, when he was at Hamburg acting as Morris's agent in the sale of American land to European investors (Scott and Rothaus, *Historical Dictionary*, II, 935; Syrett, *Hamilton*, XXVI, 735n; Frances S. Childs, *French Refugee Life in the United States, 1790-1800* [Baltimore, 1940], 96; *Windham Papers*, I, 121; Articles of Agreement between Morris, Nicholson, and Walter Stewart and J. C. Hottinguer, Philadelphia, 1 Oct. 1795, PHarH: John Nicholson Papers).

To Edmund Randolph, with Randolph's Reply

TH:J. TO E. R.   Mar. 12. 93.

Will you be so good as to tell me what answer to give to the interrogatory in the last sentence of this letter?

[*Reply by Randolph:*]

I do not see any absolute, or indeed probably[1] necessity for the *ancient* treaties. But I am not certain, that it may not be satisfactory to have those, made with the state governments; since some of the commissioners are new in this kind of business; and might be surprized by a sudden objection from a treaty, which they had never seen.

RC (CtY); with Randolph's undated reply subjoined. Not recorded in SJL. Enclosure: George Washington to TJ, 10

Mch. 1793.

[1] Thus in manuscript.

To George Clinton

SIR   Philadelphia Mar. 13.[1] 1793.

I duly recieved your favor of the 5th. inst. and have now to request transcripts of the Indian treaties made under the state of New York, as it is conceived they may be necessary to put the Commissioners in full possession of all facts relative to the subjects they have to treat of, and to prevent their being surprised by the producing of any matter whatever with which they may be unacquainted, which they might therefore be unprepared to answer, or even to correct if mistated. I have the honor to be with great esteem & respect your Excellency's most obedt & most humble servt   TH: JEFFERSON

PrC (DLC); with altered date; at foot of text: "H. E. Govr. Clinton." FC (Lb in DNA: RG 59, DL); dated 13 Mch. 1793.

Recorded in SJL under 12 Mch. 1793.

[1] Second digit reworked by TJ from "2."

From the Commissioners of Accounts for the States

SIR   Office of Accounts March 13th. 1793

We have to Request that we may be furnished with an authenticated Copy of the last enumeration in Conformity to the Sixth Section of the act of Congress pass'd the 5th: Augst: 1790, entitled An Act to provide more effectually for the settlement of the Accounts between the United States and the Individual States. We have the Honor to be sir Your Obedt: hble: servts   WM. IRVINE
                                                               JOHN KEAN
                                                               WRY: LANGDON

RC (DNA: RG 59, MLR); in a clerk's hand, signed by Irvine, Kean, and Langdon; at foot of text: "The Honorable The Secy. of State"; endorsed by George Taylor, Jr., in part: "requesting a *Census*."

Section 6 of the 5 Aug. 1790 ACT for settling the accounts of the states with the United States prescribed that each state's share of the common charges of the Revolutionary War was to be apportioned by the Commissioners of Accounts on the basis of population, as determined by the first ENUMERATION, or census, the same rule specified in Article I, section 2, of the Constitution for apportioning direct taxes and representation in the House of Representatives (*Annals*, II, 2357-9). According to a memorandum book kept by the Department of State, the Commissioners were furnished with a certified copy of the 1790 census on 14 Mch. 1793 (DNA: PCC, No. 187). The Commissioners made their final report on 29 June 1793, and President Washington submitted it to Congress on 5 Dec. 1793 (Syrett, *Hamilton*, XV, 252-3n, XIX, 37-8n; Ferguson, *Power of the Purse*, 322, 332-3).

[373]

From Gouverneur Morris

DEAR SIR   Paris 13 March 1793

In mine No. 23 of the ninth Instant I mention'd to you that the Enemy was in Possession of Brussels and so it was then asserted by Authority but it seems that he confind himself to Tongres and Liege leaving the french Army in Possession of St. Tron. At the same Time it appears that he was employ'd in pushing forward a Column on his left to turn their right Flank and had that Movement been compleated the french Army would in all human Probability have been destroy'd. To prevent the threatned Danger Miranda fell back to Louvain keeping open thereby the two Roads to Antwerp and Brussels. As the Enemy will doubtless endeavor to cut him off from the latter I do suppose that Dumouriez relinquishing his Expedition against the Netherlands will form a Junction with Miranda. In this Case a Battle must decide the Fate of Flanders and both Parties will collect for the Purpose all the Force they can muster. I do not think the Position taken at Louvain is tenable because Brussels may be reach'd by the Route of Namur towards which the Enemy will probably turn his Attention in the first Instance. Great Exertions are making here to reinforce Dumouriez and still greater to bring about a new Revolution whose Effect if successful would be I think the Destruction of what is calld here the Faction of the Gironde and which calls itself the republican Party qualifying its Enemies by the Term Anarchists. To avoid if possible the Carnage of the second to the eighth of last September a Tribunal calld the revolutionary Tribunal is organized with very large and wide Powers. It is one of those Instruments whose Operations are incalculable and on whose Direction depends the Fate of the Country. Opinion seems to set very strongly against the Convention. They are suppos'd to be incapable of steering the State Ship in the present rough Weather but it must blow yet a little harder before they are thrown overboard.

A propos I beleive I never mention'd to you that a Constitution was reported but Truth is that it totally escap'd me. A Paper of that Sort was read at the Convention but I learnt the next Morning that a Council had been held on it over Night by which it was condemn'd so I thought no more of it neither have I heard it mentiond till yesterday by one of my Countrymen which brought me to recollect that in my Correspondence I had not noticed it. I am Sir with sincere Esteem your obedient Servant   GOUV MORRIS

RC (DNA: RG 59, DD); at head of text: "No. 24."; at foot of first page: "Thomas Jefferson Esqr Secretary of State"; endorsed by TJ as received 15

May 1793 and so recorded in SJL; nota-
tion in pencil by TJ: "To be copied." FC
(Lb in DLC: Gouverneur Morris Papers).
Tr (DNA: RG 46, Senate Records, 3d
Cong., 1st sess.). PrC (DNA: RG 59,
MD). Tr (Lb in same, DD).

The REVOLUTIONARY TRIBUNAL, a court
established by the National Convention on

10 Mch. 1793 to deal with various crimes
against the state, was the judicial institution which presided over the Reign of
Terror (Scott and Rothaus, *Historical Dictionary*, II, 822-6).

TJ submitted this letter to the President on 15 May 1793, and Washington returned it the next day (Washington,
Journal, 140).

From Thomas Pinckney

DEAR SIR   London 13 March 1793

The printed copy of the Passport which I mentioned as being
inclosed in my letter of the 11th. of last month not having been sent
to me in time for that purpose I transmit it by this opportunity, and
as Mr. Morris differs from me in opinion on this subject and his ideas
may likewise prevail in America I here add extracts of my letters to
him on this subject which contain my principal reasons for adopting
this measure.

Our trade continues subject to great inconvenience both from our
seamen being impressed under the idea of their being british subjects and from their entering voluntarily on board of the King's Ships
tempted by the present high bounties. I have had frequent conversations on this subject with Lord Grenville who always expresses himself to be sensible of the inconvenience to which we are subjected and
desirous to apply a remedy but still nothing decisive is done. Our Consuls are permitted to protect from impressment such of our Seamen as
are natives of America but no others, and the difficulty of determining
by agreement who besides natives are to be considered as citizens of
the U.S. will I fear, during the present generation at least, remain an
obstacle to every other plan than that of letting the Vessel protect a
given number of men according to her tonnage. I insist upon the terms
of our act of Congress as the rule of discrimination and shew that in
point of time it accords with an Act of their own relating to seamen.

I send herewith the transcript of a representation I made on the
subject of British Officers detaining deserters from our Vessels under
pretence of their being Englishmen and extorting the payment of their
wages, on this last subject a question is now depending in the Court
of Admiralty, the former remains without an answer from the Lords
Commissioners of that department.

Lord Grenville having said that he wished me to have some con-

[375]

versation with Mr. Bond on account of his being particularly well acquainted with this subject, I told his lordship I had no objection to conversing with any person appointed by him on this subject—in a few days I received the inclosed note from Mr. Bond to which I sent the answer annexed in order to produce an explanation whereby neither more nor less than the proper degree of importance might be attached to the conference—when Mr. Bond came he said[1] no commission to treat on the subject, we therefore agreed that it was to be considered altogether as an informal conversation. We discoursed at length upon the subject, but I do not find that we are nearer coming to a conclusion on the business than we were before—he appeared not to be prepared for the extent of the reciprocity which I contended should form the basis and pervade the whole of the transaction, for when he urged the point of our Seamen or at least their Captain in their behalf being furnished with testimonials of their being Americans before they left our Ports, I told him the inconveniencies arising from this procedure would be equally felt by both nations for that we should expect their seamen to be furnished with similar testimonials when they came to our ports to those they expected our mariners would bring to theirs; he asked in what instance it could become necessary (alluding I presume to our not being in the habit of impressing). I answered that unless we could come to some accomodation which might insure our seamen against this oppression measures would be taken to cause the inconvenience to be equally felt on both sides. I have not since seen Mr. Bond but find he is ordered out to America with the Title of Consul General for the middle and southern States.

I have lately heard from Mr. Morris who informs me that he has in his possession the paper on account of the absence of which I have suffered so much uneasiness and promises to return it by a Gentleman to whom I on sunday last sent a Passport to Calais; so that I am in hourly expectation of receiving it, and am happy to find that the mistake of sending both papers instead of one to Mr. Morris is likely to be attended with no worse consequence than what may arise from a short delay.

I inclose a letter sent to me by the Prussian Minister here to be forwarded from the King to his Consul at Philadelphia—you will oblige me by informing me of its delivery.

I likewise send herewith Mr. Vanderhorsts bond, the Law having left a latitude in the quantum of the security I have taken a middle term which I beleive will be equal to any property likely to come to his hands in this line, but I shall be glad of your instruction as to the sum in case of future occurrences of this nature.

An Armament is about to sail immediately for the West Indies destined as it is said to take possession of the French windward Islands in which attempt they are to be assisted by part of the inhabitants. I hope the French are convinced how much more beneficial it would be for them, for us to remain neuter than to interfere in the present disputes.

I have as yet received no official information of any of the belligerent powers having stopped our Vessels bound with grain going to the ports of their enemy; but I anxiously expect your instructions on this subject which I hope will meet the question in various points of view: 'till I receive them I mean to contend for the amplest freedom of neutral bottoms. I have the honor to be with sentiments of the greatest respect Dear Sir Your most obedient and most humble Servt:

THOMAS PINCKNEY

RC (DNA: RG 59, DD); at foot of text: "The Secretary of State"; endorsed by TJ as received 5 May 1793 and so recorded in SJL. PrC (ScHi: Pinckney Family Papers). Tr (Lb in DNA: RG 59, DD). Tr (MHi: Timothy Pickering Papers); consists of second paragraph only. Enclosures: (1) Passport for captains of United States ships (printed form, in English and French, in DNA: RG 59, DD; Tr in Lb in same). (2) Extract of Pinckney to Gouverneur Morris, 5 Mch. 1793, defending his issuance of passports to American ships sailing from British ports on the grounds that they are required by the treaty of amity and commerce with France when either nation is at war and that it would be impractical to oblige such ships to obtain them in the United States; pointing out, with respect to Morris's fears that the practice will be abused and will endanger ships without passports, that he has enjoined consuls to issue no passports without due examination of each ship's register; stating that he cannot now stop providing such papers without casting doubts on the nationality of ships subsequently denied them and that this practice will not affect ships leaving French ports because of their clearances by French customhouses; and pressing Morris to find out whether the French government intends to honor the treaty and especially if it will require passports for American vessels leaving British ports. (3) Extract of Pinckney to Mor-

ris, 8 Mch. 1793, promising to communicate "to our friends in the City" Morris's opinion that the French government will scrupulously observe all stipulations in the treaty, noting the importance for "our carrying Trade" of French compliance with the treaty provision that "free Ships shall make free Goods," and observing that the conduct of the French will eventually convince everyone of their pure intentions but that in the interim the United States must pay for the incredulity of France's enemies. (4) Pinckney to Lord Grenville, 31 Dec. 1792, stating that after the American ship *Governor Bowdoin*, Edward Dowse master, bound from China to Ostend and thence to Boston, was recently driven into Ramsgate by a storm, several seamen under contract to make the round trip from Boston deserted to *H.M.S. Iphigenia*, Captain Sinclair commander, who not only refuses to restore them but threatens to detain Dowse's ship unless he pays their wages, which by their contract they forfeited by jumping ship; objecting to the detention by British naval officers of deserting sailors from American ships who claim to be British subjects because the British take advantage of the similarity of language and habits, and the failure of seamen to carry papers, to give more weight to the testimony of deserters than to their contracts, because in the absence of a convention defining citizenship precisely decisions on such a point ought not to be left to naval officers acting as judges in their own cases, because it can lead to violence, and because it is not practiced by Americans or by other countries against Americans; suggesting that deserters have no right to their wages because contracts made abroad are valid, a point Britain recognizes by a law encouraging the service of foreign seamen in its own merchant marine, and because by desertion seamen not only invalidate their contracts but greatly harm their employers; and urging that regulations be adopted to resolve this problem. (5) Phineas Bond to Pinckney, 22 Feb. 1793, stating that Grenville this morning directed him to confer with Pinckney regarding American seamen, "with a view to form some Arrangement that may be compatible with the Interest and Convenience of the navigation of Great Britain and the United States," and suggesting that they meet early next week. (6) Pinckney to Bond, 24 Feb. 1793, congratulating him on his diplomatic appointment and inviting him to confer two days hence (Trs in same, in the hand of William A. Deas; Trs in Lb in same). (7) Consular bond of Elias Vanderhorst, 10 Oct. 1792 (see note to Vanderhorst to TJ, 10 Oct. 1792). Other enclosure not found.

On 6 May 1793 TJ sent this letter to the President, who returned it the same day (Washington, *Journal*, 129). In discussions with Lord Grenville on the subject of OUR SEAMEN BEING IMPRESSED, Pinckney argued that Britain should recognize as American citizens not only natives, but individuals naturalized under OUR ACT OF CONGRESS of 26 Mch. 1790,

which required only two years' residence, a span agreeing IN POINT OF TIME with a 1740 British law which naturalized foreign mariners who served for two years in British naval or merchant ships in time of war. Pinckney cited the same act in his enclosed REPRESENTATION to Grenville to argue that Britain sanctioned the legality of service by foreigners in its own ships and could thus not oppose its validity in the vessels of other nations. Nevertheless, until 1870 Britain continued to maintain that the allegiance of its citizens was inalienable and could not be voluntarily relinquished (*Annals*, II, 2264; J. Mervyn Jones, *British Nationality Law and Practice* [Oxford, 1947], 64n, 75n, 80-3). The PAPER which had occasioned Pinckney so MUCH UNEASINESS was a cipher he had inadvertently mailed to Gouverneur Morris (Pinckney to TJ, 31 Jan., 5, 10 Feb. 1793; Morris to Pinckney, 2 Mch. 1793, DLC: Pinckney Family Papers).

On this date Pinckney also wrote TJ a brief note informing him that "Mr. Marshalls return to America affords me a safe opportunity of conveying the inclosed correspondence which I mentioned in a former communication" (RC in DNA: RG 59, DD, at foot of text: "The Secretary of State," endorsed by TJ as received 4 May 1793 and so recorded in SJL, which contains the notation "Sayer's correspdce"; Tr in Lb in same). The enclosures are identified in note to Pinckney to TJ, 8 Sep. 1792.

[1] Thus in RC. Here in Tr "he had" is interlined.

From Thomas Pinckney

DEAR SIR   Great Cumberland Place London 13 March 1793

I was hopeful to have been able to send to you by Mr. Marshall the model of a threshing machine which a mechanic promised to finish by this time, but I am for the present disappointed; I expect however it will be in time for the next Vessel. On further inquiry I find this machine well spoken of by all whom I have met with who are acquainted with its operation—it is said that the Mill whence your model is formed will with the force of four horses thresh eight quarters of Oats in an hour—if this be true it must be superior to the Mill I saw, after making the necessary deduction for the increase of force.

Mr. Marshal affords me no hope that you may be prevailed on to procrastinate the time of your retirement—if he is mistaken I shall of course be favord with your official communications, if not I hope soon to hear in what way I can be instrumental from this side of the Atlantic in augmenting your enjoyment of the sollicitæ jucunda oblivia vitæ— believe me to be Dear Sir with sincere respect & esteem Your faithful & obedient Servant   THOMAS PINCKNEY

RC (DNA: RG 59, DD); at head of text: "Private"; at foot of text: "Mr Jefferson"; endorsed by TJ as received 4 May 1793 and so recorded in SJL. PrC (ScHi: Pinckney Family Papers).

SOLLICITÆ JUCUNDA OBLIVIA VITÆ: "the pleasant oblivion of a busy life."

To Edmund Randolph

DEAR SIR   Philadelphia Mar. 13. 1793.

I received yesterday the inclosed letter from Mr. Hammond Minister Plenipotentiary of Great Britain on the case of Hooper and Pagan whereon you have been before consulted. I take the liberty of resorting again to you for the information which your presence in the supreme court will have enabled you to give, or which you may have otherwise obtained, and for your opinion on the case in it's present stage, so far as it concerns our nation in it's relation with others. And as illustrative of this whether the party complaining has duly pursued the ordinary remedies provided by the laws, as was incumbent on him before he would be entitled to appeal to the nation, and, if he has, whether that degree of gross and palpable injustice has been done him by the national tribunals, which would render the nation itself responsible for their conduct. I have the honor to be with great esteem & respect, Dear Sir your most obedt. & most humble servt   TH: JEFFERSON

PrC (DLC); at foot of text: "The Attorney general of the US." FC (Lb in DNA: RG 59, DL). The enclosed letter from George Hammond to TJ, dated 12 Mch. 1793 and recorded in SJL as received the same day, has not been found.

For a discussion of the Supreme Court's refusal on 16 Feb. 1793 to grant a writ of error to Thomas PAGAN, a British subject imprisoned in Massachusetts for his role in the capture in 1783 of a merchant ship owned by Stephen HOOPER of Newburyport, see note to George Hammond to TJ, 26 Nov. 1791.

To George Washington

Th: Jefferson has the honor to inclose to the President draughts of the instruments which he suggested as proper to be given formally to each tribe of Indians whose circumstances may call for such a[1] manifestation of our views with respect to them. The first is a Letter of protection of the ordinary tenor, except that it declares a protection of the lands as well as the persons and other property, and would be signed by the President[2] under the great seal. The second contains extracts from the late law of the US. and contains 1. those paragraphs which would shew to the Indians that our laws will punish injuries done them as if done to ourselves. 2. those paragraphs which may answer the purpose of directing those on the spot, when any injury is committed, how and where they are to proceed. If the furnishing such papers should be approved, it will be best to have them *printed*, on *parchment*, with the seal, and put into tin cases, so as to give them marks of solemnity which may strike those to whom they are given, or to whom they shall be shewn.

RC (DNA: RG 59, MLR); endorsed by Tobias Lear. Pr C (DLC); partially overwritten in a later hand. Tr (Lb in DNA: RG 59, SDC). Tr (same). Recorded in SJPL. Enclosure: Extracts from Act to regulate Trade and Intercourse with the Indian Tribes, 1 Mch. 1793, comprising sections 4-5, part of section 8, and sections 10-12 (Pr C of Tr in DLC: TJ Papers, 96: 16473-6; undated; in a clerk's hand, partially overwritten in a later hand). Other enclosure printed below.

With this letter and its enclosures TJ sought both to improve American relations with friendly Indians and to publicize and render effectual the criminal sanctions against unauthorized land purchases from Indians that he had helped insert in the recently enacted Indian trade and intercourse law (see enclosure to TJ to George Washington, 13 Jan. 1793). The paragraphs from the statute of 1 Mch. 1793 that TJ extracted for circulation with the presidential letter of protection included sections specifying that crimes against the persons and property of Indians were subject to the same penalties as similar crimes against whites and that pur-

chases of land from Indians without federal sanction were both invalid and grounds for fines and imprisonment, as well as sections indicating the procedures to be used in bringing offenders to justice. He understandably decided against including the sections of the law placing restrictions on who might conduct trade with Indians (*Annals*, III, 1442-5).

On this date the President circulated both enclosures among the rest of his Cabinet. Alexander Hamilton approved the extracts from the law but expressed concern that the letter of protection might "at some time produce inconveniencies." Henry Knox approved both documents, while Edmund Randolph agreed "to consider of them." Washington ultimately approved the documents (albeit with the significant change noted below), for on 23 Mch. TJ transmitted for the President's signature the "letters printed on parchmt. which are proposed to be given to the Indian tribes, together with extracts from the law regulating trade & intercourse with the Indian tribes." Seven copies were given to members of a delegation of Illinois and Wabash Indians taking their leave of the President on 7 May 1793;

the remaining copy was signed and sealed and "taken back to the Office of the Secretary of State" (Washington, *Journal*, 88-9, 102, 130). The set received by the Kaskaskias (printed texts on parchment in ICHi; letter dated 7 May 1793 signed by Washington and TJ; extracts certified by TJ on 7 May 1793) indicates that, while the extracts from the law were unaltered, the letter of protection had been changed in one important particular. TJ's draft had enjoined both citizens and non-citizens of the United States from harming the persons or infringing the property rights of Indians under the nation's peace and protection, and had similarly warned citizens and non-citizens alike against purchasing land from them. As actually issued, however, the letter of protection guaranteed Indian rights only against infringement by American citizens, although the prohibition of land purchases by non-citizens as well as citizens remained.

[1] Here TJ canceled "mark of our."
[2] Preceding two words interlined in place of "yourself."

ENCLOSURE

Letter of Protection for Friendly Indians

[13 Mch. 1793]

GEORGE WASHINGTON, President of the United States of America.
To all to whom these Presents shall come.

KNOW YE, That the Nation of Indians called the   inhabiting the Town of   and other Towns, Villages and Lands of the same community, are, in their persons, Towns, Villages, Lands, Hunting-grounds and other Rights and Property in the Peace and under the Protection of the United States of America. And all Persons, Citizens of the United States and others of whatever country or condition, are hereby warned not to commit any Injury, Trespass or Molestation whatever on the persons, lands, Hunting-grounds, or other Rights or Property of the said Indians. And they are in like manner forbidden to purchase, accept, agree or treat for, with the said Indians directly or indirectly, the title or Occupation of any Lands held or claimed by them, and I do hereby call upon all persons in authority under the United States and all Citizens thereof in their several capacities, to be aiding and assisting to the prosecution and punishment according to Law of all persons who shall be found offending in the Premises.

Given under my Hand and the Seal of the United States this   day of   in the Year of our Lord one thousand seven hundred and ninety three and of the Independence of the United States of America the

PrC of Dft (DLC: TJ Papers, 96: 16472); undated; in the hand of George Taylor, Jr., but partially overwritten in a later hand. Recorded in SJPL under 13 Mch. 1793: "form of [letter of protection to Indns.]."

From George Washington

DEAR SIR   Philadelphia 13th. Mar. 1793

The returned draught of a letter to Mr. Gouvr. Morris accords with my sentiments.—Taking it for granted, that the words "We suppose this will rather overpay the instalments and interest due on the loans of 18. 6 and 10 Millions"—means all that could be demanded by[1] the French Government to the close of last year.—This being the idea I have entertained of the payments, and engagements[2] to pay.

If it has not been done in a former letter, it would be very[3] agreeable to me, that Mr. Morris should be instructed to neglect no favorable opportunity of expressing *informally* the sentiments and wishes[4] of this Country respecting M. de la Fayette.—And I pray you to commit to paper—in answer to the enclosed letter from Madame de la Fayette to me—all the consolation I can with propriety[5] give her[6] consistent with my public character and the[7] National policy;[8] circumstanced as things are.—My last, and *only*[9] letter to her is herewith sent, that you may see what has been written heretofore.[10] I am—always Yours

GO: WASHINGTON

RC (DLC); at foot of text: "Mr. Jefferson"; endorsed by TJ as received 13 Mch. 1793. Dft (DNA: RG 59, MLR); the most significant emendations are noted below; endorsed by Washington. FC (Lb in same, SDC); wording follows Dft. Recorded in SJPL. Enclosures: (1) TJ to Gouverneur Morris, 12 Mch. 1793. (2) Madame de Lafayette to Washington, Chavaniac, 8 Oct. 1792, asking the United States to send an envoy empowered to make the necessary engagements to liberate her husband from Prussian captivity, so that the reunited family could move to the United States (Trs, in French and English, in DLC: Washington Papers). (3) Washington to Madame de Lafayette, 31 Jan. 1793, expressing concern for Lafayette's plight, sending her 200 guineas for services he had rendered but "of which I never yet have received the account," stating that the uncertainty of her situation had delayed his letter, and declaring that he wrote now more in the hope of finding "where you are, than from any knowledge I have obtained of your residence" (Fitzpatrick, *Writings*, XXXII, 322).

[1] In Dft preceding six words interlined in place of what appears to be "what was demanded."

[2] In Dft preceding two words interlined and next two words lacking.

[3] Word not in Dft.

[4] Preceding two words interlined in Dft.

[5] Preceding three words interlined in Dft in place of what appears to be "expect to."

[6] Word interlined. Word not in Dft.

[7] In Dft preceding five words interlined in place of "policy."

[8] In Dft Washington first completed the sentence with "under existing circumstances [. . .]" and then altered the passage to read as above.

[9] Word not underscored in Dft.

[10] Preceding sentence interlined in Dft in place of an estimated four canceled and illegible words.

From Delamotte

Havre, 14 Mch. 1793. A rumor is abroad here that Spain has declared war on the United States. No one has identified the source, but neither has it been discredited. Since no public paper confirms it, he considers it a chimera, albeit one which frightens him. Yet it is only too probable that England wishes to prevent America from bringing supplies to France and, rather than break relations with the United States, might induce Spain to do so under the pretext of problems concerning the mouth of the Mississippi. He will send word of what he learns about the rumor through ships that are scheduled to leave here for America. Meanwhile, TJ should attach no more weight to the news than he himself does—namely, that it seems to fit the interests of the powers at war with France, and nothing more.

RC (DNA: RG 59, CD); 2 p.; in French; in a clerk's hand, signed by Delamotte; endorsed by TJ as received 4 May 1793 and so recorded in SJL.

From Beverley Randolph

DEAR SIR   Richmond March 14th. 1793

Yours of the 18 of last month did not reach me untill the 6th. instant.

I beg you will accept my Thanks for the very favourable opinion you have been good enough to express of me. I sincerely wish I may be able to answer the expectations of my Friends. I profess myself intirely ignorant of the Business which I am calld upon to execute but have notwithstanding determined to engage in it having nothing to support me in the undertaking except a consciousness of Zeal for the Public Interest and the Hope that you and my Friend Edmund Randolph will afford me such information on the Subject of my Employment as will enable to discharge the Duties of it in a Satisfactory Manner.

I should have answered your Letter before this had an opportunity offer'd from Cumberland sooner than my own Departure for this Place.

I fear it will be impossible for me to reach Philadelphia so soon as the President wishes as I have only this Day received official notice of my appointment. This Circumstance will scarcely allow me time to be there sooner than the 10th next of month by which Day I hope to be able to accomplish the Journey. I beg you will be good enough to make my apology to the President for this Delay. You know my dear Sir how impossible it is for a man in this Country to equip himself for such an expedition in so short a time as seems to be required. I beg you to be assured that I am with great Regard Yr. Friend

BEVERLEY RANDOLPH

RC (DLC); endorsed by TJ as received 21 Mch. 1793 and so recorded in SJL.

To George Gilmer

DEAR DOCTOR Philadelphia Mar. 15. 1793.
I duly received your favor of Jan. 26. and learn with great pleasure the reestablishment of your system, in which no one takes a more sincere interest than myself. I had indeed hoped by this time to have been with you. But it seems I must stay here a little longer in penance for my sins. This will give you the start in your manufactures of porter and maccaroni, in which however I shall certainly attempt to rival you.—You will have heard of the fiscal enquiries into which the late Congress went. I send you a paper containing Madison's speech. Monroe will set out on Monday, and dropping Mrs. Monroe at Fredericksbg. will pursue his route to Charlottesville alone. We have no news from France later than the beginning of the king's trial. Notwithstanding the blustering of John Bull, I still suspect that he never intended war, but only a pretext for arming at home against Tom Paine. An unparalleled want of money here, and stoppage of discount at all the banks, obliges the merchants to slacken the price of wheat and flour. But it is only temporary. Be assured the price will be very high in a short time. Give my best respects to Mrs. Gilmer & accept assurances yourself of the sincere esteem & attachment of Dear Doctor your affectionate friend & servt   TH: JEFFERSON

PrC (DLC); at foot of text: "Dr. Gilmer." Tr (DLC); 19th-century copy. Erroneously recorded in SJL under 13 Mch. 1793.

The enclosed PAPER CONTAINING MADI-SON'S SPEECH in the House of Representatives of 1 Mch. 1793 on the Giles resolutions could have been any one of several newspapers which had printed it by this date (Madison, *Papers*, XIV, 455-68).

From Stephen Hallet

MONSIEUR Geoe Town 15 Mars 1793.
Je vous demande bien sincerement pardon pour mes Importunités. Je prends la liberté d'invoquer encor vos bons offices auprés du President des Etats unis.
Je vous Joins ici la lettre des commissionnaires qui m'annonce leur Decision avec ma reponse et une Description succincte des Dispositions generales d'un nouveau plan conforme aux données resultantes de la Conference que le President m'a accordée Sous Vos auspices. Ces pieces Vous feront connoitre le sujet de ma demarche. J'ajouterai ici un aperçu de la Conduite que Jai tenue et du tenir ici.

Etranger et presque inconnu Je n'ai du esperer la Confiance quapres que le tems m'auroit fourni les occasions de la Justifier. Jai donc du m'attacher a Saisir et a rendre les idées quil a plu au Président et aux commissionnaires de m'indiquer et Je l'ai fait. J'ai produit deux essais d après mon ancien dessein il m a paru que dans le premier Javois Surpassé les Vues d'œconomie qu'on m'avoit recommandées dans le Second que Jai produit dernierement au President en votre presence avec le dessein quil m'avoit lui meme pointé Comme ce qui lui paroissoit convenable au sujet, Je me Suis rapproché de mon original et meme Je pense l'avoir perfectionné.

Enfin depuis mon retour de Philadelphie Je me suis occupe du Plan dont la Description est ci Jointe.

Plus instruit des necessités locale et prenant pour Cette fois sur moi le Choix des formes Jesperois l'offrir au Concours Comme la premiere production qui soit reellement de ma Composition, Je me Suis proposé d'imiter la Simplicité de l'antique dont les effets resultent de l'ensemble et des proportions et non de la multitude des ornemens Cest a mon Sens le genre qui doit reussir ici.

Il Seroit facheux que le Concours fut fermé a la premiere Composition qu'il m'a été possible de produire (tout mon tems ayant été employé a travailler sur des idées Etrangeres).[1]

Les procédés honnêtes que Jai toujours eprouvés de la part des commissionaires m'obligent a l'estime et a la reconnoissance mais ces sentimens memes m'imposent peut etre le devoir d'observer que Si les vues d'œconomie dont on m'a Continuellement entretenu sont necessaires au Succes de l'etablissement on S'en est fort ecarté dans le Choix qu'on vient de faire.

Convaincu de la Justice de ma Reclamation fondé sur des faits qui vous sont connus, J'ose esperer monsieur que vous voudres bien soumettre cet exposé au President le Requerant de suspendre sil est possible son Jugement Jusqua ce que J'aye pu mettre mon ouvrage en état d'etre vu et entendu dans toutes ses parties.

Ce delai ne peut nuire aux travaux preparatoires quon pourra diriger d'une maniere utile a quelque plan quon adopte en Definitif.

Je reitere en tout evenement mes offres de services et l'assurance de mon Zele pour le succes de l'etablissement promettant d'y Concourir de mon mieux dans la partie qui pourra m'etre confiée. Jai lhonneur d'etre tres Respectueusement Monsieur Votre tres humble et obnt Serviteur. S. HALLET

Nota. J'apprends indirectement que les Commres. Se sont occupes de me faire des propositions, mais elles ne me sont point encor parvenue. Jaurai lhonneur de vous les faire Connoitre.

RC (DLC); addressed: "Mr. Jefferson Secretary of the State Dept. Philadelphia"; postmarked and franked the same day by Hallet; endorsed by TJ as received 19 Mch. 1793 and so recorded in SJL. Enclosures: (1) Commissioners of the Federal District to Hallet, Georgetown, 13 Mch. 1793, advising that, although his initial plan for the Capitol came closest to their ideas and those of the President, they have chosen William Thornton's plan, and that while neither he nor Hallet is technically entitled to the prize under the terms of the advertisement, the end has been answered and Thornton will be given a reward of $500 and a lot, and Hallet will receive £100, being the value of a lot and $500, as compensation for his time to this point because his plan had merit and they had encouraged him to continue work on it (Tr in DLC; in Hallet's hand; at head of text: "Copie"). (2) Hallet to the Commissioners, Georgetown, 13 Mch. 1793, stating that the last plan for the Capitol he submitted was only a summary without elevation or sections and thus presumably not the one they considered, announcing his intention to complete his plan and to give the sections the necessary forms to indicate the disposition of the interior so that a definitive judgment can be made when the President comes, and offering his services in any event (Tr in DLC; in French; in Hallet's hand; at head of text: "suit ma Reponse"). Other enclosure printed below.

Concerning Hallet's unsuccessful efforts to win the competition to design the United States Capitol, see note to Hallet to TJ, 21 Sep. 1792.

[1] Closing parenthesis supplied.

ENCLOSURE

Stephen Hallet's Description of His New Plan for the Capitol

[ca. 15 Mch. 1793]
Succinct description of a new Plan of a Capitol by Mr. Hallet.

The principal front is in a direct line of 320. feet in length, having in the middle a circular projection of 105. feet diameter, very nearly of the proportions of the Pantheon, and crowned in the same taste, the same Cornish, surmounted by a balustrade, crowns the whole edifice which is proposed to be covered in terrasses. The Sub-basement will raise the first floor to some steps above the level of the highest ground, and will afford a great number of offices and lodgings for doorkeepers and other conveniences. In the circular mass, a large open vestibule of nine arches, 10 feet wide, gives room[1] to enter in carriages, from whence is a communication by a circular staircase to the central vestibule on the first floor, which has an entry on the same level to the East, giving passage to the antichambers, stair-cases and other interior communications. The Representatives room is in the same stile[2] and placed in the same manner as in my preceding plan. The Senate is at the other end and disposed so that all the effects of the light are symmetrical as if it occupied the whole mass. The Conference room is in the middle in the circular projection on the second floor. It's inside is an exact sphere in imitation of the Pantheon. All the rooms, without exception, are lighted and aired directly,[3] because they have all windows in outer walls.

Tr (DNA: RG 59, MLR); translation in TJ's hand; undated; enclosed in TJ to George Washington, 26 Mch. 1793. MS (DLC); in French; in Hallet's hand; undated.

To Gouverneur Morris and Thomas Pinckney

DEAR SIR   Philadelphia March 15th. 1793.

The President has seen with satisfaction that the Ministers of the United States in Europe, while they have avoided an useless commitment of their Nation on the subject of M. de la Fayette, have nevertheless shewn themselves attentive to his situation. The interest which the President himself, and our Citizens in general take in the welfare of this gentleman, is great and sincere, and will entirely justify all prudent efforts to serve him. I am therefore to desire that you will avail yourself of every opportunity of sounding the way towards his liberation, of finding out whether those in whose power he is, are very tenacious of him, of insinuating through such channels as you shall think suitable the attentions of the Government and people of the United States to this object, and the interest they take in it, and of¹ procuring his liberation by informal solicitations, if possible. But if formal ones be necessary, and the moment should arrive when you shall find that they will be effectual, you are authorized to signify, through such channel as you shall find suitable, that our Government and Nation, faithful in their attachments to this gentleman for the services he has rendered them, feel a lively interest in his welfare, and will view his liberation as a mark of consideration and friendship for the United States, and as a new motive for esteem and a reciprocation of kind offices towards the power to whom they shall be indebted for this Act.

A like letter being written to Mr. Pinckney,² you will of course take care that, however you may act through different channels, there be still a sufficient degree of concert in your proceedings. I am, with great and sincere esteem, Dear Sir, Your most obedient and most humble Servant   TH: JEFFERSON

RC (NNC: Gouverneur Morris Papers); in the hand of George Taylor, Jr., signed by TJ; at foot of text: "Mr. Morris"; endorsed by Morris. PrC (DNA: RG 59, MLR); signed by TJ in ink. RC (NNP); in Taylor's hand, signed by TJ; at foot of text: "Mr. Pinckney." PrC of Dft (DLC); with emendation noted below; lacks part of complimentary close; at foot of text: "Mr. Morris." Tr (NjP: Andre deCoppet Collection); in Taylor's hand, signed by TJ; at foot of text: "Messieurs Morris Pinckney"; marginal note in TJ's hand: "communicated to Colo. Humphries merely for his information. Th:J." PrC (DLC); unsigned; at foot of text in TJ's hand in ink: "communicated to Colo. Humphr. Carmichl. & Short." FC (Lb in DNA: RG 59, DCI); at head of text: "To Gouverneur Morris Esqr."; note in margin: "The same to Mr Pinckney. Communicated to Col. Humphreys Mr Carmichael & Mr Short." Enclosed in TJ to George Washington, and Washington to TJ, both 15 Mch. 1793, and TJ to Washington, 5 May 1793.

TJ's instructions enunciating American policy on efforts to procure Lafayette's release from captivity reflect the tensions between the humanitarian impulse to aid the man who perhaps best personified the multiple ties of friendship between France and the United States and the diplomatic imperative to preserve American neutrality in the midst of the rapidly widening war in Europe. A strong supporter of constitutional monarchy, Lafayette had fled from France on 19 Aug. 1792, when the new revolutionary regime relieved him of his command and ordered his arrest shortly after his unsuccessful attempt to rally his army on behalf of the recently overthrown Louis XVI. While enroute to the then neutral Netherlands with a party of over fifty fellow officers, orderlies, and servants, the marquis, who had hoped to make his way to England and from thence to the United States, was arrested by a party of Austrian soldiers at Rochefort in the Austrian Netherlands. At the end of that month a special commission of agents of the Austrian and Prussian monarchs, including a French émigré representative, pronounced him guilty of lèse-majesté against Louis and sentenced him to be held as a prisoner of state until a restored French monarch could decide his fate, a judgment that led to five years of imprisonment, first in Prussian and then in Austrian custody (Madame de Lafayette to George Washington, 8 Oct. 1792, DLC: Washington Papers; Samuel F. Bemis, "The United States and Lafayette," *Daughters of the American Revolution Magazine*, LVIII [1924], 341-5; Peter Buckman, *Lafayette: A Biography* [New York, 1977], 214-19; Olivier Bernier, *Lafayette: Hero of Two Worlds* [New York, 1983], 240-7).

In addition to natural sympathy for one who had rendered such signal service to the American Revolution, the Washington administration took an interest in Lafayette's case because of his pleas for American diplomatic intervention on his behalf as an unjustly imprisoned United States citizen. Lafayette enjoyed American citizenship because Maryland and Virginia had granted him state citizenship in 1784 and 1785, respectively, and state citizens automatically became citizens of the United States after the adoption of the federal Constitution. In letters of August 1792 describing himself as "an American Citizen, an American officer—No More in the french Service," Lafayette urged William Short, then serving as minister to the Netherlands, first alone and then in conjunction with the American ministers to France and England as well as the British government, to intercede with his captors in order to secure his release (Lafayette to Short, 26, 29, 30 Aug. 1792, DLC: Short Papers). Short notified Gouverneur Morris and Thomas Pinckney of Lafayette's appeal and asked whether the three ministers could do anything practicable to comply with it. Although Pinckney initially favored the issuance of a joint declaration expressing the hope that Lafayette would be accorded all the rights due him as an American citizen, Morris, noting that the marquis was not in the service of the United States, opposed any form of official intervention as a violation of American neutrality, an opinion in which Short and Pinckney immediately concurred. All three ministers then referred the matter to TJ. While Morris opposed an official démarche, he privately helped the Marquise de Lafayette draft a petition to the king of Prussia asking for her husband's release and made personal and public funds available on his own initiative to relieve the imprisoned marquis (Morris to TJ, 27 Sep. 1792, and enclosures; Short to TJ, 28 Sep. 1792; Pinckney to TJ, 9 Nov. 1792; Bemis, "United States and Lafayette," 345-50, 407).

TJ drafted this letter at the express wish of the President, who had a paternal regard for Lafayette and had been deeply affected by a touching appeal for help from the marquis's wife. In doing so TJ departed in two ways from Washington's original request. Whereas the President had only asked him to write to the

American minister in Paris, TJ included the American minister in London; and whereas the President had only authorized informal expressions of American concern about Lafayette's plight, TJ empowered the two ministers to make formal solicitations on his behalf. Washington signified his assent to the strengthening of his original proposal when he evidently approved drafts of the letters to Morris and Pinckney this day (Washington to TJ, 13 Mch. 1793; Washington, *Journal*, 91). For a discussion of American diplomatic efforts to secure Lafayette's freedom after TJ left office, including appeals by the President to the rulers of Austria and Prussia, none of which were official and all

of which failed, see Bemis, "United States and Lafayette," 408-14, 481-7. Lafayette finally emerged from Austrian captivity in September 1797 after Napoleon Bonaparte's stunningly successful Italian campaign and the French government's resultant insistence that the defeated Austrians agree to the marquis's release as a condition of peace (same, 487-9; Buckman, *Lafayette*, 232-4).

[1] The passage "of insinuating . . . and of" interlined in Pr C of Dft.

[2] "Morris" in the RC to Pinckney; "Morris Pinckney"—with the first name written in TJ's hand—in the Tr sent to David Humphreys.

From Edmund Randolph

SIR   Philadelphia March 15th. 1793.

My communications to you in the case of Pagan against Hooper, combined with the facts, which have since occurred, will support me in saying, that as the law-officer of the United States, I have contributed every thing in my power to the relief of Pagan. You will recollect, that counsel was employed by him to move for a writ of error: that the first application was refused: that upon discovering, that only part of the record was laid before the judge, who did refuse, I recommended a second effort with a complete record, which I furnished, together with an abstract of it, as it was voluminous: and that thereupon a writ of error was granted; and issued.

At the last Session of the Supreme Court of the United States, the writ of error was not returned. Pagan's counsel, holding the record in his hands, mentioned the subject to the court; upon which the Chief-justice of the United States produced a letter from the Chief-justice of Massachusetts, informing him, that the writ, having been directed to the *Supreme Court* of Massachusetts, instead of the *Supreme judicial Court*, it could not be obeyed by any Court in Massachusetts; as none bore that name. But he added, that with this correction, it should be taken into consideration. Pagan's counsel was solicitous to leave the whole business in the hands of the Court without any specific motion, but the Court declared, that without a motion, they should consider nothing. Upon this Pagan's counsel replied, that he should make a motion for an alias writ of error, but should argue against it. One of the Justices expressed his surprize, that a gentleman should argue against his own motion; and was answered by the Counsel, that he hoped to satisfy the Court, that under the *extraordinary* circumstances of the case, he was free to do so. To this the same Judge said, that the circumstances must be extraordinary indeed, which would warrant such a procedure.

On the next day, the record was exhibited by the Counsel, and the motion made. The Court asked him, whether the subject, which gave the Court jurisdiction, was apparent on the record. He averred, that it was not. I happened to be present, and reminded the Court and the Counsel, of the delicacy of the case; and particularly requested the latter to remember, that it had been before the government of the United States, that every means ought to be tried and that instead of asking for the writ as a new thing, he should move for it, as a thing of course, after one had been already granted. But he remarked, and the Court agreed, that the propriety of the writ was as much open now, as ever; and the renewal of it was unanimously rejected.

The latter part of this representation ought probably to have come from Pagan's Counsel; but to avoid delay, I have drawn it, with a view of shewing it to him, before I forward it to you.

I pretend not to decide on the style, in which the motion ought to have been made; especially as I am no stranger to the abilities and integrity of Pagan's Counsel. But I shall leave the proceeding to your own comments, and shall turn my attention to the following aspect of the case: whether

Upon the supposition, that the most perfect mode of application for the writ of error has been adopted, the United States are not discharged from responsibility by the judgment of the Court?

FC (DNA: RG 60, Letters from and Opinions of the Attorneys General); unsigned; at head of text: "A"; endorsed by Randolph: "The letter intended for the Secretary of State, as mentioned in my letter of April 12. 1793." PrC of Tr (DLC); in a clerk's hand. Tr (Lb in PRO: FO 116/3). Tr (same, 5/1). Enclosed in Randolph to TJ, 12 Apr. 1793, and TJ to George Hammond, 18 Apr. 1793.

To George Washington

Mar. 15. 1793.

Th: Jefferson with his respects to the President, sends him the draught of a letter to Madame de la Fayette, as also the draught of a letter to Mr. Morris. If this be approved, he proposes to write a like one to Mr. Pinckney.

RC (DNA: RG 59, MLR); addressed: "The President of the US."; endorsed by Tobias Lear. PrC (DLC). Tr (Lb in DNA: RG 59, SDC). Recorded in SJPL.

Enclosures: (1) George Washington to Madame de Lafayette, 15 Mch. 1793. (2) TJ to Gouverneur Morris and Thomas Pinckney, 15 Mch. 1793.

From George Washington, with Jefferson's Note

March 15. 1793

The President approves of the enclosed draft of a letter to Mr. Morris—and wishes to know if there is any opportunity of sending it directly, as he thinks it would be best for him to send the one for Made. la fayette, to Mr. Morris at the same time, knowing that she is in France.

[*Note by TJ:*]
This was the letter of Mar. 15. 93.

RC (DLC); in the hand of Tobias Lear; addressed: "The Secr[. . .]"; with note by TJ at foot of text; endorsed by TJ as received 15 Mch. 1793. Recorded in SJPL. Enclosure: TJ to Gouverneur Morris and Thomas Pinckney, 15 Mch. 1793.

George Washington to Madame de Lafayette

DEAR MADAM   Philadelphia. Mar. 15.[1] 93.
I addressed a few lines to you on the 31st. of January, in a state of entire uncertainty[2] in what country or condition they might find you, as we had been sometimes told you were in England, sometimes in Holland, and at sometimes in France. Your letter of Octob. 8. 1792. first relieved me from doubt, and gave me a hope that, being in France, and on your own estate, you are not as destitute, as I had feared, of the resources which that could furnish. But I have still to sympathize with you on the deprivation of the dearest of all your resources of happiness, in comparison with which, others vanish. I do it in all the sincerity of my friendship for him, and with ardent desires for his relief: in which sentiments I know that my fellow-citizens participate. The measures you were pleased to intimate in your letter are perhaps not exactly those which I could pursue, perhaps indeed not the most likely, under actual circumstances, to obtain our object. But be assured that I am not inattentive to his condition, nor contenting myself with inactive wishes for his liberation. My affection to his nation and to himself are

unabated, and notwithstanding the line of separation which has been unfortunately drawn between them, I am confident that both have been led on by a pure love of liberty and a desire to secure public happiness: and I shall deem that among the most consoling moments of my life which should see them reunited in the end, as they were in the beginning, of their virtuous enterprize. Accept I pray you the same lively sentiments of interest and attachment to yourself & your dear Children, from, dear Madam, your &c.[3]   G.W.

Dft (DNA: RG 59, MLR); in TJ's hand, with emendations by Washington noted below; dateline at foot of text; at foot of first page: "Mde. de la Fayette. departement de la Haute-Loire. à Chavaniac, prés Brioude"; endorsed by Washington. PrC (DLC); entirely in TJ's hand. Recorded in SJPL. For the letter as sent by Washington under the date of 16 Mch. 1793, with only trifling variations from the emended Dft, see Fitzpatrick, *Writings*, xxxii, 389-90.

[1] Washington reworked "15" to "16" in the dateline at the foot of text and added a second dateline at the head of text: "Phila. March 16th. 1793."
[2] First part of this word written over "doubt," erased, by TJ.
[3] Reworking this abbreviation, Washington added "most Obedt. & devoted Servt."

From John Wilkes Kittera

DEAR SIR   Lancaster March 16th. 1793.

Having left the City before the receipt of Mr. Chambers' letter to me, containing the inclosed papers, I beg leave to transmit them to you. Mr. Chambers, like all other Projectors,[1] appears quite captivated with his discovery. Whether any thing, or what ought to be done with his letter to the President of the National Convention of France, I submit to you as better able to judge. I am, Sir, with Sentiments of perfect respect & esteem Your most obt. & very hble Servt.

JNO W: KITTERA

RC (DNA: RG 59, MLR); at foot of text: "Honble. Thos. Jefferson Esqr." and (immediately above in a different hand, possibly TJ's) "sign of Lamb. Market"; endorsed by TJ as received 15 Apr. 1793. Enclosures not found.

[1] Word reworked from "inventors."

From James Maury

Liverpool, 16 Mch. 1793. He encloses this month's price current at Liverpool, which remains closed to foreign wheat and flour. He lately corresponded with Pinckney on whether the irregularity of American sea captains "in furnishing the particulars required in your Instructions of the 26. Augt. 1790" requires government intervention and was advised to mention it to TJ, of whom he requests instructions. He asks for three sets of the laws of the United States for his consular agents.

RC (DNA: RG 59, CD); 2 p.; in a clerk's hand, except for signature, internal address, and part of complimentary close by Maury; at foot of first page: "Secretary of State to the United States of America Philadelphia"; endorsed by TJ as received 1 May 1793 and so recorded in SJL. Enclosure: Price current of American produce at Liverpool, 11 Mch. 1793, with subjoined extracts from Lloyd's list of quotations for stock, exchange with Paris, and gold and silver, 8 Mch. 1793 (printed form in same; signed by Maury, with prices and comments entered in a clerk's hand).

To Thomas Pinckney

DEAR SIR   Philadelphia, March 16th. 1793.

I wrote you on the 30th. of December, and again a short Letter on the 1st. of January, since which I have received yours of October 2d. and 5th. Nov. 6th. and 9th. and Dec. 13th. 14th. 15th. I now inclose you the Treasurer's second of exchange for 24,750 Guilders to be employed in the purchase of copper for the mint from Sweden or wherever else it can be got on the best terms, the first of exchange having been enclosed in my letter of December 30.

I am in hopes you will have been able to enter into proper arrangements with the British Minister for the protection of our seamen from impressment before the preparations for war shall have produced inconvenience to them. While he regards so minutely the inconveniences to themselves which may result from a due regulation of this practice, it is just he should regard our inconveniencies also from the want of it. His observations in your letter imply merely that if they should abstain from injuring us, it might be attended with inconvenience to themselves.

You ask what should be your conduct in case you should at any time discover negotiations to be going on which might eventually be interesting to us? The nature of the particular case will point out what measures on your part would be the most for our interest, and to your discretion we must refer the taking such measures without waiting for instructions where circumstances would not admit of such a delay. A like necessity to act may arise on other occasions. In the changeable scenes, for instance, which are passing in Europe, were a moment to offer when you could obtain any advantage for our commerce, and especially in the american Colonies, you are desired[1] to avail us of it to the best advantage, and not to let the occasion slip by for want of previous instruction.

You ask what encoragements are given to emigrants by the several States? No other than a permission to become citizens and to participate of the rights of citizens, except as to eligibility to certain Offices in the government. The rules, as to these, are not uniform in the States. I have found it absolutely impracticable to obtain even for my Office a regular transmission of the laws of the several States: consequently it would be more so to furnish them to our ministers abroad. You will receive by this, or the first proper conveyance those of Congress, passed at their last Session.

The appointment of your Secretary depending absolutely on yourself, no confirmation is necessary for that of Mr. Deas.

It is impossible for me to give any authority for the advance of monies to Mr. Wilson. Were we to do it in his case, we should, on the same principles be obliged to do it in several others wherein foreign nations decline or delay doing justice to our Citizens. No law of the United States would cover such an act of the Executive: and all we can do legally is to give him all the aid which our patronage of his claims with the British Court can effect.

With respect to the payment of your allowances, as the laws authorize the payment of a given number of Dollars to you, and as your Duties place you in London, I suppose we are to pay you *the Dollars* there, or other money of equal value, estimated by the par of the metals. Such has accordingly been the practice ever since the close of the War. Your powers to draw on our Bankers in Holland, will leave you the master of fixing your draughts by this standard.

The transactions of Europe are now so interesting that I should be obliged to you every week to put the Leyden Gazettes of the week under cover to me, and put them into such Ship's bag as shall be first coming to any port North of north Carolina.

Mr. Barclay's death is just made known to us, and measures are taking in consequence of it.

You will perceive by the news papers a remarkable fall in the price of our public paper. This is owing chiefly to the extraordinary demand for the produce of our Country, and a temporary scarcity of Cash to purchase it. The merchants holding public paper are obliged to part with it at any price to raise money.

The following appointments of Consuls have taken place.

Nathl. Cutting	for Havre
Edward Fox	for Falmouth
Joseph Yznardi Jr.	for Cadiz
Robert Montgomery	for Alicant
John Parish	for Hamburg

Henry Cooper   for Santa Cruz
David Matthew Clarkson   for St. Eustatia
Benjamin Hamnell Philips for Curraçoa
Samuel Cooper Johonnet   for Demarara
Michael Murphy   for Malaga
James Greenleaf   for Amsterdam

I sent you some time ago a dozen plans of the City of Washington in the Federal territory, hoping you would have them displayed to public view where they would be most seen by those descriptions of men worthy and likely to be attracted to it, and particularly in the principal towns.

I trust to Mr. Taylor to forward you the newspapers by every good opportunity so as to avoid the expense of postage. I am with much respect Dear sir, your most obedient and very humble servt.

Th: Jefferson

RC (CSmH); in the hand of George Taylor, Jr., signed by TJ; at foot of first page: "Mr.   Pinckney." PrC (DLC); unsigned. FC (Lb in DNA: RG 59, DCI). Enclosure not found. Enclosed in TJ to George Washington, 20 Mch. 1793.

¹ Word reworked by TJ from "directed," and similarly altered by him in ink on PrC.

To Benjamin Russell

Sir   Philadelphia March 16. 1793.

Be pleased to correct the following typographical error in the 1st. Section of the Act intituled "An act to alter the times and places of holding the Circuit Courts in the Eastern District, and in North Carolina, and for other purposes." To wit "for the district of Massachusetts, at Boston, on the seventeenth day of June"; strike out the word "*seventeenth*" and insert in lieu thereof the word *seventh*.

Th: Jefferson

If you have not published the above mentioned act, its publication with the above correction will be sufficient.

PrC (DLC); in the hand of George Taylor, Jr., signed by TJ; at foot of text: "Mr. Benjamin Russell." FC (Lb in DNA: RG 59, DL). Tr (MHi: Robert Treat Paine Papers); partly in Taylor's hand; lacks postscript; endorsed by William Cushing.

The ACT in question became law on 2

Mch. 1793 (*Annals*, III, 1449-50). On 16 Mch. 1793 TJ also wrote a letter to the justices of the United States Supreme Court notifying them of the ERROR and enclosing copies of his letter to "Mr. Russel of Massachusetts who publishes the laws of the United States in that District" (RC in MHi: Robert Treat Paine Papers, at foot of text: "Judge Cushing," in Taylor's hand, signed by TJ, endorsed by William Cushing; PrC in DLC, in Taylor's hand, unsigned, with "Judge Iredell" at foot of text, next to which Taylor added in ink "No. Caro." and above which he added in ink "Chief Justice Jay & associate Judges Paterson—N.J. Wilson—Penna. Cushing—Massa. Blair—Virga."; FC in Lb in DNA: RG 59, DL, at head of text: "Chief Justice Jay and associate Judges").

To Francis Eppes

DEAR SIR   Philadelphia Mar. 17. 1793.

Besides the difficulty you mentioned with respect to Jack's trip to the Indian treaty, one has occurred here from a necessity, not expected, of circumscribing the number of persons who are to go, within as narrow limits as possible. Under these circumstances it becomes necessary to consider what would be his best plan for the summer. Tho' I have promised[1] to remain here longer than I had declared, and without saying how much longer, yet my private determination, which I may confide to you, is that it shall be but little longer. I have therefore given up my house, and am now packing up my furniture to send it off to Virginia. In the mean time, to wear the appearance of remaining here I have taken a small house in the country, *for a year.* In this situation I have thought it would be best to recommend to you that Jack should go to Williamsburg, as I have ever advised students to pass the last year there, as well to go through the course of law lectures, as to acquire the habit of publick speaking in the moot-court there before they appear on the public stage. The want of this habit has sometimes struck such a panic into a new orator as that he has never got over it. This too is the only method by which a student can discover his own powers, and decide for[2] himself his future enterprizes. Jack tells me that the college vacation ènds in may, and that the lectures begin then. He will therefore return to you in time to be at their opening, if you approve of it. I directed his books to be sent from Ireland in April, and my correspondent has promised they shall. They will arrive at Richmond addressed to me to the care of Mr. James Brown. They will be known from other packages which will come from the same person under the same address, from the circumstance that they will come from *Ireland*, the others from England. From this description you can apply for and receive them from Mr. Brown without further authority from me.

I mentioned to you in my last letter that I had found that I should in fact have occasion, on winding up here, for some hundred dollars of the money expected from Carey's executor. I shall be happy to learn from you what are the prospects, as a disappointment will be a puzzling, perhaps a distressing, circumstance to me. I shall see you at Eppington when I come to Virginia. In the mean time present my affectionate respects to Mrs Eppes and love to the family, and accept yourself assurances of the warm esteem of Dear Sir Your sincere friend & servt.   THS. JEFFERSON

PrC (ViU: Edgehill-Randolph Papers); consists of first page only; at foot of first page: "Mr. Eppes." Tr (same); 19th-century copy of complete text.

The BOOKS TO BE SENT FROM IRELAND

are listed in the enclosure to TJ to Alexander Donald, 11 Oct. 1792.

[1] Word interlined in place of "determined."

[2] PrC ends here; remainder supplied from Tr.

From Horatio Gates

MY DEAR SIR   Rose Hill 17th: March 1793.

I am favoured with the receipt of your obliging Letter of the 12th: Instant and shall with pleasure Obey your Commands; Your Letters to me, during the Period you mention, are in a large Chest full of public papers; My Letters to you, are all Copied in a Book, from whence they shall be recopied, and with the others deliverd into your Hands. But what if you was to come and pass the Hot Summer Season here, and hereabouts, while this is doing; At Times we can amuse ourselves upon this, and Long Island, where much amusement is to be had; Rose Hill will do now, and then, as place of Rest; from whence we can Start, and Return, when we please. Tell Mr: Maddison he can't do better than be of the Party; You Statesmen should take all Opportunitys to relax your Minds; The best Bow will be Spoil'd, by being always bent; therefore come to New York; the best Time of the Year to Ramble, is from the Middle of June, to the last of July, for then this Country is delightfull; My Mary Joins me very Sincerely in this Invitation. The only reason I can give for discontinuing a correspondence by which I was so much obliged was, a diffidence lest I should intrude upon the Time of a Minister, and might now, and then, ask Questions, which a Man high in Office, might think Impertinent;—Trust me I shall upon every proper occasion be Glad to Testify the respect, and regard, with which I am Dear Sir Your Faithfull, and Obedient Servant;

HORATIO GATES

[397]

P.S. Mrs: Gates presents Her Compliments, and requests you will also present them to Mr: Maddison.

RC (NHi); endorsed by TJ as received 20 Mch. 1793 and so recorded in SJL.

To Edmund Randolph

Mar. 17. 93.

Th: Jefferson incloses for the examination of the Atty. Genl. the abstract form of a patent proposed under the new law, wherein will be inserted the title only of the discovery, within the body of the instrument; and the description required by law, to be in a schedule annexed to and making part of the letters patent. This will admit the very words of the petitioner to be used, without the possibility of imputing to us either it's legal defects, or grammatical improprieties. It will admit too of *printing* the whole of the letters patent with short blanks for the name of the inventor and title of his invention.

Th:J. sends an example of a patent to Saltonstall on this plan, and another prepared by Mr. Taylor on the former one, where the description was inserted in the body of the letters, from which the advantages of the former will be evident. He will thank the Atty. Genl. for his corrections of and opinion on the form, this being the first instance, and to serve as a precedent.

PrC (DLC); partially overwritten in a later hand. Recorded in SJPL. First enclosure printed below. Other enclosures not found.

The simplified NEW LAW regarding patents, enacted on 21 Feb. 1793, lifted the heavy administrative burden imposed on TJ as Secretary of State by the 1790 Patent Act it superseded (*Annals*, III, 1431-5). For a discussion of TJ's role in effecting this reform, see note to A Bill to Promote the Progress of the Useful Arts, [1 Dec. 1791]. Randolph's reaction to TJ's ABSTRACT FORM OF A PATENT has not been found, but TJ's draft served as the basis for the somewhat modified patent form the United States government used for the next seventy-three years (Karl B. Lutz, "Evolution of U.S. Patent Documents," *Journal of the Patent Office Society*, XIX [1937], 396-7; for an example of an issued patent, see the 17 Feb. 1803 patent issued by TJ as President to Elisha Bartlett and others for a nail-making machine in NjP: Andre deCoppet Collection). On 22 Mch. 1793 the President signed a patent dated 28 Feb. 1793 for a plan by Richard Roswell SALTONSTALL for "improvemt. in the manufacturing the plant called Rhus or Sumach for dying" (Washington, *Journal*, 99-100; *List of Patents*, 7).

Proposed Form for Patents

[ca. 17 Mch. 1793]

The US. of America to all to whom these[1] *letters patent* shall come:

Whereas A.B. *a citizen* of the state of _____ *in the US. hath alledged that he has invented [or discovered]* &c. *not before known or used*[2] *has made oath [or affirmation] that he does verily believe that he is the true inventor [or discoverer] thereof:* has *paid into the treasury* of the US. the sum of *30. dollars delivered a receipt for the* same, and *presented a petition to the Secretary of state signifying a desire of obtaining an exclusive property in the said invention [or improvement] and praying that a patent may be granted* for that purpose:

These are therefore to *grant* according to law to *the said A.B. his heirs administrators or assigns, for the term of 14 years, the full and exclusive right and liberty of making constructing, using and vending to others to be used the said invention [or discovery]* a description whereof is given in the words of the said A.B. himself in the schedule hereto annexed, and is made a part of these presents.

In testimony whereof I have caused these letters to be made patent, and the seal of the US. to be hereunto affixed. Given under my hand at the city of Philadelphia this __ day of ____ in the year of our lord 179_ and of the independance of the US. of A. the _____

G.W.

By the President
Tʜ:J.

The Schedule referred to in these Letters patent and making part of the same, containing a description in the words of the said A.B. himself of the &c.

PrC (DLC: TJ Papers, 96: 16471); undated; in TJ's hand, but partially over-written in a later hand; brackets in original.

[1] Here TJ canceled "presents."
[2] Preceding five words interlined.

To John Syme

Dᴇᴀʀ Sɪʀ   Philadelphia Mar. 17. 1793.

I received yesterday your favor of the 8th. covering one to Mr. Barclay, and, the moment before, I had received a letter giving me an authentic account of his death, of which a less certain one had arrived a few days before. No person more sincerely sympathizes with his family, than I do, on this melancholy event: and I should ask you to express my condolences to them, did I not know by experience that all such expressions serve but to open anew the sluices of grief, and that silence and time can alone bring a remedy. In the meantime it may be a satisfaction to them to learn what particulars we know of his death, for which reason I give the following extracts from the letter of Colo. Humphreys dated Lisbon Jan. 23. 93.

'Mr. Barclay, consul for Morocco, who arrived here from Cadiz on tuesday last, died on Saturday. His sudden death is supposed to have been occasioned by an inflammation of the lungs. On the Thursday[1] he complained of a slight fever, costiveness and raging thirst for water, for some time. That night he took medicine. On Friday he mostly kept his bed. I conversed with him however a good deal on business; and when I left him he told me he hoped to be well in two or three days. Next morning I was sent for early, and finding his life despaired of by the Physicians, I took possession of his public papers. From the time he was apprehended to be in danger, he was never able to pronounce more than a word or two at a time, or to give the least information respecting the public affairs, or his own.'

As no opportunity had yet occurred of forwarding your former letter, I have thought it best to return both to you. I am with great regard, Dear Sir your most obedt. humble servt   Th: Jefferson

PrC (DLC); at foot of first page: "Colo. Syme." Tr (DLC); 19th-century copy.

[1] Word interlined in place of "Wednesday."

To George Washington

Mar. 17. 1793.

Th: Jefferson with his respectful compliments to the President returns him Colo. Humphrey's letter and those from George town. The last are indeed disagreeable: yet there does not seem any room for the President's interposition.—Should Dr. Stewart and Mr. Johnson persist in their idea of retiring, it seems really desireable that they should do it separately, leaving such an interval between the two resignations as that the public mind may receive no unfavorable impression.

RC (DNA: RG 59, MLR); addressed: "The President of the US."; endorsed by Tobias Lear. Tr (Lb in same, SDC). Not recorded in SJL. Enclosures: (1) David Humphreys to Washington, Lisbon, 23 Jan. 1793, seeking approval of his efforts to subsist American captives in Algiers and secure the property for the Moroccan mission left by Thomas Barclay, offering to assist Barclay's successor in negotiating with Algiers and suggesting ways to facilitate these negotiations, and noting his intention to write to the Secretary of State about American wheat and flour in Portugal (DLC: Washington Papers). (2) Commissioners of the Federal District to Washington, Georgetown, 11 Mch. 1793, expressing approval of William Thornton's plan for the Capitol but suggesting a modification and indicating concern about the sufficiency of funds for the plan, requesting that their accounts be regularly inspected to rebut any criticisms of their work, announcing day of my death. but I deplore them as I should have done had they fallen in battle. it was necessary to use the arm of the people, a machine not quite so blind as balls and bombs, but blind to a certain degree. a few of their cordial friends met, at their hands the fate of enemies. but time and truth will rescue & embalm their memories, while their posterity will be enjoying that very liberty for which they would never have hesitated to offer up their lives. the liberty of the whole earth was depending on the issue of the contest, and was ever such a prize won with so little innocent blood? my own affections have been deeply wounded by some of the martyrs to this cause, but rather than it should have failed I would have seen half the earth desolated. were there but an Adam & an Eve left in every country, & left free, it would be better than as it now is. I have expressed to you my sentiments, because they are really those of 99 in an hundred of our citizens. the universal feasts, and rejoicings which have lately been had on account of the successes of the French shewed the genuine effusions of their hearts. you have been wounded by the sufferings of your friends, and have by this circumstance been hurried into a temper of mind which would be extremely disrelished if known to your countrymen. the reserve of the Presdt of the US 224. 68.1160.914.83. had never permitted me to discover the light in which he viewed it. and as I was more anxious that you should vote by him than me, I had still avoided explanation with you on the subject. but yours 113. induced him to break silence and to

The Execution of Louis XVI

Frontispiece from Jean Pierre Blanchard's Account of

Whereas Andrew Michaux, a native of France, and inhabitant of the United States has undertaken to explore the interior country of North America from the Missisippi along the Missouri and Westwardly to the Pacific ocean, or in such other direction as shall be advised by the American Philosophical society & on his return to communicate to the said society the information he shall have acquired of the geography of the said country it's inhabitants, soil, climate, animals, vegetables, minerals & other circumstances of note. We the Subscribers, desirous of obtaining for ourselves relative to the land we live on, and of communicating to the world, information so interesting to curiosity, to science, and to the future prospects of mankind, promise for ourselves, our heirs executors & administrators, that we will pay the said Andrew Michaux, or his assigns, the sums herein affixed to our names respectively, one fourth part thereof on demand, the remaining three fourths whenever, after his return, the said Philosophical society, shall declare themselves satisfied that he has performed the sd journey & that he has communicated to them freely, all the information which he shall have acquired & they demanded of him; or if the sd Andrew Michaux shall not proceed to the Pacific ocean, and shall reach the sources of the waters running into it, then we will pay him such part only of the remaining three fourths, as the said Philosophical society shall deem duly proportioned to the extent of unknown country explored by him in the direction prescribed, as compared with that omitted to be so explored. And we consent that the bills of exchange of the sd Andrew Michaux, for monies said to be due to him in France, shall be recieved to the amount of two hundred Louis & shall be negociated by the sd Philosophical society, and the proceeds thereof retained in their hands, to be delivered to the sd Andrew Michaux, on his return, after having performed the journey to their satisfaction, or, if not to their satisfaction, then to be applied towards reimbursing the subscribers the fourth of their subscription advanced to the said Andrew Michaux. We consent also that the sd Andrew Michaux shall take to himself all benefit arising from the publication of the discoveries he shall make in the three departments of Natural history, Animal Vegetable and mineral, he concerting with the said Philosophical society, such measures for securing to himself the said benefit as shall be consistent with the due publication of the said discoveries. In witness whereof we have hereto subscribed our names and affixed the sums we engage respectively to contribute.

G Washington one hundred Dollars
John Adams Twenty Dollars
Benjamin Hawkins Twenty Dollars
Ra: Izard — Twenty Dollars
Saml Johnston Twenty Dollars
Robt Morris Eighty dolrs
Jas Henry — ten dollars
G Cabot Ten Dollars
John Rutherford Twenty dollars

Knox fifty dollars
Th: Jefferson fifty dollars
Alexander Hamilton fifty dollars
Rufus King Twenty dollars
John Langdon Twenty dollars
John Edwards Sixteen dollars
John Brown Twenty dollars
Tho Mifflin Twenty dollars

Jona Trumbull Twenty dollrs
James Madison Jr. Twenty dollars
J H Parker Twenty dollars
Alex White Twenty dollars
John Page twenty dollars
John Beckle 10 drs
Wm Smith Twenty dors
Jere Wadsworth Thirty
Richard Bland Lee ten dollars
Thos Fitzsimons ten dollars
Saml Griffin Ten dollars
Wm B Giles Ten dollars
J Williams Ten dollars

First Page of Subscription Agreement for André Michaux's
Proposed Western Expedition

William Branch Giles

Tench Coxe

Mar. 2. 1793. see the papers of this date, mr Giles's resolutions. he & one or two others were sanguine enough to believe that the palpableness of these resolns rendered it impossible the house could reject them. those who knew the composition of the house 1. of bank directors 2. holders of bank stock. 3. stock jobbers. 4 blind devotees. 5 ignorant persons who did not comprehend them 6 [lazy &] good humored persons, who comprehended & acknoleged them, yet were [too lazy to examine, or] unwilling to pronounce censure. the persons who knew these characters foresaw that the 3. first descriptions [taking] making ⅓ of the house the 3. latter would make ½ of the residue, and of course that they would be rejected by a majority of 2. to 1. but they thought that even this rejection would do good, by shewing the public the desperate & abandoned dispositions with which their affairs were entrusted. the resolns were proposed, and nothing spared to present them in the fullness of demonstration. there were not more than 3. or 4. who voted otherwise than had been expected.

it is known that Murray of Maryld. deals in paper.

Mar. 23. 1793. the following list of paper-men is communicated to me by mr Beckley.

* Gilman. S.H.
† * Gerry. S.H.
  Sedgwick.
* Ames S.H.
* Goodhue S.H.
  Bourne. R.I. suspected only
* Trumbull S.H.
* Wadsworth. S.H.
* Hillhouse. S.H.
  Learned. S.H.
  Laurence. S.H. & Director
  Loudon.
† Bourbon? S.H.
* Dayton S.H.
* Fitzsimmons S.H. & Director
* D.Hunter. S.H.
  Sterret
  Murray S.H.
† * Williamson. S.H.
  Smith S.H. & Director. for himself & his proxies his vote is near ⅕ of the whole

* Cabot. S.H. & Director
* Sherman S.H.
  Elsworth qu.
* King. S.H. & Director
  Dickinson
* Morris. S.H.
* Johnson
* Izard S.H.

* these are known to Beckley
† these avowed it in person

Mar. 25. Beckley says he has this day discovered that Benson is a stockholder. also Bourne of R.I. and Key.

	H.Repr.	Senate
Stockholders	16	5
Mer paper	3	2
suspected	2	1

Jefferson's Notes on the Defeat of the Giles Resolutions

Jefferson's Residence on the Schuylkill

Draft of Jefferson's Dispatch to Carmichael and Short Withdrawing
Authorization for an American Guarantee to Spain

[22 April 1793]

By the PRESIDENT of the United States of America.

A PROCLAMATION.

WHEREAS it appears that a ſtate of war exiſts between Auſtria, Pruſſia, Sardinia, Great-Britain, and the United Netherlands, of the one part, and France on the other, and the duty and intereſt of the United States require, that they ſhould with ſincerity and good faith adopt and purſue a conduct friendly and impartial toward the belligerent powers :

I have therefore thought fit by theſe preſents to declare the diſpoſition of the United States to obſerve the conduct aforeſaid towards thoſe powers reſpectively ; and to exhort and warn the citizens of the United States carefully to avoid all acts and proceedings whatſover, which may in any manner tend to contravene ſuch diſpoſition.

And I do hereby alſo make known that whoſoever of the citizens of the United States ſhall render himſelf liable to puniſhment or forfeiture under the law of nations, by committing, aiding or abetting hoſtilities againſt any of the ſaid powers, or by carrying to any of them thoſe articles, which are deemed contraband by the *modern* uſage of nations, will not receive the protection of the United States, againſt ſuch puniſhment or forfeiture : and further, that I have given inſtructions to thoſe officers, to whom it belongs, to cauſe proſecutions to be inſtituted againſt all perſons, who ſhall, within the cognizance of the courts of the United States, violate the Law of Nations, with reſpect to the powers at war, or any of them.

(L.S.) *IN* TESTIMONY WHEREOF *I have cauſed the Seal of the United States of America to be affixed to theſe preſents, and ſigned the ſame with my hand. Done at the city of Philadelphia, the twenty-ſecond day of April, one thouſand ſeven hundred and ninety-three, and of the Independence of the United States of America the ſeventeenth.*

G°. WASHINGTON.

By the Preſident.

TH: JEFFERSON.

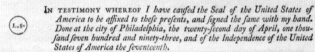

Washington's Proclamation of Neutrality

the Quest.

H's reasoning.

admitted that this is real i.e. national treaty

L. Nations 1. Moral law. 2. Usage. 3. Conventions
this Qu. depends on 1.st branch.

nature of Moral Oblign on individuals
                                    societies   aggregate
evidence of. moral sense & reason of men.

Oblign of Contracts.— self destruct. — head & heart — there written — useless
impossible.
non-compliance for danger.   — of this ourselves to judge.
                                        judge rigorously.

Restrictions on this right of self liberation from treaty

1. danger great, inevitable, imminent.
    is the present one so?
        1. if issue in military despotism.
        2.   republic
        3. possibility of Rank & W. Bloody bones
            possibility always exists — existed at signature
            must wait moment then imminent.
            is this the last moment.
    4. is the danger from guarantee?
        does the guarantee engage us to enter &c.
        this danger then not certain enough, nor imminent.
    5. is it from 17.th art. asylum. Holl.d & Prussia have not sent
                                        Engl.d same art. agt us.
    6. 2.nd art. prohib. enemies of France to fit out has not sent too.
                                                privateers in our ports
        we may prohibit France the same
    7. the Reception of Minister is act of election; & loses right
        qualified
                    no connection with treaty
    8. to elect the continuance of a treaty is = makes treaty &c.
        no act necessary. — treaty goes on.

2.d Restriction. liberate from infraction of neutral?
                    no act
                    the residue non
    3. limin. Comparison clause of guarantee — option then in opposite treaty
    self-libern without just cause or comparison gives cause of war to France
    Examine authorities — how far they weigh. — danger of understg Vattel with
    Grotius — Puff. — Wolf — Vattel
    Vattel. 2. 160.
            158.   163. 219.220.

their intention to dismiss Andrew Ellicott for slowness and inaccuracy in surveying the Federal District and to redo much of his work, and concluding with a postscript of 12 Mch. 1793 announcing the arrival of Ellicott, his brother Benjamin, and Isaac Briggs, enclosing an exchange of letters with Ellicott, and stating that they have taken possession of the large plat and will reorganize the Surveyor's department tomorrow (DNA: RG 42, DCLB). (3) Same to same, 13 Mch. 1793, enclosing a further exchange of letters with Ellicott as well as his handbill, reporting that yesterday Ellicott tried to give them the plan of the territory Washington had sent him with orders for revisions but that they refused it and told him to complete it as specified by the President, and announcing that they have "nearly arranged the Surveying Business with Checks, and expect on trial it will produce dispatch" (same).

Washington had received these enclosures on 16 Mch. 1793 and sent them to TJ for "perusal & consideration" the same day (Washington, *Journal*, 91). Nos. 2 and 3 enclosed in turn twelve letters between the Commissioners and Andrew Ellicott pertaining to their dismissal of him as chief surveyor of the Federal District on 12 Mch. 1793 (Commissioners to Ellicott, 6, 7 Feb., 11, 12, and 13 Mch. 1793, DNA: RG 42, DCLB; Ellicott to Commissioners, 12, 13 Mch. 1793, same, PBG). This controversy is discussed in Ellicott to TJ, 9 Jan. 1793, and note.

To George Wythe

DEAR SIR   Philadelphia Mar. 17. 1793.

Your seal not being finished till this morning I was not able to send it by any of the gentlemen bound directly to Richmond. I now put it into the care of Mr. Madison and Colo. Monroe, who go to Fredericksburg and there will find some person going on to Richmond. It has been delayed by an error in the engraver, who in engraving the word *EYΘEIAN*, mistook the *Y* for a *Ψ* and had engraved the latter character. On discovering the error I sent it back to him, and he had to erase two or three of the neighboring letters to get the whole to stand right. The price is sixty four dollars. Brass has been preferred to steel, because of the liableness of the latter to rust, and to silver for it's liableness to be stolen. I am with great & unceasing affection, my dear sir, your sincere friend & obedt. servt   TH: JEFFERSON

P.S. Rapahanae is the orthography of the drawing.

PrC (DLC); at foot of text: "G.   *EYΘEIAN*: "on a straight."
Wythe." Tr (DLC); 19th-century copy.

To Joseph Fay

DEAR SIR   Philadelphia Mar. 18. 1793.

I received your kind favor of the 26th. Ult. and thank you for it's contents as sincerely as if I could engage in what they propose. When I first entered on the stage of public life (now 24. years ago) I came to a resolution never to engage while in public office[1] in any kind of enterprize for the improvement of my fortune, nor to wear any other character than that of a farmer. I have never departed from it in a single instance: and I have in multiplied instances found myself happy in being able to decide and to act as a public servant, clear of all interest, in the multiform questions that have arisen, wherein I have seen others embarrassed and biassed by having got themselves into a more interested situation. Thus I have thought myself richer in contentment than I should have been with any increase of fortune. Certainly I should have been much wealthier[2] had I remained in that private condition which renders it lawful and even laudable to use proper efforts to better it. However, my public career is now closing, and I will go through on the principles on which I have hitherto acted. But I feel myself under obligations to repeat my thanks for this mark of your attention and friendship.

We have just received here the news of the decapitation of the king of France. Should the present ferment in Europe not produce republics every where, it will at least soften the monarchical governments by rendering monarchs amenable to punishment like other criminals, and doing away that aegis of insolence and oppression, the inviolability of the king's person. We I hope shall adhere to our republican government, and keep it to it's original principles by narrowly watching it. I am with great & sincere affection Dear Sir your friend & servt

TH: JEFFERSON

PrC (DLC).

[1] Preceding four words interlined.
[2] Word interlined in place of "richer."

To Alexander Hamilton

SIR   Philadelphia March 18. 1793.

The contingent account of the Department of State down to the 9th. instant, having been delivered to, and passed by the Auditor, and being at present in want of a further sum to satisfy demands against my Office, I must request the favor of you to order a warrant to issue payable to George Taylor Junior for Twelve hundred Dollars, and am, with respect Sir, Your most obedt. servt.

PrC (DLC); in the hand of George Taylor, Jr., unsigned; at foot of text: "The secretary of the Treasury of the United States of America." FC (Lb in DNA: RG 59, DL).

The CONTINGENT ACCOUNT is described in Vol. 17: 377, No. 3.

To Thomas Mann Randolph, Jr.

DEAR SIR   Philadelphia Mar. 18. 93.

I have to acknolege the receipt of your two favors of Feb. 20. and 29. on the 9th. instant. I wrote to my daughter the last week (the 10th.) as usual.

I thank you for your information respecting my affairs. I counted little on Ronald or his affairs for my debt. I took a mortgage of the land sold, and of a moiety of his Beverdam land. I previously had the Goochld. records examined in my own presence and found no previous mortgage there of the Beverdam lands. I procured some friend (I do not remember who) to search the general court in like manner. I shall rather hope that executors will be for making immediate provision by sale of the lands, and so hasten my remedy.—I see no possibility of defect in my title to the Natural bridge. It was king's land, entered and surveyed for me by old Tom Lewis, who was too attentive a surveyor to have done this if it had not been vacant. I received the patent in the usual time and form. I believe the taxes were regularly paid while I was in Europe. Since my return Mr. Stuart promised to do it annually, to be reimbursed from time to time when the sum should become worth note.—You doubt whether I do not let my lands too low. I try this two ways, and think I do not. First, every 100 acres with one negroe[1] will bring me 50 dollars, which is more than I ever made, and is 10. Dollars more than Garth and Mousley paid me; and it is certain they made a very small profit. Secondly suppose a tenant and his wife and four negroes to occupy a farm of 400. acres, or a tenant and his wife and 2 negroes to have one of 200. acres, the rent will be about 15. dollars on each labourer, which I believe is as much as the labourer can spare for the land he works, reserving a moderate and reasonable price for the labour he bestows on it. I was allowed but 50/ a hand by my father's executors for the hands of my brother who in 6. or 7. years totally destroyed the upper tract of my land on the East side of the river, when it was the richest peice of tobacco land in the neighborhood. I think it will always be best to let tenants pay rather too little than too much. Otherwise they will remove or break.— I doubt whether it will not be better to leave the renewal of the lease to be negociated during it's course, as circumstances may change so materially.—I will certainly endeavor to procure some tenants for you if I find it practicable to extend the thing at all. As you do not mention the two young men who went to see my lands, I hope they arrived after I apprised you of my proposal and that you would be able to encourage them. In my letter last week I expressed my wishes that you would apply the force in your hands to the accomodation of the family with whatever convenience they can, as a first object; and after that only, to what I had planned. It is my earnest wish you should do so, as the former is the first object in my mind.—My love to my dear Martha, and am sincerely & affectionately Dear Sir your's &c.

TH: JEFFERSON

RC (DLC); addressed: "Thomas M. Randolph junr. esq. Monticello." PrC (MHi).

The second of Randolph's FAVORS was actually dated 27 Feb. 1793.

[1] TJ first wrote "two negroes" and then altered the phrase to read as above.

From William Loughton Smith

March 18th. [1793]

Mr. Smith requests the favor of Mr. Jefferson to inform him of the annual amount of the following items, viz.

Salaries[1] of foreign Ministers &c.

Treaties—(conjectural.)

Annual Contingencies (conjectural.)

RC (DLC); partially dated; endorsed by TJ: "Smith Wm. (S.C.)."

William Loughton Smith (1758-1812), a staunchly Federalist congressman from South Carolina, 1789-97, and minister to Portugal, 1797-1801, authored vitriolic pamphlet attacks on TJ in 1792 and 1796 (Editorial Note on opinions on the constitutionality of the Residence Bill, in Vol. 17: 178-80). The leading defender of Alexander Hamilton during the recent debates in the House of Representatives on the Giles resolutions, Smith around this time also requested detailed state-

ments from the Treasury Department on the domestic and foreign debt for "his own Information," probably hoping to use this data, as well as what he requested from TJ, to counteract Republican criticisms of Hamilton's fiscal management during a forthcoming visit to South Carolina (Syrett, *Hamilton*, XIV, 212-13, 338-41). See also George C. Rogers, Jr., *Evolution of a Federalist: William Loughton Smith of Charleston (1758-1812)* (Columbia, S.C., 1962), 241-6.

[1] Before this word and "Treaties" on the next line Smith canceled "Anl."

To William Loughton Smith

Mar. 18. 93.

Th: Jefferson presents his compliments to Mr. Smith. Supposing his enquiries to go to the *ordinary* foreign establishment (not to the extraordinary respecting the Barbary powers) he has the honor to inform him that the salary of our Min. Plenipo. is 9000. D. per ann. and their secretaries 1350. D. That of a Minister Resident is 4500. D. and no secretary allowed, because the fund not sufficient. Treaties and other contingencies (which include Outfit and Return) may be set down at nearly the balance remaining of the 40,000 D. a year; that fund being about 5, or 10,000 D. less than would have sufficed for the establishment desired by the Executive. The establishment has consequently been reduced just within the limits of the fund.

RC (DLC: William Loughton Smith Papers); endorsed by Smith. PrC (DLC). Tr (DLC); 19th-century copy. At foot of RC Smith wrote:

"Minis. P. to England		9000
Outfit		9000
Secretary		1350
Min. P. to France		9000
Outfit		9000
Secrety		1350
Minis. Resident Holld		4500
Do.	Portugal	4500
Do.	Spain	4500
		52200
Deduct Outfit		18000
		34000."

To George Washington

Mar. 18. 93.

Th: Jefferson has the honor to inclose to the President the copies of the Algerine papers which have been made out to form the basis of instructions for the Commissioner to be appointed. The President will be pleased to consider whether he would chuse to have them altered in any particular.

RC (DNA: RG 59, MLR); addressed: "The President of the US."; endorsed by Tobias Lear. Tr (Lb in DNA: RG 59, SDC). Not recorded in SJL.

The enclosed ALGERINE PAPERS—which the President approved without alteration the same day and TJ enclosed in his 21 Mch. 1793 letter to David Humphreys— consisted, with suitable modifications, essentially of those sent to John Paul Jones and Thomas Barclay the year before (Washington, *Journal*, 93).

From Stephen Cathalan, Jr.

Marseilles, 19 Mch. 1793. He encloses and confirms a copy of his last letter of 17 Feb. The *Aurora* of Baltimore, André L. Burgain (a French native) master, bound for J. Baptiste Guide in Nice, and for Marseilles, laden with tobacco, flour, staves, and coffee, was taken near Barcelona by the privateer *Patriote* of Marseilles, Captain Neel, and brought here on 27 Feb. Unaware that war at sea had broken out in Europe and assuming that an Algerine privateer was chasing him, Burgain burned his American ship papers, hoping that French papers procured in St. Domingo and confirmed by the French consul in Baltimore would protect him. He declared this to Neel but disputed too much and was put in irons. Neel avers that Burgain told him that he had escaped from France, where he was under sentence of death on matters related to the Revolution. As a naturalized American citizen whose ship and cargo belong to Zacharie Coopman & Company of Baltimore, Burgain while in quarantine claimed his assistance as vice-consul. After taking Burgain's sworn statement that he was a naturalized citizen of the United States with a wife and three children at Philips point, Baltimore, where he owns 250 acres granted him by Congress for service during the Revolution, he took his oath of allegiance, acknowledged him as an American citizen, and obtained a municipal order for his release from irons. The ship had a free *pratique* on 15 Mch., but Burgain has been imprisoned "for his Individual affair" on Neel's charges, a matter for the judicial system, though Burgain's memoir appears to vindicate him. At the request of Burgain and Guide, who has arrived here, he attended the opening of the ship's papers and letters in the commercial court that will determine its status as a prize. His paraphrase of them, signed by himself, the judge, the privateer's owner, and Guide, was inserted in the procès-verbal along with Cathalan's protest on behalf of all Americans concerned. He has sent Gouverneur Morris an account of the matter and extracts from the procès-verbal to be forwarded to TJ if necessary. A letter from Zacharie & Company to Guide indicates that French papers were obtained solely for protection from the Algerines, a common practice that no maritime power can sanction and that is more harmful than beneficial. He will act prudently to save American property in this complicated affair, but it will take a long time if as is likely the privateer sues for condemnation. If the ship is released, he is at a loss how to furnish proper papers to get her safely home, but will do his best. On 3 Mch. the American brig *Bacchus*, Roger Robbins master, laden with wheat and flour belonging to Zacharie & Company and addressed to Guide at Nice, was taken by a French privateer and carried into Cette, where it was released, the captain having shown the ship's American papers and hoisted American colors at sea; as Cette needed wheat, it purchased the wheat and flour at the price they would have fetched in Nice. He hopes that American vessels will visit the Mediterranean, where Portuguese naval ships are cruising while at war with Algiers, and that TJ will take proper measures in this favorable circumstance to protect them. France has favored American ships lately. In 1778 he obtained an abatement on foreign bacalao from Necker, and he has urged Morris to apply for abatement of the prohibitive duty on American imports of bacalao, as French fishermen will not risk going to Newfoundland during the war with England, Holland, and Spain. On the first motion in the National Convention such a decree will be made, since only bread and meat are more necessary. Americans should thus be encouraged to send bacalao next fall and winter, when it will obtain high prices in ready money. American flour is now worth £100ᵗᵗ a barrel, and wheat would fetch £98ᵗᵗ to £100ᵗᵗ per charge now and soon much more. During the war American ships will find freight here for all parts of the world at extravagant terms. [P.S.] He asks that Dunlap's gazette be sent when it contains material useful to the consulate or trade with France.

RC (DNA: RG 59, CD); 4 p.; at foot of first page: "The Secretary of State at Philadelphia"; endorsed by TJ as received 16 July 1793 and so recorded in SJL. Enclosure: Cathalan to TJ, 17 Feb. 1793.

From David Humphreys

Lisbon, 19 Mch. 1793. He acknowledges TJ's dispatch of 2 Jan., accompanied by others for Carmichael and Short which the Spanish ambassador will forward, and by plans of the Federal City which will be disposed of as requested. In his No. 60 he reported that Portugal will probably grant no monopoly in wheat to Naples, and in No. 65 he described his efforts to expand American commerce here. His enclosed letters to the Secretary for Foreign Affairs document his continuing efforts in these areas since returning from Gibraltar. He has obtained no reply as yet, but will keep this letter open until the vessel sails. Freire is still here, but still plans to go to America this spring. Besides Freire's desire for a better appointment, the Portuguese government is peculiarly prone to delay. For example, the man chosen to congratulate the newly elected Emperor of Germany left Lisbon soon after that event but had not reached Vienna when the Emperor died. The Queen of Portugal's health reportedly worsens. The kingdom is very quiet, but hostile preparations go on apace and the Prince of Brazil has enhanced his popularity by visiting several posts and showing unusual activity and concern for the state's welfare. The common people are much irritated against the French since the execution of the king. Portugal must soon decide whether to let Spain and England draw it into war, and the decision whether to admit a French *"Agent Negociateur"* now arrived at the border will bring matters to a crisis. He encloses a list of Barclay's papers left sealed under Simpson's care at Gibraltar. Two letters for TJ from Short go by this conveyance, but he has heard nothing from Carmichael. Church has not arrived, but an American ship chartered here by his order has gone to Bordeaux for him and his family. P.S. The latest information from the court gives little reason to expect favorable responses to the two subjects addressed in his applications to the Secretary for Foreign Affairs, but he consoles himself with the conviction that he has done everything possible.

RC (DNA: RG 59, DD); 4 p.; at head of text: "(No. 68.)"; at foot of text: "The Secretary of State &c. &c. &c."; endorsed by TJ as received 17 May 1793 and so recorded in SJL. Tr (Lb in same). Enclosures: (1) Humphreys to Foreign Minister Luis Pinto de Sousa Coutinho, 4 Mch. 1793, urging a favorable response to his earlier requests that American flour be freely admitted into Portugal and that the Portuguese government refrain from compelling grain vessels which land in Portugal to sell their cargoes there. (2) Humphreys to Pinto de

Sousa Coutinho, 16 Mch. 1793, again requesting a response to these requests (Trs in Humphreys's hand in same; Trs in Lb in same). (3) List of "Papers found in Mr Barclay's small Mahogany case" and "sealed in a Packet at Gibralter 8th Feby 1793," n.d. (MS in Humphreys's hand in same; Tr in Lb in same).

On 17 May 1793 TJ sent this letter and its enclosures to the President, who returned them the next day (Washington, *Journal*, 142-3).

From Thomas Pinckney

DEAR SIR   London 19 March 1793

Finding Captn. Loxley still detained I avail myself of the opportunity thereby afforded, to inform you that I have received the paper concerning which I was sollicitous from Mr. Morris, to whom it had been sent by mistake, and that I shall observe the directions contained in your favor of the 1st. Jany. I am happy to find that circumstances have not occasioned the detention of this paper to be attended with any inconveniencies, nor is it probable from present appearances that it would have been the case for some time to come. I have the honor to be with great respect Dear Sir Your faithful and most obedient Servant   THOMAS PINCKNEY

Gardner has no transports nor troops with him nor can any be spared from hence yet.[1]

RC (DNA: RG 59, DD); lacks ciphered postscript, supplied from TJ's decipherment on verso (see note 1 below) with prefatory note in his hand: "passage on a separate paper in cypher"; at foot of text: "The Secretary of State"; endorsed by TJ as received 3 May 1793 and so recorded in SJL. PrC (ScHi: Pinckney Family Papers); with postscript in unidentified code on separate sheet. Tr (Lb in DNA: RG 59, DD); includes deciphered postscript.

The PAPER Pinckney received was the cipher he had inadvertently sent to Gouverneur Morris and which he used to encode the postscript to the present letter. Rear Admiral Alan GARDNER had sailed from England the month before in command of a British naval squadron headed for the West Indies (DNB).

[1] Sentence as deciphered by TJ on verso.

From George Washington

March 19th. 1793

The President returns to the Secretary of State the letter and enclosures from Colo. Humphreys—and sends him a letter just received from Mr. Ellicott.

The President wishes the Secretary's opinion whether the direction to the Director of the Mint for collecting and assaying certain foreign Coins agreeably to the law—"regulating foreign Coins" &c—should go directly from the President to this Officer—or whether it should go through the Secretary of State.

RC (DLC); in the hand of Tobias Lear; endorsed by TJ as received 20 Mch. 1793. Recorded in SJPL. Enclosures: (1) David Humphreys to TJ, 25 Jan. 1793, and enclosures. (2) Andrew Ellicott to Washington, 16 Mch. 1793, reporting his dismissal as surveyor by the Commissioners of the Federal District and demanding that the accuracy of his work be judged by "men of known professional abilities in that way" (printed in Sally K. Alexander, "A Sketch of the Life of Major Andrew Ellicott," *Records of the Columbia Historical Society*, II [1899], 189-90).

TJ had sent the President the letter from Humphreys earlier the same day (Washington, *Journal*, 94).

From Thomas Auldjo

Cowes, 20 Mch. 1793. He encloses an account of the imports and exports of American ships within his district from 1 July to 31 Dec. 1792, hoping it will suffice, even though it is not so correct as he could wish because his unpaid agents in the outlying ports lack incentive to be very exact, and ship captains sometimes refuse to show their papers and detail their cargoes. The ambassador will have told TJ that, as England is at war, he is furnishing passports to protect American ships. Nothing detrimental to American trade has occurred in this district since the war began. He has successfully resolved several disputes with impressment officers over seamen, but can not suggest a remedy for this troubling problem. Subjoining a list of expenses—£9.1.6 for obtaining a royal warrant approving his commission as consul and £2.12.6 for a seal of office—he leaves it entirely to TJ to decide whether he should be reimbursed, though he thinks he should be allowed something for postage costs, which have lately been heavy. Corn prices are rising. Wheat brings 6/ sterling a bushel and rice 19/ a hundred deliverable in France or Holland. The former price can be sustained but the latter must fall.

RC (DNA: RG 59, CD); 3 p.; at foot of text: "The Secretary of State"; endorsed by TJ as received 31 May 1793 and so recorded in SJL. Enclosure not found.

From John Gregorie

Paris, 20 Mch. 1793. He solicits the consulship for Dunkirk, which has never had one even though it is among Europe's more important ports and enjoys a considerable trade with the United States. Although French by birth, he is recognized as an American citizen and has kept an establishment at Petersburg since 1785, taking the oath of allegience, owning land, paying taxes, and generally acting as a good citizen until embarking for Europe last

September. Inquiry will show his character to be irreproachable; if appointed, his abilities will enable him to carry out his duties satisfactorily. The European war enhances the value of neutral, particularly American, ships, and a consul is needed at Dunkirk to prevent violations of the Navigation Act. Incentives granted by France to Nantucket whalers who settle in that country and outfit a ship for the whale fishery under its flag have lured great numbers of them to Dunkirk, many of whom had retained their American ship registers when hostilities commenced and, he believes, may have sold or disposed of them, a practice which violates American law and should be stopped. He requests that an answer be sent to him in Dunkirk, or to the care of Charles Herrias & Company in London or Gregorie & Barksdale in Petersburg.

RC (DLC: Washington Papers, Applications for Office); 3 p.; at foot of text: "His Excellency Thomas Jefferson Secretary of State"; endorsed by TJ as received 17 July 1793 and so recorded in SJL. Dupl (same); dated 7 Apr. 1793; at head of text: "(Copy)"; on verso of last page: "Duplicate of a Letter from Paris 7 April 1793."

This letter, together with David Meade Randolph's letter of 28 June 1793 from Presque Isle supporting Gregorie's aspirations for the Dunkirk appointment (RC in DLC; endorsed by TJ as received 17 July 1793 and so recorded in SJL), was enclosed in William Barksdale to TJ, dated 10 July 1793 at Petersburg, which also vouched for Gregorie's character, asserted that he owned American

property worth several thousand pounds, and named William Davies of Virginia as one of his friends (RC in DLC: Washington Papers, Applications for Office; endorsed by TJ as received 17 July 1793 and so recorded in SJL). On 1 June 1793 Gregorie wrote TJ enclosing a Dupl of the above letter and arguing that his claim to the Dunkirk consulate was superior to that of Francis Coffyn, who was acting as consular agent under a commission from Silas Deane but was not an American subject and was overly beholden to men likely to violate American navigation laws (RC in same; endorsed by TJ as received 6 Sep. 1793 and so recorded in SJL). Gregorie's bid for this post ended with Coffyn's appointment as consul in December 1794 (JEP, I, 165).

To Thomas Pinckney

DEAR SIR   Philadelphia Mar. 20. 1793.

The death of Mr. Barclay having rendered it necessary to appoint some other person to proceed to Algiers on the business of peace and ransom, the President has thought proper to appoint Colo. Humphreys, and to send on Capt. Nathaniel Cutting to him in the character of Secretary, and to be the bearer of the papers to him. I am to ask the favor of you to communicate to Colo. Humphreys whatever information you may be able to give him in this business, in consequence of the agency you have had in it. I have given him authority to draw in his own name on our bankers in Amsterdam for the money deposited in their hands for this purpose according to the letter I had the honor of writing to you July 3. 1792. I have now that of assuring you of the sincere sentiments of esteem & respect with which I am Dear Sir Your most obedt. & most humble servt   Th: Jefferson

RC (InHi); at foot of text: "Thomas Pinckney esquire." PrC (DLC). FC (Lb in DNA: RG 59, DCI). Enclosed in TJ to George Washington, 21 Mch. 1793, and approved and returned by the President the same day (Washington, *Journal*, 98).

To Jean Baptiste Ternant

Sir   Philadelphia March 20th. 1793.

I have to acknowledge the receipt of your note of the 6th. instant, on the claim of an inheritance of lands in North Carolina, supposed to have devolved from M. Giroud on Monsr. Preau, a Citizen of France, by virtue of the 11th. article of our treaty of Commerce. I have not received any letter on the subject from the President or Trustees of the University of North Carolina, or any other person. Indeed I could hardly expect to receive such a letter, as it would be quite improper in the Executive to give an opinion on the subject. It is purely a question of property which must be decided by the tribunals of the Country, who alone in litigated cases are competent to expound the laws of the land, among which, and of a paramount nature, is the treaty in question. To these tribunals therefore Mr. Preau must appeal, and I can refer him to them with the more satisfaction from my entire confidence that he will receive at their hands the most perfect justice. I am with great and sincere esteem, Sir your most obedient & most humble Servant.

PrC (DLC); in a clerk's hand, unsigned; at foot of text: "The Minister of France." FC (Lb in DNA: RG 59, DL).

Ternant's note of the 6th, recorded in SJL as received the same day, has not been found. Evidently Preau was seeking to recover escheated lands in North Carolina which the state had granted to the University of North Carolina under an act of 21 Dec. 1789. In December 1792 he had petitioned the University, whose trustees decided to defer action and ask "some of our members in Congress" to obtain a ruling from the Secretary of State on whether Article 2 of the 1778 treaty of commerce with France, which gave French subjects rights of inheritance in the United States, applied to real as well as personal property (R. D. W. Connor and others, eds., *A Documentary History of the University of North Carolina, 1776-1799*, 2 vols. (Chapel Hill, 1953), I, 45-7, 182, 186-7; Miller, *Treaties*, II, 11-12). There is no evidence that TJ was ever consulted in this matter by representatives of the University and the ultimate fate of Preau's appeal is unknown.

To George Washington

Mar. 20. 93.

Th: Jefferson, with his respects to the President, observes in answer to the note of yesterday respecting directions to the Mint for the assay of the new coins, that the Departments being instituted to relieve the President from the details of execution, it will be sufficient that the directions go from the head of the department, the President's approbation being known. They shall accordingly be given.

RC (DNA: RG 59, MLR); addressed: "The President of the US."; endorsed by Tobias Lear. PrC (DLC); partially overwritten in a later hand. Tr (Lb in DNA: RG 59, SDC). Recorded in SJPL.

From George Washington

Sɪʀ   United States, March 20th: 1793

I have to request that it may be given in charge to the director of the mint, to take measures for collecting samples of foreign coins issued in the Year 1792, of the species which usually circulate within the United States, to examine by assays at the mint whether the same are conformable to the respective standards required, and to report the result, that the same may be made known by proclamation—agreeably to the Act entitled "An Act regulating foreign Coins, and for other purposes."   Go: Washington

RC (DLC); in the hand of Tobias Lear, signed by Washington; at foot of text: "The Secretary of State"; endorsed by TJ as received 20 Mch. 1793. Dft (DNA: RG 59, MLR); in Lear's hand. FC (Lb in same, SDC). Recorded in SJPL.

To George Washington

Mar. 20. 1793.

Th: Jefferson, with his respects to the President incloses him the draught of a letter to Mr. Pinckney: also some Canada gazettes, with the letter from Colo. Fay accompanying them. He perceives from this letter that Colo. Fay had not awaited his approbation to make use of the name of Th:J. in the land-job. He thinks it possible the government of Canada may get hold of this, and perhaps make some use of it, if they should suppose any purpose may be answered by it. He is the more happy therefore in having made the first communication to the President, which at that time had others only in view, and not all Th:J. himself.

RC (DNA: RG 59, MLR); endorsed by Tobias Lear. PrC (DLC); partially overwritten in a later hand. Tr (Lb in DNA: RG 59, SDC). Recorded in SJPL. Enclosures: (1) TJ to Thomas Pinckney, 16 Mch. 1793. (2) Joseph Fay to TJ, 12 Mch. 1793.

Fay's FIRST COMMUNICATION to TJ, inviting him to participate in a land speculation venture in Canada, was dated 26 Feb. 1793. Apparently TJ had shown it to the President after receiving it on 12 Mch. and before receiving Fay's second letter on 19 Mch. 1793, but evidence on the date of transmittal is lacking.

From George Washington, with Jefferson's Note

March 20th. 1793

The President returns the enclosed draft of a letter to Mr. Pinckney, the contents of which meet his approbation.

The President will thank Mr. Jefferson to send him a map of the Federal City, if he has any by him.

[*Note by TJ:*]

The above was the letter of Mar. 16. 93. to Mr. Pinckney.

RC (DLC); in the hand of Tobias Lear, except for note by TJ at foot of first page below dateline; second paragraph written on verso with address; addressed: "The Secretary of State"; endorsed by TJ as received 20 Mch. 1793. Recorded in SJPL.

To Willink, Van Staphorst & Hubbard

GENTLEMEN   Philadelphia Mar. 20. 1793.

In a letter of July 3. 1792. I remitted you a bill of exchange drawn on you by the Treasurer of the US. for 123,750 current gilders, and desired you to enter it to the credit of the Secretary of state for the US. and to answer draughts which should be made on it by Mr. Pinckney for purposes unconnected with those of his general mission. I have now to inform you that Mr. Nathaniel Cutting will immediately draw on you a bill for one thousand dollars part of this money, and that the whole power over the residue of it not drawn for by Mr. Pinckney, is transferred to Colo. David Humphreys, our resident at

Lisbon, whose draughts therefore to the amount of that residue you will be pleased to honour. I am gentlemen your most obedt. humble servt   Th: JEFFERSON

RC (NjP: Andre deCoppet Collection); at foot of text: "Messrs. W. & J. Willink Nichs. & Jac. Van Staphorst & Hubbard Amsterdam." PrC (DLC). PrC of Dupl (DLC); at foot of text: "Duplicate." Tr (Lb in DNA: RG 59, DCI). Tr (DLC); 19th-century copy. Enclosed in TJ to George Washington, and TJ to David Humphreys, both 21 Mch. 1793.

From Brown, Benson & Ives

SIR   Providence 21st March 1793

The design of this address being of great Consequence to the Commercial interests of our Country, we shall attempt no apology while we beg leave to solicit your attention to the following statement of facts.

On the 15th of Decemr. last we dispatch'd our Brig Commerce Capt. James Munro Jr. with a Valuable Cargo for the French West Inda. Islands, with instructions to the Captain to Proceed to Windward and there dispose of part or all of the Cargo if it could be sold to advantage, but if the sales were not Compleated at Windward he was to Proceed to Cape Francois or Port au Prince, in order to finish the business; the Vessel arriv'd at Martinico where the Captain sold his Codfish only, not being able to obtain the original Cost for the remainder of his Cargo—he therefore in pursuance of our Orders proceeded to Leeward, and unfortunately stopt off Port au Prince, at which Place he landed, in order to ascertain the state of the Markets, but finding no demand for his Cargo, he intended to proceed to the Cape but was forcibly prevented, a Guard being put on board his Vessel and she brought into the harbour, and 'tho he produc'd his Invoice to the Assembly, and offer'd them his Cargo at a Discount of ten ℔ Cent from the Cost, they refused to purchase, and Persisted in their refusal to Permit his Departure, in Confirmation of all which, and for a detail of his Proceedings, you will please to peruse two Original Letters which we have received from the Captain, also a Coppy of his Petition to the Municipality which are here inclosed. It appears that many other American Vessels were in the same unhappy situation, and as our Exports to the Islands are usually Compos'd of Perishable articles, which was the Case with the Cargo of our Brig, we need not suggest how ruinous such detention must be to the Voyages, and as the Proceedings are totally repugnant to the Laws and Practice of all

Nations, except in Cases of Actual hostility, we Persuade ourselves Sir, that you will impart the Circumstances to the French Minister at Philadelphia, and Prevail on him to adopt such Measures as will speedily and effectually relieve the suffering Americans at Port au Prince, any Delay will Operate very Injurious, and Perhaps Issue in the total loss of many Cargoes, and Cause great injury if not ruin to the Vessels.

As we have not the honour of a Personal acquaintance with you, our Friends Mr. Foster and Mr. Bourne are so Obliging as to Accompany this address with a Letter; Permit us to Commend the subject to your early attention and be assured that We are Sir, very respectfully, Your Obedt. Friends & Servants, BROWN BENSON & IVES

RC (DNA: RG 59, MLR); at foot of text: "Honble. Thomas Jefferson Esq Philadelphia"; endorsed by TJ as received 30 Mch. 1793 and so recorded in SJL. PrC of Tr (DLC); in a clerk's hand. Tr (Lb in DNA: RG 59, DL). Enclosures: (1) James Munro, Jr., to Brown, Benson & Ives, Port-au-Prince, 11 Feb. 1793, describing the arbitrary detention of his ship and other American ships by French authorities at this port and calling for action by Congress to obtain redress. (2) Same to same, 23 Feb. 1793, enclosing his petition to the municipality of Port-au-Prince and reporting the continued detention of his ship and that of ten other American ships since his arrival two weeks ago (RCs in DNA: RG 59, MLR; PrCs of Trs in DLC, in a clerk's hand; Trs in Lb in DNA: RG 59, DL). (3) Petition of Munro to the Municipality of Port-au-Prince, n.d., requesting permission to sail to Cape François so that he can sell the cargo he has been unable to sell in Port-au-Prince (Tr in DNA: RG 59, MLR, in Munro's hand; PrC of Tr in DLC, in a clerk's hand; Tr in Lb in DNA: RG 59, DL). Enclosed in TJ to Jean Baptiste Ternant, 5 Apr. 1793.

The letter to TJ of 21 Mch. 1793 from Senator Theodore FOSTER and Representative Benjamin BOURNE is recorded in SJL as received from Providence on 30 Mch. 1793, but has not been found. An earlier letter from Foster, dated 31 Aug. 1790 and recorded in SJL as received 26 Sep. 1790, is also missing.

Circular to Consuls and Vice-Consuls

SIR   Philadelphia March 21st. 1793.

Present appearances in Europe rendering a general war there probable, I am to desire your particular attention to all the indications of it, and on the first imminent symptoms of rupture among the maritime powers, to put our vessels on their guard. In the same event the patronage of our Consuls will be particularly requisite to secure to our vessels the rights of neutrality, and protect them against all invasions of it. You will be pleased also in the same case to give no countenance to the usurpation of our flag by foreign vessels, but rather indeed to aid in detecting it, as without bringing to us any advantage, the usurpation will tend to commit us with the belligerent powers, and to subject those vessels which are truly ours to harrassing scrutinies in order to distinguish them from the counterfeits.

The law requiring the Consuls of the United States to give bond with two or more good sureties for the faithful performance of their duties, I enclose you a blank bond for that purpose. According to a standing regulation which places our Consuls in Europe in relation with the minister of the United States in the same Country with them, if there be one, and if none, then with their minister in Paris, and our Consuls in America in immediate relation with the Secretary of State, you will be pleased to have your sureties approved by the person to whom you stand thus refferred, and to send [the] bond when executed, by a safe conveyance, to the Secretary of State, to [be] disposed of according to law; and this with all the expedition the [case] will admit: provided this should not have been done before.[1]

A copy of the laws of the last Session of Congress is[2] sent to [Mr.] Pinckney, Minister plenipotentiary of the United States in London to be forwarded to you.[3]

PrC (DLC); entirely in a clerk's hand, unsigned; at head of text: "Circular to the Consuls of the United States"; bracketed words lost in frayed right margin of first page supplied from FC; includes one minor correction in ink by TJ; lacks substitute third paragraph to Samuel Shaw given below. FC (Lb in DNA: RG 59, DCI); contains postscript to James Maury and substitute third paragraph to Samuel Shaw. SJL does not record the text to Shaw, but indicates that a text was sent to Benjamin Joy, consul at Calcutta. At foot of text in PrC and FC are listed, individually or in groups, twenty-four recipients (twenty-three in PrC) to whom the circular was sent and the additional paragraphs, some with clerical directions, that were to be incorporated into their letters immediately following the text of the circular. Except where noted, the paragraphs given below are taken from the PrC:

(1) To Thomas Auldjo, vice-consul at Poole: "With acknowledgments of the receipt of your letter of Decr. 6th. and a desire that you will continue the address recommended in my letter of Novr. 14th. I have to add assurances of the esteem with which I am Sir, your mo. obt. hble. Servt."

(2) To Joshua Johnson, consul at London: "I have to acknowledge the receipt of your letter of October 9th. and am sincerely sorry that the provisions made by Congress relative to our Consuls have not been such as you expected, and still more so that this or any other circumstance should induce you to decline giving the bond which they require, and which in your case is a mere formality. We have been sensible that your services have been faithful and useful, and have no reserve in giving you the fullest assurances of it; and if this has not been done before it has proceeded from the circumstance that the multiplicity of business in this Department puts it out of my power to correspond with the Consuls but by Circular letters, except as to particular and urgent circumstances. I am persuaded that on a review of my letter of August 7. 1790. you will find no promise but what Mr. Pinckney is fully authorized to comply with, there being none in it beyond what the laws authorize. To return to the circumstance of the bond, I cannot but hope you will be sensible that the law in prescribing cautions proper for the generality of cases, cannot give offence to the particulars in whose case they would be unnecessary and would therefore have been unprescribed if such case had stood alone, and that reconsidering your resolution expressed in your letter of October 9th. you will by a compli-

ance with this formality before Mr. Pinckney, still give us the benefit of your services; with which I can assure you the President is so well satisfied that it would be with regret he should proceed to the nomination of a successor as proposed in your letter, and as the precepts of the law would require, with which he has no power to dispense. I beg you to be assured from myself personally of those sentiments of perfect esteem and respect with which I am, Sir Your most obedient and most humble Servt." (RC in DNA: RG 59, CD, in a clerk's hand, signed by TJ, at foot of text: "Joshua Johnson Esqr.," endorsed on separate sheet as received 17 June 1793 and answered 24 Aug. 1793 "℗ the Pigou Capt Loxley"; Tr in Lb in DNA: RG 360, FL, subjoined to Tr of TJ to Johnson, 7 Aug. 1790). This paragraph was substituted for the second and third paragraphs of the circular in accordance with the bracketed clerical direction given in the PrC: "In this letter the Circular passage respecting the bond must be omitted."

(3) *To James Maury, consul at Liverpool*: "With acknowledgments of the receipt of your letters of Septr. 19. Novr. 13. and Decr. 1. (the first of which however did not cover any bond) and a desire that you continue to use the address recommended in my letter of Novr. 14. I am with great esteem Dear Sir your &c." (FC in DLC; in Taylor's hand; consists only of postscript: "I have sent the blank bond agreeably to your desire to your Brother Mr. Fontaine Maury requesting him to execute it"; at head of text: "P.S. to Mr. Maury").

(4) *To Benjamin Hamnell Philips, consul at Curaçoa; John Street, vice-consul at Fayal; Nathaniel Cutting, consul at Le Havre; Edward Fox, consul at Falmouth; Joseph Yznardi, Jr., consul at Cadiz; John Parish, consul at Hamburg; Henry Cooper, consul at Santa Cruz; David Matthew Clarkson, consul at St. Eustatia; Samuel Cooper Johonnet, consul at Demerara; Michael Morphy, consul at Malaga; Fulwar Skipwith, consul at Martinique; James Greenleaf, consul at Amsterdam*: "You will be pleased to address your letters always to 'the Secretary of State for the United States of America at Philadelphia,' with-

out adding the name, in order to prevent the casualties to them which changes in the office might otherwise occasion. I have the honor to be, Sir Your most obedient and most huml. Servant" (RC owned by George Green Shackelford, Orange, Virginia, 1961, on deposit ViU, in a clerk's hand, signed by TJ, lacks third paragraph of circular, at head of text in the hand of George Taylor, Jr.: "Circular," at foot of text in a clerk's hand: "Saml. Cooper Johonnet Esqr."; RC owned by Mrs. Henry M. Sage, Albany, New York, 1954, in a clerk's hand, signed by TJ, lacks third paragraph, at head of text in Taylor's hand: "Circular," at foot of text: "Fulwar Skipworth, Esq."; RC in PWacD: Feinstone Collection, on deposit PPAmP, in a clerk's hand, signed by TJ, containing variant of third paragraph recorded in note 2 below, at foot of text: "James Greenleaf Esqr.").

(5) *To Robert Montgomery, consul at Alicant*: "to the preceding clause add, in the case of Montgomery as follows. Acknowledging the receipt of your letters of July 17. and 24. I have the honor to be Sir &c." (The letters from Montgomery were dated 1791.) The "preceding clause" is the one quoted in No. 4 above.

(6) *To Elias Vanderhorst, consul at Bristol*: "Same as preceding, only as to dates, which are Octr. 10. Decr. 24. and 31."

(7) *To Delamotte, vice-consul at Le Havre*: "According to what was mentioned in my letter conveying your Commission to you, the case has occurred wherein a respectable native (Captn. Cutting) proposing to settle at your Port has received the appointment of Consul there; This you will be pleased to observe does not revoke your Commission, nor otherwise affect you than by a suspension of your functions while he is within the limits of his jurisdiction. Acknowledging the receipt of your letter of Octr. 5 I have the honor to add every assurance of personal esteem and respect from Sir your &c."

(8) *To Stephen Cathalan, Jr., vice-consul at Marseilles; Edward Church, consul at Lisbon; Joseph Fenwick, consul at Bordeaux; John M. Pintard, consul at Madeira; Hans Rodolph Saabije, consul at Copenhagen*: "Desiring a continuance of the address recommended in my letter of

Novr. 14. I have the honor to be with great esteem & respect, Sir Your most obedient & most humble Servant" (RC owned by André de Gasquet, Paris, 1978; in a clerk's hand, signed by TJ; contains variant of third paragraph recorded in note 2 below; at foot of text: "Stephen Cathalan Esqr.").

(9) *To Samuel Shaw, consul at Canton*: "A set of the laws of the United States is likewise herewith enclosed together with copy of a former circular letter, intended as a standing instruction to our Consuls. I am with esteem, Sir, Your most obedient, and most humble servant" (PrC in DLC; in a clerk's hand, unsigned; at foot of text in ink in Taylor's hand: "Saml Shaw—Consul at Canton in China"). This paragraph was substituted for the third paragraph of the circular in accordance with the bracketed clerical direction given in

FC: "in lieu of the last paragraph in the Letter." The "former circular letter" was TJ's Circular to American Consuls, 26 Aug. 1790.

TJ submitted this circular to the President on 22 Mch. 1793, and he approved it the same day (Washington, *Journal*, 99).

[1] This paragraph omitted in RC addressed to Joshua Johnson. See notes above for substitute paragraph.
[2] Word reworked to "will be" in RCs addressed to James Greenleaf and Stephen Cathalan, Jr.
[3] This paragraph omitted in RCs addressed to Joshua Johnson, Samuel Cooper Johonnet, and Fulwar Skipwith. See No. 9 above for substitute paragraph to Samuel Shaw.

To Joseph Fay

DEAR SIR   Philadelphia Mar. 21. 1793.

Before you receive this, mine of the 18. inst. will have reached your hands, in answer to yours of Feb. 26. The purpose of the present is to acknolege the receipt of yours of the 12th. inst. with the Canada papers, and to thank you for them as for others received on former occasions. I have not been able to take any measures for the regular transmission of these papers to my office, as I have no correspondence in either of those two governments. If you could do it by any means it would oblige me, as there seems now to be a regular post between us. They should be directed 'to the Secretary of state for the U.S. at Philadelphia' without his name, as this would save the trouble of ever changing the superscription. We can always readily order payment through the nearest port of collection to Canada. In the mean time if you can any otherwise furnish those papers I shall thank you, and desire you to make known to me their cost that it may be replaced. I am with great esteem Dear Sir Your most obedt. humble servt

TH: JEFFERSON

PrC (DLC); at foot of text: "Colo. Joseph Fay." Tr (DLC); 19th-century copy.

To Horatio Gates

Dear General   Philadelphia Mar. 21. 1793.

I received yesterday your friendly letter of the 17th. and thank you sincerely, as well as Mrs. Gates, for the kind invitation to Rose-hill. Nothing would be more pleasing to me than such a visit: but circumstances will not admit so long an absence from hence. Mr. Madison had set out for the Southward before the receipt of your letter. I am much indebted for the readiness with which you are so good as to honor my request concerning our correspondence; and as your letters to me, being in a book, cannot be sent here, I have thought I could do no less than save as much trouble as possible in the business of copying, by examining the files of Congress to whom I had forwarded some of your letters. I find there the following letters, which of course need not be copied from your book. viz.

Genl. Gates to T.J. dated Hillsborough. Sep. 9. 1780.
do.   to do.   Hillsborough Oct. 3. 1780.
the following inclosures.

General orders. June 1.	These inclosures are on
a letter of Ld. Cornwallis's without date.	the files, but if Genl.
Colo. Preston to Martin. Sep. 18.	Gates wrote a letter
Hooper to Genl. Gates. Sep. 27.	covering them, that let-
Williams to do. Oct. 2.	ter is not on the files.
Davidson to Summer. Oct. 3.	

Genl. Gates to T.J. Oct. 12. 1780. with it's inclosures.
do.   to do. Nov. 1.   with do.
do.   to do. Nov. 2.   with do.

Such only therefore as are not in this list are now necessary to complete the collection of your letters to me. Of mine to you there does not exist a single copy on the files of Congress: I presume indeed they were not sent hither; and therefore I must ask the whole of them, which being in bundles you can send to me, and they shall be immediately copied and faithfully returned to you. I shall ever be happy to hear of your health and welfare, and know nobody who has more wisely combined the otium cum dignitate in retirement than yourself. I thought it a real misfortune to me that I missed seeing you when I was last at New-York, as my own plans of retirement rendered it hardly probable I should pass that way again. Be this as it may, you possess every sentiment of respect & affection, under every situation, of Dear General your sincere friend & humble servt   Th: Jefferson

RC (NHi: Gates Papers); addressed: "Major-General Gates at Rose-hill near New York"; franked, stamped, and post-marked; endorsed by Gates. PrC (DLC).

[419]

The FOLLOWING INCLOSURES were actually covered by Gates to TJ, 6 Oct. 1780; all except the letter from William HOOPER to Gates (DNA: RG 360, PCC) are accounted for in the note to TJ to Samuel Huntington, 14 Oct. 1780, where the addressee of William Preston's letter to Martin Armstrong (incorrectly listed here by TJ as PRESTON TO MARTIN) is erroneously given as Gates. A letter from Gates to TJ of 2 Nov. 1780 has not been found; the intended reference was almost certainly Gates to TJ of 8 Nov. 1780, which TJ forwarded to Congress in a letter to Huntington of 19 Nov. 1780. OTIUM CUM DIGNITATE: "leisure with dignity."

To David Humphreys

SIR   Philadelphia, March 21. 1793.

The deaths of Admiral Paul Jones first, and afterwards of Mr. Barclay, to whom the mission to Algiers explained in the enclosed papers was successively confided, have led the President to desire you to undertake the execution of it in person. These papers, being copies of what had been delivered to them will serve as your guide. But Mr. Barclay having been also charged with a mission to Morocco, it will be necessary to give you some trouble with respect to that also.

Mr. Nathaniel Cutting, the Bearer hereof, is dispatched specially, first to receive from Mr. Pinckney in London any papers or information, which his Agency in the Algerine Business may have enabled him to communicate to you: He will then proceed to deliver the whole to you, and accompany and aid you in the Character of Secretary.

It is thought necessary that you should, in the first instance settle Mr. Barclay's accounts respecting the Morocco Mission, which will probably render it necessary that you should go to Gibraltar. The communications you have had with Mr: Barclay in this mission will assist you in your endeavors at a settlement. You know the sum received by Mr. Barclay on that account, and we wish as exact a statement as can be made of the manner in which it has been laid out, and what part of it's proceeds are now on hand. You will be pleased to make an inventory of these proceeds now existing. If they or any part of them can be used for the Algerine Mission, we would have you by all means apply them to that use, debiting the Algerine fund, and crediting that of Morocco with the amount of such application. If they cannot be so used, then dispose of the perishable Articles to the best advantage, and if you can sell those not perishable for what they cost, do so, and what you cannot so sell, deposite in any safe place under your own power. In this last stage of the Business return us an exact account 1st. of the specific Articles remaining on hand for that mission, and their value. 2d. of it's cash on hand. 3rd. of any money which may be due to or from Mr. Barclay or any other person on account of this mission, and take measures for replacing the clear balance of cash in the Hands of Messrs. W. & J. Willincks and Nichs. & Jacob Van Staphorsts and Hubbard.

This matter being settled, you will be pleased to proceed on the Mission to Algiers. This you will do by the way of Madrid, if you think any information you can get from Mr. Carmichael, or any other may be an equivalent for the Trouble, Expense, and delay of the Journey. If not, proceed in whatever other way you please to Algiers.

Proper powers and Credentials for you addressed to that government are herewith enclosed. The Instructions first given to Admiral Paul Jones are so full that no others need be added, except a Qualification in one single article, to wit: Should that Government finally reject peace on the terms in *money* to which you are authorized to go, you may offer to make the first payments for peace and that for ransom in *naval stores*, reserving the right to make the subsequent annual payments in money.

You are to be allowed your travelling expenses, your Salary as minister Resident in Portugal going on. Those expenses must be debited to the Algerine Mission, and not carried into your ordinary account as Resident. Mr: Cutting is allowed one hundred Dollars a month, and his expenses, which as soon as he joins you, will of course be consolidated with yours. We have made choice of him as particularly qualified to aid under your direction in the matters of account, with which he is well acquainted. He receives here an advance of One thousand Dollars by a draught on our Bankers in Holland in whose Hands the fund is deposited. This and all other sums furnished him, to be debited to the algerine fund. I enclose you a letter to our Bankers giving you complete Authority over these funds, which you had better send with your first Draught, though I send a copy of it from hence by another opportunity.

This business being done, you will be pleased to return to Lisbon, and to keep yourself and us thereafter well informed of the transactions in Morocco and as soon as you shall find that the succession to that Government is settled and stable so that we may know to whom a Commissioner may be addressed, be so good as to give us the information that we may take measures in consequence. I have the honor to be, with much respect Sir, Your most obedient and most humble servant   TH: JEFFERSON

RC (NjP: Andre deCoppet Collection); in the hand of George Taylor, Jr., signed by TJ; at foot of first page: "Colo. D. Humphreys"; endorsed by Humphreys. PrC (DLC); unsigned. FC (Lb in DNA: RG 59, DCI). Enclosures: (1) TJ to John

Paul Jones, 1 June 1792, and Enclosures Nos. 1-2 listed there. (2) Commission to Humphreys to negotiate a treaty of peace and friendship with the Dey and government of Algiers, 21 Mch. 1793 (RC in NHyF, in Taylor's hand, signed by George Washington and TJ; FC in Lb in DNA: RG 59, Credences). (3) Commission to Humphreys to negotiate the ransom of American captives with the Dey and government of Algiers, 21 Mch. 1793 (RC in NjP: Andre deCoppet Collection, in Taylor's hand, signed by Washington and TJ; FC in Lb in DNA: RG 59, Credences). (4) Letter of credence for Humphreys to the Dey and Regency of Algiers, 21 Mch. 1793 (PrC of Tr in DLC, in Taylor's hand but partially overwritten in a later hand, at head of text: "(Copy)"; FC in Lb in DNA: RG 59, Credences; recorded in SJPL in clerk's hand). (5) TJ to Willink, Van Staphorst & Hubbard, 20 Mch. 1793. Letter and

Enclosure No. 5 enclosed in TJ to Washington, 21 Mch. 1793. On 22 Mch. 1793 TJ sent Nos. 2, 3, and 4 to the President, who signed and returned them the same day (Washington, *Journal*, 99). Washington to Thomas Barclay, 11 June 1792, which had been among "what had been delivered" to Barclay, may also have been among the papers enclosed to Humphreys.

Humphreys never reached Algiers. In September 1793 he left Lisbon in connection with this mission and chartered a Swedish vessel at Alicante, but returned to Lisbon when the Dey denied him a passport. No American diplomat reached Algiers until September 1795, and the American captives were not ransomed until October 1796 (H. G. Barnby, *The Prisoners of Algiers: An Account of the Forgotten American-Algerian War, 1785-1797* [London, 1966], 101-10, 159-60, 264-303).

From John M. Pintard

Madeira, 21 Mch. 1793. The Hope of London, a British privateer, arrived today. The captain reports that when he left Portsmouth fourteen days ago rumors were current that the American minister at Paris had been murdered, that Dumouriez had shot himself after being defeated by the Prussians, and that France had declared war on Spain and Portugal. The merchant to whom this ship was sent has no newspaper confirming the minister's death, which is said to have been inflicted by the King's friends, and he leaves TJ to judge the reliability of the report. The privateer captured a French ship bound from Toulon to L'Orient laden with oil, rice and wine, and an English ship previously taken by the French; both prizes are expected daily. French privateers cover the seas and have captured many valuable British ships. He will write whenever he has news of interest.

Dupl (DNA: RG 59, MDC); 3 p.; endorsed by TJ as received 6 May 1793 and so recorded in SJL. Tr (same, CD); in a clerk's hand, except for signature and part of complimentary close in Pintard's hand; conjoined with Pintard to TJ, 27 Mch. 1793.

TJ submitted this letter to the President on 13 May 1793 and received it back the same day (Washington, *Journal*, 136-7).

To David Rittenhouse

Mar. 21. 1793.

Th: Jefferson with the approbation of the President begs leave to draw the attention of Mr. Rittenhouse to the latter part of the 1st. section of the inclosed act, and to request that he will take measures for collecting samples of foreign coins issued in the year 1792, of the species which usually circulate in the US. to examine by assays at the Mint whether the same are conformable to the respective standards required, and to report the result, that the same may be made known by Proclamation.

PrC (DLC). FC (Lb in DNA: RG 59, DL).

For the INCLOSED ACT, see note to Report on Acts of Congress, 10 Mch. 1793.

To George Washington

Mar. 21. 93.

Th: Jefferson with his respects to the President incloses him draughts of letters in the Algerine business. In that to Colo. Humphreys he proposes a modification of the former instructions in one point,[1] on a presumption that the President will be disposed to approve it. He will wait on him to-day to know his pleasure, as also to submit to his consideration the question of Mr. Genet's reception in case of his arrival during the absence of the President.

RC (DNA: RG 59, MLR); addressed: "The President of the US."; with penciled notation by Tobias Lear as noted below; endorsed by Lear. PrC (DLC); partly overwritten in a later hand. Tr (Lb in DNA: RG 59, SDC). Recorded in SJPL. Enclosures: (1) TJ to Thomas Pinckney, 20 Mch. 1793. (2) TJ to Willink, Van Staphorst & Hubbard, 20 Mch. 1793. (3) TJ to David Humphreys, 21 Mch. 1793.

The President approved the enclosed DRAUGHTS OF LETTERS and returned them to TJ this day (Washington, *Journal*, 98).

[1] To this word Tobias Lear keyed the following penciled notation with a cross: "which is that payment may be made in Naval stores."

George Washington to the Cabinet

GENTLEMEN   United States, March 21st: 1793

The Treaty which is agreed to be held on or about the first of June next at the Lower Sandusky of Lake Erie, being of great moment to the interests and peace of this Country; and likely to be attended with difficulties arising from circumstances (not unknown to you) of a peculiar and embarrassing nature; it is indispensably necessary that *our* rights under the Treaties which have been entered into with the Six Nations—the several tribes of Indians now in hostility with us—and the claims of[1] others, should be carefully investigated and well ascertained, that the Commissioners who are appointed to hold it may be well informed and clearly instructed on all the points that are likely to be discussed: thereby knowing what they are to insist upon (with or without compensation, and the amount of the Compensation, if any[2])—and what, for the sake of peace, they may yield.

You are not to learn from me,[3] the different views which our Citizens entertain of the War we are engaged in with the Indians, and how much these different opinions[4] add to the delicacy and embarrassments[5] alluded to above—nor the criticisms which, more than probable, will[6] be made on the subject, if the proposed Treaty should be unsuccessful.

Induced by these motives, and desireous that time may be allowed for a full and deliberate consideration of the subject before the departure of the Commissioners, it is my desire that you will, on the 25th. of this month, meet together at the War Office (or at such other time and place as you may agree upon) where the principal documents are, with whatever papers you may respectively be possessed of on the subject, and such others as I shall cause to be laid before you, and then and there decide[7] on all the points which you shall conceive necessary for the information and instruction of the Commissioners. And, having drawn them into form, to revise the same and have them ready, in a finished state,[8] for my perusal and consideration when I return—together with a digest of such references as shall be adjudged necessary for the Commissioners to take with them.

And, as it has been suggested to me, that the Society of Quakers are desireous of sending a deputation from their Body, to be present at the aforesaid Treaty (which, if done with pure motives, and a disposition accordant with those sentiments[9] entertained by Government respecting boundary, may be a mean of facilitating the good work of peace) you will consider how far, if they are approved Characters, they ought to be recognized in the Instructions to the Commissioners[10]—

and how proper it may be for them to participate therein or to be made acquainted therewith.   Go: Washington

RC (DLC); in the hand of Tobias Lear, signed by Washington; at head of text: "(Circular) To The Secretary of State—The Secretary of the Treasury—The Secretary of War and The Attorney General of the United States"; endorsed by TJ as received 22 Mch. 1793. Dft (DNA: RG 59, MLR); dated 22 Mch. 1793; in Washington's hand except for dateline and "(Circular)" in Lear's hand at head of text and one revision in Lear's hand noted below; unsigned; only the most important emendations are noted below; endorsed by Lear. FC (Lb in same, SDC); dated 22 Mch. 1793; wording follows Dft. Recorded in SJPL. Washington evidently did not send this circular until 22 Mch. 1793, the date TJ received his copy (Washington, *Journal*, 99). The later date on the other surviving texts suggests that Lear either misdated the text sent to TJ or prepared the texts to the recipients over a two-day period.

TJ, Alexander Hamilton, and Edmund Randolph met on the appointed date but, owing to an illness of Henry Knox, postponed discussion of the issues raised here until 2 Apr. 1793 (Washington, *Journal*, 106; TJ to Knox, 26 Mch. 1793; TJ to Washington, 7 Apr. 1793). The instructions to the commissioners of 26 Apr. 1793 ultimately specified that THE SOCIETY OF QUAKERS could send a delegation to the Lower Sandusky conference, provided that its members discussed no matters of importance with the Western Indians without the prior approval of the commissioners (ASP, *Indian Affairs*, I, 340-2). For an account of the ensuing unsuccessful peace conference, see

Reginald Horsman, "The British Indian Department and the Abortive Treaty of Lower Sandusky, 1793," *Ohio Historical Quarterly*, LXX (1961), 189-213.

[1] Preceding three words interlined in Dft.
[2] Preceding eight words interlined in Dft.
[3] Preceding two words interlined in Dft in place of "at this time."
[4] Preceding two words interlined in Dft, with "these" reworked from "they."
[5] Preceding two words interlined in Dft.
[6] Remainder of sentence interlined in Dft by Lear in place of "accompany an unsuccessful Treaty."
[7] In Dft Washington initially wrote "will . . . meet together with such papers as you may respectively possess—then and there, or at such other time or place as you may agree upon, decide," before emending the passage to read "will . . . meet together at the War Office (where the documents are) with such papers as you may respectively be possessed of and which I shall cause to be laid before you then and there, or at such other time or place as you may agree upon, decide." The FC follows this emended text almost verbatim, but the passage was revised again for the RC.
[8] Preceding four words interlined in Dft.
[9] Word interlined in Dft.
[10] Washington first wrote the remainder of the sentence in Dft as "—and how far they may be made participators thereof or become acquainted therewith," and then altered it to read virtually as above.

To Andrew Ellicott

SIR   Philadelphia Mar. 22. 1793.
    Your letter of the 16th. to the President has been duly recieved, wherein you require an examination into the execution of the gen-

eral plan of the city by men of known professional abilities. If this be addressed to the President under an expectation that he should order such an examination, I have to observe to you that it would be out of the line of his interference to originate orders relative to those employed under the Commissioners. Their plans come to him for approbation or disapprobation but every thing concerning the execution is left to themselves, and particularly the President declines all interference with those employed by them, or under them: the President is sincerely concerned at the difference which has taken place: but does not suppose it to be open for any interposition on his part. To these expressions of his sentiments on the subject of your letter I have only to add those of regard & esteem from Sir Your most obedt. humble servt   TH: JEFFERSON

PrC (DLC); at foot of text: "Mr. Andrew Ellicot." FC (Lb in DNA: RG 59, DL).

TJ enclosed both this letter and Ellicott's letter to George Washington of 16 Mch. 1793 in a brief note to the President dated 22 Mch. 1793, commenting

that the letter to Ellicott "if approved may go by to-day's post" (RC in DNA: RG 59, MLR, addressed: "The President of the US.," endorsed by Tobias Lear; Tr in Lb in same, SDC; not recorded in SJL). See also Washington to TJ, 19 Mch. 1793, and note.

To David Humphreys

DEAR SIR   Philadelphia Mar. 22. 1793.

I have to acknolege the receipt of your letters from No. 60. to No. 67. inclusive. You cannot be too vigilant against any such treaty as that mentioned in No. 60. which by giving the exclusive supply of wheat to Naples, would altogether debar[1] the US. from it. This would bear so hard on us, that not only an exclusion of their wines from the US. ought to be expected on their part, but every other measure which might open to us a market *in any other part of the world*, however Portugal might be affected by it. And I must for ever repeat it that, instead of excluding our *wheat*, we must continue to hope that they will open their ports to our *flour*, and that you will continue to use your efforts, on every good occasion, to obtain this without waiting for a treaty.

As there appears at present a probability of a very general war in Europe, you will be pleased to be particularly attentive to preserve for our vessels all the rights of neutrality, and to endeavor that our flag be not usurped by others to procure to themselves the benefits of our[2] neutrality. This usurpation[3] tends to commit us with foreign nations, to subject those vessels truly ours to rigorous scrutinies and delays to distinguish them from counterfeits, and to take the business of transportation out of our hands.

Continue, if you please, your intelligence relative to the affairs of Spain, from whence we learn nothing but thro' you: to which it will be acceptable that you add any leading events from other countries, as we have several times received important facts thro' you, even from London, sooner than they have come from London directly.

The letters inclosed for Mr. Short and Mr. Carmichael are of a very secret nature. If you go by Madrid, you will be the bearer of them yourself; if not, it would be better to retain them than to send them by any conveyance which does not command your entire confidence. I[4] have never yet had a letter from Mr. Carmichael but the one you brought from Madrid. A particular circumstance will occasion forbearance yet a little longer.

Capt. Cutting will bring you a copy of the laws of the last session of Congress, and of the gazettes to the time of his departure.

Not yet knowing the actual arrival of Mr. Church at Lisbon, I believe it will be safer that I direct letters for you during your absence[5] to Messrs. Bulkeley & son, with whom you will leave what directions on the subject you shall think proper. I am with great & sincere esteem & respect, Dear Sir Your most obedt. & most humble servt

Th: Jefferson

P.S. Be so good as to inform Mr. Simpson at Gibraltar how he is to direct his letters to my office, to wit 'to the Secretary of state &c.'

RC (NjP: Andre deCoppet Collection); at foot of first page: "Colo. Humphreys"; endorsed by Humphreys. PrC (DLC). FC (Lb in DNA: RG 59, DCI). Enclosures: (1) TJ to William Carmichael and William Short, 23 Mch. 1793. (2) TJ to William Short, 23 Mch. 1793 (two letters).

On 22 Mch. 1793 TJ submitted this letter to the President, who approved and returned it the same day (Washington, *Journal*, 99).

[1] Preceding two words interlined in place of "exclude."
[2] Word interlined.
[3] Word interlined.
[4] Word reworked from "we."
[5] Preceding three words interlined.

To David Humphreys

DEAR SIR   Philadelphia Mar. 22. 1793.

I thank you sincerely for your friendly letter of Jan. 8. Particular circumstances have forced me to protract awhile my departure from office, which however will take place in the course of the year. Continue therefore if you please the general address of your letters to 'the Secretary of state &c' as recommended. Be assured that I shall carry into retirement and retain the most affectionate sentiments towards you. I am in truth worn down with drudgery, and while every circumstance relative to my private affairs calls imperiously for my return to them, not a single one exists which could render tolerable a continuation in public life.

I do not wonder that Capt. Obrian has lost patience under his long-continued captivity, and that he may suppose some of the public servants have neglected him and his brethren. He may possibly impute neglect to me, because a forbearance to correspond with him would have that appearance, tho it was dictated by the single apprehension, that if he received letters from me as M.P. of the US. at Paris, or as Secretary of state, it would increase the expectations of the captors and raise the ransom beyond what his countrymen would be disposed to give, and so end in their perpetual captivity. But in truth I have labored for them constantly, and zealously in every situation in which I have been placed. In the first moment of their captivity, I first proposed to Mr. Adams to take upon ourselves their ransom, tho' unauthorized by Congress. I proposed to Congress and obtained their permission to employ the order of Mercy in France for their ransom, but never could obtain orders for the money till just as I was leaving France and was obliged to turn the matter over to Mr. Short. As soon as I came here I laid the matter before the President and Congress in two long reports, but Congress could not decide[1] till the beginning of 1792. and then clogged their ransom by a previous requisition of peace. The unfortunate deaths of two successive Commissioners have still[2] retarded their relief, and, even should they be now relieved, will probably deprive me of the gratification of seeing my endeavors for them crowned at length with success by their arrival while I am here. It would indeed be grating to me if, after all, I should be supposed by them to have been indifferent to their situation. I will ask of your friendship to do me justice in their eyes that to the pain I have already felt for them, may not be added that of their dissatisfaction. I explained my proceedings on their behalf to a Dr. Warner whom I saw at Paris on his way to Algiers, and particularly the reason why I did not answer Obrian's letters, and desired him to communicate it to Capt. Obrian. But I do not know whether he did it.—I think it more probable that Mr. Carmichael will impute to me also an event which must take place this year. In truth it is so extraordinary a circumstance that a public agent, placed in a foreign court for the purpose of correspondence, should in three years have found means to get but one letter to us, that he must himself be sensible that if he could have sent us letters, he ought to be recalled as negligent, and if he could not, he ought to be recalled as useless. I have nevertheless procured his continuance in order to give him an opportunity which occurred of his rendering a sensible service to his country, and thereby drawing some degree of favor on his return. Wishing you every circumstance of success & happiness I am with great esteem Dear Sir Your sincere friend & servt

TH: JEFFERSON

RC (NjP: Andre deCoppet Collection); at head of text: "(Private)"; at foot of first page: "Colo. David Humphreys"; endorsed by Humphreys. PrC (DLC).

and printed in Vol. 18: 423-36 as part of a group of documents on Mediterranean trade and Algerine captives. See also note to TJ to Pierce Butler, 2 Dec. 1791.

The TWO LONG REPORTS were the Report on American Trade in the Mediterranean and the Report on American Captives in Algiers, both dated 28 Dec. 1790

[1] Preceding three words interlined in place of "provided no means."
[2] Word interlined.

From James Monroe

DEAR SIR   Baltimore March 22. 93.

This will be presented you by Judge Symes of the western territory, with whom I served in the former-Congress and whom I deem a sensible and honest man. He was of service in repelling the attack upon the Missisippi in 1786 by Gardoqui and company. As he is well acquainted with the affairs of that country I have thought it might be useful for you to know him.

We arrived here last night, the roads having almost exhausted ourselves and horses. We stay to day and move on tomorrow early.

JAS. MONROE

RC (DLC); endorsed by TJ as received 25 Mch. 1793 and so recorded in SJL.

For what Monroe perceived as THE ATTACK UPON THE MISSISSIPPI growing out of negotiations on the navigation of that river between Secretary for Foreign Affairs John Jay and Spanish representative Diego de GARDOQUI in 1786, see Monroe to TJ, 19 Aug. 1786, and note.

To James Simpson

SIR   Philadelphia Mar. 22. 1793.

Your favor of Feb. 12. has been duly recieved, and I am to make you my acknolegements for your attention to the affairs of Mr. Barclay, and of the public in his hands. Colo. Humphreys is now authorised to settle those matters finally, to receive and dispose of all the public effects and monies confided to Mr. Barclay, and to him therefore I will refer you as to those remaining in your hands. The present unsettled state of the succession in Morocco, rendering it useless to renew as yet Mr. Barclay's mission, your correspondence on the progress of events there, will be thankfully recieved. I have the honor to be with much regard Sir Your most obedt. humble servt   TH: JEFFERSON

PrC (DLC); at foot of text: "Mr. James Simpson. Gibraltar." FC (Lb in DNA: RG 59, DCI).

This day TJ submitted the above letter to the President, who approved and returned it the same day (Washington, *Journal*, 99).

To William Carmichael and William Short

GENTLEMEN   Mar. 23.[1] 1793.

It is intimated to us, in such a way as to attract our attention, that France means to send a strong force early this spring to offer independance to the Spanish American colonies, beginning with those on the Missisipi: and that she will not object to the receiving those on the East side into our confederation.[2] Interesting considerations require that we should keep ourselves free to act in this case according to circumstances, and consequently that you should not, by any clause of treaty, bind us to guarantee any of the Spanish colonies against their own independance,[3] nor indeed against any other nation. For when we thought we might guarantee Louisiana on their ceding the Floridas to us, we apprehended it would be seised by Great Britain who would thus completely encircle us with her colonies and fleets. This danger is now[4] removed by the concert between Great Britain and Spain: and the times will soon enough give independance, and consequently free commerce to our neighbors, without our risking the involving ourselves in a war for them.

Dft (DLC); *en clair* text written and signed by TJ on 21 or 22 Mch. 1793, then substantially revised and date reworked on 23 Mch. 1793 (see note 3 below); at head of text: "to be in cypher"; at foot of text in the hand of George Washington: "The above meets the approbation of Go: Washington"; enclosed as emended in TJ to Washington, 24 Mch. 1793. RC

(William M. Elkins, Philadelphia, 1945); unsigned; with reworked date (see note 1 below); in code except for salutation, dateline, and names of addressees, with interlined decipherment in Short's hand; at foot of text: "Messrs. Carmichael & Short." PrC (DLC); with date reworked in ink by TJ. FC (Lb in DNA: RG 59, DCI); entirely *en clair*; includes "Philadelphia" in dateline and contains complimentary close and TJ's name at foot of text. The Editors have verified the Dft against the encoded RC and Short's interlinear decipherment using partially reconstructed Code No. 10. RC enclosed in TJ to David Humphreys, 22 Mch. 1793.

This instruction to the American commissioners in Madrid, triggered by intelligence recently received from William Stephens Smith that France would SEND A STRONG FORCE EARLY THIS SPRING to liberate the Spanish colonies in America, reflected a significant change in the Washington administration's policy toward Spain (see Notes on Conversations with William Stephens Smith and George Washington, 20 Feb. 1793). When Great Britain and Spain nearly went to war in 1790 over the Nootka Sound crisis, TJ had instructed Carmichael to explore the prospects of obtaining all Spanish territory east of the Mississippi in return for an American guarantee of her trans-Mississippi possessions. The peaceful resolution of this confrontation made such an agreement very unlikely. Although TJ did not withdraw the authorization to Carmichael, he did not mention the scheme in later letters to him and gave it only passing reference in the otherwise comprehensive report on Spanish negotiations he sent to the commssioners in March 1792 (TJ to Carmichael, 2 Aug. 1790, and enclosure, Document II in a group of documents on the war crisis of 1790, in Vol. 17: 111-17; Report on Negotiations with Spain, 18 Mch. 1792).

If the original guarantee was no longer in the forefront of the Secretary of State's thinking, he was nevertheless still prepared to sanction a more limited guarantee as late as 22 Mch. 1793, when he sent the President a draft of the present letter offering, in exchange for the Floridas, to guarantee Spanish possession of Louisiana against Britain, though not against a bid for independence by its own inhabitants. The decision only a day later to abandon the guarantee altogether very likely resulted from the President's initiative, for he did not approve the draft when the Secretary of State submitted it on 22

Mch. Two days later, however, after reading the draft as revised by TJ, Washington took the unusual step of inscribing it with his formal approval, which was also registered emphatically in the President's journal. Although the growing CONCERT BETWEEN GREAT BRITAIN AND SPAIN, capped by their treaty of alliance of 25 May 1793, would soon remove any need by Spain to negotiate such a guarantee, TJ had received no foreign dispatches about this rapprochement between writing and revising the draft that might have led him to change his strategy. Rather it seems likely that Washington had become wary of any guarantee that might lead to war with Britain, even in exchange for major territorial advantages (TJ to Washington, 24 Mch. 1793; Washington, *Journal*, 99, 104; Bemis, *Pinckney's Treaty*, 169).

With this dispatch TJ sent another copy of a 15 Nov. 1781 letter from Lachlan McIntosh to Edward Telfair and Noble Wymberly Jones, then Georgia delegates to the Confederation Congress, supporting the American position on the disputed Florida-Georgia boundary (PrC of Tr in DLC; in a clerk's hand, but partly overwritten in a later hand; at head of text in TJ's hand in ink: "Copy" and "3plicate sent by Capt. Cutting. Mar. 23. 93."; recorded in SJL under 23 Mch. 1793). TJ had previously enclosed a copy of the letter with his 18 Mch. 1792 instructions to the commissioners (see note to Report on Negotiations with Spain, 18 Mch. 1792).

[1] Second digit reworked from "1" or "2" in Dft and RC. TJ made the same alteration in ink on the PrC.
[2] TJ first wrote "confederacy" before altering the word.
[3] Remainder of text substituted for "but only ⟨*against Gr*⟩ that of Louisiana against those who hold Canada also, and that only in consideration of their ceding the Floridas to us. We are very anxious to hear from you. Th: Jefferson." TJ canceled this passage, together with the subjoined address to "Messrs. Carmichael & Short," after conferring with Washington.
[4] Word interlined.

To Alexander Hamilton

S<small>IR</small>   Philadelphia Mar. 23. 1793.

I inclose you the order of the President for 39,500. Dollars to complete the third year's allowance under the act concerning intercourse with foreign nations, which third year will end on the last day of June next. I have the honor to be Sir Your very humble servt

T<small>H</small>: J<small>EFFERSON</small>

PrC (DLC); at foot of text: "The Secretary of the Treasury." FC (Lb in DNA: RG 59, DL). Enclosure: George Washington to Hamilton, 23 Mch. 1793 (Syrett, *Hamilton*, XIV, 241).

To Alexander Hamilton

S<small>IR</small>   Philadelphia Mar. 23. 1793. Saturday.

The Attorney general has just informed me that on a conversation with you it has been found convenient that we should meet at 9. aclock tomorrow at his house as Commissioners of the Sinking fund. I will attend there and shall hope the honor of meeting you. I have that of being Sir your most obedt. servt.   T<small>H</small>: J<small>EFFERSON</small>

PrC (DLC); at foot of text: "The Secretary of the Treasury." Tr (DLC); 19th-century copy.

Notes on Stockholders in Congress

Mar. 23. 1793. The following list of paper-men is communicated to me by Mr. Beckley.

*	Gilman.	S.H.
† *	Gerry.	S.H.
	Sedgwick.	
*	Ames	S.H.
*	Goodhue	S.H.
	Bourne. R.I.	suspected only.
*	Trumbul.	S.H.
*	Wadsworth.	S.H.
*	Hillhouse.	S.H.
	Learned.	S.H.
	Laurence	S.H. & Director

Gordon.
† Boudinot.   S.H.
  * Dayton.   S.H.
  * Fitzsimmons. S.H. & Director
  * D. Heister. S.H.
   Sterret
   Murray   S.H.
† * Williamson S.H.
   Smith   S.H. & Director. for himself & his proxies his vote is near $\frac{1}{5}$ of the whole[1]

---

  * Cabot.   S.H. & Director
  * Sherman S.H.
   Elsworth. qu.
  * King.   S.H. & Director
   Dickinson.
  * Morris. S.H.
  * Johnson.
  * Izard S.H.

	H. Reprs.	Senate
Stockholders	16[2]	5
other paper	3	2
	19	7[3]
suspected	2	1

* these are known to Beckley
† these avowed it in presence of Th:J.

MS (DLC); entirely in TJ's hand; written with "Anas" entries for 2 and 25 Mch. 1793 on the other side of a sheet bearing "Anas" entries for 30 and 31 Mch. 1793. Included in the "Anas."

This list of twenty-eight known or suspected PAPER-MEN—members of Congress who held stock in the Bank of the United States or public securities—and the brief addendum TJ wrote on 25 Mch. 1793 confirming one name and adding two others, mirrored the efforts of key Republicans to document their conviction that Alexander Hamilton had established a fiscal system that corrupted Congress and threatened representative government (see Notes on Stockholders in Congress, 25 Mch. 1793; TJ to Washington, 23 May, 9 Sep. 1792; Notes of a Conversation with Washington, 10 July, 1 Oct. 1792). This political accounting had actually begun before 27 Aug. 1792, when John BECKLEY, the fiercely Republican clerk of the House of Representatives,

informed Benjamin Rush that "a member of Congress had examined the Register's books and found 26 members of the House of Representatives and 8 of the Senate certificate holders" (George W. Corner, ed., *The Autobiography of Benjamin Rush: His "Travels Through Life," together with his Commonplace Book for 1789-1813* [Princeton, 1948], 227). The decisive defeat of the Giles resolutions censuring the Secretary of the Treasury on 2 Mch. 1793, however, evoked fresh expressions of TJ's concern and sparked Republican efforts to demonstrate that their intended rebuke to Hamilton had been thwarted by a phalanx of congressional speculators with a personal interest in sustaining his fiscal system (Editorial Note on Jefferson and the Giles resolutions, at 27 Feb. 1793; Notes on the Giles Resolutions, 2 Mch. 1793; TJ to Thomas Mann Randolph, Jr., 3 Mch. 1793).

At the time that Beckley supplied TJ with the names recorded in this "Anas" entry, he was also involved in preparing a somewhat longer list of thirty-four names that appeared in *An Examination of the Late Proceedings in Congress, Respecting the Official Conduct of the Secretary of the Treasury* [Philadelphia, 1793], 26n. This pamphlet attack on Hamilton and defense of the Giles resolutions carried a date of 8 Mch. 1793, but was first published on 9 Apr. 1793 and reprinted as late as 20 Oct. 1793. Its authorship, once ascribed to John Taylor of Caroline, is still in dispute, but Beckley probably wrote most or all of it, possibly with the assistance of James Monroe (Edmund and Dorothy Smith Berkeley, "'The Piece Left Behind': Monroe's Authorship of a Political Pamphlet Revealed," VMHB, LXXV [1967], 174-80, and same, *John Beckley: Zealous Partisan in a Nation Divided* [Philadelphia, 1973], 88-9, conclusively refuting earlier attributions to John Taylor of Caroline, assign joint authorship to Monroe and Beckley but argue for Monroe's predominant role; Ammon, *Monroe*, 596n, regards the degree of Monroe's involvement as uncertain; Robert E. Shalhope, *John Taylor of Caroline: Pastoral Republican* [Columbia, S.C., 1980], 218-19, shares Ammon's doubts as to Monroe's coauthorship). Whether TJ knew of the preparation of this pamphlet is unclear, but there can be no doubt that he approved of its sentiments and publication (TJ to James Madison, [24 Mch. 1793], and note; TJ to Peter Carr, 14 Apr. 1793; TJ to Monroe, 5 May 1793).

Although the Editors have made no attempt to verify the accuracy of TJ's lists or the list in *An Examination*, the substantial overlap between the names in both tabulations should not obscure the important discrepancies between them. Twenty-six legislators described as holders of bank or public stock were recorded in both, but four names in TJ's lists did not appear in *An Examination*, while eight names printed in the latter were not listed by TJ. Twenty-four of the paper holders listed by TJ were identified as stockholders in the bank, but only twenty-two in *An Examination* were so designated. Of the twenty-six names common to both lists, eighteen were described as bank stockholders in both lists, five were so recorded in TJ's enumeration but not in *An Examination*,

two were listed in the pamphlet but not by TJ, and one was not listed as a stockholder in either compilation. These discrepancies suggest that Beckley continued to revise and supplement his list almost up to the date of publication.

Shortly after TJ recorded his "Anas" entries of 23 and 25 Mch. 1793, but before the publication of *An Examination*, the Republican allegation that Hamilton had been exonerated of Giles's charges through the agency of a corrupt squadron in the House of Representatives was aired by "Timon." In a letter of 10 Mch. 1793 published in the *National Gazette* seventeen days later, "Timon" impugned the integrity of the votes on the Giles resolutions in the House by asserting that three of the Secretary of the Treasury's supporters were directors and fifteen or twenty more were reputedly stockholders in the Bank of the United States. Returning to this theme in a 2 Apr. 1793 letter published eleven days later, "Timon" offered a new breakdown of House members with a personal stake in Hamiltonian policies, maintaining that twelve stockholders in the Bank of the United States (five of whom were also directors) and an additional ten to twelve substantial holders of public securities had voted against the Giles resolutions. "Take away the votes of bank-directors and stockholders," he asked rhetorically, stating the gravamen of his case, "and is the Secretary fairly acquitted or condemned?" (*National Gazette*, 27 Mch., 13 Apr. 1793). Edmund and Dorothy Smith Berkeley have suggested that Beckley probably wrote the "Timon" essays ("'The Piece Left Behind,'" 176; *John Beckley*, 87-8), but the evidence for this attribution is tenuous at best, and the numerical discrepancies between the "Timon" letters and *An Examination* with respect to bank directors and stockholders further suggest that they were not written by the same person.

[1] Below this line TJ erased one line of text so completely as to obliterate it and partially remove the surface of the paper. The obliterated line, which evidently contained the name of another congressman and a comment about him, must have been effaced after TJ calculated a total of

twenty-nine such members in the tabulation below. This erasure may be related to a similarly thorough cancellation TJ made in Notes on the Giles Resolutions, 2 Mch. 1793.

[2] Number written over what appears to be "21," erased.

[3] This line interlined.

To William Short

DEAR SIR   Philadelphia Mar. 23. 1793.

As my public letter of Oct. 14. 1792. required you to leave the Hague immediately on another business, I have addressed no other to you since that date. In the mean time I have received your Nos. 103. 107 to 117 inclusive and 119 to 122. inclusive and it is chiefly to acknolege these, and place your mind at ease with respect to them, that I write the present, as it is so uncertain how it may be conveyed to you from Lisbon that nothing confidential can be trusted to it. Tell Mr.[1] Carmichael that I have still[2] but one letter from him.[3] Newspapers for yourself and Mr. Carmichael will go to Lisbon, whatever their fate may be afterwards.

Appearances indicate a very general war in Europe. If the powers there leave us in the full enjoyment of the rights of neutrality, neutrality will be our plan. We expect from our ministers and consuls their utmost vigilance to protect our vessels in these rights, and to prevent other vessels from usurping our flag, which usurpation tends to commit us with foreign nations, to provoke rigorous scrutinies of the vessels truly ours in order to discover the counterfeits, and to take business from us.—Joseph Yznardi junr. is appointed our Consul at Cadiz, Robert Montgomery at Alicant, and Michael Murphy at Malaga. Be pleased to remember to forward your account immediately after the 30th. of June. I am with great & sincere esteem Dear Sir your friend & servt   TH: JEFFERSON

RC (DLC: Short Papers); contains one sentence written in code (see note 3 below), with Short's interlinear decipherment; at foot of text: "Mr. Short"; endorsed by Short as received 5 May 1794. PrC (DLC). Dft (DLC: TJ Papers, 83: 14394); en clair text entirely in TJ's hand; undated; consists only of sentence encoded in RC; at head of text: "publick"; written on same sheet as Dft of TJ's private letter to Short of this date. FC (Lb in DNA: RG 59, DCI); entirely en clair. Enclosed in TJ to David Humphreys, 22 Mch. 1793.

[1] Short's decipherment: "Master."
[2] Here in Dft TJ canceled "received."
[3] This sentence is in code; it has been supplied from the Dft and verified by the Editors against both Short's decipherment and partially reconstructed Code No. 10. In the Dft TJ canceled the remainder of the sentence: "and that the ⟨cases of⟩ individuals on whose cases he has never given any answer are strong."

To William Short

DEAR SIR   Philadelphia Mar. 23. 1793.

My last *private* letter to you was of Jan. 3. Your private letters of Sep. 15. Oct. 22. Nov. 2. Nov. 20. Nov. 30. and Dec. 18. have been received and shall be attended. Particular answers cannot be hazarded by this conveyance. But on one circumstance it is so necessary to put you on your guard that I must take and give you the trouble of applying to our cypher.[1] Be cautious in your letters to the Secretary of the treasury. He sacrifices[2] you.[3] On a late occasion when called on to explain before the Senate his proceedings relative to the loans in Europe, instead of extracting such passages of your letters as might relate to them, he gave in[4] the originals in which I am told were strong expressions against the French republicans: and even gave in a correspondence between G. Morris and yourself which scarcely related to the loans at all, merely that a long letter of Morris's might appear in which he argues as a democrat himself against you as an aristocrat. I have done what I could to lessen the injury this did you, for such sentiments towards the French are extremely grating here, tho they are[5] those of Hamilton[6] himself and the monocrats of his cabal.— Particular circumstances have obliged me to remain here a little longer: but I certainly retire in the summer or fall. The next Congress will be strongly[7] republican. Adieu[8]

RC (ViW); unsigned; partly in code (see note 1 below), with Short's interlinear decipherment; at head of text: "Private"; at foot of text: "Mr. Short"; endorsed by Short as received 5 May 1794. PrC (DLC). Dft (DLC: TJ Papers, 83: 14394); *en clair* text entirely in TJ's hand; undated; consists only of portion encoded in RC; with penciled note by TJ at foot of text (see note 8 below); at head of text: "private"; subjoined to Dft of TJ's official letter to Short of this date. Enclosed in TJ to David Humphreys, 22 Mch. 1793.

The LATE OCCASION took place on 6 Feb. 1793, when Alexander Hamilton—in response to a Senate resolution of 23 Jan. 1793 calling upon the President to submit copies of the powers given by him for the negotiation of loans under acts of Congress of 4 and 12 Aug. 1790—submitted a report on foreign loans to the Senate enclosing copies of various letters on this subject that William Short had written to him and exchanged with Gouverneur Morris. The report was designed to defuse Republican charges that Hamilton had unduly delayed payment of the American debt to France (*Annals*, III, 633; Syrett, *Hamilton*, XIV, 5-6; concerning the acts in question, see Notes on Alexander Hamilton's Report on Foreign Loans, [ca. 20 Feb. 1793], and note). In addition to disclosing Short's unflattering assessment of the government that assumed power in France after the overthrow of Louis XVI and his initial delay in paying the next installment on the debt to France, the letters appended by Hamilton also revealed Morris's insistence that Short make the payment to the revolutionary regime as the legitimate government of France (Syrett, *Hamilton*, XII, 293-7, 425-80). The LONG LETTER was undoubtedly Morris to Short, 20 Sep. 1792, wherein

Morris emphasized the legality of the new French government (same, XII, 462-6). Morris had expressed similar views on the government's legitimacy in his 22 Aug. 1792 letter to TJ. See also note to TJ to Short, 3 Jan. 1793.

[1] The remainder of the text is in code; it has been supplied from the Dft and verified by the Editors against both Short's decipherment and partially reconstructed Code No. 10.

[2] Deciphered by Short as "sacrificed," but encoded in the present tense by TJ.

[3] Here in Dft TJ canceled "infamously," the last word in the sentence.

[4] Here TJ wrote code 1096, which Short deciphered as "wick," instead of code 1093 for "in," the word TJ used in Dft.

[5] At this point in Dft TJ canceled what appears to be "exactly."

[6] Here TJ canceled two illegible ciphers which correspond to no word in Dft.

[7] For the last syllable of this word TJ inadvertently wrote code 284, whose meaning is unknown, instead of 287, the code for "ly," but Short correctly deciphered the word.

[8] At foot of Dft TJ wrote the following note so lightly in pencil that it is partly illegible: "See hurry of Hs proceedings under the pressure of Congress to [place his?] defence [before?] the session expired [as the?] answer [to this?] base charge⟨d⟩. But it is *characteristic* of its *Author*."

From John Syme

DEAR SIR   Richmd. 23d. March 1793.

I came down here Yesterday, and am this moment favor'd with your melancholy Letter, of 17th. Currt. with the Inclosures. After returning you My sincere thanks, for your very Freindly Communications of poor Barclay's Death, I am to request You'll Advise me, soon as possible, of the readiest Method, of Obtaining for His Family, the Moneys Due, for His Services to the publick, and which They are really in Want of. I am sure, Mrs. Barclay will be so much Affected, by the Sad Tidings, that She Will not be able, to think of Business, which Hope Will plead My Excuse, for Giving you this additional, Or any other Trouble, that may arise, on this Truly Afecting Occasion, and in which your real Goodness of Heart, Simpathizes with His Conections and Freinds. I Have the Honor to be, in Great Haste, My Dear Sir, Your Oblig'd & Obedt. Servt.   J SYME

NB. No Doubt, the Family would Wish to Know, if there is a Will among the papers which probably, will Come through Your Hands, and to Myself, as Heretofore.

RC (MHi); endorsed by TJ as received 30 Mch. 1793 and so recorded in SJL.

To George Washington

SIR Philadelphia Mar. 23. 1793.

Before your departure, it becomes necessary for me to sollicit your orders on the Treasury for the third year's allowance under the act concerning intercourse with foreign nations. This act commenced July 1. 1790. Two years allowance have been furnished and a sum of 500. Dollars over. Nine months of the 3d. year are now nearly elapsed, and according to an estimate I had the honor of giving in to you the 5th. of Nov. last, the expences to the 3d. of Mar. last probably amounted to about 90,785.09 D. from which deducting the sums received, to wit 80,500. D. the bankers would be in advance at that day upwards of 10,000. D. and near 20,000. D. by the time this remittance can reach them. They could feel no inconvenience from this, because they had in their hands the Algerine fund. But now that that is to be drawn for by Colo. Humphreys, it becomes necessary to pay up the arrearages of the foreign fund, and to put them moreover in cash to answer the current calls of our ministers abroad, in order to prevent any risque to the honor of Colo. Humphreys's bills. I must therefore sollicit your orders for 39,500. D. which will compleat the allowance for the 3d. year, ending June 30. A summary view of the account is stated below. I have the honor to be with the most perfect respect & esteem, Sir, your most obedt. humble servt.　　　　　　　　　　　　　　TH: JEFFERSON

	D	D.
Actual expences incurred from 1790. July 1. to 1792. July 1.	64,485.09	
Probable do. as by acct. given in　　to 1793. Mar. 3.	26,300.	90,785.0
1790. Aug. 14. Cash to Colo. Humphreys.		500.
1791. Mar. 19. Bill on the bankers in favr. of Secy. of state. 99,000ƒ =		40,000.

	ƒ		D.		
do. on do. in favr. of G. Morris	2 475	=	1 000.		
do. on do. in favr. of J. B. Cutting	577.10	=	233⅓		
1792. Jan. 23. do. on do. in favr. of Secy. of state. 95,947 ⁄ 99,000		=	38,766⅔	40,000	80,500.

RC (DNA: RG 59, MLR); endorsed by Tobias Lear. PrC (DLC); at foot of text in ink by TJ: "⟨Short Wm.⟩" and "Secy. Treasy."; lengthwise in left margin in ink by George Taylor, Jr.: "To the President of the U.S." FC (Lb in DNA: RG 59, DL); lacks subjoined account. Tr (Lb in same, SDC). Not recorded in SJL.

As requested, the President gave TJ ORDERS ON THE TREASURY this day (TJ to Alexander Hamilton, 23 Mch. 1793; Washington, *Journal*, 102). For the relevant statutes CONCERNING INTERCOURSE WITH FOREIGN NATIONS, dated 1 July 1790 and 9 Feb. 1793, see *Annals*, II, 2292, III, 1411-12.

¹ Tr: "80,000."

To C. W. F. Dumas

Dear Sir   Philadelphia Mar. 24. 1793.

I have to acknolege the receipt of your favors of Sep. 20. Nov. 13. and Jan. 9. I shall hope your continuance to send us the Leyden gazette as usual, but all the other gazettes which you have hitherto usually sent, may be discontinued. The scene in Europe is becoming very interesting. Amidst the confusions of a general war which seem to be threatening that quarter of the globe, we hope to be permitted to preserve the line of neutrality. We wish not to meddle with the internal affairs of any country, nor with the general affairs of Europe. Peace with all nations, and the rights which that gives us with respect to all nations, are our objects. It will be necessary for all our public Agents to exert themselves with vigilance for securing to our vessels all the rights of neutrality, and for preventing the vessels of other nations from usurping our flag. This usurpation tends to commit us with the belligerent powers, to draw on those vessels truly ours, rigorous visitations to distinguish them from the counterfeits, and to take business from us. I recommend these objects to you. I have done the same to Mr. Greenleaf lately appointed our Consul at Amsterdam. Be so good as to remember to send your account immediately after the 30th. of June. I forward for you to Mr. Pinckney a copy of the laws of the last session of Congress: and am with very sincere esteem Dear Sir, your most obedt. humble servt.   Th: Jefferson

RC (PHi: Gratz Collection); addressed: "A Monsieur Monsieur Dumas à la Haye"; postmarked; endorsed by Dumas. PrC (DLC). FC (Lb in DNA: RG 59, DCI).

From Alexander Hamilton

Sir   Philadelphia March 24. 1793

I have the honor of your two notes of yesterday and today, respecting a proposed Meeting of the Commissioners of the Sinking Fund. The first came to hand only within a half hour.

As you mention, that the Attorney General has informed you, that "*on a conversation with me*, it has been *found convenient*" that a Meeting should take place—I cannot help inferring, there has been some misapprehension: Since it certainly is not my opinion, that a Meeting at the present moment is necessary; there being several depending and undecided circumstances which put it out of my power at this time, to pronounce that there are monies to be invested in purchases. Add to this that a Meeting must *of course* take place within the ensuing Month of April—when further information may afford better data for operation.

I understood on Saturday from the Attorney General, that it was your wish a Meeting should be had—to which I replied, in substance, that I considered it as in your power to convene one; and should attend if called upon; but that I did not perceive the utility of one at this time. As we shall meet at the War Office tomorrow on another business, there will be an opportunity for further explanation. I have the honor to be Sir Your Obedient servant A HAMILTON

RC (DLC); at foot of text: "The Secretary of State"; endorsed by TJ as received 24 Mch. 1793 and so recorded in SJL.

TJ's note to Hamilton of TODAY has not been found and is not recorded in SJL, but it probably inquired why Hamilton was not at the PROPOSED MEETING OF THE COMMISSIONERS OF THE SINKING FUND that the Secretary of State had called for this morning. Hamilton's presence was required to form a quorum because all the commissioners except TJ and Attorney General Edmund Randolph were out of town, but he evidently feared that at the meeting TJ intended to ask inconvenient questions about the foreign loan of $2,000,000 that had been authorized by an act of 12 Aug. 1790 for use by the Commissioners in reducing the domestic debt. On 2 Apr. 1793 Hamilton commented to Rufus King: "A meeting of the Commissioners has lately been called by Mr. Jefferson out of the course heretofore practiced, in which I have been pressed to declare whether *I had or had not funds applicable to purchases.* I answered so as to be safe." No evidence that the Commissioners actually met between 24 Mch. and

2 Apr. 1793 has come to light, although they were obliged by law to meet at the end of each quarter and thus sat as a matter OF COURSE on 6 Apr. 1793 (see Hamilton to TJ, 4, 5 Apr. [1793]). In the interim TJ may have "pressed" the Treasury Secretary at the OPPORTUNITY FOR FURTHER EXPLANATION on 25 Mch. 1793 when the Cabinet gathered as scheduled at the War Office but deferred transacting business because Henry Knox was ill. Although the minutes of the 6 Apr. meeting record no discussion of the availability of the foreign loan, TJ may have raised the matter informally to pave the way for his unsuccessful attempt at a special meeting of the Commissioners on 7 May 1793 to have the matter laid before the President (Syrett, *Hamilton*, XIV, 276, 292-3; *Annals*, II, 2369-70; note to George Washington to the Cabinet, 21 Mch. 1793; Notes on the Sinking Fund and the Proclamation of Neutrality, 7 May 1793). See also Notes on Alexander Hamilton's Report on Foreign Loans, [ca. 20 Feb. 1793], and note; and Editorial Note on Jefferson and the Giles resolutions, at 27 Feb. 1793.

From David Humphreys

SIR   Lisbon March 24th. 1793.

I have the honour to transmit a Copy of the Official Answer of the Secretary of State for foreign Affairs, respecting the two Subjects on which I had applied to him. A Translation is also annexed.

As the Papers containing the circumstances relative to this business will be before you, I will not trespass on your time by offering comments. I even forbear to remark on the *policy of State* that has operated in the forcible detention of all vessels from America, laden with grain, which have arrived here since the month of Decr. last; as well as on the idea which seems to be held forth of its being fraudulent for Merchants to dispose of their articles of commerce in the best markets and to the best advantage. Yet I must frankly confess the information is new to me, that any of our Merchants should have such a predilection for the Port of Lisbon as to order their Cargoes to be sold unconditionally there, at a lower price than might be obtained at Cadiz or other nieghbouring Ports.

I never entertained very sanguine hopes that any thing but the imperious dictates of necessity would induce that Class of Persons alluded to in the letter from the Secretary of State, to consent to the importation of flour into the Ports of Portugal. The Nobility, whose influence you are not insensible of, being the principal Mill-Owners, constitute that Class. However, I have no doubt we should already have obtained our object, had it not been for the arrival of so many Cargoes of wheat from America within the last two months. A crisis more favorable to the accomplishment of our wishes may still come. And if the superior prices which are now offered for flour in other Countries (and particularly in some of the Ports of Spain) should continue a little longer, perhaps that period is not so far distant as may have been imagined by this Government.

In submitting to the Executive, the profession on the part of the Court of Lisbon, "of its constant dispositions of cordial friendship and good correspondence towards the U.S. of America; as well as of its perpetual readiness to listen to all propositions which may tend to draw more closely those ties, and to establish a solid and permanent System of Commerce, reciprocally beneficial for the two States:" I have the honour to remain, with the highest esteem & respect Sir Your most obedient & Most humble Servant   D. HUMPHREYS

P.S. Since finishing this letter M. d'Arbot the New French Minister has arrived. France, we understand has declared war against Spain.

RC (DNA: RG 59, DD); at head of text: "(No. 69.)"; between signature and postscript: "The Secretary of State &c. &c. &c."; endorsed by TJ as received 17 May 1793 and so recorded in SJL. Tr (Lb in same). Enclosures: (1) Foreign Minister Luis Pinto de Sousa Coutinho to Humphreys, 20 Mch. 1793, reporting in response to his petitions of 18 Jan. to 16 Mch. 1793, which were referred to the Prince of Brazil, that his court has not altered its liberal policy respecting American ships with grain that are positively bound for other countries, and that any temporary exceptions to this system had been dictated by "either a momentary urgency or rather a well founded presumption," demonstrated by the enclosed extract, that many American ships fraudulently try to take advantage of high prices elsewhere contrary to the real intention of their owners to sell the cargoes in Lisbon; explaining that there would be no change in the policy of refusing admission to American flour because the prohibition protects Portuguese interests and applies impartially to all foreign powers; and avowing his court's cordial friendship and desire to strengthen commercial ties with the United States. (2) Extract from the Secretary of State for the Home Department to the Administrator General of the Custom House, 23 Dec. 1792, directing him not to permit the export of flour or wheat from Lisbon without the permission of the Administrator of the Corn Market, similarly instructing him not to allow the re-export of grain in order to prevent ships from feigning entry in distress so as to purchase and export grain "destined for the consumption of this Court," and ordering him to stop the practice whereby Lisbon pilots advise ship captains either to avoid the port or enter it only while claiming to do so in distress, so that "we may not be reduced by negligence from our present abundance to want" (Trs in same, in Portuguese, in Humphreys's hand; Trs in same, in English; Trs in Lb in same, in Portuguese and English).

On 17 May 1793 TJ sent this letter and its enclosures to the President, who returned them the next day (Washington, *Journal*, 142-3).

To James Madison

Th: Jefferson to J. Madison   [24 Mch. 1793]

The idea seems to gain credit that the naval powers combining against France will prohibit supplies even of provisions to that country. Should this be formally notified I should suppose Congress would be called, because it is a justifiable cause of war, and as the Executive cannot decide the question of war on the affirmative side, neither ought it to do so on the negative side, by preventing the competent body from deliberating on the question. But I should hope that war would not be their choice. I think it will furnish us a happy opportunity of setting another precious example to the world, by shewing that nations may be brought to do justice by appeals to their interests as well as by appeals to arms. I should hope that Congress instead of a denunciation of war, would instantly exclude from our ports all the manufactures, produce, vessels and subjects of the nations committing this aggression, during the continuance of the aggression and till full satisfaction made for it. This would work well in many ways, safely in all, and introduce between nations another umpire than arms. It would relieve us too from the risks and the horrors of cutting throats. The death of the king of France has not produced as open condemnations from the Monocrats as I expected. I dined the other day in a company where the subject was discussed. I will name the company in the order in which they manifested their partialities, beginning with the warmest

Jacobinism and proceeding by shades to the most heartfelt aristocracy. Smith (N.Y.) Coxe. Stewart. T. Shippen. Bingham. Peters. Breck. Meredith. Wolcott. It is certain that the ladies of this city, of the first circle are all open-mouthed against the murderers of a sovereign, and they generally speak those sentiments which the more cautious husband smothers.—I believe it is pretty certain that Smith (S.C.) and miss A. are not to come together. Ternant has at length openly hoisted the flag of monarchy by going into deep mourning for his prince. I[1] suspect he thinks a cessation of his visits to me a necessary accompaniment to this pious duty. A connection between him and Hamilton seems to be springing up. On observing that Duer was secretary to the old board of treasury, I suspect him to have been the person who suggested to Hamilton the letter of mine to that board which he so tortured in his Catullus. Dunlap has refused to print the peice which we had heard of before your departure, and it has been several days in Bache's hands, without any notice of it.—The President will leave this about the 27th. inst. and return about the 20th. of April. Adieu.

RC (DLC: Madison Papers); undated, but recorded in SJL under 24 Mch. 1793 and postmarked "25 MR"; addressed: "James Madison junior Orange. to the care of Mr James Blair Fredericksburg"; franked and stamped. PrC (DLC: TJ Papers, 83: 14443-4). Tr (same, 14441); 19th-century copy.

THE PIECE WHICH WE HAD HEARD OF BEFORE YOUR DEPARTURE was probably either the essay by "Timon" attacking Alexander Hamilton's fiscal policies that appeared under the date of 10 Mch. in the *National Gazette* of 27 Mch. 1793, or the equally critical pamphlet, *An Examination of the Late Proceedings in Congress, Respecting the Official Conduct of the Secretary of the Treasury* [Philadelphia, 1793], which was published on 9 Apr. 1793 (see note to Notes on Stockholders in Congress, 23 Mch. 1793). For Hamilton's attack on TJ in September 1792 under the pseudonym of CATULLUS, see note and enclosure to TJ to George Washington, 17 Oct. 1792.

[1] TJ initially began the sentence with "he," then canceled the word.

From James Madison

DEAR SIR   Alexanda. Mar: 24: 93

I wrote at Baltimore, but the letter being too late for the mail, I have suppressed it. It contained nothing of consequence. We arrived here to day (2 OC) and shall proceed to Colchester to night. Our journey has been successful; tho' laborious for the horses. The roads bad generally from Head of Elk; on the North of Baltimore, and thence to George Town, excessively so. I am just told by Mr. R. B. Lee here, that Rutherford is elected, so is Griffin, Nicholas, and New. The other elections are unknown here. Yrs. always & affecy.

Js. MADISON JR

RC (DLC: Madison Papers); endorsed by TJ as received 30 Mch. 1793 and so recorded in SJL. Madison's next letter to TJ, dated 31 Mch. 1793 and recorded in SJL as received 9 Apr. 1793, has not been found, but it concerned the Virginia elections (Madison, *Papers*, xv, 3).

To Martha Jefferson Randolph

MY DEAR DAUGHTER   Philadelphia Mar. 24. 1793.

I have nothing interesting to tell you from hence but that we are well, and how much we love you. From Monticello you have every thing to¹ write about which I have any care. How do my young chesnut trees? How comes on your garden? How fare the fruit blossoms &c. I sent to Mr. Randolph, I think, some seed of the Bent-grass which is much extolled. I now inclose you some seed which Mr. Hawkins gave me, the name of which I have forgotten: but I dare say it is worth attention. I therefore turn it over to you, as I should hope not to reap what would be planted here. Within about a week I remove into the country. Tell Mr. Randolph that I send Fenno's papers thro' Mr. Madison, who left this place with Colo. and Mrs. Monroe on the 20th. Give my best attachments to Mr. Randolph and kiss the little ones for me. Your's affectionately my dear   TH: JEFFERSON

RC (NNP); at foot of text: "Mrs. Randolph." PrC (MHi). Tr (ViU: Edgehill-Randolph Papers); 19th-century copy.

¹ TJ here canceled "say."

To George Washington

Mar. 24. 93.

Th: Jefferson presents his respects to the President and submits to his approbation an addition to the letter to Messrs. Carmichael and Short. The circumstances and prospects under which the guarantee of Louisiana had been suggested are so changed, as in his opinion to render it better to retract that suggestion, and to forbid the guarantee.

RC (DNA: RG 59, MLR); addressed: "The President of the US."; endorsed by Tobias Lear. PrC (DLC: TJ Papers, 81: 14058); partially overwritten in a later hand which reworked the faded date to "Jan. 93." Tr (Lb in DNA: RG 59, SDC). Recorded in SJPL between 21 and 25 Mch. 1793. Enclosure: Corrected Dft of TJ to Carmichael and Short, 23 Mch. 1793.

From William Barton

Fifth Street, No. 36 North, 25 Mch. 1793. Today he received a letter from Rodolph Vall-Travers of Hamburg which had been mistakenly delivered to his brother, Dr. Barton. A small box marked R.V. described as accompanying the letter has not come to hand. He asks through which channel the letter reached TJ, in hopes that this will help him find the box.

RC (DLC); 2 p.; at foot of text: "Thomas Jefferson, Esq. Secretary of State"; endorsed by TJ as received 25 Mch. 1793 and so recorded in SJL.

C. W. F. Dumas had previously asked TJ to forward a box and two packages from Vall-Travers to their respective addresses (Dumas to TJ, 13 Nov. 1792).

From Richard Harrison

SIR   March 25. 1793.

I have reflected on the subject of our conversation of the other day, and beleive I can state your Accounts in a manner that will be satisfactory to yourself, and at the same time conformable to law. Such at least will be my endeavour, being with sentiments of real Respect and esteem Sir Your Obed hble St   R. HARRISON

RC (DNA: RG 59, MLR); endorsed by TJ as received 26 Mch. 1793 and so recorded in SJL.

For a discussion of the settlement of

TJ's French ACCOUNTS, see the Editorial Note on the settlement of Jefferson's accounts as minister plenipotentiary in France, at 8 July 1792.

From George Meade

SIR   [25 Mch. 1793]

Permit me to Recommend Mr. Blake to you, should you want a Person in your office, I know him well, or I would not undertake to give him this Recommendation, I would if it was thought necessary be his Security, to the Amount [of] One thousand Guineas. I am very Respectfully Sir Your devoted hble St.   GO. M[EADE]

RC (DLC: Washington Papers, Applications for Office); undated; frayed at bottom; at foot of text: "[Honbe] Thomas Jefferson Esqr"; subjoined to brief note of James Blake to TJ, 25 Mch. 1793, from 177 Race Street in Philadelphia: "I beg leave to offer myself for the next vacancy for a clerk, that may happen in your Office"; mistakenly endorsed by TJ as received 23 Mch. 1793.

Blake did not receive a State Department clerkship during TJ's tenure in office, but Meade's willingness to commit himself to such a sizable sum as SECU-RITY must have impressed TJ, who later employed Blake as a confidential courier to the American commissioners in Spain (TJ to Blake, 12 July 1793). Blake also assisted TJ in his prolonged but ultimately successful efforts to acquire an edition of the letters of Cortés to Charles V on the conquest of New Spain (Blake to TJ, 6 June, 20 Oct., 8 Dec. 1795; TJ to Blake, 29 Feb. 1796).

Three letters exchanged by Meade and TJ between 19 May 1795 and 8 June 1795 are recorded in SJL but have not been found.

Notes on Stockholders in Congress

Mar. 25. Beckley says he has this day discovered that Benson is a stockholder, also Bourne of R.I. and Key.

MS (DLC); entirely in TJ's hand; partially dated; inserted opposite "Anas" entry for 23 Mch. 1793 and written with it and 2 Mch. 1793 entry on the other side of a sheet bearing "Anas" entries for 30 and 31 Mch. 1793. Included in the "Anas."

From David Rittenhouse

SIR   March 25th. 1793

I am again obliged to request you to make application to the President for a further Sum of money to defray the Expences of the Mint (5000 Dolls. if he shall think proper) and have enclosed a concise Statement of the expenditure of sums heretofore granted, which you will be pleased to communicate to him. The accounts, as preparing by the Treasurer of the Mint for settlement to the end of this month, will be much more particular and bulkey. But I thought it best to arrange them for the Presidents View in such a manner as should exhibit the whole at once with as much regularity as possible. I am, Sir, with great respect Your very humble Servant   DAVD. RITTENHOUSE
                                                                                    Directr. of the Mint

RC (DNA: RG 59, MLR); at foot of text: "T. Jefferson, Secretary of State"; endorsed by TJ as received 25 Mch. 1793 and so recorded in SJL. Tr (Lb in same, SDC). Enclosed in TJ to George Washington, 25 Mch. 1793.

Account of Expenditures for the Mint

[25 Mch. 1793]

Account of Expenditures for the Purposes of The Mint of the United States

		Dolls. Cents
For purchasing two Lots of Ground together with a Dwelling House, Still House, with two large Copper Stills &ca.		4266.67

	Dolls Cts	
For erecting two New brick buildings, Furnaces, a Frame Mill House & Stable &c.		
Vizt. Scantling, Boards, plank, Shingles	775.44	
Stone	106 56	
Lime &ca.	184 22	
Bricks	751 21	
Sand, Haling	72 88	
Bricklayer's Bill	688.12	
Carpenter's Do.	683 44	
Stone Cutter's Do.	21 65	
Nails, Hinges &ca.	128 83	
Iron Stoves, Sheet Iron	77 81	
Painting & Glazing	92 13	
Pump Maker	36 31	
		3618.60
Smith's work done out of The Mint for the buildings and Machinary[1]		760.06
Castings of Iron, Brass, wooden Patterns for Do. Bar Iron and Steel		843 33
Mill-Wright's Bill, not yet complete		345 75
Ironmongery		148.28
Coals and Fire wood		275 13
Provisions, Spirits &ca. for raising The several Buildings and for Labourers		158 80
Horses, Oxen, and Harness for Do.		194 78
Hay, Oats, Shorts &ca. for Do.		74.61
Lead, Tin, Black Lead Muffles & Pots, Weights, Brushes, Expence of Assaying &ca.		121.68
Incidental Expences of Offices, Advertisments &ca.		111.02
Labourers employed at The Buildings & Works & Mechanics including many small Articles from July 1st. to December 31st. 1792		924.16
Labourers, Mechanics &ca. Employed from January 1st to March 16th. 1793		725 44
Cash advanced for Sundry Articles[2]		50.00
For Copper purchased		1920 17
Officers Salaries and Clerk's Pay in part to December 31st. 1792		1694 88
		$16,233.46

Received on The Presidents warrant of July 10th. 1792	10,000	
" on Do. Do. November 29th 1792	5,000	
" for Sundry Appurtenances of The Distillary, sold	170 21	
Ballance, The Mint in advance	1063.25	
		$16,233.46

MS (DNA: RG 59, MLR); undated; in a clerk's hand; digits torn away in right margin supplied from Tr. Tr (Lb in same, SDC).

[1] Second digit in cents column in this and the next eleven entries supplied from Tr.
[2] Dollar total for this line in Tr: "30.–"

To George Washington

Mar. 25. 1793.

The Director of the mint having given in to the Secretary of state a general statement of the monies hitherto received for the mint, to wit 15,000 Dollars from the Treasury, and 170.25 D. the proceeds of certain articles sold, as also of the expenditures of the mint amounting to 16,233.46 D. with an application for a further sum of 5000. Dollars the same are respectfully laid before the President.

Th: Jefferson

RC (DNA: RG 59, MLR); endorsed by Tobias Lear. Pr C (DLC); overwritten by a later hand. Tr (Lb in DNA: RG 59, SDC). Enclosure: David Rittenhouse to TJ, 25 Mch. 1793, and enclosure. Recorded in SJPL.

From George Washington

March 25th: 1793

The President encloses a draft for the Director of the Mint to receive five thousand dollars for the purposes of that establishment—likewise a letter for Mr. G. Morris, which he requests the Secretary of State will be so good as to forward with the public dispatches he may send to that Gentleman.

RC (DLC); in the hand of Tobias Lear; addressed: "The Secretary [. . .]"; endorsed by TJ as received 25 Mch. 1793. Recorded in SJPL. Enclosures: (1) Washington to Alexander Hamilton, 25 Mch. 1793 (Syrett, Hamilton, xiv, 245). (2) Washington to Gouverneur Morris, 25 Mch. 1793 (Fitzpatrick, Writings, xxxii, 402-3).

From John Carey

Sir   March, 26: 1793.

I have the honor of submitting to your inspection the enclosed draught of an index to the laws—mortified, at the same time, to reflect, that, notwithstanding my earnest wishes and efforts to render it complete and satisfactory, it is yet so very far from being adequate to the liberal reward offered for it. I can therefore only add, that, to the utmost of my power, I am ready to make whatever alterations you may please to direct, either in the plan or the execution; and have the honor to be, with perfect respect, Sir, Your most obliged, humble servant, JOHN CAREY

RC (DLC); at foot of text: "The honble. the Secretary of State"; endorsed by TJ as received 26 Mch. 1793 and so recorded in SJL. Enclosure not found.

From Andrew Ellicott

SIR   Geo. Town March 26th 1793

I have been most injuriously treated by the commissioners: Accused, and dismissed on a charge of errors where there were none, and my character degraded so far, as they could degrade it. In this situation I thought the most respectful mode of obtaining redress, was by an appeal to the President: but by your letter of the 22d. I am cruelly disappointed. Has a man in public service, tho' under the direction of the commissioners, no resource for vindication from calumny, and oppression, but in an appeal to the candid public? If the President will have the patience to inform himself fully of the truth of the charges made against me by the commissioners, I would chearfully submit to his decision. I am the more sanguine in the hope of this indulgence, from having seen a letter from the commissioners to a gentleman in this place[1] dated the 14th. saying. "Having taken our resolution with respect to Major Ellicott, and on a very different state of facts than he has communicated to you, we have laid them before the President, and with candour, and an effectual decision on our conduct, can come only from him." This is the very decision I wish for. I am Sir with much regard and esteem Your Hbe. Serv.   ANDW. ELLICOTT

RC (DLC); at foot of text: "Honble. Thos. Jefferson Esqr."; endorsed by TJ as received 28 Mch. 1793 and so recorded in SJL.

The LETTER FROM THE COMMISSIONERS of the Federal District of 14 Mch. 1793 was addressed to Uriah Forrest (DNA: RG 42, DCLB).

[1] Preceding six words interlined.

To Henry Knox

DEAR SIR   Philadelphia Mar. 26. 1793.
    The President having desired a meeting at the War-office yesterday,
as you were apprised by his letter of the 21st. the Secy. of the Treasury,
Attorney general and myself met, but knowing you were too unwell
to attend, we agreed not to enter on the business submitted, till you
should be well enough to assist us. I will beg the favor of you therefore
whenever you shall be well enough, to be so good as to fix the time of
meeting and give us notice. That it may be soon is the sincere prayer
of Dear Sir your very humble servt   TH: JEFFERSON

PrC (DLC); at foot of text: "Genl. Knox." Tr (DLC); 19th-century copy.

From Henry Knox

March 26th: 93.
General Knox has received Mr: Jefferson's kind note of this day, and
hopes to be well enough, in a very few days, to attend to the business
alluded to; when he will inform Mr: J thereof. At present, HK's
indisposition prevents his attending to any serious business.

RC (DLC); in a clerk's hand; endorsed
by TJ as received 26 Mch. 1793.

    A letter from Knox to TJ of 1 Apr.
1793, recorded in SJL as received the
same day, has not been found, but it probably announced his ability to join with the
rest of the Cabinet on 2 Apr. to consider
the instructions for the commissioners to
the forthcoming conference with the Western Indians (see note to George Washington to the Cabinet, 21 Mch. 1793).

From Gouverneur Morris

DEAR SIR   Paris 26 March 1793
    The last Letter which I had the Honor to write was of the thirteenth
Instant, of which I enclose a Copy, as well as of No. 21. 22. and 23 of
the seventh eighth and ninth Instant. I also enclose a Copy of the Letter
from Dumouriez to the Convention, of the twelfth Instant, which not
having been publickly read he has caus'd to be printed in Flanders,
and the enclos'd is from Brussels. This Letter, and the Proclamations
which accompanied it, form a singular Contrast with the Conduct
pursued by that General on entering Victoriously into the Country,
which I had the Honor to communicate in mine No. 14 of the twenty

first of December. It accords but badly also with a later Transaction. He had opened a large Loan, on his private Credit and Account, at Antwerp; but the Capitalists having no great Confidence in him, it went on slowly, and to stimulate their Zeal he threatned them with some thing very like military Execution. Having mention'd here my Letter of the twenty first of December, I cannot avoid observing to you that the Correspondence between Pache and Dumouriez as publish'd by the latter, shews that the orders given by Pache to reinforce Custine were far more extraordinary than I had conceiv'd; seeing that he was directed to March in midWinter across the Pathless Mountains of the Ardennes, in which he could have found neither Food Forage nor Shelter from the Storm. Similar orders to Beurnonville had push'd him (as I therein inform'd you) on the Road to Treves. No good Opportunity offering, I did not then communicate the Result of that Expedition; which by the bye was never made public here, but the Fact is that he lost one Half his Army, and those which return'd were as fit for the Hospital as for the Field almost, so that the Austrian General Beaulieu push'd his advanc'd Posts forward with Impunity to the french Frontier. There are in the enclosd Letter of Dumouriez three Things worthy of Notice 1st. the great Diminution of the french Armies in that Quarter, 21y. The violence used to obtain an Appearance of Union with France, and thirdly the Temper and Disposition of the Flemish Nation. On the first of these Points I refer (for the Force which he commanded in Entering the low Countries) to the abovementiond Correspondence with Pache, mutilated as it is; and from which you will find that the Accounts I had given you of his Numbers were exact. Between one hundred and one hundred and ten thousand french men broke into the low Countries last Autumn, and yet what I told you on the first Day of the present year, viz. that the Effectives under Miranda and Valence when united did not exceed 35000 is strictly true. But there were sundry Posts and Garrisons spread thro the Country and all along to the Sea Coast, making up about ten thousand More. And it is true that many have come out of the Hospitals, and many Recruits have been sent on; but some have gone into the Hospitals, and straggling Parties have constantly returnd, so that 45000 Men was about the existent Force previous to the Efforts for the Expedition to Holland; about all which I shall say more presently, and only observe here that he states the Army as being reducd by Sickness Skirmishes and Desertion to less than one Half of their Force. Such says he was our Situation, when on the first of February you declar'd War against England and Holland. The 2d. Point viz. the Manner of obtaining the *free* Vote of the Belgic People for an Union with France, I had mention'd to you in mine of the 7th. Instant No. 21, upon very full Information from various Quarters of that Country. The Account which Dumouriez gives is a curious Piece for History. The Conduct which may naturally be expected from Men so abus'd I had mentiond to you on the twenty fifth of January, and assign'd on the thirteenth of February the Reason why they had not already aveng'd the Injuries they had receivd. But no sooner did the Movements towards Holland lessen the Garrisons distributed among them, than the smotherd Flame began to break out, and the french have already paid pretty severely for a Conduct, of which the Instances in modern Times are rare.

In my last I mentioned to you that a Battle appeard probable, and that it would decide the Fate of the low Countries. This battle took Place definitively on the eighteenth, having been preceeded by some warm Skirmishes on the preceeding Days. As I mentiond on the 9th., the whole Force of the French as not being more than from 50 to 60000 Men, it may be not amiss to give here some general State of the Force now at the Disposition of the Republic. Speaking in round Numbers, the Force requird was about 500000; to compleat which, an Apportionment was made on the first Instant of near 300000 (viz. 296.553) on the Different Departments, exclusively of the Army of Reserve which we may suppose to consist of the Paper-Surplus beyond 500000, whatever that may be. Thus it would seem that the existent Force on the first Instant (as borne on the Returns) was about 200000. Note here that this Force is divided and to be divided, into eight different Armies: viz. That of the North commanded by Dumouriez, the Ardennes by Valence, the Mozelle by Beurnonville, the Rhine by Custine, the Alps by Kellerman, Italy by Biron, the Pyrenees by Servan, and the Sea Coast by Labourdonnay. Deducting from the supposd existing Force, for Garrisons, Sick, Posts and Communications, and the numberless Contingencies of Service, eighty to ninety thousand we have remaining a Total of 110000 to 120000 in the different Armies under Arms. So much for a general View, To give a more particular one coincident therewith: The Army of Dumouriez may be stated at 90000, that of Custine at 54000, that of Biron at 18000, Those of Valence and Beurnonville each 7000, those of Kellerman Servan and Labourdonnay each 9000, together 203000. But of these there are only the three first worth noting here, as the others are all in different Posts and Garrisons. And, by the Way, that we may finish at once with Biron's Army (intended to be about 50000 Strong but avowedly defective the first Instant about 32000) As it has been in a Kind of small Action for the last three Months and must keep up sundry

Posts in the Country of Nice, and on the Communications, the Total operative Force cannot exceed 12000 Men. We shall come to Custine by and bye, but at present we will return to the northern Army. As this was to be exposd to the greatest Efforts of the Enemy, and as the Government counted on success in that Quarter for the Means to dictate its own Terms of Peace, the Force of it was to be 140000; but the avowd Deficiency being 50000, leaves the above Number of 90000. Deducting therefrom twenty five thousand for the several Garrisons (of which there are at least a dozen) and for the sick, we have a Remainder of 65000, of which 15000 were under Dumouriez in Holland. The Armies then of Miranda and Valence did not exceed 50000 and the Enemy give an Account of above ten thousand of these in the Affairs of the 28 Feby. to the 4th. of March, besides what may have gone off in different Directions. The Army therefore which Dumouriez commanded at Louvain (on the fifteenth Instant) could not exceed 40000. His Loss, between that and the nineteenth, was at least 20000. He cannot therefore on the twentieth have had more than 20000 left. Probably about 15000. From the Dutch Expedition, if ever they get back, not more than 10000 can ever join him, because the Losses in that Quarter also have been considerable. When the Want of Discipline, and the Desertion are considered, you will see that there remains but a very trifling Force to be scatterd thro the Frontier Towns in Addition to the very weak Garrisons above mention'd. If this Army be cut off it seems to me that the Towns cannot be all defended, and if ever it should return a very very strict defensive is the utmost which can be expected.

It is proper, in this Place, to say Somewhat about the Plans and Movements of the Enemy. From the best Information I have been able to procure, it seems that the Allies intended to open the Campaign in the first Fortnight of April, at which Period the different Armies were to be compleat. The Austrians under the Prince de Cobourg, including those on the Moselle under the Prince de Hohenloe, were to be near 90000 strong, the british and Hanoverians were to be 20000, the prussians (with some Troops of the Empire) about 20 to 30.000. The Dutch contingent depended on Circumstances. The scattering Bodies of Emigrants also formd an eventual Force. The whole might perhaps be carried to 150000, from which it might be well to deduct one third for Posts, Garrisons, Contingencies, Maladies, and Deficiencies. On the first of April therefore the Prince de Cobourg would have been at the Head of at least one hundred thousand Men, altho not all united. He was oblig'd to commence his Operations a Month or six Weeks sooner than had been agreed on, because the Prince of

Hesse (commanding in Maestrecht) inform'd him that he could not answer much longer for the Defence of that Place, a great Part of his Garrison being illy disposed, and the Citizens unwilling to resist while their Houses were crumbling about their Ears. I have Reason to beleive that the Information I recievd of an Offer to surrender was unfounded. In this State of Things a Council of War was held, and it was resolv'd to undertake, at all Hazards, the raising of the Siege. This was done by the Prince de Cobourg at the Head of about 25000 Men. The Prussians (under Prince Ferdinand of Brunswic) came up the Meuse on the Side of Cleves and Wezel, with a Body of ten to fifteen thousand, and drove the french from Ruremonde. The French lost in these Affairs not less than twelve thousand Men killd Wounded and taken, besides the Dispersion of their Troops in different Directions. The Stores taken at Liege were immense. Of Artillery alone, above one hundred pieces of different Caliber as is said. The Austrians suffered very little, since it was rather a Route than a Battle. The Prussians lost some Men. These last marched (soon after) to Bois Le Duc, to affect a Junction with the british Troops. The Austrians prepar'd for Action again as soon as they were recover'd from their Fatigue, and had made the needful Dispositions. To this Effect, Orders seem to have been given to General Beaulieu to advance towards the Meuse from Luxemburgh, and to the Prince de Hohenloe to replace the Force of Beaulieu: but this Line being long and parallel to the french Frontier, the Movements must be made with Caution; and the more so as a Month was to elapse before the Corps of Beaulieu and Hohenloe were to be compleated. The Prince de Cobourg seems to have sent off however a Column of between eight and ten thousand Men on the Side of Namur, for the Purpose of dislodging the French, opening the whole Course of the Meuse up to the french frontier, forming a Junction with the Army of Beaulieu, and eventually cutting off the Retreat of the french Army by possessing a Post in their Rear between Mons and Brussels, should they retire towards Valenciennes. Such was the State of Things when Dumouriez join'd the Army which had fallen back to Louvain. He sent off, I presume, his Orders immediately to evacuate Holland, so as to form a Junction with those Troops and make good his Retreat; but shortly after, finding that the Column of Austrians just mention'd was advancing rapidly on his right, Sensible that his Enemy would (if suffered quietly to collect his Force) be soon superior in Number, and that his whole Army must (in Consequence) be cut off; he determin'd as a last Ressource to fight them, because a Victory would give him Time to receive Reinforcements, and secure the doubtful Junction with the Army in Holland. The

Army of the Prince de Cobourg must, at this Time, have been inferior to Dumouriez, because even supposing that he had collected from
the Rhine Men sufficient to occupy the Posts in his Rear and to carry
his Army to a compleat of near 30000, Yet the Detachment on his
left had reduc'd it to 20000. He had push'd forward his advanc'd
Posts to Tirlemont, but the Army of Dumouriez drove them back,
and this latter General marchd forward by his Right so as to cut
off the Communication between the main Body of the Austrians and
the Corps which had been detach'd on their left. If, under these Circumstances, he had gain'd a Victory it would have been decisive.
It was on the same Field that the Marechal de Luxembourg beat
King William the 29 July 1693, and nearly in the same respective
Positions. The Event however was revers'd. The Action was very
warm, and altho Dumouriez writes to one of his Officers that the
Retreat was a knowing or skilful one (savante) he appears to have
been more indebted to the Night than to his Generalship, or to the
Manœuvres of his Troops: for his left Wing was cutt to Pieces and
his right very severely handled. The great Superiority of the Enemy's Cavalry would, in these Circumstances, have wholly destroy'd his
Army had the Day light continued. Altho we have no Account of the
Enemy's Loss, we may well suppose it to have been considerable, and
of Course much was to be done before they could attack the french
who had taken a strong Post near Louvain; and the more so as by
persisting in his Movement to the left the Prince de Cobourg might
hope to prevent Dumouriez from getting back to the Frontier Towns,
and in the mean Time his Reinforcements were coming on. It was
under these Circumstances that Dumouriez prepar'd for his Retreat.
To that Effect after having collected his scatterd Forces at Cumptich he
retird to Louvain and sent off his Stores and Artillery from Brussels.
The Sick were taken away (as I am told) by Water on the twenty
second, when the Commissioners from the national Assembly also
left Brussels, and then some Parties of the Austrians had, it is said,
appeard in the Neighbourhood. It would seem then that the Plan of
Dumouriez, who is said to be on his Retreat towards Mons, is to go
to Tournai in order to form there a Junction with the Troops from
Holland to whose Protection it would seem that he has committed
his sick and Wounded, who may be forwarded to Ghent, and thence
by the Canals along thro west Flanders to the french Territory. In
this Way he will cover the Retreat of the Troops from Holland by the
Scheldt, and the Reinforcements intended for his Army will be thrown
into Valenciennes, and he himself will take Post eventually near Lisle.
This Plan supposes the Evacuation of all Flanders, which indeed seems

to be indispensible for in three Weeks from the present Time the Enemy will be in compleat Force. He may as it were immediately collect 50000 Men by bringing up the Prussian and british Troops, and these again may be follow'd by the Dutch and Hannoverians. Now on the Supposition that Dumouriez should extricate himself in the Course of ten Days, he would not on the Whole Frontier from Valenciennes to Dunkirk, have more than 50000 Men: and that in the Supposition that the Recruits should have joind to the Number of ten thousand so as to replace Deserters and supply the Deficiencies of Sick and unfit for Duty, which bear daily a greater Proportion to the whole Number as Losses in Action and by desertion encrease.

I expect that in a very few Days the Campaign will open on the Side of the Rhine, and this Circumstance will leave the Prince de Hohenloe more Master of his Motions, seeing that a Column of Troops under the Orders of the Duke of Brunswic will be of Course sent to occupy the Passes along the Rhine above Coblentz; and as the two Armies of the Ardennes and the Mozelle (which on the first of the Month did not exceed sixteen to twenty thousand Men) cannot be encreasd in any reasonable Time, beyond what may be necessary for the Garrisons on that Frontier, and to prevent the Enemy from entering by the Meuse, the left of the Prince de Cobourgs Army may bend all its Efforts that Way, and I daily expect to hear of a Stroke in that Quarter. What may be the Fate of Custine I know not. He has taken great Pains to fortify himself, and to defend the Banks of the Rhine from Switzerland to below Mayence; but these very Precautions would seem to render the Passage certain, because it is next to impossible that a Line so long should be defended, thro all its Extent. The King of Prussia seems determin'd to take Mayence let it cost what it may. The Inhabitants are universally in his Favor, and should Custine (who is a brave but a blundering Soldier) be taken with his Army, the whole Province of Alsace is lost. It may indeed fall in a different Way, for I am well convinc'd that the imperial Troops will make a serious Effort in the upper End of it; and here the Conduct of Switzerland becomes important. People differ much on that Subject, but I beleive that England will have a very large Body of Swiss in her Pay, to act in Conjunction with the Austrian Troops, and that having penetrated to Befort, which is but about thirty miles from Basle, the ulterior Movements will depend on the existent State of Things between the Armies at Mayence. In one Contingency an Effort may be made to penetrate to Besancon, distant about fifty miles, and thence to Lyons, which is distant from Besancon along the Rivers Doux and Saone by Dole and Chalons about one hundred and fifty Miles, but by the common Road seventy. I need not say that the Possession of Lyons would oblige both Kellerman and Biron to retreat, and open the whole of that Country to the Troops of Savoy, whatever might have been the previous Situation of those Armies: for you know that on that Quarter the Difficulty of Subsisting *in* the Country, is much greater than that of Keeping the Enemy *out* of it.

I had mention'd to you (in mine No. 21 of the seventh Instant) my Idea as to the Recruiting, if forc'd forward immediately. It has been tolerably successful. In some Places very much so. In others it has met with serious Opposition. Upper Britanny is in Revolt, and both Nantz and Rennes are menaced, while a Descent is apprehended at St. Malo. Does the Insurrection proceed from a Plan laid by the Enemy, or from Impulses of the Moment? Both may have concurr'd, but I think that (like the Campaign) it has happen'd sooner than was expected. It is however very serious and should they take St. Malos and receive a Supply of Arms Ammunition and Provisions, with a few Troops and a little Money from England, it is not possible to calculate the Extent of the Mischeif; for Normandy is I am perswaded ready to revolt as soon as a fair Opportunity offers, and it is in that Quarter that I did suppose a Descent would be made, and I am still of that Opinion, and that the Movements mention'd in mine of the thirteenth of last Month will take Place. In the Midst of these Troubles, with an Expence which last Month exceeded the Receipts near two hundred Millions of Livres (worth at present Prices at least four Millions Sterling) the Insurrection which I formerly mentiond, as likely to take Place against the Brissotines, is still in Agitation and will in a few Days most probably take Effect.

I enclose, herewith, a Copy of my Letter of the 24th. Instant to Monsieur Le brun, respecting Captures of American Vessels, which will sufficiently explain itself. I ought also to mention to you, which I omitted in its due Season, that Monsieur Génést before he went hence calld to take Leave, and apologiz'd for Mr. Lebrun on Account of his constant Business, for not calling on me to present Mr. Genest &ca. &ca. The Truth is that I attach very little Importance to these Matters, whether of Compliment or Inattention, and I beleive that I estimate them at their true Value. With sincere Esteem & Respect I am my dear Sir your obedient Servant   GOUV MORRIS

RC (DNA: RG 59, DD); at head of text: "No. 25"; at foot of first page: "Thomas Jefferson Esqr. Secretary of State"; endorsed by TJ as received 21 June 1793 and so recorded in SJL. FC (Lb in DLC: Gouverneur Morris Papers); with corrections in Morris's hand. Tr (DNA: RG 46, Senate Records, 3d Cong., 1st sess.). PrC (DNA: RG 59, MD). Tr (Lb in same, DD). Enclosures: (1) Morris to TJ, 7, 8, 9, 13 Mch. 1793. (2) Morris to Lebrun, 24 Mch.

1793, complaining of the violent seizure of the ship *Aurora* of Baltimore by the privateer *Patriote* of Marseilles, of the brig *Bacchus* of Baltimore by a privateer from Cette, and of the ship *Lawrence* of Charleston by the privateer *Sans Culotte* of Honfleur, and requesting that orders be given to prevent the recurrence of such acts, which violate the law of nations as well as Article 15 of the 1778 treaty of amity and commerce between France and the United States (Tr in same, DD, in French, endorsed by TJ as "enclosed in No. 25"; Trs in DNA: RG 46, Senate Records, 3d Cong., 1st sess., in French and English; PrCs in DNA: RG 59, MD; Trs in Lb in same, DD, in French and English). (3) Charles François Dumouriez, *Lettre du Général Dumouriez, général en chef de l'Armée du Nord, á la*

Convention nationale, Louvain ce 12 Mars 1793 . . . [Brussels, 1793].

THE CORRESPONDENCE BETWEEN PACHE AND DUMOURIEZ was *Correspondance du Général Dumourier avec Pache, Ministre de la Guerre, Pendant la Campagne de la Belgique, en 1792* (Paris, 1793). The BATTLE of Neerwinden TOOK PLACE DEFINITIVELY on 18 Mch. 1793 ON THE SAME FIELD where WILLIAM III was defeated on 29 July 1693. The REVOLT which broke out in Brittany during 10-16 Mch. 1793 marked the beginning of the protracted Vendée insurrection (Scott and Rothaus, *Historical Dictionary*, II, 1000-3, 1039).

TJ submitted this letter to the President on 21 June 1793 (Washington, *Journal*, 185-6).

Edmund Randolph's Notes on Jefferson's Letter to Alexander Hamilton

[ca. 26 Mch. 1793]

Would it be amiss to anticipate a suspicion, that the paper, mentioned in the 6th. line, was prepared and[1] reserved for a fit opportunity of disgust? Suppose it to be designated, as an official paper?

That the two loans were not consolidated by your opinion does not sufficiently appear. I understand the fact to be, that this was fixed, without calling in your judgment.

If the two loans had not been consolidated, would or would not the application of the *third* million of florins to the purchase of *foreign paper* in Amsterdam been a diversion from the the appropriation? If so, does not this circumstance render necessary some fuller[2] exposition of motives as to that *third* million, so as to get clear of the animadversion? It may be asked, why did you not suggest any impropriety, which occurred to you, in applying money borrowed under the act of the 12th. of August to the purchase of foreign paper in *Amsterdam*?

MS (DLC: TJ Papers, 83: 14410); undated and unsigned; entirely in Randolph's hand; endorsed by TJ as received 26 Mch. 1793.

In these notes Randolph commented on the unrevised Dft of TJ to Alexander Hamilton, 27 Mch. 1793. TJ relied heavily on Randolph's notes in putting his letter to Hamilton into its final form.

[1] Preceding two words interlined.
[2] Word interlined.

To George Washington

Mar. 26. 93.

Th: Jefferson with his respects to the President, incloses a description of a new plan of a Capitol in which Mr. Hallet is engaged, who has expressed very earnest wishes that the ultimate decision may not be pronounced till he can bring it forward.

RC (DNA: RG 59, MLR); addressed: "The President of the US."; endorsed by Washington. Tr (Lb in same, SDC). Not recorded in SJL. For the enclosure, see Stephen Hallet to TJ, 15 Mch. 1793.

From Giuseppe Ceracchi

SIR   Mûnich the 27 Marzy 1793

As sun my arrival to Urope I didn't fall to give my self the plaesure of addressing you tow letters dated from Amsterdam the 16. july last, I am affraid Sir that your ansered is not come to me because I didn't point out a place for my direction, but if you please to give me this honour you might send it to Amsterdam at Mr. Stapolster, Goll, or Alstorphius this three Gentilmens been equaly my friends they will let me have it. In few weeks I shall set of to Legorne for a commission of this Elector Palatine which loves the Arts, I shall find in this sea port, at the banker Mr. Combiagio my boxes that contaned the models I did in America. I shall have then the plaesure to cut your bust in marbre, and present it to you as a patern of my cisel and a little mark of my estime.

I scould be glad to Know somthink about the new Election, and if Congress as rememberd my projet of the national Monument; I remenber Sir that before my departure from Philadelphia jou was pleased to tel me that Congress in the session of this eayr would have certenly decreed the exccuetion of the President equestrian figure in bronse and honoured me with that commission in Urope; I dont doubt

[459]

this resolution is passed, your influence, upon this subjet, as a Man of tast in the fines Artes could not have falled.

The Article of *Liberty* as produced graet combustion in Urope, I dont doubt that this *Divinity* will trionfe at Last, while the oppinions upon the wrights of Man pleases every body. I beg to [presente][1] my respects to the President and Mr. Maddison. I am Sir Your Most Obbidient and most Humb Servent   JOSEPH CERACCHI

RC (DLC); endorsed by TJ as received 30 July 1793 and so recorded in SJL. Dupl (DLC); contains minor variations in spelling and phraseology; endorsed by TJ as received 2 Oct. 1793 but mistakenly annotated by him as a letter of 17 May 1793.

[1] Word supplied from Dupl.

To Alexander Hamilton

SIR   Philadelphia Mar. 27. 1793.[1]

In compliance with the desire you expressed, I shall endeavor to give you the view I had of the destination of the loan of three millions of florins obtained by our bankers in Amsterdam previous to the acts of the 4th. and 12th. of Aug. 1790. when it was proposed to adopt it under those acts. I am encouraged to do this by the degree of certainty with which I can[2] do it, happening to possess an official paper[3] whereon I had committed to writing some thoughts on the subject, at the time, that is to say, on the 26th. of Aug. 1790.[4]

The general[5] plan presented to view, according to my comprehension of it, in your Report and Draught of instructions, was 1. to borrow, on proper terms, such a sum of money as might answer all demands for principal and interest of the foreign debt due to the end of 1791. 2. to consider *two* of the three millions of florins already borrowed, as if borrowed under the act of Aug. 4. and[6] so far an execution of the operation beforementioned.[7] 3. to consider the *third* million of florins so borrowed, as if borrowed under the act of the 12th. of Aug. and[8] so far an execution of the powers given to the President to borrow two millions of Dollars for the purchase of the public debt. I remember that the[9] million of Dollars surplus of[10] the Domestic revenues, appropriated to the purchase of the public debt,[11] appeared to me[12] sufficient for that purpose *here*,[13] for probably a considerable time. I thought therefore,[14] if any part of the three millions of florins were to be placed under[15] the act of the 12th. of Aug. that it should rather[16] be employed in purchasing[17] our *foreign paper* at the market of Amsterdam. I had my self observed[18] the different degrees of estima-

[460]

tion in which the paper of different countries was held at that market, and wishing that our credit there might always be of the first order, I thought a moderate sum kept in readiness there to buy up any of our *foreign paper*, whenever it should be offered below par, would keep it constantly to that mark, and thereby establish for us a sound credit, where, of all places in the world, it would be most important to have it.

The subject however not being within my department, and therefore[19] having no occasion afterwards to pay attention to it,[20] it went out of my mind altogether, till the late enquiries brought it forward again. On reading the President's instructions of Aug. 28. 1790. (two days later than the paper beforementioned) as printed in your Report of Feb. 13. 1793. in the form in which they were ultimately given to you, I observed that he had therein neither confirmed *your* sentiment of employing a part of the money *here*, nor *mine* of doing it *there*, in purchases of the public debt;[21] but had directed the application of the whole to the *foreign debt*: and I inferred that he had done this[22] on full and just[23] deliberation, well knowing he would have time enough to weigh the merits of the two opinions, before the million of dollars would be exhausted *here*,[24] or the loans for the foreign debt would[25] overrun their legal measure *there*.[26] In this inference however[27] I might be mistaken; but[28] I cannot be[29] in the fact that these instructions gave a sanction to neither opinion.

I have thus, Sir, stated[30] to you the view I had of this subject in 1790. and I have done it because you desired it. I did not take it up then as a Volunteer, nor should now have taken the trouble of recurring to it, but at your request, as it is one in which I am not particularly concerned, which I never had either the time or inclination to investigate, and on which my opinion is of no importance. I have the honor to be with respect, Sir, Your most obedt humble servt

TH: JEFFERSON

RC (DLC: Hamilton Papers); addressed: "The Secretary of the Treasury"; several words torn away supplied from PrC; endorsed by Hamilton. PrC (DLC). Dft (DLC: James Madison Papers); originally dated "Mar.   1793" (see note 1 below); lacks final page with signature sent to Edmund Randolph; contains numerous revisions, based in part on Randolph's comments of 26 Mch. 1793, as noted below; enclosed in TJ to Madison, 31 Mch. 1793. PrC (DLC); signed; lacks all revisions except those recorded in notes 1, 11 and 21 below; at head of text by

TJ in ink: "not sent." Tr of PrC of Dft (DLC); 19th-century copy.

Carefully amended in light of Edmund Randolph's suggestions (see Randolph's Notes on Jefferson's Letter to Alexander Hamilton, [ca. 26 Mch. 1793]), this letter was TJ's response to what amounted to an effort by the Secretary of the Treasury to undermine one of the most serious accusations against him in the resolutions of censure offered to the House of Representatives exactly a month before by William B. Giles—that Hamilton had exceeded his authority from the President by applying to the domestic as well as to the foreign debt a loan of 3,000,000 florins for partial payment of the American debt to France provisionally arranged in January 1790 by Willink, Van Staphorst & Hubbard, OUR BANKERS IN AMSTERDAM. For a discussion of Hamilton's retrospective approval of this loan under the authority of the ACTS OF THE 4TH. AND THE 12TH. OF AUG. 1790, which authorized the President respectively to borrow up to $12,000,000 for the payment of the foreign debt and $2,000,000 for the redemption of the domestic debt, and TJ's sanction of Hamilton's action at the time, see note to Notes on Alexander Hamilton's Report on Foreign Loans, [ca. 20 Feb. 1793]; see also Editorial Note on Jefferson and the Giles resolutions, at 27 Feb. 1793.

Although the House overwhelmingly defeated the Giles resolutions, Jefferson and other Republicans refused to allow the issue of Hamilton's alleged misuse of the 1790 loan to die. Writing as "Franklin," the Virginia Republican leader John Taylor of Caroline raised it in an essay published in the *National Gazette* early in March 1793, as did John Beckley five weeks later in an anonymous pamphlet charging that Hamilton's administration of the Treasury Department was rife with corruption ("Franklin," *National Gazette*, 2 Mch. 1793; TJ to Jean Baptiste Ternant, 25 Feb. 1793, and note; Beckley's pamphlet is discussed in note to Notes on Stockholders in Congress, 23 Mch. 1793).

In the meantime Hamilton became convinced that TJ planned to raise the issue at a special meeting of the Commissioners of the Sinking Fund, the body responsible for supervising the redemption of the domestic debt. To counter this move, as well as to prepare himself for an anticipated resumption of the Republican assault on his management of public finances during the next congressional session, Hamilton apparently took advantage of their joint attendance at what proved to be an abortive Cabinet meeting on 25 Mch. 1793 to press the Secretary of State for a statement of his original understanding of the intended use of the 1790 loan.

Hamilton justified this request by informing TJ that he wished to use this statement to satisfy "some friends" about the disposition of the loan and to assist his plan "to revive this subject"—a veiled reference to his intention of calling himself for another congressional investigation of his administration of the Treasury in order to rebut once and for all Republican allegations of official misconduct, a strategy he actually followed soon after the Third Congress convened in December 1793 (Editorial Note on Jefferson and the Giles resolutions, at 27 Feb. 1793; TJ to James Madison, 31 Mch. 1793; see also Hamilton to TJ, 24 Mch. 1793, and note). Hamilton's approach to TJ suggests that he either knew or suspected that the Secretary of State had originally approved his proposal to apply the 1790 loan to the foreign and domestic debts and that he hoped by this stratagem to elicit an admission that would serve to undermine Republican attacks on him. In any event, TJ parried Hamilton's maneuver by distinguishing between his original approval of the Treasury Secretary's proposed application of the 1790 loan and his subsequent conviction that the President's instructions had confined the use of the loan to the foreign debt. As a result, there is no evidence that Hamilton sought to make use of TJ's letter in the continuing polemics over his handling of this loan.

[1] TJ originally dated the Dft "Mar. 1793." After Randolph returned the Dft with his comments, TJ filled in the blank with "27" and inserted the same date in ink on the Pr C of Dft.

[2] Word interlined in Dft in place of "am enabled to."

[3] In Dft TJ first wrote "a paper" and then altered the phrase to read as above.

[4] In Dft TJ originally did not begin a new paragraph at this point, but during revision he inserted a paragraph symbol.

[5] Word interlined in Dft.

[6] Dft: "if . . . and" interlined.

[7] In Dft TJ first wrote "this operation under the act of Aug. 4." and then altered the phrase to read as above.

[8] Dft: "if . . . and" interlined.

[9] Preceding eleven words interlined in Dft in place of "under the act of the 12

of August. This I thought expedient *if* this third million of florins were to be employed in buying up our *foreign paper* on the exchange of Amsterdam. The surplus of a."

10 Preceding two words interlined in Dft in place of "from."

11 In Dft TJ first wrote "to purchases of that debt" before reworking the phrase to read "to purchases of the public debt." After Randolph returned the Dft, TJ altered the wording of the passage to read as above.

12 Preceding three words interlined in Dft in place of "being."

13 Word not underscored in Dft.

14 "I thought it better" in Dft before TJ altered the passage to read as above.

15 Preceding two words interlined in Dft in place of "allotted to."

16 Word interlined in Dft.

17 Preceding two words interlined in Dft in place of either "on" or "in."

18 Preceding four words interlined in Dft in place of "I was disposed to think this from having seen."

19 Paragraph to this point interlined in Dft.

20 Word interlined in Dft in place of "this subject as being out of my department."

21 Preceding six words interlined in Dft and Pr C of Dft.

22 Here in Dft TJ canceled "of design, and."

23 Preceding two words interlined in Dft.

24 Word not underscored in Dft.

25 Word interlined in Dft.

26 Word not underscored in Dft, where TJ canceled "But," the first word in the next sentence.

27 Word interlined in Dft.

28 Word interlined in Dft.

29 Here in Dft TJ canceled "however."

30 In Dft remainder of letter is added to foot and right margin of verso. Pr C of Dft contains final page with remainder of TJ's original ending: "to you my view of the destination of these monies in 1790. and have the honour to be with sentiments of due respect, Sir, Your most humble servt. Th: Jefferson."

From James Monroe

DEAR SIR   Fredericksburg March 27. 93.

We arrived here on the 25. and set out to morrow for Albemarle. We have had a more comfortable trip than could well have been expected.

Mr. Madison informed you from Alexa. of the fate of several elections since which we have heard that Mr. New of Caroline was preferred to Corbin of Middlesex. Heth for the Northumberland district. Walker for Albemarle (this latter only a report). If we should hear of any others you will be informed by Mr. M. before we set out. Mr. M. without opposition for orange.

In every respect, so far as we have heard, we find the publick mind perfectly sound in regard to those objects of national policy, at present most interesting. Every member is either as he should be, or has gained his place by fraud and imposition.

We find likewise the sentiment universal in favor of your continuance thro' the present crisis, and of course that a contrary conduct would have proved a publick as well as a very serious private detriment to your self. Be so kind as send the enclosed to Mr. Beckly and believe me affectionately yr. friend servant   JAS. MONROE

RC (DLC); endorsed by TJ as received 2 Apr. 1793 and so recorded in SJL. Enclosure not found.

From John M. Pintard

Madeira, 27 Mch. 1793. The foregoing is a copy of his letter of 21 Mch. The French consul here has since asked him to help the French prisoners brought in by the British privateer mentioned therein. Lest the captains of the two American ships in port be blamed, he encloses copies of the letters exchanged in this matter, since which he has spoken with Samuel L. Parker of Boston, charterer of the brig *Jerusha* of Boston, who still refuses to grant any of the prisoners passage. However, John Light Banjer, a British merchant here, persuaded Richard Brush & Company to let the French captain and his servant go in the brig *Polly and Sally*, Captain Elisha Ritch, and they sailed today for Charleston.

RC (DNA: RG 59, CD); 2 p.; subjoined to Pintard to TJ, 21 Mch. 1793; endorsed by TJ as received 13 May 1793 and so recorded in SJL. Dupl (same, MDC); in a clerk's hand, signed by Pintard. Enclosures: (1) M. de La Tuellier, the French consul at Madeira, to Pintard, 26 Mch. 1793, invoking the alliance and friendship between France and the United States to request that eleven French prisoners with no other way of leaving the island be taken to the United States by the two American vessels in port, six on the ship bound for Boston and five on that headed to Charleston, the prisoners to carry their own provisions and pay suitable passage. (2) Pintard to La Tuellier, 26 Mch. 1793, stating that he has written to Captains Gamaliel Bradford of the brigantine *Jerusha* and Elisha Rich of the brigantine *Sally and Polly* and that he is fairly confident of success. (3) Pintard to Bradford and Rich, 26 Mch. 1793, requesting them to transport the prisoners on the terms outlined by La Tuellier and stating that he would provide free passage were the vessel his own. (4) Bradford to Pintard, 26 Mch. 1793, asserting that he would gladly comply with his humane request, but that the man who has chartered his ship has refused to consent. (5) Rich to Pintard, 26 Mch. 1793, stating that he would willingly provide transport to help our French allies if Pintard could secure the consent of Brush, who chartered the vessel, without which he would be liable for any ensuing difficulties. (6) Pintard to Bradford, 26 Mch. 1793, urging him to seek the consent of Parker, the charterer, to transport the captain of the French vessel and his servant. (7) Bradford to Pintard, 26 Mch. 1793, reporting that Parker has agreed to discuss the matter with Pintard. (8) Pintard to Rich, 26 Mch. 1793, challenging the right of Brush, a British merchant on this island, to prevent him from taking on his ship whomsoever he pleased, deploring the refusal of a request by a nation which "so nobly assisted in obtaining our Liberty" to pay the prisoners' passage to the United States "in an American Vessell duly Registerd and wholly Owned by Citizens of the United States," and asking him to reconsider taking up to three of the prisoners, who would carry explanatory certificates from the English, French, and American consuls (Trs in DNA: RG 59, CD; Trs in same, MDC).

TJ submitted this letter and its enclosures to the President on 13 May 1793 and received them back the same day (Washington, *Journal*, 136-7).

From Peter Carr

MY DEAR SIR   Monticello. March. 28. 1793.
I wrote you some time in December last, from Richmond, but am informed by Mrs. Randolph that the letter has not been received. I am sorry for this on one account principally. I wished to have your approbation to a measure, which I had in contemplation respecting some negroes, formerly claimed as my property under my Grandfather's will. Your opinion with respect to the *right* I knowe—tis only with regard to the propriety and expediency of my bringing it forward again that I would ask your opinion. Though I can conceive nothing improper in an attempt to regain this property yet perhaps in my own case I am not the proper judge. Any hint from you therefore on the subject either way would determine me.

In expectation of seeing You here early this spring, I have hitherto said nothing of the business of the law. My intention is to commence the practice early this summer. I have yet however fixed on no place, and must remain undetermined untill I hear from you. My mother wrote to you some time ago and wishes to know if you have received her letter. With hearty wishes for your prosperity and happiness, believe me to be Dear Sir yr. affectionate friend and Servt.

                                                            P: CARR

RC (ViU: Carr-Cary Papers); endorsed by TJ as dated "[28]" Mch. and received 1 Apr. 1793 and so recorded in SJL.

The letter MY MOTHER WROTE TO YOU SOME TIME AGO was Martha Jefferson Carr to TJ, 15 Dec. 1792.

Notes on the Payment of the Public Debt

[ca. 28 Mch. 1793]

In how many years will a Debt bearing int. @ 6 pr. Ct. be extinguished by equal annual payments of 7. 8. 9. or 10. pr. ct. on acct of principal & interest?

Answer.

	pr ct		y m D
By annual payments of	7.	in	$33-4-22\frac{436}{693}$
	8.		$23-9-15\frac{57}{693}$
	9.		$18-10-7\frac{420}{693}$
	10.		$15-8-21\frac{259}{693}$

[465]

Example of the calculn, easily performed in 5 minutes.
Annual payment 8
Interest pr. ct.   6
Annual excess   2. principal for do. $33\frac{1}{3}$ Log. = 1.5228787
debt to be redeemed Add 100. makes $133\frac{1}{3}$ Log = 2.1249387
divide by Log. of ratio   y m d
   of int. 1.06 =   .0253059) diff. = .6020600 (23–9–1
                                              506118
                                              959420
                                              759177
                              $.21088\frac{1}{4}$) 200243
note the first divisor divided by   189794
12 gives $21088\frac{1}{4}$ the division   692.8) 10449
for months, which divided by $30\frac{7}{16}$ 6928
gives 692.8 divisor for days   3521
                                               3464
                                              57 remaind

If the question be reversed the solution is equally easy. viz.
What must the equal annual payments be to extinguish a debt in 20
years at 6. per cent?   Answer 8.71845 pr. cent on the debt.

See Bache's paper Mar. 2. 93. The rule thus expressed.
from the log. of 8. (the annual payment)
subtract the log. of 2. (the part of the principal paid the first year)
divide ye remr by the log. of 1.06 (the amount of 1. dollar in 1. year)
the quotient 23.79 or 24. years will be the time required.

see Bache's paper, Mar. 28. 93.

MS (DLC: TJ Papers, 96: 16484); undated; entirely in TJ's hand; endorsed by TJ: "Finance. public debt. 1793. an idea for paying off public debt"; printed literally.

Benjamin Franklin BACHE'S PAPER, *The General Advertiser*, began printing mathematical questions posed by correspondents on 19 Feb. 1793. Readers who answered correctly were invited to pose new questions in their turn. This initially innocent exercise assumed political overtones on 22 Feb. 1793 when, in the midst of the Republican attack in the House of Representatives on Alexander Hamilton's management of public finances, "E" answered the third question and asked: "In how many years would Congress pay off the whole of their 6 per cent national debt, supposing them to pay every year (as the funding act allows) 8 per cent on the original principal, both on account of principal and interest?"

On MAR. 2. 93. "Q" responded that "If the six per cent national debt be supposed to amount to 100 dollars (and whether more or less will not affect the present question) then the following rule is easily demonstrated, viz.

"From the logarithm of 8 (the annual payment) subtract the logarithm of 2 (the part of the principal paid the first year) and dividing the remainder by the logarithm 1.06 (the amount of 1 dollar in 1 year) the quotient, 23.79, or 24 years, will be the time required."

The potential of this method of calculation for providing a date certain on which the nation could aspire to be free of public debt—a Republican political imperative—must have appealed to TJ. With characteristic rigor he expanded on the response in the newspaper by posing the same question based on payments of varying size, extending the calculation to give the answer in months, days, and fractions of days, and successfully inverting the method so as to obtain the size of payment which would pay off a debt in a given number of years. For TJ's continuing interest in rapidly extinguishing the

national debt, see Editorial Note on proposals for funding the foreign debt, in Vol. 14: 190-7.

The article in *The General Advertiser* of MAR. 28. 93. which evidently caught TJ's eye was a response to another mathematical question with political overtones: "To find the value of a six per cent annuity, *with the interest paid quarterly*, calculating the market rate at 5, 6, and 7 per cent per annum." This question had been posed by "A.B." in the 21 Mch. 1793 issue of the paper.

From Benjamin Rush

DEAR SIR   28th march 1793.

The bearer Mr. Parry Hall wishes to reprint your notes on the state of Virginia. He is One of our most correct printers, and a worthy man. Should you incline to add any thing to the work, or to make any Alterations in it, he will gladly obey your instructions. From Dr Sir Yours sincerely   BENJN. RUSH

RC (DLC); endorsed by TJ as received 30 Mch. 1793 and so recorded in SJL.

Hall, a printer, bookseller, and stationer at 149 Chesnut Street, Philadelphia, did not publish an edition of TJ's NOTES ON THE STATE OF VIRGINIA, although he went so far as to print a proof sheet (James

Hardie, *The Philadelphia Directory and Register* [Philadelphia, 1793], 58; Hall to TJ, 25 July 1793). The next edition of this work was published in Philadelphia by Mathew Carey in 1794 (Coolie Verner, "Some Observations on the Philadelphia 1794 Edition of Jefferson's *Notes*," *Studies in Bibliography*, II [1949-50], 201-4).

From Rodolph Vall-Travers

"*Rotterdam, Haring's Vliet, in Lodgs. at the Widows Hamilton & Habercrafft; Friday March 29th. 1793.*" He requests TJ to take care of "the various Contents of the inclosed Letters and Dispatches" addressed to the President.

RC (DNA: RG 59, MLR); 1 p.; endorsed by TJ as received 1 July 1793 and so recorded in SJL. Enclosures: (1) Vall-Travers to George Washington, Rotterdam, 16 Mch. 1793, with two postscripts of 29 Mch. 1793, describing his intercessions with various Dutch authorities to secure the release of eight American

ships detained in the Netherlands as a result of a general trade embargo begun on 22 Feb. 1793 in consequence of the war with France, one of which (the *Hope*) was to have borne this letter, announcing (in the first postscript to the Dupl) that the States General had decided to detain foreign ships under the embargo for no longer than thirty-five days, and citing (in the second longer postscript) the detention of these ships in the Netherlands as an example of the need for the appointment of a consul general or other representative of the United States in that country, offering to serve in various capacities, and describing recent diplomatic and military developments in Europe (RC in same, lacking first postscript of 29 Mch. 1793 but containing elements of it in body of text; Dupl, with some variations in wording and containing two postscripts of 29 Mch. 1793, the second undated; long postscript to both texts filed with Vall-Travers to TJ above). (2) Petition of American sea captains to the States General, Rotterdam, 3 Mch. 1793, and Amsterdam, 6 Mch. 1793, protesting the detention of three American ships at Rotterdam and five at Amsterdam under a Dutch trade embargo as a violation of the 1782 treaty of amity and commerce with the United States (Tr in same; in Vall-Travers's hand, signed by twelve petitioners, including Herman Hend Damen on behalf of two of the original eight sea captains and three other American sea captains whose ships arrived later). (3) Vall-Travers to Van Son, Procurator at The Hague, Rotterdam, 8 Mch. 1793, requesting the release of the five American ships at Amsterdam (Tr in same; in French; in Vall-Travers's hand). (4) Van Son to Vall-Travers, The Hague, 12 Mch. 1793, reporting that the States General had provisionally declined to release these five American ships (Tr in same; in French). (5) Van Son to the States General, [ca. 12 Mch.] 1793, recit-

ing a request by Captain Miller that the embargo be lifted on the *Hope* so that he can sail from Rotterdam for Pennsylvania (Tr in same; in Dutch). (6) Extract from the Register of Resolutions of the States General, 14 Mch. 1793, stating that the *Hope* will be provisionally included in the Dutch embargo and referring documents relating to this matter to the Dutch minister in the United States so that he can justify this embargo (Trs in same; in Dutch, French, and English, the last in Vall-Travers's hand). (7) Queries by Vall-Travers respecting the 1782 Dutch treaty of amity and commerce with the United States, neutral rights, and the Dutch trade embargo, Rotterdam, 26 Mch. 1793 (MS in same, in Vall-Travers's hand; Dupl in same, with variant heading, dated 27 Mch. 1793). See also F. P. Van Berckel to TJ, 22 May 1793, and TJ to Van Berckel, 29 May 1793.

On 2 Apr. 1793 Vall-Travers wrote TJ from Amsterdam advising that after the packet for the President which he directed to TJ and entrusted jointly to Captain James Miller, commander of the Philadelphia-bound *Hope*, and Captain Benson Forster, a passenger, left Rotterdam three days ago, he returned there to deliver the enclosed duplicate and a new Dutch regulation on contraband, and that if Dumas, Willink, Van Staphorst & Hubbard, or Van Berckel do not furnish an English translation of the latter, he will send one in his next letter (RC in DNA: RG 59, MLR; endorsed by TJ as received 17 May 1793 and so recorded in SJL).

To David Humphreys

DEAR SIR   Philadelphia Mar. 30. 1793.

Having very short notice of a vessel just sailing from this port for Lisbon, direct, I think it proper to inform you summarily that powers are made out for you to proceed and execute the Algerine business committed to Mr. Barclay. Capt. Cutting, who is to assist you in this special business as secretary, leaves this place three days hence, and will proceed in the British packet by the way of London, and thence to Lisbon where he will deliver you the papers. The instructions to you are in general, to settle Mr. B's Marocco account and take care of the effects provided for that business, applying such of them as are proper to the Algerine mission, and as to the residue converting the perishable part of it into cash, and having the other part safely kept. You will be pleased therefore to be preparing and doing in this what can be done before the arrival of Capt. Cutting, that there may be as little delay as possible. I am with great & sincere esteem & respect Dr. Sir your most obedt. & most humble servt   TH: JEFFERSON

RC (NjP: Andre deCoppet Collection); addressed: "Colo. David Humphreys Minister Resident of the US. of America at Lisbon"; endorsed as forwarded by Goodair & Company of Lisbon on 9 May 1793; endorsed by Humphreys. PrC (DLC). FC (Lb in DNA: RG 59, DCI).

On 18 Apr. 1793 TJ submitted this letter to the President, who approved and returned it the next day (Washington, *Journal*, 110, 114).

Notes on the Reception of Edmond Charles Genet

Mar. 30.[1] 93. At our meeting at the Presid's Feb. 25. in discussing the question whether we should furnish to France the 3,000,000.[tt] desired, Hamilton in speaking on the subject used this expression 'when Mr. Genet arrives, whether we shall recieve him or not, will then be a question for discussion.' Which expression I did not recollect till E.R. reminded me of it a few days after. Therefore on the 20th. inst. as the Presidt. was shortly to set out for M. Vernon, I observed to him that as Genest might arrive in his absence, I wished to know before hand how I should treat him, whether as a person who would or would not be received? He said he could see no ground of doubt but that he ought to be received. On the 24th.[2] he asked E.R.'s opinion on the subject; saying he had consulted Colo. Hamilton thereon who went into lengthy considerations of doubt and difficulty, and viewing it as a very unfortunate thing that the Presidt. should have the decision of so critical a point forced on him, but in conclusion said, since he was brought into that situation he did not see but that he must receive Mr. Genest. E.R. told the Presidt. he was clear he should be received and the Presidt. said he had never had any doubt on the subject in his mind.—Afterwards on the same day he spoke to me again on it, and said Mr. Genest should unquestionably be received, but he thought not with too much warmth or cordiality, so only as be satisfactory to him.—I wondered at first at this restriction; but when E.R. afterwards communicated to me his conversation of the 24th. I became satisfied it was a small sacrifice to the opinion of Hamilton.

MS (DLC); entirely in TJ's hand; written with "Anas" entry for 31 Mch. 1793 on the other side of a sheet bearing "Anas" entries for 2, 23, and 25 Mch. 1793. Entry in SJPL: "[Notes] on the opns as to the reception of Genet." Included in the "Anas."

[1] Second digit reworked, possibly from "1."

[2] Reworked from "23d."

To George Turner

SIR   Philadelphia Mar. 30. 1793.

Having received letters from Mr. Sargent, Secretary and acting governor of the North Western territory, stating the extreme inconveniences which the people of that territory are experiencing from the absence of that body which constitutes both their legislature and Judiciary, I think it my duty, to inclose you copies thereof, not doubting but that you will duly feel the urgency of their calls for your presence. I have the honor to be with great respect, Sir your most obedt. & most humble servt   TH: JEFFERSON

PrC (DLC); at foot of text: "The honble Judge Turner." FC (Lb in DNA: RG 59, DL). For the enclosures, see Winthrop Sargent to TJ, 7 Feb. 1793, and note.

On 18 Apr. 1793 TJ submitted this letter and its enclosures to the President, who approved and returned them the following day (Washington, *Journal*, 110, 114).

To Nathaniel Cutting

SIR   Philadelphia. Mar. 31. 1793.

The Department of state, with the approbation of the President of the United States, having confidential communications for Mr. Pinckney, our Minister Plenipotentiary at London, and Colo. Humphreys our Minister Resident at Lisbon, and further services to be performed with the latter, you are desired to take charge of those communications, to proceed with them in the first American vessel bound to London, and from thence, without delay, to Lisbon in such way as you shall find best. After your arrival there, you are appointed to assist Colo. Humphreys, in the character of Secretary, in the business now specially confided to him; and that being accomplished, you will return directly to the US. or receive your discharge from Colo. Humphreys, at your own option.

You are to recieve, in consideration of these services, one hundred dollars a month, besides the reasonable expences of travelling by land and sea (apparel not included) of yourself and a servant: of which expences you are to render account and receive payment, from Colo. Humphreys, if you take your discharge from him, or otherwise from the Secretary of state if you return to this place: and in either case Colo. Humphreys is authorised to furnish you monies on account within the limits of your allowances: which allowances are understood to have begun on the 20th. day of the present[1] month, when you were engaged on this service, and to continue till your discharge or return. You receive here one thousand dollars on account, to enable you to proceed.   Th: Jefferson   Secretary of state

RC (PHi); at head of text: "To Captain Nathaniel Cutting"; endorsed by Cutting. PrC (DLC). FC (Lb in DNA: RG 59, DCI).

TJ's check for ONE THOUSAND DOLLARS drawn on the cashier of the Bank of the United States in Cutting's favor is dated 12 Apr. 1793 (MS in DLC). On 18 Apr. 1793 TJ submitted this letter to the President, who approved and returned it the same day (Washington, *Journal*, 110, 114). On 31 Mch. 1793 TJ also wrote Cutting the following note: "Th: Jefferson considering the prospect of war between France and Gr. Britain, recommends to Capt. Cutting to consider whether it will not be better for him to look out for an American vessel going to England, rather than venture in the Packet" (RC in ViU: McGregor Library; PrC in DLC, on same sheet as PrC of TJ to Alexander Hamilton, 31 Mch. 1793; Tr in DLC, 19th-century copy, on same sheet as Tr of TJ to Hamilton, 31 Mch. 1793). Only one of the 31 Mch. 1793 letters to Cutting is recorded in SJL.

[1] Word written over "last," erased.

To Alexander Hamilton

Mar. 31. 1793.

Th: Jefferson presents his compliments to the Secretary of the Treasury, and is obliged to recall to his mind the order of the President inclosed to him on the 23d. inst. Tuesday being the last day allowed Th:J. for transmitting bills by the packet.

PrC (DLC); on same sheet as PrC of TJ to Nathaniel Cutting of this date. Tr (DLC); 19th-century copy; on same sheet as Tr of TJ to Cutting of this date.

From Alexander Hamilton

Sunday March 31. 1793

Mr. Hamilton presents his Compliments to Mr. Jefferson. The warrant for the sum in question will be forwarded to him tomorrow. Mr. J may therefore count on finding the money ready to pay for the bills which he may engage, as early as he pleases tomorrow.

RC (DLC); endorsed by TJ as received 31 Mch. 1793 and so recorded in SJL.

Hamilton sent the WARRANT this day rather than TOMORROW (Report on the Fund for Foreign Intercourse, 18 Apr. 1793).

From John Garland Jefferson

DEAR SIR   Goochland March 31 1793.

I have been driving on since I wrote to you last post haste in my old pursuit. I have almost finished Tracy Atkins in the first collumn, I have finished Smith's wealth of nations in the second, and Burnet's history in the third. I have besides these perused the grecian history and Ferguson's philosophy. The roman history I have not yet been able to procure, but intend to read it as soon as possible. I shall soon begin Hawkin's pleas of the crown, and Beccaria. After having finished them, there will be no great many more to read. So I flatter myself, I shall be qualifyed[1] next fall to appear at the bar. I have not yet sent all the books I have read to Monticello, but only occasionally such as Peter wanted. I expected you woud be in this spring, and rather chose to wait for your return, that I might give you a particular account of those I might send, and of such as I have delivered to Mr. Peter, or Samuel Carr. I have been so particular as to keep a list of the books, and the date they were received, put back in the library, or delivered to Peter, or Sam. As I have now reason to believe you will not be at Monticello as soon as you expected, I only wait for your further directions, to dispose of the books I have in possession, as you shall order. I coud wish the revised code of laws was finished. It woud save much trouble. I long to see the day when I shall begin the practice of the law. I fear I have been troublesome to you. But I think I am well enough acquainted with you to know, that it gives you pleasure to befriend the unfriended, and to succour those in want. What ever may be said of the bar's being overstocked, which I often hear, I confess my prospects are flattering. I have not even a doubt. I see my way, and my resolutions are taken, for tho it must be owned that the bar is crouded, yet I conceive that a man of strict integrity, of close application, and one who will consider his client's money as sacred, and never to be touched unless when called for by him, will not want employment. I hope to see you at any rate in the fall. I wish to have your advice respecting my practice &c. I am more fond of Chancery, than common law. The decisions which are founded on natural justice, are peculiarly engaging. I am come now, my dear Sir, to a part, which I am always willing to put off to the last. The wants of the spring call for a supply, and you are the only person to whom I can apply. Your generosity affords an assylum, which from the ill management of some of my father's executors, and the rascality of others, I shoud have wanted. I expect that 12£. exclusive of board, one quarter of which will soon be due, will serve till the fall. You gave an order last fall for 75 dollars. 5£. was appropriated to a quarter's board, and the rest was laid out in winter clothes, and other unavoidable expences. I have become indebted in the neighbourhood two or three pounds, for trifling necessaries. A person who is obliged to pay for making up linnen, and every little thing that is done, is obliged to expend more than one who was never in the same circumstances, or who never made a calculation of these expences, is aware of. I shall take no step towards satisfying the wants of spring, till I hear from you. In the meantime, believe to be, dear Sir, Your most grateful, and obt. servant.　　Jno G: Jefferson

RC (ViU: Carr-Cary Papers); at foot of first page: "Mr. Thomas Jefferson"; endorsed by TJ as received 9 Apr. 1793 and so recorded in SJL.

TJ had prescribed a course of readings by collumn in his letter to John Garland Jefferson of 11 June 1790. For the

revised code of laws adopted by Virginia in the autumn of 1792 but not published until 1795, see Editorial Note on the revisal of the laws 1776-1786, in Vol. 2: 324.

[1] MS: "quafyed."

To James Madison

Th:J. to J. Madison　　　　　　　　Philada Mar. 31. 1793.

Nothing remarkeable this week. What was mentioned in my last respecting Bache's paper was on misinformation, there having been no proposition there. Yours of the 24th. from Alexandria is received. I inclose you the rough draught of a letter I wrote on a particular subject on which the person to whom it is addressed desired me to make a statement according to my view of it. He told me his object was perhaps to shew it to some friends whom he wished to satisfy as to the original destination of the 3. mill. of florins, and that he meant to revive this subject. I presume however he will not find my letter to answer his purpose.—The President set out on the 24th. I have got off about one half my superfluous furniture already and shall get off the other half within two or three days to be shipped to Virginia: and shall in the course of the week get on the banks of the Schuykill. Ham. has given up his house in Market street and taken a large one in Arch. street near 6th.

RC (DLC: Madison Papers). PrC (DLC). Tr (DLC); 19th-century copy. Enclosure: revised Dft of TJ to Alexander Hamilton, 27 Mch. 1793.

Washington actually SET OUT from Philadelphia for a visit to Mount Vernon on 27 Mch. 1793 (Washington, *Journal*, 107).

Notes on Alexander Hamilton and the Bank of the United States

Mar. 31. Mr. Beckley tells me that the merchants bonds for duties on 6. mo. credit became due the 1st. inst. to a very great amount. That Hamilton went to the bank on that day and directed the bank to discount for those merchants all their bonds at 30. days, and that he would have the Collectors credited for the money at the Treasury. Hence the Treasury lumping it's receipts by the month in it's printed accounts these sums will be considered by the public as only received on the last day, consequently the bank makes the month's interest out of it. Beckley had this from a merchant who had a bond discounted and who supposes a million of dollars were discounted at the bank here. Mr. Brown got the same information from another merchant who supposed only 600,000 D. discounted here. But they suppose the same orders went to all the branch banks to a great amount.

eod. die. Mr. Brown tells me he has it from a merchant here that during the last winter the Directors of the bank ordered the freest discounts. Every man could obtain it. Money being so flush, the 6. percents run up to 21/ and 22/. Then the Directors sold out their private stocks. When the discounted notes were becoming due, they stopped discounts, and not a dollar was to be had. This reduced 6. percents to 18/3 then the same directors bought in again.

MS (DLC); entirely in TJ's hand; written with "Anas" entry for 30 Mch. 1793 on the other side of a sheet bearing "Anas" entries for 2, 23, and 25 Mch. 1793. Possibly recorded in a torn and virtually illegible entry for this date in SJPL. Included in the "Anas."

TJ's interest in the apparent abuses of discounting by Alexander HAMILTON and the BANK of the United States was shared by other Republicans. The bank's practice of discounting the notes of merchants purchasing Treasury bills of exchange had been singled out for criticism as a mechanism which generated "a regular and continual influx of moneys into the Bank" by William B. Giles in a speech to the House of Representatives on 23 Jan. 1793 attacking Hamilton's management of Treasury funds and foreign loans. Hamilton defended discounting—"the great profitable business of a bank"—in a report to the House of 19 Feb. 1793 on the state of the Treasury, explaining that the discounting of merchants' notes at a credit of 30 days or more was a customary and reasonable practice and that those who criticized the bank's policy simplistically confused notes with cash, an error which "could not be long acted upon without ruin to the institution" (Syrett, *Hamilton*, XIV, 106-8; *Annals*, III, 837-8).

To Thomas Mann Randolph, Jr.

DEAR SIR   Philadelphia Mar. 31. 1793.

I wrote to my daughter on the 24th. since which Maria has received yours of the 13th. Some cold nights lately make us fear for the fruit in Virginia. We have nothing remarkeable from abroad but what you will see in Freneau's paper. Fenno's will go to you through Mr. Madison. Private letters strengthen the idea of a civil war in England, and of a very general war through Europe. I am in hopes that the first step of France will be to open her colonies to our commerce freely. This with the situation of Europe must ensure a great price for our wheat for years to come. The present price here is 120 cents, and there being a hope that the distresses for money will begin soon to abate, we may expect the sale to become very brisk. The spring sales of wheat are so much higher than those made in the fall that I think we should submit to any degree of distress to gain the advantages of the former. My love to my dear Martha and am with greatest attachment Dear Sir your's affectionately   TH: JEFFERSON

RC (DLC); at foot of text: "Mr. Randolph." PrC (CSmH). Tr (DLC); 19th-century copy.

Six days earlier TJ received the following weather diary written by Randolph on the verso of an address cover that may have enclosed his missing letter to Maria Jefferson OF THE 13TH:

"March. 1. 30. f.   40. c.
         2. 30. c.   50. c.
         3. 48. c.   56. f.
         4. 53. c.   55. r.
         5. 55. f.   52. f.
         6. 46 f.   52. f.
         7. 51. r.   50. r.
         8. 54. r.   54. r.
         9. 38. f.   45. f.
        10. 38. f.   48. c.
        11. 46. r.   52. f.
        12. 40. snow   43. f.
        13. 41. clouds 45. f.
        14. 34. c."

(MS in MHi; torn; addressed: "Thomas Jefferson Secretary of State Philada."; in an unidentified hand: "Free"; in the hand of George Taylor, Jr.: "Private examd."; endorsed by TJ as received 25 Mch. 1793).

To Archibald Stuart

DEAR SIR   Philadelphia Mar. 31. 1793.

The bearer hereof Mr. John Nancarrow comes to Staunton on some view respecting a mine, in which line of business he has been brought up. He has been engaged in Philadelphia in that of making steel. He is a sensible, scientific and worthy man, and such as is rarely found in the walk of the arts, or even of the sciences. I take the liberty of recommending him to your notice and especially to your counsel in his dealings with persons known to you. I am ever with great and sincere esteem Dear Sir Your affectionate friend & humble servt.

TH: JEFFERSON

PrC (DLC); at foot of text: "Mr. Archibald Stuart." Tr (DLC); 19th-century copy.

To Archibald Stuart

DEAR SIR   Philadelphia Mar. 31. 1793.

I have written you a line this day by Mr. John Nancarrow to recommend him to you as a man of worth and science. What I say therein of him is religiously true, and I recommended him sincerely as a man I esteem. But lest you should be off your guard I mention in this, which goes by post, that I have understood his circumstances here to be bad, so that you must not be led into any money matters on his account. I had avoided saying any thing on that subject in my other letter, but apprehensive you might not infer that it was done of design, I have thought it my duty to be more particular in this special letter. I wish Mr. Nancarrow could be persuaded to set up with you some more hopeful business than that of mining. I should imagine his former one of making steel would be gainful.—I take for granted you receive Freneau's paper from hence regularly, and therefore I write you no news, there being nothing in that way but what the papers mention. I hope to be at home in the summer or autumn where I shall always be happy to see you. I am with sincere esteem Dr. Sir your affectionate friend & servt   TH: JEFFERSON

RC (ViHi); addressed: "Archibald Stuart esquire at Staunton in Virginia"; franked, stamped, and postmarked. PrC (DLC). Tr (DLC); 19th-century copy.

To Timothy Pickering

SIR   Philadelphia Apr. 1. 1793

Having from time to time through the winter and down to the present day received repeated information that the post rider between Richmond and Charlottesville, and consequently along the rest of that line, has been and continues extremely unpunctual, sometimes not going even as far as Charlottesville (only 75 miles of the route) for three weeks, and often missing a fortnight, I have thought it a duty to mention it to you, as I am sure you will always be glad to be informed of what is going amiss in any part of[1] your[2] establishment. This happens to lie under my particular notice because through that my neighbors[3] my family and myself exchange weekly notices of our health &c. Whether the correction depends on Mr. Davies at Richmond or Mr. Millar at Charlottesville I know not. I believe both are punctual men, I know the latter is: and therefore should hope a recommendation from you to them would procure a reformation of the evil. I am with great esteem Sir Your most obedt. humble servt

TH: JEFFERSON

P.S. Observe that the road between Richmd. and Charlottesville is at all times practicable on horse-back: rarely otherwise for a carriage.

PrC (DLC); at foot of text: "Colo. Pickering." Tr (ViU: Edgehill-Randolph Papers); 19th-century copy.

[1] Preceding three words interlined.
[2] TJ here canceled "departme."
[3] Preceding two words interlined.

To George Washington

DEAR SIR   Philadelphia Apr. 1. 1793.

The Report brought by a captain of a ship from Lisbon just in the moment of your departure that France had declared war against several nations, involved in that declaration almost every power of Europe. I therefore suspect that it has arisen from Kersaint's proposition to declare war against every nation, which a pilot may not have distinguished from a declaration. Still I have thought it adviseable that Capt. Cutting should prefer going in an American ship. He therefore has written to know the precise day of sailing of two or three vessels bound from New York to London, and will go in the first.   I am told that private letters from Gr. Britain render civil war a more probable thing there than would be concluded from the papers.—I received from Mr. Sargent a letter complaining of the absence of the judges from the N. Western territory; and inclosed a copy of it in a letter from myself on the subject to Judge Turner. I have not yet any answer. General Knox continues still too unwell to meet us on the subject of your circular letter. I have the honour to be with the most perfect respect & attachment Dear Sir Your most obedt: & most humble servt TH: JEFFERSON

RC (DNA: RG 59, MLR); at foot of text: "The President of the U.S."; endorsed by Washington. PrC (DLC). Tr (Lb in DNA: RG 59, SDC). Tr (DLC); 19th-century copy.

KERSAINT'S PROPOSITION: a reference to the proposal made in the National Convention on 1 Jan. 1793 by Armand Guy Simon de Coetnempren, Comte de Kersaint, for the issuance of a general proclamation "à tous les peuples" stating that "dans une guerre des rois contre des hommes, nous ne pouvons connaître que des amis ou des ennemis" (Archives Parlementaires, 1st ser., LVI, 114). An English translation of the lengthy speech by Kersaint containing this proposal was printed in the 23 and 27 Mch. 1793 issues of the National Gazette. The President's CIRCULAR LETTER to the Cabinet is printed above at 21 Mch. 1793.

From Timothy Pickering

SIR   General Post Office April 2d. 1793.

I am honoured with your letter of yesterday's date, respecting the delinquency of the post rider between Richmond and Charlottesville. Mr. Davis had some time ago informed me of his irregularities and defects: but soon afterwards wrote me that it appeared he had been so poor as to be unable to provide suitable horses: tho' he had then accomplished it; and expected such assistance as would enable him to be punctual in future.

Thus the matter rests on my mind; and I have not since received information (as I recollect) of any delinquencies, except what the roads or waters rendered unavoidable. I am respectfully sir, Your most obedt. servt.   TIMOTHY PICKERING

I shall write Mr. Davis to-morrow: he negociated the contract in my behalf.

RC (DLC); at foot of text: "Thomas Jefferson Esqr."; endorsed by TJ as received 2 Apr. 1793 and so recorded in SJL.

From William Short

DEAR SIR   Aranjuez April 2. 1793

Since my arrival in this country I have written to you in your public character Feb. 3 and March. 6.—and M. Carmichael and myself have written to you also Feb. 19. I have delayed[1] for some time resuming my private correspondence because I wished to know a little more of this residence before speaking to you of it—and because I have been indisposed ever since my arrival in this country—and have for some time past been confined to my room, by an indisposition of the climate—or a seasoning which I have always gone through in every new country I have been to. I was getting out and going to write to you on my subject in relation to my mind, when I received on the 25th. ulto. your private letter of Jan. 3. with a postscript of the 15th. This letter excited a variety of emotions in my breast, so new and so unexpected, particularly the postscript, that I found myself incapable of taking up my pen—the only soothing circumstance that presented itself was the eminent proof, it contained my dear Sir of your friendship and so far from its style needing any kind of apology as you seem to suppose[2] I do assure you, it is the most pleasing circumstance I have experienced for a long time—and probably the most pleasing I shall experience for a long time to come. If as I understand your letter a certain person has thus cleared himself and another in throwing blame on me—or leaving me exposed to blame, where he and he alone had all the means in his hands of shewing the position in which I had been insensibly and gradually placed—if I say he has kept out of sight my correspondence in a case of this kind, it can only have been to have left an object to feed public ill-humour in order to divert it from himself or his favorite. Whether the one or the other be to blame is a question that I am fully disposed to leave to the public judgment—to have stated a part of the truth only in a case of that sort is safer than advancing a direct falsehood—but it is not less infamous—as it is equally decieving those to whom it is pretended to give explanations. I was preparing to state the whole of this matter to you and to shew you by what means the delay had happened—as all my letters had done to the Sec. of the treasury—and to prove that situated as I was and had been from the month of Jany.—every consideration both of honor and delicacy forced me to begin this delay and to follow it, until M. Morris was installed in his office, into whose hands I then considered it as passed (and who willingly undertook it)—until I received a letter from the Sec. of the Treasury on the 17th. of Aug.—when it was too late to do any thing. I was preparing this business in a very agitated and enraged

[479]

state of mind when I received on the 29th. a letter informing me that the house of Donald & Burton had failed more than[3] a month ago[4] for £150,000 stlg. As you know that they had almost the whole of my fortune in their hands, you will readily concieve what an effect that had produced on me. It seems as if all the misfortunes that can befall the human lot were reserved for me and to be crowded on me at once. This has forced me to abandon the painful and provoking subject I was engaged in to take up another still more painful and distressing. The three days which have passed since I have recieved that information are such as I have never passed before. Although little in a condition to write or do any thing else, I set down to communicate to you this disquieting event, and under the authority of your former friendly offer to ask your aid and assistance. In a few days I will forward to you the state of the other business mentioned in the postscript of your letter— and you may rest assured beforehand that it will be such as must be approved by every body. I do not mean to say that either of the other persons in question is culpable—but this I will venture to affirm that the most prejudiced will agree I was not in fault—and indeed could not have acted otherwise whatever my dispositions might have been. I will then answer the other parts of your letter also begging you to be assured also in the mean time that you are very right in your opinion as to my principles of government—whatever I may think of the means made use of to set up and pull down governments employed in another country, and of which it appears my opinions or expressions have been dissatisfactory.

I proceed now to state my situation with respect to Donald & Burton. Tied down as I am here by public duty I can do nothing but write, both to London and America, fearing too much however it will be of little avail. I have written there to M. Donald begging him to let me know in what situation I am—and how much I count on his personal honor and friendship—and to let me know also whether Mr. Browne will be involved, and in general what I am to expect. M. Donald's having never written to me to inform me of this disaster, seems an extraordinary and an alarming circumstance.

In my private letter to you from the Hague of Nov. 30—I stated to you how my affairs stood in the hands both of M. Browne and M. Donald—and left it to you [to][5] decide on the propriety of having them placed in my name. In my letter of Dec. 18—I repeated the same subject to you and enclosed a letter open for Mr. Browne with the proper power of attorney to be used in the case you should have the funds then standing in his name converted and placed in mine. These letters give me some glimmering of hope that that part may have been rescued—as I hope you recieved my letters in time. Yet as the business was there left optional, I fear that Mr. Browne may if he desired it have found means to delay it. I now inclose you a general power of attorney asking the favor of you to take whatever measures you may judge best for me in my affairs, which however may perhaps be already desperate.

I have already on former occasions informed you how these funds had passed into Mr. Browne's hands—and what kind of stupid false delicacy, which I shall rue as long as I live, had prevented my having them placed in my own name. I will now briefly repeat it. When M. Donald was in Richmond Colo. Skipwith placed a certain sum in certificates belonging to me, in his hands—these certificates as you know proceeded from the sale of my patrimonial state. When M. Donald left Richmond he left them in M. Browne's hands and informed me of it. I afterwards corresponded with Mr. Browne on the subject, so that he alone I suppose became answerable for them. Still I fear he will be involved of course by Messrs. D. & B. He wrote me in the year 1791. that he had subscribed them being state certificates to the federal loan—and had kept them in his name for the convenience of recieving the interest—their amount as he stated them to me was 15000 dollars 6. per cts. 11,256. do. 3. per cts. and 7500 do. deferred. I know not what more to add on this distressing and distracting subject than to beg you my dear Sir to be so good as to secure me if you can. If Mr. Browne is a man of honor or delicacy he will certainly have kept this deposit inviolate and sacred. It seems to me now I must have been infatuated not to have had them placed in my name. Nothing but a false delicacy arising from my having the misfortune to be in public employment (for I shall ever consider it the greatest misfortune that has ever befallen me, and which now perhaps the total ruin of my fortune may force me to desire the continuance of) prevented my doing it. How differently I should now be situated! how much pain and anxiety I should have saved myself! These are sensations that no person can judge of who has not felt himself as I now do, almost under the certainty of ruin, with all his prospects for a settlement in life, blasted. Besides this sum M. Donald kept in his hands a part of that which had been saved as I have already informed you from Mr. Parker's. This arose as you know from money which I had in Paris, that had been remitted to me from home, and which I had entrusted to Mr. Parker to lay out for me. It seems as if it was destined to run the gauntlet. I have great confidence in Mr. Donald's honor—and it seems to me if he deserves it he will have kept this deposit sacred and untouched by his disaster—but his having not written to me since it has befallen him, staggers me much. The sum in his hands was about 6000 dollars of the several descriptions of 6. per ct. 3. per ct. and deferred.

I have heard from the commissioners at Amsterdam that you have given public notice of your intention to resign last month. I am a little embarassed how to send you this letter—but I have determined to address it to Monticello hoping it will get safe to your hands. It will go by[6] Cadiz—another shall go[7] by Lisbon, and I will thank you to be so good as to say whether you recieve the one or the other[8] or both. I am in the most pained & afflicted state both of mind and body, my dear Sir, your constant & unalterable friend   W Short

RC (DLC); at head of text: "*Private*"; at foot of first page: "Mr Jefferson"; endorsed by TJ as received 20 June 1793 and so recorded in SJL. PrC (PHi). Enclosure not found.

CERTAIN PERSON: Alexander Hamilton. HIS FAVORITE: Gouverneur Morris. For a discussion of the roles of Morris and Short in the temporary suspension of debt payments to the French government in the summer of 1792, see note to TJ to Short, 3 Jan. 1793. COMMISSIONERS AT AMSTERDAM: Willink, Van Staphorst & Hubbard.

[1] Word interlined in place of "postponed."
[2] Preceding five words interlined.
[3] Preceding two words interlined.
[4] Short here canceled "at least."
[5] Word inadvertently omitted by Short.
[6] Short here canceled "duplicate by."
[7] Preceding three words interlined in place of "This goes."
[8] Preceding four words interlined in place of "duplicate or original."

From William Short

DEAR SIR   Aranjuez April 2. 1793

I wrote to you this morning by the way of Cadiz informing you of the distressing account which I have just received of the bankruptcy of the house of Donald & Burton. As you know that their agent Mr. Browne has in his hands, the whole of the funds for which my patrimonial estate was sold you will judge of the state of mind in which this places me. I wrote to you from the Hague Nov. 30—and Dec. 18—mentioning my desire that these funds should be entered on my name and asking you to be so good as to have it done—although I then had no suspicion of the disaster which was to arrive. If this should not have been providentially done, I fear I shall suffer much, unless indeed Mr. Browne's delicacy and honor protect me. The funds in his hands amounted agreeably to his letter in the summer of 91. to thirty odd thousand dollars subscribed to the federal loan in 6.

and 3. per cts. and deferred. It seems to me now I must have been infatuated not to have had them placed in my name—but destined to all sorts of misfortune it would seem it was not given to me to avoid my fate—but condemned to be tortured from fear to anxiety and from anxiety to despair. I send herein inclosed a double of the power of attorney I inclosed in my letter of this morning asking the favor of you to do whatever you can for me—but I fear before its arrival it will be too late for any thing. Besides these funds Mr. Donald had in his hands a considerable sum arising from the cash which I put into M. Parkers hands in June 89.—and which was near being lost with him. I have heard nothing from Mr. Donald—which makes me fear every thing. I counted so much on his honor and his long established reputation, that I could never have supposed he would have allowed this deposit to be blended with his speculations—indeed I never suspected that he was a speculator. My letter of this morning being very long and I being still very weak, and my mind a good deal disordered—I close this letter here—it being sent merely by precaution. I shall ever remain my dear Sir, however unfortunate or afflicted—your unalterably grateful friend

W SHORT

RC (DLC); at head of text: "*Private*"; at foot of first page: "Thos Jefferson"; endorsed by TJ as received 11 June 1793 and so recorded in SJL. PrC (DLC: Short Papers). Enclosure not found.

From Jacob Hollingsworth

SIR   Elkton 3 Aprile 1793

Yours of 3 March I Reciev'd, and thank you for your freindly attention to my Busines Respecting my Lost Certificates, My Brother Stephen is now in town, I Expect Ere this the avent of my small Pappers are Knone to him, I Should have wrote you Soonar tho Mr. Biddle was Unfortunatly been very ill with the Pleuecarecy, tho now Recovered, and was here on Sunday Last, he wishes to be informed in time, when you will be here or at Wilmington, when he will wait on you, About Eight Days Since a Sartain Mr. Noble Boulding a Cozen of Mr. Biddls, Left this Nighbourhood with a Small famaly on his way to the Westard, I Made free to Give him a Line to your Lands in your Name, or to Such of your friends as weare ajaicent to the Lands, Mr. Boulding I have Knone Since a Boy and have Ever Considerd him a Honest Man, as is the Charracter of all his famaly, and Understands farming Wheat and Coarn well and tolarably well Aqueunted with

Small Seeds of all Sorts, if your Lands meet[1] the approbation of my Neghbours I Doubt not their being Soon Settled. Sr your Huml Servt
JACOB HOLLINGSWORTH

RC (MHi); addressed: "Thomas Jefferson Esqr Philada." and "Post"; franked; endorsed by TJ as received 6 Apr. 1793 and so recorded in SJL.

[1] MS: "mee."

To Benjamin Rush

Apr. 3. 93.

Th: Jefferson being engaged in packing his books will thank Dr. Rush for the volumes lent him if he had done with them. He presents him his best compliments.

Douignan de la vie humaine. 2. vols.
Compendium of Physic.

RC (DLC: Rush Papers); addressed: "Dr. Rush"; endorsed by Rush. Not recorded in SJL.

The first book TJ requested was Guillaume Daignan, *Tableau des Variétés de la Vie humaine* ..., 2 vols. (Paris, 1786). The second was [Joseph Flowerden], *A Compendium of Physic, and Surgery* (London, 1769). See Sowerby, Nos. 909, 892.

From William Davies

SIR   Philadelphia Apr. 4th.[1] 1793.

I beg leave to introduce to your notice Mr. James Murray, a grandson of the late President Yates of William and Mary. He has written in my office for some time past, and has given me satisfaction. My public business here being near a termination, he appears desirous to obtain a commission in the army, and more particularly in the line of the artillery. As I know him to be possessed of many amiable and valuable qualities, I feel an interest in recommending him to those, who have in their power the accomplishment of his wishes of obtaining an appointment in the service. With this hope, I have taken the liberty of presenting him to you; and am, sir, with very respectful esteem Your obedient & most humble servt.,   WM. DAVIES

RC (DLC); endorsed by TJ as received 4 Apr. 1793 and so recorded in SJL.

There is no evidence that James Murray ever received a commission in the United

States Army. MY PUBLIC BUSINESS: Davies was the Virginia commissioner responsible for settling the state's accounts with the federal government (Madison, *Papers*, XIII, 190-2).

¹ Digit written over "3."

From Alexander Donald

DEAR SIR   London 4th. April 1793.

My last respects to you were under date of the 10th. Ultimo, to which I beg you to refer.

On the 14th. there was a meeting of D. & B.'s Creditors, when it appeared to be the general opinion that they should be allowed time to wind up their business, to collect their debts, and to pay off the Creditors as quickly as possible. An Instrument for this purpose has been drawn out, and is now in the progress of signing. Whether it will be carried into effect I cannot positively say—but I am still determined to do business for myself in future, and I therefore repeat the request made to you in my last that your Tobacco should be put into the hands of my nephew to ship for you, and not into Mr. Brown's, who I suspect will rather attach himself to Mr. Burton.

The Orrery you ordered from Jones is gone by the Camilla, Service into James River, and I trust it will get safe to hand, The order for venetian blinds &ca. were given in agreeable to your directions, but were not shipped on account of our situation. I hope to be able to send every thing to you in the course of this summer.

It requires a considerable strength of mind to enable me to bear up under what has lately happened to me. Well Born, Genteely brought up and educated, and left a Fortune by my Father when I was only fourteen years of age of upwards of Five Thousand Pounds Stg., having always been industrious, Free from gameing and every kind of extravagance, and at a time when I thought my self independent, and in a fair way of making a Fortune, to be brought to distress and ruin by improper conduct in my Partner, and at my time of Life is what does not fall to the Lot of many People. My dependence on my Friends in America has enabled me to consider my misfortunes as an aweful lesson, from which I hope to derive great advantages in future.

Was you to desert me I would indeed dispair, but this I know you cannot do, Because it is contrary to your nature. I will always be proud to receive your commands and I remain Dear Sir Your Faithful & obt. Sert.   A DONALD

[485]

RC (MHi); at head of text: "Thomas Jefferson Esqr."; endorsed by TJ as received 20 May 1793 and so recorded in SJL.

From Joseph Fenwick

Bordeaux 4 April 1793

I had the honor of writing you the 25 February past inclosing a Decree of the national Convention relative to American Vessels. I now Send an additional one concerning Vessels carrying provisions in to the french Islands, to which they have Since added the permission of trading to Senegal in American Vessels fitted out of the Ports of France, to return back with their Gum into France.

American Vessels receive here the greatest favor and protection from the Government. The commercial People have more confidence in their neutrality than in those of any other Nation, and give them a decided preference in freights, which are now very high, and demanded both for the North of Europe and the W. Indias.

American produce continue very high here, and much wanted particularly Grain. The Government is giving prices equal to 35/ Str. per Barrl. for Flour, and 7/ Str. per Bushel for Wheat 20 a 22/. Str. for Rice, and appear to have no means at present of procuring any provision from foreign Countryes excepted the United States. Tobacco is 60 a 80tt per Ct. Exchange 13½ and 14d. Str. per 3tt with England.

We are perfectly quiet in this Departement and the late insurrections in the former Province of Britany are nearle Subsided or quitted. The french Armies it is Said has evacuated Austrean flanders. With the highest respect I have the honor

Tr (DNA: RG 59, CD); in Fenwick's hand, unsigned; at head of text: "To the Honarble Secretary of State"; endorsed by TJ as a letter of 14 Apr. 1793 and as received 25 July 1793, but this probably refers to a covering letter of 14 Apr. from Fenwick recorded in SJL as received 25 July 1793 but not found. RC recorded in SJL as received 13 June 1793. Enclosure: Decree of the National Convention, 26 Mch. 1793, granting an exemption from customs duties to ships of the United States bringing provisions to French colonies in the Americas and setting forth the conditions under which these ships could carry away certain tropi-

cal products of these colonies (printed text in same; contained in last two pages of an issue of the Bordeaux *Journal de Commerce, de Politique et de Littérature*). See also *Archives Parlementaires*, 1st ser., LX, 574-5.

On 29 Mch. 1793 the National Convention granted permission for ships of the United States and other countries not at war with France to engage in the gum trade between France and its trading posts in SENEGAL if they outfitted themselves first in French ports (*Archives Parlementaires*, 1st ser., LX, 692-3).

From Alexander Hamilton

Thursday April 4h. [1793]

The Secretary of the Treasury presents his respects to the Secretary of State, and proposes, if convenient to him, a Meeting of the Commissioners of the Sinking Fund, on Saturday. The Secretary of State will please to name the hour and place.

RC (DLC); partially dated; endorsed by TJ as received 4 Apr. 1793 and so recorded in SJL.

For the background, see Hamilton to TJ, 24 Mch. 1793, and note.

From David Humphreys

Lisbon, 4 Apr. 1793. Since his letter of 24 Mch. he has repeated his application to the Secretary of State for Foreign Affairs about "the hardship of refusing our vessels laden with wheat, after requesting *Franquia*, to proceed to their destination." He has succeeded in this instance, as his letter to the Secretary and its enclosures indicate, and will continue to be unremitting in his efforts to protect American trade. Bountiful rains promise an improved harvest in Portugal. European affairs become more critical every day. After a conference with the Secretary of State for Foreign Affairs, M. d'Arbot, the National Convention's "Agent Negociateur to this Court," is returning to France on the first neutral ship, not having been officially acknowledged. War with France will probably ensue after Arbot's return, despite the assertions of English gazettes that it exists already. The celebrations planned for the Princess of Brazil's childbirth will overshadow the Queen. He encloses a letter from Short for TJ and another for the Secretary of the Treasury.

RC (DNA: RG 59, DD); 2 p.; at head of text: "(No. 70.)"; at foot of text: "The Secretary of State"; endorsed by TJ as received 31 May 1793 and so recorded in SJL. Tr (Lb in same). Enclosures: (1) Bill of Lading, Petersburg, Virginia, 2 Feb. 1793, for shipping 7,218 bushels of wheat to Cadiz on the *Mary* for Gurdon Bachus of Petersburg (printed form in same; signed by Joseph Perkins; endorsed on verso: "Copy of Original left at Belleam Custom House"). (2) Joseph Perkins to Humphreys, Lisbon, 23 Mch. 1793, stating that the brig *Mary*, owned by Moses Brown of Newburyport and commanded by himself, put into Lisbon for safety on the way to Cadiz and was being unjustly detained on the pretended grounds that its cargo of wheat "was order'd to this market" and "invested entirely to my care independent of any Consignee"; that he would sail to his destination come what may unless the vessel and cargo were confiscated, thereby enabling him to justify himself to his employers; and that he should be paid the price of the market he is bound for if bread is urgently needed in Lisbon, where the price is only four-fifths of that in neighboring ports and will not cover the freight and charges of the voyage (Tr in same; signed by Perkins). (3) Humphreys to Luis Pinto de Sousa Coutinho, 25 Mch. 1793, promising to transmit to his government as soon as possible Pinto's 20 Mch. answer to several communications on the subjects of grain and flour, transmitting Nos. 1 and 2 to verify the destination of the *Mary*

[487]

and document the hardship caused by its detention, and requesting that the ship be allowed to proceed on her voyage before her perishable cargo was ruined (Tr in same, in Humphreys's hand; Tr in Lb in same). (4) Pinto de Sousa Coutinho to Humphreys, n.d., enclosing an advisory for the *Mary* to be released from customs so that it may continue its voyage (Tr in same, in Portuguese, in Humphreys's hand; Tr in Lb in same).

The enclosed letter from William Short to TJ has not been identified; its receipt was not recorded in SJL on 31 May 1793 when TJ registered Humphreys's letter. Short's letter to Alexander Hamilton was dated either 22 or 30 Mch. 1793 (Syrett, *Hamilton*, XIV, 235-6, 261-3). TJ submitted Humphreys's letter to the President on 31 May 1793 (Washington, *Journal*, 157).

From Gouverneur Morris

DEAR SIR   Paris 4 April 1793

My last No. 25 was of the twenty sixth of March. Enclos'd you have Copies of Mr. Lebrun's Letter to me of the twenty sixth of March, Mine to him of the twenty eighth and his to me of the twenty ninth. I also enclose under this Cover the Journal of the Debates and Decrees No. 195. 196. 197 and 198. These will give you the present State of our News up to the last Evening. You will perceive that all my Conjectures respecting the Army of Dumouriez are more than realiz'd. From the Letters of Custine you will perceive that he has been totally Defeated for he found it necessary to fall back about forty Miles leaving a Garrison in Mayntz which must fall of Course, and we may hourly expect to hear of farther Misfortunes in that Quarter. Perhaps the Prussian Army may stop to beseige Mayntz but I think a Part of their Force will be sufficient for that Purpose. The Country as I have mentioned in a former Letter is universally indispos'd to France and I can say on good Information the same Thing of Savoy. It is now very fine Weather in this City and if the Season be proportionately advanced in other Quarters the Campaign will be soon opened on every Side. There will be a great Want of Bread before we have another Harvest unless Peace should take Place. If Lisle and Valenicennes should surrender at once the Campaign on that Quarter will not be so much advanc'd as might be apprehended because as yet the Magazines are not brought up and Time must be allowd for that Purpose. It seems indeed probable that the Enemy have taken considerable Magazines belonging to France but even these are at some Distance. I expect every Hour to hear of an Attempt upon Givet or Maubeuge and it would seem from the best Information to be had that neither of these Places can be defended long. In short on every Side the Horizon looks darkly. Whether Dumouriez will be able to lead his Army against Paris seems as yet uncertain. Perhaps he may experience a similar Fate to that of la fayette but he is in much better Circumstances for a high Game and much abler to play it. At any Rate the Enemy derive Advantage from the Squabble between him and the Convention. Here they are not yet fully appriz'd of their Danger. Like those who die of a Hectic Hope gleams to the last and the latest Breath is spent in Expression of some splendid Fancy. In the expiring Struggles however, let them happen when they may, we shall experience new Horrors. Such at least is the probable Chance. The constant Complaints on account of the Capture of American Vessels and the Necessity of giving Protection to such of our Countrymen as are here have prevented me hitherto from leaving Paris. At present the Barriers are strictly guarded, and those who have applied lately for Pasports have been disappointed; but in a few Days we shall know Something more upon this Subject. The Ministry seems to be in a fair Way towards an entire Dissolution. In Short every Thing here is in almost as much Confusion as on the Frontiers. Adieu my dear Sir I am truly yours   Gouv Morris

RC (DNA: RG 59, DD); at head of text: "No. 26"; at foot of first page: "Thomas Jefferson Esqr. Secretary of State"; endorsed by TJ as received 21 June 1793 and so recorded in SJL. FC (Lb in DLC: Gouverneur Morris Papers). Tr (DNA: RG 46, Senate Records, 3d Cong., 1st sess.); copy made early in 1794 by State Department; with omissions; at head of text: "Duplicate." PrC (DNA: RG 59, MD); more complete text with first two pages not corresponding to Tr. Tr (Lb in same, DD). A Dupl recorded in SJL as received on 9 Sep. 1793 has not been found. Enclosures: (1) Lebrun to Morris, 26 Mch. 1793, stating that he had submitted to the Minister of Marine Morris's letter of 24 Mch. on the capture of American vessels by French privateers and was sure that Morris would soon receive a satisfactory response. (2) Morris to Lebrun, 28 Mch. 1793, requesting that he direct agents of the Republic at Morlaix to settle the claim for damages, expenses, and interest made by Captain George Todd in consequence of the capture of his ship, the *Mercury*, by the French frigate *La Proserpine* in violation of the treaty of amity and commerce with the United States. (3) Lebrun to Morris, 29 Mch. 1793, stating that he had requested the Minister of Marine to render such satisfaction as Captain Todd was due and to

prevent future French attacks on American ships; that these attacks resulted from the difficulty of distinguishing between English and American vessels, and from the probable collusion between Americans and Englishmen in disguised expeditions; that it was in the interest of the American government to prevent such fraud so as to preserve to its citizens the benefit of neutrality; that he needed Congress's last regulation defining the ownership of American vessels in order to transmit it to French port officials and naval commanders; and that the recent decrees of the National Convention in favor of American commerce were proof of France's desire to tighten fraternal connections with the United States (Trs in same, in French; Trs, in French and English, in DNA: RG 46, Senate Records, 3d Cong., 1st sess., with note by Edmund Randolph at foot of English translation of Enclosure No. 3: "Note: The Journals are not sent to the Senate, upon a supposition that they do not come within their desire"; PrCs in DNA: RG 59, MD, lacks Randolph's note; Trs in Lb in same, DD, in French and English).

TJ submitted Morris's letter to the President on 21 June 1793 (Washington, *Journal*, 185-6).

To David Rittenhouse

Apr. 4. 93.

Th:J. returns to Mr. Rittenhouse the treatise of De la Sauvagere and Keith's pamphlet which he had presented him before, as he had also De la Lande which he insists on his keeping, as he has copies of them all.   The other books received from Mr. Rittenhouse belong to the Department of state, but more immediately are for the Mint. He therefore returns them for the use of the Mint, to which also belong the two books retained by Mr. Rittenhouse, to wit Traité des Monnoyes 2. vols. and Abregé de la theorie chymique. So that Mr. Rittenhouse has now nothing of Th:J's unless perhaps he lent him Sancho's letters, which he finds not among his books and has some idea of having lent to Mr. R.

RC (NjP); addressed: "Mr. Rittenhouse." Not recorded in SJL.

DE LA SAUVAGERE: Félix François Le Royer d'Artezet de La Sauvagère, *Recueil de Dissertations, ou recherches historiques et critiques sur le temps où vivoit le solitaire saint Florent au Mont-Glonne, en Anjou, sur quelques ouvrages des anciens Romains nouvellement découverts dans cette province et en Touraine ... avec de nouvelles assertions sur la végétation spontanée des coquilles du chateau des Places ...* (Paris, 1776). KEITH'S PAMPHLET: George Skene Keith, *Tracts on Weights, Measures, and Coins* (London, 1791). DE LA LANDE:

Joseph Jérôme Le Français de Lalande, *Astronomie*, 2d ed., 4 vols. (Paris, 1771-81). See Sowerby, Nos. 647, 3766, 3796. THE TWO BOOKS RETAINED by Rittenhouse were: Jean Boizard, *Traité des Monoyes, de Leurs Circonstances & Dépendances*, new ed., 2 vols. (Paris, 1711); and *Abrégé de la théorie chymique, tiré des propres écrits de M. Boerhaave, par M. de la Métrie. Auquel on a joint le Traité du vertige, par le même* (Paris, 1741). SANCHO'S LETTERS: Ignatius Sancho, *Letters of the Late Ignatius Sancho, an African. In Two Volumes. To which is prefixed, Memoirs of His Life* (Dublin, 1784). See Sowerby, No. 4640.

From Willink, Van Staphorst & Hubbard

SIR   Amsterdam 4 April 1793
We had the pleasure to address you our last Respects the 17 August past, and have now the honor to transmit you Abstract of your Account Current with us for the Department of State up to this Date, the Balance whereof due unto us Holld. cy. ƒ13,255.6. augmenting constantly by fresh Disposals, for the Objects to be supplied by your Department. We are persuaded You will have attended, to provide us with further Remittances, to be placed to the Credit of this Account. We are respectfully Sir Your most obedient and very humble Servants
WILHEM & JAN WILLINK
N & J. VAN STAPHORST & HUBBARD

RC (DLC); in the hand of Van Staphorst & Hubbard, signed by the two firms; at foot of text: "Thos. Jefferson Esqr."; endorsed by TJ as a 2 Apr. 1793 letter received 17 May 1793 and so recorded in SJL. Dupl (DLC); in a clerk's hand, signed by the two firms; at head of text: "Copy"; endorsed by TJ as received 7 June 1793 and so recorded in SJL. Enclosure: Account of Department of State with Willink, Van Staphorst & Hubbard, 2 Apr. 1793, containing entries for 30 June 1792-2 Apr. 1793 (MS in DLC, in a clerk's hand, signed by the two firms; PrC of Tr in DLC, in a clerk's hand; PrC of another Tr in DLC, in a clerk's hand; Tr in MHi, 19th-century copy).

TJ submitted this letter and its enclosure to the President on 8 June 1793 (Washington, *Journal*, 164).

To Brown, Benson & Ives

GENTLEMEN   Philadelphia, April 5th. 1793.

Your Favor of March 21, is just received. I have enclosed a copy of it to the Minister of France, with the Letter I now communicate to you. As you did not state precisely whether any and what Loss had accrued to you ultimately, I could only write to him in general Terms as to that matter. If you propose to solicit an indemnification, it will be necessary for you to employ some Person on the Spot to follow it up, in which Case I take for granted the Minister's Interposition will have secured you a just Attention. I am, with great Respect, Gentlemen, Your most obedient humble servant,

PrC (DLC); in the hand of George Taylor, Jr., unsigned; at foot of text: "Messrs. Brown, Benson & Ives merchants Providence." FC (Lb in DNA: RG 59, DL). Enclosure: TJ to Jean Baptiste Ternant, 5 Apr. 1793.

From C. W. F. Dumas

The Hague, 5 Apr. 1793. The lifting of the embargo in the Dutch ports enables him to resume his dispatches. He encloses a statement of his disbursements for the last half of 1792, two copies of which he furnished to the bankers at Amsterdam when he drew on them for the sums of ƒ301.16 and ƒ204.15 mentioned in it. The poorly conceived French campaign strategy of maintaining separate corps instead of concentrating them on the Meuse and the Rhine has just had the most disastrous results for them. At the same time civil war is breaking out in earnest in France itself. He veils his face like that of the king whose daughter was being sacrificed and prays daily that God may protect the United States, its Congress, the President, and the Secretary of State.

RC (DNA: RG 59, MLR); 1 p.; in French; at head of text: "No. 95. à S. E. Mr. ____ Secretaire d'Etat & des Aff. Etr. en Congrès genl. des Et. Un. d'Am." Dupl (same, MDC); at head of text: "Dupl."; endorsed by TJ as received 19 July 1793 and so recorded in SJL. Enclosure: Statement of Dumas's official disbursements for July-December 1792, dated 18 Mch. 1793 and sent to Willink, Van Staphorst & Hubbard on that date, showing expenditures of ƒ301.16 and ƒ204.15 (MS in same; entirely in Dumas's hand).

Dumas also wrote a brief letter of 14 Apr. 1793 to the Secretary of State congratulating the United States on its good fortune in not being entangled in the current European crisis (RC in DNA: RG 59, MLR, at head of text: "No. 96. a Son Exce. M. ____ le Secretaire d'Etat & pour les Affaires Etr. en Congrès-genl. des Et. un. d'Am."; endorsed by TJ as received 29 July 1793 and so recorded in SJL; Dupl in same, MDC, at head of text in part: "Dupl.," endorsed by TJ as received 19 July 1793 and so recorded in SJL).

From Alexander Hamilton

Friday April 5 [1793]

Mr. Hamilton presents his Compliments to the Secy. of State—elects his office as likely to be most convenient to him where Mr. H will accordingly attend tomorrow at 10 OClock.

RC (DLC); partially dated; endorsed by TJ as received 5 Apr. 1793 and so recorded in SJL.

For the minutes of the ensuing meeting of the Commissioners of the Sinking Fund, at which TJ registered his continued dissent "from any estimate of the true value of . . . 3 pr. Ct. stock at more than 10/– in the pound," see Syrett, *Hamilton*, XIV, 292-3.

From Gouverneur Morris

DEAR SIR
Paris 5 April 1793

I did myself the Honor of writing to you No. 26 Yesterday. Colo. Touzard who takes Charge of my Letters having been detain a Day longer it furnishes the Opportunity of sending this Day's Gazettes and such Intelligence as is now arriv'd. It appears that the Army of Dumouriez is attach'd to him and will go all the Lengths which he desires. What is worse is that the Militia also adhere so that he has all Chances now in his Favor and probably as soon as the Magazines are duly replenished he will advance for under such Circumstances we are not to expect much Resistance from the frontier Towns. The Affair of Custines has been very serious: the Garrison of Mayence is shut up in that Town and if it Capitulates the Enemy derive from the Magazines lodg'd in it the Means needful for ulterior Operations. Hence I conclude that such Terms will be offered as will [be]¹ accepted of. Custines left Flank is entirely open and in all human Probability the several Passes in the Vosge Mountains will be occupied by the Column of Hessians and in that Case his Retreat to France becomes impossible and he must make the best of it in Alsace. Every Hour is now big with important Events and how Matters will go in this City the Lord knows. I am with Esteem and Respect Dr Sir Your obedient Servant   GOUV MORRIS

RC (DNA: RG 59, DD); at head of text: "No. 27"; at foot of first page: "Thomas Jefferson Esqr Secretary of State"; endorsed by TJ as received 21 June 1793 and so recorded in SJL. FC (Lb in DLC: Gouverneur Morris Papers); with correction by Morris. Tr (DNA: RG 46, Senate Records, 3d Cong., 1st sess.); at head of text: "Duplicate." Pr C (DNA: RG 59, MD). Tr (Lb in same, DD). A

Dupl recorded in SJL as received on 9 Sep. 1793 has not been found.

TJ submitted Morris's letter to the President on 21 June 1793 (Washington, *Journal*, 185-6).

[1] Omitted word supplied from FC, where it is interlined in Morris's hand.

From Thomas Pinckney

DEAR SIR   London 5th. April 1793.

In a Conversation I had this day *with*[1] *Lord Grenville I conclude that no Ship coming to the ports of the King of Gt. Britn. will be permited to proceed to ports under French dominion with grain or other provisions or naval stores or any goods called contraband: that this government intends to make prize of enemies property on board of neutral Ships and all provisions going to ports blockaded.* These points are not however finally determined and endeavours are making to obviate what may bear hard on us. A Bill for preventing traitorous Correspondence is[2] now before the House of Commons which if it passes into a Law will materially affect our commercial Intercourse with this Country. Although these Matters are at present incomplete I thought it adviseable to give this Intelligence that our Merchants may be on their guard against the probability of their being carried into effect, and in particular may not rely upon Insurances to be made here on any species of Goods sent to the Dominions of France. *One regiment is to sail from Ireland to the W. Indies.* The late Successes of the combined Armies in the Netherlands *may enable Gt: Britn. to send more troops that way.* I have the honor to be with the utmost respect Dear Sir Your most obedient and most humble Servant   THOMAS PINCKNEY

P. S.[3] I have not been able to procure Copies of the Bill mentioned in this Letter but it declares in substance that any Person being or residing within any of the Dominions of his Britannic Majesty who shall directly or indirectly supply, or cause, direct, authorise or procure any Person or Persons whomsoever or wheresoever residing to supply or to send for the purpose of being sold or supplied to any of the dominions of France or place in their Possession or to the Armies Fleets or Vessels employed by the French Government any naval or military Stores, Gold or Silver in Bullion or Coin, Forage or Provision of any kind and various other Articles shall be deemed guilty of Treason. All Insurance made on any Goods and Vessels bound to or from the Ports under French dominion made null and void and Parties guilty of misdemeanor.

RC (DNA: RG 59, DD); in the hand of William A. Deas, with complimentary close, signature, and inside address by Pinckney; written partly in code; decoded interlinearly by George Taylor, Jr. (see note 1 below); at foot of text: "The Secretary of State"; with penciled notation by TJ (see note 3 below); endorsed by TJ as received 20 May 1793 and so recorded in SJL. PrC (same, MD); lacks complimentary close, signature, and decipherment. Dupl (same, Duplicate Dispatches); written partly in code, but lacks decipherment; varies slightly in wording; endorsed by TJ as "Duplicate." PrC of Tripl (ScHi: Pinckney Family Papers; in Deas's hand, unsigned; written partly in code, but lacks decipherment. Tr (Lb in DNA: RG 59, DD); entirely *en clair*, with encoded words in brackets. Enclosure: Extract of Gouverneur Morris to Pinckney, 2 Mch. 1793: "I am informed in a way that precludes doubt that the executive Council here sent out by Genet three hundred blank commissions for privateers to be given clandestinely to such persons, as he might find in america inclined to take them" (Tr in DNA, RG 59, Duplicate Dispatches, written entirely in unidentified code by Deas and decoded interlinearly by Taylor, at head of text: "Ex-tract of a Letter from Mr. Morris"; PrC in same, MD, lacks decipherment; Tr in ScHi: Pinckney Family Papers, written entirely in code by Deas, at foot of text: "Extract from Mr. Morris's Letter of 2d. March 1793, inclosed in the above"; Tr in Lb in DNA: RG 59, DD, entirely *en clair*).

Parliament passed the bill for PRE-VENTING TRAITOROUS CORRESPONDENCE in May 1793 (Sir Thomas Edlyne Tomlins and John Raithby, eds., *The Statutes at Large, of England and of Great-Britain . . .*, 20 vols. [London, 1811], XVIII, 15).

TJ submitted this letter to the President on 21 May 1793 (Washington, *Journal*, 146).

[1] This and subsequent words in italics are written in unidentified code, the text being supplied from Taylor's decipherment.

[2] The sentence to this point initially began "I inclose a Bill" before it was revised to read as above.

[3] Above the postscript TJ penciled: "Extract of a letter from a well informed correspondent dated Lond. Apr. 5. 1793." This extract was printed in the 22 May 1793 issue of the *National Gazette*.

From William Short

DEAR SIR   Aranjuez April 5 1793

I wrote you two letters on the 2d. inst. via Cadiz and Lisbon, each inclosing a power of attorney to you and asking the favor of you to do what you could for me in a case where I may be perhaps totally ruined—I mean the bankruptcy of Donald & Burton and consequently I fear of Mr. Browne. I was about answering your letter of Jan. 3d. and postscript 15th. in a disordered state both of body and mind when I recieved this alarming intelligence, which forced me to postpone it in order to trouble you with the letters abovementioned. I will say no more respecting them at present, but proceed to the answer of your letter recieved here, from the Duke de la Alcudia's office, the 25th. ulto.

I will begin with the postscript as being what affects me the most, although I am by no means indifferent to the subject of the letter. The loans in Europe have been a constant source of pain and anxiety to me, ever since I had the weakness to allow myself to be employed in them. For some time things went to the satisfaction of every body, except myself, who from instinct was averse to meddle with money matters— and uniformly wrote to the Sec. of the treasury, begging him to join some other to me if I were to be continued therein. When I received this employment I felt that I should repent of it—but being then in a state of probation as I considered it, for the place I desired at Paris, I felt that to refuse this burthen, and thereby disappoint government by subjecting them to delay until they could name another, would be a sure means of excluding me from the appointment at Paris—and hoping if this business were well executed it might procure me that place, I determined to undertake it. According to my usual fortune the events have been such as to make me undergo all the pain, without acquiring any thing desired—and moreover to be so entangled in the service of government, as not to have known how to have withdrawn myself, although I felt sorely their neglect and mortification. In fine nothing was wanting to complete the measure of my ill fortune, but to see public censure like to fall on me, in order to remove it from the shoulders of others, after having seen the munificence and confidence of government bestowed on others also without their having done any thing but attend to their own speculations and concerns, whilst I was forced as it were by that government to engage in a business which being of a dangerous kind and subject to public censure, they did not chuse to commit to their favorites—chusing to reserve them for more agreeable and less dangerous occasions—of this I think you will see a proof in the following state of facts, which I give you, as the best way of letting you see whether Mr. Hamilton had a right to throw blame on me, in the affair of the suspension of the payments. I do not pretend to say that either he or his favorite is to blame— all that I shall do is to shew that I could not do otherwise than I did. He had in his hands at the time of his acting as mentioned in the postscript of your letter, numberless letters from me repeating and repeating with prolixity and satiety, the position in which I was placed and my anxiety thereon. Not to have brought those letters forward was a cruel conduct and particularly with respect to me. I had thought that letters addressed to one department would have been open to the head of the other—or I should have written to you more fully on the painful situation in which I was kept, with respect to these payments. Still I think I must have touched on it in some of my letters to you. Of this I cannot be sure having left the greater part of my letters in Holland—this obliges me also to give the following statement from memory, although I am sure of its exactitude.

Facts as to the delay of payment to France from the year 91. until the agreement made by Mr. Morris with the Commissaries of the National treasury in Aug. 92.

1. At the time of the loan being opened which is dated Jan. 1. 92. there remained no monies in the hands of the bankers at Amsterdam, except $2\frac{1}{2}$ million of florins, which the Sec. of the treasury had directed me should be kept there to answer his draughts from America—these $2\frac{1}{2}$ millions were ordered to be reserved out of the preceding loan of six millions opened in Sep. 91—the rest of this loan was paid to France as it came in.

2. Loans when opened are paid in monthly portions—that opened in Jany. 92. was to be paid by the undertakers at the rate of 500,000 florins a month for six months—these were the monies to come in, and out of them were to be paid the large sums for interest and premium, on former loans during the months of Febry. and march.

3. Previously to this loan being opened I had received a letter from the Sec. of the treasury, informing me that the U.S. intended making up the depreciation on the assignats in their payments to France and authorising me to settle that depreciation. This became a preliminary step therefore to future payments—immediately on the reciept of that letter from the Sec. of the treasury (in Nov. 91. a little before my setting out for Holland) I gave notice of this intention to the French government, desiring them to consider of what would be the proper data for fixing this depreciation—we had at that time no money to pay them—but I told them it was certain we should soon have—and that the payments would necessarily be delayed until the principles for settling the depreciation should be fixed by them. A loan was opened the month after at Antwerp, by a banker whom Mr. Morris had recommended to me in such a manner as had induced my placing this confidence in him without knowing him myself—on my arrival at Antwerp some reason was given me to make me apprehend he was

not so sure as he should be—and fearing to let the money remain in his hands until the depreciation should be fixed I directed him to make the payments as he should recieve them, to the agent whom the commissaries of the treasury named for this purpose at Antwerp. I prevailed on them to do this in order to avoid the risk of bills of exchange, during a moment of uncommon fluctuation and when several capital houses at Brussels were failing—and also to avoid that loss of the depreciation which occured from the time of the bill being drawn until it was paid at Paris and which would have been the pure loss of the U.S. I have mentioned this to shew why there was not the same delay at Antwerp as at Amsterdam—the uncertainty of the banker there being the principal cause—the depreciation on these payments is not yet settled as you will see below.

4. At the time I recieved the letter from the Sec. of the treasury confiding to me the additionally delicate and dangerous task of fixing a depreciation where there was so much latitude, I knew that the President must be about nominating the Minister for Paris—the imperturbable silence and reserve which had been observed with me on this subject, for so long and painful a period,[1] made it at least doubtful whether this mark of the Presidents confidence was not reserved for some other—that alone would have made me forbear to have undertaken the settlement of the depreciation—as it was evident that so short a delay could not be prejudicial (the time of the meeting of Congress giving every reason to believe we should be immediately made acquainted with the nomination)—but another consideration presented itself which must have been conclusive with every person of delicacy, even if the task had been of the most agreeable and flattering kind. In the Presidents instructions to the Sec. of the treasury of which he sent me a copy there is a clause, which enjoins him *in making the loans to employ W. Short—and in all arrangements with France respecting their debt to employ the Minister of the U.S. at Paris for the time being.* (This is the substance and I believe the very words, although I have not the paper here with me.) Now I would ask whether with any kind of decency I could have undertaken in the face of this clause so delicate an arrangement with respect to this debt after having received the Secretary's letter relative thereto in Novr.—when I had every reason to believe that the nomination of the minister must have been previously made or at least making at that very moment[2]— but as I have observed, at the time of recieving this letter, I was setting out for Holland—and therefore nothing could have been done in it by me before my return which was on the 15th. of Janry. At that advanced season of the session of Congress I expected every day

not only to hear of the nomination being made but the arrival of the person—even if he were to come from America. I considered that if the choice fell on me, the delay from the 15th. of Jany., until I should be able to proceed to this[3] business of the French debt, would be of no importance—and that if the choice should not fall on me both duty and delicacy required that I should leave so delicate a business to the person who should possess a greater share of the President's confidence. On my return to Paris I did every thing I could with propriety to prevent delay in this business. I waited on the commissaries of the treasury, to see whether they had considered of the data for settling of this depreciation in a manner agreeable to them so as not to discredit their assignats (the Sec. of the Treasury having informed me that the matter was to be arranged so as not to create embarassment to them on this head). I told them that I expected every day a minister for Paris from the U.S.—and that that minister would settle the business with them and pressed them to be ready for him, as monies were accruing at Amsterdam, which would be detained for that purpose. They renewed their expressions of satisfaction—and told me they would not fail to be prepared.

5. As yet I have only mentioned the settling of the depreciation, as the cause of delay, (though not a sufficient cause to prevent the payments from Antwerp where I feared there was danger in leaving it in the hands of the banker)—this was however by no means the only cause of delay as you will see. Mr. Morris, from meer motives of desire to benefit the U.S. and serve the public before he was publicly employed, had had it much at heart that some method should be devised of our debt to France being appropriated to the purchase of the productions of the U.S. for the French colonies—for which kind of relief the colonists had petitioned the national assembly. It appeared to me so evidently advantageous that the debt of the U.S. should be employed in this way, that I desired it also, and was willing to do whatever was in my power to forward the design. Whilst I was absent at Amsterdam, Mr. Morris settled I believe some plan of carrying this into execution with M. de Bertrand the then minister of marine. M. de Bertrand made a report to the assembly on the subject, which I received whilst at Amsterdam and forwarded to America. M. Morris also at the request of that minister as he informed me, desired that the money might be kept at Amsterdam, until the decision of the assembly; observing that if once paid into the French treasury it might prevent the assemblys appropriating it to that object. Thus when I left Amsterdam to return to Paris, the cash in hand and coming in was inconsiderable. It was necessary and proper that the

depreciation should be settled before its being paid to France—because it then might be paid in florins to the French agents at Amsterdam—instead of being remitted by bills of exchange, at a time where there was great risk from the numerous bankruptcies[4]—in a manner where the charges were greater—and finally where there was an unavoidable loss for the U.S.—being the depreciation through which assignats passed from the day of the bill being drawn at Amsterdam until paid in Paris, which depreciation was then considerable every day[5]—and further there was evident propriety in settling the depreciation whilst the money was in our own hands rather than after the payment, in which sentiment the Sec. of the Treasury concurred as appeared by a letter received a long time after. (To understand this it should be observed that there were two sorts of depreciation, one which might be called of exchange, and the other of assignats—as it was this latter only that the U.S. were to make up, they would have had a right to have claimed more than par for their payments viz., more than six livres for every 2. florins 14. sous of Holland—this however was fully and often explained to the Sec. of the treasury—and is immaterial at present.) The reasons I have given for not settling myself this depreciation I trust will appear to you as they did to me—and besides I have shewn that I could not have done it before the 15th. of Jany. at which time the sums on hand were not greater than the demands accruing for Febry. and March. The bankers therefore were directed to suspend the payments out of the monies which were recieving on the loan until they should recieve further orders. It was then expected also daily that the assembly would adopt M. de Bertrand's report—in which case those monies would have been appropriated thereto—either being remitted to the Sec. of the treasury—or by some plan which M. Morris would have, and probably had, settled with him.

I have said that the sum in the bankers hands was inconsiderable when I left Amsterdam. I at that time considered as at my disposition only the 500,000 florins a month which were to be paid up on the loan opened in Jany. I have mentioned that $2\frac{1}{2}$ millions of the preceding loan were by the orders of the Secretary kept in their hands to answer his draughts. Under that idea I left Amsterdam, having given the orders for the suspension of the payments then supposing the suspension would be[6] unavoidably removed in a very short period, either by the nomination of the Minister for Paris—who would settle the depreciation—or by the decision of the assembly expected daily in favor of M. de Bertrands proposition for applying the debt of the U.S. to the purchase of their productions for the colonies. The Sec. of the treasury however had changed his mind as to the appropriation he had directed of the $2\frac{1}{2}$ million of florins—this change took place during the month of Nov. 91. The first of that month he wrote me in confirmation of his former letters notifying that he had drawn for one million thereof—and towards the close of that month should draw for another million counting that the loan would have been received in time to answer these draughts—this letter I received on my return to Paris the 15th. of Jany. He wrote to me a following letter on the 30th. of Nov. informing me he had changed his mind and should not draw for more than one million of florins; leaving thereby $1\frac{1}{2}$ million of his appropriation to be applied to the French debt. This letter however I did not recieve until my return to the Hague in June last, the original never came to my hands—the duplicate which I received had been sent to the Hague and kept there by M. Dumas, in the most stupid manner, because as he informed me he thought I was in Spain, and should daily arrive there—but in truth because he was in his dotage—of this delay the Sec. was informed in due time—although it was of no consequence—because had I known at the time of my leaving Amsterdam that this $1\frac{1}{2}$ million was added to the sum at the disposition of the bankers, still I should have proceeded in the same manner—viz. have suspended the payments to France therefrom, until the nomination of the Minister to Paris (to whom I then supposed under the instructions from the Prest. to the Sec. of the treasury, the settlement of the depreciation would belong) or until the assembly should have decided on M. de Bertrands proposition relative to this debt.

Thus matters stood on the 15th. of Janry.—and I think no person with the smallest spark of delicacy would have acted otherwise however great the sums on hand might have been—but it should be remembered that I acted in giving orders for suspending the payments under the idea—that there was at that time no disponible cash in fact—and could be very little—before the events daily expected to remove this suspension—for greater exactitude it should be observed that over and above the large payments to be made for interest and premium on former loans—during the months of febry. and march—a considerable sum also (I think about 300,000 florins) were to be deducted to make up the $2\frac{1}{2}$ million to be reserved out of the preceding loan for the Sec. of the treasury, as the calls on the bankers had not admitted of their keeping the complete sum of $2\frac{1}{2}$ millions out of that loan. It remains now to be seen whether I am to blame for these payments having been suspended after the 15th. of Janry.

6. At this time I was in daily expectation of hearing of the nomination of the minister—and although this had been postponed much to my astonishment, (and as things turned out still more to my humiliation)

at the preceding session of Congress, yet the arrival of the French minister in America, did not leave a doubt that it would take place at this session, and it was natural to suppose it would be early in the session. The demands which I then contemplated as existing against the cash arising on the loan were 300,000 florins to complete the sum of $2\frac{1}{2}$ million—and for which bills from the Sec. of the treasury might arrive daily—payments to be made the first of febry. for interest and premium I think about 330,000 florins. To answer these demands the undertakers were only obliged to pay by the end of Janry. 500,000 florins, although it was probable they would pay something more—and from that time no other payments could be expected till about the end of febry.—as by the usages established at Amsterdam, the undertakers have the same commencement of interest viz. from the 1st. of each month, whether the payment be made on the first or last day of the month—and of course they keep the money in their hands generally until the last of each month. Consequently it would not have been until towards the end of febry. that the bankers would have had disponible cash, and as consequently even if the causes above mentioned had not existed I could not be blamed for not having had payments made prior to that epoch. It may be observed also that 125,000 florins of the cash to be then on hand were to be paid the 1st. of March, for interest due on a former loan. In the middle of february I learned that the Prest. had placed his confidence in M. Morris with respect to French affairs and nominated him to the Senate as Minister at Paris. M: Morris was then in London and might be expected daily in Paris. No earthly consideration would have tempted me after that to have taken on me any thing in that department, which the public welfare did not imperiously and instantly exact—this could not be the case with respect to the payments to France as there was not yet disponible cash on hand. Independent of the indelicacy that there would have been in taking advantage of the distance I was removed from government, to act in a case where the head of the government had so solemnly announced that he did not repose his confidence in me, I was by no means (after being kept in[7] so long and painful a suspense and as it now appeared for the convenience of others) in a condition of mind to meditate on a subject which required calm, contentment and encouragement from an idea of governmental confidence. A rich banking house at Paris as their own agent and that of the house of Hope at Amsterdam, and others had made overtures to me for paying off our whole debt to France at one stroke and taking the bonds of the U.S. for the amount at 4. per cent interest in London and Amsterdam—and at the then rate of exchange—the advantages of this plan struck the

Sec. of the Treasury, and he expressed to me his desire it should be effectuated—which certainly would have been done if government had been less reserved with me and had let me know that I had so much of the Prest.'s confidence, as to be nominated for Paris—or even if I had not learned that that confidence was transferred to another. On that I suspended entering into the arrangement, advising that house to treat there of with Mr. Morris whom I expected daily at Paris—before his arrival a revolution took place in the exchange which frightened the bankers and deterred them from engaging in the propositions which they had made me. Such an opportunity can never again occur—and such advantages in paying off the debt—aiding France—and enlisting in the support of the American credit, the richest houses of Europe will probably never again be within our reach. Mr. Morris's nomination prevented this. Still I do not doubt his talents abilities, and services, will much more than compensate it.

I wrote to press Mr. Morris's arrival at Paris informing him of the state of affairs and the necessity of his presence. Before he arrived, a decision was taken by the assembly relative to the succours to S. Domingo and the then Minister of marine applied to me on the subject. As it did not admit of delay, it being necessary that he should know immediately whether and to what amount he could count on the American debt for immediate succour, I did not think myself justifiable in postponing it absolutely—mentioning to him therefore that I expected my successor without delay, and could wish that it should be with him that the rate of this payment should be settled (viz. what sum in livres the U.S. were to be credited for each florin or dollar paid, which was virtually settling the depreciation). That the U.S. might not however lose the advantage of having this debt laid out in their own productions, I immediately engaged that the sum of 800,000 dollars should be held by the Sec. of the treasury for this purpose at the disposition of the minister of marine—and instantly gave notice thereof to the Sec. of the treasury, that he might draw on the bankers for that sum, which I contemplated would be in hand before his draughts could arrive. In my situation I considered it a considerable effort for me to act at all in this business, as I regarded whatever related to the French debt as absolutely within Mr. Morris's jurisdiction—but knowing that he wished the debt to be applied towards succours to the French islands (although I did not know what mode he would chuse to adopt, or had formerly settled with M. de Bertrand for carrying it into execution) I thought myself bound to take the step I did, leaving the settlement of the rate of payment, to his better intelligence in all cases, and particularly one of this kind.

Immediately on taking the arrangement abovementioned with M. de la Coste the then minister of marine[8] I announced it to the Sec. of the treasury that he might commence his draughts and be ready for the demands of the minister. I did this even too soon, as it turned out, for at the next meeting which I had with M. de la Coste in order to settle the business finally, some difficulty having arisen between his department and the commissaries of the treasury, and one of his assistants having observed to him that S. Domingo having already drawn bills on the treasury, which perhaps the assembly might consider as the succour voted, and thereby preclude the ministers right of applying this additional sum, he determined to suspend this until he could obtain from the assembly an explanation of their decree—so as to enable him to apply this additional sum at least—which explanation he added he was sure he should obtain in a few days. I observed to him that I expected Mr. Morris also in a few days—and would therefore commit the matter to him,[9] as I did not doubt he would arrive before the explanatory decree. With this he was perfectly satisfied and thus the matter stopped between him and me—of which suspension I gave immediate notice to the Sec. of the treasury, that he might regulate his draughts accordingly. It having become by this means, by no means certain in my mind that the assembly would grant what the minister desired and if not it would have been improper that the Sec. of the treasury should have drawn this sum to America, it being destined for the debt to France.

Things remained in this[10] posture from April the 25th. (the date I think of my letter to the Sec. of the treasury informing him of this stoppage by the ministers chusing to have an explanatory decree) until Mr. Morris's arrival at Paris the 7th. of May. From that time I considered the business as no longer under my control and Mr. Morris seemed to consider the subject as I did and took it up as belonging to him. (This however it appears was not the intention of the Sec. of the treasury although I did not learn it from him until after the kings suspension as you will see below.) I communicated to Mr. Morris fully what I knew on these several subjects and particularly respecting the settlement of depreciation, which was now growing urgent from the apparent approach of the end of the then existing government (although we did not then suppose it was to be succeeded by a republic). Mr. Morris seemed sensible of this—and promised that no time should be lost after having been presented to the King. He observed also I think that he expected some further explanation from you, as in a letter from you which he recieved, I believe on his arriving at Paris, it appeared as if your idea was that the depreciation was to be thrown on France.[11] However this might be it was evident to me that it concerned me no further.

Mr. Morris was waiting to be installed in his functions—and M. de le Coste, for the explanatory decree, as I had given him notice of M. Morris's arrival, in order to proceed to the appropriation of the cash on hand to the succours of S. Domingo—when I recieved (on the 11th. of May previous to my leaving Paris) Mr. Hamilton's letter of I think March 21st. shewing that he should have occasion to draw a considerable sum from Amsterdam for domestic purposes[12] having changed his mind again since the date of his letter of Nov. 30. which letter had not yet come to my hands, as mentioned above. In consequence of this M. Morris and myself determined that it would be proper to hold the loan (then going on at Amsterdam, and which had been intended for France) at his disposition. This was suggested by Mr. Morris, he observing that should the minister obtain the explanatory decree and demand the 800,000 dollars in consequence of what had passed, he (Mr. Morris) would parry it by observing that the long silence of M. de le Coste had made him suppose he had changed his mind—and that the sum had been otherwise disposed of for the moment—and also that having learned that our treasury had already made advances to the French minister for succours to the islands, it became necessary to recieve further advices from thence. Of all this, notice was immediately given to the Sec. of the treasury by me I think on the 14th. of May.

Previous to my leaving Paris on the 2d. of June I recieved advices from the bankers at Amsterdam that they had succeeded in opening another loan at 4. per cent interest, to date from the 1st: of June—this placed at our disposition during the ensuing six months the additional sum of 3,000,000 of florins—so that a part of the cash on hand might again be considered as applicable to France; counting on the entry of sums on the new loan to answer such of the draughts of the Sec. of the treasury for domestic purposes[13] as might then arrive. Mr. Morris was made acquainted with this and when I left Paris matters stood as follows. (Thus far I think the delay of the payment cannot be imputed to me as a fault unless it be my fault that the Prest. should have instructed the Sec. of the Treasury, to employ the minister at Paris for the time being in arrangements to be made with respect to the French debt—that he should have given that ministry to M. Morris—and that payments under present circumstances should require a previous arrangement, to settle the depreciation—or unless it be my fault that M. de le Coste should have chosen to have an explanation on a decree passed by the assembly after so long a delay and after[14] having given

[504]

reason to expect it should be passed daily from the time of M. de Bertrands report).

When I left Paris, I say, Mr. Morris was to have fixed the basis on which payments were to be made and I was to order no further payment until that should be done—this was perfectly settled and understood between us—neither the one or the other doubted an instant of its being proper to settle the depreciation before making any further payment—and neither of us doubted (and I think no other person on earth could have doubted) of that settlement being a part of his functions, and particularly under the instructions of the President above alluded to. I did not then suppose that those instructions would be changed in order to save Mr. Morris as much [as][15] possible from such business as might expose him to public censure and to put others less favored, in this line of forlorn hope, where there was evidently much more danger than honor.

Notwithstanding I considered this business as now entirely in Mr. Morris's hands, yet wishing it to be settled advantageously for the U.S.—and feeling that it would be much better to settle it with the then existing government than any other—and being anxious also that the payments should be recommenced, I urged these points with him in the most earnest manner before leaving him—and after my arrival at the Hague, never ceased pressing and importuning him thereon by letter after letter. He gave me different causes of the delay owing to the changes of ministry. I advised him to address himself directly to the commissaries of the treasury, being a permanent body. In fine I informed him that if the depreciation were not immediately settled, I should not think myself longer authorized to suspend the payment and should give orders to the bankers to commence the remittances by bills of exchange, leaving the depreciation to future settlement between the two countries. He informed me that he had determined if the commissaries (from whom I think he had at length recieved the statement of the account he had been solliciting) did not immediately enable him to settle the business, he should direct Mr. Grand to draw on the bankers and pay into the national treasury. As this was doing nothing but employing an house the more in the business, I informed him of what had passed between the Sec. of the treasury and me on the subject of employing Mr. Grand—and advised his not doing it, but to treat himself with the commissaries, as the Sec. had formerly authorized me to do. The commissaries decided this matter by enabling Mr. Morris to direct the payment at Amsterdam—and accordingly he wrote to me on the 6th. and 9th. of August, informing me that he had at length come to an agreement with the commissaries of the treasury for ƒ1,625,000 bo.—and desiring that I would direct our bankers to pay that sum to their agent at Amsterdam. No mention was made to me of the nature of the agreement— or of the sum in livres which the U.S. were to be credited for these florins. As this depended on the rate of exchange and depreciation to be allowed, which I considered altogether under Mr. Morris's control at present, I should have proceeded immediately to have directed the payment, and the more so as the delay which had already taken place had given me a great deal of anxiety, which was increasing daily by the daily increase of the cash on hand for which the U.S. were paying a dead interest. But by a combination of unlucky circumstances I did not recieve these letters of Mr. Morris until after I knew of the King's suspension. I had gone to Amsterdam for the purpose of signing the contract and bonds of[16] the last loan. I returned from thence on the 15th.—the letters which had come to my address at the Hague and among them Mr. Morris's were forwarded to me by mistake the same day, so that I crossed them on the road from Amsterdam. They were returned to me to the Hague, the next day. My perplexity was, as you may suppose, very great, and my mortification also—to be placed under those circumstances, after so long a delay. The intelligence of the King's suspension and confusion at Paris— the knowlege that the Duke of Brunswic was to enter France the 15th.—my belief (although time has shewn it to be erroneous) that he would arrive at Paris and that the then government would cease and disperse—all this left not a doubt in my mind that the payment should not be made. I think no person on earth in his senses would have determined otherwise at that moment, there was every reason to believe that this payment would become private spoil—and that the government to come would refuse giving credit for it. I determined therefore to wait to the next day at least, being the post from France— before deciding fully—expecting I should be aided therein by a letter from Mr. Morris. I accordingly recieved a letter from him, dated the 13th. three days after the suspension, in which no hint of a counter-order of this payment, being given, I determined to direct its being made, although absolutely against my opinion, considering myself therein merely the instrument of M. Morris. It appeared to me however advisable that the precaution should be taken of expressing in the receipt that this payment was on account of the debt due by the U.S. to France and to be held at the disposition of *H. M. Christian majesty* (I should more properly have said perhaps the *King of the French* but this misnomer escaped me and could not have had any bad effect whatever M. Morris may think or say now to the contrary). I did suppose the French agent (being a Dutch banking house)[17] would consent with out difficulty to that kind of clause, for several reasons—and in that case the U.S. were as safe as they could be placed, under whatever kind of government should [emerge?][18]—and at the same time stop the interest on the amount of the payment. Should the French agent pay the sum to the commonwealth immediately—and the counter-revolution have taken place—it became an affair between that agent and the monarch. Should the agent have stopped the money in his hands until the establishment of a government, still the dispute was placed by our reciept between him and France—and the U.S. could claim credit for the payment from the time of having paid the money to that agent. Should the commonwealth be established, the same principle would have held good—or at worst they would have consented to have given credit from that time in order to purchase our consent to have removed the scruples of the French agent by changing the expression of the receipt. The agent contrary to my expectation, declined giving that kind of receipt immediately—and asked time to consider of it—which our bankers gave. This occasioned delay during which time I received several letters from M. Morris—as he was uniform in favor of the payment being made (our bankers were of the same opinion, at least one of them Mr. V. Staphorst who pressed me much thereon) I yielded my opinion and directed it to be done on the 4th. of Sep. It was executed the 5th.—although I had learned from M. Morris in the mean time that the U.S. were to have credit for 6,000,000 of livres for this payment, which shewed that it was according to the current exchange of the day in assignats, without the depreciation having been settled, and which was therefore nothing more than I could have done from the moment there were disponible cash on hand. As soon as M. Morris found there was like to be some difficulty, on account of the change of government and affairs in France, he wrote me that on examining his powers more minutely he had found that this business was committed wholly and of course exclusively to me, and of course that he would meddle no further in it—this was after the payment had been made by his desire and in consequence of his agreement—and after the matter was thus put out of my reach he refused for a long time going to the commissaries to see that they had given credit for the 6,000,000 of livres agreeably to their agreement with him—and did not do it until after our bankers had obtained that acknowlegement from the commissaries. With his usual address he directed the suspension, the payment, and every thing else respecting this debt, and in such a manner as that if necessary he may say he had nothing to do with it—and has already as it appears from your postscript, so contrived this that the Sec. of the treasury says this for him—notwithstanding all my letters to the Sec. stated and restated the matter as I have done to you, and shewed that both Mr. Morris and myself at the time of his arriving at Paris, considered the settlement of the depreciation as belonging to him absolutely—and future payments by that means, virtually, as it was proper to settle the depreciation before making them.

If it were possible I wish you would run over my correspondence with the Sec. of the treasury for the year 92. that you might see how little candor and justice there was in him to have thrown the blame of delay on me, as to these payments, and that so long after recieving my letters which stated the causes of that delay over and over again, and shewed how they did not depend on me. I have here only copies of the letters written after my arrival at the Hague in June—those written previously from Paris were dated Jan. 26. March 24. April 22. 25. May. 14. 26.—those from the Hague were June 28. Aug. 6. 30. Sep. 25. Oct. 9.—the reciepts of these were acknowleged by him Dec. 31. 92. I have read them over here and they all repeat the same thing—of course he could not be ignorant when in Jan. 93. he threw the blame on me. I hope you will be so good as to call the Presidents attention to this—what I consider still more important is the attention of my fellow citizens at large—and if necessary in order to do myself justice I shall call theirs to it—not with a desire to injure any body (notwithstanding I have been sacrificed to their promotion and honor) but that the public may know not only the truth but the whole truth. I do not suppose Mr. Hamilton has done this to injure me; but to save his favorite and that of the President, against whom he thought perhaps there would be still more malevolence than against me.

I have been so prolix in answer to the postscript of your letter that I have little space left to answer the letter itself—the fear of absolutely wearying you out at once will make me adjourn this to another opportunity, only observing for the present, that the respect which I always have had and ever shall have for your opinions, would make me now distrust mine still more with respect to the Jacobins of France, if you had been in the way of seeing and examining them with your own eyes. I will say nothing thereon at present, but appeal to time and experience—and God grant they may shew that I have been mistaken in my letters objected to. No body on earth can wish better to France than I do whatever form of government its inhabitants may give themselves—their happiness and prosperity I desire most sincerely both as a friend to humanity and citizen of America. Still I do think it was my duty in my correspondence with the government by whom I was employed to give my real sentiments and to give them freely—those letters were intended for their perusal alone—and if I decieved myself in my opinions, it was my misfortune—it would have been my crime to have given better opinions as my own, if I really possessed different ones. As to the acrimony of my style it proceeded from the sincerity of my feelings and I do think it ought not to be blamed in an official correspondence of that kind—but since it is thought otherwise, I am happy to know it, and consider it I do assure you my dear Sir, as the strongest proof of your friendship. Had I made use of the same language *in my conversations*, as the President has been informed—I should have been highly blameable, in my position. I here deny it absolutely, and, as it is difficult to prove negatives, I can only observe that I ever passed at the Hague and still am considered there by all the people with whom I kept company, as a violent Jacobin. This I did not deserve either— and indeed said as little, perhaps less than any member of the *corps diplomatique* with respect to French affairs, though I certainly felt more than any of them. I leave you to judge whether I should have had the reputation of Jacobin, if my conversations had been such as the Prest. was informed. I have some right I think to know from whence he got this very officious information—and it seems to me a little odd that he should so soon know my conversations from the Hague and blame them, from the supposition of censuring the French Jacobins, whilst he remained ignorant of Mr. Morris's words at Paris not only against the Jacobins but against the principles of the revolution— and his deeds against the constitution itself—or if he was not igno- rant of them thought proper to reward them by giving him his[19] confi- dence and making him the representative of the U.S. with the King of that constitution he always ridiculed, and went further in intrigu- ing to destroy—these things were public in Paris and published in their gazettes. Still they were unknown to the Prest. it seems.[20] I sus- pect how and why he got the information as to me. I should have supposed his caution and sagacity would have made him suspicious of the chanel—but it seems things which come through a favorite chanel, are recieved with[21] too much favor to be examined even by the most cautious. A thousand pardons for so much ennui—but unhappy, neglected and mortified, as I am, it is my only consolation to unbosom myself and disclose my feelings to a real friend. Yours   W Short

RC (DLC); at head of text: "*Private*"; at foot of first page: "Mr. Jefferson— Monticello"; with penciled note by TJ (see note 11 below); endorsed by TJ as received 21 Nov. 1793 and so recorded in SJL. PrC (DLC: Short Papers).

THE PLACE I DESIRED AT PARIS: a reference to Short's ambition to become TJ's successor as minister to France, a post that went to Gouverneur Morris instead. For a discussion of the AFFAIR OF THE SUSPENSION OF THE PAYMENTS of the American debt to France, see note to TJ to Short, 3 Jan. 1793. Alexander Hamilton's 2 Sep. 1791 letter to Short on the DEPRECIATION ON THE ASSIGNATS is in Syrett, *Hamilton*, IX, 158-62. Charles John Michael de Wolf was the Antwerp banker MR. MORRIS HAD RECOMMENDED TO ME (same, 481-2). For TJ's role in the drafting of the PRESIDENTS INSTRUCTIONS TO THE SECRETARY OF THE TREASURY on the negotiation of new foreign loans, see Opinion on Fiscal Policy, 26 Aug. 1790, and note. The letter from the SEC. OF THE TREASURY, which Short RECEIVED A LONG TIME AFTER and which he apparently construed as prospective approval of his handling of the matter of depreciation in relation to the payment of an installment on the debt to France in September 1792, was evidently that of 25 July 1792 (Syrett, *Hamilton*, XII, 103-5). Boyd & Kerr was the RICH BANKING HOUSE AT PARIS which had sought to assume the American debt to France (Short to Hamilton, 24 Mch. 1792, same, XI, 181). THE SUCCOURS TO S. DOMINGO: a reference to various abortive efforts by the French ministry in 1792 to devise a plan for using the American debt

to purchase provisions for the colony of Saint-Domingue as part of its attempt to suppress the great slave revolt there (see Gouverneur Morris to TJ, 30 Aug. 1792, and note).

¹ Preceding seven words interlined.
² Preceding eight words interlined.
³ Short initially wrote "complete the" before revising the passage to read as above.
⁴ Preceding four words interlined.
⁵ Preceding three words interlined in place of "daily augmenting."
⁶ Short here canceled "duly."
⁷ Preceding three words interlined.
⁸ Preceding five words interlined.
⁹ Short here canceled what appears to be "after the advance."
¹⁰ Short here canceled "unsettled."
¹¹ Next to this sentence TJ penciled in the margin: "no foundation for such an opinion."
¹² Remainder of sentence interlined.
¹³ Preceding three words interlined.
¹⁴ Preceding six words interlined.
¹⁵ Word omitted by Short.
¹⁶ Preceding five words interlined.
¹⁷ Parenthetical phrase interlined.
¹⁸ Word written over an erased word.
¹⁹ Remainder of text written in margin.
²⁰ Preceding two words interlined.
²¹ Short here canceled "favor."

To Jean Baptiste Ternant

SIR   Philadelphia April 5th. 1793.

I take the Liberty of enclosing to you the Copy of a Letter with the papers it refers to which I have received from Messrs. Brown, Benson & Ives, merchants of Rhode Island, complaining that their Brig Commerce commanded by Capt. Munroe with a valuable Cargo, was forcibly carried into Port au Prince, where not being able to sell the Cargo, nor permitted to proceed to any other market, a very considerable Loss was incurred. If their Case has been as is therein stated, you will be sensible, Sir, that an Indemnification from the Administration of the Colony will be no more than right, and I hope you will interpose your good Offices to procure their attention to it, and that Justice which the Complainants shall be found entitled to.

We are thoroughly sensible of the Difficulties of an Administration rigorously exact in the midst of such Troubles as at present distress the Colonies of France; We are willing to make every reasonable allowance for such Difficulties, and disposed to every friendly Office in our power. But we must be permitted to hope that they will prevent in every possible Instance all acts of irregularity and force on our Citizens and their Property, and where these cannot be avoided that a just Indemnification will be granted: these being in Truth the most certain means of securing to the Colonies the supplies of Provision they need and on the best terms. The merchant must calculate all his risks and be paid for them. To lessen these therefore, will be to cheapen his Supplies.

I will beg the Favor of you to represent to the Colony administration how much on principles both of Friendship and Interest their just patronage of our mutual Commerce is an object of desire with us. I have the Honor to be with great respect Sir, Your most obedient and most humble servant

PrC (DLC); in the hand of George Taylor, Jr., unsigned; at foot of first page: "The Minister of France." PrC of Tr (DLC); in Taylor's hand, unsigned. FC (Lb in DNA: RG 59, DL). Enclosure: Brown, Benson & Ives to TJ, 21 Mch. 1793, and enclosures thereto.

From George Washington

DEAR SIR   Mount Vernon April 5 1793.

Your Letter of the 1st instant, came to my hands[1] yesterday. I regret the indisposition of General Knox; but hope, as there is yet time for consideration of those matters I referred to the heads of the Departments, no inconvenience will result from the delay, occasioned thereby; unless it should continue much longer. At George Town, I met Mr. Randolph; and by a Letter just received[2] from Mr. Lear, I am informed that General Lincoln was expected to be in Philadelphia about the middle of this week.

I am so much surprized, and mortified at the conduct of Judge Turner, that if he should be in Philadelphia at the receipt of this Letter, and not the best evidence of his proceeding to the North-Western Territory immediately; it is my desire[3] that you will, in my name, express to him, as far as my powers will authorise you to do, that I can no longer submit to such abuses of public trust without instituting (if I have powers to set it on foot) an enquiry into his conduct. The same with respect to the Governor of that Territory. Such remissness in those Gentlemen[4] not only reflects upon the common rules of propriety; but must[5] implicate me, in the shamefulness of their conduct, in suffering it.

I *hope* the account brought by the Captain from Lisbon, had no better[6] foundation than that suggested in your Letter; for I should be sorry to receive a confirmation of it. It was prudent, however, to guard against an event which might have proved unfortunate in case of the capture of the Packet. With esteem & regard, I am Dr. Sir, Your very hble Servant   Go: WASHINGTON

RC (DLC); in the hand of Bartholomew Dandridge, Jr., signed by Washington; at foot of text: "Thos. Jefferson Esqr. Secretary of State"; endorsed by TJ as received 9 Apr. 1793 and so recorded in SJL. Dft (DNA: RG 59, MLR); in Washington's hand, except for complimentary close and signature in Dandridge's hand; the most important emendations are noted below; endorsed by Dandridge. FC (Lb in same, SDC).

[1] Preceding four words interlined in Dft in place of "I received."
[2] Preceding two words interlined in Dft.
[3] Preceding four words interlined in Dft.
[4] Preceding four words interlined in Dft in place of "conduct."
[5] Here in Dft "inevitable" is canceled.
[6] Word interlined in Dft in place of "other."

From Thomas Pinckney

DEAR SIR   London 6th. April 1793.

I inclose the Copy of a Letter from Mr. Holloway an Engraver here who by the Enquiries I have made would answer very well as Engraver to our Mint. He would be satisfied with the Salary annexed to that Office, but wishes to have some Engagement that a Provision will be made him for life in case old Age or Infirmity should incapacitate him from continuing the Duties of his Office. He has a Brother also whom he wishes to carry with him to America every way qualified according to his account for any Office in the Bank, having been employed many Years in the Bank of England; if a Person is wanted for our Bank well acquainted with the mode of transacting Business here I will make the necessary Enquiries concerning him and if judged expedient endeavour to engage him for our Establishment. I have the honor to be with great respect Dear Sir Your most obedient and most humble Servant   THOMAS PINCKNEY

RC (DNA: RG 59, DD); in the hand of William A. Deas, with complimentary close and signature by Pinckney; at foot of first page: "The Secretary of State"; endorsed by TJ as received 3 June 1793 and so recorded in SJL. PrC (ScHi: Pinck- ney Family Papers). Tr (Lb in DNA: RG 59, DD). Enclosure: Thomas Holloway to Pinckney, Newington Green near Islington, 2 Apr. 1793, setting forth his qualifications for the position of engraver to the United States Mint and the conditions under which he was willing to serve in this capacity, the most important being a pension in case of infirmity, and describing the talents of his brother in the banking business (Tr in same; Tr in Lb in same).

For the rejection of Holloway's application, see TJ to George Washington, and Washington to TJ, both 4 June 1793.

This day Pinckney also wrote a brief letter to TJ enclosing a "Copy of a Letter sent by various Conveyances" and introducing the bearer of it, "Captn. Beaulieu who served long in our Army," and whose "Services and Sufferings in our Cause engage me to give him this Introduction to you and I doubt not you will promote his Establishment among us by your Advice and Countenance" (RC in DNA: RG 59, DD, in the hand of William A. Deas with complimentary close and signature by Pinckney, at foot of text: "The Secretary of State," endorsed by TJ as received 3 June 1793 and so recorded in SJL; Tr in Lb in same). The enclosed letter has not been identified.

To James Brown

DEAR SIR   Philadelphia Apr. 7. 1793.

I expect from Mr. Donald a very small parcel of books from London this spring, and a larger one from Dublin. Both will be addressed to me, to your care. The latter one being intended for Mr. Eppes, I will beg the favor of you to deliver it to him as soon as it comes to hand. It will be certainly known by it's coming from Dublin directly.—Having intended to have gone home this spring I had not taken sufficient measures to be informed of the progress of affairs there. I have not learned whether my Bedford tobacco is got down to you, and if down whether it is shipped. If it be not shipped I should wish it to go in an American bottom if possible, or if that be impossible, then that it be ensured; as I think the information now merits credit that war is declared between France and Great Britain. This circumstance may render the market more advantageous for what gets safely to it.—I inclose you a letter I have received from Mr. Short.—Having determined to remove from this city into a small house in the country, I have packed my superfluous furniture and am putting it on board the sloop Union Capt. Bradford, which will sail from this port for Richmond the day after tomorrow. I have taken the liberty of addressing it to you, and as it is very bulky (about 1200. cubical feet) must ask the favor of you to rent or procure for me room for it in a dry[1] warehouse, as much of it can only go to Monticello[2] by water, and of course must wait till next winter, and I am not yet decided whether the whole shall not await that mode of transportation. I shall submit it to Mr. Randolph's orders. I must give you one special trouble respecting it. There are 4. particular boxes, Nos. 25. 26. 27. and 28. which contain looking glasses of very large size and value. They are carried by hand to the waterside here, and will need to be taken in a scow from on board the vessel at Rocket's,[3] to be landed as near as possible to the warehouse, and carried from the landing to the warehouse by hand. The boxes are of such a size as to require three pair of porters, who should take them on long handspikes. To this I must ask the goodness of your attention. The Captain will receive his freight here. Any other expences there I must ask you to answer. I am with great esteem Dear Sir Your most obedt. humble servt   TH: JEFFERSON

PrC (DLC); at foot of first page: "Mr. Brown." Tr (ViU: Edgehill-Randolph Papers); 19th-century copy. Enclosure not found.

[1] TJ here canceled "magazine, [or?]."
[2] Preceding two words interlined.
[3] Preceding two words interlined.

From Tench Coxe

Sunday [7 Apr. 1793]

Mr. Coxe has the honor to inform Mr. Jefferson that he has been attentive to the State of Exchange on Holland and Britain since last Monday Morning. He found that bills on England sold on that day and Tuesday at par on a credit of 60 days the *buyer* allowing the interest—and for cash at small discounts, about 1 ℔Ct. or £165 currency for £100 stg. Dutch bills were about 3/ ℔ guilder at the same time, and have continued so thro the week, tho Mr. Coxe thinks it not improbable that they might have been procured on Friday or Saturday a little lower for Cash. British Bills sold after the packet went away at $162\frac{1}{2}$ to 165 ℔Ct., par is $166\frac{2}{3}$.

The certainty of war renders it highly probable that bills will be lower early in this week, and Mr. Coxe doubts not purchases may be made as low on Monday, Tuesday and Wednesday as at the lowest Moment of the past week. He should not be at all surprized, if the orders by the British mail just received should produce great Bill drawing, and a considerable reduction of the rate of Exchange. He proposes to communicate to Mr. Jefferson the appearances of to Morrow and the next day.

He begs leave to suggest an Attention to the State of things in Holland, where the payers of bills will most probably be unable to keep themselves in order if an Invasion, and motion of the people should take place—Events, which may perhaps be indicated by the accounts by the packet.

RC (DLC); partially dated; endorsed by TJ as received 7 Apr. 1793 and so recorded in SJL.

To Francis Eppes

DEAR SIR   Philadelphia Apr. 7. 1793

According to the information contained in my letter of Mar. 17. Jack now sets out for Virginia. The circumstances which have determined the moment of his departure have been, the commencement of a term at Wm. and Mary should you accede to the proposition of his going there, and my relinquishing my house here and retiring to a small one in the country with only three rooms, and from whence I shall hold myself in readiness to take my departure [for][1] Monticello the first moment I can do it with due respect to myself. I can give you the most consoling assurances as to Jack's temper, prudence, and excellent dispositions. On these points I can say with truth every thing a parent would wish to hear. As far too as his backwardness would ever give me an opportunity of judging I can pronounce a very favorable verdict on his talents, in which I have been entirely confirmed by those who have had better opportunites of unreserved conversations with him. After all, the talent for speaking is yet untried, and can only be tried at the moot courts at the college, which I propose for his next object.

My papers being packed for removal, I am not able to look to your last letter: but I think you say in it that, instead of money, we are to receive from Cary's executor only bonds of 6. 9 and 12 months, this being the case of an execution, I do not well understand it: however I will solicit your attention to it, on my behalf, to avail me of this resource for any sum of money which it may yeald, and as early as it can be yeilded (I mean my proportion only) for a disappointment from another quarter in Virginia has so far abridged the provision I had made for winding up my affairs here, as that it will fall considerable short, and will really distress me, and perhaps subject me to mortification.—We may now give credit to the information that war is declared between France and England. If you have not sold your wheat, the moment will be favorable but It should not be overpassed, as the purchases will of course cease as soon as the chance ceases of getting them to Europe before their harvest. I hope they will let us work in peace to feed them during the continuance of their follies. Present me most affectionately to Mrs. Eppes and the family, as also to our friends at Hors du monde when an occasion offers, and believe me to be most sincerely Dr. Sir Your friend & servt.

                                              THS. JEFFERSON

Tr (MHi); 19th-century copy; at foot of text: "Mr. Eppes."

[1] Word supplied by the Editors for space left blank by copyist.

To James Madison

Th:J. to J. Madison   Philadelphia Apr. 7. 93.

We may now I believe give full credit to the accounts that war is declared between France and England. The latter having ordered Chauvelin to retire within eight days, the former seemed to consider it as too unquestionable an evidence of an intention to go to war, to let the advantage slip of her own readiness, and the unreadiness of England. Hence I presume the first declaration from France. A British packet is arrived. But as yet we learn nothing more than that she confirms the accounts of war being declared. Genest not yet arrived.—An impeachment is ordered here against Nicholson their Comptroller general, by a vote almost unanimous of the house of Representatives. There is little doubt I am told but that much mala fides will appear: but E.R. thinks he has barricaded himself within the fences of the law. There is a good deal of connection between his manoeuvres and the *accomodating* spirit of the Treasury Deptmt. of the US. so as to interest the impeachors not to spare the latter. Duer now threatens that, if he is not relieved by certain persons, he will lay open to the world such a scene of villainy as will strike it with astonishment.—The papers I *occasionally* inclose you, be so good as to return, as they belong to my office. I move into the country tomorrow or next day. Adieu your's affectionately.

RC (DLC: Madison Papers). PrC (DLC).

John NICHOLSON, comptroller general of Pennsylvania since 1782, was notorious for taking advantage of his office to engage in land and securities speculation on a grand scale. On 5 Apr. 1793 the Pennsylvania House of Representatives voted to impeach him on the grounds that he had violated a state law enacted in 1789 to reduce the Continental debt Pennsylvania had assumed in 1786 when it issued new state loan certificates in exchange for Continental securities held by its citizens. Nicholson was accused of contravening the 1789 act—which encouraged holders of the new state certificates to surrender them for federal securities—by subsequently certifying new state loan certificates he had subscribed in his name and for others as debts assumable by the state and redeeming them at the state treasury. Although the Pennsylvania Senate

acquitted him in April 1794 of all the charges, Nicholson resigned from office soon thereafter, apparently to forestall further legislative inquiries into his conduct as comptroller general (Robert D. Arbuckle, *Pennsylvania Speculator and Patriot: The Entrepreneurial John Nicholson, 1757-1800* [University Park, Pa., 1975], 5-38, 52-60; Ferguson, *Power of the Purse*, 228-30; 331). E.R.: Attorney General Edmund Randolph, who was in debt to Nicholson, subsequently refused to serve as a counsel to the prosecution or the defense in the impeachment trial. Randolph, however, did act as Nicholson's attorney before the Pennsylvania Supreme Court in the summer of 1793 in a separate suit brought by the state to recover the more than $60,000 Nicholson had received from the redemption of the abovementioned state certificates (same, 57-8). TJ had long been convinced that William DUER, the former assistant secretary of the treasury who had been confined in debtor's prison in New York since March 1792, could implicate Alexander Hamilton in unlawful speculative activities as Secretary of the Treasury (see Appendix on the first conflict in the cabinet, Vol. 18: 648-58).

Notes on Conversations with Tobias Lear and John Beckley

Apr. 7. 93. Mr. Lear called on me and introduced of himself a conversation of the affairs of the US. He laughed at the cry of prosperity and the deriving it from the establishment of the treasury: he said that so far from giving into this opinion and that we were paying off our national debt he was clear the debt was growing on us: that he had lately expressed this opinion to the Presidt. who appeared much astonished at it. I told him I had given the same hint to the P. the last summer, and lately again had suggested that we were even depending for the daily subsistence of government on borrowed money: he said that was certain, and was the only way of accounting for what was become of the money drawn over from Holland to this country.—He regretted that the Pr. was not in the way of hearing full information, declared he communicated to him every thing he could learn himself: that the men who vaunted the present government so much on some occasions were the very men who at other times declared it was a poor thing, and such a one as could not stand, and he was sensible they only esteemed[1] it as a stepping stone to some thing else, and had availed themselves of the first moments of the enthusiasm in favor of it, to pervert it's principles and make of it what they wanted: and that tho' they raised the cry of Antifederalism against those who censured the mode of administration, yet he was satisfied whenever it should come to be tried that the very men whom they called Anti federalists were the men who would save the government, and he looked to the next Congress for much rectification.

---

eod. die. Mr. Beckley tells me that a gentleman, heartily a fiscalist, called on him yesterday, told him he had been to N. York and into the prison with Duer, with whome he had much conversation. That Pintard, Duer's agent has about 100,000 D. worth of property in his hands and bids defiance: that this embarrasses Duer much, who declares that if[2] *certain persons* do not relieve him shortly, he will unfold such a scene of villainy as will astonish the world.

MS (DLC); entirely in TJ's hand; written on the other side of a sheet bearing "Anas" entry for 18 Apr. 1793 that was written on 6 May 1793. Recorded in SJPL under 5 May 1793: "Notes—nationl. debt—Lear—Beckly—Duer." Included in the "Anas."

TJ described his HINT TO THE P. in Notes of a Conversation with George Washington, 10 July 1792. He suggested LATELY AGAIN that the government was subsisting on BORROWED MONEY in his

Observations on the Questions about the Application of France, one of a group of documents on that subject printed under 12 Feb. 1793. PINTARD: John Pintard, a New York speculator and business associate of William Duer (Richard A. Harrison, *Princetonians, 1776-1783: A Biographical Dictionary* [Princeton, 1981], 93-5).

[1] Word interlined in place of "praised."
[2] TJ here began to write "some" but canceled it after writing only the first two letters.

To George Washington

SIR   Philadelphia Apr. 7. 1793.

The accounts of the last week from Lisbon, announcing an actual declaration of war by France against England and Holland, when applied to the preceding note of the British court ordering the French minister to leave London (which is generally[1] considered as preliminary to a declaration of war) now render it extremely probable that those powers are at actual war, and necessary in my opinion that we take every justifiable measure for preserving our neutrality, and at the same time provide those necessaries for war which must be brought across the Atlantic.—The British packet is arrived, but as yet we hear nothing further of the news she brings than that war is declared, and this is only a rumour here as yet. If any letters are come by her for me, they are not yet received.—You will learn by this post that our intelligence from the South as to the Indians is discouraging. We met on Tuesday last on the subject of your circular letter, and agreed in all points, except as to the power of ceding territory, on which point there remained the same difference of opinion as when the subject was discussed in your presence.—We have no further news of Mr. Genest. Mr. Dupont leaves town for France on Wednesday next. By him I shall send my dispatches for Mr. Morris.—Stocks are down @ 17/10. We determined yesterday to lay out the interest fund (about 25,000. Dollars) the only money at our disposal.—I have the honour to be with sincere attachment & respect, Dear Sir, your most obedt. & most humble servt.   TH: JEFFERSON

RC (DNA: RG 59, MLR); at foot of text: "The President of the US."; endorsed by Washington. PrC (MHi). Tr (Lb in DNA: RG 59, SDC).

The INTELLIGENCE FROM THE SOUTH consisted of reports from James Seagrove, the United States agent to the Creeks, to Secretary of War Henry Knox and the President. In the former Seagrove described two Indian raids—one by a party of thirty Lower Creeks on a store owned by Robert Seagrove in western Georgia, which resulted in the theft of goods worth more than £2,000 sterling, the murder of two Georgians, and the disappearance of a third—and noted his inability to apprehend the perpetrators. In the latter Seagrove blamed William Panton, a Spanish agent in Florida, for instigating this raid and claimed that it was part of a larger effort by Spanish authorities in East and West Florida to provoke a war between the Creeks and the United States (Seagrove to Knox, 17 Mch. 1793, and enclosures, ASP, *Indian Affairs*, I, 373-4; Seagrove to Washington, 17 Mch. 1793, DNA: RG 59, MLR; Washington, *Journal*, 108).

YOUR CIRCULAR LETTER: Washington to the Cabinet, 21 Mch. 1793. For the Cabinet's previous discussion of the POWER OF CEDING TERRITORY to the Western Indians, see Cabinet Opinions on Indian Affairs, [25 Feb. 1793], and Notes on Cabinet Opinions, 26 Feb. 1793. MR. DUPONT: François Dupont, the brother-in-law of Brissot de Warville, was the French vice-consul in Philadelphia (Eloise Ellery, *Brissot de Warville: A Study in the History of the French Revolution* [Boston, 1915], 398-401). The minutes of the meeting of the Commissioners of the Sinking Fund recording their decision to LAY OUT THE INTEREST FUND for the purchase of stock in the national debt are in Syrett, *Hamilton*, XIV, 292-3.

[1] Word interlined in place of "ever."

To Gouverneur Morris

DEAR SIR   Philadelphia Apr. 8. 1793.

My letters of the 12th. and 15th. of Mar. with your newspapers and laws were to have gone in the care of a gentleman bound to London. The papers and laws being bulky, he had sent them on to New-York, being still here himself. In the mean time Mr. Dupont's departure for France directly takes place. Of course I deliver to him the letters beforementioned and the present one. Whether we shall be able to get back the papers &c. is doubtful.—Your latest letter received is of Oct. 23. five months and a half old. In the mean time the public papers tell us the king of France has been suspended, tried and executed, a republic established, another Minister appointed to us,[1] and war declared between France, England and Holland. I have no doubt but difficulties exist for the conveyance of your letters, and I mention these things that you may be apprised of the delays, if any happen to them after they get out of your hands, and may be on your guard how you send your future letters.—There were made at Paris, partly while I was there, and partly afterwards, a set of dies for the medals given by Congress to officers, I believe they were 12. or 13 in number. There was also one made since to strike medals to be given to diplomatic characters on their taking leave of us. They were all under the care of Mr. Short, and I think he deposited them in Mr. Grand's office. They have cost the US. a great deal, and have particular value because the purposes for which they were made are not yet fulfilled. The diplomatic dies are[2] particularly wanting. I must beg the favor of you to enquire for them, and to send them here by the first very safe conveyance. Should none occur from Paris, I should think they might be sent to Mr. La Motte at Havre, with an express charge not to forward them but in an *American* vessel bound to this port, New York or Baltimore.—We have received accounts of considerable injuries lately done by the Indians on our Southern frontier. This strengthens the suspicion, not only that the Northern Indians do not mean peace, but that the Southern are leagued with them. Our Commissioners will set out in a few days for Sanduskey to try the event of negociation. I am with great esteem & respect Dear Sir Your most obedt. & most humble servt TH: JEFFERSON

RC (NNC); addressed: "A Monsieur Monsieur Morris Ministre Plenipotentiaire des E.U. d'Amerique à Paris"; endorsed by Morris. Not recorded in SJL.

For a discussion of the DIES FOR THE

MEDALS, see Editorial Note on American medals struck in France, Vol. 16: 53-66.

[1] Preceding clause interlined.
[2] TJ first wrote "medal is" before revising the passage to read as above.

From Timothy Pickering

SIR   General Post Office April 8. 1793.

To remove objections at the auditors office to the settlement of my demand for the repayment of the money paid S. Bradshaw who went express to Kentuckey for the return of the election there of President and Vice-President—be pleased to favour me with a certificate that I employed and paid him at your request. I am respectfully sir Your most obedt. servt.   TIMOTHY PICKERING

RC (DLC); at foot of text: "The Secretary of state"; endorsed by TJ as received 9 Apr. 1793 and so recorded in SJL.

To Martha Jefferson Randolph

MY DEAR MARTHA   Philadelphia Apr. 8. 1793.

Since my letter of the last week, Maria has received one from Mr. Randolph which lets us know you were all well. I wish I could say the same. Maria has for these three or four weeks been indisposed with little fevers, nausea, want of appetite, and is become weak. The

Doctor thinks it proceeds from a weakness of the stomach, and that it will soon be removed.—I learn from the head of Elk that a person of the name of Boulding set out from thence some days ago, to view my lands with an intention to become a tenant. He carried a letter from Mr. Hollingsworth, whom I had desired to procure tenants for me; not addressed I beleive to any particular person. I am in hopes he will apply to Mr. Randolph. The lands I should first lease would be the upper tract joining Key: but if enough of them would join to take the whole lands on that side of the river, they might divide them as they pleased.—I have never heard yet whether you got the servants' clothes which were sent by water. I have got all my superfluous furniture packed and on board a vessel bound to Richmond, to which place she will clear out to-day. I have written to Mr. Brown to hire a Warehouse or rather Ware-room for it, there being 1300. cubical feet of it, which would fill a moderate room. Some packages containing looking glass will have to remain there till next winter I presume, as they can only be trusted by water. Indeed I do not know how the rest will be got up. However, on this subject I will write to Mr. Randolph the next week.—War is certainly declared between France, England and Holland. This we learn by a packet the dispatches of which came to hand yesterday.   J. Eppes sets out for Virginia to-day, to go and finish his course of study at Wm. and Mary. Tell Mr. Carr his letter is just now received, and shall be answered the next week, as I am now in the throng of my removal into the country. Remember me affectionately to him, to Mr. Randolph and kiss the little ones for me. Adieu my dear. Your's most affectionately   Th:J.

RC (NNP); at foot of first page: "Mrs. Randolph"; endorsed by Mrs. Randolph. PrC (ViU: Edgehill-Randolph Papers); consists of second page only. Tr (same); 19th-century copy. Recorded in SJL under 7 Apr. 1793.

From Tench Coxe

April 9. 1793

Mr. Coxe has the honor to inform Mr. Jefferson that Dutch Bills remain difficult to procure, and that English Bills can be obtained at $162\frac{1}{2}$ ⅌Ct. being a Discount of £4.3.4 Curry. upon the £100 Stg. Mr. Coxe continues to think it extremely hazardous to remit by bills on Holland. Indeed he takes the liberty to say he would by no means risque them.

Mr. Jefferson will be able to procure such part of the sum as may not be immediately necessary upon as good or lower terms a few days hence.

The Bank is not drawing on Britain or Holland.

RC (DLC); endorsed by TJ as received 9 Apr. 1793 and so recorded in SJL.

Coxe also wrote the following note to TJ on 10 Apr. 1793: "Mr. Coxe has the honor to inclose to Mr. Jefferson a Note just received from Mr. Vaughan. He takes the liberty to observe that the bills are such as he should deem good" (RC in DLC). The enclosed note of the same date from John Vaughan to Coxe

stated: "I have ingaged Three thousand Pounds Willing Morris & Swanwicks Bills four hundred pounds Genl. Stewart and Expect to Complete the whole this afternoon. Whose order Must the Bills be to and how am I to call for the Needful. WMS I beleive would be glad of some Money immediately" (RC in DLC; at foot of text: "Exe. 162½"). See also Vaughan to TJ, with Jefferson's Note, 11 Apr. 1793.

To Alexander Hamilton

SIR   Philadelphia Apr. 9. 1793.

Having received full authority from Mr. William Short to superintend and controul the disposal of his property in the public funds, I take the liberty of desiring that no property of his of that kind, whether standing in his own name or in that of Mr. James Brown or any other person in trust for him may be permitted to be transferred or to [be][1] paid to any person whatever. I have the honor to be Sir your most obedt. humble servt   TH: JEFFERSON

PrC (DLC); at foot of text: "The Secretary of the Treasury." Tr (ViU: Edgehill-Randolph Papers); 19th-century copy.

[1] Word inadvertently omitted by TJ.

From George Hammond

SIR   Philadelphia 9th April 179[3]

On the 12th of March last I had the honor of addressing a letter to you on the subject of Mr. Pagan. As you have never *acknowledged the receipt of that letter*, I am apprehensive it may not have reached you: if that shall have been the case, I will transmit you a copy of it, and am with due respect, Sir, Your very humble servant,

GEO. HAMMOND

RC (DNA: RG 59, NL); in the hand of Edward Thornton, signed by Hammond; mutilated date supplied from Tr; at foot of

text: "The Secretary of State"; endorsed by TJ as received 9 Apr. 1793 and so recorded in SJL. Tr (Lb in same).

Concerning Hammond's 12 Mch. 1793 letter, see TJ to Edmund Randolph, 13 Mch. 1793. The present letter from Hammond, and TJ's reply printed below, may have been included in the correspondence with the British minister on the Pagan case that TJ submitted to the President on 18 Apr. 1793 and that was returned to him the next day (Washington, *Journal*, 110, 114). The case is discussed in note to Hammond to TJ, 26 Nov. 1791.

To George Hammond

SIR   Philadelphia Apr. 9. 1793.

Immediately on the receipt of your letter of March 12th. on the subject of Mr. Pagan, I referred it to the Attorney general of the US. for his opinion. As soon as I receive that opinion from him, I will do myself the honor of addressing you thereon. I am with due respect Sir your very humble servt.   TH: JEFFERSON

PrC (DLC); at foot of text: "The Minister Plenipotentiary of G.B." FC (Lb in DNA: RG 59, DL).

From Rodolph Vall-Travers

Rotterdam, Haring's Vliet, 9 Apr. 1793. By Captain William Callahan, commander of the brig *Jn. Pringle*, bound for Charleston, he encloses a copy, which he officially received yesterday morning from van Sohn, Attorney General to their Highmightinesses, of the capitulation of the French garrisons in Breda and Gertruidenberg to the Dutch, English, Prussian, and Imperial armies. The humane treatment of these plundering invaders by the allies provides a striking contrast to the "Maxims and Characters" of the French. He has also received an official communication from President De Loches of this city concerning the certain defection of General Dumouriez after the National Convention dispatched four commissaries to his army to bring him back to Paris or, as it is said, to murder him on the road thither. One of them, his friend M. Beurnonville, warned him of the danger, whereupon Dumouriez arrested the other three at camp and sent them, through the Imperial general Clerfayt, to Prince Saxe-Coburg, commander in chief of the German armies, who incarcerated them in the Mons fortress. Dumouriez has donned the white cockade of the Royalists, "who now make up the two Thirds of the Inhabitants of France, detesting the Convention and its bloody Faction of the Jacobins," and has offered to join the allied armies and restore the crown to Louis XVII, with suitable changes in the ancient form of government "in Favor of the Bulk of the People, groaning under all Kinds of Oppressions and Miseries." He hopes that this, as well as his packet of 31 Mch. by the *Hope*, Captain James Miller of Philadelphia, along with the first sketch of the latter sent as a secondary duplicate by the *Peggy*, Captain Elliot, from Amsterdam, will arrive safely. P.S. All ten provinces of the Austrian Netherlands and the bishopric of Liège have been evacuated by the French and restored to their former sovereigns and constitutions. The Austrian Netherlands would soon become a thriving state, emulating the Dutch in industry, if their governor, Archduke Charles, brother of the Emperor, became their sovereign hereditary Duke independent of Vienna, thus saving the tribute of 14 million florins sent there annually.

RC (DNA: RG 59, MLR); 3 p.; at head of text: "In Mrs. Hamilton's Lodgs.— recommended to the friendly Care of Thos. Brown Esqr. Mercht. at Rotter-dam, or of Messrs. Beerenbrock & van Dooren, at Amsterdam"; endorsed by TJ as received 27 June 1793 and so recorded in SJL.

To James Brown

DEAR SIR   Philadelphia Apr. 10. 1793.

I wrote you by the post of the day before yesterday on the subject of my furniture sent by the Union sloop, Capt. Bradford. I now inclose the bill of lading indorsed by Mr. Finlay the owner 'the freight to be paid at Philadelphia on notice of the delivery of the goods.' This was to correct the error in filling up the bills of lading as if the freight was to be paid in Richmond. The copy of the bill which the Captain has is uncorrected, because it was in his possession and he not then in the way, but he concurred in the arrangement. I will pray you to give me notice of the arrival of the goods, early, and to have attention paid to the four boxes No. 25. 26. 27. 28.

I cannot express to you the grief with which I learned yesterday the calamity of the house of my friend Mr. Donald. It was announced here by Mr. Morris's attaching their property wherever he could find it. I do not know your exact degree of connection with that house. But I sincerely wish it to be such as may make you feel the shock as little as possible. Knowing the importance, to my friend Mr. Short, of the stock which has been managed for him through that house and yourself, I know the distressing anxiety into which he will be thrown by this news. I shall have an opportunity of writing to him within a short time and should be rendered extremely happy to be able to inform him that all his public stock stands in his own name. This was the footing on which he desired it to be placed in his last letter to me, and in that which I forwarded you from him, and I shall consider it as a most particular mark of your esteem for him, and of the integraty of your character to enable me, by the return of post, to give him the consoling information that his property, the whole of his dependance, is placed in his own name, beyond the reach of all accident and claim.

With respect to my little accounts with yourself or the house of

Donald & Burton, if my tobacco is not yet shipped, I would wish it to be so in an American vessel, because I count on a fine price, considering it's quality, and the moment of war. But I would not chuse it to be so consigned as to go into the hands of Commissioners, who would not pay that attention to my interest for which I counted on the friendship of Mr. Donald. It shall be sacredly applied to cover the monies advanced on it, and I shall be glad to concert[1] with you by letter how this may be best done for all our just interests. If it could fall in my way to render any services to yourself or my friend's house it would give me pleasure, being with great & sincere esteem Dr. Sir your friend & servt   TH: JEFFERSON

PrC (DLC); at foot of first page: "Mr. Brown." Tr (DLC); 19th-century copy. Enclosure not found.

[1] TJ first wrote "consult" and then altered it to read as above.

From James Brown

DEAR SIR   Richmond 10h: April 1793
I have the satisfaction to inform you of the safe arrival of the Four friends Cap. Valance from Lisbon, by which Vessell I have letters from Messrs. John Bulkely & Sons covering Bill Loading for 3 Pipes Lisbon Wine for your Account deliverable to my Order. I have Ordered my friend to have the said Wine Entered and Sent forward to this place, judging it is intended for Montichello. I have received 18 Hhds. of your Tobacco, nothing new here. I am with Respect Sir Your Obt Hle St   JAMES BROWN

RC (MHi); endorsed by TJ as received 17 Apr. 1793 and so recorded in SJL.

From Thomas Pinckney

DEAR SIR   London 10 April 1793
I avail myself of the delay of the Ship James, by which I have already written, to send the news papers up to the present time as they contain intelligence of some importance.[1] The Armament of this country both by sea and land continues with spirit. A divi[si]on of the dominions of France is talked of in which the French W. Indies will be again allotted to Great Britain.

I have no hope of obtaining at present any convention respecting Seamen as lord Grenville now says it is necessary for them to make enquiries as to some points in America which object is given in charge to Mr. Bond. The impressment on the present occasion has not been so detrimental to our trade as it was on former occasions, though several instances of hardship have occurred which I have endeavor'd to remedy but not always with success. I send herewith a box of coins and some letters received from Mr. Diggs of Virginia now at Birmingham. You will also receive herewith the Account of Mr. Johnson our Consul at this Port—there being some articles in it which altho' they appeared to me to be equitable charges against the United States I did not think myself authorised by my instructions to pass I recommended it to him to receive payment for such part of the account as I could pass and to refer the other charges to you, he however preferred my sending the whole account to you, which you will be pleased to return with your instructions thereon. I have the honor to be with the utmost respect Dear Sir Your most faithful and obedient Servant

THOMAS PINCKNEY

I send herewith the certificate of register of the Ship Philadelphia Packet lately lost in the European Seas. I took it at the Captains request to forward to the Secretary of the Treasury and gave the Captain a receipt for it: be pleased, Sir, to obtain a receipt from the Treasury for it on my account.

Mr. Philip Wilson continues here in the utmost distress. I have urged his claim with all my industry. The treasury have at length made him an offer of £2000 on the score of compassion which he declines, his demand being for more than £18,000. I wrote not long after my arrival that I had obtained a loan of £100 for him, but I have not heard whether that measure was approved or whether I should allow him any thing for support 'till his claim shall be finally admitted or rejected which I am given to understand will take up a long time.

RC (DNA: RG 59, DD); written partly in code; decoded interlinearly, with one anomaly, by George Taylor, Jr. (see note 1 below); at foot of second page: "The Secretary of State"; endorsed by TJ as received 31 May 1793 and so recorded in SJL. PrC (ScHi: Pinckney Family Papers); lacks decipherment. Tr (Lb in DNA: RG 59, DD); written en clair with encoded sentences in brackets. Enclosures: (1) Thomas Digges to TJ, 10 Mch. 1793. (2) Same to Pinckney, Birmingham, 21 Mch. 1793, advising that "a Book of medals and Coins," intended for TJ and sent by coach from Birmingham eight days ago, would not arrive in London until this day or the day after; cautioning Pinckney to conceal from Matthew Boulton that specimens of the half pence minted by Obadiah Westwood were also being sent to TJ; and describing methods used in England to debase the Spanish dollar, as well as the coins and paper of other countries, that threatened to have adverse consequences for America. (3) Same to same, 6 Apr. 1793, stating that Boulton's coining apparatus would be the best security against counterfeiting in the United States and recapitulating his account of counterfeiting practices in England (RCs in DLC; printed in Robert H. Elias and Eugene D. Finch, eds., *Letters of Thomas Attwood Digges [1742-1821]* [Columbia, S.C., 1982], 449-56). For the certificate of registry, see TJ to Pinckney, 4 June 1793, and note. Other enclosure not found.

For a discussion of the case of PHILIP WILSON, see TJ to Thomas McKean, 23 Dec. 1790, and note. TJ submitted this letter to the President on 1 June and the enclosures on 12 June 1793 (Washington, *Journal*, 158-9, 169).

Pinckney also wrote a brief note to TJ on 15 Apr. 1793 in which he enclosed

"the Gazette containing the Proclamation on our Intercourse and the Leyden Gazette received since my last" (RC in DNA: RG 59, DD, endorsed by TJ as received 5 June 1793 and so recorded in SJL; PrC in ScHi: Pinckney Family Papers; Tr in Lb in DNA: RG 59, DD). One of these enclosures was the 9-13 Apr. 1793 issue of the *London Gazette*, which contained the text of a royal proclamation of 10 Apr. setting forth the conditions under which United States ships could trade with Great Britain (DNA: RG 59, MLR; endorsed by Pinckney).

[1] The remainder of the paragraph is in unidentified code, the text being supplied from Taylor's decipherment.

From David Rittenhouse

Dr. Sir   Wednesday Morn [10 Apr. 1793]

Mr. Misho called on me Yesterday, he wishes to know whether he is to prepare for his journey, and that instructions be prepared for him if he goes. This I hope you will do. Will it be proper to call a meeting of the Society, or shall we have a meeting of a few individuals who are interested in this business? He says 3 or 4 Hundred dollars put into his hands at present will be sufficient. Yours &c

D. RITTENHOUSE

RC (DLC); partially dated; addressed: "Mr. Jefferson"; endorsed by TJ as received 10 Apr. 1793 and so recorded in SJL.

MR. MISHO: André Michaux. THE SOCIETY: American Philosophical Society.

To Henry Skipwith

My dear Sir   Philadelphia Apr. 10. 1793.

I have but a moment before the departure of post to inform you that we learnt from Mr. Morris yesterday the failure of the house of Donald & Burton. Keep it secret if you please, my only object in communicating it being to induce you to go post to Richmond on behalf of our friend Mr. Short and induce Mr. Brown to place all Mr. Short's paper in the public funds in Mr. Short's own name. It stands at present I believe in that of Mr. Brown himself or of Donald & Burton.

[527]

You know his all depends on this, and I am sure will not begrudge the trouble of a journey which may save his all. You know the efficacy of personal sollicitations, and that a moment sooner or later saves or loses every thing on these occasions. I have written to Mr. Brown by this post, as I know that Mr. Short had desired the transfer of his stock to be made to his own name in a late letter. My best love to Mrs. Skipwith & family & am with great & sincere esteem Dr. Sir your affectionate friend & servt   TH: JEFFERSON

PrC (DLC); at foot of text: "Mr Skipwith." Tr (DLC); 19th-century copy.

From Elias Vanderhorst

Bristol, 10 Apr. 1793. He has not heard from TJ since sending his last letter of 31 Dec. by the *Charles* via New York and a duplicate by the *Fabius* via Philadelphia. The enclosed accounts of imports and exports in American ships here for the last half of 1792 would have been sent sooner, but he only recently learned that TJ expected them. To ensure more accurate accounts, he suggests that TJ consider requiring masters of American vessels to show their registers and manifests to consuls upon arrival in England, as they have no authority to demand these documents and must take much trouble and expense to obtain the information from the customhouses. He encloses a price current for American products in Bristol, which will remain open for wheat at a duty of 2/6 per quarter until 15 May, although there is no telling how much longer it will be admitted. In the last two months there has been, in addition to a stagnation in commerce and construction here, an uncommon number of business and banking failures here and throughout the kingdom, which must lead to an increase in immigration to America. The enclosed letter from Pinckney received on 6 Apr. will save him the trouble of communicating political news. *12 Apr. 1793.* He cannot send the shipping accounts by the *Dolphin* with this letter and three of the latest newspapers because the customs collector refuses to deliver them without permission from the Commissioners of the Customs, a clog which is symptomatic of the delay and expense entailed in dealing with almost all the public offices here. He did not procure his exequatur from Lord Grenville's office until 10 Feb., although he had submitted his commission long before, and then had to pay £6.16.6 for it. These circumstances show the propriety of obliging masters of American vessels to bring their registers and manifests to the consuls.

RC (DNA: RG 59, CD); 3 p.; addressed: "Thomas Jefferson Esquire. Secretary of State, Philadelphia"; endorsed by TJ as received 4 June 1793. Enclosures: (1) Thomas Pinckney to TJ, 5 Apr. 1793. (2) "Price Current of American produce at Bristol," 12 Apr. 1793 (MS in same; in a clerk's hand, signed by Vanderhorst).

To Thomas Leiper

SIR   Philadelphia Apr. 11. 1793.
   According to an arrangement with Mr. Wilson, who was to succeed
me in your house, I have continued in it till now. We have at length
got every thing out of it except an article which will be taken away
to-day or tomorrow. The coachman's wife also who happened to lay
in on Sunday last, has Mr. Wilson's permission to remain till she can
safely remove.   I have had every repair made which according
to the information of the workmen ought to be made by the tenant,
and have employed, where I could do it, the very workmen who built
the house, taking it for granted they would make a point of restoring
things to the best state. They have all finished except the plaisterer
who had some nail holes to fill in two rooms this morning. I shall be
obliged to you to visit the house, and drop me a line if you think I
have put it into a proper state, in which case I shall immediately give
you an order for the rent. If the note is lodged at my office I shall get
it at whatever hour I may happen to come to town. I am Sir your very
humble servt   TH: JEFFERSON

PrC (DLC); at foot of text: "Mr. Lieper." Tr (DLC); 19th-century copy.

MR. WILSON: United States Supreme Court Justice James Wilson, to whom TJ was relinquishing the Market Street residence where he had lived while in Philadelphia since 1790 (TJ to James Wilson, 17 Apr. 1793).

To Fontaine Maury

SIR   Philadelphia Apr. 11. 1793.
   The law concerning Consuls requiring that they should give bond
and security for the due discharge of their office, Mr. James Maury has
inclosed me his own bond, and referred me to you to obtain security
for him. I therefore take the liberty of inclosing to you a blank bond
which I shall be obliged to you to have filled up by two responsible
persons and to be so good as to return it to me. I am Sir your very
humble servt   TH: JEFFERSON

PrC (DLC); at foot of text: "Mr. Fontaine Maury. Fredericksburg." Tr (DLC); 19th-century copy.

Fontaine Maury (1761-1824), a Fredericksburg merchant, was the brother of James Maury, the American consul in Liverpool (VMHB, XXVII [1919], 376). For the consular bond signed by Fontaine Maury on his brother's behalf, see note to James Maury to TJ, 19 Sep. 1792. According to SJL, Fontaine Maury wrote

[529]

a letter to TJ on 16 Jan. 1794; the same source records that TJ wrote three letters to Maury between 6 May 1799 and 21 Apr. 1800 and that Maury wrote four to TJ. None of these letters have been found.

From Gouverneur Morris

DEAR SIR   Paris 11 April 1793

An Opportunity presents itself which I make Use of to transmit Copy of my Letter of the first to Monsieur Lebrun with that of his Answer of the eighth and of the Decrees which were therein enclos'd viz of the eighteenth of February and twenty sixth of March. I have not sufficient Confidence in the Conveyance to give you any Information beyond what you will derive from the News Papers of which I shall send a Packet. Accounts from the Northward are contradictory and uncertain. The Enemy was however ready for Action three Days ago and therefore I presume that we shall hear of him presently. I am with Esteem & Respect Dear Sir your obedient Servant

GOUV MORRIS

RC (DNA: RG 59, DD); at head of text: "No. 28"; at foot of text: "Thomas Jefferson Esqr Secretary of State"; endorsed by TJ as received 9 Sep. 1793 and so recorded in SJL. FC (Lb in DLC: Gouverneur Morris Papers). PrC of Tr (DNA: RG 59, MD); in a clerk's hand; at head of text: "Duplicate." Tr (Lb in same, DD). Enclosures: (1) Morris to Lebrun, 1 Apr. 1793, enclosing the forms of the certificates of registry for American vessels, describing the conditions under which the United States grants such certificates in accordance with a 1789 act of Congress, promising to forward a copy of a 1793 registration act as soon as he has received one, and asking for a copy of the decrees of the National Convention mentioned in Lebrun's 29 Mch. 1793 letter. (2) Lebrun to Morris, 8 Apr. 1793, promising to forward Morris's letter to the Minister of Marine so that it can be made known in French ports, observing that it would be desirable for American vessels to be furnished with passports similar to the model annexed to the 1778 treaty of commerce, and stating that he had requested Genet to ask the United States to issue a regulation to this effect. (3) Decree of the National Convention regulating the trade of American vessels with France and her colonies, [19] Feb. 1793. (4) Decree of the National Convention regulating American trade with French colonies in America, 26 Mch. 1793 (Trs in DNA: RG 46, Senate Records, 3d Cong., 1st sess., in French and English; PrCs in DNA: RG 59, MD; Trs in Lb in same, DD; in French and English).

To David Rittenhouse

DEAR SIR   Philadelphia Apr. 11. 1793.

I received yesterday your note on the subject of Michaud's instructions, and think it would be better to have a meeting of the society that they may accept the charge proposed to them by the subscribers, and may appoint a committee to draw instructions, and a person to collect the fourth of the subscriptions and pay it to Mr. Michaud. My attendance on the society will be precarious, as it must depend on the weather: but I hope you will attend and have the thing done right. I am Dear Sir your's affectionately   TH: JEFFERSON

RC (PPAmP); addressed: "Mr. Ritten-house." PrC (DLC). Tr (DLC); 19th-century copy.

For the sequel, see Editorial Note on Jefferson and André Michaux's Proposed Western Expedition, at 22 Jan. 1793.

From John Vaughan, with Jefferson's Note

Thursday. 11 April 1793

M. Vaughan informs Mr. Jefferson that he has purchased Bills for about 15,000 Dollars and expects in an hour to complete the 20,000. He wishes to know to what order they are to be drawn, and as the parties only draw to answer pressing demands, M. V. will request that he may know as early as Convenient this morning, where to send for the money.

3000	13,000	Willing Morris & Swanwick
400	1 733.33	Walter Stewart
600	2 600.	Robt. Gilmore favor Mordecai Lewis
4000	17 333.33	

[*Note by TJ:*]
Apr. 11. 1793. drew checks on the bank for the above sums, in favor of W. M. & S. of W.S. and of M.L. or bearer, and delivered them to Mr. Vaughan.

RC (DLC); dateline precedes list of bills of exchange; with note at foot of text by TJ.

Vaughan enclosed the above letter in an undated note written from "No 115 So Frt Street" to the Department of State requesting that it "may be Sent out to M. Jefferson if he is not likely to be in Town by Ten O'Clock unless some of the Gentlemen in the Office may have received Directions which May enable them to reply" (RC in DLC; addressed: "To be opened At Secretary of States Office";

endorsed by TJ as a letter to the Department of State received 11 Apr. 1793). Vaughan, a Philadelphia merchant, was purchasing BILLS of exchange on TJ's behalf for remittance to England in order to carry out the act for intercourse with foreign nations, which provided for the overseas expenses of the Department of State (Report on the Fund for Foreign Intercourse, 18 Apr. 1793, and note; TJ to Thomas Pinckney, and to Willink, Van Staphorst & Hubbard, both 12 Apr. 1793). The three checks drawn by TJ on the cashier of the Bank of the

United States, all dated 11 Apr. 1793, were, respectively, for $13,000 payable to Willing, Morris & Swanwick for their bill of exchange of £3,000 sterling; for $1,733.33 payable to Walter Stewart for his bill of £400 sterling, and for $2,600 payable to Mordecai Lewis for Gilmor's bills totaling £600 sterling (FCs in DLC; entirely in TJ's hand).

To David Humphreys

DEAR SIR   Philadelphia Apr. 12. 1793.

As your drawing for the whole sum of 123,750. florins placed in the hands of our bankers at Amsterdam for the purpose now committed to your care, would, if done at short notice, leave a void for the ordinary purposes of our foreign legations, I must beg the favor of you to draw your bills for the last half of that sum, at *so many days sight* as may give them time to provide themselves by draughts on a fund which I now place in London for that as well as other purposes, and I subject it to the orders of Mr. Pinckney. I think that for this part of your draughts you would do well to give advice both to him and our Amsterdam bankers, as early as you can after drawing, that there may be full time to transfer the money from London to Amsterdam should it be necessary.

Capt. Cutting has been delayed, in order that he might go by an American ship, as the war between France, Great Britain and Holland became known here before his departure. Nothing new has occurred since my last. I am with great & sincere esteem Dear Sir your most obedt. & most humble servt   TH: JEFFERSON

RC (NjP: Andre deCoppet Collection); at foot of text: "Colo: Humphreys"; endorsed by Humphreys. PrC (DLC). FC (Lb in DNA: RG 59, DCI). Enclosed in Report on the Fund for Foreign Intercourse, 18 Apr. 1793.

For the PURPOSE NOW COMMITTED TO YOUR CARE, see TJ to Humphreys, 21 Mch. 1793.

TJ submitted this letter to the President on 18 Apr. 1793, and Washington returned it the next day (Washington, *Journal*, 110, 114).

From James Madison

DEAR SIR   Orange April 12. 1793

Your favor of the 31. ult: and the preceding one without date have been received. The refusal of Dunlap in the case you mention confirms the idea of a combined influence against the freedom of the Press.

If symtoms of a dangerous success in the experiment should shew themselves, it will be necessary before it be too late to convey to the public[1] through the channels that remain open, an explicit statement of the fact and a proper warning of its tendency. In the mean time it is perhaps best to avoid any premature denunciations that might fix wavering or timid presses on the wrong side. You say that the subject of the 3 Mil. flos. is to be revived. Have you discovered in what mode; whether through the next Congs., or thro' the press; and if the latter, whether avowedly or anonymously. I suspect that the P. may not be satisfied with the aspect under which that and other parts of the fiscal administration have been left.

As far as I can learn, the people of this country continue to be united and firm in the political sentiments expressed by their Reps. The reelection of all who were most decided in those sentiments is among the proofs of the fact. The only individual discontinued, is the one who dissented most from his colleagues. The vote at the election stood thus—for R. 886—S. 403—W. 276. *It is said* that the singular vote on assuming the balances, gave the coup de grace to his popularity. We were told at Alexa. that if the member for that district had been opposed, his election would have failed; and at Fredg. that a notice of G's vote on the resolutions of censure had nearly turned the scale against him. I have seen and conversed with Mr. F. Walker. I think it impossible he can go otherwise than right. He tells me that I. Cole, and not Clay as in the Newspaper is elected for the Halifax District. Hancock, is the new member from the district adjoining Moore; and Preston for that beyond him. I fell in with Mr. Brackenridge on his way to Kentucky. He had adverted to Greenup's late vote with indignation and dropped threats of its effect on his future pretentions.

The sympathy with the fate of Louis has found its way pretty generally into the mass of our Citizens; but relating merely to the man and not to the Monarch, and being derived from the spurious accounts in the papers of his innocence and the bloodthirstyness of his enemies, I have not found a single instance in which a fair statement of the case, has not new modelled the sentiment. "If he was a Traytor, he ought to be punished as well as another man." This has been the language of so many plain men to me, that I am persuaded it will be found to express[2] the universal sentiment whenever the truth shall be made known.

Our feilds continue to anticipate a luxuriant harvest. The greatest danger is apprehended from too rapid a vegetation under the present warm and moist weather. The night before last it received a small[3] check from[4] a smart frost. The thermometer was down at 37° and we were alarmed for the fruit. It appears however that no harm was done. We have at present the most plentiful prospect of every kind of it.

Will you be so good in case an opportunity should offer to enquire of Docr. Logan as to the plows he was to have made and sent to Mrs. House's; and to repay there what may have been advanced for those and two or three other Articles that were to be forwarded to Fredg. by water. I forgot to make the proper arrangements before I left Philada. Adieu Yrs. Affy.

RC (DLC: Madison Papers); unsigned; endorsed by TJ as received 22 Apr. 1793 and so recorded in SJL.

R.: Robert Rutherford, a Virginia member of the House of Representatives from 1793 to 1797 (*Biog. Dir. Cong.*). S.: John Smith, a Virginia state senator who subsequently served in the House of Representatives from 1801 to 1815 (same). W.: Alexander White, the defeated incumbent congressman for the district consisting of Frederick and Berkeley Counties, was the only member of the Virginia delegation to vote on 28 Jan. 1793 in favor of a bill for the additional assumption of state debts (JHR, I, 683-4). Richard Bland Lee, a moderate supporter of Hamiltonian measures in the House of Representatives, was the candidate whose bid for reelection supposedly WOULD HAVE FAILED if Republicans had opposed it (Norman K. Risjord, *Chesapeake Politics*, *1781-1800* [New York, 1978], 346, 391, 405-6). G'S VOTE: Samuel Griffin, a Federalist congressman from Virginia, had voted against two, abstained on three, and supported only one of William B. Giles's RESOLUTIONS OF CENSURE against Alexander Hamilton (JHR, I, 727-30). GREENUP'S LATE VOTE: apparently a reference to Kentucky Representative Christopher Greenup's opposition to two and abstention on four of the Giles resolutions on which the House of Representatives voted (same). Greenup continued to serve in the House until 1797 (*Biog. Dir. Cong.*). For a more detailed description of these electoral matters, see Madison, *Papers*, XV, 8n.

[1] Preceding three words interlined.
[2] Preceding five words interlined in place of "expresses."
[3] Word interlined.
[4] Madison here canceled "the attack of."

To Thomas Pinckney

DEAR SIR   Philadelphia Apr. 12. 1793.

Since my letters of the 15th. 16th. and 20th. of Mar. which go by Capt. Cutting I have received yours of Jan. 31. Feb. 10. and 11. You will recieve with this a new Cypher, as it would be improper to use the old one again should it come back to you. The cyphered paragraph of Jan. 1. was to desire you to be very watchful over the embarcation of troops to Canada, and to give us immediate and constant information thereof. A determination will soon be formed as to the manner of furnishing our ships with passports. It will occur to you that some danger would attend the trusting blank passports across the sea in a time of war.

We now learn with certainty that Gr. Britain and Holland are engaged in the war. The dangers which this may bring on Amsterdam render caution necessary in making new deposits of money there: and as the draughts of Colo. Humphreys, should they extend to the whole 123,750. florins deposited in the hands of our bankers for a particular purpose, would leave a void for the current purposes of our foreign legations, I am endeavoring to make a remittance by the present occasion of about 20,000 Dollars. This I find can only be done to advantage in London bills; and considering the incertainty in which we are as to the present security of Amsterdam from invasion, I find myself obliged to have this remittance made subject to yourself altogether, to deposit it wheresoever safety and advantage shall direct. If these are in favor of Amsterdam, equally with any other place, that is to be preferred; because no change should be made of the place and persons of deposit, without a preponderance of cause. But if that place be not safe, or if the money cannot be transferred there without sensible loss, then place it in some safe deposit in London, and take such arrangements for remitting any advances our bankers at Amsterdam may have made, or may hereafter make for the department of state, as may be approved by them and yourself. Notify also, in this case, Messrs. Morris, Carmichael and Short how, and on what place and person they are to draw in future, as also Colo. Humphreys as to the expences of his legation at Lisbon: and be so good as to apprise the department of state of your arrangements that a proper correspondence may be opened with the persons with whom you make the deposit, should future remittances be made in the same way. Indeed some further remittance will be necessary before I can hear from you on this subject.

I recommended to you in a late letter the sending the Leyden gazettes brought by every Dutch mail, to be put immediately into the letter bag of the first ship bound from London to this place, Baltimore or New York: to which may be added every other port from N. Hampshire to Virginia inclusive, our posts being so far well regulated. In the present interesting times, it is most desireable to receive this gazette as quickly as possible to relieve us from the torment of the English newspapers, whose lies suffice to teaze while their truths (because doubted) can give no satisfaction.

The letter you inclosed to Mr. Genest shall be taken care of: but as yet we have not even heard of his embarcation. I am with great & sincere esteem Dear Sir Your most obedt. & most humble servt

TH: JEFFERSON

P.S. Apr. 12. Your letter of Jan. 3. is this moment received. I now inclose herein the following bills of exchange, viz.

Willing Morris & Swanwick for	£3000	13,000 Doll.
on John & Francis Baring & co. London.		
Walter Stewart on Joseph Birch. mercht.		
Liverpool	400	1,733.33
Robert Gilmer & co. on James Strachan &		
James Mackenzie London, indorsed by		
Mordecai Lewis	200	
do.	150	2 600.
do.	250	
	4000. =	17,333.33

RC (William M. Elkins, Philadelphia, 1945); at foot of first page: "Mr. Pinckney"; endorsed by William A. Deas. PrC (DLC); lacks postscript. PrC (DLC); consists of last page only with postscript; at foot of text in ink: "Pinkney Thos." FC (Lb in DNA: RG 59, DCI). Enclosures: Bills of exchange payable to Pinck-ney, as listed above by TJ, 2, 11 Apr. 1793 (printed forms, with amounts, drawers, payers, and payees inserted, in DLC; consisting of second and later sets of exchange). Enclosed cipher not found. Letter enclosed in Report on the Fund for Foreign Intercourse, 18 Apr. 1793.

To Thomas Pinckney

DEAR SIR   Philadelphia Apr. 12. 1793.

I have duly received your *private* letter of Feb. 10. and am very sensible of the friendly sentiments you are so good as to express on the event of my retiring. I have, for particular reasons, deferred it for some time, but not for a long one. However I am sure you will be secure of a friendly correspondence with my successor, whoever he may be. I think it very certain that a[1] decided majority of the next Congress will be actuated by a very different spirit from that which governed the two preceding Congresses. Public faith will be cherished equally, I would say more, because it will be on purer principles: and the tone and proceedings of the government will be brought back to the true spirit of the constitution, without disorganising the machine in it's essential parts.—Continue if you please the general address I formerly recommended 'to the Secretary of state &c.'   I shall thank you most sincerely for the model of the threshing machine, besides replacing the expence of it. The threshing out our wheat immediately after harvest being the only preservative against the weavil in Virginia, the service you will thereby render that state will make you to them a second

Triptolemus. Adieu my dear Sir, & be assured of every sentiment of friendship & respect from your's affectionately   TH: JEFFERSON

RC (Henry Myers, Detroit, Michigan, 1949); at head of text: "Private"; at foot of text: "Mr. Pinckney"; endorsed by William A. Deas. PrC (DLC). Tr (DLC); 19th-century copy.

TRIPTOLEMUS: the inventor of agricul-

ture and the plow in classical mythology (H. B. Walters, ed., *A Classical Dictionary of Greek and Roman Antiquities, Biography, Geography, and Mythology* [Cambridge, Eng., 1916], 1026-7).

[1] TJ here canceled "very."

From Edmund Randolph

SIR   Philadelphia April 12th. 1793.

You will perceive from the two letters marked A and B, of which I enclose copies, that the subject of Mr. Pagan has been for some time in my view. The former of those letters being intended for you, and containing a summary of facts; I determined to shew it to Mr. Tilghman, who was Pagan's Counsel, before it was sent to you, in order that he might correct any mistatement. This produced the latter letter from him to me; and I have thought it more adviseable to forward both of them to you, even in the unfinished state of my own, than to reduce the case into a form, which might be supposed to be less accurate.

As I do not discover an essential difference between Mr. Tilghman and myself, I shall not discuss any seeming variance, but proceed upon his ideas.

It is too obvious, to require a diffusive exposition, that the application for a writ of error was not only prudent, but a duty, in Pagan. To this Mr. Tilghman explicitly assents, when he says, that he was perfectly "satisfied of the prudence of applying for the writ of error, as Pagan could not complain of a defect of justice, until he had tried the writ of error and found that mode ineffectual." This remark becomes the more important, as it manifests, that the process was not suggested, as an expedient for shifting any burthen from the Government. Indeed I may with truth add, that the proceedings, taken collectively, appeared to me to present a sufficient intimation of the main question, to serve as a ground of decision.

However, take the case under either aspect, as excluding, the consideration of the main question by an omission in the pleadings and record; or as exhibiting it fully to the cognizance of the Court.

It never was pretended, that a writ of error ought to have been granted, unless the matter was apparent on the record. Whose Office was it to make it thus apparent? Of the attorney who managed the pleadings. If therefore he has failed to do so, we may presume, that he considered the ground untenable, or was guilty of inattention. Either presumption would be fatal to a Citizen of the United States; and the condition of a foreigner cannot create a new measure in the administration of justice. It is moreover certain; that those, who have been consulted on Pagan's behalf, as well as others, have seriously doubted, whether a cause, which has been pursued to the extent which his had reached before the commencement of our new Government, was susceptible of federal relief.

The last observation opens the inquiry, what remedy ought the Supreme Court of the United States to have administered, even if the question had been fairly before them? My opinion is, that the very merits are against Mr. Pagan. In America the construction of the Armistice has been almost universally to compute the places, within which different times were to prevail, by latitude only. Am I misinformed, that such an interpretation has been pressed by *our* Ministers, and not denied by those of *London*? A second mode has been adopted by describing a circle; and thereby comprehending longitude as well as latitude: Now let either rule be adopted; and the position of the Capture in this case will be adverse to Pagan's pretensions.

But what can be exacted from our Government, after repeated trials, before various jurisdictions, none of which can be charged with any symptom of impropriety, and upon a subject, which to say no more, is at least equipoised? Nothing—And I appeal to the British reasoning on the Silesia loan as supporting this sentiment in the following passages. "The law of nations, founded upon justice, equity, convenience and the reason of the thing, and confirmed by long usage, do not allow of reprisals, except in case of violent injuries, directed and supported by the State and justice absolutely denied, in re minime dubiâ, by all the tribunals and afterwards by the prince." "Where the Judges are left free, and give sentence according to their conscience, tho' it should be erroneous, that would be no ground for reprisals. Upon doubtful questions different men think and judge differently; and all a friend can desire is, that justice should be as impartially administered to him, as it is to the subjects of that prince, in whose Courts the matter is tried." Under such circumstances, a Citizen must acquiesce. So therefore must Pagan; against whom even the Court of Nova Scotia, within the dominions of his own sovereign, has once decided.

There are many smaller points, arising from the controversy, which might be relied on. But I pass them over, from a hope, that the observations, already made, will induce you to think with me, that

Government is not bound to interpose farther in the behalf of Pagan. I have the honor, sir, to be with respect & esteem yr. mo. ob. serv.

EDM: RANDOLPH

RC (DNA: RG 60, Letters from and Opinions of the Attorneys General); in a clerk's hand, with complimentary close and signature by Randolph; at foot of text in Randolph's hand: "The Secretary of State." PrC of Tr (DLC); in a clerk's hand. Tr (Lb in PRO: FO 116/3). Tr (same, 5/1). Enclosure: Randolph to TJ, 15 Mch. 1793. Other enclosure printed below. Letter and enclosures enclosed in TJ to George Hammond, 18 Apr. 1793.

For a discussion of the case of the Loyalist Thomas Pagan, which hinged on the issue of whether or not one of his privateers had captured an American merchant ship in conformity with the terms of the January 1783 Anglo-American ARMISTICE agreement, see George Hammond to TJ, 26 Nov. 1791, and note. On 18 Apr. 1793 TJ submitted Randolph's letter, and the letter from Edward Tilghman to him printed below, to the President, who returned them the next day (Washington, *Journal*, 110, 114).

SILESIA LOAN: In 1752 Frederick the Great refused to pay British bondholders the final installment of £45,000 on a loan

that the Emperor Charles VI had originally contracted in 1735 on the security of his revenues from the Duchy of Silesia. The Prussian monarch, who had assumed the obligation to repay this loan in connection with his conquest of Silesia, took this step in retaliation for the British government's failure to redress his grievances about British captures of Prussian ships and cargoes in the latter years of the War of the Austrian Succession. The British contended, in turn, that their admiralty courts had properly decided the cases in question according to prevailing norms of international law. This matter was finally resolved in 1756 when, as part of the celebrated reversal of alliances that heralded the coming of the Seven Years War, Frederick agreed to make the final payment on the loan in return for a payment of £20,000 by the British government in compensation for Prussian maritime claims (Ernest Satow, *The Silesian Loan and Frederick the Great* [Oxford, 1915], 1-46, 73-6, 179-99). The BRITISH REASONING on this dispute comes from a 1753 report of the law officers of the crown (same, 73, 82-3).

ENCLOSURE

Edward Tilghman to Edmund Randolph

Sir   Philadelphia March 19th. 1793.

The first application to me on the part of Mr. Pagan was accompanied with the proceedings of the Supreme judicial Court of Massachusetts to the 3d. Tuesday of June 1789 inclusive; my opinion was requested, whether the Judgment then given was liable to an appeal to, or writ of error from, the Supreme Court of the United States. I was clearly of opinion, that there could with propriety be no such appeal made or writ of error granted. When my opinion was thus requested I knew not that application had been made on Pagan's behalf to the Government of the United States. I received the first intimation of such application from yourself, when you informed me that there had been subsequent proceedings in Massachusetts of which you shortly afterwards furnished me with an abstract. Before the abstract came into my hands I wrote Messrs. Jos. Anthony & Son, that you was to let me have an abridgement of all the documents in your possession relative to the business, which might possibly induce me to think that a writ of error ought in strict legal propriety to be sued out; that from your verbal communication I was perfectly satisfied of the prudence of applying for the writ of error, as Pagan could not complain of a defect of justice, until he had tried the writ of error and found that mode ineffectual. Accordingly application was made to a Judge— the writ was refused—I rather think, the Record, as it was exhibited to me, was laid before the Judge, with your abstract of the subsequent proceedings; of this however I am not positive. Be it as it may, you recommended a second application, and that it should be made while the Supreme Court was sitting, in order to give the Judge an opportunity to consult his Brethren on the subject. The writ was then awarded, but the Clerk of the Supreme Court having omitted the word "Judicial" in the stile of the Court of Massachusetts, no return was made to the writ. When the Clerk called the action on the first Tuesday of the last Supreme Court, Chief Justice Jay read a letter from the Chief Justice of Massachusetts, stating the misdirection of the writ, and adding in very respectful terms, that when a writ came properly directed, it should be taken into consideration. I then briefly mentioned that I should during the Session address the Court on the subject. On the second friday of the Supreme Court after you had closed your argument in Pepoon a Jenkins, I broke the business to the Court without making any specific motion, but the Court said that without a motion, they should consider nothing. I then replied that in the morning I should move for a writ of error (not an alias) but should wish to be heard against my own motion. One of the Justices expressed his surprise that I should argue against my own motion, and I answered I hoped to be able from the particular circumstances of the case to satisfy the Court of the propriety of my conduct; to this the same Judge replied in the very words you have used. At this time one of the Justices observed that he had been for granting the writ under the idea that a writ of error was of right, but that now he was of opinion, it ought to appear that the Court had Jurisdiction. On the next day I moved for a writ of error, having in my hand all the proceedings in Massachusetts, declaring that out of respect to what fell from one of the Justices, the day before, I would not ask to be heard against my motion, but would barely mention the two reasons which influenced Pagans Counsel in Massachusetts and here to entertain the opinion that there was no jurisdiction in the Supreme Court. To the best of my recollection, those reasons were mentioned. The Chief Justice ordered me to read the record—I did so—that is of the 3d. Tuesday of June 1789 and stated the subsequent proceedings briefly. The Chief Justice then asked me whether I said (perhaps the word was "thought") there appeared any thing on the record to give the Supreme Court jurisdiction. My answer was that in my opinion there was nothing of the sort, that such was the opinion I at first entertained, and that I never had a doubt except from the Courts granting the writ. You being present addressed the Court and myself in substance as you have stated.

I think I mentioned to the Court the propriety of *applying* to them for the writ of error, and urged as a reason that on Pagan's application to Government, it had been recommended to him that he should make such application— whether this was on Friday or Saturday I do not recollect.

One of the Judges declared he had ever been of opinion that the Court had not jurisdiction, but as other members of the Court thought the writ was grantable, he acquiesced. The writ was refused.

[540]

Thus Sir you have the history of Pagan a Hooper to the best of my recollection. Be pleased to accept my thanks for your favorable mention of Abilities and Integrity and believe me Your most obedt. hble Servt.

EDWD. TILGHMAN

Tr (DNA: RG 60, Letters from and Opinions of the Attorneys General); at head of text: "(copy)" and "B"; at foot of text: "E. Randolph Esqr." PrC of another

Tr (DLC); in a clerk's hand. Tr (Lb in PRO: FO 116/3). Enclosed in TJ to George Hammond, 18 Apr. 1793.

From George Washington

DEAR SIR   Mount Vernon April 12 1793.

Your letter of the 7 instant was brought to me by the last Post. War having actually commenced[1] between France and Great Britain, it behoves the Government of this Country to use every means in it's power to prevent the citizens thereof from embroiling us with either of those powers,[2] by endeavouring to maintain a strict neutrality. I therefore require that you will give the subject mature consideration, that such measures[3] as shall be deemed most likely to effect this desirable purpose[4] may be[5] adopted without delay; for I have understood that vessels are already designated as Privateers, and preparing accordingly.

Such other measures[6] as may be necessary for us to pursue against[7] events which it may not be in our Power to avoid or[8] controul, you will also think of, and lay them before me at my arrival in Philadelphia, for which place I shall set out Tomorrow; but will leave it to the advices which I may receive tonight by the Post,[9] to determine whether it is to be by the most direct Rout, or by the one I proposed to have[10] come—that is, by Reading, the Canals between the Rivers of Pennsylvania,[11] Harrisburgh, Carlisle &ca. With very great esteem & regard I am, Dear Sir, Your mo: hble Servt.

GO: WASHINGTON

RC (DLC); in the hand of Bartholomew Dandridge, Jr., signed by Washington; at foot of text: "Thomas Jefferson Esqr."; endorsed by TJ as received 17 Apr. 1793 and so recorded in SJL. Dft (DNA: RG 59, MLR); entirely in Washington's hand; contains numerous emendations, the most significant of which are noted below. FC (Lb in same, SDC).

This day the President also instructed the Secretary of the Treasury, but not the Attorney General or the Secretary of War, to consider ways and means for the United

States to preserve A STRICT NEUTRALITY in the war between France and Great Britain (Fitzpatrick, *Writings*, XXXII, 416). See also Washington to the Cabinet, 18 Apr. 1793, and note to the enclosure thereto.

[1] In Dft Washington first wrote "having been actually declared" and then altered it to read as above.
[2] Remainder of sentence interlined in Dft.
[3] Word interlined in Dft.
[4] Preceding three words interlined in Dft in place of "us."

⁵ In Dft Washington here canceled "point."
⁶ Word interlined in Dft in place of "steps."
⁷ Preceding two words interlined in Dft in place of a canceled and illegible passage.

⁸ Preceding two words interlined in Dft.
⁹ Preceding three words interlined in Dft.
¹⁰ Word interlined in Dft.
¹¹ Preceding two words interlined in Dft.

To Willink, Van Staphorst & Hubbard

GENTLEMEN   Philadelphia. Apr. 12. 1793

In my letter of Mar. 20. (which goes by the same opportunity with the present one) I informed you that Colo. Humphreys was now authorized to draw on you for the 123.750ƒ deposited in your hands on a former occasion on account of the Department of state. As this would probably be over the balance which the Department has now in your hands, I make a remittance, by London bills, payable to the order of Mr. Pinckney. Had we been assured that Amsterdam was now in it's usual state of tranquillity and correspondence, I should have directed the money to be transferred to your coffers, as usual, at once. But the accounts we receive give us much to apprehend for the present situation of Amsterdam. It became my duty therefore to let the remittance halt at London under the discretion of Mr. Pinckney, who will make arrangements with you according to circumstances. I also write to Colo. Humphreys to give so many days sight, on a proper proportion of his bills, as will enable you to be furnished with cash by Mr. Pinckney in time to honour them, in such way as shall be arranged between yourselves and Mr. Pinckney. He will write to Mr. Morris, Mr. Carmichael and Mr. Short to do the same should it be necessary. I shall hope however to receive your letters soon, and to be assured that all is safe with you, that our money transactions may return as soon as possible into their former channel. I am with great esteem Gent. your most obedt. humble servt   TH: JEFFERSON

P. S. Instead of Capt. Cutting's drawing on you for a thousand dollars as proposed in my last, I have found it better to furnish him the cash.

PrC (DLC); postscript written in margin; at foot of text: "Messrs W. & J. Willinck N. & J. Van Staphorst & Hubbard." Tr (CSmH); in the hand of George Taylor, Jr. PrC (DLC). FC (Lb in DNA: RG 59, DCI). Enclosed in Report on the Fund for Foreign Intercourse, 18 Apr. 1793.

From Jean Baptiste Ternant

Philadelphie 13 avril 1793 l'an 2 de la République française

Je ne puis me dispenser de faire encore auprès du gouvernement des Etats unis, une Sollicitation dont la copie cy jointe d'une lettre du Consul général de la République expose completement l'objet. Vous jugerez vous même qu'il est fondé sur des besoins réels, ainsi que sur des obligations d'humanité et de Service, extrêmement imperieuses. Je n'ajouterai au contenu de cette lettre, qu'une seule reflexion, c'est qu'elle me parait de la plus exacte vérité, et qu'en accordant les fonds Sollicités à titre de remboursement courant, le gouvernement des Etats unis fera, j'en suis persuadé, une chose utile et agréable à la nation française. Cette consideration me fait espérer, que le Président accueillera la demande que j'en fais; et je vous prie de vouloir bien la mettre aussitot sous ses yeux.

Tr (AMAE: CPEU, xxxvii); at head of text: "Le Ministre plénipotentiaire de France au secrétaire d'Etat des Etats unis." Recorded in SJL as received 14 Apr. 1793. Enclosure: Antoine René Charles Mathurin de La Forest to Ternant, 12 Apr. 1793, requesting payment by the United States government of French consular salaries and expenses in America (Tr in same; in French).

A letter from Ternant to TJ of 8 Apr. 1793, recorded in SJL as received that date, has not been found.

To Thomas Bell

DEAR SIR   Philadelphia Apr. 14. 1793.

My business here is of such a nature as to oblige me for long intervals to put aside all my private matters, and only to take them up at times when I have a little glimmering of leisure. Hence an almost total abandonment of my pecuniary interests, in cases often of real magnitude: and hence the long delay of answering your favor of Jan. 30. received two months ago. Tho' I cannot view Mary's hire as an insignificant thing as was done by one of the valuers as mentioned in your letter, yet I know we shall have no difficulty in settling it finally when I come to Virginia. In the mean time I am desirous of furnishing my kinsman J. Garland Jefferson with necessaries for the summer, and some small matter of money. I have thought it would be a convenient thing to you as well as myself that I should desire him to apply to you. I should have furnished him in Richmond with 75. Dollars but I have no funds there:[1] and as your goods will of course be dearer than he would have got them in Richmond, I desire him to go beyond that sum to make up the difference. I will therefore thank you to accomodate him, and debit me with the supplies.—Mr. Derieux' affairs are still stagnant here. So astonishing has been the dearth of money, that nothing has prevented a general bankruptcy among the merchants,[2] but a general indulgence by mutual consent. We are told the circulation will not be free again till May. Mr. Derieux may be assured not a moment shall be lost which I can prevent. Present me affectionately to all my neighbors, particularly at Mr. Lewis's and Dr. Gilmer's, and believe me to be very sincerely Dr. Sir Your friend & servt   Th: Jefferson

PrC (MHi); at foot of first page: "Colo. Bell." Tr (ViU: Edgehill-Randolph Papers); 19th-century copy. Enclosed in TJ to John Garland Jefferson, 14 Apr. 1793.

[1] Preceding six words interlined.
[2] Preceding three words interlined.

To Dabney Carr

Dear Dabney   Philadelphia Apr. 14. 1793.

Having expected to have seen you in Virginia before this, I had not proposed the plan of your law reading to you: but as I do not now expect to be there till the summer or fall, I think it will be necessary for you to begin it without awaiting my return. Mr. Maury thought you were ripe for leaving him last fall. I would now therefore advise you to go to your mother's and pursue there through the summer the first stages of law reading. Apply to Peter for[1] Coke's institutes, a Law dictionary, and Kennet's history of England. These will suffice till I come; especially if you fill up the intervals of the day with reading such good writers in greek and Roman history as you have not yet read. When I come home I shall propose your coming to Monticello, and pursuing your studies there, at least the Summer half of the year.— Present my friendly respects to Mr. Maury. Tell him I had expected to have given him an order, for what is due to him, on the same person on whom I gave him the last; but that a derangement in the affairs of that house renders it nugatory: and that I fear I shall not be able to pay him till the fall. I will certainly do it the first moment it shall be in my power. Adieu my Dear Dabney, be industrious, be learned, and be always just and honorable, and you will be sure to succeed. Your's affectionately   Th: Jefferson

PrC (DLC); at foot of text: "Mr. Dabney Carr." Enclosed in TJ to Peter Carr, 14 Apr. 1793.

KENNET'S HISTORY OF ENGLAND: White Kennett and others, *A Complete History of England: with the Lives of all the Kings and*

Queens thereof; from the Earliest Account of Time, to the Death of His late Majesty King William *III*, 3 vols. (London, 1706). See Sowerby, No. 377.

¹ TJ here canceled "Coke Littleton."

To Martha Jefferson Carr

DEAR SISTER   Philadelphia Apr. 14. 1793.

Your bill for £10–5 in favor of Mr. Austin has been presented and paid. It greives me to inform you I am not able to furnish the residue of the sum you desired in any short time. I never in my life had such a *right* to be flush in money as at present, and yet never was so mortifyingly bare and helpless. I had a right to receive £800. in Richmond under an execution, and by some evasion of law, I understand I am not to count on it till the fall. The occasion of your want too renders it particularly afflicting to me. I can in this case only recur to Mr. Myers's indulgence with an assurance that he shall have the money the first moment it shall be at my command. I am so far from having any funds to spare here, that I am obliged to receive aids from Virginia. In fine I shall see you in the summer or fall, and once more be able to take my own affairs into my own hands.—I now write to Dabney to advise his joining you and beginning a course of law reading; and to Peter and Garld. Jefferson to furnish him the requisite books. As soon as I come home I shall propose his coming to Monticello.—I am happy to hear of your recovery. Maria has for some time been unwell. Doctors always flatter, and parents always fear. It remains to see which is right. My love to your family and am Dear Sister your's affectionately   TH: JEFFERSON

PrC (CSmH); at foot of text: "Mrs. Carr." Martha Carr responded in a letter to TJ of 8 May 1793, recorded in SJL as received 18 May 1793 but not found.

To Peter Carr

DEAR SIR   Philadelphia Apr. 14. 1793.

The letter you mention to have written, never came to my hands; and indeed I have thought you a very lazy fellow to have let me hear from you so seldom. But if you will never give any other proof of laziness, I will pardon you this one. I have duly received my sister's letter, and have written to her to-day a second time in answer to it. I also write to Dabney the inclosed letter, advising him to apply to you for Coke's institutes, a Law Dictionary, and Kennet's English history, and retire to his mother's till I come to Virginia and commence his law reading. You will be so good as to contrive the letter to him immediately. With respect to the scene of your practice, you must be a much better judge than I am. I have been so long out of the state, and the system of practice is so totally changed there, that I am utterly incompetent to form any opinion on the subject. This I am sure of, that you may succeed where you please, if you please, as you can command application, and have every thing else. My anxiety on your behalf is great and sincere.

With respect to your right to the negroes, I think myself bound to say nothing, but that the arrangements I took with your family were expressly mentioned to be obligatory on myself alone, that I observed to them that you would be perfectly free to pursue your rights when you should come of age, that I would do nothing to diminish your right, (as I observed to them I had not the power to do) and that I would neither encourage nor discourage your reviving the question. You are therefore as free to act in this as if nothing had ever been done in it.

Present my affections to Mr. Randolph and my daughter. I should have written to the former to-day, but am so excessively busy that I can only inclose the newspapers and a pamphlet for him. The author of the latter is not known. There are some peices in the papers under the signature of Timon which are among the most unanswerable things that have ever yet appeared on the questions they discuss. I am sincerely & affectionately Dear Sir your friend & servt   TH: JEFFERSON

RC (ViU: Carr-Cary Papers); slightly torn, resulting in loss of addressee's name at foot of first page. PrC (DLC); at foot of first page: "Mr. Peter Carr." Tr (ViU: Edgehill-Randolph Papers); 19th-century copy. Enclosure: TJ to Dabney Carr, 14 Apr. 1793.

The enclosed PAMPHLET was probably *An Examination of the Late Proceedings in* *Congress, respecting the Official Conduct of the Secretary of the Treasury* [Philadelphia, 1793], which was first printed on 9 Apr. 1793. The PEICES IN THE PAPERS UNDER THE SIGNATURE OF TIMON appeared in the 27 Mch. and 13 Apr. 1793 issues of the *National Gazette* (for the circumstances giving rise to these attacks on Alexander Hamilton, see note to Notes on Stockholders in Congress, 23 Mch. 1793).

To John Wayles Eppes

DEAR SIR   Philadelphia Apr. 14. 1793.

Your departure hence is so recent that nothing has occurred worth communicating to you. The object of the present letter is merely to inclose to you an account presented me by Peter Gordon the shoe-maker, who supposed you had forgotten him. As I know that there is sometimes a forgetfulness on the side of the Creditor, I told him I would pay the account if you should admit it to be just. You have therefore only to drop me a line of acknolegement, and I will discharge it.

We learn that Mr. Beverley Randolph is stopped at Baltimore with the gout. The President is expected in town within three or four days. Present me affectionately to Mr. and Mrs. Eppes. Maria joins me in this. Her health is still disquieting. I am my dear Sir your's sincerely & affectionately   TH: JEFFERSON

PrC (DLC); at foot of text: "Mr. J. W. Eppes." Tr (ViU: Edgehill-Randolph Papers); 19th-century copy. Enclosure not found.

To John Garland Jefferson

DEAR SIR   Philadelphia Apr. 14. 1793.

Your letter of Mar. 31. came duly to hand on the 9th. inst. Having been induced, for particular reasons, to continue a while longer in my office, I should have written to you but that I have been occupied with removing from the town a little way into the country. I am much pleased to see that you are so nearly through the course of reading I had proposed to you. It proves your industry, because I know that that course requires three years industrious reading. With respect to the Roman history, if you have read Suetonius and Tacitus, Gibbons's will be sufficient to conduct you down to the time when that empire broke to peices, and the modern states of Europe arose out of them. As I do not suppose you can get a copy of Gibbons, you may leave him for the next winter when I shall have mine in Virginia. In the mean while study well Blair, Mason, Quinctilian, and endeavor to catch the oratorical stile of Bolingbroke. I should imagine that at the courts of the next fall you might venture to take your stand at the bar of such of them as you conclude to enter into, and argue some cause, judiciously selected for you by some friendly gentleman of the bar. This will present you to the view of clients and bring in something perhaps during the winter to begin on in the spring. In the mean time the winter may be employed in finishing your course of reading, and studying the forms of pleading.

My expectation was to have been in Virginia in time to have provided a resource for the supply of the 75. Dollars for the spring. Having no means of doing it here, and no fund in Richmond on which I could rely with certainty, I am obliged to take the only measure which remains in my power, that of referring you to Colo. Bell in Charlottesville. This I know cannot be as desireable to you, because you cannot have such a choice of supplies there and because they are dearer. The latter objection however I get you over by desiring you to consider yourself free to go beyond the sum as far as the difference of prices between Richmond and Charlottesville. The former objection will remain, and as to that I must only pray you to take the will for the deed. In or before the fall I shall certainly see you.—I shall recommend to Dabney Carr to begin a course of Law-reading at his mother's immediately: so that you may deliver my books to him as you finish them. I am with great & sincere esteem Dr. Sir your affectionate kinsman   TH: JEFFERSON

P.S. I inclose you a letter of credit to Colo. Bell.

PrC (DLC); at foot of first page: "Mr. J. Garland Jefferson." Tr (ViU: Carr-Cary Papers); 19th-century copy. Enclosure: TJ to Thomas Bell, 14 Apr. 1793.

From J. Wheatcroft

SR.   Havre Apl. 14th. 1793

I do my self the honour to inclose you a series of News papers, from the date of my last *envoy*. It is a new established paper and reckoned an exceedinly good one, I have changed it for the Moniter, as our inteligence in this paper is generaly a Day newer.

If you should have received the same paper from any other Friend, hope this will still be an acceptable present to any of your acquaintance in the Country. You will find a great change has happened in the situation of French politics since my last.

In No. 60 and suite you will see an interesting Trial, respecting the Lawrence Capt. White an American Vessel brought in here by the Sans cullotte, which turn'd out in favour of the Captain.

These papers will be forwarded by Capt. Lowe of the Swanwick of Philadelphia who sails this Day. I am Sr. Your most Obedt. Servt

J WHEATCROFT PÈRE

P.S. We are always perfectly tranquil at Havre.

RC (DLC); endorsed by TJ as received 10 Sep. 1793 and so recorded in SJL.

The LAST ENVOY from Wheatcroft, an English merchant in Le Havre who had assisted TJ in his departure from France in 1789, was undoubtedly his letter to TJ of 9 Feb. 1793, recorded in SJL as received 4 May 1793, but not found. See also Extract from the Diary of Nathaniel Cutting at Le Havre and Cowes, 28 Sep.-12 Oct. 1789; and Cutting to TJ, [12 Oct. 1789].

From James Brown

DEAR SIR   Richmond 15th: April 1793

I have just time to acknowledge receipt of your favors of the 8th: and 10th: Currt. and to assure you that every attention shall be paid to the contents. I pray you at same time to write Mr. Short that his Stock with Other matters in my hands is Safe and shall remain so, subject alone to his order, however I will write you and hand a letter for Mr. Short in a day or two, at present my whole frame is so agitated that I little Know what I am about. The late unfortunate failure of D. & Burton, deranges me much, yet I will weather the gale with honor and save all my American friends from loss. With much respect I am Dear Sir Your Obt: Hbl: St   JAMES BROWN

RC (MHi); endorsed by TJ as received 22 Apr. 1793 and so recorded in SJL; with TJ's notes for his 23 May 1793 reply to Brown penciled beneath signature: "Camilla. Service
        Young Eagle. Elias Lord
        2. workmen.
        shippg. tobo.
        wine."

Tr (ViW); extract of second sentence in TJ's hand on same sheet with extract of Brown to TJ, 3 June 1793; enclosed in TJ to William Short, 11 July 1793. PrC (DLC). Tr (ViU: Edgehill-Randolph Papers); 19th-century copy of extract.

The first of TJ's FAVORS was actually his letter to Brown of 7 Apr. 1793.

To Richard Dobson

SIR   Philadelphia Apr. 15. 1793.

I had fully expected to have been ere this returned to Virginia, where I knew I should have the materials and leisure to settle with you the balance due from me to Mr. John Dobson. Circumstances unforeseen have deferred my quitting this place till some time in the summer or autumn. If you think the settlement can be effected by way of letter, I am willing to try it. I am only apprehensive that as the payments have been very much in detail, in money, in tobacco in orders, and by various persons and I am here without the documents necessary, it may[1] occasion a more lengthy and extensive correspondence than will consist with a speedy settlement; and the rather as there occur often considerable intervals during which the affairs of my office do not permit me to turn a thought towards my private affairs. Still it shall be at your option whether to try this method or let it lye till my return, when it shall be my first object. I had destined for it's payment part of a judgment which is to be obtained this present month. But I apprehend it may be doubtful whether the money will be actually levied before the fall. This is the earliest and most certain resource of paiment it is in my power to provide. I shall be happy to hear from you on this subject. I am Sir your very humble servt   TH: JEFFERSON

PrC (DLC); at foot of text: "Mr. Richard Dobson."

Dobson's reply of 29 Apr. 1793,

recorded in SJL as received 6 May 1793, has not been found.

[1] Word interlined in place of "will."

From Horatio Gates

DEAR SIR   Rose Hill 15th: April 179[3]
   In compliance with your request, I have Inclosed you all The Letters I was Honoured with from you, during my Command to the Southward; and during your Administration of The Government of Virginia; Those from me, To You; shall, as soon as they can be Transcribed out of my Letter Book, be forwarded in like manner to your Hands: Mrs: Gates Joins me in Compliments and in the Hope, that you will be able to make a Visit to Rose Hill in the course of the approaching Summer. With Sentiments of Sincere Esteem, I am Dear Sir your very Obedt: Servant   HORATIO GATES

RC (NNP); partially dated; at foot of text: "His Excellency Thomas Jefferson"; endorsed by TJ as received 17 Apr. 1793.

To James Lyle

DEAR SIR   Philadelphia Apr. 15. 1793.
   According to what I mentioned to you in a former letter, I have had, in January past, a sale of negroes made for the purpose of paying my bonds to Henderson & co. The amount of the sales returned to me is £700–1–6 besides which there is one other bond not yet taken which will be about £100. so that the whole is about £800. Virginia currency, the one half payable the next christmas, the other half christmas twelvemonth. The ensuing winter I hope to be able to

add from another source £200. or a little upwards, so as to compleat[1] the bonds payable 1791. 2. 3. and 4.[2] one half the money receivable this year and the whole by the end of 1794. I expected ere this to have been in Virginia and to have put into your hands myself the bonds for the £700–1–6 but particular circumstances defer my departure till the latter end of summer. In the mean time the bonds are lodged at Monticello.

The last bond to Henderson & co. and my mother's balance will then remain. As I have now cleared myself of Farrell & Jones by bonds in like manner to within about £100. I shall be more able to manage the last bond to Henderson and my mother's balance: but still I can by no means promise myself to do it by the times stipulated. However when I return to my own country and my own affairs I shall have time to examine into my resources for doing it. In the mean time I am with sincere esteem Dear [Sir][3] your affectionate friend & servt

TH: JEFFERSON

PrC (DLC); at foot of text: "Mr. James Lyle."

TJ's FORMER LETTER to Lyle was that of 29 July 1792.

[1] TJ here canceled "all."
[2] TJ originally completed the sentence with "and the whole money receivable by the end of 1794" before amending the passage to read as above.
[3] Word omitted by TJ.

From Edward Ryan

SIR   Philadelphia 15 April 1793

I propose to morrow (if the weather should be favourable, if not the next fair day) to erect a furnace for the purpose of melting pot ash.

If You, Sir, could make it convenient to honour me with your company for a few minutes at any time between the hours of two and five, you would have a much better opportunity of judging concerning the principles of the furnace than by any explanation which I could give you. My manufactory is in fifth street between pine and Lombard Street. With sentiments of the highest esteem I am Sir your most obdt. Servant.   EDWARD RYAN

P.S. The favour of an answer is requested by the Bearer.

RC (DNA: RG 59, MLR); dateline opposite signature; above postscript: "Thomas Jefferson Esqr"; endorsed by TJ as received 16 Apr. 1793 and so recorded in SJL.

Edward Ryan was a potash manufacturer at 106 South Fifth Street, Philadelphia (James Hardie, *The Philadelphia Directory and Register* [Philadelphia, 1793], 125). On 29 Apr. 1793 he was issued a patent for a "Furnace for pot and pearl ashes" (*List of Patents*, 7; Washington, *Journal*, 128).

To Edmund Randolph

Th:J. to E. R.   Apr. 17. 1793.

On the information received from Crosby, and which I directed him to communicate to you, I have prepared the inclosed letter to him according to the President's instructions. If you approve of it, be so good as to send it on to him. But if you are not satisfied that you can set some effectual process on foot, it would be better to hold it up till the President's return, that he may not be uselessly committed. I am not certain whether I can come to town to-day. If I do, I will see you; if not, then tomorrow.

PrC (DLC). Tr (DLC); 19th-century copy. Enclosure: TJ to George Turner, 17 Apr. 1793.

Sampson CROSBY was a factotum in the Department of State, but the LETTER TO HIM was in fact TJ's letter of this date to

George Turner, the federal judge whose prolonged absence from the Northwest Territory had recently become a matter of serious concern to TJ and the President. The PRESIDENT'S INSTRUCTIONS on this matter were given in Washington to TJ, 5 Apr. 1793.

Edmund Randolph's Opinion on George Turner

[ca. 17 Apr. 1793]

To instruct Governor St. Clair

1. To transmit to Judge Turner any authentic intelligence, which he may have received, concerning the complaints of the people against his absence:

2. Or, if no such intelligence be possessed, to represent to Judge Turner, without undertaking to *order* in any manner, the inconvenience in a judicial view,[1] which the Territory sustains by his absence: and

3. To *summon* Judge Turner to attend at the seat of government, as a member of the legislature.

RC (DLC: TJ Papers, 80: 13910); undated and unsigned; endorsed by TJ.

If this opinion embodying the Attorney General's counsel on how best to handle Judge Turner's absence from the Northwest Territory was a response to the preceding letter and its enclosure, Randolph must have submitted it to TJ soon thereafter. However, there is no evidence

that TJ issued the recommended instructions to Arthur St. Clair, governor of the Northwest Territory, or to Turner. Randolph himself wrote a letter to Turner on 11 May 1793 about his continued absence, which elicited a reply from the judge justifying his delay on the grounds of ill health and promising to return to the Northwest Territory forthwith (Washington, *Journal*, 136, 137). Neverthe-

[552]

less, Turner appears to have remained in Philadelphia until late August or early September 1793 before returning to the Northwest Territory to resume his judicial duties (TJ to St. Clair, 13 Sep. 1793).

[1] Preceding four words interlined.

To George Turner

SIR   Philadelphia Apr. 17. 1793.

The inconveniences which have resulted to the Territory of the US. Northwest of the Ohio, from the absence of the legislative and judiciary bodies, and the length of time, you have in particular been absent have rendered it necessary, in the opinion of the President, that some legal enquiry into the causes of it should be instituted: and I have it in charge from him to inform you, that the Attorney General of the US. is instructed to consider, and to do what may be proper on the occasion. I have the honor to be with great esteem & respect Sir Your most obedt. & most humble servt   TH: JEFFERSON

PrC (DLC); at foot of text: "The honble Judge Turner." FC (Lb in DNA: RG 59, DL). Enclosed in TJ to Edmund Randolph, 17 Apr. 1793.

TJ submitted this letter to the President on 18 Apr. 1793 (Washington, *Journal*, 110).

To James Wilson

Apr. 17. 1793.

Th: Jefferson presents his compliments to Mr. Wilson. He omitted to observe to him on the subject of his bookshelves that whenever he has occasion to remove them from one room to another, or one house to another, they may be taken to peices and put together again the whole of them in half an hour, as there is not a single nail, screw, nor glue used in putting them together. Carstairs, who knows their construction, would be the best person to employ in doing it. He states below, according to his desire, a note of their cost extracted from Long's and Carstair's bills. He has not noted the articles of locks, hinges, cloth-covering for one peice &c. which were not worth hunting up.

		£ s	
1791. Jan. 11. & 15.	pd. Mr. Long for 2. lengths of book-cases	7–15	
Dec. 19.	pd. Mr. Carstairs for 10. do. great & small	24–10	
	do. for 2. corner paper presses @ 21/6	2– 3	D
		£34– 8	=91.73

PrC (DLC).

[553]

From Brown, Benson & Ives

SIR   Providence, 18th. April 1793

We have the honour to acknowledge the reception of your esteem'd favour of the 5th. instant accompanied with your address to the French Minister on the Subject of the Complaints specified in our Letter to you; At present Sir we have only to express our grateful sence of your Prompt and obliging attention to our wishes. When we did ourselves the pleasure to solicit your interference it was impossible to transmit any particular estimate of the Injury we should suffer by the detention of our Vessel at Port au Prince, but in Case she ever returns we shall endeavour to Ascertain the Amount of Damages when we shall be happy to avail ourselves of your friendly and official influence to enforce our Claim.

Our last letter from Capt. Munro was dated the 20th. Ulto. at which time he was still subjected to the same restraint and mentions that "flour is on the rise and was mine fresh and good, I could easily obtain seven Dollrs. but I am sorry to say the great length of time it has been on board has proved so injurious to this Article that I can get no Purchaser." It is therefore evident that we shall experience very Considerable Detriment by the Cruel and unprovok'd Procedure of the French at that Port and for which we Certainly ought to be indemnified. Reiterating our thanks for the early and decided Measures you adopted on an Occasion so interesting to the American Trade—We have the honour to be Sir, Your most Obliged & Obedt. Friends

BROWN BENSON & IVES

RC (DNA: RG 59, MLR); at foot of text: "The Honble. Thomas Jefferson Esq Secretary of State Philadelphia"; endorsed by TJ as received 26 Apr. 1793 and so recorded in SJL.

From William Carmichael and William Short

SIR   Aranjuez April 18. 1793.

When we had last the honor of addressing you we mentioned the delay which had taken place with respect to the business with which we are charged here. We then hoped that delay had ceased as we were just informed that His Majesty had designated the person to treat with us on his behalf. We have found ourselves however much mistaken in our hope.

As soon as it was announced to us that M. de Gardoqui was the person, we waited on him and expressed to him our satisfaction that His Majesty's choice had fallen on a person so well acquainted with the subjects of which we were to treat, and also with the dispositions of the U.S. and their desire to cultivate the friendship of His Catholic Majesty. He shewed evident marks of being pleased with this nomination, and gave us the strongest assurances of his desire that a business so long depending, should be brought to a conclusion agreeable to both parties. He added that he hoped the negotiation would be carried on in the same familiar and friendly manner to which he had been accustomed in America; and other things of the sort which are always used more or less on such occasions, according to the humour of the person, and which prove nothing as to the main object.

After waiting a few days in the expectation of his announcing to us officially his nomination and fixing the time and manner of proceeding to the conferences, we learned from him that he was delayed by his powers and instructions not having been made out, which being to be done in another department was not under his control. At length we wrote him a letter on the 24th. of Febry., having concerted it with him, expressive of our desire to proceed to a communication of our respective full powers; this he desired, that he might have an opportunity of pressing the foreign department.

From that time we continued seeing him very frequently always expressing our desire to proceed to business and recieving assurances from him of his reciprocating it fully—of his having done every thing to hasten the making out his powers and instructions—of his recieving daily promises that it should be done—and of his waiting for nothing else. In this manner things passed delayed from day to day until the 23d. of March when we had our first conference.

We have now had three meetings on three successive saturdays, the ministerial occupations of M. de Gardoqui not allowing him to have them more than once a week, and not always so often; as that which was to have taken place on the last saturday was postponed by him. Although such conferences are meer conversations in order that the two parties may settle as many previous points as possible and find out what will be the best mode of discussing between them such as present the greatest difficulty, yet we think it proper to give you a general idea of what has passed in those which have already taken place, as they have discovered a disposition in this court very different from what we imagine was expected in America at the time of our commission being formed.

We begun, after having communicated the originals of our respective full-powers and interchanged copies of them, by mentioning that although they embraced a variety of objects of mutual concern to the two countries, we would confine ourselves in the first instance to the two leading ones—namely the navigation of the Mississipi, and the territorial limits. We stated these points and supported them by the arguments which are contained in your report to the President—considering always the *right* to the former as unquestionable, and of course the *means of exercising it* as the only object of negotiation.

M. de Gardoqui discovered evident signs of impatience under this statement, and much surprize, either real or feigned, at it. He assured us that no consideration whatever would ever induce his Majesty to acknowlege a right in us to this navigation—and he seemed to consider our claim to the limits under the treaty with England as extravagant and unwarrantable, regarding this treaty as an agreement made between two people to dispose of the property of a third. You will see lower down his ideas as to the acquisition of this property by Spain.

We observed to him on what he said was the determination of H M, as to the navigation, that we knew not how to suppose that H M so conspicuously remarkable among the sovereigns of Europe for his love of justice, would refuse to acknowledge a right, as soon as that right should be exhibited to his view established by proofs as unquestionable as those of a geometrical truth, and founded equally on what all men hold sacred—both natural and conventional law.

As to the former, he held the very extraordinary doctrine, for a diplomatic negotiator, of its deserving no attention, having never yet bound any power further than suited their convenience. As to the second, he considered the treaties as not giving us a right, or at least as not being obligatory on Spain, in the instance where she was not a party. You will easily suppose that such opinions were not attempted to be supported by argument. The most general and desultory assertions only were brought forward—such as that the King would never hear of the treaty made between us and England, to dispose of what belonged to him—that we had no right to navigate any where on the Mississipi but on our own shore—that he would never consent to advise H M to acknowlege our right to navigate it throughout its extent &c. &c. He would hardly agree that the exclusive right of Spain to this navigation had any beginning—and could not be brought to say precisely at what time this exclusive right did commence or how. Indeed it really appeared a point about which he was uncertain at that moment.

He was less scrupulous in affirming the origin of the right of Spain to the territory within our limits. He stated it to be by conquest during the late war. On its being observed to him that by the usages of nations hitherto respected, conquest could give only an inchoate right in any case,[1] and that its accomplishment depended on treaty—and that the treaty so far from comprehending, did expressly exclude the conquest now contended for—and that Spain not being at war with us, no right of any kind could be claimed against us—the doctrine was neither acknowleged or denied, though there appeared an evident ignorance of it. It was replied to by sometimes pretending that all that was now claimed by Spain was comprehended in the cession by England of the Floridas (their previous treaty with us being considered as null and void) and sometimes by positions which would lead to a very new and unexpected system—that Spain until she had acknowleged our independence had a right to make conquests within our limits. This was laid down as the great difference between the rights of Spain and of France derivable from the successes of their arms within any part of the U.S. It was acknowleged that France for instance had no right to York town—but given clearly to be understood that if the Spanish forces had taken possession of Charleston or any other place, the case as to Spain would have been different. We could only observe thereon that we did suppose that Spain would be the last power to set on foot seriously such an unlimited system of conquest, as being certainly at least as dangerous for her as any other. And indeed we are persuaded that the length to which this doctrine was carried was more the result of the heat of conversation than of cool reflection.

When it was observed to him that this court had formerly entertained different ideas with respect to the limits, as was demonstrable from what had passed between the Count de Florida Blanca and the Mis. de la fayette, he treated that subject in the most contemptuous manner—adding that he had written to the Count on it from America, who had affirmed it to be the grossest misrepresentation on the part of M. de la fayette. We observed to him that the letters which had passed between them on that subject being in their office of foreign affairs would shew how far this had been a misrepresentation and that we must refer him to them.

It would have been evidently useless to have pressed this subject any further at that time. Had Count de Florida Blanca been still more explicit on this head, still it would probably have no weight with the present ministry. It could only serve to give additional force to argument hereafter and shew in a clearer view the injustice of the present system of this court as to that question.

M. de Gardoqui afterwards went into some detail of the manner in which this subject had been conducted with respect to him whilst employed therein in America. He complained in more clear terms of the delay which had been made use of, and which he had mentioned to us previously whenever we had pressed him and taken notice of the delay here. We observed to him that the expiring stages of a government and the transition from one form to another would unavoidably have produced that delay. To this he replied that he had remained a long time after the establishment of the new government—and that he should have remained still longer to have continued the negotiation if he had not acquired full proof that the system had been adopted on the part of the U.S. of taking no other step then, and of leaving the subject to time.

He proceeded in telling us that he and Mr. Jay had for a long time meditated on the difficulties which presented themselves—that they both had been as desirous of removing them as any persons could be expected to be in future, and that he thought they had by sacrifices on both sides succeeded as far as could be done. He said they had agreed on the basis of the treaty between themselves—but that Mr. Jay chusing to take the opinion of Congress on some parts of it (those with respect to the navigation and limits) had consulted them thereon and was to have given him their answer—that he, on his part, had announced this to his court who had from that time been expecting in vain the answer. He gave us to understand that he expected that we should be charged with this answer. He endeavored to give us from recollection the substance of what had been agreed on between him and Mr. Jay. It was as follows.

Commerce—Conformable to the articles annexed to his letter to Mr. Jay of the 25th. of May 1786. which you forwarded to us—he stated them as being the propositions of Mr. Jay, to which he had assented. Limits—to begin somewhere about the mouth of the Yazou—from thence a straight line in that parallel to the Apalachicola, from thence towards St. Mary's river by a line about the direction of which he seemed uncertain, and down that river to the ocean. The Navigation of the Mississipi—to be used in the following manner: our citizens to carry their productions in their own vessels to the limits agreed on where magazines should be constructed—from thence they should be taken by Spanish boats and carried to N. Orleans—if there should not be Spanish boats enough for that purpose (although he was convinced there would be) then he thought the American boats passing on to N. Orleans would be connived at. Whether our vessels were to be allowed to come from the sea to recieve these productions at N. Orleans was to be the subject of further negotiation, as well as the toll to be paid. And all this they could not consent to insert in a public treaty, lest other nations should claim a like admission into this colonial possession; and was therefore to have been a private article. He took the precaution of adding that no answer having been given by Congress on Mr. Jay's reference to them no decision therefore had been taken thereon by his court; and of course he could not pretend to say that H.M. would consent to these conditions at present, although he would have done it formerly.

He was assured that no decision on such articles would ever be asked from him by us—nothing respecting such having been communicated to us by you was a convincing proof that government had considered them not capable of being deliberated on.

In the course of these conferences he had mentioned that the limits and navigation were objects of much less importance than we appeared to make them—both Spain and the U.S. having much more territory than they knew what to do with, and the use of the river against stream being impracticable even if allowed by Spain. We observed thereon that taking these positions for granted, he must agree that the King of Spain was much more the uncontrolled arbiter of limits, and much less obliged to consult the prejudices (as he seemed to consider them) of the inhabitants, than was the government of the U.S.—that moreover by our constitution the limits of each state were guaranteed to them— and therefore not under the control of the general government—that as to the navigation, if impracticable, it would not be exercised, and consequently that Spain should have no objection to recognize our right thereto, and that not doing it under that view of the subject, shewed that much less importance was annexed to the friendship of the U.S. than we had hoped.

It was replied to this that the admission of foreigners to any of the Spanish colonial possessions was an innovation, and that Government was much more averse to the smallest innovation, in any of their colonial regulations, than in those at home (the exception in favor of French vessels for a limited time being a case of necessity which of course did not admit of its being taken as a general rule)—and further that although it was evident the current of the river would not admit of its being ascended for the purposes of commerce, yet it facilitated the descent; and that European manufactures carried through the U.S. into the Western country would be brought down the river, and smuggled into their possessions, if our vessels were allowed to go there. He seemed also to fear much the propagation of principles of independence among them by communication with our citizens. We obviated both objections as we thought, and shewed that the U.S. would have an interest to see the Spanish possessions dependent on

Spain if they enjoyed all they claimed, which was the navigation of the river. He said this would be the case if men were reasonable enough to follow what was their interest, but that there were so many instances to the contrary (he cited the attempts of France to propagate their own principles as a living instance) that such considerations were little to be relied on.

The conduct of their agents in America with respect to us in at least exciting the animosity of the Indians towards us, was incidentally touched on—it was roundly denied and affirmed on the contrary that their standing instructions were directly opposed thereto. We told him the U.S. had no doubt of the dispositions of H.M. on such subjects and of course were persuaded that the conduct of those agents was not warranted thereby—but that the proofs of their conduct were established on the strongest testimony. It was evident however that it did not appear so to him. We shall have occasion necessarily to bring forward this subject in more serious terms and accordingly it was not pushed further at that time.

M. de Gardoqui deviated from it to complain in very bitter terms of the manner in which the Spanish navigation and commerce had been treated by the regulations of the U.S. He said that the few vessels of this country which were formerly employed were completely expelled from thence. When we observed to him that whatever regulations had been made, were common to all foreign countries, and that Spain though without a treaty was treated as the most favored nation there, he insisted that whatever might be the appearance the effect was not so, since as the Spanish commissaries had informed them, their vessels had ceased going to the ports of the U.S. whilst those of other nations went there. Spain he observed was a country *sui generis* as to commerce—that there was no reciprocity in the treatment respectively of Spanish subjects and American citizens in America and Spain. He advanced that Spain had no need of the U.S.—whereas the U.S. having no mines of gold and silver[2] could not do without Spain in order to procure these indispensable articles. However absurd this may appear, and whatever ignorance it may betray of the true principles of commercial and political economy, yet we are persuaded they are his real sentiments.

It would have been lost labor to have combated rooted prejudices of that kind by serious argument. We only replied to them therefore by observing that as long as food should continue to be an indispensable ingredient in the wants of men, we trusted that cornfields would be found to be the surest and most inexhaustible mines of gold and silver. We added that we were persuaded however that nothing hostile had been intended against the commerce of Spain—and that he would find that the U.S. had the fullest disposition on the contrary to cultivate and increase the commercial relations of the two countries.

He told us (which he seemed to desire we should consider as a proof of his frankness) that he had advised His Majesty, immediately on being informed of our regulations, to levy an additional duty on our fish and flour, as the surest means of making us treat them differently. This additional duty was intended as an excess to be paid by us above other foreigners; and he informed us that it was only delayed to take place with a general regulation of their commercial system which he was about forming. We doubt however whether what he told us of the additional duty has been hitherto seriously intended—although we cannot assure you, should the growing connexions between this country and England be carried to the degree of which they seem susceptible under present circumstances, that this menace would not be realized in favor of the English fishery.

From this general statement of what has hitherto passed here you will see that their ideas at present with respect to the two leading objects of our commission are out of the circle of negotiation under the instructions we received from you. It was matter of embarrassment therefore to us not to have been informed what overtures had been made from this court and induced the President to send a commission for treating here, after Mr. Carmichael had informed you of their intention to send a minister for that purpose to America.

We found ourselves placed therefore under circumstances of much delicacy arising from the explicit declarations of M. de Gardoqui,[3] and the present *unsettled relations of this country with England*.[4] Had we insisted on the *sine quibus non*[5] of your instructions as preliminaries we should inevitably have been obliged to have broken off the conferences which could not have been done without eclat, as an express commission had been sent here for the purpose of treating. It was evident that *this would have been playing into the hands of England by exciting alarm* in this *court* with respect *to us*. We have therefore thought it our duty to *temporize* and without giving any hope of *our abandoning* any part of *our rights* we have proceeded to canvass the subjects of our commission in general as has been stated to you. Under other circumstances we should have proceeded immediately to have[6] supported them by the arguments which your report to the President furnishes, and which could have been opposed only by an open and manifest refusal of incontrovertible right and of course exhibited to the view of all the world *the justice of resorting to other means for obtaining it*. At present we should unquestionably *obtain nothing by urgency*. And as we have full conviction that *they would now refuse what we* should insist on, we should not be the wiser for⁷ *forcing them to express this determination by writing.*

We think it our duty therefore to give it as our opinion *that whatever preparatory⁸ steps would be taken by government in the case of this refusal of our right,* should be taken under *present circumstances* as we consider unquestionable *the determination of this court to refuse it when pressed.* Our intention is not to *press this determination until* we shall see with more certainty the *influence of French affairs on them and their connexions with England.* As great changes have taken place therein (since *your instructions were given*) with which you will have been duly made acquainted, we flatter ourselves also with *learning soon the further intentions of the President* arising therefrom. Should the *conferences in the meantime come to a close* we shall endeavour that it be without recieving⁹ *such a refusal* as it might be difficult for them to *retract from hereafter.*

No body can say what changes may take place in the relations of European powers nor in how short a time. We do not scruple however to say that *until some considerable change shall take place* from the *present and excite the alarms of this country* with respect to *England, they* will not be *induced by meer negotiation to yield our rights. Such a position* however we believe did exist *at the time of the Nootka negotiation and we think it probable that such will occur again.*¹⁰

Whatever may occur, or whatever progress may be made in any direction you may count on being informed of with as much expedition and punctuality as may depend on us. This would be done sooner and more regularly if we were not obliged to wait for such conveyances¹¹ as it may be proper to make use of. This will be sent under cover to Colo. Humphreys by an express despatched from hence by the Portuguese Ambassador. We have the honor &c.   (signed) W.C.
                                                                W.S.

PrC (DLC: Short Papers); in Short's hand, with conclusion of letter added in ink by him (see note 11 below); written partly in code (see note 4 below); at foot of first page: "The Secretary of State for the United States. Philadelphia." Dft (same); in Short's hand; consists of small sheet pasted to PrC containing several paragraphs written *en clair* with words to be encoded underscored (see notes 3 and 10 below); only emendations affecting content have been noted below. Tr (CtY); entirely *en clair*; at head of text: "(Duplicate)"; contains minor varia-

tions in wording. PrC (DLC). Tr (DNA: RG 46, Senate Records, 3d Cong., 1st sess.); entirely *en clair*; at head of text: "(Duplicate)"; contains minor variations in wording. Tr (Lb in same, TR); entirely *en clair*. Recorded in SJL as received 22 July 1793. Enclosed in TJ to Thomas Pinckney, 11 Sep. 1793.

YOUR REPORT TO THE PRESIDENT: see Report on Negotiations with Spain, 18 Mch. 1792. For a discussion of Spanish claims to the TERRITORY WITHIN OUR LIMITS, see Bemis, *Pinckney's Treaty*, 41-3.

The exchange of views in 1783 BETWEEN THE COUNT DE FLORIDA BLANCA AND THE MIS. DE LA FAYETTE on the boundary dispute between the United States and Spain is described in note to Report on Negotiations with Spain, 18 Mch. 1792. For Gardoqui's negotiations on this and other issues with then Secretary for Foreign Affairs John Jay WHILST EMPLOYED THEREIN IN AMERICA during the latter years of the Confederation Congress, see Bemis, *Pinckney's Treaty*, 66-108. TJ had complained of the conduct of various Spanish AGENTS IN AMERICA in inciting the Creeks to hostilities with the United States in his 14 Oct. and 3 Nov. 1792 letters to Carmichael and Short.

TJ submitted this letter to the President on 23 July 1793 (Washington, *Journal*, 205-6).

[1] Preceding three words interlined.

[2] Preceding two words interlined.
[3] Dft begins here.
[4] Except where noted, these and subsequent words in italics are in code, the text being supplied from Short's Dft and verified by the Editors using partially reconstructed Code No. 10.
[5] Words written *en clair* and underscored by Short.
[6] In Dft Short wrote "reduced our claims to writing and."
[7] Here in Dft "making" is canceled.
[8] Word interlined in Dft.
[9] Sentence to this point and preceding sentence interlined in Dft in place of heavily emended section which originally read "Should that be delayed too long, to bring the conferences to a close without exacting a positive re."
[10] Dft ends here.
[11] From this point Short completed the Pr C in ink.

To George Hammond

SIR   Philadelphia Apr. 18.[1] 1793.

I have now the honor to inclose you the answer of the Attorney General to my letter covering yours of Mar. 12. on the case of Hooper and Pagan, wherein he has stated the proceedings of Pagan for obtaining a writ of error from the Supreme court of the US. for revisal of the judgment of the inferior court pronounced against him; and also his opinion on the merits of the question, had the writ of error been procured, and the merits thereby been brought into question. From this statement you will be able to judge whether Pagan has bonâ fide complied with the rule which requires that a foreigner, before he applies for extraordinary interposition, should use his best endeavors to obtain the justice he claims from the ordinary tribunals of the country. You will perceive also that had the writ been pressed for and obtained, and the substantial justice of Pagan's claim thereby brought into discussion, substantial justice would have been against him, according to the opinion of the Attorney General, according to the uniform decisions of the courts of the US. even in the case of their own citizens, and according to the decision of this very case in the British provincial court where the evidence was taken and the trial first had. This does not appear then to be one of those cases of gross and palpable wrong ascribable only to wickedness of the heart, and not to error of the head,

[563]

in the judges who have decided on it, and founding a claim of national satisfaction. At least, that it is so, remains yet to be demonstrated.

The readiness with which the government of the US. has entered into enquiries concerning the case of Mr. Pagan, even before that case was ripe for their interposition according to ordinary rules, will, I hope, satisfy you, that they would with equal readiness have done for the redress of his case whatever the laws and constitution would have permitted them to do, had it appeared in the result that their courts had been guilty of partiality or other gross wrong against Mr. Pagan. On the contrary, it is hoped, that the marked attentions which have been shewn to him by the government of Massachusets, as well as by that of the US. have evinced the most scrupulous dispositions to patronize and effectuate his right had right been on his side. I have the honor to be with due respect Sir Your most humble servt TH: JEFFERSON

PrC (DLC); with blank space in date-line completed in ink (see note 1 below); at foot of first page: "The Min. Plenipy. of Gr. Britain." FC (Lb in DNA: RG 59, DL). Tr (Lb in PRO: FO 116/3). Tr (same, 5/1). Enclosures: Edmund Randolph to TJ, 12 Apr. 1793, and enclosures.

TJ submitted this letter to the President on this day, and Washington returned it with his approval the next day (Washington, *Journal*, 110, 114).

¹ Digits added in ink.

Notes for Reply to Jean Baptiste Ternant

Substance of the¹ answer proposed to the letter of the French Minister of Apr. 13.

Before the new Government of France had time to attend to things on this side the Atlantic, and to provide a Deposit of money for their purposes here, there was a necessity that we, as their friends and debtors, should keep their affairs from suffering, by furnishing money for urgent purposes. This obliged us to take on ourselves to judge of the purpose, because on the soundness of that we were to depend for our justification. Hence we furnished monies for their colonies and their agents here; justified, in our own opinion, by the importance and necessity of the case.

But that necessity is now at an end. The Government has established a deposit of money in the hands of their minister here. We have nothing now to do but to furnish the money, for which their order is our sanction. We are no longer to look into the purposes to which it is to be applied. Their minister is to be the judge of these, and to pay the money to whom, and for what he pleases.

If it be urged that they have appropriated all the money[2] we are advancing to another object, that he is not authorised to divert any of it to any other purpose, and therefore *needs a further sum*; it may be answered that it will not lessen the stretch of authority to add an unauthorized payment by us, to an unauthorised application by him, and that it seems fitter that he should exercise a discretion over their appropriations, standing, as he does, in a place of confidence, authority, and responsibility, than we who are strangers, and unamenable to them.

Private reasons of weight which need not be expressed to the minister

That these applications make us in some sort a board of Auditors for French accounts, and subject our payments to question:

That it is known to us that the present minister, not having the confidence of his government, is replaced by another, and consequently the authority of his application lessened:

That it is rather probable the whole establishment of their consuls here will be suppressed as useless and expensive to them, and rather vexatious to us.

Apr. 18. 1793.

PrC (DLC); frayed and partly over-written in a later hand. Recorded in SJPL.

This document was probably intended for submission to the President for his approval of TJ's proposed reply to Ternant's 13 Apr. 1793 letter on the subject of French consular salaries and expenses.

TJ incorporated a modified text of the first three paragraphs in his 20 Apr. 1793 reply to Ternant, which internal evidence suggests was approved by Washington.

[1] Preceding three words interlined in place of "Draft of."
[2] TJ here canceled "in his hands."

Report on the Fund for Foreign Intercourse

The Secretary of state thinking it his duty to communicate to the President his proceedings of the present year[1] for transferring to Europe the annual fund of 40,000 Dollars appropriated to the department of state (a report whereof was unnecessary the two former years, as monies already in the hands of our bankers in Europe were put under his orders)

Reports

That in consequence of the President's order of Mar. 23. he received from the Secretary of the Treasury Mar. 31. a warrant on the Treasurer for 39,500. Dollars: that it being necessary to purchase private bills of exchange to transfer the money to Europe, he consulted with persons acquainted with that business, who advised him not to let it be known that he was to purchase bills at all, as it would raise the exchange, and to defer the purchase a few days till the British packet should be gone, on which event bills generally sunk some few percent. He therefore deferred the purchase, or giving any orders for it till Apr. 10. when he engaged Mr. Vaughan (whose line of business enabled him to do it without suspicion) to make the purchase for him: he then delivered the warrant to the Treasurer, and received a credit at the Bank of the US. for 39,500. D. whereon he had an account opened between 'The Department of state and the Bank of the US.' That Mr. Vaughan procured for him the next day the following bills

	£ sterl.	Doll.
Willing, Morris & Swanwick on John & Francis Baring & co. London	3000.	for 13,000
Walter Stewart on Joseph Birch. mercht. Liverpool.	400–0 =	1,733.33
Robert Gilmer & co. on James Strachan & James Mackenzie, London, indorsed by Mordecai Lewis	£ 200– 150– } 600–0 = 250–	2,600.
	4,000–0 =	17,333.33

averaging 4s–7$\frac{38}{100}$d the dollar, or about 2$\frac{1}{2}$ per cent above par, which added to the 1. per cent loss heretofore always sustained on the government bills (which allowed but 99 florins, instead of 100. do. for every 40. dollars) will render the fund somewhat larger this year than heretofore: that these bills being drawn on London (for none could be got on Amsterdam but to considerable loss, added to the risk of the present possible situation of that place) he had them made payable to Mr. Pinckney, and inclosed them to him by Capt. Cutting, in the letter of Apr. 12.[2] now communicated to the President, and at the same time wrote the letters of the same date to our bankers at Amsterdam and to Colo. Humphreys, now also communicated to the President, which will place under his view the footing on which this business is put, and which is still subject to any change he may think proper to direct, as neither the letters nor bills are yet gone.

The Secretary of state proposes hereafter to remit in the course of each quarter, 10,000 D. for the ensuing quarter, as that will enable him to take advantage of the times when exchange is low. He proposes to direct at this time a further purchase of 12,166.66 D. (which with the 500. D. formerly obtained and 17,333.33 now remitted, will make 30,000 D. of this year's fund) at long sight,[3] which circumstance with the present low rate of exchange will enable him to remit it to advantage.

He has only further to add that he delivered to Mr. Vaughan orders on the bank of the US. in favor of the persons themselves from whom the bills were purchased, for their respective sums.

Th: Jefferson
April. 18. 1793.

RC (DNA: RG 59, MLR); endorsed by Tobias Lear. PrC (DLC); partly overwritten in a later hand. FC (Lb in DNA: RG 59, SDR). Tr (Lb in same, SDC). Entry in SJPL: "Report on the fund for foreign intercourse." Enclosures: (1) TJ to David Humphreys, 12 Apr. 1793. (2) TJ to Thomas Pinckney, 12 Apr. 1793. (3) TJ to Willink, Van Staphorst & Hubbard, 12 Apr. 1793.

For the circumstances that led TJ to draw upon the fund for foreign intercourse, which provided for the overseas expenses of the Department of State, see TJ to George Washington, 23 Mch. 1793. Washington, who had arrived back in Philadelphia from Mount Vernon only the day before, returned this report and its enclosures to TJ with his approval on 19 Apr. 1793, the day after TJ submitted them to him (Washington, *Journal*, 107, 109, 110, 114).

[1] Preceding four words interlined.
[2] Preceding number and two words interlined.
[3] TJ here canceled "as it will be wanting in Europe through the months."

To Edward Stevens

Dear Sir   Philadelphia Apr. 18. 1793.

You recollect that the British destroyed our records during their invasion of our state in the year 1781. Among these were all the letters I had written or received during my administration; that is to say the originals of the latter and copies of the former. These being chiefly interesting to myself, I am endeavoring to recover the most important of them by applications to the individuals with whom I had a public correspondence. I have recovered those written to the President of Congress, to Genl. Washington and Genl. Gates, and expect those written to Genl. Greene. As during your commands I wrote several to yourself also, I am to sollicit the favor of you to confide them to me to be copied; which being done, the originals shall be faithfully returned. They will come to me as safely by post, as if put at once into my own hands. Your speedy compliance will oblige Dear Sir your friend & servt.   Th: Jefferson

PrC (DLC); at foot of text: "General Stephens." Tr (DLC); 19th-century copy.

From Rodolph Vall-Travers

Amsterdam, 18 Apr. 1793. By the *Neptune* of Baltimore, Captain William Montgomery, he sends the enclosed resolution of their High Mightinesses concerning the mutual security of the fisheries of Holland and France during the present war received last week from van Sohn at The Hague and hopes it will be of service to the United States whether they sign a new treaty or suffer a rupture with Britain. Tomorrow he returns to Rotterdam and then goes to Antwerp and Brussels for a few weeks to collect information about trade, navigation, duties, and customs at Ostend, Antwerp, and Nieuwpoort in the Austrian Netherlands—now returned to their ancient constitution and governed by the Emperor's beloved brother Prince Charles, Archduke of Austria—that might pave the way for a treaty of commerce with them. He hopes soon to receive directions from "the Father of Your illustrious Republicks." P.S. Messrs. Beerenbroek & Van Dooren of this place will forward any letters directed to him during his absence from Rotterdam.

RC (DNA: RG 59, MLR); 3 p.; endorsed by TJ as received 20 July 1793 and so recorded in SJL. Enclosure not found.

George Washington to the Cabinet

Sir   Philadelphia April 18th. 1793.

The posture of affairs in Europe, particularly between France and Great Britain, places the United States in a delicate situation; and requires much consideration of the measures which will be proper for them to observe in the War between those Powers. With a view to forming a general plan of conduct for the Executive, I have stated and enclosed sundry questions to be considered preparatory to a meeting at my house to morrow; where I shall expect to see you at 9 'o clock, and to receive the result of your reflections thereon.

Go: Washington

RC (DLC); at foot of text: "The Secretary of State"; endorsed by TJ as received 18 Apr. 1793. PrC (DLC: Washington Papers); lacks addressee at foot of text. FC (Lb in DNA: RG 59, SDC); at head of text: "(Circular)" and "The Secretary of State, the Secry. of the Treasury, the Secretary of War, and The Attorney General of the U States." Tr (AMAE: CPEU, xxxvii); in French; at foot of text: "Pour traduction conforme, P. A. Adet." Entry in SJPL: "G.W. to Th:J. with questions relative to France & England."

ENCLOSURE

Questions on Neutrality and the Alliance with France

Question I. Shall a proclamation issue for the purpose of preventing inter-ferences of the Citizens of the United States in the War between France and Great Britain &ca.? Shall it contain a declaration of Neutrality or not? What shall it contain?

Question II. Shall a Minister from the Republic of France be received?

Question III. If received shall it be absolutely or with qualifications—and if with qualifications, of what kind?

Question IV. Are the United States obliged by good faith to consider the Treaties heretofore made with France as applying to the present situation of the parties. May they either renounce them, or hold them suspended 'till the Government of France shall be *established*.

Question V. If they have the right is it expedient to do either—and which?

Question VI. If they have an option—would it be a breach of Neutrality to consider the Treaties still in operation?

Question VII. If the Treaties are to be considered as now in operation, is the Guarantee in the Treaty of Alliance applicable to a defensive war only, or to War either offensive or defensive?

VIII. Does the War in which France is engaged appear to be offensive or defensive on her part?—or of a mixed and equivocal charac-ter?

IX. If of a mixed and equivocal character does the Guarantee in any event apply to such a War?

X. What is the effect of a Guarantee such as that to be found in the Treaty of Alliance between the United States and France?

XI. Does any Article in either of the Treaties prevent Ships of War, other than Privateers, of the Powers opposed to France, from coming into the Ports of the United States to act as Convoys to their own Merchantmen?—or does it lay any other restraints upon them more than would apply to the Ships of War of France?

Question XII. Should the future Regent of France send a minister to the United States ought he to be received?

XIII. Is it necessary or advisable to call together the two Houses of Congress with a view to the present posture of European Affairs? If it is, what should be the particular objects of such a call?

Philada. April 18th. 1793.   Go: WASHINGTON

MS (DLC); entirely in Washington's hand. PrC (DLC: Washington Papers); endorsed by Tobias Lear. FC (Lb in DNA: RG 59, SDC). Tr (AMAE: CPEU, xxxvii); in French; at foot of text: "pour traduction fidelle, Signé P. A. Adet." For the provenance in 1796 of the French Trs of this document and the

accompanying circular letter, see Turner, *CFM*, 815.

TJ immediately detected the fine hand of Alexander Hamilton behind these ques-tions, and the weight of the evidence generally supports his suspicion of Ham-iltonian authorship. On 9 Apr. 1793, shortly after the arrival in Philadelphia of reliable news of the French declaration of war on Great Britain, Hamilton wrote two letters to Chief Justice John Jay in New York about measures necessary for preserving American neutrality in this epochal conflict. In them Hamilton touched upon the points raised in questions 1-6 and 12 above, often in almost the same language as that employed by the President, and two days later Jay even sent him a draft declaration of neutrality, though it does not seem to have had any direct bearing on the one issued by the President on 22 Apr. 1793. Moreover, Attorney General Randolph subsequently informed TJ that on the day before Washington transmitted these questions to the Cabinet (and presumably prior to Washington's return to Philadelphia late that day from a visit to Mount Vernon) Hamilton had discussed with him "the whole

chain of reasoning of which these questions are the skeleton." Randolph deduced from this that Hamilton was the author of the questions, a judgment in which TJ concurred on the basis of their literary style and implied reservations about the French alliance (Notes on Relations with France, 6 May 1793; Syrett, *Hamilton*, XIV, 297-300, 307-10). Although it now seems indisputable that Hamilton inspired the form and content of the President's queries on neutrality, especially in view of the complete lack of evidence of similar advance preparations on the part of other Cabinet members, it is still impossible to determine whether he did so in conversation with Washington or by actually providing him with a now missing draft of the questions (Thomas, *Neutrality*, 26-30, 41-50; Freeman, *Washington*, VII, 43-7). See also the following document.

Cabinet Opinion on Washington's Questions on Neutrality and the Alliance with France

[19 Apr. 1793]

At a meeting of the heads of departments and the Attorney general at the President's Apr. 19. 1793. by special summons[1] to consider[2] of several questions previously communicated to them in writing by the President.

Qu. I. Shall a Proclamation issue &c.? [see the questions][3]

agreed by all[4] that a Proclamation shall issue, forbidding our citizens to take part in any hostilities on the seas with or against any of the belligerant powers, and warning them against carrying to any such powers any of those articles deemed contraband according to the modern usage of nations, and enjoining them from all acts and proceedings inconsistent with the duties of a friendly nation towards those at war.

Qu. II. Shall a Minister from the Republic of France be recieved?

agreed unanimously that he shall be received.

Qu. III If received, shall it be absolutely &c.[5]

⟨*The Attorney general and Secretary of state are of opinion he should be received absolutely and without qualifications.*

The Secretaries of the Treasury and War⟩

This and the subsequent questions are postponed to another day.[6]

MS (DLC: Washington Papers); entirely in TJ's hand, with canceled passage restored; undated; square brackets in original. Tr (Lb in DNA: RG 59, SDC); varies significantly (see textual notes below) and represents final form of opinion. In the absence of a PrC, it is impossible to determine whether TJ, acting on his own initiative or someone else's—Washington, a secretary or clerk acting under the President's direction, or another member of the Cabinet—was responsible for making the cancellation before or after the document was submitted to the President.

TJ's notes barely hint at the deep differences that emerged when the Cabinet met this date to consider the thirteen questions on neutrality posed by the President the day before (see Washington to the Cabinet, 18 Apr. 1793, and enclosure). In regard to the first question, which was whether to issue a PROCLAMATION declaring American neutrality in view of the outbreak of war between France and Great Britain, TJ differed with his colleagues in the Cabinet. Though he wished to follow a policy of strict neutrality, TJ opposed the issuance of a presidential proclamation to this effect on constitutional and diplomatic grounds. He contended that since the Constitution had authorized Congress to declare war, the executive was incompetent to proclaim a state of peace. He also argued that delaying a formal proclamation of the nation's neutral status would force Great Britain and France to make significant concessions to the United States on the issue of neutral rights. To these arguments Alexander Hamilton, with the support of Henry Knox and Edmund Randolph, replied by upholding the constitutional authority of the President to declare neutrality and by asserting that in the absence of such a declaration the well known wish of many Americans to take an active part in support of the French cause would lead to grave diplomatic complications with the British. Not wishing to weaken his position on the question of the mode of receiving the new French minister, TJ yielded to these arguments and acquiesced in the issuance of a proclamation on condition that it omit the word *neutrality*. In deference to TJ's wishes, the resultant proclamation, which Randolph drafted at Washington's behest and showed to TJ before the President approved it on 22 Apr. 1793, virtually declared the United States to be in a state of neutrality without using the word itself. Despite this concession to TJ, the President from the beginning regarded this document as a proclamation of neutrality (Notes on Washington's Questions on Neutrality and the Alliance with France, [6 May 1793]; Notes on the Sinking Fund and the Proclamation of Neutrality, 7 May 1793; TJ to James Madison, 23, 29 June 1793; TJ to James Monroe, 14 July 1793; Fitzpatrick, *Writings*, XXXII, 430-1; Syrett, *Hamilton*, XV, 33-43; Washington, *Journal*, 117, 118, 120).

After unanimously agreeing to receive the new French minister to the United States, Edmond Charles Genet, the Cabinet divided evenly over the President's third question—whether his reception should be absolute or qualified. For the ensuing debate over this issue, see Editorial Note on Jefferson's opinion on the treaties with France, at 28 Apr. 1793. See also Notes on the Reception of Edmond Charles Genet, 30 Mch. 1793.

[1] Preceding three words not in Tr.
[2] Remainder of sentence in Tr: "the foregoing questions proposed by the President."
[3] This line not in Tr.
[4] Tr to this point: "It was agreed by all on Question I (to wit, 'shall a proclamation issue' &ca.)."
[5] This line and the canceled passage below it not in Tr.
[6] Sentence in Tr: "The remaining questions were postponed for further consideration."

From Horatio Gates

DEAR SIR   Rose Hill 19th: April 1793.
   By this post I have sent you Seald Up under Cover, my Letter
Book; containing Copies of the Public Letters which I wrote during
my Command to the Southward and some few after my return from
thence; You will in the Index, find those addressed to You, regularly
numbered, and Paged; this, will save your Amanuensis some trouble
in Selecting them; I shall be obliged by your keeping the Book intirely
in your Own Care, and by your not confiding it to any Clerk but one,
in whom you repose the greatest Trust; as soon as you have done with
the Book, I desire you will favour me by returning it by the Post. With
high regard, I am Dear Sir your Obedt: Servant

                                                    HORATIO GATES

RC (DLC); endorsed by TJ as received 20 Apr. 1793 and so recorded in SJL.

To Thomas Greenleaf

SIR   Philadelphia Apr. 19. 1793.
   Being desirous of making a collection of the best gazettes which
have been published at the seats of the present general government
I take the liberty of troubling you to make up for me a collection of
your's of the years 1789. and 1790. either unbound or half-bound.
The stages will furnish the best method of conveying them to me, the
price of which conveyance shall be paid here, and that of the papers
remitted to you as soon as you shall be so good as to notify it to Sir
your very humble servt   TH: JEFFERSON

PrC (DLC); at foot of text: "Mr. Greenleaf. New York." Tr (DLC); 19th-century copy.

During the years mentioned by TJ Greenleaf's newspaper was first known as the *New-York Journal, and Weekly Register*, and then as the *New-York Journal, & Patriotic Register* (Brigham, *American Newspapers*, I, 656-7).

From Gouverneur Morris

DEAR SIR   Paris 19 April 1793
   Enclosed you have Copies of mine of the fourth fifth and eleventh
Instant No. 26. 27. and 28. Also Copies of my Letters to Mr. Lebrun
of the first and third with Copy of Captn. White's Memorial. You have

furthermore Copies of a Letter from the Minister of the Marine to the Minister of foreign Affairs of the seventh Instant and of two Letters of the eighth from the Latter to me, the one covering a Circular from the former to the Officers of his Department in the different Ports, and the other, two Decrees of the Convention the Purport of which I have already communicated.

Since mine of the fifth I learn that the Militia have in general quitted the Standard of Dumouriez, but he has about twelve thousand of the regular Troops, and there is Reason to beleive that others mean to join him. The Terror excited by his Defection begins to subside, or rather it is suspended untill some great Blow shall be struck. There seems to be more of Treason in this Country than was imagind, and every Day increases Suspicion, which whether well or ill founded has always the Effect of distracting the public Councils. Most People wonder at the Delay of the Prince de Cobourg, but besides the Necessity of collecting his Magazines Artillery &ca., which is a very heavy Affair, I have Reason to beleive that he waits untill some other Schemes are ready for Execution, and therefore it may be yet four or five Days before he commences the Siege of Valenciennes. Condé is a needful Preliminary, as in that Place he must receive the various Supplies which come up the Scheldt. It cannot hold out long.

You will observe that Dumouriez, and after him the Prince de Cobourg, declare themselves in favor of the late Constitution with such Alterations as the Nation may adopt; and the latter gives the most solemn Assurances that he will not meddle with the internal Affairs of France. This Conduct is wise, and will doubtless gain them a considerable Party in the Country, if they act consistently with those Declarations. It is said here (and those who say so to me tell me that they speak on good Authority) that the Powers allied against France begin already to be disunited. That they will disagree (if very successful) there can be little Doubt, because they are actuated by different Interests and Motives, but I think that at present those who assert the Disunion rather speak from Induction than from Information. Custine has retired you see to Weissembourg, and there he has a bad Position. The Enemy will probably attempt to cut off his Retreat before they attack him in Front. As yet we do not learn that the Austrians have cross'd the Rhine in upper Alsace, and that will be perhaps a Preliminary to the Operations against him.

As far as I can judge the public Mind, it seems that there is a general State of Suspense. Success on either Side will fix the Opinions of a very great Number, who will then act to shew their Sincerity. Here they hang People for giving an Opinion in favor of Royalty (that is they cut off their Heads) but yet I am told that such Opinion is openly avowed and supported in the Streets. I am told that there is a Majority even of the Convention who think a King necessary, but as they see the Loss of their own Lives in Connection with the ReEstablishment of the Throne, it is not to be suppos'd that they would tell such Thoughts; and therefore the Information may well be suspected. Time will shew that there are among them some false Brethren, and certainly the most intelligent must be convinc'd that the republican Virtues are not yet of Gallic Growth. The Duke of Orleans is in the Way of reaping the Fruits of his Conduct; being as you will see sent a Prisoner to Marseilles. The Storm thickens all round us, but as yet one cannot certainly determine how it will burst. The Attempts made to excite Disturbances in Paris have hitherto prov'd ineffectual, but that Stroke seems to be reserv'd for the Moment when the Deputies now on Commission in the Departments shall return. It is possible, meerly possible, that all may go off smoothly, but the Chances are greatly the other Way. I am my dear Sir with Esteem & Respect your obedient Servant   GOUV. MORRIS

P.S. I should have mention'd that I am told there is a Plan in Operation here to detach Great Britain from the Confederation and make a seperate Peace with her but I am perswaded that the Attempt in itself vain must fail from the Parties said to be employ'd if from no other Cause.

RC (DNA: RG 59, DD); at head of text: "No. 29"; at foot of first page: "Thomas Jefferson Esqr. Secretary of State"; endorsed by TJ as received 9 Sep. 1793 and so recorded in SJL. FC (Lb in DLC: Gouverneur Morris Papers). Tr (DNA: RG 46, Senate Records, 3d Cong., 1st sess.); copy made early in 1794 by State Department; with omissions. PrC (DNA: RG 59, MD). Tr (Lb in same, DD). A Dupl recorded in SJL as received 5 Sep. 1793 has not been found. Enclosures: (1) Morris to TJ, 4, 5 Apr. 1793. (2) Morris to TJ, 11 Apr. 1793, and enclosures. (3) Morris to Lebrun, 3 Apr. 1793, enclosing a copy of a memorial of Captain Thomas White and a proclamation of Congress pertaining to the treaty of amity and commerce with France, especially Article 15, and urging that violators be prosecuted. (4) Memorial of Thomas White to Morris, 3 Apr. 1793, protesting the seizure of the *Laurence*, a ship under his command that was bound from Charleston to London with a cargo of rice and indigo, by the *Sans-culotte*, a French privateer from Honfleur, in the latitude of Portland on 21 Mch. 1793, its removal to Le Havre, and his mistreatment by the captor's crew. (5) Monge, Minister of Marine, to Lebrun, 7 Apr. 1793, stating, in response to a letter from Morris to Lebrun respecting French captures of American vessels in violation of American neutrality and the treaty of alliance, that he has issued orders directing that American neutral rights be honored, and that Morris should be assured of satisfaction in every case provided American vessels conform to laws relative to contraband prohibited on neutral vessels in time of war. (6) Lebrun to Morris, 8 Apr. 1793, stating that he has requested the Minister of Marine to secure justice for Captain White and enclosing a circular letter from that minister to the civil ordonnateurs of the ports of the Republic. (7) Monge's Circular to the Civil Ordonnateurs in the Ports of the Republic, 30 Mch. 1793, ordering them to stop the capture of American vessels by French privateers and calling their attention to a 1 Mch. 1793 decree of the National Convention admitting all non-prohibited articles on neutral vessels (Trs in same, DD, in French; Trs in DNA: RG 46, Senate Records, 3d Cong., 1st sess., in French and English; PrCs in DNA: RG 59, MD; Trs in Lb in same, DD, in French and English).

HIS DEFECTION: On 5 Apr. 1793 Charles François du Perier Dumouriez, the commander of the Army of the North, defected to the Austrians after the failure of a treasonous plot whereby, in return for an Austrian promise to refrain from attacking his force, he planned to march his army to Paris in order to reestablish the monarchy (Scott and Rothaus, *French Revolution*, I, 332-3). On 5 Sep. 1793 TJ submitted this letter to the President, who returned it the same day (Washington, *Journal*, 238).

From Tobias Lear

Saturday Afternoon [20 Apr. 1793]

T. Lear has the honor to return to the Secretary of State the letter which he this day sent to the President—and to inform him that the President expects the Gentlemen to be at his house on Monday at nine o'clock to decide upon the other questions which are before them.

T. Lear begs leave to observe to the Secretary (if it has slipped his memory) that Colo. Humphreys mentions in his letter of the 8th of Feby. that he found *two Cyphers* among Mr. Barclay's papers—one of which is very probably Mr. Pinckney's.

RC (DLC); partially dated; endorsed by TJ as received 20 Apr. 1793.

The LETTER returned to the Secretary of State was probably one of the following: Thomas Pinckney to TJ, 30 Jan., 5 Feb.

1793, TJ to Pinckney, 20 Apr. 1793, or TJ to Gouverneur Morris, 20 Apr. 1793 (Washington, *Journal*, 115-16). For the Cabinet meeting of 22 Apr. 1793 UPON THE OTHER QUESTIONS relating to neutrality, see same, 117.

To Gouverneur Morris

DEAR SIR   Philadelphia Apr. 20. 1793.

Since my letters of the 12th. and 15th. of the last month, which went by Mr. Dupont, I have received one from Mr. Pinckney wherein he informs me that being unable to procure us a Chief Coiner in England he had written to you to desire you to engage Mr. Droz, whom he understood to be employed at Paris, not much to his satisfaction. We shall be glad, very glad, to receive Droz. But this matter has already been so long retarded that we are obliged to bring it to an issue, as the officer who is employed in the interim, and who answers pretty well, will not consent to remain on so indefinite a footing. We wish you therefore to bring Mr. Droz to an immediate decision, and we must place the matter on this footing, that if he be not embarked by the 1st. day of July, we shall give a permanent commission to the present officer, and be free to receive no other.

No country perhaps was ever so thoroughly disposed against war, as ours. These dispositions pervade every description of it's citizens, whether in or out of office. They cannot perhaps suppress their affections, nor their wishes. But they will suppress the effects of them so as to preserve a fair neutrality. Indeed we shall be more useful as neutrals than as parties, by the protection which our flag will give to supplies of provision. In this spirit let all your assurances be given to the government with which you reside. I am with great & sincere esteem Dear Sir your most obedt. humble servt TH: JEFFERSON

PrC (DLC); at foot of text: "Mr. Morris." FC (Lb in DNA: RG 59, DCI).

Henry Voigt was currently EMPLOYED IN THE INTERIM as chief coiner of the

United States Mint (TJ to Washington, 9 June 1792, and note). TJ submitted this letter to the President on this day (Washington, *Journal*, 116).

From Thomas Paine

MY DEAR FRIEND   Paris April 20th 2d year of the Republic

The Gentleman (Dr. Romer) to whom I entrust this letter is an intimate acquaintance of Lavater, but I have not had the opportunity of seeing him as he had sett off for Havre prior to my writing this letter, which I forward to him under cover from one of his friends who is also an acquaintance of mine.

We are now in an Extraordinary Crisis, and it is not altogether without some considerable faults here. Dumouriez, partly from having no fixed principles of his own, and partly from the continual persecution of the Jacobins, who act without either prudence or morality, has gone off to the Enemy and taken a considerable part of the Army with him. The expedition to Holland has totally failed and all Brabant is again in the hands of the Austrians. You may suppose the Consternation which such a sudden reverse of fortune has occasioned, but it has been without commotion. Dumouriez threatened to be in Paris in three weeks. It is now three weeks ago. He is still on the frontiers near to Mons with the Enemy who do not make any progress. Dumouriez has proposed to reestablish the former constitution in which plan the Austrians act with him. But if France and the National Convention act prudently this project will not succeed. In the first place there is a popular disposition against it, and there is force sufficient to prevent it. In the next place, a great deal is to be taken into the calculation with respect to the Enemy. There are now so many powers accidentally Jumbled together as to render it exceedingly difficult to them, to agree upon any common[1] object. The first object, that of restoring the old Monarchy, is evidently given up by the proposal to reestablish the late Constitution. The object of England and Prussia was to preserve Holland, and the Object of[2] Austria was to recover Brabant, while those separate objects lasted, each party having one, the Confederation could hold together each helping the other; but after this I see not how a common object is to be formed. To all this is to be added the probable disputes about apportioning the expence, and the projects of reimbursements. The Enemy has once adventured into France and they had the permission, or the good fortune to get back again. On every military calculation it is a hazardous adventure, and Armies are not much disposed to try a second time the ground upon which they have been defeated.

Had this revolution been conducted consistently with its principles there was once a good prospect of extending liberty through the greatest part of Europe, but I now relinquish that hope. Should the Enemy by venturing into France put themselves again in a condition of being captured, the hope will revive, but that is a risk that I do not wish to see tried, lest it should fail.

As the prospect of a general freedom is now much shortened, I begin to contemplate returning home. I shall wait the event of the proposed constitution, and then take my final leave of Europe. I have not written to the President as I have nothing to communicate more than in this letter. Please to present to him my affection and Compliments, and remember me among the Circle of my Friends. Your sincere and Affectionate Friend &c.   THOMAS PAINE

P.S. I just now received a letter from General Lewis Morris who tells me that the house and Barn on my farm at N. Rochelle are burnt down. I assure you I shall not bring money enough to build another.

RC (DLC); endorsed by TJ as received 9 Sep. 1793 and so recorded in SJL.

[1] Paine here canceled "cause."
[2] Paine here canceled "Pruss."

To Thomas Pinckney

DEAR SIR   Philadelphia. Apr. 20. 1793.

In a Postscript to my letter of the 12th. I acknoleged the receipt of yours of Jan. 3. since which those of Jan. 30. and Feb. 5. have been received by the William Penn.

[577]

With respect to our negociation with Mr. Hammond, it is exactly in the state in which it was when you left America, not one single word having been received in reply to my general answer (of which you had a copy). He says he waits for instructions, which he pretends to expect from packet to packet. But sometimes the Ministers are all in the country, sometimes they are absorbed in negotiations nearer home, sometimes it is the hurry of impending war, or attention to other objects, the stock of which is inexhaustible, and can therefore never fail those who desire nothing but that things shall rest as they are. Perhaps however the present times may hasten justice.

We shall be glad to receive the Assayer you hope to procure, as soon as possible; for we cannot get one in this country equal to the business in all it's parts. With respect to Mr. Droz, we retain the same desire to engage him, but we are forced to require an immediate decision as the officer employed in the interim, and who does tolerably well, will not continue much longer under an uncertainty of permanent employment. I must therefore desire you to press Mr. Morris to bring Droz to an immediate determination: and we place the matter on this ground with him, that if he is not embarked by the 1st. day of July next, we shall give a permanent commission to the present officer and be free to receive no other.   We are likely to be in very great distress for copper for the mint, and must therefore press your expediting what we desired you to order from Sweden.

You may on every occasion give assurances which cannot go beyond the real desires of this country to preserve a fair neutrality in the present war, on condition that the rights of neutral nations are respected in us, as they have been settled in *modern* times, either by the express declarations of the powers of Europe, or their adoption of them on particular occasions. From our treaties with France and Holland, and that of England and France, a very clear and simple line of conduct can be marked out for us, and I think we are not unreasonable in expecting that England shall recognise towards us the same principles which she has stipulated to recognise towards France, in a state of neutrality. I have the honor to be with great & sincere esteem Dr. Sir Your most obedt & most humble servt   TH: JEFFERSON

RC (NjGbS); at foot of first page: "Mr. Pinckney"; endorsed by William A. Deas. PrC (DLC). FC (Lb in DNA: RG 59, DCI).

MY GENERAL ANSWER: TJ to George Hammond, 29 May 1792. TJ submitted the above letter to the President on this day (Washington, *Journal*, 115-16).

To Jean Baptiste Ternant

SIR   Philadelphia April 20. 1793.

Your letter of the 13th. instant, asking monies to answer the expenses and Salaries of the Consular Offices of France, has been duly laid before the President, and his directions thereon taken.

I have, in consequence, to observe to you that before the new Government of France had time to attend to things on this side the Atlantic, and to provide a deposit of money for their purposes here, there appeared a degree of necessity that we, as the friends and debtors of the Nation, should keep their affairs from suffering, by furnishing money for urgent purposes. This obliged us to take on ourselves to judge of the purpose, because on the soundness of that we were to depend for our justification. Hence we furnished monies for their Colonies and their Agents here, without express authority, judging from the importance and necessity of the case, that they would approve of our interference.

But this kind of necessity is now at an end: The Government has established a deposit of money in the hands of their minister here, and we have nothing now to do, but to furnish the money, which we are in the course of doing, without looking into the purposes to which it is to be applied. Their minister is to be the judge of these, and to pay it to whom, and for what he pleases.

If it be urged that they have appropriated all the money we are furnishing to other objects, that you are not authorized to divert any of it to any other purpose, and therefore that you *need a further sum*; it may be answered that it will not lessen the stretch of authority to add an *unauthorized payment by us* to an *unauthorized application by you*, and that it seems fitter that their minister should exercise a discretion over their appropriations, standing, as he does, in a place of confidence, authority, and responsibility, than we who are strangers, and unamenable to them. It is a respect we owe to their authority to leave to those acting under that, the transaction of their affairs, without an intermedling on our part which might justly appear officious.

In this point of light I hope you will view our conduct, and that the Consular Officers will be sensible that in referring them to your care, under which the national authority has placed them, we do but conform ourselves to that authority. I have the honor to be with sentiments of great respect and esteem, Sir Your most obedient and most humble Servant.   TH: JEFFERSON

RC (Goodspeed's Bookshop, Boston, Massachusetts, 1950); in a clerk's hand, signed by TJ; at foot of text: "The Minister Plen: of France." PrC (DLC); at foot

[579]

of first page by TJ in ink: "Mr. Ternant."
FC (Lb in DNA: RG 59, DL).

For the antecedents, see Notes for Reply
to Ternant, 18 Apr. 1793, and note.

To Richard Curson

DEAR SIR   Philadelphia Apr. 21. 1793.
  The ship Four friends, Capt. Volans, received three pipes of wine
for me at Lisbon, to be landed in Virginia, at Norfolk, and I had taken
measures in Richmond to have them received, duties paid &ca. He has
however carried them to Baltimore, where it becomes necessary for
me to provide for their entry &ca. A recollection of your very friendly
readiness to do me kind offices, has induced me to recur to you to have
these wines entered, and sent to Richmond by the first safe conveyance
to the care of Mr. James Brown merchant there. I inclose you the bill
of lading and[1] a bank post note of 12.D. to pay the freight from Lisbon
to Baltimore. I asked of the custom house officer here a blank bond for
the duties which I would have executed and inclosed to you. But he
writes me he has no blank bonds. If therefore the collector at Baltimore
will send me one by post I will execute and return it immediately, and
in the mean time stand responsible by virtue of this letter for paying
the duties in due time, which I believe is 6. months. I have had so
much experience of your goodness that I will not add to your trouble
by an apology. Accept assurances of the sincere esteem with which I
am Dear Sir your most obedt humble servt   TH: JEFFERSON

PrC (DLC); at foot of text: "Mr.
R. Curson. Baltimore." Enclosures not
found.

The letter from Sharp Delany, the CUS-
TOM HOUSE OFFICER HERE, has not been

found and is not recorded in SJL. For
the substance of Curson's reply, see TJ to
Archibald Moncrief, 28 Apr. 1793, and
note.

[1] Preceding five words interlined.

To Thomas Mann Randolph, Jr.

DEAR SIR   Philadelphia Apr. 21. 1793.
  I have intended this fortnight to make out a list of the packages of
furniture I have sent to Richmond, with the contents of each, that if
there was any thing which would be convenient to yourself or Martha,
you might have it brought up immediately; but an eternal hurry of
business prevents me from thinking of that or any thing else of a private
nature but just in the moment of setting down to write to you, and

then does not give me the time. I must still therefore put it off: and thus I go on, like a horse under whip and spur from the start to the poll, without time to look to the right or left, my mind eternally forbidden to turn, even for a moment, to any thing agreeable or useful to my self or family.—I informed you some time ago that I had sold Brimmer, and that Matchless was killed, so that I am reduced to a pair. Tarquin must be sold here if possible, because his hoofs are so tender that he would be absolutely useless at Monticello. Consequently I must have a third horse before I can get home: and I think it will be better to get a good one at once in Virginia, than to buy an indifferent one here. I will therefore ask the favor of you to purchase one for me, if you can meet with one a match for mine,[1] of fine form, full sized, young, sound[2] broken to a carriage and without tricks in it. I would rather give latitude in the price, than dispense with any of these qualities. But it would be necessary for me to have a credit till the tobacco of the present year can produce money. Should you be able to procure me such a horse, I will take arrangements for having him got here.

Mr. Genest, the new minister from the Republic of France, is arrived at Charleston. The frigate in which he came, brought into that port an English prize.—Mr. Pinkney has seen the Scotch threshing machine. He says that three men and three horses get out from 8. to 16. bushels an hour. He promises I shall have a model in time to get out the crop of this year. My love to my dear Martha, and kiss the little ones for me. I am my dear Sir yours affectionately   TH: JEFFERSON

P.S. You will doubtless have heard that Donald & Burton have stopped payment. If you have not, say nothing of it.

RC (DLC); at foot of first page: "Mr. Randolph." received 1 Apr. 1793, that has not been found.

Randolph had written a letter to TJ on 21 Mch. 1793, recorded in SJL as

[1] Preceding four words interlined.
[2] Word interlined in place of "and."

From John Carey

SIR   Tuesday April 23: 1793

I have the honor of presenting, for your inspection, the remainder of what I have been able to copy of general Washington's correspondence. The whole of those 808 pages, and the best part of what has been copied by two of the gentlemen in your office, has been carefully compared with the originals. One of the original letters, of a particular nature, I take the liberty of enclosing. The index, that accompanies the papers, will shew where to find my copy, if you wish to cut it out: and if this be the case, I presume I will not do amiss, in striking out every passage (for several occur in other letters) pointing out even the existence of such pieces.

I am extremely sorry, that it is not in my power to complete the correspondence of the commander in chief, as I expect to embark on Sunday next. However, if I might, without impropriety, request your interference, I am confident that a single word from you, would considerably expedite the business, and induce the two gentlemen in your office to hasten the part they have in hands—which was undertaken on a presumption that I was to sail by the first of April, is already paid for in advance—and not yet finished. Indeed the difficulties and delays that have been unnecessarily thrown in my way, since I first employed an *extern* to assist me, and dropped hints that I might probably complete the work, would render it necessary for me to request your interference in another manner, if I were to stay and continue it. But this being wholly out of my power, I think it needless to particularize them.

Before I conclude, Sir, I would beg leave to remind you of the utility of a certificate, under the seal of your office, purporting in general terms, that I have, under the proper authority, had access to the original papers, have made oath (which I am ready to do) that I have diligently and carefully copied, have not wilfully perverted the text in any instance—and that my copies have been compared with, and corrected by the originals.

As to sealing up my papers, and directing them in the manner I had the honor of mentioning to you some time ago, you alone, Sir, are a competent judge of the propriety of the measure. I shall therefore only observe (as perhaps this circumstance may make some difference) that the vessel, in which I sail, is to touch first at Lisbon, and thence, in 4 or 5 days, proceed to Dublin. With Sentiments of sincere respect & gratitude, I have the honor to be, Sir, your most obliged, & most obedient, humble servant, JOHN CAREY

RC (DLC); addressed: "The honble. the Secretary of State"; endorsed by TJ as received 24 Apr. 1792 and so recorded in SJL. Enclosure not found.

For Carey's subsequent edition of GENERAL WASHINGTON'S CORRESPONDENCE, see Carey to TJ, 30 June 1792, and note.

To Archibald Moncrief

SIR   Philadelphia Apr. 23. 1793.

I am much obliged by your kind attention to the three pipes of wine brought to Baltimore for me. Capt. Volans had called on me here, and I had in consequence written to Mr. Curson of Baltimore, inclosing to him the bill of lading, and a bank note for the freight, and desiring him to send me from the Custom house the usual form of the bond for the duties which I would execute and return by post. The wine to be sent by the first safe conveyance to Richmond *direct*. As I presume Mr. Curson has been so obliging as to proceed in this as I had requested, I have only to repeat my thanks for your friendly notice, and assure you of the regard with which I am Sir your most obedt. humble servt

TH: JEFFERSON

PrC (DLC); at foot of text: "Mr. Archibald Moncrief. Baltimore." Tr (DLC); 19th-century copy. Recorded in SJL under 22 Apr. 1793.

Archibald Moncrief was a Baltimore merchant whose home and counting house were located at 14 Water Street ([William] Thompson and [James L.] Walker, *The Baltimore Town and Fell's Point Directory* ... [Baltimore, 1796], 55, s.v. "Moncrieff"). Moncrief's letter to TJ of 18 Apr. 1793, recorded in SJL as received 22 Apr. 1793, has not been found.

To Jean Baptiste Ternant, George Hammond, and F. P. Van Berckel

SIR   Philadelphia April 23rd. 1793.

As far as the public Gazettes are to be credited, we may presume that war has taken place among several of the Nations of Europe, in which, France, England, Holland and Prussia, are particularly engaged. Disposed as the U.S. are[1] to pursue steadily the ways of Peace, and to remain in Friendship with all Nations, the President has thought it expedient, by Proclamation,[2] of which I enclose you a copy, to notify this disposition to our Citizens, in order to intimate to them the Line of conduct for which they are to prepare: and this he has done without waiting for a formal notification from the belligerent powers. He hopes that those powers, and your Nation in particular, will consider this early precaution as a proof, the more candid, as it has been unasked, of the sincere and impartial intentions of our Country, and that what is meant merely as a general intimation to our Citizens,

[583]

shall not be construed to their prejudice in any Courts of Admiralty, as if it were conclusive evidence of their Knowledge of the existence of war, and of the Powers engaged in it. Of this we could not give them conclusive information, because we have it not ourselves; and till it is given to us in form, and so communicated to them, we must consider all their acts as lawful which would have been lawful in a state of Peace. I have the honor to be, with great respect Sir, Your most obedient and most humble servant,

PrC (DLC); in the hand of George Taylor, Jr., unsigned, with additions by TJ; at foot of text in ink by TJ: "M. de Ternant." PrC (DLC); in a clerk's hand, unsigned; at foot of text in ink by TJ: "Mr. Hammond." PrC (DLC); in a clerk's hand, unsigned; at foot of text in ink by TJ: "Mr. Van Berkel." FC (Lb in DNA: RG 59, DL); at head of text: "The Ministers of France and Great Britain and the Resident of the United Netherlands"; at foot of text: "Copy of this sent to all our Ministers." Tr (NjP: Andre deCoppet Collection); in a clerk's hand, except for note at foot of text by TJ: "Mr. Ternant Mr. Van Berkel Mr. Hammond." Tr (DLC: Short Papers); in a clerk's hand, except for note at foot of text by Taylor: "Mr. Ternant Mr. Van Berckel Mr. Hammond." PrC of another Tr (DLC); in a clerk's hand; at foot of text: (by Taylor) "Mr. Ternant [Mr.] Van Berckel [Mr.] Hammond" and (by TJ in ink) "copy sent to all our ministers." Tr (Lb in PRO: FO 116/3). Tr (same, 5/1). Enclosure: Proclamation of Neutrality, 22 Apr. 1793 (Fitzpatrick, *Writings*, XXXII, 430-1). Enclosed in TJ to Gouverneur Morris, Thomas Pinckney, and William Short, 26 Apr. 1793, and TJ to William

Carmichael and David Humphreys, 26 Apr. 1793.

TJ submitted a draft of the above letter with a brief covering note to Washington of this date (RC in DNA: RG 59, MLR, addressed "The President [. . .]," endorsed by Tobias Lear; Tr in Lb in same, SDC; recorded in SJPL). On the same day Tobias Lear wrote a brief note to TJ returning the draft and informing him that the President had approved it (RC in DLC; addressed: "The Secret[. . .]"). See also Washington, *Journal*, 118; and Notes on the Sinking Fund and the Proclamation of Neutrality, 7 May 1793.

A letter from Ternant to TJ of 25 Apr. 1793, which Washington described as an answer to this letter, is recorded in SJL as received 26 Apr. 1793 but has not been found (Washington, *Journal*, 125).

[1] Preceding four words interlined in ink by TJ in place of "ourselves," a change made or reflected in all other texts except the FC and the Trs in NjP and DLC.
[2] FC, Trs in NjP and DLC, and PrC of another Tr in DLC: "President of the United States has thought it expedient, by the proclamation."

To Alexander Hamilton

SIR   Philadelphia April, 24th: 1793.

Nearly the whole of the last draft of contingent money for the Department of State being expended, I must request the favor of you to cause a warrant to issue payable to Geo. Taylor Junr. for the sum of six hundred, fifty one Dollars, sixty seven Cents, the Balance of the appropriation for my office, to be applied to defray it's contingent

expenses; and am with respect Sir, Your most obedient & most humble servt.   (signed) TH: JEFFERSON

PrC (DLC); in the hand of George Taylor, Jr., with signature added in ink by him;
at foot of text: "The Secretary of the Treasury." FC (Lb in DNA: RG 59, DL). Not
recorded in SJL.

From George Hammond

SIR   Philadelphia 24h April 179[3]
I have the honor of acknowledging the receipt of your letter of
yesterday inclosing a copy of the President's proclamation. I beg you to
be persuaded that I entertain a proper sense of this spontaneous proof
of the disposition of the United States to observe a generally friendly
and impartial conduct towards the belligerent powers: But as you seem
to be of opinion that, in order to give this measure immediate and
complete operation, it is necessary for this government to obtain some
more formal knowledge of the existence of hostilities than such as is to
be collected from the public Gazettes, I think it my duty to inform you,
Sir, that I have received from my Court an official notification that, on
the 1st. of February last, the French national convention declared war
against Great Britain and the United Netherlands. I have the honor
to be, with great respect, Sir, your most obedient humble Servant,
                                              GEO. HAMMOND

RC (DNA: RG 59, NL); dateline torn;
at foot of text: "[The] Secretary of state
&c &c &c"; endorsed by TJ as received
24 Apr. 1793 and so recorded in SJL.
FC (Lb in PRO: FO 116/3). Tr (same,
115/2). Tr (same, 5/1). Tr (Lb in DNA:
RG 59, NL).

TJ submitted this letter to Washington
this day, and the President immediately
returned it (Washington, *Journal*, 118).

To Gouverneur Morris

DEAR SIR   Philadelphia Apr. 24. 1793.
Mr. Robert Leslie a watchmaker of this city goes to establish himself
at London. As his curiosity may lead him to Paris, I take the liberty
of asking your patronage of him, so far as may be necessary to enable
him to see what may be serviceable to him in his way. He is without
exception one of the greatest mechanics I have ever known in any
country, he is modest, and of pure integrity, and will fully merit any
service you can render him. The rod-pendulum, an entire new method

of making the repeating apparatus of a watch, with one eigth of the peices heretofore used, two different constructions of marine clocks which he carries with him, are some of many inventions of his. I am with great respect & esteem Dr Sir your friend & servt

TH: JEFFERSON

PrC (DLC); at foot of text: "Mr. G. Morris." Tr (DLC); 19th-century copy.

Three days later TJ drew an order on the Bank of the United States for $115.30 to pay Robert Leslie for the "great clock" and for cleaning a small one (MB, 27 Apr. 1793). The order, signed and dated 27 Apr. 1793 by TJ, is in the Riggs Historical Collection, Riggs National Bank, Washington, D.C.

To Thomas Pinckney

DEAR SIR   Philadelphia Apr. 24. 1793.

The bearer hereof Mr. Robert Leslie, a watchmaker of this city, goes to establish himself in London. His great eminence will unquestionably ensure his success, if he can but be known. I have considered him and the deceased Mr. Rumsey (both born in the same neighborhood) as the two greatest mechanics I have ever met with in any country. Not to mention many other useful inventions, we are indebted to Mr. Leslie for the idea of the rod-pendulum for a measure, for an entire new method of making the repeating apparatus of a watch with about one eigth of the number of peices hitherto used, and he carries with him two different constructions of marine clocks, to try on his voyage. I take the liberty of recommending him to your patronage and protection, and can assure you that as a man of the purest integrity of modesty and talents he will fully merit it. I am with great & sincere esteem Dear Sir your friend & servt   TH: JEFFERSON

PrC (DLC); at foot of text: "Mr. Pinckney." Tr (DLC); 19th-century copy.

To John Brown Cutting

DEAR SIR   Philadelphia Apr. 25. 1793.

The bearer hereof, Mr. Robert Leslie, a watchmaker of this city goes to establish himself in London. I consider him and the late Mr. Rumsey as two of the most ingenious mechanics I have ever known. Having been a witness to your patronage of Mr. Rumsey I have thought I could not more befriend Mr. Leslie than to make him also known to you.

6

55

Your knowlege of London may enable you to give very useful counsel to one who knows nothing of it, and whose modesty and candor might make him a prey to the place. His real worth and pure integrity will do justice to any recommendations you may be so kind as to give of him. I am with great esteem Dear Sir your most obedt. humble servt

TH: JEFFERSON

PrC (DLC); at foot of text: "Mr. J. B. Cutting." Tr (DLC); 19th-century copy.

From Lord Wycombe

DEAR SIR   London April 25. 1793.

I trust you will excuse the liberty I take in introducing to your acquaintance Mr. Godfrey who proposes making a tour for the purpose of amusement and information only in the United States. He is a gentleman of highly respectable connections and of large property in this country, and is accompanied by Mr. Archdeken who has the same motives for visiting America. These gentlemen are naturally desirous of the honour of becoming acquainted with the President, and I shall esteem it as a particular favor if you will put them into the best mode of being presented to him. It is unnecessary for me to assure you how happy I shall at all times be to recieve your commands in this country as well as how sincerely I am Dear Sir Your obliged friend & Humble Serv   WYCOMBE

RC (MHi); endorsed by TJ as received 6 July 1793 and so recorded in SJL.

On the following day Thomas Pinckney wrote a letter of introduction to TJ: "Lord Viscount Hampden has done me the honor to request Letters of Introduction for Mr. Archdekne and Mr. Godfrey who purpose travelling through some parts of the United States. This respectable Recom-

mendation will I am convinced insure them your good Offices in procuring them such a Reception as will enable them to effect their purpose to the best Advantage" (RC in DLC; in the hand of William A. Deas, with complimentary close and signature by Pinckney; at foot of text: "Mr. Jefferson. Secretary of State"; endorsed by TJ as received 6 July 1793 and so recorded in SJL).

To William Carmichael and David Humphreys

SIR   Philadelphia, April, 26th. 1793.

The public papers giving us reason to believe that the War is becoming nearly general in Europe, and that it has already involved Nations,

[587]

with which we are in daily habits of Commerce and friendship, the President has thought it proper to issue the Proclamation of which I enclose you a copy, in order to mark out to our Citizens the line of conduct they are to pursue. Uninformed whether the government where you reside, will take a part in the War, or remain neutral, I transmit you this paper, as also, copies of the letters written on that subject to the representatives of the belligerent powers here, and to ours, with them. Should the nation where you are, remain neutral, these papers will serve merely for your information: should they take a part in the War, you will be pleased to make to them the same communication, which our Ministers at Paris, London, and the Hague, are instructed to make. I am, with great esteem and respect, Sir, Your most obedient and most humble servant   TH: JEFFERSON

RC (NjP: Andre deCoppet Collection); in the hand of George Taylor, Jr., signed by TJ; at foot of text: "Colo. Humphreys Minister Residt. at the Court of Portugal"; endorsed by Humphreys. FC (Lb in DNA: RG 59, DCI). PrC of RC (DLC); in Taylor's hand, signed by TJ; at foot of text: "William Carmichael Esqr." FC (Lb in DNA: RG 59, DCI). Enclosures: (1) Proclamation of Neutrality, 22 Apr. 1793

(Fitzpatrick, *Writings*, XXXII, 430-1). (2) TJ to Jean Baptiste Ternant, George Hammond, and F. P. Van Berckel, 23 Apr. 1793. (3) TJ to Gouverneur Morris, Thomas Pinckney, and William Short, 26 Apr. 1793.

TJ submitted a draft of this letter to the President on this day (Washington, *Journal*, 120).

Circular to the Governors of the States

SIR   Philadelphia April 26th: 1793.

The war in Europe having now become nearly general, and involving some nations with whom we are in intimate habits of commerce and friendship, The President of the United States has thought it expedient to put our citizens on their guard as to the line of conduct they are to observe towards the parties at war. He has for this purpose issued the proclamation of which I have the honor to inclose you a copy; and entertains no doubt but that injunctions so interesting to the happiness and prosperity of the United States, will have the benefit of Your Excellency's aid towards their general and strict observance by the citizens of the State over which you preside. I have the honor to be with great respect and esteem Your Excellency's most obedient and most humble servant   TH: JEFFERSON

RC (R-Ar); in a clerk's hand, signed by TJ; at foot of text, with last two words in the hand of George Taylor, Jr.: "To his Excellency the Governor of The State of

Rh. Island." RC (Mrs. Henry M. Sage, Albany, New York, 1954); in a clerk's hand, signed by TJ; at foot of text, with last word in Taylor's hand: "To his Excellency the Governor of The State of Connecticut"; endorsed as received 10 May and answered 15 May 1793. RC (Nj); in a clerk's hand, signed by TJ; at foot of text: "His Excellency the Governor of The State of New Jersey." RC (DLC: Shelby Family Papers); in a clerk's hand, signed by TJ; addressed by Taylor: "His Excellency The Governor of the State of Kentucky Lincoln County near Danville"; franked; postmarked 29 Apr. 1793. Dft (DLC); in TJ's hand, unsigned, with note at foot of text in Taylor's hand: "to all the Governors except of Penna."; endorsed by Taylor: "April 26—1793 Circular To the Governors"; with directions on verso in TJ's hand:

"a copy to the Gov. of each state.

have 50. proclamations *immediately* printed on a quarto peice of paper.

prepare a copy of this letter without delay & inclose a proclamation in it to Govr. Mifflin.

as those to the other governors cannot go till Monday's post, they may lie till the letters to our foreign ministers are pre-

pared because there is an opportunity of sending them tomorrow."
FC (Lb in DNA: RG 59, DL); at head of text: "The Governors of the several States." Tr (Lb in PHarH); at foot of text: "His Excellency the Governor of the State of Pennsylvania." Recorded in SJPL. Enclosure: Proclamation of Neutrality, 22 Apr. 1793 (Fitzpatrick, *Writings*, XXXII, 430-1).

Two days earlier Washington had instructed TJ to write a circular letter to the state governors enclosing the PROCLAMATION of neutrality, and on 26 Apr. TJ submitted a draft of this letter to the President (Washington, *Journal*, 118, 120). In a brief note of the same date returning the draft to TJ, Tobias Lear wrote: "The President approves of the enclosed" (RC in DLC; addressed: "The Secre[...]"; note at foot of text in TJ's hand: "to wit the letter of this day to the Governors"; endorsed by TJ as received 26 Apr. 1793).

To Ernst Frederick Guyer

SIR   Philadelphia Apr. 26. 1793

I have duly received your letter of the 24th. inst. inclosing a Memorial to the President on the subject of an instrument and table of your invention for ascertaining the longitude at sea, and desiring that the patent-board might appoint a time for examining into the same. I suppose it had escaped your notice that that board was discontinued by the late Congress, and that the business of issuing patents was referred to the department of state, from which they are given out as a matter of right on the party's complying with certain conditions required by the law. As neither the President, nor any other officer of the US. has been particularly authorized to refer applications of this kind to any persons whatsoever, nor otherwise to act on them, my wish to see whatever may be useful brought forward with advantage, and to encourage the inventors, induces me to suggest to you the Philosophical society as the body whose approbation of your invention would be the most likely to give it such a sanction as might be advantageous to you. I am Sir Your most obedt. servt   TH: JEFFERSON

[589]

PrC (DLC); at foot of text: "Mr. Frederick Guyer." Tr (DLC); 19th-century copy. Enclosure not found.

Guyer's letter of 24 Apr. 1793, recorded in SJL as received the same date, has not been found. For the change made in the BUSINESS OF ISSUING PATENTS, see A Bill to Promote the Progress of the Useful Arts, [1 Dec. 1791], and note. There is no evidence that Guyer ever submitted his invention to the American Philosophical Society.

From John Mason

SIR   George Town 26th Aprl. 1793

Having lately Seen it was proposed in france to make Applications to the Executive of the United States to furnish in American Produce part of their Debt, and Supposing it probable if such a measure is adopted Some of the purchases might be made to greater advantage on Potomac, Rappahanok and James River than North of them, I take the Liberty thro' you Sir to Offer my Services (Say those of my House) to make any purchase or Shipments in this part of the Country; and may I be allowed if you Judge me Adequate, to Sollicit Your friendly Influence in the Choice of an agent, should one be named for Such purposes.

I should not presume to ask this, if I was not fully persuaded I can serve the public as well as any Merchant whoever in such a Commission, and flatter myself the line of Business I have been engaged in for Several Years has given me a perfect Knowledge of the produce of this Country and made me equal to any Negotiation with France. I have Sometime Since Established a House in this Town, under the Same firm with that in Bordeaux.

Wheat and flour can always be Shipped on better terms, generally by 3/ a 4/ ℔ bll. and 6d at 1/ ℔ bushel from this River, than from Philadelphia, or even Baltimore; flour is at this time from 35/ to 37/6 Maryland Currency ℔ barrell, Wheat 7/6 to 8/9 ℔ Bushel. With assurances if any thing of this kind should be entrusted to us of our best Endeavors to Convince You, Your Confidence will not be misplaced—I have the honor to be Sir with great respect your Very Obt. Servt.

J: MASON

RC (DLC); at head of text: "Thomas Jefferson Esqr. Secretary of State"; endorsed by TJ as received 30 Apr. 1793 and so recorded in SJL.

To Gouverneur Morris,
Thomas Pinckney, and William Short

SIR   Philadelphia 26th. April, 1793.

The public papers giving us reason to believe that the war is becoming nearly general in Europe, and that it has already involved nations, with which we are in daily habits of commerce and friendship, the President has thought it proper to issue the Proclamation of which I enclose you a copy, in order to mark out to our citizens the line of conduct they are to pursue. That this intimation, however, might not work to their prejudice, by being produced against them as conclusive evidence of their knowledge of the existence of war and of the nations engaged in it, in any case where they might be drawn into courts of Justice for acts done without that Knowledge, it has been thought necessary to write to the representatives of the belligerent powers here, the letter of which a copy is also enclosed, reserving to our citizens those immunities to which they are entitled, till authentic information shall be given to our government by the parties at war, and be thus communicated with due certainty to our citizens. You will be pleased to present to the government where you reside,[1] this proceeding of the President, as a proof of the earnest desire of the United States to preserve peace and friendship with all the belligerent powers, and to express his expectation that they will in return extend a scrupulous and effectual protection to all our citizens, wheresoever they may need it in pursuing their lawful and peaceable concerns with their subjects or within their jurisdiction. You will at the same time assure them that the most exact reciprocation of this benefit shall be practised by us towards their subjects in the like cases. I have the honor to be, with great esteem & respect Sir, Your most obedient and most humble servant   TH: JEFFERSON

RC (NNC: Gouverneur Morris Papers); in the hand of George Taylor, Jr., signed by TJ; at foot of first page: "Mr. Morris"; endorsed by Morris. PrC (DLC). RC (NjP); in Taylor's hand, signed by TJ; at foot of text: "Thomas Pinckney Esqr. Minister plenipotentiary of the U.S. of am. at the Court of Great Britain"; with variation recorded in note 1 below. PrC (DLC). RC (DLC: Short Papers); in a clerk's hand, signed by TJ; at foot of first page: "Wm. Short Esqr."; endorsed by Short as received 12 July 1793. PrC (DLC). FC (Lb in DNA: RG 59, DCI); at head of text: "To G. Morris, T. Pinckney & W. Short." Tr (NjP: Andre deCoppet Collection); in a clerk's hand, signed by TJ. PrC of another Tr (DLC); in a clerk's hand, signed by TJ; at foot of first page in ink in TJ's hand: "Gouvr. Morris T. Pinckney Mr. Short." Enclosures: (1) Proclamation of Neutrality, 22 Apr. 1793 (Fitzpatrick, *Writings*, XXXII, 430-1). (2) TJ to Jean Baptiste Ternant, George Hammond, and F. P. Van Berckel, 23 Apr. 1793. Letter and enclosures enclosed in TJ to William Carmichael and David Humphreys, 26

Apr. 1793; letter enclosed in TJ to Gouverneur Morris, 13 June 1793.

TJ this day submitted to the President drafts of the above letter to each of the three ministers in question, but Washington made no recorded comment on them (Washington, *Journal*, 120).

[1] At this point the text addressed to Thomas Pinckney contains the phrase "as also to the representatives of Austria and Prussia at the same place." This variation is recorded in the margin of the FC.

To George Clinton

SIR   Philadelphia Apr. 27. 1793.

I have the honor to acknolege the receipt of your Excellency's favor of the 19th. inst. with the exemplification of the treaties accompanying it as also the Bill of the secretary, amounting to $12\frac{1}{2}$ dollars, for which I take the liberty of inclosing him a bank post note thro' your Excellency, as I know not his particular address. Be pleased to accept my thanks for your attention and assurances of the esteem & respect with which I have the honor to be your Excellency's Most obedt & most hble servt.

TH: JEFFERSON

PrC (DLC); at foot of text: "H.E. Govr. Clinton." FC (Lb in DNA: RG 59, DL). Enclosure not found.

Governor Clinton's letter of 19 Apr. 1793, recorded in SJL as received 22 Apr. 1793, has not been found. The EXEMPLIFICATION OF THE TREATIES ACCOMPANYING Clinton's letter consists of certified copies of five treaties, concluded between various members of the Iroquois Confederation and the New York Commissioners of Indian Affairs on 28 June 1785, 12 and 22 Sep. 1788, 25 Feb. 1789, and 30 June 1790, conveying certain tribal lands to the state of New York (PrC of Tr in DLC: TJ Papers, 85: 14624-50; dated 11 Apr. 1793; in a clerk's hand). Attached to it is the following statement by TJ:
"Department of State, to wit.
"I hereby certify that the foregoing sheets, consisting of twenty six pages

4to., and containing Deeds and other acts of certain Nations of Indians conveying Lands to the State of New York, are truly copied from an original exemplification thereof, under the Hand of His Excellency George Clinton Esquire, Governor of the said State, and with the Great Seal of the same appendant, which original exemplification is deposited in the office of the Secretary of State.
"In Testimony whereof I have caused my seal of Office to be here unto affixed. Given under my Hand this twenty six day of April, one thousand seven hundred and ninety three. Th: Jefferson" (PrC in same, 14651; in the hand of George Taylor, Jr., signed by TJ). TJ had requested copies of these treaties for the use of the commissioners appointed to treat with the Western Indians at the forthcoming Lower Sandusky conference (TJ to Clinton, 13 Mch. 1793).

From Josef de Jaudenes

DEAR SIR   Philada. 27th. Apl. 1793.
By my private Letters from Madrid of the 1st. March, just received
via Baltimore, I have the pleasure to learn that His Excelly. Don Diego
de Gardoqui had been authorized by his Majesty on the 27th. feby. to
negociate with the American Plenipotentaries, which news as I supose
will please you, I hasten to communicate them to you in this friendly
manner.

War was not declared at that period, but seemed to be unavoidable,
particularly as the Letters of the 3rd. of March from Cadiz mention
that the french had captured some Spanish vessells, and there were
orders at Cadiz to stop all the french vessells in that Harbour.

If you have received any news communicable, I will be very much
obliged to you for the recital of them. I have the honor to be with
sentiments of very great esteem and high respect Dr. Sir Your most
obedt. most hbl. Se[rvt?]   JOSEPH DE JAUDENES

RC (DNA: RG 59, NL); mutilated in part; at foot of text: "Thomas Jefferson Esqr.
&ca. &ca."; endorsed by TJ as received [27] Apr. 1793 and so recorded in SJL.

From John Garland Jefferson

DEAR SIR   Goochland April 27. 1793.
Your favor of the 14. instant, I received yesterday. It gives me real
pleasure to find that my efforts meet with your approbation. And as
this is an object I have ever had in view; so through life, will it prove
a powerful stimulus to close application, and whatever may be best
suited to procure your esteem and entire confidence. I have not yet
determined in what courts I shall practice. This is a matter I have
defered till I coud get your opinion, and counsel. It is you my dear Sir,
by whom I am to be govened. I have however, thus far determined;
that if you do not recommend some other place, I intend to board in
some private family between Petersburg, and Richmond; to practice in
the Districts of these courts, or of Petersburg, Brunswick, Lunenburg
&c. and the county courts adjoining the place where I shall reside. I
shall still adhere to this plan if approved by you, if not, I am willing
to change it for a better. I am come to that part of your letter where
you refer me to Colo. Bell, for my spring supply. It has ever been
my wish to put you to as little inconvenience as possible. I therefore
embrace with chearfulness, your proposition, but let me first suggest

to you, a method, more agreeable to me, if equally so to you, and I trust if it shall appear to be as little, or less inconvenient, you will come into it. The Gentleman with whom I live, is a merchant of a considerable capital. He imports his goods from London; Colo. Bell gets his from Richmond. Added to this the carriage to this place, is much less than the carriage to Charlottesville, so I may with reason suppose that goods may be had here, on much better terms, than there. I may even say with propriety, that Mr. Shelton can afford to sell goods almost as cheap as Mr. Bell can get them himself. Besides, the difficulty of getting to Charlottesville, is almost insurmountable. I have tryed to get to almost every D. court held in Charlottesville, and have effected it in but instance.[1] Mr. Shelton has solicited me to deal with him. He will expect no payment till the fall. Then he will take country produce at the price it sells at in Richmond. I shall keep the letter you were so good as to give me to Colo. Bell till I know your mind. In my wish to deal with Mr. Shelton, I consult your interest as well as mine. Mr. Shelton expects payment for board quarterly. He agreed on this account, to board me for less. One quarter next month is due. In this I hope you can accomodate me, especially as it is but small. My occasion also for about five pounds is great. Three or four pounds, I mentioned in my letter to you, I was indebted in their neighbourhood. Nothing but the expectation of a supply of money this spring, coud have induced me to incur this little debt, tho for necessaries; all I want besides this, and the five pounds for board, is enough to pay my shoemakers, taylors &c. As to pocket money, I want none. I shall be glad to hear from you as soon as possible. In the mean time I shall be passive. Believe me to be with all possible esteem, Your affectionate and grateful Servant.   JNO. G: JEFFERSON

RC (ViU: Carr-Cary Papers); endorsed
by TJ as received 6 May 1793 and so
recorded in SJL.

[1] Thus in manuscript.

From Thomas Leiper

SIR   Philad April 27 1793

I have yours of the 11h and observe you and Mr. Wilson have settled the time when you was to remove and he to take possession. This is a matter between you and him which I have nothing to do with only to have it fixed for as your rent and his are the same it can make no difference to me.

But what respects myself and my interest I think I ought to have an opinion. It would appear from yours of the 11h that the Carpenter who built the house has given it as his opinion that things are restored to their best state. In my opinion it is not so. I am also of the opinion from your letter to me a Copy of which I sent you some time ago you are oblidged to finish the inside of the small House in the Garden. As their is a difference of opinion suppose these matters were reffered and I beg to give you the names of the men whom I think would be the best Judges in this case. If they are not agreeable to you any other carpenter you please I except none but the carpenter who has given his opinion already—Mr. Joseph Ragstraw Mr. Robert Allison and Mr. Jones. The two former of these men were appointed by Mr. Carstairs and myself to examine the work when it was finished. The later was the person sent by the Fire insurance company to examine the House before the Insurance was made. These are the persons whom I think are most likely to judge right in this case. Iff these men are agreeable to you please inform me as soon as you can make it convenient and I beg leave to inform their judgement I will concur in. I am Sir Your most Obed St

FC (Lb in Leiper Papers, Friends of Thomas Leiper House, on deposit PPL); at foot of text: "To the Honorable Thos Jefferson Secretary of State for the United States."

TJ's 24 Aug. 1791 LETTER to Leiper was apparently the basis for Leiper's asser-
tion that TJ had obligated himself to finish the interior of the SMALL HOUSE IN THE GARDEN of the dwelling he had formerly rented from the Philadelphia merchant. Evidently Leiper had enclosed a copy of this letter in his missing letter to TJ of 14 Dec. 1792, on which see TJ to Leiper, 16 Dec. 1792, and note.

To Thomas Pinckney

DEAR SIR   Philadelphia Apr. 27. 1793.

Mr. John Carey having had permission to copy and publish such parts as might be interesting to the public, of the correspondence of the Commander in chief, the officers commanding in separate departments &c. and proposing to print them in Europe, it has been thought safer to put the M.S.S. books under cover to you. There go with this letter about 12. or 13. packets of them. I have to ask the favor of you to receive and keep them till he shall apply for them in person, and then to deliver them to him. Should any accident happen to him, be pleased to retain them till further orders as it is not meant to trust the publication to persons unknown. I have the honor to be with great & sincere esteem Dear Sir Your most obedt. & most humble servt

TH: JEFFERSON

PrC (DLC); at head of text: "Private"; at foot of text: "Mr. Pinckney." Tr (DLC); 19th-century copy. Enclosures not found.

From Thomas Pinckney

MY DEAR SIR   Great Cumberland Place 27th April 1793

I send herewith the Gazettes to the present time which contain all the public intelligence.

I fear that some of your dispatches intended for me must have miscarried as your last letter received by me was dated the first day of this year and I have only got the newspapers up to the 17th. November 1792—although there are letters here from Philadelphia of the 18th. March.[1] I am well informed that negociations are now on foot with a prospect of success to form a closer and more permanent connection between this country and Prussia and Austria. If the combined crowns should succeed against france it is impossible to tell what their detestation of popular governments, added to the intoxication of[2] success, may induce them to attempt. I hope we keep a supply of articles essential for military uses; such as nitre &c. There are very few regular troops left in this island—so that none can yet be spared for distant expeditions.

I am induced to get the copper for our mint from hence and hope to send it by an early opportunity from Bristol. The French privateers have carried several of our Vessels into their ports but they have been dismissed and the captors awarded to pay damages. I have the honor to be with the utmost respect My dear Sir Your most faithful and most obedient Servant   THOMAS PINCKNEY

[1st. May 1793

I have only to add to the above duplicate that I send herewith the newspapers received since that date and a packet which Mr. Richard Penn requested me to send with my dispatches which as it is of considerable importance to him and the papers must go by the mail coach I take the liberty of troubling you with.]

RC (DNA: RG 59, DD); written partly in code; decoded interlinearly by TJ and George Taylor, Jr. (see note 1 below); at foot of text: "The Secretary of State"; lacks postscript, supplied from Dupl; endorsed by TJ as received 27 June 1793 and so recorded in SJL. PrC (ScHi: Pinckney Family Papers); lacks decipherment. Dupl (DNA: RG 59, Duplicate Diplomatic Dispatches); in the hand of William A. Deas, with signature and postscript by Pinckney; written partly in code, but lacks decipherment; at head of text: "(Duplicate)." PrC (ScHi: Pinckney Family Papers); consists of postscript only. Tr

(Lb in DNA: RG 59, DD); entirely *en clair*, with deciphered words in brackets; includes postscript.

For a discussion of British efforts to form a MORE PERMANENT CONNECTION with PRUSSIA AND AUSTRIA in order to prosecute the war against France with greater vigor, which led to the signing of separate conventions for this purpose with these two powers in July and August 1793, see John Ehrman, *The Younger Pitt: The Reluctant Transition* (London, 1983), 270-4.

¹ The remainder of the paragraph is in unidentified code, the first sentence being supplied from TJ's decipherment, the rest from Taylor's.

² Pinckney here canceled five codes.

To George Wythe

DEAR SIR   Philadelphia Apr. 27. 1793.

I received not till yesterday your favor of the 12th. Mr. Poupard was paid the 64. Dollars agreed for, on the delivery of his work. As draughts on Richmond cannot be disposed of here, take any opportunity at your convenience of remitting the sum here. The Custom house officers can generally give post-bills of the bank of the US. here: but these must not be confounded with branch-bank bills which the bank here will not receive.—We understand that a French frigate has taken several English vessels off the capes of Delaware, within two or three days after they had left Philadelphia. We shall be a little embarrassed occasionally till we feel ourselves firmly seated in the saddle of neutrality. I am with great & sincere esteem & respect Dr. Sir your affectionate friend & servt.   TH: JEFFERSON

PrC (DLC); at foot of text: "Mr. Wythe." Tr (DLC); 19th-century copy.

Wythe's FAVOR of 12 Apr. 1793 from Richmond simply stated: "Be pleased, my dear sir, to inform M. Poulard [Poupard] that his money shall be paid on sight of his order" (RC in MHi; endorsed by TJ as received 27 Apr. 1793 and so recorded in SJL).

Jefferson's Opinion on the Treaties with France

I. NOTES ON WASHINGTON'S QUESTIONS ON NEUTRALITY AND THE ALLIANCE WITH FRANCE, [BEFORE 28 APR. 1793]

II. NOTES FOR OPINION ON THE TREATY OF ALLIANCE WITH FRANCE, [BEFORE 28 APR. 1793]

III. THOMAS JEFFERSON TO GEORGE WASHINGTON, 28 APR. 1793

IV. OPINION ON THE TREATIES WITH FRANCE, 28 APR. 1793

E D I T O R I A L   N O T E

Thomas Jefferson's carefully qualified opinion in favor of the continued validity of the 1778 treaties of alliance and commerce with France was designed to resolve a neutrality question of fundamental importance raised by Alexander Hamilton in response to the arrival in Philadelphia early in April 1793 of reliable intelligence of the French Republic's declaration of war on Great

Britain and the Netherlands. This development gave a maritime dimension to a war that hitherto had been confined to the European continent and emboldened Hamilton to question whether continued adherence to the French treaties was compatible with the preservation of American neutrality.

In addition to his general antipathy to revolutionary France, Hamilton was concerned that three provisions of the treaties might lead to hostilities with Britain, an eventuality he dreaded because of the dependence of his financial system on the revenues generated by Anglo-American trade. Article 11 of the treaty of alliance obliged the United States to guarantee French possessions in America and thus might lead to a request from France for American assistance in defending the French West Indies against the British. At the same time, French efforts at sea against Britain and her allies stood to benefit immensely from two provisions of the commercial treaty—Article 17, which gave French warships and privateers the right to bring enemy prizes into American ports while denying this right to those of her enemies, except in carefully defined emergencies, and Article 22, which forbade nations at war with France to fit out privateers, sell prizes, or purchase more than a minimum amount of provisions in American ports without specifying whether France herself could exercise these rights (Miller, *Treaties*, II, 16-17, 19-20, 39-40; Syrett, *Hamilton*, xv, 55-63, 65-9). Although Jefferson and Hamilton both resolutely opposed any American military involvement in the European conflagration, the debate generated by Hamilton's criticisms of the French treaties exposed for the first time the enormous gulf between the two secretaries over the form American neutrality should take. Whereas Jefferson wished to honor the treaties with France while avoiding any of the provisions in them that might provoke British retaliation, Hamilton sought to avoid war with Britain by effectively nullifying the French treaties. This conflict between a policy that worked to the advantage of the French and one that favored the British remained at the heart of the recurring disputes between Jefferson and Hamilton over the conduct of American neutrality in 1793.

With characteristic boldness, Hamilton wasted no time in launching a frontal attack on the French treaties. On 18 Apr. 1793—only a day after hurriedly returning from Mount Vernon to Philadelphia in order to put the nation on a neutral footing in the face of the expanded European war—President Washington submitted to Cabinet members thirteen Hamilton-inspired questions on American neutrality that among other things asked them in effect to consider whether the United States could honor the treaties with France and still be truly neutral (Questions on Neutrality and the Alliance with France, 18 Apr. 1793, and note, enclosed in Washington to the Cabinet, 18 Apr. 1793). After deciding during a 19 Apr. meeting that the President should issue a proclamation of neutrality and receive the French Republic's first minister to the United States, Edmond Charles Genet, the Cabinet turned its attention to the momentous issue raised by Hamilton. Dividing along sectional lines, it debated whether the President should receive Genet conditionally or unconditionally. Hamilton and Secretary of War Henry Knox supported a conditional reception, arguing that the downfall of the French monarchy and the uncertain future of the French Republic created a situation sufficiently dangerous to American interests to justify Washington in informing Genet at the time of his reception that the United States reserved the right to suspend or renounce the treaties with France. Unconditional reception, they maintained, would amount to an irrevocable decision that the treaties should remain in force and, further, be tantamount to forming a new treaty with a guarantee clause that would make the United States a belligerent. Jefferson and Attorney General Edmund Randolph, in contrast, contended that the treaties were valid and favored an unconditional reception of Genet. But Randolph wavered when Hamilton offered to produce a citation from that formidable authority on international law, Emmerich de Vattel's *Le Droit des Gens* (1758), in support of his position that a treaty might under certain circumstances be suspended or renounced after a change of government by one of the contracting parties. The Attorney General thereupon announced that he wished to prepare a formal written opinion of his views on the status of the French treaties, and so the Cabinet adjourned without resolving the question. When it reconvened to consider neutrality again on 22 Apr. 1793, Randolph's opinion was still not ready and the Cabinet again adjourned without deciding the treaty issue. It was probably either at this meeting or the one of the 19th that the President requested the other Cabinet members to follow Randolph's suggestion and submit separate written statements of their views on this highly contentious question (Cabinet Opinion on Washington's Questions on Neutrality and the Alliance with France, [19 Apr. 1793], and note; Notes on Washington's Questions on Neutrality and the Alliance with France, [6 May 1793]; Washington, *Journal*, 114, 117; the President's request for written Cabinet opinions is cited in the opening sentence of Document IV below).

Despite the two broadly divergent lines of argument in the 19 Apr. Cabinet meeting, in their written opinions Hamilton and Knox shared two assumptions with Jefferson and Randolph. The first, that the people of a nation are the source of authority and may change their form of government, was a postulate that Jefferson, with the President's approval, had officially communicated to the American minister in London in December 1792 and affirmed to the American minister in France in connection with the resumption of debt payments to that country in March 1793 (Notes on the Legitimacy of Government, 30 Dec. 1792; TJ to Thomas Pinckney, 30 Dec. 1792; TJ to Gouverneur Morris, 12 Mch. 1793). They were also united in the assumption that the French treaties were agreements between nations rather than heads of state—that is, that they were, in eighteenth-century terms, *real* as opposed to *personal* treaties. To a significant degree, therefore, the question on which the President's advisers divided was the extent to which the present situation of France satisfied the conditions under which Vattel and other authorities on international law would sanction suspension or renunciation of the treaties by the United States.

Jefferson was the first Cabinet member to submit a written opinion on the French treaties to the President. He prepared his rebuttal of Hamilton's arguments in favor of suspending or renouncing these compacts with unusual care, as befitted the magnitude of the stakes involved. The French alliance was the cornerstone of Jefferson's diplomacy, and it was highly unlikely that this partnership could survive an American suspension of the treaties at a time when the French Republic was engaged in a mortal struggle with most of the great powers of Europe. France, in Jefferson's view, was America's only reliable European ally, the only one she could count on as an effective counterweight to a British nation he deeply distrusted on ideological and diplomatic grounds. At the same time, he felt a profound affinity for revolutionary France, seeing in her the champion of republicanism and liberty and fearing that the triumph of her royalist and aristocratic enemies would further the allegedly monarchical designs of his own Federalist adversaries. Yet much as Jefferson hoped that France would triumph in the current war, he was unalterably opposed to any American military involvement in that conflict. He realized that it would be more advantageous for the United States to serve France as a neutral carrier of provisions than as an active belligerent and thus looked forward to the great economic benefits he expected American farmers, merchants, and shippers to reap by virtue of the nation's neutrality. Hence he wished neither to risk war with France by nullifying the alliance nor to provoke Britain by fulfilling some of the more inconvenient provisions of the French treaties.

In order to present a carefully balanced argument to the President, Jefferson first made a rough outline of the principles he intended to invoke and the treaty obligations he would address in his opinion on the questions of neutrality and the treaty of alliance (Document I below) and then wrote a more detailed outline of the opinion itself, compiling the arguments that would sever link by link the chain of reasoning employed by Hamilton during the Cabinet meeting of the 19th (Document II below). Only then did he write the opinion in its final form, dealing therein with both treaties, and submit it to Washington on 28 Apr. 1793 with a covering letter of that date responding to other neutrality questions the President had asked the Cabinet to consider ten days before (Documents III and IV below; Washington, *Journal*, 124). The opinion is especially noteworthy for the vigor and cogency of its argument in favor of the proposition that the treaties with France remained in force despite the overthrow of the Bourbon monarchy and the establishment of the French Republic. Although Jefferson tacitly acknowledged Hamilton's theoretical point that a change of government in France could justify the United States in renouncing or suspending the treaties if this alteration made continued adherence to these agreements extremely dangerous to American interests, he assembled evidence from authorities on international law to show that the doctrine held only in extraordinary cases—analyzing Vattel in particular to demonstrate that Hamilton had quoted the Swiss jurist out of context—and vigorously denied that matters had reached this critical point in France. In this connection, Jefferson's opinion is also remarkable for its effort to minimize America's treaty obligations by downplaying the likelihood that France would ever invoke the guarantee provision of the alliance treaty and by suggesting that Article 22 of the commercial treaty left the United States free to forbid France, as well as her enemies, to fit out privateers and sell prizes in American ports.

Hamilton and Knox were the next Cabinet members to submit a written opinion to the President. Whereas Jefferson feared that nullifying the French treaties would lead to war with France, they feared that adhering to them would bring on hostilities with Britain; and whereas Jefferson viewed France as the standard-bearer of republican liberty, they viewed her as the harbinger of political license and social chaos. Accordingly, in an opinion written and signed by Hamilton but jointly endorsed by him and Knox in a covering letter to Washington of 2 May 1793, one day before these documents actually reached the President, they advised him to receive Genet but at the same time to inform him that the United States reserved the right to suspend the treaties with France as circumstances dictated. Provisional suspension of the treaties, they argued, was justified on grounds of principle and national interest. Adducing the writings of Vattel and other authorities on international law, they contended that the law of nations gave the United States the right to judge whether circumstances attending the transition from monarchy to republic in France justified suspension of the treaties on the ground that the change in form of government could be highly dangerous and disadvantageous to American interests. The French Republic, they noted, had already set the precedent of repudiating certain treaty obligations entered into by the monarchy and had blemished the sacred cause of liberty with numerous crimes and excesses. By endorsing the treaties before it knew whether the forces of revolution or royalism would finally prevail in the highly unstable political and military situation of France and Europe, the United States would jeopardize its own character and reputation as a nation of "sobriety, moderation, justice, and love of order," thereby implicating itself as an associate regardless of the outcome. Honoring the treaties, with their "stipulations of military succours and military aids in certain cases which are likely to occur," they argued, would also constitute a serious breach of neutrality and might even bring the United States into conflict with France's enemies, especially Britain. Suspending the treaties, on the other hand, would earn the United States the gratitude of France's opponents and spare it the humiliation of having to plead military and naval weakness in case France tried to invoke the American guarantee of the French West Indies. Finally, they denied that the decision in March 1793 to resume debt payments to France implied an acknowledgment that the United States intended to fulfill the treaties under the present circumstances (Syrett, *Hamilton*, XIV, 367-96; Washington, *Journal*, 126). Despite their ostensible emphasis on the need for suspending the treaties until a stable government was established in France, it seems clear that Hamilton and Knox's real objective was to break the alliance with France and draw the United States closer to Britain. Hamilton had been looking for such an opportunity since at least 1791, when France was still a monarchy, and as Jefferson and Edmund Randolph pointed out to Washington in their own opinions, the suspension of these agreements while the French Republic was battling for its survival would almost certainly have led to war between France and the United States (Syrett, *Hamilton*, VIII, 43-4).

In the end, the Cabinet member who suggested the desirability of written opinions on the French treaties was actually the last to submit one to the President. Under prodding from Washington, who doubtless wished to settle this matter before Genet arrived in Philadelphia, Attorney General Randolph handed in his opinion on 6 May 1793, the day he completed it. Addressing all of the questions posed on 18 Apr., Randolph, like Jefferson, strongly endorsed the unconditional reception of Genet and the continued validity of the French treaties. A qualified reception, he argued, was not necessary because Genet's claim to be received did not depend on the treaties and they gained no confirmation from his reception; neither was it expedient, for the right to renounce the treaties would not be impaired by "prudent forbearance" toward an issue that, if not prematurely provoked, might never arise. "Vigilance in government is undoubtedly wisdom," Randolph advised the President, in an obvious criticism of Hamilton, "but it is equally wise not to create an evil for the gratification of subduing it." Quoting Vattel at length, Randolph echoed Jefferson's contention that the treaties could not be invalidated simply because France had changed its form of government, and that present circumstances and future eventualities were insufficient grounds for announcing their provisional suspension. Randolph also followed the Secretary of State in insisting that fidelity to the treaties would be consistent with American neutrality. In view of the naval and military weakness of the United States, Randolph predicted that France would prefer the United States to act as a reliable neutral trading partner rather than as an ineffectual ally. At the same time, he contended, the United States could justifiably refuse to carry out the guarantee provision of the treaty because the French-American alliance was entirely defensive in character, and compliance with this obligation would involve it in a war that would be overwhelmingly disadvantageous to American interests. Randolph also denied that honoring Articles 17 and 22 of the commercial treaty would lead to war with France's enemies, noting that the United States had entered into this agreement more than a decade before the present European war began, that these articles had been recognized as valid in American commercial treaties with the Netherlands and Prussia (two countries presently at war with France), and that Britain had similar provisions in her own 1786 commercial treaty with France. In contrast to Jefferson, however, Randolph laid greater stress on the diplomatic and political aspects of the treaty question. Not only did he urge Washington to consider that France was America's most reliable and only proper European ally, but he also warned him that the French cause was so popular in America that government opposition to the French treaties would produce serious internal divisions as well as war with France. The only substantive point on which the Attorney General and the Secretary of State differed was the meaning of Article 22 of the commercial treaty, which Randolph interpreted as inferentially allowing France to fit out privateers and sell prizes in American ports (Opinion of Randolph, 6 May 1793, DLC: Washington Papers; Washington, *Journal*, 127; the date Randolph submitted his opinion may be inferred from Notes on Washington's Questions on Neutrality and the Alliance with France, [6 May 1793]).

With Randolph's opinion in hand, and without consulting further with the Cabinet as a group or circulating all the opinions among its members, Washington informed Jefferson on 6 May 1793 that the treaties would remain in force and thus by inference that he would receive Genet unconditionally, as indeed he did twelve days later. At the same time, the President indicated to Jefferson that personally he had always accepted the continued validity of the French treaties, but it is difficult to believe that Hamilton had not caused him to have at least some temporary doubts (Notes on Washington's Questions on Neutrality and the Alliance with France, [6 May 1793]; Washington, *Journal*, 143; Turner, *CFM*, 214, 245). In any case, Jefferson had little time to savor his victory over his great antagonist at the Treasury on the issue of the treaties, for on 8 May 1793 British minister George Hammond dispatched a series of memorials to him that forced the Cabinet to begin consideration of a new constellation of neutrality issues that was destined to bedevil French-American relations for the duration of Jefferson's tenure as Secretary of State.

I. Notes on Washington's Questions on Neutrality and the Alliance with France

[before 28 Apr. 1793]
On the Questions of Apr. 18. 93.[1]

1st. Principle. the people the source of all authority
the Constituent[2] in all treaties
this answers Qu. II. III. IV. V. VI. XII.

2d. Principle. the Legislature alone can declare war
the question of Guarantee is a question of war.
this answers Qu. VII. VIII. IX-X.

Qu. XI. Art. 17. French ships of war & privateers with prizes[3] may
come & go freely, ⟨with prizes⟩
English do.[4] may not. If they put in distress, must
go as soon as possible
Dutch. 22.5. Prussian. 19.[5]
Art. 22. English privateers may not be fitted out, nor sell
prizes here.
no stipuln that French do. may.
nor that French ships of war may.
⟨French⟩

Armed neutrality
free vessels free goods et econtre.
free commerce to places not besieged.
certificate of officer of convoy prevents searches.
contraband defined.
_____
Vattel. 2. 157. the validity of treaties
158. lezion does not annul them.
159. duties of nations in this ⟨particular⟩ matter
160. nullity of treaties ruinous to a state.
163. oblign to observe treaties
164. the violn of a treaty is an injury.
218.
219.
220.
221
222.

OPINION ON FRENCH TREATIES

232
233.

160
157. 158. 159. 163. 219. 220. 233.

MS (DLC: TJ Papers, 84: 14559); written entirely in TJ's hand on one side of a small sheet; undated; printed literally. Recorded in SJPL under 18 Apr. 1793: "notes on those questions [relative to France & England]" (see Questions on Neutrality and the Alliance with France, enclosed in George Washington to the Cabinet, 18 Apr. 1793).

Despite the date TJ later assigned in SJPL to these rough notes for his 28 Apr. 1793 Opinion on the Treaties with France (Document IV below), internal evidence indicates that the MS consists of as many as four sections written at different times, but presumably no earlier than 19 Apr. 1793. The first section, which includes everything below the heading and above ARMED NEUTRALITY, was probably written soon after the 19 Apr. Cabinet meeting that first considered the thirteen questions Washington had posed on neutrality and the French alliance (see Cabinet Opinion on Washington's Questions on Neutrality and the Alliance with France, [19 Apr. 1793]). The remainder of the manuscript, judging from the subject matter, less careful penmanship, and space separating it from the first section, is composed of two sections that were proba-

bly written, perhaps at different sittings, closer to the time of TJ's opinion. Despite TJ's notes on the issue of ARMED NEUTRALITY in the second section, this subject was not covered in the list of questions the President submitted to Cabinet members on 18 Apr. 1793 or in the opinion TJ transmitted to him ten days later (see Document IV below). TJ's citations from Vattel's *Le Droit des Gens* in the third section all relate to the subject of the OBLIGN TO OBSERVE TREATIES; the Secretary of State cited several of these passages in his opinion to counteract the lone passage from this eighteenth-century authority on international law that Hamilton adduced at the 19 Apr. 1793 Cabinet meeting in support of his proposal for suspending or renouncing the treaties with France (TJ to Madison, 28 Apr. 1793). The final section, the heading interlined at the very top of the page in a small, fine hand, was almost certainly added significantly later, perhaps at one of the times later in life when TJ organized his papers.

[1] Heading interlined at a later date.
[2] Word written over "principal," erased.
[3] Preceding two words interlined.
[4] Word written over "shi," erased.
[5] This line interlined.

II. Notes for Opinion on the Treaty of Alliance with France

[before 28 Apr. 1793]

the Quest.

H's reasoning.
Admitted that this is real i.e. national treaty
L. Nations 1. Moral law. 2. Usage. 3. Conventions
this Qu. depends on 1st. branch.

[604]

nature of Moral oblign on individuals

        societies ⟨*aggrete*?⟩ aggregate[1]

  evidence of moral sense & reason of men.

oblign of Contracts.

    impossible.—self-destruct.[2]

non-compliance for DANGER. appeal to ⟨*feelings*⟩ head & heart—

  there written—*useless, disag.*[3]   —of this ourselves to judge.

                  judge rigorously.

Restrictions on this right of self liberation from treaty

  1. danger great, inevitable, imminent.

    is the present one so?

      1. if issue in military despotism.

      2.   republic

      3. possibility of Rawhead & Bloody bones

        possibility alwais exists—existed at signature

        must wait moment when imminent.

        is this the last moment.

      4. is the danger from guarantee?

          does the guarantee engage us to enter &c.[4]

        this danger then not certain enough, nor imminent,

      5. is it from 17th. Art. ASYLUM. Holld. & Prussia have

                subscribd.

          Engld. same art. agt us.

          has subscribed too.

      6. 22d. art. prohib. enemies of France to fit out privateers

        in our ports.

        we may prohibit France the same.

      7. the Reception of Minister is act of election, & closes

        right

          qualificns

        no connection with treaty

      8. to elect the contince. of a treaty is = makg treaty &c

        no act necessary. —treaty goes on.

        if no act done, no infraction of neutraly.

      deny that explicit declaration now bars us hereafter.[5]

2d. Restriction. liberate from only so much of treaty as is dan-

    gerous.

        the residue remns. — option then in op-

        posite party.

        clause of guarantee only dangerous one.

3. limn. Compensn.

self-libern without just cause or compensn gives cause of war to France.

Examine Authorities. —how far they weigh. —danger of understg. Vattel witht restrn.
    Grotius — Puff. — Wolf — Vattel
    Vattel. 2. 160.[6]
        158. ⟨*159.*⟩ 163. 219. 220. ⟨*233.*⟩

[Lengthwise in the margin in darker ink:]
Do[es the] guarantee en[gage us to en]ter into the war in any event?
    Are we to enter into it before called on by our allies?
    have we been called on?—shall we be called on?—is it yr interest?
    Can they call on us before invasion, or immintly. threatened?
    if they can save them themselves, can they call on us?
    are we to go to war at once witht. trying peaceable negocns?
    Are we in a condn to go to war?
    can we be expected to begin before we are in condn?
    will the islds. be lost if we do not save them?
    have we the means of saving them?
    if not, are we bound to go to war for a desperate object?
    will not 10. years forbearce in us, entitle to some indulgce. from them?

MS (DLC: TJ Papers, 84: 14560); written entirely in TJ's hand on one side of a sheet; undated; left margin torn, obliterating several words conjectured in brackets; printed literally.

These rough notes form the outline for a rebuttal of the REASONING employed by Alexander Hamilton at the 19 Apr. 1793 Cabinet meeting to justify the right of the United States to suspend or renounce the French treaties. To judge by the words, interlineations, and marginalia he added in a darker ink, TJ apparently made the notes at two different sittings sometime after the meeting and before 28 Apr. 1793 (see Document IV below). In his opinion, as in these notes, TJ originally focused on the treaty of alliance, but he altered the opinion to encompass the commercial treaty with France before transmitting it to the President. See also Document I above.

RAWHEAD & BLOODY BONES: an imaginary horrific figure in English folklore, especially to children, used here by TJ to ridicule Hamilton's expressed concerns about the possible dangers to the United States of honoring the treaty of alliance with France (OED). HOLLD. & PRUSSIA HAVE SUBSCRIBD: a reference to clauses in the 1782 Dutch and 1785 Prussian treaties of commerce with the United States that replicated Article 17 of the American commercial treaty with France (Miller, *Treaties*, II, 64-5, 78, 175). SAME ART. AGT US: a reference to Article 40 of the 1786 treaty of amity and commerce between France and Great Britain, whereby each nation agreed to open its ports to ships of the other nation and the prizes they captured from third-party belligerents (Clive Parry, ed., *The Consolidated Treaty Series*, 231 vols. [Dobbs Ferry, N.Y., 1969-81], L, 90).

¹ Word inserted in darker ink.
² This line interlined in darker ink.
³ Preceding ten words interlined in darker ink.
⁴ TJ subsequently developed this and other questions in the marginal notes printed at the end of the document; he adhered to this logical order in Document IV below.
⁵ This line interlined in darker ink.
⁶ This and the following line added in darker ink.

III. Thomas Jefferson to George Washington

SIR   Philadelphia. Apr. 28. 1793.

According to the intimation the other day, and indeed according to my own wish in a question, if not difficult, yet very important, I have the honor to inclose you a written opinion on the question Whether the US. ought to declare their treaties with France void, or suspended?

This contains my answer to the 2d. 3d. 4th. 5th. and 6th. of the written queries.

The 1st. had been before answered and acted on.

The 7th. 8th. 9th. and 10th. are questions on the Guarantee, which it may possibly never be necessary to answer; or if we should be called on,¹ we may then take due time to give in the answer, which must always be framed in a considerable degree on the circumstances existing at that moment.

The 4th. page of the inclosed contains my answer to the 11th.

The 12th. I answer by saying that if the nation of France shall ever reestablish such an officer as Regent (of which there is no appearance at present) I should be for receiving a minister from him: but I am not for doing it from any Regent, so christianed, and set up² by any other authority.

The 13th. has been decided negatively. I have the honor to be with the most entire respect & attachment, Sir, your most obedt. & most humble servt   TH: JEFFERSON

RC (DLC: Washington Papers); addressed: "The President of the US."; endorsed by Bartholomew Dandridge, Jr. Pr C (DLC); partially faded and overwritten in a later hand. Tr (Lb in DNA: RG 59, SDC). Recorded in SJPL. Enclosure: Opinion on the Treaties with France, 28 Apr. 1793 (Document IV below).

The WRITTEN QUERIES were enumerated in the enclosure to Washington to the Cabinet, 18 Apr. 1793. Washington's thirteenth question on neutrality—whether to summon Congress to consider the implications of the outbreak of war between France and Great Britain—was probably DECIDED NEGATIVELY at a Cabinet meeting held on 22 Apr. 1793. At that meeting the Proclamation on Neutrality was approved, and once the President had thus decided on the basic course the nation was to follow in the European war, there was no need to consult Congress about the matter (Washington, *Journal*, 117). The Cabinet meeting of 19 Apr. 1793 had resolved only the first two of the President's questions on neutrality (Cabinet Opinion on Washington's Ques-

tions on Neutrality and the Alliance with France, [19 Apr. 1793], and note).

¹ Word interlined.
² Preceding two words interlined in place of "established."

IV. Opinion on the Treaties with France

I proceed, in compliance with the requisition of the President, to give an opinion in writing on the general Question, Whether the US. have a right to renounce their treaties¹ with France, or to hold them suspended till the government of that country shall be established?

In the Consultation at the President's, on the 19th. inst. the Secretary of the Treasury took the following positions and consequences. 'France was a monarchy when we entered into treaties with it: but it has now declared itself a Republic, and is preparing a Republican form of government. As it may issue in a Republic or a military despotism, or in something else which may possibly render our alliance with it dangerous to ourselves, we have a right of election to renounce the treaty altogether, or to declare it suspended till their government shall be settled in the form it is ultimately to take; and then we may judge whether we will call the treaties² into operation again, or declare them³ for ever null. Having that right of election now, if we receive their minister without any qualifications, it will amount to an act of election to continue the treaties;⁴ and if the change they are undergoing should issue in a form which should bring danger on us, we shall not be then free to renounce them.⁵ To elect to continue them is equivalent to the making a new treaty at this time in the same form, that is to say, with a clause of guarantee; but to make a treaty with a clause of guarantee, during a war, is a departure from neutrality, and would make us associates in the war. To renounce or suspend the treaties therefore is a necessary act of neutrality.'

If I do not subscribe to the soundness of this reasoning, I do most fully to it's ingenuity.—I shall now lay down the principles which according to my understanding govern the case.

I consider the people who constitute a society or nation as the source of all authority in that nation, as free to transact their common concerns by any agents they think proper, to change these agents individually, or the organisation of them in form or function whenever they please; that all the acts done by those agents under the authority of the nation, are the acts of the nation, are obligatory on them, and enure to their use, and can in no wise be annulled or affected by any change in the form of the government, or of the persons administering it. Consequently the Treaties between the US. and France, were not treaties between the US. and Louis Capet, but between the two nations of America and France, and the nations remaining in existence, tho' both of them have since changed their forms of government, the treaties are not annulled by these changes.

The Law of Nations, by which this question is to be determined, is composed of three branches. 1. the Moral law of our nature. 2. the Usages of nations. 3. their special Conventions. The first of these only concerns this question, that is to say the Moral law to which Man has been subjected by his creator, and of which his feelings, or Conscience as it is sometimes called, are the evidence with which his creator has furnished him. The Moral duties which exist between individual and individual in a state of nature, accompany them into a state of society, and the aggregate of the duties of all the individuals composing the society constitutes the duties of that society towards any other; so that between society and society the same moral duties exist as did between the individuals composing them while in an unassociated state,[6] their maker not having released them from those duties on their forming themselves into a nation. Compacts then between nation and nation are obligatory on them by the same moral law which obliges individuals to observe their compacts. There are circumstances however which sometimes excuse the non-performance of contracts between man and man: so are there also between nation and nation. When performance, for instance, becomes *impossible*, non-performance is not immoral. So if performance becomes *self-destructive* to the party, the law of self-preservation overrules the laws of obligation to others. For the reality of these principles I appeal to the true fountains of evidence, the head and heart of every rational and honest man. It is there Nature has written her Moral laws, and where every man may read them for himself. He will never read there the permission to annul his obligations for a time, or for ever, whenever they become 'dangerous, useless, or disagreeable.' Certainly not when merely *useless* or *disagreeable*, as seems to be said in an authority which has been quoted. Vattel. 2.197. And tho he may under certain degrees of *danger*, yet the danger must be imminent, and the degree great. Of these, it is true, that nations are to be judges for themselves, since no one nation has a right to sit in judgment over another. But the tribunal of our consciences remains, and that also of the opinion of the world. These will revise the sentence we pass in our own case, and as we respect these, we must see that in judging ourselves we have honestly done the part of impartial and rigorous judges.

But Reason, which gives this right of self-liberation from a contract in certain cases, has subjected it to certain just limitations.

I. The danger which absolves us must be great, inevitable and imminent. Is such the character of that now apprehended from our treaties with France? What is that danger. 1. Is it that if their government issues in a military despotism, an alliance with them may taint us with despotic principles? But their government, when we allied ourselves to it, was a perfect despotism, civil and military. Yet the treaties were made in that very state of things, and therefore that danger can furnish no just cause. 2. Is it that their government may issue in a republic, and too much strengthen our republican principles? But this is the hope of the great mass of our constituents, and not their dread. They do not look with longing to the happy mean of a limited monarchy. 3. But says the doctrine I am combating, the change the French are undergoing may possibly end in something we know not what, and bring on us danger we know not whence. In short it may end in a Raw-head and bloody bones in the dark. Very well: let Rawhead and bloody bones come, and then we shall be justified in making our peace with him, by renouncing our antient friends and his enemies. For observe, it is not the *possibility of danger*, which absolves a party from his contract: for that possibility always exists, and in every case. It existed in the present one at the moment of making the contract. If *possibilities* would avoid contracts, there never could be a valid contract. For possibilities hang over every thing. Obligation is not suspended till the danger is become real, and the moment of it so imminent, that we can no longer avoid decision without for ever losing the opportunity to do it. But can a danger which has not yet taken it's shape, which does not yet exist, and never may exist, which cannot therefore be defined, can such a danger, I ask, be so imminent that if we fail to pronounce on it in this moment we can never have another opportunity of doing it?

4. The danger apprehended, is it that, the treaties remaining valid, the clause GUARANTEEING[7] their West India islands will engage us in the war?   But Does the Guarantee engage us to enter into the war in any event?

Are we to enter into it before we are called on by our allies?

Have we been called on by them?—shall we ever be called on?

Is it their interest to call on us?

Can they call on us before their islands are invaded, or imminently
threatened?

If they can save them themselves, have they a right to call on us?

Are we obliged to go to war at once, without trying peaceable negociations with their enemy?

If all these questions be against us,[8] there are still others behind.

Are we in a condition to go to war?

Can we be expected to begin before we are in condition?

Will the islands be lost if we do not save them?

Have we the means of saving them?

If we cannot save them, are we bound to go to war for a desperate
object?

Will not a 10. years forbearance in us to call them into the guarantee
of our posts, entitle us to some indulgence?[9]

Many, if not most of these questions offer grounds of doubt whether
the clause of guarantee will draw us into the war. Consequently if this
be the danger apprehended, it is not yet certain enough to authorize
us in sound morality to declare, at this moment, the treaties null.

5. Is the danger apprehended from the 17th. article of the treaty of
Commerce, which admits French ships of war and privateers to come
and go freely, with prizes made on their enemies, while their enemies
are not to have the same privilege with prizes made on the French?
But Holland and Prussia have approved of this article in our treaty
with France, by subscribing to an express Salvo of it in our treaties
with them. [Dutch treaty 22. convention 6. Prussian treaty 19.] and
England in her last treaty with France [art. 40.] has entered into the
same stipulation verbatim, and placed us in her ports on the same
footing on which she is in ours, in case of a war of either of us with
France. If we are engaged in such a war, England must receive prizes
made on us by the French, and exclude those made on the French by
us. Nay further, in this very article of her treaty with France, is a salvo
of any similar article in any anterior treaty of either party, and ours
with France being anterior, this salvo confirms it expressly. Neither of
these three powers then[10] have a right to complain of this article in our
treaty.

6. Is the danger apprehended from the 22d. Art. of our treaty of
commerce, which prohibits the enemies of France from fitting out
privateers in our ports, or selling their prizes here. But we are free to
refuse the same thing to France, there being no stipulation to the contrary, and we ought to refuse it on principles of fair neutrality.

7. But the reception of a Minister from the Republic of France, without qualifications, it is thought will bring us into danger: because this, it is said, will determine the continuance of the treaty, and take from us the right of[11] self-liberation when at any time hereafter our safety would require us to use it. The reception of the Minister at all (in favor of which Colo. Hamilton has given his opinion, tho reluctantly as he confessed) is an acknolegement of the legitimacy of their government: and if the qualifications meditated are to deny that legitimacy, it will be a curious compound which is to admit and deny the same thing. But I deny that the reception of a minister has any thing to do with the treaties. There is not a word, in either of them, about sending ministers. This has been done between us under the common usage of nations, and can have no effect either to continue or annul the treaties.

But how can any act of election have the effect to continue a treaty which is acknoleged to be going on still? For it was not pretended the treaty was void, but only voidable if we chuse to declare it so. To make it void would require an act of election, but to let it go on requires only that we should do nothing. And doing nothing can hardly be an infraction of peace or neutrality.

But I go further and deny that the most explicit declaration made at this moment that we acknolege the obligation of the treaties[12] could take from us the right of non-compliance at any future time when compliance would involve us in great and inevitable danger.

I conclude then that few of these sources threaten any danger at all; and from none of them is it inevitable: and consequently none of them give us the right at this moment of releasing ourselves from our treaties.

II. A second limitation on our right of releasing ourselves is that we are to do it from so much of the treaties only as is bringing great and inevitable danger on us, and not from the residue, allowing to the other party a right at the same time to determine whether on[13] our non-compliance with that part they will declare the whole void. This right they would[14] have, but we should not. Vattel 2. 202. The only part of the treaties[15] which can really lead us into danger is the clause of guarantee. That clause is all then we could suspend in any case, and the residue will remain or not at the will of the other party.

III. A third limitation is that when a party from necessity or danger witholds compliance with part of a treaty, it is bound to make compensation where the nature of the case admits and does not dispense with it. 2. Vattel 324. Wolf. 270. 443. If actual circumstances excuse us from entering into the war under the clause of guarantee, it will be a question whether they excuse us from compensation. Our weight in the war admits of an estimate; and that estimate would form the measure of compensation.

If in witholding a compliance with any part of the treaties, we do it without just cause or compensation, we give to France a cause of war, and so become associated in[16] it on the other side. An injured friend is the bitterest of foes, and France has not discovered either timidity, or over-much forbearance on the late occasions. Is this the position we wish to take for our constituents? It is certainly not the one they would take for themselves.

I will proceed now to examine the principal authority which has been relied on for establishing the right of self liberation;[17] because tho' just in part, it would lead us far beyond justice, if taken in all the latitude of which his expressions would admit. Questions of natural right are triable by their conformity with the moral sense and reason of man. Those who write treatises of natural law, can only declare what their own moral sense and reason dictate in the several cases they state. Such of them as happen to have feelings and a reason coincident with those of the wise and honest part of mankind, are respected and quoted as witnesses of what is morally right or wrong in particular cases. Grotius, Puffendorf, Wolf, and Vattel are of this number. Where they agree their authority is strong: but where they differ, and they often differ, we must appeal to our own feelings and reason to decide between them.

The passage in question shall be traced through all these writers, that we may see wherein they concur, and where that concurrence is wanting. It shall be quoted from them in the order in which they wrote, that is to say, from Grotius first, as being the earliest writer, Puffendorf next, then Wolf, and lastly Vattel as latest in time.

Grotius. 2. 16. 16.

'Hither must be referred the common question, concerning personal and real treaties. If indeed it be with a free people, there can be no doubt but that the engagement is in it's nature real, because the subject is a permanent thing. And even tho the government of the state be changed into a kingdom, the treaty remains, because the same body remains, tho' the head is changed, and, as we have before said, the government which is exercised by a king, does not cease to be the government of the people. There is an *exception*, when the object seems peculiar to the government as if free cities contract a league for the defence of their freedom.'

Puffendorf. 8. 9. 6.

'It is certain that every alliance made with a republic, is real in it's nature, and continues consequently to the term agreed on by the treaty, altho' the magistrates who concluded it be dead before, or that the form of government is changed, even from a democracy to a monarchy: for in this case the people does not cease to be the same, and the king, in the case supposed, being established by the consent of the people, who abolished the republican government, is understood to accept the crown with all the engagements which the people conferring it had contracted, as being free and governing themselves.— There must nevertheless be an *Exception* of the alliances contracted with a view to preserve the present government. As if two Republics league for mutual defence against those who would undertake to invade their liberty: for if one of these two people consent afterwards voluntarily to change the form of their government, the alliance ends of itself, because the reason on which it was founded no longer subsists.'

Wolf. 1146.

'The alliance which is made with a free people, or with a popular government, is a real alliance; and as when the form of government changes, the people remains the same, (for it is the association which forms the people, and not the manner of administering the government) this alliance subsists, tho' the form of government changes, *unless*, as is evident, the reason of the alliance was particular to the popular state.'

Vattel. 2. 197.

'The same question presents itself in real alliances, and in general on every alliance made with a state, and not in particular with a king for the defence of his person. We ought without doubt to defend our ally against all invasion, against all foreign violence, and even against rebel subjects. We ought in like manner to defend a republic against the enterprises of an oppressor of the public liberty. But we ought to recollect that we are the ally of the state, or of the nation, and not it's judge. If the nation has deposed it's king in form, if the people of a republic has driven away it's magistrates, and have established themselves free, or if they have acknoleged the authority of an usurper, whether expressly or tacitly, to oppose these domestic arrangements, to contest their justice or validity, would be to meddle with the government of the nation, and to do it an injury. The ally remains the ally of the state, notwithstanding the change which has taken place. *But if this change renders the alliance useless, dangerous or disagreeable to it, it is free to renounce it. For it may say with truth, that it would not have allied itself with this nation, if it had been under the present form of it's government.*'

The doctrine then of Grotius, Puffendorf and Wolf is that 'treaties remain obligatory notwithstanding any change in the form of government, except in the single case where the preservation of that form was the object of the treaty.' There the treaty extinguishes, not by the election or declaration of the party remaining in statu quo; but independantly of that, by the evanishment of the object. Vattel lays down, in fact, the same doctrine, that treaties continue obligatory, notwithstanding a change of government by the will of the other party, that to oppose that will would be a wrong, and that the ally remains an ally, notwithstanding the change. So far he concurs with all the previous writers. But he then adds what they had not said, nor would say 'but if this change renders the alliance *useless*, dangerous, or *disagreeable* to it, it is free to renounce it.' It was unnecessary for him to have specified the exception of *danger* in this particular case, because that exception exists in all cases, and it's extent has been considered. But when he adds that, because a contract is become merely *useless* or *disagreeable*, we are free to renounce it, he is in opposition to Grotius, Puffendorf, and Wolf, who admit no such licence against the obligation of treaties, and he is in opposition to the morality of every honest man, to whom we may safely appeal to decide whether he feels himself free to renounce a contract the moment it becomes merely *useless* or *disagreeable* to him? We may appeal too to Vattel himself, in those parts of his book where he cannot be misunderstood, and to his known character, as one of the most zealous and constant advocates for the preservation of good faith in all our dealings. Let us hear him on other occasions; and first where he shews what degree of danger or injury will authorize self-liberation from a treaty. 'If simple lezion,' (LEZION means the loss sustained by selling a thing for less than half value, which degree of loss rendered the sale void by the Roman law) 'if simple lezion, says he, or some degree of disadvantage in a treaty, does not suffice to render it invalid, it is not so as to inconveniences which would go to the *ruin* of the nation. As every treaty ought to be made by a sufficient power, a treaty pernicious to the state is null, and not at all obligatory; no Governor of a nation having power to engage things capable of *destroying* the state, for the safety of which the empire is trusted to him. The nation itself, bound necessarily to whatever it's preservation and safety require, cannot enter into engagements contrary to it's indispensable obligations.' Here then we find that the degree of injury or danger which he deems sufficient to liberate us from a treaty, is that which would go to the absolute *ruin* or *destruction* of the state; not simply the lesion of the Roman law, not merely the being disadvantageous, or dangerous. For as he says himself

§.158. 'lezion cannot render a treaty invalid. It is his duty, who enters into engagements, to weigh well all things before he concludes. He may do with his property what he pleases, he may relinquish his rights, renounce his advantages, as he judges proper: the acceptant is not obliged to inform himself of his motives, nor to weigh their just value. If we could free ourselves from a compact because we find ourselves injured by it, there would be nothing firm in the contracts of nations. Civil laws may set limits to lezion, and determine the degree capable of producing a nullity of the contract. But sovereigns acknolege no judge. How establish lezion among them? Who will determine the degree sufficient to invalidate a treaty? The happiness and peace of nations require manifestly that their treaties should not depend on a means of nullity so vague and so dangerous.'

Let us hear him again on the general subject of the observance of treaties §.163. 'It is demonstrated in Natural law that he who promises another confers on him a perfect right to require the thing promised, and that, consequently, not to observe a perfect promise, is to violate the right of another; it is as manifest injustice as to plunder any one of their right. All the tranquillity, the happiness and security of mankind rest on justice, on the obligation to respect the rights of others. The respect of others for our rights of domain and property is the security of our actual possessions; the faith of promises is our security for the things which can not be delivered or executed on the spot. No more security, no more commerce among men, if they think themselves not obliged to preserve faith, to keep their word. This obligation then is as necessary as it is natural and indubitable, among nations who live together in a state of nature, and who acknolege no superior on earth, to maintain order and peace in their society. Nations and their governors then ought to observe inviolably their promises and their treaties. This great truth, altho' too often neglected in practice, is generally acknoleged by all nations: the reproach of perfidy is a bitter affront among sovereigns: now he who does not observe a treaty is assuredly perfidious, since he violates his faith. On the contrary nothing is so glorious to a prince and his nation, as the reputation of inviolable fidelity to his word.' Again §.219. 'Who will doubt that treaties are of the things sacred among nations? They decide matters the most important; they impose rules on the pretensions of sovereigns: they cause the rights of nations to be acknoleged, they assure their most precious interests. Among political bodies, sovereigns, who acknolege no superior on earth, treaties are the only means of adjusting their different pretensions, of establishing a rule, to know on what to count, on what to depend. But treaties are but vain words if nations do not consider them as respectable engagements, as

rules, inviolable for sovereigns, and sacred through the whole earth.'[18]
§.220. 'The faith of treaties, that firm and sincere will, that invariable
constancy in fulfilling engagements, of which a declaration is made
in a treaty, is then holy and sacred among nations, whose safety and
repose it ensures; and if nations will not be wanting to themselves,
they will load with infamy whoever violates his faith.'

After evidence so copious and explicit of the respect of this author
for the sanctity of treaties, we should hardly have expected that his
authority would have been resorted to for a wanton invalidation of
them whenever they should become merely *useless* or *disagreeable*. We
should hardly have expected that, rejecting all the rest of his book, this
scrap would have been culled, and made the hook whereon to hang
such a chain of immoral consequences. Had the passage accidentally
met our eye, we should have imagined it had fallen from the author's
pen under some momentary view, not sufficiently developed to found a
conjecture what he meant: and we may certainly affirm that a fragment
like this cannot weigh against the authority of all other writers, against
the uniform and systematic doctrine of the very work from which it
is torn, against the moral feelings and the reason of all honest men.
If the terms of the fragment are not misunderstood, they are in full
contradiction to all the written and unwritten evidences of morality:
if they are misunderstood, they are no longer a foundation for the
doctrines which have been built on them.

But even had this doctrine been as true as it is manifestly false, it
would have been asked, to whom is it that the treaties with France
have become *disagreeable*? How will it be proved that they are *useless*?

The conclusion of the sentence suggests a reflection too strong to be
suppressed. 'For the party may say with truth that it would not have
allied itself with this nation, if it had been under the present form of it's
government.' The Republic of the US. allied itself with France when
under a despotic government. She changes her government, declares
it shall be a Republic, prepares a form of Republic extremely free, and
in the mean time is governing herself as such. And it is proposed that
America shall declare the treaties void, because 'it may say with truth
that it would not have allied itself with that nation, if it had been under
the present form of it's government'! Who is the American who can
say with truth that he would not have allied himself to France if she
had been a republic? Or that a Republic of any form would be as
disagreeable as her antient despotism?

Upon the whole I conclude

That the treaties are still binding, notwithstanding the change of
government in France:

that no part of them, but the clause of GUARANTEE, holds up *danger*, even at a distance, and consequently that a liberation from no other part could be proposed in any case:

that if that clause may ever bring *danger*, it is neither extreme, nor imminent, nor even probable:

that the authority for renouncing a treaty, when *useless* or *disagreeable*, is either misunderstood, or in opposition to itself, to all other writers, and to every moral feeling:

that were it not so, these treaties are in fact[19] neither useless nor disagreeable:

that the receiving a Minister from France at this time is an act of no significance with respect to the treaties, amounting neither to an admission nor denial of them, forasmuch as he comes not under any stipulation in them:

that were it an explicit admission, or were an express declaration of their obligation now to be made, it would not take from us that right which exists at all times of liberating ourselves when an adherence to the treaties would be *ruinous*, or *destructive* to[20] the society:

and that the not renouncing the treaties now is so far from being a breach of neutrality, that the doing it would be the breach, by giving just cause of war to France.   TH: JEFFERSON

Apr. 28. 1793.

RC (DLC: Washington Papers); entirely in TJ's hand; brackets in original. PrC (DLC); torn and partly overwritten in a later hand. Tr (Lb in DNA: RG 59, SDC). Tr (ViU); in the hand of Martha Jefferson Randolph; at foot of text in the hand of Nicholas P. Trist: "The foregoing was copied from the original Press Copy in the possession of Thos. J. Randolph, by Mrs. Martha Randolph for N. P. T. at Edgehill, Octr. 1834." Tr (ViU); incomplete 19th-century copy. Recorded in SJPL under 26 Apr. 1793: "Opn. on the Queries of Apr. 18." Enclosed in TJ to George Washington, 28 Apr. 1793 (Document III above).

GUARANTEE OF OUR POSTS: a reference to the decision of the United States government not to invoke Article 11 of the treaty of alliance with France, which bound that kingdom to guarantee the territorial integrity of the United States, in connection with its efforts to secure the evacuation of the posts on American soil still held by the British in contravention of the Treaty of Paris (Miller, *Treaties*, II, 39-40). In preparation for this opinion,

TJ transcribed on a single sheet the parallel passages from GROTIUS, PUFFENDORF, WOLF, AND VATTEL in the languages of the editions he used before translating them for Washington's benefit (MS in DLC: TJ Papers, 84: 14561, entirely in TJ's hand, undated; PrC in same, 14562). TJ drew the passages from *Hugonis Grotii de Jure Belli ac Pacis Libri Tres* ... (Amsterdam, 1651); Samuel von Pufendorf, *Le Droit de la nature et des gens* ..., trans. from the Latin, 3 vols. (London, 1740); Christian Wolff, *Institutions du Droit de la Nature et des Gens* ..., trans. from the Latin, 6 vols. (Leyden, 1772); and Emmerich de Vattel, *Le Droit des Gens, ou Principes de la Loi naturelle, appliqués à la conduite & aux affaires des nations & des souverains*, 3 vols. ([Neuchâtel?], 1758). See Sowerby, Nos. 1404, 1406, 1410-11. The sheet also contains one sentence, which TJ did not quote, from Jean Jacques Burlamaqui, *Principes du Droit Politique* (Amsterdam, 1751), concerning the obligation of heads of state to honor treaties made by their predecessors. See Sowerby, No. 1408.

[1] Word altered from "treaty."

2 Word altered from "treaty."

3 Word written over "it."

4 Word altered from "treaty."

5 Word substituted for "the treaty" here and in the next sentence.

6 TJ here canceled "and if our atia," the last word being the Greek term for *source* or *cause*, used in classical philosophy and theology to signify the ultimate source, or deity.

7 TJ first wrote "of GUARANTY" and then altered it to read as above.

8 TJ here canceled what appears to be "I will establish."

9 Sentence interlined.

10 Word interlined.

11 TJ here canceled "non compliance."

12 Word altered from "treaty."

13 Word interlined.

14 Word reworked from "will."

15 Word altered from "treaty."

16 Word interlined in place of "with."

17 Preceding seven words interlined.

18 This and the following quotation mark supplied.

19 Preceding two words interlined.

20 Word written over "of."

To James Madison

DEAR SIR   Philadelphia Apr. 28. 1793.

Yours of the 12th. inst. is received, and I will duly attend to your commission relative to the ploughs. We have had such constant deluges of rain and bad weather for some time past that I have not yet been able to go to Dr. Logan's to make the enquiries you desire, but I will do it soon. We expect Mr. Genest here within a few days. It seems as if his arrival would furnish occasion for the *people* to testify their affections without respect to the cold caution of their government. Would you suppose it possible that it should have been seriously proposed to declare our treaties with France void on the authority of an ill-understood scrap in Vattel 2.§.197. ['toutefois si ce changement &c—gouvernement'] and that it should be necessary to discuss it?—Cases are now arising which will embarras us a little till the line of neutrality be fairly understood by ourselves, and the belligerant parties. A French frigate is now bringing here, as we are told, prizes which left this but 2. or 3. days before. Shall we permit her to sell them? The treaty does not say we shall, and it says we shall not permit the like to England? Shall we permit France to fit out privateers here? The treaty does not stipulate that we shall, tho' it says we shall not permit the English to do it. I fear that a fair neutrality will prove a disagreeable pill to our friends, tho' necessary to keep us out of the calamities of a war. Adieu, my dear Sir your's affectionately   TH: JEFFERSON

RC (DLC: Madison Papers); at foot of text: "Mr. Madison"; brackets in original. PrC (DLC). Tr (DLC); 19th-century copy.

During the Cabinet meeting of 19 Apr. 1793, Alexander Hamilton had cited this ILL-UNDERSTOOD SCRAP IN VATTEL, a noted eighteenth-century authority on international law, in support of his contention that the overthrow of the French monarchy justified the United States government in suspending or renouncing its treaties with France. For TJ's interpretation of this passage from Vattel, see Opinion on the Treaties with France, Document IV in a group of documents on that subject at 28 Apr. 1793. See also Notes on Washington's Questions on Neutrality and the Alliance with France, [6 May 1793].

To Archibald Moncrief

Sir   Philadelphia Apr. 28. 1793.

By a letter I have just received from Mr. Curson, I find that the duties of my wine had been bonded by yourself on behalf of Mr. James Brown of Richmond. It was to him I had applied to do what was necessary for me, and he had written to me that he had desired his correspondent to enter them: but (conceiving from the bill of lading that they were landed in Norfolk) I imagined he meant a correspondent in Norfolk, and therefore on learning they were at Baltimore took the measures I did for their entry there. These being rendered unnecessary, nothing further I presume, need be done for the present. I will carefully account in due time to Mr. Brown, or any other person for the duties. I would thank you in the mean time for information of their amount. I am with much regard Sir Your most obedt humble servt   Th: Jefferson

PrC (DLC); at foot of text: "Mr. Moncrief."

The 25 Apr. 1793 letter from Richard curson, recorded in SJL as received 27 Apr. 1793, has not been found.

To Beverley Randolph

Dear Sir   Philadelphia Apr. 28. 1793.

You will perceive by the inclosed letter from Mr. Harry Innes that some time the last year the Indians carried off, from a farm of his, three negro men. The method proposed for their recovery, in his letter, I knew would produce nothing, and therefore did not move in it at all. I presume that one of the subjects of your ensuing treaty will be the restoration of all prisoners, without regard to colour or condition. This will open a door for the recovery of Mr. Innes's negroes, and as it is not a question[1] whether they shall be free, or slaves, but whether they shall be slaves among the savages, or in the country of their birth and connections, I know no ground of scrupling to endeavor to recover them. It is probable that the Indians of the very towns where these negroes are understood to be (Kickapou and Eel river) will be at the treaty, and these towns are so little remote from Kentuckey that there seems a better probability that they may be heard of, and conducted home. I take the liberty of putting these papers into your hands, and of solliciting your endeavors for the restoration of the persons they describe. You will observe that Mr. Innes is willing to meet any reasonable expence which may attend their recovery. I am with great & sincere esteem Dr Sir your friend & servt   Th: Jefferson

PrC (DLC); at foot of text: "Beverley Randolph esq." Tr (DLC); 19th-century copy.

Harry Innes to TJ, 30 June 1792, which is recorded in SJL as received 25 Aug. 1792, but has not been found.

The INCLOSED LETTER was probably

[1] Preceding two words interlined.

To Martha Jefferson Randolph

MY DEAR MARTHA   Philadelphia Apr. 28. 1793.

I am now very long without a letter from Monticello, which is always a circumstance of anxiety to me. I wish I could say that Maria was quite well. I think her better for this week past, having for that time been free from the little fevers which had harrassed her nightly.— A paper which I some time ago saw in the Richmond gazette[1] under the signature of R.R. proved to me the existence of a rumor, which I had otherwise heard of with less certainty. It has given me great uneasiness because I know it must have made so many others unhappy, and among these Mr. Randolph and yourself. Whatever the case may be, the world is become too rational to extend to one person the acts of another. Every one at present stands on the merit or demerit of their own conduct. I am in hopes therefore that neither of you feel any uneasiness but for the pitiable victim,[2] whether it be[3] of error or of slander. In either case I see guilt but in one person, and not in her. For her it is the moment of trying the affection of her friends, when their commiseration and comfort become balm to her wounds. I hope you will deal them out to her in full measure, regardless of what the trifling or malignant may think or say. Never throw off the best[4] affections of nature in the moment when they become most precious to their object; nor fear to extend your hand to save another, lest you should sink yourself. You are on firm ground: your kindnesses will help her and[5] count in your own favor also. I shall be made very happy if you are the instruments not only of supporting the spirits of your[6] afflicted friend[7] under the weight bearing on them, but of preserving her in the peace and love of her friends. I hope you have already taken this resolution if it were necessary; and I have no doubt you have: yet

[621]

I wished it too much to omit mentioning it to you. I am with sincere love to Mr. Randolph & yourself, my dear Martha your's affectionately

TH: JEFFERSON

RC (NNP); at foot of first page: "Mrs. Randolph"; endorsed by Mrs. Randolph; accompanied by a separate sheet bearing the following notes by Nicholas P. Trist, the first two sentences of which are undated and were written at a different time: "Jefferson Thomas Apr. 28. '93 To his daughter Mrs. Randolph. This letter is a fair Specimen of the truly christian Spirit of charity and moral courage which ever actuated him. This letter was once shewn to me by Mrs. R, on the occasion of her making a search among her father's letters to her, at my request, with a view to finding a suitable one to send to Mr. Aaron Vail at London. (He had been requested by Princess Victoria to procure for her an autograph of Mr. Jefferson). I was so much struck with this letter, as a specimen of her father's character, that I asked it of her, and she gave it me. N.P.T. Phila. June 11. '55. It has come under my hand today, in searching for an autograph for Dr. Dunglison." Tr (ViFreJM); 19th-century copy; at foot of text in Trist's hand: "Note by N. P. Trist. The original of the above was given to me, at my request, upon its being shown to me by Mrs. Randolph at Washington, on the occasion of a Search among her father's letters for one to be sent to Mr. Aaron Vail (then Secretary of Legation at London) for Princess Victoria. I now place this in its place on the file. Phila. June 5. '56." Tr (Mrs. Thomas O. Gamble, Albany, New York, 1950); 19th-century copy.

The PAPER . . . UNDER THE SIGNATURE

OF R.R. was a letter to the public from Richard Randolph, printed in several Virginia newspapers early in April 1793, in which he announced that he planned to appear before the Cumberland County Court to answer any charges anyone might think fit to bring against him. Randolph, the husband of Martha Jefferson Randolph's sister-in-law, Judith Randolph, took this step to counteract widespread rumors that he had fathered a child by his wife's sister, Ann Cary Randolph, THE PITIABLE VICTIM of these reports, and murdered it after birth. The court subsequently examined various witnesses, including Martha Jefferson Randolph, and on 29 Apr. exonerated Richard Randolph of any wrongdoing. For a detailed description of this episode—which suggests that Randolph's younger brother Theodorick, who died soon after Ann Cary Randolph's child was conceived, was the father and that the baby either miscarried or was stillborn—see Marshall, *Papers*, II, 161-78. See also John Wayles Eppes to TJ, 1 May 1793, and note, and Martha Jefferson Randolph to TJ, 16 May 1793.

[1] Word interlined in place of "papers."
[2] TJ here canceled what appears to be "of this crime" or "of this rumor."
[3] Preceding two words interlined.
[4] Word interlined.
[5] Preceding three words interlined.
[6] Word altered from "our."
[7] Word interlined in place of what appears to be "guest."

From F. P. Van Berckel

MONSIEUR   à Philadelphie Ce 28e. Avril 1793.

Venant de recevoir la Lettre que Vous m'avez fait l'honneur de m'adresser en date du 23e. dernier avec la Copie d'une Proclamation du President des Etats Unis, je m'empresse à Vous faire part de la Sensibilité avec laquelle je m'assure que Leurs Hautes Puissances recevront les temoignages des dispositions Amicales des Etats Unis envers Elles, aussi bien que des intentions Sinceres et impartiales que les Etats Unis desirent de manifester.

Quoiqué je n'aye jusques içi reçu aucune notification directe de la Hollande d'une declaration de Guerre par la France aux Etats Generaux des Provinces Unies, je ne Saurois Cependant me dispenser de Vous informer, Monsieur, que j'en ai reçu telle information, qué je Considere Comme egalement authentique, m'ayant été donnée par le Ministre de Sa Majesté Britannique, l'Allié de Leurs Hautes Puissances. J'ai l'honneur d'etre avec la plus parfaite Consideration Monsieur Votre très humble & très Obeïssant Serviteur

F: P: van Berckel

RC (DNA: RG 360, PCC); at foot of text: "Monsieur Jefferson, Secretaire d'Etat à Philadelphie"; endorsed by TJ as received 29 Apr. 1793 and so recorded in SJL.

TJ submitted this letter to the President on 1 May 1793, and Washington returned it the next day (Washington, *Journal*, 125).

From David Humphreys

Lisbon, 29 Apr. 1793. He has received no direct intelligence from America since his last dispatch. The birth of a daughter to the Princess of Brazil this morning will require the diplomatic corps to attend court for ten successive days beginning tomorrow and lead to the suspension of all business for some days so that the Portuguese can celebrate the arrival of this eagerly awaited successor to the reigning family. There is no reliable news from France because of the suspension of land communications with it. M. d'Arbot, the proposed French minister mentioned in his last, left a few days ago for Le Havre in an American vessel, his departure having been hastened by certain intimations from this court. At the captain's request, he has asked Pinto to indemnify his expenses in being detained here by the government, but owing to the minister's illness Mr. Seabra has laid the matter before the Prince. Captain Perkins, for whom he obtained permission to leave Lisbon, sailed to Cadiz and sold his cargo for a much higher price than he could have obtained here. He has just seen a despondent letter of 20 Mch. from Captain O'Bryen to a gentleman here stating that the plague has broken out again in Algiers, that the Swedish consul had ransomed George Smith, an American captive, for 2,696 dollars, that five Dutch ships worth 1,500,000 dollars have been condemned and 63 people enslaved, that it will cost the Dutch 350,000 dollars more to make peace, and that the French consul has been ordered to leave Algiers in 55 days. A late letter from Simpson at Gibraltar mentions that Moroccan affairs remain in the same state they have been for a long time, and this day's post brings a letter from Short in Spain with no significant information.

RC (DNA: RG 59, DD); 4 p.; at head of text: "(No. 71.)"; at foot of text: "The Secretary of State &c. &c. &c."; endorsed by TJ as received 10 June 1793 and so recorded in SJL. Tr (Lb in same).

TJ submitted this letter to the President on 10 June 1793, and he returned it the next day (Washington, *Journal*, 165-6, 167).

American Philosophical Society's Instructions to André Michaux

[ca. 30 Apr. 1793]

To Mr. Andrew Michaud.

Sundry persons having subscribed certain sums of money for your encouragement to explore the country along the Missouri, and thence Westwardly to the Pacific ocean, having submitted the plan of the enterprize to the direction of the American Philosophical society, and the Society having accepted of the trust, they proceed to give you the following instructions.

They observe to you that the chief objects of your journey are to find the shortest and most convenient route of communication between the US. and the Pacific ocean, within the temperate latitudes, and to learn such particulars as can be obtained of the country through which it passes, it's productions, inhabitants and other interesting circumstances.

As a channel of communication between these states and the Pacific ocean, the Missouri, so far as it extends, presents itself under circumstances of unquestioned preference. It has therefore been declared as a fundamental object of the subscription, (not to be dispensed with) that this river shall be considered and explored as a part of the communication sought for. To the neighborhood of this river therefore, that is to say to the town of Kaskaskia, the society will procure you a conveyance in company with the Indians of that town now in Philadelphia.

From thence you will cross the Missisipi and pass by land to the nearest part of the Missouri above the Spanish settlements, that you may avoid the risk of being stopped.

You will then pursue such of the largest streams of that river, as shall lead by the shortest way, and the lowest latitudes to the Pacific ocean.

When, pursuing these streams, you shall find yourself at the point from whence you may get by the shortest and most convenient route to some principal river of the Pacific ocean, you are to proceed to such river, and pursue it's course to the ocean. It would seem by the latest maps as if a river called Oregan interlocked with the Missouri for a considerable distance, and entered the Pacific ocean, not far Southward of Nootka sound. But the Society are aware that these maps are not to be trusted so far as to be the ground of any positive instruction to you. They therefore only mention the fact, leaving to yourself to verify it, or to follow such other as you shall find to be the real truth.

You will, in the course of your journey, take notice of the country you pass through, it's general face, soil, rivers, mountains, it's productions animal, vegetable, and mineral so far as they may be new to us and may also be useful or very curious; the latitude of places or materials for calculating it by such simple methods as your situation may admit you to practice, the names, numbers, and dwellings of the inhabitants, and such particularities as you can learn of their history, connection with each other, languages, manners, state of society and of the arts and commerce among them.

Under the head of Animal history, that of the Mammoth is particularly recommended to your enquiries. As it is also to learn whether the Lama, or Paca of Peru is found in those parts of this continent, or how far North they come.

The method of preserving your observations is left[1] to yourself, according to the means which shall be in your power. It is only suggested that the noting them on the skin might be best for such as are most important, and that further details may be committed to the bark of the paper birch, a substance which may not excite suspicions among the Indians, and little liable to injury from wet, or other common accidents.   By the means of the same substance you may perhaps find opportunities, from time to time, of communicating to the society information of your progress, and of the particulars you shall have noted.

When you shall have reached the Pacific ocean, if you find yourself within convenient distance of any settlement of Europeans, go to them, commit to writing a narrative of your journey and observations and take the best measures you can for conveying it by duplicates or triplicates[2] thence to the society by sea.

Return by the same, or such other route, as you shall think likely to fulfill with most satisfaction and certainty the objects of your mission; furnishing yourself with the best proofs the nature of the case will admit of the reality and extent of your progress. Whether this shall be by certificates from Europeans settled on the Western coast of America, or by what other means, must depend on circumstances.

Ignorance of the country thro' which you are to pass and confidence in your judgment, zeal, and discretion, prevent the society from attempting more minute instructions, and even from exacting rigorous observance of those already given, except indeed what is the first of all objects, that you seek for and pursue that route which shall form the shortest and most convenient communication between the higher parts of the Missouri and the Pacific ocean.

It is strongly recommended to you to expose yourself in no case to unnecessary dangers, whether such as might affect your health or your personal safety: and to consider this not merely as your personal concern, but as the injunction of Science in general which expects it's enlargement from your enquiries, and of the inhabitants of the US. in particular, to whom your Report will open new feilds and subjects of Commerce, Intercourse, and Observation.

If you reach the Pacific ocean and return, the Society assign to you all the benefits of the subscription beforementioned. If you reach the waters only which run into that ocean, the society reserve to themselves the apportionment of the reward according to the conditions expressed in the subscription.[3]

They will expect you to return to the city of Philadelphia to give in to them a full narrative of your journey and observations, and to answer the enquiries they shall make of you, still reserving to yourself the benefits arising from the publication[4] of them.[5]

Dft (PPAmP: Caspar Wistar Papers); undated; entirely in TJ's hand except for marginal note (see note 1 below) and endorsement in unidentified hand: "Philosophical Soc: to Michaud"; one line of canceled text lost through clipping (see note 3 below). PrC (DLC: TJ Papers, 81: 14054-7); lacks emendations recorded in textual notes below. Recorded in SJPL under 23 Jan. 1793: "instructions to [Michaux]."

These instructions were drafted by TJ sometime between 19 Apr. 1793, when the American Philosophical Society formally accepted responsibility for Michaux's expedition and appointed TJ to a five-member committee charged with preparing them, and 30 Apr. 1793, when they were submitted, amended, and approved at a special meeting of the Society that TJ attended (Rough Minutes of the American Philosophical Society, 19,

30 Apr. 1793, PPAmP). For a discussion of their provenance, see Editorial Note on Jefferson and André Michaux's proposed western expedition, at 22 Jan. 1793.

[1] An unidentified hand drew a brace encompassing the sentence to this point and the preceding two paragraphs, and next to it in the margin wrote "here it is proposed to insert the Contents of the annexed paper." The "paper" referred to has not been identified.
[2] Preceding four words interlined.
[3] Here TJ canceled "If you do not reach even those waters, they [refuse all reward, and reclaim the money you may have received] here under the subscription." The words in brackets are clipped and have been supplied from the PrC.
[4] Here TJ canceled "of such parts."
[5] TJ inserted the period after canceling "as are in the said subscription reserved to you."

From Tench Coxe

April 30. [1793]

Mr. Coxe has the honor to inclose to the Secretary of State a letter from Mr. Stephen Kingston relative to a foreign built Ship, which is stated to belong to Mr. Kingston of Philadelphia. This Vessel is not now in the United States but in Jamaica, Honduras or on the High Seas between them. She is British built, and has now a British register, it is presumed, as she could not without one enter the Ports of Jamaica.

RC (DLC); partially dated; endorsed by TJ as received 30 Apr. 1793 and so recorded in SJL. FC (PHi: Coxe Papers).

Stephen Kingston to Tench Coxe

DEAR SIR   Monday 29 April 1793
To you I will not attempt to suggest any thing to give force to the thoughts already alive on the subject of this mornings conversation—your mind will readily embrace and combine every Idea of strength, but the variety of Publick Business which may require your attention may also divert it at present from the object, which may justify what my immediate situation furnishes thereon.

You observ'd that we have not ourselves a sufficiency of tonnage to take away all our produce which I find the opinion of all the Merchants to whom I have spoken on the subject. Accounts are already received of several Vessells belonging to this Port being taken up to perform Voyages from and to different ports in Europe and elsewhere, thereby diverting 'em from the more immediate service of our own general Trade *and National* advantage, the carrying *our own* produce. And upon terms so very beneficial as to make it probable many more will be employed in the same way by the Merchants giving directions to their Captains now sailing to accept such good offers as may be made 'em in Europe. This will be to the Individuals a source of Wealth but to the Agricultural Interest very injurious and very speedily felt unless some recourse or remedy be soon applied. Accounts from the Eastward and Southward announce a distressing want of Vessells which has already reduced the value of many Exports and rais'd Exchange to a degree actually threatning *Specie being sent away!* which the high price of Silver in Europe will also operate to induce!

To prevent is universally allow'd to be better than to remedy an Evil, I therefore conceive in the present exigency the permission to purchase foreign built Vessells remaining subject to foreign tonage wou'd be as Politick as it seems necessary and must become very soon unavoidable.

In contemplating all the effects of this relief the possible objections of our Ship Carpenters must be consider'd—but as I take it for granted that we can build *Cheaper* than any other Nation we have nothing to fear.

Is it probable we shou'd by this means become so rapidly possess'd of an adequate number of Vessells as to injure impede or prevent our own Building? I answer no. It is not probable and scarcely possible and even if shou'd, every degree of encrease to our Navigation will require additional hands to keep them in repair for which they are better paid than for new work by about 20 per Ct!

Our own *built* Vessells will still continue to enjoy the advantage of tonage duty and the additional duties payable on all goods imported in foreign built Vessells, as *they* must come in ballast and the *whole return* freight to America be enjoy'd by the home built Vessells, or the Duties payable on Goods Imported in foreign built Vessells &c. be willingly paid *into our Treasury* instead of going for a more uncertain end into the Pockets of the English Underwriters—for it is evident the Premiums of Insurance on their Vessells will generally be more than the additional Duty to be paid here *if American bottom'd* and yet much more uncertain in effect and production, as they are less able to calculate on a well plan'd Voyage being perfected and if not—they hazard the stability of the Insurers—upon the whole then it seems evident they had better pay our Treasury the additional Duties and have their Business transacted with American protection than hazard all the uncertainties that are inseperable from the Business conducted in their own Bottoms.

With regard to foreign Vessells Bona fide owned by the Citizens of the U States *previous to the commencement of the present War* for the purposes of partaking of those beneficial branches of Trade from which our own Vessells were excluded—I conceive they ought to be register'd without delay subject to the foreign tonage Duties &c. as every Loss of property to an individual Citizen is so far an injury to the society or Government.

I need not observe that if the advantage this *carrying Trade* holds out is not embraced by us without delay, immediate recourse will be had to the Danish, Swedish and any other flag that is in a situation and disposed to embrace it, by which their Citizens and subjects will pocket that Wealth which wou'd otherwise come into the possession of our Merchants and Farmers. For it is a self evident Truth that the general riches of any Country enhance the value of it's produce and the soil thereby becomes it's greatest source of encrease, by the competition of the buyers and not of the sellers.

Under those impressions I beg leave to apply for Sea Letters for my Ship Robert of 260 tons of which I now appoint Capn. West Master a *native American* and in my employ who goes down in a small Vessell to the Bay of Honduras where she is at present. Having gone considerably into a Trade thither I found myself led into a deposit of too large a property there to remain subject to the disappointments and uncertainties of freights being obtain'd and to such excuses being given me from time to time for not sending my effects. I therefore Bought this Ship Robert for £2118 Stg. She arrived here in Decr. last and I sent her round to Norfolk in Virginia, where she was sheath'd and loaded for Jamaica and arrived the 22 March from whence she was to proceed without delay to Honduras there to wait the collection of a Cargo, the whole of which with the Ship is bona fide mine and no other Person has any share, right, Interest or Concern therein directly or indirectly to which I am ready to make Oath. I Remain very truly Dear Sir Your Obed H Servt.

STEPHEN KINGSTON

RC (DLC); in a clerk's hand, with dateline, complimentary close, and signature by Kingston.

From Sharp Delany

SIR   30th Aprl. 1793

I have distributed the Passports which I received Yesterday by Your directions, and there are now applications for a considerable number.

In Your Letter of Instruction there is no mention of any Charge, which led me to tell the Merchants I had no authority to receive any fee or emolument, but that I should make the proper inquiry and inform them accordingly. I would therefore beg leave to observe that almost every Vessell bound to a Foreign Port will require a Sea Letter—the Expence and trouble of which will be considerable, and I make no doubt on demand would be paid willingly. On this head I beg to have your opinion, and if any more are in readiness I request they may be delivered to the bearer. I am Sir with great Respect your Obedient Servant   SHARP DELANY

RC (DLC); endorsed by TJ as received 30 Apr. 1793 and so recorded in SJL.

TJ's LETTER OF INSTRUCTION to Sharp Delany, the federal customs collector in Philadelphia, has not been found and is not recorded in SJL. According to a later statement by TJ, this letter instructed Delany to fill out and deliver on TJ's behalf to the ships in question passports certifying American ownership of seven merchant vessels about to leave Philadelphia (TJ to Alexander Hamilton, 8 May 1793). On the need for passports for American ships, whether built abroad or in the United States, in the wake of the outbreak of war between France and Great Britain, see Opinion on Ship Passports, 3 May 1793.

To Sharp Delany

SIR   Philadelphia Apr. 30. 1793.

The arrangement taken with respect to sea-letters was that they should be delivered to the collectors of the customs at every port of the US. as the persons who might the most conveniently countersign and deliver them out, and for this purpose that they should be sent from my office to the Commissioner of the revenue to be distributed, as being particularly within his department. Understanding that several vessels were waiting yesterday at this port I took the liberty of troubling you with the passports directly without sending them thro' the Commissioner of the revenue. He is now supplied with a number and will hereafter be kept in a state of supply.   With respect to the fee it is not within my province to decide any thing. A moderate fee seems reasonable, and whether any law prohibits the taking it is a question which it belongs to the gentlemen of the law to decide, at least till the meeting of Congress when this article may be placed regularly on the fee-bill. I am with great esteem Sir Your most obedt. hble servt   TH: JEFFERSON

PrC (DLC); at foot of text: "Mr. Delaney." FC (Lb in DNA: RG 59, DL).

Tench Coxe was COMMISSIONER OF THE REVENUE, the official in the Department of the Treasury to whom Alexander Hamilton had deputed general oversight over the "security of Navigation" (Syrett, *Hamilton*, XI, 416-17; Jacob E. Cooke, *Tench Coxe and the Early Republic* [Chapel Hill, 1978], 239-47).

From James Simpson

Gibraltar, 30 Apr. 1793. He last wrote on 19 Feb. by the schooner *Fredericksburgh Packet.* Muley Suliman left Mequinez to quell disturbances in Tetuán and Tangier but was halted at Great Alcázar by Sidi Muhammad and deputies from the midland provinces, who invited him to proceed from thence to Morocco. If Muley Suliman follows this course there is a good chance he will soon win sole control of the Empire, but in the unexpected event he does not the midland provinces will seek another Emperor, being tired of Muley Ischem, who continues at Morocco. Muhammad Ben Absadack, who made himself obnoxious to the mountaineers, has been removed from the government of Tangier by Muley Suliman. He will inform TJ by the earliest conveyance of the outcome of the succession struggle.

RC (DNA: RG 59, CD); 2 p.; at foot of first page: "The Honble Thomas Jefferson"; endorsed by TJ as received 27 June 1793 and so recorded in SJL. Enclosed in Tobias Lear to TJ, 15 July 1793.

TJ submitted this letter to the President on 11 July 1793 (Washington, *Journal*, 191).

From John Carey

SIR   May 1st. 1793.

I have the honor of presenting to you the remainder of my manuscripts; and beg leave to observe, that there are a few of the concluding books of each of the two parcels, which you have not yet inspected.

I refrain, Sir, from expressing here my obligations, as well for the many favors I have received from you, as for the polite and easy condescension with which they were conferred, well aware, that expressions of thanks, however pleasing to the grateful heart from whence they flow, are least acceptable to those who are best entitled to receive them. I shall therefore content myself with declaring, in the plain language of sincerity, that, with unfeigned respect and gratitude, I have the honor to be, Sir, Your most obliged, and most obedient humble Servant,   JOHN CAREY

RC (DLC); endorsed by TJ as received 1 May 1793 and so recorded in SJL.

From Henry Cooper

St. Croix, *1 May 1793*. He expresses thanks for the correspondence covering his consular commission for this island and promises at the earliest opportunity to attend to TJ's general letter of instructions and communicate to him such information as may be required.

RC (DNA: RG 59, CD); 1 p.; addressed: "Honble. Thomas Jefferson Esqr."; endorsed by TJ as received 27 May 1793 and so recorded in SJL. Enclosed in TJ to George Washington, 27 May 1793.

From Joseph Dombey

MONSIEUR   Lyon Le 1er. may 1793. l'an 2. de la république
La lecture de votre ouvrage Sur la virginie enflame mon Courage et me fait désirer voir Les Sites que vous avez Si bien décrits. Je viens de faire demander la permission au gouvernement pour aller botaniser Deux à trois années dans l'amerique Septentrionale. Je me rejouirai beaucoup, Monsieur, de pouvoir avant de mourir vous temoigner tous les Sentiments que vous m'avés inspirés pendant mon Séjour à paris ou vous m'avés Comblés de bontés.

Le Citoyen gauthier qui vous presentera, monsieur, ma Lettre S'embarque pour philadelphie, pour dela aller à St. Domingue ou Ses affaires l'appellent. Je vous Suplie de vouloir Le proteger pendant Son Séjour à philadelphie et Luy faciliter Son embarquement pour St. Domingue. Je Suis avec respect Monsieur Votre très humble et tres obeissant Serviteur   DOMBEY

RC (DLC); addressed: "Monsieur De Jefferson ministre des affaires etrangeres à philadelphie"; endorsed by TJ as received 17 Dec. 1793 and so recorded in SJL.

Joseph Dombey (1742-94), a French physician and botanist who had undertaken a noted botanical expedition to South America on behalf of the French crown from 1777 to 1785, was currently serving as surgeon of the Lyon military hospital. In December 1793 Dombey was commissioned by the Committee of Public Safety to journey to the United States in order to deliver the standards for the new metric system and purchase grain for the French Republic, but while on his way to America he was captured at sea by the British and died in a prison on Montserrat (*Dictionnaire de Biographie Française*, 17 vols. [Paris, 1933-], XI, 468-70; DSB, IV, 156-7).

From C. W. F. Dumas

The Hague, *1 May 1793*. Providence alone can foresee the final end of this unprecedented and almost general war. Correspondence with France is again interrupted, and he and many other good people in this country suffer because France pays neither incomes nor pensions abroad. People in this province suffer further from the forced imposition, which they must swear is not forced, of what is called a free gift, payable in four installments every six months, making altogether the fiftieth denier of everything they possess, except as usual for the military and a number of the high and low-privileged. Add to this the decline of commerce, the high and increasing prices, the falling real estate values, and the increasing inquisition and financial distress, and the unhappy situation can be imagined. He can say nothing about the even more unhappy condition of Poland or the rest of Europe, of which this city is kept in distressing ignorance. He consoles himself with the certainty that God loves the United States and that the governors and the governed there render themselves worthy of it by loving one another in the manner described by Paul in the thirteenth chapter of 1 Corinthians. *P.S. 10 May 1793.* Papers from France have not come here since 13 Apr.

Dupl (DNA: RG 59, MLR); 2 p.; in French; at head of text: "No. 97. A Son Excellence M. ... le Secretaire d'Etat, et pour les Affrs. étrangeres, en Congrès-genl. des Et. Un. d'Amerique" and "Dupl."; endorsed by TJ as received 19 July 1793 and so recorded in SJL. Another text of this letter, not found, is recorded in SJL as received 2 Dec. 1793. A second letter of 1 May 1793 from Dumas is also recorded in SJL as received 2 Dec. 1793, but no text has been found.

From John Wayles Eppes

DEAR UNCLE   Eppington May: 1st. 1793.

I received two days ago your favor of the 14th. of April, and although I am apprehensive I have already trespassed too far on your goodness, must accept of the offer you have been kind enough to make of discharging Gordons account. Forgetfulness on the part of the Creditor is but too general, and the present instance of negligence may afford you just grounds for supposing, I am not altogether clear of a foible, so common with my countryman.

My father expects on the 12th. of May a final decree with regard to Cary's Executors until which time he has postponed writing.

I am happy to inform you that the reports so injurious to the reputation of Miss Randolph, which have for some time[1] engaged the public attention are now found to be absolutely false. Richard Randolph delivered himself up at last Cumberland Court, has been since tried by a call court, and acquitted with great honour. Mr. Marshall and Mr. Campbell were present at the trial and declare, that nothing was proved which could even afford grounds for a suspicion, that either of the parties accused had acted even imprudently, much less criminally. His own relations were his prosecutors and particularly active. The people of Cumberland who carried their prejudices so far that a strong guard was necessary to protect Mr. Randolph on his way from the prison to the court house unanimously cried out shame on the accusers after the evidence was heard. It is a striking instance of the length to which the inveteracy and malice of relations may be carried when they once depart from that line of conduct which should ever be[2] observed among near connections.

I inclose a letter for my Cousin with my best wishes for her health. I am Dr. Sir with the greatest affection & respect Yours sincerely

JOHN: W. EPPES

N.B. I fear you will suppose from this letter I have forgot your injunctions with regard to my hand writing, but the badness of the hand will be excused when I inform you I had no knife that could make a pen.

I hope Petit is well, for I shall ever remember him esteem.[3]

RC (ViU: Edgehill-Randolph Papers); endorsed by TJ as received 14 May 1793 and so recorded in SJL. Enclosure not found.

Eppes's assertion that John Marshall WAS PRESENT AT THE TRIAL on 29 Apr. 1793 at which a Cumberland County call court determined that evidence was lacking to charge Richard Randolph with infanticide corroborates circumstantial evidence offered by the most detailed study of this controversial case. For a discussion of Marshall's attendance as it concerns his revealing note of the evidence given at the hearing, see Marshall, *Papers*, II, 161-8. MY COUSIN: TJ's daughter Mary.

[1] Preceding two words interlined.
[2] Eppes here canceled "preserved."
[3] Sentence thus in manuscript.

From Samuel Freeman

SIR   Portland May 1. 1793

Considering it of the utmost importance that a knowledge of the Laws of the United States should be generally circulated—and that they are printed in no part of this extensive and increasing District (the District of Maine) I readily joined in an Application to you Sir, which I signed yesterday requesting that they might be printed in the *Gazette of Maine*. As the Gentlemen who have signed the same Application are probably all Strangers to you, I take the liberty to assure you that they are Gentlemen of the first Character in this Town, and many of them the most eminent Merchants here. You will doubtless consider me as no less a Stranger than the other Gentlemen. I beg leave therefore to refer you to the Honorable Timothy Pickering Esqr. Post Master

General, under whom I have the Honor to serve as a Deputy Post Master in this place.

Mr. Titcomb the Printer of the abovementioned Paper is a worthy young Gentleman who would be happy to serve the Public in any way within his Power. His Paper is well executed and has a general[1] circulation, particularly among the mercantile part of the Community and excepting the Eastern Herald, which I am told[2] is not so generally taken by the Merchants[3] in this Town, is the only Paper printed within the District.

The expediency of the measure is pointed out in the Application. Your own Judgment, will doubtless concur therein. I need not therefore add but that I am with the most profound respect Your most obedient, and very humble Servant   SAML FREEMAN

RC (DNA: RG 59, MLR); endorsed by TJ as received 10 May 1793 and so recorded in SJL.

Samuel Freeman (1742-1831), a native and lifelong resident of Portland, Maine, served as delegate to and secretary of the Massachusetts Provincial Congress in 1775-76 and 1778 and had lengthy, concurrent tenures as clerk of Cumberland County's courts, register and later judge of probate, postmaster, town selectman, and parish deacon. He wrote several popular legal handbooks and edited the journal of the pioneering Maine clergyman Thomas Smith (William Willis, *The History of Portland*, 2d ed. [Portland, Me., 1865], 745, 746-7n).

[1] MS: "generally."
[2] Preceding three words interlined.
[3] Preceding three words interlined.

Petition from Merchants and Citizens of Maine

To the Honorable Thomas Jefferson, Secretary of State for the United States.

The PETITION of the Subscribers, Merchants and Others, citizens of the United States, in the District of Maine, Humbly shews:

That many of the inhabitants of this District, labor under great inconveniencies for want of a more general circulation of the Laws of the United States: none being published in said District; and few copies coming to the knowledge of the people here—scarce any indeed, excepting what are printed in the Boston Centinel, which has but a small circulation in this part of the State of Massachusetts. Not more than fifty or sixty are generally taken, on this side the State of New-Hampshire.

That many of your petitioners are largely concerned in trade, and all in some degree interested therein. That it is of the greatest importance, and indeed absolutely necessary, that the Laws of the Union (many of which nearly concern the mercantile part of the Community) should be known generally among those on whom they more immediately operate; as well that they may have an opportunity to comply with them, as that they may not have it in their power to plead ignorance thereof, in the violation of them.

This Territory extends more than two hundred miles upon the sea coast. It contains at least one hundred thousand inhabitants. A very considerable Trade is now carried on therein: more than seventy Sail of Vessels are now employed in the Town of Portland, only; and a still greater number in the other parts of the District collectively. In consequence of which, large sums are annually paid into the public Chest, from the Merchants of this District. The people here depending upon the circulation of their own Newspapers, for the knowledge of public affairs, in many places are utterly uninformed respecting them.

For this, and many other reasons which might be offered, your Petitioners humbly think, that provisions ought to be made for the circulation of the Laws therein. They therefore humbly pray, that you would order the Laws of the United States, to be published in the Gazette of Maine, now published at Portland, by Benjamin Titcomb junr. in this District—and Your Petitioners will ever pray.

District of Maine, April 29th: 1793.

SAML FREEMAN	JOHN BAKER	SAML. BUTTS
DAVID MITCHELL	SALMON CHASE	JOSIAH COX
STEPHEN HARDING	ENOCH ILSLEY	STEVENS & HOVEY
DANL DAVIS	DANIEL ILSLEY	JOSEPH NOYES
W SYMMES	JOHN MUSSEY	JOHN HOBBY
EBENEZER STORER	WOODBURY STORER	ABNER BAGLEY
JOSEPH COFFIN BOYD	JOSEPH MCLELLAN	JOSEPH JEWETT
LEMUEL WEEKS	HUGH M LELLAN	THOMAS HODGES
EDWARD WATTS	WILLM. MOULTON	HENRY SCOLL
NATHEL DEERING	ARTHUR MCLELLAN	DAVID SMITH
RALPH CROSS	THOMAS BECK	JESSE PARTRIDGE
ROBERT BOYD	JACOB & JNO W. QUINCY	JOHN FOX

RC (DNA: RG 59, MLR); endorsed by George Taylor, Jr.

From Grand & Cie.

Paris, 1 May 1793. Recalling with pleasure their association with TJ in France and hoping that he will continue to remember them and to avail himself of their services, they introduce M. Desdoity, a merchant who has already been established for some time in New York and is trusted by a person in France with whom they are intimately connected, and ask TJ to welcome and be of service to him.

Dupl (DLC); 2 p.; in French; at head of text: "Duplicata"; endorsed by TJ as received 2 Aug. 1793 and so recorded in SJL. Enclosed in Desdoity to TJ, 31 July 1793.

To Alexander Hamilton

SIR   Philadelphia May. 1. 1793.

When you mentioned to me yesterday that M. de Ternant proposed to apply for a sum of money, and founded himself on a letter of mine which gave him reason to expect it, I thought I could not have written such a letter, because I did not recollect it, and because it was out of the plan which you know had been adopted that when we furnished one sum of money we should avoid promising another. I have now most carefully examined all my letters to M. de Ternant, as far back as Mar. 7. 1792. the date of the first on the subject of furnishing money, and can assure you there is not a word, in one of them, which can be construed into a promise, express or implied, relative to the present subject, or which can have committed the government in the smallest degree to a departure from the rules it has laid down. I am equally confident that I have never said a word which could do it. Upon the ground therefore of any such commitment by me, the proposition will not be supported.

With respect to these applications in general, they were of course to pass through me: but I have considered them as depending too much on the arrangements of your department to permit myself to take and be tenacious of any particular ground, other than that whatever rule we adopt, it be plain and persevered in uniformly in all cases where the material circumstances are the same, so that we never refuse to one what has been done for another. It is, and ever has been my opinion and wish that we should gratify the diplomatic gentlemen in every way in which we can do it, without too great inconvenience or commitment of our own government. I think it our interest to do so; and am under this impression in the present case so much that I should readily concur, if it be the pleasure of the President, in reconsidering the rule adopted on a late occasion, and substituting any other consistent with our public duties, more adapted to the gratification of the diplomatic gentlemen, and uniformly to be applied where the material circumstances shall be the same: for it would reverse our aim were we to put ourselves in the case of disobliging one by refusing what we have done to gratify another. In these sentiments, I will hand to the President any application which M. de Ternant shall think proper to communicate to me in writing. I have the honor to be with great respect, Sir, Your most obedt. humble servt.   TH: JEFFERSON

PrC (DLC); at foot of first page: "The Secretary of the Treasury."

On 30 Apr. 1793 Jean Baptiste Ternant wrote a brief note to Hamilton requesting an advance of 20,000 livres tournois on the American debt to France in the manner previously approved by the President (Syrett, *Hamilton*, xiv, 360). Although this note did not specify the purpose of the advance and made no mention of a LETTER OF MINE, its reference to a manner of payment previously sanctioned by the President suggests that Ternant was probably alluding to TJ's letter to him of 14 Jan. 1793 advising that the President had authorized the French minister to obtain further advances on the debt, not only to pay for the purchase of supplies for Saint-Domingue, but also to meet certain French consular expenses. Although it is not clear which of these two uses of the debt to France approved by Washington was at issue in the present letter, by the time Hamilton received it on the afternoon of the following day, he had already caused to be issued to Ternant, with the President's approval, a warrant for the exact amount of money requested by the French minister (TJ to Ternant, 20 Apr. 1793; Hamilton to TJ, 3 May 1793; Syrett, *Hamilton*, xvii, 536).

Memorial from George Hammond

The undersigned, his Britannic Majesty's Minister Plenipotentiary to the United States of America, has the honor of submitting to the Secretary of State the following particulars relative to the capture, in the Bay of Delaware, of the British ship Grange commanded by Edward Hutchinson and bound from this port to Liverpool.

On Thursday the 25th. of April last at 11 o'clock A.M. as the Ship Grange, *having a Delaware pilot on board, was lying at anchor near the Buoy of the Brown* in the Bay of Delaware, a Frigate appeared off the Capes under British colours, which she continued to display until she approached within half a mile of the Grange, at which time they were struck, the colours of France hoisted in their place, and the frigate proved to be the French frigate Embuscade ____ Bompart Commander. On the Grange's shewing the colours of her nation, the frigate fired a shot over her as a signal to surrender, which Captain Hutchinson immediately obeyed. The Captain of the frigate then sent his boat with thirty or forty men, who took possession of the Grange as a prize to the French Republic, and sent the crew prisoners on board of the Frigate. The Grange arrived in the harbour of this city Yesterday Evening, but her crew still remain in confinement on board of the Embuscade.

From this statement, corroborated by the annexed affidavit of the Pilot, and the affirmations of Two respectable passengers on board of the Grange, it is manifest that the French frigate Embuscade captured the British Ship Grange, as she was lying at anchor within the territory and jurisdiction of the United States, in direct violation of the Law of Nations. The Undersigned therefore can entertain no doubt that the executive government of the United States will consider this infringement on its neutrality and this aggression on its jurisdiction as a sufficient ground of compliance with the requisition which the Undersigned has now the honor of formally and respectfully making— that the executive government of the United States will adopt such measures as to its wisdom may appear the most efficacious for procuring the immediate restoration, to the agent for the owners residing in this city, of the British Ship Grange, and for obtaining the liberation of her crew now illegally and forcibly imprisoned on board of the French frigate l'Embuscade. Geo. Hammond

Philadelphia 2d. May 1793

RC (DNA: RG 59, NL); in the hand of Edward Thornton, signed by Hammond; at foot of first page: "The Secretary of State"; endorsed by a clerk as received 2 May 1793 and so recorded by TJ in SJL. FC (Lb in PRO: FO 116/3). Tr (same, 115/2). Tr (same, 5/1). PrC of Tr (DLC); in a clerk's hand. PrC of Tr (DNA: RG 59, MD); in the hand of George Taylor, Jr.; lacks final page. Tr (Lb in same, NL). Tr (DLC: Genet Papers). Tr (same); in French. Tr (AMAE: CPEU, xxxvii); in French. Enclosures: (1) Affidavit of Gilbert Macraken, Philadelphia, 2 May 1793, stating that he was a pilot from Lewes, Delaware, who had been hired by Captain Edward Hutchinson on or about 18 Apr. 1793 to guide the Grange from Philadelphia to the sea; that Captain Hutchinson at length ordered the Grange to "proceed to the Anchorage within Cape Henlopen, and wait there for a fair wind, to carry him clear off the coast"; that at about 5:00 A.M. on the 25th, while the Grange lay at anchor "in about thirteen fathom water, within about a mile to the westward of the Buoy of the Brown, with the Light house on Cape Henlopen in view, at the distance of about twelve miles, and bearing South and by East half East from them, and Cape May bearing to the southward of East," a large ship hove in sight flying English colors; that this ship struck English colors when it came within about two miles of the Grange and then hoisted French colors when it was within hailing distance, leading Captain

Hutchinson to hoist English colors; that the French ship then fired a shot over the Grange, took possession of it with a boarding crew, declared it to be a prize of the Embuscade, and took aboard all the officers and crew except for the steward; and that the Embuscade brought the Grange up to Philadelphia, where it was in possession of a prize master and several crewmen from its captor. (2) Affidavit of Joshua Sutcliff, Philadelphia, 2 May 1793, of the same general import as No. 1, but adding that at about 11:00 A.M. on 25 Apr., with the pilot still on board and no colors flying, the Grange was lying at anchor "near the Buoy of the Brown a sand Bank in the Bay of the River Delaware" when it was approached from the sea by a frigate flying English colors and seized as a prize of the French Republic; that only after being taken to the frigate did the crew learn that it was the Embuscade, commanded by Citizen Bompard; that the Grange had not sailed past the spot in Delaware Bay where she was captured; that her captain, officers, and passengers believed themselves to be on neutral ground under United States protection; and that, contrary to reports, no alterations had been made in the Grange's name on its stern or in its registry certificate. (3) Affidavit of George Dillwyn, Philadelphia, 2 May 1793, of the same general import as No. 1, but adding that the Grange was anchored "within about a Mile of the Buoy of the Brown" and first sighted the Embuscade at about 10:00 A.M. on 25 Apr.; that he and the other three cabin passengers (including his wife) remained on board the *Grange* and received civil treatment from the French until the 28th, when the French captain allowed them to go ashore with their effects; and that he did not "discover that Captain Hutchinson had provided any false papers whereby to impose [the *Grange*] on Strangers as an American Vessel" (MSS in DNA: RG 59, NL, in various clerical hands, signed by the respective deponents, and attested by Mayor Matthew Clarkson of Philadelphia; PrCs of Trs in DLC: TJ Papers, 85: 14697-703, in various clerical hands; Trs in Lb in PRO: FO 116/3; Trs in same, 5/1; Trs in DLC: Genet Papers; Trs in AMAE: CPEU, xxxvii, in French). Memorial enclosed in TJ to Edmund Randolph, 2 May 1793, TJ to Jean Baptiste Ternant, 15 May 1793, TJ to Gouverneur Morris, 13 June 1793, and TJ to Thomas Pinckney, 14 June 1793; enclosures transmitted in TJ to Ternant, 3 May 1793.

The capture in Delaware Bay on 25 Apr. 1793 of the *Grange*, an English merchant ship, by the *Embuscade*, the French frigate that had brought Edmond Charles Genet to Charleston, was the first French challenge to the neutrality policy of the Washington administration to come to the attention of the Secretary of State. Although TJ privately exulted at the scene that occurred in Philadelphia on 1 May when the *Grange* was brought up the Delaware flying French colors (see TJ to James Monroe, 5 May 1793; TJ to John Wayles Eppes, 12 May 1793), Hammond's prompt protest forced the President and the Cabinet to begin the task of formally defining the maritime limits of the United States.

Despite the pleasure Hammond took in the Proclamation of Neutrality as a sign of "the determination of this government to entangle itself in no new or closer connexion with France, and consequently to observe as strict a neutrality as might be consistent with its existing engagements," the British envoy decided to take advantage of the *Grange* case to test the Washington administration's commitment to a truly neutral foreign policy, hoping "to ascertain the real views of the government by the manner in which it might regard this aggression on its territory" (Hammond to Lord Grenville, 17 May 1793, PRO: FO 5/1). Recognizing the gravity of the issues raised by the British minister, TJ submitted his memorial to the President almost immediately upon receipt of it and at the same time asked Attorney General Edmund Randolph to report on it to the Cabinet the following day. There is no record of the report Randolph presumably made to the Cabinet on 3 May, but perhaps it was not entirely coincidental that on that day TJ referred Hammond's representation to the French minister with a request for any information he could provide respecting the British minister's complaints (Washington, *Journal*, 125; TJ to Edmund Randolph, 2 May 1793; TJ to Jean Baptiste Ternant, 3, 7 May 1793). In the absence of any response from TJ to these complaints, Hammond on 8 May reiterated his requests for the restoration of the *Grange* and the liberation of her crew, and on the following day Jean Baptiste Ternant submitted an official French response to TJ in the form of a report by Antoine René Charles Mathurin de La Forest, the French consul general in Philadelphia. Although La Forest conceded the accuracy of Hammond's account of the circumstances of the capture of the *Grange* by the *Embuscade*, he denied that the seizure violated American neutrality on the grounds that it took place in a section of Delaware Bay that was not part of American territory—a contention that rested, in turn, on the lack of a universally accepted standard in international law for determining territorial jurisdiction over a bay (Memorial from Hammond, 8 May 1793; Ternant to TJ, 9 May 1793, and enclosure; Philip C. Jessup, *The Law of Territorial Waters and Maritime Jurisdiction* [New York, 1927], 355-82, 388-91, 395-7). Washington thereupon instructed TJ to refer these French claims to the Attorney General for a legal opinion and to submit Hammond's counterclaims to the consideration of the Cabinet. Randolph held that the United States exercised jurisdiction over all of Delaware Bay, thus taking the first official step in the definition of the nation's maritime limits, and that the capture of the *Grange* therefore violated American neutrality. TJ took the same position in letters to the British and French ministers that were approved by the President and the Cabinet—a stance applauded by Hammond as an expression of American determination to steer a genuinely neutral course in the current European conflict and one which led Genet, Ternant's successor, to accept American jurisdictional claims over Delaware Bay and arrange for the release of the *Grange* as a gesture of good will to the United States government (Edmund Randolph's Opinion on the *Grange*, 14 May 1793; TJ to Hammond, 15 May 1793; TJ to Ternant, 15 May 1793; Hammond to Grenville, 17 May 1793, PRO: FO 5/1; Genet to TJ, 27 May 1793; Washington, *Journal*, 132, 138-41; Thomas, *Neutrality*, 91-9). But the relative ease with which the *Grange* incident was resolved did not prove to be typical of the successive disputes over neutrality that preoccupied the Secretary of State for the remainder of his climactic year in office.

From Philip Mark

New York, 2 May 1793. As a citizen and longtime resident of New York soon to return to his native Germany, he offers himself as a consul with the intention of aiding German families there and in America because "some known Organ of communication between the two Countries" is needed on account of the extensive emigration from the Rhine region to the United States. Such an appointment would serve to assist people in remitting property to those presently settled in America and to foster future emigration, but he also wishes to promote the trade already underway between the United States and several cities on the Rhine. He hopes the letter from "Messr. Murray, Sands, Bache, W. Laight and Verplank" will aid his claim, and Senator Rufus King assures him that he will promote the application. Through TJ he asks the President to appoint him consul at Nürnberg in Franconia, Frankfurt am Main, or the Palatine Electorate including the bishopric of Franconia, the countries from which most of the immigrants have come, but an appointment comprehending all these jurisdictions would enable him to be more useful.

RC (DLC: Washington Papers, Applications for Office); 2 p.; at foot of text: "Thomas Jefferson Esqr Secretary of State."

Mark was a principal in the mercantile firm of Jacob and Philip Mark located at 241 Queen Street, New York City (Syrett, *Hamilton*, xvii, 438n; William Duncan, *The New-York Directory, and Register, for the Year 1792* [New York, 1792], 89). Neither the supporting letter mentioned by Mark, nor the letters from him of 12 May 1793 and from Rufus King of 17 July 1793, both recorded in SJL as received 25 July 1793 in support of Mark's consular aspirations, have been found. The New York merchant John Murray also backed Mark's appointment in a letter to Alexander Hamilton of 3 May 1793 (Syrett, *Hamilton*, xiv, 410-11). Mark did not receive the post he sought at this time, but was nominated consul at Franconia on 28 May 1794 and confirmed the next day (JEP, i, 157-8).

From Thomas Pinckney

DEAR SIR   London 2d. May 1793

Having already written by this opportunity I have only to request the favor of you to forward the inclosed. The accounts you will see in the last news papers of the destruction of Marat, Robertspierre and other leaders of the Jacobine party in Paris and of french troops being landed in Jersey are without foundation. I have the honor to be with great respect Dear Sir Your faithful and obedient Servant

THOMAS PINCKNEY

RC (DNA: RG 59, DD); at foot of text: "The Secretary of State"; endorsed by TJ as received 27 June 1793 and so recorded in SJL. PrC (ScHi: Pinckney Family Papers). Tr (Lb in DNA: RG 59, DD). Enclosure not found.

To Edmund Randolph

SIR   Philadelphia May 2d. 1793.

Having this moment received and communicated the inclosed Memorial from the British Minister to the President, relative to the Capture of the British vessel the Grange, by a French Frigate, I must ask the favor of you to consider the Case, and to give your opinion of the law arising thereon. These questions seem particularly material— By whom is the validity of the Capture to be decided? By what order are things to be arrested and kept in their present state till the decision? If the Capture be decided to be illegal, by what order or officer is the Prize to be liberated? Does not the liberation of the persons taken on board depend on different principles from that of the vessel and Cargo, and by what order or officer are they to be relieved?

As there is to be a Consultation to morrow morning at 9. oClock on another subject, it is desirable that your opinion could be communicated then. I have the honor to be with great and sincere esteem and Respect, Dear Sir, &c: TH: JEFFERSON

FC (Lb in DNA: RG 59, DL); at head of text: "The Attorney General of the United States." Enclosure: Memorial from George Hammond, 2 May 1793.

TJ submitted this letter to the President before sending it to the Attorney General this day (Washington, *Journal*, 125). The CONSULTATION was a Cabinet meeting of the following day on the issue of granting passports to American-owned ships built abroad (see Opinion on Ship Passports, 3 May 1793; TJ to George Washington, 4 May 1793). Randolph must have communicated his OPINION orally to the Cabinet, since no written reply by him to TJ's questions about the capture of the *Grange* has been found.

[641]

From Edmund Randolph

E. RANDOLPH TO MR. JEFFERSON   May[1] 2. 1793.

There is, without doubt, a protection due to foreign built vessels, owned by American citizens; altho' they cannot claim the privileges, belonging to Vessels of the U.S. For the former are no less neutral property, than the latter.

The usual evidence of the neutral ownership of vessels is a certificate from the officers of the customs; who may and in the papers, granted on clearing out, generally do, I believe, express, in whom, of what country, the property resides. If I do not err in this, the security to such vessels would seem to be sufficiently provided for already. In the instances of the French and Dutch, the sealetters add a further assurance.

Is it then expedient to call upon the President to take a part in this business? For the facts, he must appeal to the certificate from the customhouse; the seal of the customhouse is current and authentic every where; and if the President is to interpose now, in order to make the thing more authentic, into what may he not on other occasions be led?

The President's name would not go farther in a court, than that of a collector under the seal of office; cruisers would therefore be as free to dispense with his testimonial, as that of the collector, and if he should happen to certify, that a vessel is neutral property, when in truth she is not, will not the character of government be committed?

RC (DLC); endorsed by TJ as received 2 May 1793 and so recorded in SJL.

TJ must have solicited this opinion in connection with the debate in the administration over the PROTECTION DUE TO FOR-EIGN BUILT VESSELS, OWNED BY AMERICAN CITIZENS. See Opinion on Ship Passports, 3 May 1793, and note.

[1] Word written over "April," erased.

To Tench Coxe

May. 3. 1793.

Th: Jefferson presents his compliments to Mr. Coxe—and informs him it has been determined to issue passports to all vessels *belonging* wholly to American citizens, whether home, or foreign-built: to endeavor to give them only to those which are *bonâ fide* our own, to prevent all collusion, the prevalence of which might draw rigorous examinations and embarrasments on the vessels truly ours, and as a means to prevent[1] such collusion and it's ill effects, to grant passports only to vessels within the ports of the US. where they and their destinations will be under the eye of our own officers. Mr. Coxe will be pleased to give directions accordingly to the collectors of the customs in the different ports, when he shall distribute the passports to them.

PrC (DLC). FC (Lb in DNA: RG 59, DL).   [1] TJ here canceled "the detention of."

From Alexander Hamilton

Sir   Treasury Department May 3d. 1793

I regret extremely, that I did not receive your letter respecting Mr. Ternant's application till two oClock yesterday; after a warrant had issued in his favour for the sum requested.

Agreeing entirely in opinion with you, that all applications from Diplomatic characters, as well those relating to pecuniary matters as others, ought to be addressed to your Department—I should have taken no step on the present occasion had it not been put on the footing of a previous arrangement (as you will perceive by the copy of Mr. Ternant's note to me)—and had I not myself carried along in my mind a general impression, that the spirit of what had passed would comprise the advance requested . . . in the *individual case.*

For greater caution, however, I thought it adviseable to mention the matter to the President—which was followed (if I remember right upon my own suggestion) by the conversation which I had with you.

You will remember that though your recollection, at the time, of what had passed from you agreed with what has been the result of your subsequent examination—yet you expressed an opinion that in the special case (adhering as a general rule to the spirit of your late communication) it might be adviseable to make the advance desired— as it would be well "*to part friends.*" And it was at my request, subsequent to this declaration, that you engaged to review your communications to Mr. Ternant.

Having told Mr. Ternant that the matter would be terminated the day succeeding his application—not having heard from you on that day—understanding it to be your opinion that on the whole it would be well to make the advance—I waited on the President yesterday Morning, stated what had passed between us, and obtained his consent for making the advance.

I am thus particular from a desire that you may see the ground upon which I have proceeded; as it would give me pain that you should consider what has been done, as the infringement of a rule of official propriety. I assure you this was not my intention. With great respect I have the honor to be Sir Your Obed se   A HAMILTON

RC (DLC: James Madison Papers); at foot of text: "The Secretary of State"; ellipsis in original; endorsed by TJ as received 3 May 1793 and so recorded in   SJL. Enclosure: Jean Baptiste Ternant to Hamilton, 30 Apr. 1793 (Tr in same; see note to TJ to Hamilton, 1 May 1793).

To George Hammond

SIR   Philadelphia May 3. 1793.

I received yesterday the representation and requisition which you were pleased to make on the capture of the British ship Grange by the French frigate L'Embuscade within the bay of Delaware, and immediately laid it before the President. The US. being at peace with both parties, will certainly not see with indifference it's territory or jurisdiction violated by either, and will proceed immediately to enquire into the facts and to do what these shall shew ought to be done, with exact impartiality. The collection of evidence may require some small time, but measures are taken to keep things in the mean time in their present state. I have the honor to be respectfully Sir Your most obedt. & most humble servt   TH: JEFFERSON

PrC (DLC); at foot of text: "The Minister Plenipotentiary of Great Britain." FC (Lb in DNA: RG 59, DL).

From Phineas Miller

SIR   Mulberry Grove (Georgia) May 3d 1793

The keen and afflicting grief of the Sisters and the inconsolable distress of Maternal sensibility at the late untimely death of Master George W. Greene, induced me to open and answer your obliging letter to him, of March 12th. rather than risk adding a wound to their feelings by shewing it to them. It came alas! too late to meet that attention he would have gladly given it, and to excite that gratitude of which his heart was sufficiently susceptible.

The letter you mention to have sent by Mr. Peale I am sure was never received, as it must have been shewn to one, who from a long residence in the family had his particular friendship and confidence.

The correspondence with which you wish to be furnished is at present in Charleston, but will be brought here some time in the ensuing summer—when, a regard to the gratification I should be sure of giving to the feelings of Mrs. Greene and family, as well as my own wishes, will lead me to a particular attention to your request. With the most perfect respect I am Sir, your very Obedient & humble Servant

PHINS. MILLER

RC (MHi); at foot of text: "The Honbe. Thos. Jefferson Esqr. Secretary of State"; endorsed by TJ as received 31 May 1793 and so recorded in SJL.

Phineas Miller (1764-1803), a native of Connecticut and a 1785 Yale graduate, tutored the children of General Nathanael Greene, whose widow Catharine Lit-

tlefield Greene he married in 1796. He became a Georgia planter, justice, and state senator, and the sponsor and business partner of Eli Whitney in his invention of the cotton gin (Dexter, *Yale*, IV, 430-1; Jeannette Mirsky and Allan Nevins, *The World of Eli Whitney* [New York, 1952], esp. 54-5, 66, 96; Miller to TJ, 27 May 1793).

Opinion on Ship Passports

It has been stipulated in our treaties with the French, Dutch and Prussians that when it happens that either party is at war, and the other neutral, the neutral shall give passports of a certain tenor to the *vessels belonging to their subjects*, in order to avoid dissension. And it has been thought best that passports of such high import to the persons and property of our citizens should have the highest sanction, that of the signature of the President, and seal of the US.—The authority of Congress also, in the case of Sea-letters to East-India vessels, was in favor of this sanction.—It is now become a question whether these Passports shall be given only to ships *owned and built* in the US. or may be given also to those *owned* in the US. though *built* in foreign countries.

The persons and property of our citizens are entitled to the protection of our government in all places where they may lawfully go. No law forbids a merchant to buy, own, and use a *foreign-built* vessel. She is then his lawful property, and entitled to the protection of his nation wherever he is lawfully using her.

The laws indeed, for the encouragement of ship-building, have given to home-built vessels the exclusive privilege of being registered and paying lighter duties. To this privilege therefore the foreign built vessel, tho owned at home, does not pretend. But the laws have not said that they withdraw their protection from the foreign built vessel. To this protection then she retains her title, notwithstanding the preference given to the home built vessel as to duties. It would be hard indeed, because the law has given one valuable right to home built vessels, to infer that it had taken away all rights from those foreign built.

In conformity with the idea that all the vessels of a state are entitled to it's protection, the treaties beforementioned have settled that Passports shall be given, not merely to the vessels *built* in the US. but to the vessels *belonging* to them: and when one of these nations shall take a vessel, if she has not such a Passport, they are to conclude she does not *belong* to the US. and is therefore lawful prize. So that to refuse these Passports to foreign built vessels *belonging* to our merchants, is to give them up to capture with their cargoes.

The most important interests of the US. hang upon this question. The produce of the earth is their principal source of wealth. Our *homebuilt* vessels would suffice for the transportation of a very small part of this produce to market: and even a part of these vessels will be withdrawn by high premiums to other lines of business. All the rest of our produce then must remain on our hands, or have it's price reduced by a war-insurance. Many descriptions of our produce will not bear this reduction, and would therefore remain on hand.

We shall lose also a great proportion of the profits of navigation. The great harvest for these is when other nations are at war, and our flag neutral. But if we can augment our stock of shipping only by the slow process of building, the harvest will be over while we are only preparing instruments to reap it. The moment of breeding seamen will be lost for want of bottoms to embark them in.

France and Holland permit our vessels to be naturalised with them. Not even to suffer theirs to be purchased here might give them just cause to revoke the privilege of naturalization given to ours, and would inflict on the shipbuilding states and artisans a severe injury.

Obj. To protect foreign built vessels will lessen the demand for ship building here.

Answ. Not at all. Because as long as we can build cheaper than other nations, we shall be employed of preference to others.—Besides shall we permit the greatest part of the produce of our feilds to rot on our hands, or lose half it's value by subjecting it to high insurance, merely that our ship-builders may have brisker employ? Shall the whole mass of our farmers be sacrificed to the class of ship-wrights?

Obj. There will be collusive transfers of foreign ships to our merchants merely to obtain for them the cover of our Passports.

Answ. The same objection lies to giving passports to home-built vessels. They may be owned, and are owned by foreigners, and may

be collusively retransferred to our merchants to obtain our passports.—
To lessen the danger of collusion however, I should be for delivering
passports in our own ports only. If they were to be sent blank to
foreign ports to be delivered there, the power of checking collusion
would be small, and they might be employed to cover purposes of no
benefit to us, which we ought not to countenance, and to throw our
own vessels out of business. But if issued only to vessels in our own
ports, we can generally be certain that the *vessel* is our property, and
always that the *cargo* is of our produce.—State the case that it shall be
found that all our shipping, home-built and foreign-built, is inadequate
to the transportation of our produce to market, so that after all these
are loaded, there shall yet remain produce on hand. This must be put
into vessels owned by foreigners. Should these obtain collusively the
protection of our passport, it will cover their *vessel* indeed, but it will
cover also our *cargo*. I repeat it then, that if the issuing passports be
confined to our own ports, it will be our own *vessels* for the most part,
and always our *cargoes* which will be covered by them.

I am therefore of opinion that passports ought to be issued to all
vessels *belonging* to citizens of the US., but only on their clearing out
from our own ports, and for that voyage only.   TH: JEFFERSON
                                                    May. 3. 1793.

MS (DNA: RG 59, MLR); entirely in TJ's hand. PrC (DLC); first page slightly torn; with two notations added at a much later date in ink by TJ to correct an error in placement after text had been bound, probably as part of the "Anas": (at foot of second page) "go back for pa. 3. 4" and (at head of third page) "for pa. 1. 2. see after 4." Tr (DLC: Madison Papers); made ca. 20 June 1801 in a clerk's hand, signed and with minor corrections by TJ; at head of text: (in TJ's hand) "Opinion given to President Washington" and (in an unidentified hand) "1793. by T.J."; at foot of text: "(copy)"; enclosed, with subjoined [ca. 20 June 1801] note on passports in TJ's hand, in TJ to James Madison and Albert Gallatin, 20 June 1801. Tr (Lb in DNA: RG 59, SDC). Entry in SJPL: "Opn on the Privileges of home built & home owned vessels." Enclosed in Tench Coxe to TJ, 4 May 1793, and TJ to George Washington, 4 May 1793.

The French declaration of war on Great Britain and the Netherlands in February 1793 gave the European war a mar-

itime dimension with obvious ramifications for the American carrying trade. According to commercial TREATIES the United States concluded with France in 1778, the Netherlands in 1782, and Prussia in 1785, when either party was at war, vessels belonging to citizens of the nation remaining neutral were to be issued sea letters or PASSPORTS to confirm their neutral status. Prussia had been at war with France since 1792, but passports were not considered necessary for American vessels until the expansion of hostilities to England, Europe's dominant naval power. TJ knew of the new combatants by 7 Apr. 1793 and issued at least one pass three days later requesting safe passage for every American member of a crew without calling for protection of the ship itself—evidently as a stopgap until he received official notification of hostilities and could obtain approval for the exact wording of the ship passports. By late April he had received official notification of the state of hostilities between France and Britain but still awaited a decision on whether the treaty with France was to be suspended in whole or in part. Until 6 May, when the President decided that the treaties of commerce and alliance with France would remain in force, TJ accordingly issued a few passports which followed the form prescribed by the Dutch treaty (Miller, *Treaties*, II, 23-4, 28-9, 80-2, 85-8, 172-3; TJ to George Washington, 7 Apr. 1793; passport to Philip Atkins, master, and ten members of the crew of the ship *Sussex* of Philadelphia, 10 Apr. 1793, Tr in DNA: RG 59, Letters Requesting Passports; George Hammond to TJ, 24 Apr. 179[3]; Notes on Washington's Questions on Neutrality and the Alliance with France, [6 May 1793]; TJ to Alexander Hamilton, 8 May 1793).

TJ prepared this opinion in connection with a Cabinet meeting held this day which dealt with the format and scope of the new passports. His use of the first person suggests that he composed this statement before the executive officers met, but his language in his letter transmitting it to the President the next day indicates that the Cabinet adopted his viewpoint. The antecedents to the meeting are obscure, but clearly Attorney General Edmund Randolph had been consulted prior to it and had raised doubts about whether the documents should carry THE SIGNATURE OF THE PRESIDENT (TJ to Edmund Randolph, 2 May 1793; Randolph to TJ, 2 May 1793; Tench Coxe to TJ, 4 May 1793). Under the Articles of Confederation sea letters had been granted by THE AUTHORITY OF CONGRESS to American ships bound for remote ports in EAST-INDIA and China, starting with that for the *Empress of China* in January 1784, but by a resolution of 12 Feb. 1788 Congress delegated responsibility for issuing these papers to the Secretary for Foreign Affairs. This authority was still considered valid under the Constitution, and the Secretary of State continued to dispense sea letters as late as 15 Mch. 1793, when a passport was issued to the ship *Sampson*, bound from Philadelphia for Canton (JCC, XXVI, 58-9; XXXIV, 39-40; "Fair Copies of Applications for Sea Letters," DNA: RG 360, PCC; Certification to the President of issuance of a passport to the *Sampson*, 15 Mch. 1793, MS in DNA: RG 59, MLR, in the hand of George Taylor,

Jr., signed by TJ, endorsed by Tobias Lear; Tr in Lb in same, SDC). These papers were signed by the President and countersigned by the Secretary of State, and the first paragraph of TJ's opinion and subsequent practice show that despite Randolph's opposition it was concluded that the precedent should be followed for wartime passports.

In view of the expanded European war the Cabinet must also have taken up the more important issue of whether such passports were to be issued to foreign-built ships owned by Americans. The language both of the East Indian sea letters and of the treaties concerned itself only with the verification of ownership, but LAWS passed in September 1789 and December 1792 had put the status of foreign-built ships OWNED AT HOME in doubt by restricting registration to "ships or vessels of the United States" built in the United States or already owned by Americans prior to 16 May 1789 (*Annals*, II, 2217, III, 1397). TJ argued that the statutes defined a privilege for customs purposes but should not be interpreted as denying government countenance and protection to other American-owned vessels. Washington must have agreed, for this day TJ informed the Commissioner of the Revenue that sea letters were to be issued to all American-owned vessels (TJ to Coxe, 3 May 1793). This liberality in granting sea letters probably contributed to the very rapid expansion of the carrying trade of the United States which ensued, despite restrictions imposed by England and France, during the years preceding the embargo of 1807 (Anna C. Clauder, *American Commerce as Affected by the Wars of the French Revolution and Napoleon, 1793-1812* [Philadelphia, 1932], 25, 67-79). For continuing doubts about the status of American-owned, foreign-built ships, which led to their being denied the Mediterranean pass, a different form of passport issued to protect American ships under the terms of a treaty with Algiers, from their first issuance in 1796 until TJ as president acted to extend the coverage of this document to such vessels, see TJ to James Madison and Albert Gallatin, 20 June 1801, and its enclosure. See also Moore, *Digest*, II, 1007-69.

To Thomas Pinckney

DEAR SIR   Philadelphia May. 3. 1793.

The bearer hereof Dr. Edwards, a citizen of the US. proposing to visit London, I take the liberty of presenting him to you. Tho I have not the honor personally of a particular acquaintance with him, yet his reputation, and the recommendations I receive of him from several persons and particularly from Colo. Burr and Doctor Rush authorise me to ask your attentions and good offices to him with the same confidence as I would on my own knowlege being assured from these sources that he will justify whatever we can say or you do in his favor. I am happy in every occasion of repeating to you assurances of the sincere esteem & respect with which I am Dear Sir your friend & servt   TH: JEFFERSON

PrC (DLC); at foot of text: "Mr. Pinckney." Tr (DLC); 19th-century copy.

To Jean Baptiste Ternant

SIR   Philadelphia May. 3. 1793.

The Minister Plenipotentiary of his Britannic Majesty has represented to the government of the US. that on the 25th. of April last the British[1] ship Grange, while lying at anchor in the bay of Delaware, within the territory and jurisdiction of the US. was taken possession of by the Embuscade, a frigate of the French republic, has been brought to this port where she is now detained as prize and the crew as prisoners, and has made a requisition in form for a restoration of the vessel and liberation of the crew. I have the honor to furnish you with copies of the evidence given in by the British minister, and to observe that the US. being at peace with all parties cannot see with indifference it's territory or jurisdiction violated by either: that the government will therefore proceed to enquire into the facts, and for that purpose will receive with pleasure and consider with impartiality any evidence you will be pleased to have them furnished with on the subject: and the President hopes that you will take effectual measures for detaining here the vessel taken, her crew and cargo, to abide the decision which will be made thereon, and which is desired to be without delay. I have the honor to be with great respect Sir Your most obedt. humble servt
                                           TH: JEFFERSON

PrC (DLC); at foot of text: "The Minister Plenipotentiary of France." FC (Lb in DNA: RG 59, DL). Tr (DLC: Genet Papers). Tr (AMAE: CPEU, xxxvii); in

French. For the enclosures, see note to
Memorial from George Hammond, 2 May
1793.

¹ Word interlined.

From Tench Coxe

Sir   Treasury Department Revenue Office, May 4th. 1793.

I have the honor to return to You the Opinion (of the 3d. instant,) prepared for the President, on the subject of the Sea-letters, to which my instructions shall conform. Applications for these documents having been made by Merchants of Philadelphia, for Vessels lying in several other Ports, I thought it best to transmit by yesterday's Southern and Northern Mails a few of the letters to Alexandria, Baltimore, New-York and Boston, which were enclosed in a circular letter of which the enclosed is a copy. You will perceive, Sir, that in draughting that letter, I have avoided to give any complexion to the instruction, favorable to either side of the question, in regard to Ships owned by our fellow-Citizens, but built in foreign Countries. After the transmission of those letters, Your note of the third instant was received; in consequence of which, a particular instruction in conformity with Your directions, and with Your communication to the President, will be forthwith given. I have the honor to be, With great Respect, Sir, Your most obedient Servant   TENCH COXE
Commissioner of the Revenue

RC (DLC); in a clerk's hand, signed by Coxe; at foot of text: "The Secretary of State"; endorsed by TJ as received 4 May 1793 and so recorded in SJL. Enclosures: (1) Opinion on Ship Passports, 3 May 1793. (2) Coxe's Circular to Collectors of the Customs of Alexandria, Baltimore, New York, and Boston, 2 May 1793, enclosing to each six sea letters signed by the President and the Secretary of State to be issued to captains of American vessels who made the requisite oath before a properly qualified official, preferably the chief magistrate in the jurisdiction where custom house was located, and promising to send more particular instructions soon (Tr in DLC).

To George Logan

May. 4. 1793.

Th: Jefferson presents his compliments to Dr. Logan, and is sorry that a great mass of business just come on him will prevent him the pleasure of waiting on him tomorrow. The hope of dryer roads is some consolation for postponing his visit a while.

RC (PHi: Dickinson-Logan Papers); addressed: "Dr. Logan"; with penciled note by TJ, presumably intended for the bearer of the letter: "inquire at Mrs. Morris's in Chestnut Street for Mrs. Logan—they may be [there?]." Not recorded in SJL.

Dr. George Logan (1753-1821) of "Stenton," near Germantown, Pennsylvania, a founder of the Philadelphia Society for Promoting Agriculture in 1785 and a member of the American Philosophical Society since January 1793, was a physician by training who devoted much of his life to the practice and dissemination of scientific agriculture, an interest he shared with TJ. A critic of Hamiltonian finance and a friend and political ally of TJ, he served as a Republican in the Pennsylvania legislature in 1795-96 and 1799 and in the United States Senate from 1801 to 1807. As a Quaker pacifist Logan undertook a controversial private peace mission to France in 1798, which led to the passage of the "Logan Act" in 1799 prohibiting private citizens from conducting diplomatic negotiations without government sanction, a measure which did not deter him from pursuing an unsuccessful peace mission to England in 1810. He corresponded frequently with TJ during his presidency and retirement (Frederick B. Tolles, *George Logan of Philadelphia* [New York, 1953]; Editorial note on Jefferson, Freneau, and the founding of the *National Gazette*, in Vol. 20: 734-6).

From David Sewall

"York (in the district of Maine)," 4 May 1793. Acknowledging receipt under TJ's frank of the laws of the United States for the most recent session of Congress, received this week, and those for the preceding one, received about a year ago, as well as various acts of the First Congress before that, he recommends that the statutes, or at least those of general concern beginning with the second session of the Second Congress, be printed in the *Gazette of Maine*, a Portland weekly published by Benjamin Titcomb, Jr. He also recommends Captain John Hobby of Portland for the post of federal marshal in this district, reportedly made vacant by Henry Dearborn's election to the House of Representatives. The Judiciary Act provides that deputies can act after a marshal dies, but whether they can do so after a resignation is unclear. It would be best if a successor were appointed and commissioned by the next session of District Court, on the third Tuesday in June.

RC (DNA: RG 59, PDL); 1 p.; at foot of text: "mr. Secretary Jefferson"; endorsed by TJ as received 13 May 1793 and so recorded in SJL.

David Sewall (1735-1825), a 1755 Harvard graduate, attorney, and lifelong resident of York, served as United States District Court judge for Maine from 1789 to 1818 (John L. Sibley and Clifford K. Shipton, *Sibley's Harvard Graduates: Biographical Sketches of Those Who Attended Harvard College*, 17 vols. [Cambridge and Boston, 1873-1975], xiii, 638-45).

To George Washington

May. 4. 1793.

Th: Jefferson having prepared a written opinion on the Question Whether Passports should be granted to vessels belonging to American citizens, but of foreign built, has the honor of inclosing it to the President as an explanation of the principles on which the affirmative was adopted yesterday.

RC (DNA: RG 59, MLR); addressed: "The President of the US."; endorsed by Tobias Lear. Tr (Lb in same, SDC). Not recorded in SJL. Enclosure: Opinion on Ship Passports, 3 May 1793.

TJ also wrote Washington a brief note this day asking for "a dozen Passports for present use" (RC in DNA: RG 59, MLR, addressed "The President of the US.," endorsed by Lear; Tr in Lb in same, SDC; not recorded in SJL).

From William Carmichael and William Short

SIR   Aranjuez May 5. 1793

Since our last of the 18th. ulto. we have had the honor of recieving the duplicate of yours of the 3d. of Novr. (the original has not yet come to our hands). The papers severally alluded to therein were recieved inclosed. Mr. Morris had forwarded them to us from Paris on the 4th. of March. The person he had charged with them having determined not to proceed further than Bayonne, these papers were detained there, for a proper conveyance which not presenting itself sooner, they were not delivered to us here until the 28th. ulto.

Our last letter in informing you generally of the conferences which had then taken place here, on the subjects of our commissions, stated also the manner in which that of the conduct of their agents towards us and the Indians had been particularly touched on. That conduct was absolutely denied in behalf of their agents, who, it was affirmed, had positive instructions to the contrary, and who could have no interest to depart from them. We observed on the facts which had taken place and the nature of the testimony which had authenticated them to the government of the U.S. M. de Gardoqui let us see clearly that he considered the presumed obedience of their agents to the orders given them, as a stronger proof of their having not interfered than any that was adduced by us to the contrary. He saw as clearly that we were of a different opinion—and as we have had already the honor to inform you, we judged it unnecessary to push that subject further in that stage of the business.

Yesterday being the first day of conference which has intervened since the receipt of your letter abovementioned it was our intention to have brought it forward again with the additional circumstance mentioned therein—but M. de Gardoqui being called off by the King at the hour appointed for the conference, it was postponed by him.

In the two which have taken place since our last, we spoke of the conduct which should be observed by the U.S. and Spain towards the several nations of Indians within or adjoining to their respective possessions. The sentiments which he expressed were perfectly conformable to humanity and good neighbourhood. He came readily into the idea suggested in your letter of October the 14th. of neither party keeping agents among the Indians. We thought it proper to sound him on this subject, although it appeared to us that a clause in our treaty with the Creeks was of a contrary tendency. He expressed his sincere desire that strict justice should in all cases be observed towards the Indians, as being the surest means of rendering them pacific and useful neighbors. We assured him that our government was actuated by these sentiments, observing the steps which had been taken since the reins were committed to the President, were an uniform proof thereof, confirmed by the treaties made with the Creeks and Cherokees.

This necessarily brought under consideration these treaties, which to our very great surprize, he declared an entire ignorance of. Although they have been certainly transmitted to the foreign department here, yet the several departments are kept so separate and distinct, that we deem it highly possible, added to what we have seen of M. de Gardoqui himself, that they may not have come under his inspection.

When we mentioned to him the substance of these treaties he expressed much satisfaction at the articles securing the Indians in their rights of property, and fixing the mode of punishment for crimes committed towards them, as well as the encouragement to be held out to them to dispose them to agriculture and civilisation. The clause declaring them under our protection he apprehended might create difficulty, as they had a previous treaty with Spain to the same effect. He seemed to wish us to believe that he considered the favourable[1] disposition of our government towards the Indians as the most likely means to remove the difficulties existing with respect to the settlement of boundary.

We are persuaded however that the same difficulties would still remain and that they do not rest in our treaties with the Indians or our conduct towards them, but on the fixing the limits between us and Spain. Humanity and justice towards the Indians may be the pretended, but the acquisition of territory, the domineering, though extravagant passion of this court, will be the real motive by which they will be actuated. Were it possible for us to agree upon the limits, no difficulties would be made by them with respect to the inhabitants within those assigned to us. We think you may rely therefore on their commissaries having siezed the true principle of the interference of their court, in their conversation with you, as stated in your letter to the President of Nov. 2.

We mentioned in our last that M. de Gardoqui had declined absolutely precising the origin of their claim to the exclusive navigation of the Mississipi. He has since then by acknowleging in conversation that the English were entitled to navigate that river also previous to the late war, fixed the epocha of their exclusive right. Even this acknowlegement of what must strike every body as unquestionable he was brought to with evident reluctance.

In our last we had the honor of stating to you the embarrassment in which we found ourselves, 1. from the explicit declarations of M. de Gardoqui, shewing the dispositions of this court to be opposite to what we are convinced must have been expected at the time our commission was formed—and 2. from the change of circumstances which have taken place among several European powers since that epoch. As yet we can only confirm what we then said on these subjects.

Situated as we are under these circumstances we concieve it will be the wish of the President that we should not at this moment press the negotiation in a manner which might produce an effect directly opposite to our interests and wishes, and which could not render any service under the present crisis the most inauspicious that could have taken place for our business. We have already full conviction of the sentiments of this court and know that they will not at present assent to what we must insist on. Should we immediately push the negotiation it could produce no other effect than to make them acquainted with the *fixed determination of the U.S. to exact their full right*.[2] This would unavoidably only make *them more tractable* with respect to *England*, and would tend joined to the influence of the *French war*[3] to make them take a *ground that they might repent of* hereafter in vain as well as *ourselves*. It might *make them also take preparatory measures* with respect to *us which they would not* otherwise do, and which we must desire that *they should not do*, whatever may be the *intentions of our government*.

Other considerations also weigh with us in *favor of delay* under our *circumstances* and particularly that of leaving thereby *time to recieve further instructions* after the *Prest. shall have been made acquainted with the changes* which have taken place in the *relations between France England and this country*. From what we conjecture of the time that this will have been announced to you as inevitable we imagine we may ere long be made acquainted with the Presidents sentiments thereon. We will not take on ourselves to suggest any thing on a subject which will have been placed so amply under his contemplation.

We should not perhaps omit mentioning a circumstance which is particularly unfavorable to our negotiation, arising from the actual situation of this cabinet, and the business we are charged with being in consequence thereof exclusively committed to M. de Gardoqui. As he is fully known in America we need not delineate his character here. It will suffice to say that notwithstanding his protestations of good will towards the U.S. and desire to see this business terminated to their satisfaction we have very full evidence of his sentiments being absolutely opposed thereto. As to those of the Duke de la Alcudia whose power and influence are unlimited here, we can only judge of them, from what M. de Gardoqui tells us, being precluded ourselves by the character in which we are admitted here, from that kind of intercourse with him which would enable us to judge for ourselves. He assures us that the sentiments of that minister are conformable to those expressed to us in the conferences. We should rather apprehend however that he had not given himself the trouble to form any ideas on the subject. So far as M. de Gardoqui can have influence on him, the impressions he will recieve will certainly not be such as we should wish.

Being young and without experience but at the same time well disposed to recieve information, and having no other source so ready or so natural to recieve it from as M. de Gardoqui, it is probable that it is from him that he will take his ideas thereon. He cannot have time and certainly will not have inclination under his present occupations to attend to any course of argument on these subjects. He will ask only for the result and that result he will recieve implicitly from the person to whom he may give his confidence respecting it. It may be expected also that at this moment the English Ambassador in his close and constant communications with him, will not let slip opportunities of giving such insinuations as he may think likely to produce effect— and when we consider the situation of the two countries and compare the two men, we cannot doubt they may have a considerable effect.

We do not let M. de Gardoqui percieve the idea we have formed of his hostility to the business of this negotiation. We recieve with calmness the constant protestations of his particular good will which he takes every opportunity of repeating. He assures us often that there is no person in Spain who would be disposed to go so far in advising the King to make sacrifices for the termination of this business, as himself. These sacrifices consist in what we stated to you in our last as the result of the agreement between him and Mr. Jay.

These assurances however by no means convince us. And although we have no direct opportunities of ascertaining the ideas of the other ministers (should they have formed any) on the subjects of our negotiation, still it appears to us that there are several causes which would contribute to render M. de Gardoqui, on the contrary, more hostile than others. His ideas of the rights of Spain and of the U.S. were formed a long time ago; and as too often happens, he was probably much influenced by the comparative power of the respective parties in considering their respective rights. The view he had of the U.S. during his residence there has manifestly not yet given place to those impressions which their present situation ought to have produced. He still sees them divided among themselves—and without efficient government—and although he now and then recollects the change, yet in general it seems to have escaped him. Having been formerly charged with this business, and having probably at that time given assurances to his court of being able to procure different terms he may not know now how to come forward and propose others to them. This circumstance added to a considerable obstinancy of character we concieve would have much weight with him. It is possible also that being little accustomed to generalise his ideas, and having viewed this subject only on one side, and meditated on it in that point of view alone, he may have brought himself to have regarded these extraordinary pretensions of Spain as just; and indeed he affirms this to us with so much warmth that we cannot help attributing it in some degree to that kind of error. His having been educated also and still being in the mercantile line is by no means an indifferent circumstance—that class of people in those European countries which have colonies, being more than any other prompt to take the claim at whatever may tend to facilitate the intercourse of foreigners with those possessions.

Another source of error which we observe in M. de Gardoqui is that of drawing general conclusions from particular cases. He conversed with some individuals in America, who expressed their wishes to see the navigation of the Mississipi prohibited, and our limits narrowed, in order to have the productions of the Western country brought through the Atlantic States, and to have our population more concentrated. He saw some individuals of the Western country, or going to settle there, who treated their adhesion to the rest of the union as visionary. From hence he has formed an opinion which he has not concealed from us—that the U.S. do not desire this navigation and the limits we ask, or at least do not desire it so generally as that they would be brought to make any general effort to attain it—and also that the Western inhabitants whenever they shall acquire force will separate from the Atlantic states. Under the influence of these opinions it is probable that the navigation may be held back *in petto*, in order to purchase this separation if too long delayed—or to purchase the friendship of those inhabitants after being separated from us—and perhaps still further in order to purchase the promise of their allegiance to the crown of Spain.

What we have said will give you an idea of M. de Gardoqui's sentiments and influence on these subjects so far as he may act of himself. We should add however that the general opinion of him here is that no minister has ever given more constant proofs (notwithstanding the natural obstinacy of his character) of facility in relinquishing his own sentiments in favor of those of persons at the fountain of power. Should the present principal minister for instance, be by any means disposed[4] to treat these subjects of negotiation differently, nobody entertains apprehension that M. de Gardoqui would make opposition thereto, after being made acquainted with that disposition.

There is another event also which may take them out of the hands of M. de Gardoqui. It is known that he has no weight in the cabinet, and that he is counteracted in all his operations by the persons employed under him. It has therefore been for some time believed that his place would not be long tenable. The exigencies of war naturally increase the difficulties of a minister of finance, and add to the probability of change in such a department. We have some reason to believe that M. de Gardoqui himself feels this and that he is endeavouring to provide for a retreat by obtaining a foreign embassy. It has been reported that he is to have that at Turin. It is more probable however that it is not yet decided on. Still the usage of this court with respect to dismissed ministers gives good reason to believe he would be provided for—and as the diplomatic line is that which he desires it would be probably in that. Should he be thus removed from hence, what we have observed with respect to the manner of doing business here, gives reason to believe he would have little influence on that which concerns us.

In speaking of M. de Gardoqui we should not omit the opinion which he seems to have imbibed, and still retains with respect to the faculties of the U.S. in relation to foreign powers—either of injuring their enemies or aiding their friends. He did not conceal from us that he thought it impossible that the Northern, middle and Southern States should ever be brought to act in concert with respect to a foreign enemy out of their territory—and even if they should, that they had no means of acting efficaciously until they should have a marine; an event which he regarded as never to take place, or at least to be so far off as not be worthy of present consideration. These sentiments of M. de Gardoqui are probably consonant to those of his court.

He seemed fully impressed with the danger to which Spain was exposed from the balance of maritime force being absolutely destroyed by the present situation of France. He acknowleged his apprehensions on that subject—and his desire to see a sufficient number of maritime powers united with Spain, to restore that balance. It was evident however he did not count on this—he observed on the impossibility of several distant powers uniting their interests and still more of their acting in concert. He did not deign to take the U.S. into this account, and on this subject said he would quote to us an English proverb "that whilst the grass was growing the horse would starve." All this seemed to confirm a truth with which we were fully impressed before—that a few ships of the line would have more weight in securing peaceably the territorial rights of the U.S. and those with respect to the Mississipi than all the most unanswerable arguments and incontestable proofs that could be adduced in support thereof.

We are much mortified not to be able to give you more agreeable intelligence with respect to the commission with which the President has done us the honor to charge us jointly. We trust you will see that this situation of the business has depended and still depends on circumstances, which do not and never could have depended on us. And we hope you will be persuaded that should the present crisis of European affairs, bring about any change in the *relations of this country which may render her* less indifferent to the *friendship or enmity of the U.S.* whilst we remain here, we shall make the most pressing use of it in endeavouring to obtain by pacific means those rights which we are persuaded the United States *will never abandon the pursuit of* and which we flatter ourselves the *progress of their union and force will enable them to obtain with usury if withheld at present.* We have the honor to be with the most perfect respect & sincere attachment Sir your most obedient & most humble servants   [WM. CARMICHAEL]

W SHORT

PrC (DLC: Short Papers); in Short's hand, with Carmichael's name as signatory supplied from Tr in CtY; written partly in code (see note 2 below); at foot of first page: "The Secretary of State for the United States—Philadelphia." Dft (same); in Short's hand; entirely *en clair*; consists of small sheet interfiled with PrC bearing only the three sections with encoded passages; at head of text: "C & S. to Sec. of State—May 5. 93." Tr (CtY); entirely *en clair.* PrC (DLC). Tr (DNA: RG 46, Senate Records, 3d Cong., 1st sess.); entirely *en clair.* Tr (Lb in same, TR); entirely *en clair.* Recorded in SJL as received 22 July 1793. Enclosed in David Humphreys to TJ, 29 May 1793, and TJ to Thomas Pinckney, 11 Sep. 1793.

THEIR AGENTS: Francisco Luis Hector, Baron de Carondelet, the governor of Louisiana and West Florida, who was seeking to form a Spanish-led confederation of Southern Indians to deter American expansion into the Southwest, and Pedro Olivier, Carondelet's agent to the Creeks (TJ to Josef Ignacio de Viar and Josef de Jaudenes, 9 July 1792, and note; Notes of Cabinet Meeting on the Southern Indians and Spain, 31 Oct. 1792, and note). The CLAUSE IN OUR TREATY WITH THE CREEKS that Carmichael and Short interpreted as justifying the United States government in keeping an agent among the tribe was Article 12 of the 1790 Treaty of New York, which gave the United States the right to station up to four agents to live with the Creeks in order to aid them in making the transition from hunting to herding and farming (ASP, *Indian Affairs*, I, 82). Article 14 of the 1791 Treaty of Holston with the CHEROKEES contained an identical clause (same, 125). The CLAUSE DECLARING THEM UNDER OUR PROTECTION was Article 2 of the Treaty of New York, whereby the Creeks declared themselves to be "under the protection of the United States of

America, and of no other sovereign whatsoever" (same, 81). For a conflicting provision in Spain's PREVIOUS TREATY of Pensacola with the Creeks in 1784, see note to TJ to Carmichael and Short, 3 Nov. 1792. THEIR COMMISSARIES: Josef Ignacio de Viar and Josef de Jaudenes, the Spanish government's representatives in Philadelphia. Despite Carmichael and Short's belief that his dismissal was imminent, Diego de Gardoqui remained in charge of negotiations with them throughout TJ's tenure as Secretary of State and beyond (Bemis, *Pinckney's Treaty*, 188-94, 221-9).

TJ submitted this letter to the President on 23 July 1793 (Washington, *Journal*, 205-6).

[1] Preceding two words interlined in place of "the."

[2] These and subsequent words in italics are in code; they have been supplied from Short's Dft and verified by the Editors using partially reconstructed Code No. 10.

[3] Preceding eight words interlined in Dft.

[4] Word interlined in place of "willing to treat [. . .]."

From Thomas Greenleaf

SIR   New York, May 5, 1793.

I have to apologize for not replying earlier to yours of the 19th. ultimo—the reason of this delay was, the uncertainty whether a *file* for '89 and '90 of the N. Y. Journal, &c. could be completed or not. The file is now complete with the exceptions of *4 papers*, viz. Jany: 15—Augt. 20—Dec. 17 of 1789—and Oct. 5, 1790. They are now *half binding* agreably to your Order, and I have directed a strip of white paper bound in the stead of the missing papers, that they may be pasted in if found hereafter. They will be sent on by the stage on Tuesday or Wednesday.

I am Sir, yr. obedient Servant

File	Dols. 4:	$\frac{66}{100}$
Binding	1	$\frac{50}{100}$
	£6–16 Cts.	

THOS: GREENLEAF

P.S. This Receipt is inclosed to your Address by request of Mr. Taylor.

RC (MHi); endorsed by TJ as received 7 May 1793 and so recorded in SJL.

To James Madison

Th:J. to J. Madison   May. 5. 93.

No letter from you since that of Apr. 12.—I received one from Mr. Pinckney yesterday informing me he expected to send me by the next ship a model of the threshing mill. He had been to see one work, which with 2. horses got out 8. bushels of *wheat* an hour. But he was assured that the mill from which my model was taken gets out[1] 8 quarters (i.e. 64 bushels) of *oats* an hour with 4. horses.—I have seen Dr. Logan. Your ploughs will be done in a week and shall be attended to.—Seal and forward Monroe's letter after reading it. Adieu your's affectly.

P.S. I inclose a Boston paper as a proof of what I mention to Monroe of the spirit which is rising. The old tories have their names now raked up again; and I believe if the author of 'Plain truth' was now to be charged with that pamphlet, this put along side of his present Anglomany would decide the voice of the yeomanry of the country on his subject.

RC (DLC: Madison Papers); dateline between body of letter and postscript; addressed: "James Mad[. . .]." PrC (DLC). Tr (DLC); 19th-century copy. Enclosure: TJ to James Monroe, 5 May 1793.

Thomas Pinckney's private letter to TJ concerning A MODEL OF THE THRESH-ING MILL was dated 13 Mch. 1793. The BOSTON PAPER has not been identified: possibly TJ sent either the *Independent Chronicle*'s extra issue of 19 Apr. 1793, in which an unsigned article headed "The French" compared American opponents of the French Revolution to the Massachusetts loyalist governor Thomas Hutchinson "and his *coadjutors*," or the *Columbian Centinel* of 20 Apr. 1793, which carried a similar letter by "Freeman." For TJ's mistaken belief that Alexander Hamilton had written the 1776 loyalist pamphlet *Plain Truth*, see Notes on Alexander Hamilton, 19 Nov. 1792, and note.

[1] MS: "get outs."

To James Monroe

Dear Sir   Philadelphia May 5. 1793.

The expectation that you are always from home, prevents my writing to you with regularity; a matter of little consequence to you, as you probably receive Freneau's paper regularly, and consequently all the news of any importance.—The fiscal party having tricked the house of representatives out of the negative vote they obtained, seem determined not to lose the ground they gained by entering the lists again on matters of fact and reason. They therefore preserve a triumphant silence notwithstanding the attacks of the pamphlet entitled 'an examination &c.'[1] and of Timon. They shew their wisdom in this if not their honesty. The war between France and England seems to be producing an effect not contemplated. All the old spirit of 1776. is rekindling. The newspapers from Boston to Charleston prove this; and even the Monocrat papers are obliged to publish the most furious Philippics against England. A French frigate took a British[2] prize off the capes of Delaware the other day and sent her up here. Upon her coming into sight thousands and thousands of the *yeomanry* of the city crowded and covered the wharfs. Never before was such a crowd seen there, and when the British colours were seen *reversed*, and the French flying above them they burst into peals of exultation. I wish we may be able to repress the spirit of the people[3] within the limits of a fair neutrality.—In the mean time H. is panick struck if we refuse our breach to every kick which G. Brit. may chuse to give it. He is for proclaiming at once the most abject principles, such as would invite and merit habitual insults. And indeed every inch of ground must be fought in our councils[4] to desperation in order to hold up the face of even a sneaking neutrality, for our votes are generally $2\frac{1}{2}$ against $1\frac{1}{2}$. Some propositions have come from him which would astonish Mr. Pitt himself with their boldness. If we preserve even a sneaking neutrality, we shall be indebted for it to the President, and not to his counsellors.—Immense bankruptcies have taken place in England. The last advices made them amount to 11. millions sterling, and still going on. Of the houses connected with America they have fallen only on those who had dealt in American paper. The beginning of the business was from the alarm occasioned by the war, which induced cautious people to withdraw their money from the country banks. This induced the bank of England to stop discounting, which brought on a general crush, which was still going on. It is said that 2. millions of manufacturers &c. would be put out of employ by these failures. This is probably exaggerated.—The stocks are very low here now, and an immense mass of paper is expected to be returned immediately from England, so that they will be still lower. Notwithstanding this, the sinking fund is idle, not having had a shilling to lay out (except the interest of the part sunk).—You will see in Freneau's next paper a most advantageous decree of the French National assembly in our favor. They have lately sustained some severe checks. The papers will confuse you on the subject. The truth is that in a combination of three operations Clairfayt killed and wounded 1400. took 600. Saxe Cobourg killed and wounded 4000. and took 1600. Brunswick killed and wounded 1300. and took 700. This is the sum. Their defeats are as sensibly felt at Philadelphia as at Paris, and I foresee we are to have a trying campaign of it.—Great Br. has as yet not condescended to notice us in any way. No wish expressed of our neutrality, no answer of any kind to a single complaint for the daily violations committed on our sailors and ships. Indeed we promise beforehand so fast that she has not time to ask any thing.—We expect Genest daily. When Ternant received certain account of his appointment thinking he had nothing further to hope from the Jacobins,[5] he that very day found out something to be offended at in me (in which I had been[6] made ex officio[7] the ostensible agent in what came from another quarter, and he has never been undeceived) attached himself intimately to Hamilton[8] put on mourning for the king, and became a perfect Counter-revolutioner. A few days ago he received a letter from Genest giving him a hope that they will employ him in the army. On this he has tacked about again, become a Jacobin, and refused to present the Viscount Noailles and some French aristocrats arrived here. However he will hardly have the impudence to speak to me again. From what I learn from Noailles, la Fayette has been more imprudent than I expected, but certainly innocent.

Present my best affections to Mrs. Monroe and accept them for yourself also. Yours sincerely   TH: JEFFERSON

RC (NN); at foot of first page: "Colo. Monroe." PrC (DLC). Enclosed in TJ to James Madison, 5 May 1793.

TJ maintained that the FISCAL PARTY supporting Secretary of the Treasury Alexander Hamilton had TRICKED THE HOUSE OF REPRESENTATIVES into its NEGATIVE VOTE of 1 Mch. 1793 on the Giles resolutions, with the trick presumably being the participation in the vote of a cadre of congressmen whose investments in federally funded debt and stock in the Bank of the United States constituted a conflict of interest (Editorial Note on Jefferson and the Giles resolutions, at 27 Feb. 1793; Notes on the Giles Resolutions, 2 Mch. 1793). The FRENCH FRIGATE was the *Embuscade*, and its BRITISH PRIZE was the *Grange* (see Memorial from George

Hammond, 2 May 1793). H: Alexander Hamilton. $2\frac{1}{2}$ AGAINST $1\frac{1}{2}$: a reference to Attorney General Edmund Randolph's oscillation in the Cabinet between the views of Hamilton and Secretary of War Henry Knox on the one hand and TJ on the other. The MOST ADVANTAGEOUS DECREE, printed in the *National Gazette* on 8 May 1793, was a proposal to the National Convention by the Committee of General Defense on 3 Feb. 1793 that resulted in a decree of 19 Feb. opening American trade with French colonial ports (see note to Joseph Fenwick to TJ, 25 Feb. 1793).

The occasion when Jean Baptiste Ternant found SOMETHING TO BE OFFENDED AT IN ME cannot be identified with certainty, but it evidently took place on 25 Feb. 1793 when TJ asked the French minister to produce his powers to nego- tiate the advance of three million livres tournois on the American debt to France he had requested on 8 Feb. The subse- quent arrival of Colonel William Stephens Smith from France with a proposal from the Provisional Executive Council that the entire debt be paid off in American pro- duce under Smith's auspices, and of word that Edmond Charles Genet had been cho- sen to replace Ternant, coupled with Ter- nant's initial ignorance of both develop- ments, evidently led to concern in the administration over whether he was in fact authorized to obtain the payment. TJ's request to see Ternant's authorization was no doubt related to the Cabinet meet- ing of that day to consider the French minister's application. Although Ternant regarded it as an affront to the French diplomatic service and initially refused to comply, the Cabinet nonetheless approved the payment, after which Ternant did pro- duce his authorization for the Secretary of State (Turner, *CFM*, 180-1; Editorial Note on Jefferson's questions and obser- vations on the application of France, at 12 Feb. 1793; Notes on Conversations with William Stephens Smith and George Washington, 20 Feb. 1793, and note; TJ to George Washington, 25 Feb. 1793). The person for whom TJ was MADE EX OFFICIO THE OSTENSIBLE AGENT may have been the President.

[1] Closing quotation mark supplied.
[2] Word interlined.
[3] Preceding three words interlined.
[4] Preceding three words interlined.
[5] Preceding ten words interlined.
[6] Word interlined.
[7] Preceding two words interlined in place of "of necessity."
[8] Preceding five words interlined in place of "to."

From Rodolph Vall-Travers

Rotterdam, 5 May 1793. In hopes that his exertions on behalf of the United States, described in his letters of last year and this to the President and TJ, have been well received, he calls a new emergency to the administration's attention. The Netherlands, which has hitherto favored North America with loans and the fruits of its West Indian colonies and plantations, will now suspend though not repeal, for the duration of the war and the benefit of "neutral, especially N. american, Vessels," its regulations excluding all but Dutch ships from the carrying trade with its colonies, and will connive to admit such vessels to Surinam, Demerara, Essequibo, Berbice, and St. Eustatius so they can carry the products of these places to Holland and return with Dutch cargoes, subject to payment of the usual duties to West Indian agents of the directors for remission to their principals in Europe. Directors here and at Amsterdam and Middelburg will issue proper passports to all North American captains willing to participate in this temporary trade. Nicholas Foster of Baltimore, captain of the frigate *Anne*, built in North America and flying American colors, is the first to sail from Amsterdam; he carries a Dutch cargo for Berbice and will return from thence to Holland with cotton, sugar, coffee, and indigo. Another countryman of his will reportedly do the same. The report in English papers of the capture by an English priva- teer of a large North American ship bound to France with a cargo of 2,600 barrels of flour provides one more grievance among many for Pinckney and Morris, "your Ministers in England," to protest. The government of poor France is as unstable and inhuman as ever. Its vicissitudes will be exhibited in a magic lantern now being contrived by Mr. Euler, an excellent genius and philanthropist at The Hague. Some of the lately published satirical prints enclosed may enrich his work. Throughout Europe royalists are unstinting in their efforts to prop up their tottering power. "True Liberty, like yours, requires a more diffused Light of Truth and better Manners, than the present too neglected Age will admit of." This week he will repair to the Austrian Netherlands for a month or two to investigate prospects for a mutually beneficial commercial relationship between them and the United States. He will transmit his findings to the President when commissioned as embassy counsellor or as some other officer by the United States. Messrs. Beerenbroek & Van Dooren, his respectable friends at Amsterdam well known to Staphorst & Hubbard, will always forward TJ's commands to him.

RC (DNA: RG 59, MLR); 4 p.; at foot of text: "To Thos. Jefferson, Esqe. Secretary of State to the united & confederate Free states of N. America In Philadelphia"; endorsed by TJ as received 19 July 1793 and so recorded in SJL. Dupl (DLC: Washington Papers); dated 4 May 1793; varies slightly in wording. Enclosures not found.

To George Washington

May 5. 93.

Th: Jefferson has the honor to inclose to the President a letter delivered him this day by Mr. de Noailles.

RC (DNA: RG 59, MLR); addressed: "The Presid[. . .]"; endorsed by Tobias Lear. Tr (Lb in same, SDC). Not recorded in SJL.

Louis Marie, Vicomte de Noailles, a brother-in-law of the Marquis de Lafayette who had served with the French army in America during the Revolutionary War and distinguished himself at Yorktown, arrived in Philadelphia on board the *New Pigou* with a group of other French émigrés on 3 May 1793 and was immediately received by the President, who among other things inquired about the condition of the imprisoned marquis. The LETTER DELIVERED by Noailles for the President has not been found, but evidently it led Washington and TJ to believe that Noailles had come to America to second Lafayette's request that the United States intervene to secure his release from Prussian captivity—for on 6 May TJ took the unusual step of sending the President a copy of a letter on this subject he had written to the American ministers in Paris and London seven weeks before. However, there is no evidence to indicate that Noailles raised the issue at a subsequent meeting he claimed to have had with the President. The letter from Noailles came through TJ's hands apparently because Washington this day asked the Secretary of the Treasury, one of the vicomte's old comrades in arms, to inform Noailles that the President preferred to receive any written or oral communications he might wish to make on public matters "through the proper channel," which in this case could only have meant the Secretary of State (Noailles to Washington, [3 May 1793?], DLC: Washington Papers, which does not appear to be the enclosed letter; TJ to Washington, 5 May 1793; Syrett, *Hamilton*, XIV, 414-15; *Windham Papers*, I, 122; AHR, XXXVIII [1933], 633).

To George Washington

May. 5. 1793.

Th: Jefferson with his respects to the President has the honour to inclose him the following papers.

1. a letter from Mr. Pinckney, with the papers it refers to, on the subject of Mr. Albion Coxe, employed as Assayer, who is arrived.

2. a copy of the letter written to Mr. Morris and Mr. Pinckney, on the subject of M. de la Fayette,[1] copies of which were sent to Messrs. Humphreys, Carmichael and Short. The two former were to act on the subject, because nearer the proper scene. The communication was made to the three latter merely for their information, and that they might know the views of the government in case they should have occasion to say or do any thing on the subject.

3. Mr. Fox's pamphlet.

RC (DNA: RG 59, MLR); endorsed by Tobias Lear. PrC (DLC). Tr (Lb in DNA: RG 59, SDC). Recorded in SJPL. Enclosures: (1) Thomas Pinckney to TJ, 12 Mch. 1793, and enclosures. (2) TJ to Gouverneur Morris and Thomas Pinckney, 15 Mch. 1793. (3) Charles James Fox, *A Letter from the Right Honourable Charles James Fox, to the Worthy and Independent Electors of the City and Liberty of Westminster* (London, 1793), the third edition of which was owned by TJ (Sowerby, No. 2829).

TJ submitted this letter and its enclo- sures to the President on 6 May 1793, and Washington returned them the same day (Washington, *Journal*, 129). Later that day TJ wrote a brief note to the President returning "the copy of the letter on the subject of M. de la Fayette, supposing it might be agreeable to keep it by him," since another copy was retained for the office (RC in DNA: RG 59, MLR, addressed "The President of the US.," endorsed by Tobias Lear; Tr in Lb in same, SDC; not recorded in SJL).

[1] Preceding clause interlined.

Notes on Washington's Questions on Neutrality and the Alliance with France

[6 May 1793]

Apr. 18. The President sends a set of Questions to be considered and calls a meeting. Tho those sent me were in his own hand writing, yet it was palpable from the style, their ingenious tissu and suite that they were not the President's, that they were raised upon a prepared chain of argument, in short that the language was Hamilton's, and the doubts his alone. They led to a declaration of the Executive that our treaty with France is void. E.R. the next day tells[1] me, that the day before the date of these questions, Hamilton went with him[2] thro' the whole chain of reasoning of which these questions are the skeleton, and that he recognised them the moment he saw them.

We met. The 1st. question whether we should receive the French minister Genest was proposed, and we agreed unanimously that he should be received, Hamilton at the same time expressing his great regret that any incident had happened which should oblige us to recognize the government. The next question was whether he should be received absolutely, or with qualifications. Here H. took up the whole subject, and went through it in the order in which the questions sketch it. See the chain of his reasoning in my opinion of Apr. 28. Knox subscribed at once to H's opinion that we ought to declare the treaty void, acknoleging at the same time, like a fool as he is, that he knew nothing about it. I was clear it remained valid. E.R. declared himself of the same opinion, but on H's undertaking to present to him the authority in Vattel (which we had not present) and to prove[3] to him that, if the authority was admitted, the treaty might be declared void, E.R. agreed to take further time to consider.—It was adjourned.— We determined Unanimously the last question that Congress should not be called. There having been an intimation by E.R. that in so great a question he should chuse to give a written opinion, and this being approved by the Pres. I gave in mine Apr. 28.—H. gave in his. I beleive Knox's was never thought worth offering or asking for. E.R. gave his May 6.[4] concurring with mine. The Presidt. told me the same day he had never had a doubt about the validity of the treaty: but that since a question had been suggested he thought it ought to be considered. That this being done, I might now issue Passports to sea vessels in the form prescribed by the French treaty. I had for a week past only issued the Dutch form; to have issued the French would have been presupposing the treaty to be in existence.—The Presidt. suggested that he thought it would be as well that nothing should be said[5] of such a question having been under consideration.

May 6. written

MS (DLC); entirely in TJ's hand; partially dated, but with last line written in a different shade of ink and possibly at a later date; written on verso of sheet containing "Anas" entry for 7 Apr. 1793. Recorded in SJPL under 5 May 1793: "[Notes] on the questions of Apr. 18.— Passports to be now issued." Included in the "Anas."

For the President's SET OF QUESTIONS

on neutrality, see enclosure to Washington to the Cabinet, 18 Apr. 1793. MY OPIN-ION OF APR. 28.: see Document IV of a group of documents on Jefferson's opinion on the treaties with France, at 28 Apr. 1793. Although Secretary of War Henry KNOX's opinion was not submitted separately to the President, he concurred in the opinion written and signed by the Secretary of the Treasury arguing for the right of the United States to suspend or void the French treaties (see Editorial Note at same). See also Cabinet Opinion on George Washington's Questions on Neutrality and the Alliance with France, [19 Apr. 1793], and note.

[1] Reworked from "told," or vice versa.
[2] Preceding two words interlined.
[3] TJ first wrote "and prove it" and then altered it to read as above.
[4] Reworked from "7."
[5] TJ here canceled "about."

Notes on Alexander Hamilton and the Enforcement of Neutrality

1793. May 6. The President shews me a draught of a letter from Colo. H. to the Collectors of the customs, desiring them to superintend their neighborhood, watch for all acts of our citizens contrary to laws of neutrality or tending to infringe those laws, and inform him of it; and particularly to see if vessels should be building pierced for guns.—I told the Pr. that at a conference a few days before Colo. H. and E.R. had concurred in opinion against me that for us to build and sell vessels fit for war would be a breach of neutrality, but that I understood them as agreeing that no opinion should go from the public on that question as not being now necessary: that as to the 1st. part of the letter I did not of a sudden decide it to be improper.—He, on this, returned the letter to Ham. with a desire that he, E.R. and myself would confer on it.

MS (DLC); entirely in TJ's hand; written on same sheet as "Anas" entries for 7 and 12 May 1793. Entry in SJPL: "[Notes] on Ham's lre to collectors to watch over neutrality." Included in the "Anas."

These notes of a conference with the President represent an early example of the disputes between the Secretary of State and the Secretary of the Treasury over the conduct of American neutrality that were to be a recurring feature of Washington's second administration until TJ retired from office at the end of 1793. Two days before this meeting, in a preemptive bid to assert control over the enforcement of American neutrality, Hamilton wrote a letter to the President enclosing for his approval a draft circular letter on this matter to federal customs collectors that has since disappeared. On the following day Washington instructed

Hamilton to refrain from dispatching this circular to the collectors until they had discussed "a particular clause in it," but if such a conversation ever took place there is no record of it. Although the President did not identify this clause, he seems to have been primarily concerned about the adverse impact on domestic shipbuilding of a provision in the draft circular that would have made the sale to belligerents of a vessel built in the United States and pierced for guns a violation of neutrality (Syrett, *Hamilton*, XIV, 412, 414, 422). TJ shared the President's concern on this point, but for political and constitutional reasons he explained at length in an 8 May 1793 letter to Attorney General Edmund Randolph he was even more alarmed by another part of the circular that required collectors to report violations of American neutrality directly to the Secretary of the Treasury. The President also showed Hamilton's draft to Randolph at about this time. After conferring with these two officials, Washington instructed Hamilton on 7 May 1793 to withhold his circular until the Cabinet had reconsidered that portion of it "respecting the building of Vessels in our Ports wch may be converted into armed ones" and asked (apparently on the basis of a suggestion by the Attorney General) whether it would not be expedient to write to the federal district attorneys "requiring their attention to the observance of the Injunctions" of the Proclamation of Neutrality (Syrett, *Hamilton*, xiv, 422-3; Edmund Randolph to TJ, 9 May 1793). No minutes of the ensuing Cabinet meeting have been found, but it is clear from other evidence that Hamilton yielded on both points. In deference to the President, he agreed to delete from the circular the provision relating to the ban on vessels pierced for guns, and in response to a proposal by the Attorney General, he amended the circular so that collectors would report violations of neutrality to the federal district attorneys instead of to the Secretary of the Treasury. Although the latter change sharply curtailed the role of the Secretary of the Treasury in enforcing American neutrality, TJ accepted it with reluctance because he preferred to entrust federal judges and grand juries with primary responsibility for monitoring American violations of neutrality. However, owing to the Washington administration's delay in adopting a precise set of rules of neutral conduct for American citizens, Hamilton did not dispatch the revised circular to the collectors, who were also instructed to report violations to the state governors, until early in August 1793 (TJ to Randolph, 8 May 1793; Randolph to TJ, 9 May 1793; TJ to James Madison, [13 May 1793]; Syrett, *Hamilton*, xv, 168-9, 178-81). In the meantime, anxious to preserve the nation's neutral stance in the epochal struggle between Great Britain and France, the President directed the Attorney General on 10 May 1793 to instruct the district attorneys "to require from the Collectors of the several Ports, within them, information of all infractions of neutrality that may come within their perview at the different ports, requiring the interposition of Government, particularly as to building & equipping Vessels for war." Two days later Randolph dispatched a circular letter to the district attorneys ordering them to prosecute violators of American neutrality vigorously and particularly to rely on the collectors for information in ferreting out offenders (Washington, *Journal*, 135; Edmund Randolph to William Channing, 12 May 1793, NN: Emmet Collection).

To Thomas Mann Randolph, Jr.

Dear Sir   Philadelphia May. 6. 1793.

The inclosed papers will inform you of some checks the French have lately received. They are confounded and multiplied in the papers. The truth is that a combined operation in three different parts took place the first days of March, under Clairfayt, Saxe-Cobourg and Brunswick, every one of which succeeded. The first killed and wounded 1400, and took 600. The second killed and wounded 4000. and took 1600. The third killed and wounded 1300. and took 700. In consequence of these the French lost Liege and raised the siege of Maestricht.—A French frigate has brought 2. prizes up to Philadelphia. The *yeomanry* of the city (not the fashionable people nor paper men) shewed prodigious joy when, flocking to the wharves, they saw the British colours reversed and the French flying above them.—I very much fear that France will experience a famine this summer. The effects of this admit of no calculation.—Grain is the thing for us now to cultivate. The demand will be immense, and the price high. I think experience shews us that to sell it before the spring is an immense sacrifice. I fear we shall experience a want of vessels to carry our produce to Europe. In this case the tobacco will be left, because bread is more essential to them.   Mr. Beverley Randolph left this a few days ago in pretty good health. Maria I think is getting[1] into better health. I hope you are all well, tho' having no letter later than the 28th. of March we are uneasy. My love to my dear Martha and am Dear Sir sincerely & affectionately Your's   Th: Jefferson

RC (DLC); at foot of text: "Mr. Randolph." PrC (DLC). Tr (DLC); 19th-century copy.

The LETTER since which TJ had not heard from Monticello was Peter Carr to TJ, 28 Mch. 1793.

[1] MS: "getter."

From F. P. Van Berckel

Monsieur   à Philadelphie Ce 6e. Mai 1793.

Ayant Compris par Ce qué Vous m'avez fait l'honneur de me dire Ce matin, qué Vous ne Consideriez pas ma Lettre du 28e. dernier, Comme une notification formelle d'une Guerre declarée entre la France et les Provinces Unies; je Crois de mon devoir de Vous informer Sans delai qué J'ai recu d'une Maniere officielle la Confirmation de Ce qui m'avoit été Communiqué par le Ministre de Sa Majesté Britannique, l'Allié de Leurs Hautes Puissances; Savoir qué la Convention Nationale par Son decret du 1er. Fevrier 1793, a déclaré, au nom de la Nation Francoise, qu'elle est en Guerre avec le Roi de la Grande Bretagne, et avec le Stadhouder des Provinces Unies. J'ai l'honneur d'etre avec les Sentimens de la plus parfaite Consideration Monsieur Votre très humble & très Obeïssent Serviteur

F: P: van Berckel

RC (DNA: RG 360, PCC); at foot of text: "à Monsieur Jefferson, Secretaire d'Etat a Philadelphie"; endorsed by TJ as received 7 May 1793 and so recorded in SJL.

On 8 May 1793 TJ submitted this letter to the President, who recorded in his journal that after receiving it the Secretary of State had personally asked the Dutch minister "if he had recd. information of Holland having declared War agt. France," to which Van Berckel replied, "No—he was informed they had not & it was doubtful whether such a declaration would be made or not." TJ also took back the letter on that day (Washington, *Journal*, 131).

From Tench Coxe

SIR   Treasury Department Revenue Office May 7th 1793

In addition to the short letter of last week for Boston, New-York, Baltimore and Alexandria; I have now the honor to inclose you two copies of my instructions to the Collectors (to accompany the Sea letters) 200 of which have been this day delivered to me from the Press. All the sea letters which have been received are disposed of, in consequence of applications, as fast as they came to my hands.

I beg leave to remark, that a considerable degree of anxiety will probably arise in all the Ports of the United States for these documents, upon its being known that they have been issued and that it therefore appears necessary to have a full supply of them transmitted to every customhouse without delay. The fishing Vessels upon whaling voyages, which depart for some of the latitudes at all seasons, will likewise want them, and the little fleets, which go to the Banks and which have begun to depart, will want them in large Numbers. Not less than 500 will be wanted by the Eastern States for those two descriptions of Vessels, besides the supply for their foreign traders.

I beg leave to submit to your consideration these two points of instruction, which I intend to give to the Collectors.

1st: That all foreign built ships (not registered) which have been or may be acquired by our Citizens after the 15th. of May 1789 shall be measured by our officers and have their names and the place to which they belong painted on their Sterns respectively, prior to the issuing Sea letters for them.

2dly. That a duplicate of the bill of Sale shall be endorsed on the Back of their national register and duly executed before the Collector of the Customs (or his Deputy), and the Naval Officer (or his deputy) if there be one in the Port.

This will be a pretty efficacious method of preventing frauds injurious to our Merchants and dangerous to the Peace of the United States. I have the honor to be with great Respect, Sir, Your most Obedient Servant   TENCH COXE

Commissioner of the Revenue

RC (DLC); in a clerk's hand, with signature and a minor correction by Coxe; at foot of text: "The Secretary of State"; endorsed by TJ as received 7 May 1793 and so recorded in SJL. Enclosure: Coxe's Circular to Collectors of the Customs, 7 May 1793, enclosing three copies of sea letters received from the Department of State and signed by the President and the Secretary of State that were to be issued to every vessel wholly and bona fide owned by United States citizens once the captain had sworn to that effect under oath on the certificate annexed to the sea letter; giving instructions for filling in the blanks on the English and Dutch copies of the sea letters; cautioning that sea letters, though issuable to foreign-built ships owned by American citizens on 15 May 1789 or actually acquired since then, were not to be given to vessels owned in any part, directly or indirectly, by foreigners and ordering the collectors to *"take the most especial care to prevent deceptions and collusions in that respect"*; advising that the French copy of the sea letters had been delayed but will probably be completed before this circular went out and will appear "on the back of the present form" to be filled in the same way; and giving directions for keeping records and submitting a quarterly return of sea letters issued (two printed forms in DLC; addressed respectively to James M. Lingan, collector for Georgetown, Maryland, and John Fitzgerald, collector for Alexandria, Virginia; with blanks for the day, the port, Coxe's signature, and the collector's name filled in by a clerk).

The SHORT LETTER OF LAST WEEK was enclosed in Coxe to TJ, 4 May 1793. Alexander Hamilton issued a revised version of Coxe's INSTRUCTIONS TO THE COLLECTORS in his own name around the middle of May, differing from the enclosed circular mainly in its inclusion of directions on how to fill in the French form of the ship passports (Syrett, *Hamilton*, XIV, 442-7). Acts passed in September 1789 and December 1792 stipulated that FOREIGN BUILT SHIPS acquired by United States citizens after THE 15TH. OF MAY 1789 were not entitled to registry as American vessels, and were thus ineligible for the reduced customs duties which this designation carried with it (*Annals*, II, 2217, III, 1397). Coxe was concerned with setting up procedures for establishing that such unregistered vessels were bona fide American owned and accordingly entitled to receive sea letters.

From C. W. F. Dumas

The Hague, 7 May 1793. A fortnight ago he received TJ's letter of 2 Feb. and a fortnight before that the plans of our beautiful Federal City, eight of which he sent to Amsterdam to be displayed in the counting houses of great merchants friendly to us and in patriotic clubs. He is preparing ten others for Dort, Rotterdam, Leyden, and Haarlem and has reserved five for North Holland and Utrecht and one for himself, but it would be useless and odious to show it here and in Delft. The leading figures in this place, which Short left about five months ago, are definitely not our friends. They regard the United States as the cause of the entire upheaval of Europe. TJ's letter was very precious to him, and he hopes for the continuance of such favors.

Dupl (DNA: RG 59, MLR); 1 p.; in French; at head of text: "A S. E. Mr. Ths. Jefferson, &c." and "Dupl."; endorsed by TJ as a letter of 1 May 1793 received 19 July 1793 and so recorded in SJL.

From Enoch Edwards

SIR   Philadelphia May 7th. 1793

I will be exceedingly obliged if you will excuse my asking one Letter from you to Some Gentleman in France, whether it be to Mr. Morris our Minister there, or some private Gentleman—I submit that to you.

Doctor Rush at the Time He asked the one you have been so kind as to write, did not know that I certainly meant to visit France. The Agriculture of this Country as well as England I intend to see as far as Circumstances will admit—these Objects next to my Health are among the first I have in view.

Your Sources of Information on Subjects of this as well as other Kinds are I expect so abundantly numerous—that an Offer on my Part to do any thing that might either be useful or agreeable to You while abroad, can only appear Complimentary—should I however be mistaken you will gratify me not a little, by chearfully commanding my Services.

That I may unfeignedly wish my Country well, I shall very sincerely wish for your Health and Happiness—and for the Establishment of those political Sentiments, which I believe have a Residence in your Heart. I am Sir with Respect & Gratitude Your obedt: Sert.

ENO: EDWARDS

P:S: I go down to Chester on thursday by Land.

RC (DLC); dateline between signature and postscript; beneath signature: "Honl. Thomas Jefferson Esqr."; endorsed by TJ as received 7 May 1793 and so recorded in SJL, with both endorsement and SJL erroneously identifying the writer as George Edwards.

Dr. Enoch Edwards (1751-1802) of Philadelphia County, Pennsylvania, was Benjamin Rush's first medical student. An army surgeon in the Revolution, Edwards was a member of the Pennsylvania convention to ratify the United States Constitution in 1787 and the state constitutional convention in 1789-90, and served as associate justice of the court of common pleas from 1791 until his death. He went to Europe partly in order to act as an agent in the sale of Pennsylvania land belonging to the speculator John Nicholson (William Henry Egle, "The Federal Constitution of 1787: Sketches of the Members of the Pennsylvania Convention," PMHB, XI [1887], 74-5; George W. Corner, ed., *The Autobiography of Benjamin Rush* [Princeton, 1948], 311-12; James S. Biddle, ed., *Autobiography of Charles Biddle, Vice-President of the Supreme Executive Council of Pennsylvania, 1745-1821* [Philadelphia, 1883], 309-11). The letter TJ had been SO KIND AS TO WRITE was his letter to Thomas Pinckney of 3 May 1793.

From Joseph Fay

DEAR SIR   Bennington 7th. May 1793

Your favours of the 18th. and 21t. March, I had the honor to receive, and altho I should have been happy to have had you joined our Company, yet the reasons you offer against it are highly satisfactory and such as I sincerely wish Governed all our public Servants.

I send two of the last Quebec papers, and shall send more as they come forward. If it will not give you too much trouble I should be glad to recieve the Philadelphia papers in Return. And whatever the difference in the expence shall appear I will chearfully pay.

The Acts of the last Session of Congress, and the journals of the Senate have not yet been received, those which are designed for Vermont, I would thank you to direct to my Care as I have the Governors directions to keep one set for the use of the Council, and to forward the other to him. I am Dear Sir with Sentiments of Gratitude and respect your obedient Servant   JOSEPH FAY

RC (DLC); at foot of text: "Mr. Jefferson"; endorsed by TJ as received 14 May 1793 and so recorded in SJL; notations adjacent to signature in the hand of George Taylor, Jr.: "Send Mr. Freneau's paper" and "sent Saturday May 18. 1793."

TJ did not reply to this letter, and Fay's next one to him, recorded in SJL as dated 28 Nov. 1795 and received 2 Dec. 1795, has not been found.

Notes on the Sinking Fund and the Proclamation of Neutrality

May 7. We met as trustees of the sinking fund. For the opinion I delivered see my note of May 8. to E. R.[1] and for his see his answer of May 9.—On the business of the sinking fund, we had meant to have come to a resolution to ask of the Pres. if there was any money under the loans at our disposal, the occasion of laying it out being favorable. But H. produced a letter just received from our bankers informing him of the impossibility[2] of[3] effecting the new loan which had been ordered (and of which I had not heard before). On this I declared it as my opinion that if the money on hand was not sufficient to pay our next installment to France and also to purchase public debt, (of which I could not be a judge, only knowing that our next installment would be of between 6. and 700,000 D. and was approaching) I should be against failing in the payment which was a positive engagement whereas the purchase of public debt was voluntary. So nothing was done.

When the question was whether the proclamation of Apr.[4] 22 should be issued, E. R. observed that there should be a letter written by me to the ministers of the belligerent powers to declare that it should not be taken as conclusive evidence against our citizens in foreign courts of Admiralty for contraband goods.—Knox suddenly adopted the opinion before Hamilton delivered his. Hamilton opposed it pretty strongly. I thought it an indifferent thing but rather⁵ approved E.R.'s opinion. The President was against it: but observed that *as were three for it,*⁶ *it should go.* This was the first instance I had seen of an opportunity to decide by a mere majority including his own vote.

MS (DLC); entirely in TJ's hand; partially dated, but first paragraph obviously set down no earlier than 8 or 9 May 1793 and second paragraph, in a different shade of ink, probably on 12 May 1793 with "Anas" entry of that date; written on same sheet as "Anas" entries for 6 and 12 May 1793. Entry in SJPL: "[Notes] on proceedings on sinking fund. [Notes] on proclamn—decision by majority." Included in the "Anas."

For the background to this meeting of the TRUSTEES OF THE SINKING FUND, see note to Alexander Hamilton to TJ, 24 Mch. 1793. TJ's OPINION related not to sinking fund business but to the propriety of ordering federal customs collectors to report violations of American neutrality directly to the Secretary of the Treasury (TJ to Edmund Randolph, 8 May 1793; see also Notes on Alexander Hamilton and the Enforcement of Neutrality, 6 May 1793). The LETTER JUST RECEIVED was Willink, Van Staphorst & Hubbard to Alexander Hamilton, 26 Feb. 1793, which reported the IMPOSSIBILITY OF EFFECTING THE NEW LOAN of two million florins for the payment of the foreign debt which Hamilton had authorized in letters of 5 Nov. 1792 to them and to William Short (Syrett, *Hamilton*, XIII, 19-23, XIV, 166-7). TJ's letter to THE MINISTERS OF THE BELLIGERENT POWERS was dated 23 Apr. 1793.

¹ Remainder of sentence interlined.
² First syllable interlined.
³ TJ here canceled "borrowing."
⁴ Reworked from "Mar."
⁵ TJ here canceled "joined E."
⁶ TJ here canceled "*he should.*"

To Thomas Pinckney

DEAR SIR   Philadelphia May 7th. 1793.

Since my Letter of April 26th. yours have been received of March 12. 12. 13. 13. and 19. Before the receipt of these, one of which covered the form of your passports, it had been determined here that passports should be issued in *our own ports* only, as well to secure us against those collusions which would be fraudulent towards our Friends, and would introduce a competition injurious to our own vessels, as to induce these to remain in our own service, and thereby give to the productions of our Soil, the protection of it's own flag in it's passage to foreign markets. As our citizens are free to purchase and use *foreign-built* vessels, and these, like all their other lawful property, are entitled to the protection of their Government, passports will be issued to them as freely as to *home-built* Vessels. This is strictly within our Treaties, the letter of which as well as their spirit, authorizes passports to all vessels *belonging* to Citizens of the United States. Our laws, indeed, indulge *home-built* vessels with the payment of a lower Tonnage, and to evidence their right to this, permit them alone to take out registers from our own offices; but they do not exclude foreign-built vessels owned by our Citizens from any other right. As our home-built vessels are adequate to but a small proportion of our Transportation, if we could not suddenly augment the stock of our Shipping, our produce would be subject to war-insurance in the vessels of the belligerent powers, though we remain at peace ourselves.

In one of your letters of March 13th. you express your apprehensions that some of the belligerent powers may stop our vessels going with grain to the Ports of their Enemies, and ask instructions which may meet the Question in various points of view, intending, however, in the meantime to contend for the amplest freedom of neutral Nations. Your intention in this, is perfectly proper, and coincides with the Ideas of our own Government in the particular case you put, as in general cases. Such a stoppage to an unblockaded port would be so unequivocal an infringement of the neutral rights, that we cannot conceive it will be attempted. With respect to our conduct, as a neutral nation, it is marked out in our Treaties with France and Holland, two of the belligerent Powers: and as the duties of neutrality require an *equal* conduct to both parties, we should, on that ground, act on the same principles towards Great Britain. We presume that this would be satisfactory to her, because of it's *equality*, and because she too, has sanctioned the same principles in her Treaty with France. Even our 17th. Article with France, which might be disagreeable, as from it's nature it is unequal, is adopted exactly by Great Britain in her 40th. Article with the same power; and would have laid her, in a like case, under the same unequal obligations against us. We wish then that it could be arranged with Great Britain, that our Treaties with France and Holland, and that of France and Great Britain (which agree in what respects neutral nations) should form the line of conduct for us all, in the present war, in the cases for which they provide. Where they are silent, the general principles of the law of nations, must give the rule. I mean the principles of that law, as they have been liberalized in latter times by the refinement of manners and morals, and evidenced by the Declarations, Stipulations and Practice of every civilized Nation. In our Treaty with Prussia, indeed, we have gone ahead of other nations in doing away restraints on the Commerce of peaceful nations, by declaring that nothing shall be contraband, for, in truth, in the present improved State of the Arts, when every Country has such ample means of procuring Arms within and without itself, the regulations of contraband answer no other end than to draw other nations into the war. However, as nations have not given sanction to this improvement, we claim it, at present, with Prussia alone.

You are desired to persevere till you obtain a regulation to guard our vessels from having their Hands impressed, and to inhibit the British navy-officers from taking them under the pretext of their being British subjects. There appears but one practicable rule, that, the vessel being American, shall be conclusive Evidence that the Hands are so, to a certain number proportioned to her tonnage. Not more than one or two Officers should be permitted to visit a vessel.—Mr. Albion Coxe is just arrived. I have the honor to be, with great and sincere esteem, Dear sir, Your most obedient and most humble servant, TH: JEFFERSON

RC (William M. Elkins, Philadelphia, 1945); in the hand of George Taylor, Jr., signed by TJ; at foot of first page: "Mr. Pinckney"; endorsed by William A. Deas. PrC (DLC). FC (Lb in DNA: RG 59, DCI). Tr (MHi: Timothy Pickering Papers); extract consisting of first three sentences of final paragraph. Enclosed in TJ to George Washington, 7 May 1793.

TJ had received Pinckney's 13 Mch. 1793 letter covering THE FORM OF YOUR PASSPORTS on 5 May 1793. Within the next two days he submitted a draft of his reply, which has not been found, to Alexander Hamilton and Edmund Randolph. After altering the draft in light of their suggestions, TJ submitted a revised text to the President, who immediately approved it (TJ to Washington, 7 May 1793; Washington, *Journal*, 129).

For OUR 17TH. ARTICLE WITH FRANCE in the 1778 commercial treaty with that country, which was closely replicated in the 40TH. ARTICLE of France's 1786 commercial treaty with Great Britain, see, respectively, Editorial Note on Jefferson's opinion on the treaties with France, at 28 Apr. 1793, and note to Document II there.

To Jean Baptiste Ternant

SIR   Philadelphia, May 7th. 1793

I had the honor of addressing you on the 3d. instant, on the subject of the British Ship Grange, reclaimed on behalf of the Owners as having been taken by the frigate Embuscade, within the capes of Delaware, as is said. If this fact is to be controverted, permit me to hope that the counter evidence may be produced without delay; besides the confinement of the Crew, which is a circumstance of consideration, any unnecessary delay may be imputed by the party reclaiming to an unwillingness on our part to do them justice. If the fact is not to be controverted, I will ask the favor of your answer to that effect, and the President will then take measures for having the question decided, Whether the Capture has been consistent with the territorial jurisdiction of the United States. I have the honor to be with great Respect, &c: TH: JEFFERSON

FC (Lb in DNA: RG 59, DL); at head of text: "The Minister of France." Tr (DLC: Genet Papers). Tr (AMAE: CPEU, xxxvii); in French.

From Josef Ignacio de Viar and Josef de Jaudenes

MUI SEÑOR NUESTRO   Philadelphia 7. de Mayo de 1793.

En contestacion al Oficio que pasàmos à la Superioridad, incluiendo Copia del que V.S. nos escrivò, quexandose de que el Govierno de la Luisiana huviese embiado un Comisario, ò Agente à la Nacion Creek, nos Manda S. M. (despues de aprovar en un todo la Respuesta que dìmos à V.S.) pasar à manos de V.S. (como lo hacemos ahora) Copia del Tratado concluido entre España, y la Nacion Creek el Año de 1784, para que por el pueda V.S. venir en conocimiento de la anticipacion con que aquellos Indios se hicieròn Nuestros Aliados, y que como à tales, pudo embiar el Govierno persona que Resida entre ellos, con el unico fin de Mantenerlos en paz, asi como los Estados Unidos embian à quien quieren sin quexa, ni oposicion Nuestra, pero ofrece S. M. sin embargo hacer este punto uno de los que se traten con los Plenipotenciarios de los Estados Unidos.

Los contenidos del citado Tratado al paso que impondràn¹ a V.S. de nuestros Convenios con los consavidos Indios, confiàmos seràn mui oportunos para evitar, el que los Estados Unidos por falta de conocimiento de ellos, entren en lo venidero en Negociaciones con los Indios, que se opongan à lo que tienen estipulado con Nosotros, y al mismo tiempo contribuirà à Rectificar los concluidos anteriormente, siendo estos pasos los mas eficazes para precaver qualesquiera discenciones en aquella Nacion, y no interrumpir la buena harmonia, y perfecta amistad, que reina entre España, y los Estados Unidos, de lo qual tiene aquella dadas pruevas bien convincentes en todas ocaciones, y aùn en el mismo Tratado en el Articulo 7°.

Tenemos la honrra de pasar à V.S. este aviso, en cumplimiento de la orden del Rey, y con el fin, de que se sirba enterar al Presidente de los Estados Unidos, y nos Subscrivimos con gusto à la disposicion de V.S. Rogando à Dios guarde su vida muchos años. B l mo. de V.S. Sus mas atentos, y seguros Servidores.

JOSEF IGNACIO DE VIAR   JOSEF DE JAUDENES

EDITORS' TRANSLATION

DEAR SIR   Philadelphia, 7 May 1793.

In reply to a memorandum which we transmitted to higher authority, enclosing a copy of the one which you wrote to us complaining that the government of Louisiana had sent a commissioner or agent to the Creek Nation, His Majesty (after approving the answer we gave you) commands us to transmit to you (as we do herewith) a copy of the treaty concluded between Spain and the Creek Nation in the year 1784, so that you may become aware of the priority with which those Indians became our allies, and so that you may understand how it was that to such allies the government might send a person to live among them, for the sole purpose of keeping peace among them, just as the United States sends out anyone it pleases, without complaint or opposition from us, but His Majesty nevertheless offers to make this one of the points to be treated in discussions with the ministers plenipotentiary of the United States.

We trust that the contents of the treaty referred to will both inform you of our agreements with the aforesaid Indians and serve to prevent the United States from entering into negotiations with the Indians in the future which might conflict with the Indians' agreements with us, and at the same time contribute to the rectification of earlier agreements, these measures being the most effective ones for forestalling any kind of dissension in that nation and for maintaining the harmony and perfect amity that prevails between Spain and the United States, of which Spain has given convincing proof on every occasion and even in Article 7 of the treaty itself.

We have the honor to transmit to you this advisory in compliance with the King's orders, and so that you may kindly inform the President of the United States. It is the pleasure of the undersigned to place ourselves at your disposition, with the prayer that God may preserve and keep you for many years. Respectfully yours, your most attentive and assured servants,

JOSEF IGNACIO DE VIAR   JOSEF DE JAUDENES

RC (DNA: RG 59, NL); in Viar's hand, signed by Viar and Jaudenes, with one phrase translated interlinearly in pencil by TJ (see note 1 below); at foot of text: "Señor Dn Thomas Jefferson &ca." Tr (AHN: Papeles de Estado, legajo 3895); in Viar's hand, attested by Viar and Jaudenes. Recorded in SJL as received 7 May 1793. Enclosure: Treaty of Pensacola between Spain and the Creek Indians, 1 June 1784 (Tr in DNA: RG 59, NL, in Spanish, attested by Viar and Jaudenes, endorsed by George Taylor, Jr.: "Communicated with a Letter from de Viar & Jaudenes commissioners on the part of Spain dated ____ May 1793" and "Copy of a treaty between Spain & the Creek Indians"; Tr in same, English translation in TJ's hand, with notation at head of text in Taylor's hand: "Translation"; Tr in same, English translation in a clerk's hand; all three texts filed with 12 May 1793 letter from Jaudenes and Viar to TJ regarding Creek Indians; Tr in DNA: RG 46, Senate Records, 3d Cong., 1st sess., English translation in a clerk's hand; printed in ASP, Foreign Relations, I, 278-9; recorded in SJPL between 16 and 22 May 1793: "Convention between Spain & Talapuche Indians").

This letter from the Spanish government's agents in Philadelphia, which TJ submitted to the President on the following day and took back the same day, was their official response to the complaints in the Secretary of State's letter to them of 9 July 1792 about the appointment of a Spanish agent to Creek Indians living in territory claimed by the United States (see Washington, Journal, 131). ARTICULO 7 of the enclosed treaty bound the Creeks to deliver to the governors general of Louisiana and the Floridas all white citizens of the United States held prisoner by that tribe (ASP, Foreign Relations, I, 279).

[1] Preceding four words translated interlinearly by TJ as "while they will apprise."

To George Washington

May 7. 93.

Th: Jefferson presents his respects to the President and incloses the draught of a letter to Mr. Pinckney in answer to one lately received from him. As Colo. Hamilton, the Attorney General and Th:J. had a meeting on another subject, Th:J. took the liberty of consulting them on it, and has altered it agreeably to their minds.

RC (DNA: RG 59, MLR); addressed: "The President of the US."; endorsed by Tobias Lear. Tr (Lb in same, SDC). Not recorded in SJL. Enclosure: TJ to Thomas Pinckney, 7 May 1793.

To Brissot de Warville

DEAR SIR   Philadelphia May 8. 1793.

The bearer hereof, Doctor Edwards, a citizen of the United States proposing to visit Paris, I avail myself of that occasion to recall myself to your recollection, and to recommend to your notice a person whose ta[lents?] information and worth will merit it. As the cause of freedom in one country is dear to the free of every other, and your partialities for our states may still interest you in their situation, he will be able to give you the true state of republicanism with us, which I apprehend to be imperfectly known with you. We too have our aristocrats and monocrats, and as they float on the surface, they shew much, though they weigh little. For their more particular description, as well as that of our real republicans, I refer you to him, as perfectly able to give it, with the weight and numbers of each description. I am happy in a safe occasion of assuring you that I continue eternally attached to the principles of your revolution. I hope it will end in the establishment of some firm government, friendly to liberty, and capable of maintaining it. If it does, the world will become inevitably free. If it does not, I feel that the zealous apostles of English demi-despotism here will increase the number of it's disciples.—However, we shall still remain free. Tho' they may harrass our skirts, they can not make impression on our center.—A germ of corruption indeed has been transported from our dear mother country, and has already borne fruit, but it's blast is begun from the breath of the people.—Adieu, my dear Sir, & accept assurances of sincere confraternity with your citizens, and affection & respect for yourself from your cordial friend & servant   TH: JEFFERSON

[679]

PrC (DLC); faded; at foot of text: "M. Brissot." Tr (DLC); 19th-century copy. Enclosed in TJ to Enoch Edwards, 8 May 1793.

This letter, which closed TJ's correspondence with the Girondist leader, never reached its intended recipient, for Edwards was still in England when Brissot was executed on 31 Oct. 1793 (Scott and Rothaus, *Historical Dictionary*, I, 126; Edwards to TJ, 28 Oct. 1793).

To Enoch Edwards

SIR   Philadelphia May. 8. 1793.

It was under the idea that you meant to go to England only that I gave you a letter only to that country. I have now the honor to inclose you one for Mr. Morris and another for Mr. Brissot. The former is a letter of mere general introduction, because you will find Mr. Morris living in the country at some distance from Paris, and consequently not in the way of being much seen by you. The letter to Mr. Brissot is more particular. I have addressed you to him because he speaks English well, knows this country, loves it, and is a true disciple of liberty. I have taken the liberty of referring him to you for a true state of republicanism here, and for the characters, objects, numbers and force of our parties. It is really interesting that these should be well understood in France, and particularly by their government. Particular circumstances have generated suspicions among them that we are swerving from our republicanism. Nobody is more capable of being set to rights on this subject, or more disposed to be so than Mr. Brissot. I hope therefore you will take some pains to make him master of the state of things, persons and principles here, that he may explain them to others, and understand the train of our proceedings hereafter. Do not be deterred in London for your personal safety in France. You will be as safe there as here. Wishing you a pleasant journey & happy return I am with great esteem & respect Sir your most obedt. humble servt   TH: JEFFERSON

PrC (DLC); at foot of text: "Doctr. Edwards." Tr (DLC); 19th-century copy. Enclosures: (1) TJ to Brissot de Warville, 8 May 1793. (2) TJ to Gouverneur Morris, 8 May 1793.

To Alexander Hamilton

SIR   Philadelphia May 8. 1793.

I had wished to have kept back the issuing passports for sea vessels, till the question should be decided Whether the treaty with

France should be declared void, lest the issuing the Passport prescribed by that treaty might be considered as prejudging the question. The importunities however of the owners obliging me to give out a few, I had them printed in the Dutch form only. Not then having sufficiently considered on the best mode of distributing them, I took the liberty, as an expedient of the moment, of sending 7. (the number of vessels then waiting in this port) to Mr. Delaney, asking the favor of him to fill them up and deliver them for me. Application for another parcel coming, and the applicant not being able to wait himself till I could send them to be signed by the President, he desired I would lodge them with Mr. Coxe on whom it would be convenient for him to call for them. I did so: and afterwards sent a second parcel of a dozen, which were pressingly requested.

The President having now decided that the French passport may also be issued, it is at this time in the press, and the whole instrument compleat, with the two passports, sea-letters, and certificates in it's final form, will be ready for signature tomorrow. It has therefore now become necessary to determine on the ultimate channel of distributing them. I am not the judge whether the task of distribution might interfere too much with the other duties of the collectors of the customs. If it would not, their position seems best accomodated to that distribution. I took the liberty therefore to-day of proposing to the President that, if you should think there would be no inconvenience in charging them with the distribution, the blanks might be lodged with them; of which he approved: and I have now the honor of submitting that question to you. If you find no inconvenience in it, I will send 500 blanks, as soon as they shall be signed, either to your office or to that of the Commissioner of the revenue, whichever you shall prefer, to be forwarded to the collectors of the different ports; and from time to time afterwards will keep up a supply. Should it however, in your opinion, interfere too much with the other duties of those officers, I will submit to the President the depositing them with the deputy marshals appointed or to be appointed in every port. I will ask the favor of your answer, as the applications are numerous and pressing, and I am unwilling to be further troublesome to the gentlemen who have hitherto been so kind as to fill up and deliver them for me till some arrangement could be made which might relieve me personally from a business with the details of which I was not acquainted. I have the honor to be with great respect, Sir, Your most obedt & most humble servt   TH: JEFFERSON

PrC (DLC); at foot of first page: "The Secretary of the Treasury."

The documents issued by governments to protect neutral ships in wartime were uniformly identified as "Sea Letters or Passports" in American commercial treaties with France, the Netherlands, and Prussia, and both terms were used interchangeably by TJ, Washington, and others at this time to describe what the Secretary of State in this letter more precisely called the THE WHOLE INSTRUMENT COMPLEAT, WITH THE TWO PASSPORTS, SEALETTERS, AND CERTIFICATES. But even TJ's description reflects the ambiguity in nomenclature which reigned at the time (Miller, *Treaties*, ii, 23-4, 80-2, 172-3; TJ to Sharp Delany, 30 Apr. 1793; Tench Coxe to TJ, 4, 7 May 1793; Washington, *Journal*, 122, 138). See also Moore, *Digest*, ii, 1045-69.

The document being readied by the Department of State actually consisted of two sections. The first—a proclamation that permission had been granted to a ship to leave a given American port after it had been visited and its captain had sworn to the ship's American ownership—was signed by the President and countersigned by the Secretary of State, and was sometimes referred to as the "passport" or "sea letter" in its own right. Below it was a certification of the captain's oath by the mayor or magistrate of the port; this certificate followed the wording of the "Form of the Sea-Letter" appended to the 1782 Dutch treaty and the sea letters granted by the Confederation Congress to ships bound for the East Indies and China before 1789 (Miller, *Treaties*, ii, 86-7; jcc, xxvi, 58-9). For an example of the less obsequious form of the certificate used between 1789 and the outbreak of war in 1793, see the "sea letter" issued for the ship *Fair American* on 23 Nov. 1791 (printed form with blanks filled in a clerical hand, Mrs. Frank B. Crowninshield, Montchannin, Delaware, 1954; signed by Washington, countersigned by TJ).

Three different forms of this composite document were issued successively. Between 29 Apr. and 14 May 1793 Washington signed a total of 109 passports printed in parallel columns in Dutch and English, but by 10 May he was signing passports in French, Dutch, and English (Washington, *Journal*, 122, 123, 128, 133, 136, 137, 138). At first the Dutch and English forms were printed on one side of the document and the English and French forms on the other. Since the French and Dutch treaties both contained appendices giving the forms to be followed in making out passports, as well as one for sea letters in the Dutch case (Miller, *Treaties*, ii, 28-9, 85-8), this design allowed the language called for in both treaties to be given almost verbatim (passport for schooner *Amazon*, 23 Sep. 1793, printed form with blanks filled in a clerical hand, in NjP: Andre deCoppet Collection; in Dutch and English on one side and English and French on the other; signed by Washington, countersigned by TJ; lacks certificate). See also Syrett, *Hamilton*, xiv, 443-5n, for the text of a Dutch-English part of a complete 18 June 1793 passport of the same type. However, by June 1793 the two-sided passport had been replaced by a single-sided passport containing French, English, and Dutch versions in parallel columns, with the English and Dutch texts following the form given in the Dutch treaty and the French text following that prescribed in the French treaty (passport for brig *Polly*, 24 Aug. 1793, printed form with blanks filled in a clerical hand, in MeB; in parallel columns of French, English, and Dutch; signed by Washington, countersigned by TJ). See also TJ to Gouverneur Morris, 13 June 1793. This format continued into TJ's presidential administration, by which time a fourth column in Spanish had been added in accordance with the Pinckney Treaty of 1795 with Spain (passport for schooner *Lucy*, 14 July 1801, printed form with blanks filled in a clerical hand, in MH; in French, Spanish, English, and Dutch parallel columns; signed by TJ, countersigned by James Madison). See also Miller, *Treaties*, ii, 332-4, 339-43.

Memorial from George Hammond

The undersigned, his Britannic Majesty's Minister Plenipotentiary
to the United States of America, requests permission to recall to the
attention of the Secretary of State the memorial which was presented
to him on the 2nd. curt., relative to the capture of the British Ship
Grange by the French frigate the Embuscade. The subject of that
memorial being merely a question of fact, the Undersigned entertained hopes that the confirmation or contradiction of the testimony
he adduced might have been so easily procured as to have enabled the
executive government of the United States before this time to have
formed some determination upon it. But having been disappointed
in these hopes, he ventures to indulge the expectation that the delay
may not be of much longer duration, and that he may receive an early
answer on a matter, in which he cannot but conceive the two countries
deeply interested. Indeed he trusts that this renewal of his solicitation
cannot be regarded as too importunate, when it is considered that
a British ship has been a week in the harbour of Philadelphia in a
state of arrest and detention under a capture, which he presumes to
be illegal, and in consequence of which a number of his Majesty's
subjects remain in a condition of rigorous and unjust confinement.
The undersigned is farther impelled to desire as speedy an answer
as may be convenient by the consideration of his great anxiety to
transmit to the King's government in England the final resolution
of the executive government of the United States on this important
point—on the decision of which is to rest the degree of future security
and protection, which vessels belonging to the subjects, of the King
his Master and of the other powers now engaged in war with France,
may expect to receive in the ports and harbours of the United States.
Philadelphia   GEO. HAMMOND
    8th May 1793.

RC (DNA: RG 59, NL); in the hand of
Edward Thornton, signed by Hammond;
at foot of first page: "The Secretary of
State"; endorsed by TJ as received 8 May
1793 and so recorded in SJL. FC (Lb
in PRO: FO 116/3). Tr (same, 115/2).
Tr (same, 5/1). Tr (Lb in DNA: RG 59,
NL).

TJ laid this and the following three
memorials from Hammond before the
President on 8 May. Washington the following day directed TJ to submit the
present memorial, together with the 8
May letter TJ received from Jean Baptiste Ternant on the subject of the Grange,
to Attorney General Edmund Randolph
for his opinion, and to lay the other
three memorials before the heads of the
departments and the Attorney General
and report to him "their opinions thereon" (Washington, Journal, 131, 132). For
the outcome of the Cabinet's deliberations,
see TJ to Hammond, and TJ to Ternant,
both 15 May 1793. The memorials are
printed here in the order TJ entered them
in SJL.

Memorial from George Hammond, with Jefferson's Notes

The Undersigned, his Britannic Majesty's Minister Plenipotentiary to the United States of America, has the honor of representing to the Secretary of State that he has received information from various respectable quarters that a considerable quantity of arms and military accoutrements, which an agent of the French government has collected and purchased in this country, is now preparing to be exported from New York to France.

The secrecy, with which a transaction of this nature is generally conducted, has rendered it impossible for the Undersigned to procure precise proof of it. Entertaining however no doubt of the existence of the fact, he esteems it his duty to lay it immediately before the executive government of the United States, which he trusts will deem it more expedient (if any measures for the purpose can be devised) to prevent the execution of this contravention of the President's proclamation than to expose vessels belonging to its citizens to those dangers and difficulties which may result from the circumstance of their carrying articles of the description above mentioned.

Philadelphia   GEO. HAMMOND
8th May 1793.

[*Notes by TJ:*]

expressions of our desire that no aids of arms or other contreband
        goods should be furnished by our citizens

but that such are the difficulties of interfering that we must leave it on

H. and J. pro.
R. reluctant
K. contre
    the footing of the L. of nations, by abandoning private adventurers to the external penalty, and at the same time, that all the belligerent parties shall have equal liberties on this subject.

disdain responsibility for acts of citizens
government has reported in proclamation it's abandonment of individuals

RC (DNA: RG 59, NL); in the hand of Edward Thornton, signed by Hammond; at foot of first page: "The Secretary of State"; with subjoined penciled notes by TJ; endorsed by TJ as received 8 May 1793 and so recorded in SJL. FC (Lb in PRO: FO 116/3). Tr (same, 115/2). Tr (same, 5/1). PrC of Tr (DLC); in the hand of George Taylor, Jr. PrC of

Tr (DNA: RG 59, MD); in Taylor's hand. Tr (Lb in same, NL). Tr (DLC: Genet Papers). Tr (same); in French. Tr (AMAE: CPEU, xxxvii); in French. Enclosed in TJ to Jean Baptiste Ternant, 15 May 1793, TJ to Gouverneur Morris, 13 June 1793, and TJ to Thomas Pinckney, 14 June 1793.

William Stephens Smith, the son-in-law of Vice President John Adams, was the AGENT OF THE FRENCH GOVERNMENT referred to by Hammond. Sir John Temple, then the British consul general stationed in New York City, had recently informed Hammond that a French agent there was seeking to procure 50,000 stand of arms for France, but Temple identified him as Smith only in a subsequent letter to the British foreign minister (Temple to Hammond, 23 Apr. 1793, to Lord Grenville, 24 Apr. 1793, PRO: FO 5/2). Hammond himself had been aware for some time of Smith's arms-purchasing activities in New York City for the French government (Hammond to Grenville, 7 Mch., 2 Apr. 1793, same, 5/1). In writing the above memorial to TJ, as Hammond subsequently explained to the British foreign minister, "I was well aware that it could not operate to the prevention of these arms from being exported, but I judged it proper to obtain from this government a formal and explicit assurance that it would not protect its citizens in these proceedings: And I further thought that the knowledge of the circumstance of my having communicated the fact might induce the persons concerned in the pro-

ject, if not to abandon it, at least perhaps to postpone its execution" (same to same, 17 May 1793, same). For the outcome of Hammond's complaint, see TJ to Hammond, and TJ to Jean Baptiste Ternant, both 15 May 1793.

TJ's subjoined notes consisted of points to be included in the sections of his 15 May 1793 letters to Hammond and Ternant on the official attitude of the United States government toward arms purchases by American citizens for a belligerent power. Internal evidence clearly shows that the Cabinet considered the issues recorded in these notes during its deliberations on the drafts of the letters to the British and French ministers, which apparently took place between 13 and 15 May 1793. Hammond himself, who was regularly informed of Cabinet proceedings by Secretary of the Treasury Alexander Hamilton, claimed that the Cabinet pondered TJ's letter to him for three days, and other evidence suggests that two of these meetings took place on 14 and 15 May 1793 (Hammond to Grenville, 17 May 1793, PRO: FO 5/1; Henry Knox to Washington, 16 May 1793, DLC: Washington Papers; Washington, *Journal*, 132, 137).

Memorial from George Hammond, with Jefferson's Notes

The Undersigned, his Britannic Majesty's Minister Plenipotentiary to the United States of America, has the honor of submitting to the consideration of the Secretary of State the following information which he has received from his Majesty's Consul at Charleston South Carolina.

On the 22nd. ulto. the two brigantines the Four Brothers and the Morning Star, belonging to subjects of his Majesty, and which had been previously captured by the French frigate the Embuscade, were condemned as legal prizes by Mr. Mangourit the French Consul at Charleston, and, under his authority, together with their cargoes exposed to sale.

The Undersigned is advised that this judicial act of the French Consul at Charleston is not warranted by the usage of nations or by the stipulations of any existing treaties between the United States and France, and may lead to the most dangerous consequences. The undersigned therefore presumes to hope that, if his opinion should be so fortunate as to receive the sanction of the executive government of the United States, the latter will adopt such means as to its wisdom may seem best adapted to the purpose of preventing similar exertions of illegal authority on the part of the French Consuls resident within the territory of the United States.

Philadelphia   GEO. HAMMOND
8th May 1793.

[*Notes by TJ:*]
The adjudication a nullity as to title
write to Fr. Min. that it is unwarrantable to decide between Fr. and Eng. parties

RC (DNA: RG 59, NL); in the hand of Edward Thornton, signed by Hammond; at foot of first page: "The Secretary of State"; with subjoined penciled notes by TJ; endorsed by TJ as received 8 May 1793 and so recorded in SJL. FC (Lb in PRO: FO 116/3). Tr (same, 115/2). Tr (same, 5/1). PrC of Tr (DLC); in the hand of George Taylor, Jr. PrC of Tr (DNA: RG 59, MD); in Taylor's hand. Tr (Lb in same, NL). Tr (DLC: Genet Papers). Tr (same); in French. Tr (AMAE: CPEU, xxxvii); in French. Enclosed in TJ to Jean Baptiste Ternant, 15 May 1793, TJ to Gouverneur Morris, 13 June 1793, and TJ to Thomas Pinckney, 14 June 1793.

The account that George Miller, the British CONSUL AT CHARLESTON, sent to Hammond of the capture of the TWO BRIGANTINES by the *Embuscade* and their condemnation by a French prize court in Charleston presided over by Michel Ange Bernard de MANGOURIT, the French consul there, has not been found, but Miller included another account of these events in

a 6 May 1793 dispatch to Lord Grenville (PRO: FO 5/2). As Hammond himself noted to the British foreign minister, he was moved to write this memorial "not only by a consideration of the daring and lawless conduct of the French Consul at Charleston, but also by the desire of establishing upon record this sort of proof and admission that the vessels immediately in question had been illegally condemned as prizes" (Hammond to Grenville, 17 May 1793, same, 5/1).

TJ's subjoined notes consisted of points to be included in the sections of his 15 May 1793 letters to Hammond and Jean Baptiste Ternant on the French usurpation of admiralty jurisdiction in Charleston. Although there is no firm evidence indicating that the Cabinet considered these notes, as it did the ones appended to the preceding memorial from the British minister, this possibility cannot be excluded. For a general discussion of the Washington administration's response to the issue raised by Hammond, see Thomas, *Neutrality*, 206-19.

Memorial from George Hammond

The Undersigned, his Britannic Majesty's Minister Plenipotentiary to the United States of America, has the honor of informing the Secretary of State that he has received intelligence from his Majesty's Consul at Charleston South Carolina, that two privateers have been fitted out from that port under French Commissions. They carry six small guns and are navigated by forty or fifty men, who are for the most part citizens of the United States. One of these privateers left the harbour of Charleston on the 18th. ulto., and the other was on the 22nd. ready to depart.

The Undersigned does not deem it necessary to enter into any reasoning upon these facts, as he conceives them to be breaches of that neutrality which the United States profess to observe, and direct contraventions of the proclamation which the President issued upon the 22nd. of last month. Under this impression he doubts not that the executive government of the United States will pursue such measures as to its wisdom may appear the best calculated for repressing such practices in future, and for restoring to their rightful owners any captures which these particular privateers may attempt to bring into any of the ports of the United States.

Philadelphia   GEO. HAMMOND
8th. May 1793.

RC (DNA: RG 59, NL); in the hand of Edward Thornton, signed by Hammond; at foot of first page: "The Secretary of State"; endorsed by TJ as received 8 May 1793 and so recorded in SJL. FC (Lb in PRO: FO 116/3). Tr (same, 115/2). Tr (same, 5/1). PrC of Tr (DLC); in the hand of George Taylor, Jr. PrC of Tr (DNA: RG 59, MD); in Taylor's hand. Tr (Lb in same, NL). Tr (DLC: Genet Papers). Tr (same); in French. Tr (AMAE: CPEU, xxxvii); in French. Enclosed in TJ to William Rawle, 15 May 1793, TJ to Jean Baptiste Ternant, 15 May 1793, TJ to Gouverneur Morris, 13 June 1793, and TJ to Thomas Pinckney, 14 June 1793.

The letter to Hammond with the INTELLIGENCE from George Miller, the British CONSUL AT CHARLESTON, has not been found, but Miller discussed the TWO PRIVATEERS commissioned there by Edmond Charles Genet in a 6 May 1793 dispatch to Lord Grenville (PRO: FO 5/2). The privateers in question were the *Citoyen Genet* and the *Sans Culotte* (Hammond,

"List of British Ships captured on the coast of America," n.d., enclosed in Hammond to Grenville, 17 May 1793, same, 5/1). Hammond deliberately avoided a detailed account of the activities of these privateers in this memorial so that he could "obtain an explanatory answer upon the general principle" of the validity of commissioning French privateers in American ports "rather than such an one as might afterwards have been perverted, as being applicable solely to the particular circumstances of the instances adduced" (Hammond to Grenville, 17 May 1793, same). For the outcome of this approach, see TJ to Hammond, 15 May, 5 June 1793; and TJ to Jean Baptiste Ternant, 15 May 1793. For an informative account of the various privateers commissioned by Genet, see Melvin H. Jackson, "The Consular Privateers; an account of French Privateering in American waters, April to August, 1793," *American Neptune*, XXII (1962), 81-98. See also Thomas, *Neutrality*, 118-59, for a discussion of the Washington administration's response to the problems arising from this practice.

From Henry Lee

SIR   Richmond May 8th. 1793.

I did my self the honor to write to the President of the United States, a few days past relative to the defenceless situation of Norfolk and beg leave now to forward to you, for his information, a copy of a letter received from Colonel Newton.

Your letter of the 26th. of April is come to hand and will be duely regarded. I have the honor to be sir with perfect respect your most ob: sert.   HENRY LEE

RC (DNA: RG 59, MLR); in a clerk's hand, with complimentary close and signature by Lee; endorsed by TJ as received 14 May 1793 and so recorded in SJL. FC (Vi: Executive Letterbook). Enclosure: Thomas Newton, Jr., to Lee, Norfolk, 29 Apr. 1793, stating that Norfolk had no guns mounted nor militia formed and could be taken by a very small armed force; that a few of the twenty six-pound cannon belonging to Virginia and the larger cannon belonging to the United States in his care could be readied quickly if shot were supplied; that instructions were needed because the treaties with France and Holland apparently gave those countries the right to arm vessels and sell prizes in America; and that companies of artillery and light infantry could be immediately raised if commissions were sent (Tr in DNA: RG 59, LGS).

On 15 May 1793 TJ submitted this letter and its enclosure to the President, who returned them without comment the next day. On 21 May he showed the letter to the President again while obtaining his approval for the reply to Lee (Washington, *Journal*, 140, 146; TJ to Lee, 21 May 1793). Governor Lee's letter asking for advice from Washington on THE DEFENCELESS SITUATION OF NORFOLK was dated 2 May 1793 (Vi: Executive Letterbook; see also Washington, *Journal*, 132).

From James Madison

DEAR SIR   Orange May 8th. 1793.

Your last received was of the 28 Apl. The receipt of all the preceeding is verified by the uninterrupted dates of the Gazettes inclosed. I anxiously wish that the reception of Genest may testify what I believe to be the real affections of the people. It is the more desireable as a seasonable plum after the bitter pills which it seems must be administered. Having neither the Treaty nor Law of Nations at hand I form no opinion as to the stipulations of the former, or the precise neutrality defined by the latter. I had always supposed that the terms of the Treaty made some sort of difference, at least as far as would consist with the Law of Nations, between France and Nations not in Treaty, particularly G. Britain. I should still doubt whether the term *impartial* in the Proclamation is not stronger than was necessary, if not than was proper. Peace is no doubt to be preserved at any price that honor and good faith will permit. But it is no less to be considered that the least departure from these will not only be most likely to end in the loss of peace, but is pregnant with every other evil that could happen to us. In explaining our own engagements under the Treaty with France, it would be honorable as well as just to adhere to the sense that would at the time have been put on them. The attempt to shuffle off the Treaty altogether by quibbling on Vattel is equally contemptible for the meanness and folly of it. If a change of Government is an absolution from public engagements, why not from those of a domestic as well as of a foreign nature; and what then becomes of public debts &c &c. In fact, the doctrine would perpetuate every existing Despotism, by involving in a reform of the Government a destruction of the Social pact, an annihilation of property, and a compleat establishment of the State of Nature. What most surprises me is that such a proposition should have been discussed.

Our weather has not been favorable of late, owing more to want of sun, than excess of rain. Vegetation of all sorts even the wheat, nevertheless continues to flourish: and the fruit having no longer any thing to fear from frost, we are sure of good crops of that agreeable article. Yrs. Always & Affy.   Js. Madison Jr.

Will you send me a copy of the little pamphlet advertised under the title of an Examination of the proceedings in the case of the Secy. of the Treasy.?

RC (DLC: Madison Papers); endorsed by TJ as received 16 May 1793 and so recorded in SJL. For the enclosure, not mentioned here, see TJ's reply of 19 May 1793.

To Gouverneur Morris

Dear Sir   Philadelphia May. 8. 1793.

The bearer hereof Doctor Edwards, a citizen of the US. proposing to visit Paris, I take the liberty of presenting him to you as a gentleman of talents, information and worth. He will do ample justice to any attentions you may shew him and merit any services you can render him. His objects being health and information, it is uncertain what stay these may induce him to make in Paris. Should he find them promoted by travelling, you will of course favor him with such documents of protection as the state of things may render necessary for his safety. As it will be some time before he will have the honor of handing you this,

I shall only add assurances of the sincere esteem & respect with which I have the honor to be Dear Sir Your most obedt. & most humble servt   TH: JEFFERSON

PrC (DLC); at foot of text: "Mr. Morris." Tr (DLC); 19th-century copy. Enclosed in TJ to Enoch Edwards, 8 May 1793.

To Thomas Pinckney

DEAR SIR   Philadelphia May. 8. 1793.
  I took the liberty, some short time ago, of putting under cover to you some packets containing copies of official papers which Mr. John Carey had been permitted to take and publish, accompanying them with a request that you would be so good as to deliver them to him particularly, but to no other person should any accident happen to him. I now trouble you with another packet of the same kind and with the same request. It completes what Mr. Carey has prepared, I believe, for present publication. I have the honor to be with great esteem & respect Dear Sir Your friend & servt   TH: JEFFERSON

PrC (DLC); at foot of text: "Mr. Pinckney." Tr (DLC); 19th-century copy. Enclosure not found.

To Edmund Randolph

[8 May 1793]
  I understood Colo. H. yesterday that he should confer again with the President on the subject of our deliberation. As that is not exactly the channel thro' which I would wish my objections to be represented, should the President mention the subject to you, I will thank you to communicate to him this note, or it's substance.

PrC (DLC); undated; unsigned; letter-pressed upside down at foot of TJ to Randolph, 8 May 1793, the document enclosed with it. Internal evidence suggests that the missing RCs of these documents were written on separate sheets.

For the SUBJECT OF OUR DELIBERATION, see Notes on Alexander Hamilton and the Enforcement of Neutrality, 6 May 1793, and note.

To Edmund Randolph

Th:J. to E.R.   May. 8. 1793.

I have been still reflecting on the draught of the letter from the Secretary of the Treasury to the Custom house officers, instructing them to be on the watch as to all infractions or tendencies to infraction of the laws of neutrality by our citizens and to communicate the same to him. When this paper was first communicated to me, tho' the whole of it struck me disagreeably, I did not in the first moment see clearly the improprieties but of the last clause. The more I have reflected, the more objectionable the whole appears.

By this proposal the Collectors of the customs are to be made an established corps of spies or informers against their fellow citizens, whose actions they are to watch in secret, inform against in secret to the Secretary of the Treasury, who is to communicate it to the President. If the action and evidence appear to[1] justify a prosecution, a prosecution is to set on foot on the *secret information of a collector*. If it will not justify it, then the only consequence is that the mind of government has been poisoned against a citizen, neither knowing nor suspecting it, and perhaps too distant to bring forward his justification. This will at least furnish the collector with a convenient weapon to keep down a rival, draw a cloud over an inconvenient censor, or satisfy mere malice and private enmity.

The object of this new institution is to be to prevent infractions of the laws of neutrality, and preserve our peace with foreign nations. Acts involving war, or proceedings which respect foreign nations, seem to belong either to the department of war, or to that which is charged with the affairs of foreign nations. But I cannot possibly conceive how the superintendance of the laws of neutrality, or the preservation of our peace with foreign nations can be ascribed to the department of the treasury, which I suppose to comprehend merely matters of revenue. It would be to add a new and a large feild to a department already amply provided with business, patronage, and influence.—It was urged as a reason, that the collectors of the customs are in convenient positions for this espionage. They are in convenient positions too for building ships of war: but will that business be transplanted from it's department, merely because it can be conveniently done in another?

It seemed the desire that if this means was disapproved, some other equivalent might be adopted.—Tho we considered the acts of a foreigner making a capture within our limits, as an act of public hostility, and therefore to be turned over to the military, rather than the civil

[691]

power; yet the acts of our own citizens infringing the laws of neutrality, or contemplating that, are offences against the ordinary laws and cognisable by them. Grand jurors are the constitutional inquisitors and informers of the country, they are scattered every where, see every thing, see it while they suppose themselves mere private persons, and not with the prejudiced[2] eye of a permanent and systematic spy. Their information is *on oath*, is public,[3] it is in the vicinage of the party charged, and can be at once refuted. These officers taken only[4] occasionally from among the people, are familiar to them, the office respected, and the experience of centuries has shewn that it is safely entrusted with our character, property and liberty. A grand juror cannot carry on systematic persecution against a neighbor whom he hates, because he is not permanent in the office.—The Judges generally, by a charge, instruct the Grand jurors in the infractions of law which are to be noticed by them; and our judges are in the habit of printing their charges in the newspapers. The Judges having notice of the proclamation, will perceive that the occurrence of a foreign war has brought into activity the laws of neutrality, as a part of the law of the land. This new branch of the law they will know needs explanation to the grand juries more than any other. They will study and define the subject to them and to the public. The public mind will by this be warned against the acts which may endanger our peace, and foreign nations will see a much more respectable evidence of our bonâ fide intentions to preserve neutrality, and society will be relieved from the inquietude which must for ever be excited by the knowlege of the existence of such a poison in it as secret accusation. It will be easy to suggest this matter to the attention of the judges, and that alone puts the whole machine into motion. The one is a familiar, impartial and precise instrument, the other, not popular in it's present functions, will be odious in the new ones, and the odium will reach the Executive who will be considered as having planted a germ of private inquisition absolutely unknown to our laws.—I am not quite certain what was considered as agreed upon yesterday.—It cannot be too late however to suggest the substitution of the Judges and grand-jurors in place of the collectors of the customs.

PrC (DLC); dateline added in ink; with covering note letterpressed upside down at foot of text. Enclosed in TJ to Randolph, [8 May 1793].

For the provenance of this document, see note to Notes on Alexander Hamilton and the Enforcement of Neutrality, 6 May 1793.

[1] Preceding two words interlined in place of "will."
[2] Word interlined.
[3] Preceding two words added in margin.
[4] Word interlined.

From Thomas Mann Randolph, Jr.

DEAR SIR   Monticello May 8: 1793.

We returned to Monticello on the evening of the sixth inst. Our journey has only increased our relish for retirement and our fondness for
this charming spot which we quit allways with the greatest reluctance.
Patsy and the children are well. We are unhappy at Maria's indisposition but put much confidence in the strength of her constitution.

Your desire respecting a horse shall be particularly attended to: upon
the first information of your set being broken I began to look out and
soon fixed on one having all the qualities apparently which I knew you
would require. I purchased it immediately but upon trial have reason
to think that it is too delicate for the long journeys you are obliged to
make. I have hopes of meeting with another more fit, shortly.

From the dullness with which the operations you directed to be
performed by your Carpenters were carried on during my absence
altho' I placed them immediately under the command of Clarkson I
think it would be better to employ some industrious white-person
to labor with them and lay off their work for them. It will be of
the greatest advantage to them to be superintended by one who is
a tolerable carpenter as they are more awkward and clumsy than you
can conceive and are really incapable of raising the coarsest building
without some one to direct them in every part of the work. It will
be easy to contrive a mode of compensation for the services of such
a person that will stimulate him to perform any piece of work in
the shortest time and my attention will insure its being well done.
A variety of little jobs will appear in the neighbourhood which may
be done with out any great interference with your business and these
will afford a sum sufficient for the pay of the superintendant. I am
convinced that the gain in the quantity not considering the quality
of the work would be considerable after the deduction of as much as
would discharge the wages of the Overseer. Clarkson is so constantly
occupied in directing the hands employed in agriculture and so totally
ignorant of every thing else that he is of little accompt. I shall not
hezitate to take any step in this matter which it is manifest will advance
your interests but shall be extremely cautious not to enter into any
engagements which may not be dissolved, without giving umbrage,
immediately upon your intimating your dislike.

Clarkson goes on very well with the crop: the wheat is remarkably
fine and the quantity great enough to make it worth your while to
procure the new threshing machine immediately. Your most sincere
and aff: friend   TH: M. RANDOLPH

RC (MHi); endorsed by TJ as received 18 May 1793 and so recorded in SJL.

The Randolphs RETURNED TO MONTICELLO after Martha Jefferson Randolph testified on 29 Apr. 1793 at a Cumberland County call court which was considering a charge of infanticide against Richard Randolph (see note to TJ to Martha Jefferson Randolph, 28 Apr. 1793).

From Jean Baptiste Ternant

Philadelphie 8 May 1793 l'an 2 de la République française

J'ai reçu hier au soir votre lettre du 7e. concernant la prise contestée qui a fait le sujet de votre précédente du 3. Dès que cette première lettre m'est parvenue, j'en ai sur le champ, donné communication officielle au Consul général de notre République, en le chargeant d'en informer aussitôt le Commandant de l'Embuscade, et de m'adresser le plus promptement possible les témoignages et observations nécessaires, pour me mettre en état de repondre au Gouvernement des Etats unis. Cette marche est de devoir strict pour moi. Le Consul général, quoique pressé d'accélerer son examen, ne m'en a pas encore fait parvenir le résultat. Je viens de le lui demander de nouveau: et si je l'obtiens aujourd'hui, comme j'en ai le plus vif désir, j'aurai l'honneur de vous l'adresser sur le champ. Soyez persuadé que je sens trop les inconveniens du délay, pour ne pas mettre tout mon zèle à l'abréger. Au reste, la Conduite franche et loyale du Citoyen Bompard en amenant ici le Grange, doit vous être un Sûr garant qu'il ne disposera de cette prise, que quand elle aura été décidément prononcée bonne et valide.

S. TERNANT

Tr (AMAE: CPEU, xxxvii); at head of text: "Le Ministre plénipotentiaire français au sécrétaire d'Etat des Etats unis." Tr (DLC: Genet Papers); in

English. Recorded in SJL as received 8 May 1793.

TJ submitted this letter to the President this day (Washington, *Journal*, 131).

From Mary Barclay

SIR The Retreat 9 May 1793

You have heard of the irreparable loss I and my family have Sustained. Your friendship to me formerly emboldens me to trouble you at this time. In a letter I lately received from Coln. Humphreys he advises me to make application to you, that the person who should be authorised to take possession of the public property that was in

Mr. Barclays charge, may be directed to deliver his private effects to the order of the person or persons empowerd to receive them. John Barclay Esqr. of Philadelphia is the person to whom I would wish Mr. Barclays private effects to be sent, and your giving directions that they may be delivered to his order will add to the obligations, confer'd on me by your attentions to myself and family in France, and with them will be ever gratefully acknowledged by Sir your most obedt humble Servant   MARY BARCLAY

RC (DLC); endorsed by TJ as received 17 May 1793 and so recorded in SJL.

From Tench Coxe

May 9th. 1793

Mr. Coxe has the honor to transmit the foregoing to the Secretary of State. He forgot to mention this morning that he had written particularly to Mr. Seton on the Subject communicated by the Secretary yesterday noon.

RC (DLC); subjoined to enclosure; endorsed by TJ as received 9 May 1793 and so recorded in SJL. Enclosure: Vincent Gray, the Deputy Collector of Customs at Alexandria, Virginia, to Coxe, 6 May 1793, acknowledging receipt of his 2 May letter with its enclosures and requesting him to send about ten or fifteen more as soon as possible, as some may be needed even before they can arrive (Tr in DLC).

The FOREGOING letter from Gray was a response to Coxe's circular letter transmitting six sea letters to each of certain customs collectors (see note to Coxe to TJ, 4 May 1793). For the object of Coxe's letter to William SETON, see Coxe to TJ, [11 May 1793], and note.

From Alexander Hamilton

SIR   Treasury Department May 9. 1793

I have this moment received your Letter of yesterday.

It appears to me, as it does to you, that the position of the Collectors of the Customs will render them the most convenient channel of distribution for the Passports; nor do I perceive, that it can interfere with their other duties.

It will be equally agreeable to me, that they be transmitted either directly from your office, or through this department. If you prefer the latter, which I shall with pleasure facilitate, I will request you to cause them to be sent in the first instance to me . . . when I will put them in the usual course of conveyance. With great respect I have the honor to be Sir Your obedient servant   ALEXANDER HAMILTON

P.S. Inclosed is the copy of a letter from the Collector of New York to Mr. Coxe of the 7th instant, which is transmitted for your consideration.

RC (DLC: Madison Papers); ellipsis in original; at foot of text: "The Secretary of State"; endorsed by TJ as received 9 May 1793 and so recorded in SJL. Enclosure: John Lamb to Tench Coxe, New York, 7 May 1793, acknowledging Coxe's letter of 2 May 1793 transmitting ten sea letters for American vessels, asking for a further supply as soon as possible for the great number of such vessels about to sail, and passing on the inquiry of merchants

here as to whether they will receive "similar papers to prevent their vessels from being carried into the ports of the other belligerent powers" (Tr in DLC).

On this day Tench Coxe transmitted another copy of the enclosure to TJ directly (RC in DLC; subjoined to Tr of Lamb to Coxe, 7 May 1793; in Coxe's hand; endorsed by TJ as received 9 May 1793 and so recorded in SJL).

From James Monroe

DEAR SIR   Fredericksburgh May 9th.[1] 1793.

I came here a few days past to attend the district court and shall leave this place on the 10th. for the chy. in Richmond which commences on the 12. In Charlottesville in the case of Barrett the verdict and judgment were against you, deducting the interest as you had proposed during the war. He had no proof except that of Colo. Lewis to establish his claim (at the trial). Upon confering with this latter gentleman I found he had an imperfect recollection of what had passed between him and Barrett, whether he had refused to pay him the whole interest, as well during as since the war, and upon shewing him the paper containing your instruction, and upon which his proposition must have been founded, he expressed a wish it might be shewn the court and jury in the trial, as he could not say he had made any other proposal, and the presumption would then be satisfactory that he had not. To this I agreed. Upon the trial I took the opinion of the court whether, without my consent they could avail themselves of Colo. Lewis's evidence, he being your trustee—which was that they could not. I then admitted it with an assurance to the court and jury, that if the claim could in any mode be established it would be allowed. Colo. Lewis referred to the paper in my possession and which I then producd, making it a point whether that paper amounted to an assumpsit, being only a conditional proposition, with an absolute declaration you did not believe the debt was due. Tucker

[696]

was of opinion it was no assumpsit. Roane doubted, but both were of opinion it might go to the jury—and their verdict was founded upon your apparent willingness to pay it under certain modifications, which were regarded in it. I moved the court for a new trial as against evidence, and it lay over till the next day. Then Roane had left the bench for the residue of the term. Finding that if the verdict had been in your favor, you were resolved to pay the money, in case Barrett would prove his account, by affidavit only, and he upon conference assuring me that he would not only do it in that mode[2] but by some orders, he was well assured you had forgotten, I saw no benefit resulting from a success in the motion for a new trial[3] especially as in any event you would be forced to pay the costs of the proceeding. I then proposed to Barrett that if he would permit me to state to the court that if he had known the real contents of your instruction to Colo. Lewis (for he declared that Colo. Lewis had refused to pay any interest) he never would have brought suit against you, but waited your accomodation, I would withdraw the motion, and to which he agreed—observing further that he knew nothing of the transaction about [Sheys?] bond untill after the suit was over—that it was bought up by a brother of his, suit brought, and every operation conducted by his brother and absolutely without his knowledge. I accordingly stated the affair as above agreed and withdrew the motion. Barrett said he would wait till the fall for the money but expected interest of which I informed him I would advise you. Of your other business I will write you from Richmond.

In my rout I scarcely find a man unfriendly to the French revolution as now modified. Many regret the unhappy fate of the Marq: of Fayette, and likewise the execution of the king. But they seem to consider these events as incidents to a much greater one, and which they wish to see accomplished. The sphere of the opposit policy may be considered (exclusive of the tory interest of the Late war) as confined to Alexa., a city which certainly comprehends no enlightened man, and Richmond. At the bar here two gentlemen only are in this sentiment, Chs. Lee and Bushrod Washington, the former of Alexa. and the latter Richmd.—and tis manifest that their opposition to the general sentiment of their country, is not confined to the principles of the French revolution only, but extends to the general policy of the representation in Congress, and particularly the late proceedings and enquiries respecting the use and application of the publick monies. It was declared by the former, and in a manner that shewed it was no recent conception, that Mr. Madison in stating[4] the disobedience of the Secry. of that department to the orders of the President, had placed the merits of the controversy on an improper footing. Col: Mercer, who conducted the argument against him, affirmed the contrary, with other declarations expressive of the strongest disapprobation of his conduct and distrust of his rectitude.

I left Mrs. M. in Alb: not well recovered from the fatigue of the journey but in other respects tolerably well. Mr. R. and family were and had been absent since our return—Gilmer and others well. You have probably heard of a charge of a very heinous kind against R. Rand.; and that before the examining court he was acquitted 12. to 2. of the magistrates in his favor, and upon the question for his enlargement. The accounts here are universally in his favor, and seem to have removed impressions that were before deeply fixed. Very affectionately I am yr. friend & servant JAS. MONROE

PS. I have not received a line from any person there since I left Phila.

RC (DLC); illegible word conjectured; endorsed by TJ as a letter of 8 May 1793 received 14 May 1793 and so recorded in SJL.

CHY.: the Virginia High Court of Chancery. The details of the case are lacking, but THE CASE OF BARRETT, probably the Richmond merchant and sometime mayor John Barret, involved a disputed debt over which TJ had been sued. The action wounded TJ's pride, and his primary goal in contesting the case was to demonstrate that Barret had had recourse to the law unnecessarily without first seeking relief through arbitration or other extralegal means (TJ to Nicholas Lewis, 7 Mch. 1790; TJ to Monroe, 16 Sep. 1792, 4 June 1793; Monroe to TJ, 27 June, 23 July 1793; Marshall, *Papers*, I,

356). A letter from TJ to John Barret of 29 Sep. 1794, recorded in SJL, has not been found; nor has Barret's response of 11 Oct. 1794, recorded in SJL as received 21 Oct. 1794.

The occasion for which James Madison was faulted for STATING THE DISOBEDIENCE of Alexander Hamilton TO THE ORDERS OF THE PRESIDENT was his speech in the House of Representatives on 1 Mch. 1793 in support of resolutions censuring the Secretary of the Treasury (Madison, *Papers*, XIV, 455-69).

[1] Digit reworked from "3."
[2] Preceding three words interlined.
[3] Remainder of sentence interlined.
[4] Word interlined in place of "observing."

From William Vans Murray

DEAR SIR   Cambridge. E.S. Maryland 9th. May 1793.

As it is not improbable that either the French minister, or Some one of the ministers of the Combined powers may apply to you on a transaction which took place in this District, yesterday, you will I am Sure excuse me in this trouble.

A Prize, taken from the British, by a French Privateer, lately a packet from this town, was sent up the Choptank, within the District of the port of Oxford, a few days since. The Custom house officer, Col.

Banning called on me for my advice and the construction of the 17th. article of the Commercial Treaty. Hearing that the prize was then commanded by a citizen of Maryland, of this county, and considering the Rights of Neutrality I advised the Naval officer to detain the prize, provided No *commissioned officer* could "show his commission" which by the article 17th. he is bound to do—and that only.

On going on board the prize (a large Schooner) Capt. John Hooper was in possession of her and show'd a written paper in French, purporting to be a copy of a Commission to a Capt. Ferey a french citizen from the Executive Council of the French Republic. This copy was by way of recital, no name that I remember of any of the Executive Council—and then follow'd his orders to Hooper to carry in the prize to any port of the US.—(So on my memory.) This the Officer did not think a sufficient commission even had it been in the hands of a French Citizen, much less so in the hands of a Citizen of Maryland—and seized the Vessel as deficient in papers—and having been three or four days in port without entering. This accorded really with my own ideas of the duties of good faith under the rights of Neutral States—supposing that if Mr. Hooper had even had a commission from the French Republic or any of its agents, authorised, the Commission would be divested of its powers and rights under the 17th: article the moment that he a citizen came within the reach or operation of the rights of Dominion of the U.S.

If the U.S. are to join, the Government must say so—till that however, as a citizen I thought myself bound to aid the discharge of Neutral duties.

As to my wishes—my affections and my whole Soul are devoted to the success of the French Republic and the establishment of their Republican Government.

By possessing you as early as possible of some of the particulars of this business I thought you might without much delay see the ground on which any complaint would stand on either side. Hooper is said to be a holder of an 8th. of the privateer—Capt. Tucker commanded the prize when taken.† I am Dear Sir with every Sentiment of Sincere respect & esteem yr. mo. obt.   W. V. MURRAY

†She was from New Providence, bound for Philada.

RC (ViW: Tucker-Coleman Collection); addressed: "The Honble Thomas Jefferson Esqre. Secretary of State. Philadelphia"; postmarked; endorsed by TJ as received 15 May 1793 and so recorded in SJL.

On 15 May 1793 TJ submitted this letter to the President, who returned it without comment the next day (Washington, *Journal*, 140). A day before writing TJ, Murray, a Federalist congressman from Maryland, sent Alexander Hamilton a fuller account of the events surrounding the detention by Jeremiah BANNING, collector of customs for the Oxford district on Maryland's Eastern Shore, of the LARGE SCHOONER *Eunice*, a prize of the FRENCH PRIVATEER *Sans Culotte*, which had been commissioned at Charleston by Edmond Charles Genet (Syrett, *Hamilton*, XIV, 425-8; JEP, I, 14).

From Edmund Randolph

E.R. TO MR. J.   Philadelphia May 9. 1793.

I cannot suffer my engagements in business, to interfere with a reply to the observations, with which you favored me, on the proposed letter to the collectors. For while I shall support, within my limited sphere, every just energy of government; I am solicitous, that my friends should ever believe, that I do support it, because it contributes to the essence of republicanism, and our fœderal safety.

You recollect, that I was on the point of making Your very objection, as deserving consideration, when you mentioned it. It was impossible not to have heard, that the revenue-officers have been suspected to be a corps, trained to the arts of spies, in the service of the Treasury. Awake as I was to this conjecture, I wished not only to guard against the practice, but to submit it to an accurate inquiry.

I accordingly[1] asked Colo. H. whether his correspondence has[2] at any time been directed to the prying into the conduct of individuals, or even an inspection over the legislatures. He solemnly appealed to his letter-books for a proof of the negative.

Viewing then his draught, as[3] unconnected with past suspicions, I could discover nothing, opposed to my judgment.

Was there ever a government, which hesitated to gather information from its *executive* officers? If their duties are defined; still it may reasonably be expected, that they will readily transmit *general* intelligence to the fountain head. A refusal might not be the ground of an impeachment; but under the strictest[4] constitution it would be deemed an indecorum, unless public duties absorbed too much of their time. In truth, when I consider, that government cannot proceed blindfold; that it must proceed blindfold in general cases,[5] if it does not retain[6] intelligencers, catch flying reports, or correspond with persons of confidence, and that of these three expedients, the last[7] is intitled to a preference; a letter to almost every officer in the U.S. would scarcely be censurable, if it promised to be effectual.

But it is thought best to waive so universal an instruction, and select those, who are most capable of furnishing the desired information. What is this desired information? The U.S., conscious of their love of neutrality, are anxious to afford proofs, by deeds as well as words. They have reason to suppose, that the preponderance of affection in the people towards[8] the French will subject the conduct of government to harsh constructions. The natural remedy against such a mischief is to watch the violations of neutrality, to punish them, and, if necessary, to provide further legislative arrangements. In this last object, the collectors are, from their position near the water, the scene of those violations, best qualified to assist congress. To stop here would at least be innocent; but more probably[9] useful.

Why too, may not the collectors be requested, to represent any unlawful actions, which fall more immediately under their notice, to the district attornies? It is the right, nay duty of every citizen to enforce the laws. This has been the constant opinion of governments in most proclamations, which call upon the officers at large to cooperate in bringing offenders to[10] justice. It would be a vain pretence, and wholly unsatisfactory to the warring powers, to make a request of the kind to all officers so as to comprehend the very excise officers[11] on the top of the Allegany. But it is direct and wears the aspect of fidelity, to point the attention of those, who are most likely to know the facts, to the communication of them to the efficient authority.

You ask, why this class of offences may not be left to the usual course of offences? They will not be wrested from the usual course. For as a collector might always inform the attorney, consistently with law, without being required to do so; the stimulus to his vigilance would be no otherwise different, than to infuse a warmer[12] incentive, unknown to the cold duty[13] of a private citizen. As soon as the Attorney possesses the case, the grandjury, judges, and rest of the judicial apparatus, which I esteem with you, as bulwarks, will[14] travel in the work according to the forms, which you have delineated.

It is true, that the original draught proposed, that a report should be made to the Secretary of the treasury. But this was agreed to be[15] erased upon my suggestion; so that the intercourse was confined to the attorney alone. This correction goes very far into your main objection.

The impropriety of the treasury-department, entering into this business, was so slightly hinted by you during the consultation, that it did not pass thro' any discussion in my mind. It is a misfortune, that the line of partition is not always obvious between the different departments. In this particular instance,[16] the correspondence, as being relative to infractions of law, committed by our own citizens, might seem to devolve on the *domestic*[17] branch of the department of state; or, as relative to the violation of the rights of[18] foreign nations, on the *foreign* branch of the department of state; or, as being directed to the collectors, to whom the secretary daily writes, was barely important enough to be turned out of that channel.[19] At the same time, it will be better, I believe, that on those occasions, which do not *evidently* belong to one department rather than another, the President should specially[20] instruct, whom he pleases; and that the letters should express, that they are written by his direction.

RC (DLC); endorsed by TJ as received 10 May 1793 and so recorded in SJL.

For the provenance of this document, see Notes on Alexander Hamilton and the Enforcement of Neutrality, 6 May 1793, and note.

[1] Randolph here canceled "inquire."
[2] Randolph here canceled "ever."
[3] Randolph here canceled "uninfluenced."
[4] Randolph here canceled "form."
[5] Preceding three words interlined.
[6] Randolph here canceled what appears to be "to furnish."
[7] Randolph here canceled "will."
[8] Preceding three words interlined in place of "favor of."

[9] Randolph here canceled "serviceable."
[10] Randolph here canceled "punishment."
[11] Randolph first wrote "to such a description of officers, as may comprehend the excise officers" and then altered the passage to read as above.
[12] Word interlined in place of "stronger."
[13] Word altered from "duties."
[14] Word interlined.
[15] Preceding three words interlined.
[16] Randolph here canceled "on the one hand."
[17] Word interlined in place of "*home.*"
[18] Randolph here canceled "neutrals."
[19] Preceding six words interlined in place of canceled and illegible phrase.
[20] Word interlined.

From Jean Baptiste Ternant

Philadelphie 9 May 1793. l'an 2 de la République française
J'ai l'honneur de vous adresser cy jointe une copie du rapport que le Consul général de notre République vient de me remettre concernant la prise et la réclamation du navire Anglois le Grange. Si ce rapport qui contient l'exposition des principes et des raisons que j'ai à faire valoir vous laisse encore quelques éclaircissemens à désirer, je m'empresserai de les donner dans une conférence particuliére, à l'heure que vous voudrez bien m'indiquer. Mon Successeur étant journellement attendu, et ayant lieu de croire qu'il sera muni d'instructions applicables au cas dont il s agit, il me reste à vous prier de n'y Statuer définitivement qu'après son arrivée dans cette residence.

Signé TERNANT

Tr (AMAE: CPEU, xxxvii); at head of text: "Le Ministre plenipotentiaire de france au secretaire d'Etat des Etats unis." Tr (DLC: Genet Papers); in English. Recorded in SJL as received 9 May 1793.

TJ submitted this letter and enclosure on this date to the President, who instructed him to submit them to the Attorney General for an opinion (Washington, *Journal*, 132).

La Forest's Report on the *Grange*

[ca. 9 May 1793]

Le Consul général au Ministre plénipotentiaire de la République française près les Etats unis.

J'ai reçu et je m'empresse de vous remettre les papiers que vous avez bien voulu m'envoyer avec votre lettre du 3 de ce mois. J'en ai donné communication au Citoyen Bompard commandant l'Embuscade. Le Batiment Anglois le Grange, son equipage et Sa Cargaison resteront dans ce port, conformément à la demande du sécrétaire d'Etat des Etats unis, en attendant décision ultérieure, et il ne Sera rien changé à Sa situation présente.

Le Citoyen Bompard a pris le Grange, dans la ferme persuasion que ce batiment n'étoit plus sous la protection d'un territoire neutre. Il pouvoit l'envoyer en france, ou dans les Colonies, et rien ne prouve mieux sa confiance dans l'impartialité du Gouvernement americain, que la bonne foi avec laquelle il a fait remonter sa prise à Philadelphie.

Le Ministre plénipotentiaire de la Cour de Londres reclame le Grange, dans la Supposition que ce batiment a été pris dans l'étendue *du territoire* de la Jurisdiction des Etats unis. J'ai comparé les dépositions Sur lesquelles il se fonde avec les procès verbaux produits par le Citoyen Bompard. Je n'y vois aucune différence materielle quant aux faits. Le Capitaine de l'Embuscade admet que le Batiment Anglois a été pris à l'ancre ayant encore un pilote à Bord, étant à un mille à peu près dans l'ouest de la Bouée du banc de Sable appellé *le Brown*. Le Cap James restant au Sud 4 dégrès est distant de quatre lieues 10 parties environ, le Cap May restant à l'Est 3 dégrès sud distant de 5 lieues environ, la terre la plus proche étant le point appellé *Draper's inlet* distant d'environ 3 lieues. Il s'agit donc d'appliquer les principes aux faits reconnus par les deux parties, et rien n'empêche que la question ne puisse être bientôt déterminée.

J'observerai avant tout, qu'il faut établir le Sens des mots *territoire* et *jurisdiction* qui sont liés ensemble dans la reclamation du Ministre plénipotentiaire Britannique. La jurisdiction de tout état Maritime S'étend très loin. Elle prend connoissance par exemple des délits commis en haute mer à bord d'un batiment Marchand quelconque et à quelque distance que ce soit, dès que ce que ce batiment entre dans les limites du territoire. Ce genre de jurisdiction est étranger au Sujet. Le mot jurisdiction même s'y trouve mélé mal à propos, il dénature l'idée à laquelle Seule on doit S'attacher. La question se réduit en effet à Savoir Si le Grange étoit encore Sous la protection d'un *territoire neutre* à l'endroit où il a été pris.

Plusieurs puissances ont manifesté des prétentions exagérées sur l'étendue de leur domination maritime: Presque toutes ont eu dans le cours des guerres Européennes, occasion de S'expliquer sur la ligne neutre de leurs côtes. À la verité, ces actes particuliers d'un souverain n'obligent les autres qu'autant qu'ils veulent bien les reconnoître. Mais leur effet est d'indiquer l'intention du souverain et les égards qu'il attend des nations belligerantes; leur effet est encore au moins une base pour Statuer sur les reclamations respectives de ces nations, dans les cas semblables à celui du Grange. J'ai cherché inutilement dans les journaux du Congrès sous le régime fédéral et dans les actes des Etats unis sous le Gouvernement consolidé, l'expression de quelqu'opinion

Sur la limite des côtes et Sur le fait des prises. Tout ce que je trouve, c'est des resolutions nombreuses, qui prononcent bonne prise [un] batiment pris en pleine mer, où sur les côtes *entre le plus haut et le plus bas point des marées*, ai[nsi que] la recommandation aux batimens armés des Etats unis de s abstenir de capturer les vaisseaux ennemis Sous *la protection des côtes neutres*. Les Etats unis n'ont donc prononcé aucune intention particuliére pour l'information des puissances disposées autant que la République française à faciliter leur neutralité. Ils paroissent s'en rapporter aux principes du droit des gens.

Ces principes sont, que tout espace de mer qui est à portée du Canon le long des côtes, est regardé comme faisant partie du territoire; que toutes les eaux Salées qui ne sont point *eaux closes*, ne peuvent être regardées que comme des extensions de mer; que les eaux Salées communiquant avec la mer peuvent être appellées *Eaux closes*, Si les deux caps qui les terminent sont assèz rapprochés pour en défendre l'entrée; que la neutralité des rivages qui bordent les eaux de la mer, ne s'étend pas au delà de la portée du Canon. Plusieurs traités récens particularisent la généralité de ces principes, les font entrer dans le droit public des puissances contractantes, les rendent obligatoires pours elles à double titre et donnent à cet égard un excellent exemple aux autres puissances. Par l'article 12 du traité de commerce entre la france et la Grande Brétagne du 26 Septembre 1786, les deux pays S'engagent à ne pas souffrir que sur leurs côtes *à la portée du canon* les batimens respectifs Soient pris par un ennemi. Par l'article XXVIII du traité de navigation et de commerce entre la france et la Russie du 11 Janvier 1787 chacune des deux parties contractantes promet 1°. de n'attaquer jamais les vaisseaux ennemis que hors *de la portée du canon des côtes* de son allié; 2°. d'observer la plus parfaite neutralité dans les ports, havres et autres eaux comprises *sous le nom d'eaux closes*.

Il resulte de l'application de ces principes aux faits admis concernant la prise du Grange 1°. que ce batiment étoit à 3 lieues de la terre la plus voisine et par conséquent hors de la portée du canon et de toute protection du territoire, 2°. que la Baye de Delaware large de 21 milles à l'entrée des caps, bientôt après, large de 30 milles, et dans laquelle se vuident les eaux de la rivierre du même nom à Bacon's neck et Bombay hook, ne peut entrer dans la classe des Eaux closes; 3°. que la Baye, longue d'environ 38 milles ne présentant à Son entrée, ni dans aucun des points de sa prolongation aucun signe de neutralité qui puisse indiquer la volonté des Etats unis, laisse un libre accès aux vaisseaux des puissances belligerantes, 4°. Que le batiment anglois le Grange, a donc pu être pris par la frégate l'Embuscade dans la Situation cy dessus décrite.

On pourra objecter que la Boüée établie sur le bas fond dit le Brown, à un mille de laquelle le Grange étoit mouillé, indique une occupation territoriale mais on voit sur différentes côtes des Boüées établies jusqu'à 20 lieues au large pour la Sureté de la navigation: Ces boüées sont un bienfait, et non point un Signe d'occupation.

On pourra objecter qu'un fond couvert de 13 brasses d'eau Seulement, tel que celui ou le Grange étoit mouillé, est une annexe de territoire. Mais sans S'éloigner des côtes des Etats unis, ne voit-on pas des bas fonds s'étendre à une grande distance des terres? Dès qu'un fond est couvert d'eau c'est sa distance de la terre la plus voisine, et non point le produit de la sonde qui détermine la position neutre.

On pourra objecter que le Grange avoit encore Son pilote à Bord: Mais on

Sait qu'il est beaucoup de Bayes, de Golphes, et meme des côtes d'ailleurs peu Sinueuses, où les bancs de Sable sont tellement multipliés, qu'un pilote est obligé de mener un batiment très loin en haute mer, avant de pouvoir l'abandonner aux soins du Capitaine. Jamais l'étendüe nécessaire du pilotage n'a prolongé la protection d'une côte neutre.

Telles sont Citoyen Ministre plénipotentiaire les observations qu'il étoit de mon devoir de mettre sous vos yeux pour que vous puissiez faire au Gouvernement des Etats unis la reponse que vous jugerez convenable. Je crois qu'il est heureux, que cette question se soit élévée dès le commencement des hostilités. Elle donnera lieu à des explications et à des mesures utiles dans toute neutralité.

Signé DELAFOREST

Tr (AMAE: CPEU, xxxvii); undated; faded; at head of text: "Rapport du Consul général."

From Robert Gamble

SIR Richmond May 10th. 1793

A subject of considerable importance to myself as an individual, and probably to our part of Virginia, has been proposed to me to day, by Monsr. Genet, The French Ambassador now on his way to Philadelphia.

In consequence of Governor Lee, introducing me to *him*, as a fit person to act as Agent, in this State, to purchase Flour, and other supplies for France—Monsr. Genet has taken in writing from me an Estimate of the quantity of Flour on hand on this River, Alexandria &c. But as he can make no decision until he arives with you—He can only Say that I Shall be on the same footing as to compensation say, Commission &c. as others he may appoint.

As our intercourse with France is in a manner not begun, and the War in Europe wholly prevents negociations thro' our British Correspondents, as usual to that Country, for Supplies we might send to the French Republic—Add to this every Measure, that can be adopted by Certain Characters *influential in the Commercial line*, will be used to Counteract my efforts to make purchases, (I being a Virginian,)—and also refuse Mr. Genets Bills should he have no other Resource but drafts on the French Government.

Therefore, should it Coincide, with the disposition, and appropriations made by the American Government to pay any part of the debt we owe to France in the produce of our Country So much wanted by them, Treasury drafts on the Collectors—or Loan officer of this state, will enable me to secure the Flour, and ship it as fast as American Vessells, or *others* He may direct, can be obtained to carry if off. Or, if a

[705]

Certain proportion of money can be advanced in the manner Specified, And Monsr. Genets Bills be authenticated in such a Manner, in any official way that will inspire Confidence, that those Bills will be paid in Paris, in gold and silver Coin—Specifying the rate of the Milled Dollar &c &c, no difficulty appears that can impede supplies being obtained from Pensylvania, Maryland *and Virginia* sufficient for the present exegincy, from the remains of the present crop, on hand—and the Growing Crop in this state has the most flattering appearance.

As a Virginian, I am truly anxious, that our Markets Should not be always dependant, on Philadelphia or any other port. Our Planters are turning Farmers. Our Mills make flour that is not surpassed by any in america—in 4 years the 3 little Counties of Augusta Rockbridge, and Rockingham, which is contigious to your seat—from having but one Manufacturing Mill only has upwards of 100 Merchant Mills, in great perfection. And our adventuring farmers are coming with their Batteaus loaded down James River thro' the Blue Ridge within 3 and 4 miles of Lexington. Yesterday and to day I have received upwards of 500 Barrels sent to me by that mode. And the men assure me 2,000 will come the same route in this month—exclusive of the quantities that now Come to Milton and Warren in your Neighborhood Over Rockfish Gap.

I trust sir, the liberty I have taken with you on this subject, will not be displeasing, to you. *To you* I write in Confidence, being assured your efforts will not be wanting to enable such Agents as Monsr. Genet may apoint, to obtain the supplies which His Nation are in such want of—and which we so much abound in.

I have not the honor of a personal acquaintance with, you, but the *important office you fill*; induces me with frankness, and familiarity, to communicate, a matter I feel interested in, as a Citizen of the United States, and particularly as a Virginian. Governor *Lee*, Colo. Harvie, Willson C. Nicholas, and many others, of your acquaintances will be surety for my faithful performance of any Contract I undertake, respecting the matter mentioned. I am with regard & Esteem Your mo. Ob Hue Servt   Ro. Gamble

RC (DLC); addressed: "Honble. Thomas Jefferson Esq Secretary of *State* Philadelphia"; franked; endorsed by TJ as received 16 May 1793 and so recorded in SJL.

The Washington administration subsequently rejected Edmond Charles Genet's proposal that it repay THE DEBT WE OWE TO FRANCE IN THE PRODUCE OF OUR COUNTRY (see Genet to TJ, 22 May 1793, and note).

From James Monroe

DEAR SIR   Fredbg. May 10. 1793.

I could wish Mr. Beckley might receive [this?] immediately. But if he should not[1] be in town will you be so kind as possess him of it as soon as possible, adverting to the consideration that it requires of him to perform something in Phila.

I wrote you a few days past and shall again from Richmd. whither I am just sitting out. Yrs. affectionately   JAS: MONROE

RC (MHi); torn; addressed: "[. . .] of State Philadelphia"; franked; endorsed by TJ as received 16 May 1793 and so recorded in SJL.

The enclosed letter to John BECK-LEY, not found, covered "a political Jeu de Esprit of a friend" intended for the *National Gazette* (Monroe to TJ, 28 May 1793).

[1] Word interlined.

INDEX

A., Miss: relations with William Loughton Smith, 443

"A.B.": and public debt, 467n

Abbeville, France: and British military plans, 191

Abram (TJ's slave): and canal for Monticello, 138

Abrégé de la théorie chymique (Hermann Boerhaave and Julien Offroy de La Mettrie): for Mint, 490

Académie des sciences: impact of French Revolution on, 226; report on weights and measures, 226, 227n

acid, vitriolic: and Blanchard's balloon flight, 42; price, 42

Adam, 14, 349

Adams, John: letter to, 306; electoral vote for as vice-president, 9; letter from cited, 11n; and U.S. debt to France, 50; and sinking fund, 56, 63, 261; and French Revolution, 63-4; and Michaux's proposed western expedition, 78, 82; and criticism of Franklin, 274; and Ky. electoral votes, 306, 310; and captives in Algiers, 428

Adet, Pierre Auguste, 568n, 569n

Admiralty Court, British: and deserting British seamen, 151; and deserting seamen, 375

Aesop: fables, 334, 335-6n

Agoult (Dagout), Louis Annibal de Vincens de Saint Michel, Comte d': discusses royal veto, 58

agrarian law: support for in France, 129

Ailhaud, Jean Antoine: commissioner to Saint-Domingue, 34n

Aimable Antoinette (ship), 84, 120, 133n

air: and Blanchard's balloon flight, 43; and temperature of snowfall, 304-5

Alcudia, Duke of. *See* Godoy Alvarez de Faria, Manuel, Duque de la Alcudia

Alexander, Caleb: letter from, 235; copyright for, 235; *Grammatical System of the English Language*, 235; identified, 235n

Alexander the Great: and Gordian knot, 335

Alexandria, Va.: passports for U.S. ships in, 650, 670; and French Revolution, 697

Algiers: Barclay's mission to, 7, 86-7, 278-9, 319n, 400n, 405n, 420, 429-

30, 468-9; proposed treaty with Portugal, 29; relations with France, 88n; relations with Portugal, 88n; Spanish consul in, 88n; Lamb's mission to, 143; J. P. Jones's mission to, 144n, 405n, 420, 421; British consul in, 160; Dutch consul in, 161; relations with U.S., 161, 214, 359n; war with Netherlands, 161, 327, 358-9, 623; Cathalan's proposed mission to, 278-9; reported declaration of war on U.S., 327; Humphreys's mission to, 400n, 405, 413-14, 420-1, 423, 429-30, 438, 468-9, 532, 535, 542; piracy of, 406; war with Portugal, 406; proposed treaty with, 421; French consul ordered to leave, 623; plague in, 623; Swedish consul in, 623; treaty with U.S., 648n

Algiers, American captives in: subsistence of, 29, 86, 87-8n, 400n; ransom of, 86, 88n, 111, 143-4, 161, 421, 422n, 428, 623

Algiers, Dey of. *See* Ali Hassan, Dey of Algiers

Alicante, Spain: U.S. consul at, 203, 227, 238, 369, 394, 435

Ali Hassan, Dey of Algiers: relations with U.S., 161, 422n; reported declaration of war on U.S., 327; and war with Netherlands, 327, 331n

Allison, Robert: and TJ's Philadelphia house, 595

Allport, Thomas: partnership with Robert Crew, 252-3; letter from cited, 253n

almanacs: TJ's comments on, 54

Alps, 190

Alsace, France: evacuated by Prussians, 130-1; opposition to French Revolution in, 190; and allied military strategy, 191, 456

Alstorphius, Mr., 459

Amazon (ship): passport for, 682n

American Oracle (Samuel Stearns): copyright for, 100n

American Philosophical Society: and Michaux's proposed western expedition, xl, 18n, 71-2, 75-84, 85, 527, 530-1, 624-6; receives plaster bust of TJ, 31n; and viniculture, 93n; and hemp production, 256n; praised by R. R. Livingston, 304; Dugald Stewart elected to, 357; mentioned, 589, 651n

[709]

INDEX

Bachus, Gurdon: cargo detained in Portugal, 487n

bacon: as salted provisions, 146; duties on in Great Britain, 187; export to Great Britain, 187

Bagley, Abner: petition from, 634-5

Baker, John: petition from, 634-5

Baldwin, Abraham: and Republican effort to censure Hamilton, 290

balloons: Blanchard's flight in, 42, 43-4, 50; TJ's notes on, 42

Baltimore: lottery in, 263; French consul in, 406; roads, 443; passports for U.S. ships in, 650, 670

Banjer, John Light: and transport of French prisoners to U.S., 464

Bank of England: stops discounting, 661

Bank of the United States: stockholders in Congress, xli, 154-5, 281, 290-1, 311, 313-14, 432-4, 446; relations with Hamilton, 20-23, 178, 284, 285, 292, 293, 474; and speculation, 20-23, 474; U.S. debt to, 21, 22, 23n, 282-3, 293, 295, 369n; directors in Congress, 154-5, 281, 290-1, 311, 313-14, 432-4; federal deposits in, 283; TJ's comments on unconstitutionality of, 318; check for Nathaniel Cutting, 471n; discounts merchants' bonds, 474; TJ's notes on, 474; and drawing of bills on Great Britain, 522; and drawing of bills on Netherlands, 522; and bills of exchange for Department of State, 531n, 566, 567; and branch bank bills, 597; and post bills, 597; mentioned, 586n

banks: discontinue discounting, 318, 384

Banks, Henry: and purchase of Elk Hill, 69-70

Banning, Jeremiah: and case of *Eunice*, 699-700

Baradone, Laurence: property confiscated by G. R. Clark, 251n

Barbaroux, Charles Jean Marie: and dethronement of king, 125

Barbary States: and French war with First Coalition, 191; and U.S. trade with France, 213; relations with U.S., 358-9, 405

Barcelona, Spain: need for U.S. consul lessened, 203

Barclay, Capt.: and Natural Bridge, 299

Barclay, John, 694-5

Barclay, Mary (Mrs. Thomas Barclay): letter from, 694-5; correspondence with husband, 217n; widowed, 319n, 437, 694-5; mentioned, 216

Barclay, Thomas: letter from, 7; mission to Algiers, 7, 86-7, 278-9, 319n, 405n, 410, 420, 429-30, 468-9; lack of correspondence from, 9; death, 86-7, 159-60, 166, 169, 182, 319, 394, 399-400, 407, 410, 420, 428, 437, 694-5; mission to Morocco, 87, 88n, 143, 159-60, 182, 234, 319n, 400n, 420, 429-30, 468-9; cipher for, 106-7, 150, 167, 575; letter from cited, 155n; and Moroccan civil war, 161, 234-5; and T. Pinckney's cipher, 169; consul at Morocco, 202; naval intelligence, 203; correspondence with wife, 217n; letters from submitted to Washington, 265, 276n; account with Willink, Van Staphorst & Hubbard, 421; mentioned, 107n, 151n

Baring, John & Francis, & Co.: and bills of exchange for Department of State, 536, 566

bar iron: duties on in Great Britain, 187, 201; export to Great Britain, 187; for Mint, 447

Barksdale, William: letter from cited, 410n; recommends John Gregorie as consul at Dunkirk, 410n

barley: import from U.S. to Netherlands forbidden, 237

Barlow, Joel: letter from, 336-7; and French Revolution, 336-7; *Lettre adressée aux habitants de Piémont*, 336-7

Barnave, Antoine Pierre Joseph Marie: discusses royal veto, 58

Barnwell, Robert: and Republican effort to censure Hamilton, 289

barrel staves: duties on in Great Britain, 202

Barret, John: debt to TJ, 696-7, 698n; letter from cited, 698n; letter to cited, 698n

Barrett, Nathaniel: recommends consular agent for Rouen, 53; resigns as consul at Rouen, 202

Bartlett, Elisha: patent for nail-making machine, 398n

Bartlett, Josiah: letter to, 588

Barton, Benjamin Smith: letter to, 8; letters from, 17-18, 361-2; and Michaux's proposed western expedition, 17-18; requests loan from TJ, 361-2; mentioned, 445

Barton, William: letter from, 445; and Currie v. Griffin, 86, 346

Bartram, William: botanical garden in Philadelphia, 347

INDEX

Basle, Switzerland, 456
Bassett, Richard: and grass seed for TJ,
112-13
Bavaria: proposed cession of, 190
Bavaria, Elector of. *See* Charles Theodore,
Elector Palatine and of Bavaria
Beaulieu, Johann, Baron von: and inva-
sion of Rhineland, 451; and invasion of
Netherlands, 454
Beaulieu, Louis de: moves to U.S., 513n
beaver: duties on in Great Britain, 201
Beccaria, Cesare Bonesana: *Essay on
Crimes and Punishments*, 472
Beck, Thomas: petition from, 634-5
Beckley, John: and assumption of public debt, 208; and stockholders in Congress, 432-4, 446; *Examination of the
Late Proceedings in Congress*, 433-4n,
443n, 462n, 546, 661, 689; and Republican effort to censure Hamilton, 433-
4n; and "Timon" essays, 434n; and
discounting of merchants' bonds by
national bank, 474; and William Duer's
threats, 517; mentioned, 463, 707
Bedford. *See* Poplar Forest
beech boards: duties on in Great Britain,
201
beef: price, 69; duties on in Netherlands,
237. *See also* dried beef; pickled beef;
salted beef
beer: duty on, 149n
Beerenbroek & Van Dooren, 256n, 568,
664
beeswax, 148n
Béhague, Jean Pierre Antoine de: flees
Martinique, 271
Belfort, France, 456
Bell, Thomas: letter to, 543-4; letter from,
101; TJ's account with, 65, 90, 101,
544, 548, 593-4; and sale of TJ's slaves,
91; account with Monroe, 101; and hire
of TJ's slave, 543
Bellanger, Mme. *See* Plumard de Bellanger, Mme.
Benson, Egbert: stockholder in national
bank, 446
Berbice, Dutch Guyana: opened to U.S.
ships, 663
Bergen, N.J.: Michaux's nursery in, 76
Bertrand de Molleville, Antoine François,
Marquis de: and U.S. aid to Saint-
Domingue, 498-9, 500, 502
Besançon, France, 456
Beurnonville, Pierre de Ruel, Marquis de:
and invasion of Rhineland, 451; military

command, 452; and Dumouriez's defection, 523
Biddle, Clement: letter from, 337; and
diplomatic immunity for servants, 337;
identified, 337n
Biddle, Samuel: overseer for Monticello,
225, 313, 483; health, 483
Big Miami river: and boundaries with
Western Indians, 355
Billet, Pierre: letter to, 249-50; and trade
duties, 249-50, 254; identified, 250n
bills of exchange: drawn on Saint-
Dominque, 20, 33-4, 49, 51-2, 368; for
Department of State, 514, 521-2, 531-
2, 536, 542, 565-7
Bingham, William: and Michaux's pro-
posed western expedition, 83n; as secu-
rity for Stephen Cathalan, Jr., 212; and
execution of Louis XVI, 443
Birch, John: and bills of exchange for
Department of State, 536, 566
Bird, Savage & Bird: and Mint, 371n
Birmingham, England: copper coinage in,
347-50
Biron, Armand Louis de Gontaut, Duc
de: military command, 452; retreat pre-
dicted, 457
Blackwell, Jacob: salary, 10
Blackwell, Robert: and Michaux's pro-
posed western expedition, 82n, 83n
Blacons, Henri François Lucrecius d'Ar-
mand de Forest, Marquis de: dines with
TJ, 58; discusses royal veto, 58; iden-
tified, 58-9n
Blair, Hugh: recommended by TJ, 547
Blair, James, 443n
Blair, John: letter to quoted, 395-6n
Blake, James: seeks clerkship in Depart-
ment of State, 445; courier to Spain,
446n; and edition of Cortés letters for
TJ, 446n; letter from quoted, 446n
Blanchard, Jean Pierre: balloon flight in
America, xxxix-xl, 42, 43-4, 50, 400
(illus.)
Bleakley, John: and Michaux's proposed
western expedition, 82
blockade: TJ's comments on, 675
Blodget, Samuel, Jr.: and lottery for Fed-
eral District, 25; as superintendent for
Federal District, 25, 45n
Blount, John Gray: relations with Mount-
florence, 132n
Blount, Thomas: relations with Mount-
florence, 132n
Blount, William: relations with Mount-

INDEX

florence, 132n; mentioned, 84
Board of Treasury, U.S.: and survey of
Northwest Territory, 332, 338
Bob (TJ's slave): and clothing for TJ's
slaves, 257
Bodega y Quadra, Don Juan Francisco de
la: and John Kendrick's land purchases,
307
Boerhaave, Hermann: *Abrégé de la théorie
chymique*, 490
Bois le Duc, Austrian Netherlands: and
invasion of Austrian Netherlands, 454
Boizard, Jean: *Traité des Monnoyes*, 490
Bolingbroke, Henry St. John, Viscount:
recommended by TJ, 547
Bolling, Powhatan: and Natural Bridge,
299
Bompard (Bompart), Citizen (captain of
Embuscade): captures *Grange*, 637-40,
694, 702-5
Bonaparte, Napoleon: TJ's attitude
toward, xxxix; and Lafayette's captivity,
389n
Bond, Phineas: and TJ's negotiations
with Hammond, 150, 151n; British
consul general for middle and southern
states, 376; and deserting seamen, 376,
378n; and impressment, 525-6
Bonnet, John: settles in U.S., 371-2;
identified, 372n
Borda, Jean Charles: report on weights
and measures, 226
Bordeaux, France: exchange rate, 69, 486;
U.S. consul at, 202; trade with U.S.,
262, 486; and Federal District, 369
Bordley, John Beale: and Michaux's proposed western expedition, 82n, 83n
Boston: J. W. Eppes's proposed trip to,
19; French consul in, 39; passports for
U.S. ships in, 650, 670
Boudinot, Elias: and Republican effort to
censure Hamilton, 289; stockholder in
national bank, 433
Boulding, Noble: recommended as tenant
farmer for TJ, 483, 521
Boulton (Bolton), Matthew: and copper
coinage, 347-50, 526n
Bourgoing, Jean François de: banished
from Spain, 327, 328n
Bourne, Benjamin: and case of *Illustrious
President*, 296-7; and case of *Commerce*,
415; letter from cited, 415; stockholder
in national bank, 432, 446
Bourne, Sylvanus: resigns as consul at
Saint-Domingue, 202

Boyd, John Coffin: petition from, 634-5
Boyd, Robert: petition from, 634-5
Boyd & Kerr: and U.S. debt to France,
501, 510n
Brabant, Austrian Netherlands: French
withdrawal from, 576, 577
Brackenridge, Mr. *See* Breckinridge,
John
Bradford, Capt. (master of *Union*), 513,
514, 524
Bradford, Gamaliel: master of *Jerusha*,
464n; and transport of French prisoners
to U.S., 464n
Bradley, Mr., 302
Bradley, Stephen R., 184
Bradshaw, Samuel: messenger to Ky.,
302, 306, 310, 520
Brandywine, Pa.: TJ's proposed visit to,
313
brass: for Mint, 447
Brazil, Prince of. *See* John Marie Joseph
Louis, Prince of Brazil
Brazil, Princess of. *See* Charlotte
Joachime, Princess of Brazil
bread: shortage in Europe, 28-9; duties
on in Great Britain, 187; export to
Great Britain, 187; export from U.S. to
Netherlands forbidden, 188, 237; short-
age in France, 407; shortage in Paris,
488
breadstuff: export to France, 146, 186;
and grain, 149n; export to Spain, 185;
export from U.S. to French West Indies
forbidden, 186; export to British West
Indies, 188
Breck, Samuel: and execution of Louis
XVI, 443
Breckinridge (Brackenridge), John: and
Republican effort to censure Hamilton,
533
Breda, Netherlands: captured by French,
262n, 335; captured by allies, 524
Bremen: and workmen for Federal District, 24
Brest, France: and naval warfare, 165
bricklayers: for Mint, 447
bricks: for Monticello, 315; for Mint, 447
Briggs, Isaac: assistant to Andrew Ellicott, 152, 153n, 268, 401n; and survey
of Federal District, 267n
Brimmer (TJ's horse): sale of, 134, 230,
581
Brissot de Warville, Jean Pierre: letter to,
679; praised by TJ, 680; execution of,
680n; mentioned, 518-19n

INDEX

Brissotines: conflict with Jacobins, 457
Bristol, England: U.S. consul at, 202;
economic distress in, 528; trade with
U.S., 528
Brittany, France: revolt in, 457, 458n,
486
Brodie, William Douglas: recommended
for consular appointment at Malaga,
309n
Brown, Andrew: edition of U.S. laws,
106
Brown, Benson & Ives: letter to, 491;
letters from, 414-15, 554; and case
of *Commerce*, 414-15; ship detained at
Port-au-Prince, 491, 510-11, 554
Brown, James: letters to, 513-14, 524-5;
letters from, 3, 525, 549; and sale of
TJ's tobacco, 3, 351, 485, 513, 524-
5; TJ's account with, 3, 101, 138,
524-5; and Wayles estate debt, 8; and
wine for TJ, 28-9, 235, 525, 580, 620;
and clothing for TJ's slaves, 91, 230,
257; and books for J. W. Eppes, 396,
513; and Short's business affairs, 479-
82, 495, 513, 522, 524, 527-8, 549;
and books for TJ, 513; and TJ's furniture, 513, 521, 524
Brown, John (Eng.): medical system, 97
Brown, John (Ky.): and Michaux's proposed western expedition, 82; and
discounting of merchants' bonds by
national bank, 474; and speculation by
national bank, 474
Brown, John (R.I.): and case of *Illustrious
President*, 297n
Brown, Moses: ship detained in Portugal,
487n
Brown & Francis: and case of *Illustrious
President*, 296-7
Brunetta, Italy: fortress at, 359
Brunswick, Karl Wilhelm Ferdinand,
Duke of: and invasion of France, 8, 97,
128, 130, 239, 506; proposed assassi-
nation of, 128; and invasion of Nether-
lands, 454, 662, 668; and invasion of
Rhineland, 456
Brush, Ebenezer: resigns as consul at
Surinam, 202
Brush, Richard, & Co.: and transport of
French prisoners to U.S., 464
brushes: for Mint, 447
Brussels: and French invasion of Nether-
lands, 335; reportedly captured by
allies, 343, 374; and invasion of Aus-

trian Netherlands, 454; banking failures
at, 497
Bulkeley, John, & Son: letters from, 28-
9, 235-6; letter to cited, 28-9; and wine
for TJ, 28-9, 235-6, 525; and captives
in Algiers, 86, 88n; and Barclay's mission to Morocco, 160n; TJ's account
with, 235-6; letters from cited, 236n;
mentioned, 427
Buoy of the Brown, 638n, 703, 704
Bureau de Pusy (de Puzy), Jean Xavier:
Lafayette's aide de camp, 124
Burgain, André L.: captured by *Patriote*,
406; detained in Marseilles, 406; land
grant from Continental Congress, 406
Burgoyne, John, 8, 97
Burlamaqui, Jean Jacques: *Principes du
Droit Politique*, 618n
Burnet, Gilbert: *History of My Own Time*,
472
Burr, Aaron: letter to, 66; and Depart-
ment of State records, 66-7; relations
with TJ, 66-7; identified, 67n; recom-
mends Enoch Edwards, 649
Burton, Robert: business failure, 351,
485; and sale of TJ's tobacco, 485
Butler, John: letter from, 40; *Vindication of the planters of Martinique &
Guadaloupe*, 40
Butler, Pierce: and appointment of minis-
ters to Europe, 102
butter: duties on in Netherlands, 237
Butts, Samuel: petition from, 634-5

Cabinet, U.S. *See* United States: Cabinet
Cabot, George: and U.S. debt to France,
50; and Michaux's proposed western
expedition, 82; recommends William
Douglas Brodie for consular appointment at Malaga, 309n; director of
national bank, 433; stockholder in
national bank, 433
Cadiz, Spain: U.S. consul at, 102, 203,
227, 238n, 369, 394, 435; trade with
U.S., 441, 487n, 623; stoppage of
French ships at, 593
Cahokia, Ill.: and boundaries with Western Indians, 355
Calcutta, India: hospital at, 71; U.S. consul at, 71, 203; sale of U.S. ship in,
297n; trade with U.S., 297n
California: and G. R. Clark's proposed
western expedition, 75

INDEX

Caligari, Sardinia: bombarded by French, 359

Callaghan (Callahan), David: and Barclay's death, 319

Callahan, William: master of *John Pringle*, 524

Calvert (Colvard), Benjamin: hires TJ's slaves, 43

Camilla (ship), 485, 549n

Campbell, Alexander: and case of Richard Randolph, 632-3

Campbell, John: delivers book to TJ, 92

Canada: British reinforcements for, 6, 534; newspapers from sent to TJ, 184, 363, 412-13, 418; immigration from Europe, 268-9; immigration from Vt., 268-9; Joseph Fay's land company in, 268-9, 412-13; and French Revolution, 363

Canary Islands: trade with U.S., 205, 219

candles: for TJ, 270-1

Canton: U.S. consul at, 203; and china for TJ, 315

Cape Henlopen, 638n

Cape James, 703

Cape May, 638n, 703

Cap François, Saint-Domingue: massacre of slaves at, 271; trade with U.S., 415n

Capitol, U.S.: Hallet's plans for, 25, 107-8, 110, 152, 384-6, 459; Thornton's plan for, 107-8, 110, 152, 386n, 400n

Carey, James: letter to, 27; newspapers requested by TJ, 27; identified, 27n

Carey, John: letters from, 105-6, 236, 448-9, 581-2, 630; *Official Letters to the Honorable American Congress*, 105-6, 236, 581-2, 595, 630, 690; and edition of U.S. laws, 106; and index for U.S. laws, 448-9

Carey, Mathew: edition of *Notes on the State of Virginia*, 467n

Carey's United States Recorder (Philadelphia): published by James Carey, 27n

Carmichael, William: letters to, 277, 400 (illus.), 430, 587-8; letters from, 232-4, 554-62, 652-8; and guarantee of La., xli-xlii, 430-1, 444; newspapers for, 9; and captives in Algiers, 29, 86, 88n; and U.S. debt to Torino, 88n; papers for, 94, 103, 407, 427; negotiations with Godoy, 139, 232, 233; and diplomatic precedence in Spain, 232-4, 323; relations with Charles IV, 233; journal of, 234; letters from submit-

ted to Washington, 234n, 563n, 659n; and case of *Dover*, 277; instructions for, 316n; negotiations with Gardoqui, 321-2, 555-61, 593, 653-7; insufficiency of diplomatic authority, 322, 324, 328n; negotiations with Floridablanca, 324; and French war with First Coalition, 339; and Lafayette's captivity, 387n, 665; expenses, 405n, 535, 542; relations with Humphreys, 407; and Humphreys's mission to Algiers, 421; irregular communications of, 427, 428-9, 435; and acquisition of East Fla., 430-1; and acquisition of West Fla., 430-1; letters to submitted to Washington, 431n, 444, 588n; and navigation of Mississippi, 556, 559-60, 653, 656-7; and U.S. boundary with Spain, 556-8, 559, 657; and Jay-Gardoqui Treaty, 558; and Spanish relations with Southern Indians, 560, 653-4; and trade with Spain, 560-1; and relations between Spain and Great Britain, 561-2; and Proclamation of Neutrality, 587-8; mentioned, 479

Carnes, Burrill: resigns as consul at Nantes, 202

Carondelet, Francisco Luis Hector, Baron de, 659n

carpenters: for Federal District, 24; recruited for French naval service, 68; and remodeling of Monticello, 138, 693; for Mint, 447

Carr, Dabney (TJ's brother-in-law): TJ's bond on estate of, 223

Carr, Dabney (TJ's nephew): letter to, 544; legal education, 544, 545, 548; mentioned, 223

Carr, Martha Jefferson (Mrs. Dabney Carr, TJ's sister): letters to, 223, 545; requests loan from TJ, 223; changes in family, 297; debt to Austin, 545; health, 545; TJ unable to lend money to, 545; letter from cited, 545n; mentioned, 465, 544, 548

Carr, Mary (Polly, TJ's niece): remains at home, 297

Carr, Peter (TJ's nephew): letter to, 545-6; letter from, 465; letter from cited, 64; plans to practice law, 465, 545-6; right to slaves, 465, 546; legal education, 472, 544, 545; mentioned, 98, 521

Carr, Samuel (TJ's nephew): settlement

INDEX

chestnut wood: for Monticello, 73
Chickasaw Indians: boundaries under Treaty of Hopewell, 209-11; and Va. land claims, 209-11
china: for TJ, 315
China: trade with U.S., 297n
Chippewa Indians: boundary with U.S., 355
Chittenden, Thomas: letter to, 588; requests congressional records, 673
Church, Angelica Schuyler (Mrs. John B. Church): letter from, 215
Church, Catherine, 215
Church, Edward: letter to, 415-18; consul at Lisbon, 202, 407, 427; letter to cited, 212
Churchman, John, 226, 227n
cifrão: Portuguese symbol for milréis, 235-6
cinnamon water: gift for Emperor of Morocco, 234
ciphers: for T. Barclay, 106-7, 575; for T. Pinckney, 106-7, 166-7, 169, 376, 378n, 408, 534, 575; for G. Morris, 167; for Humphreys, 167
circuit court act: error in, 395
"Citizen of Columbia, A": criticizes Andrew Ellicott, 267, 268
Citoyen Genet (French privateer): commissioned by Genet, 686-7
civil ordonnatueurs, French: and capture of U.S. ships by French privateers, 575n
Clairfayt, Gen. *See* Clerfayt, François Sebastien Charles Joseph de Croix, Comte de
Clark, George Rogers: proposed western expedition, 75; and French plan to liberate La., 80; confiscates property near Vincennes, 251; land grant in Northwest Territory, 355-6
Clark, William: western expedition, 75, 81
Clarke, John: patent for, 276
Clarkson, David Matthew: letter to, 415-17; appointed consul at St. Eustatius, 204, 228, 238n, 369, 395; letter to cited, 238n
Clarkson, Manoah: overseer at Monticello, 98, 138, 693
Clarkson, Matthew: and Michaux's proposed western expedition, 83n; recommends David M. Clarkson for consular appointment at St. Eustatius, 204; mentioned, 639n

Clarkson, Samuel: letter to, 134; purchases TJ's horse, 134; identified, 134n; letters from cited, 134n
Classon, Mr.: Danish consul at Tangier, 234
Clavière, Etienne: letter from, 62; and commercial treaty with U.S., 62; dismissed from office, 131-2; and U.S. debt to France, 164n; and recall of G. Morris, 248
Clay, Matthew: defeated for election to House of Representatives, 533
Clayton, Joshua: letter to, 588
Clerfayt (Clairfayt), François Sebastien Charles Joseph de Croix, Comte de: and Dumouriez's defection, 523; and invasion of Netherlands, 662, 668
clergy, Roman Catholic: requested by Illinois and Wabash Indians, 118; oaths for in France, 122-3, 127; banishment from France, 190; reserved land for in Canada, 268-9; opposition to French Revolution among Spanish, 325-6
Clerici, Gaudenzio: letter from cited, 60
Clinton, George: letters to, 215-16, 373, 588, 592; letter from, 317; and Indian treaties, 215-16, 317, 373, 592; and cession of Montauk Point, 265; letter from quoted, 265n; letters from submitted to Washington, 317n, 344; letter from cited, 592
clocks: paid for by TJ, 586n
clothing: for TJ's slaves, 51, 91, 230, 257, 521
coal: for Mint, 447
Coates, Samuel: and Michaux's proposed western expedition, 83n
Coblentz. *See* Koblenz
Cobourg, Prince of. *See* Saxe-Coburg, Friedrich Josias, Prince of
cocoa: export to U.S., 188
codfish: export to Martinique, 414
coffee: export to U.S., 145, 188; export to France, 406
Coffin, Laben, 53n
Coffyn, Francis: U.S. agent at Dunkirk, 53, 410n; letters from cited, 53n; appointed consul at Dunkirk, 410n
coinage: assay of foreign, 31-2, 37-9, 40, 354, 409, 412, 423; TJ's report on, 37-8; act on, 38n. *See also* copper coinage; Mint, U.S.
Coke, Sir Edward: *Institutes of the Laws of England*, 544, 546

Coles, Isaac: elected to House of Representatives, 533

Colle (Philip Mazzei's plantation): and Antonio Giannini's claim on Mazzei, 299

Collin, Nicholas: and Michaux's proposed western expedition, 78, 82, 83n

Columbian Centinel (Boston): and printing of U.S. laws, 634; prints "Freeman" essay, 660n

Columbia Rediviva (ship): voyage to Pacific Northwest, 308n

Colvard, Mr. *See* Calvert, Benjamin

Combiagio, Mr.: banker in Leghorn, 459

Commerce (ship): detained at Port-au-Prince, 414-15, 510-11, 554

Commerce, Report on: preparation of, xl, 145-9, 158-9; T. Coxe's notes on, 145-9, 237; submitted to Washington, 168, 183, 212; submitted to foreign ministers in U.S., 184-9, 198; extracts from draft of, 185-9; Hammond's comments on, 199-202, 206-7, 212, 224; Viar and Jaudenes's comments on, 205-6, 219; Ternant's comments on, 211, 217-18; submission to House of Representatives deferred, 246-7; Van Berckel's comments on, 253-4

Commissioner of the Revenue, U.S.: and passports for U.S. ships, 629, 681. *See also* Coxe, Tench

Commissioners of Accounts, U.S.: letter from, 373; request census, 373; final report, 373n

Commissioners of the Customs, British, 528

Commissioners of the Federal District. *See* Federal District Commissioners

Commissioners of the Sinking Fund, U.S.: and public debt, 21, 22, 283, 293, 294n, 295, 439-40, 518-19n, 661, 673; report of, 22, 23n; meetings of, 56, 63, 432, 439-40, 487, 492, 673; and foreign loans, 178, 462n, 673; letter to Jonathan Trumbull, 261

Commissioners of the Treasury, French: and U.S. debt to France, 17n, 496, 498, 505, 507; and U.S. aid to Saint-Domingue, 503

Commissioners of the Treasury, U.S.: and captives in Algiers, 143

Commissioners to Spain. *See* Carmichael, William; Short, William

Committee of Public Safety, French, 631n

common law: J. G. Jefferson's comments on, 473

Como (Potawatomi chief): peace conference with Washington, 114, 115-16

Compendium of Physic (Joseph Flowerden): requested by TJ, 484

Complete History of England (White Kennett and others): recommended by TJ, 544, 546

Comptroller of the Treasury, U.S. *See* Wolcott, Oliver, Jr.

Condé, France: allied siege of, 573

Congress, Continental: and Ky. Indian expeditions, 99; and survey of Northwest Territory, 332, 338n; and military land bounties in Northwest Territory, 355, 356; and captives in Algiers, 428; and diplomatic medals, 519-20; and military medals, 519-20; and Jay-Gardoqui Treaty, 558; TJ seeks copies of correspondence with president of, 567; and passports for East Indian ships, 645, 648n, 682n

Congress, U.S. *See* United States: Congress

Connecticut: wages in, 24; and workmen for Federal District, 24

Connecticut, Governor of. *See* Huntington, Samuel

Constitutional Diary (Philadelphia): published by James Carey, 27n

Constitution of the United States: and appropriations, 292, 294-5; and appointment of members of Congress to federal office, 300n, 303; Henry Knox's comments on, 301-2; and state debts, 373

consular establishment: act for, 212

consuls, French: salaries, 6-7, 51-2, 543, 564-5, 579; and supplies for France, 39; in N.Y., 226; admiralty jurisdiction in U.S., 685-6

consuls, U.S.: letter to (circular), 415-16; fees in Portugal, 13; and register certificates, 55-6; security requirements for, 68, 69n, 71, 202, 212, 262, 365, 376, 416, 417n, 529; TJ's instructions to on neutrality, 365, 415-16; and impressment, 375; letter to submitted to Washington, 418n; and U.S. ship papers, 528. *See also* Auldjo, Thomas; Cathalan, Stephen, Jr.; Church, Edward; Clarkson, David Matthew; Cooper, Henry; Cutting, Nathaniel; Delamotte, F. C. A.; Fenwick, Joseph; Fox, Edward; Greenleaf, James; Johnson, Joshua; Johonnet, Samuel Cooper; Joy, Benjamin; Maury, James; Montgomery, Robert; Morphy, Michael; Parish, John; Phillips, Benjamin Hamnell; Pintard, John Marsden; Saabÿe, Hans Rodolph; Shaw, Samuel; Skipwith, Fulwar; Street, John; Vanderhorst, Elias; Yznardi, Joseph, Jr.

Continental Army: land bounties for, 171

Continental Congress. *See* Congress, Continental

contraband: Dutch regulation on, 468n; British restrictions on export to France, 493-4; debated in Cabinet, 673-4; TJ's comments on, 675; and U.S. arms sales to France, 684; mentioned, 574n, 603

Cook, James, 75

Cooper, Henry: letter to, 415-17; letter from, 631; appointed consul at St. Croix, 204, 228, 238n, 369, 395; letter to cited, 238n

Coopman, Zacharie, & Co.: and capture of *Aurora*, 406; and capture of *Bacchus*, 406

Copenhagen: U.S. consul at, 203; trade with U.S., 237n

copper: for Mint, 151, 204, 393, 447, 578, 596; price, 350

copper coinage: in Birmingham, 347-50, 526n; machinery for, 348-9; in Paris, 349; production costs, 350

copyrights: for Samuel Stearns, 100; for Caleb Alexander, 235

Corbin, Mr.: returns to U.S., 336-7

Corbin, Francis: defeated for election to House of Representatives, 463

corn: production in Md., 230, 263; shortage in France, 358-9; shortage in Levant, 358-9; shortage in Papal States, 358-9; shortage in Sicily, 358-9; shortage in Venice, 358-9; price, 409. *See also* Indian corn; maize; wheat

Cornwallis, Charles, Earl: surrender at Yorktown, 122; mentioned, 8, 419

Correspondance du Général Dumourier avec Pache: sent to TJ, 451, 458n

corruption: TJ's comments on, 154-5, 311, 313-14, 318, 679

Cortés, Hernán: TJ seeks edition of letters of, 446n

Course of Experimental Philosophy (John Theophilus Desaguiliers): and fire engines, 163, 164n

Courtrai, Austrian Netherlands: and conflict between Lafayette and Luckner, 124

Cowes, England: trade with U.S., 409

Cox, Albion: assayer for Mint, 370-1,

665; identified, 371n; arrives in Philadelphia, 676

Cox, Josiah: petition from, 634-5

Cox, Merle & Co.: and Mint, 371n

Cox, Moses: letters to, 332, 362; rents house to TJ, xlii, 332, 362; identified, 332n

Cox, William: and Mint, 371n

Coxe, John: and Michaux's proposed western expedition, 83n

Coxe, Tench: letters to, 149, 158-9, 337-8, 642-3; letters from, 145, 159, 237, 332, 338, 514, 521-2, 626-7, 650, 670, 695; portrait of, xl, 400 (illus.); relations with Hamilton, xl; *Plan for encouraging Agriculture*, 136, 159; and TJ's report on commerce, 145-9, 158-9, 168n, 237; and British trade restrictions, 158-9; and TJ's report on boundaries with Western Indians, 332, 337-8; and execution of Louis XVI, 443; and bills of exchange for Department of State, 514, 521-2; letter from quoted, 522n; and foreign-built U.S. ships, 627-8, 642-3, 650, 670-1; letter from Stephen Kingston, 627-8; commissioner of the revenue, 629n; and passports for U.S. ships, 642-3, 650, 670-1, 681, 695; and Mint, 695; letter from cited, 696n

Creek Indians: conflict with in Ga., 518-19, 520; and Treaty of New York, 653; and U.S. agents, 653, 659n; relations with Spain, 677-8

Crew, Robert: letter from, 252-3; partnership with Thomas Allport, 252-3; letter from cited, 253n

Crooked legs (Wiaw chief): and peace conference with Washington, 113, 116

Crosby, Sampson: salary, 10; factotum in Department of State, 552

Cross, Ralph: petition from, 634-5

crown, English: assay of, 32

crown, French: assay of, 32

Culnan, John: appointed consul at Tenerife, 204n

Cumberland County Court: and case of Richard Randolph, 622n, 632-3, 698

Cumberland river: as Chickasaw boundary, 209; and Iroquois land claims, 210

Curaçao: U.S. consul at, 204, 228, 238n, 369, 395; trade duties at, 253

Currie, Ann Inglis (Mrs. James Currie), 172

Currie, James: letter to, 346; letters from, 86, 171-2; financial affairs, 86, 171,

INDEX

Currie, James (*cont.*)
346; land claim, 171, 346
Curson, Richard: letter to, 580; and wine for TJ, 236n, 580, 583, 620; letter from cited, 620
Cushing, William: and Washington's second inaugural, 302n; letter to quoted, 395-6n
Custine, Adam Philippe, Comte de: and allied military strategy, 191; and invasion of Rhineland, 451, 488, 492, 573; military command, 452
customs collectors, U.S.: and post bills, 597; and passports for U.S. ships, 629, 642-3, 650, 670-1, 681, 835; and foreign-built U.S. ships, 642, 670-1; and enforcement of neutrality, 667-8, 691-2, 700-2
Cutting, John Brown: letter to, 586-7; expenses, 438
Cutting, Nathaniel: letters to, 415-17, 470-1; letter from, 102; recommends Joseph Yznardi for consular appointment at Cadiz, 102, 203, 204n; appointed consul at Le Havre, 203, 227, 238n, 369, 394, 417n; letter to cited, 238n; secretary to Humphreys, 410, 413-14, 420, 421, 427, 468-9, 470-1, 477, 532, 534, 566; expenses, 421, 471, 542; letter to quoted, 471n; letter to submitted to Washington, 471n

Dagout, M. *See* Agoult, Louis Annibal de Vincens de Saint Michel, Comte d'
Daignan (Douignan), Guillaume: *Tableau des Variétés de la Vie humaine*, 484
Daily Advertiser (Philadelphia): published by James Carey, 27n
Dana, Francis: and Pagan v. Hooper, 389, 540
Dandiran, Mr.: plan for hemp production, 256n
Darcel, Nicolas: and Derieux's business affairs, 44
Darguilleur, John: property confiscated by G. R. Clark, 251n
D'Arot, Gov. *See* Arrot, René Marie d'
Davidson, William, 419
Davies, William: letter from, 484; recommends James Murray for military commission, 484; identified, 485n; mentioned, 410n
Davis, Daniel: petition from, 634-5
Davis (Davies), Augustine: and postal service at Richmond, 477, 478
Davy (TJ's slave): and canal for Monticello, 138
Dayton, Jonathan: and Republican effort to censure Hamilton, 290; stockholder in national bank, 433
deals: duties on in Great Britain, 202
Dearborn, Henry: elected to House of Representatives, 651
Deas, William Allen: secretary to T. Pinckney, 394
debt payment act: and Republican effort to censure Hamilton, 177-9, 240, 241n, 242n, 283, 285, 289, 292, 294n, 295, 460-2; and Senate investigation of foreign loans, 436n
debt redemption act: and Republican effort to censure Hamilton, 177-9, 240, 241n, 242n, 243n, 261n, 283, 285, 289, 292, 293, 294n, 295, 440n, 460-2, 463n; and Senate investigation of foreign loans, 436n; and foreign loans, 458
Declaration of Independence, 226, 354
Decline and Fall of the Roman Empire (Edward Gibbon): recommended by TJ, 547
De Coin, John Baptist. *See* Ducoigne, Jean Baptiste
deeds: probate of, 70
Deering, Nathaniel: petition from, 634-5
De Hart, Jacob: master of *Dominick Terry*, 28-9
De Jure Belli ac Pacis (Hugo Grotius): and French treaties, 606, 612-15, 618n
Delamotte, F. C. A.: letter to, 415-17; letters from, 53, 340, 341, 362-3, 383; and case of *Euphrasie*, 5, 362-3; and payment of foreign officers, 55; and case of Rochefontaine, 59; letter to cited, 59n; letter to quoted, 151; consul at Le Havre, 202; and U.S. trade with France, 340; and books for TJ, 341; and macaroni for TJ, 341; and TJ's retirement, 341; and medals, 520
Delany, Sharp: letter to, 629; letter from, 628-9; letter from cited, 580; letter to cited, 628-9; and passports for U.S. ships, 629, 681
Delaware, Governor of. *See* Clayton, Joshua
Delaware Bay: U.S. jurisdiction over, 639-40, 683, 702-5
Delaware Indians: hostility to U.S., 114; conflict with Western Indians, 118; boundary with U.S., 355

INDEX

"E": and public debt, 466n

Eagle Cent: coinage in Birmingham, 347-8, 351n

Eastern Herald (Portland), 634

East India Company, British: and hospital at Calcutta, 71; rejects Benjamin Joy's consular authority, 71n; and rice trade, 201

East India Company, Dutch: U.S. within limits of, 237

East Indies: snuff exports, 202; trade with France, 262n

Edgehill: proposed rental of, 230; tenant farmers for, 230, 298

Edwards, Dr. Enoch: letter to, 680; letter from, 671-2; travel plans, 649, 671-2, 679, 680, 689-90; identified, 672n

Edwards, John: and Michaux's proposed western expedition, 82

eggplant. *See solanum melongena*

Elements of the Philosophy of the Human Mind (Dugald Stewart): sent to TJ, 92, 357

Elk Hill (TJ's plantation): proposed sale of, 70, 72-3, 306, 347

Elkton, Md.: TJ's proposed visit to, 313

Ellicott, Andrew: letters to, 54, 425-6; letters from, 41, 266-7, 449; and survey of Federal District, 25, 52, 54, 110, 152, 169, 170, 231n, 267, 401n; and Anacostia river, 41; dispute with Federal District Commissioners, 41-2, 45n, 54, 56, 152, 199, 266-8, 316, 401n, 409, 425-6, 449; letters from submitted to Washington, 42n, 268; resigns as chief surveyor of Federal District, 42n; almanac sent to TJ, 54; letters to submitted to Washington, 54n, 199, 316, 426n; letter from cited, 55n; appointed Pa. road surveyor, 153

Ellicott, Benjamin, 401n

Elliot, Capt. (master of *Peggy*), 524

Ellsworth, Oliver: suspected holder of public debt, 433

Embuscade (French frigate): captures British prizes, 581, 597, 619, 668-9; captures *Grange*, 644, 649, 661, 662n, 668-9, 676, 683, 694, 702-5; captures *Little Sarah*, 668-9; captures *Four Brothers*, 685; captures *Morning Star*, 685

émigrés: and British military plans, 191; decree against, 192, 194n; and invasion of Netherlands, 453

Enville, Louise Elisabeth de La Rochefou-

cauld, Duchesse d': letter from cited, 60; losses in French Revolution, 60-1; Short visits, 60-1

Eppes, Elizabeth Wayles (Mrs. Francis Eppes, TJ's sister-in-law): correspondence with niece, 65; and proposed Indian peace conference, 65; mentioned, 19, 63, 279, 397, 515, 547

Eppes, Francis (TJ's brother-in-law): letters to, 19, 63, 279, 396-7, 515; letters from, 8, 65, 319; account with James Brown, 3; and Wayles estate debt, 8, 252, 279, 319, 396-7, 632; and proposed Indian peace conference, 65; mentioned, 547

Eppes, John Wayles (TJ's nephew): letter to, 547; letter from, 632-3; laziness, 8; and peace conference with Western Indians, 19, 279, 319, 396; health, 63; books for, 396, 513; education, 396, 515, 521; character, 515; returns to Va., 515, 521; account with Peter Gordon, 547, 632; and case of Richard Randolph, 632-3; relations with Mary Jefferson, 633

Escaut. *See* Scheldt river

Esperance (ship): and use of flags, 5n, 362-3

Essay on Crimes and Punishments (Cesare Bonesana Beccaria): cited by J. G. Jefferson, 472

Essequibo, Dutch Guyana: opened to U.S. ships, 663

estragon (tarragon): seeds for, 306; little known in U.S., 347

Euler, Mr.: magic lantern on French Revolution, 664

Eunice (ship): captured by *Sans Culotte*, 699-700

Euphrasie (ship): and use of flags, 5n, 362-3

Eutrusco (ship): renamed *President Washington*, 297n

Evans, Lewis: *Geographical, Historical, Political, Philosophical and Mechanical Essays*, 199

Eve, 14, 349

Ewing, John: and Michaux's proposed western expedition, 78, 82n, 83n

Examination of the Late Proceedings in Congress (John Beckley): and stockholders in Congress, 433-4; criticizes Hamilton, 462n; distribution of, 546; and Republican effort to censure Hamil-

INDEX

Examination (*cont.*)
ton, 661; requested by Madison, 689;
mentioned, 443n
exchange rate: at Amsterdam, 6, 69; of
assignats, 6, 68; at Paris, 6; at Philadelphia, 6, 514; at Bordeaux, 69, 486; at
London, 69, 340; at Madrid, 69; at Le
Havre, 340

Fabius (ship), 528
factors, U.S.: status in British colonies,
147, 188
Fair American (ship): passport for, 682n
Falmouth, England: U.S. vessel released
at, 150; U.S. consul at, 203, 227, 238n,
369, 394
Fanny (TJ's slave): and canal for Monticello, 138
"Farmer, A": criticizes Washington, 155n
Farrell & Jones: and Wayles estate debt,
70, 551
Fauchet, Jean Antoine Joseph: succeeds
Genet, 80
Fay, Joseph: letters to, 98-9, 402, 418;
letters from, 184, 268-9, 363, 672-3;
relations with TJ, 98-9; relations with
Madison, 99; sends Canadian newspapers to TJ, 184, 363, 418, 672-3; letters from cited, 184n, 673n; offers share
in land company to TJ, 268-9, 363,
402, 412-13, 672; letter from submitted
to Washington, 412-13; requests congressional records, 673
Fayal, Azores: U.S. consul at, 203
Febiger, Christian: and Michaux's proposed western expedition, 82n
Federal District: engraved plan of, 9, 135,
369, 395, 407, 413, 671; President's
House, 24; workmen for, 24-5, 152-3;
Capitol, 25, 107-8, 110, 152, 384-6,
400n, 459; lottery for, 25; superintendent for, 25, 109, 361n; survey of, 25,
26n, 45, 52, 54, 56, 110, 152, 169,
170, 231, 267, 401n; marble for, 152,
170; money for, 199n; proprietors of,
266-8
Federal District Commissioners: letters
to, 24-5, 52; letters from, 152-3, 169,
170; and machine for cutting stone, 24;
and workmen for Federal District, 24-
5, 152-3; and lottery for Federal District, 25; and superintendent for Federal District, 25, 109; and survey of
Federal District, 25, 45, 52, 54, 110,

152, 169, 170, 231, 267, 401n; letter
to cited, 25n; letters from submitted to
Washington, 26n, 169n, 171n; dispute
with Andrew Ellicott, 41-2, 45n, 54,
56, 152, 199, 266-8, 316, 401n, 409,
425-6, 449; and Capitol, 107-8, 110,
152, 384-6, 400n; letters from Washington, 107-8, 109; compensation for,
109, 152, 345, 361; sent pamphlet by
T. Coxe, 136n, 159; expenses of, 170;
dispute with L'Enfant, 266-7; planned
retirements among, 360-1, 400. *See also*
Carroll, Daniel; Johnson, Thomas; Stuart, David
*Federal Gazette and Philadelphia Daily
Advertiser*: prints Giles resolutions censuring Hamilton, 296n
Federalists: and Republican effort to censure Hamilton, xli, 284-91; alleged
monarchism, 436
Federès. *See* National Guard, French
Fenner, Arthur: letter to, 588
Fenno, John: and criticism of Franklin,
273-4; prints *Gazette of the United
States*, 444, 475; mentioned, 214n
Fenwick, George: and survey of Fed-
eral District, 267n; assistant to Andrew
Ellicott, 268
Fenwick, Joseph: letter to, 415-18; let-
ters from, 68-9, 165-6, 261-2, 486; and
Derieux's legacy, 18, 44, 49, 67, 306,
346-7; security for, 68, 69n, 262; consul at Bordeaux, 202; letter to cited,
212; letter from quoted, 262n; and wine
for TJ, 269; letter from cited, 486n;
mentioned, 61
Fenwick, Mason & Co.: as security for
Stephen Cathalan, Jr., 212; mentioned,
69n
Ferey, Baptiste André: captures *Eunice*,
699; commander of *Sans Culotte*, 699
Ferguson, Adam: *Institutes of Moral Philosophy*, 472
Feuillants: TJ's comments on, 14;
and unicameralism, 58; conflict with
Jacobins, 121; support constitution,
121; divisions among, 122; and war
with Austria and Prussia, 122
Findley, William: and Republican effort to
censure Hamilton, 290
Finlay, Mr.: owner of *Union*, 524
fire engines: in England, 163-4; Nancarrow's comments on, 163-4; in Philadelphia, 163-4
firewood: for Mint, 447

INDEX

fish: duties on in French West Indies, 187; export to French West Indies, 187; duties on in Spain, 561. *See also* codfish; salted fish

Fitzgerald, John: and passports for U.S. ships, 670-1n

Fitzhugh, Elizabeth Chew (Mrs. Peregrine Fitzhugh): marriage of, 263n

Fitzhugh, Peregrine: letter from, 262-3; lottery for, 262-3; identified, 263n

Fitzhugh, William, 263n

FitzSimons, Thomas: and Michaux's proposed western expedition, 82; director of national bank, 433; stockholder in national bank, 433

flag, Spanish: and case of *Euphrasie*, 5n, 362-3

flag, U.S.: and case of *Euphrasie*, 5n, 362-3; and case of *Illustrious President*, 297n; use by foreign ships forbidden, 365, 415-16, 426-7, 435, 439

Flanders, Austrian Netherlands: and French invasion of Austrian Netherlands, 339, 374, 455, 486; mentioned, 190

Flanders, France: opposition to French Revolution in, 190

flax: production of, 256n

flaxseed: duties on in Great Britain, 187, 202; export to Great Britain, 187

Florida, East: proposed acquisition by U.S., 245, 430-1; acquisition by Great Britain feared, 430-1; boundary with Ga., 431n; and conflict between Creeks and Ga., 518-19n; ceded to Spain, 557

Florida, West: proposed acquisition by U.S., 245, 430-1; acquisition by Great Britain feared, 430-1; boundary with Ga., 431n; and conflict between Creeks and Ga., 518-19n; ceded to Spain, 557

Floridablanca, José Moñino y Redondo, Conde de: and relations with U.S., 140; negotiations with Carmichael, 324; and U.S. boundary with Spain, 556-8, 563n

florin: value in comparison to dollar, 175; value in comparison to livre, 175

flour: demand for in U.S., 4; for Saint-Domingue, 20n; price, 68, 69, 213, 279, 358-9, 384, 407, 441, 486, 554, 590; export to Portugal, 93-4, 400n, 407n, 426, 441; duties on in Spain, 186, 205, 219, 561; reexport to Spanish colonies, 205; export to France, 213, 278, 406, 663; import from U.S. to Netherlands forbidden, 237; purchase

in U.S. for France, 266, 705; speculation in, 351; demand for in Mediterranean, 358-9; export to Liverpool forbidden, 392; export to Spain, 441; milling in Portugal, 441; export from Lisbon forbidden, 441-2n; milling in Va., 706

Flowerden, Joseph: *Compendium of Physic*, 484

forage: British restrictions on export to France, 494

Ford, Paul Leicester: and TJ's draft censure resolutions, xli, 280-1

foreign coinage act: passage of, 38n; and assay of foreign coins, 354, 409, 412, 423; provisions of, 354n

foreign intercourse: act for, 154, 155n, 432, 565-7; TJ's report on fund for, 565-7

foreign officers: payment of, 21, 143, 178, 194n, 240

Forrest, Uriah: and Federal District, 56, 449n; letter to Washington quoted, 56n

Forster, Benson: returns to U.S., 468n

Forster, Nicholas: and Dutch colonial trade, 663; master of *Anne*, 663

Forster, William, 100

Fort Harmar, Treaty of: and boundary with Western Indians, 221-2

Fort Laurence: and boundaries with Western Indians, 355

Fort Pitt, 19, 229

Foster, Theodore: and case of *Commerce*, 415; letter from cited, 415

Four Brothers (ship): captured by *Embuscade*, 685; condemned by Mangourit, 685

Four Friends (ship), 235, 525, 580

Fox, Charles James: *Letter from the Right Honourable Charles James Fox*, 665; mentioned, 253n

Fox, Edward: letter to, 415-17; appointed consul at Falmouth, 203, 227, 238n, 369, 394; mistaken consular appointment of, 228n; letter to cited, 238n

Fox, John: petition from, 634-5

Fox, Robert Weare: appointed consul at Falmouth, 228n

Fox, Samuel M.: and Michaux's proposed western expedition, 83n

FRANCE

Army
size of, 5, 191, 333-4, 452-3; in winter quarters, 5; sent to French West

[725]

INDEX

INDEX

INDEX

Francis, Thomas Willing: master of *Illustrious President*, 297n

Francis II, Holy Roman Emperor: and war with France, 121, 131; and Lafayette's captivity, 128, 389n; proposed assassination of, 128; relations with Prussia, 131; election of, 407; mentioned, 524, 568

Franconia: emigration from to U.S., 640; U.S. consul at, 640n

Frankfurt am Main: emigration from to U.S., 640

"Franklin": pseudonym used by John Taylor of Caroline, 265n, 462n

Franklin, Benjamin: criticism of, 273-4

franquia: and detention of U.S. grain ships in Portugal, 94n, 487-8

Fredericksburgh Packet (ship), 630

Frederick the Great, King of Prussia: and Silesian loan, 539n

Frederick William II, King of Prussia: proposed assassination of, 128; negotiations with Dumouriez, 130-1; relations with Austria, 130-1; and war with France, 130-1; letter to Paleske cited, 376; and Lafayette's captivity, 388n, 389n

"Freeman": supports French Revolution, 660n

Freeman, Samuel: letter from, 633-4; petition from, 634-5; identified, 634n

Free Mason's Calendar (Samuel Stearns): copyright for, 100

Freire, Cypriano Ribeiro, Chevalier: arrival in U.S. expected, 9, 407

"French, The": supports French Revolution, 660n

French Revolution: consular reports on (*see* Cathalan, Stephen, Jr.; Delamotte, F. C. A.; Fenwick, Joseph); TJ's comments on, xxxix, 14-15, 18, 30, 58, 436, 679; conflict between Feuillants and Jacobins, 14-15, 121, 122; support for in U.S., 14-15, 91, 436, 660, 661, 697, 699; opposition to in U.S., 15, 697; G. Morris's reports on, 27-8, 95; impact on French West Indies, 40; J. Adams's comments on, 63-4; Mountflorence's report on, 84, 119-33; execution of king, 95, 100, 103-4, 107, 189, 325, 327, 328n, 340, 402, 407, 442-3, 519, 533, 697; opposition to in Europe, 95, 325; impact on Sweden, 95-6; support for in Europe, 95-6; September Massacres, 120, 128-9, 374;

opposition to in France, 190; Le Roy's comments on, 226; impact on Spain, 325-7; conflict between Girondins and Jacobins, 334, 374, 457; impact on Canada, 363; Short's comments on, 509; T. Paine's report on, 577. *See also* France: War with Austria and Prussia; France: War with First Coalition

Freneau, Philip: duties in Department of State, 10; salary, 10; prints *National Gazette*, 475; mentioned, 214n

"Friend to Liberty, A": pseudonym used by J. Butler, 40-1n

Froullé, Jean François: TJ orders books from

Furant (Durant), M.: recommended as consul at St. Croix, 11, 204

fur trade: in Pacific Northwest, 307

Gallatin, Albert: letter to, 92-3; and viniculture, 92-3; identified, 93n

Gallipolis, Ohio: complaints against Scioto Company, 320

Galloway, Joseph, 103

Gamble, Robert: letter to, 65; letters from, 48-9, 90, 705-6; letter to quoted, 19n; and Derieux's legacy, 44, 48-9, 67, 306; and Thomas Bell's debt to TJ, 65, 90, 101; and purchase of provisions for France, 705-6

Gamelin, Paul: letter to, 251; and confiscation of property by G. R. Clark, 251, 254; identified, 251n

Gamelin, Pierre: identified, 251n

Gardner, Alan: expedition to West Indies, 408

Gardoqui, Don Diego de: identified, 234n; negotiations with Carmichael and Short, 321-2, 555-61, 593, 653-7; and navigation of Mississippi, 429, 556, 559-60, 653, 656-7; and U.S. boundary with Spain, 556-8, 559; and Jay-Gardoqui Treaty, 558, 656; and French Revolution, 559-60; and independence of Spanish colonies, 559-60; and Spanish colonial policy, 559-60; and Spanish relations with Southern Indians, 560, 653-4; and U.S. trade with Spain, 560-1; hostility to U.S., 655-8; relations with Godoy, 656-7; reported ambassadorial appointment to Turin, 657; and war with France, 657

Garth, Thomas: TJ's tenant, 403

Gates, Horatio: letters to, 363-4, 419; letters from, 397, 550, 572; TJ requests copies of correspondence with, 363-4, 397, 419, 550, 567, 572; invites TJ to visit Rose Hill, 397, 419, 550

Gates, Mary Vallance (Mrs. Horatio Gates): invites TJ to visit Rose Hill, 397, 419, 550

Gauthier, M.: visits U.S., 631

Gautier, Jean Antoine: and watch for William Branch Giles, 318

Gazette de Leide: requested by TJ, 394, 439, 535; sent to TJ, 527n

Gazette de Paris: editor executed, 130

Gazette of Maine (Portland): and printing of U.S. laws, 633-4, 651

Gazette of the United States (Philadelphia): and criticism of Franklin, 273-4; prints Giles resolutions censuring Hamilton, 296n, 313-14; prints extract of consular letter, 340n; distribution of, 444, 475

General Advertiser (Philadelphia): prints Giles resolutions censuring Hamilton, 296n; announces TJ's continuance in office, 305n; and public debt, 465-7; refuses to print criticism of Hamilton, 532-3; mentioned, 473

Genet, Edmond Charles: relations with Michaux, xl, 79-80; criticism of, 12; appointed minister to U.S., 57, 193, 519, 565, 663n; and commercial treaty with U.S., 57, 62, 194n; papers for, 166; and French trade concessions to U.S., 243, 244; and recall of G. Morris, 245n; arrival in U.S. expected, 331, 516, 518; privateering commissions for, 333, 494n; praised by Barlow, 336-7; reception by U.S. government, 423, 469-70, 569, 570-2, 598, 600-1, 602, 605, 608, 612, 618, 666, 688; visits G. Morris, 457; and passports for U.S. ships, 530n; arrival at Charleston, 581, 639n; arrival in Philadelphia expected, 619; and case of *Grange*, 640n; commissions privateers in U.S., 686-7, 700n; and case of *Eunice*, 699; and provisions for France, 705, 706; mentioned, 535

Geneva: diplomatic representation policy, 330n

Genoa: foreign loans, 358-9; proposed consular appointment at, 358-9; declares neutrality, 359; trade with France, 359

Geographical, Historical, Political, Philosophical and Mechanical Essays (Lewis Evans): requested by TJ, 199

George (TJ's slave): and canal for Monticello, 98, 138; tools needed by, 156

George III, King of Great Britain: and war with France, 41, 137; planet named for, 54; and enforcement of navigation act, 200, 224; and Charles Grey's peace motion, 252-3

George Barclay (ship), 169

Georgetown, Md.: survey of, 52, 54; roads, 443

Georgia: messenger to, 5; and Republican effort to censure Hamilton, 290; boundary with East Fla., 431n; boundary with West Fla., 431n; conflict with Creeks, 518-19, 520

Georgia, Governor of. *See* Telfair, Edward

Georgium sidus: TJ's comments on, 54

Germany: hostility to French, 95; trade with Netherlands, 146; immigration to U.S., 640; trade with U.S., 640

Gerry, Elbridge: letter to, 269; letter from cited, 269; stockholder in national bank, 432

Gertruidenberg, Netherlands: captured by allies, 524

Ghent, Austrian Netherlands: French retreat to, 455

Giannini, Antonio: claim on Mazzei, 298-9

Gibbon, Edward: *Decline and Fall of the Roman Empire*, 547

Giles, William Branch: portrait of, xli, 400 (illus.); and Michaux's proposed western expedition, 82; and Republican effort to censure Hamilton, 241n, 280-96, 311, 313-14, 433-4n, 461n; and seal for Va. chancery court, 276; and U.S. debt to national bank, 283; censure resolutions against Hamilton, 294-6; watch for, 318; and discounting by national bank, 475n

Gilliat, J. & T.: and Derieux's legacy, 49

Gilman, Nicholas: stockholder in national bank, 432

Gilmer, Dr. George: letter to, 384; letter from, 97; health, 4, 698; treats Anne Cary Randolph, 91; mentioned, 544

Gilmer, Lucy Walker (Mrs. George Gilmer), 97, 384

Gilmor (Gilmore, Gilmer), Robert, & Co.: as security for Stephen Cathalan, Jr., 212; and bills of exchange for Department of State, 531-2, 536, 566

Gilpin, Joshua: and Michaux's proposed

INDEX

Gilpin, Joshua (*cont.*)
western expedition, 83n
ginger: export to U.S., 188
Girondins: conflict with Jacobins, 334, 374, 457
Giroud, M.: lands in N.C., 411
Givet, France: anticipated allied attack on, 488
glazing: for Mint, 447
globes: TJ's inquiries about, 342
Godfrey, Mr.: visits U.S., 587
Godin, P. N.: opposes William Stevenson for consular appointment at St. Eustatius, 204; recommends David M. Clarkson for consular appointment at St. Eustatius, 204
Godoy Alvarez de Faria, Manuel, Duque de la Alcudia: negotiations with Carmichael and Short, 139, 232, 233; and relations with U.S., 140; and relations with Great Britain, 141; relations with Maria Luisa, 142n, 191, 194n; and relations with France, 327; hostility to U.S., 655; relations with Baron St. Helens, 655; relations with Gardoqui, 656-7; mentioned, 495
gold: British restrictions on export to France, 494
Goldsmith, Oliver: *Roman History*, 472
Goliah (TJ's slave): and canal for Monticello, 138
Goll van Frankenstein, Johan, 459
Goodale, Mr., 235
Goodhue, Benjamin: stockholder in national bank, 432
Gordon, James: holder of public debt, 433
Gordon, Peter: J. W. Eppes's account with, 547, 632
Gore, Christopher: as security for Benjamin Joy, 71, 366n
Goths, 133n
Gouvernet, M. de: criticizes Short, 249
Gouverneur, Isaac: recommends William Stevenson for consular appointment at St. Eustatius, 204
Governor Bowdoin (ship): desertion of crew, 377-8n
grain: and still for TJ, 3; price, 12, 68, 94n; demand for in Europe, 28-9; shortage in France, 68, 486, 669; export to Portugal, 93-4; embargo on in Portugal, 94n; export to Spain, 146; and breadstuff, 149n; duties on in Great Britain, 187; export to Great Britain,

187; reexport from Great Britain, 188; for horses, 269; allied trade restrictions on, 377; detention of U.S. in Portugal, 441, 487-8; reexport from Lisbon forbidden, 441-2n; British restrictions on export to France, 493-4, 675
grain spirits: duties on in Netherlands, 146, 188
Grammatical System of the English Language (Caleb Alexander): copyright for, 235
Grand, Ferdinand: and captives in Algiers, 111, 143, 144; and U.S. debt to France, 505; and diplomatic medals, 519-20; and military medals, 519-20
Grand & Cie.: letter from, 635
grand juries: and enforcement of neutrality, 692, 701
Grand Pensionary, Netherlands: and relations with France, 137
Grange (ship): captured by *Embuscade*, 637-40, 641, 644, 649, 661, 662n, 668-9, 676, 683, 694, 702-5; released from French captivity, 640n
grass: white bent, 112-13, 444; timothy, 444
Gray, Mr. *See* Grey, Charles
Gray, Vincent: and passports for U.S. ships, 695n
Gray's Ferry, Pa.: site of TJ's house, xlii, 332, 362

GREAT BRITAIN

Army
home garrisons, 596

Economy
imports wheat, 63; trade with Portugal, 94n; trade restrictions, 146; reexport trade, 188; trade with Spain, 327; distress in, 661

Finances
coinage, 31-2, 37-9

Foreign Relations
with France, 4, 12, 26, 28, 41, 53, 68, 95, 96, 100, 104, 107, 192, 516; with Austria, 96, 190; with Netherlands, 100; with Spain, 141, 142n, 322, 327, 383, 430-1, 561-2, 654; diplomatic representation policy, 324, 330n; with Portugal, 407; with Switzerland, 456; and Silesian loan, 539n

INDEX

INDEX

TJ's retirement, 36-7, 427-8; secretary to Washington, 37n; absence from Lisbon, 87, 93-4, 159-60, 166, 169, 182, 319n; and trade with Portugal, 93-4, 407, 441; letter from cited, 155n; and T. Pinckney's cipher, 167; and levees, 208; and Lafayette's captivity, 387n, 665; letter from quoted, 400; mission to Algiers, 400n, 405, 410, 413-14, 420-1, 423, 429-30, 438, 468-9, 470-1, 532, 535, 542; expenses, 405n, 421, 438, 532, 535, 542; and proposed commercial treaty between Portugal and Naples, 407, 426; relations with Carmichael, 407; and detention of U.S. grain ships in Portugal, 407n, 441, 487-8, 623; account with Willink, Van Staphorst & Hubbard, 410, 413-14, 421, 532, 535, 542; and Barclay's mission to Morocco, 420-1; and civil war in Morocco, 421; letters to submitted to Washington, 423, 427n, 469n, 532n, 566, 588n; TJ's instructions on neutrality to, 426-7; and relations with Spain, 427; account with T. Pinckney, 532, 535, 542; and Barclay's ciphers, 575; and Proclamation of Neutrality, 587-8; mentioned, 562, 694-5

Huntington, Samuel: letter to, 588

Hutchins, Thomas: and survey of Northwest Territory, 332n, 338n; *New Map of the Western Parts*, 356

Hutchinson, Edward: captured by *Embuscade*, 637, 638n; master of *Grange*, 637

Hutchinson, James: and Michaux's proposed western expedition, 82n

Hutchinson, Thomas: criticism of, 660n

Huy, Austrian Netherlands: and French invasion of Austrian Netherlands, 343

hydrogen: and Blanchard's balloon flight, xl

Hyena (H.M.S.): and case of *Illustrious President*, 103, 104n

Hylton, Daniel L.: letter to, 70; letters from cited, 70, 71n; and proposed sale of Elk Hill, 70, 72-3; and stalactite for Peale's museum, 91

Hylton, Mrs. Daniel L., 70

Illinois Indians: and Michaux's proposed western expedition, 72; peace conference with Washington, 112-19, 133-4, 136, 144, 153, 158; conflict with Delawares, 118; conflict with Shawnee, 118; request priests, 118; boundary with U.S., 356; letter of protection for, 380n

Illustrious President (ship): case referred to Grenville, 103, 104n; case referred to TJ, 296-7

Ilsley, Daniel: petition from, 634-5

Ilsley, Enoch: petition from, 634-5

immigration: from U.S. to Canada, 268; from Great Britain to U.S., 394, 528; from Rhineland to U.S., 640

impressment. *See* seamen, impressment of

Independent Chronicle (Boston): prints "The French," 660n

India: needy seamen in, 71; U.S. consul in, 71

Indian Commissioners, U.S.: appointment of, 19, 88-9, 229, 265, 383; and proposed peace conference with Indians, 65; instructions for, 220-3, 255, 354-6, 372, 373, 424-5, 450; compensation for, 229; deadline for negotiations with Western Indians, 271; departure from Philadelphia, 279, 520; mentioned, 319. *See also* Lincoln, Benjamin; Pickering, Timothy; Randolph, Beverley

Indian corn: and still for TJ, 3; export to Portugal, 28-9; price, 69. *See also* corn; maize

Indians: peace negotiations with U.S., 9, 19, 30, 65, 88-9, 215-16, 220-3, 229, 247n, 255, 258-9, 271-3, 279, 317, 354-6, 368, 372, 373, 383, 424-5, 440, 450, 478, 511, 518, 520, 592; TJ's comments on, 19; land purchases from, 46, 47-8; U.S. regulation of trade with, 47-8, 249-50; and Michaux's proposed western expedition, 72; British policy toward, 112, 114, 247n; peace conference with Washington, 112-19, 133-4, 136, 144, 153, 158; relations with Ky., 113, 114, 118; and proposed colony on Mississippi, 195n; conflict with in Northwest Territory, 215-16, 220-3, 229, 255, 258-9, 271-3, 354-6, 368, 424-5, 520; right of U.S. to cede territory to, 220, 258-9, 272-3, 518; U.S. sovereignty over lands of, 222; TJ's report on boundaries with Western, 332, 337-8, 354-6; letter of protection for, 380-1; conflict with in Ga., 518, 520; alliance between Southern and Western feared, 520; Spanish policy toward, 560, 653-4, 677-8; land

Indians (*cont.*)
  cessions to N.Y., 592n; capture slaves,
    620-1. *See also* individual tribes
Indian trade and intercourse act: TJ's
    amendment to, 47-8; and letter of pro-
    tection for Indians, 380-1
indigo: import from U.S. forbidden by
    Denmark, 146; duties on in France,
    186; export to France, 186; import from
    U.S. to Spain forbidden, 186; duties on
    in Great Britain, 187, 202; export to
    Great Britain, 187; reexport from Great
    Britain, 188
Ingersoll, Jared: and Michaux's proposed
    western expedition, 83n
Innes, Harry: letter to, 10-11; and Ky.
    electoral votes, 302, 306, 310; letters
    from cited, 306n, 620; slaves captured
    by Indians, 620-1
Inquisition: in Sicily, 120; in Spain, 120
Institutes of Moral Philosophy (Adam Fer-
    guson): cited by J. G. Jefferson, 472
Institutes of the Laws of England (Sir
    Edward Coke): recommended by TJ,
    544, 546
*Institutions du Droit de la Nature et des
    Gens* (Christian Wolff): and French
    treaties, 606, 612-15, 618n
insurance: in France, 68
Iphigenia (H.M.S.): and desertions from
    Governor Bowdoin, 377-8n
Iredell, James: letter to quoted, 395-6n
Ireland: and Portuguese restrictions on
    U.S. trade, 94n; reported French inva-
    sion of, 97; status of U.S. factors in,
    147; status of U.S. merchants in, 147;
    trade with U.S., 147, 159; iron produc-
    tion, 201; regiment from sent to West
    Indies, 493
iron: and Blanchard's balloon flight, 42;
    for Monticello, 138; for Mint, 447. *See
    also* bar iron; pig iron
Iroquois Indians: southern land claims,
    199, 209-10; treaties with U.S., 424;
    treaties with N.Y., 592n
Irvine, William: letter from, 373
Izard, Ralph: and Michaux's proposed
    western expedition, 78, 82; and criti-
    cism of Franklin, 274; stockholder in
    national bank, 433

Jackson, Francis James: British minister
    to Spain, 327, 331n
Jacobins: and constitution, 14, 121;

TJ's comments on, 14; political inten-
    tions, 28; and monarchy, 58, 121;
    and September Massacres, 120; conflict
    with Feuillants, 121, 122; and war with
    Austria and Prussia, 121; conflict with
    Lafayette, 122, 123-5, 127; and French
    army, 122; accusations against king,
    127; conflict with G. Morris, 128; and
    political assassination, 128; and agrar-
    ian law, 129; conflict with Girondins,
    334, 374, 457; Short's criticism of,
    508; unpopularity of, 524; conflict with
    Dumouriez, 576
James (ship), 525
Jaudenes, Josef de letters to, 184-5, 219;
    letters from, 205-6, 593, 677; letter
    to quoted, 16n; and U.S. negotiations
    with Spain, 140; and TJ's report on
    commerce, 184-5, 205-6, 219; letters to
    submitted to Washington, 185n, 198,
    220; letters from submitted to Washing-
    ton, 220, 678n; and Spanish relations
    with Southern Indians, 677-8; men-
    tioned, 16, 653, 659n
Jay, John: and debt to France, 197; and
    case of *Dover*, 277; and Pagan v. Hoop-
    er, 389, 540; letter to quoted, 395-6n;
    and Jay-Gardoqui Treaty, 558, 656;
    and neutrality, 569n
Jay-Gardoqui Treaty: and commercial
    treaty with Spain, 558; and navigation
    of Mississippi, 558; and U.S. boundary
    with Spain, 558; mentioned, 656
Jefferson, Jane Randolph (Mrs. Peter Jef-
    ferson, TJ's mother): debt to Hender-
    son & Co., 551
Jefferson, John Garland: letter to, 547-8;
    letters from, 472-3, 593-4; education,
    472-3, 543, 545, 547; account with TJ,
    473, 543, 548, 593-4; plans to practice
    law, 593; account with Shelton, 593-4
Jefferson, Mary (Maria, Polly, TJ's
    daughter): health, 30, 43, 353, 520-
    1, 545, 547, 621, 633, 669, 693; and
    Blanchard's balloon flight, 50-1; cor-
    respondence with aunt, 65; correspon-
    dence with brother-in-law, 91, 157n,
    230, 256, 313, 475, 520; correspon-
    dence with sister, 91, 297; relations
    with J. W. Eppes, 633; mentioned, 8,
    64
Jefferson, Peter (TJ's father): executors
    of, 403
Jefferson, Randolph (TJ's brother): and
    sale of TJ's slaves, 91; slaves of, 403

INDEX

INDEX

INDEX

INDEX

INDEX

Kuhn, Adam: and Michaux's proposed western expedition, 83n

Labourdonnaie, Anne François Auguste, Comte de: military command, 452
Lacoste, Jean de: and U.S. aid to Saint-Domingue, 503-4
Lady Washington (ship): voyage to China, 308n; voyage to Pacific Northwest, 308n
Lafayette, Marie Adrienne Françoise de Noailles, Marquise de: letter to, 391-2; and husband's captivity, 257-8, 382, 388n, 391-2; aided by G. Morris, 388n
Lafayette, Marie Joseph Paul Yves Roch Gilbert du Motier, Marquis de: discusses royal veto, 58; in Austrian captivity, 119-20, 128, 142-3, 194, 215, 257-8, 382, 387-9, 390-2, 664, 697; conflict with Jacobins, 120, 122, 123-5, 127, 129; appointed to army command, 122; conflict with Luckner, 123-4; and Legislative Assembly, 123-4; proposed assassination of, 128; conflict with Dumouriez, 130; relations with George Washington Greene, 135n; relations with king, 143n; in Prussian captivity, 258n, 382n, 388n; Md. citizenship, 388n; U.S. citizenship, 388n; Va. citizenship, 388n; and U.S. boundary with Spain, 556-8, 563n; mentioned, 489
La Forest, Antoine René Charles Mathurin de: and French consular salaries, 6-7, 543; and bills on Saint-Domingue, 20n, 34n; and supplies for France, 39; and U.S. aid to Saint-Domingue, 52n; and Michaux's bills, 72; and case of *Grange*, 639n, 694, 702-5; report on *Grange*, 703-5
Laight, William, 640
Lake Erie, 19, 229
Lake Ontario, 19, 229
Lalande, Joseph Jérôme Le Français de: *Astronomie*, 490
Lamb, John: mission to Algiers, 143; and passports for U.S. ships, 696
Lamballe, Marie Thérèse Louise de Savoie Carignan, Princess de: character of, 129; execution of, 129
Lameth, Alexandre Théodore Victor, Comte de: discusses royal veto, 58
La Mettrie, Julien Offroy de: *Abrégé de la théorie chymique*, 490
Langdon, John: and Michaux's proposed

western expedition, 82; and assumption of public debt, 208
Langdon, Woodbury: letter from, 373
Languedoc, France: and allied military strategy, 191
La Panse river: and boundaries with Western Indians, 355
La Porte, Arnaud de: execution of, 130
La Rochefoucauld, Alexandrine, Duchesse de: relations with Short, 60-1
La Sauvagère, Félix François Le Royer d'Artezet de: *Recueil de Dissertations*, 490
Latimer, George: and bills on Saint-Domingue, 20
Latour-Maubourg, Marie Charles César Fay, Comte de: discusses royal veto, 58
La Tuellier, M. de: and transport of French prisoners to U.S., 464
Laurance, John: and Republican effort to censure Hamilton, 289; director of national bank, 432; stockholder in national bank, 432
Lavater, Johann Kaspar, 576
law: TJ's comments on education in, 396
law of nations: and right of U.S. to cede territory to Indians, 272; TJ's views on, 609-10; and treaties with France, 609-10; and French captures of British ships in U.S. territorial waters, 638; and contraband, 675; and U.S. arms sales to France, 684
Lawrence (ship): captured by *Sans Culotte*, 458n, 548, 574n
lead: for Mint, 447
Leamy, John: letter from cited, 309n; letter to cited, 309n; recommends Michael Morphy for consular appointment at Malaga, 309n
Lear, Tobias: letters from, 45, 49, 56, 136, 144, 153, 216, 237-8, 255, 255-6, 270, 296-7, 300, 320, 575; letters from quoted, 9n, 47n, 250n, 584n, 589n; and assumption of public debt, 208; letter from cited, 255n; and republicanism in U.S., 302; and public debt, 517; mentioned, 423n, 511
Learned, Amasa: stockholder in national bank, 432
Lebrun-Tondu, Pierre Henri Hélène Marie: letter from, 57-8; correspondence with G. Morris, 46-7; introduces Genet, 57; and recall of G. Morris, 57, 58n, 243, 248; identified, 58n; and provisions for France, 163n, 266, 275-6;

and U.S. debt to France, 164n; and relations with Great Britain, 192; criticizes Short, 249; and capture of U.S. ships by French privateers, 457-8, 488, 489n, 530, 572-3, 574n; and passports for U.S. ships, 530n

Le Couteulx, M.: refuses consular appointment, 53

Ledyard, John: proposed western expedition, 75

Lee, Dr. Arthur: death, 16

Lee, Charles: and French Revolution, 697; and Republican effort to censure Hamilton, 697-8

Lee, Henry: letters to, 359-60, 588; letter from, 688; and Federal District, 152; and Va. dissatisfaction with federal government, 154; and Va. boundary with Southwest Territory, 359-60; and defense of Norfolk, 688; letter from submitted to Washington, 688n; and provisions for France, 705, 706

Lee, Richard Bland: and Michaux's proposed western expedition, 82; and Va. elections, 443-4; elected to House of Representatives, 533; identified, 534n

Lee, Thomas Sim: letter to, 588

Legaux, Peter: and viniculture, 92-3

Le Havre, France: market for tobacco in, 3; trade with U.S., 53, 150; U.S. consul at, 202, 203, 227, 238n, 369, 394, 417n; exchange rate, 340; Spanish consul in, 363; and Federal District, 369; privateering in, 548

Leiper, Thomas: letter to, 529; letter from, 594-5; James Wilson's landlord, 529; TJ's Philadelphia landlord, 529, 594-5

L'Enfant, Pierre Charles: dispute with Federal District Commissioners, 266-7

Le Roy, Jean Baptiste: letter from, 225-7; and French Revolution, 226

Leslie, Robert: and marine clocks, 585-6; and rod pendulum, 585-6; and watches, 585-6; praised by TJ, 586; and great clock for TJ, 586n

Letter from the Right Honourable Charles James Fox: submitted to Washington, 665

Letters of the Late Ignatius Sancho (Ignatius Sancho): loaned to D. Rittenhouse, 490

Lettre adressée aux habitants de Piémont (Joel Barlow): sent to TJ, 336-7

Lettre du Général Dumouriez: sent to TJ, 450-1, 458n

Levant: forbids export of corn, 358-9

levees: criticism of, 208

Lewis, Charles: and Antonio Giannini's claim on Mazzei, 299

Lewis, David: and Michaux's proposed western expedition, 83n

Lewis, Meriwether: western expedition, 75, 81

Lewis, Mordecai: and bills of exchange for Department of State, 531-2, 536, 566

Lewis, Nicholas: and sale of TJ's slaves, 91; and TJ's accounts, 101; manages TJ's affairs, 366; and John Barret's debt to TJ, 696-7; mentioned, 544

Lewis, Robert, Jr.: debt to TJ, 366; sued by TJ, 366

Lewis, Thomas: and Natural Bridge, 403

Leyden, Netherlands: and Federal District, 671

Leyden Gazette. See Gazette de Leide

Liège, Austrian Netherlands: and French invasion of Austrian Netherlands, 343, 374; French stores captured at, 454; French withdrawal from, 523-4, 668

Lille (Lisle), France: and invasion of Netherlands, 455; anticipated surrender of, 488

lime: for Mint, 447

limestone: for Monticello, 43, 91

Lincoln, Benjamin: appointed Indian commissioner, 229n; expected in Philadelphia, 511

Lindsay, Adam: letter from, 270-1; and candles for TJ, 270-1; TJ's account with, 270-1

linen: production of, 256n

Lingan, James M.: and passports for U.S. ships, 670-1n

Lisbon: and consular fees, 13; trade with U.S., 28-9, 441; U.S. consul at, 203; U.S. grain ships detained in, 441, 487-8; mentioned, 7

Lisle. *See* Lille, France

Little beaver (Wiatonon chief): peace conference with Washington, 116

Little Miami river: and boundaries with Western Indians, 355

Little Sarah (ship): captured by *Embuscade*, 668-9

live provisions: export to French West Indies, 186; export to British West Indies, 188

Liverpool, England: U.S. consul at, 203;

INDEX

Liverpool, England (*cont.*)
closed to foreign flour, 392; closed to foreign wheat, 392; prices at, 392-3
Livingston, Henry Walter: letter from cited, 45; secretary to G. Morris, 193
Livingston, Robert R.: letter from, 304-5; and relationship between snow and temperature, 304-5; and TJ's retirement, 304-5
livre: value in comparison to dollar, 149n, 175; value in comparison to florin, 175
llamas: and Michaux's proposed western expedition, 625
Lloyd's of London: and passports for U.S. ships, 166; and insurance for U.S. ships, 335-6n; Liverpool price list sent to TJ, 393n
Logan, Deborah Norris (Mrs. George Logan), 651n
Logan, Dr. George: letter to, 650; and plows for Madison, 534, 619, 660; TJ unable to visit, 650; identified, 651n
Logan Act, 651n
Logie, Charles: and captives in Algiers, 161
London: exchange rate, 69, 340; fire engines in, 163; U.S. consul at, 202
London Gazette: sent to TJ, 527n
Long, William: builds library for TJ's Philadelphia house, 553
longitude: Guyer's invention for ascertaining, 589
Longwy, France: captured by Prussians, 128, 130; evacuated by Prussians, 130-1
looking glasses: sent to Monticello, 513-14, 521
Lord, Elias: master of *Young Eagle*, 549n
Lords of the Admiralty, British: and deserting seamen, 375
Lords of the Treasury, British: and case of Philip Wilson, 526
L'Orient, France: coastal trade, 422
Lorraine, France: evacuated by Prussians, 130-1
lottery: for Federal District, 25; for Peregrine Fitzhugh, 262-3
Louisiana: proposed U.S. guarantee of, xli-xlii, 430-1, 444; French plan to liberate, 80, 244-5, 431n
Louis XVI, King of France: execution of, xxxix, 95, 100, 103-4, 107, 189, 325, 327, 328n, 340, 400 (illus.), 402, 407, 442-3, 519, 533, 697; trial of, 53, 131, 384, 519; appoints Michaux

royal botanist, 76; dethronement of, 84, 120-32, 239, 367, 388n, 506, 519; accusations against, 121; veto power, 121; and war with Austria and Prussia, 121, 130; and clerical oaths, 123; and National Guard, 123; unpopularity of, 123; alleged murder plot, 127; imprisonment of, 127, 129; relations with Princess Lamballe, 129; relations with Dumouriez, 131-2; relations with Lafayette, 143n; restoration of hoped for, 244; G. Morris presented to, 503; and treaties with U.S., 608-9
Louis XVII, King of France: proposed restoration of, 524
Louvain, Austrian Netherlands: and French invasion of Netherlands, 335; and French invasion of Austrian Netherlands, 343, 374, 453; French retreat to, 454-5
Lowe, Capt. (master of *Swanwick*), 548
Lower Sandusky: proposed site of peace conference with Western Indians, 229, 247n, 259n, 356n, 424, 520
Loxley, Benjamin: master of *Pigou*, 408, 417n
Lucas, Mr.: British consul in Tripoli, 160, 161
Luckner, Nicolas, Comte de: conflict with Lafayette, 123-4
Lucy (ship): passport for, 682n
Lur-Saluces d'Yquem (Luz-Saluce), Comtesse de: wine of, 269
Luxembourg: occupied by Prussians, 131; allied forces in, 343
Luxembourg, Maréchal de: and battle of Neerwinden, 455
Luz-Saluce, Countess de. *See* Lur-Saluces d'Yquem, Comtesse de
Lyle, James: letter to, 550-1
Lyons, France: and Federal District, 369; mentioned 456

Maastricht, Netherlands: and allied military strategy, 191; French siege of, 333-4, 339, 359, 454; French retreat from, 343, 668
McAllister, Matthew: and theft of slaves from Martinique, 61
macaroni: for TJ, 341; TJ's plans for, 384
McConnell, Matthew: and Michaux's proposed western expedition, 82n, 83n
Macdonald, Sir Archibald: and deserting British seamen, 151

INDEX

Mace, Mr.: British consul in Algiers, 160; and captives in Algiers, 161

McFaden, William: and use of flags, 5n, 362-3

McIntosh, Lachlan, 431n

McIntosh, Treaty of: and Indian boundaries, 355

Mackenzie, James: and bills of exchange for Department of State, 536, 566

McLellan, Arthur: petition from, 634-5

M'Lellan, Hugh: petition from, 634-5

Mclellan, Joseph: petition from, 634-5

Macon, Nathaniel: and Republican effort to censure Hamilton, 290

Macquinnah (Northwestern Indian chief): and John Kendrick's land purchases, 307

Macraken, Gilbert: and case of *Grange*, 638n

Madeira: and consular fees, 13; and needy seamen, 71; trade with U.S., 151; U.S. consul at, 203; French prisoners in, 464

Madison, James: letters to, 442-3, 473-4, 516, 619, 660; letters from, 443-4, 532-4, 688-9; and Republican effort to censure Hamilton, 23n, 241n, 283, 284, 287, 288, 289, 290, 384, 697; and Indian land purchases, 48n; and Michaux's proposed western expedition, 82; relations with Joseph Fay, 99; and second term for Washington, 155; and levees, 208; proposed appointment as minister to France, 245n; and U.S. debt to national bank, 283; and Federal District, 345, 361; invited to visit Horatio Gates, 397; and Va. chancery court seal, 401; and Va. elections, 443-4, 463, 533; returns to Va., 444; letter from cited, 444n; elected to House of Representatives, 463; and foreign loans, 473-4, 533; and freedom of the press, 532-3; and execution of Louis XVI, 533; plows for, 534, 619; and reception of Genet, 688; and Proclamation of Neutrality, 688-9; and treaties with France, 689; mentioned, 460, 475

Madison (ship), 213, 279n

Madrid: exchange rate, 69; and French Revolution, 325

Magaw, Samuel: and Michaux's proposed western expedition, 82

Magdeburg: Lafayette's captivity at, 194n

Maine: U.S. marshal for, 316n; printing of U.S. laws in, 633-4, 651; commerce, 634-5

Mainz (Mayence, Mayntz): and allied military strategy, 191; and invasion of Rhineland, 456; Prussian intention to capture, 456; anticipated French evacuation of, 488; allied siege of, 492

maize: export to French West Indies, 186. *See also* corn; Indian corn

Malaga, Spain: U.S. consul at, 308, 369, 395, 435

Malines, Austrian Netherlands: and French invasion of Austrian Netherlands, 343

Malone, Dumas: and TJ's draft censure resolutions, 286, 287

mammoth: and Michaux's proposed western expedition, 625

Mangourit, Michel Ange Bernard de: and French consular admiralty jurisdiction in U.S., 685-6

Manly Medal: minted in Philadelphia, 351n

Marat, Jean Paul: reported destruction of, 641

marble: for Federal District, 152, 170

Maria I, Queen of Portugal: health, 407; mentioned, 487

Maria Luisa, Queen of Spain: relations with Godoy, 142n, 191, 194n; and relations with France, 327

Marie Antoinette, Queen of France: TJ's attitude toward, xxxix; dethronement of, 84; and war with Austria and Prussia, 121; unpopularity of, 123, 125; and Princess Lamballe, 129; trial of, 131

marine clocks: Robert Leslie's improvements for, 585-6

Marit, M.: leaves London, 166

Mark, Philip: letter from, 640; seeks consular appointment in Rhineland, 640; appointed consul at Franconia, 640; identified, 640n; letter from cited, 640n

Marriot, Mr.: and Mint, 13n, 103

Marseilles, France: Jacobin club in, 121; National Guard of, 126; and allied military strategy, 191; U.S. consul at, 202; food shortage in, 213; trade with U.S., 213; privateering in, 214, 406, 458n; trade with Genoa, 359; and Federal District, 369

Marshall, Mr. (Eng.): and orrery for TJ, 341

Marshall, James Markham: returns to U.S., 352, 378n; and model of threshing machine for TJ, 378-9

Marshall, John: and James Currie's land

INDEX

Mercer, John Francis: and Michaux's proposed western expedition, 78, 82; and Republican effort to censure Hamilton, 289

merchants, U.S.: criticism of, 8; status in British empire, 147, 188

Mercury (ship): captured by *Proserpine*, 489n

Meredith, Mr.: and John Clarke's invention, 276

Meredith, Samuel: and drawing of foreign loans to U.S., 239, 240; and Mint, 393, 446; and execution of Louis XVI, 443

Mermaid (ship), 68

Miami river: and boundaries with Western Indians, 355

Michaux, André: proposed western expedition, xl, 17-18, 71-2, 75-84, 85, 527, 530-1, 624-6; relations with Genet, xl, 79-80; botanical expeditions, 76; identified, 76; subscription agreement for, 77-8, 81-2, 85, 400 (illus.); instructions for, 79, 527, 530-1, 624-6

Mifflin, Thomas: letter to, 588; and Michaux's proposed western expedition, 78, 82

military stores: British restrictions on export to France, 494

militia: drafting of in France, 344

mill: for Monticello, 156, 313

Millar, Mr.: and postal service at Charlottesville, 477

Miller, George: and French consular admiralty jurisdiction in U.S., 685-6; and French privateers commissioned by Genet in U.S., 686-7

Miller, James: and Dutch trade embargo, 468n; master of *Hope*, 468n, 524; returns to U.S., 468n

Miller, Phineas: letter from, 644-5; identified, 645n

millwrights: for Mint, 447

milréis: Portuguese symbol for, 235-6

Milton, Va.: flour trade, 706

Mingo (TJ's slave): and canal for Monticello, 138

minister of finance, France. *See* Clavière, Etienne

minister of foreign affairs, France. *See* Lebrun-Tondu, Pierre Henri Hélène Marie

minister of marine, France. *See* Monge, Gaspard

minister of war, France. *See* Pache, Jean Nicolas

Mint, U.S.: assayer for, 12, 13n, 103, 370-1, 578, 665, 695; chief coiner and engraver for, 12, 13n, 103, 512, 575-6; and assay of foreign coinage, 31-2, 37-9, 40, 354, 409, 412, 423; copper for, 151, 204, 393, 447, 578, 596; expenses, 446-7; machinery for, 447; raw materials for, 447; salaries for, 447; workmen for, 447; books for, 490. *See also* coinage

Mint, U.S., Director of. *See* Rittenhouse, David

Miquelon: provisions for, 39

Miranda, Francisco de: and invasion of Austrian Netherlands, 5, 451; and French plan to liberate South America, 243, 245n; and invasion of Netherlands, 374, 453

Mississippi river: and Michaux's proposed western expedition, 71-2, 81, 85, 624; and G. R. Clark's proposed western expedition, 75; navigation of, 80, 195n, 250, 556, 558, 559-60, 653, 656-7; as Chickasaw boundary, 209; and Spanish trade duties, 250; British right to navigate, 653

Missouri river: and Michaux's proposed western expedition, 76, 77, 81, 624, 625

Mitchell, David: petition from, 634-5

Mohawk river, 19, 229

molasses: export to U.S., 187, 188; distilling of, 237

monarchy: prospects for in U.S., 15, 30, 302, 436, 679; Jacobin attitudes toward, 58; abolished in France, 120-32, 218-19; and royal inviolability, 402; support for in France, 573-4, 577; TJ's comments on, 679

Moncrief, Archibald: letters to, 583, 620; and wine for TJ, 583, 620; identified, 583n; letter from cited, 583n

Monge, Gaspard: and U.S. trade with France, 340n; and capture of U.S. ships by French privateers, 489n, 572-3, 574n

Moniteur (Paris): J. Wheatcroft's assessment of, 548

Monroe, Elizabeth Kortright (Mrs. James Monroe): returns to Va., 384, 444; health, 698; mentioned, 662

Monroe, James: letters to, 50, 366-7, 660-2; letters from, 11, 50, 102, 429, 463-4, 696-8, 707; recommends Furant for consular appointment at St. Croix, 11; and U.S. debt to France, 50; account with Thomas Bell, 101; and appointment of ministers to Europe, 102; appointed minister to France,

INDEX

Monroe, James (*cont.*)
245n; remains in Philadelphia, 257; and TJ's business affairs, 366-7, 696-7; returns to Va., 384, 444; and Va. chancery court seal, 401; and navigation of Mississippi, 429; recommends John Cleves Symmes to TJ, 429; and *Examination of the Late Proceedings in Congress*, 433-4n; and TJ's continuance in office, 463; and Va. elections, 463; and French Revolution, 697; and Republican effort to censure Hamilton, 697-8; mentioned, 660

Mons, Austrian Netherlands: abandoned by French, 122; and French invasion of Austrian Netherlands, 454; French retreat to, 455

Montauk Point, N.Y.: cession to U.S., 265

Montgomery, Robert: letters to, 238, 415-17; and captives in Algiers, 88n; appointed consul at Alicante, 203, 227, 238, 369, 394, 435

Montgomery, William: master of *Neptune*, 568

Monticello: remodeling of, 26, 43, 73-4, 91, 138, 230, 314, 353, 693; stonemason for, 26; window sashes for, 26; limestone for, 43, 91; timber for, 43, 73-4, 91, 299; window frames for, 43; orchard, 91; stable, 91, 156; canal, 98, 138; overseer for, 98, 138, 225, 263, 313, 483; carpenters for, 138; gunpowder for, 138; iron for, 138; mill, 156, 313; tenant farmers for, 225, 230, 263, 298, 313, 403-4, 483, 521; bricks for, 314; roof, 315; garden, 353, 444; grass, 444; trees, 444

Moore, Andrew: elected to House of Representatives, 533

moral law: and French treaties, 609-10; TJ's views on, 609-10

Morning Chronicle (London), 252

Morning Star (ship): captured by *Embuscade*, 685; condemned by Mangourit, 685

Morocco: Barclay's mission to, 87, 88n, 143, 159-60, 182, 234, 319n, 400n, 420, 429-30, 468-9; British consul in, 160; civil war in, 160, 161n, 182, 234-5, 421, 429-30, 623, 630; U.S. consul in, 203

Morphy (Murphy), Michael: letter to, 415-17; appointed consul at Malaga, 308, 369, 395, 435; letter to cited, 309n

Morris, Caspar W.: and Michaux's proposed western expedition, 83n

Morris, Gouverneur: letters to, 367-9, 387, 519-20, 575-6, 585-6, 591, 689-90; letters from, 4-5, 27-8, 66, 95-6, 189-94, 195-6, 333-5, 338-9, 343-4, 374, 450-7, 488-9, 492-3, 530, 572-4; and French war with Austria and Prussia, 4, 95; and relations between France and Great Britain, 4, 28, 95, 96, 192; and case of *Euphrasie*, 5, 363; letters from submitted to Washington, 5n, 28n, 66n, 96n, 194n, 335-6n, 339n, 344n, 375n, 458n, 489n, 493n; and Mint, 12, 103, 370, 575-6, 578; and debt to France, 16-17, 47n, 50, 240, 368, 369n, 382, 479, 482n, 496, 498-9, 502, 503-9; and French politics, 27-8, 334, 374, 457, 489, 573-4; correspondence with Lebrun, 46-7; proposed recall of, 57, 58n, 243-5, 247-9; and equestrian statue of Washington, 66; letter from cited, 68; and French Revolution, 95, 244; and Louis XVI's execution, 95; and T. Pinckney's cipher, 107, 150, 167, 376, 378n, 408; conflict with Jacobins, 128; and Lafayette's captivity, 142-3, 194, 382, 387-9, 390-2, 665; cipher for, 167; and French finances, 189-90; and French war with First Coalition, 189-92, 333-4, 338-9, 343-4, 450-7, 488, 530, 573; and émigrés, 192, 194n; and treaty of alliance with France, 192; and commercial treaty with France, 192-3; acquires country house in France, 193; and Genet's mission to U.S., 193; and TJ's retirement, 193, 195-6; and payment of foreign officers, 194n, 240; letter from quoted, 194-5n; and proposed colony on Mississippi, 194-5n; proposed appointment as minister to Great Britain, 244, 245n; and passports for U.S. ships, 333, 335-6n, 375, 377n; and privateering, 333, 494n; and French trade concessions, 334, 530; and trade with France, 340n; and diplomatic recognition policy, 367-8, 369n; and U.S. aid to Saint-Domingue, 368, 498-9; letters to submitted to Washington, 369n, 389n, 390, 592n, 665; aids Marquise de Lafayette, 388n; expenses, 405n, 438, 535, 542; and case of *Aurora*, 406; and duties on bacalao, 406; reported murder of, 422; and foreign loans, 436-7; papers for, 448; meets Genet, 457;

and capture of U.S. ships by French privateers, 457-8, 488, 489n, 530, 572-3, 574n; appointed minister to France, 500-1, 502, 509n; presented to king, 503; and diplomatic medals, 519-20; and military medals, 519-20; instructions from TJ on neutrality, 576; and Proclamation of Neutrality, 591; mentioned, 61, 84, 103, 151, 518, 652, 671, 680

Morris, Lewis: home burned, 577

Morris, Mary White (Mrs. Robert Morris), 651n

Morris, Robert: and Michaux's proposed western expedition, 78, 82, 83n; recommends Edward Fox for consular appointment at Falmouth, 203; and Asylum Company, 372n; stockholder in national bank, 433; and failure of Donald & Burton, 524, 527

Moses (TJ's slave): and canal for Monticello, 138

Moulton, William: petition from, 634-5

Mounier, Jean Joseph: discusses royal veto, 58

Mountflorence, James Cole: letters from, 84, 119-20; and French Revolution, 84, 119-33; and Lafayette's captivity, 119-20; recommended to Short, 132n; identified, 132-3n

Mount Jura, 190

Mousley, Walter: TJ's tenant, 403

Moylan, James: recommends John Culnan as consul at Tenerife, 204n

Moylan, John: recommends John Culnan as consul at Tenerife, 204n

Muhammad Ben Absadack: and Moroccan civil war, 630

Muley Ischem: and Moroccan civil war, 182, 234, 630

Muley Suliman: and Moroccan civil war, 182, 234, 630; gifts for, 234

Muley Teib: and Moroccan civil war, 234

Muley Yezid: gifts for, 234

Mullikin (Mulligan), Samuel: proposed stonecutting mill, 24

Munro, James, Jr.: detained at Port-au-Prince, 414-15, 510-11, 554; master of *Commerce*, 414-15

Murphy, Michael. *See* Morphy, Michael

Murray, James: seeks military commission, 484

Murray, John, 640

Murray, William Vans: letter from, 698-9; holds public debt, 311; stockholder in national bank, 433; and French Revolution, 699; letter from submitted to Washington, 699n; and case of *Eunice*, 699-700

Musketon Indians. *See* Mascouten Indians

Muskingum river: and boundaries with Western Indians, 355

Mussey, John: petition from, 634-5

Myers, Mr.: Martha Jefferson Carr's debt to, 223, 545

myrtle wax: for TJ's candles, 270-1

Nagell, Anne Willem Carel, Baron Van: criticizes Genet, 12

nails: Elisha Bartlett's machine for making, 398n; for Mint, 447

Namur, Austrian Netherlands: and French invasion of Austrian Netherlands, 343, 374, 454

Nancarrow, John: letter from, 163-4; and fire engines, 163-4; mining interests in Va., 476; TJ's comments on, 476

Nancy (ship): passport for, 682n

Nantes, France: U.S. consul at, 203; and Federal District, 369; threats to, 457

Nantucket whalers: at Dunkirk, 410

Naples: proposed commercial treaty with Portugal, 407, 426

Nation, The: and TJ's draft censure resolutions, 281

National Assembly. *See* France: Legislative Assembly; France: National Assembly

national commission, French: and U.S. aid to Saint-Domingue, 33-4. *See also* Ailhaud, Jean Antoine; Polverel, Etienne; Sonthonax, Léger Félicité

National Convention. *See* France: National Convention

National Gazette (Philadelphia): prints extracts of consular letters, 69n, 214n, 340n; criticizes Washington, 155n, 208n; and Republican effort to censure Hamilton, 172, 173, 434n; prints "Franklin" essays, 265n, 462n; prints Giles censure resolutions against Hamilton, 296n; prints "Timon" essays, 434n, 443n, 546n; distribution of, 475, 476, 661; prints Kersaint's proposition, 478n; prints extract of T. Pinckney letter, 494n; mentioned, 707n

National Guard, French: and dethronement of king, 122-7; and invasion of France, 128, 130

Natural Bridge, Va.: TJ's title to, 299, 403

INDEX

New, Anthony: elected to House of Representatives, 444, 463

Newfoundland: trade with U.S. forbidden, 188; French fishermen absent from, 213, 278, 406

New Hampshire, Governor of. *See* Bartlett, Josiah

New Jersey, College of, xli

New Jersey, Governor of. *See* Howell, Richard

New Map of the Western Parts (Thomas Hutchins): and boundaries with Western Indians, 356

New Orleans: trade with U.S., 558

New Pigou (ship), 664n

Newsham, Richard: and fire engines, 163; identified, 164n

newspapers: for Department of State, 27; Canadian sent to TJ, 184, 363, 412-13, 418; British criticized by TJ, 535

New Testament: TJ acquires Greek edition of, 235n

Newton, Thomas, Jr.: amd defense of Norfolk, 688

New York: treaties with Indians, 215-16, 317, 358, 373, 592; cedes Montauk Point to U.S., 265; lack of philosophers in, 304; land sales in, 337-8

New York, Governor of. *See* Clinton, George

New York, Treaty of: and U.S. right to station agents with Creeks, 653, 659n; and U.S. protection of Creeks, 659n

New York City: passports for U.S. ships in, 650, 670

New York Commissioners of Indian Affairs: treaties with Iroquois, 592n

New-York Journal, & Patriotic Register: requested by TJ, 572, 659

New-York Journal, and Weekly Register: requested by TJ, 572, 659

Niagara, N.Y., 229

Nice: French troops in, 453

Nicholas, Wilson Cary: elected to House of Representatives, 444; and provisions for France, 706

Nicholson, John: and Michaux's proposed western expedition, 83n; and Asylum Company, 372n; impeachment of, 516; mentioned, 672n

Nieuwpoort, Austrian Netherlands, 568

Nixon, John: and Michaux's proposed western expedition, 82n, 83n

Noailles, Louis Marie, Vicomte de: and Lafayette's captivity, 215, 664; visits

U.S., 215; arrives in Philadelphia, 662; meets Washington, 664

Nootka Sound: crisis over between Great Britain and Spain, 327, 562

Norfolk, Va.: defense of, 688

Norfolk (ship), 182

Normandy, France: and British military plans, 190; danger of revolt in, 457

Norris, Joseph P.: and Michaux's proposed western expedition, 78, 82

North Carolina: and Republican effort to censure Hamilton, 290

North Carolina, Governor of. *See* Spaight, Richard Dobbs

North Carolina, University of: and Preau's land claim, 411

North river, 89

Northwest Territory: conflict with Indians in, 9, 19, 30, 65, 88-9, 215-16, 220-3, 229, 255, 258-9, 271-3, 354-6, 368, 424-5, 520; peace negotiations with Indians in, 9, 19, 30, 65, 88-9, 215-16, 220-3, 229, 247n, 255, 258-9, 271-3, 279, 317, 354-6, 368, 372, 373, 383, 424-5, 440, 450, 478, 511, 518, 520, 592; peace treaty with Indians in, 112-19, 133-4; absence of officials from, 157-8, 270, 303, 357-8, 470, 477-8, 511-12, 552-3; executive proceedings in, 270; laws of, 270, 344n; TJ's report on, 312; survey of, 332, 337-8; disorders in, 344, 357-8; military land bounties in, 355, 356

Northwest Territory, Secretary of. *See* Sargent, Winthrop

Notes on the State of Virginia: Parry Hall's proposed edition of, 467; Mathew Carey's edition of, 467n; praised by Dombey, 631

Noyes, Joseph: petition from, 634-5

Nürnberg: emigration from to U.S., 640

oak boards: duties on in Great Britain, 201

oak plank: duties on in Great Britain, 201

oak timber: duties on in Great Britain, 202

oak wood: for Monticello, 73

oars: duties on in Great Britain, 202

oaths: for clergy in France, 123, 127

oats: threshing of, 379; for Mint, 447

O'Brien, Capt. (master of *Aurora*), 235

O'Bryen (O'Brian, O'Brien), Richard: and proposed treaty between Portugal and

O'Bryen, Richard (*cont.*)
Algiers, 29, 30n; subsistence of, 29; and captives in Algiers, 86, 88n, 428; and Algerine affairs, 623
Official Letters to the Honorable American Congress (John Carey): preparation of, 105-6, 236; manuscript submitted to TJ, 581-2, 630; manuscript sent to T. Pinckney, 595, 690
Ohio: land grants in, 320n
Ohio river: as proposed Indian boundary with U.S., 113, 222n, 258-9; and boundaries with Western Indians, 356
olive culture: in S.C., 214, 278
Olivier, Pedro, 659n
onions: grown by Derieux, 307
Orange, Prince of. *See* William V, Prince of Orange
Oregon river: and Michaux's proposed western expedition, 624
Orléans, Louis Philippe Joseph, Duc d': arrest of, 574
orrery: ordered by TJ, 341, 352n, 485
Ostend, Austrian Netherlands: J. Gregorie recommended as U.S. consul at, 53; trade with U.S., 297n; mentioned, 568
Ott, David: and assay of foreign coinage, 32, 38n
Ottawa Indians: boundary with U.S., 355
Otto, Louis Guillaume: and U.S. debt to France, 197
oxen: for Mint, 447

Pache, Jean Nicolas: relations with Dumouriez, 27, 451; support for, 27; and Ternant's military command, 57; and invasion of Netherlands, 335, 451; and invasion of Rhineland, 451
Pacific ocean: and Michaux's proposed western expedition, 77, 81, 85, 624, 625, 626
Pagan, Thomas: counsel for (*see* Tilghman, Edward); dispute with Stephen Hooper, 379, 389-90, 522-3, 537-41, 564
Pagan v. Hooper, 379, 389-90, 522-3, 537-41, 564
Page, John: and assay of foreign coinage, 33n; letter to quoted, 33n; and Michaux's proposed western expedition, 82; and Republican effort to censure Hamilton, 289
Paine, Thomas: letter from, 576-7; and

execution of Louis XVI, 100; and French constitution, 131; and British radicalism, 384; and French Revolution, 577
paint: for Mint, 447
Palatinate: emigration from to U.S., 640
Palatinate, Elector of. *See* Charles Theodore, Elector Palatine and of Bavaria
Paleske, Charles Gottfried: letter from Frederick William II cited, 376
Panton, William: and conflict between Creeks and Ga., 518-19n
Papal States: forbid export of corn, 358-9
parachutes: Blanchard's experiments with, 44n
Paris: exchange rate, 6; and dethronement of king, 120-32; and French invasion of Netherlands, 344; copper coinage in, 349; and Federal District, 369; bread shortage in, 488; defense of, 489; disturbances in, 574
Paris, Treaty of. *See* Peace Treaty, Definitive (1783)
Parish, John: letter to, 415-17; appointed consul at Hamburg, 204, 228, 238n, 369, 394; letter to cited, 238n
Parker, Daniel: and Short's business affairs, 481, 483
Parker, Josiah: and Michaux's proposed western expedition, 82
Parker, Samuel L.: and transport of French prisoners to U.S., 464
Partridge, Jesse: petition from, 634-5
passports (sea letters): for U.S. ships, 104, 167n, 169, 333, 335-6n, 375, 377n, 409, 530n, 534, 628-9, 642-3, 645-8, 650, 666, 670-1, 674-5, 680-2, 695, 696; and treaty of commerce with France, 377n; for East Indian ships, 645, 648n, 682n; for trade with Dutch colonies, 663. *See also* Mediterranean passes
Patent Board, U.S.: and Joseph G. Chambers's plan for repeating firearms, 90; discontinued by Congress, 589
patents: information on ordered for Vall-Travers, 256n; act for, 276, 398; for John Clarke, 276; for Richard R. Saltonstall, 398; for Elisha Bartlett, 398n; TJ's proposed form for, 398-9; for Edward Ryan, 551n; issued by Department of State, 589
Paterson, William: appointed to Supreme Court, 300-1, 303, 320; letters to quot-

INDEX

ed, 301n, 395-6n; letter to cited, 301n
Patriote (French privateer): captures *Aurora*, 406, 458n
Paul, St., 632
Peace Treaty, Definitive (1783): and retention of western posts by British, 221; and U.S. sovereignty over Indian lands, 222; and right to navigate Mississippi, 556; and U.S. boundary with Spain, 557
Peale, Charles Willson: and Michaux's proposed western expedition, 83n; natural history museum, 136n
Peale, Raphaelle: scientific expedition to Ga., 135, 136n; mentioned, 644
Pearce, William (Eng.): relations with Richard Arkwright, 347
pearl ash: price, 69; export to France, 186; export to Spain, 186; duties on in Great Britain, 187, 201; export to Great Britain, 187; Edward Ryan's furnace for melting, 551
Peggy (ship), 524
Pendleton, Edmund, 275n
Pendleton, John, Jr.: letter to, 274-5; letter from cited, 274-5; identified, 275n
pendulum. *See* rod pendulum
Penn, John: and Michaux's proposed western expedition, 82n
Penn, Richard, 596
Pennsylvania: viniculture in, 92-3; silk production in, 93n; Andrew Ellicott appointed road surveyor for, 153; and Republican effort to censure Hamilton, 290
Pennsylvania, Governor of. *See* Mifflin, Thomas
Pennsylvania (ship), 261
Pennsylvania House of Representatives: and viniculture, 93n; and impeachment of James Nicholson, 516
Pennsylvania Senate: and impeachment of James Nicholson, 516n
Pennsylvania Supreme Court: and case of James Nicholson, 516n
Pensacola, Treaty of: and Spanish right to station agents with Creeks, 677-8; mentioned, 653, 659n
Peoria Indians: and peace conference with Washington, 113, 114
Pepoon v. Jenkins, 540
Perkins, Joseph: detained in Portugal, 487n; master of *Mary*, 487n; leaves Lisbon, 623
Perseverance (ship), 234

Peters, Richard: and execution of Louis XVI, 443
Petit, Adrien: relations with M. J. Randolph, 297-8; mentioned, 633
Pfeiffer, George: salary, 10
Philadelphia: exchange rate in, 6, 514; foreign trade, 28-9; and Blanchard's balloon flight, 43n; fire engines in, 163; cash shortage in, 318, 384, 544; and execution of Louis XVI, 443; passports for U.S. ships in, 650; and capture of *Grange*, 661, 668-9; and capture of *Little Sarah*, 668-9; trade with Va., 706
Philadelphia Packet (ship): register of sent to TJ, 526, 527n
Philadelphia Society for Promoting Agriculture, 651n
Phillips, Benjamin Hamnell: letter to, 415-17; appointed consul at Curaçao, 204, 228, 238n, 310n, 369, 395; letter to cited, 238n
Phill (TJ's slave): and canal for Monticello, 138
Piankashaw Indians: and peace conference with Washington, 112, 114
Picardy, France, 190
Pickering, Timothy: letter to, 477; letters from, 5, 302, 478, 520; letter to cited, 5; recommends Benjamin H. Phillips for consular appointment at Curaçao, 204; appointed Indian commissioner, 229n; and Ky. electoral votes, 310n; and postal service in Va., 477, 478; and Bradshaw's expenses, 520; mentioned, 633
pickled beef: import from U.S. to Netherlands forbidden, 188
pickled meat: as wet provisions, 146
pig iron: duties on in Great Britain, 201
Pigou (ship), 417n
pimento: export to U.S., 188
Pinckney, Thomas: letters to, 6, 320-1, 387, 393-5, 410-11, 534-6, 536-7, 577-8, 586, 591, 595, 649, 674-6, 690; letters from, 11-13, 103-4, 106-7, 149-51, 166-7, 168, 169-70, 370, 371-2, 375-7, 378-9, 408, 493-4, 512, 525-6, 596, 641; and British reinforcements for Canada, 6, 534; and impressment, 11-12, 13n, 375-6, 378n, 393, 525-6, 675-6; and Genet, 12; and Mint, 12, 13n, 103, 151, 370, 393, 512, 575, 578, 665; and relations between Great Britain and France, 12, 104, 107; letters from submitted to Washington,

Proclamation of Neutrality (*cont.*)
governors, 588; TJ's notes on, 673-
4; and U.S. arms sales to France, 684;
and French privateers commissioned by
Genet in U.S., 686-7; criticism of, 688-
9; enforcement of, 691
Proserpine (French privateer): captures
Mercury, 489n
Provence, France: and allied military
strategy, 191
Provence, Louis Stanislas Xavier, Comte
de: proposed assassination of, 128
Provisional Executive Council. *See*
France: Provisional Executive Council
provisions: price, 258; British restrictions
on export to France, 493-4
Prussia: relations with Netherlands, 100;
relations with Austria, 130-1; war with
France, 130-1, 165, 191, 335, 340n,
343-4, 374, 422, 453-7, 488, 524, 577;
trade with France, 165; and passports
for U.S. vessels, 167n; relations with
Poland, 190; minister to Great Britain,
376; and Silesian loan, 539n; relations
with Great Britain, 596
Prussia, King of. *See* Frederick the Great,
King of Prussia; Frederick William II,
King of Prussia
Pryor, Mr. *See* Prior, Abner
public debt: holders of in Congress, xli,
154-5, 281, 290-1, 311, 313-14, 432-
4; purchase of, 22; assumption of, 155,
208; payment of, 178; Federalist views
on, 318; Republican views on, 318;
TJ's comments on, 318, 517; TJ's
notes on retirement of, 465-7; Tobias
Lear's comments on, 517
Public Lands, Report on: preparation of,
132n; and TJ's report on boundaries
with Western Indians, 356n
public securities: depreciation, 318, 369,
394, 474, 518, 661; appreciation, 474;
speculation in by national bank, 474
Pufendorf, Samuel von: *Le Droit de la
nature et des gens*, 606, 612-15, 618n
pumps: for Mint, 447
Putnam, Rufus: peace treaty with Illinois
and Wabash Indians, 112-19, 134n,
158; absence from Northwest Territory, 158n

"Q": and public debt, 466n
Quakers: attend peace conference with
Western Indians, 424-5

Quebec: British reinforcements for, 6
Quincy, Jacob: petition from, 634-5
Quincy, John W.: petition from, 634-5
Quintilian: recommended by TJ, 547

Ragstraw, Joseph: and TJ's Philadelphia
house, 595
Ramsden, Jesse: TJ purchases telescope
from, 352
Ramsgate, England: and desertions from
Governor Bowdoin, 377-8n
Randolph, Ann Cary: alleged incest and
infanticide, 621-3, 632-3
Randolph, Anne Cary (TJ's granddaughter): health, 43, 50, 64, 91, 97, 156,
246, 297, 693; TJ's love for, 97, 257,
353, 444, 521, 581
Randolph, Beverley: letters to, 229, 620-
1; letter from, 383; appointed Indian
commissioner, 229, 383, 669; health,
547, 669; and slaves captured by Indians, 620-1
Randolph, Caroline Ramsay (TJ's great-
granddaughter): and TJ's draft censure
resolutions, 281
Randolph, David Meade: letter from cited, 410n; recommends John Gregorie
as consul at Dunkirk, 410n
Randolph, Edmund: letters to, 372, 398,
552, 641, 690, 691-2; letters from,
372, 389-90, 537-9, 642, 700-2; and
consular fees, 13; and French Revolution, 64; bonds of, 65; and Ky. Indian
expeditions, 99; and peace conference
with Illinois and Wabash Indians, 118n;
and TJ's retirement, 154; and debt to
France, 173, 260, 273, 310-11; and
provisions for France, 173, 260, 273,
310-11; and Republican effort to censure Hamilton, 173; and levees, 208;
letters from Washington, 220, 424-5,
568; and relations with Western Indians, 220, 255, 258-9, 271-3, 358, 372,
383, 424-5, 450; and right of U.S. to
cede territory to Indians, 220, 258-9,
273; and appointment of Indian commissioners, 229n; and recall of G. Morris, 245n; letter from Tobias Lear, 255;
and sinking fund, 261, 432, 439-40;
and criticism of Franklin, 273; and relations with France, 273; and military
rations, 299-300; and William Paterson's appointment to Supreme Court,
300n; and presidential inauguration,

301-2; and William Stephens Smith's mission to U.S., 310-11; and case of Gallipolis settlers, 320n; and Federal District, 345, 361; and acts of Congress, 354n; and Pagan v. Hooper, 379, 523, 537-41, 563-4; and letter of protection for Indians, 380n; and TJ's proposed form for patents, 398-9; and foreign loans, 458, 461n; notes on TJ's letter to Hamilton, 458; and reception of Genet, 469-70, 570-2, 598, 601, 666; meets Washington at Georgetown, 511; and impeachment of James Nicholson, 516; debt to James Nicholson, 516n; represents James Nicholson, 516n; letter from submitted to Washington, 539n; letter from Edward Tilghman, 539-41; opinion on George Turner, 552; and Northwest Territory, 552-3; and Washington's questions on neutrality and the French alliance, 568-71, 665-6; and Proclamation of Neutrality, 570-2, 673-4; and treaties with France, 599, 601-2, 666; and guarantee of French possessions in America, 602; and U.S. jurisdiction over Delaware Bay, 639n; and case of *Grange*, 639-40, 641, 683n, 702n; letter to submitted to Washington, 641n; and foreign-built U.S. ships, 642; and passports for U.S. ships, 648n; criticized by TJ, 662n; and congressional authority over neutrality, 666; and enforcement of neutrality, 667-8, 673-4, 691-2, 700-2; and sale of U.S. ships built for war, 667-8; and contraband, 673-4; letter to T. Pinckney submitted to, 676n, 679; and U.S. arms sales to France, 684

Randolph, Judith (Mrs. Richard Randolph), 622n

Randolph, Martha Cocke (Mrs. Beverley Randolph), 229

Randolph, Martha Jefferson (Mrs. Thomas Mann Randolph, Jr., TJ's daughter): letters to, 50-1, 97-8, 170, 256-7, 352-3, 444, 520-1, 621-2; letters from, 64, 297-8; health, 43, 156, 246, 693; and Charlottesville fire, 91; correspondence with sister, 91, 297; love for TJ, 91, 297; and TJ's continuance in office, 297; relations with Adrien Petit, 297-8; TJ's love for, 314, 353, 404, 444, 475, 546, 581, 669; letter from cited, 352; and case of Richard Randolph, 621-3; mentioned, 30, 73,

137, 139, 230, 403, 580

Randolph, Richard: alleged incest and infanticide, 621-3, 632-3, 698

Randolph, Sarah Nicholas (TJ's great-granddaughter): and TJ's draft censure resolutions, xli, 280-1

Randolph, Theodorick: and case of Richard Randolph, 622n

Randolph, Thomas Jefferson (TJ's grandson): health, 43, 64, 156, 246, 297, 693; TJ's love for, 257, 353, 444, 521, 581; and sale of TJ's papers, 281

Randolph, Thomas Mann, Jr. (TJ's son-in-law): letters to, 30, 72-3, 137-9, 230, 313-14, 403-4, 475, 580-1, 668-9; letters from, 42-3, 91, 156, 245-6, 298-9, 693; manages TJ's affairs, 42-3, 64, 70, 72-3, 91, 98, 138, 156, 230, 245-6, 298, 313, 353, 403-4, 444, 513, 521, 693; letters from cited, 50, 581n; correspondence with sister-in-law, 91, 157n, 230, 256, 313, 475, 520; and French Revolution, 91; weather diary, 156-7, 246, 299, 475n; proposes to rent Edgehill, 230; and TJ's continuance in office, 245, 297; TJ's regard for, 257, 353, 444, 521, 546; and tenant farmers, 404; and case of Richard Randolph, 621-3; mentioned, 154, 155n, 170, 196, 698

Randolph, Mrs. William Mann: and TJ's draft censure resolutions, 281

Ravara, Joseph: and Domenico's proposed consular appointment, 358-9

Rawhead and Bloody Bones: identified, 606n; mentioned, 605, 610

Reading, Pa.: road survey, 153n

Recueil de Dissertatons (Félix François Le Royer d'Artezet de La Sauvagère): returned to D. Rittenhouse, 490

register certificate: and payment of foreign officers, 55

réis: Portuguese unit of money, 28-9

religion: freedom of in France, 123

Remsen, Henry: retires from Department of State, 10; letter to quoted, 318n

Rennes, France: threats to, 457

repeating firearms: Joseph G. Chambers's plan for, 90, 392

Report of Cases Argued and Determined in the High Court of Chancery (John Tracy Atkyns): cited by J. G. Jefferson, 472

Representation of the Lords of the Committee in Council (Charles Jenkinson, Lord Hawkesbury): cited by T. Coxe, 146

republicanism: in France, 15, 121, 131,

INDEX

Sargent, Winthrop (*cont.*)
submitted to Washington, 344
Sartain, Samuel: engraving of Tench
Coxe, xl, 400 (illus.)
Saturn: rings, 341
Sauterne wine: for Elbridge Gerry, 269
Savannah, Ga.: trade of, 5
Savoy: annexed by France, 4, 5n; and
French war with First Coalition, 191;
invaded by France, 340n, 457; aversion
to French in, 488
Saxe-Coburg, Friedrich Josias, Prince of:
and invasion of Netherlands, 453-7,
662, 668; and invasion of Rhineland,
456; and Dumouriez's defection, 524;
and French constitution, 573; and inva-
sion of France, 573; and siege of Vale-
nciennes, 573
Sayre, Stephen: requests appointment as
T. Pinckney's secretary, 103, 104-5n
scantling: for Monticello, 73-4, 299; for
Mint, 447
Scheldt (Escaut) river: French demand
opening of, 4, 53
Scioto Company: complaints against,
320n; land grant to, 355
Scioto (Sioto) river: and boundaries with
Western Indians, 355
Scoll, Henry: petition from, 634-5
Scotland: and workmen for Federal District, 24; wealth, 26
Seabra da Silver, José de: and detention
of U.S. grain ships in Portugal, 623
Seagrove, James: and conflict between
Creeks and Ga., 518-19n
Seagrove, Robert: Creek raid on store of,
518-19n
sea letters. *See* passports
seals: Va. Court of Chancery, 276, 401,
597
seamen: recruited for French naval service,
68; aid to, 71, 365; desertion of British,
151; wages, 151; and desertion from
U.S. ships, 376, 377-8n
seamen, impressment of: T. Pinckney's
negotiations with Grenville on, 11-12,
13n, 375-6, 378n, 393, 525-6; in
Cowes, 409; TJ's instructions to T.
Pinckney on, 675-6
Secretary of the Treasury. *See* Hamilton,
Alexander
Secretary of War. *See* Knox, Henry
Sedgwick, Theodore: holder of public
debt, 432
Senate, U.S. *See* United States: Senate

Senegal: trade with foreign ships allowed
by France, 486
September Massacres: Mountflorence's
comments on, 120, 128-9; effort to prevent recurrence of, 374
Sergeant, Elizabeth Rittenhouse (Mrs.
Jonathan Dickinson Sergeant): donates
plaster bust of TJ to American Philosophical Society, 31n
Sergeant, Jonathan Dickinson: and Currie
v. Griffin, 346
Servan de Gerbey, Joseph: dismissed
from office, 131-2; military command,
452
servants: immunity from arrest, 337
Seton, William: and Mint, 695
Setúbal, Portugal, 7
Sewall, David: letter from, 651; and printing of U.S. laws in Me., 651; recommends John Hobby as federal marshal
in Me., 651; identified, 651n
Shaw, Samuel: letter to, 415-18; consul
at Canton, 202
Shawas (Kickapoo chief): peace conference with Washington, 114, 115
Shawnee Indians: hostility to U.S., 114;
conflict with Western Indians, 118;
boundary with U.S., 355
sheet iron: for Mint, 447
Shelby, Isaac: letter to, 588; and Ky.
Indian expeditions, 99; mentioned, 84
Shelton, Mr.: J. G. Jefferson's account
with, 593-4
Sherman, Roger: stockholder in national
bank, 433
Shey, Mr.: bond of, 697
shilling: assay of, 32
shipbuilders: and foreign-built U.S. ships,
646
ship carpenters: and foreign-built U.S.
ships, 627, 646
Shippen, Thomas Lee: and execution of
Louis XVI, 443
Shippen, Dr. William: and Michaux's proposed western expedition, 82n
ships, U.S.: and carrying trade with Great
Britain, 158-9, 187; sale of in France,
165, 186, 213, 278; passports for,
166, 167n, 169, 333, 335-6n, 375,
377n, 409, 530n, 534, 628-9, 642-3,
645-8, 650, 651-2, 666, 671n, 674-
5, 680-2, 695, 696; export to Spain,
185; and carrying trade with France,
186; and carrying trade with Spain,
186; and carrying trade with West

INDEX

Sinclair, Mr. *See* St. Clair, Arthur

Sinclair, Patrick: and desertions from *Governor Bowdoin*, 377-8n

Singleton, Anthony: and sale of TJ's tobacco, 352

sinking fund. *See* Commissioners of the Sinking Fund, U.S.

Sioto river. *See* Scioto river

Skipwith, Anne Wayles (Mrs. Henry Skipwith), 528

Skipwith, Fulwar: letters to, 331, 415-17; letter from, 183; consular authority not recognized, 183, 321; returns to Martinique, 183, 321; consul at Martinique, 202, 321; resigns as consul at Martinique, 204n

Skipwith, Henry: letter to, 527-8; and Short's business affairs, 527-8

slaves: revolt in Saint-Domingue, 9, 271, 510n; and Federal District, 25; hire of TJ's, 43, 101, 230, 543; clothing for TJ's, 51, 91, 230, 257, 521; stolen from Martinique, 61; sale of TJ's, 73, 91, 230, 550-1; work assignments for TJ's, 138; work for invalids, 138; management of, 230, 263; sale of Archibald Cary's, 319; productivity of TJ's, 403; criticism of TJ's, 403-4, 693; Peter Carr's right to, 465, 546; captured by Indians, 620-1

sleepers, triangular: for Monticello, 73-4

Smith, Adam: *Wealth of Nations*, 472

Smith, David: petition from, 634-5

Smith, George: ransomed from Algerine captivity, 623

Smith, John: defeated for election to House of Representatives, 533; identified, 534n

Smith, Jonathan Bayard: and Michaux's proposed western expedition, 83n

Smith, Melancthon: and execution of king, 443

Smith, Rev. William: criticism of, 265; seeks appointment as Indian commissioner, 265; identified, 266n; mentioned, 46

Smith, William Loughton: letter to, 405; letter from, 404; and Michaux's proposed western expedition, 82; and Republican effort to censure Hamilton, 288, 289, 404n; identified, 404n; and Department of State expenses, 404-5; director of national bank, 433; stockholder in national bank, 433; relations with Miss A., 443

Smith, William Stephens: letter from, 161-2; agent of French Republic, xli, 161-2, 174, 243-5, 258, 310-11, 431n, 662-3n, 684-5; and debt to France, 174, 243-5, 310-11; and recall of G. Morris, 243; and provisions for France, 243-5, 258, 310-11; purchases U.S. arms for France, 684-5

snow: relationship to temperature, 304-5

snuff: duties on in Great Britain, 202

Södermanland, Karl, Duke of: regent in Sweden, 95-6; identified, 96n

solanum melongena (mélongène): seeds for, 306; unknown to TJ, 347

Soldier, The (Wiatonon chief): wife speaks at peace conference with Washington, 116-17

Somme river, 190

Sonthonax, Léger Félicité: commissioner to Saint-Domingue, 34n

South America: French plan to liberate, 243, 244-5, 336-7, 431n

South Carolina: olive culture in, 214, 278; and Republican effort to censure Hamilton, 290

South Carolina, Governor of. *See* Vanderhorst, Arnoldus

Southwest Territory: boundary with Ky., 197, 359-60; boundary with Va., 197, 359-60

Spaight, Richard Dobbs: letter to, 588

Spain: British ambassador to (*see* St. Helens, Alleyne Fitzherbert, Baron); French legation secretary in (*see* Urtubize, Marques d'); French minister to (*see* Bourgoing, Jean François de); relations with France, 12, 191, 262, 322, 325-7, 562, 593, 654; U.S. debt to, 21, 241n, 242n, 283; coinage, 31-2, 37-9; imports wheat, 63; and navigation of Mississippi, 80, 195n, 250, 556, 558, 559-60, 653, 656-7; Inquisition in, 120; relations with Great Britain, 141, 142n, 322, 327, 383, 430-1, 561-2, 654; alliance with Great Britain, 142n; war with France, 142n, 336-7, 338, 340n, 358-9, 422, 441, 657; trade with U.S., 146, 148, 185-6, 441, 560-1; and TJ's report on commerce, 185-6; forbids foreign trade with colonies, 186; diplomatic precedence in, 232-4; 322-5; trade duties on Mississippi, 250; and execution of Louis XVI, 325; army recruitment in, 325-6, 330n; finances, 325-6, 330n; and French Revolution,

INDEX

Sweden (*cont.*)
with France, 340; loans from Genoa, 358-9
Swiss Guards: and dethronement of king, 125, 126, 127
Switzerland: and French war with First Coalition, 191; relations with France, 456; relations with Great Britain, 456
Sydnor, William G.: letter from, 196; seeks military promotion, 196
Syme, John: letter to, 399-400; letters from, 216-17, 437; and TJ's retirement, 217; letter from cited, 217n
Symmes, John Cleves: absence from Northwest Territory, 157-8; criticism of, 344n; land purchase by, 355; recommended to TJ, 429
Symmes, W.: petition from, 634-5
Synchong: and china for TJ, 315n

Tableau des Variétés de la Vie humaine (Guillaume Daignan): requested by TJ, 484
Tacitus, Cornelius: recommended by TJ, 547
Talon, Antoine Omer: settles in U.S., 371-2; and Asylum Company, 372n; identified, 372n
Tangier, Morocco: and Moroccan civil war, 160, 630; Danish consul at, 234
tar: export to Spain, 185; duties on in France, 186; export to France, 186; export to French West Indies, 186; export to Great Britain, 187; export to British West Indies, 188; duties on in Great Britain, 201
Tarquin (TJ's horse): sale of, 230, 581
tarragon (estragon): seeds for, 306; little known in U.S., 347
Taylor, George, Jr.: chief clerk in Department of State, 9, 27, 369, 395, 398, 403, 584-5, 660; salary, 10; and TJ's report on commerce, 168n, 185n
Taylor, John, of Caroline: "Franklin" essays, 265n, 462n; and *Examination of the Late Proceedings in Congress*, 433-4n; and Republican effort to censure Hamilton, 462n
Taylor, Thomas Augustus: and purchase of Elk Hill, 69-70
telescopes: TJ's inquiries about, 341-2; purchased by TJ, 352
Telfair, Edward: letter to, 588; mentioned, 431n

Tellier (Tillier), Rodolphe: delivers letter to T. Pinckney, 11
Temple, Sir John: and U.S. arms sales to France, 685n
tenant farmers: TJ's plans for, 225, 230, 298, 313, 403-4, 483, 521; rents for in Md., 263; for T. M. Randolph, Jr., 298, 404; for Thomas Digges, 347
Tenerife, Canary Islands: U.S. consul at, 204
Tennessee river: as Chickasaw boundary, 209; and Iroquois land claims, 210
Termo wine: for TJ, 28-9, 235; price, 236
Ternant, Jean Baptiste: letters to, 51-2, 184-5, 198, 217-18, 254-5, 264, 264-5, 411, 510-11, 579, 583-4, 649, 676; letters from, 33, 39, 61, 162, 164, 211, 218-19, 543, 694, 702; and French consular salaries, 7n, 51-2, 543, 564-5, 579; and U.S. aid to Saint-Domingue, 33-4, 49, 51-2, 264-5; and provisions for France, 39, 162-3, 164-5, 172-82, 196-7, 198, 260, 264, 266, 275-6, 286, 368, 662-3n; and Blanchard's balloon flight, 43n; letters to submitted to Washington, 52n, 185n, 198, 220, 255n, 584n; military command for, 57, 662; and recall of G. Morris, 58n, 244, 247-9; and theft of slaves from Martinique, 61; and Joseph G. Chambers's plan for repeating firearms, 90; letters from submitted to Washington, 163n, 220, 702n; and U.S. debt to France, 164-5, 172-82, 196-7, 198, 260, 264, 266, 275-6, 286, 368, 662-3n; and U.S. consular authority in Martinique, 183; and TJ's report on commerce, 184-5, 211, 217-18; and establishment of French Republic, 218-19, 254-5; criticism of, 264-5; recall of, 331, 336-7, 565; and bills drawn on Saint-Domingue, 368; letters from cited, 411, 543n, 584n; and Preau's land claim, 411; and execution of king, 443, 662; relations with Hamilton, 443; relations with TJ, 443, 662-3n; and case of *Commerce*, 491, 510-11, 554; arrival in U.S., 501; notes for letter to, 564-5; and Proclamation of Neutrality, 583-4; application for funds, 636-7, 643-4; and case of *Grange*, 639n, 649, 676, 683n, 694, 702
Terrell, Lucy Carr (Mrs. Richard Terrell, TJ's niece): marriage of, 223, 297;

INDEX

moves to Ky., 297

Terrell, Richard (TJ's nephew-in-law): marriage of, 223, 297; moves to Ky., 297

Tetuán, Morocco: and Moroccan civil war, 234-5, 630

Thatcher (Thayer), George: letters from cited, 309n, 317n; recommends Samuel Cooper Johonnet for consular appointment at Demerara, 309n; letter from submitted to Washington, 316n; recommends appointment of John Hobby as marshal in Me., 316n

Thayer, Mr. See Thatcher, George

Thomson, Charles: proposed appointment as Indian commissioner, 89n; and survey of Northwest Territory, 338

Thornton, Dr. William: and Michaux's proposed western expedition, 83n, 84n; plan for Capitol, 107-8, 110, 386n

Three-legs (Piankashaw chief): peace conference with Washington, 112, 113, 117

threshing machine: model of sought by TJ, 168, 378-9, 536, 581, 660; as defense against weevils, 536; need for at Monticello, 693

Tienen (Tirlemont), Austrian Netherlands: allied advance to, 455

Tilghman, Edward: and Pagan v. Hooper, 389-90, 537-41; letter from submitted to Washington, 539n; letter to E. Randolph, 539-41

Tillier, Mr. See Tellier, Rodolphe

timber: for Monticello, 43, 73-4, 91, 299; duties on in Great Britain, 202

"Timon": and Republican effort to censure Hamilton, 434n, 661; criticizes Hamilton, 443n; praised by TJ, 546

timothy grass: for Monticello, 444

tin: for Mint, 447

Tirlemont. See Tienen, Austrian Netherlands

Titcomb, Benjamin, Jr.: and printing of U.S. laws in Me., 634-5, 651

tithes: abolition in France, 190

tobacco: market for in France, 3; sale of TJ's, 3, 318, 351, 485, 513, 524-5, 549n, 581; export to France, 68, 186, 211, 406; price, 101, 214, 279, 340, 486; duties on in France, 146, 185, 186, 211, 213, 217-18, 278; French monopoly on, 186; import from U.S. to Spain forbidden, 186; duties on in Great Britain, 187, 201; export to

Great Britain, 187; reexport from Great Britain, 188

Todd, George: captured by *Proserpine*, 489n; master of *Mercury*, 489n

Tongres, Austrian Netherlands: and French invasion of Austrian Netherlands, 339, 343, 374

Torino, Don Joseph: U.S. debt to, 88n

Toulon, France: and naval warfare, 165; and allied military strategy, 191; coastal trade, 422

Toulon, John: property confiscated by G. R. Clark, 251n

Tournai, Austrian Netherlands: French retreat to, 455

Tousard (Touzard), Anne Louis, Chevalier de: returns to U.S., 492

Tracts on Weights, Measures, and Coins (George Skene Keith): returned to D. Rittenhouse, 490

Traité des Monnoyes (Jean Boizard): for Mint, 490

Traquair, James: and workmen for Federal District, 24, 25, 152-3; letter from cited, 110

Treasurer, U.S.: TJ's proposed reform of, 293, 294n. See also Meredith, Samuel

treaties of alliance: with France, 569, 597-618, 665-6, 689

treaties of amity and commerce: with France, 57, 411, 464, 489n, 530n, 574n, 578, 598, 606n, 611, 645, 647n, 665-6, 675, 676n, 681, 682n, 699; with Portugal, 94n; with Algiers, 421; between Portugal and Naples, 426; with Netherlands, 468n, 578, 602, 605, 606n, 611, 645, 647n, 675, 682n; with Spain, 558; between France and Great Britain, 578, 602, 605, 606n, 611, 675, 676n, 703; with Prussia, 602, 605, 606n, 611, 645, 647n, 675, 682n; between France and Russia, 704

Treatise of the Pleas of the Crown (William Hawkins): cited by J. G. Jefferson, 472

Trèves. See Trier

Trier (Trèves): and French invasion of Rhineland, 451

Trinidad, W.I.: trade with U.S., 205, 219; French refugees at, 271

Tripoli: British consul in, 160

Triptolemus, 537

Trousserau, Peter: property confiscated by G. R. Clark, 251n

Truguet, Laurent Jean François, Comte: attacks Sardinia, 359; commands

[765]

Truguet, Laurent Jean François (*cont.*)
French Mediterranean fleet, 359
Trumbull, Jonathan: letters to, 9-10, 38-9, 246-7, 310; and Michaux's proposed western expedition, 82; and assumption of public debt, 155; letter to cited, 210n; letter to submitted to Washington, 247n; letter from Commissioners of the Sinking Fund, 261; stockholder in national bank, 432; mentioned, 237
Tucker, Henry: captured by *Sans Culotte*, 699; master of *Eunice*, 699
Tucker, St. George: and John Barret's debt to TJ, 697
Tunis: relations with U.S., 359n
Turin: French plan to capture, 359; Gardoqui's reported ambassadorship to, 657
Turkey: and French war with First Coalition, 191
Turner, George: letters to, 470, 553; absence from Northwest Territory, 158n, 270, 358, 470, 478, 511-12, 552-3; letter to submitted to Washington, 470n; E. Randolph's opinion on, 552
turpentine: export to Spain, 185; duties on in France, 186; export to France, 186; export to French West Indies, 186; export to British West Indies, 188; duties on in Great Britain, 201
type foundry: proposed establishment by Guyer, 34-6

Union (ship), 513, 524

UNITED STATES

Army
recruiting service, 30; proposed reduction of, 30n; payment of, 179; rations for, 299-300

Cabinet
and treaties with France, xl, 599-602, 666; and Proclamation of Neutrality, xlii, 570-2, 673-4; and French consular salaries, 7n, 52n; and debt to France, 174, 239, 260, 273, 469-70, 663n; and provisions for France, 174, 260, 273, 286, 469-70, 663n; letters from Washington, 220, 424-5, 568; and right of U.S. to cede territory to Indians, 220, 258-9, 272-3, 518; and

relations with Western Indians, 220-3, 255, 258-9, 271-3, 356n, 424-5, 440, 450, 462n, 478, 511, 518; letter from Lear, 255; submits first corporate opinion to Washington, 259n; and military rations, 299-300; and presidential inauguration, 301-2; and letter of protection for Indians, 380n; and Washington's questions on neutrality and the French alliance, 568-71, 575, 665-6; and reception of Genet, 570-2, 601-2, 666; and congressional authority over neutrality, 607-8n, 666; and case of *Grange*, 641, 683n; and foreign-built U.S. ships, 648n; and passports for U.S. ships, 648n; divisions in, 661; and neutrality, 661; and sale of U.S. ships built for war, 667-8; and contraband, 673-4; Washington defers to majority view in, 674; and U.S. arms sales to France, 684-5; and French consular admiralty jurisdiction in U.S., 686n

Congress
stockholders of national bank in, xli; and debt to France, 16-17, 177-9; and Federal District, 45, 52, 361; and Indian land purchases, 48n; and diplomatic establishment, 61; and relief of seamen, 71; compensation for, 109; and captives in Algiers, 143, 144, 428; alleged corruption of, 154-5, 281, 290-1, 311, 313-14, 318, 432-4, 446; and land bounties for Va. soldiers, 171, 172n, 346; and debt payment act, 177; Washington's annual message to, 181n; and enforcement of British navigation act, 207n; and TJ's report on commerce, 219; and claims against U.S., 225, 263; and regulation of Indian trade, 249-50; and import duties, 250; adjournment of, 256, 368; and cession of Montauk Point, 265-6n; and U.S. debt to national bank, 283; and foreign loans, 292, 295; and military rations, 299-300; and case of Gallipolis settlers, 320n; TJ's report on acts of, 339, 354; and Mint, 348; and Domenico's proposed consular appointment, 359n; and state debts, 373; and naturalization, 375, 378n; and detention of U.S. ships in French West Indies, 415n; antic-

INDEX

INDEX

WASHINGTON, GEORGE (*cont.*)

treaties with France, xlii-xliii, 597-618, 648n, 666; and British reinforcements for Canada, 6; and French consular salaries, 6-7, 543, 579; and relations with France, 14-15, 370n, 391-2; and U.S. aid to Saint-Domingue, 33, 49, 51-2; and provisions for France, 39, 162, 164n, 172-82, 196-7, 243-5, 260, 266, 273, 275-6, 286, 310-11, 663n; criticizes T. Pinckney, 45; and debt to France, 47n, 164n, 172-82, 196-7, 198, 239, 240-1, 242n, 243-5, 260, 266, 273, 275-6, 286, 310-11, 382, 500, 663n; and diplomatic establishment, 61; and Burr's access to Department of State records, 67n; and appointment of ministers to Europe, 102, 497-8, 501; and consular appointments, 102n, 202-4, 227-8, 238, 308-9; and Lafayette's captivity, 142-3, 257-8, 382, 387-9, 390-2, 664; and neutrality, 165-6, 661; and TJ's report on commerce, 168, 183, 185n, 198, 212, 220, 237, 247n; and enforcement of navigation act, 200, 207n, 208n; and trade with Marseilles, 213; and proposed recall of G. Morris, 243-5, 247-9; and William Stephens Smith's mission to U.S., 243-5, 310-11; and case of Pierre Billet, 249-50; and establishment of French Republic, 254-5; and foreign loans, 283, 436n, 460-2, 504, 505, 508, 509, 533; and case of *Illustrious President*, 296-7; and Humphreys's mission to Algiers, 405, 420, 422n, 423, 470-1; and consular service, 417n; and reception of Genet, 423, 469-70, 570-2, 598, 602, 666; and captives in Algiers, 428; and Department of State expenses, 438, 471-2; and French War with First Coalition, 477, 512, 518, 541, 669n; instructions to TJ on neutrality, 541; instructions to Hamilton on neutrality, 541n; questions on neutrality and the French alliance, 568-71, 597-618, 665-6; and Ternant's application for funds, 636-7; and U.S. jurisdiction over Delaware Bay, 639n; and case of *Grange*, 639-40, 641, 644, 676, 683n, 702n; and foreign-built U.S. ships, 642, 645-8, 651-2; and passports for U.S. ships, 645-8, 650, 651-2, 666, 670-1n, 681-2; meets Noailles, 664; and congressional authority over neutrality, 666; and enforcement of neutrality, 667-8, 691-2, 702; and sale of U.S. ships built for war, 667-8; and contraband, 673-4; and defense of Norfolk, 688

Indian Affairs

and relations with Western Indians, 18n, 88-9, 112-19, 133-4, 136, 144, 153, 158, 216, 220-3, 229, 255, 258-9, 271-3, 354-6, 372, 383, 424-5, 450, 478, 511; and Indian land purchases, 46; and case of John Rogers, 210n; and right of U.S. to cede territory to Indians, 220, 258-9, 272-3; and case of Pierre Billet, 249-50; and boundaries with Western Indians, 354-6; and letter of protection for Indians, 380-1; and relations with Southern Indians, 518-19n; and Spanish relations with Southern Indians, 677-8

Other Correspondence

with House of Representatives quoted, 40n; with Uriah Forrest quoted, 56n; with D. Humphreys cited, 88n, 400; with Charles Carroll of Carrollton, 88-9; with Charles Thomson cited, 89n; with Federal District Commissioners, 107-8, 109, 199n, 400-1; with Arthur Young cited, 167n; with Cabinet, 220, 345, 424-5, 568; with Henry Knox quoted, 220-1n, 300n; with House of Representatives, 231n; with Senate, 231n, 303; with Rodolph Vall-Travers quoted, 256n; with Peregrine Fitzhugh cited, 263n; with William Smith cited, 265n; with Brown & Francis cited, 297n; with George Cabot cited, 309n; with David Stuart cited, 316n; with David Stuart quoted, 316n; with John Rome cited, 320n; with Marquise de Lafayette cited, 382n; with Marquise de Lafayette, 391-2; with Andrew Ellicott cited, 408; with G. Morris cited, 448; with Rodolph Vall-Travers cited, 467-8; with Noailles quoted, 664n; with Henry Lee cited, 688n

INDEX

A comprehensive index of Volumes 1-20 of the First Series has been issued as Volume 21. Each subsequent volume has its own index, as does each volume or set of volumes in the Second Series.